Yearbook on

International

Communist Affairs

1975

Yearbook on

International

Communist Affairs

1975

EDITOR: Richard F. Staar

ASSOCIATE AREA EDITORS:

Eastern Europe and the Soviet Union	Milorad M. Drachkovitch
Western Europe	Dennis L. Bark
Asia and the Pacific	Charles P. Ridley
The Americas	William E. Ratliff
Middle East and Africa	Lewis H. Gann
International Communist Front Organizations	Witold S. Sworakowski

HOOVER INSTITUTION PRESS
Stanford University
Stanford, California
1975

Hoover Institution Publications 146
International Standard Book Number 0–8179–1461–7
Library of Congress Catalog Card Number 67–31024
© 1975 by the Board of Trustees of the
    Leland Stanford Junior University
Printed in the United States of America

Yearbook on

International

Communist Affairs

1975

CONTENTS

Asia and the Pacific

The Americas

Middle East and Africa

International Communist Front Organizations (Paul F. Magnelia)

INTRODUCTION

The objective of the 1975 *Yearbook on International Communist Affairs*, the ninth volume in this series, is to provide information about organizational and personnel changes, attitudes toward domestic and foreign policies, as well as activities of communist parties and international front organizations throughout the world. Most of the data are based on primary source materials.

Profiles on each party include founding date, legal or illegal status, membership, electoral support, leadership, auxiliary organizations, domestic activities, ideological orientation, views on international issues, attitude toward the Sino-Soviet dispute, and principal news media. Although identity as an orthodox Marxist-Leninist party is the criterion for inclusion, pro-Chinese, Castroite, Trotskyite, and other rival communist movements are treated whenever applicable. Guerrilla groups and elements of the so-called New Left are noted, insofar as they affect policies and activities of major communist organizations.

Excluded from the *Yearbook* are profiles on the liberation movements, like FRELIMO (Frente de Libertação de Moçambique), MPLA (Movimento Popular de Libertação de Angola), and PAIGC (Partido Africano de Independência de Guiné e Cabo Verde). Although in orientation Marxist, none has been treated as a communist party. PAIGC governs the newly-independent Guinea Bissau, and FRELIMO probably will control Mozambique when the latter attains independence on 25 June 1975. MPLA conceivably may emerge as the dominant among three groups in Angola, which becomes independent on 11 November 1975, though it lacks the strength and cohesion of FRELIMO.

The ruling movement in the Congo People's Republic, the Congolese Party of Labor, has been excluded from the *Yearbook* even though it claims to be Marxist-Leninist. According to its Central Committee secretary Pierre Nze, it has few real communists and suffers from internal weaknesses (*African Communist*, no. 59, 1974, pp. 86-96). The National Front in the People's Democratic Republic of Yemen and the Somali Supreme Revolutionary Council are both in this same category. The small Communist Party of Lesotho, the illegal Socialist Workers' and Farmers' Party influencing a section of Nigerian trade unions, the Malagasy Communist Party, which remains a minor Maoist splinter group, and the small communist African Party of Independence (PAI) in Senegal also have been left out, despite the fact that they are recognized by Moscow as Marxist parties of tropical Africa. PAI is represented on the editorial council of *World Marxist Review*.

Some few parties publish their membership figures, and these are included. Others, in the past, had been cited from estimates in the U.S. Department of State publication *World Strength of the Communist Party Organizations*. The last annual volume of that excellent paperback covering the year 1973 appeared in November 1974. It is to be regretted that a shortage of funds precipitated the demise of such a valuable research tool.

* * *

A speech by Boris Ponomarev, candidate member of the Politburo, Communist Party of the Soviet Union (CPSU), and in charge of liaison with non-ruling communist parties, summarizes the world movement as comprising 89 parties, among which 75 are in opposition to governments in their respective countries and 37 of which operate underground or under semi-legal conditions. Twenty among the 38 legal parties have representation in parliament, and it is claimed that 40 million voters support communist candidates in capitalist countries. (Moscow radio, 22 April 1974.) On the other hand, only the governments of Iraq, Laos, the People's Democratic Republic of Yemen, Portugal, Sri Lanka, and Syria have communists in their cabinets. Pro-Soviet publications in Eastern Europe admit that rival Maoist splinter groups had been established in some 30 countries, but claim that they are disbanding. However, 21 such groups sent delegates to the thirtieth-anniversary celebration of Albania's liberation from Axis occupation, as did the communist parties of China, Indonesia, New Zealand, North Korea, and North Vietnam (Tirana radio, 27, 29 November). Another threat to Moscow-inspired unity is that presented by "right revisionist elements," like the expelled Manifesto Group in Italy, and the followers of Roger Garaudy in France, Ernst Fischer in Austria, Ota Šik in Czechoslovakia, and T. Petkoff in Venezuela. At the other extreme are the "super-revolutionary" left revisionists, the leaders of the Chinese Communist Party (*Sovetskaia Latviia*, 15 December).

International Conferences. To foster communist activism and unity, and to combat these deviations, several conferences were held during the year under review. Representatives of 67 communist parties convened in early January to discuss the work of *World Marxist Review*, the international Soviet-line theoretical journal published in Prague, Czechoslovakia. That same month, 20 West European parties sent delegates to Brussels. The topic of their discussion was "the present crisis of capitalism in Europe." Norway and Iceland did not send delegates. The declaration issued following the meeting called for unity of the communist movement and urged formation of an "alliance of the broadest social forces, of all working-class and democratic forces, to bring about a new upsurge in their common struggle." It also emphasized the need for "safeguarding and improving living standards, guaranteed employment, social security and social rights," together with "resistance to U.S. imperialism's attempts to heighten its already rigid control over the economies and policies of West European countries and 'revitalize' NATO." The declaration also drew attention to "the constant threat posed to the democratic gains of the peoples of Western Europe by authoritarian tendencies, the persecution of communists and other democrats and the persistence in Spain, Greece and Portugal of fascist regimes enjoying the support of the monopolies, NATO and the United States." (*World Marxist Review*, March.)

Several other meetings occurred during the remainder of the year. At the end of March, one was held at Lyon which focused on issues related to peaceful, democratic, and independent development of Western Europe. In attendance were representatives of the Belgian, British, French, Italian, Swiss and West German communist parties. (*Pravda*, 1 April.) Yet another conference on the present stage of competition between the two world systems, attended by delegates from 31 communist movements, met at Prague during 19-20 June.

A consultative gathering of 28 communist parties from East and West met in Warsaw on 16-18 October. Significantly present were delegates from Yugoslavia and Romania, which had not participated in the last such all-European conference of 24 parties at Karlovy Vary in April 1967. The day before the Warsaw meeting started, Tanyug reported assurances by certain other communist-ruled states that hostile activities against Yugoslavia would not be permitted from their terrritories, an obvious reference to the outside support given the 32 "Cominformists" sentenced to prison in September. Romanian representatives at the Warsaw conference were given instructions to insist on meetings open to all parties, with no binding decisions, no criticism of other parties, and full respect for elaboration of independent political lines. This position had been laid down in the new draft party program (Scînteia, 1 September) and was adopted by the party congress at Bucharest in November. Designed to establish policy guidelines over the next quarter-century, it stresses national communism rather than the Moscow version of ideological orthodoxy.

The 28 delegations agreed to hold an all-European conference no later than mid-1975 on the theme, "Struggle for Peace, Security, Cooperation, and Social Progress in Europe," with a preparatory meeting in December 1974 or January 1975 (Warsaw radio, 18 October). The preparatory meeting of eight ruling East European and 20 non-ruling West European communist parties took place at Budapest on 19-21 December. The (Maoist) Albanian Party of Labor and the communist parties of Holland and Iceland did not send representatives. The communiqué spoke of agreement on an editorial commission in which all parties could participate. It also announced that seminars would be held on problems connected with the conference theme. All delegates confirmed their "striving for cohesion and unity among all democratic and progressive forces of the continent." (Moscow radio, 21 December.) In return for agreeing to an all-European conference of communist parties, the delegates apparently won their fight against any world meeting that would openly criticize the Chinese communists.

Soviet Union and Eastern Europe. In the U.S.S.R. during 1974 political cohesion at the top appeared complete with the primacy of general secretary Brezhnev unchallenged. However, there were rumors at year's end about disagreements within the CPSU Politburo. One such rumor that Brezhnev had relinquished his duties because of illness were denied indirectly, when the Soviet leader allegedly attended the funeral of his mother on 8 January 1975. In general, the KGB has been able to check the dissident intellectual movement. On the other hand, nationalism persists among non-Russian nationalities especially in the republics of Georgia and Lithuania. Economic achievements were slightly below plan for both heavy and light industry, whereas production in the agricultural sector dropped 3.7 percent below the 1973 level. N. K. Baibakov, chairman of the state economic planning commission, admitted that the current five-year plan had not been reoriented to favor consumers' goods as promised (Izvestiia, 21 December 1974, 24 January 1975).

In state-to-state contacts, the U.S.S.R. continued to place relations with the United States on center stage. Agreements for technical and scientific cooperation as well as limitation of underground nuclear tests were signed during President Nixon's visit to Moscow in June-July. At the next summit meeting near Vladivostok between President Ford and Brezhnev on 23-24 November, an oral understanding was reached for a ten-year limitation on nuclear weapons. However, the linkage of trade and Jewish emigration issues led to a deterioration of relations between Moscow and Washington by the turn of the year. In a letter dated 26 October, Soviet foreign minister Gromyko denied that any agreement had been made linking the two. When the U.S. Congress made most-favored-nation status conditional upon a more liberal Soviet emigration policy in the December trade reform act and placed a ceiling of $300 million over the next four years on Export-Import Bank credits, the U.S.S.R. on 10 January 1975 denounced its trade agreement with the United States.

High priority is still placed by Moscow for an agreement at the 35-nation conference on security and cooperation in Europe which reconvened in Geneva at the end of January 1975. The stumbling block has been Western insistence on free movement of peoples, ideas, and information which the East regards as interference in its domestic affairs. U.S. officials, on the other hand, consider that sufficient progress has been made to begin planning for a final meeting of government heads that would take place in Helsinki during the summer (New York Times, 21 January). Soviet-American talks on mutual force reduction in Europe remained stalled due to the U.S.S.R.'s demand for a one-to-one cutback. The Soviet Union indicated its satisfaction with the new French president Valéry Giscard d'Estaing and new West German chancellor Helmut Schmidt, both of whom indicated a continuation of détente policies of their predecessors.

However, Soviet relations with China were at a stalemate, with acrimonious polemics (see, e.g., *Partiinaia zhizn*, no. 24, December 1974, pp. 60-68) balanced by offers to normalize the situation. Yet at Ulan Bator in Mongolia, on his way back from the Vladivostok summit, Brezhnev rejected the Chinese proposal for a non-aggression pact tied to a troop pullback from the border as "absolutely unacceptable." Soviet diplomacy continued at a high level of intensity throughout the Middle East, emphasizing solidarity with the Palestinian cause. To counteract the United States, U.S.S.R. spokesmen demanded convocation of the Geneva conference on the Arab-Israeli question. The reason for the indefinite postponement of Brezhnev's trip to Egypt and other Arab countries at the end of the year remains a mystery, although Gromyko was sent to Damascus and Cairo in early February 1975. Brezhnev had visited Cuba in January 1974 and an exchange of high-level visits showed a new emphasis on Soviet-Argentinian relations. Interest in Africa was shown during July, when chief of state Nikolai Podgorny visited the Somali Democratic Republic to sign a treaty of friendship and cooperation.

In contrast with the political effervescence in Western and Southern Europe, there were few signs of internal tension in communist-ruled Eastern Europe. The Soviet Union's leadership remained unchallenged, and its basic international views and diplomatic initiatives were endorsed, at least among member-states of the Warsaw Treaty Organization. Their leaders and propagandists echoed U.S.S.R. themes that détente and peaceful co-existence increased the role and significance of the ideological struggle between socialism and capitalism and that détente was opening new possibilities for the world revolutionary process. The already cited Ponomarev repeated these contentions at the Budapest meeting (*Pravda*, 21 December 1974). Likewise, Maoism was denounced by most East European parties as a threat to world peace and détente and as an enemy of the Soviet bloc and of world communist solidarity. Works of exiled writer Alexander Solzhenitsyn, especially his *Gulag Archipelago*, were assailed as reactionary tools against détente and the U.S.S.R. However, the traditional since 1971 meeting of all East European leaders did not take place in the Crimea during the summer of 1974.

As for the individual communist-ruled states, a purge of Albanian military officers accused of favoring accommodation with Moscow and epitomized by dismissal of Beqir Balluku, defense minister since 1953, was revealed only in January 1975 although it had occurred earlier. The regime of Enver Hoxha continued its ideological and cultural revolution, strengthening relations with the People's Republic of China. The Eleventh Congress of the Romanian Communist Party in November endorsed significant changes in the structure of the party leadership, resulting in further strengthening of Nicolae Ceauşescu's position. The congress also avoided any open confrontation with the U.S.S.R. by sidetracking the question of a world communist conference. It is noteworthy that Romania, of all East European countries the most favorably inclined toward Israel, during 1974 attempted to improve its relations with the Arab countries and became a staunch supporter of the Palestine Liberation Organization.

The German Democratic Republic (GDR) maintained its intransigent line. Constitutional amendments approved in September call the GDR a "socialist state of workers and peasants," instead of "a socialist state of German nation" (*Deutschland Archiv*, October, p. 1009). In this way, a national definition of the GDR was replaced by one based on the class struggle. The former objective of eventual reunification by the two German states was eliminated. The amendments also proclaim the GDR as "forever and irrevocably allied with the U.S.S.R." Extensive measures of militarization were undertaken during the year, and an antagonistic attitude toward the Federal Republic of Germany prevailed.

As for Yugoslavia, the Tenth Congress of its League of Communists (LCY) took place in May and reaffirmed greater party influence in state affairs but also strengthened the military role in LCY top echelons. A new Yugoslav constitution had been promulgated in February. Remnants of a representative parliamentary system were replaced by a complex system in which delegates to federal legislative bodies will be selected and bound by imperative mandates from lower-level assemblies. Membership in the collective state presidency was reduced from 23 to nine, with Tito reconfirmed president for life. One of the avowed aims of the new constitution is to extend the system of workers' self-management. Repression against domestic dissenters persisted throughout the year. While fluctuation characterized Soviet-Yugoslav relations, there was improvement in contacts with China and Albania. Cordial relations were also cultivated with Hungary and the GDR following Tito's visits in April and November, respectively. Yugoslavia exchanged sharp diplomatic notes with Italy over Trieste, protested twice against NATO naval maneuvers in the Adriatic, and accused Austria of alleged discrimination against Croat and Slovene minorities. However, relations with the United States appeared normal. Westinghouse Electric Corporation signed a contract in August to construct Yugoslavia's first nuclear power plant, the largest single project ever financed by American and European banks in that country. Dow Chemical Company agreed during the last week in January 1975 to construct a $500 million petrochemical complex at the north Adriatic city of Rijeka.

Western Europe. While there were no marked electoral successes during the year, which would have resulted in members of communist parties attaining cabinet posts, it did appear that certain among the West European communist parties had high expectations. Economic issues, such as inflation and the quadrupling in price of oil, posed increasingly serious problems for all countries. In Italy, the party holds 175 of 630 parliamentary seats and controls ten percent of the nation's 8,000 municipalities. Being the most flexible, ideologically and tactically, of all West European communist parties, the Italian party does not advocate withdrawal from either NATO or the Common Market.

This position is similar to that of the French Communist Party, which has pursued since 1972 a policy of unity with the socialists. As a consequence, the coalition captured 49 percent of the vote in the presidential election of 1974. In addition, there are almost 1,100 communist mayors among a total of 37,708 throughout France. The party holds 73 seats out of 487 in the national parliament. Georges Marchais, French Communist Party secretary-general, reiterated at the extraordinary congress on 24 October that communists in France had no intention of playing a subordinate role in the Union of the Left.

One of the most interesting developments during the year occurred in Portugal, where Alvaro Cunhal is the only communist with cabinet rank in a NATO government, although the party had been banned between 1933 and April 1974. Since the military coup, communists have achieved a major foothold among student organizations and in labor unions, the media, and certain ministerial bureaucracies. In this connection, a meeting of NATO dealing with nuclear planning was canceled in November 1974 following refusal by the United States to divulge classified information to an ally which has a communist cabinet minister. A recent poll, conducted by the armed forces, gave extreme leftists and conservatives five percent each, communists and popular democrats 10 percent each, and socialists 20 percent, with half of those questioned indicating no preference in an election (*New York Times*, 20 January 1975).

The socialist-communist alliance seemed to be headed for trouble when the Socialist Party withdrew from the Movement for a Democratic Portugal (MDP), a loose front of leftist and "progressive" groups, in September. The MDP reorganized itself into a full-fledged political entity in November, thus serving as an extension of the Portuguese Communist Party. Elections for a constituent assembly were scheduled for April 1975, but the Armed Forces Movement gave notice that it would continue to rule until the end of the year. A hotly debated law passed by the cabinet on 22 January 1975 established a single labor confederation, constituent federations of which already were controlled by the communists in Portugal.

Across the border, an article by the secretary-general of the illegal Communist Party of Spain

(PCE) was broadcast over the clandestine "Radio Independent Spain" on 26 October 1974, suggesting that the main lesson from events in Portugal centered on the need for unity of left and right opposition forces. Earlier in the year, the Soviet journal *Partiinaia zhizn* (February) had attacked a leading number of the PCE Central Committee for his criticism of "peaceful co-existence" as in effect condemning West European communists to stagnation. The PCE played a major role in forming an opposition alliance called the Democratic Junta, established after the coup in Lisbon, but which operates out of Paris.

Nonetheless, a broadcast by Moscow radio (19 October) claimed that Soviet détente policies had helped to "overthrow the fascist regimes in Portugal and Greece, strengthen the unity of left-wing forces in France and Italy, and ensure success of communist parties in other countries." Despite such claims, an interview with Nikolai Bragin, editor of *Pravda*'s department for European countries, elicited the existence of "doubts and reservations" on convening of a world communist conference among Romanian, French, Italian, Yugoslav, and Spanish parties (Gianni Corbi in *L'Espresso*, 18 August). This source also revealed that relations between the CPSU and certain "fraternal parties," particularly the Spanish, had become embittered. A reconciliation apparently occurred during a meeting between PCE and Soviet representatives at Moscow in October.

In Scandinavia, communist parties did not play any significant role during the year. Divisions existed within the parties of Sweden and Denmark, while in Norway and Finland the parties generally supported left-wing electoral alliances but remained without substantial influence. In Iceland, where the communist party had held two of the seven cabinet posts since 1971, the coalition collapsed in May. Nevertheless the party received 18 percent of the vote in the June national election and has 11 of the 60 seats in parliament. While the party in Ireland is small, communists in Great Britain occupy key positions in many labor unions. Although they have not had a member in Parliament since 1950, they did play a decisive role in the February-March 1974 coal miners' strike which seriously challenged the government's wage controls. Elections on 17 November 1974 in Greece saw the two communist parties and one front organization form a United Left alliance which polled less than 9.5 percent of the vote and secured eight seats in the 300-member parliament. The ban on communist activity, in force since 1947, had been lifted during the summer.

Asia and the Pacific. The Chinese Communist Party (CCP), claiming 28 million members, and thus largest in the world, appears temporarily to have solved its leadership crisis. The so-called anti-Lin Piao, anti-Confucius campaign during 1974 may have been part of the power struggle for the succession to 81-year-old Mao Tse-tung. Unexpectedly, a full plenum of the Central Committee, after none had been held in 16 months, convened on 8-10 January 1975 in Peking. This was followed by the first meeting in ten years of the National People's Congress or legislature on 13-17 January. The 2,864 delegates approved 76-year-old Chou En-lai's political report, reelected him premier, and announced a new government of 12 deputy premiers (seven of whom are Politburo members) and 29 ministers. The important defense post went to Yeh Chien-ying (age 76), who has held it on an acting basis since the alleged September 1971 coup attempt by Lin Piao. None of the three radical leaders (Wang Hung-wen, Yao Wen-yuan, Chiang Ching) received government posts. However, Wang (40) is still ranked as third in the party hierarchy.

The man ranking after Chou in the government is Teng Hsiao-ping (71), as first deputy premier. He also served as acting premier during Chou's illness. Teng was promoted on 17 January to be one of five vice-chairmen of the party and a member of the Politburo's Standing Committee. His appointment as army chief of staff was announced on 29 January. Next on the list is deputy premier Chang Chun-chiao (65), who presented the new constitution to the National People's Congress and subsequently was named director of the General Political Department in the armed forces. The third deputy premier is Li Hsien-nien, top economic administrator, followed by deputy premier Chen

Hsi-lien (62) who commands the Peking military region. Fifth-ranking deputy premier is Hua Kuo-peng (mid-50's), also named public security minister. Among the nine members of the Politburo's Standing Committee, only two are under the age of 70 and three are octogenarians.

The new constitution (*New York Times*, 20 January 1975) abolished the post of chief of state, held by Mao until 1959 and then by Liu Shao-chi until he was purged in 1967 during the Cultural Revolution, but vacant since that time. Mao was not present at either the Central Committee plenum or at the meeting of the legislature. No explanation was given for his absence. However, the new constitution is based on Maoist precepts and Mao becomes commander in chief of the armed forces as chairman of the CCP Central Committee. The functions normally performed by a chief of state will be executed by the chairman of the standing committee of the National People's Congress, to which Marshal Chu Teh (89) was appointed.

During 1974, the goverment functioned despite many vacancies at top levels. The foreign trade deficit increased due to larger imports of equipment and plants, apparently in anticipation of future oil exports. Commercial exchange also continued with the U.S.S.R., and it seemed that Chinese leaders no longer considered the threat of a Soviet attack imminent. Trade also increased with the United States, and an air link was established with Japan.

Peking's policies in Southeast Asia showed divergent trends. While the Chinese withdrew forces from Laos, they maintained troops in Burma and occupied the Paracel Islands off South Vietnam. China participated in U.N. conferences on the law of the sea, world population, and world food. In his speech to the U.N. General Assembly on 2 October, Chinese delegate Chiao Kuan-hua gave strong support to "third world" positions.

On the northeastern border of China, tension occurred between the two Koreas. The North Korean navy sank a small South Korean fishing vessel and captured another on the Yellow Sea in February. Troops from both sides fought a gun battle in November, when soldiers discovered a tunnel dug by northern forces to a point about 1,000 yards south of the military demarcation line. However, North Korea continued to avoid leaning toward either the Soviet Union or China. While it opposes both Soviet "revisionism" and Chinese "left opportunism" or "dogmatism," relations with both powers remained correct.

War continued in Southeast Asia, where the Khmer insurgents moved through much of Cambodia without challenge but could not establish an administrative capital by year's end. The People's Republic of China made a concerted effort at the United Nations during 1974 to discredit the Cambodian government and to seat the insurgents, without success. The comunist party in Laos, under its Lao Patriotic Front cover, became a full participant in the national government. While continuing to exhort its cadres to achieve the goal of complete victory of the revolution, it pursued less violent techniques as a member of the coalition, advocating police measures to control gambling and crime, and announcing plans for the development of agriculture, industry, and trade.

The year in North Vietnam saw no fundamental change. The leadership remains committed to control of the South. "Resolution 08" of the so-called Central Office of South Vietnam envisions 1975 as a turning point but not the end of the war (*New York Times*, 30 January 1975). No reduction in military capability of the People's Army of Vietnam in the south or of the People's Liberation Armed Forces in the north has occurred, and January 1975 witnessed a new offensive which occupied Phuoc Long Province adjacent to Cambodia in the Republic of Vietnam. Hanoi opposes all liberalization for itself or other communist-ruled states and is against détente or peaceful co-existence with the capitalist world. North Vietnam asserts its right of non-dependent status vis-à-vis China and the Soviet Union. Doctrinal disputes continued within the Lao Dong Party over proper strategy to achieve unification of Vietnam, on economic policy, and how to eliminate the various socio-psychological troubles known as the "quality of life problem."

The government of Thailand acknowledged that the communists had widened their range of operations, concentrating chiefly on armed struggle. Military attacks were also reported to have increased, with ambushes in the north and clashes in the northeast. More terrorist incidents occurred in the south as well, according to General Saiyud Kerdpol, director of the Internal Security Operations Command. The major development in Malaysia has been a three-way split among communists. A rival party, calling itself the Communist Party of Malaya (Marxist-Leninist), broke away and claims to have its own fighting force, the "Malaysian People's Liberation Army." Before this, yet another group had seceded in February from the original movement, this one calling itself the Communist Party of Malaya (Revolutionary Faction). The ideological or tactical differences among these three factions and the relative strength of each have not been established.

In the Philippines, both the Peking- and Moscow-oriented communist parties benefited from the belief that establishment of diplomatic relations with China and the U.S.S.R. is a matter of time. Although the (pro-Chinese) New People's Army suffered a few setbacks, military operations during the year revealed the Maoist guerrillas and their party organizational structure as representing a nationwide force which is committed to erode government strength in widely scattered areas throughout the country as it attempts to secure rural bases. The leadership of the pro-Soviet communist party surrendered to the government in October, and the group pledged its support to the Marcos reform program.

In another part of the Pacific, as a result of July 1974 elections, the Japanese communist party increased its representation in the upper House of Councillors from 11 to 20 (out of 252) and now holds 59 seats in the two chambers of parliament. It also won 65 additional seats in prefecture, city, town, and village assemblies for a total of 2,809 seats in all categories. However, in image and public opinion, communists lost ground in a public dispute over the Solzhenitsyn deportation. Little progress was made during the year toward achievement of a viable united front which could win national elections. The communist view still focuses on détente as a delusion and the United States as world leader of imperialism. It continues to reject leadership of the CPSU over the world communist movement and castigates both the CCP and the CPSU for their intervention in the internal affairs of the Japanese party.

The Americas. In the Western Hemisphere, most of the important communist groups continued to seek influence and ultimately power in their countries by non-violent methods. Pro-CPSU parties gave considerable though conditional support to a wide variety of governments during 1974, ranging from that of Juan (deceased in July) and Isabel Perón in Argentina to military regimes in such differing countries as Honduras and Peru. These and most other pro-Soviet parties insisted that the socialist revolution had to come by stages and that their countries were not yet ready for a dictatorship of the proletariat. Even the important communist parties of Chile and Uruguay, driven underground during "tragic events" in late 1973, did not call for armed struggle in order to overthrow existing regimes. Rather the emphasis remained on the formation of broad "anti-fascist" fronts, intended either to influence or ultimately replace present governments (*Pravda*, 26 December 1974).

The "lessons of Chile" were widely discussed by pro-Soviet and other Marxist-Leninist groups, above all by Chilean leftists at home and in exile, the latter with the resources of many European left-wing parties and international front organizations at their disposal. The Communist Party of Chile, the single most important member of the Chilean Popular Unity coalition which had been led between 1970 and 1973 by Salvador Allende, reached conclusions shared by most of Latin America's other pro-Soviet movements. Allende's government had been too slow in eliminating old government institutions, failed to make a strong enough political and ideological impact on the masses, and been unable to provide united leadership for the revolution due to "ultra-leftist" and "right-opportunist" deviations. As a consequence the coalition was unable to win majority support from the population and, rather than isolating the enemy, became increasingly isolated itself.

Throughout the hemisphere, the majority of pro-Soviet parties concluded that leftist unity was essential for revolutionary victory. Some of these parties (Costa Rica, El Salvador, Guatemala, Mexico, Nicaragua, Panama) proposed at a Central American regional meeting in May that a meeting of Latin American communist and workers' parties should be scheduled to consider a regional conference devoted to revolutionary strategy and tactics against reaction and imperialism. (*Information Bulletin*, no. 14, 1974.)

Whereas the pro-Soviet parties argued that assassination, kidnaping, bank robbery, and other terrorist action in general played into the hands of the enemy, some communist groups (most importantly the People's Revolutionary Army in Argentina) considered these tactics a significant element in their overall strategy of developing conditions for and launching a revolutionary civil war. The Chilean Movement of the Revolutionary Left still anticipated a long and difficult "people's war" in Chile, though it made some conciliatory moves toward at least temporary unity with more moderate leftist groups. However, despite the People's Revolutionary Army in Argentina and isolated spectacular actions by the Sandinist Liberation Front in Nicaragua, the Uruguayan Tupamaros, and several other groups, the "ultra-left" generally remained quiescent in most of Latin America during the year.

The Communist Party of Cuba, increasingly influenced in its political, economic, and military activities by the Soviet Union, held elections for "organs of people's power" in Matanzas Province during June and July 1974 and vowed to consider further elections when the ten-year-old party's first congress is convened in November 1975. Party policy called for reconciliation with "independent" and "anti-imperialist" governments in Latin America, and party propaganda claimed that de facto isolation of Cuba from the hemisphere was unmistakably broken. By year's end, ten Latin American countries (Argentina, the Bahamas, Barbados, Guyana, Jamaica, Mexico, Panama, Peru, Trinidad-Tobago, and Venezuela) had recognized the Castro regime.

The Communist Party, USA, which came out for the formation of a labor party in the United States, called for new presidential elections and support for a "united front against Watergate and for détente" (*Daily World*, 2 March, 10 April 1974). The CPUSA, the Socialist Workers Party (Trotskyist) and the Progressive Labor Party (formerly Maoist) all three individually condemned the terrorist actions of the Symbionese Liberation Army in California, including the kidnaping of Patricia Hearst at Berkeley and the shoot-out with police in Los Angeles.

Middle East and Africa. The communist movements of the Middle East are all small, with memberships ranging from not many thousands down to a few hundred or less. In 1974 legal parties operated only in Iraq, Israel, Lebanon, and Syria, with on the whole circumscribed roles in domestic political affairs. Communists held two ministerial posts each in Iraq and Syria, and five communists sat in Israel's parliament. The strategy of these parties is aimed at enhancing their influence through participation with more powerful groups in national fronts.

The principal communist movements in the Middle East were pro-Soviet. They supported the Soviet policy of advocating a settlement to the Arab-Israeli conflict on the basis of U.N. Security Council resolutions which would provide, inter alia, for continued existence of Israel, although some Palestinians in the Jordanian party appear to be unenthusiastic on this issue. A splinter faction in Syria accused Khalid Bakdash, head of the officially recognized party and long the foremost communist figure in the Arab world, of having succumbed unduly to Soviet influence. MAKI, the party in Israel with fewer Arab members than its larger rival RAKAH, criticized Moscow's treatment of Soviet Jews.

During 1974 the Soviet Union provided massive amounts of military equipment to Iraq and Syria. A radio broadcast on 19 January 1975 announced the largest arms agreement thus far between the U.S.S.R. and Iraq. As a consequence, in part, the communist parties in these countries are among the strongest in the Middle East, each being on good terms with the Ba'th party faction in control of its government. Iraqi communist leaders, including those of Kurdish origin, supported the government's military campaign against the Kurd insurgents.

In Egypt, deterioration of relations with the Soviet Union militated against any revival of the communist party. The once-strong party in the Sudan remains fractured and impotent. Repression by the ruling regime in Tunisia had stripped the clandestine party of political importance. Communists in Algeria fared better by working with the governing FLN, which maintained cordial relations with the CPSU. In August 1974, it was publicly announced that a legal Party of Progress and Socialism had been formed in Morocco, successor to the illegal communist Party of Liberation and Socialism. The Shah of Iran, apprehensive about Soviet penetration into the Middle East, maintained tight restrictions on local communists.

In June the National Front of Iraq, which includes the communist party, joined the *World Marxist Review* in sponsoring a seminar at Baghdad on the "Alliance of the Socialist World System and the National Liberation Movements," which was attended by delegates from 26 communist parties, four "revolutionary democratic parties," four "national liberation movements," and seven other organizations (*WMR*, October, November).

In sub-Saharan Africa, communist parties properly speaking exercise little influence. The South African movement operates in exile (broadcast by chairman Yusuf Dadoo, Moscow radio, 24 December), an army of officers without privates. The parties of Nigeria, Lesotho, and Senegal are devoid both of legal status and political influence. Insofar as communists wield any political power, they do so as members of the so-called liberation movements. The breakdown of the Portuguese colonial structure has greatly increased the influence of Marxists-Leninists of differing political hues. In Guinea-Bissau, the PAIGC is now the ruling party but, despite its Marxist vocabulary, will not describe itself as communist. Marxists have considerable influence within FRELIMO, now by far the dominant political movement in Mozambique. The MPLA is the organization most strongly supported by the new Portuguese high commissioner in Angola, but is divided into several factions and it also denies that it represents a communist movement.

Fronts. The year 1974 was significant in various areas for the international communist front organizations. Due to reasons which are not entirely clear, there was visible within these groups an effort to centralize decision-making authority. In several instances, constitutional changes reduced the number of required meetings for the main congresses and executive committees, thus leaving the secretariats with greater freedom and consequently more power. In contrast with this internal decision-making consolidation, the fronts appealed for wider contacts. As stated by the World Peace Council (WPC), "the key to success in a period when peace and détente have the growing support of millions will be the unity of all peace forces throughout the world, a unity bringing together diverse political forces concerned with the future of mankind." One area in particular in which these wider contacts were sought was within the United Nations and its organizations. WPC achieved "Consultation and Association—Category A" status in UNESCO, and the World Federation of Trade Unions (WFTU) increased its activities in ILO. All fronts sought and some achieved more effective working relationships with their non-communist counterparts—for example, the WFTU with non-communist labor groups.

On major international issues, the fronts took the Soviet position on all occasions. This was true with regard to South Vietnam, the Middle East, and Cyprus. As far as the Arab-Israeli question was concerned, the fronts increasingly supported the idea of the "rights of the Palestinian people." Indeed, Israel came in for a considerable amount of harsh criticism. The Chinese continued their attacks on the front organizations, but there existed little or no disruption because of Chinese activity. In fact, as one looks back at 1974 in review, it appears that most fronts increased their membership and were able to expand "contacts" with non-communist groups.

*   *   *

While it is impossible to make any definitive or all-encompassing statements on the situation of the world communist movement in 1974, two facts emerge as perhaps the most significant. First, the communist movement on a global scale remains fragmented, with the strongest—the Soviet-led—part anxiously and systematically trying to find ways and means to reassert its primacy. Second, in the 14 countries where they rule, communist parties did not show any disposition to allow genuine domestic political liberalization. And yet those movements in the non-communist world, especially in Western and Southern Europe, have been dynamic and militant. They exude confidence that the manifold crises of the capitalist world may lead, if properly exploited, to communist victory. Needless to say, that self-confidence is not an automatic guarantee of ultimate success.

*   *   *

Members of the staff and several associate editors were responsible for much of the research and writing of the *Yearbook*. Profiles were prepared also by a total of 56 outside contributors, many of whom wrote more than one. Full names and affiliations for most of them appear at the end of the individual essays. Mrs. Ica Juilland assisted in the processing and filing of research material together with Mr. Michael La Cava. Most of the final typing was done by Mrs. Louise Doying and Mrs. Esther Hewlett. Special appreciation is due the curators of the Hoover Institution and the members of its Readers' Services and Serials Department, as well as to all those organizations—government and private—which made available source material and translations. We are indebted particularly to the copy editor, Mr. Jesse M. Phillips, for putting most of the manuscript in its final form.

Sources are cited throughout the text, with news agencies normally identified by generally accepted initials. Abbreviations are also used for the following widely quoted publications:

Foreign Broadcast Information Service	*FBIS*
New York Times	*NYT*
World Marxist Review (Toronto, Canada, edition)	*WMR*
and its *Information Bulletin*	*IB*
Yearbook on International Communist Affairs	*YICA*

31 January 1975   Richard F. Staar

EASTERN EUROPE AND THE SOVIET UNION

Albania

The Albanian Communist Party was founded on 8 November 1941. At its First Congress, November 1948, the name was changed to the Albanian Party of Labor (Partia e Punës e Shqipërisë; APL). As the only legal party in Albania, the APL exercises a monopoly of power. Party members hold all key posts in the government and the mass organizations. All 250 seats in the national legislature, the People's Assembly, are held by representatives of the Democratic Front, the party-controlled mass political organization to which all Albanian voters belong.

In November 1971 the APL claimed a membership of 86,985. Approximately 69,000 were full members and 18,000 were candidates (*Zëri i popullit*, 4 November 1971). The population of Albania in 1973 was 2,322,600 (Albanian Telegraphic Agency, ATA, 18 June 1974). Since 1971 the party has made a concerted effort to expand its ranks. Of those admitted to the APL between November 1971 and November 1974, 42 percent were laborers; 40 percent, collectivized farmers; and 18 percent, white-collar workers and intellectuals. In December 1974 laborers accounted for 37.9 percent of the party membership. The APL is currently emphasizing the recruitment of women and persons in the 18-35 age bracket (*Zëri i popullit*, 5 December 1974).

Leadership. Enver Hoxha, who has served as the party's first secretary since its founding, as chairman of the Democratic Front since 1945, and as commander-in-chief of the People's Armed Forces since 1944, is the dominant personality in the ruling elite.

In theory, the highest APL authority is the party congress, which, according to the party statute, meets once every five years. In practice, however, the major APL policy-making organs are its Politburo (13 full members, 4 candidates) and Central Committee (71 full members, 39 candidates). The full members of the Politburo are Enver Hoxha, Abdyl Këllezi, Adil Çarçani, Beqir Balluku (see below), Haki Toska, Hysni Kapo, Kadri Hazbiu, Koço Theodosi, Manush Myftiu, Mehmet Shehu, Ramiz Alia, Rita Marko, and Spiro Koleka; while the candidates are Petrit Dume (see below), Piro Dodbiba, Pilo Peristeri, and Xhafer Spahiu. In addition to Hoxha, the secretaries of the Central Committee are Hysni Kapo, Ramiz Alia, Haki Toska, and Petro Dode.

For the first time since 1960, during 1974 there appear to have been several major changes within the inner circle of the Albanian leadership. Beqir Balluku, 57, a member of the APL Politburo and Central Committee since 1948, and reputedly (after Hoxha, Mehmet Shehu, and Hysni Kapo) the fourth-ranking member of the ruling hierarchy, was apparently purged during the summer. Balluku, who had served as defense minister since 1953 and deputy prime minister since 1954, was not reappointed to his government posts when the composition of the new cabinet was announced at the first session of the recently elected People's Assembly, which met on 28-29 October (*Zëri i popullit*, 30 October). Also, Balluku, for the first time since 1945, was not elected a member of the People's

Assembly. In fact, he did not appear in public, nor was he mentioned in the Albanian communications media, after 19 June. Moscow-trained, reportedly popular with the rank-and-file of the Albanian armed forces, he had been regarded as a staunch ally of Hoxha and Shehu. His political downfall apparently occurred at the Fifth Plenum (25-26 July) of the APL Central Committee, which was devoted to a consideration of recommendations for the "further strengthening of the national defense." From the fragmentary evidence available thus far, it appears that Balluku had come to regard Hoxha's policy of people's warfare (that is, arming and training the adult Albanian population to resist aggression) as unrealistic. The deposed defense minister allegedly also believed that since the Soviet Union would strengthen its position in the Balkans after the death of Tito, and, since the People's Republic of Albania (PRA) was too weak, either alone or in concert with other Balkan states, to oppose a Soviet move into the Balkans, the time had come for Tirana to seek an accommodation with Moscow. In addition, Balluku seems to have taken the position that China would not provide any direct military assistance in the event that Albania was invaded by the U.S.S.R. In major policy statements delivered during September-November, Shehu, Hoxha, and Kapo emphatically restated the Albanian opposition to a détente or rapprochement with the U.S.S.R. and reaffirmed the primacy of the Sino-Albanian alliance (ibid., 28 September, 3 October, 29 November). By inference, Balluku and other military leaders (see below) who have been purged or demoted were also accused of ignoring party directives, permitting discipline to break down, allowing the level of preparedness of the reserve forces to deteriorate, and attempting to cover up their shortcomings (ibid., 19 November, 19 December). Although the Albanians have, as a rule, identified and publicly denounced members of the leadership who have been purged, they apparently chose not to criticize Balluku and his supporters directly in order to avoid marring the celebration of the 30th anniversary of Albania's liberation from Nazi occupation.

Petrit Dume, 54, a candidate member of the APL Politburo since 1961 and a Central Committee member since 1948, was in late July relieved of his duties as chief of staff of the Albanian Armed Forces, a post he had held since 1953, and appointed a deputy defense minister (Tirana radio, 29 July). This move appears to have been a demotion for the Moscow-trained Dume, who had been the second-ranking member of the military leadership. By mid October Dume had also dropped from sight and was no longer being mentioned in the Albanian press. Thus, by mid December it seemed that he too had become a victim of the purge of the Albanian military establishment.

Todo Manço, 53, one of the original members of the APL and a member of its Central Committee since 1966, died on 6 November (Zëri i popullit, 7 November). An engineer by profession, he was serving as a "counsellor" in the Ministry of Industry and Mining at the time of his death. The recipient of numerous honors "for outstanding performances on the production front," Manço was considered a "model" communist. The Bulqize chrome mine was renamed in his honor.

Mass Organizations. As of late 1974 there were approximately 315,000 Albanians between the ages of 14-26 enrolled in the Union of Albanian Labor Youth (UALY). Of these, about 71,000 were classified as industrial laborers, 100,000 as farm workers, 133,000 as students, and 11,000 as white-color workers, teachers, or military personnel (ibid., 23 November). The UALY, which was severely criticized for its ideological and organizational shortcomings during 1973, appears to have made some progress in overcoming the "problems" that had been detected in these areas (ATA, 13 July; Rruga e partisë, August). Rudi Monari, who in June 1973 had been demoted from UALY first secretary to membership in the organization's secretariat, seems to have worked his way back into the good graces of the APL leadership. At year's end Monari was the second-ranking (after first secretary Jovan Bardhi) member of the UALY hierarchy.

On the occasion of the 30th anniversary of its First Congress, the Union of Albanian Women emphasized the "tremendous gains" registered by Albanian women under the communist regime.

Women comprised 34 percent of the People's Assembly, 40 percent of village and city councils, 47 percent of the nation's work force, and 24 percent of the APL (*Zëri i popullit*, 3, 4 November).

The Ideological and Cultural Revolution ("Revolutionization" Movement). The reintensification of the Ideological and Cultural Revolution initiated by Hoxha in February 1973 (see *YICA, 1974*, pp. 3-5) continued to be a major feature of the domestic scene during 1974. Indeed, as the year drew to a close, spokesmen for the regime underscored the importance the APL leadership attached to this movement by asserting that the fate of socialism in Albania hinged on the success or failure of the Ideological and Cultural Revolution. They also stressed that the party would persevere in its efforts to eliminate manifestations of both "conservatism" and "liberalism" in the country (e.g., *Rruga e partisë*, October; *Zëri i popullit*, 14 December).

Intellectuals and students continued to be prime targets of the cultural crackdown which has affected virtually every aspect of Albanian life. The regime has made an especial effort to eradicate the "bourgeois-revisionist ideas, influences, and traits" which had allegedly been "implanted" within both these groups by the activities of Fadil Paçrami and Todi Lubonja, who were expelled from both the APL Central Committee and the party in June 1973 for espousing "anti-party and anti-national viewpoints." After more than a year-long round of "meetings, discussions, educational sessions, and confrontations," the leadership appears to have brought, at least superficially, the erring intellectuals and students back into line both in their professional and their personal lives (e.g., *Rruga e partisë*, July, August, October).

Dhimitër Shuteriqi, who was ousted as chairman of the Albanian Union of Writers and Artists in July 1973, had rehabilitated himself to the point where he was permitted to present one of the major papers at the "National Conference of Studies on the Anti-Fascist War of National Liberation of the Albanian People" (*Zëri i popullit*, 12 November). There was also by year's end favorable mention and public exhibition of the art works of Vilson Kilica and Ksenefon Dilo for the first time since their ouster in July 1973 from their respective positions as secretary-general and secretary of the Writers and Artists Union (ibid., 8 December).

It was also reported that "bourgeois-revisionist" influences in behavior and dress which had been especially pronounced among students enrolled in the faculties of architecture, journalism, law, and literature at the Tirana State University had been almost totally eliminated. "Unauthorized student absences" at the university for the first semester of the 1973-74 academic year amounted to only 2 percent of the average daily enrollment, as opposed to 20 percent for the same period during the previous academic year. For the same periods, the student failure rates had dropped from 21 to 3 percent in medicine, 49 to 20 percent in history-geography, and 25 to 6 percent in geology and mining (*Rruga e partisë*, May).

Although the regime seems to have enjoyed considerable success in its efforts to "further revolutionize" Albanian education at all levels, it did acknowledge that problems still existed—especially in secondary and higher education. Too many students applying for training in such fields as medicine, foreign languages, and electronics, while fewer were studying in such areas as animal husbandry, general agriculture, and geology-mining than were required to meet the nation's needs. From the standpoint of the APL leadership, it appeared that many students did not yet appreciate the fact that the nation's educational system was primarily designed to provide the trained and indoctrinated personnel necessary to modernize and communize the country, rather than satisfy their intellectual and personal interests. For this reason, the regime reiterated its position that the selection of individuals for advanced training would be governed by such factors as national requirements for certain categories of personnel, ideological orthodoxy, and academic preparation (ibid. October).

The reintensification of the "revolutionization" movement does not seem to have stilled the demand of a small but vocal segment of the country's youth that the government make a greater effort to provide additional recreational equipment and programs for young people. On the other hand, spokesmen for the regime continue to express their disapproval of those younger generation Albanians who spend "4-5 hours per day in front of their television sets" and waste their time in "unproductive activities of various sorts" (ibid.).

The campaign against "bureaucratism" which was launched in 1966 continued to meet with opposition from "some bureaucrats and cadres." Specifically, the bureaucrats were accused of such "errors" as disregarding party directives, ignoring violations of law and labor discipline, resisting reassignment to areas outside Tirana, intimidating their subordinates and the public, and attempting to cover up their mistakes (ibid., May; *Zëri i popullit*, 15 October, 10 December). In an effort to bring this group to heel, the APL leadership warned bureaucrats and cadres that they would be evaluated on the basis of "their attitude toward the party line, as well as the manner in which they struggle in the interest of the revolution and socialism, and not on the length of their service or the height of their position" (*Zëri i popullit*, 15 October).

Despite some ten years of fairly intensive effort, the APL leadership continues to encounter difficulties, especially in the rural areas of the country, in implementing the social and cultural programs associated with the "revolutionization" movement. By early 1974 family and personal feuds in several areas of northern Albania had reached such proportions that they hampered the work of the party and Democratic Front organizations in these regions (*Bashkimi*, 15 January). Although all churches and mosques in Albania were destroyed or closed in 1967, the regime was forced to admit it had "still not achieved the total emancipation of the workers from the opiate of religion." It also asserted that the struggle against religion was entering "a new decisive stage" as Albania's "internal and external enemies" attempted to "undo the work of the APL in the struggle against religion" (ibid., 30 January; *Zëri i popullit*, 6 July).

The Albanian leaders also acknowledged that they had not yet been able to uproot "bourgeois" and "micro-bourgeois" attitudes and behavior even among some party members and cadres. They observed that there were communists who were "modern" and "scientific" in their outlook and conduct outside their homes, while they "kept alive outmoded customs and practices within their homes." Still others, as a consequence of "foreign influences," had developed a mania for "filling their homes with all sorts of things" (*Rruga e partisë*, October). By the end of the year, the APL had called for an "intensification of the class struggle" as the most effective means of guaranteeing the success of the Ideological and Cultural Revolution (*Zëri i popullit*, 14 December). It thus appeared that Albania's cultural crackdown would continue in high gear for the immediate future.

Political Developments. On 19 June the People's Assembly approved a constitutional amendment permanently setting its membership at 250. This action ended the practice of apportioning Assembly seats in the ratio of one representative per 8,000 inhabitants and resulted in a 14 seat reduction in the size of the body (ibid., 20 June). The election campaign for the People's Assembly began on 6 August, and by mid-September the nomination process was completed. As usual there was only one nominee for each place in the Assembly. The national elections were held on 6 October. According to the official returns, 100 percent of the registered voters (1,248,530) went to the polls, and all but two of them cast ballots for the Democratic Front candidates (ibid., 8 October). It was subsequently reported that 50 percent of the newly elected members of the People's Assembly were in the 18-40 age bracket, 81 percent had graduated from either secondary schools or institutions of higher education, 36 percent were elected for their first term, and 32 percent were either workers or peasants directly engaged in production (ibid., 29 October).

The first session (28-29 October) of the new People's Assembly was mainly devoted to the selection of its officers, the Council of Ministers, and the president and members of the Supreme Court. Haxhi Lleshi was reelected chairman of the Presidium of the People's Assembly, and Telo

Mezini was again chosen Secretary of this 15-member body which exercises legislative power when the Assembly is not in session. Iljaz Reka was again named to the largely honorary post of chairman of the People's Assembly (ibid.).

Mehmet Shehu was reelected prime minister and was appointed defense minister in place of Balluku. The other members of the Council of Ministers are Adil Çarçani (first deputy prime minister), Spiro Koleka (deputy prime minister), Abdyl Këllezi (deputy prime minister and chairman, State Planning Commission), Xhafer Spahiu (deputy prime minister), Kadri Hazbiu (Interior minister), Nesti Nase (Foreign Affairs), Koço Theodosi (Industry and Mines), Myqerem Fuga (Light and Food Industry), Piro Dodbiba (Agriculture), Thoma Deliana (Education and Culture), Rahman Hanku (Construction), Kiço Ngjela (Trade), Luan Babamento (Communications), Lefter Goga (Finance), and Llambi Zicishti (Health). Aranit Çela was reelected president of the Supreme Court (ibid., 30 October).

Perhaps the most significant change in the composition of the cabinet was the removal of Balluku from his posts as deputy prime minister and defense minister. Shehu's assumption of the Defense post in addition to his duties as prime minister indicates the gravity with which the APL leadership views the problems that have arisen within this ministry. It is also noteworthy that Petrit Dume, the second-ranking member of the Albanian military establishment, who might have been expected to succeed Balluku, was (aside from Balluku) the only member of the Albanian leadership who did not attend the October People's Assembly session. Given the fact he had been reelected to the Assembly, Dume's absence suggests that he too may have been purged. There were also several major leadership changes in the Defense Ministry during July. The most important of these were the appointments of Sami Mecollari, an unknown, as chief of staff replacing Dume, and Dilaver Poçi, an APL Central Committee member, as director of the Political Directorate in place of Hito Çako. Çako, like Dume, was designated a· deputy defense minister at this time (Tirana radio, 27, 30 July). In December it was revealed that the APL Central Committee Sixth Plenum (16-17 December) had been devoted to a consideration of the measures that had been taken since July to strengthen the effectiveness of the armed forces (*Zëri i popullit*, 18 December).

The designation of Adil Çarçani, 52, as first deputy prime minister marked the first time that this title had been used since 1966, when it was abandoned in conjunction with the campaign against bureaucratism. This move seems to represent a promotion for Çarçani, who will most likely be given added responsibility for overseeing the economy and state administration, while Shehu devotes greater attention to defense matters. Abdyl Këllezi, 55, was apparently given the additional title of deputy prime minister to enhance his prestige in the areas of economic planning and management. Çarçani and Këllezi appear to have emerged as the leading spokesmen within the ruling elite for the rapidly growing Albanian technocracy.

Three members of the previous cabinet were not appointed to the new government. They are Milo Qirko (Communications minister since 1966), Aleks Verli (Finance minister since 1954), and Sulejman Baholli (minister without portfolio since 1970). Their dismissals stemmed from the unhappiness of the APL leadership with the quality of their performances in their areas of responsibility. The shortcomings of this trio were presumably administrative rather than political in nature, since all were reelected to the People's Assembly and they have continued to carry out mainly ceremonial assignments for the party and government (ibid., 29 October; 7, 10 December). In addition, Qirko has been designated an "adviser" to the Council of Ministers (ibid., 10 December).

The two new cabinet members are Babamento and Goga. Both appear to have been charged with the responisibility of providing dynamic leadership for two ministries (Communications, Finance) that have had difficulties in fulfilling party and state directives in recent years. Babamento has fairly extensive experience in economic management at both the plant and regional levels. A former minister of deliveries, prosecutor general, and director of the State Inspectorate, Goga has been charged with the task of effecting economies and efficiencies in all state operations through a tight-fisted control of expenditures (*Rruga e partisë*, October).

Economic Developments. It was estimated that by the end of 1974, the fourth year of the current five-year plan, industrial production would be 44 percent greater and agricultural output 26 percent higher than in 1970 (*Zëri i popullit*, 30 October). Although the pace of industrial growth has slackened during the 1971-75 plan period, it appears that this sector will probably achieve its projected 61-65 percent production increase. There is, however, little likelihood that the planned 65-69 percent rise in agricultural output can be realized.

In 1974 laborers comprised 34 percent, white-collar workers 13 percent, and farmers 53 percent of the working population. Of the laborers, 55 percent were skilled workers; 50 percent worked in non-mechanized operations; 75 percent worked under production norms; and 35 percent worked under technical norms (*Rruga e partisë*, July, August). The membership of the United Trade Unions of Albania in 1974 was reportedly "in excess of 400,000" (*Zëri i popullit*, 4 May).

The Albanian economy continues to be plagued with a variety of problems. As a consequence of the shortfall in agricultural production, the PRA in 1974 imported "approximately 20 per cent" of the food and animal products required for the consumer trade and the raw material needs of the Ministry of Light and Food Industry. Despite the steady rise in the cost of these items, "in order not to erode the standard of living of the Albanian people" the regime did not increase retail prices. (*Rruga e partisë*, February, September.) It thus appeared that the slowdown in Albania's overall economic growth rate was in part attributable to the diversion of investment funds to cover the rising costs of food and commodity imports.

Other major concerns of Albania's leaders were the waste and inefficient use of the nation's economic resources, and the low level of labor discipline. During 1974 the regime initiated a campaign to eliminate the "abuse and destruction of socialist property." This effort was designed to cut down on the theft, neglect, and deliberate destruction of tools, machines, and vehicles as well as other equipment and material owned by the state (ibid., July). The government also launched a drive to effect "strict economies" in every sphere of activity by carefully screening all requests for labor, capital, and other resources (*Probleme ekonomike*, January-February). It appeared as if some progress had been made toward reducing unauthorized worker absences when it was announced that unexcused on-the-job absences for the first half of 1974 were 50 percent less than for the similar period in 1973 (*Rruga e partisë*, August).

During the current five-year plan, the APL leadership has striven to improve the quality of industrial production for both the foreign and the domestic market. There are indications, however, that the Albanian public has become increasingly impatient with both the shortages and the poor quality of consumer goods. In addition to its efforts to make more and better quality goods available, the regime has sought to stem rising mass economic expectations by publicizing widely what has been termed "the deepening crisis of the capitalist system." Albanian commentators have been harshly critical of what they have branded as the "twin myths" of the "post-industrial" and "consumer" societies (e.g., *Bashkimi*, 25 September; *Zëri i popullit*, 14 August, 12 December). They have also noted that in contrast to the "runaway" inflation which the capitalist and "revisionist" countries have experienced in recent years, retail prices in the PRA had on the average declined by 8 percent between 1960 and 1973 (*Probleme ekonomike*, March-April).

On 11 January the final section of the Elbasan-Prrenjas railroad (48 km.), constructed largely by "volunteer" labor, was completed, and in March work on the Fier-Ballsh line (about 20 km.) was begun (*Zëri i popullit*, 12 January, 12 March). After some initial difficulties satisfactory progress is being made on the nation's three major construction projects—the Fierza hydropower station, the Elbasan metallurgical complex, and the Ballsh oil refinery (ibid., 25 July, 1 December). It was also reported that the production of spare parts for industrial and agricultural machinery had increased by 74 percent between 1971 and 1974 (ibid., 13 December).

Foreign Relations. During 1974 Albania established diplomatic relations with Lebanon, Dahomey, Mexico, Guinea-Bissau, and Gabon, and at year's end had diplomatic ties with 69 countries. The PRA and Mexico seemed especially anxious to cement their relationship. A cabinet-level Mexican delegation visited Albania on 18-20 November (*Zëri i popullit*, 19, 21 November), and Mexico was represented by its minister of communications at the 30th-anniversary celebration of Albania's liberation from Axis occupation (ibid., 29 November). Mexico and Algeria were the only non-communist states officially represented on this occasion.

On 3 October, Hoxha delivered a major foreign policy address (ibid., 4 October) in which he reaffirmed and defended Albania's international positions. The Albanian leader stressed that the PRA was determined to chart its own international course, and declared that it would never be intimidated by the policies and attitudes of the two "superpowers," whose "collaboration," in his view, posed the greatest present-day threat to world peace. Hoxha claimed that contrary to the "lies" spread by the "Soviets, Americans, and other enemies of Albania," the PRA was not isolated from the rest of the world and would continue to expand its international contacts. On the other hand, he stated that the Albanians would continue to be selective in admitting foreigners to their country. The APL leader emphasized that Albania would remain closed to foreigners who might "corrupt" the Albanian people or engage in subversive activities. He left no doubt that the Sino-Albanian ideological and economic alliance remained the "cornerstone" of the PRA's foreign policy, and ruled out any reconciliation with the Soviet Union so long as he remained in power.

There were no significant shifts in attitudes regarding such matters as the SALT negotiations, the European Security Conference, or the Middle Eastern, Vietnamese, and Chilean situations. The PRA was especially distressed by the Cyprus conflict, which was attributed to Soviet-American "machinations," and urged the nations of the eastern Mediterranean region to act in concert to prevent the "superpowers" from imposing their will on Cyprus (ibid., 24 July). Albania also strongly supported the efforts of the "developing nations" to break the "stranglehold" of the great powers on the U.N. General Assembly and on the operations of the world organization itself (ibid., 12 December).

Albanian-Chinese Relations. The Sino-Albanian relationship seemed to be firmer during 1974 than at any time since the phasing-out of China's Great Proletarian Cultural Revolution in 1969. It would appear that the APL leadership had received sufficiently convincing assurances of continued Chinese economic, diplomatic, and ideological support to cause it to reaffirm the primacy of its ties with Peking and perhaps to act against those within Albania who might have questioned the wisdom of this course.

Hoxha indicated the importance he attached to Albania's relationship with China by attending the Chinese Embassy reception in honor of the 25th anniversary of the founding of the People's Republic of China (PRC) (ibid., 1 October). Albanian commentaries regarding the PRA's ties with China were lavish in their praise of the Chinese leadership and effusive in their thanks for the economic and technical assistance rendered by the PRC (e.g., ibid., 29 September, 4 October, 5 November). Furthermore, the APL leadership underscored its determination to persevere in its pro-Peking line by declaring that it would not be moved from this position by "counter-revolutionary tempests from whatever quarter they might come, be it from within as a consequence of the class struggle, or from abroad as a consequence of the pressures, blackmail, and intrigues of the imperialists, revisionists, and other reactionaries" (ibid., 23 November).

The PRC also seems to have made an effort to reassure the Albanians of the importance it attaches to the ties with the PRA. Mindful, perhaps, of the conjecture regarding the state of Sino-Albanian relations that their failure to send a representative to the Sixth Congress of the APL in

1971 had inspired, the Chinese dispatched a delegation headed by Politburo member Yao Wen-yuan and candidate member Wu Kuei-hsien to participate in the ceremonies marking the 30th anniversary of Albania's liberation (ibid., 28 November). Mao Tse-tung, Chou En-lai, Tung Pi-wu, and Chu Teh all signed the warm congratulatory message sent to the Albanians on this occasion. The Chinese leaders endorsed the policies of the APL, expressed their confidence in Hoxha, and acclaimed the Albanians "for their resolute struggle against the aggressive, hegemonistic policies of the United States of America and the Soviet Union, and especially for the manner in which they are waging a life-and-death struggle against modern Soviet revisionism." They concluded by reaffirming the "deep revolutionary friendship" and "warlike unity" of the Albanian and Chinese parties, nations, and peoples (ibid., 30 November).

Sino-Albanian cultural exchanges continued to increase during 1974. It also appeared that the Chinese were fulfilling their economic commitments to the Albanians. On 29 November weekly air service between Peking and Tirana via Teheran and Bucharest was inaugurated in accordance with the March 1972 Sino-Albanian civil aviation agreement (ibid.).

Albanian-Soviet Relations. In January the Soviet Union issued another call for the normalization of Soviet-Albanian relations (*Novoe Vremia*, Moscow, 18 January), which the Albanians routinely rejected (e.g., *Zëri i popullit*, 19 March). In its broadcasts to Albania, Radio Moscow (e.g., 2 April) continued to charge that the Sino-Albanian alliance was not in the best interests of the Albanian people and to recount the many benefits that had allegedly accrued to Albania when the country was a part of the Soviet camp. Moscow's propaganda campaign, the Soviet naval build-up in the Mediterranean, and a heightening concern about Soviet intentions in the Balkans following the eventual death of Tito—coupled, perhaps, with a conviction that the Chinese would not come to the aid of Albania in the event of an invasion by the Soviets—appear to have caused some Albanians to favor a rapprochement with the U.S.S.R. The length and tone of Hoxha's discussion of Soviet-Albanian relations in his 3 October speech suggest that this portion of his remarks was directed more to the domestic advocates of détente with Moscow than for foreign consumption.

In his address Hoxha unequivocally rejected all Soviet offers of friendship and made it clear he would not be intimidated by Soviet threats or displays of power when he declared:

> We tell these enemies of socialism and Leninism, these avowed enemies of our people and of the Albanian Party of Labor, that we will never become reconciled with them. We will never be their friends. We will always be their enemies. They should also not think this is merely the opinion of some Albanian leaders who are alive today, but will be gone tomorrow. . . . Neither your cannons, nor your missiles, nor your airplanes, nor your atomic bombs will make us change our stand either today or tomorrow.

Albanian Relations with Eastern Europe and Greece. There were no significant changes in Albania's relations with the pro-Soviet East European communist states. The PRA's ties with her neighbors, Yugoslavia and Greece, in 1974 could be best characterized as "correct," but not cordial.

Albania and Romania continued their modest cultural exchange programs, and in September the two countries signed a civil aviation agreement (ATA, 11 September). Romania was the only East European party state to send a delegation to the PRA for the 30th anniversary of Albania's liberation. Albania's relations with Poland and Bulgaria continued to be especially strained. An Albanian commentary characterized Poland's growing economic ties with the United States and Western Europe as an attempt on the part of a "degenerate, anti-popular regime to save itself" (*Zëri i popullit*, 12 October). The Bulgarian leaders were accused of turning their country into a "Soviet colony and military base," and the Bulgarian people were warned that they would be nothing more than "Soviet cannon fodder" in any war that might break out in the Balkans (ibid., 4 October).

In his 3 October speech Hoxha invited Yugoslavia and Greece to join Albania in resisting any act of aggression that might be directed against one or more of these Balkan states. He also pledged that

Albania would not permit the establishment of foreign military bases on its soil nor allow foreign warships to anchor in its territorial waters, and called on Albania's neighbors to do likewise. The Yugoslav foreign minister, Miloš Minić, responded by expressing Belgrade's desire to cooperate with the PRA "in all areas where objective and real possibilities exist" (TANJUG, Belgrade , 12 November). Greece, which was experiencing a political transformation during the autumn of 1974, did not respond publicly to the Albanian overture.

Albanian Relations with Western Europe and the United States. Although the Albanians widely publicized the economic and social problems confronting the Western European nations in 1974, they nevertheless sought to expand their economic and cultural ties with these countries—especially with France and the Scandinavian states. The PRA, however, indicated it would not even consider normalizing relations with Great Britain until the British government agreed to return the Albanian gold it received in compensation for the destruction of several warships in the 1946 Corfu Channel incident. An apparently non-negotiable precondition for the establishment of Albanian-West German relations was a German reparations payment of "several billion marks" for damages caused to Albanian life and property during the German occupation of the country during World War II (*Zëri i popullit*, 4 October). Although the Albanians strongly protested the explosion of a bomb on the grounds of their Rome Embassy "by fascist elements," the PRA did not sever relations with Italy (ibid., 22 May).

In his 3 October speech, Hoxha shot down what he termed recent U.S. "trial balloons" for the restoration of U.S.-Albanian diplomatic ties. While Hoxha was clearly opposed to the normalization of relations between the two countries at this time, he did not rule out the possibility he might change his position on this matter sometime in the future. The PRA did not expect any changes in U.S. foreign policy following the elevation of Gerald Ford to the presidency, since Ford was "a loyal follower of the imperialist policy of oppression and expansion" (ibid., 15 August).

International Communist Contacts. Albania during 1974 increased its contacts with the "Marxist-Leninist" parties and "revolutionary forces" in all parts of the world. The PRA also gave wide publicity to the views and activities of these organizations both on Tirana radio and in the press (e.g., ATA, 10 August).

The APL's current position within the world communist movement was reflected by the foreign representation at the celebration commemorating Albania's World War II liberation. A total of 27 communist parties or Marxist-Leninist organizations sent delegations to Albania on this occasion and another six dispatched messages of greeting and support to the APL. Only four ruling parties—the Chinese, North Vietnamese, North Korean, and Romanian—were represented, but Marxist-Leninist parties or revolutionary groups from the following countries also sent delegates: Brazil, Italy, Poland (Albania-based Communist Party of Poland), France, New Zealand, Bolivia, German Federal Republic, Australia, Indonesia, Ecuador, Great Britain, Spain, Argentina, Japan, Chile, Sweden, Belgium, Colombia, Norway, Uruguay, Austria, Switzerland, and Holland. Messages were received from the Marxist-Leninist parties of Burma, Finland, Malaya, Thailand, and San Marino and from the Lao Patriotic Front. (*Zëri i popullit*, 28 November-10 December.)

A delegation of the Royal Government of Cambodian National Unity headed by Khieu Samphan, deputy prime minister and defense minister, visited Albania on 20-26 April (ATA, 26 April). Between 16 and 20 September a South Vietnamese delegation led by Nguyen Huu Tho, chairman of the Presidium of the Central Committee of the National Front for the Liberation of South Vietnam and of the Advisory Council of the Provisional Revolutionary Government of the Republic of South Vietnam, toured the PRA (ibid., 22 September).

Publications. The APL daily newspaper (with a claimed average circulation of 101,000) is *Zëri i popullit*. The party's monthly theoretical journal is *Rruga e partisë*. Another major publication is *Bashkimi*, the daily organ of the Democratic Front (claimed average circulation, 30,000). The newspapers of the Union of Albanian Labor Youth, *Zëri i rinisë*, and the United Trade Unions of Albania, *Puna*, are published twice weekly.

Western Illinois University   Nicholas C. Pano

Bulgaria

The Bulgarian Communist Party (Bulgarska Kommunisticheska Partiya; BCP) traces its beginning back to 1891, when the social democratic movement originated. In 1903, it split into "narrow" and "broad" groups which differed in their interpretation of Marxism. The former advocated communist policies based on an industrialized economy, whereas the latter considered that the primarily agrarian economy would not support a classical Marxist approach. The Bulgarian Workers' (Communist) Party came to power after World War Two through the coalition Fatherland Front as a result of Red Army occupation. Stalinization probably took hold more aggressively in Bulgaria than in any other East European country. Todor Zhivkov has been BCP first secretary during the past two decades.

Party-Government Interlocking Directorate. In addition to being Party leader, Zhivkov is chairman of the State Council or titular chief of state. Most other members (12) and candidates (6) for membership on the top policy-making organ or Political Bureau also hold government positions. At a Central Committee plenum on 3 July, the youngest candidate members (Ivan Abadzhiev, Venelin Kotsev, Kostadin Gyaurov) were dropped from the Politburo. They also lost their positions as secretary of the Central Committee, deputy premier, and Central Council of Trade Unions' chairman, respectively.

Two new members and four candidates for membership were added to the Politburo by the same plenum. The full members are also secretaries of the Central Committee: Grisha Filipov (born 1919) is a leading economist, and Alexander Lilov (b. 1933) has been chief ideologist for several years. The four new Politburo candidates are defense minister Dobri Dzhurov (b. 1916), foreign minister Petar Mladenov (b. 1936) and the first secretaries of the two most important district Party committees, Drazha Valcheva (b. 1930) and Todor Stoychev (b. 1920). The counterparts to Dzhurov and Mladenov had been elevated to full membership on the CPSU Politburo in April 1973, namely A. A. Grechko and A. A. Gromyko.

Personnel changes also occurred during the end of October, at which time the National Assembly transferred Politburo member Ivan Popov from deputy premier to deputy chairman of the State Council. In addition, Politburo member Pencho Kubadinski was elected chairman of the Fatherland Front's national council on 20 November. At year's end, the interlocking directorate looked as shown on the table.

PARTY-GOVERNMENT ELITE

Politburo members (12)	Other positions held
1. Zhivkov, Todor	BCP First secretary; chmn., State Council
2. Dragoycheva, Tsola	Chmn., Natl. Comm. for Soviet Friendship
3. Filipov, Grisha	BCP secretary (economy)
4. Kubadinski, Pencho	Dpty. premier; chmn., Fatherland Front
5. Lilov, Alexander	BCP secretary (ideology)
6. Mihailov, Ivan	Army general (civil defense chief)
7. Pavlov, Todor	Hon. chmn., Academy of Sciences
8. Popov, Ivan	Dpty. chmn., State Council
9. Todorov, Stanko	Premier
10. Tsolov, Tano	1st dpty. premier
11. Velchev, Boris	BCP secretary (cádres)
12. Zhivkov, Zhivko	Dpty. premier

Politburo Candidates (6)

Dzhurov, Dobri	Defense minister
Mladenov, Petar	Foreign minister
Stoychev, Todor	BCP 1st secr., Varna district
Takov, Peko	Dpty. chmn., State Council
Trichkov, Krastyu	1st dpty. chmn., State Council
Valcheva, Drazha	BCP 1st secr., Plovdiv district

Central Committee Secretariat
(in addition to 1, 3, 5, 11 among Politburo members)

Secretaries	Members
Kiratsov, Penyu	Bokov, Georgi
Pramov, Ivan	Bonev, Vladimir
Tellalov, Konstantin	Dalbokov, Sava
	Yordanov, Georgi

It is difficult to interpret the foregoing changes in the top BCP leadership. Performance could have been the criterion applied in at least two cases. Gyaurov had been responsible for trade unions and may have been made the scapegoat connected with difficulties in organizing socialist competition. Kotsev had been in charge of raising the standard of living, a difficult proposition under any circumstances. It is Abadzhiev's removal that remains most intriguing. He had been responsible for science and higher education. Considered a likely successor to the Party leader, Abadzhiev may have been removed as a prophylactic measure by Todor Zhivkov. All three of those ousted received ambassadorships in August.

Party Activities. A plenary session of the BCP Central Committee took place on 7-8 February. Alexander Lilov, secretary for ideology, presented the main report which emphasized the uncompromising struggle against deformation of Marxism-Leninism and distortions about the communist-ruled states, especially emanating from Peking. He also called for strengthening ideological cohesion of the East European countries around the CPSU and the USSR, noting that peaceful coexistence does not and cannot be applied to ideology. The plenum adopted a resolution along these lines, calling for improvement of patriotic and internationalist education. A new Central Committee department for mass information media will supervise all government activities in this field.

The first national BCP conference in 24 years convened on 20 March in Sofia. Only one item appeared on the agenda, "Toward high social labor productivity," rather than the anticipated review of decisions implemented since the 10th Party congress in April 1971. Zhivkov admitted in his speech that sufficient achievements had not been made. He identified labor productivity as the key to victory over capitalism, apart from helping to attain a positive balance in foreign trade. Manpower shortages and incomplete utilization of production capacity were mentioned. A joint Party-government document in May enumerated both "spiritual" and non-material incentives for greater productivity. The preceding month, new regulations had appeared which allow more flexibility in economic organizations.

The 30th anniversary of the *coup* which brought the BCP to power was celebrated on 9 September. Nikolai Podgorny, chairman of the USSR Supreme Soviet's presidium, came to Sofia for the festivities. More than 30 new construction projects were inaugurated, including a pipeline that will supply Bulgaria with five billion cubic meters of Soviet natural gas during 1975 and a nuclear power station. In his address, Zhivkov complained about lagging construction. A few days later, the Central Committee secretariat and the government issued a joint declaration which urged completion of all unfinished projects before the end of 1974.

In a speech to the Young Communist League or Komsomol during the same 30th anniversary celebrations, Zhivkov castigated young people who refuse to work and those under foreign influence. The Central Committee secretariat had issued a resolution in mid-August on alienation of youth. It is hoped that educational reform will combat these negative tendencies. By merging two types of secondary schools, all students will be exposed to a new curriculum that links education with productive labor.

Toward year's end, a Central Committee plenum convened to discuss the brigade cost accounting method inaugurated by Soviet construction worker Nikolai Zlobin. A number of measures were agreed upon to propagandize and implement this technique which "will contribute to improving construction work in the country" (Sofia radio, 9 December). The Zlobin method is being used in the USSR, East Germany, and other unidentified countries of the Soviet bloc.

No figures on BCP membership have appeared since the 10th Party congress, when the total was just under 700,000 or about 11 percent of the adult population (*World Strength of the Communist Party Organizations*, 1974, pp. 49-50). This would seem to indicate that only a light increase, if any, has occurred over the past three years. The same is probably true of the Komsomol which had about 1,161,000 members last year (*YICA* 1974, p. 11). More than 70 percent of those eligible reportedly belong to this official youth organization (G. A. Chernenko, ed., *Narodnaya Respublika Bolgariya*, 1974, p. 67). Alienation of youth was the topic of a BCP secretariat resolution in mid-August, as mentioned in the foregoing.

Domestic Affairs. Election to people's councils for all administrative levels on 13 January resulted in 52,429 deputies being chosen. Members of the BCP comprise 51.3 percent; Bulgarian National Agrarian Union, 18.9 percent; and Komsomol, 16.5 percent. Other statistics released on social composition indicate that 25.8 percent of the deputies are industrial laborers and 23.4 percent work in agriculture. Over one-fourth of the total is under 30 years old, and 36.4 percent are women (*Otechestven Front*, 16 January).

Abandonment of the promised five-day work week indicated shortcomings throughout the economy. The State Council issued a document which sharply criticized violation of rules and established disciplinary measures. This was followed in May by a joint Party-government directive on utilization of incentives for greater productivity in all fields. The preceding month, new regulations appeared which allow state economic organizations greater flexibility.

The Council of Ministers issued a decree in July on cutting the bureaucracy by reducing managerial and administrative personnel. A second decree dealt with measures to combat the loss of labor time and to make hours at work more productive. The BCP Central Committee itself demanded that economic agencies place limits on their use of raw materials, fuel, and electricity. The gravity of the situation received extensive publicity, following a joint session on 20 September of the BCP secretariat and Council of Ministers. That same day, a national conference on the economy was held also in Sofia.

The secretariat resolution to transform construction "into a cause for the whole nation" and to fulfill the program for commissioning construction projects in 1974 and 1975 appeared in print two days later (*Rabotnichesko Delo*). This resolution centers on mobilizing white-collar employees. Still in effect is a 1973 decree allowing 45 days per year of leave with pay plus additional compensation for the manual labor undertaken on a voluntary basis. The plan calls for 1,700 production enterprises and 1,800 houses to be built during 1975. The Committee for State Control will systematically check and take action in cases where goals are not achieved. Among the first to be penalized were BCP functionaries in Gabrovo district (*Balkansko Zname*, 22 October) and heads of industries (Sofia radio, 14 November). Also related to the foregoing is the reform, currently being implemented and aimed at compulsory secondary education by 1980. The other objective involves a merger between general educational and vocational schools, to culminate in a unified polytechnic school. A new curriculum includes a subject, called "Knowledge of the Fatherland," and compulsory study of Russian from the third instead of the fifth grade as heretofore. The secondary polytechnics will link the educational process with productive and socially useful labor.

Finally, the 12th session of the National Assembly (29-31 October) adopted the 1975 economic plan and budget as well as a new penal code and a law on amnesty. The last item is offered to all Bulgarian citizens who fled the country illegally and those who did not return from trips abroad. The amnesty expires on 31 December 1975. It excludes those who left the country as "traitors," lost their Bulgarian citizenship, or are considered "dangerous recidivists." Interior minister Dimitar Stoyanov told a Sofia daily newspaper that 70 percent of the escapees were young adventurers, influenced by bourgeois ideology (*Zemedelsko Zname*, 1 November).

Foreign Affairs and Party Contacts. Relations with the Federal Republic of Germany (FRG) continued to improve since the December 1973 agreement to exchange diplomats. A Bulgarian representative at Bonn was designated the end of February, and FRG foreign minister Walter Scheel spent 25-26 March in Sofia. Discussions concerned economic, scientific-technological, and cultural contacts.

Bulgaria also stepped up its activities in the Middle East and Africa, with a visit to Iraq in early April by Party leader Zhivkov who played host to Egypt's president Anwar al-Sadat at the end of June in Sofia. Syria's president Hafiz al-Asad came to Bulgaria in September. Numerous bilateral agreements have been signed with these and other Arab governments. Zhivkov also visited Iran where he held talks with Shah Mohammad Reza Pahlavi on relations between the two countries, according to Sofia radio, 22 November. Samora Machel, president of the front for liberation of Mozambique, signed a 1975-76 cooperation agreement with the BCP after a six-day visit (ibid., 15 December).

Contacts with the United States involved more activity, especially after ratification of the consular convention (*Darzhaven Vestnik*, 9 July) and establishment that same month of a government committee on Foreign Economic Relations. Bulgaria stopped jamming "Voice of America" broadcasts on 12 September, the last Bloc country to do so. Visits during the year included officials of Kaiser Steel, Exxon, and the Food Machinery Corporation which indicated a Bulgarian desire for

American technology in these fields. Regulations for cooperation with foreign corporations were enumerated in a decree on new production facilities, scientific research, joint manufacturing, building of complete projects in Bulgaria, and joint enterprises outside the country (ibid., 20 September).

Deputy premier Ivan Popov visited the United States from 22 September through 4 October, at the invitation of commerce secretary Frederick Dent. The only agreement, one to establish a joint economic council, was signed by the respective Chambers of Commerce during his stay, having been initiated as far back as 20 November 1973. Apart from Dent, Popov also conferred with deputy secretary of state Robert Ingersoll, treasury secretary William Simon, agriculture secretary Earl Butz, and Council of Economic Advisers' chairman Alan Greenspan. Toward year's end, President Gerald Ford replied to Zhivkov's message on relations between the two countries (Sofia radio, 23 December).

Inside of Eastern Europe, contacts with Yugoslavia improved after an initial setback. The report by secretary Lilov to the Central Committee plenum on ideology in February had raised the question of improving "patriotic" education for various minorities, without mentioning Macedonians among those he listed. Belgrade commentaries noted the omission which implied that all Macedonians, even those inside Yugoslavia, were considered Bulgarians by Sofia. During an exchange at the U.N. conference on ethnic minorities, the Yugoslav representative charged Bulgaria with refusing full rights to its Macedonian minority.

However by mid-November relations had warmed to the extent that defense minister Dobri Dzhurov arrived in Belgrade with a military delegation, the first such visit in more than eight years. A month later, a BCP study group arrived in Yugoslavia to observe the activity and attitudes of the LCY in the development of domestic commerce and tourism over an eight-day period. The delegation was received by LCY Executive Committee member, Munir Mesihović (Belgrade radio, 18 December).

On an intra-Bloc level, Bulgaria hosted the 28th Council for Mutual Economic Assistance session during 18-21 June. The organization agreed to construct a high-tension powerline, a gas pipeline, from Orenburg to the Soviet western border, and accelerate the East European nuclear energy program. It also decided to speed up coordination of the 1976-1980 economic plan and adopted standards for certain commodities. On the military side, no hard evidence exists to substantiate the rumor that the U.S.S.R. had demanded an extra-territorial corridor across Romania which could have linked the Ukraine with Bulgaria. The latter certainly would not object to such a development, if one reads between the lines of an article by the first deputy defense minister Atanas Semerdzhiev in *Armeyski Komunist* for September, pp. 12-21.

Other manifestations of friendship for the Soviet Union occurred when Zhivkov flew to Moscow and decorated L. I. Brezhnev plus 12 other dignitaries with a jubilee medal commemorating the 30 years of socialist revolution in Bulgaria. (*Rabotnichesko Delo*, 17 October.) CPSU politburo member and KGB chief, Y. V. Andropov, spent three days in Sofia where he was received by Party leader Zhivkov and internal affairs minister Stoyanov (Moscow radio, 16 November).

Nor did the Bulgarians neglect their ally Mongolia which was visited by foreign affairs minister Petar Mladenov. A joint communique expressed full agreement with all Soviet positions (*Rabotnichesko Delo*, 25 October). Poland's premier Piotr Jaroszewicz paid an official visit to his counterpart and the result was a similar communique (ibid., 7 December). Finally, the Bulgarian foreign minister traveled to Hungary, where he exchanged views on cooperation between the two countries. That same day, and in the same city, BCP secretary Konstantin Tellalov addressed participants at a meeting preparatory to the 1975 conference of European communist and workers' parties. He acclaimed the role "above all of the U.S.S.R., the CPSU and Leonid Ilyich Brezhnev personally," as having been "extremely great in the positive changes that have taken place in international life." (Budapest radio, 20 December.)

Publications. The main daily newspaper of the BCP is *Rabotnichesko Delo* (Workers' Cause). The Party also publishes two monthly magazines: *Partien Zhivot* (Party Life), to disseminate information on organizational matters, and the theoretical journal *Novo Vreme* (New Times). Publications for youth include *Mladezh* (Youth) and *Narodna Mladezh* (People's Youth). The BCP Central Committee also prints the two more specialized biweeklies *Ikonomicheski Zhivot* (Economic Life) and *Politicheska Prosveta* (Political Education).

Hoover Institution   Richard F. Staar
Stanford University

Czechoslovakia

The Communist Party of Czechoslovakia (Komunistická strana Československa; KSČ) was constituted in 1921 by the members of the dissident group of "left Socialists" who had broken away from the core of the Czechoslovak Social Democratic Party, inspired by the example of the October 1917 Bolshevik Revolution in Russia. Unlike its counterparts in other Central and Eastern European countries, the KSČ did not come to power gradually but through a coup d'état, effected in February 1948, which put an end to a multi-party system of relatively long standing. Three other parties still exist in form in Czechoslavakia, as part of the National Front of Working People, but the communist party maintains an absolute majority in this formalized coalition, a majority which is guaranteed by its statute. The president of the republic, Ludvík Svoboda, and the premier of the federal government, Lubomír Štrougal, are both members of the KSČ.

In October 1968, the constitution of 1960, second since the communist take-over in 1948, was amended to the effect of transforming Czechoslovakia into a federation composed of two states: the Czech Socialist Republic and the Slovak Socialist Republic. This constitutional reform is the only remnant of an ambitious political program introduced by party first secretary Alexander Dubček in 1968, but prevented from implementation by the Soviet-led military intervention in August of the same year. The federalization of Czechoslovakia left the KSČ unaffected: there is an autonomous party organization for Slovakia (Komunistická strana Slovenska; KSS) but it has no counterpart in the Czech Socialist Republic. This contradiction between the constitution and the structure of the party engenders a paradox of a federal polity ruled by a centralist party.

The size of the membership of the KSČ, which had remained relatively constant since the wave of resignations following the military intervention in 1968 and the great purge of 1970, began to increase again during 1973 and 1974. Between the congress in 1971, when the total number of party cardholders was about 1.25 million, and early 1974, some 124,000 new candidates were admitted. Among them, the young age classes up to 35 years constituted an overwhelming majority of almost 90 percent. Blue-collar workers accounted for 59 percent of this new addition to the party (*Rudé právo*, 26 January; *Pravda*, Bratislava, 25 July). Czechoslovakia has a population of 14,480,000 (estimated 1972).

Organization and Leadership. The two supreme policy-making and executive bodies of the KSČ are the Central Committee and the Presidium. The last party congress took place in 1971, actually fifteenth in succession but officially considered to be the fourteenth, since the emergency congress, which met on the initiative of the Dubček leadership in August 1968, is not recognized as legitimate by the present group in power. The next congress is scheduled for 1976.

There were no changes in the membership of the Presidium during 1974. The Presidium includes

11 full members and 2 candidates. The Secretariat, at present in the hands of the secretary-general Gustav Husák, is composed of 7 secretaries and 2 Secretariat members. The secretary-general of the KSS is Jozef Lenárt. (For names of other officials see *YICA, 1972*, p. 21.) Today's leadership was brought into power under Soviet pressure in April 1969 and has since then pursued the policy of unreserved obedience to the Soviet Union which Czechoslovakia had known during the era before 1968.

Party Internal Affairs. The Central Committee met in a plenary session on 14-15 May 1974 to discuss and to lay down policies in the realm of science and technology. Particular attention was paid at this meeting to the relation between the actual levels of science, technology, and production, where serious gaps were found. No less concern was shown for the present state of social sciences. Here it was not so much a possible lack of progress of scholarship that was criticized by the party supreme organ, but rather the unsatisfactory degree of ideological commitment, as an extensive document, later released by the party Presidium, seemed to indicate (*Rudé právo*, 20 June). A considerable stir among the party ranks and in the Czechoslovak public at large was caused by the publication on 14 March, in the Italian communist party review *Vie Nuove*, of the letter which the former first secretary of the KSČ, Alexander Dubček, sent to the widow of Josef Smrkovský, another prominent figure of the 1968 Prague Spring, at the occasion of the latter's death. In this letter, Dubček defended the policies pursued during his tenure of the party's most important office, and accused the present secretary-general of having lost for the KSČ the confidence of the masses. On the whole, the process of the legitimation in the eyes of the rank-and-file membership of the course imposed by the Soviets did not seem to make much headway during 1974. Repeated complaints about the shortcomings in the party's ideological work among the grass-roots organizations testified to the awareness of the leadership of this situation (*Život strany*, 4 February; *Pravda*, 13 September). Another serious internal problem of the KSČ appears to be that of assuring consensus among the various shades of the ruling pro-Soviet faction on the continuity of the present line. This problem loomed large in the late spring, when the critical illness of president of the republic and Presidium member Ludvík Svoboda suggested the need to consider important changes in the incumbency of the most crucial party functions.

Domestic Affairs. An event of great symbolic significance in 1974 was the celebration of the 30th anniversary of the Slovak national uprising. This heroic episode of the World War II had provided the communist movement in Slovakia with a unique historical opportunity, but at the same time left the KSČ with a host of deep cleavages that have lasted up to the present day—above all, strong antagonism between the Czech and the Slovak components of the party. Despite this fact, or perhaps because of it, the stress in official statements and media comments concerning the anniversary was put on proletarian internationalism, that is, on the subordination of national and local interests to the interests of the Soviet Union as the true legacy of the 1944 events. (*Pravda*, 26 August: *Rudé právo*, 27 August.)

The legitimacy ambiguities about Husák's political course were also reflected in the general domestic situation. Most of the persons convicted in 1972 for having publicly denounced the Soviet invasion and the subservient policies of the present regime were released by early 1974 (*NYT*, 4 January). Nevertheless, dissident voices have not been completely silenced, nor did repressive actions against nonconformists come to an end. Clandestine publications continued to circulate in the country. Following the Soviet example, Czechoslovak authorities in several cases resorted to the expatriation of the most obstinate opponents (*Neue Zürcher Zeitung*, 30 July). It was probably in view of these circumstances that the powers of the police were increased by legislative action. Among other provisions, the new bill enhances the position of the State Security, a secret police force for repressing political offenses whose influence and scope of action had been severely curtailed during the liberalization period of 1968 (*Tvorba*, 1 May).

Mass Organizations. The continuing lack of clarity of the political course within the party manifested itself also in the relation to mass organizations. There was a discontent on the part of the leadership with the work of the Revolutionary Trade Union Movement (*Práce*, 16 October), where indifference appeared to prevail, obviously due to the fact that the unions, after a short period of independence and acting as genuine protectors of the workers' rights, had to return to the Soviet-designed role of government-steered agencies promoting the increase of labor productivity and unpaid work. The central sports and para-military organization Svazarm held a two-day Central Committee meeting early in the year (ČETEKA, 7 February). In April, a new mass organization, the Czechoslovak Union of Women, was constituted in Prague (*Rudé právo*, 20 April).

Culture, Education and Youth. Culture remained, also in 1974, among the domains of social activities which the party leaders viewed with a good deal of apprehension. In spite of a thorough reorganization of various national unions of artists and intellectuals, the party media kept on complaining about the lack of zeal among the cultural community for works which would be more "ideologically committed," that is, would propagate the current political orientation (*Film a divadlo*, no. 7, April; *Rudé právo*, 2 May). The general mistrust toward the learned strata of the society, which found a particularly sharp form of expression in the criticism of the state of social sciences, might have been also among the motives for the contemplated closing down of the "University of 17 November," an institution of higher education reserved for students from developing countries (Reuter, 4 March), where many an intellectual supporter of the Prague Spring of 1968 had found a refuge among the faculty. However, not only the academic population was found wanting by the Husák leadership: Czech and Slovak youth in general failed to satisfy the official expectations. It was blamed for being "pacifist," "overly consumerist," and in general prone to "petty-bourgeois mentality" (Radio Hvězda, 13 July). The complaints did not stop after the national youth body, the Socialist Youth Union, elected a new chairman (*Smena*, 6 April). Party officials also continued to consider religion as a serious rival in the struggle for influence over the young generation (*Život strany*, 24 June). Antireligious campaigns, resumed in the wake of the "normalization" after the Soviet-led invasion, were continued (*Učitelské noviny*, 29 August). The anti-religious stance made difficult the talks that were conducted with the Vatican about several issues, among them the problem of filling in the vacant seat of the primate of Czechoslovakia, after the death of its last incumbent, Cardinal Štěpán Trochta (ČETEKA, 6 April; Radio Prague, 23 September).

Economy. Although 1974 was a year of bumper harvest in Czechoslovakia, with yields per hectare about 10 percent higher than in 1973, and although industrial production during the first half of the year exceeded slightly the level fixed by the plan (*Rudé právo*, 25 July; Radio Prague, 23 September), the country's economy had to face a number of problems. Among these, the productivity of labor occupied an important place, its growth lagging behind that of nominal gross income (*Svět hospodářství*, 22 March). Shortage of manpower aggravated the situation (Radio Prague, 23 January), despite the fact that the number of employed women further increased (*Svět hospodářství*, 7 March). The consumer public voiced discontent about the quality of services (*Hospodářske noviny*, 8 February). These failures of economic performance threatened the implementation of one of the party's most ambitious economic goals: the passage from the labor-intensive stage of economic development to that of an automated, highly productive economy and mass consumption. The unusually high increase in bank deposits, on the other hand, was recognized as an indicator of the insufficiency of the supply of goods and services (*Tribuna*, 30 January). In addition to specific difficulties resulting from local conditions and its type of economic organization, Czechoslovakia in

1974 shared the general economic difficulties of the world, energy shortage and inflation. Czech and Slovak consumers experienced the consequences of the energy crisis in the form of a sharp increase in the prices of petrol, approximately 80 to 90 percent (*Rudé právo*, 30 March). At the same time, the allocation of oil-based fuels for domestic consumption was reduced and lower speed limits were introduced on the highways (Radio Prague, 29 March). The opening of the first section of the Prague subway, in May, several years behind the original schedule, was praised as a feat of Soviet and Czechoslovak technology (ČETEKA, 6 May).

Armed Forces. There were no large military exercises in Czechoslovakia during 1974, nor did Czechoslovak troops participate in maneuvres on the territory of other Warsaw Pact states. The Soviet garrisons in the country continued to be estimated at some 18,000 troops, stationed chiefly outside major industrial and administrative centers.

The most important events related to the Czechoslovak armed forces were the trips of defense minister Martin Dzúr to various socialist countries. In April, Dzúr visited Yugoslavia, and in May he went to Budapest, where he met his Hungarian colleague and commander in chief of the Warsaw Pact, Marshal Ivan Yakubovski (Radio Hvězda, 23 May). In June, Dzúr traveled to the Soviet Union, at the invitation of the defense minister Marshal Grechko. Later in the same month, Dzúr visited Romania as the guest of defense minister Ion Ionita (Radio Prague, 7 June; Radio Hvězda, 24 June).

Foreign Affairs. One of the highlights in the 1974 history of Czechoslovak foreign relations was the implementation of the agreement, reached in the previous year, with the Federal Republic of Germany (FRG) on establishing full diplomatic relations. In February, Jiří Goetz, career diplomat and former deputy foreign minister, was appointed ambassador to Bonn (Radio Prague, 19 February). The ratification documents of the Czechoslovak-West German treaty, however, were exchanged only later, since the clause about the nullity of the 1938 Munich pact "ab initio"—made a condition sine qua non by the Czechoslovak partners—delayed the passage of the treaty in the FRG parliament (Radio Hvězda, 15 July). Shortly after the ratification, discussions on cultural and scientific exchanges started between the two countries. Czechoslovak mass media gave a very reserved coverage to the resignation of the federal chancellor, Willy Brandt, mostly passing over in silence the fact that it was an East German spy who compromised Brandt's position and forced him out of office (*Rudé právo*, 9 May). The comments were less inhibited when dealing with the Watergate affair and Nixon's resignation, although it was claimed, to the very last, that the movement for the U.S. president's impeachment was serving the interests of the enemies of peaceful coexistence (*Pravda*, 10 August). This claim was consistent with the line along which the Czechoslovak press, radio, and television had reported earlier on the Nixon visit in Moscow (*Lidová demokracie*, 2 July). An event concerning both countries was the initialing in Prague of the document on the settlement of U.S. property claims against Czechoslovakia, the implementation of which would mean the return to Czechoslovakia of a gold deposit from the time of the Second World War (Radio Prague, 5 July).

The year also saw the adoption by the Czechoslovak Federal Assembly of a frontier agreement with Austria which is expected to reduce the risk of border incidents, quite frequent in the recent past (ČETEKA, 25 June). On the great issues of international politics, Czechoslovak official representatives and mass media faithfully followed the course set by the Soviet Union; so, for example, on the subject of European security and disarmament, currently under discussion at the Vienna and Geneva conferences (Czechoslovak television, 10 January; Radio Prague, 14 January), or on the problem of military disengagement in the Middle East (*Práca*, 31 May). Continuing denunciation of "Zionism" in the Czechoslovak press and radio was in harmony with this policy (Radio Prague, 21 March). The two major political upheavals that occurred in Europe in 1974—the fall of the rightist dictatorships in Portugal and in Greece—were equally noted in accordance with the overall Soviet bloc position, that is, hailed with some caution, in anticipation of further developments that might be more favorable to the cause of world communism (*Rudé právo*, 26 April; *Práce*, 2 October; Radio Prague, 24 July).

The calendar of official visits paid to Czechoslovakia and made by Czechoslovak personalities to other countries was quite busy in 1974. In April, Romanian foreign minister Gheorghe Macovescu arrived in Prague for an "official friendly call" (Radio Prague, 3 April). A month earlier, Bulgarian foreign minister Petar Mladenov was guest of the Czechoslovak government (*Rudé právo*, 8 March). In September, a delegation of the Provisional Revolutionary Government of South Vietnam was received in Prague at the invitation of the Czechoslovak National Front. A non-refund economic aid program for South Vietnam in 1975 was agreed upon on this occasion (ČETEKA, 15 September). At about the same time, Gustav Husák, as federal chairman of the National Front, paid an official visit to Finland, accompanied by the foreign minister Bohuslav Chňoupek and other cabinet members (ČETEKA, 19 September). At the end of the same month, a governmental delegation of the Czech Socialist Republic went to Hungary (*Népszabadság*, 29 September). The festivities on the occasion of the 25th anniversary of the foundation of the German Democratic Republic (GDR) were attended by a large delegation of the Czechoslovak National Front (Radio Prague, 5 October). During the last week of October, Yugoslav federal secretary of foreign affairs, Miloš Minić, spent three days in Prague on an official visit with his Czechoslovak counterpart (ibid., 23 October).

International Communist Movement. Although the present leaders of the KSČ have tried very hard to avoid Czechoslovakia's being a subject of controversy in the world communist movement, the issue of the justification of the Soviet intervention of 1968 and of the legitimacy of the actual party leadership remained very lively in various quarters all through 1974. In February, a four-day conference on the Czechoslovak events of 1968 was called at Bièvres near Paris and was attended by representatives of a number of West European dissident communist groups, mainly French and Italian (*Unir-Débat*, Paris, 15 February). The very critical attitude of these leftist intellectuals towards the Soviet policies in Czechoslovakia and the publicity which West European communist media gave to recent statements of prominent personalities of the Prague Spring, such as Alexander Dubček, may have been one of the reasons why the Institute of Marxism-Leninism of the KSČ organized a joint colloquium on revisionism with the Institute of Social Sciences of the East German party's Central Committee, in Prague in the autumn (*Rudé právo*, 25 September). These and other international scholarly and artistic events, such as the consultative conference of the journalist unions of socialist countries or the international symposium of socialist writers (ČETEKA, 15 February; *Rudé právo*, 9 March), were designed to improve the image of the Soviet-imposed regime in Czechoslovakia. For the rest, the KSČ leadership carefully followed the orthodox Soviet line in the international communist movement. Party Presidium member Vasil Bilák broke a lance, early in 1974, for the Soviet project, long tabled by the world communist public, of a European conference of the "fraternal" parties (Radio Prague, 6 June). A few days earlier, the KSČ central daily *Rudé právo* stated that the time was ripening for a still larger gathering, a world meeting comparable to that of 1957 and 1960 (*Rudé právo*, 31 May). When the European talks of the communist parties actually took place, later in the year, the Czechoslovak delegation fully supported the proposal for calling a world communist summit in the GDR in 1975 (*Rudé právo*, 22 October). It was obvious that the Czechoslovak leadership contemplated without alarm one of the most likely outcomes of such a parley: the showdown between the Soviet and the Chinese parties, which has made some communist organizations rather reluctant to support the summit idea. The further escalation of the anti-Chinese campaign indicated absolute identification of the positions of the Czechoslovak party with those of their Soviet comrades (*Tvorba*, 23 January). This alignment was also documented by the way Czechoslovak media covered the Tenth Congress of the League of Communists of Yugoslavia; the reportage was on the whole positive but it deliberately ignored serious differences in the views and policies of Yugoslavia and the Soviet Union (Czechoslovak television, 30 May).

Among the official contacts during 1974 between the KSČ leadership and other communist parties, two trips of the secretary-general of the KSČ, Gustav Husák, should be mentioned: in March, Husák with a delegation of the Central Committee visited Warsaw for four days (*Trybuna ludu*, 16 March). In August, Husák traveled to Simferopol in the Crimea where he met with Soviet party chief Brezhnev for talks on "further development and intensification of all-round cooperation between the two parties" (TASS, 2 August).

Publications. The daily organ of the KSČ is *Rudé právo*. The KSS publishes in Bratislava its own daily, *Pravda*. The weekly *Tribuna*, which played an important part in the process of "normalization" after 1968, has now taken the role of the theoretical party review which previously had been filled in by *Tvorba*, a weekly of long standing but focusing at present on questions of international politics and the world communist movement. The Slovak counterpart of *Tribuna* is *Predvoj*. Problems of party work and party organization are addressed by the fortnightly *Život strany*. The Czech trade unions have their daily organ, *Práce*, and the Slovak unions publish a Slovak variant, *Práca*. The Czechoslovak Socialist Youth Union issues the daily *Mladá fronta* in Czech and *Smena* in Slovak. ČETEKA, or CTA, is the Czechoslovak news agency.

University of Pittsburgh

Zdenek L. Suda

Germany: German Democratic Republic

Shortly after the end of hostilities of World War II and the establishment of the Allied military occupation zones, the Soviet Military Administration issued on 10 June 1945 Order No. 2 which permitted the founding of "anti-fascist" political parties in the Soviet Occupation Zone. On the following day, the Communist Party of Germany (Kommunistische Partei Deutschlands; KPD) was officially reactivated in Berlin, after existing underground throughout the Hitler period. The Social Democratic Party of Germany (Sozialdemokratische Partei Deutschlands; SPD) reemerged as a legal party on 16 June 1945. The Christian Democratic Union of Germany (CDU) and the Liberal Party of Germany (LDP) also received permission to organize.

As a result of the experiences of the Germans with totalitarianism and with the behavior of the Red Army, the KPD was not able to obtain the support of the population. The Soviet occupation authorities then ordered the merger of the KPD and SPD. The new party, the Socialist Unity Party of Germany (Sozialistische Einheitspartei Deutschlands; SED) came into existence on 21 April 1946 at the "Unity Party Congress" where, according to communist sources, delegates of 620,000 communists and 680,000 Social Democrats decided "unanimously" to unite (*Tribune*, East Berlin, 19 April 1974). Numerous Social Democrats resisted the forced merger and impending subordination under the communist minority, with the result that between December 1945 and April 1946 at least 20,000 were incarcerated and some were killed. The founding congress set as its objective the creation of a "socialist Germany." Within a short time, communists assumed control of the SED apparatus and by July 1948 the party was sufficiently transformed to become a "party of the new type," modeled after the Comunist Party of the Soviet Union (CPSU).

On 7 October 1949 the "German People's Congress" unanimously adopted the proposal to establish the German Democratic Republic (Deutsche Demokratische Republik; GDR) in the Soviet Occupation Zone, following by one month the creation of the Federal Republic of Germany (FRG) in the three Western occupied zones. Old-time communist Wilhelm Pieck was unanimously elected president of the GDR. On 10 October the Soviet Military Administration transferred its administrative tasks to the GDR government. Soviet diplomatic recognition of the GDR followed on 15 October. In July 1950 the Third Congress of the SED approved the draft of the first five-year plan of the GDR, which was enacted in August of the same year.

For a few years Soviet leaders thought that their zone might be the nucleus of a reunited Germany under communist (i.e., Soviet) supremacy. To facilitate this, the first constitution of the GDR consciously followed in certain areas the constitution of the Weimar Republic, based on a federal arrangement and multi-party system, although the non-communist parties were placed under close communist supervision. The federal system was eventually abandoned for more centralized control and in 1968 the GDR received a new "socialist constitution" which proclaimed it the "first socialist state of the German nation."

The elimination of private ownership of industry, financial institutions, and agriculture, along with the traditional professional civil service and the trade unions, began as early as 1946. Mass terror, justified on ideological grounds and directed against entire social groups, gradually succeeded in changing the social and political structure into a "people's democracy."

Under the leadership of the SED, the GDR moved toward economic and military integration with the Soviet Union and the other communist-ruled countries of Eastern Europe. In September 1950 the GDR joined the Council for Mutual Economic Aid (CMEA). In May 1955 it became a member of the Warsaw Pact. About that time, the National People's Army (Nationale Volksarmee; NVA) was established from the National Armed Forces (Nationale Streitkräfte), the name given in 1952 to the armed and garrisoned units of the People's Police (Kasernierte Volkspolizei), which had received authorization from the Soviet Military Administration as early as 31 October 1945.

In 1974 the SED had some 1,900,000 full members and 46,000 candidates (see below). The population of the GDR is 17,050,000 (estimated 1972).

Government and Party Structure. The GDR from its beginning has been controlled by SED leaders who in turn have been faithful executors of Moscow's directives in most domestic and foreign issues. The function of the "government" is limited to administrative and managerial tasks. The decision-making power, including the selection of key personnel within the party and government bureaucracy, rests with the SED Politburo and the Central Committee. The most influential post, therefore, is that of the SED first secretary, held since 1971 by Erich Honecker. In official announcements pertaining to leading officials of the GDR, their party positions are given before their governmental assignments. The flag protocol of the GDR ranks the special flag authorized for the SED first secretary higher than that of the head of state. The latter, mainly ceremonial, has been held since 1973 by Willi Stoph, as chairman of the State Council.

The latest general elections to the 500-member People's Chamber (Volkskammer) were held in November 1971. The "National Front," the communist-controlled alliance of all political parties, provided a single list of candidates. In addition to the SED, four parties are represented in the National Front—the CDU, the LDP, the National Democratic Party of Germany (NDPD), and the Democratic Peasants' Party of Germany (DPD), together with the trade unions and all other "mass organizations," such as the Free German Youth (Freie Deutsche Jugend; FDJ) and the Democratic Women's League of Germany (Demokratischer Frauenbund Deutschlands; DFD). Prior to the election the seats in the People's Chamber were allotted to the different parties of the National Front and mass organizations: 127 to the SED, 52 each to the four other parties, 68 to the Free German Trade Union Federation (Freier Deutscher Gewerkschaftsbund; FDGB), 40 to the FDJ, 35 to the DFD, and 22 to the German Union of Culture (Deutscher Kulturbund; DKB). The high voting participation (98.48 percent of eligible electorate of 11,400,000) presumably was due to strong political pressure and fear of severe retaliation for abstention. The National Front list received 99.85 percent of the votes cast. (*Neues Deutschland*, 20 November 1971.) The members of the People's Chamber have voted unanimously on all issues with only one exception, which occurred, after party permission had been granted, on a bill concerning abortion in March 1972.

The People's Chamber appoints the GDR government, consisting of the State Council (Staatsrat), with 24 members plus one secretary, and the Council of Ministers (Ministerrat). The State Council, like the Soviet Presidium, handles the business of the People's Chamber when that body is not in session. Its chairman is the head of state. The SED holds 16 seats in the State Council. The Council of Ministers consists of chairman (minister president) Horst Sindermann and two first deputy chairmen, 10 deputy chairmen, and 26 members who head the various ministries.

The SED Central Committee consists of 135 full members and 54 candidates. The Politburo has

16 members, and the Secretariat 11 (for names see *YICA, 1974*, p. 23). Politburo member Erich Mückenberger is chairman of the Central Party Control Commission (eight full members and five candidates). In 1974 the Central Committee accepted the request of Ernst Altenkirch to be released from the post of member of the Control Commission because of old age. Günter Pappenheim was appointed a member of the commission, and Herbert Malcherek a candidate member. (East Berlin, domestic service, 5 July.) Kurt Seibt is chairman of the Central Audit Commission (21 full members and four candidates).

The Politburo is the power center of the GDR. The members of the Secretariat exercise considerable control within their respective areas of responsibility (such as military and security policies, economic affairs, agriculture, cadre policies, science and propaganda, and international contacts). All but one of the Secretariat members and all of the most important members of the Council of Ministers are either full or candidate members of the Politburo. The Politburo also includes the first secretaries of two district leaderships (Bezirksleitungen) in industrial districts (Halle, Rostock), the party chief of East Berlin, and the FDGB chairman.

In 1974 three leading officials of the SED received high medals for their services. The State Council on 5 March conferred the "Order of Scharnhorst" on Erich Honecker for outstanding services to the socialist defense of the GDR (*Democratic German Report*, Berlin, 27 March). Willi Stoph received the highest GDR distinction, the "Karl Marx Order," on reaching the age of 60. The Supreme Soviet of the U.S.S.R. decorated him with the Order of Lenin. (Ibid., 31 July.) Politburo member Friedrich Ebert received on his 80th birthday the GDR "Star of People's Friendship" in gold and the Soviet "Order of Peoples' Friendship" (*Die Wahrheit*, 13 September).

The mass organizations. Noted earlier as a part of the National Front, the mass organizations have the purpose of assisting the SED in its many tasks and control functions and providing a mass basis for political indoctrination. They also serve as recruiting ground for future party functionaries. The most important is the Free German Youth (FDJ), with a membership of 1.9 million, organized in more than 18,000 basic units. In 1974 the FDJ Central Council elected Egon Krenz as first secretary, replacing Günter Jahn, who received a responsible post in the SED (*SK Das Sozialistische Nachrichtenmagazin*, Hamburg, January). The FDJ supervises the communist children's organization, the Ernst-Thälmann Youth Pioneer Organization, with about 1.2 million children enrolled. The FDJ Central Council appointed Helga Labs as chairman of the Pioneers (East Berlin, domestic service, 9 January). The Free German Trade Union Federation (FDGB) has 7,828,000 members and is headed by Politburo member Herbert Warnke. Its membership represents 95.3 percent of all workers. Of its members, 3,875,400 are women and 1,211,530 young persons up to the age of 25. (*Berliner Zeitung*, East Berlin, 30 April.) The Democratic Women's League of Germany has about 1.3 million members, organized into 16,700 groups (*Neues Deutschland*, 8 February 1973). Several additional mass organizations serve specific interests, such as the German-Soviet Friendship Society and the Society for Sport and Technology. The latter is a paramilitary organization which provides pre-military training to about a half million young persons before their service in the National People's Army.

Party Internal Affairs. The decisions and resolutions of the Eighth Congress (1971) remained the guidelines for the SED leaders throughout 1974 not only for the execution of domestic and international tasks, but also for intra-party affairs. First Secretary Honecker stated that the 1973-74 party elections (1 November 1973-17 February 1974) were to serve as a "period of a specially intensive political-ideological and organizational activity for the further realization of the Eighth Party Congress decisions" (*Einheit*, October 1973).

Discussions, evaluations, and constructive criticism preceded the elections and were of greater consequence for the mobilization of the party membership "for the strengthening of the fighting power of the party" than for the alleged renewal of the SED cadre. The elections in the basic, district (*Kreis*), and regional (*Bezirk*) organizations in most cases confirmed the incumbents. The higher the organizational level, the fewer changes could be noticed. Of the 263 first secretaries of the district directorates (Kreisleitungen) 247 were reelected; the other 16 lost their positions because of age, illness, or assignment to other tasks. Of the first secretaries of the 15 regional directorates (Bezirksleitungen), 14 remained in office. The elections indicated that Honecker has the party well in his control as a result of his careful personnel policies. (*Rheinischer Merkur*, Cologne, 22 February 1974.)

Party elections were also held for the approximately 10,000 SED members in the National People's Army. The party groups in the armed forces evaluated their share in the successful fulfillment of the decisions of the Eighth Congress:

> The thesis was demonstrated, fully proved and documented, that complete and sympathetic understanding on the part of all members of the armed forces about the role of socialist military power is a fundamental condition for the permanent combat readiness of the NVA. The election directive of the Chief of the Political Main Administration of the NVA ... [called] for the mobilization of members of the army for carrying out party decisions, army orders, and service regulations primarily by means of the examples set by party members. (*Volksarmee*, November 1973.)

Between September and March, account submissions and leadership elections were held in the entire FDJ organization. Election meetings were also held for the Pioneers. (*Junge Welt*, August 1973.)

The SED continued its emphasis on the ideological schooling of the party membership. Honecker stated at the Central Committee session in July: "The political-ideological work of a party organization constitutes the key to further growth of labor productivity and production efficiency" (*Neues Deutschland*, 6 July).

Politburo member and Central Committee secretary, Kurt Hager, addressing a meeting of about 600 scientists, propagandists, cultural workers, journalists, and leading workers in the foreign policy field at the Karl Marx party college in Berlin, stressed that the SED was carrying out comprehensive, thorough, and systematic ideological work toward the implementation of the decisions of the Eighth Congress. He remarked that those dealing directly with ideological work have had a great share in the further strengthening of the socialist state and the successful development of the educational system, science and culture, and international standing of the GDR. (East Berlin, international service, 17 January.)

Politburo and Secretariat member Hermann Axen reported to the Central Committee session in July that the party membership had reached 1,907,719 full members and 46,411 candidates, organized in 73,462 basic branches and sections of the party. He also gave information on the membership drive in the first half of the year. Of the 21,858 candidates admitted in this period, 77.7 percent were workers. The proportion of workers in the party (more than 58 percent) confirmed the continuity of work in this field. Students and pupils admitted as party candidate members accounted for 13.0 percent of the total, and 82.5 percent of the newly admitted members were under 30 years of age. The political and professional educational level of the party members and candidates was continuously improving. In the past two years, Axen reported, 5,000 members of the intelligentsia were admitted into the party as candidates. The Central Committee Secretariat had instructed the district and regional leaderships further to regulate the development of the membership drive so that the percentage of the workers in the SED should constantly increase. (*Neues Deutschland*, 5 July.) It was pointed out earlier that the SED does not strive to increase its membership substantially, but to improve the party's quality as the advance guard of the working class and of all working people, and that it desires to increase the percentage of workers within the party membership. On the other hand, the SED was trying to improve its influence among the students, and in 1973 students from secondary and post-secondary institutions amounted to 13.1 percent of all new admissions to the party, compared to 4.9 percent in 1970. The percentage of workers among newly admitted candidates amounted to 78.6 percent. (*Neues Deutschland*, 23 January 1974.)

Domestic Affairs. *Constitutional Amendments.* The People's Chamber in September unanimously adopted a number of significant amendments and supplements to the 1968 GDR constitution. These came into effect on 7 October, to coincide with the twenty-fifth anniversary of the GDR. Article I, which used to read "The German Democratic Republic is a socialist state of the German nation," was changed to "The German Democratic Republic is a socialist state of workers and farmers." The intent was to eliminate for the GDR the concept of a "German nation." Another meaningful change was the entire deletion of the passage dealing with "German reunification" in Article 8 which looked to the "overcoming of the division of Germany forced by imperialism upon the German Nation," and the "bringing together step-by-step of the two German states until their unification on the basis of democracy and socialism." Other amendments effected a reduction of the powers of the State Council and extended the legislative period of the People's Chamber to five years (from four) in order to make it correspond with the country's economic five-year plans. The minimum age of a member of the chamber was lowered to 18 (from 21). One of the added articles proclaimed: "the German Democratic Republic is forever an irrevocable ally with the U.S.S.R. The close and fraternal alliance with it guarantees the people of the German Democratic Republic further advance along the road of socialism and peace" (art. 6, par. 2).

GDR Anniversary. The quarter-century anniversary of the GDR, celebrated on 7 October, was the major domestic political event of 1974. Even before the end of 1973, SED propagandists utilized the forthcoming anniversary to call for further implementation of the objectives decided by the Eighth Congress. A number of congresses were held in honor of the anniversary, such as the "Scientific Conference" on 25-26 April 1974 in East Berlin, sponsored by the Institute for Social Science, the Institute for Marxism-Leninism, the Institute for Socialist Economic Management, the "Karl Marx" party school of the SED Central Committee, and the Academy of Science of the GDR, whose theme was "Twenty-five Years GDR—Rise of Socialism in Our Country in Fraternal Alliance with the Soviet Union" (*Aussenpolitische Korrespondenz*, East Berlin, 23 May, p. 159).

The festivities on 7 October were highlighted by the presence of the CPSU general secretary Leonid Brezhnev, who reviewed together with Honecker the military parade in East Berlin. About 10,000 soldiers participated in the largest display of military power in the country's history. A display of GDR naval power was held simultaneously at Rostock on the Baltic coast. The U.S., British, and French city commandants and the Senate in West Berlin protested the parade as a renewed violation of the nonmilitary status of all Berlin. Numerous diplomats accredited to the GDR did not attend. (*The Bulletin*, Bonn, 15 October.) Brezhnev received during his visit the "Karl Marx Order."

Local Elections. Elections for district, city, and local assemblies were held on 19 May, with 98.27 percent participation by the 12,000,000-odd citizens entitled to vote. The number of valid votes was 12,028,004 or 99.98 percent. The number of votes for the list of the National Front was 12,017,693 or 99.91 percent of the valid votes cast. There were 10,311 votes or 0.09 percent against the list. Altogether 21,841 deputies were elected to the various assemblies. (*Frankfurter Allgemeine Zeitung*, 21 May.)

Youth Indoctrination. A new and wide-ranging "youth law" took effect on 1 February 1974 and is intended to increase the influence of the FDJ as the guiding organization for the participation of young persons in the building of the socialist society. Section 4 has the title: "The honorable duty of youth to protect socialism." What this duty involves is clearly spelled out in paragraph 23: "the task of youth is to obtain pre-military and technical knowledge and to serve in the armed forces and the other organs of the country's defense. . . ." (Cited in *Mitteilungen Volk und Verteidigung*, Kiel, vol. 11, June, p. 9.)

The so-called Youth Consecration (Jugendweihe) and the preparatory indoctrination serve the purpose of making young people aware of their duties as "responsible socialist citizens." Between the end of March and the end of May 1974, about 266,000 fourteen-year-old youths (96 percent of this age group) pledged their dedication to the GDR in 6,550 local ceremonies. The large percentage can be explained by the fact that the Youth Consecration is a prerequisite for admission to the upper high school grades and post-secondary education and for the advancement in any chosen profession. (*Neues Deutschland*, 20 March; *Die Welt*, 2 November.)

At the beginning of the 1974 school year, secondary school graduates had 30,000 study openings available, of which 35 percent were allotted to technical sciences, 21 percent to high school teachers' training, 12 percent to economic subjects, 8 percent to mathematics and natural sciences, and 7 percent to medicine (*Neuer Tag*, 4 December). The first obligatory foreign language in the GDR is Russian, taught from the 5th grade on. More than half of the students take a second foreign language, starting with the 7th grade. (*Norddeutsche Neueste Nachrichten*, Rostock, 10 April.) Great emphasis is placed upon polytechnical training. In the current school year, 53,700 students in the 7th through the 10th grade received this training, which includes periodic "productive" work in factories. (*Berliner Zeitung*, 1 May.)

State-church relations. They are marked by continuous and increasing pressure against the churches and those who practice their religion. Confession of Christian faith is sufficient reason to bar young people from secondary and higher education and destroy working people's careers. The League of Protestant Churches in the GDR disseminated a report expressing great concern about the discrimination against young Christians, referring to their exclusion from continuing their studies (*Die Welt*, 30 September). A meeting of the "Pastoranalyse" of the Catholic church on 8-10 November, in Dresden, declared that the Christians in the GDR are living in a socialist society with an atheistic orientation, a fact which forces many members of Catholic parishes into difficult situations (ibid., 11 November). The permanent covert anti-religious pressure has had its impact. Church membership is declining. At the beginning of 1973, according to the Lutheran World Federation, there were about 9,000,000 Protestants, and a year later the number had decreased to 8,500,000. Particular pressure is brought on parents who wish their children to receive religious instruction for confirmation. Also the number of Catholics apparently is decreasing. It is usually put at 1,300,000. In 1969 there were more than 95,000 Catholics in East Berlin. In 1974 only 79,841 remained, a reduction of 16 percent. (*Die Welt*, 11 October.) Christians in the GDR are encouraged by the East German CDU, one of the four parties in the National Front, to take a more active part in building socialism and supporting the objectives of the state. This was the position taken by the CDU chairman, who is also chairman of the People's Chamber, in an article in *Neues Deutschland* (6 September). The concept which the SED wishes to implement is that of "socialist citizens of Christian belief."

Jews in GDR. Only 800 Jews remained in the GDR in 1974. Of these, 90 percent were between 55 and 90 years of age. East Berlin has the largest Jewish community, with 450 members. For the last nine years, no rabbi has been available. In 1950 there were still 3,319 Jews in the GDR. The SED prevents any communication of its Jewish citizens with those in the Federal Republic of Germany (FRG) or other Western countries. (*Die Welt*, 18 June.)

Military Affairs. The militarization of the population was intensified during the GDR's anniversary year. Emphasis was placed on increasing the political reliability of the National People's Army and the combat readiness of the fighting forces, and on the pre-military training of young people. The editor in chief of the soldier journal *Armee Rundschau* (January 1974) wrote: "Our love for Socialism, includes our hate towards its enemy." Army General Heinz Hoffmann, Politburo member and defense minister, declared:

> The class enemy is as before strong, in spite of the fact that from an unequivocal historical and political point of view, he finds himself on the defensive. Imperialism still has at its disposal great economic and military potentials, and is still not willing to give up the aims of its aggressive policies. . . . Therefore we shall have to be most vigilant also in the future and direct our entire attention to increasing according to plans the fighting power and combat readiness of the NVA and the border troops in order not to give any chances of military success to the NATO-troops. (*Neues Deutschland*, 26 January.)

Since a clear picture of the enemy is considered an integral part of combat readiness, "socialist military education" both in preparation for service in the NVA and in the political work in the NVA is directed toward making the soldier conscious of the irreconcilability of socialism and imperialism and of the two social systems (*Junge Welt*, 29 March).

On the occasion of the NVA's eighteenth anniversary on 1 March 1974, General Hoffmann in his "Order of the Day of the Minister" declared that "the NVA has grown into a firm component of the socialist class and arms alliance in the past eighteen years," and that the common protection of the GDR's territory, air space, and territorial waters is necessary because imperialism still possesses strong and highly combat-ready armed forces. Responsiblity toward the working people, as part of international class duty, was said to demand that every army member expand his knowledge and skill and persistently strive for military mastery: "It is in this spirit that we firmly pledge to our workers and cooperative peasants to fulfill honourably our duty as soldiers of socialism at any time." (*Neues Deutschland*, 1 March.) The ministers for national defense and state security presented the troop units of the NVA with the "Karl Marx Order," and the Friedrich Engels Military Academy with the "Order of Scharnhorst" (*Die Welt*, 6 February).

The GDR military budget has increased fivefold since 1960. In 1968, it amounted to 5.8 billion marks, and in 1974 to 8.9 billion. Funds for military research and developments are not included in these figures. Neither are expenditures for the more than 400,000 men of the Combat Groups of the Working Class (Kampfgruppe der Arbeiterklasse)—formerly called factory militia (Betriebskampftruppen)—nor funds for the 480,000 members of the paramilitary Society for Sport and Technology (GST). It is believed that an additional 6.5 billion marks was provided for military purposes in 1974. (*Rheinischer Merkur*, 8 March and Easter.)

The total strength of the military and paramilitary forces is as follows:

Armed Forces

NVA — land forces	90,000
NVA — Navy	16,000
NVA — air and air defense	25,000
NVA — border troops	47,000
Security troops (under the Interior Ministry)	22,000
	200,000

Combat groups (Kampfgruppen)		400,000
People's Police and other police units		90,000
		690,000

Paramilitary Forces—Concerned with Pre-Military Training

Society of Sport and Technic (GST)	members only	480,000
Free German Trade Unions (FDGB)	male members only	3,700,000
FDJ		1,900,000
Young Pioneers		1,200,000
		7,280,000

It is believed that the following percentage figures provide a realistic presentation of the political reliability of the members of the NVA:

	Officers	NCOs	Enlisted Men
		(in percentages)	
Strong supporters of the regime	95	55	35
Undecided, opportunists	5	30	35
Opposed to the regime	– –	15	30

The relatively poor attitude of the draftees among the enlisted personnel might be partly due to their low military pay. A draftee in the GDR receives 80 marks a month. The pay of draftees serving in the NATO countries is considerably higher than 100 marks. However, as far as the other Warsaw Pact states are concerned, the GDR draftee is much better off. Examples of draftee pay, in marks, are: Soviet Union, 12.75; Romania, 3.02; Bulgaria, 2.23; Hungary, 15.90; Poland, 7.69; and Czechoslovakia, 33. (*Die Welt*, 9 January.)

Hoffmann pointed out that 88 percent of the NVA officers have completed university or technical training; above 75 percent of the NCOs and enlisted personnel have had ten or twelve years of school attendance and about 85 percent are skilled workers. There are 263 NVA members who are officials in regional or district directorates of the SED. (*Neues Deutschland*, 20 September.) SED first secretary, Honecker, called for strengthening the military power of the countries of the Warsaw Pact so long as the NATO block exists (*Die Welt*, 16 September). The chief of the NVA land forces declared that the fighting strength and combat readiness of these forces can be substantially increased by utilizing Soviet armament and combat technology (ibid., 25 October).

The more than 400,000 men of the Combat Groups of the Working Class are under the direction of the SED. They are organized in "light" battalions (each comprised of three rifle units) and in 170 "heavy" regimental reserve battalions (each comprised of two rifle units, one heavy unit armed with 82-mm. mortars, anti-tank guns, and heavy machine guns) and engineer and signal units. They are trained for security and guard duties and as flank protection for the regular offensive military forces. (Ibid., 15 October.) Conscientious objectors are not recognized in the GDR and every citizen is obliged to contribute to the defense of the GDR (art.13, par. 1 of the GDR constitution).

The pre-military training of young people constitutes an important part of the militarization process in the GDR. The FDJ made propaganda for pre-military training in the GST and for volunteering for the service in the NVA. About 1,500,000 boys and girls participated in various military competitions. (Ibid., 5 June.) During 1974 some 400,000 youths obtained the markmanship badge of the GST (ibid., 4 October).

The GDR also expressed intentions to expand its system of civil defense in order to guarantee for all GDR citizens protective accommodations in case of war (IWE *Tagesdienst*, Berlin, 2 November

1973). On 1 November 1974 a new military court order came into effect. It is intended to be a part of the overall court system of the GDR. The entire legal system is to operate on the basis of the decisions of the SED, with the constitution playing a secondary role. (Ibid., 11 November.)

Security Matters. As result of the exodus of millions of persons from the GDR before the building of the Wall in Berlin and the erection of formidable obstacles along the entire border between the GDR and the FRG, the SED is much concerned with so-called security matters, as is evident in the continuous efforts to make the borders even more difficult to cross and the long prison sentences given persons guilty of the crime of attempted "flight from the Republic" (Republikflucht) and those aiding them. In spite of the GDR's admission to the United Nations and acceptance of the U.N. Charter provisions, which include the right of people to leave their country, the SED has declared:

> [It is] the sovereign right of each state to determine the provisions for travel into and out of its territory in the interest of its citizens. Protecting the interests of the citizens, for example, means protection against pirating of personnel (the pirating of one college graduate, for example, cost all of us, who paid for his education, around 50,000 marks). It also means protection against currency speculations. (*Leipziger Volkszeitung*, 17 November 1973.)

NVA border troops and the Ministry of State Security and its subordinate military formations are charged with implementing this policy. So-called voluntary border helpers, primarily recruited within the party, are attached to the border troup units (*Die Welt*, 7 October 1974). A commentary in *Neues Deutschland* (13 August) on the thirteenth anniversary of the Wall emphasized that the effective securing of the GDR's state border with the FRG and West Berlin served the cause of peace in Europe. The border fortifications include by now automatic firing devices, metal and barbed-wire fences, and at least 1.5 million mines (*Soldat und Technik*, no. 4, 1974, p. 187). The order to shoot at persons trying to leave the country across the fortified borders (Schiessbefehl) remained in force and was justified by the chief of the GDR Coastal Border Brigade in the October issue of *Militärwesen*. He stated that the soldiers of his brigade must be "educated" in order to obtain a realistic picture of the enemy and must realize that violence might be used by those who violate the border. (*Die Welt*, 22 October.) The result has been that only about every eleventh flight-attempt succeeded in 1974. Since the building of the Wall and the other border fortifications at least 164 refugees have been killed. The number of refugees dropped in 1974 by 30 percent, as compared with 1973. From January till December of this year, 898 persons succeeded in getting across the fortified borders. In the same period in 1973, the figure was 1,756. Refugees who escaped through other East European countries brought the total of all refugees from January to November 1974 to 4,803. During the same period in 1973, there were 6,092 who came to the West. (Ibid., 11 December.) During the first half of 1974, 14 members of the NVA fled, bringing the total of NVA soldiers coming to the West since August 1961 to 2,668 (ibid., 13 August). The GDR authorities, in order to stop these flights, have cracked down on what they refer to as "trafficking in human beings," and since the Transit Agreement of June 1972, until December 1974, there have been arrests of almost 300 persons for alleged misuse of the transit roads. Heavy sentences up to 15 years were given to about 200 of these "offenders." (Ibid., 10 August and 31 December.)

Political Prisoners. In October 1974 there were at least 6,500 political prisoners in the GDR, kept in more than 63 penal institutions and labor camps. The last great amnesty took place in 1972, when 600 political prisoners were released. About 1,000 remained in the various jails. In connection with *Republikflucht* about 4,000 persons were arrested. (Ibid., 12 October.) A statistic for the twenty-five years since the founding of the GDR shows that about 190,000 political trials have been held. Official organs of the FRG estimate that 194 death sentences were given and most of them carried out. In 75 cases, the crimes carrying the death sentence were in connection with the Hitler period. After the uprising of 17 June 1953, at least 20 resistance fighters were executed. An additional 1,400 alleged participants received together a total of 4,100 years in jail. During the period from 1945 to 1954 Soviet Military Tribunals also operated. They passed 536 death sentences, some of which were commuted to 25 years' forced labor. (Ibid., 5 October.)

The "buying" of the freedom of political prisoners by the government of the FRG continued in 1974. An average price of 50,000 West German marks (slightly less than $20,000) was paid per prisoner. Through 1973, the number bought increased steadily: 1,715 in 1969, 2,306 in 1970; 2,292 in 1971; 3,115 in 1972; and 4,952 in 1973. That means that in 1973 alone, East Berlin received about DM 200,000,000 (about $80,000,000) for its political prisoners. (Ibid., 11 October 1974.) There has been an apparent drop during 1974. In the first half of this year, 272 prisoners were bought. By the end of October, the total was supposed to reach 600. (Ibid., 10 August.)

The Economy. The GDR National Economic Plan for 1974 anticipated a continuation of the fast pace of economic development shown in the good fulfillment of the plan of the previous year. In the first six months, compared with the same period in 1973, industrial goods production rose by 7.8 percent (*Neues Deutschland*, 5 July), the produced national income by 5.5 percent, "labor productivity within the scope of industrial ministries by 6.7 percent, building industry production by 6.3 percent, the supply of animal products by 6.7 percent, goods transported by the GDR's transport system by 3.4 percent, foreign trade turnover with the CMEA countries by 11.6 percent, net income of the population by 5.6 percent, and retail turnover of industrial goods by 8.1 percent" (Report of the Central Board of Statistics, Dresden, 1974, p. 3).

Good results were also noted in agricultural production. In 1970, one person employed in agriculture provided food for 23 people in the GDR; in 1973 this number went up to 28 and in 1974 was expected to be about 30 (East Berlin, domestic TV, 16 July). The richest grain harvest in 25 years was expected (*NYT*, 8 September). Egg production was up by 12 percent, milk by 10 percent, and meat by 6 percent (*Democratic German Report*, East Berlin, 17 July 1974). The SED recognizes individual and collective achievements by awarding the order of the "Flag of Wrok" (Banner der Arbeit) and has increased the number of orders that may be bestowed annually from 160 to 2,000 (*Die Welt*, Hamburg, 31 August). More than 30,000 FDJ-students worked during the summer vacation in important economic projects. FDJ and SED officials regard these activities as tests of participation in the productive process. (Ibid., 2 July.)

The 13th plenum of the SED Central Committee (12-14 December) approved the economic plan and budget for 1975 followed by unanimous confirmation in the People's Chamber on 19 December 1974. Income and expenditure will balance at 121.2 billion marks of which 9.5 billion (i.e., an increase of 600 million over the preceding year) are earmarked for defense. National income is supposed to grow by 5.5 percent, although expenditure for economic investments will be reduced from 5.3 percent to 4.4 percent or 39.6 billion marks. (*Die Welt*, 21 December.)

Foreign Affairs. *Relations with the Federal Republic of Germany.* Although the "Treaty on the Basis of Relations between the GDR and FRG" (Basic Treaty) came into force on 21 June 1973, the "normalization" of mutual relations has made little progress beyond the establishment of permanent representations in the capitals of both states. The protocol was signed on 14 March 1974 and went into effect on 2 May. The chiefs of the permanent representations, Michael Kohl (GDR) and Günter Gaus (FRG), were accredited on 20 June by the respective heads of state in keeping with the provisions of the Vienna Convention. Also an agreement concerning the field of health service and two partial accords on a non-commercial payment and clearing system between the two governments were signed in East Berlin on 25 April. Commissions comprised of representatives from both countries, dealing with border problems, transportation, and transit traffic, according to Politburo member Hermann Axen, were performing business-like and useful work. In his report to the SED Central Committee on 4 July, Axen stated that these agreements and actions were proof of progress. He stressed that all the possibilities for good neighborly relations existed so long as these were based on the principle of peaceful coexistence and on the implementation of the concluded treaties in letter and spirit. (*Neues Deutschland*, 5 July).

However, this statement and similar remarks like those made by SED first secretary Honecker, in an interview with the West German communist newspaper *Unsere Zeit* (31 May), which also referred to the "headway in the normalization of relations," do not coincide with the antagonistic attitude of East Berlin toward Bonn. While Erich Honecker emphasized the contributions made by his government to the implementation of the peace program worked out by the Twenty-fourth Congress of the CPSU, he accused Bonn of pursuing a policy hostile to détente. At an SED conference in February he made this position clear:

> It is in fact in accord with the laws of class struggle in our time that the most aggressive imperialist circles do not want to accept in any way the change now taking place in international relations. They would like to return to the "Cold War." That is the reason for the accelerated armaments programs in a number of imperialist states. The arms budget of the FRG, according to information given by the Social Democratic-led government, will reach the record level of over 30 billion DM in 1974. This policy of accelerated armaments goes hand in hand with the activation of those forces that are always ready to strengthen bourgeois democracy. (East Berlin, international service in German, 10 February.)

Later, Axen stated his party's views by saying that relations between the GDR and the FRG would be characterized not by any "fictitious mutualities," but by "the irreconcilable class antagonism between socialism and capitalism" (ibid., in English, 3 October).

When the GDR obtained international recognition during 1973, the SED leaders achieved one of their most important foreign policy objectives. They were determined to utilize this accomplishment for at least two further objectives: first of all, to place further pressure on Berlin by willfully misinterpreting the Four-Power Agreement and the subsequent intra-German treaties, and second, to intensify the implementation of their policy of delineation (Abgrenzung) from the FRG. The establishment of a Federal Environment Office in West Berlin, subordinated to the Interior Ministry in Bonn, gave the SED leaders "justification" for protesting the alleged violation of the Allied agreement on Berlin and harassing the traffic on the transit roads to West Berlin. Especially in the Berlin issue, the role of the SED as an instrument of Soviet foreign policy was obvious:

> It is known that the FRG government received repeated, emphatic warnings against such a grave breach of the Four-Party Agreement. This step by the FRG government is a gross infringement of the principle of the Four-Party Agreement that West Berlin is not a constituent part of the FRG and must not be governed by it. It is at variance with the stipulation that the Federal presence must be reduced and that the situation in this city must not be changed unilaterally. It is significant that the FRG government's decision has been welcomed by those elements which for months have tried by all means to bloc the process of détente in Europe. . . (Ibid., 23 January.)

The objective of reducing the Federal presence was restated by both East Berlin and Moscow. Two typical examples of these efforts were the protest against the holding of a meeting of the Bundestag Committee on Intra-German Affairs in West Berlin on 21-22 February and the request that the Federal Administrative Court be removed from West Berlin (*Die Welt*, 20 February, 1 March). The Soviet interpretation of the Berlin agreement is based on the assumption that West Berlin is an "independent political entity" and that the Soviet Union has a veto right concerning West Berlin. Moscow attempts to establish for West Berlin a four-power status. (Ibid., 1 February, 2 August). The Western Allies took exception to the transit restrictions applied by the GDR even though Moscow apparently approved them (*NYT*, 22 July), and also rejected the notion that East Berlin had the authority to make any judgments about the Four-Power Agreement and to decide on retaliation for alleged violations, not being a party to the agreement (*Die Welt*, 1 August).

The delineation of the GDR from the FRG is pursued on two levels, the terminating of the concept of the "unity of the German Nation" and the implementing of the policy of decreasing substantially the physical and ideological contacts between the Germans on both sides of the fortified "state border." As mentioned earlier, the People's Chamber has eliminated from the GDR constitution the term "German Nation" and the objective of eventual reunification of the existing two German states. This "new" policy is apparently intended to further the integration of the GDR with the Soviet Union. The long-range objective of a reunification of the GDR with the FRG, after the latter is purged of its imperialistic and capitalistic character, has been placed at least for the time being into cold storage. (See Eric Waldman, *Die Sozialistische Einheitspartei West Berlin und Die Sowjetische Berlinpolitik*, Boppard am Rhein, 1972, pp. 19-39.) Oskar Fischer, acting minister of foreign affairs, stated in his address to the U.N. plenary meeting in September 1974:

> Today, on German soil exist a socialist state, the German Democratic Republic, in which a socialist nation is developing, and the capitalist Federal Republic of Germany . . . Between the socialist and capitalist states only relations of peaceful coexistence can be the case. (*Die Welt*, 27 September.)

> At present the relations between the GDR and the FRG are not characterized by any "national unity" but are defined in the first place by the irreconcilable conflict between socialism and capitalism. (*Die Wahrheit*, 17 September.)

The rejection of the "unity of the German Nation" provided East Berlin with the argument for demanding recognition of independent citizenships for the populations of the GDR and FRG. (The Basic Treaty did not regulate the issue of German citizenship.) The renouncement of reunification was also the reason for eliminating in the new regulations for awarding of orders, dated 3 May, "contribution in the struggle for a unified, independent, peace-loving, democratic Germany" as grounds for awarding the "Order of Merit of the Fatherland" (*Die Welt*, 26 June). The State Bank of the GDR is replacing "Mark of the German Currency Bank" (Mark der Deutschen Notenbank) with the designation "Mark of the GDR" on the new issues of currencies (ibid., 15 September).

Delineation appeared also in the numbers of persons who are prohibited from maintaining any contacts with the West, including not only members of the armed forces but an ever increasing group of "carriers of state secrets." Practically all security and party organs are involved in supervising and controlling the execution of this policy. Mail and telephone censorship reveals the names of all who carry on contacts with individuals in the West. Scientists were advised and warned not to keep up contacts with colleagues in the West. The president of the Technical University in Dresden, for example, stated at a regional SED conference that it was "essential to prepare the entire teaching staff for the struggle with imperialism," because "the enemy attempts with increasingly improved methods to exert influence upon the universities by means of the so-called all-German scientific contacts" (ibid., 23 February). It is certainly not accidental that in 1974, up to October, more than 16,000 registered letters and packages from the FRG disappeared. During the first half of the year, 208,224 packages were returned to the FRG. (Ibid., 24 October.) Bonn's foreign minister criticized the noncompliance by the GDR with the telephone agreement, which included the installation of a self-dial system with East Berlin (ibid., 11 November). A continuing campaign against receiving TV and radio programs from the FRG was carried on by the SED and its "mass organizations," which frequently demanded that the entire personnel of enterprises sign "voluntary" commitments not to listen to West German propaganda (*Deutsches Monatsblatt*, Bonn, vol. 21, no. 4, April 1974).

The number of visitors from West Berlin and the FRG substantially decreased for at least two reasons. One was the doubling of the amount of West German currency (DM 20 per day) that visitors were forced to exchange for East German currency, beginning 15 November 1973. The other was the pressure placed upon the GDR population not to receive visitors from the West. There were 881,042 West German visitors to the GDR during the first half of 1974, and 1,020,000 in a same period during 1973. (*Die Welt*, 12 October.) The GDR decided as a friendly "gesture" to reduce the currency exchange quota to DM 13 per day (from DM 20) for visits to the GDR and to DM 6.50 per day (from DM 10) for visits to East Berlin, effective 15 November 1974. For senior citizens, who were not excluded from this regulation until 20 December, this constituted a serious obstacle to visiting relatives in the east. The number of one-day visitors between 8 February and 16 July 1974 went down by 40 percent, compared with 1973, and visits for several days declined by 52 percent. (Ibid., 27 July.) Apparently the GDR's notion of "normalization" means recognition that the process of delineation has been accomplished under international law once and for ever (*Frankfurter Allgemeine Zeitung*, 20 April).

The arrest of GDR intelligence agent Günter Guillaume (alias Peter Lohse), the personal assistant to Chancellor Willy Brandt, followed by the latter's resignation on 7 May, was an indication that East Berlin's intentions toward the FRG had not changed. It is believed that Guillaume, who not only furnished the GDR with vital secret information but also operated as an "agent of influence," was working directly for the SED Central Committee's Security Department, headed until 1971 by Erich Honecker and probably still supervised by him in spite of the fact that Politburo member Paul Verner is officially in charge of security matters (ibid., 7 May). *Neues Deutschland* (2 May) declared that the arrest of Guillaume was being used as occasion for an attack against the GDR with the purpose of poisoning the political climate between the GDR and the FRG and destroying the encouraging beginnings of a process of normalization between the two states. A spokesman of the GDR Ministry of Foreign Affairs said on 7 May with regard to the resignation of Chancellor Brandt that the party and state leadership of the GDR regarded the events in the FRG as an internal affair of Bonn (*Foreign Affairs Bulletin*, East Berlin, vol. 14, no. 14, 13 May).

There was strong indication that the so-called West Activities (Westarbeit) of the SED continued during 1974. The observation and influencing of the psychological situation and domestic policies of the FRG apparently was proven by the fact that the West Activities apparatus of the SED continued to operate independently from the "International Contacts" apparatus which carries on relations with the (West) German Communist Party (DKP) and supports "leftist" activities in the FRG. The purpose of these efforts, expensive in terms of personnel and money, is to strengthen the DKP, split the Social Democratic Party, and increase the communist influence within the trade unions.

Only within the trade area is the GDR anxious to maintain the "special relationship" with the FRG. As a result of appendixes to the 1957 Treaty of Rome (the Common Market Charter), trade between the FRG and German territory not governed by Bonn is considered internal German trade. Thus products from the GDR or other East European countries, shipped to the West via the GDR, are entering without tariffs into the FRG and can move from there into other Common Market countries. According to French assertions, this trade amounts to about half of the "intra-German trade." The other Common Market countries intend to restrict the so-called internal German trade to the area of the FRG, West Berlin, and the GDR. (*Bayernkurier*, Munich, 31 August.)

Another substantial advantage enjoyed by the GDR is the "Swing" agreement going back to the Interzone Trade Treaty of 1951. At present the GDR is making use of an interest-free permanent loan of approximately DM 660 million resulting from the imbalance of the intra-German trade. East Berlin is most anxious to prolong the "Swing" beyond 1975, a fact which Bonn might utilize as a bargaining point in its negotiations. The SED leaders already are claiming that a refusal to renew the Swing would constitute a violation of the Basic Treaty. (*Deutsches Monatsblatt*, Bonn, vol. 22, no. 9, September.) Bonn and East Berlin agreed to extend the Swing Agreement until 1981 and raise the interest-free credit to 850 million marks. (*Die Welt*, 16 December.)

Saving on interest on the "Swing" amounts to about DM 56 million per year. As a result of the transit arrangement, East Berlin receives DM 235 million. (Ibid.) The GDR obtained from the FRG and West Berlin between 1970 and 1973 about DM 1.4 billion (*Deutsche Zeitung*, Stuttgart, 1 February), plus about DM 300 million during the same period from West German industries and private persons, including the forced exchange of currency (*Die Welt*, 28 January).

Intra-German trade increased substantially during 1974. Until the end of September, the total for imports and exports had increased by 22.5 percent and amounted to 4.85 billion marks (as compared with 3.96 billion during the same period in 1973). Exports valued at 2.51 billion by the Federal Republic of Germany exceeded imports from the GDR amounting to 2.33 billion marks. (*Die Welt*, 17 December.)

The GDR and the Soviet Bloc. Numerous statements by SED leaders in 1974 emphasized the everlasting integration of the GDR with the socialist community of states. It appears that the political leaders of the GDR depend in all political, economic, and military issues upon direction and "advice" received from Moscow, even in such a matter as the renunciation of a reunified "Socialist German Reich." Solidarity with the other Soviet bloc states figures only as a secondary priority.

The distinctive relationship with the U.S.S.R. was codified in one of the supplements to the GDR constitution approved by the People's Chamber on 27 September 1974:

> The German Democratic Republic is forever and irrevocably allied with the U.S.S.R. The close and fraternal alliance with it guarantees the people of the German Democratic Republic the further advance along the road of socialism and peace. The German Democratic Republic is an inseparable component of the socialist community of states. Loyal to the principles of socialist internationalism, [it] cultivates and develops friendship, all-sided cooperation, and mutual assistance with all states of the socialist community. (Art. 6, par. 2.)

The sessions of the Joint Government Commission for Economic and Scientific-Technical Cooperation between the GDR and the U.S.S.R., in Moscow on 18-22 March and Berlin on 16-18 September, made plans for further interlinkage of the two states' national economies. Increasingly close economic and scientific-technical relations, extended over many years, are considered an important factor in the deepening of the alliance. (*Foreign Affairs Bulletin*, vol. 14, no. 10, 3 April: *Neues Deutschland*, 19 September.) In 1974, trade between the two countries was expected to reach 4.3 billion rubles, an increase of 7 percent over 1973 (Moscow radio, in German, 22 February).

The major event in GDR-U.S.S.R. relations during 1974 was the visit of CPSU general secretary Brezhnev, Soviet foreign minister Gromyko, and defense minister Grechko during the celebration of the GDR anniversary. As early as 15 September, the GDR acting minister of foreign affairs commented in *Neues Deutschland*: "The relationship with the Soviet Union and the CPSU has been, is and will remain the decisive touchstone of loyalty to Marxism-Leninism, to proletarian internationalism. Thus the history of the GDR is primarily the history of the continuously closer friendship and cooperation with the party of Lenin and with the U.S.S.R." As noted earlier, the highest GDR decoration was conferred up on Brezhnev, who at the Jubilee Session of the People's Chamber praised the achievements of the GDR and of socialist economic integration (TASS, in English, 6 October).

In addition, numerous meetings were held by SED and CPSU officials either in Moscow or in East Berlin. Also during 1974, under an exchange program, 2,300 GDR students studied at Soviet universities and a similar number of Soviet students studied or did practical work in the GDR (*Democratic German Report*, vol. 23, no. 5, 27 March). The Tenth Congress of the German-Soviet Friendship Society, in Dresden on 11-12 May, attended by a delegation from the SED Central Committee, headed by Honecker, was a demonstration of "class fraternity and friendship with the Soviet people" (*Neues Deutschland*, 5 July). The GDR ambassador to the U.S.S.R. received the Soviet "Order of Friendship of Peoples" for his contribution toward the development of friendship and cooperation between the two countries (East Berlin, international service in German, 19 February).

The "Group of Soviet Armed Forces in Germany" (GSSD) was strengthened during the year as additional personnel and new equipment, such as the T-62 tank, arrived in the GDR. Soviet strength in the GDR is estimated at 40 motorized rifle regiments, 40 armored regiments, and 21 divisions organized into 5 armies. Armament and equipment is stored for an additional 7 divisions and ammunition for 40 combat days. (*Die Welt*, 29 August.) U.S. military intelligence claims that the Soviet Union has 533,000 men stationed in the GDR.

On 17-18 April, the Political Consultative Committee of the Warsaw Pact states took place in Warsaw. A joint meeting of the SED Politburo and the GDR Council of Ministers gave approval to the decisions taken in Warsaw.

At the anniversary session of the CMEA in Berlin on 10 July, it was noted that the CMEA, with the inclusion of the Mongolian People's Republic and Cuba, now extends into three continents. The GDR represents only 5 percent of the population of the CMEA countries, but produces 10 percent of the total industrial products of the member countries and thereby occupies, together with Poland, the second position within the CMEA, after the Soviet Union (*Die Wahrheit*, 2 October).

Other International Positions. The year 1973 was highlighted by the admission of the GDR to the United Nations and success in the GDR's long fight for international recognition. By December 1974 a total of 112 foreign governments had diplomatic relations with the GDR, after John Sherman Cooper presented his credentials (*Die Welt*, 21 December). The U.S.-GDR negotiations started on 15 July but were interrupted by the interference with the traffic from the FRG on the highways leading to West Berlin. The GDR's refusal to acknowledge the possibility of its obligation to pay compensation to the Jewish and the other victims of Nazism and for U.S. property seized by the Nazis or nationalized by the GDR were obstacles which had to be overcome before the final agreement on the exchange of diplomatic representatives could be reached (*Christian Science Monitor*, 5 September). Reportedly, East Berlin agreed to hold discussion on these sensitive issues after it was made clear that failure to make progress in this area would prevent the granting of U.S. credits or nondiscriminating tariffs (*NYT*, 8 September). By establishing diplomatic relations, the United States in effect recognized the division of Germany. The only NATO country which has not yet given diplomatic recognition to the GDR is Canada. Although negotiations between Ottawa and East Berlin were begun as early as 22 December 1972, Canada is holding out until the GDR will agree to permit citizens, if they wish, to join relatives in Canada (*Die Welt*, 18 January).

The improved international reputation of the GDR, and hence the SED, is being utilized by Soviet leaders to prepare a new all-European conference of communist parties, but further improvement of the SED's contacts with the Scandinavian parties, the Italian Communist Party, and the French Communist Party will be required. It appears that the SED has been used also to strengthen ties between the socialist bloc and countries in the Middle East and, especially, with the Palestine Liberation Organization (PLO). This is an all probability the reason for the official statement made by Prime Minister Horst Sindermann that, in spite of U.S assertions to the contrary, the GDR refuses to pay reparations to Zionist organizations or Israeli authorities (Hamburg radio, 27 September). At least four visits by GDR notables to the Middle East occurred during 1974: to Egypt, Syria, Iraq, and the People's Democratic Republic of Yemen in February; to Iraq in March and June; and to Syria and Kuwait in November. Agreements on economic and scientific cooperation were made with Iraq (*Foreign Affairs Bulletin*, vol. 14, no. 19/20, 3 July) and Syria (*Die Welt*, 26 November). A PLO delegation led by its chairman, Yasir Arafat, visited the GDR on 6-8 August. The SED affirmed support for the PLO's struggle for the right of the Arab people of Palestine to self-determination as laid down in the U.N. Charter. (*Foreign Affairs Bulletin*, vol. 14, no. 24, 21 August.)

The GDR faithfully supported every position taken by the Soviet Union in the United Nations. The U.N. Anti-Apartheid Committee met in East Berlin on 27-28 March. The SED declared that this meeting manifested that the most reliable allies of the peoples fighting against colonialism, racism, and apartheid were the countries of the socialist community (*Neues Deutschland*, 5 July). The GDR foreign minister approached the U.N. secretary-general with his government's position on convening a world disarmament conference and completely endorsed the Soviet submission of 1971 (*FBIS*, 11 June). An informal session of the Conference Committee on Disarmament on 20 August decided to invite the GDR to committee membership (*Foreign Affairs Bulletin*, vol. 14, no. 25, East Berlin, 3 September), and the U.N. General Assembly unanimously confirmed this on 9 December.

The Executive Committee of the World Council of Churches met for the first time in the GDR, on 18-22 February. The committee decided to support organizations which fight against racism and colonialism and supplied $450,000 to aid 29 organizations in southern Africa. (*Democratic German Report*, vol. 23, no. 4, 13 March.)

A delegation of SED and government officials headed by Honecker paid a first official visit to Cuba on 20-26 February (*Foreign Affairs Bulletin*, vol. 14, no. 8, 12 March). The GDR continued its campaign against the military junta in Chile and utilized this issue as a replacement for the former anti-Vietnam War propaganda.

With regard to China, the SED leaders followed Moscow's lead in charging the Chinese communists with anti-Sovietism and with favoring the intensification of the arms race (*Neues Deutschland*, 7 July). Especially, Chinese policy toward Europe was heavily criticized because China allegedly regards NATO as a useful counterbalance to the Soviet bloc (*Berliner Zeitung*, 27 September). A visit of high GDR and party officials to Czechoslovakia in October produced a communiqué declaring that the SED and the Czechoslovak communist party will carry on a "decisive struggle against the ideology and policy of the Maoist leadership of China" (*Die Welt*, 19 October).

Willi Stoph, chairman of the GDR Council of State, paid an official visit to Finland in October and one to India (29 November-3 December).

International Party Contacts. As a result of the mission assigned to the SED by Moscow, to operate as a catalyst and organizer for a new world conference of the communist parties, the SED continued in 1974 to intensify its contacts with communist parties throughout the world by means of bilateral visits and multi-lateral meetings. Between mid-December 1973 and early July 1974, a total of 102 delegations of communist and workers' parties, socialist parties, and revolutionary-democratic parties and organizations visited the GDR. Among these were 42 delegations from fraternal parties of the socialist countries (*Neues Deutschland*, 5 July). At various times during the year the GDR was visited by the heads of the French Communist Party, the pro-Soviet party of Peru, and the Communist Party, USA.

The Chairman of the DKP paid an official visit in November, but contacts in the FRG were not restricted to the DKP and its subsidiary organizations, and also included the participation of FDGB and FDJ delegations in events sponsored by trade unions and a number of Social Democratic organizations, such as the Young Socialists (Jusos), Nature Friend Youth, and the Falcons.

Near the end of 1973 and during 1974 a number of regional communist meetings took place, all attended by representatives of the SED, which in spite of apparent differences in their respective main subjects, appeared to prepare an all-European communist conference (like the Karlovy Vary conference of April 1967) and a fourth world conference on the pattern of the Moscow "consultations" of 1957, 1960, and 1969. Central Committee secretaries of nine governing communist parties (Warsaw Pact states plus Cuba and Mongolia) met in Moscow on 18-19 December 1973 and 22-23 January 1974. Party secretaries of 67 communist parties met in Prague on 7-9 January under the auspices of the international communist periodical *Problems of Peace and Socialism*. In Brussels, the conference of 21 West European communist parties on 26-27 January dealt with the "crisis of West European capitalism," but reportedly also discussed relations between the CPSU and the Chinese Communist Party (*Die Welt*, 28 January). The consultative meeting of European communist parties in

Warsaw, 16-18 October, drew representatives from 28 parties (only those of Albania, Iceland, and the Netherlands were absent); Yugoslavia, after a long absence from international communist meetings, participated. It appears that the European communist party conference will probably be held in East Berlin in May 1975 (ibid., 19 October) and the world conference, in which the Soviet Union wishes to reassert its leadership position and to condemn the Chinese communist leaders, may be scheduled for the end of 1975, if it can be arranged at all.

The SED seems to have also a special assignment from Moscow to assist in bringing Yugoslavia back into the socialist community of states. As early as 22 December 1973, the League of Communists of Yugoslavia and the GDR reached an accord in East Berlin to intensify their relations and cooperation during 1974 and 1975. The agreement provided, among other things, for periodic meetings of prominent leaders of the two parties and for cooperation between cities, such as is already carried on between Dresden and Skopje, and Leipzig and Zagreb. An exchange of lecturers was also agreed upon. (Tanyug, Belgrade, in English, 22 December 1973.) An article in the *Foreign Affairs Bulletin* (Vol. 14, no. 17, 11 June 1974) paid tribute to the process of consolidation of friendly relations between the two states. Especially in the economic sphere, great progress has been made since the establishment in May 1964 of the Joint Committee for Economic and Scientific-Technical Cooperation. In November 1974, Tito paid a four-day visit to the GDR. He was highly praised by Honecker for his contribution to "peace, socialism, and friendship among peoples" and was awarded the "Karl Marx Order." (*Die Welt*, 14 November.)

Publications and Broadcast Media. The official organ of the SED, *Neues Deutschland*, has a daily circulation of about 800,000. The *Berliner Zeitung* (circulation 500,000) and a number of dailies in other GRD cities are also published by the SED. The parties of the National Front and the mass organizations have their own publications, using officially approved material. The SED publishes a semi-monthly magazine, *Neuer Weg*, dealing primarily with party issues, and a monthly journal, *Einheit*, mainly concerned with theoretical and practical problems of "scientific" Marxism-Leninism. Military publications include the *Armee Rundschau*, the *Volksarmee*, and the official publication of the Defense Ministry, *Militärwesen*.

The FDJ and the Pioneer Organization "Ernst Thälmann" have their own publishing business and issue a total of 15 newspapers and magazines (total circulation above 5,000,000). The FDJ daily newspaper, *Junge Welt*, has a circulation of over 600,000 copies. The FDJ official magazine is *Junge Generation*. The FDJ biweekly theoretical organ *Forum* is concerned with intellectual problems faced by young people in the GDR.

A number of publications, some in foreign languages, serve the purpose of propaganda abroad. *Neue Heimat* and the *FDGB Review* are well-prepared publications for foreign consumption. The *Democratic German Report*, and the *Foreign Affairs Bulletin* are mailed to recipients in England and North America.

All broadcasting and TV stations of the GDR are considered important instruments of "political education" and are therefore under strictest party control. The main propaganda radio transmitter, since 15 November 1971, is the "Voice of the GDR," which replaced the former "Deutschland-sender" and "Berliner Welle."

University of Calgary
Canada

Eric Waldman

Hungary

Hungarian communists formed a party in November 1918 and became the dominant force in the left-wing coalition that established the Republic of Councils the following March and ruled for four months. Subsequently the party was proscribed and functioned sporadically in exile and illegality. With the Soviet occupation at the end of World War II the Hungarian Communist Party emerged as a partner in the coalition government and exercised an influence disproportionate to its limited electoral support. Communists gained effective control of the country by 1947, and the following year absorbed left-wing social democrats into the newly named Hungarian Workers' Party. On 1 November 1956, during the popular revolt that momentarily restored a multi-party government, the name was changed to Hungarian Socialist Workers' Party (Magyar Szocialista Munkáspárt; HSWP). The HSWP rules unchallenged as the sole political party, firmly aligned with the Soviet Union. Coordination of formal political activities, such as elections, is the function of the Patriotic People's Front.

The HSWP has about 770,000 members. The population of Hungary is about 10,400,000 (estimated 1972).

Party Leadership. Ultimate political power in the party, and therefore in Hungary, remains in the hands of the first secretary, János Kádár. Politburo members were Kádár, György Aczél, Antal Apró, Valéria Benke, Béla Biszku, Lajos Fehér, Jenö Fock (who is also prime minister), Sándor Gáspár (also head of the National Council of Trade Unions), Gyula Kállai, Dezsö Nemes, Károly Németh, and Rezsö Nyers. Continuing members of the Central Committee Secretariat were Kádár, Biszku, Miklós Óvári, and Árpád Pullai. Newly appointed to the Secretariat during 1974 were Imre Györi and Károly Németh, replacing Aczél and Nyers (see below). Politburo and Secretariat member Zoltán Komócsin died on 28 May, aged 51, after a long illness. At one time rumored to be Kádár's heir, Komócsin had been since June 1965 Central Committee secretary in charge of international and intraparty affairs (duties assumed by Pullai in 1973), and in that capacity had acquired a reputation for unquestioning loyalty to the Soviet Union. In March 1974 he was named chief editor of the party daily newspaper *Népszabadság* (a position that he held also in 1961-65). His place in the Secretariat will likely be filled at the party's Eleventh Congress in March 1975. János Brutyó continued as chairman of the Central Control Committee.

Party Policy. On 28 November 1973 the HSWP Central Committee passed a resolution on "cadre policy" aiming to reassert the party's role in setting guidelines for the selection and performance of leaders in all sectors. The qualifications for leadership—political reliability, professional competence, and leadership ability—were stated in a 1967 Politburo resolution. These, it was said, must be raised to combat negative tendencies in the growing managerial-technocratic class, such as neglect of political and social duties, indifference to the views of workers, failure to combat petty bourgeois and Western trends, the pursuit of material gain and narrow interests, and the abuse of power. The eligibility of non-party members for all non-party offices was reaffirmed. The resolution recommended less arbitrariness and more collective decisions in cadre questions, and more planned cadre exchanges and training. It was noted that the party's full cadre authority (nomenclatura) over 90,000 posts and the basic party organizations' advisory right over 350,000 posts were generally respected and that these lists should be revised and perhaps reduced. (*Társadalmi Szemle*, January 1974.)

The correctness of the middle-of-the-road line followed by the party under Kádár was defended in an article by Biszku on "Some Topical Issues of Our Party's Policy" (ibid., March). He acknowledged the existence of "conflicting interests among the classes and layers in our society," but argued: "These are of a secondary character as compared with the basic and lasting community of interests, and can be solved." Noting the uncertainty and frequent questions regarding the party's role in economic work, Biszku said that some critics would make economics independent of politics, but this would be as wrong as a return to the excessive political direction of the economy in the Rákosi era. Instead, the party must ensure the primacy of politics as a broad guide for the economy. Warning against complacency and urging vigilance—defined not as a generalized mistrust but as a political struggle against enemies and a sensitivity to internal faults—Biszku concluded that in elaborating guidelines for domestic policy, the HSWP was responsible not only to the Hungarian working class but also to the fraternal community of socialist countries, and there existed no contradiction between the two.

The theme of consolidating Kádár's reforms through emphasis on the dominant role of the working class received full play at the important enlarged plenum of the Central Committee, 19-20 March 1974.

The report on international questions, by Pullai, was unusually grim. It noted the economic and political difficulties in the capitalist world. The "fundamental characteristic" of the international situation was the "peaceful coexistence of states with different social systems," but reactionary circles, aided by such diverse elements as Solzhenitsyn, Mindszenty, and the Maoists, were harming détente and progress in the Conference on Security and Cooperation in Europe and the Mutual (Balanced) Force Reductions negotiations.

The major concern of the party, the leading role of the workers and the restoration of their confidence in the HSWP and the New Economic Mechanism (NEM), was evident in the set of guiding principles adopted at the meeting. These were aimed at: improvement in the ratio of workers in the party and leading bodies "to strengthen the process through which workers experienced in public life occupy systematically more leading posts in our society"; the development of shop-floor democracy; a "deliberate effort . . . to develop workers eminent in their jobs into public-spirited people whose work carries weight"; greater respect for workers, especially industrial workers who "form the most stable nucleus of the working class"; and improvements in the living conditions, education, and training of workers.

A report by Aczél gave rise to a resolution on the further development of public education, particularly in rural areas and among working women, with emphasis on molding a socialist attitude.

Kádár was named chairman of the preparatory committee for the Eleventh Congress. The congress is expected to produce a new party program that will preserve the basic Kádár reforms with greater stress on the role of the workers and with modifications in the NEM's system of economic regulators.

The personnel shuffle announced at the Central Committee meeting aroused comment in Hungary and abroad. Nyers and Aczél were removed from the Secretariat. Nyers, the principal architect of the NEM within the party hierarchy, was clearly demoted by his appointment as director of the Institute of Economics of the Hungarian Academy of Sciences. The move may have been caused more by his inflexible proprietary view of the NEM than by party dissatisfaction with any major aspect of the system. Aczél, whose main responsibility has been cultural policy, was appointed a deputy premier and appears to have retained his influence over education and culture. Both remained members of the Politburo.

Newly appointed to the Secretariat were Károly Németh and Imre Györi. Németh, age 52, joined the party in 1945 and became a Central Committee member in 1957, first secretary of the Budapest party committee in 1965, and Politburo member in 1970. He has taken over Nyers's supervision of economic policy, and his moderately conservative record may prompt a greater concern for workers' interests. The promotion and Németh's subsequent visits to the Soviet Union led to speculation that he is being groomed to succeed Kádár, possibly at the Eleventh Congress. Kádár has in recent years indicated a desire to retire. Györi was formerly first secretary of the Csongrad county party committee.

Lajos Fehér and Miklós Ajtai were retired as deputy premiers and replaced by Aczél and by János Borbándi, former head of the Central Committee's Administration Department. Imre Katona replaced Németh as first secretary of the Budapest party committee.

Following the Central Committee plenum, the party launched a major propaganda effort to dispel speculation, notably in the Western press, that the personnel changes and the stress on the workers' leading role indicated a shift in policy away from liberalization in the economic and cultural spheres. An article signed by Komócsin (*Népszabadság*, 23 March) stressed that the main lines of HSWP policy remained unchanged, but warned against a dogmatic adherence to established practice: "It is precisely to safeguard our correct principles and system of economic management that we must improve our practical work without delay." The article praised the other economic management systems in the Soviet sphere, whose results "do not lag in any way behind our successes."

Kádár, in a speech on 28 March (*Népszabadság*, 30 March), proclaimed Hungary's loyalty to Moscow: "In foreign politics, we have always openly sided with the Soviet Union even in the most difficult times." He added that "also our capitalist partners know that the Hungarian People's Republic is a reliable partner." Assessing the Central Committee meeting, he concluded that "the development of Hungarian society is balanced, even, and dynamic in certain respects," and that the party's task was to ensure that this development continued undiminished into the future. The personnel changes were "a cadre regrouping in certain leading positions in accordance with the requirements of practical work." He added: "We are going to continue the policy we have been pursuing so far; our domestic and foreign policy, our agricultural policy and our cultural policy remain unchanged; we will maintain our tested system of economic management, but we will have to improve practical implementation in every area."

Népszabadság (14 April) indicated some of the shortcomings to be corrected, including "giving group interests too much prominence," sometimes "at the expense of social interests"; an "increase in materialistic attitudes"; "exaggerated profit-centrism"; and some "managerial laxness." It rejected criticism that the party's agrarian policy had favored agriculture over industry and the workers.

The Central Committee session of 20 June announced the appointment of István Katona, former head of the Agitprop Department, as chief editor of *Népszabadság* to replace the deceased Komócsin. New Central Committee department heads were Dr. János Berecz (foreign relations), Károly Grósz (agitprop), and Sándor Rácz (public administration). The Central Committee recommended the split of the Ministry of Education and Culture (united in 1957). Károly Polinszky became minister of education, László Orbán minister of culture.

The issue of religious practice by party members continued to be of concern. A survey in Tolna county showed that families of party members—frequently at the instigation of grandparents—often participate in religious ceremonies such as baptisms, confirmations, weddings, and funerals. Members were enjoined to combat this and to advise the party if participation was unavoidable. Non-members were also upbraided. It was noted that religious practices compromise the required political commitment to socialism and set a bad example. (*Pártélet*, December 1973.)

Government and Administration. The principal state and government figures are unchanged. Pál Losonczi is head of state as chairman of the Presidential Council, Jenö Fock is prime minister, and Antal Apró is chairman of the National Assembly.

At its 1973 winter session, 19-20 December, the National Assembly debated the 1974 budget submitted by Finance Minister Lajos Faluvégi (see below). Former foreign minister János Péter was elected deputy speaker, replacing the deceased Catholic priest Miklós Beresztóczy. A new family law aiming to strengthen the institution of marriage by providing for a waiting period, minimum age, and enhancement of the status of women, was passed at the 1974 spring session, 24-25 April.

The fall session, 3-4 October, approved a foreign trade bill, which emphasizes the principle of state monopoly in trade and the subordination of all economic units engaged in international commerce. It upholds the principle of fulfilling interstate commitments, allows for the limited establishment of offices in Hungary by foreign companies, and encourages cooperation in production. The Assembly also heard a report on the 1971 Local Council Law. The intent of the law had been to enhance the autonomy of local councils, and the record is largely positive apart from some difficulties in developing independent decision-making in village councils and a shortage of specialists needed to assist the councils.

New regulations taking effect 1 July were intended to upgrade the status and remuneration of civil servants and thereby promote stability and professionalism. One measure revived the old titles of counselor and chief counselor. (*Magyar Közlöny*, 27 December 1973.)

A State Population Record Office began operations 1 July. On the basis of a new census on 1 January 1975, basic personal data will be recorded in a central data bank and new certificates of identity will be issued. In 1977 an eleven-digit number is to be assigned to each citizen.

The Economy. The head of state, Pál Losonczi, reported in his 1974 New Year address that the "level of national income, industrial and agricultural production, and labor productivity exceeded plans [for 1973]. Our economic results have made possible a more rapid rise in the standard of living, especially that of workers at large-scale industrial enterprises, an improvement in housing conditions, and expansion of the health, social, and cultural services" (Budapest radio, 1 January).

According to official statistics for 1973, most key indicators showed positive change. The budget deficit was lower than planned. Net industrial production increased by 7 percent (planned, 6 percent), with some 80 percent of this due to higher productivity. In keeping with the planned restructuring of the industrial profile, the best performance was in chemicals, crude-oil processing, synthetics, and light industry. Agricultural production was far above planned goals, thanks to record wheat and maize crops. Exports (in real terms) were up 14 percent, imports 4 percent, but the government is acutely concerned by the asymmetry underlying this positive result: in contrast to a manageable deficit in the non-socialist balance of trade, in the socialist sector Hungary has accumulated a huge but non-convertible surplus. Real wages in 1973 rose by 5.5 percent (*Népszabadság*, 3 February; *Magyar Nemzet*, 28 June).

The most remarkable facet of Hungary's economic growth in recent years has been agricultural production, which by the end of 1973 had reached the level planned for the end of the fourth five-year plan in December 1975. A major contributing factor has been the introduction of industrialized, closed-production systems—a modernization program that the government is planning to pursue but which is hampered by the costs of the essential Western technology. The government has also encouraged the reduction in the number of cooperative farms (from a high of 4,500 in the early

1960s to the current 1,950), largely through mergers, in order to achieve economies of scale. As a result Hungary has once again become a grain-exporting country. The remaining problem of weak but indispensable agricultural cooperatives has prompted new Politburo directives for their further subsidized technological development (*Társadalmi Szemle*, September). Small farms and private plots account for 53 percent of horticultural and 49 percent of livestock output. A decline in this sector, due partly to an aging peasant population and a rise in the living standard of cooperative employees, has prompted recommendations for the provision of marketing and technological assistance from the cooperatives, and local party organizations have been instructed to promote such cooperation (*Pártélet*, January; *Társadalmi Szemle*, June).

The 1974 budget included measures to limit the impact of Western inflation on consumers through state subsidies for enterprises dependent on imports; the further reduction of wage discrepancies by centrally-directed selective increases; and the continued restructuring of industrial production. The finance minister Faluvégi warned that the favorable trade imbalance in the socialist trade sector in 1972 and 1973 must be redressed by increased imports, and announced credit incentives to spur machinery and equipment purchases from socialist suppliers. He criticized enterprises for neglecting market research within the CMEA countries and preferring to buy from the West at a time when inflation in capitalist countries was making their goods more expensive. The inclination of Hungarian enterprises to buy from the West is of course largely attributable to their quest for superior quality and technology.

The virtual impossibility of satisfying simultaneously all categories of wage earners was indicated by the government's periodic "special" raises. In 1973 workers in state industries were the chief beneficiaries. On 28 February 1974, a Council of Ministers resolution provided special wage increases, effective 1 April, for some 300,000 workers including the skilled workers who had been left out of the 1973 raise, "auxiliary" semi-skilled and unskilled workers, theater employees, and scientific researchers. Another resolution, on 15 March, established a national "occupational wage schedule" for manual workers, to be implemented gradually in all sectors, with the aim of eliminating excessive disparities without excluding all wage differentiation. On 9 May the Council of Ministers adopted new regulations defining the "socially acceptable" limits of private property (such as real estate and water-craft), beyond which a highly progressive tax is applied.

Despite the growing problems caused by world market trends (see below), the economy performed generally above plan in the first nine months of 1974; industrial output was up 9.1 percent, productivity rose by 7.9 percent, and there were record wheat and maize crops.

Preparations are under way for the fifth Five-Year Plan, which will come into effect 1 January 1976. In contrast to recent rates of growth (the annual rate for 1966-70 was 6.8 percent, and 1971-73, 6.1 percent), the initial forecasts are for a somewhat lower rate in view of a foreseeable decline in the size of the labor force after 1975, the high capital requirements of further technological improvements to productivity, and the problems of raw material and energy shortages and external inflation. No major new centrally directed development programs are envisioned.

Energy and Trade. The relative stability in domestic prices through 1973 was helped in part by state subsidies cushioning imported inflation and by the unexpected increase in agricultural production, of which 20 to 25 percent was exported at inflated prices to the benefit of the overall trade balance. In the longer term, however, the effect of world market trends on an economy with a high dependence on trade and external sources of raw materials and energy demanded more drastic compensating measures. The chairman of the National Materials and Price Board indicated the government's view that in the long run the impact of capitalist inflation could not be subsidized. Major increases in producer prices for hydrocarbons, chemicals, cloth, and other materials as of 1 January 1975 are part of an "active price policy" designed to approximate world market prices. A compensating measure is the 30 percent reduction in the levy on the fixed and working capital of enterprises. The chairman expressed dissatisfaction with the CMEA quota system and the inflexibility of contractual prices, and noted regretfully that since most CMEA countries are only beginning to link domestic and foreign trade prices, the desirable creation of a convertible currency as envisaged under the "comprehensive program" is not imminent (*Figyelö*, 14 August).

In 1974 some 44 percent of Hungary's energy requirements had to be met through imports, including 5.7 million tons of Soviet oil (the major part of the required 6.7 million tons) (*Népszabadság*, 18 April). Satisfaction of future needs presents a growing problem. The principal supplier, the Soviet Union, appears reluctant to meet long-term requirements, partly because of domestic demand and partly because of its inclination to trade raw materials for the higher prices and superior technology offered by capitalist countries. An article in *Népszabadság* (23 January) indicated that while the CMEA's comprehensive program provided for various forms of cooperation and credit to improve raw material supplies, the smaller members must improve the quality of their exports if the Soviet Union is to be "interested in satisfying the increasing raw material requirements of the CMEA countries." Other remedial measures are cooperation with developing countries (it is estimated that the CMEA countries will need 150 to 170 million tons of crude oil from outside sources by 1980, compared with imports from developing countries of some 15 million tons in 1972); changes in the structure of production by regrouping heavy industrial users of raw materials closer to the sources; more efficient use of raw materials (CMEA countries use 70 to 80 percent more energy than advanced countries to produce the same unit of national income). Only by the turn of the century is nuclear power expected to contribute as much as one-third of the energy used in the CMEA countries.

The Soviet Union accounts for 34 percent of Hungary's trade, and the overall pattern is the exchange of Hungarian processed products for energy sources and raw materials. To promote further raw material imports, Hungary participates in various joint investments, including contribution to a new wood-pulp combine, an asbestos separation plant, and the enlargement of a phosphorite plant at Kingisepp in the Soviet Union. Agreement has been concluded on a second high-capacity long-distance power line between the two countries, and negotiations are under way on cooperation on the new CMEA 3,000-kilometer gas pipeline and the production of ferro-alloys (*Magyar Hirlap*, 4 April.)

The agreement on construction of the joint Yugoslav-Hungarian-Czechoslovak "Adria" pipeline project has been signed after many delays. The line, to be operational by 1977, is designed to carry 34 million tons of oil, including 5 million tons each to Hungary and Czechoslovakia. There is less certainty about the source of supply. Hungarian missions have been visiting various Arab states, and economic cooperation agreements were concluded with Libyan and Syrian delegations at Budapest in February and March.

In an analysis of Hungary's trade with the West, deputy foreign trade minister Béla Szalai noted that although European Economic Community members had promised to lift all quota restrictions by the end of 1974, progress was very slow and the export of textiles, leather goods, rolled steel, and some foodstuffs was still subject to discrimination (*Népszabadság*, 6 March). Hungary protested at the lack of warning and consultation when the EEC imposed a July-November embargo on beef and beef cattle imports (*Magyar Hirlap*, 25 July).

Szalai also anticipated that limitations on trade with the United States due to mutually discriminatory tariffs would be eliminated when the U.S. Congress authorized extension of most-favored-nation treatment (the likelihood of which increased with the Jackson-Kissinger compromise on the issue of free emigration, though it remains to be seen how this qualification will affect tariff negotiations with Hungary). As a follow-up to the visit by the U.S. secretary of commerce in 1973, a specialized U.S. government-business delegation spent two weeks in Budapest in April to discuss trade expansion. (In 1973, U.S. exports to Hungary reached a modest postwar high of $33 million, with Hungarian exports amounting to half that sum.) The talks concluded with agreement on the desirability of long-term cooperative ventures and on the early return visit of a similar Hungarian delegation.

The Federal Republic of Germany is Hungary's foremost Western trading partner, accounting for 6.5 percent of its foreign trade. Some 150 cooperative ventures are in force, the most recent being the agreement between Siemens A.G. of Munich and a Hungarian foreign trade enterprise to establish a joint company, Sicontact Ltd., with 51 percent Hungarian capital, designed to undertake joint industrial and marketing projects and service Siemens installations in Hungary (*Népszabadság*, 10 July). On 2 July a ten-year agreement was signed with the Swedish Volvo company establishing a joint enterprise to supervise the production in Hungary of a cross-country vehicle.

An agreement was signed by the Hungarian National Bank for a $100 million eight-year loan, underwritten by U.S. and Canadian banks at a floating interest rate and intended to modernize production and increase export capacity. In the first nine months of 1974 imports to Hungary rose by 36.7 percent and exports by 14.7 percent (at current foreign exchange prices), an imbalance due largely to Western inflation.

In 1974 for the first time two international trade fairs were held in Budapest, one in May devoted to investment goods, another in September for consumer products.

Labor. The manpower problem remains a prime concern of the government—a combination of a shortage of skilled workers in production, a surpius of white-collar employees, low productivity, and declining manpower reserves. Improvements in productivity and a reduction of inflated administrative staffs are indicated, although the latter measure is hampered by a widespread prejudice against manual work. Between 1967 and 1972 the number of workers hired in the socialist sector increased 10 percent, of white-colar employees 26 percent. In order to promote the importance of the workers' role in improving productivity and to celebrate the upcoming HSWP congress, a campaign was announced in April 1974 to revive work competitions, a tool neglected in recent years by economic leaders because of its past propagandistic purpose and limited economic effectiveness. The special wage settlements for industrial workers in March 1973 and April 1974 eased discontent in that sector, leaving white-collar employees as the current disadvantaged group.

The inadequacies of the trade union structure were the subject of periodic comment. *Társadalmi Szemle* (February) reported on a discussion session with trade unionists and enterprise leaders on the question of protecting craft interests and the inadequacy of the existing branch union in this sphere. The labor monthly *Munka* (March) indicated why the unions' right of veto is seldom exercised: in many enterprises the union barely exists as an entity independent of management, and the few union officials are too cautious; insufficient information makes union men reluctant to provoke conflict; and inadequate training of union officials. Thus instead of trying to implement enterprise democracy the officials resort to informal compromises. The HSWP's efforts to enhance the status of the workers through enterprise democracy are characterized by accusations that managers misuse their authority, disregard workers' opinions, and retaliate against justifiable criticism. "Despite repeated warnings by the party's leading organs, tolerance of such phenomena is still encountered." (*Pártélet*, January.)

During 1974 some 8,000 Hungarian *Gastarbeiter* worked in East Germany. For the first time, 200 young East German workers were sent to Hungary for "professional training."

Demographic and Social Patterns. According to the "microcensus" carried out in 1973, the population of Hungary grew by 1.1 percent between 1970 and 1973 to 10,416,000. Of those aged 18 and older, 18 percent are high school or university graduates. Nearly half (5,086,000) of the population are active wage earners, of whom 58 percent are workers, 15 percent cooperative farmers, 3 percent small producers, and 24 percent in "intellectual" occupations. Forty-eight percent of the women are employed.

Rural society has undergone a drastic transformation since the communist takeover. In 1949, 40 percent of the wage earners were small-scale farmers. Now even among the village dwellers more than half do not have farming as their principal occupation. Many work in industry, and only half of cooperative members are engaged in peasant activities, the rest filling white-collar or auxiliary jobs resulting from larger collectives, mechanization, and product diversification. The standard of living of cooperative members has in recent years reached and even surpassed that of urban industrial workers (*Magyar Nemzet*, 9 February 1974).

A new demographic policy came into effect 1 January 1974, aiming to reduce the earlier reliance on induced abortions as the principal method of family planning. This, together with the recently increased family and child welfare allowances and maternity grants, is expected to increase the birth rate, which stood at 14.7 per thousand in 1972 (16 per thousand is considered necessary to maintain the present population level). These measures will require new efforts in housing, nurseries, and kindergartens, and may in the short run have a negative effect on the manpower supply by taking more women out of the labor force, but are regarded as essential to ensure adequate human resources.

A new decree law on state and public safety was promulgated in October, replacing a 1956 law. It is designed to provide a more systematic framework for the activities of the Ministry of Interior, and assigns to the police (along with other state and social organizations) the task of fighting anti-social manifestations that can lead to criminal acts. The *Népszabadság* commentary (27 October) claimed that thanks to public cooperation, police in socialist countries solve 90 to 95 percent of the "most serious crimes," compared with 30 to 40 percent in the West, and that in Hungary anti-state (political) crimes accounted for only 1 percent of all criminal acts in 1973.

Youth. The apparent ineffectiveness of the Communist Youth League (KISZ) as an agent of political indoctrination has prompted a number of remedial measures. A Politburo resolution on 5 November 1973 criticized the inadequacy of ideological education among young persons as reflected in the persistence of patriotic, Western-oriented, and religious sentiments at the expense of appreciation for the achievements of socialism and friendship for other socialist states. Party organizations were instructed to assign better qualified members to work with the KISZ (*Pártélet*, January 1974). At the April meeting of the KISZ Central Committee, attended by Aczél and Pullai, a resolution was introduced to increase the KISZ's ideological-political effectiveness and the activity and discipline of the basic organizations. A test of political and practical knowledge is to raise requirements for admission. Beginning in 1975, membership cards will be exchanged annually to weed out undesirable members. (*Népszabadság*, 18 April.) Currently the KISZ has some 800,000 members, accounting for 35 percent of young industrial workers, 30 percent of agricultural youth, 60 percent of young skilled workers, 72 percent of secondary school students, and 93 percent of students in higher education.

In keeping with the requirements of the 1971 Youth Law, "youth parliaments" were organized in places of work and educational institutions during 1974 with the assistance of KISZ. Intended to be a forum for discussions on the implementation of the Youth Law and on problems and future tasks, the youth parliaments do not appear to offer a particularly successful mobilizing technique. The widespread popularity of beat music and the proliferation of independent youth clubs (regarded by the authorities as uncontrolled purveyors of Western fads and attitudes) have prompted measures to bring such groups and clubs under KISZ supervision. (*Magyar Ifjuság*, 29 March.)

Culture. The relatively tolerant cultural policies pursued by the regime in recent years, manifested in such diverse spheres as satirical political revues and historiography, appear to be undergoing some revision as the outward campaign for détente brings its corollary of domestic ideological retrenchment into focus. Reacting to what they consider a neglect of the problems and achievements of socialism, the authorities are providing a variety of incentives for writers to produce works "committed to socialism," especially sociographic studies of workers and of village life (*Népszabadság*, 28 December 1973).

A Council of Ministers resolution on the development of the social sciences stressed the need to improve the quality of sociological research, citing "dilettantism" and slipshod techniques of data collection (*Magyar Hirlap*, 18 January 1974). A new law regulating statistical activity is to be applied to the survey work of sociologists. In an address to the annual meeting of the Academy of Sciences in May, Aczél endorsed research directly related to production and socioeconomic needs, and warned that freedom of research must be tempered by ideological responsibility and that views deliberately opposing Marxism must be rejected.

A small "New Left" group, consisting of a few students and intellectuals and exercising a certain attraction for a broader stratum of the disillusioned, continues to draw the ire of the regime. The young writer Miklós Haraszti, who had been arrested in 1973 on charges of anti-government incitement, was given a suspended sentence. His arrest had come after radical left activities in KISZ, including attacks on anti-egalitarian tendencies of the new wage system, and distribution of *samizdat* copies of his critique. The third week in October brought a secret police sweep against dissident intellectuals and the arrests of the noted writer-sociologist György Konrád, the sociologist Iván Szelényi, and the avant-garde poet Tamás Szentjóby on charges of anti-socialist agitation. Konrád and Szelényi had produced studies of alienation in an urbanized society. After a brief detention the three men were instructed to leave the country within three months.

State-Church Relations. After consultation with the regime, the Vatican announced in February 1974 a number of new appointments in the Hungarian Catholic hierarchy, including an apostolic administrator of Esztergom, Cardinal Mindszenty's former archbishopric. As a necessary first step, Pope Paul had relieved Mindszenty of his de jure church offices in Hungary, a concession to the regime in the interests of filling the vacancies, but he did not go so far as to name a new archbishop-primate. Mindszenty, who since his departure from Hungary has been outspokenly hostile to the regime and to the Vatican's policy of accommodation (notably in his recently published memoirs), announced that the decision was entirely the Pope's. Kádár, for his part, remarked: "Those who claim that it was under our pressure that Pope Paul VI relieved Mindszenty of the archepiscopal seat of Esztergom overestimate our means and underestimate the Vatican" (*Népszabadság*, 30 March).

The chairman of the State Office for Church Affairs termed the present situation "essentially satisfactory." He claimed that "sober-minded and far-sighted church leaders are able effectively to overcome obstructionist churchmen and church groups bent on forcing on the churches a political line at variance with the socialist state and society," that smaller Protestant denominations received equal treatment, and that the state was providing "provisionally" some 70 million forints annual support to the churches as well as assistance in the restoration of buildings. (*Magyar Hirlap*, 19 August.)

Foreign Relations. During 1974, official pronouncements and press reports continued to follow Moscow's lead in advocating at great length the nebulous concept of détente. The Watergate affair received relatively little comment until U.S. President Nixon's resignation, whereupon the stress was again on the preservation of détente and the new administration's commitment to maintain the momentum of SALT and other East-West negotiations. Solzhenitsyn's *Gulag Archipelago* was denounced as a tendentious, demagogic political pamphlet the release of which was part of a psychological campaign against détente (*Magyar Nemzet*, 16 January). The resignation of Chancellor Brandt was attributed to spy hysteria promoted by West German rightists hostile to détente and Ostpolitik (*Népszabadság*, 12 May).

In his report to the HSWP Central Committee meeting in March, Pullai condemned the alleged

U.S.-supported cease-fire violations by the Thieu regime and demanded enforcement of the Paris agreements; advocated a final Middle East settlement entailing Israeli withdrawal from the occupied territories and the "complete restitution of the Palestinian Arab people's rights"; and denounced the repressive measures of the Chilean junta, repeating the Soviet bloc demand for the release of Luis Corvalán and other communists. In an effort to show objectivity, *Magyar Hirlap* (26 October) noted that "the foundation and existence of Israel is justified" but disapproved of its activities on behalf of "international imperialism"; the article stressed that Hungary's 100,000 Jews enjoy full rights and have old age homes, synagogues, etc. At the United Nations, in November, Hungary voted with the majority to grant participant status to the Palestine Liberation Organization.

The foreign ministers of Hungary's two principal Western trading partners visited Budapest in 1974. Walter Scheel was the first high West German official to come to Hungary since World War II (7-9 April). The official communiqué on the talks stressed the positive aspects of détente and noted that the establishment of diplomatic relations would facilitate wider economic cooperation. László Hamburger, an economic specialist, was appointed Hungary's first ambassador to Bonn in December 1973. The Soviet bloc's traditional mistrust of West Germany and fears of excessive economic influence remain factors in Hungarian-West German relations. The visit of Italian Foreign Minister Aldo Moro in May produced a ten-year agreement on industrial, economic, and technical cooperation and a civil aviation agreement.

International Party Contacts. Hungarian press reports of party visits are generally laconic statements of departures, arrivals, and fruitful and cordial exchanges of views, with little indication of substance. In March 1974 Sándor Gáspár led a trade union delegation to Moscow. In June, János Berecz, new head of the Central Committee's Foreign Relations Department, led a party delegation that was received by secretaries B. N. Ponomarev and K. F. Katushev of the Central Committee of the Communist Party of the Soviet Union (CPSU). Kádár held his annual informal meeting with CPSU general secretary Leonid Brezhnev on 2-5 August; the talks were characterized by "cordial friendship" and "full unity of views." Németh on 3-6 September took part in talks on economic management policy and economic, scientific, and technological cooperation in the context of the CMEA's comprehensive integration program; he also had "warm and friendly" talks with Brezhnev.

The major contact was the "official friendly visit," to the U.S.S.R. 25-30 September of a party-state delegation including Kádár, Németh, Premier Fock, *Társadalmi Szemle* editor Valéria Benke, Deputy Premier István Huszár (chairman of the Soviet-Hungarian Intergovernmental Committee on Economic and Technological-Scientific Cooperation), and Foreign Minister Frigyes Puja. The concluding communiqué referred to agreements on scientific and technological cooperation, ideology, and political coordination. Presumably policy and personnel questions related to the forthcoming HSWP congress also came under discussion.

The HSWP participated in the consultative meeting of 28 European communist parties at Warsaw, 16-18 October, which produced agreement on holding the much-discussed conference of European communist parties in the German Democratic Republic by mid-1975.

Hungary's cordial relations with Yugoslavia were reasserted in Tito's visit to Budapest, 28-29 April, and the attendance of a party delegation led by Biszku at the congress of the League of Communists of Yugoslavia in May. Close economic relations are aided by similarities in the system of economic management of both countries; trade is cleared in convertible currencies, and direct contact between enterprises is allowed. Allegations, made public in September, of Hungarian, along with the Soviet and Czechoslovak, involvement in a "Stalinist" plot against the Tito régime prompted diplomatic denials, ultimately by both sides. According to unofficial Yugoslav sources, some seditious material had been printed in Hungary, presumably as part of a Soviet-directed subversive operation.

Friendly relations between Kádár and Czechoslovak party leader Gustav Husák were in evidence once again during the former's visit to Prague, 10-12 April.

An HSWP delegation visited North Vietnam and the "liberated" areas of Laos in February. At the beginning of April a North Vietnamese delegation made a brief stop in Budapest; its leader, Pham Van Dong, met Kádár "in an atmosphere of friendship and militant solidarity."

HSWP policy regarding the Chinese Communist Party follows Moscow's lead. The visit of a Bulgarian delegation in December 1973 provided the occasion for a typical denunciation of the "great-power chauvinism, rabid anti-Sovietism, and schismatic activities" of the leaders of the Chinese party, and of their "anti-Marxist and nationalist views" (*Népszabadság*, 7 December). An analysis in *Társadalmi Szemle* (December 1973) accused the Maoists of seeking hegemony within the socialist system and urged further research into the circumstances allowing for the rise of this ideological distortion. During 1974 the Chinese were periodically excoriated for opposing and hindering détente in Europe.

Publications. The principal HSWP organs are the daily newspaper *Népszabadság* ("People's Freedom"), the theoretical monthly *Társadalmi Szemle* ("Social Review"), and the monthly organizational journal *Pártélet* ("Party Life").

University of Toronto   Bennett Kovrig

Poland

The communist party in power in the Polish People's Republic is officially the Polish United Workers' Party (Polska Zjednoczona Partia Robotnicza; PUWP). It dates back to the Communist Workers' Party of Poland, founded in December 1918, and outlawed and forced underground in early 1919. The name Communist Party of Poland was taken in 1925. For reasons still not entirely clear, the Comintern dissolved the party in 1938, and many members perished in the great Soviet purge. In January 1942 it reappeared as the Polish Workers' Party, and in 1944-45, following the advance of the Red Army into Poland, it quickly achieved dominance of the coalition government that was set up to appeal to the broad masses. After undermining the non-communist parties in the coalition, the Polish Workers' Party in 1948 merged with left-wing remnants of the old Polish Socialist Party to form the PUWP. Since then the PUWP has controlled all elections and other formal political activities through the Front of National Unity (FNU), ostensibly a coalition with two "independent" parties, the United Peasant Party (UPP) and the Democratic Party (DP), the one officially representing the peasantry and the other the working intelligentsia and small entrepreneurs. Representatives of "progressive" non-party organizations and several Catholic groups are also allowed to run candidates on the FNU "preferred lists."

In the latest national elections, in 1972, the FNU received 99.53 percent of the valid votes for the 460 seats in the parliament (Sejm). The distribution of seats, exactly the same as in the previous election, gave the PUWP 255, the UPP 117, the DP 39, and the independents 49 (including 10 for Catholic groups). Polish elections since 1956 have permitted more candidates than seats, on ballots headed by the preferred FNU names: in a district with 6 seats, for example, there might be 8 candidates, and the first 6 names would be those of the FNU choices. To vote against any of the preferred candidates, the voter would cross out a name (or names), thereby voting for the candidate (or candidates) immediately below the invisible line dividing the preferred candidates from those in excess of the seats in the district. Since the PUWP decides who gets on the ballot, the choice allowed has little meaning, but it provides for the expression of a vote of protest.

The PUWP has about 2,330,000 members, including candidate members. The population of Poland is estimated at about 33,700,000. Social composition of the PUWP has remained fairly steady for some years: approximately 40 percent manual workers, 43 percent white-collar workers, 11 percent peasants, 6 percent "other" (see below).

Organization and Leadership. The basic PUWP unit is the primary party organization, set up in places of work (factories, stores, schools, military units, etc.) and in residential locations (villages and small towns in rural areas, streets or housing units in the cities). There are about 72,600 civilian and 3,400 military primary party organizations. The next level consists of district units: all or part of a county (powiat), or parts of large cities. On the next higher level are the 19 province (voivodship) organizations, including those for the two largest cities, Warsaw and Łódż. The highest authority is PUWP congress, which meets every four years according to the party statute. It elects the Central Committee and the Central Party Audit Commission. The Central Committee elects the Politburo—the supreme policy-making body—and the Secretariat, which is the executive organ of the Central Committee and the Politburo. There are separate Central Committee departments for Administration, Culture, Economic Affairs, Foreign Relations, and so on. The Central Party Control Commission oversees party discipline and maintains ideological correctness. The province and district levels have similar but simpler structures.

Edward Gierek, Politburo and Secretariat member has headed the PUWP as first secretary since 1970, when he replaced long-time leader Władysław Gomułka. (For others in the top party leadership see *YICA, 1974*, p. 48. Changes in personnel are indicated below.)

The PUWP relies heavily on mass membership and smaller, more specialized organizations to (1) maintain its legitimacy, (2) disseminate propaganda and mobilize support for its political and economic objectives, (3) mold socialist attitudes and control mass behavior, (4) provide a party-controlled substitute for every organization normally found in modern society and preempt the field for potential opposition organizations, (5) undermine existing organizations not under party control (e.g., the Catholic church), and (6) mobilize the population for socially useful work over and above regular employment. The publications, mass meetings, rallies, campaigns, and other activities of these specialized organizations supplement the direct work of the PUWP activists and press. Further, they create the appearance of a more pluralistic society and provide outlets for the energies of a great many citizens who otherwise might not work for the party's goals.

The most important of the mass organizations are the trade unions, enrolling some 10 million members and controlled by the Central Council of Trade Unions (CCTU). Government employees, health service personnel, and schoolteachers are organized within the CCTU, but other segments of the intelligentsia have independent associations, such as the Association of Polish Lawyers, the Association of Polish Journalists, the Polish Writers' Union, and the "ZAIKS" Association of Authors. In addition are unions for those working in the cooperative sector of the economy.

In rural areas, in addition to the CCTU farm workers' union, the UPP, and the central union of agricultural producers' cooperatives (collective farms), there is a "Peasant Self-Help Cooperative," with some 2,500 separate co-ops and more than 4.5 million members, along with a network of more than 35,000 "agricultural circles" having more than 2.6 million members. The latter are coordinated under the Central Union of Agricultural Circles (CUAC).

Poland's five youth organizations—the Socialist Union of Polish Students, Socialist Youth Union, Union of Socialist Rural Youth, Polish Scouting Union, and Socialist Military Youth Union—were united in 1973 in the Federation of the Socialist Unions of Polish Youth (See *YICA, 1974*, pp. 49-50). Other important mass organizations include the Women's League, the patriotic veterans' organization known as the Union of Fighters for Freedom and Democracy (or ZBoWiD), the Volunteer Militia Reserve (ORMO), and organizations for civil defense, assistance to children, adult and working-youth education, and volunteer welfare work. "Polonia," the Society for Ties with Poles Abroad, promotes the interests of the Polish People's Republic among emigrés.

Party Internal Affairs. There were no major organizational changes in the PUWP during 1974. Party work was principally directed toward (1) fulfillment of the economic program set at the Sixth Congress in 1971 and amplified in the party's first National Conference in October 1973, (2) closer cooperation with the Communist Party of the Soviet Union (CPSU) on ideological and international questions, and (3) increasing the ideological preparedness of the cadres and strengthening the influence of Marxism-Leninism—as interpreted by the party leadership—in the surrounding society.

Turnover in the upper hierarchy of the PUWP was moderate. On 31 May, Franciszek Szlachcic was removed from the Secretariat of the Central Committee. He remained in the Politburo, however, and on 25 June became a deputy premier. There was speculation in Warsaw that his demotion was due to his associations with the former minister of the interior, General Mieczysław Moczar, and perhaps with General Ryszard Matejewski, a Moczar supporter who is under sentence to a 12-year jail term, allegedly for conspiring to oust Gierek in May 1971.

On 26 June, the Sejm elected Stanisław Wronski member of the Council of State; he simultaneously left the Council of Ministers. Wronski's portfolio, the Ministry of Culture and the Arts, had been taken over in February by Józef Tejchma. Wronski, too, was considered a Moczar supporter and, therefore, relieved.

On 18-19 May the Union of Fighters for Freedom and Democracy held its national congress in Warsaw. The gathering was addressed by leading party figures, including First Secretary Edward Gierek and Premier Piotr Jaroszewicz. Moczar, who led the organization for many years until his ouster in May 1972, was not mentioned.

On 26 February, Kazimierz Barcikowski was relieved of his Secretariat position and appointed minister of agriculture, replacing Józef Okuniecki.

At the end of September, Central Committee member Jan Mitręga was replaced as minister of mining and power by Jan Kulpiński. Manpower shortages and a series of mine disasters were blamed for Mitręga's fall. Secret wage increases, rumored to range up to 30 percent, and the administrative shake-up apparently were offered to the miners in the hope of achieving a planned increase in coal exports, largely to Western countries, and thereby increasing Poland's hard-currency earnings abroad.

The "Polish Institute on Basic Problems of Marxism-Leninism," attached to the Central Committee, was established by a Politburo decision on 26 February. Central Committee Secretary, Andrzej Werblan, was put in charge of this organization. Its official mission is to deepen and intensify ideological work of party cadres in cooperation with the Polish Academy of Sciences and institutions of higher learning, prepare analyses and forecasts, and study domestic and international problems relevant to communist and workers' parties. In late May, a new law extended the jurisdiction of the Ministry of Foreign Affairs to matters involving the "Polonia" organization (see above and *YICA, 1974*, p. 50), and to the coordination of various domestic activities pertaining to relations with foreign powers.

Ideological warfare was the theme at a conference held in Warsaw in January to commemorate the fiftieth anniversary of Lenin's death. Central Committee secretary Jerzy Łukasiewicz denounced the Maoist leadership of China's communist party for allegedly waging war on the international communist movement. He claimed that détente had opened up new possibilities for "peaceful revolutionary processes" and increased the significance of ideological warfare. Denouncing the notion of a "free flow of people and ideas," as being directed against détente, Łukasiewicz made it clear that in the field of communications, the party saw an opportunity in détente which it would not extend to its adversaries.

This position on détente was vigorously reaffirmed by foreign minister and Politburo member Stefan Olszowski at a party ideological conference in Warsaw on 25 March. He denounced Western suggestions of a "free flow of people, thoughts, and ideas" as being intended to deprive the socialist states of their sovereign right to solve internal problems and to pursue their own policies on the dissemination of information. Simultaneously, Olszowski demanded that détente be institutionalized through treaty arrangements and that the socialist states must somehow reach people "where for political reasons we cannot maintain official contacts or exchange high-level visits." He charged the Chinese with splitting and sabotaging the efforts of the other socialist states.

An article by Politburo member and Central Committee secretary Jan Szydlak (*Nowe drogi*, May) also emphasized that détente and peaceful coexistence increased the role and significance of ideological warfare. Szydlak wrote that the socialist countries were guided by the CPSU. Détente "opened new possibilities for the world revolutionary process," and peaceful coexistence was "a formula for further revolutionary transformation." It was necessary to unmask capitalism, he said, and the opportunism of social democracy, too, "even if we sometimes cooperate with it." Szydlak denounced Maoism as a threat to world peace and détente, as well as an enemy of the socialist bloc, and indicated that the time for a world conference of communist parties, presumably intended to oust the Maoists from the international movement, was at hand. He demanded that the party take increasing care to eliminate from the televised programs and youth publications "everything which, directly or indirectly, popularizes moral values and individual human models that are alien to us," and he pointed to the Church as the chief institutional structure supporting opposition and petty bourgeois ideology, still with a considerable social foundation in Poland.

In a programmatic speech to the Central Committee plenum on 26 June, Edward Babiuch, Politburo and Secretariat member, announced that 40 percent of the party members were of worker background, 10 percent were peasants, and fully half were drawn from the new middle class—the intelligentsia. He stated that it was important to continue to increase worker membership, and hinted at a possible purge of the PUWP ranks through an exchange of membership cards, in which "to obtain a new card every PUWP member will have to present a good report on his party attitude and activity."

Party organs in February and March carried articles and editorials attacking Aleksandr Solzhenitsyn, whose books, particularly *The Gulag Archipelago*, were said to be aimed at obstructing détente, unifying reactionary forces against the U.S.S.R., and providing pretexts for imperialist interference in the domestic affairs of the socialist states. In January there were attacks on Soviet physicist Andrei Sakharov for anti-Soviet, pro-imperialist views and activities.

In February, substantial personnel changes were announced in the radio and television organization, with the object of improving the ideological quality of the labor force; also an agreement was announced concerning ideological-political cooperation between the Main Political Administration of the Polish Armed Forces and the Political Administration of the Soviet Army's Northern Group (stationed in Poland); the agreement was said to be designed to strengthen brotherly cooperation between Polish and Soviet troops.

The need for military preparedness in the face of NATO, particularly certain West German, attitudes was urged in a speech by General Wojciech Jaruzelski, minister of national defense, in a speech on 9 May to the meeting of the Union of Fighters for Freedom and Democracy. He emphasized that the Polish-Soviet alliance was the keystone of Poland's position in the world.

A conference of editors of party historical journals was held in Warsaw on 9-10 April. Romania was the only Warsaw Pact state not represented. The theme was increasing interbloc cooperation on all ideological questions. In April, the editor in chief of the PUWP historical journal, *Z pola walki*, Professor Antoni Czubiński, was removed from his post, probably because of insufficiently orthodox writings. His 1973 book, *USSR, Years of Struggle and Victory*, had been criticized for an insufficiently positive treatment of Soviet-Polish relations during World War II.

At the meeting of the Polish Film Makers' Association on 27-28 April, Politburo member, deputy-premier, and minister of culture, Józef Tejchma, emphasized the party's interest in the increased ideological utilization of the Polish film industry. An organizational shake-up like that in radio and television appeared to be under way.

At the 12 June national meeting of the Socialist Youth Union, party leaders made particularly strong appeals to the young. Gierek called upon them to outdo previous generations in respect to dedication to socialism, patriotic commitment, social attitude, productive work, and manner and style of life—they were to make increasingly rational use of Poland's material resources—and to provide themselves with the "unfailing compass of Marxism-Leninism." The 1 July meeting of the

Polish Journalists' Association, in Lublin, issued a declaration in support of increased ideological efforts to "tap the production, and the social and cultural militancy of all the working people in Poland" in behalf of the party's goals.

PUWP observances of the thirtieth anniversary of the Polish People's Republic included awards to distinguished intellectuals, much publicity for the restoration of the Royal Castle in Warsaw (to be completed in 1978), emphasis on links to Poland's émigrés, and great emphasis on Polish gratitude to and indissoluble friendship with the Soviet Union. CPSU general secretary Leonid Brezhnev was frequently singled out for special personal praise and on 21 July was awarded Poland's highest military decoration by Gierek, following a Brezhnev speech to the Sejm. In July, the newspapers *Trybuna ludu* and *Życie Warszawy* reviewed party history in Poland, with a good deal of unexpected praise for Władysław Gomułka's activities, particularly those between 1943 and 1948.

On 1 October further decentralization of various policy jurisdictions over such matters as agriculture, education, health care, social welfare, finances and land consolidation was enacted by the Sejm. Greater responsibility thus devolved on local PUWP secretaries.

The Economy. Considerable expansion, modernization, and increased wages and social welfare benefits continued to characterize the economy in 1974. But these gains appeared threatened by an increasing imbalance between imports, aimed at improving and modernizing the Polish economy, and exports needed to finance them; the situation was aggravated by worldwide inflation, and particularly by increased fuel prices. Poland depends on non-communist sources for at least 15 percent of its oil supplies. At the Central Committee plenum on 19 January, Premier Jaroszewicz called for 25 percent higher taxi and long-distance bus fares to promote more economical use of gasoline. He promised, however, to maintain current price levels in public municipal transportation, and said that Poland would expand both production and import of automobiles. He claimed that cooperation with CMEA and the USSR was at the core of Poland's successful economic development.

In 1970, the last year of the Gomułka leadership, imports valued at nearly 14.5 billion zlotys and exports at nearly 14.2 billion left a deficit of 250 million. At the end of 1973, exports were up to almost 21.4 billion and imports to 26.1 billion, for a much more serious deficit of more than 4.7 billion zlotys.

At the 19 January plenum, Gierek and Jaroszewicz declared that general improvement in living conditions was the principal long-term objective. Specific measures urged or promised toward this objective in 1974 called for raising the minimum wage, raising the wages of certain key-sector employees, increasing old age and disability pensions, and liberalizing family allowances and other social welfare benefits. Wage increases were pledged to some 500,000 coal, copper, iron ore, and other mine workers amounting to 2.4 billion zlotys a year, to begin 1 February. About a million persons engaged in transportation and technical services to agriculture, ranging from tractor drivers to scientific research workers, were slated to receive 5.8 billion zlotys in annual increases beginning in April; more than a million in internal and foreign trade and various maritime jobs were slated for increases in excess of 4.5 billion zlotys beginning in mid-year. The minimum wage was to be raised from 1,100 zlotys, beginning 1 August, to 1,200. These and other wage increases, scheduled to go into effect before the end of 1974, amounted to an annual cost of 13.4 billion zlotys, with still more projected for 1975. Increases in 1974 pensions paid to the aged, the veterans, and the disabled involved additional annual costs of 2.1 billion. Families qualifying for supplementary income allowances would be permitted to earn 1,400 zlotys a month, up from 1,000 previously. On 1 August the minimum old-age pension was raised from 960 to 1,100 zlotys; disability and family pensions were raised by an average of 130 zlotys a month.

Another indication of the party's new commitment to meeting consumer demands was reflected in the 1971-75 housing construction plan. It called for completion of 1.1 million apartments, where

Poland had built only 2.5 million during 1945-71. According to Gierek and Jaroszewicz, the new consumer-oriented policies would contribute to creating a "correct social atmosphere in the country, and would unite the efforts of the whole community."

In order to achieve planned objectives, however, Jaroszewicz called for greater efforts in rationalizing the economy, the import of 1.5 million tons of Soviet grain, and substantially increased prices for petroleum products and for alcohol and services of catering establishments. He pledged that stable prices would be maintained on all basic food items, and that the stability of working people's budgets would be preserved. He claimed that the economic progress of the last three years was unprecedented in the thirty-year history of People's Poland. The national income had increased allegedly by about one-third, and the economy was growing at a rate of about 9 percent annually; industrial production had risen by 36 percent and agricultural production by almost 19 percent; and the country was in the midst of the largest investment program in its history. Between 1971 and 1973 real wages had risen four times as fast as in 1966-71, at an annual average of 7.6 percent. Jaroszewicz indicated that the government has succeeded in paying higher wages during the current five-year plan to some 6.4 million workers (about two-thirds of the labor force), as compared with a projected 4.6 million, and had increased incomes of the lowest stratum, narrowed down income disparities, increased rural incomes, increased scholarships and family allowances, provided more generous maternity and sick leaves, and extended free medical care to more rural areas.

Still, some 4 million workers would not have any wage increases till 1 January 1976, Jaroszewicz pointed out. He justified the raises to miners principally on the need for coal, both for domestic uses and for export; increases in transport, retail trade, services, and agriculture were also described as serving the highest priorities of Poland's economic development. Jaroszewicz took credit for increasing the minimum wage from 850 zlotys in 1970 to 1,200 in 1974, and for the fact that in 1970 the minimum was earned by 2.2 percent of the labor force, and now by less than one percent. By 1980, people in the 1,500-2,000 zlotys wage bracket would receive not 55 but 80 percent of their salary in retirement pensions; there would also be increases in the higher brackets, Jaroszewicz said, from 60 to 75 percent for those earning 3,200 zlotys or more per month. He also promised six Saturdays free from work in 1974 and 12 in 1975, and a general reduction of the work week from 46 hours to 42 for most workers. There would also be work-free days for those on 42-hour schedules. (In one respect, however, the PUWP undercut its promises, at least in 1974, by demanding "voluntary work" from employees, including Sunday work on some occasions.)

To increase food production, Jaroszewicz indicated that Poland would purchase some 10,000 tractors from the U.S.S.R. in addition to the 1.5 million tons of grain. More chemicals and machinery would be deployed in agricultural production. Farmers would be paid higher prices for live stock and sugar beets. Also, farmers who donated their land to the state would be given higher retirement pensions. The magnitude of the agricultural problem was indicated by the revelations of Warsaw Radio in February. Eighty percent of the land was under private cultivation by three million individual farmers, of whom only about a million made use of modern technology. About 230,000 farms were in hands of owners past the age of 65 years. The government estimated that farmers needed an inventory of some 60,000 zlotys per hectare for effective utilization of the land; 24,000 zlotys per hectare was the actual average. Doubled investment in agricultural machinery was scheduled for 1974.

With reference to the rationalization of the economy, Gierek in a speech at Warsaw on 30 January indicated that Poland suffered from a surplus of university graduates. It was necessary to develop better coordination between what young people wanted to study and what the economy really needed, and also to upgrade trade schools and obliterate the traditional distinctions in people's minds between physical and mental work. Meanwhile efforts had to be made to find appropriate employment for the university-trained young people. Some sectors of the economy, according to official media, appeared to have developed labor shortages. Universal secondary education is intended by the early 1980s.

At the Central Committee plenum on 13 February Gierek said that Poland was now the tenth leading industrial power in the world, and predicted a fourfold increase in national income by 1990. On 19 March the Politburo and the Council of Ministers in a joint meeting approved a long-term development plan for the Polish economy, through 1990, and also basic directives for the 1976-80 five-year plan. On 26 March, the Politburo adopted a plan for large-scale development of the city of Warsaw during the same period. The plan envisioned the construction of a subway and represented a continuation of Gierek's personal interest in the city's development, first evidenced in 1971 by his support for rebuilding the Royal Castle.

Echoing the leaders' theme of social stabilization linked to economic progress, was the 21 March statement by General Marian Janicki, commander of the volunteer Militia Reserve. Without citing actual figures, he claimed that there had been a 20 percent decline in economic crimes throughout the country over the previous year. He indicated, however, that juvenile crime was on the increase. On 11 April a new law required all persons to have identification cards indicating both citizenship and nationality, allegedly to provide more adequate records on the state and distribution of the population. In July, an amnesty honoring the thirtieth anniversary of People's Poland went into effect for thousands of persons sentenced for relatively minor crimes.

On 22 May the Polish Press Agency (PAP) reported that the productivity of Polish socialized industries was up 10.1 percent in the first four months of 1974, where 8.1 had been planned. In the building industry productivity rose 14.4 percent, compared with the target figure of 10 percent; some 81 percent of the total growth of Polish industrial production was officially attributed to increased labor productivity, said to be the best in 30 years. Factors credited for this included better organization of production, more rational employment, higher qualifications of the work force, and better utilization of the working day.

On 25 June Premier Piotr Jaroszewicz presented a report to the Central Committee plenum on the implementation of social and economic tasks set by the PUWP's first national conference, held in October 1973. He reported that the economy was experiencing the benefits of increased labor productivity; that wages in the socialized sector of the economy had increased by 17.5 percent in the first five months of 1974, and that the government expected an increase in personal income in excess of 14 percent by the end of 1974, as compared with a planned figure of 9.3. Continuing improvement in the general standard of living was said to be the government's main objective. There was an increased rate of meat consumption, up 11 kg. over 1970, at 64 kg. per capita. There was a 56 percent average increase in investment in housing during 1971-75, Jaroszewicz said, over the preceding 5-year period; in agriculture, investment was 60 percent higher. Claiming overfulfillment of planned goals in all sectors of the economy, Jaroszewicz cited a 36.5 percent increase in foreign trade during the first 5 months of 1974 over the corresponding period in 1973. He admitted, however, that although trade with non-communist states was increasing, Poland had a deficit of $180 million as a result of Western price increases. Continued imports of machinery and other vital capital goods were expected to accelerate the development and modernization of the economy and, in the long run, increase Poland's exports. The Central Committee issued a resolution emphasizing the importance of increasing fodder production in agriculture and continuing an effective investment policy in industry. The value of services, long neglected in all communist economies, was to be increased by 75 percent in 1975 in comparison with 1970 levels, according to the resolution.

On 26 June the Sejm adopted a new comprehensive labor code covering some 11 million employees. The code attempted to balance increased protection for workers against possible arbitrary mistreatment by management on the one hand, with safeguards against industrial saboteurs and malingerers on the other. It sanctioned preferential rewards to the more productive workers; it also allowed greater worker participation in administering policy relating to employees. Workers' councils were to be consulted in cases involving possible dismissal of employees, and in the supervision of various aspects of the code. The measure, unlike many previous party-imposed decrees, appears to have received a considerable amount of input from affected interests. The original proposal was drafted jointly by the government and the CCTU, with some 400 amendments offered, according to an official statement released by PAP, from a variety of sources including individual workers, economic experts, scientists, and parliamentary deputies as well as the unions and other "public organizations." The new code received public support from all the groupings represented in the Sejm, including the relatively independent Catholic Znak faction; Znak spokesman Janusz Zablocki endorsed the code as supportive of the principle of "honest work for the good of the country."

The Politburo approved on 9 July an extensive plan of development for the Silesian province of Katowice—Gierek's original power base—calling for continued modernization of its economy, a doubling of its steel production, and a substantial increase in coal extraction and in the output of other industries, consistent with "demands for the protection of the natural environment." The plan envisioned the creation by 1980 of one of the largest industrial-urban agglomerations in Europe. The Politburo also expressed satisfaction with economic achievements in all sectors of the mid-year. In September, legislation easing taxation and licensing handicaps on more efficient private stores and restaurants was enacted by the Sejm. The measure affected 6,700 out of a total of 127,000 such establishments.

Early in September, labor unrest was once again reported in the ports of Gdansk, Gdynia, and Szczecin. Dockers and shipyard workers apparently engaged in wildcat strikes and work slowdowns in protest of new wage rates and declining bonuses. In late September also, the government began a campaign against the hoarding of raw materials and spare parts by industrial firms. Involved were billions of dollars' worth of inventories, according to official estimates.

Despite increased government investments, the housing situation continued to be extremely unsatisfactory. By some estimates, a newly married couple might have to wait eight years for a new apartment. The gap between housing supply and demand has actually grown worse in the 1970s as a consequence of an earlier high birth-rate. On the other hand, relatively low costs for housing, food, and medical facilities made Poland economically attractive to some pensioners in the United States. About 6,000 elderly U.S. citizens of Polish extraction have emigrated to Poland; their Social Security pensions, exchanged at double the rate offered tourists, commanded substantially greater purchasing power than in the West.

Relations with the Catholic Church. While contacts with the Vatican continued to expand in 1974, the process of "normalization of relations" between church and state in Poland was seriously strained. The Polish episcopate was subjected to increasing pressures and denunciations by the PUWP. Agostino Casaroli, Vatican secretary of the Council for Public Affairs of the Church, visited Warsaw on 4-6 February for far-ranging discussions with government leaders on the question of diplomatic relations between Poland and the Holy See. The Polish episcopate appeared apprehensive about the possibility of agreements that might compromise its position. Polish cardinals, though invited, did not attend the receptions given by foreign minister Olszowski and Monsignor Casaroli. Comments in the official press indicated the regime's eagerness to drive a wedge between the Vatican and the Polish clergy, whose allegedly unsatisfactory attitude was attacked.

The pro-state "Pax" daily, *Slowo powszechne*, lavished attention on the Casaroli visit; the pro-church *Tygodnik powszechny* maintained a reserved attitude with brief, matter-of-fact coverage. The removal of Cardinal Mindszenty as primate of Hungary was seen by the party as a possible precedent for Stefan Cardinal Wyszyński, should he obstruct a détente between the Vatican and People's Poland. Casaroli's public remarks in Warsaw, emphasizing the need for the clergy's obedience to the Holy See, seemed to give weight to these speculations. Vice-minister of foreign affairs Józef Czyrek, repaid the visit on 4-5 July at the Vatican. Talks between Czyrek and Casaroli led to a brief official Polish announcement on 8 July that "the Government of the Polish People's Republic and the Holy See had agreed to establish permanent working contacts."

The death of Bolesław Cardinal Kominek, at age 70, in Wroclaw on 10 March, was observed with considerable ceremony. The regime dispatched a high-ranking delegation to the funeral, and Premier Jaroszewicz sent official condolences to the Vatican. Kominek had been active in Poland's western territories, and contributed much to their Polonization. In 1966 the regime had attempted, unsuccessfully, to use him against Cardinal Wyszyński, when it alleged that Kominek displayed a more patriotic attitude.

At a Warsaw party conference on 25 March, devoted to ideological problems, Politburo member and Central Committee secretary Jan Szydlak, attacked the Catholic church as the principal institutional structure of opposition to the regime. He called for vigorous measures to oppose and counter its influence. The speech was substantially reprinted in the party's theoretical journal. The Society for the Propagation of Lay Culture, meeting at Warsaw in May adopted resolutions calling for increased efforts to counter the influences of Catholicism and religion. The creation of clubs and discussion circles among youth dedicated to advancing atheism was discussed and approved.

On 22 May the government appointed Kazimierz Kakol as the director of the state Office of Religious Affairs. Kakol, a Central Committee member since December 1971, had been editor in chief of the legal weekly *Prawo i życie* and one of the editors of *Nowe drogi*. In 1968 he distinguished himself by the harshness of his attacks on so-called Zionist and liberal elements in the party, and in 1966 by his denunciation of the "capitalist and anti-socialist" character of the church. His appointment and subsequent (24 May) elevation to the rank of minister raised the specter of a new ideological campaign against the church and Cardinal Wyszyński.

The Polish episcopate at its 141st curial conference, in Warsaw on 27-28 March, presided over by Cardinal Wyszyński, objected to the requirement that new parish priests be required to swear loyalty to the state, expressed the hope for talks with the minister of public education, emphasized the need for construction of new churches, and welcomed Vatican-government contacts but emphasized the need for participation by Polish clergy in any settlement of conflicts. On 14 April, Cardinal Wyszyński celebrated Easter Mass in a converted Soviet army barracks at Warsaw in order to dramatize the need for new church buildings. He subsequently denounced Sunday "volunteer labor," demanded by the regime, as a new form of exploiting the working class. The episcopate also showed concern over the party's educational reforms which seek to phase out small rural schools and bus children to larger ones, where priestly influences would likely to lessened.

Foreign Relations. *West Germany.* The year 1974 saw a serious, rather sudden, deterioration in Polish-West German relations. In January foreign minister Olszowski still talked about a possible visit by Gierek to Bonn. Following the 11-12 February Moscow meeting between Olszowski and Gromyko, the tone in Warsaw changed. The Polish press complained that attitudes in various West German circles were not in keeping with the conciliatory spirit of the 7 December 1970 treaty. In late January, a Polish delegation opened negotiations in Bonn seeking low-interest credits in return for exit permits for several hundred thousand ethnic Germans from Poland's western territories. Poland demanded three billion marks; the West Germans refused to give more than one billion.

Sixty-four passengers on the Polish liner *Batory* defected in Hamburg on 31 January, while Polish-West German negotiations were being conducted in Bonn. This was reported to have strained the atmosphere of the talks. Including defections of other Polish passengers in ports of Denmark and Norway, fully 10 percent of the *Batory* cruise passengers fled.

The problem of German repatriation from Poland proved a thorny one. According to estimates of the Federation of Expellees in West Germany there are as many as one million ethnic Germans in Poland. Official West German figures claimed only 280,000. The Polish government put the number at about 100,000 and argued that repatriation of these people, many of them skilled workers, would hurt the Polish economy; that the Polish educational system had financed the training of much of this labor force; and that Poland was entitled to some compensation. This was eventually put forward in terms of indemnification for Polish victims of Nazi persecution. A 30 March article in PUWP weekly *Polityka* by editor in chief Mieczyslaw Rakowski called for the payment of compensation to such victims, as did several other Polish newspapers in April. According to one official source, there were still some 180,000 survivors of Nazi concentration camps in Poland in 1974, and some 1,200,000 persons who had worked as slave laborers in wartime Germany, receiving only about 10 to 15 percent of normal remuneration for their efforts.

West Germany claimed the 280,000 ethnic Germans still in Poland should be allowed to emigrate, and declared its readiness to discuss financial credits, economic cooperation, and the payment of German social security pensions to certain eligible residents of Poland. It refused, however, to discuss indemnities, claiming that the London agreement of 1949 precluded further reparations. The term "ransom" began to crop up in the West German press and parliament.

Mutual relations were inconclusively discussed on 23-24 April in Warsaw by West German Foreign Ministry official Guenther von Well and Polish deputy foreign minister Józef Czyrek. West German sources claimed that Poland had reneged on an agreement to expatriate at least 50,000 Germans in 1974, the commitment was denied in Poland. The impasse continued unresolved. Nevertheless, trade between Poland and West Germany, which has increased three-fold since 1970, continued to grow. In late July an agreement on social security coverage for Polish and West German workers employed in each other's country was concluded in Bonn.

Other States. There was a great upsurge in Polish diplomatic and economic contacts with non-communist nations during the year. Polish efforts abroad were clearly geared to an expansion of trade and the modernization of the Polish economy, and toward international recognition of the political and territorial postwar status quo in Europe. Much of the economically oriented diplomatic activity involved "Third World" developing countries. In January, ten-year pacts involving economic, scientific, technical, and cultural cooperation were concluded with Italy and Finland.

In February, Libya's premier Abdul Salam Jallud visited Warsaw at the head of a large delegation. The Polish press warmly praised Libya's anti-imperialist and anti-Zionist policies. A long-term agreement was concluded, providing for the import of Libyan oil by Poland in exchange for manufacturing plants, industrial goods, cargo ships, tankers and technological assistance.

In early April, Poland was host to Swedish premier Olof Palme. A ten-year agreement on economic, industrial, scientific, and technical cooperation, signed on 4 April provided for the construction of Volvo automobile plants in Poland in apparent fulfillment on the PUWP's pledge to provide more cars for the Polish people. The agreement included the abolition of visas between the two countries. This was likely to facilitate greater Swedish tourism in Poland, though not vice versa, on account of stringent passport controls in Poland.

On 8 April foreign minister Olszowski traveled to London for talks with Prime Minister Harold Wilson. There had been concern in Warsaw that the ten-year pact signed with Britain in December 1973 was not producing the expected share of exports for Poland. Differences on international issues were also discussed, and Wilson was invited to visit Poland. Differences on the issues of the Geneva security conference and the Vienna mutual force reduction talks remained. Poland supported the Soviet position of seeking speedy accords not linked to increased "people" contacts between East and West; Britain opposed it. Olszowski's visit met with an embarrassing snub by the Communist Party of Great Britain, which had been antagonized by Poland's failure to support the British miners' strike in

February. Despite an appeal by the British miners' union, the Polish government had decided to go ahead with the sale of 500,000 tons of coal to the United Kingdom. British communists had appealed directly to Polish miners to protest their government's decision.

On 7 May the Argentine economics minister, José Ber Gelbard, arrived in Warsaw with a large delegation of experts and officials for talks aimed at the expansion of trade. On 9-10 May, summaries of Polish-Argentine agreements were published in the official press, calling for "long-term" trade and cooperation, with Poland extending some $100 million in credit to Argentina for industrial purchases in Poland; the agreement called for a doubling of annual trade between the two nations, and for joint mining ventures to be undertaken in Argentina.

Later in May (12-23), a Polish delegation led by deputy premier and minister of mining and power Jan Mitrega visited the United States at the invitation of U.S. secretary of the interior Rogers C. B. Morton. Under the impetus of the energy shortage, Poland has considerably increased its sales of low-sulfur-content coal to the United States.

On 4 June a ten-year agreement on trade, shipping, industrial, and technological cooperation was concluded between Spain and Poland. An exchange of Polish coal for citrus fruit and leather goods from Spain was the major issue.

On 22 June a long-term agreement extending from 1974 to 1980 between Poland and Morocco was signed in Warsaw. Morocco has been one of Poland's principal developing-nation trade partners. According to the new pact, the volume of trade was to rise threefold in 1974, over 1973. Poland has been exporting sulfur, sugar, coal, capital goods, and chemical and engineering equipment to Morocco, in exchange for phosphorites, fish meal, iron and non-ferrous ores, and farm and food products. Poland will construct several industrial plants in Morocco. On 13-17 June, Poland was host to Ghana's minister of trade and tourism, Colonel David Amadu Idissa. Prospects of economic cooperation and trade were discussed by Amadu Idissa and vice-premier and foreign trade minister Kazimierz Olszewski.

Italy's foreign minister Aldo Moro visited Warsaw on 26-28 June for talks on détente and Polish-Italian economic cooperation. After West Germany, Great Britain, and the United States, Italy was Poland's fourth most important Western trading partner.

Foreign minister Olszowski and a large delegation visited Holland on 1-3 July. On 2 July a ten-year pact on economic, industrial, and technical cooperation between the two countries was signed.

On 8-10 October, PUWP first secretary Gierek visited U.S. president Gerald Ford at the White House. This was the first such visit to the United States by a Polish communist leader. The several agreements signed by Gierek and Ford were concerned with U.S.-Polish cooperation in research on methods of coal extraction and use, cooperation in medicine and joint research projects in health care, a convention removing double taxation between the two countries, cooperation in environmental protection, and institutionalized means of economic consultation by the respective chambers of commerce.

Polish-U.S. trade has expanded threefold since 1972, reaching a volume of about $700 million in 1974, with the expectation of $1,000 million by 1976 and $2,000 million by 1980. Poland alone of the Eastern Bloc enjoyed most-favored-nation treatment in the United States in 1974. Unprecedented declarations of mutual friendship were issued by the two leaders at the conclusion of Gierek's visit.

Polish foreign policy views were summarized in an August article by Stefan Olszowski in the Soviet publication *Mezhdunarodnaia zhizn'*. It emphasized Polish support of various Soviet international policies, including détente with the United States, disarmament, reduction of forces, and a European Security conference to "liquidate the remnants of the cold war."

International Party Contacts. Early in January 1974, Andrzej Werblan headed the Polish delegation to the meeting of communist parties held in Prague under the auspices of the periodical *Problems of Peace and Socialism.*

Talks between Polish foreign minister Stefan Olszowski and Andrei Gromyko in Moscow, 11-12 February, culminated in a communiqué stressing "full unity of views between Poland and the U.S.S.R." The talks appear to have set the tone for subsequent Polish foreign policy pronouncements and activities, particularly the decline in Polish-West German relations. Between 20 and 24 February, the leader of the West German communist party, Herbert Mies, visited Poland; he was accorded VIP treatment and received by PUWP first secretary Gierek. The communiqué issued by the two leaders affirmed their parties' cordial friendship and unity of outlook.

With somewhat less fanfare another Hungarian party delegation visited Poland 18-22 February, led by that party's Central Committee secretary Rezsö Nyers, father of the 1968 Hungarian economic reforms.

Close relations with the German Democratic Republic (GDR) and Czechoslovakia were maintained throughout the year. In March, a GDR party delegation met with PUWP Politburo members Franciszek Szlachcic and Ryszard Frelek in Warsaw; GDR trade union leaders visited Poland in early April. On 12 March Czechoslovak communist party leader Gustav Husák came to Warsaw on his fourth visit since 1969. He and his entourage were accorded an unusually warm welcome and great media attention during their four-day stay. Among other appearances, Husák and Premier Jaroszewicz addressed 16,000 dock workers in Gdansk. The Polish party press emphasized Czechoslovakia's key importance as Poland's third largest trading partner (after the U.S.S.R. and the GDR) and the significance of Polish Baltic ports for Czechoslovakia.

In mid-May, Gierek was host to Gus Hall, general secretary of the Communist Party, U.S.A. The two joined in a call for a world conference of communist and workers' parties. As reported in the Polish press, Hall criticized the activities of the Chinese Communist Party, citing China's recognition of the Chilean military regime as an example of collusion with imperialism.

In late May, Edward Babiuch headed a PUWP delegation to the congress of the League of Communists of Yugoslavia (LCY) in Belgrade. *Trybuna ludu* praised the LCY for reasserting its leading role in society and for purging itself of oppositional and deviationist elements.

At the meeting of the Warsaw Pact's Political Consultative Committee, in Warsaw on 17-18 April, foreign minister Olszowski outlined Poland's position toward the all-European Conference on Security and Cooperation under four basic principles: inviolability of existing frontiers, respect for the sovereignty and territorial integrity of all states, renunciation of the use or threat of force in international relations, and non-interference in domestic affairs of other states.

On 29 May, reporting to the Sejm on the Warsaw Pact meeting, Olszowski urged that détente become "irreversible," and called for a second round of meetings and agreements within the framework of the Conference on Security and Cooperation in Europe as soon as possible. He also urged the creation of a permanent consultative committee of all European states to implement agreements and to monitor and discuss mutual problems. Olszowski advocated a reduction of military forces—both national and foreign—in central Europe with no advantage to any party. He said that the improvement of Soviet-U.S. relations served the cause of world peace. On the other hand, he maintained that it was necessary to strengthen the defense capability of the Warsaw Pact in view of the continued likelihood of the existence of NATO.

In speaking of Poland's ties with other states, Olszowski listed the Soviet Union first, followed by the Warsaw Pact bloc as a whole. He mentioned friendly relations with Yugoslavia, Cuba, Mongolia, North Vietnam and North Korea, in that order, and indicated that Poland sought to "normalize" relations with Albania. In a sweeping attack he accused China (which was not even included among his category of "socialist states") of opposition to curbing the arms race, supporting Cold War trends in Europe, weakening the struggle against imperialism, and undermining the interests of peace and socialism throughout the world. He concluded, however, that in the interest of peace Poland would continue to support the development of good interstate relations with the Chinese.

GDR party chief Erich Honecker and premier Horst Sindermann visited Poland on 5-8 June. They were received with effusive expressions of friendship by Gierek. Indissoluble ties between Poland and the GDR, and of both with the U.S.S.R., were emphasized in joint statements. The GDR's role as Poland's second most important trading partner was widely publicized, along with pledges of future economic, scientific and cultural cooperation.

On 11 June, Polish and Romanian journalists' associations signed an agreement on cooperative exchanges in Warsaw. On 17 June, North Korea's deputy foreign trade minister, Pang Tae-yul, visited Warsaw and discussed expansion of cooperation and trade with deputy premier Kazimierz Olszewski. On 19 June an agreement with the Mongolian People's Republic, relating to exchanges of radio and television programs, was signed in Warsaw.

The executive committee of the World Federation of Democratic Youth met in Warsaw on 10-13 June to prepare the program for its congress, scheduled for late in the year in Varna, Bulgaria. Some 200 representatives from 60 organizations in 54 countries attended.

Yugoslav leader Edvard Kardelj visited Poland for a week at the end of June and conferred with Gierek and other top PUWP officials. Gierek, in turn, visited Tito in Yugoslavia, 5-7 July. Polish and Yugoslav relations with West Germany and an international meeting of the communist movement were believed to have been discussed.

On 26 July, Premier Jaroszewicz visited with Romanian party and government leader Nicolae Ceauşescu. Cuban communist party leaders, led by Central Committee secretary Isidoro Malmierca, visited Poland on 19 July. In August, GDR premier Sindermann vacationed in Poland and conferred with Jaroszewicz. On 15 August Gierek met with Brezhnev in the Crimea, where Gierek had been vacationing since late July. On 11 September, Politburo candidate member Zdzisław Grudzien conferred with leaders of the French Communist Party in Paris.

For several days, beginning 29 September, Soviet foreign minister Gromyko conferred with Gierek in order to "harmonize" Soviet and Polish positions before Gierek's trip to Washington. On 7 October Brezhnev also stopped in Warsaw for talks with Gierek.

On 16-18 October, a meeting of Warsaw Pact and West European communist parties took place in Warsaw. CPSU secretary and Politburo member Boris Ponomarev gave the principal address, alerting representatives of the parties to new political opportunities created by what he called the "deepening crisis of imperialism," which allegedly was reflected in inflation, energy, and agricultural crises and in a general "sharpening of social relations" in the West.

Publications. The daily organ of the PUWP is *Trybuna ludu* ("People's Tribune"); its monthly theoretical journal is *Nowe drogi* ("New Roads"). A monthly, *Życie Partii* ("Party Life") is directed at party activists, and a biweekly, *Chłopska droga* ("The Peasant Road") is aimed at rural readers. The Central Committee's Department of Propaganda, Press, and Publications puts out the fortnightly *Zagadnienia i materiały* ("Problems and Materials") for the training of party members. A party monthly, *Ideologia i polityka* ("Ideology and Politics"), has been published for several years. Seventeen dailies are printed by voivodship party organizations. Two influential Warsaw weeklies, *Polityka* and *Kultura*, deserve notice though they are not official PUWP publications.

*　　　*　　　*

The Polish Communist Party (KPP) in Albania issued a 1974 May Day manifesto which (according to Radio Tirana) was distributed in leaflet form in Poland. It called on Polish workers and communists to fight the "revisionist counter-revolution created by the shipbuilders' uprising of 1970." It called for Polish unity with the Albanian Workers' and Chinese Communist Party against "U.S. imperialism" and "contemporary revisionism," "the center of which is Soviet social imperialism." The PUWP was described by the KPP as a revisionist dictatorship of the bourgeoisie. The KPP urged illegal organization for an inevitable struggle by Polish communists against the Gierek revisionists.

University of California
Davis

Alexander Groth

Romania

The Romanian Communist Party (Partidul Comunist Român; RCP), according to official histories, was founded on 13 May 1921, following the splitting of the Social Democratic Party. From the beginning the party was harassed by government authorities, and in 1924 it was officially banned. The party lacked popular support because of its official sympathy for the idea of returning Bessarabia to Russia and the non-Romanian character of much of its membership; internal dissensions during the interwar period further weakened its influence. The economic crisis of the 1930s gave the RCP a new opportunity to exploit social and economic ills, but again it proved to be disunited, and government repression prevented it from achieving any real success. The growth of fascist elements in Romania led to further police activity against the illegal communists, and most of the party's leaders were sentenced to prison terms.

With its leaders either incarcerated in Romania or in exile in the Soviet Union, the party's role during the early war years was limited. The defeat of the Nazis on the eastern front and the arrival of Soviet troops in Romania reversed its fortunes, however. On 23 August 1944 the pro-German government was overthrown in a coup d'état, and a coalition government came to power. In October 1944, under communist leadership, the National Democratic Front (NDF) was established; this consisted of the RCP, the Social Democratic Party, the Union of Patriots, and the Plowmen's Front led by Petru Groza. At Soviet insistence, a government representing the NDF, with Groza as premier, was appointed on 6 March 1945. The RCP, with the assistance of the occupying Soviet army, continued to consolidate its position despite the opposition of the king and the British and U.S. governments. The elections of November 1946, which were held under legislation highly favorable to the RCP, resulted in an overwhelming victory for the NDF and further strengthened the communists. On 30 December 1947 the king was forced to abdicate and the People's Republic of Romania was proclaimed.

In February 1948 the RCP and the Social Democratic Party were merged into the Romanian Workers' Party (RWP). At the same time the NDF was replaced by the People's Democratic Front, which was composed of a number of political parties and various front organizations but in which the RWP had predominant influence. At its congress in July 1965 the RWP reverted to its original name, the Romanian Communist Party. This measure was taken concomitantly with the elevation of Romania from the status of a people's democracy to that of a socialist republic. In 1968, after having opposed the Soviet-led invasion of Czechoslovakia, the party sought to mobilize mass support, and the Front of Socialist Unity (FSU) was created to replace the largely inactive People's Democratic Front. The reorganized front includes trade union, youth, and women's front organizations, as well as associations representing the various national minorities living in Romania. The RCP is the only political party. The FSU provides the permanent organizational framework for mass participation in politics at all levels.

According to the report of party secretary-general Nicolae Ceauşescu at the RCP's Eleventh Congress, in November 1974, the party had "almost 2,480,000 members," or 500,000 more than at the time of the Tenth Congress, in 1969. Of this number, 48.4 percent were workers, reflecting the party's success in increasing their proportion in its membership (the corresponding figure was 42.6 percent in 1969). The proportion of peasants was 22 percent, and 21 percent were intellectuals. The party's ethnic composition remained approximately the same as that of the country as a whole—89 percent Romanian, 8 percent Hungarian, and the remaining 3 percent German and other nationalities. The proportion of women was 25 percent. (*Scînteia*, 26 November.) The population of Romania is 20,770,000 (estimated 1972).

Organization and Leadership. The party is organized into basic units or cells in factories, on farms, and in the smaller political subdivisions; in 1973 there were 69,193 such basic party units. The next higher step is represented by the party organizations in communes (rural territorial subdivisions) and municipalities, in which there were 2,706 and 235 organizations, respectively. Finally, there are party organizations for each of the 39 counties and for the municipality of Bucharest, which supervise the lower-level party organizations within their territories. (Figures from *WMR*, May 1973.) Each unit is directed by a party committee headed by a secretary or first secretary who is responsible for its activity.

According to the party statute, the supreme authority of the RCP is vested in the congress, which is held every five years and to which delegates are elected by county party organizations. The real power, however, is wielded by the Secretariat, the Executive Committee, the Permanent Bureau, and the Central Committee.

A series of significant changes in the structure of the party leadership took place in 1974. At the 25-26 March plenum of the Central Committee, the Permanent Presidium was abolished. (Created in 1965 to replace the old Politburo, this was the most powerful body in the RCP, and its nine members were the most influential individuals within the party.) The old Permanent Presidium was replaced by a Permanent Bureau, in which membership in the majority of cases was ex officio. Thus the secretary-general of the party (Ceauşescu) and all Central Committee secretaries were automatically members of the Permanent Bureau, as were the president of the republic (also Ceauşescu), a vice-president of the State Council, the premier, the first deputy premier, one or two deputy premiers, the chairman of the Central Council of Workers' Control of Economic and Social Activities, the chairman of the State Planning Committee, and the chairman of the trade union organization. The amendments to the party statute adopted at the March plenum also specified that other persons could be designated members of the Bureau by the Executive Committee.

At the Eleventh Congress, in November, further changes were made in the composition and structure of the Permanent Bureau. The party statute was again amended, and now specifies only that the Bureau is to be chosen by the Executive Committee from among its members and that it is to be led by the party secretary-general; ex officio designation of members was dropped. After the congress the new Executive Committee designated only five persons as members of the Bureau—Ceauşescu, the party leader; Manea Mănescu, the premier; Gheorghe Oprea, a deputy premier; Ion Păţan, another deputy premier and minister of foreign trade and international economic cooperation; and Ştefan Andrei, a Central Committee secretary responsible for foreign relations of the party.

A unique feature of the new organizational structure is the fact that the Permanent Bureau is responsible to the party's Executive Committee rather than to the Central Committee. The Permanent Presidium, which was abolished in these changes, and the Politburos of the other East European parties are chosen by, and responsible to, the Central Committee. No official explanation was given for this two-stage elimination of the Permanent Presidium, but it seems likely that this body, comprised of the most powerful individuals in the party, had become more influential than Ceauşescu desired, and may also have become a forum in which opposition to his programs could be expressed. The first step, replacing it by a bureau composed of ex officio members, was a graceful way to drop those whose views differed from Ceauşescu's. The further change that came about during the party congress may have been prompted by the unwieldiness of the larger bureau and a desire to increase its efficiency. It is also possible that the smaller body was what Ceauşescu originally had in mind, and that he found a two-step elimination of the old Presidium to be the most politically expedient.

The party Secretariat, composed of the secretary-general and a number of Central Committee secretaries, is responsible for various spheres of party activity. At the 1974 congress Ceauşescu was reelected secretary-general of the party (he has been party leader since March 1965), and six secretaries were reelected to the Central Committee: Dumitru Popescu (a Central Committee secretary since 1968), Gheorghe Pană (August 1969), Cornel Burtică (February 1972), Ştefan Andrei (April 1972), Ilie Verdeţ (March 1974), and Iosif Uglar (July 1974). The congress did not reelect Mihai Gere as a Central Committee secretary, although he had held that position since 1966 and no reason was given for dropping him. Verdeţ was elected to the Secretariat in March, when he was released as first deputy premier and became chairman of the Central Council of Workers' Control of Economic and Social Activities. Uglar was chosen a secretary in July, upon the death of Miron Constantinescu, who had been a secretary since November 1972 and head of the Grand National Assembly since March 1974.

As a result of the structural changes that took place in the party organization during the year, the Executive Committee has become more prominent. It was created at the RCP's Ninth Congress, in 1965, primarily to give Ceauşescu a leading party body in which his own supporters would predominate, since at that time the Permanent Presidium was composed largely of older party leaders not beholden to the new party head. The Executive Committee meets frequently between plenary sessions of the Central Committee, and supervises party affairs. Among its full and alternate members are all party secretaries and leading party and government officials. A new Executive Committee was chosen at the Eleventh Congress, and although most of its members had been on the old body, 10 full and alternate members were dropped and 5 new ones added. The Executive Committee has 23 full members (the same as previously) and 13 alternates (compared with 18 previously).

The Central Committee is elected at a party congress to direct party affairs between congresses. It meets in plenary session two to five times a year to consider and approve programs and policies. The committee chosen at the Eleventh Congress has 205 full and 156 alternate members. (The committee whose mandate expired with the holding of the congress had 181 full and 134 alternate members at the time it ceased to function.)

The Eleventh Congress. Internal party activity during the year was directed toward the party congress, held in Bucharest on 25-28 November. It was attended by some 2,450 delegates, selected by local party organizations at special meetings in the weeks before it opened, and by some 133 delegations representing communist and leftist parties of other countries invited as guests.

The opening day was devoted primarily to the report of the Central Committee (read by Ceauşescu) on the party's activity over the five years since the Tenth Congress, in August 1969. On the second and third days the congress divided into 12 sections to consider specific topics, and party leaders spoke on the various items on the agenda. On the final day the members of leading party bodies were chosen—the secretary-general, the Central Committee, and the Central Auditing Commission. The Central Committee in turn met to choose the Secretariat and the Executive Committee.

The congress itself was a routine affair, but there were two developments of a somewhat unusual nature. First, Bucharest party leader Gheorghe Cioară proposed that Ceauşescu be elected secretary-general of the party for life. The proposal was initially made at the Bucharest party organization's pre-congress meeting, which Ceaușescu attended. The party leader reportedly did not comment on the proposal at that time, but it was reported by *Scînteia* and Agerpres, and then not mentioned again until the congress, at which time, however, Ceaușescu turned down the proposal.

Why the suggestion was made and why Ceaușescu declined raise a number of interesting questions. Cioară and the Bucharest party organization may have made the proposal without higher approval, in order to curry favor with the party leader on the eve of the congress, but it is also conceivable that it was made with Ceaușescu's approval, or even at his instigation, but then dropped because of strong opposition. The way in which the matter was handled also gave Ceaușescu an opportunity to decline the honor modestly, thus allaying some of the criticism of the personality cult that has grown up around him. Some individuals took advantage of Ceaușescu's response to raise the issue of age during the congress debates, in an effort to weaken the claims made by older party activists that they had a right to be reelected to higher party positions.

The second significant development was the failure of the congress to deal fully with all items on its agenda before adjourning. The delegates approved the Central Committee report given by Ceaușescu, the party program establishing a framework for party activity during the next quarter century, the 1976-80 socioeconomic plan, and guidelines for the economy between now and 1990. As they were considering changes in the party statute, however, Petre Blajovici (Bihor County party first secretary) proposed that an age limit be established beyond which individuals could not hold membership in higher party bodies. Ceaușescu intervened in the debate, agreeing that party leaders should have the physical capacity to carry out their responsibilities but opposing the setting of specific age limits. He proposed instead that the Central Committee be empowered to give final form to the party statute, taking this problem into consideration. "Draft standards of the life and work of communism, socialist ethics, and justice" were also considered during the congress, and in this case, too, the Central Committee was authorized by the delegates to put the document in final form and publish it. Even the resolution of the congress was turned over to the Central Committee to be given final form (*Scînteia*, 29 November). The fact that these three important matters were not fully dealt with by the delegates is highly unusual and raises questions about Ceaușescu's control over the proceedings.

Of the documents adopted by the congress, three deserve special attention: the party program, the directives for the 1976-80 plan, and the economic guidelines through 1990.

The party program—a massive document covering some 13 newspaper pages when it was published in draft in early September—was drawn up under instructions issued at the National Party Conference held in July 1972. Two themes that run through the whole program are the link between Romanian national interests and the party's policies, and the application of the general truths of Marxism-Leninism to specific Romanian conditions. The impact of the ideological campaign initiated in 1971 is apparent in the preoccupation with problems of ideology and political education. Although the document reaffirms the RCP's well-known positions on such issues as national independence, autonomy in foreign affairs and interparty relations, and the importance of the nation, it does little more than restate previous positions in modest terms, and gives the impression that an effort was made to avoid straining relations with the Soviet Union or challenging the basic tenets of Marxism-Leninism.

The draft directives on the 1976-80 plan indicate that Romania's dynamic economic development is to continue in the next five-year period. Although the targets for industrial growth are in many cases lower than current rates, these are only preliminary figures, and past practice indicates that upward revision of initial targets is more than likely. National income and industrial production are both to rise by 54 to 61 percent, an annual rate of 9 to 10 percent. (The current plan calls for an annual rate of 11 to 12 percent.) Investment is to increase by 65 to 72 percent during the five-year period—a rather steep increase which is one of the more significant features of the new plan. Growth in agricultural output is to increase by a more modest 25 to 34 percent. In presenting the new plan, party leader Ceauşescu emphasized that the greater the proportion of resources devoted to accumulation and economic development, the greater the annual increase in consumption—an indication of concern to enlist popular support for the high investment rate.

The guidelines on the economy until 1990 indicate that a high rate of industrial growth is anticipated for some time. Industrial production is to by 6.5 to 7.5 times greater in 1990 than it was in 1970, and average per capita income is to be in the range of 2,500 to 3,000 dollars. Similar long-term guidelines were presented by Ceauşescu in 1971 and at the National Party Conference in 1972, although there are some interesting differences between the most recent draft and the earlier ones. The latest figures show that the goals for electric power production and cement output are lower, while that for steel production is higher. The goals for 1990 indicate that maximum efforts will be required for some time to maintain the high rate of growth.

Central Committee Plenary Sessions. The four Central Committee meetings held during the year were devoted primarily to preparing for and completing the work of the party congress. The first, on 25-26 March, approved a series of leadership changes. (For the dissolution of the Permanent Presidium and the creation of the Permanent Bureau see above.) The common denominator in the changes was the attempt by Ceauşescu to further strengthen and institutionalize his personal rule. Creation of the post of "President of the Socialist Republic of Romania," with himself as incumbent, appears to be designed to remove those institutional and procedural restraints on the power and speed of his own decision making which existed, at least formally, until now. Among the party leader's new prerogatives are the right to preside over meetings of the Council of Ministers when necessary, and the right to grant special powers to the chairman of that council and to individual ministers in respect to the conclusion of international treaties. He will henceforth be able to issue decrees without having to convene a plenum of the State Council, and will have the right to appoint and remove members of the Council of Ministers upon the proposal of its chairman at times when the Grand National Assembly is not in session.

Ion Gheorghe Maurer, premier since 1961, requested that the plenum release him from his duties for reasons of health and age. His retirement removed the most influential figure in Romania who stood for a certain moderation in Ceauşescu's more radical programs. There seems little doubt that Maurer had reservations about certain aspects of Ceauşescu's style of leadership and about his domestic policy. The plenum recommended Manea Mănescu as the new premier. A close associate of Ceauşescu, Mănescu was most recently chairman of the State Planning Committee, and before that a Central Committee secretary. He has had training in economics, and was formerly a professor in that field.

Other important personnel changes included naming Ilie Verdeţ, formerly first deputy premier, as a party secretary and chairman of the Central Council of Workers' Control of Economic and Social Activities, which had been headed by Miron Constantinescu. Constantinescu became chairman of the Grand National Assembly, but retained his position in the Secretariat until his death in July. Virgil Trofin, a former party secretary and at the time of these changes a deputy premier and minister of domestic trade, was dropped from his government post and subsequently became party first secretary of Brasov County. A number of others were also reshuffled.

The second Central Committee plenary session, on 27-29 July, approved the congress agenda, the draft party program, the draft five-year plan, and the economic guidelines up to 1990, as well as other matters related to the congress. This plenum also adopted criteria to be applied in electing party members to central and local party positions; these stipulate the length of time an individual must have been a party member, the experience in party positions, and the amount of "party education" he must have had before being elected to a position in the party. The effect may be to give older party members the advantage in regard to election to important posts, at the expense of younger members. These criteria were included in the party statute adopted at the congress.

The third plenum, on 23 November, just before the congress, approved Ceaușescu's report on party activity since the last congress, and the fourth, on 18 December, completed the tasks assigned by the congress: the changes in the party statute were adopted in final form, as was the code of socialist ethics and equity. This plenum also took steps to increase participation of Central Committee members in implementing the political and economic policies of the party, and to reorganize the Central Committee bureaucracy. Further, it approved a number of constitutional and legislative measures relating to the election of members of parliament which were subsequently adopted by the Grand National Assembly.

Domestic Affairs. The basic problems of the economy continued to cause difficulties in 1974. The high rate of industrial growth now being encouraged and called for in the next five-year plan puts a strain on the economy. The continuing forced pace appeared to be taking its toll in terms of industrial accidents. On 31 July, *Scînteia* acknowledged that accidents involving certain (unspecified) enterprises had occurred, and Western press reports said major damage had been sustained by the Pitesti Chemical Combine, the Steagul Rosu truck plant in Brasov, and the Electroputere plant in Craiova. The report in *Scînteia* and a similar one published by Moscow's *Pravda* (29 July) denied reports in the Western press that the Soviet Union was behind the accidents in Romania. The reports of Soviet involvement seem inaccurate and a more likely explanation for the disasters is carelessness on the part of workers who are apathetic and at the same time being pressed to overfulfill the economic plan.

Concern for management of the economy was a key topic during the year. At a special meeting of party and state ministerial aktifs in April, Ceaușescu expressed anxiety about economic efficiency, and linked this with the need to overfulfill the five-year plan; planning and management were specifically criticized. Later, during a tour of Dolj County, he revealed serious cases of mismanagement and falsification of records to cover up deficiencies.

The agriculture sector also had its difficulties, indicated by a number of measures that were adopted to improve organization. Statutes were published specifying conditions for cooperation between agricultural production cooperatives, and between these cooperatives and state agricultural units. New prerogatives and responsibilities were given officials and leading councils of agricultural units, and the responsibilities of people's councils in the field of agriculture were more clearly spelled out. Despite these measures, it is unlikely that the agricultural goals of the present five-year plan will be reached.

The congress of the Front of Socialist Unity was held on 23-24 May for the purpose of preparing this umbrella organization for its role in the elections to be held in the spring of 1975, and also in preparation for the party congress. In view of the increased role specified for the FSU in some of the recent constitutional amendments and the new election law adopted in December, which permits more than one candidate to be nominated for a single position in the next elections, this organization may play a more important political role in the future. Up to the present, however, its role has been limited. Although it was established in 1968, it did not hold its first congress until 1974, and only then were its statutes adopted—almost six years after the organization was created.

In his speech to the FSU congress Ceaușescu made several references to the churches in Romania. He noted that the constitution permits freedom of religion, and observed that faith is a matter of individual conscience. All religious groups, however, must respect the existing social order and must display patriotism for the country. These comments, plus the fact that a number of religious leaders were elected to the FSU Council, suggest a more conciliatory policy toward religion.

The FSU Council elected during the congress gives greater representation to the military, the agricultural production cooperatives, religious institutions, and women. There were also representatives of the minorities living in Romania. The representation of writers and cultural figures, however, was reduced.

The cultural scene continues to be dominated by party efforts to maintain careful ideological control. Ideological utility remains the foremost justification for literature and art. This was pointed up by the transformation of the Writers' Union monthly, *Viaţa românească*. Of the former 14-member editorial board, 10 were dropped, and the review will henceforth concentrate on ideological and political objectives rather than aesthetic and artistic ones. Theoretical discussions in the cultural press continued to center on the political and ideological content of literature and art, but a few brave voices were heard contesting the prevailing trend.

This ideological tightening has also been extended to the mass information media. A press law—the first in postwar times—was adopted by the Grand National Assembly at the end of March. In the context of renewed ideological emphasis in all spheres of social, political, and cultural life, the law appears to be conceived as an instrument for streamlining the operation of the press and strengthening party control over and guidance of it. The main characteristics of the new law can be summed up as follows: the entire professional activity of journalists should be oriented in such a way as to help implement the domestic and foreign policies of the RCP; the administrative structure of the mass media makes it possible for tight control and supervision to be exercised not only by the editor but also by an executive council made up of representatives of all kinds of political and mass organizations; strong limitations are set upon the freedom of the press granted by the constitution. Responsibility for the observance of these limitations is said to rest with editors in chief; a special Press and Printing Committee (in effect, a censorship office) will guarantee additional control and has the right to "prevent the dissemination" of material considered out of line with the provisions of the law.

The party's attempt to exercise greater control over the press included extensive changes in the editorship of most publications. The cultural press in particular seems to have been hard hit by the changes. A party decision designed to cut consumption of paper led to a reduction in the number of newspapers in order to avoid repetition, the combining of similar publications, and the less frequent appearance of many newspapers and journals. The paper shortage appears to have provided the party with a good opportunity, which it seized upon, to strengthen its control by making extensive changes in the editorial personnel.

A basic reorganization of the educational system, which is apparently contemplated, is also linked with efforts to strengthen ideology and to relate education more directly to production. At a major conference on the subject, held on Ceauşescu's initiative in mid-September, the party leader called for a "revolutionary turning point" in education. The main concern was that the educational system be more efficiently utilized in the process of ideological indoctrination and in applying the latest advances of science and technology. The Ministry of Education was severely criticized, but the minister, former Central Committee secretary Paul Niculescu-Mizil, was still in office at year's end. First deputy minister Virgil Cazacu, however, was discharged just a few weeks before the conference. His dismissal reflected dissatisfaction with his performance, since he was appointed to the post at the beginning of the ideological campaign in 1971 to strengthen party influence in the ministry.

Foreign Relations. Romania's relations with the Soviet Union, which have the first priority in the RCP's foreign policy, showed during 1974 a slight shift in attitude. Although differences continued to separate Bucharest and Moscow, each was anxious to avoid an open confrontation. For their part, the Romanians maintained their position on major issues, but were somewhat more flexible on the less important problems. The differing emphases that emerged in reports on the April Warsaw Pact summit suggest that Romania favored more genuine consultation among alliance members and rotation of the post of joint commander among all member states, while the Soviet Union favored closer coordination. Romania continued to cooperate with the Council for Mutual Economic Assistance, at the same time maintaining its right to limits its own participation.

A number of significant exchanges of visits underlined this improvement in relations. The Soviet delegation at the celebrations marking the 30th anniversary of the 23 August 1944 coup, which changed Romania's alliances during World War II and eventually led to the communist party's coming to power, was led by Soviet premier Aleksei Kosygin. The RCP's Eleventh Congress was also attended by a high-level Soviet party delegation, led by Politburo member and Central Committee secretary Andrei Kirilenko, accompanied by Central Committee secretary Konstantin Katushev. After the congress, Romanian foreign minister Gheorghe Macovescu paid an official visit to Moscow and met a number of the Soviet leaders. Despite these signs of improving relations, the fact that Soviet party chief Leonid Brezhnev did not lead a Soviet delegation to Romania (he attended an anniversary celebration in Mongolia at the time of the Romanian congress) suggests the continuation of differences and the existence of a certain reserve in relations.

In Ceauşescu's review of Romania's foreign relations during the party congress, which stressed relations with the socialist countries, the necessity to develop and maintain good political and economic relations with the Soviet Union was listed first. Although strengthening friendship and cooperation among the socialist states was emphasized, Ceauşescu pointed out that the greater the success of each individual state, the greater the opportunity for international cooperation and the greater the prestige of socialism. Differences of opinion among socialist states, he said, should not hamper cooperation. While observing that "in view of the contemporary international situation, relations of cooperation must be developed among the socialist member states of the Warsaw Pact, and among the armies of these states," he emphasized the need to strengthen each national army, and said that "the struggle to dissolve military blocs must be intensified." He also pledged to continue expanding cooperation "between our army and those of all the socialist countries, as well as the armies of other friendly states." (*Scînteia*, 26 November.)

One topic on which Soviet-Romanian differences were quite apparent was the question of a conference of world communist parties, raised by the Soviet and other East European parties in the last months of 1973. Initially, the RCP refused to endorse the idea of a conference, and then made its view implicitly clear in January 1974 by publishing excerpts from a resolution of the Japan Communist Party congress opposing the convening of a conference. In an interview with *Die Presse* (Vienna, 23 March) Ceauşescu outlined the Romanian tactics with regard to a world gathering: the line will be to accept the idea of a conference in principle, but to demand that certain limiting conditions be observed. In an interview with the *Manchester Guardian* (9 April) and in his address to the RCP congress (*Scînteia*, 26 November 1974), Ceauşescu expressed the party's view on an international conference. He insisted that a collective document could be drafted only "with the agreement of all," and at the same time could not be binding on anyone. Also, the full participation of all interested parties must be insured, and the policies of other parties (whether present at the conference or not) could not be discussed. At the party congress he said that, in the opinion of the RCP, cooperation and exchanges of views between parties were useful, and in this spirit Romania would participate in a conference of European communist parties. He said the RCP did not consider a world conference to be "of topical interest," but its Central Committee would consider the question at the appropriate time on the basis of the conditions that had been laid down.

Romania's continuing good relations with Yugoslavia and China were underlined by a number of visits. Tito went to Bucharest in early July for consultations with Ceauşescu. The visit was the 12th in a series of conferences that have become a tradition between the two leaders since 1965. The Romanians were more obviously sympathetic and concerned than other East European parties about the Yugoslav "Cominformist" group which was discovered during the year. The conference of

European communist parties was also a topic on which the two parties attempted to align their policies, and a visit by RCP secretary Stefan Andrei to Belgrade obviously dealt, inter alia, with this issue. The Yugoslav party's delegation to the RCP congress was led by Stane Dolanc, secretary of the Executive Committee of the party's Presidium. The high level of the delegation and the warm message sent by the Yugoslav party to the Romanian congress reflected the close political relationship between Belgrade and Bucharest.

Relations with China also appeared to be on the upswing. The Chinese delegation that came to Bucharest for the 30th-anniversary celebrations in August was a high-level one led by Li Hsien-nien, who is both a member of the Chinese party's Presidium and a deputy premier. Romanian foreign minister Macovescu paid an official visit to Peking (and Pyongyang) during August, and military exchanges between Peking and Bucharest continued; a group of Romanian officers spent a month's vacation in China, and an official Chinese military delegation visited Romania.

The second area of priority, after the socialist states, is relations with the developing countries. In this category, the Middle Eastern states took on new importance after the oil embargo that followed in the wake of the October 1973 Arab-Israeli conflict. Relations with the Arab states improved dramatically. Political and, especially, economic relations became much closer. The Romanian president and party leader made a major trip to Libya, Lebanon, Syria, and Iraq in Febuary, just a few weeks after he had been host to King Hussein of Jordan in Bucharest. Although one of his goals was to play an important and constructive role in resolving the Middle East problem, Ceauşescu's real successes lay in the area of improving bilateral political and economic relations with the countries he visited. He negotiated an important agreement under whose terms Libya will export 12,000,000 tons of oil to Romania over the next four years, in return for Romanian machinery and equipment. Economic and scientific-technological agreements were also signed elsewhere, though they appear to be of less significance. A boycott against Romanian products was apparently being considered by the Arab Boycott Office because of Romania's continuing economic and diplomatic ties with Israel, but the Ceauşescu visit may have been a factor in mitigating or postponing such a step.

Romania's active Middle East diplomacy continued with Ceauşescu playing host to Egyptian president Anwar al-Sadat in June and to Syrian president Hafiz al-Asad in September. During the visit of the Egyptian leader, Romania agreed to extend a 100,000,000-dollar credit to Egypt, and a number of other steps were taken to strengthen economic relations between the two states. Sadat pledged himself to close consultation with Ceauşescu not only on bilateral questions but also on other issues of interest, including the Middle East.

Romania has been a consistent supporter of the Palestine Liberation Organization (PLO). Bucharest was one of the first states to permit the establishment of an official PLO office on its territory, and PLO leaders have visited Bucharest on a number of occasions. During the U.N. General Assembly debate on the Middle East in November, Romania upheld the PLO and its right to speak for the Palestinian people. The Romanian stand on the Middle East conflict has always been that the Palestinian problem must be resolved in a manner consonant with the wishes of these people.

Contacts with Israel were maintained, but on a much lower level than with the Arab states. Foreign minister Macovescu paid an official visit to Israel in September, perhaps in an unsuccessful bid to mediate between that country and Syria. Also, the Israeli minister of commerce, industry, and development went to Bucharest in November for talks on economic cooperation, and was received by Ceauşescu. Although trade with Israel has expanded since 1967, the growing need for oil and increased world prices have made economic relations with the Arab states of much greater importance to Romania.

The attempt to improve relations with the developing countries was given further impetus by Ceauşescu's visit to Argentina, Liberia, and Guinea. The visit to Argentina was to have taken place in the fall of 1973, but the overthrow of Chilean president Allende and presidential elections in

Argentina forced a postponement. A number of agreements—including a 100,000,000-dollar Romanian credit to Argentina and a treaty of friendship and cooperation—were signed during the visit. En route to Argentina, Ceauşescu visited Liberia, and on his way back stopped off in Guinea. Agreements on economic and technological cooperation were signed with both countries. Ceauşescu also played host to a number of Third World leaders, including the president of Mauritania, the president-elect of Colombia, the president of Zambia, and the premier of Sri Lanka.

Romania has continued to seek an active role in dealing with foreign trouble spots, as was evidenced by the fact that it sought to play a useful diplomatic role after the Cyprus crisis came to a head in July. The government officially expressed concern over the Greek-inspired coup that had given rise to the recent problems, and over Turkish military intervention on the island. In early September Ceauşescu sent a personal representative with messages to Greek, Cypriot, and Turkish leaders, and Macovescu met with the foreign ministers of Greece and Turkey at the United Nations.

During the year Romania continued to demonstrate its desire to develop relations with Western states and to maintain strong ties with the United States. The resignation of President Nixon was greeted with regret because of his visit to the country in 1969 and the personal relationship the former president had established with Ceauşescu. The Romanian leader, however, immediately sent a special emissary to Washington with a personal message for President Ford and an invitation to visit Romania. Ford accepted, but no date was set for the visit. U.S. secretary of state Henry Kissinger went to Romania in November, as part of an extensive diplomatic tour, and the U.S. secretary of commerce also visited Bucharest.

Publications. *Scînteia* is the official daily of the RCP Central Committee. *Era socialista* is the party's popularized theoretical-political fortnightly, and *Munca de partid* is a fortnightly which deals with questions of organization and methods of conducting party activity. Other important publications include *Informaţia Bucureştiului*, the daily of the Bucharest party committee and municipal people's council; *Munca*, the daily of the trade union federation; *România libera*, the daily of the Front of Socialist Unity; *România literară*, the weekly of the Writers' Union; and *Scînteia tineretului*, the daily of the Union of Communist Youth. Agerpres is the Romanian news agency.

Radio Free Europe   Robert R. King
Munich

Union of Soviet Socialist Republics

The Communist Party of the Soviet Union (Kommunisticheskaia Partiia Sovetskogo Soiuza; CPSU) traces its origins to the founding of the Russian Social Democratic Labor Party in 1898. The party split into Bolshevik ("majority") and Menshevik ("minority") factions at the Second Congress, held at Brussels and London in 1903. The Bolshevik faction, led by Vladimir I. Lenin, was actually a minority after 1904 and, unable to regain the policy-making dominance attained at the Second Congress, broke away from the Mensheviks in 1912 at the Prague congress to form a separate party. In March 1918, after the seizure of power, this party was renamed the "All-Russian Communist Party (Bolsheviks)." When "Union of Soviet Socialist Republics" was adopted as the name of the country in 1925, the party's designation was changed to "All-Union Communist Party (Bolsheviks)." The party's present name was adopted in 1952 at the Nineteenth Congress. The CPSU is the only legal political party in the U.S.S.R.

The structure of the CPSU parallels the administrative organization of the Soviet state. There are 380,000 primary party organizations. Above this lowest level, there are 2,810 rural *raion* committees, 448 urban *raion* committees, 760 city committees, 10 *okrug* committees, 142 *oblast'* committees, six *krai* committees, and 14 union-republic committees. There is no separate subsidiary organization for the Russian Republic, largest constituent unit of the Union. At the top, the All-Union Congress is, according to the party rules, the supreme policy-making body. The Twenty-fourth Congress, in 1971, set the maximal interval between congresses at five years. Between congresses, the highest representative organ is the Central Committee. At this level, power is concentrated in the Politburo, the Secretariat, and the various departments of the Central Committee.

Party membership was in a state of flux during 1974 due to the exchange of party cards, approved by the Twenty-fourth Congress in 1971 and initiated in 1973. Although difficulties were encountered in certain areas in carrying out of the exchange (*Pravda*, 1 March, 28 May 1974), party sources claimed that more than 12 million cards had been exchanged as of April (ibid., 23 April), and it appeared likely that the low-key purge of party ranks would be completed as scheduled by the end of 1974. Reports on pre-election meetings for the Supreme Soviet campaign indicated a total CPSU membership of approximately 14,970,000 (ibid., 19 March). This represents a 1.01 per cent increase over 1 January 1973, when the party reportedly had 14,330,525 members and 490,506 candidate members (*Partiinaia zhizn'*, no. 14, 1973; *Kommunist*, 14 September 1973), and continues the trend toward stabilization of party size. Between 1961 and 1966 the average annual increase was 6.0 percent; between 1966 and 1971, 3.16 percent; between 1971 and 1973, 1.28 percent. The present party membership includes approximately 10 percent of the adult population and less than six percent of the total population, now reportedly 252 million (*NYT*, 21 July 1974).

According to party sources, almost three-fourths of the membership consists of people employed in the "field of material production" and approximately 56 percent are workers and kolkhoz members (*Pravda*, 9 June). Workers and peasants are said to account for approximately 30 percent of the membership of union republic party, *krai*, and *oblast'* committees; 40 percent of the membership of *okrug*, city, and *raion* committees; and half the membership of production party organization committees and bureaus. Party cadres include approximately 1.8 million members. The party's youth auxiliary, the Komsomol, has about 34 million members (*TASS*, 26 April).

Elections and Government. Quadrennial elections for the Supreme Soviet, the country's nominal legislature, were held 16 June 1974. The Supreme Soviet has 1,517 members and is divided into two equal chambers–the Soviet of the Union, in which each deputy represents approximately 300,000 persons, and the Soviet of the Nationalities, in which deputies represent the republics, regions, and national areas in the Soviet Union. All candidates on the single slate supported by the CPSU were elected. Of the 161,689,612 registered voters, 99.98 percent participated in the balloting. The 767 official candidates for the Council of the Union received 99.79 percent of the votes cast, against 332,664 negative votes; the 750 official candidates for the Soviet of the Nationalities received 99.85 percent, against 245,750 negative votes. Composition of the new Supreme Soviet by categories is as follows: 32.8 percent workers, 17.9 percent collective farmers, 72.2 percent party members and candidate members, 27.8 percent non-party people, 31.3 percent women, and 18.4 percent below the age of 30 (*Izvestiia*, 19 June).

The Supreme Soviet meets twice each year for two or three days to ratify decrees issued or drafted between sessions by its Presidium and the Council of Ministers and to formalize official appointments. In its opening session of 25-26 July, the Ninth Supreme Soviet unanimously ratified decrees that established a new ministry for the communications equipment industry, enabled workers dismissed from their jobs to appeal through the courts, stipulated penalties for polluters of waterways, strengthened laws against narcotics, firearms, and explosives, and provided support for civilian police auxiliaries (*NYT*, 27 July). Aleksei P. Shitikov was reelected as Chairman of the Council of the Union, and Vitali P. Rubenis, of the Latvian Supreme Soviet, was elected chairman of the Council of the Nationalities. Among the Supreme Soviet's standing committees, the most notable appointment was that of Ivan V. Kapitonov, CPSU Secretary for cadres, as chairman of the Legislative Proposals Committee. There were some changes in the 36-member Presidium due to deaths and resignations; the most prominent figure dropped from Presidium ranks was 73-year-old Anastas I. Mikoyan, formerly first deputy premier under Nikita S. Khrushchev, who was not a candidate for the new Supreme Soviet.

There had been widespread speculation concerning possible changes in the composition of the government, but all 73 incumbent ministers were retained in their posts (*Izvestiia*, 27 July). Nikolai V. Podgorny was reelected as chairman of the Supreme Soviet's Presidium and hence nominal head of state. The reappointments emphasized the aging of the Soviet leadership: Podgorny is 71, Premier Aleksei N. Kosygin 70, the youngest cabinet minister 51 and the oldest 75; the majority of cabinet members are above the age of 60.

Aleksei M. Shkolnikov was named Chairman of the People's Control Committee, filling the post left vacant since the ouster of Gennadi I. Voronov in April 1973, but vacancies in the Ministries of Wages and Prices were not filled. Nikolai S. Patolichev, foreign trade minister, and Roman A. Rudenko, prosecutor-general, who had been expected to retire for reasons of age and health, were both reappointed to their posts. The biggest surprise was the retention of Yekaterina E. Furtseva, who had been reprimanded earlier in the year for building a luxurious country house at state expense and had not been reelected to the Supreme Soviet, as minister of culture. However, Furtseva's long and controversial political career ended with her death on 25 October. Piotr N. Demichev, candidate member of the Politburo, was appointed in November as her successor in the Culture Ministry.

Party Organization and Leadership. Major activities of the party during 1974 included preparations for the Supreme Soviet elections and the meeting of the Komsomol's Seventeenth Congress in Moscow, 23-27 April. It was reported that 93 percent of party members took part in pre-election local conferences (*Pravda*, 19 March); as always, party cadres performed the functions of explaining and defending regime policies during the campaign and assuring maximum voter turnout for the uncontested elections.

Major themes of the Komsomol congress were the youth organization's role in future economic development and its responsibility for the moral and ideological direction of Soviet young people. The congress pledged a half million "volunteers" for new construction and priority projects in the period 1974-77. Yevgeny M. Tyazhelnikov, at 46 the oldest first secretary of the Komsomol in its history, was reelected by the Seventeenth Congress (*TASS*, 26 April). Komsomol membership increased by six million between the Sixteenth Congress, in 1970, and the Seventeenth Congress. Opportunism apparently accounts for much of this rapid increase, given the Komsomol's privileged position in Soviet society; it contrasts starkly with the stabilization of CPSU size during the same period. Moreover, serious charges of "hooliganism," overt corruption, and inefficiency involving Komsomol members have been made recently by senior party officials in several republics, most notably in Azerbaidzhan. CPSU general secretary Leonid I. Brezhnev noted these deficiencies in his speech to the Komsomol congress. While lavishly praising the Komsomol for its past achievements, Brezhnev delivered a ringing denunciation of frequent "signs of egoism, money grubbing, and an opportunistic attitude toward life," and of idleness, drinking bouts, and " 'merriment' for the sake of killing time" among Soviet youths (ibid., 24 April).

Shortcomings in party organization were noted during the year by party officials in several republics, including the Ukraine, Lithuania, Uzbekistan, Georgia, Azerbaidzhan, and Armenia. This was reflected in some governmental reshuffling in most of these republics. Corruption and inefficiency in Georgian government and party ranks had reached crisis proportions by September 1972 when Eduard A. Shevardnadze, the republic's top police official, was appointed first secretary of the Georgian party. Between 1972 and 1974, Shevardnadze carried out a thoroughgoing purge of both party and government ranks, but a report by him in April 1974 indicated that serious organizational problems remained (*Izvestiia*, 6 April). Lithuania, which witnessed anti-Soviet riots of religious origin in 1972, continued to be a trouble spot for the CPSU (*Sovetskaia Litva*, 24 November 1973); Piatras P. Griskiavicus, first secretary of the Vilnius City Party Committee, was appointed to succeed the late Antanas Y. Snechkus as republic first secretary in February 1974 (*Pravda*, 19 February), with the obvious mission of tightening control of the party and society in Lithuania. Vladimir V. Shcherbitsky, Ukrainian first secretary and a longtime close associate of Brezhnev, apparently had some success in strengthening party organization in the Ukraine and in consolidating Moscow's control over the republic, which had weakened during the tenure of his predecessor, Piotr M. Shelest. However, on several occasions during the year Shcherbitsky pointed out the need for more intensive party activity, particularly in ideological work.

Much of the party's organizational deficiency in the borderland republics is clearly related to nationalism, but there are indications that Soviet society in general has lost most of its revolutionary dynamism and that apathy toward ideological appeals extends to the Russian Republic and into the ranks of the party itself. This no doubt accounts for the continued strong emphasis upon ideological training and retraining of party cadres, an activity that was apparently pursued even more vigorously in 1974 than in previous years (*Krasnaia zvezda*, 31 August; *Pravda*, 2 September; *Izvestiia*, 5 September). Major themes for the year's ideological campaigns—the central role of the CPSU and the

Leninist approach to international relations—were set out in a conference on Leninism held in Moscow in January; Mikhail A. Suslov, Politburo member and CPSU secretary for ideology, gave the keynote address (*TASS*, 21 January).

While the party faced organizational and other problems in 1974, its primacy in Soviet society remained unchallenged. Tendencies toward greater autonomy for other bureaucratic structures due to the requirements of technical expertise have been checked by the technical upgrading of party cadres at all levels, by the insistence upon party supervision of the performance of economic and other social functions, and by the need for the party to perform the essential "arbitration" function among conflicting interest groups in the allocation of resources. Moreover, cohesion of top and mid-level party elites appeared to be more pronounced in 1974 than at any time since the death of Stalin. This results in part from General Secretary Brezhnev's success in securing the dismissal of major opponents such as Gennadi I. Voronov and Piotr M. Shelest. More importantly, the present leadership's policies have strengthened the privileged status of political elites and have assured generally greater job security for both party and governmental officials. Domestic control problems and bloc and world policies have served to heighten the roles of the KGB and the armed forces in intra-party politics, reflected in increasing membership for these structures in the Central Committee and increasing numbers of former police officials in important party positions at the union-republic level. The coercive forces in 1974 appeared to give full support to the CPSU leadership, with no indications of attempts to develop political power independent of the party; their representatives on the Politburo, KGB chief Yuri V. Andropov and defense minister Marshal Andrei A. Grechko, were reportedly extremely close to Brezhnev. The armed forces' participation in ideological campaigns and in the exchange of party documents was accorded highest priority by the military leadership (*Krasnaia zvezda*, 15 March, 31 May; *Voprosy istorii KPSS*, No. 5).

A coming problem for the CPSU involves matters of succession and extends far beyond any competition for the leadership mantle of Brezhnev as general secretary. The pronounced security of political elites during the Brezhnev era has produced an aging leadership, and the mobility of younger cadres has been impeded in both party and government. Key Politburo figures were near or past the age of 70 in 1974 and among the 396 Central Committee members, more than 55 percent were over 60. Within the next decade, a new generation of political leadership will emerge in the Soviet Union. These newcomers will lack the political experience in positions of high responsibility attained by their predecessors at comparable career stages. This unavoidable development may infuse new vigor into the increasingly conservative Soviet system; it may also make for a difficult transitional period.

Brezhnev continued to dominate the Soviet political scene during the year but was ill in September (*Washington Post*, 23 September), and in view of his age, 68, and past medical history, speculation rose anew as to how long he could carry the heavy burden of leadership. In any case, given the advanced ages of several Politburo members and high government officials, it was clear that the remarkable stability in upper echelons of party and government that has characterized the Brezhnev years could not last much longer. It seemed quite likely that important leadership changes were being postponed until the CPSU's Twenth-fifth Congress, which is expected to take place in 1975. High party officials who gained in prominence during 1974 included Politburo members Mazurov, Shcherbitsky, and Grishin, Politburo candidate members Solomentsev, Dolgikh, Ponomarev, and Romanov, and Secretariat members Kapitonov and Katushev. Fedor D. Kulakov is the only other full Politburo member whose age, 56, and party organizational grounding entitle him to consideration as a potential future leader. These ten men are the most obvious prospects to form the nucleus of a new governing team in the event of early major leadership changes. Thus, whatever the coming generational turnover in the party portends for Soviet politics in the long run, the next power succession is unlikely to produce the dramatic changes in style of leadership that featured the transitions of 1953-55 and 1964. Membership of the Politburo at the end of the year is shown in the accompanying list.

POLITBURO

Members:

Brezhnev, Leonid I.	General secretary, CPSU Central Committee
Podgorny, Nikolai V.	Chairman, Presidium of the U.S.S.R. Supreme Soviet
Kosygin, Aleksei N.	Chairman, U.S.S.R. Council of Ministers
Suslov, Mikhail A.	Secretary, CPSU Central Committee
Kirilenko, Andrei P.	Secretary, CPSU Central Committee
Pel'she, Arvid I.	Chairman, Party Control Committee
Mazurov, Kiril T.	First deputy chairman, U.S.S.R. Council of Ministers
Poliansky, Dimitri S.	Minister of agriculture, U.S.S.R. Council of Ministers
Shelepin, Aleksandr N.	Chairman, All-Union Central Council of Trade Unions
Grishin, Viktor V.	First secretary, Moscow City Party Committee
Kunaev, Dinmukhamed A.	First secretary, Kazak Central Committee
Shcherbitsky, Vladimir V.	First secretary, Ukrainian Central Committee
Kulakov, Fedor D.	Secretary, CPSU Central Committee
Andropov, Yuri V.	Chairman, Committee of State Security (KGB)
Grechko, Andrei A.	Minister of defense, U.S.S.R. Council of Ministers
Gromyko, Andrei A.	Minister of foreign affairs, U.S.S.R.

Candidate members:

Ustinov, Dimitri F.	Secretary, CPSU Central Committee
Demichev, Piotr N.	Minister of culture
Rashidov, Sharaf R.	First secretary, Uzbek Central Committee
Masherov, Piotr M.	First secretary, Belorussian Central Committee
Solomentsev, Mikhail S.	Chairman, RSFSR Council of Ministers
Dolgikh, Vladimir I.	Secretary, CPSU Central Committee
Ponomarev, Boris N.	Secretary, CPSU Central Committee
Romanov, Grigori	First secretary, Leningrad *oblast'* Party Committee

The composition of the Secretariat remained unchanged (except for Demichev's transfer to the Ministry of Culture): Brezhnev, Suslov, Kirilenko, Kulakov, Ustinov, Ponomarev, Dolgikh, Ivan V. Kapitonov, and Konstantin F. Katushev.

Republic first secretaries were as follows: Anton Y. Kochinian (Armenia), Geidar A. Aliev (Azerbaidzhan), Piotr M. Masherov (Belorussia), Ivan G. Kebin (Estonia), Eduard A. Shevardnadze (Georgia), Dinmukhamed A. Kunaev (Kazakhstan), Turdakun U. Usubaliev (Kirghizia), August E. Voss (Latvia), Piatras P. Griskiavicus (Lithuania), Ivan I. Bodiul (Moldavia), Dzhabar R. Rasulov (Tadzhikistan), Mukhamednazar G. Gapurov (Turkmenia), Vladimir V. Shcherbitsky (Ukraine), Sharaf R. Rashidov (Uzbekistan).

Domestic Policies. Major internal concerns of the party and government in 1974 included civil rights activism among intellectuals; the resurgence of nationalism among non-Russian nationalities; the need for improved economic efficiency and the requirements of continued economic growth; threats to ideological cohesion in a time of détente; and social problems such as drugs and crime which, from the theoretical standpoint of Marxism-Leninism, should not be associated with a mature socialist society. The regime scored some apparent successes during the year in the silencing of dissent and in a continuing recovery of the economy following the downturn of 1972. However, the major problems confronting the leadership are chronic ones and relate in large measure to the rapid and uneven modernization induced by the CPSU's policies of social transformation. Even in a society subject to such pervasive political control as the Soviet Union, processes of modernization tend to generate their own momentum, escalating demands upon the political system. As the demands are increasingly met, the basis for the political elite's dominance is undermined by the rise of new economically-based social structures; if the demands are not met, the political elite's legitimacy is rapidly eroded. Historically, these processes have generally eventuated in peaceful broadening of the base of political power or in revolution. In the Soviet Union, they have been associated instead with a remarkable expansion of CPSU power at a time when the party's status as a privileged elite has become increasingly obvious, both qualitatively and quantitatively. Basic reasons for this pertain to the absence of structural alternatives politically to the CPSU and the leadership's largely successful effort to impose greater "superstructural" control upon the social "substructure." But the dilemma posed by modernization remains, and Soviet society in 1974 showed an uneasy equilibrium between the growing centrality of the party's role and the continuing underlying social change. The party appeared to continue to enjoy broad if not enthusiastic consensual support, especially in the Russian Republic. However, it was quite clear that the consensual cohesion of Soviet society was far less pronounced than that of the party itself and that serious challenges had been posed to both the methods and aims of the political leadership.

Dissent and nationalism. After a brief period of hesitation, the Soviet leadership responded dramatically to the publication—in Paris, on 28 December 1973—of the first volume of Aleksandr Solzhenitsyn's *The Gulag Archipelago*, an account of the inception of the Soviet slave-labor empire and the terror practiced under both Lenin and Stalin. The author had not planned an early publication of his book, but decided upon it following the suicide of Yelizaveta Veronskaia, who had reportedly revealed the whereabouts of one copy of the manuscript during an interrogation by the KGB. (See *YICA, 1974,* p. 76.) In January 1974, the Soviet press mounted a campaign of intense denunciation against Solzhenitsyn (*Pravda,* 14 January; *Literaturnaia gazeta,* No. 3, 16 January), and on 13 February he was deported from the Soviet Union and deprived of his citizenship. On 14 February all of Solzhenitsyn's works that had been published in the Soviet Union were banned from Soviet libraries. Notably, the actions of 13 February came just four months after the Soviet Union's adherence to the International Convention on Human Rights and represented specific violations of Articles 13 and 15 of that covenant. Nevertheless, in June the United Nations itself subscribed to the suppression of Solzhenitsyn's work by prohibiting the sale of *Gulag* at its European headquarters in Geneva, in order "not to offend a member nation." The second volume, in Russian, of *Gulag*, dealing specifically with conditions in the forced-labor camps, was published in Paris in June. Unlike the first volume, it was not quickly translated, and it attracted comparatively little attention.

Other Soviet dissident leaders, notably Andrei Sakharov and Roy and Zhores Medvedev, rushed to Solzhenitsyn's defense following his expulsion. Even the poet Yevgeny Yevtushenko, not previously associated with the Democratic Movement, dispatched a telegram of protest to Brezhnev, for which he was punished by cancellation of an appearance in the Hall of Columns commemorating his fortieth birthday and by a public reprimand from the Writers' Union. By year's end, Yevtushenko had rehabilitated himself with the regime somewhat by publication of a poem containing oblique criticism of Solzhenitsyn.

The temporary solidarity in dissident ranks was broken by Solzhenitsyn's publication, after his arrival in the West, of his 1973 letter to the Kremlin leadership in which he had outlined his proposals for the future of the Soviet Union. In the letter he had called for abandonment of Marxist ideology, renunciation of Soviet domination of East Europe and the non-Russian nationalities, isolation from Western economic and other influences, and concentration upon the development of a simple, non-technological society in rural Siberia based upon traditional religious values with continuing authoritarian control. Sakharov responded with a 3,500-word critique issued in early April. While backing Solzhenitsyn's call for a non-Marxist Russia, Sakharov said that the "nationalist and isolationist direction of Solzhenitsyn's thinking, the religious-patriarchal romanticism characteristic of him, leads him into very substantial errors and makes his proposals utopian and potentially dangerous." Further, Sakharov said, Solzhenitsyn's ideas were "authoritarian" and could lead to the "slavish lackey spirit that existed in Russia for centuries." (*NYT*, and United Press International, 14 April.) Sakharov's own perspective is that of secular liberalism and his proposals for the future involve "convergence" between Russia and the West on such matters as technology, living standards, and especially civil liberties. In a critique of *Gulag* (*NYT*, 7 February), Roy Medvedev said that the book "contributes much to the study of the entire criminal and inhuman system of Stalinism," but that "Solzhenitsyn is wrong in assuming that this system has been preserved in its basic features up to the present day." Further, Medvedev argued, the "terror of the Civil War period did not predetermine the frightful terror of the Stalin era," and the "sum total of Lenin's activities was positive." In his response to Solzhenitsyn's 1973 letter to the leadership, Medvedev presented the view that "socialism with a human face" can be achieved in the Soviet Union through a combination of reform from above and pressure from abroad (*Washington Post*, 28 April). Sakharov had earlier denounced the Medvedev brothers' pragmatic approach to reform as immoral (ibid., 3 December 1973). The dispute among the dissident leaders, which evoked memories of the nineteenth-century Slavophil-Westernizer controversies and was unresolved at year's end, clouded prospects for a future unification of the protest movement.

The Democratic Movement, led by Sakharov, appeared to be virtually demolished in early 1974, due to the arrest and exile of most of its leaders. However, the *Chronicle of Current Events (Khronika tekushchikh sobytii)*, the movement's underground newspaper, was revived in May after a lapse of 18 months, and several issues appeared during the year, indicating that new recruits were entering the dissidents' ranks to replace earlier KGB victims. Meanwhile, the regime's campaign of repression against dissent continued unabated and took various forms. Solzhenitsyn's friend and defender Lidia Chukovskaia was expelled from the Writers' Union in January. Viktor Khaustov, who had led a protest against the treatment of imprisoned dissident Vladimir Bukovsky, was sentenced to four years in prison (*Washington Post*, 7 March.) In May the 250th-anniversary celebration of the Academy of Sciences was indefinitely postponed, apparently because the academy had failed to purge the handful of dissidents among its members. Also in May, the dissident priest Father Dimitri Dudko, whose sermons in Moscow had attracted large audiences, was punished by a transfer reportedly instigated by the local Komsomol organization; he subsequently resigned from the priesthood. The novelist Viktor Nekrasov, a one-time winner of the Stalin Prize, was granted an exit visa in August, apparently in lieu of forced exile. Approximately 50 Jewish civil rights activists were arrested in Moscow and other cities in the week before U.S. President Nixon's arrival for the summit conference in June; a similar roundup had occurred prior to Nixon's 1972 Moscow visit.

The number of political prisoners in the Soviet Union was reportedly about 10,000 in early 1974 (*NYT*, 13 January). Detention in psychiatric institutions continued to be used as a political weapon in certain cases, with new admissions of dissidents reported during the year. Prominent civil rights activists confined for psychiatric "treatment" included Leonid Plyushch, a former member of the Committee for Human Rights, and Yuri A. Shikmanovich, a former Moscow University mathematician. Former Major-General Piotr Grigorenko, one of the more prominent dissident leaders of the 1960s, was released from a mental hospital on 26 June, one day prior to President Nixon's arrival in Moscow. This was widely interpreted as a gesture to facilitate détente. If the move was intended to mollify the United States, the effect was nullified by the Soviet action in halting abruptly the television transmissions of U.S. correspondents when they sought to report the activities of Sakharov and other dissidents during the summit conference.

While agitation for civil liberties continued to be a major irritant to the Soviet leadership throughout the year, the Democratic Movement and its sympathizers posed no immediate internal threat to the regime. The movement appeared to have made no positive impact upon the Soviet masses and its support among the intelligentsia remained quite limited. The general resurgence of nationalism among the subordinate nationalities is a far more serious matter. The KGB apparently succeeded in its campaign to break linkages between the general Democratic Movement and nationalist groups, but this has not impeded the revival of nationalism in various areas. Soviet spokesmen confirmed during the year the continued existence of anti-Soviet nationalism in Lithuania, the Ukraine, Georgia, Azerbaidzhan, and Armenia. There were also indications of rising nationalist discontent in the republics of central Asia. Resistance to "Russification" on cultural grounds is compounded by economic factors. Officially reported plan results for the first quarter of 1974 indicated that the economic gap between the Russian and other republics may be widening rather than closing (*Pravda*, 21 April) and there is a continuing disparity in living standards between urbanized, more highly educated Russians and indigenous populations in the borderland republics. Despite the overwhelming evidence of failure in Soviet nationalities policy, there were no indications of reassessment of that policy by the leadership during the year. Rather, the leadership appeared more committed than ever to the "amalgamation" (*sliianie*) approach to nationalities questions.

Soviet treatment of three ethnic groups during the year posed present or potential difficulties for the regime's foreign relations. Charges of continued Soviet oppression of Jews and resistance to emigration demands constituted a major obstacle to Soviet-U.S. détente; a group of U.S. senators, led by Henry Jackson, insisted upon relaxation of emigration restrictions as a quid pro quo for most-favored-nation treatment in trade matters. In October, it was announced that U.S. secretary of state Henry Kissinger had arranged an informal agreement with the Soviets providing for substantial increases in Jewish emigration. The case of the Kirov Ballet dancers Valery and Galina Panov, which had provoked widespread protests in the West, was formally resolved in June when both Panovs were allowed to emigrate to Israel. However, Western protests against Soviet treatment of Jews continued and the Bolshoi Ballet was greeted with lively demonstrations during its summer visit to Britain. While showing some flexibility in regard to Jewish emigration, the Soviet authorities adamantly refused to accept the full freedom of emigration demanded by Sakharov and by Western delegates at the European Security Conference in Geneva. Soviet commentator Yuri Zhukov charged that the demand for "free emigration" presented an attempt by Western monopolies to buy off technical specialists and drain the socialist countries of experts in various fields (*Pravda*, 4 June).

Emigration policy also posed problems for relations with the Federal Republic of Germany (FRG) since the rapprochement between the two states in the early 1970s had been based in part upon the assumption of freer emigration for ethnic Germans. The year was marked by the appearance of an underground *samizdat* newspaper reporting the plight of the 1.8 million Soviet citizens of German origin, by public protests against assimilation and emigration policies, and by appeals from ethnic Germans in Estonia, Kazakhstan, and Kirghizia to FRG chancellors Brandt and Schmidt and to the U.N. (Hamburg radio, 8 April, 10 September). Several ethnic Germans were jailed in both Estonia and Kazakhstan for participation in the protests. A new drive against Moslem culture and religion also contained dangers for Soviet relations with the Arab world. Survival of religious traditions in the Moslem republics of central Asia was bitterly attacked by the party propaganda chief of Turkmenistan (*Pravda*, 24 June), and several chairmen of collective farms in the Adzhar Autonomous Republic were expelled from the party for taking part in Moslem religious services (*Zaria vostoka*, 5 July).

Economy. On 18 December, Nikolai K. Baibakov, a deputy premier and chairman of Gosplan, the Soviet planning agency, presented a report to the Supreme Soviet about the 1974 overall economic performance. According to the report, the national growth rate for 1974 was 5 percent.

(The plan called for 6.5 percent. The goal next year will again be 6.5 percent.) Industrial production rose 8 percent, above the revised 1974 goal of 6.8 percent but still below the 8.6 intended in the original plan. Baibakov stressed the decision to swing back in 1975 toward heavy industry. The 1974 grain harvest was 195.5 million tons, 10 million tons below the goal. Despite the shortfall, the harvest still ranks as the second largest in Soviet history. While promising better economic perform-ance in 1975, with the new plan emphasizing both quality and efficiency, the Gosplan chairman attributed to the following elements the mediocre performance in some fields of economy: poor management, inefficiency, lagging productivity, incomplete use of industrial capacity and resources, and failure to complete new facilities on time (*NYT*, 19 December).

Brezhnev announced in March an ambitious program for the agricultural development of the non-black-soil region of the Russian Republic (*Izvestiia*, 16 March). For this program, which was approved by the Central Committee in December 1973, 35 billion rubles (about $44 billion) are to be allocated in the next five-year plan. Bigger and more efficient collective and state farms are envisaged for the non-black-soil region along the lines of the conglomerates in the Moldavian Republic, which have proved to be quite successful.

Industrial development of Siberia, particularly exploitation of its oil and other natural resources, continued to be a central concern of economic planners. Serious deficiencies in planning for Siberian development, especially in housing, were noted by a party and government investigative team (*Pravda*, 11 April). Low productivity continued to be a general problem for Soviet industry and a front-page editorial in *Pravda* (16 July) charged that wastefulness and inefficiency were rampant in several branches of industry.

Production and distribution of consumer goods remained the most blatant problem area of the Soviet economy. The original goal of an 8.5 percent average annual increase in consumer-goods production for the current five-year plan had been scaled down to 4.5 percent by 1974. The rate of growth for consumer goods was only 4 percent in the first quarter of 1974, and light industry failed to meet its production goals for the month of March (*Izvestiia*, 23 April). In July, it was disclosed that the output of consumer goods in some of the largest enterprises of Ukrainian heavy industry amounted to less than one percent of the total (*Pravda*, 14 July). Quality of most consumer goods remained below acceptable standards; this has resulted in a "consumer revolt" that has produced massive unsold inventories and huge increases in savings deposits. Consistently unable to deliver on promises to consumers, the Kremlin launched a campaign in the official press against "consumerism," a "fascination with obtaining goods" (*International Herald Tribune*, Paris, 8 July).

The targets set by the directives of the Twenty-fourth Congress on the production of consumer goods proved unreachable, according to the 18 December report to the Supreme Soviet (see above). Nikolai Baibakov, chairman of Gosplan, attributed the failure to "incomplete fulfillment" of the tasks given the sectors responsible for setting up the production facilities and supplying the necessary raw materials (*NYT*, 19 December). Prospects appeared dim for an early improvement in the consumer's lot as of the end of 1974; in fact, a decline in real per capita income seemed likely over the next five years due to the expected levels of costs and productivity. Premier Kosygin admitted in April that rising costs constitute a major problem of the Soviet economy. Particularly, construction costs in the power and electrification, automobile, and chemical industries have increased (*Christian Science Monitor*, 24 July). The planned major projects for the development of remote regions require heavy investment at the outset and low initial returns; it was apparent in 1974 that these projects would be financed mostly by internal savings. With productivity rising slowly in an era of increasing costs, a reduction in real personal income thus appeared to be highly probable. If the Soviet Union continues to press for strategic nuclear superiority over the United States, as seemed likely following the successful tests of the mammoth SS-X-18 and three other types of MIRVed ICBMs in February and the refusal of Brezhnev to make concessions on strategic matters at the June summit conference, pressures on the Soviet consumer could be further intensified. The tentative agreement between President Ford and Secretary Brezhnev at Vladivostok in November probably did not mean a reduction in Soviet arms expenditures during the 1970s.

Ideology. Party spokesmen repeatedly stressed throughout the year the intensification of ideological struggle as détente proceeds and the growing importance of the party's central role in directing the offensive against bourgeois ideas. Détente was interpreted as signaling recognition by the U.S. political leadership of a tilt in the world balance of forces toward the socialist camp; Georgi A. Arbatov, director of the Institute of the U.S.A., said that U.S. adhesion to détente was "accommodation to the new realities of the international situation, to the changing foreign and domestic conditions in which U.S. policy is being conceived and shaped." While it was acknowledged that strong divisions existed in the West over questions of détente, Soviet spokesmen presented a view of general simplification of the context of ideological struggle in accord with the Leninist concept of polarization of ideology and the "two camps" analysis. Arbatov identified the enemies of détente as the U.S. "military-industrial complex, extreme imperialist reactionaries, Zionist circles, professional anti-communists of all stripes," the "ruling circles of NATO" in Western Europe, and "the Peking leaders" (*Izvestiia*, 13 July). Ukrainian first secretary Shcherbitsky extended the polarization analysis further, claiming that Ukrainian nationalist intellectuals had adopted the "bourgeois propaganda line," and that "in recent times the Ukrainian nationalist organizations abroad have begun to establish contacts with the Zionists and Maoists" (*Pravda Ukrainy*, 17 May).

General A. A. Yepishev, head of the armed forces political directorate, in a March speech to the army Komsomol secretaries explained the ideological struggle in these terms:

> We live in a world in which the battle of ideas is constantly raging. Bourgeois ideologists employ the most varied means to try to influence the minds and hearts of people, especially the younger generation. The aim of these efforts is clear: to try to weaken our society from within, to shake the Soviet people's moral-political unity and, with respect to the army, to undermine the morale of our personnel. (*Krasnaia zvezda*, 15 March).

KGB chief Andropov also pointed out the dangers of the Western anti-Soviet ideological offensive, in a speech in early June:

> It is not for nothing that reactionary forces allocate millions of dollars to intelligence and subversive services to carry out hostile activities against our country. The imperialists know that it is impossible to defeat the country of the Soviets with military means. . . . They would like to weaken the unity of the Soviet people or, as some say in the West, to cause Soviet society to corrode. There are also people in the West who would like to use détente to interfere in our country's domestic affairs. (Moscow domestic service in Russian, 5 June).

Andropov's deputy, in a 400-page pamphlet on the ideological struggle, asserted that any U.S. visitor whom Soviet citizens meet in the U.S.S.R. is likely to be a spy, and claimed that all of the 90,000 U.S. tourists in the Soviet Union during 1973 were required to submit written reports to U.S. intelligence officials upon their return. The head of the border guards charged that Western visitors were attempting to inundate the Soviet Union with a flood of "poisonous spiritual food," including the work of "sovietologists," religious pamphlets, and pornography (*Krasnaia zvezda*, 28 May).

Soviet ideologists thus continue to follow the line of an open-ended struggle between social systems that appeared with the elaboration of the Brezhnev Doctrine, and admit the vulnerability of mature socialist society in the Soviet Union to Western "bourgeois" ideas. The specific character of that vulnerability was indicated in an editorial in *Izvestiia* (5 September):

> We cannot reconcile ourselves to phenomena which are alien to our society such as egoism and philistinism with its rejection of spirituality and cult of material possessions. It is essential to wage an

irreconcilable, uncompromising struggle against the bourgeois concept of the "consumer society," and against individualism which bourgeois propaganda is trying to impose upon us.

Social Problems. Rising crime rates attracted much attention from the Soviet press during the year. No statistics are available on crime in the Soviet Union, but press reports indicated a sharp increase in "theft of socialist property," especially in the republics of Georgia, Azerbaidzhan, and Armenia, and an alarming rise in crimes of violence in those republics and in Moscow. In February, the Presidium of the Supreme Soviet issued a new gun-control law, providing five years' imprisonment for unauthorized possession of firearms (*Pravda*, 12 February). Two decrees in June and August vastly extended the jurisdiction of the voluntary auxiliary police force (*druzhinniki*).

A sweeping expansion of laws penalizing the sale and possession of narcotics was decreed in May (*NYT*, 27 May); this followed reports of rising drug abuse among young persons, particularly the use of marijuana and hashish. Alcoholism has long been recognized as one of the gravest problems of Soviet society; press reports during 1974 indicated that the campaign against alcoholism launched in June 1972 has had little effect. A regime spokesman admitted in a February article that alcoholism is growing, that it is rising faster among women than among men, and that it can no longer be attributed to bourgeois influences or survivals of Czarist society (*Literaturnaia Rossiia*, 8 February).

On 25 December the Soviet news agency TASS announced that all Soviet citizens above the age of 16 would be issued new internal passports during a change-over period between 1 January 1976 and 31 December 1981. The new documents will be for life, whereas the present policy requires passport changes at certain ages. Those affected by the decision will include the workers on collective and state farms who have been denied internal passports. The decision was made by the CPSU Central Committee and the Council of Ministers.

II

International Views and Policies. Foreign policy in 1974 again pursued the themes set forth by Brezhnev at the Twenty-fourth CPSU Congress in 1971 as the Soviet "peace program." The scope and pace of Soviet diplomatic contacts was intense, even though the top leaders traveled less widely than in the previous year. Moreover, the leaders' travel schedule symbolized the renewed concentration on relations with other communist states, as the Soviets concentrated more on shoring up the political, economic, and ideological unity of the world communist movement. Thus, of Brezhnev's six trips abroad, only one—the December visit to France—was outside the "bloc." Podgorny made only three foreign trips, and Kosygin one, reflecting the continuing dominance of the general secretary in Soviet diplomatic activity.

Brezhnev's preeminence was also symbolized in the treatment accorded him in Andrei Gromyko's speech on the anniversary of the Bolshevik Revolution. Referring to Brezhnev as "head" of the Politburo, the foreign minister cited his name ten times in the course of the speech. Praising the "many-sided and tireless work," the "great talent and enormous strength of conviction" of the general secretary, Gromyko proudly testified that at diplomatic gatherings "one can see for oneself how weighty Leonid Ilich's words are and how high his prestige is." (*FBIS*, 7 November.)

This high status, of course, was a mark of the strength and prestige of the Soviet Union itself. Though they eschewed the word "superpower," especially as it was used to equate the U.S.S.R. with the United States, the Soviet leaders clearly felt in 1974 that their country had "arrived" as a global power second to none. As Gromyko put it on another occasion: "Essentially, not a single more or less important international problem can now be solved without the participation of the Soviet Union or, furthermore, to the detriment of its interests" (ibid., 18 June). The success of Soviet foreign policy was attributed by *Kommunist* (no. 1; in a review of a collection of Brezhnev's speeches in this sphere) to the party's ability to achieve an organic combination of continuity with Leninist principles and a "creative approach toward everything new which the movement of time has brought." As Lenin himself had demanded, the party's current international objectives were based on "the study of the uniqueness of living reality, and not the reiteration of old formulas isolated from it."

Primary among these objectives was the promotion of a relaxation of tensions leading to an "irreversible" détente, founded on the principles of peaceful coexistence among states with differing social systems. The lessening of Cold War tensions between East and West was not, in Brezhnev's words, "a temporary phenomenon but the beginning of a fundamental restructuring of international relations." And the policy of peaceful coexistence was not a tactical expedient but a course rooted in objective factors, including "the very nature of the socialist system and its profound internal requirements." For the Soviet people, it was said to produce the most favorable conditions for success in building communism. But it was "just as beneficial and necessary for the West," for the changed policies of "realistic" politicians in the capitalist countries stemmed not from "well-meaning desire" but from a correlation of forces altered in favor of socialism. (*Pravda*, 7 August.)

Even "those skeptical toward détente"—of whose existence *Izvestiia* had warned in April 1973 (*YICA*, 1974, p. 78)—would now have to admit "that something had changed" as a result of the Soviet-U.S. commitments to peaceful coexistence (*SShA: Ekonomika, politika, ideologiia*, no. 7). Although détente could not preclude conflict situations—since the objective contradictions between the two systems could not be eliminated—experience had shown its effectiveness in impeding negative trends, restraining the imperialists, and promoting solutions to conflict situations. V. Matveyev pointed to the improved circumstances in Indochina and the Middle East as evidence, and cited the crisis of October 1973 in the latter area as proof of the ability of détente to survive a "serious test" (*New Times*, no. 46).

One particular manifestation of the relaxation of tensions—the limitation of strategic arms—was cited by Soviet commentators as benefiting the domestic economy. In light of the December announcement that the plan for consumer goods production had not been fulfilled, the comment of Vladimir Pozner on Moscow Radio has particular meaning: "Speaking for the man on the street, I can say that these vast [military] allocations have had adverse effect on our standard of living. By limiting strategic weapons, we are not only going to have that much more money to invest in such areas as will raise our standard of living, but we are simultaneously going to lessen the danger of war." (*FBIS*, 2 December.)

It was with a rare touch of eloquence that Brezhnev himself hailed the reduction in the threat of nuclear war as the "main thing" in the party's peace program. As he told the Soviet people in his election speech, the first generation who had not been obliged to "tread the paths of war, to live through the calamities of wartime," had now "flowered" in the U.S.S.R. "To put it quite simply, comrades, we must insure that these children and grandchildren of ours will never experience what war means." (Ibid., 17 June.)

By no means did these confident and optimistic appraisals of the international situation in 1974 signify a complacent outlook on the part of the Soviet leaders. Tributes to the achievements of the peace program were almost invariably balanced with reminders of the obstacles yet to be overcome by further struggle. Although the "imperialists" had been compelled to turn away from Cold War policies, they did not share the Soviet interpretation of what "peaceful coexistence" required. Certain bourgeois statesmen saw it not as a policy of active cooperation to insure peace, but only as a "commitment to observe the minimal mutual restraint" necessary in international conduct, "in the spirit . . . of the classic 'balance of power.' " (*SShA: Ekonomika, politika, ideologiia*, no. 2.) Others, more dangerous, sought to utilize a foreign policy of détente as an instrument for interfering in the internal affairs of the socialist countries. As G. A. Trofimenko saw it, the foreign policy of countries in contact will necessarily exert an *indirect* influence on the domestic policy of their partners, affecting resource allocation and—in the case of friendly policies—strengthening an "atmosphere of public support for a similar policy in return, which creates an additional stimulus for them to move toward each other. But attempts at direct interference arouse indignation, provoke a reply in kind, and lead to a course no different from the policy of Cold War time." (Ibid.) The strategists of anti-communism, feverishly concocting new, more outwardly respectable forms of subversive activity against socialism, would be heeded only by "short-sighted politicians" who look at relations with the U.S.S.R. "through the prism of narrow parochial interests and considerations of an election struggle" or make them "conditional on the success or failure of their interparty fights in bourgeois parliaments." With this warning, seemingly aimed at the aspirants for the French presidency, the combatants of Watergate, and the contenders over trade and immigration policy in the U.S. Congress, *Pravda* (30 April) declared that "responsible" politicians in the West will shed their illusions and hopes for the transformation of communism, just as the socialists themselves realize the unchanged ideological hostility imperialism holds for them.

Early in the year, Brezhnev sounded a relatively defensive note in insisting that "stubborn resistance from the most reactionary and aggressive circles of imperialism" had not caught the regime unprepared, and that the "sallies by the enemies of peace" had been no surprise (ibid., 16 March). Podgorny, too, in his June election speech, conceded that "it would be a mistake not to see and take account" of the remaining dangers, and to be "vigilant and take appropriate measures" to strengthen Soviet defenses. Even so, he argued, it would be a "still greater mistake" not to see that, despite the dangers, the tendency toward détente was "gaining strength more and more noticeably" and that positive changes already achieved had created more favorable conditions for "the successful progress of the cause of peace, democracy and socialism." (*FBIS*, 14 June.) In the same vein, Brezhnev, on the following day, avowing that failure to halt the arms race led the regime to "pay unrelenting attention to strengthening the defense might" of the U.S.S.R., declared: "The supporters of the arms race cite the argument that limiting arms, and all the more so reducing them, means taking a risk. In actual fact there is immeasurably more risk in continuing the unrestrained accumulation of arms." (Ibid., 17 June.)

But while Brezhnev and Podgorny saw the "greater mistake" and "greater risk" in pessimism, other Soviet voices—prominently including some in the military—were not so confident. Thus, whereas *Pravda* had asserted on 12 July 1973 that "the dark clouds of military danger [were] dispersing," the military's newspaper editorialized a year later that "the clouds of military danger still darken the sky above our planet" (*Krasnaia zvezda*, 9 July). Less frequent than such clear contradictions were distinct differences of emphasis among certain spokesmen. Marshal Grechko, for example, declared in February: "The world has changed, but the aggressive, misanthropic nature of imperialism has remained unchanged" (*Pravda*, 23 February). The previous month, prominent "Americanologist" Georgi Arbatov had stated substantially the same premise with considerably different emphasis: While the "class nature" of imperialists had not changed and could not do so, "what has changed is the world in which they have to live and operate. . . . They have been compelled to adapt their policy to these changes and to the objective realities of the international situation." (*Problemy mira i sotsializma*, no. 2.)

In effect, a sharp debate on the possibility of nuclear war—reminiscent of that which occurred two decades earlier—seemed to be taking place. In February, Rear Admiral (and Professor) V. V. Shelyag attacked assertions "in the West" that nuclear war would destroy civilization. While war would indeed be a great misfortune, the "mood of communists is far from one of futility and pessimism," he wrote. If Western powers should initiate a war, Soviet nuclear potential provided the means of "routing the aggressor and consequently defending civilization." (*Krasnaia zvezda*, 7

February.) Likewise, Marshal Grechko, refuting those "imperialist ideologues" who argue that war has ceased to be an instrument of policy, declared that "war and aggression always have been and will remain the inevitable accompaniment of capitalist society" (*Kommunist*, no. 3). Reiterating the point in his election speech a few months later, the Soviet minister of defense said: "Imperialism is still sharpening its weapons for war. . . . The danger of war is still a grim reality." (*FBIS*, 5 June.)

On the other side of the debate were some prominent civilian officials and academicians. Among them were party official V. G. Dolgin, who wrote that the growth in military potential of the two opposing systems "makes hopeless the solution of conflicts by military means" (*Problemy filosofii*, no. 1), and researcher A. Ye. Bovin, who declared that it was "impossible to find arguments and to identify a goal which would justify the unleashing of a general nuclear-missile war" (*Molodoi Kommunist*, no. 4). Arbatov was on the opposite side from Grechko on this issue as well. Quoting Clausewitz on the need for correspondence between the "political ends of war" and the means, he argued that with the emergence of nuclear missiles this correspondence was lost, "since no policy can have the objective of destroying the enemy at the cost of complete self-annihilation." Even "bourgeois figures far removed from Marxism" were now acknowledging that the sphere of applicability of military force for national political ends was "inexorably shrinking." (*Problemy mira i sotsializma*, no. 2.)

This debate virtually ceased toward the second half of 1974, and a different theme began to be sounded in some Soviet commentaries on détente. An editorial in *Pravda* (5 June), commemorating the fifth anniversary of the 1969 Moscow meeting of communist and workers' parties, was among the first to articulate the new (and yet quite venerable) note: the alleviation of international tensions, *together with* "the intensification of the political and economic instability of capitalism," *Pravda* said, influenced the deployment of class forces by opening up to the "workers and democratic movements of the capitalist countries unprecedented opportunities." In such a context, a revived version of the "popular front" strategy was appropriate, as attention should be directed to "establishing relations with socialists and social-democrats, setting up alliances with broad masses of religious believers, working with the young people, drawing the intelligentsia to the side of the workers' movement, and so forth."

Mikhail Suslov was quick to adopt this theme in his June electoral speech. Couching it in terms more reminiscent of the Stalinist era, he spoke of the "aggravation of the general crisis of capitalism" and its "deep decay" as opening up more favorable prospects for the "further advance of revolutionary forces" (*FBIS*, 18 June). Although it was to be Suslov and his associate Boris Ponomarev who were most frequently to sound this note, Brezhnev himself spoke in October of a "serious economic crisis," "unprecedented in its force and acuteness," and an ideological and moral crisis, which together were "accelerating the disintegration of the political machinery of capitalist rule" (*FBIS*, 15 October). A week later, in a speech in Warsaw at the consultative conference of European communist parties, Ponomarev cited the "conditions of détente" and the "general crisis of capitalism" as opening particular opportunities for leftist forces in Portugal, Greece, Spain, Italy, and France. "At this time, we believe, the communist parties have greater opportunities and resources than ever before for influencing the course of events in Europe." (*Pravda*, 18 October.)

Reactionary and "fascist" groups still existed, of course, and would seek to crush the advancing revolutionary forces, as they had done in 1973 in Chile. But, said Brezhnev in June, "it is not the events in Chile, but rather the events in Portugal which lie in the general trend of social development" (*FBIS,*, 17 June). Less confident, Ponomarev argued that communists must be prepared for quick changes in the forms of struggle they employ to defend their revolutionary gains, so that the use of violence by counter-revolutionary forces could immediately be repelled. The "peaceful road," he warned, could only be guaranteed by a communist vanguard prepared to utilize the "boldest" means of struggle in its defense. (*Problemy mira i sotsializma*, no. 6.)

It was in this context of the need for reassessing communist strategy in light of the new international conditions of détente and capitalist decay that the Soviet support for a joint meeting of communist parties was expressed in the final months of the year. Interestingly, however, the overt Soviet conception of both the thrust and the scope of the projected meeting had shifted over the summer. The original plan, for a world-wide meeting of parties in the near future for the purpose of strengthening the unity of the communist movement—by ostracizing the Chinese—had been promoted since the fall of 1973. To avoid the appearance of dictating from the center, the Soviets had apparently encouraged party leaders Kádár of Hungary and Zhivkov of Bulgaria to act as "stalking horses" for the idea. Only in April did the Soviets take formal cognizance of the plan for a world meeting; in his Lenin's birthday speech, Ponomarev noted that "many fraternal parties" had proposed a conference, and that the CPSU was prepared to support the suggestion (*Pravda*, 23 April). In June, in their editorials marking the fifth anniversary of the last such meeting, both *Pravda* and *Kommunist* reiterated Soviet interest. As the latter journal noted (no. 9), so much had changed in the international situation that the communist movement was experiencing the "urgent need collectively to discuss new problems and to find constructive solutions to them and jointly to determine the new tasks of united action in the struggle against imperialism." Such initiatives aimed at the "further ideological and political consolidation of the communist movement" would readily enjoy Soviet support.

But the Soviet leadership evidently became persuaded during the next few weeks that a world meeting, with its anti-Chinese overtones, would not succeed in the near future in attracting sufficient attendance. Thus, when the need for forging closer unity through joint meetings was next mentioned—by Brezhnev in Poland on 20 July—it was now phrased in terms of a new conference of *European* parties, on the pattern of the 1967 meeting in Karlovy Vary (*FBIS*, 22 July). That the Soviets had not completely abandoned their hopes for an eventual world conference was evidenced in the communiqué released following Kádár's visit to Moscow in September. Employing a formula clearly aimed at China—the demand for "uncompromising struggle against all and every manifestation of anti-communism, nationalism and chauvinism, against right and left opportunism"—the Soviet and Hungarian parties affirmed the great importance of "collective forms of work by communist and workers' parties both in the regional and global framework" and confirmed their "readiness to support practical steps in this direction." (Ibid., 1 October.)

Nevertheless, when relatively low-ranking delegates from 28 European communist parties—all save those of Albania, Iceland, and the Netherlands—assembled in Warsaw for a consultative meeting on 16-18 October, the Soviets were on their best behavior, reportedly neither dominating the proceedings nor insisting that their policies be adopted by all (*NYT*, 17 October). Supporting the convocation of a full-fledged conference in Berlin—after the conclusion of the Conference on Security and Cooperation in Europe (CSCE), but before the middle of 1975—Ponomarev declared that the documents it produces "must express the joint and agreed view of all the parties participating," though this, of course, would not "preclude any party from touching in its conference speech on any problem it deems necessary." Noting in the communiqué their satisfaction with the "atmosphere of democratism and fraternal cooperation in which work took place on the basis of the principles of equality, respect for the opinion of all parties, and with the aim of establishing common grounds," the Warsaw participants committed themselves to approach the preparatory meeting at the end of the year "in the same spirit." (*FBIS*, 21 October.)

Pravda's editorial (30 October) on the Warsaw conference termed it the "broadest" meeting of communists ever held in Europe and expressed particular pleasure at the presence of the Yugoslav delegation. In the Soviet view, the Berlin forum, "whose delegates will represent 25 million communists, has all the prerequisites of becoming a major international event." Its task would be the examination of the causes and nature of the changes brought about on the continent—and the opportunities for "social progress" opened up—by détente and the deepening crisis of capitalism. Reiterating Ponomarev's formula for the conference's proceedings, *Pravda* noted that, since each party operates in its own specific conditions, it is "perfectly understandable" that each one "often resolves dissimilar tasks" in different ways, sometimes displaying "a different approach to a given practical issue." But this relatively tolerant stance was balanced by the position that, nevertheless, "the main objectives, interests and intentions of the various detachments chiefly and basically coincide."

In a further hint of the limits to Soviet tolerance, *Pravda* concluded by reiterating a familiar formula: the conference would be a landmark in the struggle "for the further consolidation of the unity of the European and the entire international communist movement on the principles of Marxism-Leninism and proletarian internationalism." Clearly, then, while the Soviets were anxious to demonstrate their reasonableness in the interests of consolidating communist unity, they remained uncompromising in their insistence that such unity must be based on Soviet—and not Chinese—principles.

Soviet-Chinese Relations. For these reasons, the Soviets were persistent during the year in their practice of balancing shrill polemics against the Chinese party with the ostentatious display of their own willingness to normalize diplomatic relations on the basis of "peaceful coexistence." The basic thrust of the Soviet analysis of the sins of China's leaders was unchanged: Mao and his clique had abandoned socialism at home and had joined with the most reactionary forces of imperialism in struggle against the Soviet Union and its socialist brethren.

According to *Kommunist* (no. 12), in Mao's internal policies the task of building socialism had been abandoned for the sake of militarizing the country. In its foreign policies, this military-bureaucratic dictatorship aimed at sabotaging the socialist community's efforts at easing international tension and at undermining the unity of socialist forces. Having abandoned the anti-imperialist struggle in order more effectively to fight against its main enemy, the socialist community, the Chinese regime sought to enlist the United States in the anti-Soviet struggle. But its continued hegemonistic aspirations only worsened its contradictions with the United States, and both potential partners grew even more uncertain about their relationship. Nevertheless, according to another article, the Maoists were persisting in their efforts to prevent the weakening of the position of imperialist groupings, hoping at worst to gain time for strengthening their own forces, and at best to achieve accelerated growth of Chinese might as a result of assistance from imperialist regimes (*Problemy dal'nego vostoka* no. 1). By the end of the year, the Soviets had begun to characterize Peking's policy as one which was "increasingly assuming an anticommunist nature" (*New Times*, no. 39).

In the sphere of government-to-government relations, the year began with two incidents which revealed how deep the Sino-Soviet rift had become. On 15 January, five Soviet diplomats were arrested in Peking on charges of spying and subversion. According to the Chinese, the Soviet "spies" were caught red-handed under a bridge, and their scandalous activities were recorded on film. The Soviet Union in turn, accused the Chinese of seizing its diplomats and concocting an elaborate frame-up. In "blatant violation" of diplomatic immunity and the norms of international law, the Soviet citizens had been held for four days before being expelled from the country. In retaliation, a Chinese diplomat was accused of espionage in Moscow and ordered to return home. The great publicity attending the incident was taken as indicative not only of Peking's lack of interest in improving relations, but also of its desire to damage Soviet prestige in the eyes of other communist parties at a time when Moscow was seeking to convene an international communist conference.

Two months later, a Soviet frontier-troop helicopter made a forced landing inside Chinese territory and its three crewmen were arrested on charges of espionage. Early in May, Soviet ambassador Tolstikov visited the Chinese foreign ministry to demand a meeting with the arrested crewmen and the immediate return of both helicopter and crew. According to detailed accounts appearing in the Soviet press shortly thereafter, the helicopter had been dispatched on a mission of mercy—to pick up a seriously ill serviceman for delivery to a hospital—when it had encountered bad weather, lost its bearings, run out of fuel, and made an emergency landing just inside Chinese territory. Complete with heart-rending details about the emotional state of the missing crewmen's families, these accounts concluded with a denial of the "far-fetched allegations" of Peking and a warning that if China should continue to detain the helicopter and crew, it thereby would assume the "full measure of responsibility for the inevitable consequence of such a provocative stance." (*Krasnaia zvezda*, 9 May; *Literaturnaia gazeta*, 8 May.)

The extent of Soviet patience in the face of repeated Chinese "provocations" was revealed the following week in an article in *Izvestiia* (16 May) entitled "Who Is Preventing Normalization? " Using a form of content analysis to demonstrate the growing intensity of Peking's anti-Soviet campaign, the article claimed that the two central Chinese newspapers and the journal *Red Flag* had published more than 900 "slanderous" articles about the U.S.S.R. in 1973—almost twice as many as in the previous year. In the first two months of 1974, the pace had been stepped up even more. For its part, said *Izvestiia*, the Soviet Union "had to its credit" many proposals submitted to the Chinese side, whose realization could considerably improve the atmosphere and eliminate any pretext for speculation concerning the "threat from the north." Proposals for a treaty on non-use of force, a resumption of coastal trade, and a long-term trade agreement, and suggestions for scientific cooperation and the exchange of newspaper correspondents—all had been frozen or rejected on various pretexts by the Chinese, without the "slightest positive initiative" in return. Despairing at the "vicious circles" in Sino-Soviet relations, the article complained that Peking makes any improvement in relations dependent on a prior border settlement, necessitating Soviet concession to "absurd, unacceptable claims." And, it said, Peking rejects a nonagression treaty on the grounds that a Sino-Soviet treaty already exists, yet it refuses Soviet proposals to reaffirm commitments in this treaty and refers to it as "a scrap of paper" in conversations with Western diplomats.

Nonetheless, a minimal level of Sino-Soviet contact continued. A trade agreement signed on 15 May called for a total trade flow in 1974 valued at 266 million rubles, compared with 200 million rubles in 1973 (and only 42 million in 1970) (*FBIS*, 31 May). In June, the Sino-Soviet border talks resumed after a long recess, and one Soviet objective reportedly was to negotiate the release of the three helicopter crewmen. But by late July, it was reported that the talks had failed to produce any progress, and that chief Soviet negotiator Ilyichev had again returned to Moscow (Reuter, in *FBIS*, 26 July).

By autumn, the Soviets seemed resigned to the notion that prospects for improved relations would come only with the departure of the Maoist leadership in China. Thus Brezhnev, reaffirming the Soviet commitment to continued efforts at normalization of state relations and restoration of fraternal party ties, declared: "We are convinced that such an unnatural state of affairs cannot last indefinitely. This grim page . . . will inevitably be turned by the Chinese people themselves." (*Pravda*, 7 October.)

Widespread speculation in the Western press, in November, that the present Chinese leaders had taken a new initiative toward normalization in their message greeting the anniversary of the Bolshevik Revolution was quickly put to rest by the Soviets. The first denial came through the Hungarian news agency, which quoted "official circles" in Moscow as stating "with regret" that the Chinese message was only a reiteration of the earlier unacceptable view. An interesting sidelight in this account was the revelation that the Soviets had proposed to the Chinese in March that the eastern frontier, "which follows a river and is 4,000 kilometers long" be precisely delineated "in a way customary in international practice—by taking into consideration the changed river beds." By this version, the Soviet offer would have meant "the declaration of several hundred smaller islands as Chinese"—but it had nevertheless been rejected (*FBIS*, 15 November.)

Shortly thereafter, Brezhnev himself confirmed that the "new" Chinese proposal—which, he said, advanced as "preliminary conditions" no more and no less than the "withdrawal of Soviet border guards from a number of areas of our territory which [the Chinese] call disputed"—was "absolutely unacceptable." The Soviets recognized the existence of no "disputed areas." (Ibid., 27 November). Thus, at the end of the year, Sino-Soviet relations remained stalemated.

Relations with the United States. Bilateral Soviet-U.S. relations seemed for most of 1974 to be losing momentum as doubts grew concerning the possibility of further progress in arms limitation and expansion of trade. Secretary Kissinger's visit to Moscow in late March, advertised as the last opportunity to achieve a "conceptual breakthrough" on Strategic Arms Limitations Talks (SALT) in time for the June summit, was widely interpreted in the West as a failure. The communiqué itself, noting that "considerable attention" had been given to the arms problem, declared that "mutually acceptable solutions" were possible and pledged both sides to "energetic efforts" to reach a solution, as well as to continued pursuit of policies aimed at making the improvement of bilateral relations "irreversible" (*FBIS*, 28 March). Although Soviet commentaries attacked pessimistic Western press reports, Soviet experts conceded that the arms problem, affecting "the very core of national security of both sides," was "extremely complex, leaving no room for premature decisions." Hence there was "much painstaking work" ahead. (*SShA: Ekonomika, politika, ideologiia*, no. 5.)

Between March and June, a wide scope of Soviet-U.S. contacts took place. The Soviet leaders held talks in Moscow with Senators Kennedy and Scott, with Averill Harriman, and with Gus Hall and Harry Winston of the Communist Party, USA. Henry Kissinger met with Gromyko in Geneva in April. And President Nixon conferred with Podgorny the same month at Pompidou's funeral in Paris, and with a visiting delegation of the Supreme Soviet, led by Boris Ponomarev, in Washington in May.

But there were warnings from the Soviets that their desire for further progress should not be overrated. Georgi Arbatov told an Italian newspaper in May that it was a "typical feature of the American mentality" to do just that. Referring to economic relations, he charged: "Having seen that you are interested in doing business, they think they can have what they want in exchange. This is the mistake." The Soviets had done without U.S. trade for a long time, and could continue to do so. Any economic interests in this area were, after all, mutual. "Indeed, I would say that in this case, the political interest is greater than the economic interest for us. We believe that the conditions for making the détente process irreversible can be created in this way." (*L'Unità*, Rome, 10 May.)

On the arms front, Arbatov likened the present situation to that of the traveler who had raised his leg to cross over an obstacle—it was impossible to remain in this position indefinitely, and one must either cross or go back. "If other steps do not follow in the near future," he warned, "the arms race will continue and possibly even grow," leading not only to enormous expenditures but also to "serious political consequences." (*SShA: Ekonomika, politika, ideologiia*, no. 5.) The particular cause for Soviet concern was expressed in an article by V. Nikitin the same month. Stressing the particular importance of adherence by both sides to the principle of equality, Nikitin warned that U.S. dedication to the principle was being brought into question not simply by "profuse talk of traditional anti-Soviets," but by a "policy being introduced by representatives of the government" which found expression both in military-political programs and in the increased defense budget. Statements of defense secretary Schlesinger were cited as contrary "to the line of easing tensions proclaimed by U.S. leaders." Moreover, they disregarded the "fundamental change in the correlation of forces," which had produced the failure of the U.S. policy of securing decisive military superiority, and which was the cause and guarantee of détente. Attempts by U.S. circles to "activate military preparations" would not, said Nikitin, produce any "trumps" at future talks, but could complicate the solution of the problem and lead to a new spiral of the arms race. (*Mezhdunarodnaia zhizn'*, no. 5.)

In the weeks preceding the Nixon-Brezhnev summit, there were signs that, though it would produce no SALT agreement, the Soviets still valued it for other purposes. Attacking persons who were mounting an "anti-summit campaign," the journal of Soviet "Americanologists" reminded its readers that "it is not at all a question of the mere number of documents" signed at summit conferences, these meetings were useful as well "for the favorable atmosphere they create" (*SShA: Ekonomika, politika, ideologiia*, no. 6). Gromyko's election speech contained a passage noting that "some sort of zigzags" in U.S.-Soviet relations could not be excluded, due to the activities of forces in the United States who oppose improved relations with the U.S.S.R. However, he concluded, "it can be said with confidence that it will not be easy for them to reverse the course of events." (*FBIS*, 18 June.) And Brezhnev in his own election speech stated that "no one, of course, is hurriedly going to solve matters which are not yet ripe. However, comrades, one should not mark time." The Soviets were ready, he said, for new arms limitation agreements, and if the United States would adhere to the principle of equal security and reject attempts to win unilateral advantage, it would "find the Soviet Union a conscientious and active partner." (Ibid., 15 June.)

By 27 June, when Nixon arrived in Moscow, the 1973 pledge of both sides to conclude in 1974 a permanent and comprehensive agreement to control the arms race had clearly been abandoned. The United States had evidently proposed an agreement readjusting the totals of missiles included in the 1972 temporary agreement and placing a limit on the number of MIRVs to be deployed by both sides—leaving the Soviets with a small advantage in number of rockets and the United States an advantage in MIRVs. Rejecting this, the Soviets reportedly had sought a continued lead in number of missiles, parity in MIRVs, U.S. abstention from development of the Trident submarine and B-1 bomber, and inclusion of forward-based systems in the U.S. missile totals. Faced with deadlock on a permanent agreement, the two sides apparently agreed at the last minute to seek a new temporary agreement on offensive systems, to remain in force until 1985. (*NYT*, 9 July.)

Other accords reached at the summit included a further limitation on ABMs; a ban on underground nuclear tests over 150 kilotons (but excluding "peaceful nuclear explosions"), to take effect in March 1976; a ten-year agreement on facilitating economic, industrial, and technological cooperation; a new consular agreement; and agreements on cooperation in energy, housing, medicine, space, transportation, and the environment. The two sides also addressed the problems of concluding the CSCE, achieving a Middle East settlement, stabilizing the situation in Indochina, and increasing the effectiveness of the non-proliferation treaty. According to the communiqué, both sides were "deeply convinced of the imperative necessity of making the process of improving their relations irreversible" and believed that a "real possibility" had been created for achieving this goal. (*Pravda*, 4 July.)

Although a joint statement of the highest Soviet party and government bodies hailed the summit as a "major landmark" and "major new contribution" to Soviet-U.S. relations, it was clear that the danger of interrupted momentum had not been overcome. Secretary Kissinger's post-summit complaint, that both sides needed to convince their military establishments of the benefits of restraint, indicated that internal decisions would have to be made in Moscow and Washington before further progress could be assured. The Soviets evidently believed that the major burden lay with Washington. Referring to the summit accords in his speech to the Polish parliament, Brezhnev declared: "We would have liked to have gone further and were prepared to do so." The Soviets, he said, were ready for a complete ban on underground weapons tests, for the withdrawal of ships and submarines carrying nuclear weapons from the Mediterranean, for strengthening the non-proliferation treaty, for an agreement on arms and troop reductions in central Europe, and for a world disarmament conference. "In brief, the ball is not in our court." (Ibid., 22 July.)

The partial underground test ban treaty was, according to U.S. officials, likely to be renegotiated. The relatively high limits it allowed, and the exclusion of "peaceful" explosions, were reportedly obstacles to Senate ratification of the treaty. (*NYT*, 7 October.) The Soviets, however, claiming that "great economic benefits" accrued from "explosions for peaceful creative purposes" (*Pravda*, 17 August), appeared reluctant to agree to include such tests in a revised treaty. As worded, the treaty posed some embarrassment to the United States, which had sought to impress upon India in May the impossibility of distinguishing "peaceful" and "non-peaceful" explosions. That the Soviets were not oblivious to this loophole and to the risks posed by the Indian nuclear test was evident from the increasing frequency of their statements advocating greater adherence to and effectiveness of the treaty on non-proliferation of nuclear weapons.

But a far more serious concern than the possible renegotiation of a single treaty was evident in Moscow at the end of July, as the political future of Richard Nixon became more and more desperate—raising the specter of the collapse of the entire framework of Soviet-U.S. agreements. The Soviets had already signified their disapproval of the efforts during the spring on the part of some Americans to link the summit with Watergate. As V. Matveyev had posed the issue, could not this "ballyhoo" be seen as a "desire to 'trip up' responsible American figures who have embarked on the path of talks and agreements with the Soviet Union"? (*Za rubezhom*, no. 22.)

Late in July, the Soviet press broke a nine-month silence on the details of the unfolding Watergate scandals. In a report on the Supreme Court decision regarding the presidential tape recordings, *Pravda* (26 July) sought to prepare its readers for a serious Congressional effort to force the President from office. When Nixon announced his resignation, the Soviet party newspaper was quick to reaffirm the Soviet intention to maintain a policy of further improvement in U.S.-Soviet relations, and to restate the "need to observe agreements unswervingly and to fulfill pledges." Although the change of presidents was an "internal affair" of the Americans, "it makes a lot of difference to the international public just how the U.S. foreign policy and Soviet-American relations will be developed." (*Pravda*, 10 August.) The same day, Moscow Radio assured its listeners that when Nixon had signed the summit documents, he was acting on behalf of the United States—*all* its people and parties.

Even after the resignation, Soviet commentators continued to suggest that Nixon had been unfairly hounded from office. Thus highly-placed commentators Zamyatin and Zorin—never once mentioning the specific charges against him—told a Soviet television audience on 10 August that the President's resignation had resulted from an interparty struggle, a deteriorating economy, and the "brainwashing of public opinion for internal political motives" (*FBIS*, 12 August). A week later, defending himself against charges in the U.S. press of exaggerating the "persecution," Zorin reminded his listeners of past cases of Democratic Party scandal. Corruption, he concluded, is "a chronic disease in American politics," and thus could not by itself account for Nixon's fate. (Ibid., 19 August.)

In October, two events not to their liking caused puzzlement and anger on the part of the Soviets toward the new U.S. administration. Contrary to the spirit of the 1973 U.S.-Soviet agreement on exchange of agricultural information, the Soviets in late summer refused permission for a U.S. agricultural team to visit the "virgin lands." Moreover, they had not yet provided figures on their 1973 harvest—much less the current one. Thus, the U.S. government was surprised to discover in October that the Soviets had secretly negotiated a purchase of 3.4 million tons of feedgrains, and President Ford forced cancellation of the deal. Although a purchase of about a million tons less was later approved, the Soviets felt that they had been badly treated by the administration.

The Russians were even more disturbed by the publicity given in the same month to a purported compromise on the trade and emigration issue. Senator Jackson had been singled out in the Soviet media during the entire year for his "anti-Soviet attacks" and "unimaginable" attempts to pressure the Soviet regime (*Izvestiia*, 1 January, 17 June), and thus his claims of "victory" in October were particularly galling. Emigration of Jews from the U.S.S.R. had in fact slowed by about 25 percent, to a rate of about 2,000 per month in the first half of the year, probably in part as a result of uncertainties about the future of Israel and of the widely publicized difficulties in regaining Soviet citizenship, once surrendered (*NYT*, 29 May). Although the specifics of Jackson's demands were never discussed in the Soviet press, *Pravda* commentator Yuri Zhukov told a Japanese newspaper in June that "95 percent of the Jews who want to emigrate ... except for military men and those engaged in the defense industry" had been given permission (*Mainichi Shimbun*, Tokyo, 22 June). But the prospect of any further Soviet concessions appeared dim when Brezhnev, in a meeting with U.S. Treasury Department secretary Simon and a dozen U.S. businessmen on 15 October, complained of "irrelevant and unacceptable" conditions on trade (*Washington Post*, 19 October).

But on 18 October Senator Jackson announced that, in exchange for Soviet concessions on emigration, he would accept a compromise on the bill facilitating U.S.-Soviet trade. Letters exchanged between Jackson and Kissinger were released to the press. Kissinger's letter said that, "on the basis of discussions with Soviet representatives," he had been assured that no punitive actions would be taken against those Jews seeking to emigrate, that barriers would be lowered, and that applications would be processed by the Soviets in order of receipt. The rate of emigration would begin to rise promptly and would continue to correspond to the number of applications. Jackson's letter included some more specific provisions, including as a "benchmark" the figure of 60,000 emigrants a year—later formally disavowed by Ford. According to Kissinger's letter, Jackson's specific points would be among the understandings applied in testing Russian compliance with the understanding. The trade bill itself allowed the President to extend most-favored-nation treatment and credits to the Soviets for 18 months, after which the bill was renewable by vote of Congress for an additional year. (*Washington Post*, 19 October.)

Exactly two months later TASS announced that "leading circles" in the U.S.S.R. flatly rejected as unacceptable any attempt to attach conditions to U.S.-Soviet trade, or otherwise to interfere in Soviet internal affairs. Simultaneously a letter was released, purportedly given by Gromyko to Kissinger on 26 October, during the latter's visit to Moscow. The letter, charging that a distorted picture had been given out on the Soviet position, reiterated that the question was entirely within the internal competence of the U.S.S.R. It rejected the contention that emigration would increase, and noted that, to the contrary, the number of emigrants was declining. The entire episode was treated both by Senator Jackson and by U.S. diplomats as a Soviet face-saving device, aimed at registering a formal exception to the publicized arrangement, and thereby dampening the hopes of Soviet Jews, without actually denying the existence of an informal understanding. Jackson announced that President Ford had promised to withdraw trade benefits should the Russians actually fail to abide by the original "agreement" (*NYT*, 19 December). Although the trade bill finally passed the U.S. Congress on 20 December, the Soviets were clearly displeased with the ceiling set by Congress on Export-Import Bank credits—$300 million over four years. On 28 December, a Kremlin spokesman warned that the Soviet Union might reexamine its economic obligations toward the United States in retaliation against what the Russians view as discriminatory provisions of the trade bill enacted by Congress (ibid., 29 December).

Moreover, the autumn brought continuing Soviet-U.S. complaints concerning the arms race. A charge by U.S. Senator James Buckley of Soviet violations of the SALT agreement called forth an indignant denial by the chief of Soviet rocket forces, General Tolubko. Asserting that not a single new silo had been installed since May 1972, and that no tests of mobile intercontinental systems were being conducted, the general declared that "in all its history the Soviet Union has never violated obligations which it has assumed" (*Nedelia*, no. 46). For their part, the Soviets accused the Pentagon of contradicting the spirit of détente by searching for ways of making "limited" use of nuclear weapons. The civilian authors of this complaint concluded with an observation ostensibly directed toward the Pentagon, but conceivably meant to apply to their own military planners as well:

> Considerable progress in further improvements of basic missile systems, by improving the quantity and yield of warheads in conjunction with improving accuracy, can give rise to fear . . . of attempts to acquire capability for a neutralizing counterforce strike. This, even before the capability is acquired, will call forth a corresponding reaction, giving a new impetus to the arms race, [and by engendering] new suspicions regarding the other side's intentions, will affect the overall political situation. (*SShA: Ekonomika, politika, ideologiia* no. 11.)

In the midst of such foreboding, few in the West expected an arms agreement to emerge from Brezhnev's 23-27 October meeting with Kissinger and his 23-24 November "working summit" with President Ford in Vladivostok. Yet an agreement was reached at the latter meeting on provisions to serve as the basis for a new temporary SALT treaty. As determined at the summit, the new agreement: (1) would incorporate relevant provisions of the 1972 interim agreement and cover the period October 1977-December 1985, (2) would be based on the principles of equality and equal security, (3) would entitle both sides to have 2,400 strategic delivery vehicles, (4) would allow both to emplace MIRVs on 1,320 ICBMs and SLBMs (but would not limit "throw-weight"—an American concession), (5) would include in the totals bombers, but not "forward-based systems" (a Soviet concession), and (6) would provide for further negotiations on limitations and possible reductions of arms, to begin no later than 1980-81. The details of the agreement were to be negotiated in Geneva beginning in January 1975.

Moreover, the Soviet and U.S. leaders agreed to continue "without a loss in momentum, to expand the scale and intensity of their cooperative efforts in all spheres," and they reiterated previous commitments to attempt to conclude the CSCE and to solve the Middle Eastern conflict (*FBIS*, 25 November). Although the arms agreement drew considerable criticism in the United States, it was defended by Secretary Kissinger as "putting a cap on the strategic arms race," and was hailed by *Izvestiia* (30 November) as representing "undoubted progress, progress which inspires hope, progress which enables us to look with greater confidence in the future." In view of the earlier Soviet debate on the subject, it is interesting to note *Izvestiia*'s comment that "a very hard blow has been struck against the view that nuclear war is a fatal inevitability and that curbing the arms race is impossible."

Together, both the projected arms agreement and the trade bill, while raising doubts about the stability of domestic political support for détente in the United States, provided the Soviet leadership with some basis for long-term planning with respect to the Soviet-U.S. relationship. As Arbatov had noted earlier, in commenting upon the 10-year trade agreement concluded in July, a long-term pact was "particularly important at a time when work [was] proceeding on the new five-year plan and the long-term plans for national economic development." (*Izvestiia*, 13 July.)

Europe. In the communiqués issued at both the July and November summits, Soviet and U.S. leaders addressed the timetable for concluding the work of the CSCE. In both documents, the Americans qualified their endorsement for an early, high-level conclusion to the conference with the "assumption that the results achieved in the course of the conference would permit an early summit." Although it was not clear to what extent the Soviets were willing to make concessions in order to produce results deemed worthy by Western delegations, it was evident throughout the year that a 35-nation summit capping the work of CSCE was high on Brezhnev's agenda. Such a meeting, affirming the general principles of security and cooperation in Europe would, the Soviets felt, provide a fitting climax to a campaign that the U.S.S.R. and its allies had waged since 1966. In the opinion of K. Lavrov, this would signify not only the "consolidation of the results" of World War II and postwar developments in Europe, but would also clear the way for drawing a "demarcation line between the period of Cold War and a period of stable peace and irreversible détente in Europe." Thus, the conference itself was merely an "overture orchestrated for 35 instruments." (*Mezhdunarodnaia zhizn'*, no. 4.)

Similarly, the April statement of the Warsaw Pact's Political Consultative Committee regarded the conference—which was "called upon to turn Europe into a region of truly equal cooperation of all states, and to effect moves contributing to growing trust among them"—not "as a goal in itself but as a starting point of the historic work to build new relations" between all the states of Europe. In like manner, the Vienna talks on mutual force reductions in central Europe were regarded by the Warsaw Pact states as creating conditions "for holding future such talks concerning other areas of Europe." (*Pravda*, 20 April.)

What was impeding attainment of this laudable goal, in the case of CSCE, was—in the opinion of Yuri Zhukov—"absolutely unrealistic and truly laughable" Western demands seeking concessions "equivalent to legitimization of interference in internal affairs and abandonment of socialist achievements" (*Pravda*, 9 July). In Kosygin's words, individual commissions of the conference were "functioning as if they were an idling engine." It was time for every participating state to assess "at a high political level" the work to date and "adopt responsible decisions that would open the road for completion" of CSCE at the summit level in the near future. (*FBIS*, 13 June.) Brezhnev joined the chorus the following month to denounce as "unrealistic and short-sighted" those who were "striving to raise the stakes [and] to create problems that cannot yet be solved . . . given the level of trust that has been achieved." A host of "irrelevant trifles" should not be allowed to "drown those major principled questions" that were "in fact close to settlement." The solution to such problems could be found later "in the process of furthering international détente." (*Pravda*, 22 July.)

The "trifling" problems of which Brezhnev spoke were related to the so-called "Basket Three" issues concerning the east-west flow of people, ideas, and information. In the Soviet view, the solution to specific problems in this area—the "broad development of cultural ties and solution of human problems"—was possible only if the threat of war had first been eliminated. The "key problem," as the Soviets saw it, was to develop a preamble elaborating the general principles on which cooperation in this field would be based. Prominent among these should be sovereign equality and non-interference in internal affairs, and respect for differences among social systems and originality of constitutional and legal systems, national traditions, laws, and customs. Anything less would open the way for "ideological subversion" of socialist systems by Western propagandists. (*Mezhdunarodnaia zhizn'*, no. 4.)

As the conference recessed for its summer break, *Pravda* (31 July) noted "considerable progress" in the desired directions, "although not as quickly as one would have liked." But as deliberations resumed in the autumn, the conflicts over "Basket Three" continued to slow the conference's pace. One of the major objectives of Brezhnev's December trip to France—whose delegation was among those insisting on meaningful progress in the third commission—was an attempt to break this deadlock. The communiqué issued at the end of the visit noted that the two sides found "good basis for an early conclusion of the CSCE and signing of its final documents at the highest level." According to a French spokesman, President Giscard d'Estaing would not have budged on the timetable had not Brezhnev agreed to concessions on the issues of freer movement and human rights. (*NYT*, 7 December.)

Brezhnev had in January for the first time described the Vienna talks on force reductions as a venture parallel to CSCE in Moscow's peace program in Europe. In June he noted "a possibility in the near future to achieve here the first concrete results—given, of course, good will on the part of all parties to the negotiation" (*Pravda*, 15 June).

However, NATO's negotiating position, which would confine the first cuts to U.S. and U.S.S.R. ground forces and impose a heavier reduction on the latter, was viewed by Soviet commentators as aimed at shifting the "balance of forces" in favor of NATO. In response to the "geographic factor"—used by the West to justify an asymmetrical reduction—Moscow cited a number of "equally important factors" (West Europe's economic and mobilization potential, the presence of "over 300 NATO military bases" near the borders of the Warsaw Pact states, and greater Soviet vulnerability to damage in a European war) which it said necessitated equal reductions. (*SShA: Ekonomika, politika, ideologiia*, no. 7.) Only in November, after months of deadlock in the talks, did the Soviets propose a "new initiative" which "takes into account a number of elements of the Western side's position." In fact, the "new" proposal closely resembled the previous one—again calling for reductions on both sides in 1975 of 20,000 men "together with corresponding armaments and combat equipment." However, the Soviets conceded that the "chief proportion" of this first reduction could fall on the U.S.S.R. and the United States, with reductions in the contingents of other participating states to follow soon thereafter. (*Pravda*, 15 November; *Za rubezhom*, no. 48.)

In assessing the general situation in Western Europe in 1974, the Soviets perceived—in addition to the sharpening economic crisis and opportunities for "social progress" examined above—a growing rivalry with the United States and a widespread crisis of leadership. The former phenomenon was surveyed by V. F. Davydov in the context of the failure of the "year of Europe," which had climaxed in the intra-NATO conflict over the Middle Eastern war and the energy crisis. In his opinion, these events demonstrated that "the intricate knot of complex and acute contradictions between the two centers of rivalry in the capitalist world" was "being tied increasingly tightly." (*SShA: Ekonomika, politika, ideologiia*, no. 3.)

With respect to the latter phenomenon, the Soviet focus was on the removal from power of Georges Pompidou and Willy Brandt, two leaders whose foreign policies had brought general satisfaction to Moscow. Franco-Soviet relations in the last months of Pompidou's lifetime, however, had been subjected to strain. Brezhnev had met with the fatally ill French president in mid-March at Pitsunda, and despite the Soviet leader's glowing reports of the summit (*Pravda*, 16 March), it was clear that little if any substantive progress was achieved. The source of the difficulties was indirectly acknowledged by Brezhnev in his pre-summit press conference with French journalists, at which he denounced the bourgeois media for its use of the term "superpower" to equate the U.S.S.R. and the United States—a habit to which Pompidou was also given.

The Soviet position in the spring presidential elections in France—pitting the conservative Giscard against the leftist Mitterrand, the candidate of the Socialist-Communist coalition—was at best ambiguous. Soviet ambassador Chervonenko's call on candidate Giscard was interpreted in some circles as an endorsement of his acceptability to Moscow. A post-election article by a Soviet professor in *Le Monde* took pleasure in the fact that "no candidate deemed it profitable to have recourse openly, at least in person, to the poisonous weapon of anti-Sovietism." But the French communists quickly pointed out the professor's "error," contending that Giscard had not hesitated to insure a large-scale propaganda campaign containing the "crudest possible slanders" against Moscow, and alleging that the Soviet embassy had in fact delivered a protest to the candidate (*FBIS*, 12 June). At any rate, a meeting between the new French foreign minister Sauvagnargues and Brezhnev in Moscow in July was said by the Soviets to have given "every reason for looking optimistically at prospects for further deepening of friendly relations" between the two states (*New Times*. no. 29). On the whole, Giscard's continuation of an independent French policy—without the allusions to a "superpower condominium"—seemed to relieve the earlier Soviet anxieties. Brezhnev's December trip to Paris, which produced—in addition to the agreement on a CSCE summit—a major new five-year trade agreement, was hailed by the two leaders as providing "important new momentum" for European peace and for Franco-Soviet relations (*NYT*, 7 December).

The transfer of leadership in the Federal Republic of Germany (FRG) was more surprising and complex. The scandal occasioned by the discovery of an East German spy on Brandt's personal staff was initially viewed by the Soviets as just another case of "anti-communist hysteria" and "slander" by West German "ultras" (*Izvestiia*, 4 May). But when the scandal eventuated in the resignation of the architect of Soviet-West German détente, an embarrassed and surprised Moscow dropped all references to the espionage case. *Pravda* (10 May) attributed the resignation of Brandt to a "gamut of complex domestic processes" and to "enemies of détente and the Eastern treaties." But it was quick (18 May) to reaffirm Soviet commitment to Soviet-German cooperation and to reassure its readers that the new German leaders were doing likewise. Although Brezhnev could tell the Polish parliament in July of Soviet "satisfaction" at the "firm intention" of both Giscard and Chancellor Schmidt to "preserve and augment" the détente policies of "their far-seeing predecessors' (*Pravda*, 22 July). strains on Soviet-German relations soon arose over the hoary issue of West Berlin. Already on 3 June *Izvestiia* had criticized politicians who were "deliberately striving" to violate the Quadripartite Agreement. Two months later (10 August), the government newspaper specifically cited the new FRG Environmental Office in West Berlin as "most definitely flouting" the agreement. The matter was discussed the following month during Gromyko's visit to Bonn. And Brezhnev himself told the East Germans in October—in the context of a laudatory reference to the "special place" relations which the FRG had for socialist countries—that an attempt to get special advantages counter to the Berlin agreement would "play the game" of forces opposing détente: "Everything which has been achieved is too valuable and important to make it an object of a political game" (*FBIS*, 7 October).

Chancellor Schmidt's visit to Moscow later in October provided the occasion for further Soviet-West German discussions on West Berlin. In his banquet speech, Brezhnev denounced "attempts to create obstacles for mutual understanding in the areas where, it seemed, obstacles have already been overcome," and he suggested that greater mutual trust could be developed between the two states by concentrating on large-scale economic cooperation (*NYT*, 29 October). At the conclusion of his visit, Schmidt acknowledged that there had been substantial difficulties over Berlin, but contended that some progress had been made. The two sides described the talks as characterized by a common wish to strengthen trust and cooperation, and they expressed satisfaction at the favorable development of their "increasingly balanced" economic ties, which had led to a tripling of trade—to a level of $2.6 billion—since 1971. A supplemental trade agreement was signed, together with an agreement for delivery of Soviet natural gas to Germany between 1978 and 2000. Another agreement allowed West Berlin to be tied in to the West German power grid, and Schmidt also was said to have gained assurances that emigration of Soviet ethnic Germans would be increased beyond the present rate of 3,500-4,000 a year. But certain other bilateral agreements were reportedly left unsigned as a result of the continuing controversy over West Berlin. (*Washington Post*, 31 October.)

The predominant themes in Soviet contacts with other West European governments in 1974 were CSCE and the negotiation of expanded long-range economic and scientific-technological agreements. Besides those concluded with France and Germany, the Soviets signed economic agreements with Britain (May), Italy (July), the Netherlands (November), and Denmark (November), and entered into negotiations for long-term pacts with Portugal, Austria, and Norway. Visiting Moscow for talks on these issues were Austrian chancellor Kreisky (28 May-1 June), Dutch foreign minister van der Stoel (22-28 April), and Norwegian premier Bratteli (18-25 March). The visit of Bratteli was also notable for an agreement that the U.S.S.R. and Norway would open talks in November on defining their disputed boundary on the potentially oil-rich continental shelf in the Barents Sea. The two sides also discussed possible joint development and utilization of the Norwegian island of Spitsbergen.

Moscow was of course particularly attentive to the growing political instability and opportunities for leftist advance in the south of Europe. Soviet relations with Italy were marked by an exchange of visits between Gromyko (18-21 February) and Italian foreign minister Moro (24-29 July). But when the Italian government crisis developed in the early autumn, compounded by economic chaos, the Soviets were quick to deny any communist desire for the collapse of the Christian Democratic government and holding of new elections. Perceiving that "rightist forces" were seeking to exploit the crisis to their own advantage, *Pravda* quoted the Italian communists to the effect that a dissolution of parliament would paralyze the country, creating a governmental vacuum at a time when urgent problems loomed.

Soviet commentaries on revolutionary prospects in Portugal were also relatively restrained. The fall of the rightist dictatorship was greeted with pleasure, but it was stressed that the country's "lower strata were not fully prepared for mass independent action." In light of the efforts of reactionary forces to seize power, and of the tendency of left-wing extremists to play into rightist hands (as in Chile) by organizing paralyzing strikes, what was needed was a firm alliance of the "broadest popular masses" for "democratization and social progress and against the maneuvers of reaction." (*Izvestiia*, 7 May; *Mezhdunarodnaia zhizn'*, no. 11.) The latter point was underlined during the 29 October-3 November visit to Moscow of Alvaro Cunhal, minister without portfolio in the new government and leader of the Portuguese Communist Party—recently returned to his homeland from many years of exile in Moscow. The Soviets underlined the party affiliation by having Ponomarev receive Cunhal at the airport, but Cunhal himself was reportedly anxious to emphasize the governmental nature of his visit. Seeking food aid from Moscow in order to help the new leftist coalition in Portugal stave off economic collapse, Cunhal was given Soviet assurance of "appreciation of the economic problems facing Portugal and its preparedness to help with regard to the possibilities which exist for solving them." (*FBIS*, 4 November; *NYT*, 31 October.)

The overthrow of the Greek military dictatorship also aroused Soviet concern for broader cohesion of "all progressive forces" against the danger that right extremists might seek to return to power. A TASS dispatch on 25 August urged that Greece form a "government in which all political parties and organizations opposed to dictatorship would participate without exception." But the relatively poor showing of communists and the "united left bloc" in the November elections aroused no visible sorrow in the Soviet press, as *Pravda* hailed the victory of Karamanlis as an endorsement of the return to democratic norms, withdrawal from NATO, and search for a "just" solution on Cyprus.

The initial Soviet reaction to the Cyprus coup in July had been to give a "serious warning" of "grave consequences" to the Greek military government for its flagrant interference in "a region lying close to the southern regions of our country" (*Izvestiia*, 18 July). But the initial Soviet opposition to Greece and support of Turkey in demanding restoration of the legitimate government was suspended after the Turkish invasion of Cyprus and the subsequent overthrow of the Greek junta. Wishing at that point to alienate neither Greece nor Turkey, the Soviets began to place exclusive blame for the crisis on "aggressive NATO circles which nurture plans to turn Cyprus" into a strategic base directed against "progressive" forces in the Middle East (*Pravda*, 8 August)—and thus dealing with Ankara and Athens as though their interests were separate from NATO's. Accusing the British and Americans of using the Geneva conference as a framework for shifting the discussions away from the Security Council and for resolving the crisis exclusively in the interests of NATO, the Soviets sought to convene a wider forum to deal with Cyprus. They proposed an international conference within the framework of the United Nations—a "representative forum of states, mirroring the political image of the world"— including the permanent members of the Security Council and "non-aligned" countries, along with Greece, Turkey, and representatives of the legitimate government of Cyprus, this conference would bring about the withdrawal of foreign military personnel and secure the independence, sovereignty, and territorial integrity of Cyprus. (*FBIS*, 22 August.)

Soviet interest in Spain was focused primarily on a dispute between the CPSU and the leadership of the Spanish communist party regarding the value of détente and Soviet motives in urging an international meeting of communist parties. The Spanish communists, fearing that the Soviets were attempting to revive direction of the international movement from a single center (*TANYUG*, 2 April), sent a delegation to Moscow in October to confer with Suslov, Pel'she, and Ponomarev. The resulting communiqué, declaring that the continued existence of the Franco regime was an "anachronism" poisoning the atmosphere in Europe, and demanding the liquidation of foreign military bases in Spain, added that the two parties believed that "peaceful coexistence does not mean maintenance of the social and political status quo or the weakening of the ideological struggle," but on the contrary "creates conditions more favorable" to the development of class struggle and activity of communist parties in capitalist countries. Moreover, in return for the Spanish communists' support for the all-European communist conference and for the fight against "anti-Sovietism" and "all distortions of Marxism-Leninism," the Soviets agreed to state that they attached "great importance to the view" stated in the 1969 Moscow document concerning the "non-existence in the international communist movement of a directing center." (*FBIS*, 17 October.)

More cordial visits to Moscow were made in 1974 by high-level delegations from the communist parties of Belgium, Austria, and the FRG. Also a CPSU delegation headed by Ponomarev went to Italy for a meeting with Italian communists. According to the communiqué—starkly modifying the usual Soviet formulation—the two parties proceeded from the premise that "solidarity and coopera- tion" among the parties "on the basis of the great ideas of Marx, Engels, and Lenin and in the spirit of proletarian internationalism—which involves respecting the independence and equality of every party and noninterference in one another's internal affairs," constituted an important condition of successfully resolving major tasks (*Pravda*, 21 July).

An apparent violation of this principle was involved in Soviet dealings in 1974 with Finland's faction-plagued communist party. Following the visit of a Finnish party delegation to Moscow in February, at which Suslov reportedly sided with the policies of the minority neo-stalinist Sinisalo faction, a member of the Politburo majority gave a public interview accusing Sinisalo of lying to Suslov and endangering Finnish-Soviet relations. Not only was the unfortunate member reprimanded by his party, but he was also the object of the scorn of the authoritative "I. Aleksandrov," whose 18 May article in *Pravda* accused him of spreading fabrications about the existence of an "organized anti-party opposition" as well as of "violating the norms of party discipline." Another example of Soviet willingness to interfere in Finnish affairs came during Podgorny's October visit, the final communiqué of which warned that "by showing the necessary sense of responsibility and business- like attitude, the mass communications media must serve the important cause of strengthening friendship and trust . . . and refrain from harming the favorable development of friendly relations" (*FBIS*, 23 October).

The major thrust of Soviet efforts in Eastern Europe was directed toward preparing for and conducting multilateral conferences. The year began with a meeting of party secretaries concerned with ideological questions, from all the CMEA countries. With Suslov presiding, the participants "exchanged experiences" on current problems of "party construction, questions of growth of party ranks and further improvement of qualitative make-up, and Leninist norms of party life" (*Pravda*, 24 January).

In April the top party and government leaders of the Warsaw Pact states assembled in Warsaw for a meeting of the pact's Political Consultative Committee. Issuing declarations on the Middle East, Vietnam, Chile, and the CSCE—but not, in Romania's presence, agreeing on China or a world communist meeting—the delegates signed a communiqué reiterating their readiness to disband the organization or its military arm simultaneously with the dissolution of NATO. But, they declared, so long as NATO exists and effective disarmament is not achieved, they "deem it necessary to strengthen their defenses." (*FBIS*, 19 April.) The Soviet estimate of the enhanced political value of the Warsaw Pact was provided the following month by V. Aleksandrov, who hailed it as "a well-oiled mechanism of political and defense cooperation . . . an organic part of the world socialist community" which "acts as a real generator of ideas, as the creator of the European socialist countries' collective peace-loving policy" (*Izvestiia*, 14 May).

In the bilateral sphere, the Soviets in September received a Hungarian delegation headed by Kádár for six days of talks concentrating on coordination of economic policies for the period 1976-80. A reference in the communiqué to the need for further work to coordinate plans in the area of fuel and energy resources signaled possible Hungarian resistance to a Soviet effort to increase oil prices (*FBIS*, 1 October). As for the German Democratic Republic (GDR), its party chief Honecker visited the U.S.S.R. in June, and Brezhnev traveled to East Berlin in October, where he hailed the GDR's development as a socialist success story while praising cooperation between the socialist states and the FRG. On this occasion, and throughout the year, the Soviets hailed international recognition of the GDR as a victory for détente (and precedent for cessation of the boycott of Cuba). Brezhnev met with party chief Gierek of Poland twice during the summer—during his visit to that country in July, and during Gierek's vacation in the Crimea in August. High-level bilateral contacts with Czechoslovakia were limited to a visit to that country by Marshal Grechko in August, and talks between CPSU secretary F. D. Kulakov and Husák—dealing with cooperation in agriculture and other economic spheres—in November in Prague. Bulgarian leader Zhivkov was in the U.S.S.R. twice during the year—in May, with Premier Todorov to discuss long-range economic cooperation, and in October to discuss with Brezhnev the strengthening of the unity and cohesion of socialist countries and consolidation of international communist solidarity.

One possible item of discussion between the Soviets and Bulgarians was a reported request to the Romanians from the Warsaw Pact command for a military land corridor across that country linking Bulgaria and the U.S.S.R. This may have been an item for discussion in Moscow on 8 October, when Ponomarev received the Romanian ambassador for "comradely talks" while Suslov received the Bulgarian envoy for discussions in a "friendly and cordial atmosphere" (*Pravda*, 9 October). Whether or not this was the case, Soviet-Romanian relations remained less than cordial, despite a visit by Kosygin to Bucharest in late August and a trip by Kirilenko, to attend the Eleventh Congress of the Romanian Communist Party, in November.

Kirilenko also headed the Soviet delegation to the Tenth Congress of the League of Communists of Yugoslavia (LCY). While in that country, he lectured the Yugoslavs on the need to consolidate the leading role of the working class and the alliance with the working peasantry and intelligentsia, to strengthen the communist education of the masses, and to overcome the influence of bourgeois and nationalist ideology. Although *Pravda* noted on 2 June a certain amount of progress in consolidating the ranks of the LCY and rebuffing anti-socialist forces seeking to undermine the leading communist role in society, Kirilenko saw a need for even more "daily and purposeful leadership of society" on the part of a party which has "mastered Marxism-Leninism" and has strong links with the people. Reiterating the view that the "choice of the specific forms of the organization of social life is the internal affair of each communist party and each people," he added that the CPSU was "firmly convinced that the differences in these forms should not serve as the reason for any alienation or mistrust in mutual relations between socialist states." Finally, he characterized ties between the two parties as "a sort of tuning fork by which Soviet-Yugoslav relations as a whole are pitched," and urged an increasing intensification of "ties along party lines." (*Pravda*, 29 May.) A further attempt on the part of "double-dyed anti-Soviets" to complicate these relations was seen by *Pravda* on 27 September in the "provocative bally-hoo" and "giving free rein to the imagination" of those who interpreted the arrest of a group of Yugoslav communists "who opposed the existing system in the country" as an "anti-Soviet plot." It was not, *Pravda* concluded, the first time that such Western forces had undertaken to embroil Yugoslavia with the U.S.S.R.

The Middle East. The year 1974 saw very active diplomacy in the Middle East, and although Secretary Kissinger received most of the credit and publicity, the Soviets were following closely in his wake, seeking persistently to prevent a decline in their influence and to gain a recognized voice in future negotiations. The year began with Egyptian foreign minister Fahmy's visit to Moscow, following the first Israeli-Egyptian troop disengagement and growing reports of Cairo's disillusionment with its alliance with Moscow. Noting that the events of October 1973 confirmed the strength of Soviet-Egyptian friendship, the two sides reaffirmed their insistence on a fundamental settlement freeing all lands occupied in 1967 and respecting Palestinian rights. An important factor in encouraging such a settlement, they agreed, was close coordination of actions between Cairo and Moscow at all stages. (*Pravda*, 25 January 1974.)

In February and March, Gromyko followed Kissinger in his "shuttle diplomacy," traveling between Cairo and Damascus—but not, of course, to Jerusalem. Speaking in Egypt, he declared that a further deepening of relations between the two states was possible if both sides would "strive not only in words but in deeds as well." Though opponents of a just peace would like to substitute a partial settlement for a real one, and would like to split the Arabs from their allies, such a drifting apart must not be permitted, he declared. (*FBIS*, 5 March.) At the same time, Moscow Radio was stressing the point that favorable changes in the Middle East had not come automatically, nor as a result of imperialist or Israeli generosity, but only through Arab struggle and the active and decisive support provided by the Soviet Union. (Ibid.)

In April, Syria's president traveled to Moscow to hear a message similar to that given the Egyptians: friendship with the U.S.S.R. must be strengthened and attempts to strain it rebuffed, partial steps are not satisfactory, and Soviet participation in all stages of the settlement must be insured. The communiqué noted that the two sides would sign an agreement on trade and had outlined "steps for further strengthening the defense capacity" of Syria (ibid., 17 April). The following month Kissinger and Gromyko were back in the Middle East, for discussions on Israeli withdrawal on the Syrian front, and the Soviet foreign minister called in Damascus on two occasions, meeting with al-Asad, Kissinger, and Arafat.

Meanwhile Soviet discomfiture continued to grow, and Moscow's commentaries demonstrated concern over Sadat's course in Egypt, reminded the Arabs that U.S. policy was striving to incite progressive Arab states against each other and the U.S.S.R., and complained that the disengagement talks were overshadowing the Geneva conference. Articles by *Izvestiia*'s editor Lev Tolkunov on 25 July and 1 August summed up the Soviet message. (*a*) The Geneva conference—unlike "someone else's mediation"—gives the Arabs greater leverage and allows them to receive Soviet support. (*b*) Although Arabs and Soviets differ on ideological questions, "we do not wish to impose our ideology on anyone." (*c*) Not enough Arabs regard Soviet friendship as a permanent factor "which the Middle East cannot do without either in resolving urgent settlement problems or in fulfilling" tasks of national liberation. Agents of reaction and imperialism seek to sow doubts and spread misinformation concerning the quality, quantity, and delivery terms of Soviet arms, and recently these unfounded anti-Soviet rumors had shifted to the economic sphere. (*d*) But did U.S. circles really intend to raise Egypt's living standards? Could the United States really deliver a just settlement in the Middle East? How could it assist both the aggressor and his victims? If the pro-Israeli lobby in Congress could block bills regarding a powerful state like the U.S.S.R., how would it react to steps aimed at weakening the expansionist tendencies of Israel? (*e*) What was needed in the Arab World was not only friendship with the Soviet Union but also Arab unity and, since only changes in the class structure could provide a long-term guarantee of that, cooperation with the U.S.S.R. was the best guarantee of such unity.

Another theme developed by Tolkunov—that the Soviets "do not harbor enmity for the state of Israel as such" but just for its annexationist policies—was reiterated by Gromyko at the United Nations in September. Asserting Soviet support for Israel's independent existence and development, the Soviet foreign minister noted that "real" progress toward a Middle Eastern settlement would create "the preconditions for the Soviet Union to develop relations with all Middle Eastern states, including Israel" (*Pravda*, 25 September). Lack of such ties was undoubtedly hampering full Soviet participation in negotiations in the area, and was probably one reason for Moscow's continuing emphatic insistence on an immediate resumption of the Geneva conference.

But with the decision of the Rabat meeting of Arab leaders in October to recognize the Palestine Liberation Organization (PLO) as sole representative of the Palestinian peoples, and to press for its full participation in a settlement and ultimate statehood, the Soviets found themselves in possession of an asset—good contacts and relations with the PLO—shared by neither Washington nor Jerusalem. Brezhnev had come out, in a speech in Kishinev on 11 October, for a settlement which satisfied the "lawful interests of the Arab people of Palestine and their right to a national home" (*FBIS*, 15 October), and the formula had been repeated in the communiqué issued after Fahmi's fence-mending mission to Moscow the following week. In fact, Tolkunov had written in July that "many realistic Palestinians believe" that if Israel should liberate the West Bank and Gaza, "a Palestinian state may be formed on this territory." In the same article, he had asserted that these "realistic Palestinians" had abandoned the previous "irreconcilable" position regarding Israel, which advocated that "this state be destroyed and a Palestinian formation created in its place." The "progressive" sector of the Arab public, moreover, condemned terrorist actions, which only play into the hands of reactionaries, and has chosen armed struggle only because Israel was refusing to free occupied lands. The crux of the matter, Tolkunov argued, was "to choose correctly the forms of this struggle and to make them most effective." The Palestinians needed unity, close cooperation with the U.S.S.R., and a "program which would combine with international efforts to achieve a just settlement." (*Izvestiia*, 30 July.)

It was undoubtedly such matters that Soviet officials discussed with Arafat when he led a PLO delegation to Moscow the first week of August. And when he returned in late November, having won victory at Rabat and pleaded his case at the United Nations, the matter was even more pressing. The Soviets publicly reaffirmed their solidarity with the Palestinian cause and with their right to "creation of their own national home, even to establishment of their own state," and noted that "appropriate practical measures" had been taken to open a PLO mission in Moscow in the very near future, as decided during Arafat's August visit (*FBIS*, 2 December). Privately, the Soviets were reported to have tried to impress on Arafat the need to make efforts to become an acceptable participant in the negotiating process, in part by dropping his "politically unrealistic" platform calling for a "democratic secular state." The Palestinians reportedly assured the Soviets that they had already tacitly accepted Israeli existence, but Moscow was said to have backed off from supporting early creation of a provisional Palestinian government in exile—arguing that only a government offering explicit recognition of Israel would win Soviet or widespread international recognition. (*Washington Post*, 11 December.)

The fruit of the primary thrust of Soviet Middle Eastern diplomacy in 1974 would be fully revealed only by Brezhnev's scheduled visit to Egypt, Syria and Iraq in January 1975, but it seemed evident that the Russians had managed to improve their position from the low point of late spring.

Other Soviet contacts with Middle Eastern leaders during 1974 included a visit of a party and government delegation of the People's Democratic Republic of Yemen in July, and Marshal Grechko's visit to Algeria in May, both of which included discussions of Soviet military assistance. Another, more unlikely visitor to Moscow was Libya's Prime Minister Jallud, who came in mid-May for talks with Brezhnev, Podgorny, and Kosygin. Given their earlier polemics, it was to be expected that the Soviets and Libyans would not be in full agreement, and indeed the communiqué noted that "frank" discussions had occurred. A trade agreement was concluded and the two sides "pointed out with satisfaction that there are all possibilities for the further fraternal development of all-round Soviet-Libyan relations." (*FBIS*, 22 May.) But their relations seemed to cool again by year's end, as the Soviets again grew closer to Sadat.

A final high-level Arab visitor was Iraqi strong-man Hussain, who was received by Brezhnev in February. The following month Grechko returned the visit, discussing, among other topics, oil, the Middle Eastern crisis, and Soviet military assistance. There were reports at the time that Soviet pilots had begun to fly MIG-23's in Iraq in raids against the rebellious Kurds. Such activity would indicate that, especially given strained relations with Egypt, consolidation of their position in Iraq was becoming a high priority for the Soviets. Another exchange of military visits in the fall confirmed this estimate, as Grechko received the chief of the Iraqi general staff in September, and General Kulikov, his Soviet counterpart, returned the visit in November.

Such developments were of serious concern to the Shah of Iran, who traveled to Moscow for a "friendly business visit" in mid-November. Podgorny, describing Soviet-Iranian relations as "peaceful coexistence in action," nevertheless lectured his royal visitor on the need for a settlement of the Iranian-Iraqi conflict at the conference table. Stressing the need for creation of a "security system on the Asian continent," he declared that it was this path, and "not the arms race, or competition in stockpiling of the means of destruction or ostentatious shows of force" that could insure peace and tranquility. (*FBIS*, 19 November.) Underlining the point, Radio Moscow declared the following week that this "hotbed of tension" between two countries friendly to the Soviet Union was not only causing "great anxiety" among the Soviet people, but was playing into the hands of "imperialist" forces seeking to destroy the Organization of Petroleum Exporting Countries (*FBIS*, 26 November).

Asia, Africa, and Latin America. The Soviets addressed the question of the distribution of natural resources in "third world" countries in Gromyko's speech to the special session of the United Nations in April. Posing the question as one of struggle by developing countries against the exploitation of monopoly capital, he came out for "unconditional respect for the sovereign right of every state to dispose freely of its own natural resources." Countering Peking, he blasted "the false concept of division of the world into poor and rich countries, which places socialist and exploiter nations on the same level." Addressing the oil situation, he disavowed both the use of "embargo for its own sake" and the "quest for solutions . . . conducted in secret," and advocated instead bilateral and multilateral discussions on the problem with the participation of a broad circle of states. (*Pravda*, 12 April.)

Lev Tolkunov addressed the oil crisis in more detail in the fall. Declaring that the roots of the crisis were in the defects of the capitalist economies, he noted that it had not only deepened the "general crisis of capitalism" but also exacerbated contradictions between imperialism and the third world. Imperialists, he warned, would concentrate their efforts on oil, seeking to penetrate oil-producing regions to restore their political and economic positions. But, contrary to "malicious fabrications," the Soviet Union believed "that people should not be indifferent to the ever-increasing exacerbation of the oil problem," which might "lead to the disorganization of trade and economic ties [and] engender outbreaks of international tension." The Soviet Union had "advocated . . . a solution of the oil problem which would completely take account of the interests of both oil producers and consumers." (*Kommunist*, no. 16.)

The world food crisis was also perceived by the Soviets as rooted in the contradictions between imperialism and the third world. Its main causes, according to the Soviet delegate to the World Food Conference in Rome, were to be found in "socioeconomic and sociopolitical phenomena, rather than in the 'population explosion,' the impoverishment of the natural environment, or market fluctuations," and its solution was interconnected with the struggle for universal peace and security. *Pravda* (24 November) noted with satisfaction that the plan presented by "certain capitalist powers" intending to take advantage of the "young states' food difficulties" in order to consolidate imperialist hegemony had been rejected. The successful conquest of famine and poverty, concluded *Pravda*, depended upon the struggle of the third world to achieve "economic independence."

Soviet diplomacy in Asia continued to promote the idea of a "system of collective security," which Victor Mayevsky claimed had been supported by the leaders of Mongolia, India, Bangladesh, Malaysia, Sri Lanka, Iran, Syria, and Iraq (*Pravda*, 30 July). Kosygin complained in an interview with a Japanese newspaper that it was unreasonable to establish the solution of "still-unsolved local or temporary problems among Asian nations" as a prerequisite to a security system (*Asahi Shimbun*, Tokyo, 24 October). Gromyko told the United Nations that the 1973 Soviet-Indian declaration contained "important principles which could form the basis" for developing collective security

(*Pravda*, 25 September), and Brezhnev declared in Ulan Bator that "persistent and practical steps of many states and consideration for many opinions and positions is required so as to translate this idea into practice" (*FBIS*, 27 November). The Chinese, with their "slanderous" attacks on the Soviet proposal, were evidently afraid that "assertion of precise norms of international law" in Asia "would be an obstacle in the path of their great-power policy of incitement" (*Izvestiia*, 16 July).

The Soviet Union denied that its activities in the Indian Ocean constitute a threat to the peace, and it denounced the Pentagon plans, "silently supported" by Peking, to secure a military bridgehead on Diego Garcia (*Pravda*, 27 February). President Ford's public assertions that the U.S.S.R. possessed bases in the region called forth denials, published in the Soviet press, from Iraq, Somalia, and Yemen. In a joint communiqué following the visit to Moscow of Sri Lanka's prime minister, the Soviets reiterated their "readiness to participate, together with all interested countries on an equal basis, in searching for a favorable solution to the question of turning the Indian Ocean into a zone of peace, in accordance with the principles of international law" (*FBIS*, 18 November).

The Soviets continued to stress the importance of their friendly relations with India, though New Delhi showed signs of continuing coolness. The Soviet press expressed alarm at the "new fierce onslaught by reactionary forces in India" (*Pravda*, 11 April), but it refused to condemn the government for its harsh suppression of the national rail strike in May, and it reported factually on the Indian explosion of a nuclear device and denials of military intent the same month. Moscow's "Radio Peace and Progress," moreover, hailed India's no-weapons declaration as "new proof of its peace-loving policy," and pointed with alarm to Chinese plans to build a new nuclear center in Tibet as posing a "threat to India's security" and justifying India's "measures to ensure her security" (*FBIS*, 31 May). TASS announced on 3 July that Mrs. Gandhi had accepted an invitation to visit Moscow—probably to discuss the nuclear issue—but no date was subsequently announced. The Indian premier greeted the anniversary of the Indo-Soviet treaty with marked restraint ("a step forward"), and the September visit of Indian foreign minister Swaran Singh saw Gromyko denounce—a month before Kissinger's visit to the subcontinent—"foolhardy politicians" who attempt to "drive a wedge" between the Soviets and the Indians (*Pravda*, 10 September).

Mrs. Gandhi was the only major South Asian leader who did not pay a call in Moscow during 1974. In addition to Sri Lanka's Mrs. Bandaranaike, the Soviets were hosts to Sheikh Mujibur Rahman of Bangladesh (who was in the country for medical treatment), Prime Minister Bhutto of Pakistan, and President Daud of Afghanistan. Daud's visit in June featured talks with the Soviets on the growing tension on the borders of Afghanistan and Pakistan. He told his hosts "with regret" that there had been no progress on the dispute, and that "unlawful and flagrant actions undertaken by the Pakistani leaders" against Pushtun and Baluchi "patriots" had made the situation even more unstable, jeopardizing the peace of the region. The communiqué, noting Soviet efforts to "meet the Afghan side's wishes halfway" in granting economic assistance, and recording Daud's belief that "Asian people's interests would be served by creating through collective efforts of all Asian states a security system," expressed hope that "political differences between Afghanistan and Pakistan would be settled peacefully by negotiation" (*Pravda*, 9 June).

Before Bhutto's visit, the Soviet press noted that, though its path was not "bestrewn with roses," Pakistan was experiencing a "period of renewal," and "progressive forces" there were on the offensive (*Pravda*, 13 August). Kosygin told Bhutto of his satisfaction with the way bilateral relations had developed, and wished for the "speediest settlement of differences that still cloud relations between Pakistan and our friendly neighbor Afghanistan." Bhutto, whose visit had been twice postponed by the Soviets, expressed alarm at the spread of nuclear weapons and reiterated his proposal to declare South Asia a nuclear-free zone, but the final communiqué made no mention of this and simply expressed the hope "that all outstanding issues between Pakistan and India will be settled." (*FBIS*, 28 October.)

Indochina received far less attention in the Soviet media than in previous years. The Soviet position on Vietnam was stated in the April communiqué of the Warsaw Pact states, who accused Saigon, supported by imperialist forces, of trying by every means available to prevent implementation of the Paris agreement. The statement expressed support for a full cease-fire, the granting of "democratic freedoms" to the South Vietnamese people, and early talks between the two South Vietnamese sides to prepare for general elections. But it also pointed to "definite progress toward normalization" in the previous year, which had created prerequisites for strengthening the move from war to peace and for solving tasks of socialist construction in North Vietnam. (*FBIS*, 19 April.) There were a number of meetings during the year in Moscow between the Soviets and officials of North Vietnam. In November, the Soviet side pledged to "continue to do everything possible to render comprehensive assistance and effective support to the fraternal Vietnamese people's struggle," while the visiting delegation—in a formulation carefully hedged to minimize Peking's wrath—expressed hope that the U.S.S.R.'s "international role and influence in consolidating the socialist system in the interests of struggle by world revolutionary and progressive forces, and in achieving peace and national independence, democracy and socialism, would continue to grow" (*FBIS*, 25 November).

Brezhnev traveled to Mongolia, following the Vladivostok summit with Ford, for the celebration of socialist Mongolia's fiftieth anniversary. Meetings with Tsedenbal, in which the Soviets promised economic assistance and both sides pledged to support "uncompromising struggle against any manifestations of anticommunism, nationalism and chauvinism, and against rightwing and leftwing opportunism," were held in an atmosphere of "cordiality, complete mutual understanding, and unity of views" (ibid., 28 November). No high-level meetings were held in 1974 with the North Koreans, but Gromyko's speech at the United Nations demanded withdrawal of "foreign troops" in South Korea, which "constitute a source of permanent military and political tension,"all the more inappropriate in the context of efforts under the initiative of North Korea "toward peaceful unification (*Pravda*, 25 September).

Soviet-Japanese relations continued to develop in the economic sphere and to stagnate in the political sphere. Brezhnev and Kosygin's meeting with leading Japanese businessmen in March was followed the next month by a series of agreements on Japanese participation in large-scale resource-exploitation projects in Siberia and the Far East. Although these agreements were said to constitute "a worthy new page" in the history of Soviet-Japanese relations (*Izvestiia*, 5 May), Brezhnev expressed hope the following month that these relations would "develop on a parallel also in the political sphere" (*Pravda*, 15 June), and Gromyko later declared: "It is now up to Japan to show corresponding readiness" (ibid., 7 November). Early in the year, *Izvestiia*, (7 February) had characterized Japanese policy in Asia as a "policy of yesterday," placing too much emphasis on the United States and "shutting its eyes to Peking's policy of great-power hegemonism." The urge on the part of Japanese ruling circles to delay solution of Soviet-Japanese problems was largely attributable to outside influence. But Japan's foreign policy could not be "stable and genuinely national" without mutual understanding between itself and the U.S.S.R. Prime Minister Tanaka's resignation, in the Soviet opinion, achieved no change in the fundamental problems of Japanese policy.

Soviet relations with the Japan Socialist Party were strengthened during the year by an exchange of visits, during which the two sides found their positions coinciding on many issues. But relations between the CPSU and the Japan Communist Party (JCP) continued to be unfriendly. An article by an Argentine communist, criticizing the decisions of the Twelfth Congress of the JCP, was published in May by *Partiinaia zhizn'*. Especially distasteful to this observer (and to the Soviets as well) was the temerity shown by the JCP in raising the "so-called territorial question" at its congress—"an occasion unprecedented in the history of the international communist movement for a communist party of a capitalist country to submit at a congress a proposal on territorial claims on a socialist state"—and in incorrectly drawing a parallel between the Soviet and Chinese leaderships when talking about the international communist movement.

The high point of a year of relative inaction for the Soviets in tropical Africa came in July, when Podgorny visited the Somali Democratic Republic (SDR) to sign a treaty of friendship and cooperation. The treaty, which was ratified on 29 October, provided for the "development and strengthening of Soviet-Somali relations" in the field of politics, economics, and culture, and provided for regular political consultations. Podgorny's speech in this strategically located East African republic hailed the SDR as "one of the most progressive states of new Africa, which [had] set itself the aim of creating a society free from social inequality, exploitation and oppression" and had adopted the "aim of reconstructing life along socialist lines." Noting that the treaty was not directed against any third country, Podgorny took the occasion to denounce the "myth of collusion of two superpowers" and the "notorious theory of rich and poor countries." That defense cooperation was also an objective of the treaty relationship was signaled by the presence in Podgorny's retinue of Army General S. I. Sokolov, a first deputy minister of defense. (*FBIS*, 12 July.)

Two African heads of state paid official visits to Moscow in 1974. President Kenneth Kaunda of Zambia came in November for talks in an atmosphere of "friendship, frankness and mutual understanding." Discussing the problems of struggle against white minority rule in southern Africa, the two sides noted the presence of "favorable conditions for further development and consolidation" of their "relations of friendship and mutually advantageous cooperation." (Ibid., 2 December.) General Gowon of Nigeria made his visit in May, expressing Nigerian appreciation for Soviet assistance in the Biafra struggle and holding discussions regarding cooperation in the fields of geological prospecting, oil, public health, and technical education. A "specific cooperation project" agreed upon in Moscow was installation of a metallurgical complex in Nigeria. (*Pravda*, 29 May.) In the sphere of party relations, contacts took place during the year between the CPSU and the Congolese Labor Party, the Tanganyikan African National Union, and the ruling party in Sierra Leone.

The major event in Soviet relations in Latin America came in January, with Brezhnev's visit to Havana. The Soviet leader used the occasion to proclaim that the goals of superpower détente superseded, but did not contradict, the goals of revolution—in effect telling Castro that Soviet-U.S. détente did not threaten Cuba's interests. Denouncing as "inadmissible and criminal" any attempts to export counter-revolution, Brezhnev also declared: "Nor are the communists supporters of the 'export of revolution.' A revolution matures on the domestic soil of this or that country." How or when it breaks out, he indicated, and what forms and methods it employs, are matters for the people of the given country to decide. Having delivered this lecture to Castro, Brezhnev added a message for the United States: "We know well, as others evidently know too, that Soviet weapons in the hands of Cubans are not weapons for attacking anybody, not a means of aggravating the international situation," but serve the "just cause" of "defending the revolutionary gains" of Cuba. (*FBIS*, 30 January.)

On more than one occasion, the Soviets reminded the world of their solidarity with the Chilean people and their "deep anxiety" over the situation in that country. The April meeting of the Warsaw Pact states issued a declaration "condemning" the "arbitrary acts, outrages and lawlessness" and the "cruel terror," including persecution of communists, carried out by the Chilean military junta (*FBIS*, 19 April). In July, Belorussian party chief Masherov led a Soviet delegation to the All-European Conference of Solidarity with Chile in Paris.

In the first half of the year, the Soviets sought to exploit opportunities for developing cooperation with Peron's Argentina. In May, Argentina minister José Gelbard paid a visit to Moscow, leading a delegation of over 130 specialists, including representatives of the armed forces. Talks in a "warm and friendly atmosphere" explored the building of a "qualitatively new phase" of Soviet-Argentine relations. The Argentinians voiced their interest in establishing contacts with CMEA, while the Soviets promised to start purchasing Argentine agricultural products, "possibly this year, providing the quality, price and other delivery terms are competitive." Plans were announced for a visit to Moscow in the fall by Juan Peron. (*Pravda*, 11 May.)

The chaotic political situation in Argentina found the Soviets and the Argentine communist party united in opposing "disruptive elements" of the extreme left, whom they feared would provoke a military *coup* on the Chilean model. Peron's death exacerbated the situation, leading Moscow to warn of the danger of reactionary forces, directed by foreign imperialist circles, who were seeking to create chaos. A CPSU delegation headed by minister of justice Terebilov traveled to Buenos Aires at the invitation of the Argentine party to urge the strengthening of leftist unity and give support to the communist demand for formation of a "democratic coalition cabinet." (*FBIS*, 11 July.)

Publications. The main CPSU organs are the daily newspaper *Pravda*, the theoretical and ideological journal *Kommunist* (appearing 18 times a year), and the twice-monthly *Partiinaia zhizn'*, a journal on internal party affairs and organizational party matters. *Kommunist vooruzhennikh sil* is the party theoretical journal for the armed forces, and *Agitator* is the journal for party propagandists, both appearing twice a month. The Komsomol has a newspaper, *Komsomolskaia pravda* (issued six times a week); a monthly theoretical journal, *Molodoi kommunist*; and a monthly literary journal, *Molodaia gvardia*. Each U.S.S.R. republic prints similar party newspapers and journals in local languages, and usually also in Russian.

Louisiana State University   (I) R. Judson Mitchell
New Orleans

Vanderbilt University   (II) Robert H. Donaldson

Yugoslavia

Yugoslav communists put the beginning of their party in April 1919, when a "unification congress" in Belgrade established a "Socialist Workers' Party of Yugoslavia (Communists)" including both communist and non-communist elements. In June 1920, this organization disbanded and a "Communist Party of Yugoslavia" was formed. In November 1952, at its Sixth Congress, the name was changed to the League of Communists of Yugoslavia (Savez Komunista Jugoslavije; LCY). As the only political party in the Socialist Federal Republic of Yugoslavia (SFRY), the LCY exercises power through its leading role in the Socialist Alliance of the Working People of Yugoslavia (Socijalistički savez radnog naroda Jugoslavije, SAWPY), a front organization which includes all mass political organizations as well as individuals representing various social groups.

The LCY claims a membership of 1,076,711 (*Borba*, 14 May 1974), with the majority comprised of white-collar workers. The population of Yugoslavia is 21,260,000 (ibid., 3 January 1975).

Organization and Leadership. The Tenth LCY Congress, held in Belgrade on 27-30 May 1974, amended the party statutes (adopted at the Ninth Congress, March 1969) in order to reintroduce the Central Committee (166 members) and its Presidium (39 members, elected from the Central Committee), together with the Executive Committee (formerly the Executive Bureau; 12 members). Josip Broz Tito was elected president of the LCY "without limitation of mandate," i.e., for life. The presidents of the six republican central committees, the presidents of the two provincial committees, and the secretary of the LCY organization in the Army (nine altogether) are ex officio members of the Presidium. Six members were elected to the Executive Committee from among those on the Presidium, all with the title of secretary: Stane Dolanc (b. 1925), Slovene, secretary of the Executive Committee; Todo Kurtović (b. 1919), Serb, for ideology and propaganda; Mirko Popović (b. 1923), Serb, socio-political developments; Vojo Srzentić (b. 1934), Montenegrin, socio-economic relations; Jure Bilić (b. 1922), Croat, party discipline; and Aleksandar Grličkov (b. 1923), Macedonian, international relations. The remaining six members of the Executive Committee were elected from the Central Committee, without the title of secretary: Dobrivoje Vidić (b. 1918), Serb; General Ivan Kukoč (b. 1918), Croat; Dušan Popović (b. 1921), Serb; Munir Mesihović (b. 1928), Moslem; Ali Šukrija (b. 1919), Albanian; and Dragoljub Stavrev (b. 1932), Macedonian. A Statutory Commission (24 members), and a Control Commission (15 members) were also elected.

Unlike the former LCY statutes, which did not permit a person to occupy both top party and state posts (except in Tito's case), the amended statutes make such a duality possible. The following list includes 15 top party and state leaders:

Josip Broz Tito (b. 1892), Croat, president of the republic, president of the LCY, commander in chief of the Army

Dr. Vladimir Bakarić (b. 1912), Croat, member of the State Presidency and the Central Committee Presidium

Džemal Bijedić (b. 1917), Moslem, prime minister of Yugoslavia and member of the CC Presidium

Stevan Doronjski (b. 1919), Serb, member of the State Presidency and of the CC Presidium

Kiro Gligorov (b. 1917), Macedonian, president of the Federal Assembly and member of the CC Presidium

Fadil Hodža (b. 1910), Albanian, member of the State Presidency and of the CC Presidium

Edvard Kardelj (b. 1910), Slovene, member of the State Presidency and of the CC Presidium

Lazar Koliševski (b. 1914), Macedonian, member of the State Presidency and of the CC Presidium

General Nikola Ljubičić (b. 1916), Serb, Yugoslavia's defense minister and member of the CC Presidium

Miloš Minić (b. 1915), Serb, Yugoslavia's foreign minister and member of the CC Presidium

Cvijetin Mijatović (b. 1913), Serb, member of the State Presidency and of the CC Presidium

Dušan Petrović (b. 1914), Serb, president of the SAWPY and member of the CC Presidium

Mika Špiljak (b. 1916), Croat, president of the Trade Union Federation, member of the CC Presidium

Petar Stambolić (b. 1912), Serb, member of the State Presidency and of the CC Presidium

Vidoje Žarković (b. 1927), Montenegrin, member of the State Presidency and of the CC Presidium

The composition, by nationality, of 205 top party functionaries is indicated in the accompanying table.

Nationality, 205 Top Party Functionaries, Yugoslavia, 1974

Nationality	Central Committee	Statutory Commission	Control Commission	Total
Serb	46	9	5	60
Croat	25	2	2	29
Slovene	22	3	2	27
Montenegrin	22	3	2	27
Macedonian	18	3	3	24
Albanian	13	2	–	15
Moslem	11	1	1	13
Hungarian	4	1	–	5
"Yugoslav"	2	–	–	2
Romanian	1	–	–	1
Slovak	1	–	–	1
Turk	1	–	–	1
Total	166	24	15	205

The Montenegrins appear to be heavily represented, and out of proportion to their numerical strength both in the state (population) and in the party. On 31 March 1971 there were 508,843 Montenegrins in all of Yugoslavia, and 355,632 of them were in Montenegro. In early 1974 there were only 41,150

Montenegrin party members (ibid., 5 April). Yet there were 27 Montenegrins in the party hierarchy, as many as the Slovenes, who numbered 1,678,032 in March 1971, but counted only 67,069 party members (ibid., 4 April).

One of the most significant results of the Tenth LCY Congress was the strengthening of the military's position in the party's top echelons. For the first time in many years a general on active duty, Ivan Kukoč, a Croat, became a member of the Executive Committee. There are two additional generals in the 39-member Presidium: Nikola Ljubičić, a Serb, and Džemail Šarac (b. 1921), a Moslem, the leader of the army party. In the 166-member Central Committee there are 15 generals, as well as other army officers. Two weeks before the congress convened, an active-duty general, Franjo Herljević (b. 1915), a Croat, was appointed Yugoslavia's new minister of internal affairs. Another general, Dr. Vuko Goce-Gučetić (b. 1917), also a Croat, was appointed Yugoslavia's public prosecutor.

It appears that in the period between the convocation of the Ninth Congress and the Tenth, the army's influence has grown. Following the Croatian purges in December 1971, President Tito stated publicly that it was the duty of the Yugoslav Army to defend the country from foreign enemies as well as to "defend the achievements of our revolution, if needed, from internal enemies." He said that "if it comes to shooting, if there is a need to defend our achievements, the army, too, will be there. This should be made clear to all." (Ibid., 24 December 1971.) No exact figures of party membership among the military were published on the eve of the Tenth Congress, but on the basis of one delegate for every 1,000 party members, the figure of 68,000 would seem probable.

Another noteworthy result of the Tenth Congress was the disappearance from the political scene of Mijalko Todorović, who, until 15 May 1974, was president of the Yugoslav Federal Assembly in Belgrade and one of Serbia's most prominent party leaders. Although he was a delegate at the congress and an elected member of the commission for the preparation of 18 resolutions adopted at the congress, he was not among the 205 top members of the Yugoslav Party. Todorović (b. 1913) was a prominent partisan leader during the war, later decorated with the high order of "National Hero," and after the war he was one of Tito's closest collaborators. Therefore, his unexpected and unexplained "cold purge" comes as a surprise.

Party Internal Affairs. In 1974, the months preceding the LCY congress in May were marked by a struggle between party leaders and groups of Marxist intellectuals in Zagreb and Belgrade, associated with the Zagreb philosophical bimonthly *Praxis*. This conflict also involved major clashes at the universities in both cities. As a result, relations between the party and the intellectuals deteriorated considerably. The *Praxis* people came to be known as opponents of the purged Croatian leaders because of the latter's nationalistic tendencies. Their colleagues in Belgrade, meanwhile, supported the Serbian leaders Marko Nikezić and Mme Latinka Perović (both purged in October 1972) because they had advocated complete implementation of the self-management system—the basis of Yugoslavia's socialist order. When "leftist intellectuals" among the Serbs and Croats began "marching together" (an unusual phenomenon in a country periodically torn by nationalistic strife), party leaders began to attack them under the pretext that they espoused a differing interpretation of Marxism.

The conflict between the party and the intelligentsia has actually been a conflict between two groups of intellectuals—between a ruling group claiming the workers' "full support" in all spheres of life, and the "oppositional group" (so-called by their colleagues in power), requesting "real workers' self-management" which in the long run would lead not only to a withering away of the state but also to the dissolution of party monopoly. The "oppositional group" among the intellectuals has accused the "ruling group" of trying to revive "state capitalistic tendencies"—another name for Stalinism. The best-known *Praxis* professors in Zagreb are Branko Bošnjak, Veljko Cvijetičanin, Danilo Grlić, Milan

Kangrga, Ivan Kuvačić, Gajo Petrović, Žarko Puhovski, Rudi Supek, Predrag Vranicki. Prominent colleagues in Belgrade are: Svetozar Stojanović, Ljubomir Tadić, Mihajlo Marković, Miladin Životić, Dragoljub Mićunović, Mme. Zagorka Pešić-Golubović, Triva Indjić, and Nebojša Popov.

Although political pressure initially seemed to have been stronger in Zagreb than in Belgrade, the party eventually concentrated its criticism against the above professors and lecturers of the Belgrade Philosophical Faculty. Professor Stojanović seems to have become a prime target of criticism because of the articles he wrote for *Praxis* in 1972 and 1973 in which, among other things, he attacked Tito's "charismatic leadership" (*Praxis*, no. 3-4, May-August 1972) and called the LCY "a Stalinized party" (ibid., no. 5-6, September-December 1973). Popov, another contributor, compared the current situation in Yugoslavia with the rule of 19th-century princes and with the German occupation of Yugoslavia during World War Two (ibid., no. 1-2, January-April 1974). When accused of wanting to change the program of the LCY, the *Praxis* people replied, in an open letter published in a West German daily: "It is not a matter of changing this program, but rather implementing it in a more rapid and consequential way. It is not a matter of creating, along with the LCY, yet another party, but rather to democratize the LCY in a more profound way." (*Süddeutsche Zeitung*, Munich, 26-27 January 1974.)

The answer came directly from Stane Dolanc, secretary of the Executive Committee, when, in a speech he directly accused the eight Belgrade colleagues of being "anarchists" and "rightists." These people, Dolanc said, "call themselves 'the Left' even though anarchy has never belonged to the Left [and,] in essence, anarchy is a synonym for the extreme Right" (*Komunist*, 25 February).

After the Tenth LCY Congress adjourned, it appeared that the party apparatus would take a more liberal attitude toward the Belgrade professors. Instead of being dismissed from the Philosophical Faculty for their alleged "anti-party activities," they were reported to have had their passports returned after having been deprived of them since June 1968. In August 1974 they apparently pledged to authorities that they would stop teaching voluntarily if their passports were returned. On 19 November, however, the National Assembly of Serbia approved amendments to the law on higher education, strengthening its power over the universities and the teaching staffs. The new legislation gave the Assembly the right to ban any university lecturer from teaching and insures greater influence to the policy-making faculty councils. As a reaction to the amendments (which have not yet been made public), the Belgrade professors and lecturers (according to Western news agencies) stated they no longer felt bound by their August pledge to refrain from teaching.

Domestic Affairs. *New Constitution.* Yugoslavia's newest constitution was solemnly proclaimed on 21 February 1974 by the Federal Assembly in Belgrade. The country's first post-war constitution (a copy of the Soviet constitution) was proclaimed on 31 January 1946. After the break with Moscow in June 1948, President Tito favored a change and on 13 January 1953 a so-called *constitutional law* was adopted, creating an "unofficial constitution." It lasted ten years and on 7 April 1963 the third constitution, with 259 articles, was proclaimed. This document was amended three times: amendments 1-6 were adopted in April 1967, 7-19 in December 1968, and 20-42 in July 1971. Because of the extensive additions, it was decided that a completely new text should be drawn up. Thus, the fourth constitution, with an introductory chapter called the "Basic Principles" and six subsequent sections with a total of 406 articles (the draft text had 378 articles), came into being.

Although official party propaganda insisted that the new law of the land was designed to strengthen both the working class in general and the workers' self-management system in particular, it has obviously strengthened nationwide one-party control. At least three innovations in the constitution confirm this: *first*, the Presidency of the SFRY, the country's top state collective leadership, which previously had 23 members, was reduced to 9, with the president of the LCY acting as an ex officio member (as he would also be following President Tito's death); *second*, the new system of delegation is based on the so-called imperative mandate, under which elected delegates at all levels are unable (compared with previously fewer restrictions) to voice their views, but must now strictly adhere to instructions "from the base" which is controlled by the party; *third*, the Socio-Political Chamber of the three-house assemblies in the communes, provinces, and republics (the Assembly of the SFRY has only two chambers), are composed of delegates "from the socio-political organizations." Thus the SAWPY, "led by the LCY," sends it delegates to the assemblies on three levels.

Articles 313 through 332 deal with the composition, rights, and duties of the Presidency of the SFRY, referred to as the State Presidency. Article 321 stipulates that "the Presidency of the SFRY shall be composed of one member from each of the [six] constituent republics and the [two] autonomous provinces; they shall be elected by national assemblies of the republics and autonomous provinces at joint sessions of all chambers by secret ballot; the President of the LCY shall be a member of the Presidency of the SFRY ex officio." (*The Constitution of the SFRY*, Belgrade, 1974).

Listed below are the nine members of the supreme state collective leadership. These men, with the exception of Tito, but including his successor to the post of party president, will assume power on the latter's death or incapacity: Josip Broz Tito, Croat, to represent the LCY; Edvard Kardelj, Slovene, to represent Slovenia; Dr. Vladimir Bakarić, Croat, to represent Croatia; Petar Stambolić, Serb, to represent Serbia proper; Cvijetin Mijatović, Serb, to represent Bosnia-Hercegovina; Lazar Koliševski, Macedonian, to represent Macedonia; Vidoje Žarković, Montenegrin, to represent Montenegro; Stevan Doronjski, Serb, to represent Vojvodina; and Fadil Hodža, Albanian, to represent Kosovo.

The Constitution gives the State Presidency a strong position vis-à-vis the Assembly of the SFRY as well as the government. Article 319 provides that in the event of a conflict between the Assembly and the State Presidency, the latter would be superior. During the gap in time created by the dissolution of a "competent chamber" of the Assembly's two chambers and the election of a new one, the State Presidency would be free to make whatever changes it deemed necessary. The new Assembly composed of two chambers, which would seldom (if at all) meet in plenum, would be unable to threaten seriously the activities of the State Presidency, because delegates are obligated to follow orders "from the base."

Article 324 stipulates that members of the State Presidency shall be elected for a period of five years and that "nobody may be elected a member of the Presidency of the SFRY twice in succession." Also, if a member of the State Presidency is prevented from performing his functions, he would be deputized "by the president of the presidium of the [corresponding] republic or autonomous province." Concerning immunity, the constitution provides that the State Presidency shall decide on the immunity of its members (Art. 323). This again demonstrates the strength of that body, since the earlier draft text of the constitution had stated that immunity for members was to have been decided upon by the assembly of the competent republic or autonomous province.

New Electoral System. Article 284 of the new constitution states that the Assembly of the SFRY shall consist of two chambers composed of *delegates* rather than *deputies*: the *Federal Chamber*, with 220 delegates (30 from each of the six constituent republics and 20 from each of the two autonomous provinces) all delegated by communal assemblies; and the *Chamber of Republics and Autonomous Provinces*, with 88 delegates (12 delegates from each of the six republics and eight from each of the two autonomous provinces) all delegated by the republican and provincial assemblies. The spring elections of 1974 were held in *three phases* lasting altogether about two months. During *phase one*, carried out in March and April, workers in enterprises, peasants in cooperatives and individual farmers, white-collar workers, employees in various institutions, state officials, and members of the army elected "more than one million delegates" (*Politika*, 10 May) to represent them in higher bodies. During *phase two*, coming in April and the beginning of May, about 100,000 delegates were selected from the previously mentioned one million delegates to serve in communal, provincial, and republican assemblies as well as in the assembly of the SFRY. On 15 May both chambers met in a joint session and elected the president of the Assembly of the SFRY (Kiro Gligorov), five vice-presidents (Marijan Cvetković, Peko Dapčević, Sinan Hasani, Rudi Kolak, and Branko Pešić) as well as the presidents of the Federal Chamber (Danilo Kekić) and the Chamber of the Republics and Autonomous Provinces (Zoran Polič).

The following day (16 May) Josip Broz Tito was elected president of the republic by a joint session of the two chambers; in addition, the remaining eight members of the State Presidency were confirmed. *Phase three* ended when Džemal Bijedić (b. 1917) was reelected Yugoslavia's prime minister on 17 May.

There are 501 administrative units in Yugoslavia referred to as *communes*. Each of the 501 communes (some of the smaller ones combining with larger communes) has a communal assembly divided into three chambers: the Chamber of Associated Labor, in which citizens are delegated as *producers*; the Chamber of Local Communities, in which citizens are delegated as *consumers* defending interests of the localities in which they live, and the Socio-Political Chamber, in which delegates are sent from the *socio-political organizations* such as the LCY, the SAWPY, and TU.

In the provinces and republics, which also have three-house assemblies, the first and third chambers retain the same name, while the second is titled the Chamber of Communes. Here, delegates from various communes gather to defend varying interests. (A village community, for example, would have different interests from those of a town.)

According to the official Yugoslav theory, the system of delegation is more than an indirect electoral system. In this way, the "classical bourgeois and class idea of representation" is defeated and replaced by the "direct class rule of the majority" through emissaries, or delegates. (Prof. Jovan Djordjević, in his book *Demokratija i izbori*). In other words, through *indirect* elections, the working class rules in a *direct* way. Previously the deputies in national assemblies at all levels were professional politicians—they had to leave their jobs in the economy or the administration to represent people who elected them. Now, the new delegates retain their jobs in enterprises, schools, various institutes, the army, administration, and so on, and are regarded as amateur politicians.

Constitutional Court. Articles 375 through 397 deal with the function and duties of the Constitutional Court of Yugoslavia—a unique institution in a communist country. There are also constitutional courts in the six constituent republics and in the two autonomous provinces. The main task of these courts has been to determine whether the laws in force conform to the constitution and whether other regulations and general ordinances are in accord with constitutional provisions.

The Constitutional Court of Yugoslavia consists of a president and 13 judges elected by the Assembly of the SFRY (Art. 381). In practice, two members from each of the six constituent republics and one member from each of the two autonomous provinces are elected to the court. These 14 members then elect a president from among themselves. The current president is Blažo Jovanović (b. 1907). The president and judges of the court are elected for a term of eight years and may not be reelected after their term has expired.

New Defense Law. On 26 April the Federal Assembly in Belgrade adopted a new National Defense Law. Like the preceding one, this law forbids any Yugoslav to accept or sign any document ordering the country's capitulation. It also authorizes the so-called Nationwide Defense System to enlist every individual, social group, and enterprise in the fight against foreign aggression. (*Službeni list*, 4 May.) According to Yugoslav military experts, Marx's theory of an "armed nation" has found full expression in the Yugoslav self-managing socialist system and constitutes the basis of the Nationwide Defense System.

As long as Tito lives, there will be no question of who is the Armed Forces' commander in chief.

A special provision in Article 20 of the National Defense Law stipulates that "the Supreme Commander of the Armed Forces can transfer the execution of definite actions of commanding and leading the Armed Forces to the Federal Secretary of National Defense." The State Presidency is also responsible for the "realization of the Nationwide Defense" (Art. 112). The Council for National Defense actually administers the country's defense system in the name of the State Presidency. The new law also states that the six constituent republics and the two autonomous provinces will have their own defense ministers to organize the defense of their respective republics and provinces.

The Trial of the Cominformists. On 20 September the Federal Prosecutor's Office announced that the convicted "Cominformist plotters" in Peć (Kosovo) and Titograd (Montenegro) had been arrested in April 1974. This raised the question of why there had been a long interval between the discovery of the plot and the public announcement of it? One possible answer is that in April the Yugoslav leaders were preparing their Tenth Party Congress, and the revelation of a "Cominformist plot" indirectly involving the Soviet Union and other East European communist parties would have given the Tenth Congress an anti-Soviet aspect. President Tito apparently wanted to avoid this.

Three months after the congress adjourned, the "Cominformist plot" was publicly revealed. In the interim, Yugoslav leaders had apparently been attempting to solve the problem in direct talks with Moscow. These talks ended in September when Edvard Kardelj returned from a 10-day visit to the Soviet Union (1-10 September). Soon after his return, President Tito delivered a speech in the Slovenian town of Jesenice (12 September), revealing that some people were "plotting against the state." They were reported to have held a "congress" in the Montenegrin town of Bar, at which time they set up a rival communist party based on "Cominformist views." The Yugoslav leaders tried to minimize the importance of the affair by blaming Western journalists for allegedly inventing the story for the sake of sensationalism. Yugoslav sources, however, informed Western correspondents through "private channels" in Belgrade of many details which were officially denied. Thus, it was learned that the Soviet diplomat, Dimitri Sevian, had been recalled to Moscow (a farewell party was held in the Soviet Embassy in Belgrade) and that the Czechoslovak envoy, Josef Nalepka, and the Hungarian ambassador, Alek Toth, were also to be recalled from Belgrade. All this was later denied and labeled as "rumors."

The trials of the "Cominformist plotters" were held in the Kosovo town of Peć and the Montenegrin town of Titograd. Out of the 32 people tried, three were sentenced to between one and three years' imprisonment and 29 to terms of four to 14 years. Only three of the alleged plotters among those sentenced were mentioned by name: Komnen Jovović, an old-age pensioner; Momčilo Jokić, a journalist; and Dr. Branislav Bošković, a university professor from Priština. The others remained anonymous. (*Vjesnik*, 22 September 1974.)

On 26 September the Soviet news agency vigorously denied any connection between the Soviet Union and the "Cominformist plotters" in Yugoslavia. TASS charged that the Western news media, and what it called anti-Soviet elements, had tried to exploit the discovery of the "Cominformist" group in Yugoslavia to mislead world public opinion and discredit the good state of relations between Moscow and Belgrade. A week before, a Yugoslav exile living in Western Europe, former Colonel Vlado Dapčević, denied reports by Western newsmen that he was connected with the plotters. He voiced both his anti-Titoist and anti-Moscow sentiments. (*Le Monde*, Paris, 19 September 1974.) Another suspected leader of the "Cominformist group" is said to be Mileta Perović, who reportedly lives in Kiev.

Yugoslav commentators were clearly displeased that anti-Titoist exiles have been given shelter in East European countries. One editorial stated: "The Yugoslavs believe that the toleration of such activities would lead to a deteriorating relationship with these countries and to a deterioration of the international atmosphere in general" (*Komunist*, 23 September). The Yugoslav authorities continued to play down the whole affair, and by the end of 1974 there was little or no mention of it, particularly regarding the involvement of the Soviet Union and other communist countries.

Other Trials and Persecutions of "State Enemies." In addition to the trial of the "Cominformist plotters," a trial of the "Chetnik plotters" took place in Belgrade in October. A 74-year-old Serbian, Dr. Djura Djurović, a former lawyer, and his 48-year-old secretary, Mme Zagorka Stojanović, were sentenced, respectively, to five and three years' "strict confinement." They were accused of having allegedly cooperated with a Paris-based "Chetnik émigré group" and spreading hostile propaganda. In an explanation after sentencing, the court said it had been proven that Dr. Djurović had written "six hostile articles" between 1964 and 1969 and Mme Stojanović "had typed them." Dr. Djurović was alleged to have had contacts with a Chetnik organization, the "Serbian Youth Resistance Movement," one of whose leaders was Andrija Lončarić (murdered in his apartment in Paris in 1969). After World War Two, Dr. Djurović and Mme Stojanović were sentenced to 20 and 15 years, respectively, in Yugoslav prisons (of which he served 17 and she, 7 years). Dr. Djurović was a leading member of the wartime national committee of the anti-Axis and anti-communist resistance movement, led by General Dragoljub Mihajlović. (*Politika*, 24 October.)

On 22 November the trial of 15 members of a "Ustasha terrorist group" opened in the Adriatic town of Zadar. The 16th member of the group escaped and was being tried in absentia. Among the defendants were three professors and five students, all Croat nationals who were accused of having had links with Ustasha émigré groups in West Germany, France, and Canada. The defendants were alleged to have formed a self-styled "Croatian liberation army" with a program dedicated to political assassination, bombing, kidnaping, hijacking, and robbery aimed at achieving a separate Croatian state. Only a limited number of domestic journalists was admitted; foreign reporters were excluded. (*Vjesnik*, 23 November.)

On 7 October Mihajlo Mihajlov was arrested in the Vojvodina capital of Novi Sad on suspicion of anti-state activity and of spreading hostile propaganda. The author of *Moscow Summer* and *Russian Themes*—both published in the West—was released from prison in March 1970 after having served a three-and-a-half-year sentence. Mihajlov, who was born in Yugoslavia but is of Russian background, was sentenced to a one-month term in 1971 for publishing an article in *New York Times* and thus violating a publishing ban imposed on him; he never had to serve the term, however. The latest arrest apparently resulted from the publication of five articles of his in the Russian émigré periodicals *Posev* in Frankfurt (West Germany) and *Russkaia Mysl'* in Paris. Although the articles were first published in U.S. newspapers and magazines, the current charge against Mihajlov is that he contributed articles to anti-Soviet émigré newspapers. His trial is expected to take place in January 1975.

Congress of the Youth Organization. The Ninth Congress of the Federation of Socialist Youth of Yugoslavia (FSYY), previously known as the Youth Federation of Yugoslavia (YFY), was held in Belgrade on 21-23 November 1974, with 956 delegates participating. It was prepared by republican and provincial youth congresses and conferences. In 1973 the federation had more than two million members, and at that time there were some 6,500,000 persons in Yugoslavia between 15 and 34 years of age.

The congress was planned for January 1974 (Radio Belgrade, 23 July 1973), but was postponed until after the Tenth Congress of the LCY. The FSYY congress opened with a speech by President Tito, who particularly stressed the need to give priority to a Marxist education for Yugoslavia's young people, something which had been "neglected" in the past. This neglect had led "a number of young people to succumb to the influence of anti-socialist ideologies" and be manipulated "by the nationalists, anarcho-liberals, Cominformists, and other opponents of our self-managing society," Tito said. He added that he was hurt to see that "young people, born and brought up in our socialist society, have not mastered even the basic principles of the Marxist-Leninist science." (*Politika*, 22 November.)

A letter to Tito, five resolutions, an Action Program, and the statutes of the FSYY were adopted on the last day of the congress, 23 November. In a letter to Tito, the delegates pledged they would "resolutely march" along his road in order to "continue the further development of socialist self-managing relations" in the country. "We will do everything possible to turn the greatness of your ideas and your historical deeds into the strength of our action." (*Borba*, 24 November.)

The new statutes state that the FSYY is a "socio-political and educational organization" which young people can join voluntarily in order to further the overall socialist development of equality, brotherhood, unity of nationalities and national minorities, and the safeguarding of freedom and independence. In implementing its tasks, it was stated, the FSYY must above all wage a struggle to insure that young people adopt a Marxist outlook on the world. The statutes further provide that the basic organization of the FSYY shall be established in all enterprises, institutes, schools, villages, the army, and so on. Any young person up to 27 years of age can become a member of the FSYY if he (or she) accepts the statutes of the organization. The statutes permit a person over 27 to become a member of the FSYY if the basic organization agrees. (Tanjug, 23 November.)

The Action Program stresses that in the future the FSYY must, with greater speed and efficiency, eliminate the weaknesses that encumber it. The youth organization must be linked up organizationally and functionally with other "organized socialist forces" and together with them implement concrete programs. The FSYY demands, the Action Program says, that the subject of "foundations of the theory and practice of socialist self-management in Yugoslavia" be introduced as soon as possible as part of the curriculum of the higher grades in primary and secondary schools. The FSYY shall wage a "continuous struggle" against all aspects of anti-socialist and anti-self-management activities of the class enemies, that is, "against nationalistic, Cominformist, dogmatic, and anarcho-liberal forces." Concerning cadre policy, the document opposes excessive "professionalization" of the cadres. Finally the Action Program insists that training for nationwide defense should include "all young people regardless of age, sex, education, or profession."

The congress elected a new youth leadership. At its first session, the Conference of the FSYY (the highest organ of the youth organization) elected its Presidium of 29 members plus eight presidents of the republican and provincial youth federations who are ex officio members of the FSYY Presidium. The President of the FSYY is Azem Vlasi (b. 1948), an Albanian from Kosovo, who automatically is also a member of the Presidium of the FSYY Conference. The Presidium then elected a 10-member Secretariat with Matko Topalović (b. 1944), a Serb from Bosnia, as its secretary (and the 11th member of the Secretariat).

Trade Union Congress. On 17-20 December took place the seventh congress of the Yugoslav Trade Union Federation (TUF). It adopted several resolutions, the most important concerning the basic directions of union activities in implementing the new constitution and the decisions of the Tenth LCY Congress. Trade unions were urged to struggle for the development of self-management and for the consolidation of brotherhood and unity among all Yugoslav nations and nationalities. A resolution on all-people defense stated that TUF "must organize and train for activity under war conditions." Another resolution dealing with the employment of workers abroad said that "workers can only go abroad to work temporarily for the first time if organized employment and an equal position with workers in the country to which they are going is insured." Finally, a resolution on the TUF international activity affirmed the "autonomous and independent position of the TUF in the international trade union movement." At the end of its proceedings, the congress elected a new TUF Council with 144 members, and approved a new TUF statute. Mika Špiljak was reelected president of the TUF. (Tanjug, 20 December.)

Economy. As in previous years, economic stabilization was again assigned top priority in 1974. At the first session of the newly elected Assembly of the SFRY, held on 23 July, Yugoslavia's vice-premier, Dr. Berislav Šefer, read a report on the country's economy during the first half of 1974. He hailed "a dynamic development in almost all spheres of production," particularly in industry, which increased 9.7 percent as compared with the same period in 1973. Production of processing materials increased by 10.3 percent, industrial consumer goods rose 9.5 percent, and equipment goods 7.2 percent. Dr. Šefer stated, however, that industrial production had reached its peak in June and accurately predicted that it might not maintain its momentum during the second half of the year. (*Politika*, 23 July.)

Prospects for agricultural production were also good, Dr. Šefer added. This year's wheat yield was a record one, amounting to 5.4 million tons (ibid., 21 July) and maize production totaled 8.3 million tons (*Borba*, 5 October). According to the report, other sectors that have increased in output are forestry, which rose by 22 percent; construction, by 12 percent; and volume of transport, by 16 percent, with only tourism failing to show any growth. The volume of exports and imports also increased by 15 and 16 percent, respectively. These somewhat positive results were diminished by the fact that prices rose faster than was anticipated. Because of the slower growth in gross personal income there was a drop in net incomes and therefore in consumption. Big changes in export-import price relations resulted in a large payment deficit.

The negative trend appearing in the first half of the year continued during the second. In October a document titled "Basis of the Joint Policy of Long-Term Development of the SFR Yugoslavia To 1985" was submitted by the Yugoslav government for public discussion (ibid., 26 October). The preamble of the document states that "domestic economic problems had been accumulating for a long time" and that "unfavorable international economic trends" made it necessary to find "strategic solutions" which would guarantee Yugoslavia's economic and social prosperity for the future.

The economic problems dealt with in the document were discussed at the third and fourth sessions of the Presidium of the LCY's Central Committee, held in Belgrade on 30 September and 8 October. A resolution was adopted which, without quoting any statistical data, called upon all party members and the leadership to combat more resolutely the "constantly increasing inflationary trends" and collaborate with state organs in trying to solve existing problems. (Ibid., 10 October.)

After having stressed that Yugoslavia is one of the seven countries (along with the U.S.S.R., Romania, Bulgaria, Japan, Greece, and Israel) that in the postwar period have achieved the highest rate of economic growth, the above-mentioned document charged that in 1974 this picture had changed.

By the end of July, the Yugoslav trade deficit amounted to about $2 billion (*Politika*, 3 August) and by the end of September, to about $2.3 billion (*Financial Times*, London, 27 November). Despite a rather high influx of foreign currency, about $1.7 billion, due to invisible earnings—from tourism, about $950 million (*Politika*, 8 October), and from the remittances of about a million migrant workers and other sources, about $750 million—it was anticipated in July that the entire 1974 deficit in balance of payments would amount to about $720 million. The largest part of this deficit, some $600 million, was due to increased oil prices. (*Vjesnik*, 25 July.) In the first nine months of 1974, the deficit amounted to about $600 million (*Financial Times*, 27 November). It was largely covered by foreign loans and credits ($352.1 million), by using short-term credits ($50.0 million), by "other incomes" ($77.7 million), by using means achieved from trade through clearing ($68.9 million), and by diminishing foreign currency reserves ($28.9 million) (*Ekonomska politika*, 25 November).

Foreign Affairs. *The Soviet Union.* Yugoslav-Soviet relations in 1974 could best be characterized as fluctuating. Both the "Polarka Plan," revealed via the Austrian information media by former

Czechoslovak general Jan Sejna, and the "Cominformist plot" (see above) produced serious concern in the first part of the year.

Jan Sejna (who defected to the United States in February 1968) was interviewed in February 1974 by a Vienna weekly (*Profil*, 25 February, 4 March), and by Austrian television (20 February), at which time he indicated that the Warsaw Pact nations, under Soviet leadership, were contemplating in 1968 an invasion of Yugoslavia via Austria. He referred to this as the "Polarka Plan." Sejna stated that the justification for a Warsaw Pact move against Austria, together with intervention in Yugoslavia, would be provided by charges that Austria had allowed anti-communist forces to enter Yugoslavia from Austrian territory. The first Yugoslav objections came at the end of March. A Belgrade daily (*Politika*, 31 March) said that plotters in West Germany, Italy, and Austria were using the Soviets' "incomplete denials" to spread rumors that Yugoslavia was "imperiled." Another Belgrade daily (*Borba*, 29 March) commented that "Europe's most reactionary forces took the 'Polarka' plan from the icebox of the Czechoslovak exile general Sejna, a CIA guest, and resurrected irredentist pretensions." Yet, later, a Zagreb daily (*Vjesnik*, 20 June) stated in connection with the "Polarka" rumors that "Yugoslavia would defend its policy and road of development against any foreign aggression."

After the arrest of the "Cominformist plotters" in April, Yugoslav-Soviet relations reached a low point, which prompted Tito to send Kardelj to Moscow in September. It appears that Kardelj's talks with the Soviet leaders resulted in a truce. Kardelj left for Moscow on 1 September, 12 days after a Politburo message to Tito was delivered in Belgrade by the Soviet ambassador to Yugoslavia. This was the Politburo's second letter to Tito in two months, an unusual occurrence. The first was delivered on 8 July, the day Tito left for Bucharest. Several days before Tito's trip to Romania, Kardelj had been in Poland, where he had talks with Polish party chief Edward Gierek. His stay in Poland was announced only after he returned to Belgrade on 5 July. On the same day Gierek suddenly arrived in Dubrovnik, ostensibly on vacation, but on 7 July he had talks with Tito in Belgrade and then immediately returned to Warsaw. It is assumed that Gierek was acting as mediator between Moscow and Belgrade over the "Cominformist plot."

On 12 September Tito announced the discovery of the "Cominformist plot" and indirectly attacked the Soviet Union, but in October he gave an interview to the Soviet Army paper *Red Star* praising the friendship between the two countries. After hailing their joint military struggle, Tito said: "What must at present bring us together and link us more than anything else is the struggle for the common aims of socialist and communist construction, for the implementation of the great ideas of Marx, Engels, and Lenin, and the struggle for peace, international cooperation, and democratic relations in the world" (*Borba*, 10 October). Seven days before, a spokesman for the Yugoslav government denied reports that Belgrade had protested to the Soviet Union, Czechoslovakia, and Hungary about the activities of a group of the Cominformists. The spokesman stressed, however, that Yugoslavia had received assurances from Moscow, Prague, and Budapest that "hostile activities by emigrants against Yugoslavia would not be tolerated." (*Politika*, 4 October.)

Despite the "Cominformists" affair, a high-level delegation from the Communist Party of the Soviet Union (CPSU), led by Politburo member Andrei P. Kirilenko, attended the LCY's Tenth Congress in May (for details see the international views and policies section of the CPSU profile). There was marked improvement in relations between the CPSU and the LCY in the second half of 1974, stemming largely from the Soviets' conciliatory attitude at the 16-18 October meeting of 28 European communist parties in Warsaw. At this conference Yugoslav delegate Aleksandar Grličkov, a member of the Executive Committee of the Central Committee Presidium, outlined Tito's views on an independent road to socialism and his opposition to a world communist center without encountering public dissent from the Soviet delegates and their East European allies. Yugoslav satisfaction with the Soviet attitude found an expression in a *Borba* article (8 November) commemorating the 57th anniversary of the Bolshevik Revolution. Describing the revolution in Russia as having been the "inspiration of entire progressive mankind," the article said: "We are connected with the U.S.S.R. by common goals and numerous identical outlooks on most important international problems, although there exist certain differences which, however, are recognized and considered to be normal. They are caused by objective specific features in our general position and by priorities in development or historical legacy." Aleksandar Grličkov represented again the LCY at the second preparatory meeting of 28 European communist parties held in Budapest on December 19-21.

Concerning Soviet credits to Yugoslavia (on the basis of an agreement signed in Belgrade on 2 November 1972), the Yugoslavs have been promised much (almost $1,000 million) but given very little. The volume of trade between the two countries during the first nine months of 1974 amounted to $500 million (Yugoslav exports, $228 million; imports, $272 million) (Tanjug, 13 November).

People's Republic of China. Yugoslav-Chinese relations improved significantly in 1974. On 7 January *Jen-min Jih-pao* published a lengthy article on Yugoslavia praising the country's development and particularly, the "friendliness which the Yugoslav people have shown toward the Chinese." A Yugoslav party delegation headed by Kiro Gligorov, at that time a member of the Executive Bureau, spent a day in Peking while en route home from North Korea. Between 22 and 29 September a delegation of the Yugoslav Federal Assembly, headed by its vice-president, Peko Dapčević, paid an official visit to China. Following the delegation's warm reception, the Chinese praised Yugoslavia's non-aligned policy and pledged support of its "just struggle" against "subversion and interference from abroad." (*Politika*, 25 September.) On the 25th anniversary of the birth of the People's Republic of China, Tito sent a message in which he stated: "I am very glad to notice the successful development of Yugoslav-Chinese relations, and I wish continued progress in the many forms of friendly cooperation between our two countries, in the interest of our peoples and peace in the world" (*Borba*, 1 October). Between 24 October and 2 November, a Yugoslav military delegation, headed by General Branislav Joksović, assistant chief of the general staff, paid an official visit to China. The delegation was everywhere given a warm and cordial welcome. (Tanjug, 2 November.) On 3-7 November Chinese deputy foreign minister Yu Chan visited Yugoslavia on his way from Tirana. It has been assumed that Tito's upcoming visit to Peking was planned at that time.

Albania. Albanian leaders are showing some concern over the approaching end of the Tito era. Since the Soviet invasion of Czechoslovakia in August 1968, the Albanians have deliberately avoided any action which might negatively affect relations between Belgrade and Tirana. Enver Hoxha's 3 October speech, in which he called for closer cooperation between the two countries, was lauded in Yugoslavia as "certainly the only correct road toward a greater understanding and promotion of relations" (*Borba*, 8 October). In February 1971 Yugoslavia and Albania agreed to exchange ambassadors, after having been represented by chargés d'affaires since 1958; in January 1974 Tito remarked that he would like to see an improvement in Yugoslav-Albanian relations.

During the Eleventh Conference of the League of Communists of Kosovo (29-30 March), Mahmut Bakalli, the local party leader, praised Albanian relations with Kosovo, but added that only Yugoslav-Albanian relations as a whole could benefit both countries. He criticized certain articles and books published in Albania in which "historical facts from the period of our common struggle against common enemies are being falsified, and one-sided information about life in Kosovo and Yugoslavia is being spread." (Ibid., 30 March.)

In 1974 there were about 920,000 Albanians and about 230,000 Serbs living in the Autonomous Province of Kosovo. As of 31 March 1971, when the last census was taken, there were more than 1,300,000 Albanians in all of Yugoslavia. The population of Albania in 1973 was 2,322,600 (Albanian Telegraphic Agency, ATA, 18 June 1974).

Trade between Yugoslavia and Albania in 1974 exceeded $45 million. According to a protocol signed in October, the exchange of goods in 1975 would increase by 15 percent over the previous year. (*Borba*, 22 October.)

On the 30th anniversary of Albania's liberation (29 November), Yugoslav media published friendly articles particularly praising Hoxha's speech of 3 October.

Other East European Countries. On 28-29 April, President Tito paid an official visit to Budapest that was highly praised. The Hungarians spoke of the "unclouded relations between the two countries" (Radio Budapest, 29 April), and the Yugoslavs referred to "successful talks" (*Komunist*, 6 May). During the 10-16 June visit of Hungarian deputy prime minister Matyas Timar it was announced that Yugoslav-Hungarian trade would increase from $150 million in 1974 to $170 million in 1975 (*Politika*, 17 June). The two countries at present settle their accounts in freely convertible currency rather than in rubles. Once the "Adria" pipeline is completed, cooperation is expected to increase even more. The pipeline will be ready by 1977 and will carry 34 million tons of oil annually, of which Hungary and Czechoslovakia will each receive five million tons. A plan for the mutual development of the territory lying between the Danube and the Tisza rivers was also discussed, and it was announced that Hungary would grant a loan of $25 million to Yugoslavia for this purpose.

According to the March 1971 census, there were 477,374 Hungarians living in Yugoslavia, with both sides regarding these people as a "bridge" between the two countries.

A Hungarian parliamentary delegation, headed by Antal Apró, chairman of Hungary's National Assembly, visited Yugoslavia on 12-18 November and was received by Tito. Béla Biszku, a member of the Hungarian party's Politburo and Secretariat, was his party's representative at the Tenth Congress of the LCY.

Between 18 and 22 February, Budislav Šoškić, a member of the LCY Presidium, visited Czechoslovakia. Czechoslovak defense minister General Martin Dzúr, visited Yugoslavia on 22-26 April. Between 17 and 24 June, a Czechoslovak parliamentary delegation headed by Alois Indra paid an official visit to Yugoslavia. Indra "renewed" an invitation to President Tito to visit Czechoslovakia. A Czechoslovak party study delegation stayed in Yugoslavia from June 30 to July 4. Yugoslav foreign minister Miloš Minić paid an official visit to Prague on 23-25 July. The talks between Minić and his Czechoslovak colleague, Bohuslav Chnoupek, were described as "open," which generally implies that differences still exist between the two countries.

Yugoslav-Czechoslovak trade in 1974 totaled $600 million; this was $70 million more than had been anticipated (*Politika*, 15 November). Prague granted the following three loans to Yugoslavia: in March, $25 million for the "Adria" pipeline; in April, about $59 million for the construction of the Danube-Tisza-Danube Canal; and in July, $75 million for the purchase of mining equipment and consumer goods.

Of special significance in Yugoslav relations with the German Democratic Republic (GDR) was an official visit by President Tito to East Berlin on 12-15 November. This was his second trip to the GDR (the first was in June 1965). The lengthy communiqué did not specifically refer to either China or to the conference of European communist parties scheduled for 1975 in the GDR (*Vjesnik*, 17 November). In an interview broadcast by East Berlin television and in a statement after his return Tito emphasized the "exceptional hospitality" with which he and his entourage had been treated, and termed the visit "very successful." Tito repeatedly stated that his welcome in East Berlin and Leipzig had not been "organized," but that people had "spontaneously" lined the streets to greet him. (Ibid.)

While in East Berlin, Tito was awarded East Germany's highest honor, the "Karl Marx Order," at a ceremony in which Honecker praised him "for decades of untiring efforts toward achieving peace, socialism, and internationalism" (*Borba*, 14 November). The GDR party newspaper *Neues Deutschland* (11 November) carried an article by the Croatian party leader Mme Milka Planinc explaining Yugoslavia's system of "self-managing socialism." The article is believed to be the first one published in East Germany which was not followed by a critical reference from the official party press to

Yugoslavia's particular form of socialism. Trade between the two countries in 1974 reached a total of $300 million (Tanjug, 10 November). With an average of 1.5 million West German tourists visiting Yugoslavia annually (*Frankfurter Allgemeine Zeitung*, 12 November), there were only 20,000 tourists in the same period from East Germany. The Yugoslavs have pressing economic reasons for promoting better relations between the two countries. The GDR, as the most prosperous and industrialized country in Eastern Europe, could become an increasingly valuable partner for Yugoslavia in the years ahead. The SED party delegate at the LCY congress was Paul Verner, a member of the Politburo.

During the past few years, Yugoslav-Romanian relations have been particularly cordial. Following the August 1968 invasion of Czechoslovakia, these relations took on increased significance, although both Tito and Ceauşescu did their best to reassure Moscow that there was no "Belgrade-Bucharest axis" in the making. On 8-11 July, Tito paid an official visit to Bucharest—his 12th meeting with Ceauşescu since the latter assumed power in April 1965. Tito was accompanied by Prime Minister Bijedić and Foreign Minister Minić. The problems discussed by Tito and Ceauşescu were mentioned only in general terms in the final communiqué, and the agreement on future economic cooperation over a ten-year period only provided a framework for other more concrete agreements to be signed in the years ahead. The actual motive behind the meeting appears to have been the need to assess the Nixon-Brezhnev summit talks in Moscow (27 June-2 July) and their impact on an East-West dialogue in general and the European security conference in particular. On 23-25 September Romanian Communist Party secretary Ştefan Andrei, following his sudden arrival in Belgrade, talked with Tito and Kardelj and handed Tito a message from Ceauşescu (*Borba*, 25 September). Bijedić visited Bucharest on 5-7 October and was received by Ceauşescu. On 7 November, Romanian foreign minister Gheorghe Macovescu made a stopover in Belgrade on his way home from Paris. On 25 November, Stane Dolanc, Secretary of the LCY Executive Committee, read a message at the Eleventh Congress of the Romanian party in Bucharest. According to an estimate made in July, trade between the two countries in 1974 was expected to total $250 million (Radio Belgrade, 9 July).

Yugoslav-Bulgarian relations in 1974 were clouded by the quarrel over the Macedonian minority living in Bulgaria and the alleged Bulgarian claims that these Macedonians were Bulgarians. On 2 December the deputy chief of the Yugoslav mission to the United Nations, Cvijeto Job, criticized Bulgaria in connection with Sofia's "discrimination" toward the Macedonian national minority in Bulgaria. Job said that although there had officially been 178,862 Macedonians in Bulgaria in 1956, today "no Macedonian national minority is recognized at all." (*Večernje novosti*, 3 December.) Throughout the year, anti-Bulgarian articles appeared in the Yugoslav information media and concentrated largely on two topics: the denial that the Bulgarian army had "liberated" parts of Yugoslavia in 1944, and the problem of the Macedonians. The long-standing dispute over Macedonia remained an apparently insuperable barrier to closer cooperation between the two countries. From time to time individual Soviet publications were also attacked because of their pro-Bulgarian attitude (*Nova Makedonija*, 3 April; *Politika*, 19-25 September). On the other hand, Bulgarian party and state leader Todor Zhivkov spoke of the "common historical destiny and fraternal friendship between the Bulgarian and Yugoslav peoples and between Bulgarian and Yugoslav communists" (*Politika*, 27 June). Yet at the Sixth U.N. "Seminar for Furthering and Protecting the Human Rights of National, Ethnic and other Minorities," held in the Macedonian town of Ohrid on 2-8 July, there was an open clash between the Bulgarian and Yugoslav delegates (*Nova Makedonija*, 4 July; *Borba*, 5 July).

On 21 September Bulgarian foreign minister Petar Mladenov made a stopover in Belgrade and talked to some high-level functionaries in the foreign ministry. During 11-15 November Bulgaria's defense minister, General Dobri Dzhurov, paid an official visit to Yugoslavia. Several days before, Yugoslav foreign minister Minić, speaking before the Yugoslav National Assembly, admitted that "no major progress" had been made in solving "outstanding questions" between Yugoslavia and Bulgaria, though there had been cooperation in a number of separate areas (*Politika*, 6 November). The Bulgarian party delegate at the LCY congress was Zhivko Zhivkov, a member of the Politburo.

On the basis of the trade protocol between Yugoslavia and Bulgaria for 1974, the volume of mutual trade was forecast at $128 million. However, during the first six months, trade was valued at $142 million, 11 percent higher than was predicted for the entire year. (*Ekonomska revija*, Belgrade, October.)

Next to Bulgaria, Poland was the East European country most highly criticized by the Yugoslav press in 1974. Nevertheless, the Polish communist leaders, notably Edward Gierek, acted as mediators between Belgrade and Moscow. Gierek's unexpected visit to Belgrade on 5-6 July, explained as a "short rest" (*Politika*, 6 July), was actually used to speak with Tito. Gierek's visit followed Edvard Kardelj's eight-day visit to Warsaw. Moreover, Gierek and Kardelj traveled together from Warsaw to Yugoslavia and it is assumed that the "Cominformist plot" in Yugoslavia was one of the reasons for Gierek's trip. According to Polish sources, "the results of the talks between the two leaders were of great importance to the continued development of friendly relations and over-all cooperation between the two countries." (PAP, Polish news agency, 9 July.)

Yugoslav information media viewed Gierek as a "staunch standard-bearer" of a propaganda line which insisted that success be disseminated and failures hidden (*Politika*, 14 September.) The Polish leaders were criticized for having published "doctored" reports and for practicing "news management." On 1-2 October, Aleksandar Grličkov, a member of the LCY Executive Committee in charge of foreign relations, visited Warsaw and talked with Gierek about the forthcoming conference of 28 European communist parties to be held in the Polish capital (16-18 October). Later, there was a divergence of views between the Yugoslavs and Poles at the conference over the problems to be discussed. The Poles wanted to concentrate primarily on the situation in Western Europe and the Yugoslavs insisted on examining the basic questions which currently beleaguer the world communist movement. (*Corriere della sera*, Milan, 18 October.)

Yugoslav defense minister Ljubičić, paid an offical visit to Poland on 2-6 October and was received by Gierek. On 15-19 November, Ivan Franko, federal secretary for justice in the Yugoslav government, visited Warsaw to discuss economic relations. In a statement issued following his return from Warsaw, Franko said that a new Polish-Yugoslav agreement on convertible payments would help expand trade and promote other economic ties between the two countries. There were mutual assessments that Polish-Yugoslav trade was developing well and that it might be expected to reach the predicted level of $320 million in 1974.

The Polish party delegate at the LCY congress was Edward Babiuch, a member of the Politburo.

West and Central Europe. Tito made two trips to Western Europe: to West Germany (24-27 June) and Denmark (29 October-1 November). The joint communiqué issued on the last day of the visit to West Germany said that President Tito and Federal Chancellor Helmut Schmidt reached "a high degree of harmony" on both bilateral and international issues, and discussions were said to have taken place in "a frank and cordial atmosphere." The two statesmen expressed satisfaction over their countries' past economic cooperation and agreed to promote such efforts, particularly in long-term industrial cooperation, joint capital investments, and collaboration in third-country markets. The communiqué also stated that the two sides agreed that Yugoslav workers in West Germany (about 750,000 with family members) are a very important element in their relations, and all questions regarding these workers have a special place in bilateral cooperation. (Tanjug, 27 June.)

Several days before Tito's arrival, an agreement was initiated in Bonn in which West Germany gave Yugoslavia a 700-million-mark loan (about $250 million), on preferential terms. (The agreement was signed on 10 December.) Yugoslavia had asked for sums in the billion-dollar bracket to compensate for about 950,000 cases of Nazi damages. By 1973 Yugoslavia had already received 300 million marks (about $120 million).

According to a Yugoslav army newspaper, there were about six billion marks (about $2.4 billion) in West German banks belonging to Yugoslav workers—a point which Tito also reportedly discussed with the West German leaders (*Narodna armija*, 27 June). The same paper wrote that West Germany was Yugoslavia's major trade partner in 1974, accounting for 16 percent of the latter's foreign trade.

Yugoslav-Danish relations are considered to be "very friendly." In an interview on Danish television, Tito remarked that talks in Copenhagen had revealed "completely identical views on various international questions." (Tanjug, 1 November.)

While official relations with France were cordial, relations with Italy and Austria deteriorated. In March, the Italian and Yugoslav ministries of foreign affairs exchanged heated notes about the old border dispute in the Istrian peninsula. (The 1947 Treaty of Peace with Italy and the Memorandum of Understanding, concluded between Yugoslavia and Italy on 5 October 1954 in London, stipulated that Trieste and Zone "A" would become part of Italy, while Zone "B" would become Yugoslav territory.) The Italian government protested the erection of metal signs with the inscription "SFR YUGOSLAVIA" near the demarcation line of Zone "B" and claimed that "Yugoslav sovereignty has never been extended to the Italian territory designated as Zone "B" of the unrealized Free Territory of Trieste." The Belgrade government denounced Rome's calling Zone "B" Italian territory as "an attack on Yugoslavia's sovereignty and territorial integrity," and threatened to counteract the Italian reopening of the "Trieste question" by challenging the rights of Italy over Zone "A." (Texts of Italian and Yugoslav diplomatic notes, in *Yugoslav Facts and Views*, New York, no. 87, April.) An editorial in *Borba* (1 April) assailed the "anti-Yugoslav action of the Italian government," which had caused the "indignation of Yugoslav citizens not seen recently in our country." For many days Yugoslav newspapers reported on resolutions and meetings held throughout Yugoslavia against Italian "irredentism."

The tension was heightened by naval maneuvers held by the Italian and U.S. NATO forces in the northern Adriatic Sea between 29 March and 5 April. The participation of the U.S. Sixth Fleet in the maneuvers was assailed in the Yugoslav press as having a "taste of provocation," and representing a "dangerous event and precedent" (*Borba*, 3 April). NATO naval maneuvers in the Adriatic (9-16 November) were again protested by the Yugoslav government in notes sent to the Italian, U.S., British, and Turkish governments. According to the TASS dispatch of 16 November, the Yugoslav government came out resolutely against attempts to turn the Adriatic Sea into a military place d'armes, adhering to the view that the sea should remain a zone of peace, and that NATO countries should refrain from such actions in the future.

While the Italian-Yugoslav tension subsided in the second part of the year, the Austrian-Yugoslav controversy flared up toward the year's end. On 29 October the Yugoslav government presented a note to the Austrian government charging that Slovene and Croatian minorities in Austria were "exposed to permanent pressure" (*Politika*, 30 October). On 2 December the Austrian government answered the note, denying all of Belgrade's allegations (*Die Presse*, Vienna, 3 December). Although the full text of the Austrian reply was not published in Yugoslavia, Yugoslav information media continued to attack the note as "arrogant" and "completely unsatisfactory." Some Yugoslav newspapers reported that Austria had even provided "training space" for anti-Yugoslav "terrorist groups" (*Borba*, 8 December). The deputy chief of the Yugoslav U.N. mission in New York severely criticized Austria for alleged "discrimination" toward Yugoslav national minorities in that country (*Vjesnik* 5 December).

European Economic Community. On 22 November Yugoslavia's Foreign Minister Miloš Minić had talks in Brussels with the Commission President, François Ortoli, its vice-president in charge of external affairs, Sir Christopher Soames, and the commission member in charge of agriculture, Pierre Lardinois. The discussions concentrated on the EEC's ban on beef imports. Soames made an official visit to Belgrade in April. Yugoslavia concluded a nonpreferential trade agreement with the EEC which went into effect in September 1973. Yugoslav trade with the EEC accounted for 40 percent of the country's foreign trade. Minić asked the EEC leaders to take a more liberal stand toward developing countries such as Yugoslavia, but Ortoli answered that "serious difficulties were affecting the community and that it was necessary to isolate itself to a certain extent from other countries." To Minić's request that the ban be lifted on Yugoslav beef exports, Soames replied by stating that the EEC is faced with "very serious problems in this sector of agriculture" and that it would be able to get a better view of the situation only after January 1975. (Tanjug, 22 November.)

Following talks with Belgian and Common Market officials, Minić traveled to Great Britain (24-27 November). Shortly after that, Swedish Foreign Minister Sven Anderson paid an official visit to Yugoslavia (2-7 December.)

The United States. Earlier U.S.-Yugoslav tension, caused by the twin events of the Italian-Yugoslav dispute over Trieste and the NATO naval maneuvers in the north of the Adriatic Sea (see above), was apparently eased during the visit by U.S. Secretary of State Henry Kissinger to Belgrade on 4 November. He had talks with President Tito, Prime Minister Bijedić, and Foreign Minister Minić. The talks were "open and friendly" (*Borba*, 5 November), and there was "dissipation of certain clouds" in the mutual relations (*Vjesnik*, 6 November). Official Yugoslav sources admitted to differences on some international issues, "but they had existed before and nobody had expected them to disappear completely" (Tanjug, 5 November).

An article in *Washington Post* (5 November) stating that the Yugoslavs were eager to buy spare parts for weapons that the United States had supplied in the past provoked some protests in the Yugoslav newspapers (*Politika*, 8 November). These protests claimed that Tito had not discussed this purchase with Kissinger but that this topic had been touched upon in his "talks with others" while in Belgrade.

Robert Ellsworth, U.S. assistant secretary of defense, visited Yugoslavia on 11-15 December.

United Croatian and Slovenian electrical enterprises selected a U.S. firm, the Westinghouse Corporation, to construct Yugoslavia's first 632 MW nuclear power plant. The firm won the contract by offering the best crediting conditions and promises of technological cooperation. The U.S. Export-Import Bank and a consortium of 37 European banks granted an additional $380 million credit to guarantee the construction and initial operation of the plant. The $518 million project is, to date, the greatest single construction project ever financed by U.S. and European money in Yugoslavia. (*Borba*, 7 October.)

Nonalignment. One of the 18 resolutions adopted at the Tenth Congress of the LCY stated that "the policy of nonalignment and joint action by countries that have adopted it [had] become a factor of historic importance in the struggle to change substantively the present political, economic, and other forms of international relations" (*Komunist*, 3 June 1974). Despite Yugoslavia's official formula that military rather than ideological nonalignment was possible, Yugoslav leaders have continued to adhere to nonalignment as the basis of the nation's foreign policy. Visits to Yugoslavia by political leaders from nonaligned countries and trips by Yugoslav representatives to these countries, were commonplace in 1974.

The Coordinating Bureau of Nonaligned Countries met in Algeria (19-21 March), with 16 countries and 24 observers taking part, including representatives of the Palestine Liberation Organization (PLO). The Bureau appointed a seven-member committee, composed of representatives from Yugoslavia, Algeria, India, Egypt, Guyana and Nigeria, which met in Belgrade on 10-13 September and discussed economic cooperation (Tanjug, 13 September).

On 30 November-3 December, PLO leader Yasir Arafat paid an official visit to Yugoslavia, where he was received by President Tito. President Kenneth Kaunda of Zambia visited Yugoslavia on 27-29

November. The premier of Nepal visited between 4 and 8 December. On 28-30 March President Anwar al-Sadat of Egypt visited Yugoslavia, and in July Edvard Kardelj had political talks in Cairo. On 14-16 August, President Hafiz al-Asad of Syria paid an official visit.

Publications. The chief organs of the LCY are *Komunist*, a weekly magazine, and *Socijalizam*, a theoretical monthly. The daily newspapers *Borba* (Belgrade), *Politika* (Belgrade) and *Vjesnik* (Zagreb), are organs of the SAWPY of Yugoslavia, Serbia, and Croatia, respectively. The *Vjesnik* publishing house also puts out a weekly *Vjesnik u srijedu*, and *Politika* also publishes *Nedeljne informativne novine*. The Yugoslav communist youth organization publishes a weekly, *Mladost*. Tanjug is the official Yugoslav news agency.

Slobodan Stanković

Radio Free Europe
Munich

WESTERN EUROPE

Austria

The Communist Party of Austria (Kommunistische Partei Österreichs; KPÖ) was founded on 3 November 1918. Although enjoying legal status, the party plays can insignificant part in political affairs and has never had more than 3 percent of Austria's parliamentary representation. Since the election (1959) following the Hungarian uprising, it has been without a seat in the Nationalrat (lower house). Its strength reached a new low after the Soviet-led intervention in Czechoslovakia in 1968. While the party rift following that event is now healed, the KPÖ faces competition from communist (especially Maoist) splinters among students and other young people. The population is about 7,400,000 (estimated 1970).

New reports on membership figures are ambiguous. Party chairman Franz Muhri reported that membership since the last Congress had increased by 2,000 (*Pravda*, 19 January). *Die Presse* (Vienna, 23 January), on the other hand, reported a party congress document indicating that 1972 membership was 20,676, almost 2,000 less than that of 1971. The same article reported that, in 1972, 49 percent of the members were over sixty years old, and that only 23.5 percent were workers. The *World Marxist Review* (June 1974, p. 139) states, in contrast, that, of new members admitted in 1973, over 50 percent are below thirty years of age, that 68.7 percent are workers, and 5.4 percent are students. (See YICA, 1974, pp. 111-115 and YICA, 1972, pp. 117-123.)

During 1974, the party proved its weakness in various elections. The provincial election in Salzburg, 31 March, brought the party a slight gain, but only to 1.2 percent of the vote. In Lower Austria, 9 June, the past vote of one percent was maintained (with the best result apparently in Ternitz, a small steel town, at four percent). On 20 October, the party polled 1.3 percent in Styria, and on the same day, 0.9 percent in Vorarlberg, where it had not contested the previous election.

Contesting the Chamber of Labor (Arbeiterkammer) election, in September, there was an official KPÖ list (Communists) and that of a splinter, Trade Union Unity (Gewerkschaftliche Union, a designation used earlier by the official Labor wing). The official list polled 2.4 percent, as in the previous election, and the dissident list 0.3 percent. The number of communist seats on the representative bodies (total seats, 810) declined from eleven to ten (*Wiener Zeitung*, 2 October). The communists' share among foreign workers (*Gástarbeiter*), eligible to vote for the first time, was estimated at five percent (*Die Presse*, 10 October). In the election of the same month among postal employees, the communists improved their vote slightly over the previous total, ending with above two percent of the vote among civil servants and among postal workers (*Wiener Zeitung*, 27 September). Earlier, in March, in the Carinthian shop stewart election, the communists held their own, with close to two percent of the vote, and increased their representation on the shop councils from 30 to 51 (out of 3,205) (ibid., 11 April).

Most successful for the radical left, though not necessarily for the communists, were the student elections in January. Of 53 seats on the executive of Austria's post-secondary students (Österreichische Hochschülerschaft), at least five were won by candidates of groups to the left of the Socialists. However, only one of nine left radicals was on the official communist slate contesting the election, and it captured only one seat. Some of these groups' success was ascribed to foreign students, eligible to vote for the first time. (*Volkszeitung*, Klagenfurt, 20 January; Vienna radio report, 18 January.) The formerly Socialist organization of secondary students (Verein Sozialistischer Mittelschüler) announced in April that it was separating from the Socialist Party and would cooperate with the Verband Marxistischer Arbeiterjugend and the Verband Marxistischer Studenten (*Wiener Zeitung*, 20 April). Both of these associations belong to the radical left, but neither is an official communist organization.

The KPÖ did not present a candidate in Austria's major election of the year, the election for federal president on 23 June.

Leadership and Organization. The major organizational event of KPÖ in 1974 was the Twenty-second Congress of the party, held in Vienna on 18-20 January. All nominees to the Central Committee, Central Party Control, and Arbitration Commission were elected (*Volksstimme*, 22 January). In early February the newly constituted Central Committee reelected Franz Muhri chairman and Erwin Scharf, Walter Wachs, and Hans Kalt, editor in chief of *Volksstimme*, as secretaries. Veteran Friedl Fürnberg was among the ten members elected to the Politburo.

The Communist Youth of Austria (Kommunistische Jugend Österreichs; KJÖ), founded 1970, held its First Congress in Vienna on 20-21 April 1974. Its new leader is Willi Rau.

Party Internal Affairs. The Twenty-second Congress of the KPÖ was prepared at a plenary meeting of the party's Central Committee in Vienna in December 1973. The congress itself opened in Vienna on 18 January 1974, with 450 delegates in attendance and also fraternal delegates from 14 countries (TASS, 20 January). Chairman Muhri in the main address reported that the rift in the party was now healed: "After the Twenty-first Party Congress the representatives of the rightist-opportunist groups, so far as they still held certain positions here and there, were completely isolated and eliminated." Some of them, he said, had receded into a petty-bourgeois private life, while others had become the henchmen of the "rightist Social Democratic leadership" (the government of Bruno Kreisky, Socialist Party of Austria: SPÖ) or allies or Trotskyites, Maoists, and similar leftist-radical groups. Regarding the latter, Muhri reiterated that there could be no unity of action between the KPÖ and such groups. Rather he said, "We will endeavor to win over all honest leftist people in these groups for the joint struggle." (*Volksstimme*, 19 January.)

The congress adopted politico-ideological guidelines and an Action Program (*WMR*, April). Muhri emphasized that the party would seek parliamentary representation in the election of 1975.

Domestic Attitudes and Activities. Evaluating the performance of Austria's Socialist government, Muhri stated:

> The 'democratic socialism' peddled by the Socialist Party of Austria (SPA) leadership as the "alternative to communism" is a mere decoy and another futile attempt to further the restoration of capitalism in socialist countries. "The main purpose of the SPA leaders' anti-communism," the Guidelines say, "is to prevent the Austrian working class from taking the road to socialism." (*WMR*, April.)

The wide sector of nationalized industries was attacked in the Guidelines as state-monopoly capitalism which exploited workers through an increasing wage-to-profits lag. The SPÖ was being accused of governing Austria through an industrialists, trade union, and government triangle; the economy was said to be controlled by technocrats, while state monopoly capitalism was being supported by the media and higher educational establishments continued to serve the interests of the few. Austria's "social partnership" ideology, supported by the Socialists, was designed to confuse the workers' class consciousness. (Ibid.)

The KPÖ Action Program calls for a transitional stage between capitalism and socialism, which it designates as "anti-monopoly democracy," involving the democratization of all aspects of Austrian society:

> The existence of highly developed industry and agriculture, a powerful state sector of the economy and a developed cooperative system are national characteristics that will eventually facilitate Austria's transition to socialism. The guidelines note that the [KPÖ] is working for socialism without civil war, but the possibilities for this will depend on how far the front of class struggle expands in Austria and the world. We deliberately avoid using the term "peaceful road to socialism" because the Austrian Social-Democrats have been using it for decades. (Ibid.)

During Kreisky's visit to the U.S.S.R. in June, Muhri attacked him for insisting on an unreconcilable difference between socialism and communism when, Muhri declared, the unreconcilable contradiction was not "between communists and their social democratic class comrades but between the workers class and capital" (*Volksstimme*, 2 June).

Earlier, during April, Kreisky attempted to prevent any kind of common action between the communists and the SPÖ, except that common demonstrations in Vienna relating to Chile had already been approved by the local SPÖ organization and were therefore tolerated for humanitarian purposes. Common actions in Upper Austria and Salzburg were discontinued (*Die Presse*, 9 April).

There was a sharp debate about the future of Austrian broadcasting. The system had been taken out of the hands of the parties in 1967 and placed under an expert, technocratic, and essentially liberal-conservative management. In Kreisky's eventually successful effort to change the direction back to more traditional Austrian political circumstances, a parliamentary discussion with wide participation developed. Muhri demanded an arrangement whereby the KPÖ could itself present the communist point of view, rather than have it presented by opponents (*Kurier*, Vienna, 11 July).

The presidential election of 23 June was a contest between a People's Party (ÖVP candidate, Mayor Lugger of Innsbruck, and Kirchschläger, the foreign minister, a non-party candidate nominated by the SPÖ. The KPÖ opposed both. A party conference in Vienna on 11 May, attended by 233 delegates found both candidates representative of the capitalist system. A vote for Lugger, being a vote for neutrality, might be the greater evil, but a vote for Kirchschläger would constitute a support of Kreisky's anti-communism (*Volksstimme*, 12 May). Later, Kreisky called on Socialist workers to persuade their KPÖ colleagues to support Kirchschläger. Muhri answered that it was Kreisky who had refused Socialist-Communist discussions in municipalities and industrial plants (*Wiener Zeitung*, 10 June). Kirchschläger won the election by a narrow majority.

International Views and Positions. In 1974, in addition to the KPÖ's usual affirmation of Austrian neutrality and attacks on the international stance of the Chinese communists, there were new developments to face. In an interview with *Pravda* (17 January), Muhri welcomed Austria's diplomatic recognition of the German Democratic Republic and the Democratic Republic of Vietnam. He voiced alarm over a closer orientation toward the United States and the Common Market. About the latter, he said: "The agreement between Austria and the Common Market which came into force 1 January 1973 weakened the country's capabilities to resist crisis phenomena." Muhri welcomed détente as being in the interest of socialist states, and of help to the workers' struggle in capitalist countries (*WMR*, April).

One of the last major discretionary programs of the Austrian Broadcasting System (ÖRF)— (before it once again became quasi-responsible to the government) gave the KPÖ an opportunity for a foray into international affairs. The setting of the program "Polarka" was a simulated Soviet, Czechoslovak, and Hungarian occupation of Austria, in order to launch an attack on Yugoslavia. The attack of the KPÖ was directed not only against the ÖRF but also against the Austrian minister of defense, who had participated in the program (*Volksstimme*, 22, 24 February). *Izvestiia* was quick to exonerate Kreisky in the affair, and to implicate the U.S. Central Intelligence Agency instead (1 March). The episode led to further attacks on the minister in *Volksstimme* (7, 8, 20 March).

Chancellor Kreisky's official visit to the U.S.S.R. (28 May-3 June) gave his hosts an opportunity to emphasize the significance of the stability in Austrian-U.S.S.R. relations, and of the material and cultural cooperation between the two countries. Soviet premier Kosygin went beyond this emphasis. In apparent contradiction with KPÖ pronouncements, he said to Kreisky:

> The 24th CPSU Congress reiterated our party's positive attitude toward possible joint action in the international arena with social democratic parties. The three years since the congress have convincingly confirmed that this position is well-founded and correctly understood in the ranks of many social democratic parties, particularly West European ones, which are making their contribution to the easing of the international situation. (*Pravda*, 29 May.)

The replacement of Schönau castle—the transit camp for Soviet Jews that the Austrian government closed after an Arab terrorist attack—with a transit camp in Kaiserebersdorf led to a hostile comment by *Volksstimme* (20 October). The camp, so the paper claimed, was becoming just like Schönau: a center in which armed Israeli agents immediately interrogated Jewish arrivals from the U.S.S.R. and disseminated the information, in violation of Austria's neutrality.

International Activities and Party Contacts. KPÖ contacts with other communist parties early during 1974 were focused on the Twenty-second Congress. Paul Verner, Politburo and Secretariat member of the East German party, played a particularly important role at the congress, which was the first since Austria's diplomatic recognition of the German Democratic Republic (GDR). Verner thanked the KPÖ for having "insistently called for the establishment of diplomatic relations between the republic of Austria and GDR" (*Volksstimme*, 20 January). The delegation from the Soviet party was headed by Eduard Shevardnaze, first secretary of the Communist Party of Georgia. The message from the CPSU Central Committee stressed the importance, for European security, of Austria's permanent neutrality (*Pravda*, January 19).

In late April, a delegation from the Communist Party of Czechoslovakia came to Vienna for an official friendly visit.

On 14-21 May the KPÖ was host to a four-man delegation of the Communist Party of the Soviet Union (CPSU), headed by V. I. Dolgikh, Central Committee secretary for heavy industry. The delegation visited a number of nationalized industrial plants (*Volksstimme*, 22 May). Also in May, a KPÖ delegation visited East Berlin, primarily for a discussion of trade union and other economic matters.

On 29 September-6 October the KPÖ was visited by a delegation of the Bulgarian Communist Party. Both parties called for an "All-European and later, a new worldwide, conference of communist and workers' parties" (Sofia radio, 7 October).

KPÖ first secretary Scharf was awarded the Soviet "Order of People's Friendship" on the occasion of his sixtieth birthday. (TASS, 28 August.)

Publications. The KPÖ publishes the daily *Volksstimme* ("People's Voice") and monthly *Weg und Ziel* ("Path and Goal"). It was reported in 1974 that the party had succeeded in raising one million schillings (about $50,000) to support its publications and that the circulation of *Volksstimme* had increased by 1,500 (from 70,000) (*WMR*, February).

*   *   *

A sign of life in the Fischer-Marek (*Wiener Tagebuch*) group (see *YICA, 1973*, p. 122, and *1974*, pp. 114-15) came when one of its members, Leopold Gruenwald, declared in a Vienna broadcast (26 June) that only 9 of the 65 communist parties not in power, including the KPÖ, had publicly endorsed the world-wide conference called for by the CPSU. Gruenwald is the author of *The Myth of World Communism* (Graz, 1974).

Austria's Trotskyists could claim some success in the student elections in January. Their student organization, the Group of Revolutionary Marxists (GRM), received 2.5 percent of the vote, compared with 3 percent for the communist students association (Vienna radio, 18 January). Each group received one council seat. The showing of the GRM gave some justification to the claim that "in Austria, Trotskyism is anything but dead [and] is more than ever one of the most vital elements of the young communist movement" (*Intercontinental Press*, New York, 5 March 1973).

A former communist group, the "Kommunistische Bund Salzburg/Hallein," said to be pro-Maoist, was the only political group announcing the setting up of a protest information booth during U.S. President Nixon's stay in Salzburg, on his Middle Eastern trip, 11-12 June (*Wiener Zeitung*, 10 June).

The University of Alberta   F. C. Engelmann

Belgium

The Communist Party of Belgium (Parti Communiste de Belgique; PCB) was founded in 1921. Although the party is of only peripheral importance in Belgian politics, it is the largest of several contending Marxist-Leninist organizations. Other extreme-left parties include the Maoist Marxist-Leninist Communist Party of Belgium (Parti Communiste Marxiste–Léniniste de Belgique; PCMLB), the Flanders-based Alle Macht aan de Arbeiders (All Power to the Workers; AMADA), which is also Maoist in orientation, and the Trotskyist Revolutionary Workers' League (Ligue Révolutionnaire des Travailleurs/Revolutionaire Arbeiders Liga; LRT/RAL). The PCB is believed to have between 10,000 and 12,500 members; the combined total membership of the other groups is probably around 2,000. The population of Belgium is some 10 million (estimated 1974).

In terms of electoral support, the PCB received 169,668 votes (3.2 percent) in the 10 March 1974 elections to the Chamber of Representatives. Although this represented a small increase from the previous (1971) parliamentary elections, when the party received 162,463 votes (3.1 percent), the PCB obtained one seat less in the 212-member Chamber, bringing its representation down to four. In simultaneously held elections to the Senate, the party retained its single representative. The Senate has 181 members: 106 directly elected, 50 appointed by provincial councils, and 25 co-opted by secret ballot. Finally, in the elections to the nine provincial councils' 720 seats (706 in 1971), the PCB obtained 9 seats (8 in 1971). The only other extreme-left party that participated in the elections was the Flemish Maoist AMADA. Contesting only four districts (Anvers, Gand, Hasselt, and Alost), it obtained a total of 19,784 votes. Most of these came from Anvers, where AMADA obtained 14,923 votes (2.8 percent). None of AMADA's candidates was elected.

Leadership and Organization. The PCB held its Twenty-first Congress on 14 to 16 December 1973. The Congress elected a 63-member Central Committee (see *Le Drapeau Rouge*, 21 December 1973), which, in turn, elected the party's Politburo, Secretariat, president, and vice-presidents. There were no reported changes in the party leadership during 1974. The Politburo consisted of: Jean Blume, Urbain Coussement, Jan Debrouwere, Albert De Coninck, Augustin Duchateau, Robert Dussart, Georges Glineur, Claude Renard, Jef Turf, Frans Van den Branden, and Louis Van Geyt. The four-member Secretariat comprised Coussement, Debrouwere, De Coninck, and Renard. The party was headed by Louis Van Geyt, as president, with Jean Terfve and Jef Turf acting as vice-presidents for Wallonia and Flanders, respectively.

The PCB directs a youth organization, the Communist Youth of Belgium (Jeunesse Communiste de Belgique; JCB), and a student group called the National Union of Communist Students (Union Nationale des Etudiants Communistes; UNEC). The party does not have its own labor union, but exerts peripheral influence in the country's largest trade union, the General Workers' Federation of Belgium (Fédération Générale du Travail de Belgique; FGTB).

Domestic Views and Activities. With only a small base of support in the country, the PCB has repeatedly stressed the need for alliances with other "progressive" political formations. The most important of the latter has been the Belgian Socialist Party (Parti Socialiste Belge; PSB). As noted by Politburo member Jean Blume, "it is obvious that no decisive step toward anti-monopoly democracy can be made without [the PSB] or, more precisely, without the working people under its influence" (*WMR*, May 1974). The PCB's courtship of the Socialist Party had suffered a setback in 1973, when the Socialists formed a coalition government with the Christian Social Party (Parti Social-Chrétien/ Christelijke Volkspartij; PSC/CVP) and the Liberal Party (Parti de la Liberté et du Progrès/Partij voor Vrijheid en Vooruitgang; PLP/PVV), under the premiership of PSB leader Edmond Leburton. At its Twenty-first Congress, at the end of 1973, the PCB had responded by offering a complex plan of "partial alliances." According to the congress's Final Resolution, the "essential task" for the PCB was to "help the organized worker movement win its political independence from the governing class and to help it unite and become the pivot of a broad anti-monopolistic people's alliance" (*Le Drapeau Rouge*, 21 December 1973). The party's president, Louis Van Geyt, explained that the PCB's "flexible but systematic policy of alliances" should be aimed "both toward the large organized worker and democratic movement and toward structured nontraditional progressive groups" (ibid.). He claimed that in Belgium it would be impossible to "isolate and thus defeat big capital and the right" with only the support of the forces "traditionally classified on the left." What was needed was the mobilization also of "the essential core of Christian and democratic forces and at least a considerable percentage of the people's forces present at the side of the worker movement and linked with it in highly diverse ways" (ibid.).

The PCB's strategy had been elaborated to a large extent in response to a situation in which the PSB was in government. On 18 January 1974 the Socialist members of the coalition cabinet tendered their resignations. As a result of the March elections and after lengthy negotiations that extended into the second half of April, a new minority government was formed, under the premiership of Christian Social leader Léo Tindemans. It included the Liberal Party, but not the PSB.

In conformity with Van Geyt's call for an extended alliance strategy, the PCB had helped form a Democratic and Progressive Union (Union Démocratique et Progressiste; UDP), which, in addition to the party, was comprised primarily of left-wing Christians. In describing the UDP, PCB vice-president Jean Terfve explained: "Some have insinuated that the UDP is a camouflage operation. Such criticism does not hold water. The Communist Party is in no way seeking to conceal that it is the UDP's motivational force." (*Le Soir*, Brussels, 19 February.) Terfve claimed that there were "constantly growing feelings of sharp opposition" to the "class collaboration" of both the PSB and Christian Social leadership. A similar opposition, he stated, could be seen within the FGTB and the Confederation of Christian Trade Unions (Confédération des Syndicats Chrétiens; CSC—the country's second largest union). The purpose of the UDP, he concluded, was to offer this opposition a means of expression, which would not necessitate the renouncement of ideological views. Terfve admitted that the UDP was not the ultimate answer, that "a perfect solution would require an alliance of all progressive forces," but he noted that "it would be foolish to believe" that that could be achieved "in one fell swoop." There was, he stated, "too much inertia and usefulness in the old structures to expect them to yield all at once." (Ibid.)

International Views and Positions. While it has generally supported the views of the Soviet Union and the Communist Party of the Soviet Union (CPSU), the PCB has at times (as in the case of the Soviet-led invasion of Czechoslovakia) offered relatively strong criticism. The party has also tended to take a more conciliatory attitude vis-à-vis the Chinese in comparison with that of the Russians.

To a certain extent, the guarded nature of the PCB's support for Soviet policies can be seen as a reflection of the party's domestic concerns. This was brought out clearly in a lengthy discussion on the Solzhenitsyn case, published by the PCB's theoretical journal *Cahiers Marxistes* (May 1974). Claiming that "capitalist circles ... need to combat the attraction of socialism by trying to give credence to the idea that certain negative features of Soviet reality are inherent in the nature of socialism," Central Committee member Pierre Joye stated: "It is a skillful tactic because it involves precisely those problems (democratic freedoms and human rights) to which our potential and necessary allies (socialists, progressive Christians, and so on) are justly sensitive." Joye concluded:

> To counteract this effectively, we must take the goals of this campaign into account. Since it is aimed chiefly at blocking the rise of socialism in our own country—by distorting the prospects we set ourselves when we advocate socialism—we must respond by addressing ourselves first of all to our potential allies. In doing so, we must be unequivocal in explaining our conception of socialism and how we view the socialism which we are proposing that they achieve with us in Belgium. We must not hide the fact that there are various areas in which Soviet reality differs considerably from the democratic and pluralistic socialism we want to achieve in Belgium.

The PCB's reaction to the expulsion of Solzhenitsyn from the Soviet Union (on 13 February) was immediate, albeit guardedly worded. While expressing hostility toward Solzhenitsyn himself, describing his ideas as "reactionary and anti-social," an article in *Le Drapeau Rouge* (14 February) added: "There are numbers of Communist parties, including our own, which feel that the political positions of opponents of socialism must be fought by political measures rather than by administrative measures."

In addition to being host to the Brussels "Conference of Communist and Workers' Parties of Western Europe," the PCB was represented at most of the year's multi-national meetings involving European communist parties. In April, PCB vice-president Jean Terfve presided over a meeting of the Soviet-sponsored "International Committee for European Security," held in Brussels.

Publications. As of 2 January 1974, the PCB's weekly *Le Drapeau Rouge* was changed into a daily. The party also increased the frequency of its theoretical journal, *Cahiers Marxistes*, from a quarterly to a monthly.

Stanford University   Milorad Popov

Cyprus

The original Communist Party of Cyprus (Kommounistikon Komma Kiprou) was founded by Greek-trained agents in August 1926 while the island was a British crown colony. Outlawed in 1933, the party emerged in April 1941 as the Reconstruction Party of the Working People of Cyprus (Anorthotikon Komma Ergazomenou Laou Tis Kiprou; AKEL). It was outlawed again in 1955, when political organizations were proscribed by the British, but has been legal since the proclamation of the Cypriot Republic in 1959. AKEL is the oldest and by far the best-organized political party in Cyprus. Membership is estimated at 12,000 to 14,000. The population of Cyprus is 651,000 (estimated 1972). In proportion of party members to population, AKEL is second only to the Italian party among non-ruling communist parties. Virtually all AKEL support comes from among the Greek Cypriot majority (about 80 percent).

Despite the party's overall strength and legal status, AKEL has never held any cabinet posts. For tactical reasons, it played down it strength in the latest parliamentary elections, in 1970, contesting only nine of the 35 seats reserved for the Greek Cypriots. In winning all nine seats, AKEL received 39.7 percent of the actual vote (30.2 percent on the basis of the total Greek Cypriot registered electorate). Some 29 percent of the eligible Greek community voters did not turn out, which meant that apathy on the part of the nationalists was a significant factor in the communist success at the polls. The leading nationalist parties also suffered from fragmented voting because President Makarios did not express a preference among the parties.

AKEL's reluctance to make a genuine showing of its ability to win parliamentary seats takes into consideration, first, the fact that the 1959 Zurich and London agreements provide a rationale for the three guarantor powers (Greece, Turkey, and England) to intervene against an internal communist takeover of the government, and second, the probability that a legal push for power by AKEL would unite the nationalist parties against the leftists. Though AKEL continues to have friction with the four Greek Cypriot non-communist parties, the one consistent tactic in recent years has been its open support of the domestic and foreign policies of Archbishop Makarios. AKEL supported Makarios for a third consecutive term as president in 1973, and has played down its differences with the Church of Cyprus, particularly over the issues of the vast landholdings of various monasteries. The party has seen fit to avoid direct involvement in religious politics by giving lip service to whatever ecclesiastical positions the archbishop advocated. In Cyprus, the autocephalous church has traditionally been most influential in secular politics and AKEL has learned from bitter experience that it cannot appeal to the Greek Cypriot populace by attacking its Orthodox faith.

Leadership and Organization. The leading figures in AKEL are the general secretary, Ezekias Papaioannou, in the office since 1949, and his deputy, Andreas Fantis. Both were reelected in April

1974 at the party's Thirteenth Congress (TASS, 28 April). The Politburo of the Central Committee includes Pavlos Georgiou, M. Poumbouris, Andreas Ziartides, Yiannis Sofoikli, and Yiannis Katsourides; Secretariat members include Georgiou, Katsourides, and Dinos Constantinou. A notable feature of the party collective leadership is its stability and the comparatively advanced age of each individual.

The total membership for all elements within the AKEL apparatus, including various fronts and allowing for overlapping memberships, is estimated at some 60,000. AKEL controls the island's largest trade union organization, the Pan-Cyprior Workers' Confederation (Pankiprios Ergatiki Omospondia; PEO), which has come 37,000 members—49.3 percent of all those holding membership in labor unions. It is an affiliate of the communist-front World Federation of Trade Unions. Many businessmen prefer to deal with PEO because it is well run, historically trustworthy, and usually not excessive in bargaining demands. Andreas Ziartides, a labor leader since 1943, is the PEO general secretary. Influential in AKEL's decision making, he has been mentioned from time to time as a possibility for the post of minister of labor and social insurance in the Makarios cabinet.

The AKEL-sponsored United Democratic Youth Organization (Eniaia Dimokratiki Organosis Neolaias; EDON), is headed by Panikos Paionidis. EDON claims to have 10,000 members and is believed also to operated a branch in England. Through sport and social programs, EDON extends its influence to more than thrice its young membership. Its organization of secondary school students—known as PEOM—has an estimated 2,000 members, who are also members of EDON. EDON holds a seat on the Executive Committee of the communist-front World Federation of Democratic Youth.

Other AKEL-dominated organizations included the Pan-Cypriot Confederation of Women's Organization (POGO); the Pan-Cypriot Peace Council (PEE), a member of the communist-front World Peace Council; the Cypriot-Soviet Association; and the Cypriot-German Friendship Society. AKEL and its adjuncts have regularly exchanged fraternal delegations with the communist parties of Eastern Europe and the U.S.S.R.

Within the Turkish Cypriot community there are no professed communists, but some of the young people, especially those enrolled in certain Turkish universities, are Marxist-influenced. AKEL has made continual overtures for membership to the Turks in Cyprus and also has tried to infiltrate the one Turkish Cypriot labor union, without apparent success.

An adjunct to AKEL in the United Kingdom, the "Union of Cypriots in England," has an estimated 1,250 members, overwhelmingly Greek. On the other hand, of the estimated 20,000 Turkish Cypriots who reside in England, a few are open members of the Communist Party of Great Britain and some others are undoubtedly crypto-communists. Some of the leftist tension occurring in mainland Turkey is thought to be abetted by Turkish Cypriot communists living in London.

Domestic Attitudes and Activities. AKEL has consistently exploited anti-colonialist sentiment in its protest against the restrictions placed on Cyprus by the 1959 Zurich and London agreements and against the continuing presence of the two British bases in the island. Because as a mass party it seeks to attract the Turkish minority as well as the Greeks, AKEL has shown little favor for the purely Greek objective of enosis—the union of Cyprus with Greece. Before the 1967 coup in Greece, AKEL's strength as a national party was for some time precarious because, unable to advocate enosis openly, it used instead the term "self-determination" in its slogans. Since the coup on Cyprus in July 1974, which temporarily deposed President Makarios and brought on the Turkish invasion, the issue of enosis—fortunately for AKEL—has become moot.

AKEL's continuing support of independence rather than enosis are clear: the status quo ensures continuation of a non-aligned policy and prevents "NATO-ization of Cyprus," permits freedom for AKEL activities (while enosis would probably result in the legal prohibition of the party), and allows communists to reap propaganda benefits among mainland Turks and Turkish Cypriots, who fear enosis.

From 1967 throughout 1974, AKEL stressed its "patriotic" orientation and its consistent backing of Makarios against the efforts of the terrorist group (EOKA) to overthrow the government. Early in 1974, General Secretary Papaioannou stated:

> Cyprus and its people are threatened with a grave danger which has heightened in connection with the aggravation of the economic crisis of capitalism. The imperialist conspiracy against Cyprus, continues in diverse forms, but with the old aim of dividing the island and subordinating it to the strategic interests of NATO's aggressive circles. The activities of underground armed groups of Grivas and the attempts at breaking the resistance of the Cyprior people surely are nothing else but a manifestation of the imperialist plot. (TASS, 9 January.)

After the EOKA leader, General George Grivas, died from old age in January, the clandestine organization announced that it would discontinue activities (ibid., 29 January). In an olive-branch gesture, Makarios granted amnesty to all Grivas supporters who had been arrested. AKEL's statement on the amnesty offer again demonstrated its support for the archbishop:

> This decision by the president, is a gesture of great political significance and an act of patriotism. It is a new manifestation of good will by the government and of the need to end lawlessness, violence and terrorism. (Ibid., 30 January.)

EOKA's promise to stop its illegal activities was short-lived. Not only did its leaders fail to respond to the amnesty declared by President Makarios, but they embarked on a new campaign of violence. On the situation, the AKEL general secretary stated: "Imperialist circles are hatching plans for the overthrow of President Makarios, establishment of a fascist dictatorship in Cyprus and turning the island into a bridgehead for their military adventures in the Middle East" (ibid., 9 March). It was reported, he said that weapons were increasingly being stored by the underground; a further indication of the "criminal designs of the reaction" was the fact that the "new leader of the underground" was "a man from Greece, an expert in the field of subversive actions" (ibid., 7 March).

Thus, the main domestic problem in the first half of 1974 was the underground threat to the Makarios government. At AKEL's party congress, Papaioannou elaborated on the strategy and tactics of the regenerated terrorist group:

> The proclaimed aim [is] enosis. It tries to intimidate the population, to cause disorder, torpedo the talks between the two communities in Cyprus and thus give to external forces a pretext to directly interfere in the country's internal affairs. The actions of the terrorists and the Athens junta that backs them serve the interest of aggressive NATO circles that want to solve the question of Cyprus by arranging a division of the island behind the backs of the Cypriots. (Ibid., 23 April.)

The AKEL general secretary issued a warning to the EOKA activists:

> All the intrigues of the reactionary underground and its masters encounter the cohesion and unity of the Cypriot people. The people of Cyprus are ready to give the Makarios government every support in suppressing the terror and the plot, in protecting the life and security of the country's citizens. (*Pravda*, 27 April.)

Of the many routine resolutions passed at the congress, those directed toward the domestic scene were summarized as follows:

> AKEL views the ensuring of democracy and suppression of terror and violence in the country as the main task in AKEL's domestic policy. The party comes out for the continuation of the talks between the two Cyprus communities and believes that any other procedure is fraught with serious danger for Cyprus. The congress strongly opposed the preservation of foreign military bases on the island. In the economic field, the resolution says, AKEL stands for a just distribution of national income, for a revision of the tax

policy in the interests of working people in the low-income bracket, for an improvement of the pension system, for the introduction of free tuition in secondary schools and transition to free medical services. (TASS, 28 April.)

The congress closed with an appeal to all Cypriots "to rally behind the government of President Makarios and to strengthen patriotic unity in the struggle for a peaceful settlement of the Cypriot question on the basis of a single, independent, territorially integral and demilitarized Cyprus" (ibid.).

The AKEL leader later penned these self-serving words for his patrons in the Soviet Union:

> The Congress demonstrated unanimity on all major questions and confirmed the cohesion and monolithic nature of the party and its leadership. . . . Being the most serious, consistent political force of the country, AKEL has exerted and will continue to exert every effort to frustrate the imperialist plans for the dismemberment and enslavement of Cyprus. (*Pravda*, 4 July.)

AKEL's prediction of a coup against Makarios and the "dismemberment" of the island became a reality on 15 July. Acting with full knowledge of the Athens military junta, the 1,500 Greek officers of the National Guard led their pro-enosis followers against the presidential palace. Their target was Makarios. Had it not been for a dramatic escape the president would surely have been murdered at his desk, as was abortively reported that day by the insurgents. Sporadic fighting ensued between the two forces, but there was little doubt from the beginning that coup was to be successful.

Five days after Makarios was deposed and replaced initially by a newspaper publisher, Nicos Sampson, the mainland Turks mobilized. Fearing for the safety of the Turkish Cypriot community, the Ankara government launched a military invasion on the north shore of the island. The superior Turkish army met little resistance from the National Guard, and in short order, Cyprus fell under what an AKEL spokesman described as a "triple occupation by Greece, Turkey and Britain" (Dinos Constantinou, in *WMR*, September).

On 20 July the U.N. Security Council in emergency session passed a resolution calling for a cease-fire and the withdrawal of foreign military personnel from Cyprus. AKEL greeted the U.N. action with enthusiasm. Deputy general secretary Fantis said that, for the reestablishment of peace and constitutional government in Cyprus, it was "necessary to ensure without delay the implementation of the U.N. Security Council resolution." The Cyprus people, he stressed, particularly needed "support from all the progressive forces of the world so as not to allow the reactionary circles of NATO to torpedo the decisions of the U.N. Security Council." (TASS, 22 July.) In summary, AKEL expressed readiness to promote the immediate implementation of the resolution, the establishment of peace and normalization of the situation in the country, and the restoration of the constitutional system. The Central Committee further urged all political parties in Cyprus to unite efforts "to save the country" (*Pravda*, 26 July). Papaioannou hailed the "important role played by the Soviet Union in the efforts to bring about a just solution of the Cyprus problem." The Soviet Union, he went on, had "resolutely declared its support for the independence, sovereignty and territorial integrity of Cyprus." (TASS, 28 July.)

The Turkish invasion of Cyprus produced an unexpected crisis in Athens. Unprepared to send any armed force to the island to back up their staged coup, and unwilling to further provoke the Turks, who were mobilized on the Thrace border, the Greek junta fell in disgrace. The leaders of the Greek armed forces announced on 23 July that they were handing over the running of the country to a civilian government under a new prime minister, Constantine Caramanlis, who had been in exile. Replacement of the seven-year-old dictatorship by a democracy in Greece was one of AKEL's few bright spots during the month of July. The party later expressed its gratitude "to all who in those trying days raised their voice against the crime of the Greek military" (*WMR*, September).

Another event which undoubtedly gave AKEL some pleasure was the subsequent fall from the presidency of Nicos Sampson, a fanatical anti-communist, who had been installed with the blessings of the junta. In accordance with the constitution of the Republic of Cyprus, which stimpulates that in the absence of a president his duties are to be performed by the chairman of the parliament, Glafkos Clerides rightfully assumed the office on 25 July. AKEL praised Clerides' first policy declaration "that the Cypriot Government would continue the quest for the solution of the island's problems on the basis of preservation of its sovereignty" (*Pravda*, 26 July).

Soviet deputy foreign minister Illichev made an official visit to Cyprus on 18 September. He and Clerides promptly announced the "identity of views between the two countries on the Cyprus problem" (Nicosia domestic service, 18 September). Illichev also made an official call on Rauf Denktas, the vice-president of the republic and president of the Turkish Cypriot Autonomous Administration. Claiming that the meeting had been beneficial, Denktas said that Illichev wanted to "learn the Turkish Cypriot position on the Cyprus issue and to explain the views of his government on the issue" (Bayrak radio, 18 September).

The purpose of the Illichev visit was to consider the previous Soviet proposal for an eighteen-national conference on the future of Cyprus. The idea was to replace the NATO-oriented talks between Greece, Turkey, and Britain in Geneva by a broad international conference within the U.N. framework. Clerides and Illichev agreed on the proposed international parley as a promising effort to find "guarantees for the Republic of Cyprus and for the security in this zone of the Eastern Mediterranean" (Nicosia domestic service, 18 September). On the same day that the Soviet delegation was in Cyprus, Papaioannou was attending a public meeting at the Patrice Lumumba Friendship University in Moscow. During the meeting a resolution was "adopted by representatives of eighty-eight countries of Asia, Africa and Latin America approving the Soviet initiative for the international conference to settle the problem of Cyprus" (TASS, 19 September). Apparently the public relations campaign behind the Soviet foreign policy initiative was well planned in advance.

In a "warm and friendly meeting" two days earlier, AKEL representatives and members of the Central Committee of the Communist Party of the Soviet Union (CPSU) agreed on a party line about Cyprus. The CPSU representatives confirmed their continued support for the "just struggle of AKEL and the Cypriot people against intrigues of NATO in and around Cyprus, against foreign military interference and against internal reaction," and assured the Cypriot comrades that the CPSU would

> continue declaring resolutely for the withdrawal of all foreign troops, for restoration of constitutional order, specifically for return of lawfully-elected President Makarios, in defense of complete independence, sovereignty and territorial integrity of the republic of Cyprus, and for the inalienable right of the Cypriots to decide their destiny themselves. (Ibid., 18 September.)

At a press conference after his return to Cyprus, Papaioannou reasserted the Soviet stand on the Cyprus question and noted:

> the existence of good ground for making the relations between Cyprus and the Soviet Union closer, the need to disarm all those illegally carrying arms, the need for the restoration of constitutional order and sincere unity for the salvation of Cyprus, and the need for the return of Archbishop Makarios and for the formation of a government of national unity. (Nicosia domestic service, 2 October.)

Condemning violence and terrorism, Papaioannou warned: "If the Soviet efforts for the convocation of an international conference fail, the Soviet Union will consider other measures for the implementation of the Security Council resolution on Cyprus" (ibid.). What the "other measures" could be was not elaborated upon publicly by either AKEL or the Soviet Union.

Archbishop Makarios did not think the Soviet Union could do much to help solve the Cyprus dilemma. In an interview from exile in London, he declared:

> I appreciate the usefulness of certain Soviet proposals. Moscow's attitude is friendly but rather ambiguous

as far as Turkey is concerned. Practically speaking, the Russians have adopted no concrete measure. But can they do more, considering the international context and their interests in the region? (*Le Mondes*, Paris, 18 September.)

Initially, however, he did see some "merit" in the Soviet proposal (*Washington Post*, 21 August).

After the U.N. General Assembly placed the Cyprus question on its agenda for the 29th Session, the Soviets felt their proposal might be adopted. A communist journalist stated in a dispatch from New York:

> The Soviet proposal to hold an international conference on Cyprus within the framework of the United Nations is regarded here as very timely. The Soviet initiative was, as is known, supported by Cyprus and Greece. The Soviet proposal to send a Security Council mission to study the situation in Cyprus was also met with due attention. The struggle of different forces in the United Nations around the Cypriot question is going on. The efforts of the adherents of a just settlement to the Cypriot problem meet with counteraction on the part of the militaristic circles not wishing to resolve this question outside NATO. The Peking representative in the United Nations, who attacked constructive Soviet proposals, expressed his complete support of NATO. However, with every passing day forces are growing strong within the framework of the United Nations which are coming out for such a settlement, which would answer the interests of the Cypriot people and contribute to the process of détente throughout the world. (TASS, 20 September.)

A typical editorial in the U.S. press, on the other hand, criticized the Soviet proposal as a "cumbersome propaganda-prone forum . . . even if the shape of the table could ever be agreed upon," adding: "The Kremlin would dearly like a piece of the diplomatic action in the eastern Mediterranean, where it seeks to increase its influence. The Cyprus situation also is ready-made for Soviet mischief-making against NATO." (*Washington Star-News*, 28 August.)

The thrust of the Soviet effort was effectively blunted by the Cyprus resolution that the U.N. General Assembly adopted on 1 November. As a result of the U.N. action, the minority Turkish Cypriot community was recognized as an equal partner with the Greek community to determine the future status of the island. While the Turks saw this as a great "success" for themselves, the Greek differentiated the positive and negative aspects. In what could be assumed to be the view of AKEL as well, provisional President Clerides made this observation on the U.N. resolution:

> The positive elements are the respect for the independence, sovereignty and territorial integrity of Cyprus: the withdrawal of foreign troops; return of the refugees to their homes; and the beginning of talks to find a peaceful solution of the problem. The most negative point of the resolution is the equalization of the two communities which places the Greek majority on the same footing with the Turkish minority. (Athens domestic service, 7 November.)

Clerides then said: "The present circumstances do not allow for a solution based on the existence of a unitary state, but a solution based on federation." He rejected, however, any idea for federation of the island on a geographic basis. (Ibid.)

Realizing that the U.N. resolution must be lived with, the AKEL general secretary shifted his position away from the Soviet proposal:

> Our problem will be solved peacefully by the Cypriot people themselves, Greeks and Turks, at the negotiating table, and there is no doubt that, from the moment that the Turkish troops withdraw, and when all the refugees return to their homes together with those in enclaves and missing, then all the prerequisites will have been created for the successful outcome of the negotiations between the Greek Cypriots and the Turkish Cypriots (Nicosia domestic service, 6 November).

Since the statement was made in the presence of the Soviet ambassador to Cyprus, it can be surmised that the Kremlin had also shifted away from its suggestion for a multilateral conference. Thus, negotiations on the future of the island were to come back again to the domestic inter-communal level, which in the past had produced very little in the way of agreement.

During the last two months of the year, fruitless talks were held between the two community leaders, who were essentially serving as surrogates for their respective mainland patrons. A state of emergency continued on both sides, but the fighting subsided as a result of the ability of the U.N. peacemakers to enforce the cease-fire. While amnesty was not granted to the perpetrators of the July coup, prosecutions were also not ordered as Clerides felt that this action "would certainly have led to civil war" (ibid., 12 October). When Makarios returned in December he found Cyprus ravaged by war, with economic losses estimated above $10 billion. In a conciliatory tone, the president noted that if agreement could be reached soon between Greeks and Turks, "it would be possible to rebuild Cyprus within a rather short time, within five years." (*Washington Post*, 11 December.)

International Views and Positions. Before "the Greek-officered National Guard rose in a revolt directed against the people and independent state of Cyprus," Papaioannou found time to write about his party's views of the current world scene. He claimed that "a decisive turn is coming about in the international situation as tension and confrontation give way to détente and cooperation." In almost the same breath, he modified his sweeping generalization:

> The current détente does not at all mean that imperialism and neo-fascism have abandoned their aggressive plans. Reality shows that they are merely waiting for a chance to impose a reactionary, neo-fascist regime on this or that country as was the case in Chile not long ago. The tenacity of fascism is exemplified by the situation in Spain, Greece and elsewhere. Furthermore, the seats of tension in Southeast Asia and the Middle East are still there. An unrelenting struggle goes on between the partisans of peace, democracy, national independence and socialism and bellicose imperialist and neo-fascist quarters. The turn toward détente is a reality but the peoples must show vigilance and fight on if the cause of world peace and cooperation is to prevail. (*WMR*, August 1974.)

Deputy general secretary Fantis saw détente as "plainly gaining the upper hand in the contest between the old and the new in international relations." These "favorable changes" were made possible by the "appropriate initiatives on the part of the socialist community" and primarily on the part of the Soviet Union, the "vanguard force." Fantis asserted that the "principles of peaceful coexistence" form the essence of a "new moral code in the nuclear age":

> The policy of peaceful coexistence is an explicit class policy, a special form of class struggle between the working class of the world and capital, between socialism and imperialism. It accords entirely with the Marxist-Leninist world outlook and serves the real interests of the international working class and the forces of peace, national independence, democracy and progress, the fundamental interests of mankind. (Ibid., July.)

The AKEL line concerning the world scene is thus highly consistent with that of the Soviet Union.

At the party congress, Papaioannou condemned the "nationalistic, dogmatic and sectarian policy mapped by the leadership of the Chinese Communist Party," and charged that "the Chinese leadership does enormous harm to the cause of socialism and peace and to the struggle of peoples for independence, democracy and social progress" (TASS, 25 April).

In May, President Makarios made a seven-day visit to China. Upon his return Makarios described the talks as cordial and said: "The Chinese leaders, who took a particular interest in the Cyprus question, unreservedly support our efforts for a democratic solution of our problem" (*Cyprus Bulletin*, 5 June). Due to their strong support of Makarios, AKEL was on the horns of a dilemma as a result of the China trip, and avoided making any comment. AKEL does, on the other hand, support fully the neutralist nonaligned foreign policy of the government of Makarios, which gives Cyprus the opportunity to participate actively in the many conferences of the Third World countries.

Following the coup in July, AKEL was more concerned with the domestic turmoil, as were the other political parties in Cyprus. While undoubtedly pleased by such events as the cutoff of U.S. military aid to Turkey, AKEL offered little editorial comment on this and other international affairs during the latter half of the year. Despite the upheaval in the island, AKEL members managed to make exchange visits to Eastern bloc countries throughout the year.

Publications. AKEL enjoys influential press channels. Its central organ is the daily newspaper *Khravyi* ("Dawn"), but there are sympathetic writers and editors on most of the island's periodicals. AKEL's theoretical organ is *Theoritikos Dimokratis* ("Theoretical Democrat"). The party also publishes a quarterly review, *Neos Dimokratis* ("New Democrat"); a monthly journal, *Nea Epochi* ("New Epoch") and a weekly, *Neoi Kairoi* ("New Times"). The PEO publishes a weekly newspaper, *Ergatiki Vima* ("Workers' Step"). EDON publishes a newspaper, *Dhimokratia*, and a monthly, *Neolaia* ("Youth"). After the coup, the communist publications did not appear with their usual regularity.

New York, New York   T. W. Adams

Denmark

The Communist Party of Denmark (Danmarks Kommunistiske Parti; DKP) sprang from the left wing of the Social Democratic Party (SDP) during the agitated aftermath of World War I. It was organized on 9 November 1919 and has been legal ever since, with the exception of the period of German occupation during World War II. Membership has edged up to an estimated 8,000. The population of Denmark is about 5,100,000 (estimated 1973). The DKP continues to draw most of its followers from among industrial workers and farm laborers, together with leftist intellectuals in Copenhagen and other urban centers.

The DKP has been riding a crest of rising political strength and popularity since the parliamentary election of 4 December 1973. The communists capitalized on the Danish protest vote against more traditional parties and high taxes to win six seats in the Folketing (parliament). The DKP received 110,809 votes, or 3.6 percent of the votes cast. This represented a significant increase over the 1.4 percent tally in the previous election of 21 September 1971 and was the highest percentage achieved by the party since the September 1953 election, when it won 4.3 percent of the total. The victory ended the DKP's twelve-year exclusion from parliamentary power and put party chairman Knud Jespersen into the Folketing. Details of the election results for all parties are tabulated at the end of this profile.

Since that electoral victory, DKP fortunes have prospered on several fronts. Opinion polls reflect support from almost six percent of the electorate. Significantly, much of the new support is from young Danes. The DKP is making clear inroads into the intellectual and radical youth groups once considered the main domain of the Socialist People's Party (Socialistisk Folkeparti; SF). With poll support for the DKP surpassing that for the SF, there has been growing speculation that the latter rival of the communists may be the first victim of revived struggle on the Danish left. The communists scored well during the March municipal elections. The DKP jumped to 54 seats (from 6) throughout Denmark, and to seven places (from one) in the 55-member Copenhagen Municipal Assembly. The DKP also appeared to be making gains in the Danish labor movement, at the expense of both the SDP and the SF.

All of these advances contrast sharply with what had been a fairly consistent downhill slide for the DKP. Party power had peaked in 1945, owing in large part to the DKP's effective role in the Danish resistance. The expulsion of the late Aksel Larsen (party chairman, 1932-58) for "Titoist revisionism" in 1958, the formation of the SF in 1959, the emergence of the Left Socialists (Venstresocialisterne; VS) in 1967, and the DKP's continuing loyalty to Moscow had all whittled away at the communist constituency. The DKP has subsequently been able to capitalize on the pervasive malaise of Social Democracy throughout Scandinavia and the special economic challenges of burgeoning inflation, unemployment, and deficits on current account occasioned, in party, by the energy crisis.

Leadership and Organization. The congress, convened at three-year intervals and last assembled in Copenhagen on 12-14 January 1973, is the supreme party authority. It discusses the report of the Central Committee, adopts the Party Program and Rules, and elects the leading party bodies, consisting of the Central Committee (41 members and eleven alternates), a five-member Control Commission, and two party auditors. The Central Committee elects the Executive Committee (14 members) and Secretariat (five).

Knud Jespersen is DKP chairman, a post to which he was first elected in 1958 and for which he was last reelected at the 1973 party congress. John Berg Larsen is chairman of the party's youth affiliate, the Communist Youth of Denmark (Danmarks Kommunistiske Ungdom; DKU). The DKU has formed a variety of new sections, with the objective of establishing a communist student organization on the national level.

In 1974 there was no palpable change in the balance between conservative and liberal forces within the DKP. The conservatives retained control of the party's tactical lines and maintained loyalty to the Communist Party of the Soviet Union (CPSU).

Domestic Attitudes and Activities. The DKP clearly relished its new parliamentary clout and used it primarily to criticize or undermine the minority Hartling government. In his first speech to the parliament, Jespersen condemned the prime minister for presenting a "crisis line characteristic of capitalism and the Common Market countries in particular" and for favoring the haves (landed proprietors and employers) over the have-nots (workers) (*Land og Folk*, 10 January 1974).

The communists promised to work both inside and outside parliament for: effective correlation between wage and price increases, a price and profit halt on food and imports of oil and raw materials, elimination of the value-added tax on food, democratic tax reform, repeal of the construction halt, nationalization of big oil monopolies, democratic labor protection law, a rise in pensions, and an end to encroachments on social rights, health care, and education (ibid., 16, 22 January). Villy Fuglsang, veteran DKP member and a new member of parliament, spoke out against continued capitalist development of Danish agriculture and for an expansion of the cooperative movement with common management forms (ibid., 5-6 January).

The oil crisis figured prominently in parliamentary debate and communist concerns. The DKP demanded the nationalization of oil depots, imports, and trading (ibid., 19-20 January). Jespersen claimed that "the oil monopolies have misused their power to bring about crisis situations" and that "Denmark must break this power of the monopolies and carefully investigate all the possibilities for purchasing energy from the socialist countries, as well as elsewhere." He faulted both Denmark and the European Community (EC) for lacking an energy policy which gave people and their environment top priority. (Ibid., 19-20 January, 19 April).

DKP anger with the so-called black cabinet—the socialist government in Copenhagen—grew as the year progressed. The communists characterized the allegedly anti-labor moves of the government as "cynical attempts to shift the burden of the crisis of the capitalist system in Denmark and of the EC to the working people" (interview of Jespersen in *Neues Deutschland*, East Berlin, 17 May). They helped organize numerous demonstrations and strikes to protest against record levels of inflation and unemployment.

The specifics of the DKP domestic program emerged most clearly at the party's national meeting, 22-23 June. About 400 delegates from the country's local party organizations convened to discuss and adopt a manifesto entitled "For the Unity of the Working Class in the Struggle against Big Capital." The document stressed the need to fortify working-class unity in Denmark and proposed joint action to redistribute taxes equitably, stem price increases, improve the position of young people and women, and effect Denmark's withdrawal from NATO and the EC. The latter affiliation, it was argued, only aggravated the nation's difficulties and shackled Denmark to imperialist policies.

Though Jesperson said that the DKP's goal was "revolutionary transformation to socialism," he advocated recourse to parliamentary means, mass action, demonstrations, and strikes–but not armed struggle. (*Land og Folk*, 22-23, 25, 27 June, 6-7 July.)

The "revolutionary transformation to socialism" also seemed to stop short of collaboration with the Social Democrats. Jespersen refused to join forces with former SDP prime minister Anker Jørgensen and "share responsibility for the two billion kronor to the employees for compulsory savings or the housing settlement that strangled the tenants' opportunities and helped throw thousands of construction workers out of work and left the same threat hanging over the heads of even more thousands" (ibid., 13 August). The bloom was clearly off any fledgling political romance between the DKP and SDP, as rivalry for a labor following revived within Denmark's left.

International Views and Activities. Demands that Denmark quit both NATO and the EC continued to dominate DKP declarations on issues of foreign policy. The communists seized the opportunity of the twenty-fifth anniversary of NATO 24 August, to sponsor anti-NATO demonstrations. They put particular emphasis on events in Cyprus, where "two NATO countries, Greece and Turkey, may be fighting each other but are working together to subjugate the Cypriot people . . . with the United States . . . standing in the shadows and pulling the strings." (*Land og Folk*, 17-18 August.)

Two further themes recurred throughout DKP anti-NATO pronouncements. The communists linked the continuation of NATO with Cold Warriors resisting détente, particularly as exemplified in the Conference on Security and Cooperation in Europe (CSCE) (ibid., 24-25 August), and they condemned the Hartling government for increasing defense expenditures while cutting back on budgets for social welfare. The DKP vowed to "combine the fight against NATO with the fight for a better existence."

Besides its support for the CSCE, an issue on which the DKP diverged from some other leftist forces in Denmark, the party made a related point. It asserted that "the connection between European developments and relations between the Soviet Union and the United States shows that there is no conflict between relaxation of tension in one area and in another–on the contrary, they determine each other" (ibid., 28 July).

The DKP worked energetically to capitalize on the backlash from the EC referendum campaign, occasioned by economic conditions. As in its anti-NATO drive, the party argued that the "Hartling regime" honors the demands of the Alliance and the Community, "but sends the bill to the workers and consumers" (ibid., 22 January, 1 October). The communists pressed instead for more Danish affiliation and trade with socialist states (ibid., 18-19 May, 20 September).

The toppling of Allende by the military junta in Chile continued to arouse strong feelings within the DKP. The party criticized the Hartling government for not taking a clear stand against the junta's alleged violation of human rights (ibid., 11 July).

Finally, the DKP condemned reductions in aid to under-developed countries. It asserted that "Denmark's aid to the world food program, the Common Market loan to Turkey, and support of the coup regimes through the World Bank should be cut long before the aid to the U.N. development program" (ibid., 16 January).

International Party Contacts. The DKP continued in 1974 its virtually unswerving loyalty to Moscow. Party chairman Jespersen visited the Soviet Union in April and met with CPSU Central Committee member M. A. Suslov. Their exchange of opinions reaffirmed "complete unity of views and positions on all the questions discussed." Jesperson claimed that the peace program adopted by the CPSU's Twenty-fourth Congress was "an inspiration to Danish communists in their struggle for the vital interests of the working class." He said that any problems in the communist movement were started, not by the U.S.S.R., but by "dissenter anti-communist forces." Hard-liners within the DKP considered the "Solzhenitsyn case" a "cynically prepared political maneuver" and "conscious attack upon the progress made for peaceful coexistence" (*Land og Folk*, 15 February). The DKP applauded initiatives to increase contacts between Nordic and Soviet trade unions (ibid., 11 July).

The Danish communists considered the conference of Western European communist parties in January a success. They continued cordial relations with the East German party, and also the Romanian Communist Party, whose secretary-general Ceauşescu received Ib Norlund of the DKP Central Committee in March. A DKP study delegation was warmly received in East Berlin in June. Representatives of the DKP spent two weeks studying Bulgaria's "successes in socialist construction," as guests of the Bulgarian Communist Party Central Committee in June. Chairman Jespersen visited Bucharest at the invitation of the Romanian party's Central Committee in August. The DKP participated in a conference of the Nordic communist parties in Finland in September. The communiqué from that meeting stressed the struggle against the growing power of the monopolies, the need to seek higher living standards and greater democratic rights for the working people, and solidarity with the Chilean people.

Publications. *Land og Folk* ("Nation and People"), a daily newspaper, is the DKP central organ. It enjoys a daily circulation of about 8,000 and on weekends about 11,500. *Tiden-Verden Rund* ("Time round the World") is the party's monthly theoretical journal. The DKU publication is *Fremad* ("Forward").

Date of latest election: 4 December 1973

Party name	Votes received	Percent of total	Seats	Percent of seats
Communist:				
Communist Party............	110,809	3.6	6	3.4
Non-communist Left:				
Left Socialist	44,572	1.5	–	–
Socialist People's	183,273	6.0	11	6.3
Social Democrat	783,566	25.6	46	26.3
Other:				
Center Democrats	236,801	7.8	14	8.0
Radical Liberals	342,715	11.2	20	11.4
Moderate Liberals	374,802	12.3	22	12.6
Conservative	279,461	9.2	16	9.1
Christian People's	122,920	4.0	7	4.0
Justice	88,033	2.9	5	2.9
Progressive	485,482	15.9	28	16.0
Total	3,052,434	100.0	175	100.0

Finland

Exiled Social Democratic dissidents—"reds" escaping from Finland's bloody civil war—established the Communist Party of Finland (Suomen Kommunistinen Puolue; SKP) in Moscow on 29 August 1918. The SKP operated through front organizations until 1930 when, weakened by internal friction and prohibited by the Finnish government, it reverted to illegal activities. In 1974 the party celebrated the thirtieth anniversary of its elevation to legal standing. Elaborate marches and ceremonies commemorated the fact that the SKP became a legal political party in 1944, as required by the Finnish-Soviet armistice of that year. A large gathering in Helsinki's Olympic Stadium heard SKP leaders and foreign dignitaries salute the party's role in behalf of workers' rights and Soviet-Finnish friendship.

SKP members are estimated to number about 48,000. Most come from either the industrialized urban areas of southern Finland or the small farming communities in the nation's northern and eastern districts where a radical tradition thrives. The population of Finland is about 4,700,000.

The SKP has consistently received between a fourth and a fifth of the total vote in national elections since World War II. It has done so through the Finnish People's democratic League (Suomen Kansan Demokraattinen Liitto; SKDL), an electoral front established in October 1944. The SKDL won 17 percent of the vote in the most recent parliamentary election, 2-3 January 1972. It garnered 37 seats in the 200-seat Eduskunta (parliament), second only to the 55 seats of the Social Democratic Party (SDP).

Despite that significant parliamentary bloc, the communists have not participated in Prime Minister Kalevi Sorsa's coalition of Social Democratic, Swedish People's, Center, and Liberal parties. They last shared authority in a center-left coalition from 15 July 1970 to 17 March 1971. The serious rift between the liberal and Stalinist factions of the SKP and the party's distaste for sharing responsibility for difficult economic decisions have continued to discourage a communist return to power. The Soviet Union, with which the SKP maintains close communication, has given conflicting signals on whether it puts higher priority on SKP unity, communist participation in a broad-based government (such as Finland's president Urho Kekkonen would probably prefer), or greater communist loyalty to Moscow.

Leadership and Organization. Aarne Saarinen, "liberal" communist and former union leader, remained SKP chairman in 1974. First elected to that post in 1966, he had been reelected at the party's Sixteenth Congress, 31 March-2 April 1972. Both main party factions had spokesmen as vice-chairmen, in the Stalinist Taisto Sinisalo and the liberal Olavi Hänninen. Arvo Aalto, a liberal, remained secretary-general. The relative strength of the two SKP wings, established at an extraordinary congress in February 1970, stayed the same, with the ratio of liberals to Stalinists at 20-15 in the Central Committee, 9-6 in the Politburo, and 5-3 in the Secretariat. The SKP Central Committee decided on 27 September to hold the party's Seventeenth Congress in Helsinki on 16-18 May 1975.

Party Internal Affairs. The "liberal" majority and Stalinist minority of the SKP continued their rivalry in 1974, sometimes seemingly just short of pitched battle. Their "parallel activities" persisted, despite injunctions to the contrary from the Sixteenth Congress. That meeting, in fact, had all but formalized the existence of two parties within the SKP.

The conflict harked back to the ideological turmoil following the 1956 "de-Stalinization" congress of the Communist Party of the Soviet Union (CPSU). Different reactions to the Warsaw Pact invasion of Czechoslovakia in 1968, fluctuating party fortunes within Finland, and seemingly ambivalent signs from Moscow only widened the gap between the two ideological camps. Key indices to this schism were: the rhetorical pot-shots between the liberal *Kansan Uutiset* and the Stalinist *Tiedonantaja*, reports of the 11 February SKP meeting with Soviet ideologist Suslov in Moscow, the 9 May Hautala interview, and critiques of both the SKDL and Maoist splinter groups.

Chairman Saarinen condemned the parallel activities of the Taistoists around *Tiedonantaja* on numerous occasions. He condemned their violation of the decision of the Sixteenth Congress whereby "the activities of organizations not belonging to the organizational structure . . . must cease" (*Kansan Uutiset*, 26 September). He admitted, however, that "as long as the *Tiedonantaja* newspaper is able to play the role that it has been playing," it would be hard to eliminate parallel activities. The Central Committee's sharp reprimand of the Stalinist provincial newspaper *Hämeen Yhteistyö* for publishing writings and speeches which violate party decisions seemed futile. Saarinen feared that the entire communist movement would lose momentum if disunity persisted: "As long as we give the impression that as communists we do not get along with each other . . . we will naturally not be able to assure those with whom we are attempting to create the anti-monopoly front of our desire for cooperation and our ability to cooperate on the basis of equality and mutual respect" (*Kansan Uutiset*, 16 June).

The so-called Hautala affair may have been the most dramatic new development in the SKP rift during 1974. Arvo Hautala—second chairman of the Federation of Finnish Trade Unions (Suomen Ammattiyhdistysten Keskusliitto; SAK), member of the SKP Central Committee, and one of the "liberal" majority—gave a public interview on 9 May. He accused SKP vice-chairman Sinisalo of having lied to the Soviet ideologist Suslov about the situation in Finland while the SKP was visiting Moscow in February. Hautala charged that Sinisalo had engaged "in personal slander abroad and purveyed half-truths, fantasies, and unfounded disparagement as an article of export." He was particularly angered by Sinisalo's comments on the activities of the SAK and his attacks against SKDL chairman Ele Alenius.

Hautala was duly reprimanded by the SKP, even though he had expressed the feelings of the non-Stalinist majority. Alenius came to the strong support of Hautala because of the Taistoist interference in SKDL matters (ibid., 21 May). The Stalinists played up a *Pravda* article which criticized Hautala's behavior as the worst kind of blow against the communist movement and relations between the SKP and CPSU, and bemoaned rightist exploitation of the Hautala stand (*Tiedonantaja*, 21 May). The SKP liberals, obviously nervous because of the article's assertion that Hautala had acted against friendly Soviet-Finnish relations, appealed for unity (*Kansan Uutiset*, 21 May). Their appeal may have been in vain. During an October visit to Finland, Soviet president Podgorny reportedly criticized the liberal wing of the SKP and announced that the CPSU would like to send a delegation to Finland just before the SKP's next party congress.

The Stalinists did not limit their critique of the SKDL to Alenius. They claimed that it was necessary to "quash the erroneous idea about the SKDL as being some kind of a party-oriented organization having an 'overall socialist ideology' " (*Tiedonantaja*, 10 May). They printed protests from local labor organizations deploring the detrimental reformist development of the SKDL (*Tiedonantaja*, 8 January). Finally, they condemned Ilkka-Christian Björklund, a non-communist member of the SKDL, for arguing that the "super-states of the East and West" were opposing peace initiatives "all over the world as a result of the prevailing selfish interests of military policies." Björklund, they said, failed "to distinguish the Soviet Union and its policies of peace from the imperialist United States, in the same manner as the super-power theories of the current Peking leadership do." (Ibid., 7, 14 March.)

Domestic Activities and Attitudes. SKP domestic preoccupations centered on how to deal with Finland's growing economic troubles, how or if to cooperate with the SDP, and how to integrate expanded cooperation with the Soviet Union into Finland's emerging policy on energy.

Communist disenchantment with Finnish economic well-being grew during the course of 1974. Because of what the SKP called the "exceptionally strong inflationary landslide," Saarinen urged that forthcoming labor contracts safeguard the real value of wage increases (*Kansas Uutiset*, 19 January). Sinisalo condemned the Sorsa government for capitulating to reactionary forces and so increasing the strain on low-income workers. He claimed that "the EC [European Community] decision is only of economic benefit to the wood processing industry—to those who have traditionally done well." (*Tiedonantaja*, 2 February.) SKP secretary-general Aalto said that the Sorsa government had "bungled worst in economic policy and in the approval of the EC agreement which affects it," and thus proposed an SKDL interpellation on the government's incomes policy (*Kansan Uutiset*, 8 April).

Sorsa's reply to the communists' interpellation did not satisfy the SKDL parliamentary delegation. Real wages were dropping; imports were being restricted; social reforms were being curtailed (ibid., 24 April). Alenius claimed that the "basic line of economic policy must be changed" (ibid., 25 April). The communists determined to try to strengthen their position in the trade union movement by doubling their membership at places of employment (ibid., 30 June). The SKP suggested the following measures to curb the gains of big capital, improve the position of the average citizen, halt inflation, and rectify the balance of trade: impose export taxes on the large lumber firms; invest part of those tax returns in state enterprises like shipbuilding and housing construction; limit imports from capitalist countries like Western Germany, Sweden, and Japan, and increase ties with the socialist countries; supervise the activities of the commercial banks; and renounce the EC agreement (ibid., 16 June). As the government's solutions continued to fall short of economic needs—in communist eyes—the SKP called for new parliamentary elections.

The request for elections reflected, in part, the SKP's on-again, off-again efforts to seek cooperation with the Social Democrats—a recurrent theme in Finnish communist affairs. Prospects for cooperation were discussed at a meeting of the SKP Central Committee, 18-19 January (ibid., 22, 24 January). In early March, Saarinen announced the resumption of the long-suspended talks between the SKP and the SDP. The primary objective was to address the question of labor contracts. The initial talks, however, did not go well. The communists claimed that they wanted results, not just gesture (*Helsingin Sanomat*, 11 March). By April, Sinisalo said: "Objectively speaking, negotiations between the leadership organizations of the SKP and SDP can be considered fallen through" (*Kansan Uutiset*, 22 April). SDP chairman Rafael Paasio corroborated that view during May Day speeches. The talks, to quote Sinisalo, had temporarily flickered like the smallest possible pilot light.

Energy was the third item in the triad of principal SKP domestic concerns. The SKDL came down harshly on the government's handling of the fuel situation. It opposed having the workers pay for energy price hikes. It advocated developing a total energy program in cooperation with the Soviet Union, while at the same time taking into consideration the opportunities for cooperation with Poland and the other Nordic countries. (Ibid., 28 February, 16 October.) The SKP dismissed the allegation that the Soviet Union was charging exorbitant prices for its oil as "pure nonsense" (ibid., 29 March).

International Views and Activities. Finnish cooperation with the U.S.S.R., promotion of détente, concern about political prisoners in Chile, support for leftist activity in Portugal, and continuing opposition to the European Community were the central themes in the SKP's statements on foreign policy during 1974.

The communist press stressed the special importance of increased trade between Finland and the Soviet Union. It considered such a commercial relationship a stabilizing factor in the Finnish national economy (*Kansan Uutiset*, 22 April). It particularly favored the conclusion of more comprehensive energy agreements with Moscow (ibid., 14 February, 15 March; *Tiedonantaja*, 7 February). Those who objected were criticized for having an "unfounded lack of confidence in the Soviet Union" (*Kansan Uutiset*, 3 July).

Détente drew high marks from the SKP. Following the Nixon-Brezhnev summit in July, the communist press expressed full approval for the results of the meeting and the communiqué which advocated holding the third concluding stage of the Conference on Security and Cooperation in Europe at an early date. (Ibid., 5 July). At a conference held in Rovaniemi during the "Days of Peace and Friendship," 6-7 July, delegates agreed that Soviet-U.S. détente, the Vienna negotiations on arms reductions in Central Europe, and the Geneva talks on the Mideast had created favorable conditions for strengthened peace (*Tiedonantaja*, 10 July).

Condemnation of the military junta in Chile ranked high in SKP declarations. The Central Committee demanded the immediate release of the Chilean communist party's secretary-general Luis Corvalán. The emergence of the long-outlawed communist party in Portugal brought congratulations from the SKP (*Kansan Uutiset*, 14 May) and a welcome for the visit in May of Carlos Ingles, Central Committee member of the Portuguese party (ibid., 23 May).

Responding to the alleged Chinese assertion that the crisis in Cyprus reflected the power struggle between the United States and the U.S.S.R. over the Mediterranean, writers for the Stalinist press concluded that the Chinese stand was "directed solely against the Soviet Union" (*Tiedonantaja*, 22 August).

International Party Contacts. The most important contacts were nurtured in Moscow, and perhaps the most significant of such meetings in 1974 was the aforementioned one with Suslov of the CPSU Central Committee. Erkki Tuominen of the SKP Central Committee led a delegation of Finnish communist workers to Moscow for discussion of economic policy, 16-20 February. In March, a high-level Soviet honor guard accompanied the coffin at the funeral of Hertta Kuusinen, president of the Women's International Democratic Federation and honorary SKP chairman. A mid-level Soviet delegation attended events in June devoted to the thirtieth anniversary of the legalization of the SKP.

The SKP extolled the conference of West European communist parties, in Brussels on 26-28 January, as an "exceptionally significant event." It went on record in behalf of strengthening the operational unity of communist and workers parties against imperialism (*Kansan Uutiset*, 3 March). It considered the convocation of a new international communist conference "essential" and stated its readiness to participate in the broad collective preparation of such a meeting (*Pravda*, 7 March; *Tiedonantaja*, 21 August).

Members of the French and Chilean communist parties joined the Soviets as foreign speakers at the SKP thirtieth anniversary festivities. SKP secretary-general Aalto met with Edward Babiuch of the Polish communist party in late August. Gustav Husák, secretary-general of the Czechoslovak party, met with members of the SKP Central Committee in Finland, 16-19 September. It was Husák's first official visit to a non-communist country. Finland was host to a conference for nordic communists, 5-7 September, which focused on the crisis of capitalism and the need to continue the fight against the EC and its policies.

Publications. The SKP's central organ is *Kansan Uutiset* ("People's News"), published daily in Helsinki and notable for its more "liberal" orientation. *Kommunisti* is the party's monthly theoretical journal. *Tiedonantaja* and *Hämeen Yhteistyö* serve as the voices of the SKP's Stalinist faction. The weekly *Folktidningen* ("People's News") is the communist newspaper for Finland's small Swedish-speaking minority. Finnish Maoists circulate such publications as *Punalippu* ("Red Flag"), *Kiina Sanoin ja Kuvin* (China in Words and Pictures"), and *Punakaarti* ("Red Guard").

France

The French Communist Party (Parti Communiste Français; PCF) was founded in December 1920. Although it remained the largest left-wing party in France, the PCF, in 1974, appeared to be losing its electoral preeminence to an increasingly influential Socialist Party. Other small Marxist-Leninist organizations continued to challenge the PCF from the left, but their political significance was either diminishing or marginal.

For a number of years, the PCF had hidden the net total of its membership by announcing the number of cards sent to its 97 federations but not revealing how many had been actually distributed. At a meeting on 1 December 1973, Politburo member André Vieuguet broke precedence by claiming that the party's actual strength was "approaching 410,000" (*L'Humanité*, 3 December 1973). On 10 July 1974, journalists were invited to a federation secretaries' work session. During the meeting, Vieuguet claimed that the federations had by then ordered 495,300 cards, and that the number of these distributed had already reached the total given out in the entire year of 1973. "We can calculate," he added, "that the total of card-carrying members of the party, which had reached 410,000 by the end of 1973, can rise to about 450,000 by the end of 1974." (*Le Monde*, Paris, 12 July.) Non-communist observers, however, remained skeptical of the party's membership claims. Thus, following Vieuguet's first disclosure (of the 1973 figures), the fortnightly *Est & Ouest* (16-31 January 1974) analyzed other party pronouncements and concluded that the actual membership in 1973 was closer to 330,000.

The elections to the National Assembly, held on 4 and 11 March 1973, had given the PCF 5,026,417 votes (21.29 percent) on the first ballot. The Socialist Party entered the first round together with the small Movement of Left Radicals (Mouvement des Radicaux de Gauche) under the ticket of the Union of the Socialist and Democratic Left (Union de la Gauche Socialiste et Démocrate; UGSD). The UGSD ticket obtained just under five million votes (19.6 percent), of which some 350,000 (1.43 percent) were received by the Left Radicals. An electoral alliance between the PCF and the UGSD called for a withdrawal in the second round in favor of the allied candidate in any given single-member constituency who had the greatest chance of winning. The PCF obtained 73 seats, the Socialists 89, and the Left Radicals 12, out of a total of 490. (See *YICA, 1974*, pp. 133-34.)

In the presidential elections of 5 and 19 May 1974, the PCF did not present its own candidate in the first ballot. Instead it joined the Socialists and Left Radicals in the so-called Union of the Left, which presented Socialist Party leader François Mitterrand as its candidate. (For further details, see below.)

On 22 September 1974 indirect elections were held for 88 seats in the 283-member Senate. The PCF obtained 4 seats (an increase of 2), which brought its representation in the Senate to 20. The party also participated in by-elections to the Assembly, held on 29 September and 6 October (see below).

Leadership and Organization. The national leadership of the PCF was elected at the party's Twentieth Congress, held on 13-17 December 1972 (see *YICA, 1973*, pp. 143-44). The Central Committee numbered 90 full and 28 candidate members. Representing the party's Politburo were: Gustave Ansart, Guy Besse, Jacques Duclos, Etienne Fajon, Benoît Frachon, Georges Frischmann, Henri Krasucki, Paul Laurent, Roland Leroy, Georges Marchais, René Piquet, Gaston Plissonnier, Claude Poperen, Georges Séguy, André Vieuguet, and Madeleine Vincent. Mireille Bertrand, Jean Colpin, and Guy Hermier were candidate members of the Politburo. The Secretariat consisted of: Etienne Fajon, Roland Leroy, René Piquet, Gaston Plissonnier, and André Vieuguet, Georges Marchais remained secretary-general of the party. The ailing Waldeck Rochet retained the title of honorary president. A meeting of the Central Committee, held on 24-25 January 1973, appointed the heads of the Central Committee sections and persons responsible for various party activities (for details, see *L'Humanité*, 29 January 1973). In early October 1973, Paul Laurent was appointed to the Secretariat. Although the PCF held an Extraordinary Twenty-first Congress on 24-27 October 1974, the event did not include elections to the party's leading bodies. The congress was followed, however, in mid-November, by a meeting of the Central Committee, which made some changes in the party leadership. Etienne Fajon was replaced as director of *L'Humanité* by Roland Leroy, who had hitherto been responsible for relations with intellectuals and party cultural affairs. The latter's duties were given to Jacques Chambaz, who, also, was appointed to the Politburo. (For other changes, see *Le Monde*, 16 November.)

Statistics made public at the Twenty-first Congress revealed that 44.8 percent of the 1,257 delegates were working-class; there were 370 women, 61 percent of whom were under thirty years of age; the average age of all delegates was thirty (compared to thirty-three at the Twentieth Congress); and only 82 delegates had belonged to the party before 1944, in contrast to 700 who had joined since 1968 (ibid., 29 October).

At its Twentieth Congress, the PCF had claimed to have 19,520 cells in its 97 federations. Of these, 5,376 were industrial, 5,225 rural, and 8,919 local. By the end of 1973, the total had reached 20,037. At the aforementioned federation secretaries' meeting of 10 July 1974, André Vieuguet claimed that, despite the disappearance of some cells, the net total had increased to 20,700. This number included 1,519 new cells; 974 industrial (including 259 in teaching establishments), 214 rural, and 331 local. (Ibid., 12 July.)

The PCF's primary auxiliary organization is the General Confederation of Labor (Confédération Générale du Travail; CGT), the largest trade union in France, with a membership estimated at about 1,700,000. The CGT is led by PCF Politburo members Georges Séguy (secretary-general) and Benoît Frachon (president).

The other major PCF auxiliary organization is the Movement of Communist Youth (Mouvement de la Jeunesse Communiste; MJC), which comprises four groups—the Union of Communist Students of France (Union des Etudiants Communistes de France; UECF), the Union of Young Girls of France (Union des Jeunes Filles de France; UJFF), the Union of Communist Youth of France (Union de la Jeunesse Communiste de France; UJCF), and the Union of Farm Youth of France (Union de la Jeunesse Agricole de France; UJAF). The MJC's latest congress was held on 17-20 May 1973. A new 146-member national council was elected, and Jean-Michel Catala (candidate member of the PCF Central Committee) became the movement's new secretary-general. In June 1974, Catala announced the planned fusion of the UJCF and UJFF.

Among students the PCF controls a splinter group of the National Union of Students of France (Union Nationale des Etudiants de France; UNEF). Originally referred to as UNEF-Renouveau, this splinter group is now designated by the PCF simply as UNEF. The contending UNEF, which represents French students at international gatherings, is led by Trotskyists. The principal PCF-controlled high-school organization during the year continued to be the National Union of High School Action Committees (Union Nationale des Comités d'Action Lycéenne; UNCAL), a body formed in 1968.

Party Internal Affairs. During the summer months that bridged the presidential elections and the autumn by-elections to the Assembly, the PCF undertook a two-pronged policy of extensive membership recruitment and overture to its political right (see below). It also opened up the columns of its press to PCF grass-roots opinion, allowing the publication of uncustomarily candid criticism. Much of the latter was directed at the party's summer strategy, which, in a reportedly divided Politburo, had been advocated most notably by George Marchais and opposed by Roland Leroy, the PCF's chief ideologist.

By the end of October, when the PCF held its Twenty-first Congress, there had developed a marked hardening in party policy, and significant changes were made in the congress's Final Resolution, originally drafted at a Central Committee meeting at the beginning of September. Thus, as explained by Roland Leroy, the draft's statement that membership in the party was "open without restriction to all who want to play a part in the fight for democratic changes" had brought a number of militants to ask that "the nature of the party's final goal be reaffirmed." The Final Resolution was, therefore, amended to include the statement that "one adheres to the Communist Party in order to become a Communist." Likewise, Leroy noted that it was necessary to emphasize the party's "scientific definition of socialism," so as to differentiate it from other "models and utopias." Revisions were adopted that stressed the "revolutionary" nature of the party, and explained that the PCF's own "struggle for democratic changes" had to be understood within this context. Finally, with reference to the Union of the Left, an insertion was added, which expressed concern over Socialist and Left Radical attitudes, and warned against the strengthening of one group at the expense of another. The amendment stressed, in particular, the "pernicious character of any action which contributes toward reducing the influence of the French Communist Party."

Whether the party's grass-roots militants had indeed been instrumental in changing the leadership's policy became an issue of debate among French observers of the PCF. An analysis by André Laurens, in *Le Monde* (1-2 December), stated:

> The rectification was undertaken less on the initiative of the party leadership than that of the grass roots. In the opinion of all Communist militants there had never been so real a discussion at all levels of the organization. Some members of the Politburo then showed themselves more receptive than others to the aspirations of the rank-and-file members and encouraged them. In this case "democratic centralism," the alpha and omega of the party, operated from bottom to top—not a very frequent occurrence.

In contrast, Michèle Cotta, writing in *L'Express* (16-22 December), placed greater emphasis on the rivalry between Georges Marchais and Roland Leroy, claiming that the latter had orchestrated the grass-roots revolt, taking advantage of Marchais's absence from Paris during the month of August.

Whichever the correct interpretation, developments during the latter part of the year revealed an erosion in Georges Marchais's leadership of the party. As noted earlier, Leroy was appointed director of *L'Humanité* at the Central Committee meeting in November. Despite Marchais's emphasis on the need to promote young cadres, Leroy's replacement and new Politburo member was Jacques Chambaz, a party veteran. René Piquet and Paul Laurent, both strong supporters of Marchais's advocacy of a renewal and opening up of the party (see below), were notably silent during the Twenty-first Congress. Finally, Marchais had to respond to concern expressed by the leadership's pro-Soviet elements, most notably Jean Kanapa, that the PCF was engaging unduly along the way of polycentrism. This task was given, at the Twenty-first Congress, to Charles Fitermann, who delivered a speech characterized by its strong defense and praise of developments in the Soviet Union and Eastern Europe.

Marchais continued, nonetheless, to receive extensive coverage in the party press, his book, *Le Défi Démocratique* (published in 1973), was, as in the previous year, repeatedly publicized, and there was no marked waning in the personality cult that he had acquired. Moreover, the dissident communist monthly, *Unir pour le socialism*, which had repeatedly criticized him since his accession to the secretary-generalship, announced in June that it would no longer be publicly available. Finally, Pierre Daix, a leading critic of PCF policy and of Marchais's leadership (see *YICA, 1974*, pp. 135-37), announced his resignation from the party, in his preface to a book—*Prague au Coeur*—published in the autumn.

Domestic Views and Activities. With only some 20 percent of electoral support, the PCF's bid for power rests on the party's ability to persuade other elements of the left-wing opposition to coordinate their actions with communist policy. A major step in this direction had been taken in 1972 when the PCF, the Socialist Party and a splinter group from the Radical-Socialist Party, ultimately designated as the Movement of Left Radicals, adopted a Common Program and an electoral alliance for the March 1973 elections to the National Assembly.

In the second ballot of the elections of 1973 the combined left had polled a higher percentage of votes (46.6 percent) than the government parties (46.1 percent). With the death of French president Georges Pompidou, on 2 April 1974, the Communist-Socialist alliance was again put to the test. Since these were presidential elections, the left-wing parties were not handicapped by the nature of the French electoral system, which, in terms of seats to the Assembly, does not reflect accurately the constituencies' populations. (In 1973, the Communists and Socialists had a combined vote of over 9.7 million, and received 162 seats; the Gaullists obtained some 5.7 million votes, but received 186 seats.) For the PCF, the alliance posed both opportunities and dangers. Not least of the latter was the party's concern over the growing strength and influence of the Socialist Party, partly resultant from Communist-assisted electoral gains. In order to attain power the PCF had to further the interests of the alliance, but it had to do so in a manner that would preserve its own identity and influence. It had to also assure itself against a resurgent Socialist Party's temptation to realign itself with the political center. This meant that the PCF had to downplay its revolutionary aspirations (in order to broaden its own and the alliance's support), while, at the same time, endeavoring to commit the Socialist Party to move to the left so as to bind the two parties closer to one another.

An underlying source of friction between the Communists and Socialists has been the former's close identification with Soviet views and policies. At the beginning of the year, and partly in response to the publicity over the Solzhenitsyn case (see below), the PCF initiated a concerted campaign on the theme that "anti-Sovietism" was being used to "hinder the irresistible progress of the alliance of the left." Since the Socialist Party was, at that time, demonstrating exceptional caution in its pronouncements regarding the Soviet Union, the purpose of the PCF's campaign was not entirely clear. One of the party's main targets was the mass circulation left-wing weekly, *Le Nouvel Observateur* (see, e.g., Roland Leroy's attack in *L'Humanité*, 28 January). In its issue of 18 February, the journal examined various hypotheses that had been offered to explain the PCF's motivations. Its own interpretation was that, while the party was aware of the electoral burden engendered by its pro-Soviet identification, the number of "unconditional" supporters of the Soviet Union within the party was so great that the leadership could not discard the Soviet albatross. The only solution was to denounce anti-Sovietism with such vehemence that the Socialists would feel obliged to limit their own criticisms to the minimum and thus, by their silence, share the burden.

A similar move at binding the Socialists to the PCF by preemption was made by Georges

Marchais when, as early as 18 January and without prior consultations with the Socialist leadership, the PCF secretary-general announced on radio that, as far as he was concerned, the French left was sufficiently united to be able to present a single candidate in the first round of the presidential elections (originally scheduled for 1976).

The PCF's strategy on "anti-Sovietism" evoked a mixed response from the Socialists. The Socialist Party's first secretary, François Mitterrand, stated that he was at a loss to understand the PCF's "apoplectic fit" (*Le Monde*, 13 February), and he described *Le Nouvel Observateur* as "an indispensable vector for the diffusion of ideas that constitute the common bases of the left" (*L'Unité*, weekly organ of the Socialist Party, 8 February). At the same time, the Socialist Party did show unusual caution in its comments on Soviet policy. Thus, Solzhenitsyn's arrest and expulsion from the Soviet Union drew only moderately worded criticism, and, in an interview given to *Le Nouvel Observateur* (11 February), Mitterrand, while noting that he retained "the right to judge the regimes and policies of the Soviet Union and the countries of the East," added: "Anti-communism is incompatible with the union of the left, which rests on a loyal alliance. . . . As for anti-Sovietism, if some socialists were to argue today in the same manner as Foster Dulles once used to, then we would have nothing to do with them." On the same occasion, and in response to a question concerning Marchais's call for a single left-wing candidate in the presidential elections' first ballot, Mitterrand responded: "Georges Marchais's hypothesis is a serious one, and the Socialist Party is far from rejecting it. It would create, right from the outset, a powerful dynamism. But it happens to be a tactical consideration which will have to be decided by the Socialist Party when the time comes."

While maneuvering to retain the initiative in the left-wing alliance, the PCF appeared equally anxious to emphasize its unity and extend its public appeal. At the party's first Central Committee meeting of the year (18-19 January), Marchais stressed that the left was "more united every day," but warned that it was necessary to "rally the broad popular masses around a democratic policy responding to their needs and feelings. . . . Those who want to ignore this reality, the necessity of a democratic transition, can only experience bitter disappointments. The revolutionaries are those who rally the popular forces capable of going through the stages of the struggle for socialism and not those who want to bypass the stages." (*L'Humanité*, 22 January.) At the March meeting of the Central Committee, Marchais reiterated that it was "absolutely necessary" for the left-wing alliance to extend itself to "include new forces," and added: "Having said this, let me add that the Common Program is not a program for building socialism, let alone communism! It is a program for profound democratic reforms." The party's "only objective," he stated, was to "achieve the broadest possible alliance of all possible forces." (Ibid., 22 March.)

On the day of Pompidou's death, *L'Humanité*, (2 April) carried the text of a television interview in which Marchais once again brought up the issue of anti-Sovietism and reasserted the PCF's identity by declaring: "Without the PCF there would be no Common Program. There would be no victory possible." But, thereafter, for at least the duration of the electoral campaign, PCF pronouncements were of a more conciliatory nature. A meeting of the Central Committee, on 4 April, formally decided to endorse François Mitterrand as the sole candidate of the left, and a letter was delivered to Mitterrand personally by Marchais informing him of the PCF's decision (see *L'Humanité*, 6 April). In a speech on electoral strategy, delivered to a Central Committee meeting on 8 April, Marchais admitted: "Obviously, under the conditions now prevailing, the majority of the French people would not vote for a communist presidential candidate" (ibid., 9 April).

Twelve candidates presented themselves at the first ballot (on 5 May). Mitterrand received 43.35 percent of the vote, followed by Giscard d'Estaing, with 32.9 percent. The Gaullist candidate, Jacques Chaban-Delmas, obtained 14.6 percent. the PCF's tactics, which had hitherto combined strong organizational support for Mitterrand with an emphasis on their own commitment to freedom and liberty (see, e.g., Marchais's speech in Dijon, in *L'Humanité*, 24 April), now concentrated on wooing the Gaullist vote. A Central Committee resolution of 7 May, calling for a "rallying of all national and popular energies without exception," claimed that a Giscard d'Estaing victory "would eliminate all trace of the positive aspects of General de Gaulle's foreign policy" (ibid., 8 May). Marchais's press statement went considerably further:

> The Communists and the Gaullists share things which do not depend on any electoral considerations but go really deep. I refer to our attachment to the nation and its greatness and our desire to see our people rallied together with a view to insuring a fairer and more fraternal society to whose progress all French people would really contribute. (Ibid.)

Marchais then went on to evoke Gaullist-Communist cooperation "in the Resistance, later in France's reconstruction, against the European Defense Community, for Algerian self-determination and against the OAS, and against the U.S. intervention in Vietnam." Claiming that France had "always profited from this cooperation," Marchais concluded: "This is why many French people have always hoped that they would meet again. It is time this should happen." (Ibid.)

In the second round of the elections, on 19 May, Giscard d'Estaing was elected with 13,396,203 votes as against Mitterrand's 12,971,604. An editorial in L'Humanité (20 May), entitled "Inexorable Progress," answered the question "A setback for the left? " with its own interrogative response "Who could seriously support such a thesis? " The party's newspaper stated that the "power of big capital" was under "suspended sentence," that the most important aspect of the elections was the "progress of popular unity . . . and the assertion that this alliance is irreversible," and concluded: "For a France that works and thinks it will be a season of struggles and trust. And the fruits will exceed the promises of the flowers."

On 10-11 June, a meeting of the PCF's Central Committee undertook an analysis of the electoral campaign. The main thrust of the discissions (ibid., 13 June) and of Georges Marchais's report (ibid., 12 June) was that the Union of the Left had to extend itself to encompass the rest of the "great majority" of the French people who desired change. "Many French people," Marchais claimed, "were deceived by the unbridled demagogy of Giscard d'Estaing and believed that by voting for him they were voting for change. It is out of the question that we should see these people as rightists and give them up for good." At the same time, Marchais went on, one should remember that "anti-communism and anti-socialist slanders" would always be "one of the main weapons of rightist propaganda," and "even though an advanced section of the working class and some of our electorate support socialism, the majority of our people is not yet prepared to accept it." Therefore, the reforms that the PCF should advocate should be "simply aimed at democratizing French society by reducing the power of big capitalist companies and at the same time creating the necessary prerequisites for satisfying popular and national needs." The reforms, Marchais explained, "would be limited but essential." The first task was to win over supporters for "the struggle for purely democratic objectives," then, "as a result of their experience" and the party's "political and ideological action, they [would] also become supporters of socialism." This proposal for "an alliance and action for real change," was, Marchais concluded, addressed to "our entire people, all workers, and all victims of big capital." This meant, however, that the party would have to extend itself. "It is necessary," Marchais stated, "to think big and see things in terms of many tens of thousands on a national scale." One of the prerequisites, therefore, was to "put an end to a kind of merciless selection practiced by some of our organizations which, as a result, keeps away from our party, under various pretexts, men and women who have every reason to belong to it."

Other participants in the Central Committee's deliberations elaborated on Marchais's views. According to L'Humanité's report, several speakers noted that to many voters the Common Program had seemed to be too radical, and the question was raised whether one shouldn't sift out unsuitable formulations. At the same time, Etienne Fajon warned that whenever the PCF had undertaken an opening such as the one proposed it had witnessed the development of "leftist phenomena." Léo Figuères described "the pernicious role of the leftist groups during the presidential elections." They had portrayed the Common Program as bourgeois, and had syphoned off votes from Mitterrand's candidacy. "The struggle against leftism, and Trotskyism in particular, must be continued. The battlefield must not be left to them."

The Central Committee meeting coincided with the opening of a major two-week (10-25 June) PCF public relations campaign under the slogan "Le parti communiste à coeur ouvert" (the Communist Party with open heart). Through the remaining summer months massive recruitment drives were undertaken, some hitherto closed party meetings were opened to the public, and the PCF press and spokesmen repeatedly emphasized the party's commitment to a policy of furthering "the union of the people of France." In an interview given to the PCF weekly *France Nouvelle* (6 August), party secretary Paul Laurent explained:

> We have always affirmed that the unity of the working class is the nucleus, the base of the large anti-monopolistic movement, of the union of the people of France. . . . What is new is that today, for the first time in 20 or 30 years, we can speak of the unity of the working class as a goal essentially achieved, not as a goal to be achieved. There is a clear political union of the principal political groups of the left. Beginning with this decisive fact, completely new questions are coming to the forefront of the national scene.

Hitherto, the PCF had worked for the unity of parties with socialist goals, the task now, Laurent noted, was "to convince Frenchmen who do not proclaim such goals." This necessitated a modification in the party's strategy. By "sticking to a program of struggle for socialism" the extension of the alliances would not be advanced. A meeting of the party's Central Committee, held at the beginning of September, drew up a draft resolution for the upcoming Twenty-first Congress. The resolution claimed that the Union of the Left had become a "solid pivot of a gathering of forces capable of becoming a broad majority," and that to attain this end, the PCF was "determined to do everything, absolutely everything" (*L'Humanité*, 11 September). At a press conference, held on 8 September, Georges Marchais dismissed reports of division within the left, and claimed that both the PCF and the Socialist Party were "gaining strength" (ibid., 9 September).

Both parties had indeed gained strength since the presidential elections. The problem for the PCF, however, was that its principal ally's influence appeared to be growing faster. During the summer, public opinion polls gave the Socialists an electoral lead of approximately five percent (see, e.g., Sofrès inquiry, in *Le Nouvel Observateur*, 15 July), and Mitterrand's call for the holding of national "socialist assizes" (scheduled for mid-October) threatened to consolidate the Socialist Party's relations with other formations of the non-communist left at the PCF's expense. On 9 September—on the day following Marchais's above-mentioned press conference—Mitterrand predicted: "The Socialist Party will soon be the first party of France" (*Le Monde*, 11 September).

The first significant test of the two parties' respective standings occurred on 29 September and 6 October, when partial legislative elections were held in six constituencies, where former government ministers were seeking reelection to the Assembly. In the first round, the Socialists and Left Radicals made gains in every constituency; the PCF registered losses in all but two. Two former Gaullist ministers were reelected outright. In the four remaining constituencies, where the results called for a second ballot, there was only one Communist runner-up—Yves Péron, in the Dordogne. The Socialists had two remaining candidates, while the Left Radicals had one. On 6 October, one Socialist and one Left Radical were elected. Yves Péron lost by a narrow margin of 48.32 percent to the Gaullist candidate's 51.67 percent. On 29 September, Péron had obtained 30.43 percent, while the third-placed candidate, a Left Radical, had received 22.52 percent of the vote. Thus, it was evident that a significant segment of the Left Radical electorate had failed to switch its support to the PCF candidate.

The PCFs response to the results of these partial elections signaled the start of a series of polemical disputes between the Communists and their left-wing allies that was to continue through the remaining months of the year. In a statement dated 7 October, the PCF Politburo warned that "the drop in the electoral influence" of the party had to be "considered seriously by democrats." It claimed that the "primary objective of the men of big capital" was to weaken the PCF, and that they were "publicly rejoicing at the sight of other forces of the left becoming reinforced at the Communist Party's expense." "Under these circumstances," the statement continued, "we say frankly that the constantly repeated key phrase, the necessity for an alleged counterbalancing of the left, takes on an increasingly pernicious character because it, too, implies the reduction of Communist influence." The Politburo noted that "votes obtained by the left in the first round did not go to Yves Péron in the second," and claimed that, in contrast, "everywhere else, as always and with total loyalty, absolutely all the communist votes went to the joint candidates of the left." (*L'Humanité*, 8 October.) In a radio interview, a day later, Georges Marchais developed further the theme that it was in "the interest of the workers to have a powerful Communist Party," and that Socialist and Left Radical policy, with its emphasis on the need to counterbalance the left, was becoming "more and more pernicious," since it was directed against the PCF and not against the right (ibid., 9 October).

International Views and Activities. Traditionally aligned with the policies of the Soviet Union, the PCF reaffirmed this adherence during 1974. Mindful of domestic repercussions, the party guarded itself from too close an identification with Soviet views and activities by simultaneously affirming a strong French nationalist orientation.

The PCF's nationalism, with its strikingly Gaullist overtones, had been growing in fervor ever since the resignation (in 1969) of the late French president Charles De Gaulle. During the election year of 1973, the party's neo-Gaullism was particularly notable (see *YICA, 1974*, p. 141). In 1974, the PCF's apparent attempt to divide Gaullist ranks by emphasizing differences between De Gaulle's foreign policy and that of his successors was continued. With the death of Pompidou and the election of Giscard d'Estaing, the party strove to drive a wedge between the new non-Gaullist president and his Gaullist allies.

Some of the party's strongest evocations of De Gaulle's foreign policy were made during the year's presidential campaign. Thus, in a speech in Orleans, on 26 April, Georges Marchais claimed that the PCF had "emphasized and supported with a great sense of responsibility General De Gaulle's measures aimed at disengaging France from NATO and his refusal to subordinate [the] country's sovereignty to any foreign authority even if it is called Europe." Emphasizing that there could be no compromise on national independence, and that, for the PCF, "France and its independence are inseparable," the party's secretary-general declared: "It is high time to stop this sliding toward national abdication effected by the men of the right since 1969." (*L'Humanité*, 27 April.) Earlier in the month, during a television interview, Marchais claimed that the Communists had "rescued the national flag from the bourgeoisie's unsteady hands" (ibid., 2 April).

While emphasizing their commitment to French nationalism and independence, party spokesmen took care to differentiate between France's role in the world and the PCF's role in the international communist movement. In his speech to the Brussels conference of West European communist parties (26-28 January), Marchais noted: "Our party, which is highly aware of its national responsibilities, is decisively attached to proletarian internationalism, whose implementation in all circumstances it regards as the condition for the success of our own struggles" (ibid., 28 January). The PCF, Marchais added, would "spare no effort to consolidate it and render it increasingly dynamic." One of the principal tasks, Marchais stressed, was to counter anti-Sovietism. This phenomenon, the PCF leader claimed, was being promoted by "big capital and its political representatives." Faced with crisis at home, they were attempting to conceal the stability and progress in the socialist states by "falsifying the reality" and "multiplying their anti-Soviet campaigns." Marchais concluded that the PCF was countering back and would "continue to counter with increasing strength." "We are fighting," he stated, "and will always fight against anti-Sovietism from wherever it may come." (Ibid.).

The PCF's public statements on anti-Sovietism were reiterated on a number of occasions, primarily during the first part of the year at a time when Aleksandr Solzhenitsyn's *The Gulag Archipelago* (published in Paris on 28 December 1973) and the Soviet dissident's arrest and expulsion from the Soviet Union (in mid-February) were in the forefront of the news. A meeting of the PCF Central Committee, on 18 January, published a statement under the title of "Struggle against Anti-Sovietism Is the Concern of All" (*L'Humanité*, 19 January). At the beginning of February, the party's Politburo noted that the statement was being distributed throughout the country. Claiming that "the systematic mud-slinging campaign against the socialist countries" was becoming "ever more obvious," the Politburo warned that it was inflicting "serious damage" on "the dignity of France," and concluded:

> The Politburo recommends that the leaderships of the federations and sections, and all Communist cells, should, as the Central Committee has instructed, organize an offensive in order to repulse anti-Sovietism and spread the truth about the socialist countries through all possible information media and through discussions. (*L'Humanité*, 2 February.)

On Solzhenitsyn himself, the PCF's initial response to the publicity around the publication of *The Gulag Archipelago* was to denounce it as part of a campaign to discredit East-West relations and détente. An article in *L'Humanité* (23 January), entitled "The Solzhenitsyn Operation," claimed that "the operation" had been "admirably synchronized and orchestrated." However, the article went on, while the Western media had expected repression against Solzhenitsyn, their predictions had proven baseless. "Socialist reality," the article concluded, "does not correspond to the wishes of its enemies." A similar line was taken by Marchais at a party rally on 7 February, during which he stressed the Soviet Union's accomplishments and claimed: "This is what the champions of crisis-wracked capitalism want to cover up. This is why they talk so much about Solzhenitsyn." (Ibid., 9 February.) The party's response to Solzhenitsyn's expulsion from the Soviet Union came in the form of an editorial carried by *L'Humanité* (15 February), which defended the action by claiming that the writer had put himself above the laws of his own country. Claiming that the measures taken against Solzhenitsyn were in conformity with Soviet law, the editorial added that they were not the kind advocated by the PCF for France. The party concluded: "The struggle against anti-Sovietism is the concern of all, even of those who disagree with the measures taken against Solzhenitsyn."

The PCF's numerous comments on anti-Sovietism and the party's defense of Soviet policy were publicized extensively in the soviet media and in journals such as the *World Marxist Review*. This did not preclude the Soviets, however, from assuring their own state interests at the PCF's expense. Thus, on 7 May, during the final stage of the presidential campaign, the Soviet ambassador to France paid a call on Giscard d'Estaing, giving rise to speculation concerning the Soviet Union's preferences. In a brief statement, on the next day, the PCF Politburo noted that "relations between states . . . neither can nor should be affected by or even suspended during an election period," but added: "Nonetheless, the fact remains that considering that Giscard d'Estaing is one of the two candidates in the presidential elections, the démarche of the U.S.S.R. ambassador to France was inopportune. It is the more regrettable because it has been used as a pretext for political speculations which have represented it as an adoption of an attitude favorable to the candidate of the right." (*L'Humanité*, 9 May.) A month later, the PCF felt obliged to respond to another Soviet overture to the French government, which took the form of an article on Franco-Soviet relations, published in *Le Monde* (8 June) and written by Yuri Rubinsky, research director at the Moscow Institute of World Economics and International Relations. The PCF focused on two "errors": (1) that Rubinsky had asserted that during the presidential election campaign "no candidate deemed it profitable to use openly, at least in person, the poisoned weapon of anti-Sovietism"; and (2) that he had stated that coexistence would suffice to solve France's economic and social problems. With regard to the former issue, the PCF stated: "In fact, one candidate—and as names must be mentioned, let us state that that candidate was Mr. Giscard d'Estaing—did not hesitate, for example, to sponsor a large-scale publication and dissemination of propaganda material containing the crudest possible slanders against the Soviet Union and, furthermore, accusing the PCF of being 'Moscow's agent.' " On the second issue, the PCF responded: It is a grave error to suggest that coexistence will suffice to solve the great economic and social problems in a country like ours; in order to solve these problems in conformity with the interests of the French workers it is necessary first to eliminate the domination of the monopolies over national life." Therefore, the PCF asserted, "it was not a matter of indifference—whatever Professor Rubinsky's personal views may suggest in this respect—whether the candidate of the right, whose only objective is to maintain the authoritarian rule of big capital in France, or the candidate of a united left was elected." (*L'Humanité*, 9 June; *Le Monde*, 9-10 June.)

These small incidents do not seem, however, to have engendered any significant changes in the relations between the PCF and the Communist Party of the Soviet Union (CPSU). On 27 July, Marchais conferred with Leonid Brezhnev, and a subsequent communiqué noted that the meeting had taken place "in an atmosphere of cordial fraternity and profound agreement characteristic of relations between the two parties" (*L'Humanité*, 29 July).

In conformity to its alignment with the CPSU the PCF continued to be critical of the Maoist leadership in China. In his speech to the Brussels meeting, Marchais referred to developments in the European Economic Community, which were allegedly favoring its transformation into an "expanded Atlantic Alliance" led by the United States, and added: "Our delegation must note in this connection that the support which the present Chinese Communist Party leaders are giving this undertaking of the imperialist grande bourgeoisie is an eloquent illustration of their desertion of the principles of proletarian internationalism" (ibid., 28 January.) A similar stance was taken by an article in the party's weekly, *France Nouvelle* (8-13 May), which analyzed the anti-Confucius campaign in China with a preface stating: "The unacceptable international positions adopted by Chinese leaders (when they claim to be upholding Leninism), their demonstrated benevolence toward the world's least popular governments, providing those governments are anti-Soviet, and the fact that the stance adopted by the Chinese leaders toward the superpowers is in line with positions taken by our own reactionary leaders, are all sources of misgivings and outrage." In commemoration of the twenty-fifth anniversary of the People's Republic of China, *L'Humanité* (1 October) reiterated the PCF's contention that the Chinese leadership's aims were "to feed anti-Sovietism, to speed up the formation in Western Europe of a reactionary bloc hostile to the U.S.S.R., and to torpedo the European Security Conference."

The PCF's attitude toward the European Economic Community (EEC), which, the previous year, had been characterized by a tentative acceptance of the EEC's existence (see *YICA, 1974*, pp. 141-42), remained cautious and generally hostile. As noted above, the party's strong evocation of Gaullist foreign policy precluded any acceptance of supra-nationality, and this was repeatedly stressed by party spokesmen. At the same time, the PCF indicated that political changes in Europe might bring about an EEC that would be more acceptable to the party. In an interview given to *France Nouvelle* (5 February), Jean Kanapa offered an assessment of the Brussels conference of West European communist parties, by concluding:

For years now our country's grande bourgeoisie has tried to make believe that only one Europe was possible—the Europe of the monopolies, the Europe of blocs including military blocs, the Europe of a

Common Market subjected to the law of big capital. The greatest merit of the Brussels conference is to make perfectly credible in the eyes of the great masses that another Europe is possible and that it is necessary. The Brussels conference has outlined the general contours of such a Europe. It shows that another Europe is possible, a democratic, peaceful, and independent Europe: the Europe of the workers.

In the furtherance of this goal, the PCF was, together with the Italian Communist Party, a major advocate of coordination of West European communist party relations. The party defended itself, however, against speculation that this implied the establishment of a "new focus" of the communist movement. As explained by Kanapa, the policy was simply one of response to common problems.

A notable development during the year was the improvement in the PCF's relations with the Algerian National Liberation Front. Georges Marchais's visit to Algiers, on 11-15 September, was the first by a PCF secretary-general in more than a decade, which had been marked by polemics between the two parties. A joint communiqué, published following the PCF-FLN talks, noted that the latter had "proceeded in a friendly atmosphere," and that both parties had "agreed to cooperate in all fields on a basis of militant fraternity, mutual respect, and non-interference in internal affairs" (*L'Humanité*, 16 September).

International Party Contacts. During 1974, there were a number of multi-national gatherings involving West European communist parties. The PCF was a participant in all of them, often acting as a co-sponsor. These meetings included: an international symposium on the problems of foreign workers, held in Essen, 8-9 January; an international seminar on the "position of intellectuals in capitalist Europe," in Geneva, 11-13 January; a conference of communist and workers' parties of Western Europe, in Brussels, 26-28 January; a meeting of West European communist party leaders, held in Lyons, in March; a conference of West European communist parties on the "condition of women in capitalist countries," held in Rome, 15-17 November, which was preceded by a preparatory meeting, held in Luxembourg, 28-29 September; a conference of West European communist parties to "exchange information on the carrying out of decisions" taken at the Brussels conference was held in Düsseldorf on 1 October. The PCF also participated in the Consultative Meeting of European Communist and Workers' Parties, held in Warsaw in October, and in the subsequent preparatory meeting for a pan-European conference, held in Budapest in December.

PCF leaders also held a number of bilateral meetings. Gaston Plissonnier led a delegation to East Germany, from 14 to 19 January; he was followed by Marchais, who met with East German leaders on 11-19 February. In April, Soviet president Podgorny met with the PCF leadership in Paris, and party delegations were sent to Algeria, Guadeloupe, Israel, Martinique, and Réunion. In June, Roland Leroy hed a high-level delegation to Cuba, and Paul Laurent met with the leadership of the Italian Communist Party. Also, during the month, the PCF was host to a Soviet delegation, led by Secretariat member Boris Ponomarev. In July, Marchais was in the Soviet Union, Leroy in Romania, and Madeleine Vincent in Bulgaria. Marchais conferred with Romanian party leader Ceauşescu during a visit to Bucharest on 5-12 August. During the same month, Jean Kanapa, head of the PCF's International Department, visited Bulgaria, and Jean Colpin led a delegation to Sweden. A delegation of the pro-Soviet Communist Party of Greece, led by the party's first secretary, Kharilaos Florakis, visited the PCF on 22 August. In September, Jean Colpin led a delegation to West Berlin; Marchais, as noted earlier, headed one to Algeria, and the PCF was visited by a CPSU delegation, led by Politburo candidate Grigori Romanov. In November, Marchais attended a Swiss party congress, and met with the leaders of the Portuguese Communist Party in Lisbon. At the end of the month, Gaston Plissonnier met with Ponomarev in Moscow, and the PCF leadership held talks with CPSU general secretary Brezhnev, during his visit to Paris, at the beginning of December.

Publications. The main publications of the PCF in 1974 were: the daily newspaper *L'Humanité*;

the weekly *France Nouvelle*; the monthly theoretical journal *Cahiers du Communisme*; a popular weekend magazine, *L'Humanité Dimanche*; a peasant weekly, *La Terre*; an intellectual monthly, *La Nouvelle Critique*; a literary monthly, *Europe*; a bimonthly economic journal, *Economie et Politique*; a philosophically oriented bimonthly, *La Pensée*; and a historical bimonthly, *Cahiers d'Histoire de L'Institut Maurice Thorez*. In addition the party has a number of provincial newspapers. The MJC published *Nous les Garçons et les Filles*; the UJCF journal was *Le Nouveau Clarté*, a monthly. For intra-party work the Central Committee published *La Vie du Parti*, a monthly dealing with organizational, propaganda, educational, and other problems.

*   *   *

Agitational activity by groups that challenged the PCF from the left continued in 1974, but it no longer appeared to be characterized by street demonstrations. Instead, the emphasis was on proselytism among selected sectors of society, most notably immigrant laborers, the military, prisoners, and young factory workers. A number of the small groups that had hitherto thrived on "spontaneous" confrontation tactics either disappeared or were reduced to marginal insignificance. On an electoral level, the only group to make any headway was the Trotskyist Lutte Ouvrière, whose presidential candidate, Arlette Laguiller, received 595,247 votes (2.33 percent). Another Trotskyist organization, the Front Communiste Révolutionnaire, was the principal formation in extra-parliamentary activity. The Marxist-Leninist Communist Party of France remained the primary representative of French Maoism.

Revolutionary Communist Front. Formed in April 1974, the Revolutionary Communist Front (Front Communiste Révolutionnaire; FCR) brought together former members of the Communist League (Ligue Communiste), an organization banned by government decree in June 1973 (see *YICA, 1974*, pp. 144-45). On 19-22 December, FCR militants held their first formal congress, which adopted a new name for the organization–Revolutionary Communist League (Ligue Communiste Révolutionnaire; LCR)–and reestablished constitutional links with the Trotskyist United Secretariat of the Fourth International. Before its dissolution, the Communist League had claimed 5,000 members, a figure that corresponded to FCR and LCR adherence in 1974.

In addition to the veteran Trotskyist leader Pierre Frank, the most prominent spokesman for the FCR was Alain Krivine, a presidential candidate in 1969 and again in the 1974 elections. The Revolutionary Communist League's founding congress, in December, elected a 65-member Central Committee, which, in turn, was scheduled to elect a Politburo at its first meeting on 11-12 January 1975.

During the year, the FCR directed a number of auxiliary organizations. Within the labor movement, it operated through so-called Red Mole Groups (Groupes Taupe Rouge), active in individual factories and represented in most industries. With some 2,500 members, the Red Mole Groups encompassed approximately 300 small organizations. Their second annual conference, held on 1-3 June, brought together 1,300 participants, including observers from Belgium, Canada, Italy, Spain, Switzerland, and the United States. Some 60 percent of the participants were members of the FCR. Trade union affiliation was listed as follows: 39.2 percent CGT, 37.4 percent CFDT, and 4.7 percent FEN (Fédération de l'Education Nationale–National Federation of Education, the major teachers' union); 18.6 percent did not report any particular union affiliation. The division by sector of the work force was: 11 percent laborers and semi-skilled workers, 33 percent public service, 30 percent office workers, 10 percent professional workers, and 16 percent technicians and supervisors. Sixty percent of the participants were from the provinces, and 40 percent from the Paris region. Most of them were between the ages of 20 and 25. (*Rouge*, 7 June.) The Red Mole Groups offered the

FCR the means to extend itself beyond its traditional student environment, and, by the end of the year, there were signs that the strategy was working. An article in *Le Monde* (4 December) described the Red Mole Groups' activities and impact in the labor force, noting, in particular, the significant agitational work carried out during the postal strike.

Another of the FCR's major auxiliary organizations was the Front of Revolutionary Soldiers, Sailors, and Airmen (Front des Soldats, Marins et Aviateurs Révolutionnaires; FSMAR). In 1973, *Rouge* had published a pamphlet entitled *Où Va le Mouvement Antimilitariste?* (Where Is the Anti-militarist Movement Going?), which had described anti-militarist agitation as of "central importance" in the activity of revolutionaries. During the 1974 presidential campaign, *Le Quotidien Rouge* (16 May), a daily newspaper published by the FCR during the elections, carried the text of a petition signed by 100 soliders, which listed a number of alleged grievances and called for various changes in military life. The FCR and the FSMAR offered full support to the so-called Appeal of the One Hundred. Every issue of *Rouge* carried extensive coverage on the growing support for the petition, which, by the end of the year, had been signed by several thousand members of the armed forces, and the FCR was one of the principal organizers of the broadly based Committee to defend the Conscripts (Comité de Défense des Appelés; CDA). Members of a rival Trotskyist group, centered around the weekly *Revolution!*, were the principal organizers of the Anti-militarist Committee (Comité Antimilitariste; CAM), with which the CDA engaged in a number of joint actions. The PCF, which had initially expressed hostility to the anti-militarist movement, was, by the autumn, offering cautious support.

A parallel area of FCR attention was that represented by the movement for prison reform. Throughout the year, *Rouge* gave extensive coverage to agitation within France's penal institutions, and the FCR was one of the principal supporters of the Prisoners' Action Committee (Comité d'Action des Prisonniers; CAP), an umbrella organization encompassing several contending groups. More directly linked to the FCR were: the National Federation of Struggle Committees (Fédération Nationale des Comités de Lutte; FNCL), an organization coordinating college student activism, and the High School Front of Red Centers (Front des Cercles Rouges Lycéens; FCRL). With reference to international issues, the primary thrust of FCR activity was in its involvement with the Committee in Support of the Revolutionary Struggle of the Chilean People (Comité de Soutien à la Lutte Révolutionnaire du Peuple Chilien; CSLRPC), which held its first conference on 23-24 March and organized nationwide demonstrations on 11 September, anniversary of the fall of the Allende government.

In the presidential elections, the FCR initially proposed that the far left organizations present a single candidate, who would represent the forces to the left of the Union of the Left. Charles Piaget, a member of the PSU and a leader of the 1973 workers' take-over of the Lip factories, was chosen. When Piaget declined the offer, the FCR ran its own candidate, Alain Krivine. In the first ballot, Krivine received only 0.36 percent of the vote—a considerable drop from the 1.05 percent that he received in 1969. The FCR offered its support to Mitterrand in the second round.

The FCR's principal publication was the weekly *Rouge*, which appeared daily for the duration of the electoral campaign. The FCR and Red Mole Groups published a variety of news-sheets directed at specific industries or factories, including *Renault rouge, Le Rail rouge, L'Etincelle,* and *La Taupe rouge P.T.T.* The FSMAR sponsored a number of similar publications for circulation among the military.

Marxist-Leninist Communist Party of France. Orthodox pro-Chinese orientation was centered around the weekly newspaper, *L'Humanité Rouge*, which represented the views of members of the Marxist-Leninist Communist Party of France (Parti Communiste Marxiste-Léniniste de France; PCMFL), a group banned by the government in June 1968. Although the PCMLF did not operate openly, its statements were published in *L'Humanité Rouge* (see, for example, 11 April, 16 September, and 3 October). The PCMLF's leading spokesman during 1974 continued to be Jacques Jurquet.

The PCMLF advocated abstention during the presidential elections. A statement by the party's Politburo explained that: (1) in one form or another, all the contending candidates were representatives of the bourgeoisie, and that the "most dangerous of them all" was Mitterrand; (2) Soviet "social-imperialism" threatened France, and that, while there was a need for ideological and military vigilance, all the respective candidates' pronouncements were "capitulationist" in nature—Mitterrand, in particular, had taken a stand against anti-Sovietism just as the Soviet Union was massing an unprecedented level of troops and maneuvering its navy to "grasp Western Europe in a pincer hold"; and (3) the "struggle of the peoples of Guadeloupe, Martinique, Réunion and other colonies for their national independence" had not received the "imperative" support of any of the candidates. The PCMLF Politburo claimed that the "anti-electoralist and anti-imperialist" movement was gaining ground, and called for "indispensable revolutionary violence" to shatter the "state apparatus of the bourgeoisie" and install "a new power similar to the Paris Commune [of 1871]." (*L'Humanité Rouge*, 11 April.)

Despite its repeated calls for a broad revolutionary front, the PCMLF continued to follow an isolated path. It polemicized both with the parties of the Union of the Left and with other extreme-left groups, most notably the Trotskyists. With regard to the latter, the PCMLF appeared particularly concerned by the FCR's anti-militarist activities. As the Trotskyists' agitation within the military gained momentum, drawing the participation of a broad variety of groups (including the Communist Party's youth movement), the PCMLF's pronouncements became increasingly strident. Banner headlines in *L'Humanité Rouge* (see, e.g., 12, 26 September) called for a strengthening of national defense. The party justified its stance in terms of its perception of "frenetic Soviet social-imperialist preparations" for military "aggression" against Western Europe. Within this context, the party claimed, anti-militarist propaganda was "totally reactionary, for it aimed at disarming the popular masses, threatened by their worst enemies."

The PCMLF's isolation from the mainstream of left-wing activity was reflected on a number of other issues, and on no occasion did the party actively cooperate with other groups. While it did pursue a policy of proselytizing among immigrant workers—one of the few areas which corresponded to other extreme-left groups' concerns—the PCMLF acted independently, repeatedly accusing its rivals of "counter-revolutionary sabotage." Similarly, the PCMLF expressed strong denunciation of "Trotskyist maneuvers" when its own 1 May demonstrations in Paris ended up coinciding (both in time and place) with those of other leftist parties (see *L'Humanité Rouge*, 2, 9 May).

As in preceding years, most of the PCMLF's activity was of an international orientation. The party-sponsored Centre d'Information sur les Luttes Anti-impérialistes (CILA) and the Mouvement National de Soutien aux Peuples d'Indochine (MNSPI) organized several meetings in solidarity with groups supported by the Chinese, most notably Palestinian guerrilla movements and the Cambodian forces headed by Prince Norodom Sinanouk. A new departure during the year was the extent of the favorable coverage given to developments in Algeria, which the party coupled with criticisms of the French Communist Party's Algerian policies (see, e.g., Jacques Jurquet's four-volume *La Révolution Nationale Algérienne et le Parti Communiste Français*, Paris, Editions du Centenaire).

The PCMLF's alignment with and defense of Chinese policy was total. It continued to direct the Association des Amitiés Franco-Chinoise, which held its Eleventh Congress on 2-3 June. *L'Humanité Rouge* (26 September) reported on visits to China by PCMLF-sponsored "women's, youth, and worker" delegations. Earlier in the year, a party militant, Claude Lebrun, was a quest of the Albanians (*L'Humanité Rouge*, 16 May). The party also appeared to be deepening its relations with non-ruling pro-Chinese parties, with *L'Humanité Rouge* offering significant coverage on their activities and regularly reporting on exchanges of greetings between the French Maoists and their foreign counterparts.

Although the PCMLF appeared to be the only significant Maoist group in the country, and the only one to be recognized by the Chinese, it continued to devote considerable space in its newspaper to attacks against potential challengers. During the year it focused primarily on a group centered around the weekly *Front Rouge*, which, in March, formed a rival Parti Communiste Révolutionnaire (Marxiste-Léniniste) (see *L'Humanité Rouge*, 31 January, 11 and 18 April, 2 and 9 May, and 9 June).

In addition to *L'Humanité Rouge*, the PCMLF expresses its views through an irregular theoretical journal, *Prolétariat*. During 1974 it also initiated the publication of a monthly supplement to *L'Humanité Rouge*, directed at rural workers and entitled *La Faucille*.

Stanford University   Milorad Popov

N.B. Because of the French postal strike only partial information was available for the last three months of the year. The 1975 survey of France will incorporate significant developments that occurred during the last quarter of 1974.

Germany: Federal Republic of Germany

During World War I, a revolutionary group within the Social Democratic Party of Germany (Sozial-demokratische Partei Deutschlands; SPD) formed the Spartacist League under the leadership of Rosa Luxemburg and Karl Liebknecht. On 31 December 1918, following the end of the war and in the wake of the November Revolution of the same year, the Spartacist League founded the Communist Party of Germany (Kommunistische Partei Deutschlands; KPD). The attitude of the German communists toward the Republic during the Weimar period was characterized by uncompromising hostility which even went so far as to take occasional common actions with the Nazis against the Social Democrats and the other political parties of the Weimar Coalition. The KPD benefited from the severe economic depression in Germany and steadily increased its influence. In the November 1932 elections the party received almost 6 million votes out of a total valid vote of about 35 million. During the Third Reich, the KPD was outlawed. It then continued its activities underground, although with little result except in the field of espionage on behalf of the Soviet Union. For example, the Red Chapel (Rote Kapelle) was an outstanding example of communist espionage in favor of Moscow.

In 1945, the KPD was reconstituted in the Four Occupation Zones of Germany and in the area of Greater Berlin. Soviet occupation authorities forced the Social Democratic Party to merge with the much smaller KPD in their area of occupation and in the Soviet sector of Berlin. The new party thus formed was called Socialist Unity Party of Germany (Sozialistische Einheitspartei Deutschlands; SED). In the three Western zones of occupation, which in 1949 became the Federal Republic of Germany (FRG), the KPD was outlawed as an unconstitutional party on 17 August 1956 after the Federal Constitutional Court found the party's objectives and methods in violation of Article 21/2 of the FRG Constitution.

In 1949, in the first elections in the FRG, the KPD obtained 5.7 percent of the vote and was represented with 15 deputies in the Bundestag. At the next elections, in 1953, the vote for the communists dropped to 2.2 percent and the KPD therefore lost its representation in the federal legislature. After the party was outlawed, the KPD operated as an underground organization with its chairman, Max Reimann, directing the activities from East Berlin. In 1965, the German Peace Union (Deutsche Friedensunion; DFU) was founded by communists, former socialists, and pacifists. In the elections of the same year this new party polled only 1.3 percent of the vote. The DFU is still in existence and operates as an ineffective communist front organization in spite of its merger with the International of War Resisters (Internationale der Kriegsdienstgegner; IDK) and the Association of War Service Resisters (Verband der Kriegsdienstverweigerer; VK).

In 1967, German communists launched a campaign demanding that the "illegal" judgment of 1956 which outlawed their party be set aside, an effort which was still in process during 1974 in spite of the fact that a new communist party, the German Communist Party (Deutsche Kommunistische Partei; DKP), was founded on 22 September 1968. The constitutionality of the DKP is frequently under debate.

At the time of the founding of the DKP, the underground KDP was thought to have about 7,000 members. Almost all of the underground members joined the DKP, following the example set by the KPD leaders who formed the leadership of the new party. A report of the Federal Service for the Protection of the Constitution (Bundesverfassungsschutz; BVS), prepared in 1971, provided proof that the DKP is indeed a replacement and successor organization of the outlawed KPD. This report, however, did not become known outside government circles until 1973. The BVS, for example, reported that all of the nine members of the leadership group of the DKP during the initial organization phase, the "Working Committee of the Federal Committee for the Creation of a Communist Party," were known high officials of the KPD or the Free German Youth (Freie Deutsche Jugend; FDJ) prior to the time when the communist party was outlawed. There is also proof that at least seven of them continued to be active in the underground KDP. Of the 46 members of the "Federal Committee," information on underground activities is lacking only for six, and these are mostly young members. Most of the other 40 committee members held high positions in the KPD.

The committees in the *Länder* had a total of 339 members. At least 231 were working in the KPD prior to the time when the party was outlawed. At the end of 1970, the total number of DKP officials working at the federal and *Land* levels was 663. At least 440 (67 percent) of these leading officials were members of the KPD prior to the outlawing, and 523 (79 percent) were active in the underground party. Of the 103 officials working for the DKP on the federal level, at least 86 (83.5 percent) played an active part in the underground KPD. All nine members of the "Party Presidium" were active officials in the outlawed KPD. (*Die Welt*, Hamburg, 29 March 1973.) There are numerous pronouncements by DKP officials that the party considers itself a part of the communist world movement. However, the socialist-liberal government of the FRG does not intend to outlaw the DKP as a successor organization to the KPD. Former chancellor Willy Brandt, while in office, assured Soviet party chief Brezhnev, at their Crimea meeting, that the DKP is a legal party. The West German communists are receiving open support from Moscow, a policy quite contrary to the normal practice. Soviet leaders usually make a clear distinction between state and party and are quite willing to maintain close ties with governments which suppress and persecute domestic communists (as in Spain and most of the Middle Eastern countries).

Leadership and Organization. The West German communists maintain a skeleton organization of the illegal KDP, although as a result of the activities of the DKP its significance to Moscow is probably limited. Even though it is most unlikely that under the FRG's present socialist-liberal government the DKP will be outlawed as an unconstitutional party, in that event the existence of an underground organization would greatly facilitate the continuation of communist-directed operations. Also, experience has shown that an underground organization is a fertile recruiting-ground for Soviet espionage. The underground KDP is estimated to have about 6,000 members.

The DKP has made no official statement as to its overall membership in 1974. At the Third Congress of the DKP, in November 1973, it was stated that the party had 39,344 members. If the membership increase of the *Land* North Rhine-Westphalia is an indication, the party members may have risen to a figure considerably above 40,000. The Interior Ministry of North Rhine-Westphalia has reported that during the first three months of 1974 the membership of the DKP in that *Land* increased by about 2,000 to a total of 15,000 and the number of factory groups by 3 to a total of 93 (*Deutscher Informationsdienst*, Bonn, vol. 25, no. 1381, 30 March). The population of the Federal Republic is about 61,670,000 (estimated 1972).

It appears that the DKP was able to rejuvenate its membership by substantial recruitments among the young. According to DKP statistics, a third of the new members since 1972 are under 20 and 40 percent are 20 to 30 years old. The composition of the delegates attending the Third Congress can probably be taken as representative: of the 862 delegates, 318 were less than 30 years old, 196 were between 31 and 40 years, 233 were between 41 and 50, 79 were between 51 and 60, and 36 were over 60. The average was 36.5 years. Almost 90 percent of the delegates (759) were trade union members, reflecting the high priority given by the DKP to trade union activities. Of these 759 trade union members, 322 were engaged in trade union functions (shop stewards, factory delegates) and 207 worked in plant committees. (*Die Welt*, 7 December 1973). The congress decided, in order to increase party membership, to permit foreign workers, of whom there are more than 2,000,000 in the FRG, to become full-fledged members of the party. No information is available as to what extent this policy was implemented.

The headquarters DKP is in Düsseldorf. The organizational structure of the DKP follows the established communist party pattern. At the lowest level are the industrial and residential primary organization, which are coordinated by some 200 district (*Kreis*) organizations. (The latest figure as to the number of the basic organizations was supplied by the BVS, which put it at 1,350 in 1972.)

During 1974 there were no changes of personnel in the DKP leadership organs. Herbert Mies is the party chairman, and Hermann Gautier the deputy chairman. (For names of other high officers, see *YICA, 1974*, p. 149.) The Party Directorate (*Parteivorstand*) has 91 members; the Presidium 16; and the Secretariat, 7. There is also a Central Auditing Commission, with seven members, and a Central Arbitration Commission with nine. An illustration of the claimed "democratic process" in the DKP was the election of the Party Directorate at the Third Congress. The old directorate nominated the new one, 91 nominations for 91 positions. No nomination came from the more than 600 delegates. (*Die Welt*, 8 December 1973.)

Close cooperation between the DKP and the East German communist party was indicated in a report by the Interior minister of Rheinland-Pfalz, who stated that the DKP regional office was receiving supervision and material support from the SED regional office of the city of Cottbus (*Deutscher Informationsdienst*, vol. 25, no. 1386, 10 June 1974).

The youth organization of the DKP is the Socialist German Workers' Youth (Sozialistische Deutsche Arbeiterjugend; SDAJ) founded 4 May 1968, before the founding of the DKP. The SDAJ held its Fourth Congress 18-19 May 1974 at Hannover, with 375 SDAJ delegates and 203 guest delegates present. A few days earlier, the 500th SDAJ group was formed. Membership at that time was 27,442. The slogan of the congress was: "For effective co-determination of the youth, for democratic education—against arbitrariness of the entrepreneurs—join the SDAJ." Wolfgang Gehrke was elected as the new national chairman (replacing Rolf Priemer, who received new tasks as member of the DKP Presidium) and Dieter Gautier as deputy chairman. Some 20 delegations from the socialist and capitalist countries attended the congress, among them being representatives of the Soviet Komsomol and the Free German Youth (FDJ) from the GDR. A number of delegations came from youth organizations in the FRG, such as the Nature Friend Youth (Naturfreunde-Jugend), the League of German Students (Verband Deutscher Studenten; VDS), Socialist University League (Sozialistischer Hochschulbund; SHB) and the Marxist Student Union-Spartakus (Marxistischer Studentenbund Spartakus; MSB-Spartakus). The average age of the participants was 19 years; 76.2 percent were members of trade unions; 234 were active in factory committees or held trade union positions. (*Deutscher Informationsdienst*, vol. 25, no. 1386, 10 June; *Unsere Zeit*, 24 May.) Many SDAJ functionaries, the same as those of the DKP, receive training in the GDR or the Soviet Union. The SDAJ claims to be an independent youth organization and as such was able to obtain a subvention of DM 12,000 with the assistance of Social Democrats and Free Democrats in the Youth Welfare Committee in the city of Frankfurt (*Rheinischer Merkur*, Cologne, 19 July; *Die Welt*, 9 July).

The Marxist Student Union-Spartakus was founded in Bonn in May 1971. During the past three years, the MSB-Spartakus has developed into one of the strongest and most influential student organizations, represented in many student governments. At the time of its Third Congress, 22 February 1974, it has 4,428 members, organized in 106 groups. The 302 delegates which met in Frankfurt/Main elected unanimously the 58 members of the new MSB-Spartakus directorate. The directorate in turn elected at its constituent meeting Steffan Lehndorff unanimously as the new national chairman. Christoph Strawe, the former chairman, remained a member of the directorate but did not run for the chairmanship. Following the congress, the MSB-Spartakus held a conference about "the student movement in the class struggle." (*Deutscher Informationsdienst*, vol. 25, no. 1380, 15 March.) In June the MSB-Spartakus reported growing membership and increasing influence in the student mass movement, where it employed "unity of action" as the decisive element for strengthening its fighting power, in the same way as the communists do in the working class. The MSB-Spartakus was reported to be represented in all university cities and to have 135 groups. (Ibid., no. 1387, 25 July.)

The decision of the DKP congress to found a "socialist children's organization" was carried out in 1974. International Children's Day, 1 June, was selected by representatives of 22 already existing socialist children's groups for the DKP Children's Festival in Bottrop, North Rhine-Westphalia, and as the official founding day of the "Young Pioneers" (Junge Pioniere; JP). The participants at the meeting elected a 33-member national leadership with Achim Krooss as chairman. They also adopted "10 Basic Principles" for the JP, a statute for the organization, and a declaration entitled "Rights of the Children." DKP chairman Mies promised his party's support, and SDAJ chairman Gehrke gave the assurance of that of his organization and the MSB-Spartakus. The Soviet Union, the GDR, Czechoslovakia, Bulgaria, Hungary, and Poland sent representatives, as did the Belgian, French, and Austrian Communist youth organizations. The general secretary of the World's Children Organization, CIMEA, congratulated the children of the FRG in the name of all friends from abroad. (*Unsere Zeit*, 7 June.) According to the DKP newspaper, "conscientious discipline" is one of the educational objectives of the JP, which rejects anti-authoritarianism as a petty-bourgeois attitude (ibid.). It was reported later by the JP that many children groups, founded by sympathizers, had joined collectively the "socialist children's organization." For example, a group in Bonn was accepted which includes children of Italian and Spanish *Gástarbeiter*. (*Deutscher Informationsdienst*, vol. 25, no. 1391, 25 August.)

The MSB-Spartakus works closely with the Socialist University League (Sozialistischer Hochschulbund; SHB). These two organizations together completely control the National Union of Students. The SHB was originally the official student organization of the Social Democratic Party of Germany (SPD). Because of its extreme and radical Marxist views, and its close collaboration with the communists in violation of SPD decisions, the SHB is no longer permitted to use the "Social Democratic" designation; hence it refers to itself as the Socialist University League.

In addition to these openly DKP-controlled organizations, there are several DKP-affiliated groups, such as the already mentioned DFU, VK, and Nature Friend Youth, the Young German Democrats (Deutsche Jung-Demokraten; DJD), and the Union of Independent Socialists (Vereinigung Unabhaengiger Sozialisten; VUS). The de facto identity of the DKP with the outlawed KPD may be noted in the activities of a committee—the *Kuratorium* "Gedenkstaette Ernst Thälmann"—charged with the cultivation of the memory of the KPD leader martyred by the Nazis.

The overall number of orthodox—that is, Moscow-line—communists in the FRG was reported in January 1974 to be about 88,500. They were working in 115 organizations, in addition to numerous DKP-created local and national committees concerned with specific issues such as Vietnam, Chile, and "reactionary" employers' laws. (*Deutschland Magazin*, Munich, vol. 5, no. 6, December-January 1973/74.)

A former member of the DKP regional directorate in Ruhr-Westphalia and chairman of its factory group at the Hoesch-Steelworks, Dortmund, reported that the DKP depends for all important political decisions upon the direction from the West Department of the SED Central Committee, that leading DKP functionaries receive training at the Franz-Mehring Institute of the SED, and that two-thirds of the party's financial income comes from East Berlin. He also made reference to the "secret" part of the communist organization, stating that secret lists exist of "valuable" members, among them government employees. In order to maintain their effectiveness, they do not even receive their membership book. (*Bayernkurier*, 17 August.)

Party Internal Affairs. The year 1974 witnessed attempts by the DKP to implement the decisions as to the future work of the party made at the Third Congress. The main emphasis was placed on increasing the influence of the DKP among factory workers and Social Democrats. Unity of action remained the most important means to increase the party's impact, although continuous membership drives, infiltration of trade unions, direction and control of affiliated organizations, and participation in all *Land* and municipal elections in 1974, were also considered important activities pursuing the same objective.

The allegedly nonpartisan German Trade Unions (Deutscher Gewerkschaftsbund; DGB) and the Young Socialists (Jungsozialisten; Jusos) of the SPD could be penetrated with relative ease. DKP members were able to acquire leadership positions in the trade unions. In a number of instances, Jusos members, after encountering serious difficulties within the SPD, collectively joined the DKP as the only political party fighting for the interest of the working class and for the complete change of the prevailing social and economic system. Fifty-one of the 55 DKP candidates in the *Land* elections in Hesse (27 October) were trade union members, some of them holding important positions. The concentration of the political work in large factories in the Ruhr area was highly successful. As early as April, it was reported, DKP members had been elected into 93 factory councils (*Union in Deutschland*, Bonn, no. 15, 11 April).

A number of specific events organized by the DKP served among other purposes, such as propaganda and inducement for unity of action with other "progressive" forces, to improve the internal party cohesion and win new members. The fifty-fifth anniversary of the founding of the KPD was observed at a rally in Gelsenkirchen on 5 January 1974 with 1,000 persons attending, among them guests from the GDR. Chairman Mies declared that, at the present time, the DKP is the "revolutionary party of the working class in the FRG," and that it operates in "the spirit of proletarian internationalism" remaining closely allied with the Communist Party of the Soviet Union (CPSU). (*Deutscher Informationsdienst*, vol. 25, no. 1377, 20 January).

From 19 to 24 January, the DKP sponsored the "Week of the German Communist Party" throughout the FRG under the slogan "Loyalty of the Communists to the Commands of Lenin, Liebknecht, and Luxemburg" (TASS, in German, 3 January). On 1 May, more than 100 demonstrations and rallies were organized by the DKP in the FRG (*Unsere Zeit*, 3 May). The slogan for these events was "Workers Solidarity Makes Workers' Interests secure." On 16 August, the thirtieth anniversary of the murder of Ernst Thälmann, the DKP Party Directorate and the District Directorate of Hamburg organized a demonstration and rally under the slogan "For Peace, Democracy, Socialism, and International Solidarity" (*Deutscher Informationsdienst*, vol. 25, no. 1390, 15 August). The DKP "Festival of the Workers' Press," held on 21-22 September in Düsseldorf, was attended by about 250,000 people. Numerous delegations from East and West, among them representatives from *Pravda* and *Neues Deutschland*, demonstrated their solidarity with the struggle of the West German communists against "imperialism" (*Die Welt*, 23 September.)

One of the main targets of SDAJ activities was the Federal Armed Forces (Bundeswehr). "Soldier '74—Soldiers for Peace—For More Rights for Soldiers" was published by the SDAJ magazine *Elan* on 20 April. It accused the Bundeswehr of being armed for civil war against the working population. It included statements by Social Democratic members of the Bundestag and by the left-oriented

Democratic Action (Demokratische Aktion), which later changed its name to Democratic Initiative (Demokratische Initiative), referring to the military coup in Chile as a model or as a warning for the FRG. (*Deutscher Informationsdienst*, vol. 25, no. 1385, 20 May.) The primary propaganda target remained, however, the working youth and high school students.

The MSB-Spartakus congress adopted the following action-program for the summer semester 1974:

> Intensification of the international solidarity with the people of Chile and the people of Vietnam; fight for a Europe of peace and collective security. Defence and implementation of the democratic rights contained in the federal constitution. Against special disciplinary laws for the universities. For the termination of the *Berufsverbot* [i.e., the refusal by government offices to employ persons who are confessed opponents of the present constitutional form of government]. Mass actions to achieve the immediate demands against the anti-democratic overall university law which is antagonistic to the interests of the workers and students. (Ibid., no. 1380, 15 March.)

The DKP Secretariat ordered that the ideological education of DKP members in the factories and factory groups be intensified. Compulsory topics for the bimonthly educational meetings were:

> The significance of genuine socialism for the struggle of the working class in the FRG. The role of youth in the class struggle. The intensification of the general crisis of capitalism. Anti-communism and anti-Sovietism—ideological main weapons of the class enemy. The position of the DKP to the fight for reforms. For those *Länder* where in 1975 *Land* or municipal elections will take place, the additional topic: Why does the DKP participate in elections? (Ibid., no. 1382, Bonn, 15 April.)

The DKP's auxiliary "Marxist Workers Education" (MAB) institution was also ordered to intensify its activities, broaden its appeal, and improve its collaboration with the MSB-Spartakus, and the SDAJ was asked to work closely with the MAB, stimulate existing "Clubs of Young Socialists," and organize new clubs, primarily in large cities (ibid., no. 1385, 20 May).

Domestic Attitudes and Activities. Distinction between the DKP's internal affairs and its domestic views and activities is difficult to make because of their close interrelation. One of the most important DKP activities during 1974 was the implementation of the decision of the Third Congress that the party should participate in all *Land* and municipal elections as a means to increase its influence among the masses. Hence the DKP offered "constructive programs of demands" and ran its own candidates. Deputy chairman Hermann Gautier explained:

> We are not only carrying on the extra-parliamentary struggle. In the spirit of Lenin, Liebknecht, and Luxemburg, we combine the extra-parliamentary struggle with the struggle for positions in the legislatures. The present task is to place the struggle for parliamentary representation into the center of our work wherever elections are coming up. (*Unsere Zeit*, 25 January.)

Although about a dozen communists won offices in cities and rural communities, the DKP did poorly in all of the seven elections held in the FRG: city elections in Hamburg, 2.2 percent; communal elections in Rhineland-Pfalz, 0.5 percent; communal elections in Schleswig-Holstein, 0.5 percent; communal elections in Saarland, 1.7 percent; *Land* elections in Lower Saxony, 0.4 percent; *Land* elections in Hesse, 0.9 percent; and *Land* elections in Bavaria, 0.4 percent.

Nevertheless several thousands voted for DKP candidates, despite the slim chance that the party would clear the 5 percent hurdle. For example, the communist vote in Bavaria was 45,919; in Hesse 28,626; in Hamburg; 23,187; and in Schleswig-Holstein, 6,509. The party obtained better results in local than in *Land* elections in the same area. In the city of Marburg, for example, the DKP received 9 percent of the votes in the municipal elections (getting five seats in the city legislature, an increase of two), while only 5.1 percent voted for the party on the same day in the *Land* elections (*Die Welt*, 29

October). It appears that many communists supported candidates of the SPD. Since the main thrust of DKP election propaganda was against the "reactionary, revanchist" Christian Democratic Union/ Christian Social Union (CDU/CSU), a vote for the SPD had a better chance of keeping the "right-wing cartel" (*Rechtskartell*) from obtaining power. The election results, therefore, might give a distorted view of the actual strength of the support the DKP can count on. It also seems that the DKP did fairly well among the young voting population. For example, in the Hamburg elections 10 percent of the young males and 5.7 percent of the young females gave the communists their votes. (*Union in Deutschland*, no. 17, 25 April.)

As indicated earlier, the DKP strongly emphasizes its work within the German Trade Unions and asks its members to be active trade unionists. The trade unions offer the party one of the two main opportunities to gain influence among the masses, the other being its "unity of action" programs. Almost all DKP candidates in elections are trade union members. In the *Land* elections in Hesse, for example, 51 of the 55 DKP candidates were trade unionists (*Die Welt*, 2 September). Although the impact of the communists in the DGB is difficult to assess, the demands of young trade unionists for nationalization of industry and financial institutions, closer collaboration with the trade unions belonging to the communist-controlled World Trade Union League (Weltgewerkschaftsbund, WGB), and intensification of youth exchanges with all socialist states seem to indicate the existence of a widespread influence (*Die Wahrheit*, East Berlin, 13 September).

The DKP placed great importance also upon its "Unity of Action" tactic, utilizing day-to-day issues on the local level and in factories and topics of broader appeal to mobilize the "progressive forces." Numerous local and national committees and "citizen initiatives" (*Bürgerinitiativen*) were concerned with issues such as the support of the Conference for Economic Corporation and European Security, the struggle against multi-national corporations, and the demands for disarmament. Also the *Berufsverbot* remained a viable issue for unity of action in 1974. However, the fight against the "fascist military junta in Chile," replacing the former anti-Vietnam war protests, was at the center of the DKP's unity of action, together with the call for a broad alliance of all the victims of monopoly capitalism (*Deutscher Informationsdienst*, vol. 25, no. 1387, 25 June).

The Party Directorate session on 17 February discussed the growing conflict involving the social and political interests of the workers in the FRG with the deepening economic crisis. The DKP demanded a price freeze, an increase of wages and salaries, and sizable tax reductions for workers and low-income people (East Berlin, international service in German, 17 February). Later, Mies requested the nationalization of the big oil companies in the FRG and their subjection to full "democratic control" (ibid., 21 April). After the resignation of Chancellor Willy Brandt, the DKP called upon workers and white-collar workers to pursue their wage demands and prevent the imposition of restrictions upon trade union activities (*Unsere Zeit*, 24 May). Brandt's action was blamed upon the "sinister alliance of the reactionary circles of big capital and their political supporters in the CDU/CSU ... whose actions were facilitated by anti-communist and anti-democratic propaganda, launched against the policy of détente and democracy and against labor demands" (TASS, in English, 8 May). To finance social and economic demands arising from growing unemployment and part-time work, the DKP called upon the FRG to cut defense spending by 15 percent per year, stop paying for the stationing of U.S. troops in Germany, and increase taxes for higher income brackets (*Unsere Zeit*, 21 June).

Expelled Soviet author Alexander Solzhenitsyn was attacked as a reactionary and of being used to unleash a fresh anti-Soviet campaign. The MSB-Spartakus referred to him as a "creature of the West" (*Die Welt*, 23 February).

SDAJ activities among high school students were highlighted by a "Student Congress" on 16 March in Düsseldorf and by a "Solidarity Conference for Greece and Chile," 26-28 April, organized by order of the World Federation of Democratic Youth. Most of the "red cells" within the federal armed forces have been organized by the SDAJ. From the end of 1970 to April 1974 about 90 such groups had been identified (Hamburg radio, 16 May).

East-West German Relations. The DKP welcomed the establishment of permanent missions in Bonn and East Berlin in accordance with the "Treaty on the Basis of Relations between the FRG and GDR," ratified by the Bundestag in June 1973. At the insistence of the West German government, in order to emphasize the "special relationship" of the two states of one German nation, the officials heading these missions are not referred to as ambassadors but as representatives. This does not prevent the DKP from using the designation "ambassador."

Especially the CDU/CSU is attacked for alleged efforts to hinder the development of normal relations between the FRG and GDR. Chairman Mies stated at a meeting in Hannover:

> It is in accordance with the interests of the working population and the Federal Republic and the interests of peace and security in Europe that good-neighborly relations based on international law are developing between the FRG and the GDR—diplomatic relations, that is, of the kind that are usual and normal between sovereign states. . . . We are therefore not only rejecting all attempts by the CDU/CSU and the Federal Constitutional Court to torpedo the process of détente and the normalization of relations between the two German states, but we are also against the further surrendering of realistic attitudes and against the granting of concessions to the opponents of détente . . . (East Berlin, international service in German, 8 April 1974.)

He also emphasized that those who insisted on there being "intra-German peculiarities" in relations with the GDR were "disregarding the fact that the GDR is recognized in international law, that relations between our two states must be like those usual between all states" (ibid.).

International Views and Party Contacts. The international views of the DKP are the same as those of Moscow. Early in 1974 an editorial in *Unsere Zeit* (4 January) entitled "Peaceful Coexistence Is Class Warfare" presented in all clarity the communist interpretation of peaceful coexistence, which greatly differs from the Western belief that it means "live and let live":

> Peaceful coexistence between states of different social orders is a form of class warfare aimed at avoiding war between socialist and capitalist states, and at conducting the inevitable class conflict between socialism and imperialism through non-military means. In view of the pressure of the systematic competition between capitalism and socialism, the working class can make use of the successes of the socialist countries in the fight to improve their living conditions and extend their democratic rights and freedoms. Conditions of peaceful coexistence make it difficult for imperialism to export counter-revolution and suppress revolutionary liberation movements in other countries. Peaceful coexistence provides conditions more favorable to the struggle of the working class and other democratic forces for arms limitations, and for the use of liberated resources for social reforms in the workers' interest. The accomplishment of peaceful coexistence creates more favorable conditions for the struggle against anti-communism, which is the main ideological obstacle to winning over the majority of the working class to the struggle for fundamental social change and socialism. Thus the struggle for freedom is always class warfare, truly revolutionary politics.

In June, an article by DKP deputy chairman Gautier commemorated the Fifth Anniversary of the 1969 Moscow conference of communist and workers' parties and attributed to this conference the strengthening and coordination of the international working class. "Imperialism is not in the position to regain its lost historical initiative and to turn back the wheel of history," wrote Gautier, who stressed that one of the reasons for the change in the power relation between the socialist states and the imperialist ones is the successful anti-imperialist struggle for national independence and the orientation toward socialist developments of the people liberated from colonial yoke. (*Unsere Zeit*, 5 June.)

As far as the Chinese communists are concerned, the DKP stands solidly behind Moscow.

Chairman Mies stated:

> The German Communist Party passionately rejects the recent increased attempts of the Chinese leadership to undermine the détente process in Europe and the world and the process of implementing the principles of peaceful coexistence, and to split the international Communist and workers' movement. We want to stress in this respect that the Chinese Communist Party leaders have joined today the files and ranks of the most rightist extremist forces of our country . . . (Moscow radio, in German, 25 July.)

Prior to the Brussels conference of the communist and workers' parties of the capitalist countries of Europe (26-28 January), a preparatory meeting of representatives of parties in Great Britain, Belgium, Denmark, Greece, Spain, Italy, Portugal, Switzerland, Sweden, Turkey, France, and the FRG was held in Essen (8-9 January), initiated by the DKP. The outcome of the Brussels Conference was a voluminous declaration which, based on the main document of the 1969 Moscow meeting and the 1967 European communist party conference in Karlsbad, defined the strategy and tactic for unity of action and popular front politics for Europe's communists.

DKP chairman Mies on 30 March addressed a rally in Lyons, France, in which leading officials of six communist parties of Western Europe participated.

The DKP was among the 34 communist and workers' parties at the Prague conference (19-20 June), sponsored by the international communist publication *Problems of Peace and Socialism*, on the "contemporary phase of peaceful coexistence of the two world systems."

The all-European Chile congress in Paris (6-7 July), among the 700 delegates from 108 parties and associations were representatives from the DKP, VDS, and Association of Democratic Jurists (Vereinigung Demokratischer Juristen).

The DKP maintained its good relations with fraternal communist parties, as numerous mutual visits indicate. In January a DKP delegation visited Prague at the invitation of the Czechoslovak party. Chairman Mies led a delegation of Party Directorate members to Poland (20-24 February) at the invitation of Polish party chief Gierek. Mies led a delegation also to Sofia (27 February-1 March) at the invitation of the Bulgarian Communist Party. A six-member DKP study group visited Poland, 1-7 April. But also visits to communist parties in capitalist countries were made. A three-member DKP delegation agreed on close cooperation with the Italian Communist Party during a visit to Italy in April. Several delegations and party officials of the DKP visited Moscow and discussed various problems with high CPSU officials. A DKP delegation was in the Soviet Union from 4-15 March. Ten DKP factory stewards from Ruhr-Westphalia were in the Soviet Union from 18-28 June. B. N. Ponomarev of the CPSU Politburo and Secretariat received DPK chairman Mies on 13 August. In late June and early July, a delegation from the CPSU visited the FRG as guests of the DKP Party Directorate. Kurt Bachmann, Party Directorate member and former chairman of the DKP, on the occasion of his sixty-fifth birthday, received the "Order of Peoples' Friendship" from the Supreme Soviet of the U.S.S.R. and also the "Karl-Marx-Order," the GDR's highest order (*Unsere Zeit*, 24 June). Richard Scheringer, member of the Party directorate, also received the "Karl-Marx-Order," on the occasion of his seventieth birthday (*Die Welt*, 14 September).

The chairman of the South African Communist Party led a delegation of his party to the FRG in February.

The SDAJ sent delegations to Bulgaria and Poland, and participated in an "International Friendship Camp" (27 July-13 August) near Potsdam in the GDR (*Deutscher Informationsdienst*, vol. 25, no. 1379, 25 February, and no. 1388, 20 July).

Publications. The DKP's official organ is the daily *Unsere Zeit* printed in Düsseldorf, circulation about 60,000; a weekly edition was the only official DKP paper until 1 October 1973 and continues to appear in addition to the daily paper. *Unsere Zeit* also has a number of local supplements. Its "people's correspondents" number about 500. The DKP also publishes *Bonner Korrespondenten–DKP Informationsdienst* and the "theoretical-scientific" periodical *Marxistische Blätter* (Frankfurt), which started as early as November 1963 and was published by the August Bebel Society; its circulation has increased considerably, to 8,500. In 1969 this periodical became a publishing concern, producing and distributing the series of *Marxistische Taschenbuecher* and *Marxistische Lehrbriefe*, both of importance for the "educational work" of the party. The SDAJ weekly organ *Elan* (Dortmund) has a circulation of some 20,000. The communist children's organization, Junge Pioniere, publishes *Willibald*. The MSB-Spartakus has its own organ, *Rote Blätter*, in addition to about 170 institute newspapers appearing at almost all universities in the FRG, total circulation about 200,000 per semester. (*Hochschulpolitische Informationen*, vol. 5, no. 5, Cologne, 8 March, p. 16.)

Of great importance for propaganda work are the DKP's numerous district, local, and factory papers. As of February 1972, there were 326 district papers, with a total distribution of 150,000 copies, and 408 factory papers, with an undisclosed circulation. There is reason to assume that the number and the circulation have greatly increased since then. In Lower Saxony alone, in January 1974 there were 75 local and factory DKP papers (*Die Welt*, 14 January), and in Rhineland-Westphalia, in March, 164 factory and 113 local papers. (*Deutscher Informationsdienst*, vol. 25, no. 1381, 30 March). In February the first factory newspaper in the Turkish language came out, for 700 Turks working at a mine, and was supposed to set a new trend in communist efforts to influence the 2,000,000 foreign workers in the FRG (ibid., no. 1379, 25 February).

The SDAJ issues about 200 factory and apprentice newspapers, with a circulation of about 200,000 per month (*Unsere Zeit*, 17 May). The SDAJ is also responsible for the communist soldiers' paper *Links-um*, which is distributed within the Bundeswehr.

In addition to the publications of the DKP and its subordinate organizations, there are a number of leftist periodicals, such as the *Sozialistische Korrespondenz* (Hamburg), *Express* (Offenbach), and *Links-Sozialistische Zeitung* (Offenbach). Of interest with regard to the financial resources of such publications was the revelation of the former editor of the "Polit-Porno" magazine *Konkret* who stated that his paper was supported for years by East Berlin (*Die Welt*, 27 August).

An association of socialist and democratic publishers and bookstore operators is indirectly connected with the DKP. A chain of 37 bookstores throughout the FRG offers communist literature and material from the GDR and other "socialist" countries at very reasonable prices.

*   *   *

Other Leftist Groups—Rival Communists. In addition to Moscow-oriented communist organizations, following strictly the Soviet line, numerous extreme leftist groups carry on their "revolutionary" work, which even includes terrorist activities (during 1974 there were 70 terror actions in the FRG). The groups, some of which consider themselves to be political parties, are in a state of continuous flux. They emerge, merge frequently with other groups, break up in splinter groups, and often disappear as quickly as they came. Even the BVS has difficulties in keeping track of these "parties" and groups. It reported for 1973 the existence of 110 organizations of the orthodox Moscow line, with about 73,000 members and followers, and 207 groups of the "New Left," involving about 14,000 persons (*Die Welt*, 12 July). Some estimates of left extremist organizations are put even higher, owing to the great increase in the number of left radical periodicals and their circulation. The BVS reported that left extremist publications increased in 1973 from 1,183 to 1,380 and their weekly circulation from 483,000 to 880,000 (ibid.).

The DKP and its affiliated organizations are strongly opposed to the Maoists and other "ultra-left" revolutionary groups, which they accuse of giving aid and comfort to right-wing reactionaries in the FRG because they attack the DKP, the Soviet Union, and the trade unions (e.g., *Unsere Zeit*, 13 April 1974).

After the collapse of the Socialist German Student League (Sozialistischer Deutscher Studenten-bund; SDS), which was dissolved in Frankfurt in March 1970, innumerable communist groups, cadre organizations, and sects emerged. Most of the SDS followers found their way sooner or later to the Moscow-oriented communist organizations, although some remained unaffiliated and others iden-tified themselves with Maoism or Trotskyism.

The Trotskyists have lost influence since 1970, but it was reported in 1974 that several groups, among them the League of Socialist Workers (Bund Sozialistischer Arbeiter), fairly active in North Rhine-Westphalia, had decided to found a political party on the basis of Trotskyism. The preparatory conference was scheduled for October, in Bottrop. (*Die Welt*, 28 September.)

The Maoists are split into several "parties" and groups, each claiming to have the correct interpretation of Marxism-Leninism. Among the more important organizations is the Communist Party of Germany/Marxist-Leninist (Kommunistische Partei Deutschlands/ML; KPD/ML), a collection of originally up to eight factions. Its central organ is *Roter Morgen*. In February 1974, the KPD/ML commenced with the publication of a theoretical periodical, *Der Weg der Partei*. In its first issue, the German "monopoly bourgeoisie" and the GDR were accused of treason against the German nation. The paper demanded the expulsion of the occupation powers and their lackeys from German soil and the creation of a unified, independent, socialist Germany under the leadership of the working class. (*Deutscher Informationsdienst*, vol. 25, no. 1386, 10 June.) The funeral of a KPD/ML member, who had died of a natural cause (he was a registered bleeder) one week after a confrontation between followers of the KPD/ML and police in Duisburg, was made the occasion for a demonstration of about 2,000 followers. They pledged vengeance. A party official exclaimed: "Who does not wish to be destroyed, must destroy the enemy. This, however, can only be accomplished with revolutionary power." (*Rheinischer Merkur*, 28 June.) The KPD/ML managed to obtain free radio time before the elections in Hamburg and used the opportunity to propagate the necessity of an armed uprising (*Die Welt*, 2 March).

Another Maoist organization is the Communist League of West Germany (Kommunistischer Bund West Deutschlands; KBW), which publishes the *Kommunistische Volkszeitung*. It came into existence in Bremen in June 1973 through the merger of about 25 communist groups, with a political platform drawn up primarily by former Heidelberg SDS members. The KBW creed centers on the necessity of smashing the bourgeois state apparatus by means of violent revolution and the establish-ment of a proletarian dictatorship (*Deutsche Zeitung*, Stuttgart, 1 March 1974).

Also the Communist Workers' League of Germany (Kommunistischer Arbeiterbund Deutschlands) belongs in the Maoist camp. It has a central organ, *Rote Fahne* (monthly until September 1974, thereafter biweekly).

By far the most significant Maoist "party" is the new "KPD," which is not a successor organization of the outlawed Moscow-oriented KPD (which, as has been pointed out, still exists as an underground party). This KPD was recognized as a political party on 10 January 1974 by the German courts according to Article 21 of the Basic Law and the laws concerning parties. This decision was made in spite of the fact that the federal Interior minister had previously stated that the aims (e.g., proletarian armed revolution) and activities of the KPD were unconstitutional. (*Neue Zürcher Zeitung*, 13 January; *Deutscher Informationsdienst*, vol. 25, no. 1377, 20 January). The forerunner of this new KPD was the KPD Construction Organization (KPD-Aufbauorganisation; KPD/AO), founded by former left-radical students in West Berlin after the collapse of the Extra-Parliamentary Opposition. In July 1971, the "AO" part of the designation was dropped. In the beginning of 1972 the KPD moved its headquarters to Dortmund. The party has about 5,000 members, candidates, and activists, with an average age of 25 years and claims at least another 5,000 sympathizers. One Central Committee member claimed 13,000 sympathizers and 2,000 activists. (*Die Welt*, 18 March 1974).

Twenty-five percent of the members are women. The organization follows the communist pattern. The party is headed by a 15-member Central Committee, which "elects" from among its own members the eight-member Politburo and a five-member "Permanent Committee." This latter committee leads the party between meetings of the Politburo. It is planned, however, that the collective leadership of the "Permanent Committee" will be replaced by an "elected" chairman. The highest organ of the party is the party congress. It has at least four regional committees, four city committees (Nürnberg, Frankfurt, Bremen, and West Berlin), 18 local directorates, some 70 cells, and a network of Revolutionary Trade Union Opposition Groups (*Revolutionaere Gewerkschafts Opposition*) in factories and in the DGB (*Deutscher Informationsdienst*, vol. 25, no. 1381, 30 March, and no. 1389, 28 July). It publishes a weekly, *Rote Fahne*, in an edition of about 25,000. Another KPD weekly, *Rote Presse Korrespondenz*, has a circulation of 4,000. The *Kommunistische Arbeiterpresse*, in more than 40 different editions, supports the KPD's work within the factories.

The KPD leaders have decided to give their party a program. A draft was submitted to a mass rally on 16 March 1974 in Düsseldorf, attended by about 2,500 persons. One section, concerning the "proletarian state," reads:

> Since the power in the state is the basic issue of every revolution, the armed, proletarian revolution to begin with destroys completely the bourgeois state machinery. The working class establishes a proletarian state on the ruins of the old society as means for the suppression of the overthrown class of exploiters and for the victorious construction of socialism and communism. (Cited in *Deutscher Informationsdienst*, vol. 25, no. 1381, 30 June.)

Horlemann also declared that a priority task of the party and its youth organization, the Communist Youth League (Kommunistischer Jugendverband; KJV), is "to turn around politically the armed forces of the FRG" (*Frankfurter Allgemeine Zeitung*, 18 March).

The first KPD party Congress took place at a secret location in Cologne on 26-28 June. Of the 153 delegates, 34 percent were workers of large factories, 16 percent office "workers," 31 percent "working intelligentsia" (physicians, engineers, etc.), and the rest students and pensioners. On 29 June a public meeting of the party Congress was held in Cologne, attended by some 5,000 persons, mostly young. Numerous delegations from foreign Maoist and revolutionary parties and groups, along with representatives of revolutionary organizations of foreigners in the FRG, were at this meeting. (*Deutscher Informationsdienst*, vol. 25, no. 1389, 28 July).

The KJV coordinates the work of the Communist Students League (Kommunistischer Studentenverband; KSV) and the Communist High School Students League (Kommunistischer Oberschueler Verband; KOV). The KSV, with a membership of several hundred, is primarily responsible for the revolutionary disturbances at the universities during 1974. It was founded in May 1971 and is known to use violence against persons who do not share its views and against police officers. The KOV has been able to draw sympathizers into its action program. (*Die Welt* 12/13 January 1974.) The KOV publishes a bi-weekly paper (monthly until the summer of 1974), the *Schulkampf*, in about 10,000 copies. The KSV's work is to revolutionize the high school students. (*Deutscher Informationsdienst*, vol. 25, no. 1386, 10 June.) The youth organizations of the KPD work effectively under a rigid and "appointed" leadership. (*Deutsche Zeitung*, 1 March 1974.)

The KPD decided to participate in some of the elections in 1974 and in those in the following year. At the *Land* elections in Hesse on 27 October, the party's 20 candidates received 4,152 votes, or 0.1 percent. On the same day, in the *Land* election in Bavaria, the KPD obtained 6,719 votes, again 0.1 percent.

In addition to the "German" left extremist organizations, there are also several foreign left radical groups active in the FRG, such as the Iranian Students' League (CISNU), the Student Federation of Turkey in Germany (ETÖF), the Latin American Working Group (CUPLA), the

TRIKONT-organization of Italian workers abroad (FILE), and the Revolutionary Workers of Turkey (TDI). (*Deutscher Informationsdienst*, vol. 25, no. 1387, 25 June.)

University of Calgary   Eric Waldman
Canada

Germany: West Berlin

The Socialist Unity Party of West Berlin (Sozialistische Einheitspartei Westberlin; SEW) is the creation of the Socialist Unity Party of Germany (SED) of the German Democratic Republic (GDR). It was not founded by communists in West Berlin. Originally it was the SED organization in the three western sectors of Berlin. Therefore, up to the time of the alleged separation from the "mother party," it has the same history as the SED.

In the spring of 1959 a West Berlin leadership was set up to give the impression that the SED in the western sectors of the city was an independent political party. This occurred five months after Khrushchev had demanded the formation of a "free city." The proforma separation from the SED of the GDR took place on 26 April of that year, but the transformation of the West Berlin communist organization to its present form required further steps. In November 1962 the West Berlin headquarters organized a conference of delegates. This conference assumed for the party a new set of rules (*Parteistatuten*) and adopted the name "Socialist Unity Party of Germany-Westberlin" (SED-W). The building of the Wall, in 1961, separating East and West Berlin, made this organizational division, at least for the outside world, an optical necessity.

In order to remain in harmony with official Soviet policy which emphasized the "independent political entity of West Berlin," the SED-W held a special congress in February 1969 and changed the name of the party to the present form, Socialist Unity Party of West Berlin. The elimination of "Germany" from the name represented an implementation of the policy which assigns the term "Germany" only to the ruling communist party in the GDR, implying that the SED is the only communist party responsible for the whole of "Germany" and that the other German communist parties merely carry out the tasks assigned to them by the SED. (See Eric Waldman, *Die Sozialistische Einheitspartei Westberlins und die Sowjetische Berlinpolitik*, Boppard am Rhein, 1972.)

The SEW membership in 1974 is estimated to number about 8,000. The population of West Berlin, according to a 1969 estimate, is 2,134,300.

Leadership and Organization. Even though the SEW is a small party in a very limited territory, its organizational structure follows the typical communist party pattern. The 47-member Party Directorate (Parteivorstand) is the equivalent of a typical central committee. The Party Directorate, the 12-member Buro (equivalent to a typical Politburo), and the 7-member Secretariat form the leadership group. Following the administrative subdivisions of West Berlin, the party has 12 district (*Kreis*) organizations. Each of these has a District Directorate (*Kreisvorstand*) and Secretariat. Factory and residential groups (*Betriebs-und Wohngruppen*), party groups in institutions of higher learning, comprise the primary party organizations. The SEW headquarters is in Berlin 10, at Willmersdorfer Street 165.

The 12 top party leaders—the Buro—have been in office at least since the SEW's Second Congress, in 1970, including party chairman Gerhard Danelius and deputy chairman Erich Ziegler (for other names see *YICA, 1974*, p. 158). The Fourth SEW Congress dropped Gerd Ellert, unanimously reelecting the other 12 Buro members. (*Die Wahrheit*, 18 November 1974.)

Until the late 1960s a relatively small percentage of young people belonged to the party. A concentrated party effort among the young and the influx of former members of the youthful Extra-Parliamentary Opposition (see below, "Other Leftist Groups") have resulted in a downward trend in the average age. At the Fourth Congress in November 1974 the average age of the 639 delegates was 37 years, with one-fifth under 25, one-fourth between 26 and 30 and one-fourth between 31 and 40 (ibid.).

Some SEW members were concerned about the impact of the increasing number of students and intelligentsia upon the social structure of the party. Chairman Danelius attempted to dispel this concern by stating that 80 percent of the party members came from the working class and, furthermore, that the party's "experience with students, scientists, artists, and teachers who became SEW members was excellent" (ibid., 13 September 1973). According to the *World Marxist Review* (January 1974, p. 132), the social composition of the party is as follows: workers comprise 71.9 percent of the membership; employees, 14.2 percent; students, 7.0 percent; and intellectuals, 2.4 percent. Women make up 40.5 percent of the membership.

Since the SEW is a relatively small party it must to a large extent utilize mass and front organizations in West Berlin and penetrate trade union organizations in order to reach larger segments of the population than would be possible by means of the party membership alone. The Free German Youth in West Berlin (Freie Deutsche Jugend-Westberlin; FDJ) has about 1,000 members and is responsible for the communist children's organization in West Berlin and for the Pioneer groups. The FDJ has been particularly successful in the city district of Steglitz, where in November 1973 it was accepted in the district Youth Association with the support of the Falcons and the Nature Friend Youth (both Social Democratic organizations), the Youth Work of the Protestant Free Churches, the German Youth League, the Association of German Boy Scouts, and the Protestant Youth (*Die Welt*, Hamburg, 10 January 1974; *Die Wahrheit*, 9 January). The Trade Union Youth Conference for West Berlin passed with a strong majority a resolution in favor of admitting the FDJ-W (*Die Wahrheit*, 14/15 September). The FDJ-W held a city wide conference 1-3 June 1974, in which 300 elected delegates and representatives from 14 foreign youth organizations, representatives of foreign workers in West Berlin, and delegations from "democratic" and "youth" organizations took part, as did SEW leaders Danelius and Ziegler (ibid., 4 June).

The Society for German-Soviet Friendship-West Berlin, another SEW subsidiary, has made its "Club DSF" and "Mayakovski Gallery" into an information center on the Soviet Union and the GDR, featuring lectures, movies, art shows, and other cultural exhibitions. Other organizations working for the SEW are the Democratic Women's League of Berlin, the Alliance of Victims of the Nazi Regime, the "Permanent Working Committee for Peace and for National and International Conciliation, West Berlin," and the Berlin Renters' Association (see Waldman, op. cit., pp. 101-9).

The SEW recruiting effort places special emphasis not only on the proverbial "working class" but also on intellectuals, artists, and students because of their possibility to influence further segments of the population. For example, in October 1973 it established the Association of Democratic and Socialist Artists of West Berlin, defined as a union of creative artists and intellectuals who realized their responsibility to work for a democratic culture and peace (*Die Wahrheit*, 9 October). Among students the SEW has activated groups at the Free University, the Technical University, and other post-secondary educational institutions in West Berlin. These groups work closely with the Action Union of Democrats and Socialists (ADS), which is also directed by the SEW. During the past three years the ADS has become the most important political organization among students in West Berlin, in the summer semester of 1973 obtaining 70 percent of the votes in elections at the Free University.

At the same time, the ultra-left student organizations, including the Peking-oriented Communist Student Union (see below), have made gains.

Party Internal Affairs. The major intra-party event during 1974 was SEW's Fourth Congress, 15-17 November, where members were provided guidance for their work for the Berlin elections set for 2 March 1975. It was attended by 639 elected delegates.

Two other intra-party organizational activities must be noted. The first was preceded by elections (15 March to 30 May) for the directorates of the primary party groups and for delegates to the conferences of district delegates and by elections (1 September to 15 October) of the district directorates and the delegates to the Fourth Congress. The SEW Directorate pointed out the need for preparation for the West Berlin elections set for 2 March 1975, and laid down the following tasks for the party organization: (1) to develop further the unity of action of all democratic, progressive, Social Democratic, communist, and nonaffiliated forces in order to strengthen the position of the workers and reduce the power of monopoly capitalism; (2) to broaden the anti-imperialist movement in order to make peace in Europe and the world more secure; (3) to work for better utilization of possibilities of normalizing relations between West Berlin with the socialist world, simultaneously benefiting West Berlin and serving the interest of peace; and (4) to strengthen the party by getting new members. The directive also set the task of overcoming the "undemocratic" 5 percent clause and sending representatives of the SEW into the legislative bodies of West Berlin. (The West Berlin electoral law requires that a party must obtain at least 5 percent of the overall vote before its candidates are considered for an elected office.) The directive stated that the factory and residential groups were the most important link between party and the working class. (*Die Wahrheit*, 31 January.)

The "Second Organization-Political Consultative Meeting of the Party Directorate," on 15 June, and subsequent special membership meetings of all party groups had the purpose of improving work among the "masses" and winning new sympathizers, party members, and subscribers for the official party organ, *Die Wahrheit*. Some of the party groups set themselves the goal of increasing their membership one-third by the end of 1974.

There was no change in the financial situation of the SEW in 1974. The party continued to receive substantial "contributions" from the SED. A conservative estimate of the funds received from East Berlin is between 2.5 to 3 million DM per annum. The SEW continued also to put great emphasis on the ideological schooling of party members and sympathizers (see *YICA, 1974*, p. 160).

Domestic Attitudes and Activities. The "12 Basic SEW Demands" promulgated by the Party Directorate in September 1973 continued throughout 1974 to serve as the party program (*Die Wahrheit*, 10 June). The "demands" set forth long-range objectives, such as the transformation of all private monopolies and large economic enterprises into common property, and short-range ones, such as the demand for control and co-determination to be exercised by the workers, their factory councils, and trade unions over the entire management of economic enterprises. An article in the SEW organ referred to the economic difficulties of the "capitalist countries of Europe" as a "deep crisis" which was making the establishment of socialism "not only an objective possibility but an urgent requirement of the time" (ibid., 4 April). Maintaining that the socialist transformation of society is its final objective, and that the daily struggle must be combined with this aim, the party stated: "This connection is decisive for understanding of the policy of the SEW, and at the same time conveys the fundamental ideological conflict between revolutionary Marxism and social reformism on the one hand, and petty bourgeois revolutionizing on the other" (ibid., 21 March); hence "social reformism cannot solve the problems of the workers" (ibid., 15 August). It follows, therefore, that communist support for co-determination means only the "limitations of the power of monopolies and the reinforcing of the fighting strength of the working class" (ibid., 29 November 1973).

The 1974 May Day demonstration was reported by the SEW as a great success which was due to the unity of action and the collaboration of democrats and socialists. The party claimed that 80,000 marched and 5,000 attended a mass meeting which was addressed by Danelius (ibid., 2 May). A number of strikes in West Berlin, especially the strike of the transportation workers, public service employees, and postal workers on 11-13 February, when more than 40,000 workers and employees were involved, had the active support of the SEW. The party saw in these strikes also the unity of action in operation and the politicization of the anti-monopolistic struggle (ibid., 14 March).

SEW university groups were active, in collaboration with the Action Union of Democrats and Socialists, and on their own in the struggle for "democratic study program reforms" (ibid., 17, 30 May, and 18 July). The party attaches great importance to its activities at the Free University (FU). Claiming that "without Marx [there is] no genuine reform of the study program," the SEW noted: "A significant aspect of the conflict pertaining to academic policies with great importance for the political work of the SEW university groups at the FU is the struggle to obtain study programs with democratic contents." On 20 June, thousands of students and other young people, along with teaching assistants and professors, demonstrated in support of this position in study content and other aims. (Ibid., 20, 21 June.)

The military coup in Chile provided a most welcome "Vietnam substitute." Hardly a day passed that *Die Wahrheit* did not have at least one article, photograph, or political cartoon concerning the "fascist dictatorship" in Chile and its alleged wave of arrests and torture of political prisoners. The Chile issue became a means for the implementation of "unity of action" since trade unions, youth organizations, various student associations, and special Chile committees could be induced to participate in demonstrations and other protest actions. In the early part of 1974, a mass demonstration of "solidarity with the Chilean people," entirely organized by the SEW, drew more than 20,000 participants, mostly young people; a second demonstration, promoted by the SEW with Social Democrats and Protestant groups, drew 30,000 (*WMR*, March, p. 44). A Chile-Solidarity Week, 4-11 September, in West Berlin and West Germany, was marked by demonstrations, collections of signatures and money, cultural events, and rallies. On 27 September another rally in support of the "people of Chile" was held by the SEW. (Ibid., 4, 28/29 September.)

East-West German Relations. SEW pronouncements during 1974 continued to reflect Moscow's and East Berlin's policies toward West Berlin and the city's "connections" (*Verbindungen*) with the Federal Republic of Germany (FRG). (The FRG prefers to interpret *Verbindungen* as "ties.") Frequent accusations were made that the Bonn and West Berlin governments were violating the 1971 Quadripartite Agreement. When FRG president Gustav Heinemann visited West Berlin shortly before he ended his term, he was said to have "tried once again to incite and solidarize himself with the anti-GDR slander of Klaus Schütz,"[the governing mayor of West Berlin]. When Heinemann accused the GDR of attempting to incorporate West Berlin, he was "obviously trying to cover up the fact that the dominating, ruling people of the FRG and West Berlin are interpreting the Quadripartite Agreement at will and, as before, are regarding and treating our city as a component part of the FRG." (*Die Wahrheit*, 5 April.) Also the visit of newly elected FRG president Walter Scheel brought forth strong communist reactions. The SEW especially objected to Scheel's promise to continue his visits as part of the effort to maintain the Federal Presence in West Berlin. (*Die Welt*, 22 July.)

Schütz and the Berlin Senate were charged with daily violations of the agreement, which under international law stipulates that West Berlin is not a component part of the FRG. They were said to be continuing to dream of using West Berlin as a "bridgehead" and as an "imperialist spearhead" aimed at the GDR and other socialist states. Thus they were acting against the vital interests of West Berlin's population, because, it was asserted, the last twenty years had proven that West Berlin is only viable when good relations are maintained with the GDR and other socialist countries. The establishment of the Federal Office for Environment, which is under the jurisdiction of the Interior Ministry in Bonn, drew violent protests from East Berlin, Moscow, and the West Berlin communists. The SEW asserted that this was a deliberate act to increase the "Federal Presence" in West Berlin and, therefore, in violation of the Quadripartite Agreement.

Most likely, one of the main reasons for the existence of the SEW is its availability to Moscow and East Berlin as an indigenous West Berlin political party for the promulgation of their Berlin policies and for making it appear to the outside world that an articulate part of West Berlin's population is behind them. Because few people, east or west, are aware of the insignificant role played by the SEW, the propaganda value of this argument is considerable.

International Views and Party Contacts. SEW Chairman Danelius and two other Party Directorate members participated as "guests" in the Conference of Communist and Workers' Parties of the Capitalist Countries of Europe in Brussels on 26-28 January 1974. Danelius addressed the conference and referred to the main objectives which the 1969 Moscow meeting of communist and workers' parties decided to pursue:

> The inviolability of the existing borders in Europe, especially the Oder-Neisse boundary and the border between the FRG and GDR; the recognition of the GDR under international law; the prevention of West Germany's access to nuclear weapons; the FRG's renunciation to be the sole representation of all of Germany; the recognition of West Berlin as·a special political entity; the declaration that the Munich Dictate was invalid from its inception.

He stated that it was encouraging to note how communists had been able to implement many of these objectives within a few years since the meeting, referring in particular to the Moscow and Warsaw treaties, the Basic Treaty between the GDR and the FRG, the Quadripartite Agreement concerning West Berlin, the treaties between the GDR and the Senate of West Berlin, and the diplomatic recognition of the GDR. (*Die Wahrheit*, 29 January.) He also expressed support for a new conference of the world communist movement (ibid., 28 January).

From 25 April to 2 May, the SEW was host to a delegation from the Communist Party of the Soviet Union (CPSU), led by L. D. Jermin, member of the Central Committee of the CPSU and the Supreme Soviet of the U.S.S.R. The delegation participated in membership meetings and rallies such as the one on May Day.

In observance of the twenty-fifth anniversary of the GDR, the SEW held a mass rally on 4 October which thousands of persons attended.

Chairman Danelius led a SEW delegation that visited Poland on 20-23 March at the invitation of the Polish United Workers' Party. At the Sixth Congress of the FDJ-W, 1-3 June, the representative of the Czechoslovak party's youth organization presented Danelius with its highest decoration, in recognition of the great assistance rendered by the SEW to the FDJ-W (ibid., 5 June).

Deputy chairman Ziegler on his sixtieth birthday received the "Order of Friendship of the People" by decree of the Supreme Soviet Presidium for services in the struggle against fascism, for democracy, and for his great contribution in establishing friendly relations between the population of West Berlin and the peoples of the Soviet Union. He also was honored with the "Star of Friendship of the People" in gold, a high GDR decoration. (Ibid., 21 February.)

The SEW participated in an "All-European Conference of Solidarity with Chile," 6-7 July, in Paris, which drew more than 700 representatives from European communist, socialist, and Christian parties trade unions, youth groups and other democratic organizations (ibid., 9 July).

A delegation from the French Communist Party visited the SEW on 16-19 September.

Publications. The most important publication of the SEW, *Die Wahrheit*, is published 6 times weekly in about 15,000 copies (until the end of October 1973, it appeared 5 times weekly). It is printed by the party's own plant. The twice-weekly *Berliner Extradienst*, 4,500 to 5,000 copies, although not an official SEW publication, endorses practically all of the party's positions and strongly supports unity of action. The SEW publishes at irregular intervals an increasing number of factory newspapers and distributes numerous leaflets calling for demonstrations and other actions, disseminating the party action program, and reporting on special current issues. *Konsequent*, a quarterly publication of the SEW, deals with ideological issues and also provides "help for argumentation" for the political work among the masses. The SEW operates a bookshop, "Das Europaeische Buch," which handles a large selection of classic and contemporary Marxist literature, mostly printed in the GDR, at very reasonable prices.

The SEW propaganda effort is supported by the publications of its subsidiary organizations, such as the FDJ-W monthly, *Signal*; the quarterly *DSF-Journal*, published by the German-Soviet Friendship Society; the monthly publication of the Democratic Women's League Berlin, *Im Blickpunkt der Berlinerin*; and the monthly organ of the Association of Victims of the Nazi Regime, *Der Mahnruf*. The "Permanent Working Committee for Peace and for National and International Conciliation, West Berlin," publishes *Der Informationsdienst* every two months. The FDJ-W, following the example of the SEW in bringing out special papers for factory and residential areas, publishes a number of high school newspapers.

*   *   *

Other Leftist Groups–Rival Communists. The "ultra left" is represented in West Berlin by numerous groups and organizations. Their continuous organizational flux makes any up-to-date enumeration impossible. There are groups of Maoists, Trotskyists, anarchists, dissident socialists, and left communists. Most of the followers are students in the universities and high schools, or dropouts, and "professional revolutionaries." They constitute the "APO," or Extra-Parliamentary Opposition, which is a generic term and only refers to the one common denominator, the rejection of parliamentary methods in the pursuit of political objectives. Some of the outstanding activities are terrorist actions against individuals and institutions. Incendiary attacks on several court buildings in West Berlin and an attempt to poison a West Berlin senator, and the murder in November of the highest judge in Berlin, Günter von Drenkmann, were the work of an anarchist group in sympathy with the Baader-Meinhof band and were meant as demonstrations against *Klassenjustiz*—a term which implies that injustice is meted out by the judicial organs of the dominant capitalist class. (*Die Welt*, 28 October 1974). On occasion, several groups may combine in "anti-imperialist" demonstrations or attempt to take over events sponsored by the SEW, the trade unions, or the Social Democrats. The SEW rejects these "pseudo-revolutionary" organizations and vehemently opposes their inclusion in communist-sponsored "unity of action" efforts. The West Berlin communists consider them non-class elements, outside the revolutionary workers' movement, who in reality serve big capital.

An ultra-left organization with increasing influence in West Berlin's post-secondary schools is the Communist Student Union (Kommunistischer Studenten-Verband). Together with other left-radical student groups, it carries the "militant class struggle" into academic institutions.

University of Calgary
Canada

Eric Waldman

Great Britain

The Communist Party of Great Britain (CPGB) was founded in 1920. Although the oldest communist movement in Great Britain, its traditional preeminence was seriously threatened in 1974 by other Marxist-Leninist groups and the "ultra left" (see below).

The CPGB is a recognized political party in Great Britain. In 1973 the CPGB at its Thirty-third Congress (10-12 November) reported an increased membership from 28,803 (1971) to 29,943—a rise of about 3 percent, of whom only 16,000 had paid their dues. This was the party's first significant gain since 1964. In 1974 the number dropped to 28,943 (*Comment*, 18 May). The population of Great Britain is 55,347,000 (Census, 1971).

Although CPGB candidates contend for national and local offices, there have been no members in the House of Commons since 1950. In national elections in February and October 1974 the party contested 73 seats, all unsuccessfully. Overall results are shown in the accompanying table.

Great Britain National Election of 10 October 1974

Party	Votes cast	Percent of total votes	Number of seats won	Percent of total seats
Communist				
Communist Party of Great Britain	17,008	0.5	— —	— —
Non-communist left:				
Labour	11,272,762	39.6	315	50.7
Center:				
Liberal	5,228,017	18.4	11	1.7
Conservative:				
Conservative	10,255,822	36.0	271	43.6
Other parties	1,683,952	5.5	22	4.0
Totals	28,457,561	100.0	619	100.0

Leadership and Organization. The National Congress is the supreme authority and policy-making organ of the CPGB. It meets biennially when called by the Executive Committee, but a special congress can be convened under extraordinary circumstances. The National Congress elects the

42-member Executive Committee, which is the highest authority between congresses. At its first meeting, after a congress has been convened, the Executive Committee elects the party offices and the Political Committee. The Executive Committee meets every two months; the Political Committee usually meets weekly or as and when the need arises. Below the leadership level, the CPGB is organized into district committees, then area and borough committees, and finally into party branches. Wales and Scotland do not have separate parties, but have area branches of the main party. During 1974, the Political Committee consisted of Tony Chater, Gerry Cohen, Vic Eddisford, Reuben Falber, Vi Gill, Mick McGahey, Gordon McLennan, George Matthews, Alex Murray, Bert Pearce, Bert Ramelson, James Reid, William Wainwright, George Wake, and Jack Woddis. Party offices and departmental heads were: John Gollan (general secretary), Irene Swann (chairman), Reuben Falber (assistant general secretary), Bert Ramelson (industrial), Jack Woddis (international), Gordon McLennan (organization), George Matthews (press and publicity), Jean Styles (women), Betty Matthews (education), Dennis Elwand (treasurer), and Dave Cook (election agent).

The party's youth wing is the Young Communist League (YCL), which has been affiliated to the CPGB since the latter's founding. The YCL has a 40-member executive, whose principal members are Tom Bell (national secretary), Phil Green (chairman), Dave Carson (national organizer), Jon Bloomfield (student organizer), and Brian Filling (editor of *Challenge*). YCL membership, which numbered 3,200 in 1971, has declined since then and was 2,355 in 1974 (*Comment*, 18 May).

The CPGB derives its greatest strength from the trade union movement, in which it exercises perceptible influence. Although challenged by the Trotskyist organizations, the CPGB was successfully involved in industrial agitation at a level disproportionate to its size and electoral support. In 1974 the CPGB exerted critical influence in the Amalgamated Union of Engineering Workers (AUEW), Britain's second-largest union (about 1,300,000 members). The AUEW has about 175 communists in official positions. The largest union, the Transport and General Workers Union (TGWU), has a 36-member Executive Committee, of whom 15 follow the CPGB line. The party continued to promote its Liaison Committee for the Defense of Trade Unions (LCDTU), an "umbrella" organization for unofficial rank-and-file bodies set up throughout the country and in key industries, which was founded in 1966.

Party Internal Affairs. The obduracy of the hard-liners, which reappeared at the past two party congresses (see *YICA, 1974*, p. 164), had little effect on the ideological line of the CPGB. A chronic problem for the party since World War II has been to attract and retain members, especially among the younger generation. Although a Titoist party, the CPGB is inflexible, and in assessing its poor performance in the February 1974 election it looked for reasons elsewhere but added: "We must, however, strike a critical note about our election preparations. We were less prepared for this election than at any time during the past twenty years although we knew it was coming. We had no election agent. . . . In most constituencies there was inadequate organization. . . . Involvement in the mass struggle was understandably also a fact in our inadequate organizational work." (John Gollan's report to the Executive Committee, *Comment*, 23 March.)

This situation did not improve by the time of the October election, and in an attempt to conserve its resources the party only contested 29 seats instead of the contemplated 44. There were muted complaints that the contraction of the electoral efforts would be seen as a defeat for the CPGB's political strategy, but John Gollan criticized this attitude: "To accept this suggestion would mean our almost complete disappearance from the electoral field for an indefinite period. . . . We must work in existing circumstances no matter how unfavourable they may be." (Ibid., 16 November.)

The CPGB's poor performance and the resources used to contest the elections has compelled the party to consider the declining membership in the adult and youth movements, to attract more funds, and to increase the circulation of its London daily, the *Morning Star*. In his report to the Executive Committee on 11 May, George Matthews stated: "On the *Morning Star*, the latest circulation figure shows an increase of 579 on the January 7 figure. At this time last year the increase was 1,679 on the January 8, 1973 figure, and at the end of the year we were 1,000 up. It is clear that we have not succeeded so far this year in achieving the same fight for the paper that we began to develop last year." (Ibid., 18 May.)

The party and the *Morning Star* both run at a loss and the newspaper carried daily appeals for more funds. At its January meeting the Executive Committee called for a speedy completion of the full target for a £10,000 Fund appeal. The cost of contesting two elections in nine months did not improve the party's financial position (see *YICA, 1974*, p. 164).

The CPGB's youth wing closely followed the policies of the adult party. On 8-9 June the YCL organized a "Festival of Socialism" in an attempt to create a more attractive image for potential recruits. Discussion topics included Chile, Vietnam, Ireland, and South Africa. There were delegations from Vietnam, France and Ireland—the latter represented by Madge Davison of the Connolly Youth Movement (CYM). "The turnout for both days was not as big as hoped for, but this did not undermine the enthusiasm of the weekend" (*Comment*, 13 July). Attempts to revive student interest in the YCL was challenged by the "ultra left," a challenge which was unwelcome to the YCL. "The International Socialists and International Marxist Group are the main ultra-left organizations within the student movement. [They] have a common approach to students which is fundamentally counter-posed to that of the Broad left" (ibid., 19 October). YCL influence in the student movement received a setback when communist leaders of the National Union of Students (NUS) were heavily defeated at the annual NUS conference on 1-5 April. The 1,300 delegates voted overwhelmingly to censure the 10 left-wing members of the executive, among whom are four members of the YCL, for trying to conceal the extent of oppression in the U.S.S.R. (*Daily Telegraph*, London, 4 April). In subsequent elections for the executive, the YCL's representation dropped from four to two. Visits abroad were made by YCL members to Chile and the U.S.S.R. The Thirtieth Congress of the YCL is to be held in the spring of 1975.

Domestic Attitudes and Activities. In the two national elections in 1974, the CPGB adhered to its policy of seeking power by parliamentary means, but its disastrous performance removed any imminent prospects. The party campaigned on numerous themes, mainly the economic crisis, industrial relations, low-income groups, and education.

The immediate target of criticism in the party's campaign on economic affairs was the Conservative Government, but beyond that the CPGB saw the crisis as "the result of the chronic decay of the whole capitalist system" (*Comment*, 23 February). Its suggestions for ameliorating the economic crisis included strict price controls, public ownership, food subsidies, frozen rents, defense cuts, and the imposition of a wealth tax.

In February the replacement of the Conservative Government by a Labour Administration compelled the CPGB to re-think its strategy. The party has consistently argued that a Labour Government improves communist chances of attaining power, and in this vein the party produced a pamphlet—*Which Way for Labour*—in an attempt to influence the electorate. Its author was Gerry Cohen, who perceived that while a Labour Government was a good thing, right-wing Labour politicians could be harmful to the broad left: "If Labour is to sweep the country on a genuinely left programme in the next election its necessity [is] to make a much greater fight for such a programme now. . . . There are right-wing leaders who not only do not want Socialism but will do everything to impede its achievement."

The party's influence in industrial relations is usually exercised through the LCDTU (chairman, Kevin Halpin). At a meeting in London on 6-7 April the LCDTU called for a "lobby of Parliament to demand the release of the jailed Shrewsbury pickets," for a "rejection of the TUC's commitment to voluntary wage restrictions," and for "defense of trade union funds [and] total repeal of the Industrial Relations Act, including abolition of the Commission of Industrial Relations and a pledge by the government to return all fines imposed under the Act." (*Morning Star*, 8 April.)

A growing threat to the CPGB was the revival of nationalist policies in Scotland and Wales, which are traditional recruiting areas for the party: "In Scotland ... problems were made more acute by the big nationalist challenge, especially in Labour seats ... This affected all our Scottish results. But in our three Welsh contests (where we more or less held our votes) this nationalist pressure applied less, as *Plaid Cymru* was concentrating elsewhere." (*Comment*, 16 November.) A modest success of the CPGB was the election of a communist, Dai Francis, as first chairman of the Wales Trade Union Council on 28 April. As in previous years, the CPGB found itself being challenged by the ultra-left in the labor and student sectors.

International Views and Positions. In 1974, the CPGB campaigned on the Common Market, European Security, Vietnam, Chile, and South Africa.

The party is opposed to the Common Market mainly because it sees the organization as "monopoly capitalism" which will directly assist the growth and influence of multi-national companies. In agitating for withdrawal, the CPGB as part of the international communist movement is in the paradoxical situation of seeming to be the only custodian of British nationalism. This stand conflicts with that of the French and Italian communist parties. Following meetings with West European parties in February, March, and June, the CPGB did little to modify its attitude, and after the October election it remained firmly opposed to the Common Market: "The process of undermining British sovereignty has been proceeding apace.... We will campaign for Britain to come out." (*Comment*, 16 November.)

On European Security the party closely followed the Soviet line on peaceful coexistence and the devolution of NATO: "Britain should take the lead by withdrawing from NATO," by "renouncing nuclear weapons and closing down all nuclear bases in Britain," and by "supporting the Soviet proposal for a world disarmament conference" (ibid., 23 February). On 28 April the all-Britain Peace Liaison Group was formed, following talks among members of the British delegation which attended the Congress of Peace Forces in Moscow, October 1973. Acting secretary of the new group is Alfred Jones, secretary of the communist-influenced Political Committee of the London Co-operative Society.

The aftermath of the Chilean coup of 1973 still rumbled on in CPGB policy: "The British Government must be compelled to break off diplomatic relations with the fascist junta and cease all aid and credits. Every possible solidarity should be given to Popular Unity and all other forces resisting the junta." (Ibid., 23 February.) Communists are involved in the National Chile Solidarity Campaign Committee (NCSCC), set up in September 1973, and by January 1974 there were 31 local Chile Solidarity Committees linked with the National Committee. But orthodox communists were challenged by the ultra-left, and at an "Action Conference" in Birmingham on 23 March a third of the delegates walked out following dissension between Marxists and Trotskyists (*Guardian*, 27 March). This kind of conflict was similar to the split which affected the pro-North Vietnam lobby of the late 1960s.

On Vietnam, the CPGB's front organization, British Campaign for Peace in Vietnam (BCPV), continued in a desultory manner. Since the Paris agreements, the BCPV has been marginal and ineffective.

Party attitudes to South Africa were principally directed against the British connection—"End all economic, political and military support for apartheid" (*Comment*, 23 February)—but the party line was overshadowed by a government debate, part military and part doctrinal, over joint British-South

African naval exercises and the Simonstown naval base.

CPGB general secretary John Gollan's visit to Lyons, France, on 30-31 March at the invitation of the French Communist Party (PCF). The occasion was a mass rally for decisions taken at the Brussels conference of West European communist parties two months earlier. Vi Gill and Tony Chater visited Yugoslavia in May as guests of the League of Communists of Yugoslavia. In June, Gordon McLennan and John Gollan took part in discussions in Rome between the British and Italian communist parties. McLennan and Jack Woddis visited the U.S.S.R. on 4-7 August and met Boris Ponomarev, secretary of the Soviet party's Central Committee. On 2-7 December a delegate of the Communist Party of Cuba visited Great Britain for the first time.

Publications. The London daily *Morning Star* is the CPGB's principal organ. Other major publications include *Comment* (a fortnightly magazine), *Marxism Today* (a monthly theoretical journal), and *Labour Monthly*, which provides a commentary on political events. The YCL publishes *Challenge* (monthly) and *Cogilo*, a monthly theoretical journal.

*   *   *

Workers Revolutionary Party. Among the Marxist-Leninist parties and groups that challenge the CPGB's leadership in the British communist movement, the largest and most influential (particularly in the trade union movement) is the Workers Revolutionary Party (WRP). It was formed on 4 November 1973 and is the reconstituted Socialist Labour League (SLL) which was founded in 1959. The WRP is an affiliate of the Trotskyist International Committee of the Fourth International.

The WRP claims a membership between 1,500 and 2,000. Its youth movement, the Young Socialists (YS), claims to have 20,000 members and is the largest Marxist-Leninist youth organization to have existed in Britain.

The WRP is led by Gerry Healy (general secretary). Other prominent members in the movement (which does not publish complete information about itself) are Mike Banda, editor of the daily party newspaper, *Workers Press*, and Tom Kemp and Cliff Slaughter, editors of *Fourth International*, a quarterly organ. The YS is led by Maureen Bambrick (national secretary); the editor of the YS weekly organ *Keep Left* is Gary Gurmeet.

The WRP controls the All Trade Unions Alliance (ATUA), a group similar to the CPGB-controlled LCDTU. The WRP's domestic policy in 1974 was addressed mainly to industrial agitation. On 24 February the ATUA held a "Solidarity with the Miners" rally in London. More than 4,000 people attended; the agenda included discussions on the election campaign, the miners' strike, and the three-day week. The WRP saw the election as "subordinate to the struggle between the two main clsses," and declared: "The working class must learn to fight. We must build up and train new leadership in the working class." (*Workers Press*, 26 February.)

In the elections of February and October the WRP put up nine parliamentary candidates, the most publicized being the film actress Vanessa Redgrave in Newham, North East. She was unsuccessful on both occasions, gaining only about one percent of the total vote.

The WRP campaigned steadily for the release of two building workers who were sentenced to prison terms in December 1973 for intimidation and violent behavior during the building workers' strike of 1972.

Like the SLL in previous years, the WRP in 1974 was involved in doctrinal disputes with its rivals on the left, the IS and the IMG (see below). The IMG, according to WRP, is "revisionist" and "counter-revolutionary" (ibid., 28 February). The CPGB, in the same vein, was termed "Stalinist," (ibid.). There was a brief tactical alliance among the left to protest at the death of a student, Kevin Gately, who died following a clash between left-wing and right-wing demonstrators on 15 June: "If the circumstances of Gately's death are hushed up, this will amount to a cover-up between the police and the extreme right-wing National Front" (ibid., 18 June).

The YS supported WRP policies in the trade unions and increased its activities among young workers and students. The 14th Annual Conference of the YS was held at Blackpool on 30-31 March. The topics of discussion included education, the young worker, and "the struggle to train Marxist cadres" (ibid., 26 March).

*   *   *

In addition to the CPGB and WRP there are numerous Marxist-Leninist groups in Britain. None of these have been able to muster numerically significant support. There are two main groups: the International Socialists (IS) and the International Marxist Group (IMG). The IMG claims to be the British section of United Secretariat of the Fourth International. Its national secretary is Pat Jordan, who is also editor of the group's monthly organ, *International*. The IMG was active on several grants but its most public involvement was in the formation of an anti-military group, Troops Out Movement (TOM), in May, and in the June demonstrations which ended in the death of a student. The IMG's fortnightly organ is *Red Weekly*.

The IS in 1974 was led by Tony Cliff, Paul Foot, and Jim Higgins, and was mainly active in the industrial front. It has about 3,500 members. On 30 April the IS held the first conference of the Rank-and-File movement (RFM), in Birmingham. The RFM is small, but has growing support among teachers, local government officers, and blue-collar unions. The IS claims that 307 unions are represented in the RFM (*New Statesman*, London, 5 April). The IS organ is the weekly *Socialist Worker*.

The Communist Party of Britain (Marxist-Leninist)—CPBML—is pro-Chinese and is led by Reg Birch, a member of the Executive Committee of AUEW. It claims 400 to 500 members, but the number is falling. The party's main organ is a fortnightly, *The Worker*. During 1974 the party steadily lost credibility, as its programmes became increasingly doctrinaire and extreme. Following the October election, the party stated: "We are in a fight to the death—the death of a class, them or us. They will not bury us. We will bury them." (*The Worker*, 3 October.)

Institute for the Study of Conflict
London

D. L. Price

Greece

The Communist Party of Greece (Kommounistikon Komma Hellados: KKE) evolved from the Socialist Workers' Party of Greece, a basically social-democratic party which was formed in November 1918. The dominant faction of that party joined the Comintern and became the KKE in 1920. The KKE had little impact on Greek politics in the 1920s. Its fortunes seemed to improve in the early 1930s, but it was outlawed and effectively suppressed after 1936 during the Metaxas dictatorship. During World War II, while Greece was under occupation by the Axis, KKE emerged as a major political force under the guise of the National Liberation Front (EAM). In December 1944, shortly after the country's liberation, an attempt to seize power by force failed, but the party remained a legitimate organization until 1947, when it was outlawed again, because of the guerrilla campaign launched by communists the previous year—a campaign that was eventually suppressed in 1949.

During the 1950s and 1960s, the communist left was represented by a front organization known as the United Democratic Left (EDA). EDA's normal electoral strength was around 14 percent. In April 1967 the Papadopoulos dictatorship banned EDA together with all other parties.

The year 1974 was a dramatic one for Greece and especially for the communist left. The turning point must be actually traced to the student demonstrations of November 1973 which, though directed against the dictatorial regime, inadvertently opened the way for a group of hard-liners under Brigadier general Dimitrios Ioannides, chief of the military police, who led a bloodless coup, deposed Papadopoulos, and installed General Faedon Gizhikis as president of the republic and Adamantios Andhroutsopoulos, finance minister under Papadopoulos, as premier. This junta disintegrated in July 1974 when a coup to eliminate President Makarios in Cyprus, instigated by the Ioannides regime, backfired when Turkey invaded the island republic. With the return of Constantine Karamanlis in late July, the democratic process was restored and within weeks the ban on the communist party was lifted.

During the years of dictatorial rule in Greece, the communist party had split into two major factions. One, dominated until December 1972 by Kostas Koliyannis and since then by Harilaos Florakis, claimed to be the genuine party. Because its leadership and most of its followers went to Eastern Europe when the guerrilla campaign was put down in 1949, it became known as the party of the exterior, or KKE-ex. The other faction, led by Babis Drakopoulos, was primarily based within Greece and thus became known as the party of the interior or KKE-es. The first faction had the support of Moscow, while the second claimed to have a more independent existence. In recent years it has been estimated that there are some 100,000 communists and sympathizers in Greece and abroad, with party members numbering about 27,000 in Greece and 15,000 abroad. The population of Greece is about 9,000,000 (estimated 1972).

The party's Ninth Congress, long overdue, finally met in late February 1974 under the leadership of Florakis.

In addition to the two KKE factions, the communist and pro-communist left includes the EDA which is currently linked to the KKE-es; the New Greek Left which follows the teachings of Marcuse and the neo-Marxist theories current in the West; a small group of Trotskyites known as "International Workers Union"; a rather amorphous group of Maoists; a youth organization, "Rigas Fereos," linked to KKE-es and EDA; Communist Youth of Greece (KNE) linked to KKE-ex; and a university student organization also linked to KKE-ex.

At present, the New Greek Left, the "International Workers Union," and the Maoists remain marginal organizations with very limited support. The KKE-ex is referring to itself simply as the KKE, while the KKE-es is planning to change its name to "Greek Communist Party" (EKK), to signify its independence of Soviet tutelage. Eventually EDA and EKK may merge into a single organization.

Party Internal Affairs. The student demonstrations of November 1973 and the downfall of Papadopoulos convinced the communist leadership that in spite of seeming stability the dictatorship was rapidly decaying. Florakis intensified his efforts to close the party ranks and strengthen the party's ties with the Soviet Union and the other Eastern European regimes—except for Romania, which continued to maintain close ties with the communist party of the interior, KKE-es. The improvement Florakis was able to promote during 1973 was dramatically manifested by his ability to call the oft-postponed Ninth Congress in late February 1974. The congress convened somewhere in Eastern Europe. In general, the resolutions adopted by the congress appeared less dogmatic than the positions taken by the party under the Koliyannis leadership. The congress called for a "wider unity of the working class and of all anti-dictatorial forces" while avoiding any pointed attacks against the KKE-es or other rival leftist groups. Predictably, the congress called for "solidarity with the great Soviet Union and the countries of the socialist community" and for "establishment of the people's power of the working people through a new democracy." In spite of the atmosphere of unity which reportedly prevailed in the congress, certain party members residing in Poland voiced complaints that the Florakis leadership did not give them the opportunity to send delegates because their views conflicted with those of the party leadership.

In the months following the congress, Florakis accompanied by members of his Politburo and the new Central Committee visited the Soviet Union where they met with Mikhail Suslov and other leading members of the Communist Party of the Soviet Union, and various Eastern European capitals. In early April, Florakis visited Tashkent, where a large contingent of former Greek guerrillas and their families has settled since the 1950s.

In Greece, reacting to rumors that another series of student demonstrations was planned for late February, the government on 19 February arrested several key members of the KKE-ex working within Greece, including Politburo members Antonios Ambatielos, Nikos Kaloudhis, and Asimina Yiannou. Those arrested included also twenty leading cadres of the KNE. Three weeks later, several other leftists were arrested in Salonika and Piraeus, including fifteen members of the Trotskyite "International Workers Union" and twenty-seven members of KNE and Anti-EFEE. More arrests were announced on 5 May. Although there were repeated rumors that "communists" were planning "anti-national activities," the communist left limited itself to verbal attacks on the regime during the spring and early summer. Abroad, Florakis continued his contacts with "sister parties" in Eastern Europe. In early July the Romanian Communist Party, as though to underline its independence of Moscow, received a delegation of the KKE-es.

The change in the fortunes of the communist left did not result from anything the party did. The dictatorial regime collapsed on 23 July under the impact of its blunder in Cyprus (see *Cyprus*). On 23 July, General Gizhikis, the junta-appointed president of the republic since the previous November, called former premier Karamanlis in Paris and invited him to return to Greece and assume the premiership. In the early hours of 24 July, a national government under Karamanlis was sworn in.

Gizhikis stayed on temporarily as president. Although the communist left sought to be represented in the "Government of National Unity, no communists were included. Nevertheless, EDA and the two factions of KKE voiced support for the Karamanlis government. On 4 August the first issue of *Avgi*, EDA's daily, appeared on the streets in Athens. Spokesmen of the KKE-ex complained publicly against the use of the name by EDA, claiming that the newspaper belonged to the communist left as a whole, nevertheless *Avgi* continued to represent the views of EDA and KKE-es. On 9 August, KKE-ex began the publication of a weekly newspaper, *Nea Ellada*, although the party continued to be, at least technically, outlawed. In any event, the intention of the Karamanlis government to legalize KKE was already evident. In mid-September the ban was lifted and on 18 September KKE-ex quietly opened its offices in Athens. Florakis had already returned to Athens on 21 August.

Also known as "Kapetan Yiotis," Harilaos Florakis was born in Rahoula, Karthitsa, in 1914. Before WWII he was an employee of the Greek postal service. In 1943, during Greece's occupation by the Axis, he joined ELAS—the communist-led guerrilla bands. After the country's liberation he continued his clandestine work for the party and in 1947 he emerged as a "lieutenant general" in the communist-led guerrilla campaign of the "Demokratic Army" (DSE). He spent several years in prison in the fifties and sixties. Released in 1966, he was again arrested in April 1967 and was deported to the island of Leros; later he was transferred to a regular prison. He was released in 1973 following the amnesty given at that time by the Papadopoulos regime, and he immediately escaped abroad. In spite of the many years he had spent within Greece, Florakis was not identified with the KKE-es. In December 1972, at the 17th plenum of KKE-ex, he replaced Koliyannis as first secretary.

With the approval of the electoral law and the setting of election day for 17 November, 1974, the rival factions of the communist left set aside their internal disagreements and formed an electoral coalition called "United Left" (EA). The coalition made up of EDA, KKE-es, and KKE-ex, and directed by a ten-member Administrative Committee (Ilias Iliou, Harilaos Florakis, Leonidhas Kyrkos, Mikis Theodorakis, Kostas Filinis, Georgios Spiliotopoulos, Nikos Kaloudhis, Vasilis Efraimidhis, Stavros Iliopoulos, and Nikos Kyriakidhis). In the elections, EA received 9.45 percent of the total vote (464,331 out of 4,912,356) and eight seats in the 300-seat legislature (see table). With the elections over, the coalition was quietly terminated.

Domestic Attitudes and Activities—Internal Views and Positions. In its Ninth congress, KKE-ex again identified two stages of "revolutionary transformation" on the way to socialism: "During the first stage, we shall solve the unresolved democratic problems, such as the country's emancipation from foreign tutelage, its complete independence, the limitation of foreign and domestic monopolies by eliminating their privileges, and the democratization of the country's political and social life. The realization of these tanks will deal a heavy blow on the regime of exploitation and will open the way to the second stage, the socialist stage. . . . To open the way for an independent, democratic, socialist Greece, it is imperative above all to overthrow the U.S.-dominated military-fascist junta regime and to establish the new democracy."

The congress declared that the party would maintain "its alliance with the peasantry and other working and repressed urban groups" even during the stage of "socialist transformation"—to the extent possible. "The working class, the vanguard of socialist transformation, aided by this alliance, shall create its own state, the state of the dictatorship of the proletariat [which] is the highest form of democracy." The congress went on to say that "to achieve these revolutionary changes the Communist Party of Greece must be prepared itself and it must prepare the working class and the people to use every form of struggle, both peaceful and non-peaceful, depending on the attitude of the reactionary forces, and it must be able to move in time from one form of struggle to the other."

In contrast, the KKE-es, in a major policy statement by Drakopoulos on 3 Octobe4 1974, adopted a very moderate stand on the question of "socialist transformation." The KKE-es, he declared, "is determined to respect fully the democratic process at all stages of the Greek evolution toward a constantly renewed democracy and toward socialism; it is further prepared to. respect the electoral results whether it is in power or out of power; and it further declares that no change in the country's political institutions and social structures can be effected without the support of the majority of the people and even less against the will of the majority."

Drakopoulos further declared that the KKE-es rejects any "dogmatic and mechanistic imitation of foreign models" and that it is "inspired by the living and constantly renewed Marxism-Leninism adjusted to the Greek conditions." The KKE-es, he concluded, "is a party of struggle, class-oriented, democratic in its internal functions, deeply rooted in Greek realities, maintaining its autonomous existence while at the same time trying to develop its contacts with other communist parties and to fulfill its internationalist obligations."

These two statements show the key elements of disagreement between the two factions of KKE. The KKE-ex maintains the orthodox views the party has espoused since its inception. The KKE-es has adopted a reformist orientation, including a virtual rejection of violence as a means for revolutionary change; also it has put aside the concept of the "dictatorship of the proletariat."

In the circumstances one may predict that KKE-ex will emerge as the genuine Communist Party of Greece (KKE) while KKE-es—possibly renamed the Greek Communist Party (EKK) to underline its independence—will merge with EDA. These political parties will have to compete in the months ahead with Andreas Papandreou's Panhellenic Socialist movement (PASOK).

With regard to major international issues, both KKE-ex and KKE-es favor an end to Greece's membership in NATO, and both are in favor of détente. However, KKE-ex takes a more intransigent view on Greece's relations with the West, and opposes membership in the European Common Market. KKE-es favors such an association and supports "normal relations with all Western and socialist countries in a climate of political independence." Further, while KKE-ex is openly speaking of its loyalty to the "great Soviet Union," KKE-es underlines its "independence" from any foreign tutelage. With regard to China, KKE-ex naturally sides with Moscow while KKE-es hardly makes any reference to the subject. In this, its position is closer to that of the Romanian Communist party.

With regard to Cyprus, both factions support President Makarios, oppose the pro-enosis EOKA, and advocate the island's demilitarization.

Publications. Following the restoration of democratic freedoms in Greece, several publications of the communist left have begun to circulate freely. These include the daily newspapers *Avgi* speaking for KKE-es and EDA) and *Rizospastis* ("Radical," speaking for KKE-ex), and the weekly *Nea Ellada* and *Voice of the Working class* (both KKE-ex).

Howard University   D. George Kousoulas

ELECTORAL RESULTS

Date of last election: 17 November 1974   **300-seat legislature**

Name of Party	Votes cast	Percent of total vote	Number of seats	Percent of total seats
Communist:				
United Left	464,331	9.45	8	2.67
Non-communist Left:				
Panhellenic				
Socialist Movement	666,806	13.58	12	4.00
Center:				
Center Union-New				
Forces	1,002,908	20.42	60	20.00
Conservative:				
New Democracy	2,670,804	54.37	220	73.33
Other	107,507	2.28	0	0
Total	4,912,356		300	100.00

Iceland

The communist-dominated People's Alliance (Altýdubandalagid) is a socialist labor party that draws support from a disparate assemblage of trade union members, radical teachers and students, die-hard nationalists, and disenchanted Social Democrats. It has an estimated 2,500 members, out of a total Icelandic population of about 210,000. Its main strength rests in the urban areas (particularly Reykjavik) and the small fishing and processing towns along the eastern and northern coasts.

The People's Alliance—or PA—is only the most recent incarnation of the communist party in Iceland. It first developed from a secessionist left-wing splinter from the Social Democratic Party (SDP) in 1930. It has enjoyed legal status ever since. In 1938—now considered its birth year—the communist party withdrew from the Third International, reconstituted itself to include more radical social democrats, and took the name of United People's Party-Socialist Party (UPP-SP). For some time, the communist and social democratic elements sustained a semblance of joint control. By 1949, however, pro-Soviet communists assumed full control of the UPP-SP. Seven years later the communists again joined with leftist Social Democrats—primarily from the Icelandic Federation of Labor (IFL)—to form an electoral front known as the People's Alliance (PA). That front became an openly avowed "Marxist political party" in November 1968 and so replaced the UPP-SP. It split from the two other main factions in the Icelandic communist movement—Hannibal Valdimarsson's Organization of Liberals and Leftists (OLL) and the pro-Soviet, politically insignificant Organization of Icelandic Socialists (OIS).

Despite its small membership and incessant internal division, the PA has parlayed an effective organization, concentration in the Icelandic labor movement, and a sharp eye for appealing political issues into relative success. It has been one of the few Western European communist parties to participate in a democratically elected government. Since World War II, it has polled between 12 and 20 percent of Iceland's popular vote. In the 1971 parliamentary election, the PA received 17.1 percent of the vote and won 10 of the 60 seats in the Althing (parliament). The PA thus joined the OLL and the Progressive Party in a left-center coalition under Prime Minister Olafur Johannesson. Two PA veterans, Ludvik Josefsson and Magnus Kjartansson, participated in the seven-man cabinet as the ministers of commerce and fisheries and of health, social security, and industries, respectively. ·

Parliamentary elections on 30 June 1974 brought mixed blessings for the PA. On the one hand, the party gained one seat in the Althing and rose to 18.3 percent of the popular vote.

On the other hand, the PA lost direct participation in the cabinet. The mid-summer elections had resulted in a 30-30 stalemate between the opposition parties (the conservative Independence Party and the SDP) and the former coalition parties. After two months of intense political bargaining, Geir Hallgrimsson formed a new coalition of his own Independence Party (which had jumped to 42.7 percent of the popular vote) and the Progressive Party on 27 August. Together, they commanded 42 seats in the Althing. The loss of direct participation, combined with an important substantive setback on defense matters (see below), tended to overshadow the PA's modest electoral gain. Details of the election results for all parties are tabulated at the end of this profile.

Leadership and Organization. Ragnar Arnalds, former leader of the anti-NATO National Opposition Party, continued in 1974 as PA chairman and Adda Bara Sigfusdottir as vice-chairman. The Management Council is the party's highest authority between meetings of the 32-member Central Committee.

Party Internal Affairs. Like all Nordic communist organizations, the PA has suffered from a surfeit of factionalism. Its parliamentary strength has fluctuated more because of intra-party disagreement than from lost popular support. The most dramatic example was the power struggle between the communists and "Hannibalists" for control of the PA in 1968. The latter managed to hold five seats in the Althing during 1971-73 which might have gone to the PA otherwise.

Friction has also been sparked by interplay between the PA's two most influential members, Josefsson and Kjartansson. The former has often tried to score immediate political points—especially on the question of extending Iceland's jurisdiction over fishing territory—at the expense of the governmental stability and international good-will espoused by the latter. During 1973 the two had also diverged on tactics regarding the European Community (EC) and the Iceland Defense Force (IDF).

Fractionalism has taken an even clearer toll recently on that colorful remnant of the communist movement, the OLL. In 1974 it shrank to a miniature of its former might. It was, in part, the victim of internal bickering and an ill-fated effort to merge with the Social Democratic Party. In the June election it dropped from 8.9 to 4.7 percent of the popular vote and from five to two seats in the Althing. It was no longer the party of the remarkable Hannibal Valdimarsson. It attracted instead those anti-IDF voters who were disgruntled with all older parties and yet would not vote for the PA because they were anti-communist and pro-NATO.

Domestic Attitudes and Activities. Growing economic problems dominated domestic concerns in Iceland, as in most of Western Europe. Inflation alone jumped to 40 percent in 1974, the highest rate recorded among countries of the Organization for Economic Cooperation and Development. Fish prices declined sharply and foreign reserves sagged to alarmingly low levels.

For most of the year, however, the PA felt constrained from taking touch measures to combat this situation. It clearly did not want to antagonize its labor constituency. It thus refused to support the prime minister's proposals which called, inter alia, for a price freeze, disengagement of wages from the cost-of-living index, rollback of the general wage increase to 20 percent from a level as high as 45 percent, forced savings above a certain level of income, higher bank reserves, limitation on construction of homes and apartments, a flexible exchange rate or an outright devaluation of the kronur, and reduction of government expenditures. The main stumbling block for the PA was the politically explosive wage rollback and disengagement of wages from the cost-of-living index.

At one point the PA reportedly offered to support Johannessen on economic measures if he, in turn, would back a resolution calling for the United States to reply to Iceland's proposals on the Keflavik base by 1 July. Iceland was to terminate the contested defense agreement with the United States if the reply were not satisfactory. Johannesson refused to link the economic and defense questions.

In fact, the two were bound to meet in the political arena. Though economic issues underlay the fall of the Johannesson government—the OLL withdrew from the coalition in protest over its anti-inflation measures—most parties, including the PA, made defense the number one question in the campaign. The election thus served a dual function: it was at once an informal referendum on the retention of the Keflavik base and a façade behind which the parties could conceal their economic programs.

International Views and Activities. The PA remained strongly opposed to Icelandic membership in NATO and to retention of the Iceland Defense Force in any form. The PA's long-term objective has been and is an unarmed and neutral Iceland.

The Johannesson government, upon taking office in mid-1971, committed itself to review Iceland's 1951 defense pact with the United States "for the purpose of having the IDF leave Iceland" by 1975. At first the government deferred action. Then, spurred by the escalating dispute over fishing rights with Great Britain, it invoked Article VII of the U.S.-Icelandic defense agreement on 25 June 1973. That action set in motion the machinery for negotiations which operated off and on during much of 1974.

The PA fought hard to keep a tough Icelandic line in the talks. After the fall of the Johannesson coalition, it opened fire on the foreign minister for his alleged insincerity and powerlessness on the Keflavik question. The PA claimed that he ministerpreted a coalition agreement of 3 March whereby there was to be no military station at the Keflavik airport. The PA newspaper *Thjodviljiin* charged the minister with "wretched servility" toward the United States.

The fact that both the pro-IDF Independence Party and the anti-IDF PA gained in the 30 June election underscored the commingling of economic and defense issues in voter minds. Many backed the Independence Party—or "business party"—because it seemed more likely to cope effectively with the growing economic crisis and because the parties of the left seemed to be placing Iceland's only form of defense in jeopardy. The modest gain achieved by the PA, on the other hand, may have indicated some growing support for that party's clear position on the defense issue and the belief of many workers that the PA would best protect their interests in a period of economic reform. The PA thus won and lost from a polarization of opinion which undercut the middle parties most conspicuously.

Once Hallgrimsson succeeded in forming a government, he issued a statement on the defense question, 29 August. He committed Iceland to special cooperation with the United States while a defense and surveillance station continued to operate in Iceland in behalf of NATO. He pledged negotiations to that end, with only minor modifications in the prior role of the IDF. Icelanders, for example, were to assume more of the non-military functions at the base and there was to be a clearer division between the operations of the defense force and those at the public airport. This reversal of the plans set forth by the Johannesson government was effected in the new accord, signed by Iceland and the United States, 26 September. PA chairman Arnalds reacted to the new government's policy by claiming that it was consistent with the goal of those who favored permanent military occupation of Iceland.

The Halgrimsson government also went on record in behalf of extending Iceland's fishing limits to 200 miles "not later than 1975." Iceland, whose economy depends heavily on fish and fish products, unilaterally extended its fishing limits to 50 nautical miles (from 12) on 1 September 1972. The result had been the outbreak of a new "cod war" with Great Britain, reminiscent of a similar conflict in 1958-61.

The PA had been quick to seize on subsequent anti-British animus—in order both to take a tough stand in the fish talks and to channel Icelandic anger against the British into a more vigorous campaign against the IDF and NATO. When Iceland finally ratified its fishing accord with the British on 13 November 1973, the PA lost a prime tool in its tactical kit-bag. It was defeated on the IDF question and was subsequently preempted from bold initiatives on fishing territory by Hallgrimsson's own 200-mile proposal.

International Party Contacts. Since the PA has traditionally put Icelandic concerns above those of Marxist-Leninist ideology or the international communist movement, its relative aloofness during 1974 came as no surprise. Increased PA activities abroad in 1973 had reflected Icelandic interest in getting foreign support in the cod war more than a fundamental change from the pattern.

Arnalds continued to stress that the PA does not attend meetings like that held in Brussels in January 1974 for Western European communists, because "purely communist conferences are not commensurate with our goals." The PA often felt that it had more in common, for example, with the Danish and Norwegian Social Democrats than with the communists in those countries. It considered the Sino-Soviet split "idiotic and chaotic" and irrelevant to Icelandic concerns.

The PA does not maintain formal ties with the Communist Party of the Soviet Union and has made clear its condemnation of the Warsaw Pact invasion of Czechoslovakia in 1968. It has made a point of siding with communist parties (most notably those of the Romanians and Yugoslavs) known for their independent or nationalistic views.

Publications. *Thjodviljiin* ("Will of the Nation"), a daily newspaper in Reykjavik, is the PA's central organ. The party also publishes a biweekly theoretical journal, *Ny Utsyn*. Outside Reykjavik, there are at least two pro-communist weeklies, *Verkamadhurinn* in Akureyri and *Mjolnir* in Siglufjordhur. The publication of the fledgling Maoist organization is *Stettabarattan* ("Class Struggle").

Date of latest election: 30 June 1974

Party name	Votes received	Percent total	Seats
Communist:			
People's Alliance	20,922	18.3	11
Non-Communist Left:			
Organization of Liberals and Leftists	5,244	4.7	2
Social Democratic	10,321	9.3	5
Other:			
Progressive	28,388	24.9	17
Independence	48,758	42.8	25
Total	113,633	100.0	60

Ireland

The Communist Party of Ireland (CPI) was founded in 1921, but its initial existence was short lived. It was refounded in June 1933, a date adopted by present Irish communists as the original year of the party's founding. The organizational structure of the CPI was disrupted during World War II, party as a result of the fact that the southern Republic of Ireland declared itself neutral while Northern Ireland participated in the war. In 1948, the communists in the south founded the Irish Workers' Party (IWP) and those in the north, the Communist Party of Northern Ireland (CPNI). On 15 March 1970 the IWP and CPNI were reunited at a special congress as the Communist Party of Ireland. That congress adopted a Constitution and a Manifesto and elected a National Executive Committee. The CPI held its Fifteenth Congress on 16-17 October 1971. The next Congress was to be held in 1974, but no plans have been announced.

The CPI has about 25o to 300 members, and its strength is declining; it has more supporters among northern Protestants than among southern Catholics. The population of the Republic of Ireland is 2,291,000 and that of Northern Ireland is 1,500,000 (1971 census).

The CPI is not strong in the north or the south and holds no seats in any legislative body. Since the outbreak of violence in the north in 1969, the CPI has declined in influence although it wields a residual influence in the Marxist Official wings of Sinn Fein and the Irish Republican Army (see *Ulster: Politics and Terrorism*, Conflict Studies, no. 36, Institute for the Study of Conflict, London, 1973). It has greater influence within the Northern Ireland Civil Rights Association (NICRA), which is an uneasy coalition of a wide range of political groups and has communists in key positions—Edwina Stewart is honorary secretary.

The party controls a small youth organization, the Connolly Youth Movement (CYM), formed in 1965 and led by Madge Davison, who is also assistant organizer of NICRA.

Direct British rule in Ulster was renewed in May 1974 (see *Ulster: Consensus and Coercion*, Conflict Studies, no. 50, ISC, London 1974).

Leadership and Organization. The CPI's leading body, the Executive Committee, is divided into northern and southern area branches, each with ten members (for names see *YICA, 1974*, p. 180), all elected at the founding congress in 1970. They in turn elected the six-member Secretariat, which includes Andrew Barr (party chairman), Michael O'Riordan (general secretary), James Stewart (assistant general secretary), and Hugh Moore (secretary for the northern area). The party is based in Dublin.

Domestic Attitudes and Activities. The fundamental goal of the CPI is the establishment of a united "socialist republic" in Ireland—a kind of offshore British Cuba. To accomplish this, the party advocates the formation of a "Nationalist Liberation Front" in which it seeks the participation both of Protestants and of anti-unionist Catholics. Many northern Protestants also oppose unification since it would mean losing the majority position they currently enjoy there. The CPI, mainly Catholics in the south and Protestants in the north, therefore attempts to unite the two sides, especially through the labor movement, on the basis of common grievances, such inadequate housing and inflatioɪ , and opposition to the Common Market. It describes the current situation in the north and the south as one of economic exploitation as a result of British "colonial" policy and offers socialism as the remedy.

The CPI recognizes that the Ulster conflict is complex and one that does not call for the violent methods of some of its rivals. While not eschewing violence, it prefers political methods to open warfare. This relative moderation has alienated extremist groups on the far left like People's Democracy, Saor Eire, and the Communist Party of Ireland (Marxist-Leninist). Since 1971 the CPI has been concerned almost exclusively with the Ulster conflict, aspects of which sharpened in 1974. The principal terrorist organization in the north is the Provisional IRA (republican, non-communist, and Catholic) group that was strongly and steadily attacked by the CPI: "We are opposed to terror-type activities to gain political ends which we believe can only be won by mass political struggle" (*Morning Star*, London, 23 November).

On the whole the CPI cautiously welcomed the British Government's attempts to find political solutions for the conflict, but its attitude was tempered by its own proposals for "a Bill of Rights, an end to internment and Emergency Powers, [and] talks with all democratic forces in the North" (*WMR*, August).

The United Kingdom's resumption of direct rule in Northern Ireland, for the second time in two years, was a consequence of an industrial strike by the Protestant Ulster Workers' Council (UWC) which brought down the Northern Ireland administration. This Protestant "backlash" was attacked by the CPI as an attempt to "capture power in what would be a fascist, terror-ridden State" (ibid.). The CPI position was also supported by the CYM and NICRA. The latter at its annual general meeting retracted its opposition to British policy, and added: "Throughout the year, the Association [NICRA] has stuck firmly to its principles, that a mass campaign for civil rights must continue irrespective of structures set up or desertions from the cause until we achieve full civil rights and social justice" (*Morning Star*, 8 April).

A modest success for the CPI was the election of Andrew Barr as president of the Irish Congress of Trade Unions on 5 July. During the UWC strike, Barr was a "prime mover behind the trade unions' unsuccessful back-to-work marches." (*Irish Times*, Dublin, 6 July.)

In July, the official Sinn Fein organized an "anti-imperialist festival" in Dublin and Belfast. Although delegates from the Palestine Liberation Organization and Welsh, Breton, Basque, and Flemish nationalists appeared, the CPI refused to participate.

A joint statement by the CPI and the Communist Party of Great Britain on 17 June announced their program for the renewal of political activity in Northern Ireland: "the immediate enactment of a Bill of Rights; the repeal of the Emergency Provisions Act, the release of all internees and an end to the harassment by British troops and their withdrawal to barracks" (*Morning Star*, 18 June).

International Views and Positions. In contrast to its domestic activity, the CPI issued no major statements on international affairs in 1974, other than to express opposition to the Common Market and imperialism, and support for the Soviet Union's concept of peaceful coexistence. Following an agreement between the Soviet Union and the Irish Republic, the first Soviet ambassador arrived in Dublin in May.

Overseas visits by the CPI included those of Hugh Moore and Edwina Stewart to Romania, in June, and of party delegations led by Andrew Barr and Michael O'Riordan to the Soviet Union,

Bulgaria, the German Democratic Republic, and France, in August and September. No foreign delegates visited Ireland.

The CPI's youth wing, the CYM, duly followed the party's program but made no significant statements or visits.

Publications. The CPI publishes a weekly paper, *Unity*, in Belfast. In Dublin it publishes the weekly *Irish Worker's Voice* and the monthly *Irish Socialist.* There is also a theoretical quarterly, the *Irish Socialist Review*. The CYM organ is the fortnightly *Forward.*

*   *   *

The CPI and CYM have to contend with about 20 left-wing groups in Ireland, the most prominent of which are the Maoist Communist Party of Ireland (Marxist-Leninist), the British and Irish Communist Organization, Saor Eire ("Free Ireland"), and People's Democracy. Since 1971, the urban conflict in the north has obscured conventional political activity on the left.

Institute for the Study of Conflict   D. L. Price
London

Italy

The roots of Italian communism extend into the nineteenth century, when the followers of Marx, Bakunin, and Mazzini contended for the allegiance of the Italian working-class movement. Marxists were extremely influential in the Italian Socialist Party (PSI), which was formed in 1892. There was no separate communist party in Italy, however, until after the Russian Revolution of 1917. In January, 1921, as a result of a split in the PSI over whether to accept Lenin's "Twenty-one conditions" for continued membership in the Comintern, the Italian Communist Party (Partito Communista Italiano; PCI) was formed at Leghorno. In 1926, all parties save the Fascists were outlawed. In 1946, partly as a result of its leading role in the twenty-year struggle against Fascism, but also because of the political acumen of its leadership, the PCI emerged in the postwar free elections with a popular following approximately equivalent to that of the PSI. Since the elections of 1946, when it received 19 percent of the vote for the House of Deputies, the PCI has increased its share of the popular vote, in 1972 receiving 27.2 percent of the total and 179 seats. It is now the second largest party in Italy, surpassed only by the Christian Democracy party (DC), which in 1972 won 38.8 percent of the vote and 267 seats. (See table of 1946-72 elections, below.)

Antonio Gramsci, a Sardinian and brilliant Marxist theoretician in 1924 became secretary-general of the PCI and succeeded in reversing the previous policy of non-collaboration with other parties opposed to Fascism. Gramsci, while still a deputy in the Italian parliament, was arrested and imprisoned by the Fascists in 1926, to be released only shortly before his death in 1937. Always in fragile health, he nonetheless was able to write many volumes of essays on such themes as the relationship between theory and practice, the importance of ideas in bringing about historical change, and the social structure of the Italian South, the influence of Benedetto Croce, and the relevance of Machiavelli. These writings and Gramsci's extensive correspondence, smuggled out of prison and published after the fall of Fascism, constitute a major intellectual legacy of Italian communism, perhaps even overshadowing the influence of Marx and Lenin.

Gramsci eloquently and incisively criticized what he termed "vulgar" or mechanically deterministic Marxism, of the kind espoused by Bukharin and others. He insisted that the "early" Marx, of the *German Ideology* of 1844, had correctly repudiated a merely passive or "contemplative" materialism, or a materialism which espouses the automatic and "inevitable" victory of Communism. While not neglecting the importance of class structure and economic factors, Gramsci emphasized the role of intelligence and will in politics, and taught that the quality and profundity of the ideas of a political movement were vital elements in its political success. Gramsci was also keenly aware of the need to adapt abstract political principles to local conditions, and he repudiated dogmatic anti-Catholicism as a suicidal policy for a communist party in an overwhelmingly Catholic country. He was also impatient of adventurism and the glorification of violent revolution by some elements of the party, and, although scarcely a defender of liberal parliamentary institutions, he did stress the need to spread the influence of Marxism in Italy through persuasion and propaganda until it could acquire the dominant or "hegemonic" intellectual position in the country. Only when sufficient popular consent had been secured could the communists hope to attain secure control of the governmental power apparatus in the country, he argued.

Gramsci's subtle and sophisticated Marxism has had and continues to have an enormous influence on the development of Italian communism. Palmiro Togliatti, a fellow student with Gramsci at the University of Turin and his successor as party leader, was also a sensitive reader of political conditions peculiar to Italy. Togliatti frequently accommodated or modified communist dogma when that dogma threatened the PCI's steady expansion of support and influence in the postwar years. For example, breaking with Pietro Nenni's Socialist Party, he directed the party's delegates at the Constituent Assembly to vote for the inclusion of the Lateran Pacts on church-state relations, which were extremely favorable to the Catholic church, in the postwar constitution (1948, art. 7). Under Togliatti's leadership the PCI made detailed proposals for socioeconomic reform which could be carried out without revolution and within the framework of the Italian parliamentary system. By abandoning (or appearing to abandon, at least) such Marxist-Leninist goals as the "dictatorship of the proletariat" and the collectivization of agriculture, the PCI has emerged in the eyes of many Italian voters as a sincerely constitutional, rather than a totalitarian, party. In his relations with the international communist movement, Togliatti also proclaimed the necessity for an autonomous "Italian road to socialism"; later he also advocated a policy of "polycentrism" (or numerous centers of power and initiative in addition to Moscow) as an appropriate model for international communism.

When Togliatti died, in August 1964, Luigi Longo, who is today the president of the party, succeeded to the position of secretary-general. Increasingly in recent years, however, Longo has occupied an elder statesman role and the actual party leadership has passed to Enrico Berlinguer, an articulate younger man, who became secretary-general in 1972.

According to official figures, the PCI had 1,657,815 members at the end of 1974 (*Pravda*, 12 December). This total represents a substantial gain over 1970, when the membership was 1,507,047. However, it reflects a sharp decrease from the postwar high of 2,145,317 in 1954, and is still below the 1946 membership of 1,776,013. (Rossana Rossanda, ed., *Il Manifesto* (Paris, Editions de Seuil, 1971, p. 252); Ugo Pecchioli, "Politica e organizzazione nel PCI," *Critica Marxista*, May-August, 1973, p. 23.) The population of Italy is 54,350,000 (estimated 1972).

Leadership and Organization. At the national level the PCI is governed by a Central Committee of some 220 elected members, by a Central Control Commission of about 55 members, and by three smaller bodies which provide the day-to-day executive leadership: the Directorate with some 35 members; the Politburo, with 17 members; and the Secretariat (presided over by Berlinguer), with seven members. The annual party congress ratifies the platform and membership of the governing bodies.

The PCI has some 11,000 "sections," often composed of one or more party cells in factories and other places of work. Above these are some 100 provincial federations and 20 regional committees. There are six federations for Italian emigrants. The youth auxiliary, FGCI, has about 113,000 members. The largest of Italian labor union federations, the CGIL, is dominated by the PCI, but includes a sizable PSI faction.

Besides Longo and Berlinguer, among prominent PCI leaders are Giorgio Amendola, Politburo member and long-time advocate of a "popular front" strategy of cooperation with the PSI and the left wing of the DC; Pietro Ingrao, Politburo member and reportedly the most pro-Maoist member of the top party leadership; and Sergio Segré, chief of the PCI's Foreign Affairs Department. Principal party spokesmen, in addition to Berlinguer, include Armando Cossutta, Giorgi Napolitano, Giancarolo Pajetta, Carlo Galluzzi, Ugo Pecchioli, all members of the Politburo or Secretariat, or both. Luciano Lama, the secretary-general of the CGIL, is another powerful force in Italian politics; although he is a member of the PCI Central Committee, he has his own power base, and there is frequent tension between the objectives of the CGIL and the PCI leadership, with the CGIL favoring a more aggressive, militant policy in favor of working-class economic objectives.

Domestic Attitudes and Activities. In September and October 1973, Berlinguer published a series of articles in the CPI weekly, *Rinascita*, outlining a policy of "compromesso storico" with the Christian Democrats. (This term is literally translated "historic compromise," although *compromesso* carries with it more of mutual "agreement" or "co-promising" than of the English "compromise," which sounds as if basic principles might be sacrificed by one or both parties.) The immediate occasion for the "new" policy (which in many respects actually represents a continuation of the PCI's policy since the end of World War II and even in the resistance to Fascism, going all the way back to the early 1920s) was the coup in Chile resulting in the overthrow of the Allende government. Berlinguer conceded that, even if the Italian left (PCI and PSI) were to win 51 percent of the votes in some future election, the Chilean experience provided that effective government was impossible without the support of substantial segments of the middle classes, who in Italy happened to be predominately Catholic in religious orientation and to be overwhelmingly represented by the Christian Democrats. Therefore, it was essential for the communists and socialists to attempt to reach an understanding with the Christian Democratic Party and so build up a coalition of progressive forces that would set Italy on a new course and be more responsive to the needs of the people.

Berlinguer's call for a "compromesso storico" touched off an enormous political debate and continued throughout 1974 to be the focus of discussion with the PCI and between the party and other parties. In March, Berlinguer stated in an article:

> The significant fact (is) that the idea touched off . . . a discussion of a scope and interest the like of which had not been seen in years. This shows that we were answering a real need.
>
> This need—for a turn toward democracy based on convergence and an understanding among the people's forces—is still more than ever the great prospect we hold out to the nation. (L'Unita, 23 March.)

He rejected the accusation of some political leaders in other parties—notably among some Christian Democrats and Social Democrats—that the formula represented merely another communist attempt at gaining power. Thus, in the same article he declared that the party was not engaged in a "mean and shabby political calculation," but in a responsible attempt to deal with the national crisis. Although he continued to call for the "advent of new forces in the nation's political leadership," he also described the historic compromise policy as representing a "new kind of opposition" for the PCI, thereby implying that the party did not seek in the immediate future to be part of a governing coalition and to have its share of cabinet posts.

That the PCI intended to remain very much an opposition party in the immediate future was demonstrated in numerous ways. The party brought all its energies and resources to bear in an effort to defeat the 12 May referendum, sponsored by conservative Catholics, to repeal the recently enacted divorce law. With only the DC and the Italian Social Movement (MSI) favoring repeal, and with many Catholics deserting the church's official stand, the attempted repeal failed, with 40.9 percent of the vote for it and 51.9 percent against. In his report to the Central Committee and the Central Control Commission of the PCI (ibid., 4 June), Berlinguer was careful to distinguish between the different tendencies within Catholicism and chose not to interpret the results as a defeat for Catholicism per se. He expressed appreciation to the numerous Catholics who joined with the PCI, PSI and most other lay parties in voting "no" on the divorce repeal referendum. By praising the "dissenting Catholics" who defend democracy and support the provisions in behalf of religious liberty endorsed by Vatican

II, Berlinguer continued the party's policy of attempting to establish a working alliance with the "progressive" segment of Italian Catholicism. It appeared that his strategy was to reach over the heads of the DC leadership to the liberal Catholic rank and file, and through a *de facto* alliance with them eventually to influence the DC party leadership to change its *de jure* policy of non-cooperation with the PCI in forming a government. Meanwhile, the PCI could enjoy the luxury of being in opposition during Italy's worst financial crisis since the war, a period in which the ravages of inflation were inflicting the majority of voters.

On 4 August, during the simultaneous national vacation, the Rome-Munich express train was blown up south of Bologna. Twelve persons were killed and twenty injured. The tragedy is widely believed to have been the result of sabotage by certain neo-Fascist elements. The apparent resurgence of neo-Fascist terrorism brought Italy's political leaders back to the capital and caused the PCI to renew its activities in behalf of strong measures against political violence and subversion attempts by right-wing extremists. Just as the divorce issue gave the PCI the opportunity to appear in a moderate position so the presumed terrorist attack enabled the party again to emphasize its attachment law and order and to the principles of the 1948 constitution.

With the rapid deterioration of the "center-left" government, there was renewed speculation of possible communist participation in a new governing coalition. DC secretary-general Amintore Fanfani, enumerated "seven points" against any coalition of his party with the PCI. They included the objections that such an alliance would cost his party votes, be harmful to its allies in those parties which have "a clear and permanent democratic vocation," increase "Nazi-Fascist" terrorism opposed to such an alliance, and harm Italy's foreign and domestic economy. (See the account of Fanfani's objections in the *Washington Post*, 16 September.) For its part, the PCI stated that it would enter a government only if sweeping changes occurred. Giorgio Amendola, veteran PCI Politburo member and leading supporter of the "compremesso storico" policy, declared in a speech on 25 August: "Communists are laying down certain irrevocable conditions: a coherent program of reforms and a new method of government which will free the state (from) corruption. Only under these circumstances can the rapprochement between Communists, Socialists, and a DC that has been changed in terms of its trends and methods provide a positive solution to the country's serious crisis." (*FBIS*, 13 September.) The PCI interpreted Fanfani's "seven points" as a reactionary move to block attempts by progressive elements in the DC to begin discussions with the party about possible forms of cooperation in solving the country's problems. Politburo member Giorgio Napolitano declared on 19 September, while on a visit to Moscow, that nothing Fanfani could say could prevent the "growing importance" of PCI and its "ever greater role" in the life of the nation (ibid., 24 September).

On 2 October, Italy's thirty-sixth postwar government resigned. The DC's Aldo Moro, on 23 November succeeded in forming a two-party government with cabinet ministers to be drawn from the DC and the small Republican Party (PRI). The PSI and the Italian Social Democratic Party (PSDI) announced that they would support the two-party governing coalition. (This government may not last long, and it is quite possible that parliament will be dissolved and new elections called in the spring of 1975). As of late 1974, the PCI remained in opposition, and its considerable power and influence—in the committees of parliament, in the bureaucracy, in the trade union movement, in regional and local governments—appeared to have been enhanced by the economic crisis through which, in common with the rest of the West but in an even more aggravated form, Italy has been going. The non-communist Turn newspaper *La Stampa* (11 October) saw Berlinguer as content to remain "on the fence" in the governmental crisis and, without abandoning the "compremesso storico" strategy, continuing his efforts to mold a "grand alliance between Catholic, Socialist, and Communist popular forces."

Opposition Within the Communist Movement to a "Revisionist" Policy by the PCI. The PCI's postwar policy of accommodation to the constitutional political process and the official renunciation of violent revolution as the means of attaining power has met with opposition by various groups within the party and has at times resulted in expulsions and secessions from the party. Some old-line Stalinists in the past even opposed the "mellowing" of the Soviet regime under Khrushchev. More recently, younger groups have been attracted to Mao and to appeals for direct revolutionary action against the "decadent" capitalist system. The party's decision to work within the Italian parliamentary system has appeared to them as a betrayal of Marxist-Leninism.

The most noteworthy expression of dissent against the party's allegedly "revisionist" policy in recent years has been provided by the "Manifesto" group. *Il Manifesto*, a journal published by militant revolutionary members of the PCI, appeared in the wake of the tumultuous student strikes in France and Italy beginning in May 1968. At the end of 1969, the group was expelled from the PCI for "Factionalism" and "left deviationism." The leaders of the *Manifesto* group at that time included three members of the PCI Central Committee: Milan deputy Rossana Rossanda; Aldo Natoli, the head of the Rome PCI organization; and Luigi Pintor, a deputy and coeditor of *L'Unita*. Another prominent spokesman for the dissidents has been Lucio Magri. In July 1974, *Il Manifesto* held a congress which approved the fusion of the group with the Proletarian Unity Party (PDUP)–the successor to the militantly leftist Italian Socialist Party of Proletarian Unity (PSIUP)–in order to form a new party, the Party of Proletarian Unity for Communism. None of these splinter movements has been able to attract much support at the polls, however, and they have posed little threat to the unity of the PCI.

International Views and Positions. *The PCI as a Continuing Enigma.* Palmiro Togliatti is once supposed to have compared the opponents of the PCI, who refuse to acknowledge its "democratic character," to "those ignoramuses who could not believe that a giraffe was real when they first saw it because it was just too different from all the other animals" ("The Giraffe," in *Encounter*, February 1972, p. 84). However, there are many who continue to suspect a more apt zoological analogy for the communist party to be that of the wolf in sheep's clothing.

Certainly, as one reporter has observed, the Italian Communists "have sought to project a moderate image. They would not try to pull out of the Atlantic Alliance and of the European Common Market [see Armando Cossutta's speech at Brescia in early September 1974 as reported in the *New York Times*, 3 September] and they would not try to destroy private enterprise. A party spokesman has even said that some state-operated businesses might be returned to private hands." (*Washington Post*, 23 October.) The party has taken some stands critical of the Soviet Union (as on the condemnation of "abrstract art" by the Soviet leadership–see *L'Unitá*, 21 September), and has firmly resisted demands for adventurist direct action tactics by left-wing dissidents. The PCI also strongly opposed the Soviet-led military intervention in Czechoslovakia in 1968. However, there is no question that a basic contradiction remains between a party committed to peaceful, reformist, constitutional government at home, and the role of the same party as an arm (although occasionally a dissenting arm) of that part of the international communist movement remaining under Soviet hegemony. For a variety of reasons, many observers who are by no means "clerical reactionaries" and "capital imperialists" are inclined to heed the warning of Luigi Mariotti, floor leader of the PSI, that for Italian democracy to "accept the life belt that the PCI is offering would inevitably mean to become subject to its hegemony, and this would be a grave mistake" (*NYT*, 3 September).

International Party Contacts. Among the PCI's numerous meetings with other communist parties from December 1973 through late 1974 were the following.

In December 1973 a delegation from the Soviet Union, led by the rector of the Academy of Social Sciences in Moscow and middle-echelon foreign affairs specialists of the Communist Party of the Soviet Union (CPSU) visited Rome to confer with PCI officials on "information propaganda and the battle of ideas" (*L'Unità*, 2 December, 18). Also in December, a PCI Central Committee delegation visited Hungary for one week.

In February 1974, a delegation of PCI executives led by Gerardo Chiaromonte, PCI Politburo member and editor of *Rinascita*, visited the Soviet Union. Chiaromonte was received by CPSU Central Committee secretary Ponomarev. Also in February, a PCI delegation headed by Longo and Berlinguer, and including PCI Foreign Affairs Department chief Segré, was received in Moscow by Soviet foreign minister Gromyko.

At Bologna, in the heart of Italy's communist "red belt," the PCI held an international festival for two weeks in September, on the occasion of the fiftieth anniversary of its daily newspaper, *L'Unità*. According to *Pravda*, "hundreds of thousands of demonstrators . . . filled the streets and squares of Bologna" in a procession that took more than four hours to pass the rostrum. The Soviet exhibition devoted to Lenin "enjoyed enormous success" and a "flood of visitors" inundated the "large exhibition prepared by the U.S.S.R. Academy of Sciences and the U.S.S.R. Committee on Atomic Energy" (*FBIS*, 3 October).

Also in September PCI Central Committee delegation visited East Germany in September for the commemoration of the twenty-fifth anniversary of the German Democratic Republic, and a PCI Central Committee delegation visited Romania.

In October, Segré announced that the Italian and Polish communist parties would be hosts of the next conference of European communist parties, at Warsaw, in the first all-European meeting since 1967. Twenty-nine parties were invited; all except Albania accepted. Segré emphasized that there would be no final vote on documents at the conference; therefore, the Yugoslavs and Romanians had no problem in accepting. (*FBIS*, 25 October).

Publications. The principal publications of the PCI are the daily newspaper *L'Unità*, the weekly political journal *Rinascita*, the bimonthly theoretical journal *Critica Marxista*, the bimonthly *Politica ed Economia*.

The PCI continues to be confronted with competition from ultra-leftist groups varying in size and orientation. The activities of these groups differed little from the previous year (see *YICA, 1974*, pp. 189-190).

University of Virginia   Dante Germino

Elections to the Italian Chamber of Deputies, 1946-72

Party	1946		1948		1953		1958		1963		1968		1972	
	Percent of vote	Seats	Percent of vote	Seats	Percent of vote	Seats	Percent of vote	Seats	Percent of vote	Seats	Percent of vote	Seats	Percent of vote	Seats
DC (Christian Democrats)	35.2	207	48.5	305	40.1	261	42.4	273	38.3	260	39.1	266	38.8	267
PSI (Socialists)	20.7	115	31.0 (+PCI)	183	12.7	75	14.2	84	13.3	87	14.5 (+PSDI)	91	9.6	61
PSDI (Social Democrats)			7.1	33	4.5	19	4.5	22	6.1	33	14.5 (+PSI)	91	5.1	29
PRI (Republicans)	4.4	23	2.5	9	1.5	5	1.4	6	1.4	6	2.0	9	2.9	14
PLI (Liberals)	6.8	41	3.8	19	3.1	14	3.6	17	7.0	39	5.8	31	3.9	21
MSI (Neo-Fascists)	—	—	—	—	5.8	29	4.8	24	5.1	27	4.5	24	8.7	56
UQ (Common Man)	5.3	30	2.0	6	—	—	—	—	—	—	—	—	—	—
PNM (Monarchist)	2.8	16	2.8	14	6.9	40	4.8	25	1.7	8	1.3	6	—	—
PCI (Communist)	19.0	104	31.0 (+PSI)	183	22.7	143	22.7	140	25.3	166	26.9	177	27.2	179
PSIUP (Proletarian Unity)	—	—	—	—	—	—	—	—	—	—	4.5	23	1.9	0
STVP (South Tyrol Party)	—	—	0.5	3	—	3	0.5	3	0.4	3	—	3	0.5	3
Others	5.8	20	1.8	2	2.6	1	1.2	2	0.9	1	1.4	—	3.1	—
Total		556		574		590		596		630		630		630

Note: I am grateful to my colleague, Professor Robert H. Evans, who prepared this convenient compilation, for permission to reproduce it here.—D.G.

Luxembourg

The Communist Party of Luxembourg (Parti Communiste de Luxembourg; PCL) was established in January 1921. The PCL enjoys legal status and is pro-Soviet in orientation. Western sources estimate that the party has between 500 and 1,000 members. The population of Luxembourg is 400,000 (estimated 1974).

Between 1945 and 1947 one party member served as a cabinet minister in the Luxembourg government. Thereafter the party's influence diminished until the national elections of 1964. At that time the party won 5 of 56 parliament seats. In the elections of 1968 the PCL captured almost 13 percent of the vote and increased its membership in parliament by one seat.

During the latest national elections, held on 26 May 1974, the ruling conservative Christian Socialist Party (Parti Chrétien Social: PCS) suffered an unexpected loss of 3 seats. The result was the creation of a center-left coalition which ended 55 years of unbroken rule by the PCS alone or in coalition.

In the new assembly, expanded to 59 seats (1968: 56 seats), the Christian Socialists remain the largest single party, with 18 seats (1968: 21 seats). But the Socialist Party, with 17 seats (1968: 18 seats), commands a straight majoirty of 31 together with the 14 seats held by the "Liberal" party (Parti Démocratique; PD). The PCL did not fare so well. It captured approximately 10.4 percent of the vote (1968: 15.5) and 5 seats in parliament (1968: 6 seats). The electorate of about 206,000 included about 13,000 voters in the 18 to 21 years age group. (*Keesing's Contemporary Archives*, 8-14 July.)

Major party strength remains in the industrial south. Arthur Useldinger continues as mayor of Luxembourg's second-largest city, Esch-sur-Alzette, and remains a member of the PCL Secretariat and Central Committee.

Leadership and Organization. Dominique Urbany is chairman of the PCL. Party headquarters are at 71 rue du Fort-Neyperg, Luxembourg city. The party is highly centralized and remains under control of the Urbany family.

Party congresses are normally held every three years. At the most recent congress, in March 1973, 28 members were elected to the Central Committee. The Secretariat consists of party chairman Urbany, his son René as party secretary, and treasurer Arthur Useldinger.

The PCL maintains a youth auxiliary (Jeunesse Progressiste), and dominates a group of former resistance members (Le Réveil de la Résistance), headed by a son-in-law of Dominique Urbany. The League of Luxembourg Women (Union des Femmes Luxembourgeoises) is headed by the wife of the party chairman.

Domestic Attitudes and Activities. The domestic policy positions of the PCL did not undergo change during 1974. At the meeting of Western European communist parties, held in Brussels in January, Dominique Urbany advocated "unity of action" among all communist parties in an effort to combat "monopoly capitalism" and the domination of the Luxembourg economy by multi-national concerns, large foreign banks, and holding companies. The PCL consistently opposed Luxembourg's participation in the Common Market as hostile to the workers' movement and as a surrender of national sovereignty. (*L'Humanité*, Paris, 1 February.)

This position in a country which supports the Common Market strongly and whose economy is strong, may account to some extent for the small support the PCL receives from the country's populaton. Nevertheless, the PCL continued to advocate during the year, and without success, cooperation with the liberal and socialist parties in order to design a common political program for both domestic and foreign policy. At the same time the PCL asserted throughout the year that inflation in Luxembourg and elsewhere is due primarily to financial exploitation of the "workers" by the Luxembourg government. (Ibid.)

For the past several years, PCL activities have been overshadowed to a certain extent by Maoist and Trotskyist splinter groups: the Luxembourg Union of Communists (Union des Communistes du Luxembourg) and the Revolutionary Communist League (Ligue Communiste Révolutionnaire). The PCL has been especially concerned that these two parties do not strengthen their positions in the Luxembourg Labor Federation (Letzeburger Arbechterverband) in which the PCL exercises significant influence (*Intercontinental Press*, New York, 25 Febuary 1974).

International Views and Positions. The PCL's views on foreign affairs closely reflect those of the Soviet Union. In a speech before the meeting of Western European communist parties in Brussels in January, Dominique Urbany endorsed "international proletarianism" and "the policy of peaceful coexistence of the U.S.S.R." He also gave special support to convening a conference of European communist parties, a proposal strongly advocated by the Soviet Union, but which did not receive unanimous support at the Brussels meeting. Consistent with his support of Soviet positions, Urbany denounced "political chauvinism, anti-Sovietism," and Maoism. (*L'Humanité*, 1 February.)

At the preparatory meeting of the conference of European communist and workers' parties held in Budapest in December, René Urbany drew special attention to "the fact that the influence of the socialist countries over events in the world and, in particular, events in Europe had increased to a great extent and this had a great effect on the class struggle which was under way in the capitalist countries" (*Summary of World Broadcasts*, Washington, D.C., 23 December). This statement reiterated the view expressed by his father through an article in *World Marxist Review* (February):

> Assimilation of Marxist views in a society dominated by bourgeois ideology is not, of course, a smooth or automatic process. It requires of us Communists an immense propaganda and enlightenment effort. However, in this we have a strong and reliable ally, life itself. For interest in our ideas is born of the desire to understand the implications of everyday life in an exploitive society and compare them with the reality of socialism. . . .
>
> Even our confirmed opponents are constrained to admit that our scientific ideology has an immense power of attraction. Time and again bourgeois newspapers and journals report with astonishment and alarm the "Marxist renaissance," the "new coming of Marx," the "upsurge of Marxist enthusiasms."
>
> The U.S. magazine *Time* (May 7, 1973) says that "professors and students alike are thoroughly Marxist" not only in the new educational establishments of Western Europe, like the Bremen University in the Federal Republic of Germany, but that traditional Catholic centers of education also devote a much more prominent place in their curricula to Marxist philosophy, sociology and economics.

Publications. The party organ, *Zeitung vum Letzeburger Vollek*, has a daily distribution of approximately 1,200. The PCL also publishes a weekly, *Wechenzeitung*. Both newspapers are printed by the party publishing company, Coopérative Ouvrière de Presse et d'Editions.

Hoover Institution
Stanford University

Dennis L. Bark

Netherlands

The Communist Party of the Netherlands (Communistische Partij van Nederland; CPN) was founded as the Communist Party of Holland in 1918. The official founding date, however, is that of affiliation to the Comintern, 10 April 1919. The present name was chosen at the party congress in December 1935. The party has always been legal (with the exception of the war years).

CPN policy is based on the "new orientation" proclaimed at the 1964 congress, which gives primary importance to the realization of domestic political goals: Relations with the international communist movement are subordinated to the realization of a united front of communists, socialists, and progressive believers. The autonomous attitude of the CPN to the Sino-Soviet dispute has led to the formation of both pro-Soviet and pro-Chinese groups outside the party. Their influence on CPN politics is small.

The CPN does not publish figures, but the number of members is estimated at 10,000 and the number of subscribers to its daily paper *De Waarheid* at 16,000. CPN followers are irregularly spread over the country, with centers of activity in Amsterdam, the highly industrialized "Zaanstreek," and the province of Groningen. The population of the Netherlands is about 13,400,000 (estimated 1972). The number of CPN votes received in elections has been increasing since the low point of 2.4 percent in 1959, when the party was split. In the November 1972 general elections the CPN received 4.5 percent of the votes, which means 7 seats out of 150 in the Lower House of the parliament. The CPN is represented in provincial and municipal governing bodies.

Leadership and Organization. There have been no changes in the composition of the highest governing bodies of the CPN since its latest party congress, in May 1972. The principal policy-making body is the 12-member Executive Committee of the Central Committee, consisting of H. J. Hoekstra (chairman), J. Wolff (director of the party's publishing house and chief editor of the party periodical *Politiek en Cultur*), J. F. Wolff (chief editor of *De Waarheid*), M. Bakker (chairman of the CPN fraction in parliament), R. J. Walraven (secretary for propaganda), K. J. A. Hoogkamp (organizational secretary), F. J. IJisberg (administrative secretary), W. J. A. Nieuwenhuyse (charged with work in industry), F. Meis (charged with work in industry), R. Haks (political secretary for the district of Amsterdam), L. Bosch (political secretary of the district of Rotterdam), and H. Kleuver (charged with financial affairs). The Secretariat, consisting of 6 members of the Executive Committee, Hoekstra, Hoogkamp, Kleuver, Nieuwenhuyse, Walraven, IJisberg), is the organizational and adminstrative center of the party. The Central Committee, consisting of 37 members and 3 deputy members, only meets a few times per year. Former leader P. de Groot still has a strong influence on CPN politics.

The significance of the CPN front organizations has decreased considerably since the breaking of their ties with the international front organizations because of the party's autonomous policy. The most active is the General Netherlands Youth Organization (Algemeen Nederlands Jeugd Verbond; ANJV). ANJV played a stimulating role in actions for improvement of the position of young workers, which were held by a number of youth organizations in various places since March 1974. At a national conference on organization, held on 12-13 October, ways to improve cultural activities and were also discussed. The activities of the Netherlands Women's Movement (Nederlandse Vrouwen Beweging; NVB), like those of the ANJV, supported CPN demands. The organization of former resistants "Verenigd Verzet 1940-1945" is politically of no importance.

Party Internal Affairs. The party conference on 22-23 December 1973 was particularly devoted to problems of organization. It was concluded that the aims should be acceleration of the growth of membership and number of subscribers, and intensification of party life.

In order to achieve this, the members were urged to drop "suspicion against new members from new layers of society attracted by the CPN," because "It should be made possible that new members can immediately and completely take their place in all activities of the party" (*De Waarheid*, 31 January 1974). With this policy, which includes holding out prospects of party functions, the CPN hoped to attract cadres from other parties (e.g., the Labor Party). In some places the policy was successful. Recruitment activities, however, did not lead to an increase in the number of members and subscribers worth mentioning, because of a rather large falling off.

After the elections in the spring of 1974, which were disappointing for the CPN, the necessity of a "thorough investigation" into the functioning of the party was stressed. In a statement of the Central Committee (ibid., 10 April), self-criticism was expressed in regard to the shortcomings of the party. Propaganda was "too superficial and not militant enough," while the work in industry was neglected and the party was in general "too passive." According to the Central Committee, this weakening was also caused by the party's lack of initiative to take a stand on questions of the international communist movement. The actual cause, however, for organizational changes was the Cyprus crisis, which had made it clear that local CPN bodies in many places were not able to organize in a short time the demonstrations which were demanded by the party leaders. Chairman Hoekstra, addressing the Central Committee noticed "weakening of political life in the party" which he wanted to fight "through improving the division of labor in the Executive Committee and through a series of other measures." In fact this means intensified control of the local and regional bodies (ibid, 7 October). At the party congress in the spring of 1975 the effectiveness of these measures will be put to the test. The Central Committee has decided to provide more information on discussions and decision-making in the party, in order to encourage political life (ibid., 5 July).

The CPN partly blames the activity of the pro-Chinese Socialist Party (SP) for the disappointing election results. Therefore it no longer attacks only pro-Soviet dissident groups but also "so-called extreme left wing groups, which abuse the healthy fighting spirit of still inexperienced people to break down the workers' movement, and which have among them agents of reaction" (ibid.). The political line of the CPN is hardly influenced by pro-Soviet or pro-Chinese movements.

Domestic Attitudes and Activities. In the elections for the provincial governing bodies, held on 27 March 1974, the CPN received 3.5 percent of the votes, which meant 19 seats out of 670 and a loss of more than 20 percent in comparison with the general elections of November 1972. In the preceding campaign special attention was paid to the recruitment of "class-conscious members of the Labor Party." In the elections for municipal governing bodies, on 29 May, the CPN received 130 seats out of 12,000, which meant a loss of 40 seats. In 16 out of 800 municipalities the CPN has aldermen. Probably the outcome of the elections was influenced by the activity of the SP, which received in 12 municipalities about 15,000 votes in total.

Originally the CPN was inclined—in accordance with its policy of a united front of communists and socialists—to shield the present Den Uyl coalition-government—in which the Labor Party is the largest coalition partner—against the right-wing parties. After the disappointing election results, however, more emphasis was put on the CPN's own character. In CPN publications extra-parliamentary mass action was recommended, "including strikes," in order to end the identification of the CPN with government policy. Through this attitude the CPN hopes to bring it about that "the left-moving and really progressive forces in the Labor Party will join the CPN and so force the leaders of the Labor Party to cooperate with the CPN." (*De Waarheid*, 10 April.) In independent trade union activities, the CPN's role was limited to propaganda and agitation efforts in industry to back up trade union demands.

In July the party newspaper declared: "The CPN is firmly bent on pursuing its policy of a united front of communists and socialists, on defending it against all attacks and on doing everything to strengthen organizations in which communists and socialists take part" (ibid., 5 July). Where this policy would not be successful at the top, it was to be tried through mass action at the basis. A demonstration trip to Kalkar, a small place in the Federal Republic of Germany, drew 9,000 persons to protest Dutch participation in the building of a nuclear power station. It was regarded by CPN leaders as successful. According to Hoekstra, the action committees of communists and socialists that had been formed for this occasion "could form the framework for further action against the dangers of war, for disarmament and for peace" (ibid., 7 October). The CPN was also involved in demonstrations in regard to Cyprus and in demonstrations on the anniversary of the coup d'état in Chile. The CPN started independent actions in certain fields hoping that these would meet with response in socialist circles, such as committees of unemployed and committees against the increasing cost of living.

International Views and Positions. In accordance with the "new orientation" policy, as proclaimed at the party's Twenty-first Congress, in 1964, the international policy of the CPN is determined far more by the domestic political situation, than by the prevailing views in the internationalist communist movement. The party stated early in 1974: "In order to be able to pursue its national and international aims, the CPN has to orient itself, uninhibited, toward the mass struggle in its own country. To conceal or gloss over increasing revisionist movements in a number of socialist countries, or the "European" phraseology in some so-called communist parties in capitalist countries, can only harm that policy." (*De Waarheid*, 10 April.)

The national independence of the country, which the CPN wants, means above all a struggle against the influence of EEC and NATO. A statement of the Central Committee made demands for:

— drastic reduction of NATO armament;
— removal of nuclear arms from Dutch territory;
— stopping of every measure which leads to the situation of the Dutch forces within NATO becoming the foot soldiers of the West German Wehrmacht;
— a halt to the subjection to the demands of the EEC and to cooperation with measures that are harmful or will increase prices for the population or parts of it. (Ibid., 31 January.)

According to the CPN, the fight for national independence is the best contribution that the Dutch working class can make for the preservation of world peace. The CPN does not take part actively in the Soviet-led campaign for European security and cooperation. It wants the government to pursue a policy of "active neutrality" as a Dutch contribution to détente and disarmament, which forms an element of a system of collective security, and first of all in Europe. It believes that concepts on peace and security should be based on the principle of peaceful coexistence of states with different social and political systems. In regard to SALT, the CPN does not expect for a very long time any agreement that would guarantee the security of the Netherlands: "NATO is not an instrument of détente but an instrument of war against the Soviet Union. For that purpose the Americans established the alliance in 1949, and West Germany has used it for building a gigantic military apparatus." (Ibid., 22 June.)

The CPN showed its independent position in the international communist movement when it sent only an observer to the conference of West European communist parties, convened in Brussels in late January. Afterward the opinion was expressed that this conference was "wide of the mark because of a wrong assessment of the situation in the EEC" (ibid., 23 February).

The relationship with the Communist Party of the Soviet Union became ever worse through the CPN's attitude toward the expulsion of Solzhenitsyn. The editor in chief of *De Waarheid* saw the way this matter was solved as a result "of a revisionist policy, for which others cannot take any responsibility" (ibid., 15 March). The CPN did not take part in the consultative conference of European communist parties in Warsaw in October. A resolution justifying this absence stated: "The conference was meant to create a platform for attacks on the Communist Party of China, and for practices which can only deepen the split in the international communist movement" (ibid., 7 October).

International Party Contacts. Because of its autonomous policy the CPN hardly maintains bilateral relations with other communist parties. In the CPN press no discussions with other parties were mentioned in 1974. As far as the parties were mentioned, it was usually in a negative sense. The French Communist Party was treated better, as the CPN has a certain respect for the agreement between the French communists and socialists.

The CPN did not take part in the conferences of West-European communist parties which were held as a follow-up of the Brussels conference. It participated, however, in an international conference of solidarity with the people of Chile, held in Paris in July. This willingness was probably caused by the participation of non-communist parties and organizations.

Publications. The daily *De Waarheid* ("The Truth") is the main source of information for the members of the CPN. The paper is in constant financial trouble. The subscription price was raised twice and special collections were made in 1974. The bimonthly *Politiek en Cultur*, devoted to the theory and practice of Marxism-Leninism under the leadership of the CPN Central Committee, was used for training purposes. The CPN has its own publishing house and bookshop, "Pegasus." As far as the import of Russian publications is concerned, the pro-Soviet bookshop "Sterboek" competes with "Pegasus." The CPN has two commercial printing plants, one for *De Waarheid* and one for other printed matter.

*   *   *

Dissident Groups. The pro-Soviet communists in the Netherlands do not have organizational unity. Most are members of the "Nederland-USSR" friendship society, which is not engaged in domestic politics; it promotes cultural relations between the Netherlands and the Soviet Union, hoping to foster appreciation for the socialist system. Its monthly paper is *NU* (standing for "Netherlands-U.S.S.R."). An important part is played by the travel agency "Vernu BV," which organizes an increasing number of tourist visits to Eastern Europe. The chairman of the friendship society, who is also director of the travel agency, is W. Hulst. He has been awarded the Soviet "Order of the Friendship of the Peoples" for "his promotion of better relations between the peoples of the Netherlands and the Soviet Union" over many years (*NU*, no. 9, 1973).

A new organization, founded by young members of the "Nederland-USSR" society in 1973, is called "Jongeren Kontakt voor Internationale Uitwisseling" (Youth Contact for International Exchange; JKU). It has organized a number of trips to the Soviet Union but is still too weak to develop political activities of any importance. Soviet views are also presented by the "Nederlands Comité voor Europese Veiligheid en Samenwerking" ("Dutch Committee for European Security and Cooperation") and by a monthly paper *Communistische Notities* ("Communist Notes"), edited by a former CPN Executive Committee member, F. Baruch.

October 1974.

Although originally splinter groups of the CPN, the pro-Chinese groups find their followers among students and young workers who have no past or present connection with the CPN. There are six competing pro-Chinese groups in the Netherlands. The two main groups are the Netherlands Communist Unity Movement-Marxist-Leninist (Kommunistische Eenheidsbeweging Nederlands-marxistisch-leninistisch; KEN-ml) and the Socialist Party. Both are small organizations. The SP issues a monthly, *De Tribune*, and the KEN-ml a monthly called *De Rode Tribune*. The SP took part in the municipal elections in May 1974, for the first time, and received in total 15,000 votes in 12 municipalities. It is mainly concerned with problems of housing shortage and environmental protection. Most followers of the KEN-ml can be found also in the Communist Students Union (Kommunistische Studenten Bond). It has good relations with the Maoist Communist Party of (West) Germany (Maoistische Kommunistische Partei Deutschlands).

Oost-West Instituut
The Hague

C. C. van den Heuvel

Norway

The Norwegian Communist Party (Norges Kommunistiske Parti; NKP) is small but no longer suffering complete political isolation. Its chairman sits in the Norwegian parliament (Storting), and the communists are active participants in a reconstitution of the Norwegian left. Most NKP members are attracted from among industrial workers in Oslo and low-income groups in the northern province of Finnmark and the eastern region of Hedmark. Membership estimates for the NKP range from 2,000 to 5,000. The population of Norway is approximately 4,000,000.

The party was organized on 4 November 1923 when a few radical politicians and trade unionists split from the Norwegian Labor Party (Det Norske Arbeiderparti; DNA). The NKP, in contrast to the parent party, conformed to Comintern principles. It started with an inherited 14 seats in the parliament and about 16,000 members, but (except for some electoral success in 1945, due to communist participation in wartime resistance against the Germans and in the liberation of northern Norway by the Soviets) subsequently lost more of its political ground.

The communists clearly suffered from being sandwiched between the nation's traditionally strongest political organization—the DNA—on the one side, and the Socialist People's Party (Sosialistisk Folkepartei; SF) and a motley collection of tiny extremist groups, on the other. The NKP broke out of this vise in 1973 through participation in the Socialist Electoral Alliance (Sosialistisk Valgforbund; SV). Whereas in the previous parliamentary election of 1969 the NKP got only one percent of the vote and no seats, in 1973 it did get one of the 16 places won by the SV. That alliance—of the NKP, SF, and dissidents who had bolted the DNA in 1972 over the issue of Norwegian membership in the European Community (EC)—garnered 238,744 votes, or 10.1 percent of those cast). The SV holds the balance of power between the minority Labor government and the combined rightist and centrist opposition in the 155-member Storging.

The SF has seized on this new key role of the leftists and has proposed turning the electoral alliance into a united political party. Despite several obvious reservations, the communists have agreed to try this course. Whether the merger will indeed materialize over the next year or so, as projected, is not clear. So far the NKP seems to see a better chance to influence events from inside such an enlarged leftist amalgam than from outside. The prospect of self-chosen liquidation is a curious development that is being watched carefully by communist parties throughout Western Europe.

Leadership and Organization. No significant changes have occurred within the NKP since its Fourteenth Congress, held in Oslo in November 1973. Reidar Larsen remains chairman. A former editor of the party weekly *Friheten*, he replaced Emil Løvlien (the NKP's uncharismatic chairman since 1946) in 1965. Larsen heads the party Secretariat, which is elected by the Central Committee. Bjorn Naustvik chairs the NKP youth affiliate, Communist Youth (Kommunistisk Ungdom; KU).

Though strongest among workers, the NKP does not control any national labor union and does not have any national officer in the Norwegian Federation of Trade Unions (Landsorganisasjonen Norge; LO). At the local level, the NKP is most significant in the construction workers' union and, to some extent, in the metal, wood, transport, and electro-chemical fields. The party directs a "Baltic Sea Committee which sends delegations to the Workers' Conferences of Baltic Nations, Norway, and Iceland, held annually in Rostock, East Germany.

Internal party debate in 1974 concentrated on two issues, the continuing friction between the NKP's Muscovite and Maoist factions, and the NKP's role in an enlarged and formalized leftist coalition. There was frequent verbal sniping between *Friheten* and *Klassekampen*, primary voice of the more Chinese-inclined Workers' Communist Party, Marxist-Leninist, or AKP (m-l) (Arbeidernes Kommunistpartei-Marxist-Leninist). The former warned the latter against "taking part in the new anti-Soviet harassment now attempted, whipped up by NATO partisans, unfortunately with the support of the present Chinese leaders" (*Friheten*, 1-5 July). Writers for the latter termed the Soviet Union a "bureaucratic capitalistic state" and concurred with the Chinese belief that the "major contradiction in the world today lies between U.S. imperialism and Soviet socialist imperialism (the two superpowers) on the one side and the oppressed peoples and nations of the world on the other" (*Klassekampen*, 24-30 July). The Solzhenitsyn case was comparable ground for disagreement, with pro-Soviet factions calling Solzhenitsyn a "political pawn in a move to return to the days of the Cold War" (*Friheten*, 18-23 February).

Opinions were, for the most part, less clearly defined on the question of NKP assimilation into the SV. Edvard Schanche, chairman of the Finnmark NKP, was among those who believed that "obscure guarantees" about the evolution of the SV into a "revolutionary party" were inadequate.

Domestic Attitudes and Activities. Debate over the nature and timing of full "organizational unification" of the Norwegian left dominated NKP domestic considerations in 1974. According to the national conference of the SV, held in April, a program of principles for a Marxist party was to be adopted by March 1975.

Some communists stressed the need for greater "ideological clarity" before taking that big step (*Friheten*, 2-7 September). Others shared the view of NKP chairman Larsen, who asserted, "More things bind us together than divide us," and believed that a united socialist left would end internal uncertainty and organizational weakness, and help overcome the influence of right-wing Social Democrats (ibid., 22-27 April). Larsen had been favorably impressed by the "striking power" of a more unified left in both the successful campaign against Norwegian entry into the Common Market in 1972 and the winning of 16 seats in the Storting in 1973.

Shared concerns about a variety of domestic economic challenges also motivated the joint action of the four parties in the SV. Larsen singled out the problem of rising inflation and the question of how to use Norway's new oil and gas deposits. Oil constituted a particularly compelling issue for the new sheiks of the north. The NKP, for its part, stressed keeping firm Norwegian control of this new resource and a judicious utilization of the reserves. It opposed development by the large international oil companies. It proposed instead that the government quickly undertake a report on nationalization of the gas and oil sales sector in Norway. (Ibid., 10-15, 17-22 June.)

International Views and Positions. There was some spillover of the oil issue into the international arena. The SV, for example, opposed the oil distribution plan proposed for emergency situations under the auspices of the Organization for Economic Cooperation and Development. It considered such "crises" fabrications of the multinational oil companies. The plan smacked of exploitation of Norwegian national sovereignty, a theme on which the communists consistently played. The SV advocated instead that Norway parlay its oil into greater self-reliance and thus curtail dependence on the EC area. It suggested that Norway become an associate member of the Organization of Petroleum Exporting Countries and extract oil at the slowest possible tempo, despite pressure from North America or the rest of Western Europe. (Ibid., 5-10 August 1974.)

Events in Portugal and the visit of U.S. secretary of defense Schlesinger in June provided opportunities for the communists to reaffirm their opposition to Norwegian membership in NATO. The NKP maintained that Norway was supporting fascist regimes by staying in the alliance (ibid., 6-11 May, 4-8 June).

International Party Contacts. The NKP during 1974 sustained its traditionally brisk pace of fraternal visits. Nicolae Ceauşescu received an NKP delegation headed by Larsen in Romania in April. Larsen also led an NKP visit to the German Democratic Republic (GDR), in May. Erich Honecker, first secretary of the GDR party, received the Norwegian delegation. Both parties welcomed détente and paid tribute to the conference of the communist parties of the capitalist states of Europe in January as an important step toward strengthening the unit of the international communist movement.

The NKP participated in the conference of Nordic communist parties, held in Finland, 5-7 September. The communiqué from that meeting urged the earliest convocation of the third stage of the Conference on Security and Cooperation in Europe at summit level and spoke out for the restoration of democratic rights in Chile. Similar themes recurred during an NKP visit to Hungary, 5-12 September, and to Poland, 17-21 September.

The only notable lapse from fraternal hospitality occurred in the People's Republic of China. An NKP delegation had planned to travel home via Peking after visiting the Democratic Republic of Korea—but was denied a visa. The NKP, traditionally neutral in the in the Sino-Soviet dispute, concluded that "the refusal was politically motivated."

Publications. The NKP press consists of *Friheten* ("Freedom"), the party's central organ, and several "in house" publications of party district organizations. First published during the wartime resistance, *Friheten* reached a peak circulation of 100,000 in 1945. Financial hard times and dwindling demand caused its transition from daily to weekly publication in 1967. The KU publishes a bulletin, *Fremad* ("Forward"). The primary voice of the AKP (m-l) is *Klassekampen* ("Class Struggle").

Portugal

Founded in 1921, the Portuguese Communist Party (Partido Comunista Português; PCP) operated illegally between 1926 and 25 April, 1974. During its 47 years of clandestine activities the PCP maintained a tight internal discipline and was credited in recent years with being the country's best-organized party. It was especially influential in the more than 200 labor unions, mostly in Lisbon and Oporto, and among university students. Its weak rural-labor strength was mostly concentrated in the upper Alentejo area of southeast Portugal. The party claimed to have deeply infiltrated the nation's armed forces.

PCP membership was estimated in early 1974 at 1,000 to 2,000. The estimate, it is now thought, may have been considerably short of the actual number. By September the party claimed to have at least doubled its ranks and the number of its organizations ("Radio Free Portugal," 23 October). Outside estimate puts its strength at between 15,000 and 60,000 members at that time. In addition, there were said to be some 800 special agents, educated in Czechoslovakia, now operating in Portugal, as well as some communist refugees from Cuba and Brazil. A fourth of Portugal's 100,000 military draft evaders and deserters were expected by some to return from other European countries as communists or at least heavily indoctrinated (*Weekly Review*, 22 August). The PCP also operated through a front organization, the Portuguese Democratic Movement (Movimento Democrático Português; MDP), which was organized officially as a political party in November 1974.

To the left of the PCP were several small extremist organizations. These included the Maoist-oriented Movement for the Reorganization of the Proletariat Party (Movimento Reorganizador do Partido do Proletariado; MRPP); the Revolutionary Party of the Proletariat (Partido Revolucionário do Proletariado; PRP); the Trotskyite Internationalist Communist League (Liga Comunista Internacionalista; LCI); the Marxist-Leninist Revolutionary Unity (Unidade Revolucionária Marxista-Leninista; URML); the Communist Party of Portugal (Partido Comunista de Portugal; PCDP), which also professed to be Marxist-Leninist; the Socialist Left Movement (Movimento da Esquerda Socialista; MES); and the Comissões de Base Socialistas (CBS). The MRPP, with an estimated membership of 1,500—mostly students—appeared to be the most active of these groups. Prior to April, the PRP had directed the underground activities of the Revolutionary Brigades (see *YICA, 1974*, p. 203).

PCP Leadership and Organization. The party is organized into cells functioning at a local level in businesses, educational establishments, rural estates, and army barracks. Some "street cells" are formed. The highest authority is the party congress, which elects the Central Committee to guide activities between congresses. The Central Committee selects the Secretariat and other executive organs.

The Seventh Congress, convened in October 1974, was the first since 1965 and the first held legally since 1926. It was attended by 1,000 delegates, from 5,000 party cells. Half were said to be workers, a fourth white-color employees, 12 percent students, and 2 percent peasants. Some 42 percent were under 30 years of age, compared with 59 percent for the PCP membership as a whole ("Radio Clube Portuguêse," 21 October). The congress elected a Central Committee made up of Alvaro Cunhal, Blanqui Teixeira, Carlos Brito, Carlos Costa, Dias Lourenço, Jaime Serra, Joaquim Gomes, José Vitoriano, Octávio Pato, and Sérgio Vilarigues. The Secretariat included Secretary-General Alvaro Cunhal, Joaquim Gomes, Octávio Pato, and Sérgio Vilarigues. (*Diario de Noticias*, Lisbon, 21 October.)

Cunhal began acting as secretary-general in exile in 1961, when he escaped from Portugal after spending many years in jail. He returned to Lisbon in April 1974, where he was soon acknowledged as one of Portugal's cleverest and most charismatic politicians.

Domestic Attitudes and Activities. The fall of the Thomaz-Caetano government on 25 April 1974 found the PCP poised to pluck maximum advantage from the new atmosphere of political freedom offered by the Armed Forces Movement (AFM). The latter group of junior officers overthrew the government with the declared intention of installing democracy in Portugal and bringing the colonial wars to an end. The strategy of the communist party was to construct a power base within the new provisional government from which it might prepare the way for success in national elections scheduled for 1975. This approach enabled the PCP to play an influential role in political developments throughout the year. ("*Radio Free Portugal,*" 26 October.)

The party developed its power base with four tactics. (1) As the strongest and most cohesive political unit in the country, it easily mobilized an impressive show of popular support at various demonstrations. (2) It actively supported a popular front of "democratic and progressive forces" in alliance with the AFM, which it made a great point of flattering in frequent public statements. (3) It very carefully sought to present an image of moderation in order to avoid alienating military and centrist middle-class groups. (4) It became progressively more aggressive in combating "counter-revolutionary" forces, which at first were only vaguely identified in PCP statements as fascists and large monopolist business interests.

The PCP's leading position among the political forces and its unrivaled influence among industrial workers was generally attributed by analysts to the organization and discipline it had been able to maintain while operating underground since 1926. Because party secretary-general Alvaro Cunhal had in particular become for many a symbol of resistance to the deposed government, he was able to return to Lisbon in April to the acclaim of huge throngs of workers, who also cheered him wildly when he addressed a May Day demonstration of thousands.

Backed by the prestige of this impressive welcome, Cunhal pressured his way into the government organized by President António de Spínola. Though he himself accepted only a minor cabinet post, as minister without portfolio, which left him with a freer hand to organize his party for the election campaign, he was able to secure the head of the important Labor Ministry for a young and obscure party man, Avelino Pacheco Gonçalves, a former bank clerk from Oporto who had organized the bank workers' union into a communist-dominated unit. There was speculation that Spínola was persuaded to accept the communists into his government principally by the argument that this could help contain labor unrest during the critical months of organizing the country for democracy.

While some 50 or more other political parties were struggling simply to organize during succeeding months, the PCP was proceeding rapidly to recruit support and new members for itself among all groups, especially the working class. The party opened offices throughout the country, distributed posters and leaflets, and generously daubed Lisbon with communist slogans and the hammer and sickle. It staged rallies and actively advanced the party line through its no longer clandestine newspaper and radio. Cunhal also appeared frequently on television. "Radio Free Portugal," 4 May; TASS,

20 May; interview in *Horizint*, East Berlin, no. 23. Lisbon anti-communists were stunned by the PCP success at the end of June in attracting an estimated 20,000 people, despite a downpour, to a giant outdoor rally called in support of government and armed forces policies (*NYT*, 3 July).

Though observers regarded the PCP as a minority party, with some expecting that it would draw only 15 percent of the vote in the 1975 elections (in November some estimates rose to 20 or 25 percent), moderates feared that unless they organized more effectively, and soon, the communists would end up dominating political life. The likely political line-up for the elections appeared to be an alliance of Communists and Socialists—the latter secured three cabinet posts in the Spínola government—against a coalition of all the conservative and moderate forces (*Christian Science Monitor*, 26 August; radio "Lusitania," Lisbon, 10 October; *Washington Star-News*, 8 November).

Popular Front—AFM "Alliance". Even while the PCP was strengthening its organization, it was publicly calling for "political unity" of anti-fascist forces during the transitional period. It stressed that party differences should be subordinated to the need for cooperation to make elections possible and avoid counter-revolution. To left-wing critics of PCP participation in the government, Cunhal replied that the PCP was needed in the government as a "stabilizer" to prevent the emergence of a right-wing government "which most certainly would not continue the policy of democratization" (MIT domestic radio, Budapest, 3 June).

Socialist leader Pedro Soares for his part also sought cooperation with the communists. He declared in the early days following the coup that he would not join a government from which communists were excluded; he cited the prestige and strength of the PCP as justifying its inclusion and said, more significantly, that he did not want the latter to be in a position to capitalize on the economic and social difficulties of the coming months to the disadvantage of the parties attempting to govern (*Christian Science Monitor*, 6 May; *Newsweek*, 13 May). At the same time, the Socialist Party began seeking to disassociate itself from the Portuguese Democratic Movement (Movimento Democrático Portuguêse; MDP), which was formed soon after the coup as a successor to the Democratic Electoral Commission. The latter had been organized in 1969 as a focal point for the anti-government opposition (see *YICA, 1974*, pp. 203, 205). Charging that the MDP was no more than a branch of the PCP, the Socialists formally withdrew from the alliance at the end of August. The PCP chided that this decision would undermine the unity of "democratic" forces and simply serve the interests of counter-revolutionists ("Radio Free Portugal," 30 August). The MDP decided in early November to become a political party and it moved into a position, along with the PCP, as one of Portugal's five main political parties. There was some speculation that the organization would be useful to the Communists as a front for candidates they felt could not win election as representatives of the PCP or who might "take a bit" out of the electorate from whom the Socialists hoped for support ("Radio Clube Portuguès," 2 November; radio "EFE," Madrid, 5 November; *Washington Post* 11 November). In November the Popular Democratic Party (PDP) also broke with the MDP. The PCP said it understood the PDP's reasons for doing so and, in an effort to neutralize the Socialist attacks on the MDP, declared that double affiliation in both the PCP and the MDP would not be permitted ("Radio Clube Portuguès," 6 November).

The PCP was especially careful to court favor with the armed forces, whose sufferance allowed it to take part in the government. Though the Communists claimed to have deeply penetrated the ranks of both the enlisted men and the younger officers, the army high command nevertheless was said to remain essentially centrist and rightist. The dominant AFM was itself reportedly a liberal-leftist group of junior officers, but most speculation discounted the likelihood of there being many, if any, Communists in the group (*NYT*, 27 May; *Washington Post*, 11 November). The number (estimated at between 25 and 1,000) and exact ideology of members actually remained highly uncertain. The AFM denied, through its general staff, any links with political parties, but did profess to some socialistic leanings (Lisbon domestic radio, 5 November). The "politicking" of officers on the movement's coordinating committee was attacked in a letter allegedly written in September with 700 AFM signatures (*The Economist*, 7 September).

Cunhal and his party constantly proclaimed the solidarity of the "popular masses"–that is, the PCP–with the armed forces. Special stress was put on the "mass movement" nature of the April uprising. Some critics recalled that since its 1965 congress the PCP had denied the possibility that a military coup in Portugal could be organized by a handful of officers. Following an abortive armed forces rebellion on 16 March, the PCP, though predicting further military revolts, had repeated that fascism could be overthrown only through a national uprising, "with the participation of the broadest popular masses and part of the armed forces" (*Granma Weekly Review*, Havana, 31 March; "Radio Free Portugal," 7 April; Radio Free Europe Research, 13 May; *Wiener Tagebuch*, Vienna, June; *Frankfurter Allgemeine*, Frankfurt, 15 June). Party spokesmen later sought to explain the success of the April revolt by citing its "deep ties with the people" and the support it received from the "overwhelming majority" of the army. They said it should not be confused as a classic coup d'état "organized and led by a small group of conspirators cut off from the masses." (*L'Unità*, Rome, 15 May; Lisbon domestic radio, 17 May.)

The PCP claimed that the revolt, organized by a "captains' movement" involving "hundreds of officers" in all three branches of the service, began to be planned following a July 1973 call by the PCP Central Committee for mass political action (*WMR*, June). Incidentally, a special distinction was made by Trotskyist communists between career captains and the more numerous non-professional captains: the former were characterized as "petty bourgeois democrats, who could move sharply to the right when confronted by a 'red danger,' " and the latter as strongly influenced by the Socialist and Communist parties and even by far-left currents (*Intercontinental Press*, New York, 24 June).

PCP Image of Moderation. Underpinning all PCP behavior following the April revolt was an attempt by the party to present a public image of moderation, responsibility, and patriotism. It was clear from statements by Cunhal that the party intended to profit from the experience of Chile's Popular Unity government, which fell in 1973 because it had fiercely antagonized army and middle-class sectors in its haste to socialize the country (*Manchester Guardian*, 1 June; *Rudé Právo*, Prague, 7 June; Budapest domestic radio, 8 June). The PCP strategy was to proceed cautiously, giving priority for the time being to the need for cooperation with "all anti-fascists" simply to "consolidate democracy" and to bring an end to Portuguese colonialism in Africa. Apart from an occasional promise of extensive social reforms for a later date and frequent vilification of "monopolists tied to foreign imperialism," the usual Marxist rhetoric was abandoned. According to Cunhal, socialism was as yet "not on the agenda" (*O Século*, Lisbon, 12 June; *Friheten*, Oslo, 22-27 July). Another PCP Central Committee member was quoted in October as saying that the party did not favor nationalizing small and medium-sized enterprises owned by the bourgeoisie, because this would not be "in the interest of the people" (*Manchester Guardian*, 30 October). Cunhal even stated in June–though he later reversed himself–that big business, aside from banks, need not fear nationalization in the event of a leftist victory in 1975 elections, even though profits would have to be reduced (*Trybuna Ludu*, Warsaw, 10 May; *NYT*, 3 July).

A particularly unaccustomed role was played by the PCP in trying to restrain widespread wage demands and strikes. Beginning in May, thousands of workers in scores of industries went on strike, restless, with their new freedom, to improve their working conditions and at least double their wages in the face of Portugal's mounting inflation. Cunhal and Gonçalves sternly condemned the work paralysis and worked actively to dissuade workers from insisting on "unrealistic"–even though "legitimate"–demands. Cunhal warned that if the minimum wages being sought were to be received by all workers, the entire national product would be consumed. The party explained that it was necessary to prevent a severe social and economic dislocation that could be exploited by reactionaries as a pretext to restore fascist tyranny. By June many workers had been won over by this argument and thousands paraded across the city to demonstrate against strikes and in support of the government ("Radio Free Portugal," 30 May; *NYT*, 2 June; TASS, 24 June; *Friheten*, 22-27 July).

The PCP also made a show of harmony and reasonableness in its relations with President Spínola and the cabinet, the political complexion of which ranged from leftist to rightist. Differences with top government figures were generally minimized: "We have certain objections . . . but we must not lay emphasis on what separates us" (*Rudé Právo*, 25 May; "Radio Free Portugal," 19 August). During General Spínola's brief presidency, he himself was not directly criticized by the PCP though neither was he personally praised. Acknowledged but not extolled by the party, for example, was his role in precipitating the April revolt with a book he published in February condemning Portugal's colonial war in Africa.

There were important differences within the government over the solution to the colonial problem, but the PCP held back from assuming a discordant stance. Spínola cherished the idea of persuading the colonies, through a referendum, to remain aligned with Portugal in a federation of equal states. The Communists, Socialists, and Christian Democrats, on the other hand, called for immediate independence for those areas. They disagreed with the president that the African peoples were not yet prepared for complete independence. Still, to avoid estranging Spínola, Cunhal publicly stressed the common position held by all in the government: the need for negotiations to end the war and recognition that the solution to the problem had to be political rather than military (*NYT*, 30 April; Tanyug, Belgrade, 4 June). By the end of July, the president's position of trying to keep the colonies with a Portuguese confederation could no longer be sustained. He then announced as official government policy, which the PCP hailed as an "historic decision," the right of the colonies to independence (TASS, 30 July, 10 August).

PCP Campaign against the Right. Two issues did provoke very sharp public reactions of disapproval from both the Communist and Socialist parties were the government decision in May to permit the exile of ousted Premier Caetano and President Thomaz, and President Spínola's naming of "fascists and reactionaries" to several high posts. Especially criticized was the July appointment of a former "Caetanoite" minister, Veiga Simão, as ambassador to the United Nations. The PCP asserted that this would "discredit Portugal's new regime internationally and make a new dipolomacy difficult" (*NYT*, 22 May: "Radio Clube Português," 8 July).

The PCP also expressed frequent concern at the continuing widespread influence of "fascists" who had not been rooted out of the government bureaucracy, and of the powerful "potentates of big capital." It warned that these "counter-revolutionary" groups were conspiring in a campaign of anti-communism and of subversion to reverse the democratic process. The monopolies and multi-national enterprises, for example, were said to be using their control over the national economy to promote chaos and mass discontent. They were allegedly discontinuing capital investment, delaying payment of accounts refusing to grant credits, and even encouraging labor to strike for unrealistic wage demands. It was charged that big companies had promised huge wage increases—higher than those expected by labor—if all businesses would follow suit, thereby threatening the "very existence" of small and medium-sized enterprises that would not withstand such cost pressures (Tanyug, 4 June; Budapest domestic radio, 8 June; *France Nouvelle*, Paris, 11-17 June; *O Século*, 12 June; TASS, June 24).

Spínola and other moderate-to-conservative officials were for their part becoming increasingly alarmed at the tactics and growing influence of the left—especially the Communists. Interior Minister Joaquim Magalhães Motta expressed frustration at his inability to brake the rapid Communist infiltration into the civil service and the party's success in manipulating summary elections to municipal councils so that by mid-May half the councils were Communist-dominated (*NYT*, 24 June; *Christian Science Monitor*, 9 July). In July, Prime Minister Adelino Palma Carlos and the other moderates in the cabinet resigned after being unable to get more authority from the AFM to restrain such leftist moves. The new cabinet, formed under the premiership of AFM member Colonel Vasco Gonçalves, was dominated by leftist elements, even though only one Communist, Cunhal, was retained (*CSM*, 11, 17 July).

In a final attempt to counter the left, President Spínola in late September summoned a "silent majority" of moderates and conservatives to what was intended as a massive demonstration "against extremist totalitarianism that fights in the shadows." However, he was outmaneuvered by the leftists, who hastily threw up roadblocks—with the help of the military—to prevent the arrival of busloads of people streaming to Lisbon for the rally. It was charged that this "right-wing operation" represented a cover for an intended counter-revolutionary putsch: the demonstrators would demand the "savior-like intervention" of Spínola and the latter would assume full dictatorial power, declare a state of siege, and dissolve the AFM. To avoid possible bloodshed, Spínola called off the rally and, two days later, resigned, frustrated at the impossibility of building an "authentic democracy" in such a "climate of anarchy" (*CSM*, 1 October, "Radio Free Portugal," 23 October).

Spínola was replaced by his close friend, chief of staff General Francisco da Costa Gomes, who was thought to be equally moderate though his political leanings were actually unclear. The latter was not expected to be any more successful in restraining the radicalized elements within and outside the government. Even though knowledge about the views of the secretive AFM was mostly speculative, that group did not appear to observers to be alarmed at the mounting Communist influence in the nation. The Lisbon military governor asserted that, "contrary to what is feared abroad," the PCP was not strong enough to start an open struggle for power ("Lusitania," 10 October).

Non-Marxist army men and politicians were reportedly very concerned that the heavy left-wing influence over radio, television, and press would have a major effect on the national elections in 1975 (*The Economist*, 7 September). President Spínola had charged that while some political party chief spoke the language of common sense, their activists committed "psychological coercion" by using the media to slander all opponents (*NYT*, 1 October). This influence on the media could also be significant in other ways. Communist members of the radio workers' union, for example, began in October to incite fellow members to refuse to broadcast commercials on the national radio and television networks. They criticized the "economic power of the commercial radio" ("Radio Clube Português," 31 October).

Such tactics were part of the PCP's stepped-up campaign against the "entrenched" monopolists and latifundists. The party emphasized that the economic power of those groups must be liquidated if they were not to regain political power and install another dictatorship ("Radio Free Portugal," 23 October). At the PCP's Seventh Congress, in October, calls for economic and political "reforms" became more strident than during the preceding months, reflecting the increasing self-assurance of the party within the new power structure. Three priority tasks were set: the "consolidation of democracy" to "halt reaction in its tracks," the defense of economic and financial stability, and the continuation of decolonization. Actions to implement these goals were to include a purge of fascist elements remaining in the bureaucracy, police force, and army; a ban on "reactionary" organizations and activities; a reduction of government budget and trade deficits; the increasing nationalization of "key sectors" dominated by big capital; and the stimulation of "free non-monopolist private enterprise" (ibid., 22, 23 October).

Rival Communist Organizations. After the April overturn of the Caetano government, the only organized opposition was provided by several extreme left-wing groups including Maoists, Trotskyites, anarchists, and others. The Maoists (the MRPP) appeared to be the most active and vociferous. In the first days of the military junta, these groups launched vigorous campaigns against the "bourgeois revolution," even though welcoming the coup itself. Their numbers were small, but they successfully promoted widespread labor unrest and incited squatters to seize housing projects (*NYT*, 2 May; *Christian Science Monitor*, 6 May). They led strikes not only among urban workers but also among agricultural laborers in southeast Portugal. Three agitators in the latter area were reportedly passing themselves off as regular Communists but the PCP charged that they were Maoists (*NYT*, 6 May, 5, 15 July). The MRPP also organized demonstrations to assail the army, cast doubt on its intention to end the war, and encourage desertions by soldiers to avoid fighting. Early in May, a group of Maoist demonstrators abducted ten army conscripts at the Lisbon airport to keep them from being flown to Africa.

The government and army reacted to such agitation with restraint during the first month, but then with increasing toughness. Extremists were warned that they would be "severely punished" for criticizing the armed forces, and a committee of seven officers was set up to supervise all news media (*The Economist*, 29 October). A Maoist editor was imprisoned in June for urging, in his weekly *Luta Popular*, that soldiers desert. A month later, the paper itself was suspended indefinitely for "ideological aggression" against the armed forces. The police and military occupied a plaza to prevent a rally from taking place in Lisbon to protest the ban, and briefly suspended three Lisbon newspapers for reporting accounts of a provocative Maoist rally that did take place on another occasion. The government rescinded the latter suspension when other news media threatened a shutdown in protest (*NYT*, 8 June, 4, 6 August; *CSM*, 26 August). A second leftist weekly, the *Red Proletariat*, was suspended in September for two months for publishing an "offensive" article (*Ansa*, Buenos Aires, 24 September).

The crackdown against anti-army extremism became more severe than was apparently intended by the government at still another demonstration. When a rally banned by authorities was staged in August in support of an Angola guerrilla movement, police shot into the crowd, killing one man and wounding several others. The government expressed deep regrets over the killing and promised an inquiry. The PCP charged that the incident represented an effort by some lingering counter-revolutionary elements in the police force to discredit the government among the masses ("Radio Free Portugal," 18 August; *CSM*, 26 August).

The PCP joined the government in condemning the disruptive and provocative "adventurism" of the extreme left, and urged workers to "unmask the demagogues" who were pushing the country toward anarchy. It charged that the latter "do not take into consideration how much the country can afford." The influence of these "minor" groups of "students, intellectuals, and petty bourgeois who have no real contacts with the workers" was claimed to be slight, but they were still regarded as dangerous since their "irresponsibility" was playing into the hands of a "reactionary right" waiting for an excuse to try to recapture power (Moscow domestic radio, 5 May; *NYT*, 29 May; *O Século*, 12 June). The suspension of leftist newspapers was also supported by the PCP—though criticized by the Socialist Party—as a necessary restraint on an "irresponsible" abuse of freedom of the press ("Radio Free Portugal," 6 August; Lisbon domestic radio, 6 August).

The Maoists and other extremists reacted to the PCP campaign agaist them by charging the party with a "revisionist" determination to support reaction (*NYT*, 22 May). It was said sarcastically in June that the military government, preferring not to resort to violent repression, instead used the Communist and Socialist parties to restrain the masses (*Intercontinental Press*, 24 June). Strikes were urged on workers by the ultra-leftists as the only means of establishing a true dictatorship of the proletariat. The Maoists further instructed the PCP that its pro-Soviet and anti-Chinese position explained why it had no close relations with the Africa guerrilla movements, which, it claimed, were more attracted to Maoism (*NYT*, 27 May). Even so, there were continued reports of Soviet influence in the Portuguese territories through the continued supply of weapons to the rebels. In May, for example, a modern Soviet ground-to-air missile hit a Portuguese plane flying over northern Mozambique (*NYT*, 10 June).

International Views and Contacts. Even though many believed that the PCP and the Soviet Union were taken by surprise by the success of the April revolt, it seemed clear, nevertheless, that at least the broad outlines of a program of action were planned for such a contingency. It was speculated that the strategy was devised when Cunhal visited Moscow in February for a briefing with top Soviet authorities. A communiqué published in *Pravda* summed up those talks as a summons to the Portuguese people to stand for "unity of all democratic forces and popular masses and for the setting up of a democratic regime" (*Christian Science Monitor*, 9 July). At the same time, Cunhal was awarded the "Order of the October Revolution" in appreciation for his services to the international communist movement—that is, for his adherence to the Soviet line "in all fundamental questions of modern times" (*Pravda*, 23 February).

Immediately after the coup, Cunhal and his party began to press for a restoration of diplomatic relations with Soviet bloc countries, and in the first two weeks of June ties were opened with Romania, the Soviet Union, and Yugoslavia. Previously, Cuba had been the only communist country represented in Lisbon; in fact, Portugal then had relations with less than half the members of the United Nations (*Manchester Guardian*, 15 June). Portuguese businessmen began exploring market possibilities in eastern countries, and the Soviet Union and Poland announced that they would take part for the first time in Lisbon's international fair in June (*NYT*, 10 June). In November, a Portuguese delegation headed by Cunhal made a two-day official visit to Moscow to develop "economic, technical, and cultural ties." Specifically, Cunhal reportedly sought Soviet shipments of grain and meat to alleviate food shortages that might set off a wave of popular discontent in Portugal. The Soviet Union, which had itself suffered production shortfalls, vaguely declared its readiness to offer economic assistance "with regard for available resources"—that is, to the extent that it could (*International Herald Tribune*, Paris, 2-3 November; *NYT*, 3 November).

Even while Portugal's provisional government was expressing the wish for normal relations with socialist countries it was also reaffirming its allegiance to the North Atlantic Treaty Organization. Cunhal himself said that the PCP would not now raise this issue and that "at present" Portugal should not withdraw from NATO or expel the U.S. from the Azores (*NYT*, 10 June; *Corriere della Sera*, Milan, 22 October). At the PCP congress in October, references to these two previously sensitive issues were considerably softened in comparison with the party position at the Sixth Congress, in 1965. Party members explained that in the present atmosphere of peaceful coexistence, such questions were not a vital problem as they were at the time of the anti-Soviet crusade during the 1950s and 1960s. "We consider that in two or three years it will be possible to obtain a disarmament agreement in Europe," it was said (*Pretoria News* and *The Star*, Johannesburg, 31 October; *Washington Post*, 11 November).

The party's restraint on these points was in accord with its general post-April posture of moderation. At the same time, it undoubtedly welcomed the opportunity to have Portugal take part in the meetings of NATO's nuclear planning group, originally scheduled for early November but postponed indefinitely. Clearly the U.S. and other members were stalling to avoid disclosing military secrets to a left-leaning Portugal. When U.S. secretary of state Henry Kissinger was reported to have warned privately of the Portuguese security risk, the Lisbon response was that the United States was trying to treat Portugal as a "second-class" alliance member (*The Star*, Johannesburg, 31 October; *Washington Post*, 11 November).

At the same time that the PCP was seeking to give reassurances in matters of détente, it found it useful to exploit publicity over U.S. Central Intelligence Agency covert operations. There was much fear that the CIA was striving to create "another Chile" in Portugal by promoting chaos in order to precipitate a rightist coup. The PCP reported rumors, "confirmed by a person closely connected with the American Government," that the CIA had been involved in the planning of the "fascist coup" that was supposed to have installed President Spínola as dictator in September ("Radio Free Portugal," 9 October; *Washington Post*, 11 November).

PCP Media. The PCP has its own press, Edições Avante, which prints *Avante*, the official organ; *O Militante*, a bimonthly theoretical bulletin; *O Textil*, a textile workers' paper; *A Terra*, a small paper for peasants; *UEC*, organ of the Communist Students Union; and various occasional publications. *Avante*, which had come out once or twice monthly as an underground paper, began in May to appear weekly and openly on the newsstands. It was claimed that 300,000 copies of the first legal issue quickly sold out, followed by another printing of 200,000. A British communist newspaper claimed that *Avante* had been the "longest-lived clandestine political paper ever" (Radio Free Europe Research, 13 May).

The PCP broadcasted from abroad until 26 October 1974 over "Radio Free Portugal." It was explained that transmissions were being suspended because the station's mission had been accomplished and conditions had been created for the free flow of information "by other means and in new forms." In other words, the party was able to broadcast over a domestically based station, "Radio Clube Português."

Elbert Covell College
University of the Pacific

H. Leslie Robinson

San Marino

The tiny republic of San Marino has an area of twenty-four square miles and a population of 19,000. The local communist party (Partito Communista di San Marino; PCS) is basically an offshoot of the Italian Communist Party. In the San Marino elections of 8 September, 1974, the PCS polled 3,246 votes, about 23 percent of the total and won 16 seats in the Great and General Council, one more than in the 1969 election. The Socialists polled 1,914 votes and have 8 seats. The Christian Democrats and Social Democrats each lost a seat, but together they retain an absolute majority in the 60-member governing council. (*NYT*, 10 September.)

The chairman of the PCS is Ermenegildo Gasperoni. He has pursued a left-of-center domestic program calling for economic, social, and legal reforms, and has also proposed that a new treaty with Italy be negotiated giving San Marino greater economic independence. In foreign policy the party tends to follow the Soviet line (see Gasperoni's statement in *WMR*, May 1974, pp. 91-94).

University of Virginia   Dante Germino

Spain

The Communist Party of Spain (Partido Comunista de España; PCE) was founded in 1920 and has been illegal since 1939. Among underground organizations, it is the strongest and most effective in the country, and one of the most active in the world. Since the Soviet-led invasion of Czechoslovakia in 1968, the PCE has frequently censured the U.S.S.R. It has also insisted on independent policies for itself, in which it has received strong backing from the Italian and French communist parties and the communist regimes in Yugoslavia and Romania. Its number of hard-core militants has been estimated at 5,000 within Spain and 20,000 outside Spain, some 10,000 of whom reside in France. Carrillo has ridiculed an alleged United States State Department estimate of 30,000; he said it was really closer to the 150,000 cited by "a newsman." The higher figures no doubt actually refer to sympathizers rather than members. ("Radio Independent Spain," 1 June 1974). There are also said to be thousands of Spanish communist exiles living throughout Europe. The party membership comprises mostly urban intellectuals in Madrid, Barcelona, and Bilbao and farm and industrial workers in and around Seville, Cadiz, Córdoba, and Malaga. The population of Spain is about 34,500,000 (estimated 1972).

A dissident pro-Moscow faction of the party, headed by Enrique Líster, was expelled in 1970. This faction formed a rival party with the same name and later became the Spanish Communist Workers' Party (Partido Comunista de Obreros Españoles; PCOE). This rival group received the financial backing of the Soviets but apparently has no more than a few hundred members in Spain and some 2,000 to 3,000 followers in exile. Carrillo's PCE allegedly has financed its activities with contributions from anti-Franco exiles in Latin America and Western Europe.

Trotskyist militants, active in Spain since 1969, are divided between the Communist League of Spain (Liga Comunista de España; LCE) and the Revolutionary Communist League of Spain (Liga Comunista Revolucionaria de España; LCR). The latter group, claiming about 1,000 members and sympathizers, merged in early 1974 with a branch—of about equal size—of the Basque separatist movement, ETA-VI. The fused party, under the name of LCR–ETA-VI, adopted a single central committee, with a third of its members coming from the ETA-VI.

ETA (Euzkadi ta Askatasuna, "Basque Homeland and Liberty") has acted since 1959 as a guerrilla group seeking "national liberation" for the Basque region. A Maoist-Stalinist group split from ETA in 1966 to become the Communist Movement of Spain (Movimiento Comunista de España; MCE). At ETA's Sixth Assembly, in 1970, the movement separated again into ETA-V, which espoused radical nationalism and military activism in line with resolutions of the Fifth Assembly, and ETA-VI, which opposed terrorism and favored more identification with social causes. It was the ETA-V which claimed to have assassinated Premier Carrero Blanco in December 1973 (*Bandiera Rossa*, Rome, 25 February 1974).

A small, aggressive pro-Chinese group, organized in 1964, is the Marxist-Leninist Communist

Party of Spain (Partido Comunista de España, Marxista-Leninista; PCE-ML). It is the principal organization, along with five others, within the Patriotic and Revolutionary Anti-Fascist Front (Frente
Revolucionario Antifascista y Patriótico; FRAP) which includes five other groups. (See *YICA, 1974*,
p. 210).

The PCE. Leadership and Organization. The PCE has party cells in each of Spain's 50 administrative provinces. These are directed at the national level by a 7-member Secretariat, 24-member Executive Committee, and 118-member Central Committee. The PCE chairman is 78-year-old Dolores
Ibarruri ("La Pasionaria" of Civil War days); the secretary-general and actual party leader is Santiago
Carrillo.

Shunning terrorism, party strategists now seek alliances with opponents of the Franco regime
through the Junta Democrática de España, which was formed in July 1974. Party members also
occupy positions of leadership in the clandestine trade unions called Workers' Commissions (Comi-
siones Obreras, or "CC OO"), which they use to promote strikes and other labor agitation. The CC
OO are illegal rivals of the government-sponsored National Confederation of Trade Unions.

Domestic Attitudes and Activities. Describing 1974 as a "crisis year" for the Franco regime, PCE
secretary-general Carrillo predicted its overthrow "in less than several years." He saw the "senile
dictator" gradually losing his authority among the military, the Falangists, and the Opus Dei technocrats, with these groups splintering into multiple factions. Some of the factions, he said, supported
traditional policies, some were opportunistic, while others claimed to have centrist or even "leftist"
views on social matters. (*L'Humanité*, Paris, 28 December, 1973; *Intercontinental Press*, New York,
22 July.)

Carrillo saw the disintegration of the system as being accentuated by the slaying of the premier,
Admiral Luis Carrero Blanco in December 1973. Carrillo did not accept the police identification of
the assassins as six members of ETA, the Basque separatist and extremist movement, and none of this
group was subsequently apprehended during the year. Carrillo asserted that the police version lacked
credibility, not only because it was full of contradictions but also because of the haste with which it
was made public—within 24 hours of the killing—and because three of the alleged suspects quickly
denied from abroad any involvement. He stated also that the mystery was not dispelled by the claim
to responsibility made at a press conference in France by four masked individuals claiming to be ETA
militants, who insisted that they were not among the suspects cited by the Spanish police. He instead
accused the government of covering up the real culprits—a "wealthy and power-hungry clique" of
Franco's relatives that was intent on perpetuating the family's domination. He implied that Franco's
son-in-law, the Marquis of Villaverde, was ambitious to become premier and was plotting as well to
have Prince Juan Carlos replaced as heir to the throne by Alfonso Bourbon Dampierre, the prince's
cousin. Alfonso is a son-in-law of Villaverde. The alleged intrigue involved the elimination of Carrero
Blanco in favor of a new premier and cabinet less sympathetic to the succession of Juan Carlos.
According to Carrillo, the impression of such a plot was reinforced by Franco's choice of a new
Premier, Carlos Arias Navarro, as the new premier: Arias was minister of the interior under Carrero
Blanco and "responsible for the failure of the police to foil the attempt" against the slain premier.
Carrillo commented that one of the most distinctive traits of the new cabinet appointed by Arias was
that "campaigners for the Juan Carlos solution" were replaced by others "not particularly known for
their affection toward the Prince." (*NYT*, 19 January; *Christian Science Monitor*, 2 February; "Radio
Independent Spain," 19 February.)

Recalling the "police truncheon" wielded by Arias as interior minister, the PCE pictured the new
premier as another figure molded in Franco's image and as the "last hope" of the regime's ultra-right-
wing sectors. The party did not share the optimism expressed by moderate opposite forces over

Arias's promise of liberal political reforms or over what might be expected from officials belonging to a younger generation allegedly more open to change. These "naive illusions," said the PCE, were quickly shattered by the government's renewed acts of repression. Arias warned that those practicing violence or other subversion should not expect to benefit from the program of liberalization and that they would be dealt with "rigorously."

According to the PCE, the campaign of repression began to be stepped up as a backlash to the assassination. Right-wing demonstrators at the funeral of Carrero Blanco demanded a crackdown on "the Reds," a term apparently used to cover all moderate to far-leftist opponents of the regime. On the day of the murder, a trial began for ten underground labor leaders arrested in mid-1972 for holding a meeting to set up a national coordinating center of the illegal Workers' Commissions; ten days later they received 12- to 20-year sentences. Some of the accused were PCE representatives within the Workers' Commissions. Communists said that because of the heightened repressive atmosphere they had to abandon demonstrations and work stoppages planned to protest the trial. This was an example, they said, of how Basque acts of terrorism—assuming the assassins were Basques—interfered with PCE programs of mobilizing the masses. The communists claimed that their party sought to organize mass support through slow, patient action in factories and neighborhoods rather than with acts of violence. ("Radio Independent Spain," 29 December, 1973; *NYT*, 19 January 1974.)

The PCE was implicated by police, along with the Basque ETA, in a September 1974 explosion in Madrid that killed eleven persons and wounded more than seventy. Eight persons were arrested by police and charged with the bombing and with belonging to ETA and the PCE. Communists commented that such joint membership was absurd considering the "well-known" political differences of the two organizations. Carrillo described the bombing instead as a "typically fascist act"; he declared that his party was opposed to terrorism and that, moreover, the crime did not even "have anything in common with the known activities of ETA up to now." (*Intercontinental Press*, 21 October). Spanish authorities announced that one of the arrested had been trained in Buenos Aires in subversive techniques by Argentine and Uruguayan terrorists, the Montoneros and Tupamaros (*La Prensa*, Buenos Aires, 25 September).

Throughout the year hundreds of Spaniards were arrested in various parts of the country for subversion or on charges of belonging to or being connected with communist, regional separatist, or other leftist groups. A Catalan anarchist, Salvador Puig, of the Iberian Liberation Movement was executed by garroting in March for having killed a policeman while resisting arrest (*NYT*, 3 March; "Radio Independent Spain," 12 March). Repression also took the form, according to communists, of the dismissal of thousands of workers. Allegedly, in Barcelona alone more than 700 workers lost their jobs and more than 5,000 were penalized (*Intercontinental Press*, 5 September). In April the PCE was badly hurt by the arrest of Francisco Romero Martín, a member of the party's Executive Committee. It was suspected that his identity may have been disclosed to police by a dissident communist group. (*Christian Science Monitor*, 16 April.)

The PCE charged that the alleged liberalization intentions of the Arias government were stained by the house arrest and attempted expulsion from Spain of the bishop of Bilbao, Antonio Añoveros Ataún, for championing Basque autonomy. The government relented only after the entire Spanish episcopacy came to the support of Añoveros. ("Radio Independent Spain," 12 March).

During the year liberals grew increasingly discouraged about the prospects that Arias would be able to fulfill his promise of giving Spaniards broader political expression, which the PCE from the beginning dismissed as "lip service to reform." Party spokesmen said that Arias's hands were tied by the orthodox Falangists, who were "even more rightist than he," and by Franco's family (*Népszabadság*, Budapest, 19 October). Through much of the year, however, communications minister Río Cabanillas did allow a much freer press than had been customary. Full coverage of the Portuguese revolution in April and relatively complete accounts of the church-state confrontation over the bishop of Bilbao, for example, appeared in the Spanish press. Right-wing opponents of such freedom were able to force the dismissal of Río Cabanillas in November. (*NYT*, 7 June, 18 November.) Thus, when Arias in December unveiled his promised draft law on "political associations," there was little surprise that it fell short of expectations. Only associations giving their unconditional support to the Franco regime and authorized by the Falangist-dominated National Movement would be allowed to function. Also, religious, professional, and labor groups would not be permitted to form political associations. (*Christian Science Monitor*, 6 December.)

The PCE continued during 1974 to urge "national reconciliation against Francoism," a call that was first made in 1958 and articulated as a "Pact for Freedom" in 1972 at the party's Eighth Congress (see *YICA, 1973*, p. 217). Carrillo reiterated that his party would take whatever action was necessary to achieve "convergent action" by all "civilized" forces of the right and left that wanted a democratic change. Such a common front was now more viable and necessary than ever, he said. No one should be deluded, he insisted, that Juan Carlos, on the impending death of Franco, would bring a liberal hue to government; he was a person "without any special qualities" and would be "either a dictator or a puppet juggled by others," his monarchy a "continuation of Francoism without Franco." This was precisely what happened in mid-year, it was pointed out, when for a month and a half Juan Carlos became chief of state while the critically ill Franco was hospitalized with phlebitis ("Radio Independent Spain," 1 June, 23 July; *Népszabadság*, 19 October).

Carrillo instructed the fragmented and weak "bourgeois" opposition groups that they should realize that "convergence" was a vital necessity for them. That is, they could build strength only in a democracy, since Franco had made a "clean sweep" of all their political parties. He urged them to abandon their squeamishness about cooperation with the well-organized communists, since there was no other way to bring about a democratic Spain than through a broad opposition front. (*L'Humanité*, 28 December 1973.) He warned that the only alternative to a national reconciliation would be violent confrontation between fascism and the masses ("Radio Independent Spain," 23 July).

During the summer the PCE did succeed in bringing together disparate left and right-wing elements, first in various provincial "mesas democráticas" and, finally, in a "Democratic Junta of Spain." The latter formation was announced in Paris on 30 July by Carrillo and Rafael Calvo Serer, an exiled monarchist of the Carlist Party and one of the founders of the Catholic Opus Dei. Calvo, an opponent of the Juan Carlos monarchy and a former adviser to Don Juan, the prince's father, said that he had agreed to join the Junta because the Spanish people must be allowed to decide their future. (Ibid., 30 July.) No other persons associated themselves by name with the Junta, but the organization claimed to be composed of communists, socialists, and Workers' Commissions members, as well as liberal monarchists, right-wing leaders, and industrial and financial representatives of "Spanish dynamic neo-capitalism" (*Washington Post*, 3 July). A "financial leader" was quoted in an anonymous interview as saying that since the capitalist bourgeoisie and the communists were the two decisive forces in Spain, their cooperation was essential to the success of any real anti-Francoist convergence (*L'Unità*, Rome, 8 August).

The pro-government *Ya* (Madrid, 3 August) was skeptical about how "broad" the united front was. No one, it said, could seriously believe the "nebulous references to some vague forces" that were claimed to have joined the Junta. Instead, here was another "masquerade" of communists in the "sheep's clothing of national reconciliation," seeking the "greater glory" of their own party.

The Junta announced that its role was to establish a provisional coalition government in Spain to succeed Franco and to give the country elections within 18 months of the restoration of freedom. It called for political, trade union, and press freedom, total amnesty for all political and trade union prisoners, and the legalization of all political parties. It also recognized the right of Catalonia, the Basque region, and Galicia to self-determination.

The PCE held that "convergence" could be further strengthened by contacts with moderate government and military figures who might "carry real weight" in facilitating political change. Such groups were said to favor some liberalization at this time as a safeguard against "too much democracy" after the death of Franco. ("Radio Independent Spain," 12 March; *NYT*, 7 June). Carrillo claimed that the Portuguese example had stimulated the beginning of a military "democratic movement" among junior officers who were "offended" by the regime. He also said that the so-called liberal elements in the high command had concluded that the best way to maintain army unity was to have the army "assume the role of arbiter in a rapid democratic solution to the Spanish political problem." (*Rinascita*, Rome, 6 September.) He praised such "moderate" thinking and hailed one of the group, General Manuel Diez Alegría, who was fired by Franco in July as chief of the general staff, as a "modern military man." (*Intercontinental Press*, 22 July; "Radio Independent Spain," 23 July.)

Though recognizing that the army would probably not take the lead, as in Portugal, in overthrowing the government, the PCE indicated that it had embarked on a program of infiltrating the rank and file. The purpose was to "neutralize" the army by making it aware of the need not to oppose the "popular national will." The party urged young communists going into the service to acquire the "greatest possible military knowledge," which could prove useful one day "to confront a counter-revolution." ("Radio Independent Spain," 6 December 1973; 18 May 1974.)

The PCE also stressed during the year that "national reconciliation" must be combined with a broadening of "mass action"—that is, militant campaigns by workers for freedom and for better wages and working conditions. According to party leaders, management was with increasing frequency, during strikes, negotiating with the Workers' Commission leaders rather than with the official trade unions, in order to reach effective agreements. They also stated that the strike movement had become as extensive in Spain as in capitalist countries where there was trade union freedom. Numerous work stoppages, slowdowns, demonstrations, and prolonged strikes took place throughout the country, especially in Madrid, Barcelona, Bilbao, Pamplona, and Valladolid. In some car factories there were fires attributed to sabotage by strikers. (Ibid., 12 March; *L'Unità*, 13 August; *NYT*, 17 November.)

International Views and Positions—Party Contacts. The PCE's continued insistence on independence from the party line of the Communist Party of the Soviet Union (CPSU) provoked a blunt though brief confrontation between the two parties early in 1974. In a January issue of a leading Soviet party journal, PCE policies were fiercely denounced by the indirect means of a personal attack on a party leader, Manuel Azcárate, who had delivered what was called a "misleading and insulting" report about CPSU policy to the PCE Central Committee, which in turn had approved the document. The Soviets scored Azcárate for "falsely" calling the U.S.S.R. undemocratic, for criticizing Soviet foreign policy, and for allegedly siding with the Chinese in the Sino-Soviet conflict. What immediately precipitated the Soviet anger was thought by analysts to be Azcárate's insistence on a Western Europe free of Soviet hegemony and the PCE's resistance to a Soviet proposal for a new international conference of communists. The PCE was opposed to such a meeting because it perceived that the purpose would be to try to restore CPSU authority in the world communist movement and to mobilize a collective denunciation of the Chinese. (Radio Free Europe Research, 27 February, 6 March.)

In March, the PCE Executive Committee responded firmly, though not belligerently, that it would not alter its stand. It issued a pamphlet that combined the texts of the Soviet article and of Azcárate's report, along with explanatory remarks showing how the latter had been distorted. The PCE said, however, that "this polemic must not hinder the efforts of our party constantly to improve relations with the CPSU on the basis of Marxism-Leninism, proletariat internationalism and the non-interference of one party in the internal affairs of another." (Ibid., 11 April; *Nuestra Bandera*, Madrid, 4th quarter, 1973.)

Also in March, Polish and Italian communists appeared to side with the PCE in the dispute. The Poles received a PCE delegation for a cordial week-long visit during which the two parties planned a summit meeting to expand relations further. An Italian communist group visited the Barcelona area for talks with local and national communist leaders and with various non-communist anti-Franco representatives. They seemed thereby to be giving support to the PCE position in favor of "pluralistic democracy," a notion that had been assailed by the Soviets. (Radio Free Europe Research, 22 March; "Radio Independent Spain," 2 April.) In September, a Spanish delegation was welcomed effusively by Romania.

In October, the Spanish and Soviet parties backed off from their feud. Perhaps by then the Soviets, impressed by the pace of events in Portugal and by the establishment in Spain of the anti-Franco Democratic Junta, had reappraised PCE prospects. Both parties agreed in a joint statement that the time had come for "further victories of all anti-imperialist forces." Concessions by the CPSU were evident in the statement that "voluntary coordination of fraternal parties" activities was more effective when the international communist movement had no leading center, with each party formulating its own policy to conform to its own country's specific conditions. In an apparent reversal of its previous support for Enrique Líster's pro-Moscow rival PCOE, the Soviet party also joined the PCE in condemning "any splintering activity aimed at undermining the internal unity of the fraternal parties." The PCE was likewise conciliatory, expressing its "deep satisfaction at the successes of the Soviet Union" and its "important contributions to the development of the revolutionary process." More significantly, anti-Sovietism, "regardless of where it originates," was condemned, and the two parties were said to have restated "their determination to fight for the restoration of unity [of] the international communist movement." Support was also expressed for the proposal to convene an all-European conference of communist and workers' parties. ("Radio Independent Spain," 16 October; *Pravda*, 16 October; *Christian Science Monitor*, November 12.)

The PCE drew much encouragement from communist successes in Portugal following the overthrow of the dictatorship in April. A party spokesman hailed the "winds from the mouth of the Tagus" that were "breathing new life and vitality into the lungs of Spanish society." He also expressed satisfaction that the Portuguese experience confirmed the "correctness" of the PCE's policy of seeking a "pact for freedom" and the support of the armed forces. ("Radio Independent Spain," 18, 26 May.)

PCE leaders Dolores Ibarruri and Santiago Carrillo were banned indefinitely from Switzerland after ignoring a government order not to speak at a June rally of Spanish emigrant communists in Geneva. At first the injunction was evaded by having their prerecorded speeches delivered over loudspeakers; finally, they spoke briefly, "to the immense excitement of the crowd," estimated by the communists at 20,000 to 25,000 and by other observers at 10,000. The workers allegedly came from all over Europe. (Ibid., 24 June, 3 July; Madrid domestic radio, 23, 24 June; *Intercontinental Press*, 22 July.)

During negotiations in 1974 for renewal of the agreement regulating U.S. use of military installations in Spain, the PCE expressed "gloomy forebodings." In exchange for use of the bases, it was said, the United States was prepared to make political concessions to Franco, secretly committing itself to back up the regime in the event of a domestic threat against it. The party asserted that the U.S. technical, economic, military, and cultural aid previously extended to Spain had not amounted to much. ("Radio Independent Spain," 12 January, 18 April, 5 November.)

The PCE continued to support Moroccan claims to the Spanish enclaves of Ceuta and Melilla and to demand Spain's withdrawal from the territory of Spanish Sahara. Denying Franco government charges that this position made them traitors, communists claimed that the country's occupation of those areas was actually harmful to Spanish interests. Spanish fishermen, for example, were banned from waters off Morocco because Spain refused to cede the enclaves. Also, the real profiteers from the occupation of the Sahara were the "great capitalistic monopolies" that exploited the rich deposits of phosphate in the territory. The PCE scorned the announcement in August that Spain would permit self-determination for the Sahara territory in 1975. The Franco regime, it said sarcastically, was "such a great guarantor of self-determination," a phrase that "neo-colonialism always uses." It asked whether Spaniards would accept a British plan for a referendum in Gibraltar, "the purpose of which would be to sanction the independence of the rock." It further asserted that the "so-called Spanish Sahara" was just as African and non-Spanish as Gibraltar is Spanish and non-British." (*Mundo Obrero*, 17 October, 1973, quoted in *al-Bayane*, Casablanca, 14 November; "Radio Independent Spain," 22 August 1974.) Carillo, incidentally, claimed that a high-ranking British official had assured him that a democratic regime in Spain could induce Britain to review its stand on the Gibraltar question ("Radio Independent Spain," 1 June).

Publications. The PCE publishes a semimonthly official organ, *Mundo Obrero*, and a quarterly theoretical journal, *Nuestra Bandera*. Party sources claim a circulation of 60,000 to 70,000 for *Mundo Obrero* and 205,000 for *Nuestra Bandera*. Both are published abroad and distributed clandestinely in Spain. There are allegedly 30 other PCE publications as well, including the semi-monthly *España Republicana*, put out in Havana by the Cuban-Spanish Friendship Society, and *Realidad*, a monthly journal published in Rome. Party messages are also broadcast to Spain from Romania over "Radio Independent Spain."

The Rival PCOE publishes another *Mundo Obrero*, with a red rather than black masthead. The LCR-ETA-VI puts out a central organ called *Combate* and the Basque-language *Zutik*. The PCE-ML publishes *Vanguardia Obrera* and *Mundo Obrero Revolucionario*.

*   *   *

Rival Communist Organizations. There were no reports that any of the communist groups outside the PCE had joined the Democratic Junta set up in July 1974. The Maoist-Leninist FRAP dismissed the organization as scarcely democratic but rather "the latest oligarchic maneuver in the context of business as usual." Carrillo's party was scorned as "only a residue of what used to be the Spanish Communist Party" and Serer as a "well-known fascist trying to jump the sinking ship." The anti-Francoism of Serer's Carlist Party had developed, it was said, only because the "successor" was not chosen from among the princes of the Carlist branch. In place of this "union with the fascist oligarchs to salvage the Franco regime," FRAP proposed the formation of "popular union committees" to defeat the dictatorship through "struggle and action." FRAP warned against nourishing "illusions" on the basis of what happened in other countries—that is, Portugal: "It only helps sustain a passive and uncertain attitude for the purpose of preventing popular struggles." (*Nuova Unità*, Rome, 3 September.)

The Trotskyist LCE mobilized thousands of students in protest demonstrations during the year, especially in Barcelona following the sentencing and execution of Salvador Puig. A number of bomb explosions were also set off in Barcelona in reprisal by anarchists of the Iberian Liberation Movement. The LCE complained that students were not joined in their demonstrations by the working class because the latter's PCE leaders "refused" to mobilize them. (*Daily Telegraph*, London, 12 January; *Intercontinental Press*, 8 April.)

Elbert Covell College   H. Leslie Robinson
University of the Pacific

Sweden

The Swedish Communist Party (Sveriges Kommunistiska Parti; SKP) grew from a left-wing dissident faction of the Social Democrats. It has been legal ever since its establishment in 1921. Most of its support comes from organized workers in the urban industrial areas of Stockholm, Gävleborg, and Göteborg, and from Sweden's northernmost province of Norrbotten.

The party name was changed in 1967 to Left Party-Communists (Vänsterpartiet Kommunisterna; VPK) in an effort to broaden appeal to young Swedes of the New Left. The change was in vain. Young leftists have either gravitated toward Maoist splinter groups or found satisfaction in Sweden's politically savvy Social Democratic Party (Socialdemokratiska Arbetarparti; SDP). In early 1973, the Communist League, Marxist-Leninist (Kommunistiska Förbundet Marxist-Leninisterna; KFML) compounded the insult of waning VPK allure by appropriating the SKP name for its own party.

Despite Maoist and SDP incursions into its natural constituency, the VPK has managed to achieve some significant political leverage. Though the party claims an estimated membership of only 17,000 out of the total Swedish population of about eight million, it has often parlayed its parliamentary representation into a pivotal role. During 1970-73, Prime Minister Olof Palme, with only 163 seats to the non-socialist opposition's 170 in the 350-seat Riksdag (parliament), sometimes had to use the VPK's 17 votes for crucial legislation or the survival of his government.

The VPK edged up to 19 seats in the latest parliamentary elections, 16 September 1973. Since the SDP dropped back to 156 places, there was a 175-175 split in the unicameral Riksdag between the socialist left and the three so-called bourgeois parties, but the VPK's hopes for advantage from this situation did not materialize. First, though the party did improve its representation in the Stockholm area, it lost some of its traditional support in the northern "forest" districts. Second, Palme was able to effect an alliance of sorts with the Liberals, thus splintering fledgling non-socialist unity and curtailing the need to invoke VPK assistance. He may thus be able to retain power until the next scheduled parliamentary election in September 1976.

Leadership and Organization. Carl-Henrik Hermansson remained VPK chairman, the post to which he was unanimously reelected at the party's Twenty-third Congress, October 1972. He first became party chief in January 1964, when he replaced a long-time Stalinist. He has continued to stress the VPK's role as an independent Swedish organization, committed to maintaining democratic institutions and pursuing left-socialist policies.

Theoretically, all important questions of policy and organization are decided at the triennial party congress. That meeting elects the 35-member Central Committee, known since 1964 as the Party Board. The Board supervises party activities and selects the eight-member Executive Committee (Politburo), which controls daily operations.

There are 28 party districts, which correspond to the nation's 28 electoral regions. Below these are the workers' communes, which are the main local units responsible for the coordination of fund raising, propaganda, and training.

Despite reliance on support from "the workers," the VPK enjoys control neither over a national trade union nor in Sweden's powerful Federation of Trade Unions (LO). The VPK controls about 80 of the nation's 9,000 union locals, primarily in the construction, forestry, and mining industries.

The VPK regained a more or less viable youth wing in 1973. The Communist Youth (Kommunistisk Ungdom) held its founding congress and so replaced the Leftist Youth League (Vänsterns Ungdomsförbund), which had broken from the VPK in 1970 and practically withered away in the wake of the pro-Chinese "Marxist-Leninist Struggle League" (Marxist-Leninistiska Kampförbundet).

Party Internal Affairs. Ideological and tactical scuffles between the VPK and SKP continued in 1974. The in-fighting was most conspicuous in exchanges between their respective newspapers, *Ny Dag* and *Gnistan*.

VPK chairman Hermansson claimed that he spent much of his time answering the questions of "the organization that illegitimately and misleadingly calls itself the SKP." He stressed four points: the VPK's unchanged critical attitude toward the Warsaw Pact invasion of Czechoslovakia in 1968; its "fundamental solidarity with the people in all socialist countries" and rejection of "petty bourgeois hatred of the Soviet Union; its opposition to the allegation that there are increasing differences between the Soviet Union and the Third World (especially, as charged, on the issue of ocean rights); and its commitment to total world-wide disarmament (including the military forces of the U.S.S.R., China, and Sweden). (*Ny Dag*, 23-27 August.)

Hermansson objected to an SKP campaign "spearheaded against the socialist states" and not focused on issues of interest to the Swedish working class. He chastised the *Gnistan* group for shifting emphasis from Vietnam with its feature editorial, "Biggest War Menace Lies in Europe." The SKP had contended: "Our tactics must be based on the fact that the reason for the trouble in Europe and in the world is the fights of both superpowers against the people and against each other, and that the most important factor at present is the offensive of the Soviet Union against the European continent." The conflict between the VPK and SKP exemplified in microcosm the ironic implications of a Sino-Soviet split which could appear to put the most revolutionary Maoists in bed with proponents of NATO or the European Community.

Given the depth of the schism, there was little prospect by year's end that the VPK and SKP would or could bridge their perceptual gap. Rhetorical war was, in effect, declared in their party press as the VPK launched preparations for its Twenty-fourth Party Congress, 12-16 March 1975.

Domestic Activities and Attitudes. A meeting of the VPK Party Board in Linkoping, 23 August, was significant—both as a reflection of the above factionalism and as a precursor of the themes dominating debate before the next party congress. Two documents approved by the Party Board were most important in this respect: "Major Tasks in the Political Campaign before the 1975 VPK Party Congress," and a presentation by VPK chairman Hermansson entitled "Solidarity, Revolution, Reforms."

The first document stressed concentration in three areas: the campaign for international solidarity, the fight against employers in behalf of better wages and working environment, and the fight against monopoly capital and state exploitation exemplified by rising prices, unjust distribution of taxes, and high housing costs (*Norrskensflamman*, 18 September 1974). It hoped to attract the support of women and young people in particular in behalf of "political mass activity" to build a socialist society. Interestingly enough, the VPK linked "Swedish imperialism" with exploitation of workers both inside and outside Sweden. Inflation was cited as a means of "big capital's exploitation" of blue- and white-collar workers, farmers, and small businessmen.

Hermansson reiterated many of the same themes in his presentation. Starting with the assertion that "imperialism is the international major enemy" and that the United States is the "leading force within the imperialist world camp," he, too, underscored the need to fight against Swedish capitalism (ibid., 19-21 September). He admitted the difficulty in evaluating developments in the socialist nations and resolving conflicts between different communist parties (especially the Soviet and Chinese). His apparently conciliatory stance vis-à-vis Peking provoked a rash of criticism from party ranks. Hermansson asserted that the VPK had failed to "analyze and clarify sufficiently the concrete form it thinks socialism should take in Sweden." This socialism, he maintained, must reflect Swedish conditions—not those of the U.S.S.R., China, or Cuba—and must reflect true popular rule. It could well be achieved via reforms which just happened to be revolutionary in impact.

Such reform suggested cooperation with other elements of the Swedish labor force. Hermansson identified the three main components of that movement—the SDP, VPK, and SKP. He condemned the SKP for playing the "role of provocateurs against the objectives of the labor movement." While acknowledging the preeminent strength of the Social Democrats among workers, he criticized them for "directly promoting the development of state monopolistic capitalism." He hoped to "bring about unity of action with the Social Democratic workers for a class policy aimed at breaking the power position of big finance."

The Liberals' capitulation to Palme on such economic issues as tax reform tended, however, to isolate the communists on the left as much as it put the moderates out on a limb to the right. In protest against the Social Democrats' alleged "march toward the right," Hermansson charged Palme with having sacrificed the interests of low-income groups to those of the wealthy.

Oil, finally, was a prime target for VPK consternation. Here, as in other areas, the communists linked domestic and international considerations. The party argued for battling the "enemy in the oil war"—namely, the big international oil companies—with a "socialist planned economy." It advocated a state takeover of private oil interests so that the people need not depend on the oil trusts for either supply or information on reserves. (*Ny Dag*, 1-5 February.)

International Views and Activities. Distinctions blurred as domestic concerns melded with international issues and the VPK took positions that either overlapped with those of the SDP establishment or conflicted with other factions within communist ranks. Developments in Southeast Asia and Chile, the plight of the Third World in general, shifting interpretations of Soviet policy, and the international energy crisis were the dominant issues during 1974.

With regard to Southeast Asia, VPK chairman Hermansson stressed that "the struggle in behalf of the people of Vietnam must continue" (*Ny Dag*, 19-27 June). The Swedish government pleased leftists by upgrading the information office operated by the Viet Cong in Stockholm to a "general delegation" in August. When Richard Nixon resigned the U.S. Presidency, Hermansson commented that the system which created Nixon remained and that he, his assistants, Gerald Ford, and Henry Kissinger should be sentenced by an international court as war criminals for the battle against the people of Vietnam, Laos, and Cambodia. General Swedish interest in Vietnam, however, seemed to wane. "Vietnam Week" events aroused less response than the "Save the Animals" campaign.

The more interesting change vis-à-vis the Vietnam question came within the communist constituency itself. The Maoists of the United National Liberation Front Groups (De Förenade FNL-Grupperna; DFFG) concluded that the Vietnam War was as good as won, following the signing of the Paris accords, and decided that the main task of the Swedish Indochina movement was to "study the world situation." This shift implied a new scrutiny of the U.S.S.R. as a super-power opposed to the struggle of Third World peoples. (The DFFG pointed particularly to Soviet objections to lesser-developed-countries positions on raw materials and the law of the sea.)

The DFFG's new campaign evoked an extensive public airing in a debate conducted in *Afton-bladet*, the largest Social Democratic daily newspaper, and in the communist press. The VPK charged that the DFFG had abandoned what little Marxist position it may have had, and expressed the hope that the *Gnistan* group would not betray the Vietnamese people in favor of a distorted view of the international class struggle (ibid., 5-11 July).

Otherwise, Chile continued to take up the slack of waning fervor about Vietnam. This interest spanned all shades of political opinion in Sweden. There were frequent visits by prominent Chilean refugees, to the accompaniment of rallies and massive media coverage. The United States got considerable attention because of stories about Central Intelligence Agency involvement in Chile. Communist representatives from Chile addressed a VPK conference, 23-24 March, and urged Swedish support for the "struggle by the democratic forces of Chile against the fascist junta." Hermansson linked that struggle with the need to battle Swedish "imperialist" policy throughout Latin America, South Africa, and Spain (ibid., 19-27 June, 30 August).

At the invitation of the VPK, energy policy was discussed prior to the meeting of the Nordic Council in Stockholm in February. The VPK, the People's Alliance of Iceland, the Republicans of the Faeroe Islands, the Communist Party of Denmark, the Socialist People's Party of Denmark, and the Socialist Election Alliance of Norway presented a joint declaration to the council. They agreed that "it is today of decisive importance for the national independence of the small countries, and for the labor movement's struggle for a socialist development in the individual countries, that the power of the multinational companies be broken." They urged that the oil monopolies' present refineries and distribution systems in the individual countries be nationalized and that the Nordic countries establish direct contacts with the oil-producing countries and develop international cooperation on energy policy on an equal basis, "aimed at satisfying the people's real needs." (Ibid., 20-21 February.)

On a related issue, the Swedish Maoists charged that the "Soviet social imperialists" were making absurd demands in their negotiations with Sweden concerning the Baltic Sea floor." They repeated the theme that Sweden was a small country threatened by the superpowers and should thus side with other small nations or developing countries in forums like the Conference on the Law of the Sea in Caracas. (*Gnistan*, 14-20 June.)

The Solzhenitsyn case was another focal point for conflicting communist views on Soviet policy. The VPK said: "We cannot struggle for democratic freedoms and rights here and at the same time accept their violation in socialist states" (*Norrskensflamman*, 23 February). To do so risked losing the confidence of the majority of the people. Stalinists within the party countered with the legalistic contention that Solzhenitsyn had broken Soviet laws passed for the protection of socialism.

International Party Contacts. Despite the disagreements among Swedish communists, the VPK kept up an active pace of consultations with fraternal parties in 1974. Hermansson visited North Vietnam in April. During talks with Le Duan, first secretary of the Workers Party, he accused the United States and Saigon government of flagrant and systematic violations of the Paris agreement and expressed full support for the 22 March proposals of the Provisional Revolutionary Government of the Republic of South Vietnam on a solution to South Vietnam's internal problems.

A study delegation of the VPK, headed by Central Committee member Gunvor Ryding, visited Poland at the invitation of the Polish ruling party on 3-9 June. VPK deputy chairman Lars Werner and a delegation visited the German Democratic Republic (GDR) 25 June-2 July. Both the VPK and the GDR party hailed détente and peaceful coexistence, and urged that the Conference on Security and Cooperation in Europe should be concluded swiftly at the highest level (*Neues Deutschland*, East Berlin, (3 July).

Other visits were made to Romania (early August), Czechoslovakia (August), and Bulgaria (September). A second VPK delegation visited the GDR (mid-August) to share thoughts on détente and express firm solidarity with the people of Chile and Chilean communist leader Luis Corvalán. The VPK also participated in a conference of Nordic communist parties in Finland, 5-7 September.

Publications. The VPK's central organ, *Ny Dag* ("New Day"), is published twice weekly in Stockholm; it appears under the name *Arbetar-Tidningen* ("Worker News") in western Sweden. The party's only daily is *Norrskensflamman* ("Blaze of Northern Lights"), published in Luleå. Its theoretical quarterly is *Socialistisk Debatt*. The weekly voice of the new SKP is *Gnistan* ("Spark").

Switzerland

The Swiss Communist Party (Kommunistische Partei der Schweiz; KPS / Parti communiste suisse; PCS), founded in 1921, was banned in 1940 and re-formed in 1944 as the Party of Labor (Partei der Arbeit; PdA / Parti du Travail; PdT / Partito de Lavoro; PdL). Ideologically, the PdA is pro-Soviet; organizationally, it is a party of cadres dedicated to "democratic centralism" and its membership of about 5,000 does not indicate its actual following; politically, it is a party with legal status that tries to use parliamentary institutions to achieve a socialist society through peaceful means, while it also tries—without always succeeding—to maintain essential tactical co-ordination with the main groups of the proliferating New Left.

The Party is not represented in the executive cabinet of the Swiss coalition government. In the last national elections (1971), the PdA received 2.7 percent of the total vote. Accordingly, it obtained 5 seats in the 200-member National Council (Nationalrat). It is not represented in the Council of States (Ständerat) of 44 members, to which two councillors (senators) are elected from each canton. All five PdA representatives in the National Council come from French-speaking Switzerland: 3 from Geneva, 2 from Vaud. In the canton of Neuchâtel it lost, in 1971, the seat won in 1967.

The PdA holds some seats in several cantonal parliaments, the largest group being 17 out of 100 seats in Geneva, twice as many, proportionately, as in its next best position, Vaud (16 out of 197). In 17 cantonal legislatures it is not represented. The population of Switzerland is 6,420,000 (estimated 1972.)

Leadership and Organization. The PdA held its tenth Congress in Basel on 1-3 June 1974. The congress elected a new Central Committee of 50 members and 10 (formerly 5) candidates, including 20 young party members who were elected for the first time. Of the Central Committee members 32 are French-speaking, 15 German-speaking, and 3 Italian-speaking. Although French-speaking members are twice the number of the German-speaking, in the national population there are ten times as many German-speaking Swiss. The new committee elected a Political Bureau of 14 members, and a 5-member Secretariat (formerly 3). The three incumbents on the Secretariat, Jean Vincent (of Geneva), André Muret (Lausanne), and Jakob Lechleiter (Zurich), were reelected, and Hansjörg Hofer (Basel) and Armand Magnin (Geneva) were added. Jean Vincent, acting chairman, was elected president of the party, replacing Edgar Woog (1898-1973), one of the last old-timers and a former executive (alias Stirner) of the Comintern.

At the congress there was marked self-criticism and a reorientation in the diffuse party program, which is essentially an "opening" on many fronts. Acting chairman Vincent said in his report: "Party leadership was mediocre, insufficient in its work, there were few meetings of the Central Committee, the activities of the Political Bureau were poorly co-ordinated and the Secretariat's work even more so."

The party vowed to fight "dogmatism, leftist deformation, [and] opportunistic rightist deviationism," and to be the "avant-garde of the working class that recognizes the necessity of a struggle to change our society radically."

Domestic Views and Positions. The PdA program that emerged in 1974–at a time of underlying threat of recession, of the energy crisis, and of the party's maneuvering with dissident New Left groups–had few clear-cut lines. The PdA recommended fighting inflation by freezing rents and prices of necessities while letting salaries adapt to cost-of-living indexes. But it reserved implicitly the right to set its own indexing by regularly accusing the capitalist establishment of publishing incomplete and twisted statistics. The party launched an initiative against rising prices which was "in all its essential points taken almost verbatim from the Socialist Party program of 1959" (*National-Zeitung*, 11 November). The PdA welcomed nuclear energy, but criticized safety standards as being far below those observed in the Soviet Union, and demanded national control and financing of all energy sources, instead of investments by "big capital." Conservationism with its "alarmist slogans" and "apocalyptic predictions" was rejected (*Voix Ouvrière*, 7 August). The PdA was no longer opposed to national defense, but wanted to "give back to our militia army its exclusively defensive and popular character" and "develop the civic consciousness of the citizen-soldier" (*Vorwärts*, 5 May).

Confrontation, as practiced by the PdA, was largely rhetoric on festive occasions throughout the year, and always linked with efforts to show a "fighting, common front" of "all enemies of big capital." But when young squatters, who had lived for 11 months in condemned buildings in Zurich, barricaded themselves, threw stones and Molotov cocktails and succeeded in bringing to the scene 300 police in riot gear to evict them on 25 July, the Zurich PdA, in a press release had already condemned the "thoughtless and violent" action of these "few pesudo-revolutionists": "Such spectaculars achieve the opposite of what they claim to want. Tenants fighting for their rights aren't helped and the Left is generally discredited." (Ibid., 18 July.)

The rivalry within the Left showed on 1 May. Parades and meetings had been planned to present a "united Left." Strong New Left groups gave the parades "a radical leftist color" (ibid., 9 May). In Zurich, Switzerland's biggest city, the PdA was but one of many groups, among which three competing bodies emerged: (1) The "Stalinists' cartel" (*Bresche*, No. 31, May), consisting of the PdA, POZ (Progressive Organizations Zurich; see below), CPI (Italian foreign workers' communist party in Switzerland), and CPE (Spanish foreign workers' communist party in Switzerland); (2) the more radical New Left groups like RAZ (Revolutionare Aufbauorganisation Zurich), the Committee for Chile and Greece, and the committee of revolutionary (teen-age) students of the Merchants' Association Trade School and the city's Arts and Crafts High School, led by the Trotskyist LMR (Ligue Marxiste Révolutionnaire); and (3) the KPS/ML (Communist Party of Switzerland/Marxist-Leninists), who tried to avoid contact with the other two aggregations, while a vocal group thought to be its extreme wing and consisting of "Maoists, semi-radical, pseudo-revolutionary loudmouths" (*Vorwäerts*, 9 May), tried to disrupt the parade.

The KPS/ML is called Maoist by some observers, but it has a rival–the KPS (Kommunistische Partei, Schweiz; Communist Party, Switzerland)–which calls itself Peking-oriented. The latter seems to advocate Western European strength against Soviet subversion. The KPS calls the KPS/ML, "useless agitators and petty-bourgeois chauvinists," and the KPS/ML calls the KPS "neo-Trotskyists and anti-communist parasites."

Only two groups of the New Left have shown structures permanent enough to have a small impact, next to the PdA, on the political scene. The POCH (Progressive Organizations, Switzerland–CH being the car number-plate letters for Switzerland) has grouped numerous local splinter organizations–exact number unknown. POCH succeeded in getting one city councillor elected in Zurich (September 1974) and one cantonal parliamentarian in Berne (May). The LMR, a member of the Fourth International, ideologically Trotskyist, has nominated candidates for local elections, but unsuccessfully so far. In Geneva (November 1973) it polled 2,345 out of 174,000 votes; and in Berne (September 1973), 728 out of 28,000 votes.

National parliamentary elections will be held in 1975.

Altogether, there were fewer loud demonstrations on and off the streets than in 1973. The major national issues in 1974 were the subject of nationwide voting in October and December, the latter on economic policy. The former gave all parties ample opportunity for a flurry of activities, and the New Left was particularly active. Swiss citizens had to vote on a proposal by a right-wing group to expel within three years half of Switzerland's foreign work force (about 550,000 persons) "to save national values." About 37 percent of Switzerland's work force, or a sixth of the country's population, consist of foreigners, mostly from Southern Europe, and resentment against the massive presence of ethnically different groups has been accumulating during twenty-five years of increasing immigration. The proposal was defeated by a 2 to 1 margin—more heavily than a milder proposal in 1970, when 46 percent of the voters were in favor of a less drastic reduction of foreign labor. The LMR was most active during the campaign, organizing numerous meetings with as many New Left groups as possible. According to *bresche* (5 November), the LMR held a meeting in Lausanne with 24 organizations, attended by 2,000 workers and young people, some not of voting age, and half of them foreigners and thus non-voting; a meeting in Zurich with 11 organizations, attended by 500; and one in Geneva with 6 organizations, attended by "more than 200." In meetings in smaller towns, attendance ranged between 50 and 100.

When the proposal was rejected in a turnout of more than 2.5 million voters, groups congratulated themselves for having led the fight, and PdA received congratulations from the Communist Party of the Soviet Union for having greatly contributed to the proposal's defeat.

The LMR program on foreign labor policy called for abolition of limitations for immigrant workers, "Immigration for a revolutionary internationalism" (*Focus*, June), abolition of the "foreigners' police" (the police branch in charge of foreign residents), and equal political rights for all people working in Switzerland.

In general, both PdA and the New Left seemed to seek consolidation rather than loud action in 1974. Subversion activities were especially visible in two fields. The LMR youth movement stepped up its attempts to infiltrate schools and high schools, its first aim being to further "revolutionary anti-militarism" at an early age. Then, there were increased attempts to form "soldiers' committees," especially during the four-months' basic training period. Mostly groups calling themselves Maoist were active. The Swiss militia army has peculiarities that make copying foreign models for agitation somewhat difficult. Observers believe that agitation in the army began rather late for this reason. But the New Left seems to have recognized the Swiss type of universal military training as an ideal meeting place for young people, whence new ideas can fan out into the populace.

Faced with the headline-stealing activities of New Left groups, the PdA seemed to withdraw increasingly into a staunch parliamentary attitude; it continued also in 1974 to seek tactical alliances with the Socialists (Social Democrats) despite unsuccessful bids in local elections in 1973 (see *YICA, 1974*, P. 223). The PdA's language has become increasingly moderate; it rejects all extremism and violence, and supports most national programs with reservations that—although significant in principle—have little immediate impact. Specialists interpret this as a symptom of the new role assigned to the PdA—and to the parliamentary communist parties in the West generally—namely, that of an "evolutionary" wing of the communist movement whose aim is to project a constructive image, create confidence, and catch on the rebound left-leaning people who are antagonized by the more violent radicals. According to this theory, the "revolutionary" groups will absorb youthful dissidents, weaken radical competitors in general, and create a confrontation that should, by contrast, make the PdA look even more respectable. Indications are still inconclusive, according to those specialists, as to whether or not there is a third party created for a tactical aim: that of working against a real rapprochement between Western Europe and Peking. Recruiting genuine local Maoists who would expect to act in Peking's best interests, the movement's top cadres would be receiving directives from the Soviet Union. The conflict situation between KPS and KPS/ML, and similar situations in other Western countries, lead observers to think that a movement of fake Maoists, inspired by the U.S.S.R. to create anti-Chinese sentiment, is afoot in Western Europe.

On 28 November, the PdA's weekly *Vorwärts* announced the planned creation, on 8 December, of an all-Swiss communist youth movement, consisting of nine former regional organizations from all three linguistic regions. It was to be called KJVS (Kommunistischer Jugendverband der Schweiz [Communist Youth Union of Switzerland]). The announcement was headlined: "Youth Will Gets Its Fighting Organization." The aim is to fight, "together with progressive youth organizations of the whole world," against imperialism and for equal rights, social security and work for the young, intellectual and professional training regardless of origin, participation in decisions in schools and factories, and meaningful leisure activities, in order to realize socialism fully. Observers see in this new, centralized organization, as well as in the opening of the ranks of the party's Central Committee to young party members, an attempt to regroup young leftists away from the more extreme splinter groups of the New Left. Regardless of the above-mentioned theory of several communist parties, the role of the PdA seems increasingly that of a respectable party, anchored in parliamentary legality, acting as a clearinghouse and possible legal aid center for all the various New Left groups, and as a fall-back opportunity for young radicals when they grow older and wiser.

International Views and Positions. The PdA, along with all other parties represented in parliament, supports Swiss neutrality, but it would like to see a more "active" neutrality in support of freedom causes, against right-wing authoritarian regimes, and for European and global security, disarmament, and world peace. It demands U.N. membership for Switzerland. It adheres to the principles formulated at the consultative meeting of European communist parties in Warsaw on 16-18 October: Europe's present borders are final; the Conference on European Security and Cooperation has chances of achieving positive results soon with a first European Summit; détente and peaceful coexistence between countries of different social systems are possible.

Publications. PdA publishes journals in three languages: *Vorwärts*, Basel, weekly (circulation 10,900), in German; *Voix Ouvrière*, Geneva, daily (circulation 8,000), in French; and *Il Lavoratore*, Lugano, weekly (circulation 1,000), in Italian.

New Left groups publish two or three dozen periodicals and occasional pamphlets. The most important are: *POCH-Zeitung*, weekly since 1974, formerly bi-monthly, contents revolutionary, Soviet line in world affairs, no clear ideology except violent opposition domestically, but never critical of the U.S.S.R. (circulation about 3,000); *Bresche* ("The Breach"), fortnightly, published by the LMR, Trotskyist, Fourth International (circulation about 3,000); *Zürcher Student*, incorporating *Konzept*, distributed to all registered university students, nine issues per year, a former nonpolitical publication taken over by a radicalized student body executive (circulation 37,000); and *Focus*, an illustrated monthly magazine on glossy paper, edited by a "collective . . . who are part of the New Left and cooperate with all groups of this movement" (masthead of *Focus*). Two smaller publications serve specific aims: *Maulwurf* ("Mole") published by the LMR youth organizations, is directed toward schools and high schools, with heavy emphasis on anti-militarism; and *Offensiv*, a quarterly "edited by soldiers for soldiers," which criticizes the army as an "instrument of repression of the bourgeois state." [All circulation figures, PdA included, are estimates, except for the *Zürcher Student*, supposed to be approximately correct.]

Martigny, Switzerland   Richard Anderegg

Turkey

Leftist activities in Turkey in 1974 were conditioned by the national elections held on 14 October 1973, and by the chain of events stemming from the inconclusive results of those elections. In general, the stringent controls imposed by the military forced many leftist activists to tone down their propaganda and work through the existing system to consolidate their position. The closing of the Turkiye Isci Partisi, (Labor Party of Turkey) and of many smaller groups, left the rank-and-file members free to join other organizations and undertake activities in order to assure the survival of their movement.

Since the government prohibited the establishment of new radical organizations, and the few surviving ones were either unsuitable, such as DISK (the leftist trade union) or too passive for militant activity, the radical left attempted to take advantage of the existing party structure. The People's Republican Party obviously was a natural target for reasons explained farther on. This party, under the influence of its social-democratic faction, moved decidedly to the left after 1965 and, through its commanding influence among the bureaucracy, intelligentsia, and the universities, succeeded in liberalizing the state of mind in society and the government in favor of the left. However, the party remained faithful to parliamentary democracy, political freedoms and private property; its main leftist ideas consisted of plans to expand economic activity through government initiative, to implement social justice and to provide greater socioeconomic and political benefits to workers and peasants. (The shift to the left in 1965 caused internal strife and led the right-wing members to form the *Güven Partisi* –Reliance Party– in 1967, and later *Cumhuriyetçi Halk Partisi*. These fused later into one party, *Cumhuriyetçi Güven Partisi*–Republican Reliance Party). However, after 1965, the extreme left wing in the mother party, consisting largely of younger and dynamic elements who controlled the party's youth organizations, could not reconcile themselves to the leaders' moderate stand. These eventually joined the Marxist Labor Party and other militant leftist radical organizations. About the end of 1970, the Republican Party's student organization, the Sosyal Demokrat, was barely holding its own against the relentless drive of the militant Dev-Genç.

After the military intervention of 12 March 1971 all radical leftist organizations were closed and consequently, the Republican Party and, especially, its youth organizations remained as the only major leftist groups in the country. Consequently, it was natural that the members of the various leftist groups whose leaders had been arrested should join or at least lend their support to the Republican Party. The latter, eager to regain the backing of its former youth groups and thus to become the main spokesman for leftism in Turkey, welcomed tacitly the unexpected political windfall. After 1971, the Republican Party, especially through its leader. Bülent Ecevit, criticized the military intervention and stood as the lone defender of democratic principles and freedom in general. Talking in December 1972 with the present writer, Ecevit stated that the military were dissatisfied and had no contacts with him despite the fact that he was the chairman of the second-largest Turkish political party at that time.

There is no question that the Republican Party worked subtly in 1972-73 to form under its aegis a united leftist front in order to enhance its own power and to control and channel the dynamism of the left toward creative democratic ends. And since the Republican Party and its possible success at polls appeared as the only major promise to salvage the radical leftist movement, the latter did not hesitate to lend its own organizational talent and intellectual prowess. Moreover, a visible trend toward moderation among radicals, resulting from a forced return to reality and the realization of the absurdity of their ambition to capture government power in 1969-71, made easier the reconciliation between the Republican Party leaders and the recanting—or so it seemed—leftist militants.

A firm decision to hold national elections was reached in the spring of 1973—that is, after an effort to elect General Faruk Gürler, the strongman, as president, failed, and the political parties combined their forces to elect their own candidate, Admiral Fahri Korutürk. Subsequently, the leftist front built around the Republican Party, whose leader gained additional momentum. The main short-term objective for the militant left was not government power but rather the establishment of an atmosphere of freedom which would permit it to regain its vitality. Consequently, notwithstanding sharp internal dissensions, the radicals ignored the calls of the *Türkiye Birlik Partisi* (Union Party of Turkey), and voted for the Republican Party. The Union Party had quickly espoused some of the slogans of the defunct Labor Party and enlisted even the support of that party's former leader, Mehmet Aybar, in order to attract the radical left but failed to achieve its ends.

The results of the elections held on 14 October 1973, are shown in the accompanying table.

Electoral Results, Turkey, 1973

Voters and Parties	Number of votes	Percent of total	Number of deputies elected
Eligible voters	16,798,164	- -	
Participating voters	11,223,843	66.8	
Valid voters	10,723,658	63.0	
Justice	3,197,897	29.8	149
People's Republican	3,570,583	33.3	185
National Action	362,208	3.4	3
Nation's	62,377	0.6	- -
Democratic	1,275,502	11.9	45
Republican Reliance	564,343	5.3	13
National Salvation	1,265,771	11.8	48
Union Party	121,759	1.1	1
Independents	303,218	2.8	6
Total	10,723,658	100.0	450

Source: *Resmi Gazete* (Official Gazette), 31 October 1973

The election results reflected a major political and ideological change in Turkey's internal politics. For the first time since the inception of the multi-party democracy in Turkey in 1945-46, the Republican Party was able to poll a plurality of votes over other parties. The reverse was also true, that for the first time, the liberal (in economy) and conservative (in ideology) group represented by the Democratic Party in 1950-60 (not to be confused with the existing one which was formed in 1969-70) and the Justice Party in 1961-74, lost. Finally, this was the first time in the history of Turkey that a leftist party won an electoral victory. It is true that the combined vote of the right exceeded by far the Republicans' total. In fact, even the votes received by the Justice Party and its offspring, the Democratic Party (which had split only four years earlier, largely because of personality conflicts), would have given the rightist group a comfortable majority in the parliament. The fact that this did not happen allowed the Republican Party to assume leadership in the parliament and to satisfy some of the most urgent demands of the left, as shall be explained later.

The election drew some attention to two other parties whose relative success is worthy of mention for the purposes of this article. First, the vote for the militant-secularist-nationalist party of Alparslan Türkes, the National Action, went up about 50 percent above the total received in 1969 (275,091). The success of this party, long regarded with contempt and derision, indicated in fact that a certain regrouping and polarization of the extreme right was occurring, largely as a reaction to the potential emergence of the extreme left. One may assume that this party, like others of its kind, will gain additional power and popularity in proportion to the rise of a truly Marxist movement in Turkey. Second, there emerged as a significant factor in Turkish politics the National Salvation Party, headed by Necmeddin Erbakan, a professor of engineering and former head of the National Chamber of Commerce. This party was supported by small merchants, craftsmen in small towns, upper-class villagers, and religious conservatives. Economically speaking, it was opposed to big capital interests, and consequently it had some appeal both for the conservative peasants and lower urban classes, and for certain small entrepreneurs still believing that their fortune lay in a revitalized free enterprise system. Ideologically speaking, Erbakan's party also appealed to the religious conservatives who had finally abandoned the Justice Party as having degenerated into a materialistic money-minded organization. Moreover, the conservatives were disturbed by continuous government repression against the extreme religious groups and various religious sects, despite the existence of broad constitutional rights guaranteeing them freedom of thought and expression.

Thus, both the leftists and the religious conservatives agreed that freedom of thought and expression in Turkey was curtailed, although each group sincerely detested the other and in their specific grievances, aside from the basic constitutional principle dealing with freedom of thought, had nothing in common with each other. The leftists were prosecuted and jailed under provisions of the penal code that forbade class struggle, while the religious conservatives were prosecuted and jailed under provisions of the same code that were designated to protect the secular character of the republic. Moreover, the National Salvation Party ideologically resembled somewhat the Republican Party because of its defense of the small farmers and craftsmen, and its leftist propaganda directed to the lower income groups, which became more pronounced during the last week of the election campaign. Interestingly enough, Erbakan pointedly refrained from putting the "communist" label on the Republican Party and its leader Bülent Ecevit as other party leaders did with great delight.

After the elections, efforts by the chairmen of each major party to form a government failed. An earlier effort, on 6 October, by Bülent Ecevit to form a coalition government with the National Salvation Party failed too, largely because the religious conservatives were bitterly opposed to any collaboration with the Republican Party, which they considered the source of antireligious secularism in Turkey. Public pressure, however, and the death on 25 December of Ismet Inönü, the former president and chairman of the People's Republican Party in 1938-72, and regarded by the religious conservatives as their arch foe, helped bring together the two parties. Finally a coalition cabinet was formed on 25 January 1974. Bülent Ecevit became premier and Necmeddin Erbakan his deputy. The important Ministry of Justice also went to the National Salvation Party, while the coveted Ministry of National Education remained with the Republicans.

The key issue which provided ground for understanding between the two parties was agreement over the need to enact a liberal amnesty law which would pardon both the leftists and the rightists; mainly these were the religious conservatives indicted or jailed supposedly in violation of the constitutional freedom of thought. The need for amnesty, it should be repeated, was also the only major issue that brought together the Republican Party and various other leftist groups ranging from rank-and-file activists to university professors, journalists, and trade unionists. As mentioned, the radicals were largely willing to lend their support to the Republicans in exchange for a promise of amnesty rather than dedication to that party's principles, despite the existence of some ideological moderation among them.

In fact, it was the need for amnesty, to be secured if possible through an election victory, which seemed to have induced some radicals within the Republican party to feign moderation and display obedience toward party leaders in the hope that the liberation of the jailed radicals would change the atmosphere in the party in their own favor. Actually, unreported in the press and well concealed by the Republican Party leaders, there was throughout 1973 a sordid struggle between leftist radicals seeking to infiltrate the party councils in the countryside and incumbent leaders struggling to maintain a social-democratic stance as well as their own control over the party. In a number of cases the radicals were removed from positions of influence through the intervention of upper party echelons. Ironically, it was the same hope of amnesty which caused some of the leftists not only to tolerate but even to praise the National Salvation Party as a sort of redeemable rightist but populist organization.

The amnesty bill freeing all leftists and religious rightists was drafted and brought to the parliament soon after the government was formed. However, in the last hours of the final debate in May, a group of about 22 conservative deputies belonging to the National Salvation Party sided with the opposition and killed the provisions granting amnesty to political prisoners sentenced under the provisions of articles 141, 142, and 146 of the penal code. This was an extraordinary volte-face which preempted the coalition of its binding foundation. Premier Ecevit immediately threatened to resign since the amputated amnesty law negated all his public and private promises to liberate all political prisoners and institute an integral regime of freedom of thought, a matter he considered of utmost urgency and priority. The rift was temporarily patched after Erbakan promised to establish a stricter discipline in his party and cooperate fully in enacting a second law to include the leftists excluded in the first law. The issue was eventually solved by the Constitutional Court, which issued an opinion to the effect that the spirit of the law was in fact much broader than its letter and covered all the indicted and sentenced leftists, except for a few cases which shall be mentioned later.

After this event the coalition remained on the verge of collapse. Its life was assured temporarily, but was doomed in the long run, by the Cyprus dispute and the landing of Turkish troops on that island on 20 July. The Cyprus crisis, which began in July with the Greek junta's attempt to oust Archbishop Makarios as president and achieve enosis with Greece, is an event of major importance in the complex struggle between the East and West in general, and between leftism and conservatism in the Mediterranean in particular. The junta's intervention, among other things, was precipitated by Makarios's leaning toward some sort of leftism, or so it appeared, in contrast to the rightist dictatorship of the military junta in Greece, and especially by his growing friendship with the U.S.S.R. The junta's intervention in Cyprus dashed Moscow's hopes for consolidating Soviet influence in the island. Thus Turkey, when it landed troops in Cyprus, found in the U.S.S.R. not only a strong supporter but also a generous friend ready to supply money and arms. The leftists in Turkey immediately capitalized on this Soviet gesture and on the enormous patriotic burst of emotions in the country by claiming that the Soviet Union had sent dozens of ships, loaded with equipment, which were being unloaded in Turkish ports on the Black Sea, and stood ready to help Turkey with men, if need be. However, after the failure of Turkish-Greek talks in Geneva and the second Turkish advance in Cyprus in August, and the declaration of President Fahri Koruturk that Turkey was in Cyprus to defend its own interests rather than to play the game of some big power, the Soviet attitude hardened. The U.S.S.R. insisted on both the withdrawal of all foreign troops from Cyprus and its own inclusion in an international settlement conference, which it had proposed. The Communist Party of Turkey abroad, through its radio station, attacked Turkey vehemently as a warmonger and a tool of NATO intent on destroying Cyprus.

In Turkey proper, the Cyprus crisis shifted attention from the amnesty law to international problems and created a new charismatic hero: the premier Bülent Ecevit. It was clear that Bülent Ecevit and his party would sweep the polls if elections were held before the euphoria created by the Cyprus victory had dissipiated. Moreover, an early election and an electoral victory would allow the Republican Party to implement its entire program without having to deal with the whims of an unreliable coalition partner.

Thereafter, the relations between Ecevit and Erbakan cooled noticeably and finally the premier resigned in September on some rather flimsy pretext in the hope of finding a new coalition partner to agree to dissolve the Parliament and hold new elections soon. However, all these blueprints proved unworkable as none of the parties that were approached would agree either to form a government or to hold national elections, lest they might underwrite four years of a social-democratic regime in Turkey. The coalition government continued as a caretaker until mid-November, when Sadi Irmak formed a cabinet composed largely of technicians mostly unaffiliated with any political party.

Domestic Attitudes and Activities. General political developments and the establishment of a somewhat leftist government—the first of its kind during the fifty years of the Turkish republic—threw the courts trying the various leftist groups in complete confusion. Practically throughout 1973, the three courts in charge of dealing with so-called subversive—that is, communist—activities, namely the civilian penal courts, the military penal courts, and the state security courts, were occupied with the trials of various leftist political groups. Actually the bulk of these cases stayed with the military courts; these were referred to as *orfi idare*, or martial courts, because they had been established under the provisions of martial law and were given jurisdiction to conclude the trial of the leftists, despite the abolition of the martial law itself before the elections. The main organizations on trial were the Türkiye Ihtilalci Isçi-Köylü Partisi (Revolutionary Workers-Peasants Party of Turkey; RWPPT), Turkiye Halk Kurtulus Ordusu (People's Liberation Army of Turkey; THKO), Türkiye Halk Kurtulus Partisi (People's Liberation Party of Turkey; THKP), Turkiye Isçi-Köylü Kurtulus Ordusu (Workers and Peasants Liberation Army of Turkey; TIKKO), and a small group belong to the Turkiye Isçi Partisi (Labor Party of Turkey). The latter group was the chief organization which was closed by court order in mid-1971. In addition, members of several student or professional organizations such as Dev-Ğenç (Revolutionary Youth), Turkiye Ögretmenler Sendikasi (Teachers' Trade Union of Turkey; TOS), and several individuals belonging to ad hoc groups accused of sabotage were on trial. For instance, according to a reliable report, in Istanbul alone a total of 1,035 persons had been sentenced or brought to trial since the introduction of martial law. All these cases were tried under provisions of the penal code dealing with subversive activities. The election results, however, showed that the population supported the People's Republican Party and rejected at least implicitly the policies pursued by the military in 1971-73. The interpretation of the legal provision prohibiting class struggle was essentially a political decision directly rooted in the social philosophy of the party in power. Thus, if a rightist government adhered to a rigid interpretation of the penal code, a leftist government was likely to adopt a more lenient approach. The premier was known to favor a liberal approach and aim at pardoning all the prisoners as soon as possible, while the minister of justice, who belonged to the National Salvation Party, favored a more strict interpretation of the code. And since according to the Turkish legal system the public prosecutors are under the justice minister's authority, and often initiate actions according to his instructions, the minister's views carried heaver weight, at least for immediate purposes, than the premier's. Yet, the course of events, as well as the premier's moral authority and prestige greatly enhanced by the handling of the Cyprus crisis, favored the liberal cause. Consequently, a number of judges seemed to lean toward a more liberal interpretation of the law. This liberal attitude was aided also by frequent press reports criticizing the torture inflicted upon political prisoners and the confessions extracted from them under duress. Criticism stemmed from professional organizations, such as the Chamber of Construction Engineers, known for its leftist sympathies, but also from middle-of-the-road medical and bar associations. In fact, the physicians' association of Ankara revoked for two months the license to practice of a member, a captain, who had been accused of torturing prisoners. The Union of Bar Associations issued a report at the end of its eighth general convention criticizing the state security courts, established in large measure in order to deal with radical activities, as likely to become subject to political controversy and ultimately to harm justice.

The result of all these conflicting political tendencies and ideologies was a series of confusing court decisions. Some courts continued to impose harsh sentences on the indicted. The third martial court condemned 33 army officers to jail sentences of 6 to 12 years for having engaged in violent actions. A court in Ankara trying a case involving Irfan Solmazer, a member of the ruling military junta in 1960-61, and his associates, asked that the sentences of four men, already condemned to 30 to 36 years in jail, be changed to death sentences. The 265 members of the Revolutionary Workers-Peasants Party of Turkey were condemned, in March 1974, to sentences ranging from 2 to 20 years. The sentence of Can Yücel, a writer who was condemned to seven and a half years in jail because of the translation of a Marxist book in 1968, was upheld while Professor Mumtaz Seysal, who had become the symbol of the leftists' struggle against political prosecutions, was condemned in a second trial to a new jail term of six years and eight months.

During the same period, a group of about 25 persons, among whom were eight teachers and fifteen students, was arrested in Sivas, a city in eastern Turkey, for engaging in communist propaganda, and the publishers of Yeni Adimlar ("New Steps"), a literary review, were indicted for the same crime. However, the liberal current seemed to be stronger. A number of teachers, members of Tüm Öğretmenler Bütünlesme ve Dayanisma Dernegi (All-Teachers Association for Unity and Solidarity; TOB-DER), on trial for leftist activities, were acquitted. Similarly, twenty-one persons indicted for sabotage acts such as the sinking of a boat and arson, were freed for lack of evidence. Of twenty accused of having organized a "Kurdistan Democratic Party," half were acquitted and half were condemned. A number of persons belonging to THKP and others involved in a rather vague plot to bomb the newly built bridge on the Bosphorus were freed. A well-known folk singer, accused of using the lyrics of his songs to make communist propaganda, was acquitted, and the death sentences of two members of the so-called Second Turkish Liberation Army were commuted to life terms.

Parallel to the trend of liberation and the freeing of political prisoners, mostly leftists (although a well-known extreme Turanist was also pardoned by the president), a series of other developments occurred. The rightist student organizations known as "komandolar" and affiliated mostly with Alparslan Türkes's National Action Party began to attack rival and mostly leftist student groups in Istanbul and other cities. The attacks abated only after the premier issued vigorous warnings and after a number of people were arrested. The Union of Trade and Industrial Chambers of Turkey, a large and powerful organization of business groups, was criticized bitterly for investing large sums (it purchased and distributed books worth 500,000 liras) in a program designated to combat communism. Meanwhile the chairman of Türk-Is, the largest trade union confederation, in a public speech, defined leftism as a movement designed to defend the workers against their employers and involve the state in economic activity. He urged DISK, the leftist trade union, whose membership is barely one-twentieth of the former, to join forces. DISK refused by saying that it envisaged itself as engaged in a political and economic struggle without class considerations, and called attention to the efforts of the capitalist class to maintain itself in power at all costs.

All these developments, including the trial of various leftist groups, reached a turning point with the passage of the political amnesty law in May. The entire month of April was taken up by long debates in the House of Deputies and the Senate—as well as conflicts between the two houses and the government—over the scope of the amnesty law.

The Issue of Amnesty. The amnesty law of 18 May 1974, was comprehensive. It commuted death sentences to 30 years, and life terms to 24 years in jail. However, article 5 of the law exempted from pardon those condemned in accordance with articles 141, 142, 146, and 149 of the penal code—that is, all leftist political prisoners. The exemption to the amnesty law was passed, as mentioned before, through a coalition formed between the opposition deputies and a group of 22 deputies belonging to the National Salvation Party, the Republican's coalition partner. Though Premier Ecevit's immediate resignation was awaited, since the action of the NSP deputies violated the basic condition of the coalition agreement, he did not resign. Instead, the premier and 137 Republican deputies claimed in a petition addressed to the constitutional court that the section of article 5 of the amnesty law exempting political crimes from pardon was in violation of the principle of legal equality recognized by the constitution, and asked the court to nullify it. The petition also capitalized on a technical conflict between articles 2 and 5 of the same law and a few minor points. Eventually, on 2 July, the supreme court in an 11-4 decision invalidated that section of the amnesty law. The practical effect of this action, which became enforceable ten days later, was to extend pardon to practically all those condemned under the provisions of articles 141, 142, 146 and 149—that· is, to all the leftist organizations and groups for crimes and offenses committed before 7 February 1974. Although the opposition protested vehemently that the action of the supreme court was a usurpation of the pardon authority vested in the National Assembly, the decision was soon carried out. Some 2,000 political prisoners were freed during the following days. This was in addition to a few hundred who had been freed in May, when the original amnesty law was enacted. (Those freed earlier included a number of persons who had been tried under the provisions of articles 151 and 296 of the penal code, including some 300 who belonged to the People's Liberation Army). Some of the major leftist political groups and an approximate number of their members benefitting from the amnesty were the following: Labor Party of Turkey, 25; Dev-Genç, 257; People's Liberation Party of Turkey, 465; Workers and Peasants Liberation Army and Front of Turkey, 26; Proletarian Party (established in Adana), 34; Kurdistan Democratic Party, 15; Teachers Trade Union of Turkey (TÖS), 147; United Front, 57; and Revolutionary Cultural Association of the East, 20. The leftists tried under the so-called Safak case, which included the Revolutionary Workers-Peasants Party of Turkey, and writers, translators, and professors sentenced or tried for communist or leftist activities, were also pardoned and freed. Meanwhile, Mihri Belli, the militant organizer, surfaced and was promptly released. Since a large number of the pardoned were students, measures were soon taken to readmit these into their respective institutions and allow them to take examinations to make up for the time lost in prison. The net result of all these activities, which captured public attention for two months, was to restore freedom to all the major leftist groups and to their leaders, all active in the political turmoil in 1968-71, minus several dozen who had been killed in various skirmishes with the army or the police or had been executed as a result of court sentences. A number of cases for which jail sentences of five years or more were asked continued to be tried, even though the sentences were rather lenient as in the case of the People's Liberation Army.

Reorganization and Resumption of Activity. The Cyprus crisis, which erupted in mid-July, the massive outpouring of popular sentiment in favor of the landing of troops on the island, and the initial Soviet support for Turkey's action, prevented the leftist groups from deciding on a specific line of action. Notably lacking were demonstrations and writings similar to those staged by the left when Turkey decided to send troops to Korea in 1950.

A rather interesting event in 1974 was the establishment of the Socialist Workers Party of Turkey on 21 June, largely as a consequence of the freedoms brought about by Ecevit's government. Ahmet Kaçmaz, an engineer, and Yalçin Yusufoglu became chairman and general secretary, respectively. Oya Baydar (Sencer) a maverick woman with great political ambitions but hardly popular among hard-core leftists, was also a member of the party. The party proposed to organize the entire population for political action and opposed all restrictions imposed upon democratic rights and freedoms since these were basic to its own survival. In the economic field, the party proposed to nationalize all large establishments at present in the hands of the foreign owners, banks, and insurance enterprises. It was clear, however, that this party, although quite active, was far from representing all the leftist groups and trade unions in Turkey.

Meanwhile the courts continued to act leniently toward and free those leftists still being tried. In the case of Sarp Koray, an officer accused of siding with the leftists, even the military prosecutors agreed that the law under which he and his friends were tried was anti-constitutional, and the indicted were freed. A few months earlier, the prosecutor had asked the death sentence for the same group. The case against general Cemal Madanoglu, a hero of the military junta of 1960-61, and his 24 friends, who included some of the well-known leftist writers, such as Dogan Avcioglu, Ilhani Soysal, Cemal R. Eyuboglu, Ilhan Selcuk and several others accused of organizing a revolutionary society, was dismissed.

Meanwhile, Turkish-Soviet relations showed some improvement, especially after the press and especially the Congress of the United States began to put pressure on Turkey to withdraw from Cyprus or at least to make major concessions. Meanwhile, by mid-October the Soviet Union agreed to grant credit to Turkey for building a series of industrial plants, and the Turkish minister of finance prepared to discuss a Soviet loan which would finance a major steel plant. On 19 October, Soviet president Podgorny received a Turkish parliamentary delegation and expressed his satisfaction with the improving relations between the two countries (but opposed geographical federation in Cyprus as demanded by Turkey). It is interesting to note that just about the same time many U.S. congressmen and senators were competing with each other to make the harshest statements against Turkey, and eventually the Congress passed a law cutting military aid to Turkey, despite President Ford's and Secretary Kissinger's opposition. And all this happened regardless of the fact that Turkey had been a member of NATO and thus an ally of the United States since 1952.

The resignation of Bülent Ecevit in September, as mentioned before, was caused by the growing antagonism between the Republicans and the National Salvation Party. No doubt it was precipitated also by Ecevit's growing confidence in his ability to sweep the polls in an early election. All this undermined the government's authority and allowed Turkey's internal political problems to come to the surface. Moreover, the continual governmental crisis and economic difficulties of all kinds, including soaring inflation, further fueled the discontent among the public and exacerbated mutual fears among the extreme left and right. Meanwhile, the smoldering conflict within the Republican Party between the moderate social-democrats and the radical leftists, surfaced gradually in the form of attacks directed against the party's general secretary, Orhan Eyuboglu, and of demands for infusing young talent into the party leadership. This meant that the left wing wanted to strengthen itself by bringing young and more militant members, whose ideological stand ranged from Fabian socialism to Marxism, to positions of leadership in the party. This group supported Deniz Baykal, a professor of political science and minister of finance, who seemed to be aiming for the chairmanship of the party. However, at the convention of the youth branches of the Republican Party, held on 9 November, the radical group lost the election to those supported by the party's central organization. The losers, claiming that the elections had been manipulated, accused the leaders of "trying to take away the leadership of the youth branches from revolutionary democratic-minded leftists and push the party to conservatism and prevent its progress." These claims have not been answered yet. If the present efforts of the party leadership to maintain a moderate social philosophy continues, the radical youth branches could desert the party once more and join Marxist organizations which may be established soon.

Meanwhile some student groups began to boycott classes and schools for a variety of seemingly professional reasons, such as the unsatisfactory system of examinations. This, in fact, was the first step used in the past to mobilize a large number of students by exploiting legitimate academic grievances before the second step—politicization and radicalization of the students—was achieved. Already a number of students at the School of Political Science in Ankara, one of the major centers of student unrest in the past, have demonstrated against the planned visit of the U.S. secretary of state to Turkey by displaying posters where Kissinger was denounced as an "imperialist killer" and by setting fire to his effigy and the U.S. flag. The extreme left apparently feared the visit because it might lead to a quick settlement of the Cyprus dispute and do away with an excellent emotional issue suitable to exploitation, and, incidentally, enhance the prestige of the United States in Turkey. These demonstrations ceased after the government crisis worsened and Kissinger's visit was canceled for lack of a minister to talk to.

The most violent action taking place in November, however, was staged by the ultra-nationalists of the Ülkü Ocaklari (Ideal Patriotic Hearths), affiliated with the National Action Party. These feared that the boycotts organized by the leftists were designated to insure them leadership on various campuses. Consequently the Ocak groups occupied the Middle East Technical and Hacettepe Universities in Ankara. In the ensuing clashes, security forces were compelled to intervene and to restore order. Later, several leaders of the Ülkü Ocaklari were arrested and brought to court, while the martial law authorities (several provinces were under martial law because of the Cyprus crisis) prohibited gatherings and demonstrations. It seems that once normal conditions are established and freedom of assembly is restored, the rightist-leftist clashes will resume. The left, which has a great deal of power in the academic institutions, will probably attempt to regain the strong position it had secured before the military intervention in 1971. The situation of the left and its potential line of action in Turkey depend now on at least four major considerations. First, it needs time to reorganize its forces and to seek the most suitable areas of activities, since the shift of the country as a whole toward the left, and the bankruptcy of the militant anarchist policies pursued in 1967-71, have discredited or preempted many of the arguments used by the extreme left. Second, there is the difficult choice of deciding what policy to pursue in the elections to be held probably sometime in 1975. The question here is to decide whether the cause of the radical left will be better served by supporting the Republican Party and seeing its own ideology diluted in the social democracy defended by this party, or by organizing a new party which may divide the left but preserve the orthodoxy of the Marxist groups. Some extreme leftist groups which have no sympathy for the Republican Party have already started their activities; on 20 November the police in Istanbul arrested 16 persons belonging to the Workers and peasants Party, which claims to be a Marxist, Leninist, and Maoist organization. Third, there is a new set of conditions resulting from the departure of Bülent Ecevit as premier and the establishment in November of a new Cabinet under the premiership of Sadi Irmak, a seventy-year-old professor of medicine. His cabinet is made up of senators, independents, and technicians not affiliated with any party. It failed to obtain a vote of confidence and the premier designate resigned but was asked to stay as a caretaker. The possible decision of this government to resign itself to the role of a caretaker until elections are held—there is no agreement yet on this basis issue—or to assume wider responsibilities if that is possible at all without proper parliamentary support, will have considerable bearing upon the tactics of the Turkish radicals. Fourth, and finally, there is an unanswered question as to the future position and policies of the liberal and rightist parties toward leftist activities. The

Justice Party held its convention and, despite some expectation that it would choose another leader, gave an overwhelming endorsement to the incumbent chairman, Suleyman Demirel. Moreover, it seems that some deputies who left the Republican Party and formed the Cumhuriyetçi Güven Partisi are willing now to rejoin their mother party, either because their election chances would thus be bolstered or because they see there some ideological moderation.

International Views and Activities. A considerable number of leftist activities connected with Turkey were carried out abroad in 1974, especially among the Turkish workers and students in Western Europe. Practically every major leftist group in Turkey tried to infiltrate and to establish some following among these workers and students—usually, in the case of the latter, in order to use their organizational skills. For instance, the radicals arrested in November in Istanbul on the charge of establishing a revolutionary party had been operating also in West Germany for two years. Activists abroad make special efforts to find workers of Kurdish origin and imbue them both with nationalist and Marxist ideas in order not only to overthrow the existing regime upon return home, but also to promote the establishment of a Kurdish state. Interestingly enough, the terms *Turk* and *Türkiyeli* ("Turk" and "from Turkey") are often used abroad among workers and students to distinguish between those who have an ethnic from those who have only a geographical identification with their country of origin.

The relations of Turkish leftists abroad with a variety of revolutionary organizations continued throughout 1974. For instance, early in the year the French authorities arrested nine Turks who carried arms and explosives. Eventually it was discovered that these were Turkish commandos who had been armed and trained by the Algerian and Palestinian revolutionary organizations, possibly for action on behalf of either the Palestinians or the leftists jailed in Turkey (one of the arrested was the wife of Mahir Cayan, who had been killed in a clash with the police in Turkey). A French court sentenced them to several months in jail.

Meanwhile the basic organization, the underground Communist Party of Turkey, located abroad in East Germany and the U.S.S.R., which directs many but hardly all of the militant activities, celebrated its fifty-fourth anniversary. It mentioned its main immediate tasks as being (1) to obstruct the assault launched against Cyprus, (2) to rid the trade union movement of yellow trade unionists, (3) to strengthen the resistance of the national force within the framework of the bourgeoisie, (4) to wage continuous struggle against the Maoists (since these seem to dominate the radical left in Turkey), and (5), naturally, to strengthen solidarity within the Soviet Union. As usual, Bizim Radyo ("Our Radio") continued its broadcasts from East Germany throughout the year.

University of Wisconsin   Kemal H. Karpat

ASIA AND
THE PACIFIC

Australia

The ideology of laborism and practice of reformism, strengthened by the advent of a progressive Labor Government, is the greatest single obstacle to the advance of the Communist Party of Australia (CPA). Its central proposition is that the immediate economic and social grievances (wages and conditions) of workers may be alleviated within the framework of Australia's capitalist economy and liberal democratic institutions. Amongst the latter are registered trade unions, the Australian Industrial Court, and the Conciliation and Arbitration Commission. Any attempt by trade unions to move beyond the area of wages and conditions is considered by this ideology as a violation of the authority of some other institution or an invasion of the rights of a particular person or group.

The most recent attempts by the CPA to surmount this obstacle to a socialist future were outlined in the policy statement adopted by its Twenty-second Congress in 1970—at enormous cost, for it split the party—and elaborated at the Twenty-third Congress in 1972. By 1973 it was clear that these had failed also. Contrary to the official figure cited in *YICA, 1974* (p. 394), a reliable and highly placed party source stated that membership had dropped below 2,000 and was continuing to decline. Moreover, the CPA was perilously close to being supplanted by the Socialist Party of Australia (SPA) in the International Communist Movement.

It was these problems that a National Executive meeting discussed in January 1973. This marathon (five-day) session was conducted in a highly acrimonious atmosphere. At various stages of the discussion, national secretary Laurie Aarons, party president and Victorian state secretary John Sendy, and Joe Palmada threatened to resign from their posts. At its conclusion, two points of view were discernible.

One, hopefully anticipating a sharpening crisis of capitalism, advocated challenging its ideas and political instrumentalities, after the fashion of the N.S.W. branch of the Australian Building Construction Employees and Builders' Labourers' Federation (BLF) (see *YICA, 1974*, pp. 391-92). It also advocated downgrading or even severing relations with the Communist Party of the Soviet Union (CPSU), believing its activities to be a bad advertisement for socialism in Australia. This was the viewpoint of Laurie Aarons, Jack Mundey (at that time secretary of the N.S.W. branch of the BLF), and Charlie Gifford.

The other, impressed by the strength of the laborist tradition, favored a united front policy, developing mass support, especially within the trade union movement, for the more progressive of Labor's policies. It was expected that such action would raise working-class expectations to include demands for radical social change. It also urged the improvement of relations with the CPSU, lest the CPA be read out of the international communist movement. The main adherents of this view were John Sendy, Victorian state president Bernie Taft, and Mavis Robertson.

In September 1973 the CPSU responded to a request made by the CPA twenty months previously, shortly after the formation of the SPA, for bilateral talks. It suggested that they be held immediately. Accordingly, a CPA delegation departed for Moscow with unseemly haste. Both sides of the division within the National Executive were represented on it, made up as it was of Laurie Aarons, Bernie Taft, and Mavis Robertson.

The first session of talks was held on 28 September. The CPSU delegation consisted of B. Ponomarov, A. S. Chernayev, G. A. Zhukov, N. Matkowski, and E. Lagutin as interpreter. (This and the following information is based on a classified CPA document entitled *Transcript of CPSU-CPA Talks*.) Aarons was the first speaker. Among other things, he said that CPA criticism of policies and actions of the Soviet government was not "anti-Soviet." He continued:

> We consider that it is both legitimate and necessary for other Communist Parties to state their views in a comradely manner on policies and actions which they believe affect the world revolutionary process and their own revolutionary activity. . . . In the struggle for socialism in developed capitalist countries such as Italy, France, Britain (and Australia), it is necessary to stress the close relationship between democracy and socialism, and to show that the aim of socialism is human liberation–economic, social, moral and political. [Therefore] the ideological struggle cannot, and should not, be dealt with administratively. . . . We raise strongly the view that the current actions against people like Dr. Sakharov, Major-General Grigorenko and others are harmful to the interests of the USSR and to the socialist cause. (P. 9.)

In short, Aarons believed the CPA had to criticize the arbitrary actions of the CPSU in order to enhance its position in democratic Australia.

Also, Aarons accused the CPSU of supporting the breakaway CPA group, which later established the SPA, while it was still a factional grouping within the CPA (P. 5). Finally, he said that if the CPSU withdrew all its support from the SPA then the nromalization of relations between the two parties would be both desirable and feasible. (P. 13).

It was a tough opening gambit. He justified the CPA's critical stance towards the Soviet Party, offered no concessions, and even demanded that it abandon the SPA as the price of improving relations. As if the CPA was more important to the CPSU than vice versa.

On the Russian side, Ponomarov was no less intransigent: "The question of normalization depends on whether you continue your anti-Soviet stand. . . . Our attitude to normalization depends on Tribune not publishing . . . anti-Soviet articles" (P. 21). Then, drawing on the Stalinist formula which equates the interests of international communism with those of the Soviet state, he declared that "there should be no anti-Soviet articles in a paper which claims to be communist" (P. 21).

The first day's talks ended at this inconclusive point. Resumption was left up in the air. That night, Bernie Taft and Mavis Robertson left for the "International Conference on Solidarity with Chile" at Helsinki. On 1 October, while the others were still away, Laurie Aarons had a working lunch with all members of the CPSU delegation except Ponomarov. Upon its conclusion he wrote a note to the other two stating that "there can be no normalization unless we retract the statement [made in *Statement of Aims, Methods and Organization: The Party's Objectives as Adopted by the 22nd Congress, 1970*] that the USSR is not a socialist country, but a socialist-based society." (P. 22).

That night, Taft and Robertson rejoined Aarons in Moscow. The following morning they sent a letter to the Central Committee of the CPSU requesting a continuation of the talks that afternoon and expressing a "genuine desire to normalize relations between our parties" (P. 22a). As requested, the talks did resume that afternoon. But Ponomarov was again absent.

Bernie Taft spoke for the first time at this session. He was far more conciliatory than Aarons. He declared: "We want to make it quite clear that we believe that the U.S.S.R. and the other socialist countries are socialist countries" (P. 24). He then quoted the formulation of the 1972 congress: "Congress declares its unconditional support of all countries now on the socialist road against U.S. and world imperialism." This, he said, "constitutes our party's authoritative statement on this question" (P. 24) He then undertook the extremely difficult task of explaining away the conception of the U.S.S.R. as a "socialist-based" society. The notion was, he said, "an attempt [to] come to grips with some of the problems posed by socialist development that have a direct bearing upon the image and attraction of the socialist system, especially in industrially advanced countries such as ours" (P. 24). Although tactfully phrased, the implication is unmistakable. The party had adopted this formulation to convey that the socialist future for which it strove would not resemble the unpleasant reality of the U.S.S.R. The one feature they would have in common would be the social ownership of the means of production.

He concluded that as the notion might be wrong, was clearly inadequate, and was certainly offensive to the CPSU, the delegation would undertake to present the Soviet view to the CPA and raise it in the pre-congress discussion. For, he reminded his counterparts, only the party congress, to be next convened in June 1974, had the authority to make a final decision on this formulation. (P. 25.)

The CPA Congress, 1974. Thus, the question of whether the CPA was to regard the Soviet Union as a socialist or socialist-based society was placed on the agenda of the Twenty-fourth Congress. And, as the Russians made clear in their response to Taft, the normalization of relations depended on the restoration of this socialist mantle.

The question had many ramifications. Some treated it as a matter to be determined factually (see, for example, Eric Aarons, *The Nature of Soviet Society Today: A Contribution to Discussion for the 24th Congress, CPA*). Others viewed it more philosophically. This line of enquiry was best summarized by the phrase: "revolution for what? " For many party members, the type of society existing in the Soviet Union was not worth making a revolution for in Australia. "If that's socialism," one member commented, "I don't want it." And others explicitly and everyone implicitly, drew conclusions as to whether making this concession to the CPSU in order to restore fraternal relations would enhance or weaken the influence of the CPA at home and, for those who saw value in it, within the international communist movement.

Upon his return to Australia, Laurie Aarons called a National Committee meeting to discuss the matters raised in Moscow. Beforehand, the left-leaning South Australian State Committee, under the youthful secretaryship of Rob Durbridge, forcefully intervened in the debate by adopting an anti-CPSU resolution for submission to the National Committee meeting. It declared tha the U.S.S.R. showed no prospect of developing socialism under "the dictatorship of the CPSU." It continued:

> Our party must conclude [that] the USSR cannot be described as "socialist" or even "socialist-based," [that] the CPSU cannot be assumed to be furthering the cause of socialism, let alone leading it, [and that] any close association with it would seriously damage our relations with revolutionary progressive forces here and overseas, and could lay us open to opportunist manipulation by the CPSU. (*Tribune*, 20-26 November 1973.)

At the National Committee meeting, 3-4 November 1973, Aarons sounded a similar but less extreme note: "Should we move back from our present position [concerning, *inter alia*, the definition of the Soviet Union as a "socialist-based" country]? The only answer we can possibly give to that is no." Otherwise, he suggested, the party would be saddled with an image of socialism based on the state of affairs in the U.S.S.R. This would make the CPA's efforts to disabuse working-class people of laborist assumptions and convert them to socialism well-nigh impossible. (Ibid., 13-19 November.)

Also giving expression to his own polarizing style of leadership, as well as revealing the parlous state of party unity, he raised the possibility of a split within the party over the issue of relations with the CPSU: "If it has to be, I believe we have to face it." (See Bernie Taft, *A Crisis in the Party? Letters to Comrades, Letter I: A Contribution to Discussion for the 24th Congress, CPA*, January 1974, p. 1.)

Mavis Robertson and Bernie Taft presented a joint statement (not separate ones as incorrectly reported by this writer in *YICA, 1974*, p. 394) to the same session of the National Committee. They proposed making the necessary concession to the CPSU in order to maintain the CPA's standing within the international communist movement. Unlike Aarons and the South Australian State Committee, they did not consider that this move would weaken the CPA's standing in Australia. Rather, it was fanciful, they declared, to believe that condemnation of the CPSU would halt and even reverse the party's declining domestic fortunes. As Mavis Robertson pointed out at a later date: "... various other left groups have always dissociated themselves from the U.S.S.R., have never promoted its model of socialism and have always been critical of communist parties, but not one of them has become an effective political force" (*Why Not Call Them Capitalist? A Contribution to Discussion for the 24th Congress, CPA*, p. 7).

The Aarons forces won the day. The National Committee overwhelmingly rejected the CPSU's condition for the normalization of relations. However, it was up to Congress to make a final pronouncement on the matter.

Bernie Taft did not let the matter rest there. He was clearly instrumental in the Victorial State Committee's subsequent adoption of a resolution which expressed:

> grave concern at some of the extraordinary veiws voiced by a small minority of NC [National Committee] members and others invited to attend the meeting. We refer to such views expressed as the USSR is not a socialist country at all nor even socialist based, and that the international communist movement is not a revolutionary force. [Therefore] we urge the National Committee to wage a vigorous ideological campaign against such irresponsible stances and for the defence of the Party's political line as decided at the last two Party Congresses. (*Tribune*, 13-19 November 1973.)

Then John Sendy wrote a highly critical open (for party members) letter to Aarons and the whole debate turned several shades darker. Like Mavis Robertson, he attacked the assumption that CPA-CPSU relations hinder the party's growth. He wrote: "the masses of people will still regard us in the same way unless we prove our mettle in the Australian political scene." (*The Real Issue Before the Party and the Congress: Open Letter, John Sendy to Laurie Aarons, November 16, 1973*, p. 3.)

He then took issue with the "blame others" approach of "leading comrades." (This was an oblique reference to Laurie Aarons and his closest supporters.) They had said, he alleged, that "most trade union officials were reformist and no good" and that it would be necessary to start again from scratch in the trade union movement. (Ibid., p. 5.) Also, he claimed, they described a sizable proportion of party members as being "not much good" (ibid., p. 8).

Thus, if the leadership is to be believed, it is the CPSU, reformist trade union officials, and the bulk of party membership who are to blame for the party's decline, which leaves very few unsullied (except, of course, the "leading comrades" in general and Laurie Aarons in particular). In 1973, Aarons had been general secretary of the party for eight years. During that period, membership continued its post-war decline and the party split for the second time in ten years, suffering a considerable loss of influence as a consequence. Planning to serve only one more term as general secretary, if reelected at the 1974 congress, he presumably felt a strong need to justify his leadership in the face of these unimpressive facts and figures. He did this in the familiar way of projecting misgivings about his own abilities onto others—communist trade union officials and party members— even to the extent of contemplating with equanimity yet another split within the party. Plausibly, it is this process which explains, in part, why factionalism is endemic among political groups of declining power.

Sendy criticized the party for going from one unsatisfactory extreme to the other in policy formulation and implementation. Concerning the ALP, he said that the party had swerved sharply from the righist attitude of the early 1960s to a sectarian approach in the 1970s which had made the CPA "shy about any semblance of support for the ALP" (ibid., p. 5). Like Taft, he suggested that the party should develop mass struggles "in support of the progressive aspects of ALP election policy" (ibid., p. 7).

Equally sharp shifts, he noted, characterized party organization. "In our fight against bureaucratic leadership," he wrote, "we have virtually done away with all meaningful office bearers of the National level except that of National Secretary" (ibid., p. 7). As for the National Executive, he noted that this body only meets every four to eight weeks. "Between meetings of the Executive [i.e., for weeks on end] we have no clearly designated body or group of comrades whose job it is to administer the work of the Party. Obviously that is left to those comrades who just happen to be around the National Office at any particular time." (Ibid., p. 7.)

Sendy's letter gives the impression of a party thrashing around first to the right and then to the left in a desperate bid to reverse its declining fortunes. Once obsequious to the CPSU, it is now rebellious. Once cooperative with the ALP, especially in the trade union movement, it now stands aloof. Once it conducted its own affairs according to the theory of Lenin (democratic centralism) and practice of Stalin; now it conducts them on an ad hoc basis. It had, in short, tried a number of revolutionary strategies, and all to no avail. It seems plausible to conclude, therefore, that Australian society at present is impervious to revolutionary overtures in whatever key they are played. This, of course, was not John Sendy's conclusion. He blamed the party's left line: "[It] can isolate us and ruin the Party for years to come." (Ibid., p. 10.)

In his reply (*Letter to a Comrade: An Open Letter from Laurie Aarons to John Sendy, December 6, 1973*) Aarons vigorously contested Sendy's gloomy conclusion. As proof of the correctness of party policy, he cited some recent left/progressive or communist victories in trade union elections. These took place, he wrote, in the Sydney branch of the Waterside Workers Federation (WWF), the N.S.W. Ship Painters and Dockers, the Builders' Labourers' Federation, and the N.S.W. Teachers' Federation (p. 2).

What the party was trying to do, Aarons stated, was overcome the reformism and conservatism of the trade unions. For these had proved major problems in the development of militant unionism and revolutionary politics in the workers' movement. (Pp. 2-3.) "Developing real change in the trade union movement," he admitted, "is not easy. There are real pressures of economism, reformism and bureaucracy; there is a constant pull to arbitration and negotiation in a class collaborationist manner." (P. 3.) Especially, he implied, under a Labor government (p. 7). Nevertheless, he concluded, there was a way forward, and it was the one taken by the N.S.W. branch of the BLF, which had demonstrated in practice how to overcome reformism (p. 4).

Following up their radical move before the National Committee meeting in November 1973, Rob Durbridge, other members of the South Australian branch and members of the Glebe-Balmain (Sydney) and Carlton (Melbourne) branches, among whom were represented the editors of and contributors to the fundamentalist Marxist Journal *Intervention*, wrote in December 1973 the so-called Adelaide document. To the left of Aarons's position, it was an alternative party program drawn up for consideration at the congress.

Opposed to united front policies, it predicted that the working class would eventually uncover the true (capitalist) motive of the ALP government. And it was the task of the CPA to hasten this process by exposing and explaining its true nature. This would be one step along the road to winning its adherents to a revolutionary position. (*Discussion Document: A Contribution to Discussion for the 24th Congress, C.P.A.*, pp. 4, 6.)

It was this document and especially its attitude to the ALP which Bernie Taft attacked in his *A Crisis in the Party?* "The ultra-lefts," he wrote, referring to the authors of the Adelaide document, "concentrate almost solely on the negative side, on the 'danger' of Labor, without at the same time stressing and above all developing and acting on the positive possibilities created by Labor in office (p. 13). One such possibility, he made clear, was the existence of an ALP left wing which can exert some pressure on the Government and which, in turn, can be pushed by "a powerful and growing mass movement." This, he asserted, "can be an important stage on the long road towards ultimate social change." (P. 11.)

While John Sendy concluded his letter with a condemnation of the leftism of the Aarons leadership, Taft reserved his fire for this more recent and more extreme manifestation of leftism: "It is late, but it is not too late for the Party to rally and overcome what is today the most serious threat to its independence and indeed its future as a viable revolutionary alternative—ultra-leftism"(P. 14.) Fellow Victorian Henry Zimmerman in his *Left Wing Communism: The Second Childhood of the Australian Left (A Contribution to Discussion for the 24th Congress, CPA)* supported Taft's stand, as did National Executive member and *Tribune* editor Alec Robertson, (whose death on 15 March 1974 was widely mourned), and, of course, Mavis Robertson.

Eric Aarons, the brother of the national secretary, responded to Taft by characterizing his strategy as one of seeking out lowest-common-denominator demands ("Comrade Taft's Strategy" *Praxis*, April 1974, p. 2). Rather, he wrote, "radical (revolutionary) alternatives" should be advanced within mass movements in order to make the ideological break with capitalism. (Ibid.) Moreover, he asserted, "there is evidence today (different from the 'fifties and early 'sixties) that radical alternatives do strike a chord." Despite this fact, Eric Aarons complained, Taft wanted the CPA to support "the progressive, but un-radical and un-revolutionary (to say the least) aspects of the Labor Government's policy." (Ibid., p. 3.) If Taft's proposal involved the danger of entangling the CPA in lowest-common-denominator demands, as Eric Aarons claimed, his proposal, very similar in thrust to his brother's, threatened to isolate the party on the left of the laborist tradition.

Although these tendencies within the party withdrew from the brink of a formal split, a party official admitted in January 1974 that the CPA was, for all intents and purposes, divided. This, he said, effected the daily conduct of party affairs, which was haphazard at best if John Sendy's letter is to be believed. *Tribune* sales, which had been steady for many months, suddenly began to fall, especially in Sydney, after September 1973. And tension rose between members who had been comrades for years (Alec Robertson, *Unfinished Contribution, 24th National Congress, CPA*, p. 3). Thus deeply scarred, the party limped forward to its congress.

A National Committee meeting in Sydney on 1-3 March decided that each state or district should elect one National Committee member for each 80 members (or part thereof greater than 40) (*Praxis*, March 1974, p. 1). This was the first time the National Committee was to be elected directly by state and district conferences (*Tribune* 11-17 December 1973). These conferences were held at the end of May and the begining of June. The names of the new national committee members elected by them and the numerical strength of each district or state, based on the ratios of National Committee to party members quoted above, are contained in table 1.

The state and district conferences also elected one congress delegate for each 30 members (or part thereof greater than 15). And at the Congress, the delegates—of whom there were 103 (*Tribune*, 2 July), implying on the above ratios a party membership between 1,545 and 3,090—elected a new National Executive from the National Committee.

Jack Mundey, former secretary and current treasurer of the N.S.W. branch of the BLF was elected president. He is the first trade union official to hold this high party office. An Aarons supporter, he defeated Mavis Robertson for the position. (Former president John Sendy, reportedly deeply offended by personal recriminations, did not stand for party office.) Laurie Aarons was reelected national secretary unopposed. Eight additional members were elected to form a national executive of ten: Charlie Gifford (Queensland), Darrell Dawson (Newcastle, N.S.W.) Laurie Carmichael (Sydney), Joe Palmada (Sydney), Mavis Robertson (Sydney), Joyce Stevens (Sydney), Bernie Taft (Victoria), and Rob Durbridge (South Australia). Durbridge defeated Victorian state executive member and Taft supporter Dave Davies in a run-off ballot for last position on the executive.

TABLE 1. Communist Party of Australia, New National Committee Members and Party Membership by State or District, 1974

District/State	Names of National Committee members elected	Number of National Committee members	Ratio of National Committee to party members	State/District membership
Queensland	Frank Bishop			
	Marie Crisp			
	Charlie Gifford			
	Hugh Hamilton	4	1:40-80	160-320
Newcastle	Darrell Dawson			
(N.S.W.)	Bob Adamson	2	,,	80-160
Sydney	Brian Aarons			
(N.S.W.)	Laurie Aarons			
	Laurie Carmichael			
	Denis Freney			
	Jack Mundey			
	Judy Mundey			
	Joe Palmada			
	Pierina Pirisi			
	John Rainford			
	Mavis Robertson			
	Joyce Stevens			
	Richard Walsham	12	,,	480-960
South Coast				
(N.S.W.)	Reg Wilding	1	,,	40-80
Victoria	Dave Davies			
	Lesley Ebbels			
	Philip Herington			
	Max Ogden			
	Bernie Taft			
	Mark Taft			
	George Zangalis	7	,,	280-560
Tasmania	Barbara Bound	1	,,	40-80
South Australia	Pat Vort-Reynolds			
	Rob Durbridge	2	,,	80-160
Western Australia	Vic Slater	1	,,	40-80
Total		30		1,200-2,400

Sources: *Praxis*, March 1974; *Tribune*, 28 May-3 June, 4-10 June 1974.

In terms of personnel, clearly an association of the Aarons supporters and the Adelaide document group had won the congress. Robertson and Taft, elected secretary of the Victorian branch at its recent state Conference, could expect no more than occasional support from Laurie Carmichael on the executive, and on the National Committee they and their supporters were outnumbered three to one by the victorious alliance.

Just as the composition of the National Executive, elected by the delegates, reflected the dominance of the Aarons group, so too did the Congress documents, adopted by the same delegates. For example, they all but ignored the dangers of leftism, devoting considerable space instead to the problems reformism poses for revolutionary action. One of these problems, the document on the workers' movement noted, was its pervasiveness: "Reformist ideas can also affect militants and those who consider themselves part of the left" ("The Workers' Movement," *The Socialist Alternative: Documents of CPA 24th National Congress 1974*, pp. 8-9).

Such considerations led the Congress to an ambivalent view of the Labor government. On the one hand, the documents point out, it offers the opportunity to conduct mass campaigns around its more progressive policies as a means of raising working-class expectations to include more far-reaching social change. On the other hand, "reformist illusions can be strengthened; appeals to workers to leave it to the government find some response in the movement" ("Strategy for Socialism," ibid., p. 8).

In order to destroy this laborist or reformist tradition or, what it amounts to in practice, namely, bourgeois hegemony, it is necessary, the congress stated, to combine revolutionary consciousness and experience in action (ibid., p. 10). And it goes on to argue, as Aarons had done beforehand, that it is the N.S.W. branch of the BLF, with its policy of confronting the instrumentalities (e.g., the Arbitration Commission) and assumptions of the laborist tradition, which provides the best examples of such activity in the workers' movement. "The N.S.W. Builders' Laborers have shown concretely what is meant by the leading role of the working class and the possibility of broad class alliances [with Resident Action Groups] of immediate and long-range significance." (Ibid.) Given the hopes that Aarons leadership places on the type of actions adopted by the N.S.W. BLF to lead it out of the reformist quagmire, attention will be focused later on this union and its N.S.W. branch in particular.

On the question of the character of Soviet society, Robertson and Taft were also defeated. So too were the supporters of the anti-CPSU resolution of the South Australian State Committee quoted above. The congress maintained its 1970 formulation of the Soviet Union as a "Socialist-based Country" ("The CPA and The International Communist Movement," ibid., p. 31). This was quite sufficient, of course, to ensure a break-down in relations with the Soviet party. What effect, if any, this step will have on the CPA's domestic political standing remains to be seen.

The CPA's international political standing had already been affected by its well-established critical posture toward the CPSU. The only parties loyal to the Soviets that sent greetings to the congress were the inconsequential Communist Party of Canada, Swiss Party of Labor and Communist Party of Israel (RAKAH). The communist parties of Italy, France, and Great Britain, all critical of the CPSU to some extent, also sent greetings. So too did four ruling parties: The Vietnamese Workers' Party, always anxious to foster anti-U.S. and revolutionary forces of whatever political hue, which sent a two-man delegation as well; the Korean Workers' Party, which maintains good relations with both the CPSU and the Chinese Communist Party; the Romanian Communist Party; and the League of Communists of Yugoslavia—the last two of which have good reason to disapprove of the CPSU. Warmest greetings came from the North Vietnamese, the Central Committee of the National Front for the Liberation of South Vietnam, the Japan Communist Party (resentful of CPSU support for the Shiga Yoshio faction of the JCP), the Communist Party of Spain (disappointed by the international communist movement after East Germany recognized the Franco regime in 1973), the anti-CPSU Communist Party of Greece-interior, and, lastly, the tiny, isolated Communist Party of Israel (MAKI). (*Tribune*, 25 June, 2, 16 July.)

The 1974 General Election. Elections always bring the CPA's relations with the ALP to a head.

This has involved a great deal of hair-splitting over campaign slogans. When the Liberal-Country Party coalition was in power, the purists advocated the slogan: "Elect Communists, Defeat Liberal Government." More practical souls argued that this would isolate the party from the workers who support the ALP. Accordingly, they advocated the slogan: "Put Communists into Parliament. Elect a Labor Government." Whatever the outcome of these arguments, the CPA always gave its second preference to the ALP. In the 1972 federal election, in the Division of Sydney, it departed slightly from this practice, by giving its second preference to the SPA and its third preference to the ALP.

In the N.S.W. state election of 17 November 1974, Joe Owens, secretary of the N.S.W. BLF and CPA candidate for Phillip, ignored this convention and, indeed, Lenin's injunction that communist parties should support the election of Labor or Social Democratic governments in order to reveal their true "social-chauvinist" character (*Left-Wing Communism*, chap. 9), by advocating a second preference for the Australia Party (*Tribune*, 13-19 November, 1973). He received 614 votes or 3.1 percent of the 20,113 votes cast (see *YICA, 1974*, p. 387).

In the 18 May 1974 election for both houses of the Australian parliament, the CPA reverted to its former practice. First taking care to define its own independent position, it then unequivocally advocated the return of the Labor government. For example, one of its slogans said: "Put Paid to Conservatism—Vote CPA for the Senate—Put Labor Back!" This change reflected the CPA's preference for the progressive Federal Parliamentary Labor Party over the conservative N.S.W. one. It also reflected the vastly different circumstances under which the two elections were fought. The N.S.W. ALP was making a half-hearted effort to unseat the Liberal-Country Party coalition government in that state. The federal ALP was fighting for its political life, having been forced into an election by opposition senators who, for the first time in the history of the federal parliament, blocked government appropriation (supply) bills.

Earlier in the year, the CPA had put together three Senate teams to contest the next election for half the Senate, which was expected to be held in May. However, the dramatic action of the opposition senators, and the events that ensued, led to a (double) dissolution of all the Senate and the House of Representatives. An election for both houses was scheduled for 18 May. This development caught the CPA unprepared. Thus, it only managed to field one candidate for the lower house. The SPA fielded two but stayed out of the Senate election.

The CPA's choice of Senate candidates underlined some of the policy preoccupations of the party. The N.S.W. team consisted of Jack Mundey in number one position, radical ecologist and architect of the green bans (see *YICA, 1974*, p. 391), Pat Miller, Aboriginal activist, and Brian McGahan of Gay Liberation. The Victorian one was made up of Bernie Taft, women's liberationist Lyn Hovey, and Max Ogden, an educational officer of the Amalgamated Metal Workers Union (AMWU). In South Australia the party was represented by Elliot Johnston Q.C., Yuri Jacomedes, a railway worker and union activist, and Rob Durbridge (*Tribune*, 2-8 April 1974). Paul Marsh, vice-president of the party's West Australian branch, stood for the House of Representatives seat of Perth. He cited "radical changes in education and preservation of the environment" as the issues upon which he would campaign. (*Tribune*, 30 April-6 May.)

The SPA, like the Victorian branch of the CPA, looks favorably upon and advocates close cooperation with the ALP. Accordingly, it was incensed by the opposition's refusal of supply to the government. "The general election," its newspaper said, "... will determine whether the general forward and progressive policies of the Labor movement are to continue and be strengthened by more resolute anti-monopoly policies or are to be stopped dead by the return to the caveman policies of the Liberal-Country Party coalition." Its two candidates were Pat Clancy, SPA president and federal secretary of the Building Workers Industrial Union (BWIU), who stood for the seat of Sydney, and J. Mitchell, chairman of the South Australian State Committee and waterside worker, who stood for Port Adelaide. (*The Socialist*, May.) Like the CPA, the SPA, of course, allocated its second preferences to Labor candidates. (Ibid.)

The Communist Party of Australia (Marxist-Leninist) maintained its view that parliamentary polices are a sham and its consequent policy of not contesting parliamentary elections. More sectarian than the other two parties, it did not specifically advocate a vote for the ALP. However, it did concede Prime Minister Whitlam the back-handed compliment that he "broke from much of the diehard policy because the more realistic section of the bourgeoisie saw that diehard policy was untenable in Australia and the world today" (*The Vanguard*, 18 April).

In the campaign, the CPA tried to wring electoral gain from the N.S.W. BLF's green bans. Its former secretary, Jack Mundey, as noted above, was number one on its N.S.W. ticket. And its main election slogan was: "Vote Red for a Green Australia." By communist standards, Mundey ran a very successful campaign, addressing a large number of well-attended meetings. Indeed, on the eve of the election, the party was hopeful about his chances of election. (See *Tribune*, 14-20 May.)

These hopes, however, were rudely dashed. The CPA performed abysmally in the Senate election (see table 2). It is not clear whether this indicated that communist electoral stocks had fallen to an all-time low or whether potential communist voters, in their anxiety to return the government, recorded a first preference vote for the ALP. Whatever the case, the *Tribune* (21-27 May) put a brave face on it. (The only other alternative is despair.)

TABLE 2. Communist Party of Australia, First Preference Votes in the 18 May Senate Election

State and total Vote	CPA candidates	1st preference votes (percent of total vote)	Total (percent of total vote)	Number of seats
N.S.W.	J. Mundey	10,888 (0.4)		
	P. Miller	187 (0.0)	11,202 (0.4)	0
2,702,903	B. McGahen	127 (0.0)		
Victoria	B. Taft	2,128 (0.1)		
	L. Hovey	248 (0.0)	2,595 (0.13)	0
2,070,893	N. M. Ogden	219 (0.0)		
South Australia	Y. Jacomedes	5,786 (0.8)		
	E. Johnston	569 (0.0)	6,786 (0.94)	0
722,434	R. Durbridge	431 (0.0)		

An indication of just how poorly the CPA did in the Senate election is gleaned from the fact that a party or a candidate requires 9.1 percent of the vote in order to gain one seat in an election for the whole Senate. The best the CPA could manage was 0.94 percent of the first preference votes in South Australia (S.A.)!

The party performed no better in the House of Representatives election for the safe Labor seat of Perth. Its candidate gained only 539 votes, or 0.87 percent of 61,829 votes cast.

The SPA's showing was equally unimpressive. In the 1972 election, Clancy gained 1,062 votes, or 2.26 percent of the total vote of 46,806 in the Division of Sydney. At that time he was competing against Laurie Aarons of the CPA who, from the top of the ballot paper, garnered 2,236 votes, or 4.77 percent of the total. In 1974, despite the fact that he was the only communist running in Sydney, Clancy was unable to improve on his 1972 percentage. He received 996 votes which was again 2.26 percent of the total vote of 44,164 (cf. the inaccurate report in *The Socialist*, July). In

Port Adelaide, J. Mitchell did little better. He polled 1,424 votes, or 2.43 percent of a total vote of 58,632.

The Australian Building Construction Employees and Builders' Labourers' Federation (BLF). It is no exaggeration to say that the CPA leadership regards the practice of the N.S.W. BLF as a panacea for its ailing political fortunes. This practice has involved a go-it-alone policy of confrontation. The BLF is openly contemptuous of other unions in the building group of the N.S.W. Trades and Labour Council and of the Council's moderate ALP leadership. In industrial disputes, it strikes first (if possible, during a concrete pour) and talks later, refusing for the most part the proffered hand of the Australian Arbitration Commission. In its relationship with employers, it has arrogated to itself the right to decide which buildings it will construct and knock down.

Laurie Aarons believes that to confront, as the BLF has confronted, the institutions and assumptions of the laborist tradition, offers a way of leading the working class out of the mire of reformism and into the garden of revolutionary politics. However, events in the building industry in 1974 suggested that such hopes are ill-founded. The BLF's actions provoked a sharp, damaging reaction from employers, whose assumed rights had been violated, from the Australian Industrial Court, which enforces the assumptions of laborism, and from the federal secretary of the union, Norm Gallagher, who, although a vice-chairman of the CPA(M-L), is steeped in the laborist tradition. (See *YICA, 1974*, pp. 391-92.)

At the end of 1973, the Master Builders Association commenced deregistration proceedings against the federation. This step was taken largely in response to the actions of the N.S.W. branch, especially its green bans. Gallagher, concerned about the prospects of deregistration, threatened to take action against the branch. Fearful of a federal takeover, it withdrew its funds from the bank. (See *YICA, 1974*, p. 392.)

Gallagher continued to toy with this idea. When the N.S.W. president, ALP member Bob Pringle, asked Gallagher over the telephone in early 1974 what he intended to do about the N.S.W. branch, the federal secretary replied: "We're going to eat you" (*Direct Action*, 23 February). His initial action, however, was less drastic. On 6 February his Federal Management Committee withdrew the right of entry onto job sites of officials of the N.S.W. branch (*Tribune*, 12-18 February).

Then, in April, he tried another tack. The Federal Management Committee restored the right of entry of N.S.W. officials and donated $1,000 to the N.S.W. Green Ban Fighting Fund (ibid., 16-22 April). Moreover, Gallagher warned the Master Builders Association of Australia that the federation would not tolerate the attacks being made on it by the N.S.W. Master Builders Association (the applicant in the deregistration proceedings). He declared that the work of its members in other states would, therefore, become, as from 7 May, the targets of industrial action. He implied that the price of industrial peace would be the suspension of the deregistration move. But all to no avail, for the N.S.W. MBA continued to press its case. Furthermore, it was successful. The Australian Industrial Court ordered the cancellation of the union's registration for continued breaches of its award, thereby hindering the objectives of the Conciliation and Arbitration Act. The judges took particular exception to the green bans and policy of industrial confrontation of the N.S.W. branch.

As a result of deregistration, the BLF lost the right to obtain awards in the Conciliation and Arbitration Commission. Nevertheless, Ms. Justice Evatt, a deputy president of the commission, allowed Builders Labourers in September to participate in proceedings for a national award for building workers. However, Building Employers successfully challenged this action in the High Court. They were granted temporary orders staying the decision of Evatt. (*Australian Industrial Law Review*, 6 September). There could be no doubt about it. Deregistration was hurting the union badly.

It seems that it was this factor that finally led Gallagher to try and seat the N.S.W. branch as the first step back on the road to reregistration. On 9 October the Federal Management Committee decided to take over the branch. (*The Age*, 8 October.) It is too early to tell what success this move will have, but not too early to realize the desperate situation into which the N.S.W. BLF's policies had led it. And these were the very policies hailed by the CPA for showing the way forward to a socialist future! The party had underestimated the strength of laborism, which even pushed Gallagher's Maoism into second place, and the ability of the Industrial Court to enforce its assumptions. The CPA had reached an impasse. The only way out was back.

Industrial Relations. Life-style issues such as green bans are an economic luxury. In 1974 the Australian economy lacked the strength to sustain them. For example, in August, one of the country's largest construction groups, Mainline Corporation, collapsed, partly as a result of a government credit squeeze (*Australian Financial Review*, 20 August, 3 September). As a result, about 3,000 building workers lost their jobs (see *The Age*, 12 September). In early September, the BLF lifted its black ban (as they are called in Victoria) on the demolition of two buildings on the Melbourne City Square site. After this step was announced Gallagher said: "We are happy to have reached an agreement [with the Lord Mayor] over the buildings. It will create more work for building workers." (*The Herald*, 2 September.) And on 30 September, Jack Mundey told this writer that a number of the green bans in N.S.W. were negotiable. Confronted with the choice between green bans or jobs, the union leadership understandably chose the latter (cf. *YICA, 1974*, pp. 391-92).

Of course, bread-and-butter demands (for better wages and conditions) are the specialty of reformist trade union leaders like Gallagher who, by their very success, have helped to integrate their union members into Australia's capitalist economy. However, in 1974 this economy was unable to absorb these demands, which were made in response to an annual rate of inflation approaching 20 percent. This enabled the CPA to ridicule the central tenet of laborism, namely, that working class grievances can be alleviated within the capitalist economy. Unable to negotiate the laborist tradition on the left in the company of the N.S.W. BLF, the CPA leadership now envisaged riding directly over its inflated carcass.

The Labor government, for its part, was appalled by Treasury advice that a sharp recession, involving a high rate of unemployment for a sustained period, was the only way to break inflationary expectations. Prominent party members showed a loss of nerve. The Labor minister considered resigning. R. Hawke, president of both the Australian Council of Trade Unions (ACTU) and the Labor Party declared that if the only possible solution to inflation was unemployment then "let it be done by a party other than the Labor Party" (*The Australian*, 13 August).

Just as caucus unity was about to crumble under the political weight of these draconian proposals, the deputy prime minister, Dr. Jim Cairns, salvaged the situation by advocating a policy which did not involve the deliberate creation of unemployment. Moreover, it was economically respectable. It proposed that the Arbitration Commission grant automatic cost-of-living adjustments for wages and salaries (indexation) and that the government use taxation and other means to discourage higher increases. Also, taxation rates would be reduced on lower incomes to ensure that increases acquired along the lines above would largely remain in the pocket of the wage or salary earner.

It was this strategy which underlay the budget, handed down on 17 September. Its success depended on the trade unions' acceptance of indexation. Failing this, hyper-inflation in 1975 appeared a probability, accompanied by grievous social and political consequences. Mr. Hawke said, for example, that the Whitlam government could not survive continued, growing inflation. Moreover, its fall would reinforce the conviction of Australians that capitalist governments could no longer look after their needs. He added grimly: "We are looking at the distinct possibility of the breakdown of the Western capitalist system, especially in this country. . . . This would be good for the extreme Left or Right who want to see [the] destruction of Western society." (*The Australian*, 22 August.)

It was this situation, both ripe with opportunity and fraught with danger, if Hawke's prognosis is to be believed, into which the CPA stepped. It opened on an offensive note. In *Tribune* (26 March), Laurie Carmichael, assistant Commonwealth secretary of the AMWU, advocated the development of "our own Australian style of the Japanese and Italian workers' offensive. If such a co-ordinated offensive gets the interest of enough unions, wide-ranging issues of great social significance could be raised." (Quoted by Fred Wells in *Sydney Morning Herald*, 6 August.)

Laurie Aarons embroidered this theme in his address to the CPA congress: "We should work for a total class offensive for national economic and social demands. . . . It was suggested [by Laurie Carmichael] that we should adapt the Japanese Spring Offensive in Australia. Why not an Autumn Offensive [i.e., March-May] —a national workers' action for economic aid social demands? " (Ibid.)

Jack Mundey then gave wide publicity to the idea in a television program. Led on by the interviewer, he presented a highly colored picture of the original CPA notion and made exaggerated claims of communist party influence within the trade unions. He described the autumn offensive as a "national strike." He made the inordinate claim that at the shop-steward level the CPA was the most influential political party "together with the left wing sections of the Australian Labor Party." He listed, more realistically, the unions within which the party had marked influence. They were, he said, "the Builders Labourers, the Metal Workers, [and] in some areas the plumbers, in other areas, the BWIU, [and] other areas, miscellaneous workers." Then asked about the CPA's influence among transport, power, oil, and mining workers, he replied, not to be outdone: "Oh, well in all four, we have substantial influence at grass roots level, and certainly when periods of strike action take place, they would plan an extremely important role." (*Federal File*, Channel 9, Sydney, 3 August.) Of course, nobody could be blamed for taking Mundey's extravagant claims at face value. An editorial in *The Herald* (5 August) stated: "The Communist Party chairman (sic) has come out for . . . greater industrial action, fending off his critics with cries of 'McCarthyism.' All unionists should think of what his party really promises." Malcolm Fraser, the federal opposition spokesman on industrial relations, claimed that the present strike situation gripping Australia was not merely industrial in origin—it had been organized by communists. He described the communist party call for a national strike as "nothing short of a disaster" and urged Australian workers to revolt against "communist dominance." (*The Age*, 6 August.)

The Victorian state secretary of the CPA, Bernie Taft, was appalled by Mundey's statement and the reaction it provoked. In a letter to the editor of *The Age* (9 August), he asserted (correctly): "The Communist Party of Australia had made no . . . call [for a general strike]." The *Tribune* (6 August) also swept Mundey's idea of a national strike under the carpet. However, it continued to give strong backing to an autumn offensive. An editorial declared: "Working people today face a massive capitalist offensive aimed at making them shoulder the burden [by wage restraint] of the biggest economic crisis since the 30's. . . . That is why we suggest the workers' movement discuss preparing an 'autumn offensive.' " Later in the month, the prime minister made an oblique contribution to the debate. In an address to the N.S.W. ALP State Council, he urged unionists who wanted to keep Labor in power to scrutinize the results of the action of some of their officials who were not Labor supporters and did not particularly want a Labor Government (*The Age*, 26 August).

It was at this point that the CPA backed down, apparently fearful of the reaction it had provoked. Laurie Aarons denied that the communist party was unconcerned about the fate of the Labor government. "A workers' offensive," he said lamely, "will strengthen the government's position, not weaken it" (*Tribune*, 27 August).

The party continued to back-pedal. Carmichael, who had been the first to call for a Japanese Spring-type offensive, now lent his support to the ACTU executive in its appeal to the government to restructure taxation scales and support a major increase in the minimum wage in addition to the introduction of quarterly cost of living adjustments. He covered his retreat in harsh language: "The ACTU demands on the Australian Government provide a basis for a workers' counter-offensive to the attack being carried out to load the effects of the growing crisis of the system on the worker's back." (Ibid., 3 September.) However, the shift in emphasis was unmistakable. His Japanese Spring Offensive had now become a "counter-offensive." Moreover, the CPA, in cooperation with other militant groups, was not to conduct it. Rather, it was to be carried out under the auspices of the moderate, ALP-dominated ACTU Executive.

The CPA was in a difficult position, partly of Jack Mundey's making. Having claimed influence within the trade union movement which it does not possess, it will be incorrectly blamed, as it was by Mr. Fraser, for industrial disruption over which it has no control. Hitherto, the CPA has existed on sufferance within Australia's liberal democratic form of government. However, if this should grow sour under economic stress, as it grew sour under international stress in the early fifties, then the communist party may go to the wall, as it nearly did in 1951. (See L. Webb, *Communism and Democracy in Australia: A Survey of the 1951 Referendum*. Melbourne, 1954.)

On 23-24 September the 131 unions affiliated with the ACTU convened to discuss their attitude to wage indexation. In the September budget, the government had offered them a carrot in the form of tax cuts on lower incomes. At the conference itself, ACTU President Hawke held a stick over them. He warned that the failure of the trade unions to cooperate with the Labor government's strategy would lead to its downfall and replacement by "the most Tory, reactionary Government in Australia since World War Two" (*Australian Financial Review*, 24 September).

The plausibility of this forecast created an atmosphere of conciliation. The demands of Laurie Carmichael and other left-wing unionists for a 35-hour week and nationalization of key industries were quietly forgotten. On the issue of taxation, however, cooperation faltered, whatever the political hue of the trade union. L. Short, the anti-communist secretary of the Federated Ironworkers Association, said: "The tax cuts in the Budget did not go nearly far enough and, to get full cooperation from the unions, the Government must provide more tax relief" (*The Australian*, 23 September). The reasonableness of this objection could not be denied. On the Treasurer's own estimates of the increase in earnings average wage earners will be paying more in tax for the financial year 1974-75, despite the tax cuts announced in the September budget (*The Age*, 18 September).

Accordingly, the conference made tax indexation the condition for its acceptance of wage indexation. The final resolution stated: ". . . until indexation of taxation is introduced, there can be no adequate protection against the erosive effects of inflation on real after-tax income. This effect has continued to be a significant factor in the level of wage and salary demands." (*Australian Financial Review*, 25 September.) However, it seems unlikely that the Government will accept this condition. Both the prime minister, Mr. Whitlam, and the deputy prime minister, Dr. Cairns, expressed misgivings. Dr. Cairns said the government would prefer to cut taxes once or twice a year than accept tax indexation. He said that it was an untried economic control. No one knew where it would take the economy. (*The Age*, 30 September.)

And no one knew where the economy, if it continued to inflate at such an alarming rate, would take the polity. However, there were a few clues. One was provided by the formation of the country-based National Action Group (NAG). It consisted of graziers, inexperienced in the ways of capital city politics, who had come together to protest what it called "industrial anarchy," inflation, and "the raw deal being handed out to people in the country." Its significance, for our purposes, lay in the alacrity which it, an essentially moderate organization, revived the dormant anti-communist themes of the fifties. At a NAG rally in September, for example, one of the speakers had this to say: "The Communist Party of Australia has convinced this nation that it has Australia at heart when in fact it is after the heart of Australia" (*National Times*, 23-28 September).

In the same month, reliable sources reported the formation of an extreme right-wing political organization (toying with the title "Save Free Australia"). Allegedly, it is sponsoring a small commando-style anti-communist strike force to combat Jack Mundey's "national strike" (see *The Bulle-*

tin, 14 September). That souring of the liberal-democratic process of government, with its dire implications for the well-being of the communist party, may already be in progress.

International Relations and the International Communist Movement. Laurie Aarons, Victorian state president Leslie Ebbels, and Malcolm Salmon, *Tribune* correspondent in the Democratic Republic of Vietnam, visited the DRV in April 1974 at the invitation of the Vietnam Workers' Party. They were accorded VIP treatment, being greeted at the airport by Le Duan, first secretary of the Central Committee and Xuan Thuy, secretary of the Central Committee (*Tribune*, 23-29 April. During its stay, the CPA delegation "pledged to do all in its power, together with other democratic and progressive forces in Australia, to promote the movement for support and assistance to the Vietnamese people and to demand of the Australian Government the recognition of the Provisional Revolutionary Government of the Republic of South Vietnam" (statement issued by the Vietnam News Agency, 20 April, quoted in *Tribune*, 30 April-6 May). The delegation departed for Australia on 20 April.

The CPA was delighted by the turn of events in Portugal. Laurie Aarons expressed this sentiment, as well as pledges of international solidarity, in a letter he wrote to Alvaro Cunhal, secretary-general of the Portuguese Communist Party (*Tribune* 7-13 May). In a television interview, Prime Minister Whitlam expressed his pleasure at the fall of the Caetano dictatorship. However, if the CPA and Mr. Whitlam agreed on this point, they expressed opposed views on another, namely, the future of Portuguese Timor. During a visit to Indonesia in September, the Prime Minister told President Suharto that he favored its inclusion within the Republic of Indonesia. On the other hand, the CPA, which has good reason to hate the Suharto government, favors independence for the colony. The *Tribune* (24 September) declared: "It is a duty of all progressive forces in Australia to come to the aid of the Timorese people and force a change in Australian Government policy."

Since its adoption of an independent posture within the international communist movement, the CPA has enjoyed close relations with the League of Communists of Yugoslavia (LCY). In November 1973, the National Committee, anxious to disown its Stalinist past, adopted a resolution which contained an unconditional retraction and apology for "CPA statements falsely attacking and slandering Yugoslavia, President Tito and other Yugoslavian leaders, made in 1948, and following years" (Quoted in Mavis Robertson, op. cit., p. 5.) No doubt this step enhanced relations between the two parties. Then the LCY invited the CPA to attend its Tenth Congress, in May. Unable to send a delegation, the CPA leadership wrote a letter of greeting which was marked both by its warm regard for the Yugoslavs and its implicit criticism of the CPSU. "Development of self-managed socialism," it stated, "and the struggle against bureaucratic distortions is a major contribution by Yugoslav Communists to revolutionary theory and to the international communist movement" (*Tribune*, 21-27 May).

In August, the U.S. government refused to grant Laurie Carmichael an entry visa on the grounds that he is a communist. The Untied Auto Workers had invited him to the United States to discuss the problems of working-class struggle against multi-national corporations. The decision to refuse him a visa was made in Washington against the advice of embassy officials in Canberra to waive, in this instance, the anti-communist sections of the Immigration and Nationality Act. Presumably, the embassy feared what, in fact, occurred: the U.S. government appeared to credit the CPA and one of its members with far more influence than either possessed. (*Tribune*, 27 August; *The Australian*, 22 August.)

In March, a delegation of the CPA(M-L) visited Peking at the invitation of the Central Committee of the CPC. It consisted of party chairman E. F. Hill and vice-chairman Norm Gallagher, taking time off from the internecine struggle within the BLF (see *The Vanguard*, 14 March). The Chinese laid out the red carpet for them. Chou En-lai, Chang Chun-chiao, and Madame Chiang Ching were the hosts at a banquet in their honor (ibid., 4 April). The Peking *People's Daily* made the greetings sent by the

Central Committee of the CPC to the CPA(M-L), on the occasion of its tenth anniversary, its front page lead story. This unusual treatment for a fraternal greetings message caused comment in Western diplomatic circles. (*The Age*, 19 March.)

In May, a major controversy blew up over the screening in Australia of Antonioni's documentary film *Chung Kuo* [*China*]. Gallagher and Hill fired the first shots. Having noted that the Sydney and Melbourne Film Festivals intended to show this film, they declared: "No person with the cause of Australia-China friendship at heart would in any way support these Film Festivals showing Antonioni's film." Promoters of the film were termed "nothing but diehard reactionaries." (*The Vanguard*, 23 May.) Jack Lazarus, President of the CPA(M-L)-dominated Australia-China society chimed in on a similar but less strident note (letter to the editor,*The Age*, 3 June).

The affair became heated when two left-wing ALP members (George Slater, secretary of the Postal Workers Union, and George Crawford, secretary of the Plumbers Union) and Norm Gallagher issued a leaflet demanding that this film be withdrawn by the festivals. Threats of physical violence, emanating presumably from the same sources, were made against the projectionists of the Melbourne Film Festival. As a result of these threats, the film was withdrawn. Because the Maoists are smaller in size and have fewer friends in Sydney, the festival there escaped intimidation and was able to show *Chung Kuo*. Whatever the Chinese attitude to such thuggery, it would be politic for them to distance themselves from their rough-and-tumble Australian friends. After all, they will be judged to some extent by the type of company they tolerate.

This was not the end of the affair. The Australian Broadcasting Commission, at some risk, apparently, to its correspondent in Peking, decided to screen *Chung Kuo*. Hill responded in his predictable manner: "The ABC is simply doing its class job by putting this film on. In the guise of 'independence' it carries out the anti-China policy of the diehards." (*The Vanguard*, 13 June.) The wide publicity that the film received as a result of the opposition of the Maoists guaranteed it a large television audience. Having seen it, most television viewers, it appears, wondered what all the fuss was about.

The SPA, having supplanted the CPA as the CPSU's most favored Australian Party, continued to hound it within the international communist movement. For example, presumably at SPA instigation, M. Farooqi, a member of the Central Committee of the Communist Party of India, published a highly critical article entitled "The Communist Party of Australia—Whither" in the CPI's journal *Party Life* in February (republished in *IB*, October). The Communist Party, USA, with which the SPA enjoys excellent relations, joined the attack. It published a strong critique of the CPA's leadership policies in its *Daily World* (8 June). It also savaged Eric Aaron's book, *Philosophy for an Exploding World* (see *YICA, 1974*, p. 386) in its theoretical journal, *Political Affairs*. The Novosti Press Agency circulated an article from *Questions of Philosophy* (November 1973) which analyzes Eric Aaron's efforts to "water down dialectics," "attack materialism," and "make short work of the real existing Socialism in an off-hand way common to countless bourgeois 'defenders' of individuality" (*The Socialist*, October 1974).

The SPA sent greetings to the Second Congress of the Communist Party of Bangladesh (*SPA*, February) and received a visit from George Meyers, a member of the Political Committee of the CPUSA, who brought greetings from Henry Winston, the party's president, and Gus Hall, general secretary (ibid.). The appointment of Edgar Ross as Moscow correspondent of *The Socialist* and the *NZ Tribune*, published by the New Zealand Socialist Unity Party, underlined the close ties existing between the CPSU and the SPA (ibid., August).

University of Melbourne

Angus McIntyre

Bangladesh

Communism in Bangladesh consists of one pro-Moscow oriented party, the Communist Party of Bangladesh (CPB), and at least five smaller Maoist groups, or which the Bangladesh Communist Party (Marxist-Leninist) is the most important. The other Maoist groups are the Banglar Communist Party, the Proletarian Party of East Bengal, the East Bengal Communist Party, and the Bangladesh Communist Party-Leninist. There is continuous discussion in Maoist circles of possible mergers of these groups as well as of further splits. Additionally, general pro-Moscow and pro-Peking sentiments animate the leaderships of two other, formally non-communist groups, the National Awami Party faction led by Muzaffar Almad (Soviet oriented), usually called NAP(M), and the National Awami Party faction directed by Maulana Bhashani (Chinese oriented) and referred to as NAP(B). The CPB and the NAP(M) today are considered the allies of the ruling Awami League (AL) government of premier Sheikh Mujibur Rahman. In October 1973 the AL, the NAP(M), and the CPB formed the "People's Unity Alliance," a loosely structured alliance, more significant as an expression of broad adhesion to a vaguely defined socialistic policy for the country than for adoption of a concrete course of implementation of specific priorities. All but one of the Maoist factions operate underground and advocate violent resistance or otherwise refuse to participate in regular politics. All, too, complain of police harassment and inhibiting surveillance.

History. The CPB is the successor to the East Pakistan organization of the Communist Party of Pakistan, which was banned by the Pakistani government in 1954. Functioning underground as the Communist Party of East Pakistan (CPEP) since then, the party surfaced in 1971 calling itself the CPB and claiming to be the country's only legal communist party. During the later fifties and most of the sixties CPEP cadres had infiltrated or identified with other parties, and ideological differences among them contributed to the division between Moscow and Peking factions in the National Awami Party in 1967. During the struggle for independence in 1971-72 the CPEP underground supported Rahman's leadership and participated in the irregular anti-Pakistani resistance of the Mukti Bahini (Bureau of Intelligence and Research, U.S. Department of State, *World Strength of the Communist Party Organizations, 25th annual report*, 1973 edition, Washington, D.C., 1973, p. 101).

Even before the 1971-72 Bangladesh freedom struggle, however, elements of the Maoist faction of Indian communism, the so-called Naxalites, active in the Indian state of West Bengal, had begun to win a scattered following in East Pakistan. Bangladesh Maoists were placed in a difficult position because of Peking's official friendship with the Pakistani government, although Chinese leaders apparently cautioned the Rawalpindi government through much of 1971 to seek a political solution to its problems in East Pakistan "according to the wishes of the people of East Pakistan" (*Far Eastern Economic Review*, 4 October 1974, p. 36). A few Maoists in Bangladesh supported the Rahman-led independence movement, but most others appear to have been committed to a revolutionary "people's war" directed against, in effect, both the Pakistanis and Rahman's Awami League. The latter was considered "bourgeois" and "reactionary" by the Maoists. After Bangladesh independence was achieved Maoist guerrillas in a generalized context of persistent depredations by armed gangs throughout the country have periodically continued their armed resistance (Justus M. van der Kroef, "Indian Maoism, Peking and Bangladesh," *Studies in Comparative Communism*, Summer-Autumn 1972, pp. 127-162).

Even during the Bangladesh struggle for independence the CPEP had joined the NAP(M) and NAP(B) in a "Cabinet Consultative Committee" that was advising the Bangladesh government in exile, then as now dominated by the Awami League in Calcutta. With independence a reality and Sheikh Mujib ensconced formally as premier of Bangladesh, the now CPB has been calling consistently for a more effective united front and coalition government (*World Strength of the Communist Party Organizations*, p. 101). The CPB ran four candidates in the 1973 general parliamentary elections but none were successful. Though the CPB had made an occasional point of alleged government inefficiency and corruption, its fundamental political position, like that of the Moscow-oriented NAP(M), seemed—and it is today—all but indistinguishable from the ruling Awami League. Indeed, both the CPB and NAP(M), because of their identity with the League, acquired the nickname of being the League's "B team," its second-string organization (Rounaq Jahan, "Bangladesh in 1973: Management of Factional Politics," *Asian Survey*, February 1974, p. 131).

Organization and Tactics. The basic tactic of the CPB today is to stay within the broad policy of the AL-dominated government, yet also to be sufficiently left of it and on occasion critical toward it so as to retain credibility and a measure of operational independence.

The Second Congress of the CPB, held in Dacca on 4-8 December 1973, adopted a new party program. The CPB is described as a party of "scientific socialism guided by Marxist-Leninist teaching" and aims at building "socialism" in Bangladesh. However, according to the program, considering the "existing backward socio-economic conditions," socialism cannot be built at once, so that "the people" should first move forward on the road of "non-capitalist development" and initially accomplish a "national democratic revolution" for the eventual sake of "achieving socialism." The "revolutionary process" is, however, under way in Bangladesh, according to the CPB program, as a result of the fact that Bangladesh has established good relations with the U.S.S.R. and "socialist countries," and also because it is pursuing an "independent, neutral policy." The obstacles that stand in the path to socialism are the result of the nation's colonial past and the "devastations" of the war in 1971.

Mass unemployment, a "tremendous number of peasants," an economy that is "of a semifeudal, semicapitalist nature," and an administrative and legal system which has remained unchanged are some of the basic hindrances to socialist development, according to the CPB program, while the nation also has been "penetrated" by many "pro-imperialist, corrupt, reactionary elements" which are hindering the government's "progressive measures." In effect, the prevailing legal and administrative system in Bangladesh is considered to be impeding the country's progress, according to the CPB. In order to achieve the party's objectives there must be unity among all "national democratic forces" and there must be a rebuff of "the onslaughts of imperialism and the Chinese Maoist leadership and their agents." Consolidation of "friendly ties and cooperation with the Soviet Union and other socialist countries and India," must, on the other hand, continue. Party members, according to the new CPB program, are urged to perform active work to further the national democratic revolution, heighten mass political awareness, and further the cause of "scientific socialism." Abroad, the CPB is a party of "proletarian internationalism," struggling for "peace and freedom" (*Pravda*, 9 December 1973; *FBIS*, 20 December).

The Second Congress was addressed by premier Rahman, who declared that the "People's Unity

Alliance" between the AL, the NAP(M), and the CPB had "become a bulwark" in the struggle against domestic "reaction" that was trying to divert Bangladesh "from its socialist road" (*IB*, 1974, no. 4, p. 16). In an obvious attempt to placate CPB concern over rising anti-Indian and anti-Soviet sentiments in the country, Rahman reportedly said also that "imperialists" and "left extremists" were trying to isolate Bangladesh from the U.S.S.R. and India, but the premier added, "I wish to tell them that the government knows the real friends and enemies of our country very well" (ibid., p. 17).

At the congress, on behalf of the CPB Central Committee, Secretariat member Abdus Salam presented reports which praised the "historic achievement" of the alliance established by the AL, the NAP(M), and the CPB, urged resolute support for the Rahman government, praised the U.S.S.R. in "successfully carrying out its ninth five-year-plan as it advances to communism," and berated the "Chinese leadership" for allegedly completely abandoning Marxist-Leninist precepts and for dividing the "international Communist movement" (ibid., p. 18). In a political resolution adopted by the congress, "socialist construction" in Bangladesh is described as a long-term process requiring definite social and economic preconditions. Hence the CPB, "at this stage," is advocating the "implementation of the government programme of progressive measures" summarized by the four principles of socialism, democracy, nationalism, and religious freedom (ibid., p. 19). The same resolution demands vigilance against both the "imperialists" and the "Maoists," and the latter are charged with being the "direct accomplices" of the "most reactionary forces," concerned with stirring up anti-Russian and anti-Indian feelings in the country. Local reactionary forces, aided by the United States, China and Pakistan, are obstructing the fulfillment of the government's progressive policies, particularly "in the foreign policy sphere," and are using political "terror" tactics to bring about a civil war in Bangladesh. In meeting this threat the CPB, according to the resolution, appeals to workers, students, and intellectuals in order to promote industrial and agricultural development, to "combat banditry, terrorism and corruption," to advance the cause of law and order, bring down prices, and "reorganise the state apparatus." Especially among the peasants the cause of the alliance represented by the AL, the NAP(M), and the CPB should be widely publicized, because the farming community represents the greater part of the population (ibid., p. 19-20).

A number of special resolutions were also passed at the congress. One expressed close solidarity with the Arabs' struggle to free Israeli-held territories, another protested the Chilean junta's "white terror" and demanded the release of Luis Corvalán, secretary-general of the Communist Party of Chile, and yet another one identified the CPB with the "intensified struggle" of the people and Communist Party of Pakistan for "national rights and democracy" against the reactionary government (ibid., p. 22).

On 7-9 May the CPB's Central Committee, which speaks for the party in between national congress meetings, met and passed a number of resolutions. A resolution on the international situation "resolutely" denounced the U.S. plan to establish a military base on the island of Diego Garcia in the Indian Ocean. Further, the resolution demands strict adherence by "the Saigon authorities" to the Paris agreement ending the war in Vietnam, and expresses support for the proposals of the Provisional Revolutionary Government in South Vietnam for "settling the Indochina problem." The resolution also declares its solidarity with the people of Chile against the allegedly "reactionary junta" in that country and, repeating a previous party demand, urges again the release of Corvalán. Finally, this resolution voiced adhesion to the aims of the "Arab progressive forces" fighting against "imperialism and the Israeli expansionism" and for peace in the region (*IB*, 1974, no. 12, p. 34).

Earlier, at the December 1973 CPB congress, the party had adopted a resolution supporting the proposal of Soviet party chief Leonid Brezhnev in 1969 for a new system of collective security in Asia. (On the Soviet proposal see Alexander O. Ghebhardt, "The Soviet System of Collective Security in Asia," *Asian Survey*, December 1973, pp. 1075-91.) This resolution also had expressed concern over "U.S. imperialism" and over its alleged building up of "tensions" in the South Asian region, "specifically in the Indian Ocean." Serious alarm was also voiced in this resolution about the "activities of Maoist China, which resists all efforts to create an atmosphere of friendship and cooperation." (*IB*, 1974, no. 4, p. 21.)

The May 1974 Central Committee plenum also passed a resolution on the Bangladesh domestic condition and on party organization. It is noted in the domestic resolution that conditions in the country have been aggravated by "speculative price increases for staple consumer goods" and by "subversive activity." Alleged conspiracies and "pressure tactics" by "Imperialism and internal reaction" are preventing the implementation of the government's progressive programs. The CPB calls on the population of Bangladesh fully to support the decision of premier Sheikh Mujibur Rahman to use the armed forces of the country in a campaign to confiscate weapons, discover and seize "hoards of food and other products," and arrest "criminals," anti-social forces" and "persons engaged in subversive activities against the state." Unity and common action of all honest and patriotic elements in society are needed to solve the country's problems, according to this resolution. Another resolution on party organization urged "Communists to strengthen and expand the Party's ranks." (Ibid., no. 12, p. 34.)

Bangladesh's problems with food supply and other products are a favorite oratorical theme of party leaders. At a CPB mass meeting in early April, for example, party chairman Moni Singh declared that while there was enough food in the country, difficulties arose because of "plots of Maoists and imperialists" and obstruction by wholesale dealers and landowners (*World Affairs Report*, Stanford, vol. 4, 1974, no. 3, p. 262). The CPB's own economic program remains essentially that on which the party ran its candidates in the general elections of March 1973. This program notes that "socialism has been declared as the objective of the country," and that if socialism is established poverty and deprivation of the masses will be removed. The program calls for "proper management of nationalised industries" and for turning to the Soviet Union in the acquisition of requisite managerial skills to run such industries, but also talks of encouraging and rendering assistance to the "private capitalists to establish industries" in fields other than the nationalized ones. At the same time, workers and employees are to be encouraged in managing "all enterprises." Specific recommendations include encouragement for cottage industries, increased output of electric power, and establishment of new industries producing tractors, tube wells, and pharmaceuticals. As for agriculture, the CPB program calls for necessary reforms to end the "feudal land system," set limits on size of holdings, and redistribute excess land of "big feudals to the landless." "Collective farming" is also to be introduced, but the thrust of the CPBs agrarian approach is toward support of the small cultivator, including the latter's emancipation from the "fetter of moneylending exploitation." Agrarian public works, such as effective flood controls ("with the help of India") and re-excavation of canals, are to be undertaken. Finally, the CPB economic program calls for development of the transportation system, expansion of international commerce "on the basis of equality with all countries," introduction of food rationing, and mobilization of popular action against black market operators, hoarders, and those engaged in corrupt activity. (*IB*, 1973, no. 6, p. 33.)

During April 1974 the steadily worsening economic plight of the Bangladesh people offered the CPB a tactical opportunity for the development of mass actions. Hence, the party called again on the government to take "resolute measures against the forces of reaction," because, according to a Moscow Radio correspondent in Dacca, "under the prextext" of a shortage of goods "the most bellicose ranks of the reaction and the extremist Maoist groupings" had formed an alliance to arrange anti-government demonstrations (*FBIS*, 30 April). The CPB organized its own meetings and demonstrations, or participated with the Awami League and the NAP(M) in urging joint action to ameliorate the rural misery. At one such gathering in Dacca, in June, CPB chairman Moni Singh appeared, together with the head of the Awami League, and the ministers for food, educaton, and jute production, on the same rostrum. Singh on this occasion called for the wiping out of the "last remnants of feudalism" and said there were still "five thousand jotdars (big landlords) and 34,000 affluent peasants in the country," whose lands needed to be taken away and distributed among landless peasantry (*The People*, Dacca, 3 June). Party spokesmen have also claimed that their organization is in the forefront in meeting the problems created by the devastating floods that regularly ravage the country. Toward the close of August, for example, CPB secretary-general Muhammad Farhad claimed that communist volunteers were organizing relief efforts for the flood-stricken population, and that, according to a TASS correspondent, in most administrative centers of Bangladesh one could see "tents with Communist flags flying over them," which presumably were being used in relief work. Farhad reportedly also warned against "speculators seeking to grow rich" in this period of national calamity for the country (*FBIS*, 28 August).

Although the CPB has now two national congresses behind it, its organizational structure is still relatively in a state of flux, in part because local branches and party offices are still being established. The opening of such CPB branch offices (e.g. at Jaipurhat and at Naogdon, toward the close of May) has customarily been utilized by CPB officials for the staging of mass political meetings, to which representatives of other parties that are part of the "People's Unity Alliance" or others who support the government are invited. Thus at the opening of the Jaipurhat CPB office representatives of the Awami League and of the NAP(M) were in attendance, as the CPB local district secretary emphasized the need for unity in achieving the goal of socialism "in our country" (*Bangladesh Observer*, Dacca, 1 June).

Constitutionally, the CPB follows the standard pattern of internal organization for communist parties. Its Central Committee (26 members) and Politburo (about five) are entrusted with the leadership between the periods of national party congresses. A CPEP veteran, the aged Moni Singh, is CPB chairman, but day-to-day executive decisions are usually made by secretary-general Muhammad Farhad. Abdus Salam and Kamrul Hossain are the most prominent secretaries of the Central Committee. Total CPB membership, according to party sources in conversation with this author last June, is "more than twenty thousand." But most non-party estimates place the actual size at about a third that figure. There is, however, no denying the CPB's considerable additional "silent" support, especially in university, trade union, and civil service circles, estimated at about ten thousand. Bangladesh has a population of about 75 million.

The still relatively unstructured state of the CPB may be gleaned from the fact that it was not until 14 July that the first CPB party cards were issued, a development which, according to Farhad in an interview with a TASS reporter, "will help to rally the Communists' ranks even further and to strengthen the party organisation." Farhad, according to the same source, on this occasion also reaffirmed that the CPB was working in a bloc with the "progressive wing of the Awami League and the National Awami Party" (presumably the NAP(M)), and was mobilizing the masses in a struggle against "domestic reaction" while at the same time the party was "propagandizing" the successes of cooperation with the socialist countries, "above all the Soviet Union." (*Pravda*, 15 July; *FBIS*, 29 July.)

By mid-1974 the CPB had, as yet, made only limited headway in developing its own student, trade union, or peasant front-group organizations, although the party's influence has remained considerable in the Awami League-dominated Bangladesh Chatra Union perhaps the largest and most influential student organization. CPB claims to be the author of the existence of wholly separate party fronts proved difficult to substantiate, largely because of the extremely volatile, schism-prone character of the trade union, peasants, and student movement in Bangladesh. Both CPB chairman Moni Singh and NAP(B) chairman Maulana Bhashani lead their own peasants' organizations, not all of whose members, whatever their radicalism, necessarily share their leaders admiration for Moscow and Peking, respectively, however. Two rival factions of the Bangladesh Chatra ("student") League support, respectively, premier Rahman and his opponent M. Bhashani, while the NAP(B) also has principal support in another student organization, the Bangladesh Biplobi ("Revolutionary") Chatra Union (*YICA, 1974*, p. 396).

Among the various Maoist-oriented communist groups, five of some significance can be clearly identified. The Bangladesh Communist Party (Marxist-Leninist) (BCP-ML), with an estimated following of about 500 committed supporters, is a continuation of a Maoist splinter group, the CPEP-ML, that broke off from the CPEP in 1969 (some sources claim as early as 1967). Mohammad Toaha, formerly active in the NAP(B), has been chairman since the party's founding. During the 1971 independence struggle the BCP-ML was accused of opposing the Bangladesh freedom fight, reportedly after the Awami League, the CPB, and the NAP(M) refused to collaborate with it in a proposed joint National Liberation Front. BCP-ML sources claim that not just independence, but a social and economic revolution needed to be achieved in Bangladesh and that the "reactionary" AL and the "social imperialist" CPB and NAP(M) refused to support this desired broader objective of the 1971 independence war. CPB critics allege that Toaha and other Maoists were prevented from siding with the independence struggle because of their overriding allegiance to Peking, which supported the Pakistan government in Rawalpindi. BCP-ML sources claim, however, that the party organization did participate in the freedom struggle.

The BCP-ML, reportedly, retains contact with the dispersed, shattered "Naxalite" organization of Maoist Indian communists (Communist Party of India-Marxist-Leninist, or CPML), and there has been speculation that the BCP-ML and other Maoist splinter factions continue to favor the creation of a single, independent "Red" Bengal state, combining Bangladesh with the Indian state of West Bengal. Reduced primarily to furtive underground activity today, the BCP-ML does not have the resources for an effective guerrilla resistance (although it has claimed to be engaged in "people's war"), notwithstanding the favorable circumstance of a continuing condition of banditry and lawlessness in much of Bangladesh. The growing potential of a future improvement in the diplomatic relations between Dacca and Peking probably acts as another brake on overt organized anti-government "people's war" resistance by the BCP-ML.

A second Maoist group is the Banglar Communist Party, formerly known as the Purba Banglar Communist Party (Communist Party of East Bengal, or CPEB). It is led by Deben Lal Sikdar as chairman and Abdul Bashar as general secretary. The Banglar party was, reportedly, established in 1968. It participated actively in the independence struggle, establishing at one time a "free zone" with its own courts and local administration, presumably dominated by its adherents, in the Rajshahi district in Northern Bangladesh (Sirajul Hossain Khan, "National Democratic Revolution in Bangladesh," *Journal of Contemporary Asia*, vol. 3, 1973, no. 2, p. 182.) The present size of the Banglar party is uncertain; the highest estimate is about 200. The party has been described as committed to the development of a united front of all social classes "which present themselves as the main forces or as the allies of the national democratic revolution" in Bangladesh (ibid., p. 190). The Banglar party, unlike the other Maoist groups, is not underground, nor is it known to be engaged in a systematic armed resistance. Indeed its spokesmen profess to support the present program of the Rahman government. But official sources in Dacca are not agreed as to the party's legality by government standards, in part because its revolutionary rhetoric often appears to make it indistinguishable from the Marxist underground groups.

The remaining three Maoist-oriented Communist organizations are the East Bengal Communist Party (EBCP), led by Abdul Matin and Mohammad Alauddin; the Bangladesh Communist Party-Leninist, led by Kazi Zafar and R. K. Menon; and the Purba Bangla Serbhara Party (Proletarian Party of East Bengal—sometimes called "Have Not Party"), led by Siraj Sikdar. The last group claims to be engaged in an avowed "national liberation" struggle against the AL-dominated government and is said to maintain relations with underground Maoist extremists in the Calcutta area. The EBCP, like the Bangladesh Communist Party-Leninist, reportedly is primarily an offshoot of leadership rivalries within the BCP-ML and does not differ from that party in its fundamentally Mao-flavored program. Both the EBCP and Sikdar's organization are considered to be in a state of open insurrection against the government, according to Dacca officials, but the position of the Bangladesh Communist Party-Leninist is less clear; the party had reportedly approached the "People's Unity Alliance" to fashion a common front. The EBCP, according to some sources, is believed to be the smallest of the Maoist groups (estimates range from fewer than 100 to 150 hard-core supporters) and not a great deal is known of or heard about it at present, unlike Sikdar's group, which has been much more active and violent and a greater object of official concern.

Virtually all Bangladesh political parties, in some degree, use or support Marxist concepts, or avow their dedication to unspecified "socialist" principles. The NAP(B)'s leader, the nonagenarian Maulana Abdul Hamid Khan Bhashani, has at various times openly admired Maoist and Chinese domestic and foreign policies, and urged a militant course on the peasant movement. But he also has repeatedly emphasized his commitment to lawful and constitutional principles. Nothing is to be gained from "subversive activities or armed insurrections," Bhashani has warned (*Eastern Herald*, Dacca, 11 May 1974), adding on another occasion: "I was never a Communist and I am not a Communist at present, and—by the grace of Allah—shall never become a Communist" (*Holiday*, Dacca, 26 May). Still, the Maulana has done little to dispel the Maoist aura that hangs about his party and his program. The NAP(B)'s anti-Indian and anti-Hindu position strikes a responsive chord among those inhabitants of Bangladesh convinced today that since 1971 India has been exploiting the Bangladesh economy. Anti-Indianism in Bangladesh, as utilized by the NAP(B), also redounds adversely on the U.S.S.R., India's ally, and on the Moscow-oriented CPB. A rising opposition group, the Jatiyo Samajtrantric Dal (JSD) or "National Socialist Group" is formally concerned with "the establishment of "scientific socialism" through a "social revolution" (*YICA, 1973*, p. 396). Its popularity in some parts of Bangladesh today makes it a much more formidable opponent than the NAP(B), particularly in the urban centers, but the JSD is not considered a doctrinaire Marxist group.

The volatile nature of Bangladesh politics makes a sudden resort to violent protest or demonstrations likely and frequent. On 15 December, 1973 Molotov cocktails were thrown at the Soviet Cultural Center, at the Indian Airlines offices, and at the premises of a principal pro-government newspaper, *Banglar Bani*, in Dacca. Sikdar's "Proletarian Party" had warned earlier that it would take such action, and the firebomb attacks were widely attributed to Sikdar's group (*Far Eastern Economic Review*, 7 January 1974). Since the elections of 7 March 1973 the parliamentary representation of all opposition groups, and of all pro-government groups other than the AL, is negligible (the JSD has two seats, the NAP(M) and NAP(B) each one, the CPB none, while the AL holds 291 seats out of the total of 300 in the House, the remainder going to independents and to another minor party). Hence the tendency of non-government parties especially to resort to extra-constitutional pressures, a tendency further accentuated by the tradition of violence in Bengal political life.

Domestic Developments. Threatened by floods, famine, smuggling, dacoity, and an uneven economic development, the government of Banghabandhu ("Father of Bangladesh") Sheikh Mujibur Rahman, during 1974, sought to find new means of stabilizing itself. On 24 January, Mohammadullah, the speaker of the Jatiyo Sangsad (National Assembly) was formally elected president of Bangladesh by the Assembly, replacing the nation's first president, Abu Sayeed Chaudhury, who had become increasingly disenchanted with the government's inability to meet economic problems and combat corruption, and with its politically repressive security policies. The latter, based on the executive powers granted by Presidential Orders 8 and 9, which replaced Order 50 with similar provisions, permit unlimited detention of those accused of "anti-state" activities (*Far Eastern Economic Review*, 4 February, 1974, p. 20).

The AL, the CPB, and the NAP(M) were targets of popular frustration over the allegedly too great and too one-sided influence of India and the U.S.S.R. on national Bangalee affairs. Widespread suspicion that India is benefiting from the smuggling of Bangladesh jute with the connivance of Bangladesh officials, and that the Soviets are gaining a hold on the Chittagong harbor region where, until mid-year, the Soviet Navy was engaged in salvage operations, have also aggravated Rahman's problems (ibid.). On 8 July the premier carried out an extensive cabinet reshuffling, accepting the resignation of six ministers, and of three ministers of state the following day. On 18 July, in an apparent move to link the cabinet changes to a new posture of vigilance against public wrongdoing, six police officers were suspended on charges of corruption and misconduct, and on 19 July premier Rahman requested prosecution of 16 officials and employees of two state-owned corporations (*Keesing's Contemporary Archives*, 2-8 September, p. 26693).

The CPB applauded these moves, just as it had earlier supported the premier's decision, announced on 24 April, that the Bangladesh armed forces would be ordered to conduct operations all across the country, side-by-side with duly constituted civil officials, against all "anti-social and subversive elements." Specifically, this campaign resulted in scores of arrests of smugglers, hoarders, merchants, and alleged price-manipulators (who had held back commodities from local markets in order to reap higher profits), and recovered various caches of weapons and supplies for the use of alleged dacoits or political extremists. A ban on strikes, lock-outs, and all processions and demonstrations was also instituted. It met with considerable criticism from opposition parties, and even with some mild remonstrances from the CPB. The CPB also complained that in the army's anti-corruption campaign the government was playing an ambiguous role, setting free some arrested for various malversations after they had been caught by the army (*Ekota*, Dacca, 24 May). The CPB throughout seemed to be at pains to stay on the side of the army, but tried also to keep its distance from the civilian component in the leadership of the anti-corruption campaign. This tactic was in keeping with much of the prevailing state of mass opinion, as expressed, though cautiously, also in other public media.

The campaign against "anti-social and subversive elements" gave the CPB particular trouble because it opened the dangerous prospect of an eventual delegitimization of *all* radical groups, perhaps even of the CPB. Prior to its repeal in February 1974, Presidential Order 50 had resulted in the arrest of "large numbers of members of the left-wing opposition," especially members of the JSD. Its replacement by Orders 8 and 9, by which the government retained the same broad powers of arrest, was sharply attacked in many quarters, including by Bangladesh bar associations (Amnesty International, *Annual Report, 1973-74*, London, 1974, p. 50). Moreover, while the Rahman government attacked the operations of various armed groups, most claiming to be veterans and volunteers in the fight for independence, it gave wide powers in February 1974 to the Rakkhi Bahini, a para-military "civil defense group," largely AL-directed and -dominated. The Rakkhi Bahiri were granted immunity from scrutiny by the courts of their acts conducted in the course of the "anti-social" campaign. Prominent journalists and JSD activists were among those subsequently arrested, while in one JSD protest demonstration, on 17 March in Dacca, at least five JSD supporters were killed (ibid.)

This kind of political violence, however, had seemingly become a part of Bangladesh political life. By November 1973 one authoritative Indian weekly estimated that in the preceding eighteen months some 7,700 murders (nearly a third of them political assassinations involving members of the AL) and some 143,000 cases of theft and robbery had been registered in Bangladesh (*Economic and Political Weekly*, Bombay, 17 November, p. 2033). Criminality generally was assuming alarming proportions. By April 1974, according to official sources, 1,313 murders and 2,021 dacoities alone had occurred in the district of Dacca, which includes the capital city, since "the emergence of Bangladesh" at the close of 1971 (*Morning News*, Dacca, 29 May). Particularly the universities, with their highly politicized and contending students' organizations, most of them affiliated to the principal parties, were often the scene of political violence. During student electons on 6 September 1973 at the University of Dacca, 24 student activists were killed by a gang of masked armed marauders, and on 5 April 1974, apparently because of rivalry between factions of the student organization of the AL, seven students were assassinated by another gang. The violence continued at a markedly lower level after the Army began its drive against "anti-social elements" on 24 April. (*Keesing's Contemporary Archives*, 2-8 September, p. 26693.)

Political opposition against the Rahman government continued to build, however, coming, significantly, from senior officers within the Army, as well as from within Rahman's own Awami League. On 17 March a popular war of independence hero, Major M. A. Jalil, principal JSD leader, was arrested after the previously noted JSD protest demonstration before the home minister's residence, and in May one of the country's senior officers, Lieutenant Colonel M. Ziauddin, former Dacca Army Brigade commander, disappeared, reportedly to join the "revolutionary underground." Leaflets distributed in Dacca subsequently announced that he had joined Siraj Sikdar's "Proletarian Party of East Bengal (*Far Eastern Economic Review*, 16 August, p. 14-15).

In October the dismissal of finance minister Tajuddin Ahmed, a major power in the ruling Awami League, was apparently linked to premier Rahman's interest in bringing about a presidential-style constitutional structure similar to that prevailing in Tanzania and Egypt (ibid., 22 November p. 11). The planned constitutional change, which would abandon the present essentially Westminster style of parliamentary government in Bangladesh, would vastly increase executive powers. Both within the premier's own party and among the opposition there has been sharp protest. The CPB's position is, however, ambiguous: much of the party's present strength derives from its identification with Rahman and the prevailing power structure; so long as Rahman remains in power the CPB's position is likely to remain reasonably secure and hence the party's support for Rahman at this juncture may well come to be considered as a critically necessary act of loyalty by the AL. But in the event of Rahman's passing from the political scene a successor, wielding presidential style executive power, could become a major threat to the party. The demise of the still popular though increasingly criticized Rahman is likely to precipitate a major power struggle, which the harrowing condition of the nation's economy and the rising public demand for meaningful improvements are likely to aggravate.

Deteriorating socio-economic conditions in Bangladesh may in fact prove to be the most important political and radicalizing dynamic across a broad spectrum of opinion and action. It is particularly likely to affect the CBP, the two factions of the NAM, and the Maoist splinter groups, opening opportunities also for the more moderate but left-of-center JSD. One prominent correspondent for the European press wrote from Bangladesh early in November that "In Dacca and in other towns of Bangladesh there occur daily demonstrations against hunger, shootings, assaults on food storage facilities, and other forms of social protest" (Revo Conti in *De Volkskrant*, Amsterdam, 2 November). Already Gross Domestic Product in 1972-73 was estimated to be 12-14 percent lower in real terms than the 1969-70 GDP, and per capita GDP was estimated to be one fifth lower than the GDP per capita in "preliberation" days, i.e. before 1971 (Rounaq Jahan, op. cit., p. 126). Rising import costs during 1974 created further grave dislocations: for example, oil imports, which had consumed 19 percent of export earnings in 1973 now consumed 50 percent, and other necessary imports, from cotton yarn to cement, now had doubled in price (*Keesing's Contemporary Archives*, 2-8 September, p. 26694). Throughout the country in 1974 shortages of spare parts forced closings of manufacturing concerns, adding to an alarming unemployment rate. On 10 June, official sources disclosed that out of a working population of 25.9 million about 7.8 million were either unemployed or underemployed (ibid.). Meanwhile, the present population density of 1,360 persons per square mile is one of the highest in the world and per capita availability of gross cropped land acreage is only 0.44 acres, the size of farm holdings averaging only 3.54 acres (I. N. Mukherji, "Economic Problems and Prospects of Bangladesh," *International Studies*, New Delhi, April-June 1974, pp. 278-80).

The ravaging floods and soaring prices deepened the general misery. By October, mass famine was apparent everywhere, evidenced by hordes of "human beings who have become walking skeletons," but a group of the nation's leading scholars, lawyers, and journalists, joined in a "Committee for Civil Liberties and Legal Aid," blamed corrupt and inefficient government officials in league with rapacious merchants for improper food and aid distribution and for the deepening human crisis (*Far Eastern Economic Review*, 25 October, p. 28, and 8 November, p. 26). Meanwhile inflation was reportedly running at the rate of about 50 percent per year and the country faced a balance of payments deficit of about $1 billion (*Wall Street Journal*, New York, 26 November). The floods that struck Bangladesh in mid-June resulted in heavy crop and other losses, estimated by the government at more than $2 billion (*Sarawak Tribune*, Kuching, 5 September), and yet new devastation was wreaked by a cyclone and tidal wave which leveled thousands of dwellings along the country's southeastern coast on 28 November.

Notwithstanding these catastrophes the country's birthrate has continued to soar. In early June the Bangladesh health and family planning minister predicted that the country's population would double in twenty-three years if the present population growth—which adds 10,000 births a day—continues (*Morning News*, Dacca, 4 June 1974). The education and cultural affairs minister estimated that 40 percent of children of school-going age were "now deprived of all facilities of education," while at the same time there is public complaint that university graduates in such critical fields as agricultural science cannot employ their skills because of poor public administration (*Sunday People*, Dacca, 2 June; *Bangladesh Observer*, 30 May).

In such an environment radical and revolutionary appeals continue to find favorable reaction, particularly among the young. An example is Sikdar's "proletarian Party," recruited initially very largely from Sikdar's covert Maoist study club among Dacca students in the later 1960s and many of whose members eventually committed themselves to open insurrection. Already by the close of 1973 the Bangladesh government had ordered the Army to take all-out repressive action against the Maoist insurgent elements operating in the Sunderbans near the Indian border. In preceding months, amidst reports that Sikdar had succeeded in welding some degree of unity among the different Maoist factions, there had been insurgent attacks, largely led by Sikdar's followers, on scores of police posts. Nearly half the insurgent assaults on police outposts had been successful, with the guerrillas overrunning the posts, killing policemen, and capturing more than 26,000 rounds of ammunition (*Far Eastern Economic Review* 17 December 1973, p. 24). In subsequent months, with the Army taking the offensive, and with new dissension in Maoist ranks, the insurgent threat diminished. Yet by Early December 1974, amidst the deepening social havoc of famine and in the aftermath of flood destruction, Maoist insurgent activity resumed, rebel ranks being supplied with fresh and desperate recruits from the ravaged Bangladesh countryside and reportedly aided by the scattered but still active Maoist underground from across the border in the nearby Indian state of West Bengal.

International Aspects. Driven by widening popular anti-Indian feeling caused by alleged Indian exploitation (via jute smuggling across the porous Bangladesh-Indian frontier) of the Bangladesh economy, and by suspicion of undue Soviet influence in the country, premier Rahman was reported by the beginning of 1974 to be attempting to realign Bangladesh's foreign policy so that four major powers, India, the U.S.S.R., the United States, and People's China "would have equal status in Dacca" (*Far Eastern Economic Review*, 4 February, p. 20). In consequence the Moscow-oriented CPB has been much concerned with praising the Soviets and with emphasizing the danger allegedly coming from "Maoist" and "U.S. imperialist" directions. The CPB also has made it a point to strengthen its relations and those of the Rahman government with the communist parties of East European nations through reciprocal vists of party delegations. During the national congress of the Awami League, in Dacca, in January 1974, a visiting delegation from the East German communist party (SED) attended, and its spokesman, Central Committee secretary Werner Jarowinsky, in an address to the congress on 19 January (1) attacked People's China for denying Bangladesh "its place" in the United Nations, (2) emphasized the need to apply principles of "peaceful co-existence and the consolidation of peace" in Asia, and (3) asserted that the Awami League, led by premier Rahman, and "in alliance with the Bangladesh Communist Party" and with the NAP(M), would bring unity and "bring the anti-imperialist, national democratic revolution to a successful conclusion in Bangladesh." A protocol on SED-CPB "cooperation" was also signed in Dacca on 20 January, between Jarowinsky and CPB secretary-general Mohammad Farhad (*FBIS*, 21 January).

In July, a CPB delegation visited Bulgaria and Hungary. Representatives of the Hungarian ruling party, in talks conducted with the CPB delegation, reportedly pledged their support for Bangladesh's "economic and social progress and the consolidation of national independence." Both parties declared support also for Soviet policy "in the interests of détente" and resolved to help efforts directed at establishing "collective security and cooperation between Asian countries." After other assurances of mutual support for "the Vietnamese people's fight for the implementation of the Paris agreements" and for the "national and social liberation movements" of the African, Asian, Latin American peoples, together with condemnation of the "fascist terror" in Chile and of "Israel's reactionary expansionist policy," the two parties' announcement declared that "bilateral and multilateral meetings between Communist and workers parties" are deemed to be "useful," adding that "conditions for a new international conference of the fraternal parties are ripening" (Budapest domestic service, 16 July; *FBIS*, 17 July.

Support by the CPB, for Soviet party leader Brezhnev's plan for an Asian collective security system was, as noted earlier, expressed again at the CPB's Second Congress in early December 1973. Coupled to such support has been the CPB's condemnation of U.S. policies in the Indian Ocean, particularly in connection with the planned expansion of military facilities on Diego Garcia Island. These U.S. policies, according to the CPB, are a direct threat to the sovereignty and security of the developing countries of Asia and Africa (Radio Moscow, TASS report in English, 30 March; *FBIS*, 1 April). On 7 November 1974 the Soviet paper *Izvestiya* gave space to an article by Mohammad Farhad, the CPB secretary-general. According to Farhad, "U.S. imperialism and the Maoist leadership of China" acted against the Bangladesh liberation movement, while, on the other hand, "our struggle found understanding and support in the Soviet Union—the cradle of the October Revolution." Friendly relations with the Soviet Union and other socialist countries were said to be aiding Bangladesh in creating an independent economy and in implementing the "progressive" policies of the Rahman government. (*FBIS*, 11 November. The Soviet press, meanwhile, had picked up the CPB's contention that the Rahman government is beleaguered by extremists from both sides. One Soviet commentator, reporting on the Bangladesh Army's anti-corruption campaign, wrote that "extreme right-wing reactionary forces" had allied themselves with "Maoist extremist groups" in Bangladesh, terming this alliance "a highly indicative phenomenon" (Aleksandr Filippov in *Pravda*, 16 June, cited *Current Digest of the Soviet Press*, 10 July).

During the past two years Bangladesh has figured prominently in Soviet efforts to promote trade and educational and cultural contacts in the Third World. A protocol signed between the two countries in December 1973 provides for trade of about $80 million in value, 60 percent in cash transactions and the rest in barter, and Moscow has seemed concerned to redirect Bangladesh trade in a Russian direction. The Soviets have promised help with a radio transmitter, railway bridge construction, and oil and gas prospecting, and have supplied at least ten MIG-21 jet fighters. In 1972 Soviet aid was reported to have been valued at about $50 million, one sixth of that given Bangladesh by the United States and one fifth of that provided by India ("The Soviet Effort in Bangladesh," *Asian Analysis*, February 1974, p. 2). The number of students from Bangladesh in communist countries increased from 205 in 1972 to 233 in 1973, and 110 Soviet scholarships alone were offered in

1973-74. Reportedly more than 300,000 copies of 16 Soviet magazines, double the number during the previous years, were distributed by the Russian Embassy in Bangladesh during 1973 (ibid., pp. 2-3).

Countering this Soviet and East European (especially East German) influence, however, is a maturing popular realization that Dacca's official hostility toward Peking may have been misplaced, and that while People's China formally sided with the Rawalpindi government in its 1971 dispute with then East Pakistan, the Chinese, in fact, may well have attempted to restrain the Pakistanis in their Bangladesh conflict. Worsening public attitudes toward India in Bangladesh have lent new importance to Chinese premier Chou En-lai's alleged warning on 12 April 1971 to the Pakistan government (then headed by Yahya Khan) that "The question of East Pakistan should be settled according to the wishes of the people of East Pakistan," and to newly circulating reports that Chinese officials condemned the Pakistani military intervention in Bangladesh at the time (Lawrence Lifschultz, "Bangladesh–A New Bogeyman," *Far Eastern Economic Review*, 4 October 1974, p. 35).

The role of dissident Maoist groups at present does not appear to be a major obstacle to improving relations with Peking, not least because one of these groups, the Banglar Communist Party, has declared its commitment to supporting the government. Peking's approval of Bangladesh's entry into the United Nations in 1974 has removed the last major diplomatic obstacle to a betterment of mutual relations. It is widely believed that Indian pressure was responsible in 1972 for the failure to consummate a reported Chinese offer to purchase 40,000 bales of Bangladesh jute at about $300 a bale, about 25 percent above the then world price (ibid., p. 37), but Bangladesh officials feel that the Chinese remain ready to purchase jute.

Soviet charges that "the Maoists in Bangladesh" are sowing disorder and confusion and planning religious and communal strife (*FBIS*, 19 April, p. 73) find little support in Bangladesh outside the CPB and the government coalition of supporters. The Chinese media have responded in kind, however, sometimes by quoting criticisms of the Rahman government appearing in Bangladesh publications. An attack appearing in the left-of-center weekly *Holiday*, much read in Bangladesh intellectual circles, to the effect that the U.S.S.R., despite Bangladesh's current disastrous food shortage, has been pressing the Rahman government for the immediate return of wheat that the Russians had loaned, was summarized in the *Peking Review* (27 September). There is some indication that the continuing Sino-Soviet rift is appreciated in broad layers of the Bangladesh public as offering tactical advantages to the nation, as does the expected gradual improvement in relations with the United States. It is significant that prominent U.S. oil companies (e.g., Atlantic Richfield and Union Oil) are playing a leading role in a projected $1.5 billion investment in the exploration of petroleum reserves in the Bay of Bengal's continental shelf. Dacca's contracts with the oil companies, however, exclude any Russian participation, an indication of the changes that may be in the offing in Rahman's foreign policy. (Revo Conti in *De Volkskrant* 2 November).

Publications. The Maoist communist factions rely primarily on cyclestyled or mimeographed pamphlets. The weekly paper *Ekota*, published in Dacca, is the chief organ of the CPB. The English-language weekly *Freedom* describes itself as the "Voice of Democratic Secular Socialist Bangladesh" and like the weekly *Holiday*, also published in Dacca, accommodates moderately radical, including independent, Marxist views.

University of Bridgeport   Justus M. van der Kroef

Burma

The Burma Communist Party (BCP) was established on 15 August 1939 with probably 13 members and Thakin Soe as secretary-general. After participating in the struggle for the liberation of Burma under the leadership of the "Anti-Fascist People's Freedom League" (AFPFL), the communists more and more disagreed with the socialists in the AFPFL. In March 1946, Thakin Soe and some followers split from the BCP, where Thakin Than Tun had taken over the leadership, and founded the Communist Party of Burma, also known as the "Red Flag" (here designated as the CPB-RF). The Red Flag soon went underground and its armed insurrection against the British resulted in its being declared an unlawful association in January 1947.

The BCP or "White Flag" communists (BCP-WF) under Thakin Than Tun collaborated for some time with the AFPFL, though without much success, even after Burma attained independence on 4 January 1948. With arrest threatening, the communist leaders went underground at the end of March 1948. Although the BCP-WF was declared illegal in October 1953, some communist activities could still be carried on legally with other organizations until the Burma Socialist Programme Party (BSPP)—founded after the coup of 2 March 1962 by General Ne Win—was declared the only legal party in the Union of Burma on 28 March 1964.

Between 1948 and 1950 the armed insurrection by both factions of the communists, together with other groups, brought the Burmese government of Prime Minister U Nu near to collapse. In the following years communist actions were confined to certain areas (especially the Irrawaddy delta, the Pegu Yoma, and the Shan State) and therefore were a local, but constant, harassment to the Union government. After 1967-68 the communist strongholds in the delta and the Pegu Yoma were, step by step, reduced to unimportant rebel camps by large-scale counter-insurgency operations of the Burmese army, undertaken in cooperation with the local "People's Militia." At the same time the internal party struggle and the purges of "revisionists" reached its climax and resulted, after the death of Thakin Than Tun in September 1968, finally in a take-over of leadership at most levels by leaders subservient to Peking. With Chinese aid given openly after the anti-Chinese riots of June 1967 and continued secretly after the resumption of full diplomatic relations between Burma and the People's Republic of China, the BCP(WF) stepped up its guerrilla activities in the Shan State, first north of Lashio and now since about 1971 in the Kunlong area east of the Salween river. Toward the end of 1973, the BCP(WF) had won absolute control over the northern areas east of the Salween, where the government troops hold hardly more than the towns of Kunlong and Hopang and the road between these two towns.

The Red Flags, whose main base was in the Arakan region and for some time also in the Irrawaddy delta, did not reach any major importance. Labeled as Trotskyist by the other communists, the CPB(RF) had no relations with communist parties outside Burma. Cooperation with the

BCP(WF) was restricted to a very few actions and a silent agreement on areas of influence. The capture of Thakin Soe and the loss of other leaders at the end of 1970 critically weakened the CPB(RF). The Arakan Communist Party, a CPB(RF) splinter group, has also lost even the small local importance it was able to claim during the mid-1960s.

Reliable figures on the membership in the communist parties in Burma are not available. According to the government, the BCP(WF) was able to assemble an army of 4,000 men in December 1973 in the area north of Kengtung. This would confirm the estimate made in the 1974 *Yearbook* (p. 405) that the strength of the BCP(WF) in the Shan State (including Lashio area, Wa State, Kengtung district, and others) is at least 6,000 men under arms, to which another 1,000 should be added from other parts of the country. A further increase of the overall strength cannot be presumed. Membership in the Red Flag and the Arakan group together probably does not exceed 200. The population of Burma is 28.8 million (census of April 1974).

The new constitution of the "Socialist Republic of the Union of Burma" was adopted in a nationwide referendum by 90.19 percent of the 14.7 million people with voting rights and came into force on 3 January 1974. Between January and February, elections were held for the 450 seats in the Pyithu Hluttaw, the new assembly; most of its members belong to the Burma Socialist Programme Party, the only legal party in Burma. Besides the names of the elected representatives, no results of the elections were published. On 2 March the Revolutionary Council (RC) handed over power to the Pyithu Hluttaw. U Ne Win, up to then chairman of the RC, was elected chairman of the State Council and president of the state, with General San Yu, the chief of the army, as secretary of the State Council. U Sein Win became prime minister.

Leadership and Organization. The Central Committee of the BCP(WF) is thought to consist, as in 1973, of Thakin Zin (chairman), Thakin Ba Thein Tin (first vice-chairman and head of the group's permanent delegation in Peking), Thakin Chit (secretary and Politburo member), Bo Thet Tin (Politburo member), Aung Myint, Ba Myint, Kyaw Mya, Naw Seng (leader of the "Northeast Command," established together with a Kachin rebel group), Thakin Pe Tint (second representative in Peking), Than Shwe, and Ko Thet. The organizational structure extends from the Politburo through the Central Committee, divisional committees, and district committees, down to the township and, in some areas, even ward committees. Divisional committees are thought to exist still, at least in name, for all parts of Burma, but other committees only in the regions where the BCP(WF) is active. Its "People's Army" is structured along traditional communist lines with party political cadres superior to military commanders at all levels. The BCP(WF) apparently did not lose any higher-ranking members in 1974.

The CPB(RF) has hardly any organizational structure left. The former leader Thakin Soe, captured in November 1970, was condemned to death in September 1973 and his appeal rejected on 27 February 1974 (*Guardian*, Rangoon, 28 February); the death sentence should, however, have been reduced to life imprisonment by the general amnesty of 19 March. As the CPB(RF) obviously is wiped out in the Irrawaddy delta, it is only for Arakan that party committees could exist, but no details or names are known.

According to a newspaper report of October 1973, "the Arakan Communist Party led by Chairman Kyaw Zan Rhee has split into two groups—a pro-Thakin Soe and a pro-Arakan Communist Party group. The pro-Thakin Soe group is being led by Kyaw Zan Rhee while the pro-Arakan Communist Party group is led by Major Maung Han of the Politburo." (*Botataung*, Rangoon, 27 October.) Both groups are very small and, especially after this split, without importance. "On 25 February [1974] Yeni Aung Tun Sein, who is a Central Committee member of the Arakan Communist Party, surrendered in Buthitaung township." With Yebaw Chit Tin another Central Committee member was killed on 3 March. (Ibid., 7 March.) Further details were not published.

Internal Affairs and Programs. The total absence of remarks on internal party affairs in the statements and speeches of BCP(WF) leaders should indicate that the party has recovered from the purges of "revisionists" after 1967. Although the government reported in October 1973 that on "17 September Bo Saw Lwin alias Tun Hla alias Shein was beaten and stabbed to death in front of the troops of the Burma Communist Party central headquarters in the Pegu Yoma mountain range by the group led by Party Central Committee Chairman Thakin Zin and Thakin Chit" (Burma Broadcasting Service, 12 October), the party's organization seems to have strengthened militarily as well as politically. In the delta and the Pegu Yoma, hwoever, heavier losses occurred in the lower cadres which caused the National Democratic United Front (NDUF)—formed by the BCP(WF) and the Karen National United Party (KNUP)—to broadcast a call to "Maintain the tradition of the revolutionary Karen and Burmese people of the delta region by replacing those who have fallen" ("Voice of the People of Burma [VPB]," 10 January 1974). The communists themselves, however, refrained from such calls, presumably with the aim of evoking, in the eyes of the Burmese people, the image of a well-settled and fully functioning party, a party free of the weaknesses and internal rivalries which it criticizes in the "military clique" (e.g., in a VPB broadcast on 10 January). Similarly, the communists have described how they built up an administrative structure in the "liberated area" of the northern Wa State (VPB, 18 October 1973).

Throughout 1974, the "Voice of the People of Burma," the clandestine radio station of the BCP(WF), tried to put the finger especially on the economic difficulties of Burma. However, the communists' critiques did not include a feasible program of their own, aside from praising generally the Chinese for their way of aiming at total self-sufficiency and their economic successes (e.g., in Thakin Zin's anniversary speech, VPB, 15 August). This attitude corresponds to the one of an opposition party which covers its own unimaginativeness purely by exploiting and profiting from the mistakes of the government.

In the economic sector such criticism is quite easily made in present-day Burma, as in the following commentary on the opening address of U Ne Win to the Second Congress of the BSPP:

> Ne Win minimized the economic crisis in Burma. He said it was a normal and temporary economic problem. In truth, the economic crisis Burma is facing is grave and chronic. It is not a temporary one caused by bad weather nor by world economic and financial difficulties, as stated by Ne Win. Today's crisis is a result of the [words indistinct] policy of depending on imperialism, maintaining landlordism-feudalism and practicing the bureaucrat capitalism pursued by the former reactionary governments and by Ne Win and his colleagues. This crisis will persist so long as the reactionary line and the military government exist. (VPB, 11 October 1973.)

About the same time, an NDUF statement addressed to the "farmers of various nationalities" urged: "Do not sell rice and crops to the fascist Ne Win-San Yu military clique, but trade only among the people; determine your own destiny" (ibid., 4 November). The economic situation worsened considerably during the first months of 1974 with prices especially for rice and cooking oil soaring. There were various reasons for it which cannot be explained in this context, but those offered by the NDUF were surely not among them. The situation climaxed in May and June with strikes and riots spreading from Mandalay over the oilfields of Chauk and Yenanchaung to Rangoon. The government had to use the army to restore order in Rangoon. According to its announcement, 22 workers were killed and 60 wounded (*Guardian*, 9 June). The BCP(WF) sought an easy way to profit from those developments by accusing the government of betraying the workers and by transforming the dead workers into martyrs of the "people's revolutionary struggle":

> From the beginning the military government had decided to kill the workers in order to crush their uprising. The so-called cabinet had decided to kill the workers to prevent the strike from developing into a general strike. They had decided to kill a hundred, a thousand, or more people in order to crush the

uprising. . . . The military government pretended to play the role of a saint by making it appear that the killing was done against its will. It made excuses because of its guilty conscience. (VPB, 16 June.)

Comrade workers and people: The martyrs' glorious bloodshed will not be in vain. The banner erected by you, comrades, will forever fly high. The reactionary military government must pay for this blood debt. Transform your mourning for the fallen martyrs into anger for struggle. Bravely march on and continue to hold high the banner of the martyrs. (Ibil., 9 June.)

The government, on the other hand, accused the communists and their followers of having instigated the strikes:

Elements of CPB [read: BCP-WF] lineage calling themselves the "Proletarian Revolutionary Front" [are] perpetrating anti-Government activities, making it appear as if they were championing the workers' cause. . . . These elements had distributed anti-Government leaflets and circulated them through the post in Magwe, Yenanchaung, and Chauk, and had done agitation work with anarchic agitation posters (*Guardian*, 24 June).

Several arrests followed and trials began soon. It can be ascertained that the strikes were caused by economic grievances. The communists never pretended that they had played any role in the outbreak or development of the workers' unrest, and they evidently only dwelt on it after the government itself had admitted that there were strikes and riots. However, it may well be that their sympathizers were involved in spreading and maintaining the unrest.

In 1974 the main political events for Burma were the adoption of the new constitution in a nationwide referendum and the following elections to the first Pyithu Hluttaw or people's assembly. The BCP(WF) denounced the referendum and the new constitution as a means of retaining power: "The military clique is bound to ratify the constitution in order to maintain its rule. to put it briefly, the military government will secure supporting votes at the so-called referendum through various kinds of preparations and various methods." (VPB, 4 November 1973.) Afterward the BCP(WF) announcements referred to the elections and the new Pyithu Hluttaw as "sham elections" and a "sham assembly," and attacked only the government and U Ne Win and General San Yu personally in its broadcasts, not the Pyithu Hluttaw or the new prime minister, U Sein Win.

In its relations with the minorities and their insurgent groups, the BCP(WF) obviously has gained better control over the Shan State Nationalities Liberation Organization, which joined the NDUF "effective 25 July 1974" (ibid., 1 September). By the end of March this Shan insurgents group had already agreed with the Shan State Progressive Party on a sort of mutual non-aggression agreement (ibid., 6 June).

Domestic Activities and Armed Struggles. During 1974 the communists continued their armed struggle against the "Ne Win-San Yu military government" and for the "liberation" of Burma as in former years. Neither the government nor the BCP(WF) has published figures summarizing the encounters during the period.

The main battles took place in November and December 1973 in the area north of Kengtung. After a first attempt in April the BCP(WF) forces

regrouped and made a second attempt, this time via Mong Pawk. The enemy forces, belonging to those same battalions of their "north-east region," heavily outnumbered the Tatmadaw [Burma Army] units out there. The latter were forced to withdraw, and Mong Lwe fell on October 25. Next fell Mongs, Yang—on October 31, but not before inflicting heavy casualties on the enemy. Mong Ma too fell. The enemy tried to push further onwards but the Tatmadaw forces stood from Mong Hkak and stopped them. (*Guardian*, 20 December 1973.)

The strength of the communists, led by one Tun Lin, was "about 2,500 men when they seized Mong Yang" and "swelled to about 4,000 men when they joined forces with Kaw insurgents under the notorious Ike Myint" (ibid., 19 December). According to government reports, "two thirds were boys round about the age of 13 who were just armed with seven grenades each and placed at the forefront of the fighting" (ibid.).

The government troops started their main counter-operation, called Ye Yan Aung, on 3 December. The troops, which were supported by planes in some operations, recaptured Mong Lwe on 6 December, Mong Yang the following day, and Mong Ma on the 11th.

> So far Tatmadaw columns taking part in Operation Ye Yan Aung have fought 31 big and small battles and 19 skirmishes with the CPB [read: BCP-WF] insurgents. . . . Thirty of the Tatmadaw men have given up their lives for the country and 143 others have been wounded in the clashes. The enemy has suffered heavy casualties with over 350 killed and over 500 wounded. . . . The number of CPB rebels who have so far surrendered to the troops is 24. (Ibid., 9 January).

If the government figures should be right, they surely only refer to the counter-operation, because the communists claim to have killed more than 90 soldiers and wounded more than 100 in their attack at the three Shan towns (VPB, 15 November 1973).

The BCP(WF) had to retreat to the Chinese border and to the northern Wa State, which they are presumed still to dominate outside Kunlong and Hopan towns. Nevertheless the military actions of both sides continued at least up to March.

In the press conference on the operations the government speaker accused the communists of having

> oppressed and exploited the people, taking away their property while shouting their so-called motto "Don't take anything, even a pin, from the people without their consent" at the top of their voices to deceive the people.
>
> They "bought" from the people pigs and cattle at the rate of Kyat 8 per ox and Kyat 3 per pig. . . . They seized all the property from deserted houses, forcing the women to carry the property to their camps. . . . They took away over 600 baskets of paddy belonging to the people there. (Ibid., 19 December 1973.)

Similarly the communists accused the government troops as in former years:

> They burned down villages, unjustly [? arrested] people, forcibly moved villages, and looted food under the pretext of military operations. Lootings, robberies, murders, and rapes broke out wherever the mercenary army went. (VPB, 11 April 1974.)

The aim of the communists in moving into the Kengtung area has supposedly been the establishment of a "people's government" in a liberated area. This may be true, since the date of the offensive was about two months before the national referendum on the new constitution. Another intention could be the domination of the "Golden Triangle," where Kuomintang remnants still play a major role. The communists and their collaborating Shan organizations attacked the "Kuomintang spy troops" on several occasions (e.g., ibid., 27 January).

In the other regions of Burma, the BCP(WF) dominates only the jungles north of Myitkyina and around Lauhkaung. In Arakan they are operating with a force of altogether perhaps 250 to 300 men, but only as one among other small rebel groups. Their attempt to regain a strong foothold in the Pegu Yoma, their traditional headquarters, most evidently failed. The government launched an offensive there, beginning 1 June, with the help of the People's Militia (Burma Broadcasting Service, 21 October). During those operations the government resettled several villages to make them less vulnerable to communist attacks. The BCP(WF) was able to carry out several guerrilla operations on the eastern slopes of the Yoma, but without lasting success. In Tenasserim, communist splinter groups clashed with the forces of the rightist expatriates, earlier led by former prime minister U Nu.

As a sort of counter-insurgency measure, the new State Council granted an amnesty to insurgents on 19 March. Up to 16 June when the amnesty ran out, a total of 1,415 rebels responded to this call (Hong Kong, Agence France Presse, 17 September). There are no figures on the number of communists among them.

International Ties and Positions. The BCP(WF) has been firmly aligned with the People's Republic of China in spite of the officially good diplomatic relations between the governments in Peking and Rangoon. Thus, it sent an admiring and quite enthusiastic address to the Chinese Communist Party on the occasion of the 25th anniversary of the PRC:

> They have also won brilliant victories in their struggle against modern revisionism along with the true Marxist-Leninist parties and organizations throughout the world. The PRC is a growing socialist country in the Third World. The PRC's prestige has soared and continues to soar daily in the international arena. We are very happy about this. Your victories are ours. Meanwhile, these victories bring joy and inspiration to the proletarian class and oppressed people throughout the world. (VPB, 1 October 1974.)

The Burmese communists receive not only ideological training, but are getting some military support as well, as was revealed after the battles in the Kengtung area:

> According to witnesses, the communists' heavy guns and sophisticated wireless equipment were manned by Chinese. Four of the Chinese who tried to gun down Burma Air Force fighters from the nunnery [at Mong Yang] were caught in rocket fire and killed. Their graves, with epitaphs written in Chinese characters, now lie in the nunnery compound. That these Chinese, as well as one non-Chinese who fell with them, were men of some rank could be gauged from the fact that about 100 communist troops (out of the town's garrison of 200) turned up to pay their last respects at the burial.
>
> Slogans written in Chinese characters in chalk were also found at many places in town. (*Far Eastern Economic Review*, 14 January.)

As the ethnics at both sides of the border are nearly identical in this area, it is hard to blame the Peking government on the basis of those facts. The *New York Times* correspondent, however, commented earlier on this issue:

> The Burmese say that the Chinese have indicated to them that the Government in Peking does not support the local rebels, but that the Chinese Communist party does. To the Government in Rangoon the distinctions are too subtle to take seriously. (*NYT*, 20 September 1973.)

In much stronger language, a Moscow broadcast in English declared in an editorial on the anniversary of Ne Win's take-over and on the opening of the new assembly:

> The Burmese know well now actively China's leaders support the insurgents. Ignoring the 1960 treaty on friendship and nonaggression between China and Burma, Peking is frankly meddling in the domestic affairs of a sovereign neighbor. Servicemen of the People's Liberation Army of China regularly infiltrate northern Burma from Yunnan Province. They act as instructors in the rebel detachments. Peking has also sent advisers to the Kachin separatists, who want to dismember the Burmese Union ("Radio Peace and Progress," 2 March 1974.)

The reason for such support of the BCP(WF) may be to maintain pressure on the Ne Win government and to prevent it from becoming too friendly with either the United States or the Soviet Union. Nevertheless, there seems to be also a special interest of China in the domination of this area bordering on Laos and Thailand. Some observers say that the Chinese have shifted troops from Laos into eastern Burma (see *Christian Science Monitor*, 18 March); this is, however, denied by the Burmese. The VPB's mentioning of a long road built by some 200,000 people in the northern Wa State (18 October 1973) could mean in this context that the Chinese are now trying to extend into Burma the strategic roads built in Laos.

On foreign policy in general, the BCP(WF) attacked the Rangoon government on several occasions for allegedly department from its policy of non-alignment, accusing it of cooperating with the Soviet Union (e.g., VPB, 4 November 1973) or of obeying the United States: "It is clear that the military government's independent foreign policy only follows the imperialists' tune and dances according to their will. [This] foreign policy of a semicolonial nature cannot be called neutral or independent." (Ibid., 27 December 1973.) The "Voice of the People of Burma" of course never mentions that the Chinese government is also giving aid to Burma, and that, for instance, China's long-term loans in 1973-74 were ten times higher than the ones accepted from the United States, or the U.S.S.R.

Besides the Chinese party, the BCP(WF) maintains friendly relations with the Malaysian communists, whom they congratulated on their foundation anniversary this year (VPB, 27 April 1974).

Publications. The only first-hand information on the BCP(WF) comes from the broadcasts of its clandestine radio station, the "Voice of the People of Burma," inaugurated on 28 March 1971. No regular publications are known. Occasional leaflets are distributed illegally and therefore not available.

Köln-Weiss   Klaus Fleischmann
Federal Republic of Germany

Cambodia

After five years of fratricidal war, there is still no widely accepted name for the coalition of forces seeking to dislodge President Lon Nol's Government of the Khmer Republic (GKR) from its capital, Phnom Penh, and from other provincial towns in Cambodia. As in 1973, a great deal of effort was exerted by Peking, in the name of the anti-GKR forces (whom we will call "Khmer insurgents," or KI, for want of a better name) in an unsuccessful attempt to oust the GKR from Cambodia's U.N. seat.

On 28 November 1974, the General Assembly voted 56-54, with 24 abstentions, to defer the question of Cambodian representation until 1975. This resolution was strongly supported by Great Britain, Japan, and the five ASEAN states: Thailand, Malaysia, Singapore, Indonesia, and the Philippines. The United States, which has provided more than $1 million a day in aid to the GKR, made a major behind-the-scenes effort to prevent the GKR from being unseated by China and the African bloc.

The Khmer insurgents are probably led by a small group of ethnic Khmer communists, possibly numbering a thousand or more, who were trained in the Democratic Republic of Vietman (DRV) between 1954 and 1970. The Khmer communist element within the KI may be considerably more pro-DRV than members of the KI who have not been to North Vietnam for training. (This latter group is referred to as "Khmers rouges" in this article.) Undoubtedly the DRV-trained Khmer communists have little or nothing in common with Prince Norodom Sihanouk, who has headed an exile regime in Peking since 1970, or with Prince Sihanouk's supporters in Cambodia.

These impressions of the Khmer communists have been developed by U.S. officials on the basis of interrogations of a few KI defectors, none of whom held senior rank in the movement. The view that the insurgents are led by Khmer communists is also supported by the statements of refugees from KI-controlled areas, which point to the determined ruthlessness of the KI in trying to regiment the lives of Cambodians in these sparsely populated district. (Well over three quarters of Cambodia's estimated 7 million people live in GKR-controlled areas, including at least 1.5 million in Phnom Penh.)

The insurgents' ruthlessness suggests that their first priority is the radical reshaping of the Cambodian way of life. Vietnamese communists, if they controlled the KI, might be more rational in their use of terror tractics, particularly if operating among the Khmer people whose hostility toward Vietnam is deeply ingrained. Presumably Hanoi and Peking are mainly interested in Cambodia as it relates to the struggle for South Vietnam or to China's third world diplomacy.

Through the end of 1974, the KI had almost no opportunity to communicate with the outside world except through North Vietnamese and Chinese-controlled media. (See "Media" below. Thus, what is known about the KI outside Cambodia is largely what Peking and Hanoi want the world to know. This is supplemented by refugee reports and by what is known in Phnom Penh about a few personalities among the KI; in addition, a few Western journalists have described the experience of being captured, held, and released by insurgent bands.

In addition to a relatively small number of DRV-trained communists, the KI includes a much larger number of so-called Khmers rouges. The term was coined by Sihanouk in the late 1950s as a derogatory name for leftist critics of his regime who took to the bush. The term is now often rather confusingly applied by journalists to the KI movement as a whole, whether recruited before or after Sihanouk's overthrow in 1970 and whether nominally loyal to Sihanouk or not. The term Khmers rouges, to repeat, is used in this article to denote members of the KI who have not been trained in the DRV. They are not personally committed to Sihanouk. There may well be many factions and sub-groups within this broad category. Among the more obvious bases for cleavage are: age, ethnic composition of one's family (e.g., part Chinese, part Vietnamese, and so on), education (the main determinant of class), date of entry into the *maquis*, tactical preferences, and loyalty to a particular regional commander of the KI. Unfortunately, there is not enough data to attempt a description of KI politics in terms of such cleavages.

A third major element in the KI appears to be a dwindling faction óf Sihanouk supporters. The only well-known personality in this group (in Cambodia) is Prince Norodom Phurissara. Sihanouk may have hoped to begin rebuilding his political base in Cambodia in November 1973, when he announced that he was disbanding his exile government (Royal Government of National Union; GRUNK) and that henceforth its ministers would have to reside in Cambodia. If this was his hope, it appears to have failed. Prince Norodom Phurissara was the only known Sihanouk supporter to receive a portfolio in the revised GRUNK "cabinet." A brief summary of political developments over the past two decades will help to place the various elements of the Cambodian scene in perspective.

In the latter stages of the first Indochina war, King Norodom Sihanouk skillfully applied various pressures that led the French to grant his country its independence in 1953. Sihanouk next had to overcome two great domestic challenges to his leadership: ethnic Khmer insurgents in rural areas (called Issaraks) and a contentious, faction-ridden Khmer elite in Phnom Penh.

Viet Minh units were also present in Cambodia, mainly raising funds for the war in Vietnam. In 1954, most of them went underground or left for North Vietnam. They may have recruited and taken with them a thousand or more Khmer and Vietnamese-Khmer youths for training. Although the Issaraks were loosely allied with the Viet Minh, few of them were pro-communist, because the Indochinese communist movement had been Vietnamese-dominated since Ho Chi Minh began it in 1929. Once having gained their chief aim—independence from France—few Cambodians could see the need to cooperate with their mortal enemies, the Vietnamese.

Sihanouk abdicated his throne in 1955 and began a successful campaign to rally the support of rural and urban Cambodians behind his new mass party, the Sangkum ("Community"). He coined the terms *Khmer rouge* and *Khmer bleu* for leftist and rightest intellectuals who refused to take part in his centrist Sangkum movement. Although Sihanouk preferred to find ways to include even his critics in the political system, he was not above using the police to harass opponents when they got out of hand; more than likely, some were executed. Rather than toe the line or go to prison, a few dozen "reds" and "blues" chose to go abroad or join guerrilla bands in Cambodia's less accessible border areas.

Meanwhile, a small "Peoples Revolutionary Party of Cambodia" (PRP), had been established as early as 1951. Although supposedly separate from the Indochina Communist Party (ICP), most Khmers who were aware of its existence probably assumed it to be a de facto branch of the ICP, fully as Vietnamese-dominated as the parent organization had been. Most of the PRP's leaders, including Sieu Heng, were Khmer Krom (ethnic Khmer or part-Khmer families long settled in South Vietnam). Many, perhaps most, of the few hundred people who joined the PRP were either Khmer Krom or ethnic Vietnamese who had lived in Cambodia. Both groups, particularly the latter, were disliked and distrusted by most ethnic Khmers in Cambodia.

A second communist front, the Pracheachon (People's) Party, was formed in 1955, but it failed to rid the communist movement in Cambodia of its Vietnamese taint. The Pracheachon was allowed by Sihanouk to contest most Cambodian national elections from 1955 to 1962, and it was recorded as polling a small and diminishing fraction of the vote. Since every step in the electoral process was carefully staged by Sihanouk and his massive Sangkum organization, the Pracheachon's percentage was exactly what Sihanouk wanted it to be (presumably to appease domestic leftists and foreign communist powers). In 1962, Sihanouk grew tired of playing cat and mouse with the Pracheachon. He attacked it openly, arrested some of its leaders, and forced the front group underground.

Later the same year, Sihanouk placed a group of young and able leftist intellectuals in senior government posts for the avowed purpose of "seasoning" them by making them cope with the nation's economic problems instead of criticizing his administration from the sidelines. The group included Khieu Samphan, Hou Yuon, and Hu Nim. There followed a period of four years of experimentation with a centralized economy.

Sihanouk broke relations with Saigon in 1963 and expelled the U.S. aid mission; he then allowed North Vietnam and the Viet Cong to establish large embassies and logistical operations in Cambodia. The predominantly conservative older Khmer elite became alarmed over the degree of Vietnamese influence Sihanouk was allowing in the country. They were hardly reassured when he broke diplomatic relations with the United States in 1965. In 1966, conservative elite members won a relatively unrigged National Assembly election by a large margin. After asking his right-of-center defense minister, Lon Nol, to form a new government, Sihanouk went abroad for a rest.

In early 1967, Hou Yuon, Hu Him, and Khieu Samphan disappeared from their homes—causing speculation that they had been killed by Cambodian police or had joined the Khmers Rouges. At about the same time, a peasant rebellion broke out in Battambang Province, and Lon Nol carried out intensive air and ground attacks against villages that he believed were Khmer rouge strongholds. (Beginning in the early sixties, a small but growing number of Khmers rouges had established base areas in the hill country of the large western provinces of Battambang and Pursat.) Sihanouk probably authorized Lon Nol's attacks in 1967, which caused large-scale destruction of life and property and probably added many new supporters to Khmer rouge ranks.

During 1968 and 1969, Sihanouk's cautious swing to the right was confirmed in many ways. He resumed relations with the United States, downgraded relations with China, and gave the impression of hoping that the Vietnam war would end with restoration of a balance of major-power influence in the area. But Sihanouk was not prepared to adjust his leftist economic and security policies to accord with his increasingly anti-communist rhetoric. When Premier Lon Nol and his deputy, Sirik Matak, began to press for a major reorientation of Cambodian policies, Sihanouk first reacted defensively, then went off to France leaving the main issues unresolved.

During February 1970, Lon Nol authorized some anti-Viet Cong demonstrations in eastern Cambodia. Sihanouk seemed not to object strongly until anti-Viet Cong riots in Phnom Penh led to the sacking of the North Vietnamese Embassy. Then Sihanouk chose to gamble his own political future on an open bid for major-power support in controlling the Viet Cong. After Sihanouk had been turned down by the French and the Russians, and warned by the Chinese not to expect much aid, Lon Nol finally cut his ties with him and allowed a cautiously "legal" coup to be carried out by unanimous vote of the National Assembly.

Lon Nol also ordered the Vietnamese communists to leave Cambodia as quickly as possibly and recklessly incited the Khmer people against their country's large Vietnamese minority. Within days, a series of bloody attacks on the helpless Vietnamese residents had blackened the new government's name. Several pro-Sihanouk uprisings were suppressed, and Lon Nol began maneuvering his tiny army against the Vietnamese communist garrisons near the South Vietnamese border.

In May 1970, the U.S. incursion into eastern Cambodia drove North Vietnamese, Viet Cong, and Republic of Vietnam divisions into the heart of Cambodia for the first time. Once there, both North and South Vietnamese forces proceeded to exact revenge on the Cambodian people for their earlier treatment of the country's Vietnamese minority. The U.S. incursion also ended private contacts that had been taking place between the Lon Nol and Peking governments (and delayed the Sino-U.S. détente). Less than a week after U.S. forces entered Cambodia, Peking authorized Prince Sihanouk to form his government in exile (GRUNK).

Several divisions each of North Vietnamese, Viet Cong, and Republic of Vietnam forces stayed in Cambodia until the Easter 1972 communist offensive in South Vietnam. Thus, during 1970 and 1971, Cambodia served as a major battleground in the Vietnam war. Both Vietnamese sides worked hard to develop their Khmer clients into effective military organizations (armed with weapons supplied by the United States and by China).

After the great majority of North and South Vietnamese forces transferred their struggle back to Vietnam in the spring of 1972, Khmer insurgents assumed the main burden of harassing Lon Nol's army. In 1974, authoritative GKR officials estimated that one-tenth of the entire Cambodian population had been killed or wounded during the war. U.S. officials estimated that there were 50,000 to 65,000 combat-effective Khmer insurgents, in addition to those serving as local police and porters and in other supporting roles. At the same time, U.S. officials said that the Phnom Penh government's army contained around 115,000 combat soldiers; an additional 110,000 or so men and women were in uniform but not regularly involved in combat.

Although heavy fighting continued during 1974, it was increasingly evident that neither side had the military leadership, morale, or trained manpower to win a decisive military victory. Neither side appeared to have a coherent strategy for victory; both sides often failed to exploit tactical advantages. It was increasingly difficult to predict whether the United States, China, and North Vietnam would continue to make available large quantities of military aid, which had fueled the war since 1970.

Leadership and Organization. The Khmer communist movement is believed to be led by a Central Committee composed of around twenty members, including four who are known to Phnom Penh Cambodians: Khieu Samphan, Ieng Sary, Saloth Sar, and Son Sen. All are around forth years old and would probably be classified as Khmers rouges. None are pro-Sihanouk; Ieng Sary and probably Son Sen have visited North Vietnam, but none of the four men belong to the shadowy group of Khmers who spent 1954-70 in North Vietnam. Only Son Sen is believed to have had enough military training and experience to qualify as the possible overall military leader of the resistance.

Khieu Samphan is well and favorably known to Khmer elite members on both sides in the current struggle. Raised by his widowed mother in Kompong Cham, he was one of the brightest members of his generation, winning scholarships all the way up to university level in France, where he received a doctorate in the 1950s. His asceticism has distinguished him rather sharply from most of his contemporaries. Although KI propaganda portrays him as the military leader of anti-Lon Nol forces, acquaintances in Phnom Penh strongly doubt that he fills that role. (For one thing, it would be very surprising if the actual military leader would have gone abroad for the last two months of the dry season, as he did in 1974.) More than likely, his image as a guerrilla fighter is part of the effort to groom him for a front-man position, corresponding somewhat to that of Prince Souphanouvong in Laos.

Ieng Sary is a Khmer Krom (i.e., was born and raised in South Vietnam). He was a notably bad student during that part of his schooling which took place in Cambodia; he failed his baccalaureate more than once. With this background, he became a teacher in a relatively obscure school. He probably joined the Khmer rouge in the early or mid-sixties, and is thought to have visited Hanoi in the late 1960s. After Sihanouk established his exile government in Peking in 1970, it was announced that Ieng Sary had been sent to Peking by the resistance forces in Cambodia to serve as their liaison with Sihanouk.

Sary accompanied Sihanouk on his foreign travels, and the prince (in talking with journalists) made no secret of his thorough dislike for Sary as a person and for his officious efforts to supervise Sihanouk's contacts with the press. It was evident that Sary had been assigned a watch-dog role, and most observers seemed to conclude that he was working on behalf of Hanoi. One of Sihanouk's motives in announcing, in November 1973, the transfer of GRUNK ministers to Cambodia was probably to get rid of Sary, who was the only one to leave Peking.

Saloth Sar, like Khieu Samphan, is known to the Phnom Penh elite as anti-Vietnamese. He is thought to have neither the brilliance nor the charisma of Samphan. He comes from a wealthy family, and he has been in the *maquis* since the early 1960s. He is thought to be a determined, rather plodding organizer. He and Ieng Sary are brothers-in-law, having married the Khieu sisters, daughters of an elite family. Both women are frequently mentioned in KI propaganda announcements.

Son Sen is less well known than the others in Phnom Penh elite circles. He is of Khmer Krom origin like Ieng Sary, and he is believed to have joined the Khmer rouge around 1960. He is described in KI propaganda as the "chief of staff" of the liberation armed forces. Some officers of Lon Nol's army regard him as possibly the real military leader of the KI.

Other members of the KI who are well-known to the Phnom Penh elite are: Prince Norodom Phurissara, Thiunn Mum, and Thiunn Prasith, Hou Yuon and Hu Nim. Phurissara served as Sihanouk's minister of foreign affairs for several years before 1970. He was named head of the "Phnom Penh Committee" in KI propaganda around 1972, and more recently has been named GRUNK minister of justice. He is one of the few KI personalities known to be pro-Sihanouk. The Thiunn brothers are well known as leftist intellectuals and members of a very wealthy and prominent Phnom Penh family; they joined the Khmer rouge sometime in the 1960s. Hu Nim and Hou Yuon fled Phnom Penh in 1967, as recounted above; Hou Yuon is considered one of the most talented Khmers of Khieu Samphan's generation. The actual roles of Nim and Yuon in the KI are unknown; both hold nominal cabinet posts in GRUNK.

Domestic Attitudes and Activities. There were no elections in Cambodia in 1974. Although KI units can move through much of Cambodia without challenge by Lon Nol's forces, they had not established an administrative center or capital (as of November 1974), and they exercized continuous administrative control over very few of the Cambodian people. The KI evidently tried and failed to take Siem Reap, the provincial town nearest Angkor Wat, in the hope of establishing a capital there. If they had gained Siem Reap and a U.N. seat, they might have installed Sihanouk at Siem Reap as ceremonial chief of state. This may remain one of their objectives.

As noted earlier, substantial numbers of Cambodians have fled the areas under KI occupation when they have found the opportunity to do so. These refugees report that people in KI areas have been forced into a communal pattern of living, with all land and other property owned in common, and cooking and eating done in mess halls. There is said to be a serious effort to reduce the central role of Buddhism in the people's lives. Early marriage and "unrevolutionary behavior" (e.g., the wearing of bright colors and jewelry and the singing of non-revolutionary songs) are severely penalized. Criticism of the KI movement is reportedly a crime that may be punishable by death.

While the KI have access to large areas of fertile land in Cambodia, much land that was cultivated before the war has been abandoned, and the KI (whose cadres are spread very thin in many areas) probably have a serious problem in finding and motivating enough people to produce a food surplus to feed the guerrilla units and to barter for medicine and other necessities in neighboring countries. Although the war has brought major damage and neglect to the rubber plantations, some rubber is still harvested and bartered by the KI for needed supplies, particularly medicine.

International Views and Policies. As indicated above, the KI within Cambodia and China at the United Nations continued during 1974 their concerted effort to discredit the GKR internationally and to seat a GRUNK representative at the United Nations. Prince Sihanouk, whose status and contacts in the third world are valuable for this purpose, continued to lend himself to the effort, although he often complained publicly that he was being used as a mere figurehead. More than likely, Peking and the KI believed that unseating the GKR would complete the regime's demoralization and lead to the curtailment of U.S. aid, thus gaining for the KI a victory they could not win on the battlefield.

In November 1973, Sihanouk declared that all GRUNK cabinet portfolios would be transferred to people in Cambodia (except for a small group in his immediate entourage). His motives were probably several: (1) the need to reduce his own official duties in Peking so he could spend more time with his ailing mother, who had just arrived in China; (2) a strong desire to send Ieng Sary back to Cambodia; (3) a hope of rebuilding his political base in Cambodia; and (4) an attempt to counter the impression that GRUNK was an exile government before the 1973 U.N. vote on Cambodian representation.

Sihanouk had just attended the October 1973 nonaligned nations conference in Algeria, where President Boumedienne had arbitrarily ruled that it was the "consensus" of those present that GRUNK was the government of Cambodia—placing those who wished to disagree in an awkward position. The Soviet Union and East European bloc countries then broke relations with the GKR and closed their embassies in Phnom Penh.

However, a motion essentially to postpone voting on the Cambodian representation question for a year was adopted in the U.N. General Assembly in December 1973 by a small margin. The sponsorship of many Asian countries and the strong support of the United States and Great Britain were crucial.

In April and May 1974, Khieu Samphan made a two-month trip to Hanoi, Peking, and a number of third world countries. One of the most startling features of this exercise was the fact that he was treated as Sihanouk's superior by Mao Tse-tung, who allowed Sihanouk the dubious honor of serving as Samphan's interpreter when they met. Efforts were later made to assuage Sihanouk's pique, but it appeared that Samphan was being groomed for the senior role. His visit to many third world countries was clearly aimed at lining up votes on the Cambodian representation issue by proving that the KI movement had some degree of substance.

However, in spite of intensive lobbying by China and various third world countries (notably Algeria), the GKR gained another one-year respite in November 1974. The solidarity of most East Asian and Southeast Asian nations on this issue was impressive. This was, of course, the General Assembly over which the Algerian foreign minister presided and which granted observer status to the Palestine Liberation Organization and refused South Africa's credentials. Hence, it is extremely unlikely that the United States could have prevented the unseating of the GKR if most East Asian countries had not been willing to fight hard on the Cambodian issue.

Media. GRUNK's major role during the five-year Cambodian war has been in the area of public relations, and Prince Sihanouk has been one of the main public relations assets of the KI movement. At his headquarters in Peking and on occasional trips abroad he has granted numerous press interviews in which he has demonstrated his flair for dramatizing his own and his associates' causes.

The GRUNK information service is known as AKI (for its French' title, Agence Khmère d'Information). AKI and the New China News Agency (NCNA) transmit a heavy volume of statements attributed to Sihanouk and other notables of the GRUNK or KI movement. Khieu

Samphan has been increasingly featured as a spokesman for the KI. AKI's electronic broadcasts are believed to originate from a low-powered transmitter located near where the borders of Cambodia and South Vietnam meet; the transmitter is believed to be owned and operated by North Vietnam. AKI broadcasts include one or two hours a day of teletype transmissions in French and about five hours a day of voice transmissions in Cambodian. The latter are known as the "Voice of the United National Khmer Front" (French acronym, FUNK). FUNK is a name sometimes used to describe the KI; another is the "Peoples Liberation Armed Forces."

AKI also publishes a daily mimeographed bulletin summarizing GRUNK and FUNK statements and press releases. This bulletin follows the format of the daily bulletins issued since the 1950s by the Cambodian Ministry of Information in Phnom Penh. Chau Seng (a former information minister and member of Sihanouk's entourage before 1970) is believed to supervise AKI public relations activities in Paris.

American University

Peter A. Poole

China

The First Congress of the Chinese Communist Party (Chung-kuo kung-ch'an tang; CCP) was held in Shanghai in July 1921. Mao Tse-tung, the present party chairman, who turned 81 years of age in December 1974, was one of the twelve delegates known to have attended. The party celebrates its anniversary each 1 July.

The People's Republic of China (PRC) was established 1 October 1949. State organs and all other organizations of society are in all important respects given leadership by the CCP, which is the sole legal party. The Tenth Party Constitution, adopted in 1973, makes this clear: "State organs, the People's Liberation Army (PLA) and the militia, labour unions, poor and lower-middle peasant associations, women's federations, the Communist Youth League, the Red Guards, the Little Red Guards and other revolutionary mass organizations must all accept the centralized leadership of the Party" (chap. II, art. 7).

The CCP is the largest communist party in the world. It had 28 million members as of August 1973, an increase of 11 million members since the previously reported figure of 17 million in 1961. The population of China was officially reported at the World Population Conference in Bucharest, August 1974, to be "nearly 800 million." The United Nations in November estimated the figure to be 838 million.

Organization and Leadership. According to the party constitution, the "highest leading body" of the CCP is the national party congress, which is to be convened every five years, although under often-invoked "special circumstances" the congress may be convened early or postponed. The party congress elects the Central Committee, which leads when the congress is not in session and which elects the Politburo, the Standing Committee of the Politburo, and the chairman and the vice-chairmen of the Central Committee. The Tenth Central Committee, elected at the party's most recent national congress, in August 1973, consists of 193 members and 124 alternate members (319 total). There were 170 members and 109 alternates (279 total) in the previous Ninth Central Committee, elected in 1969. The Tenth Politburo has 26 full and alternate members (one more member added to the original 25 in January 1974). The current Standing Committee of the Politburo was enlarged to nine members, from five. The Tenth Central Committee has five vice-chairmen; previously there had been only one. Membership in these high offices is said to embody the combination of the old, the middle-aged, and the young, constituting a variant of the "three-in-one combination." This is said to reflect the determination to have the three generations of leaders work together in a way showing that while experience is still respected and utilized, there is in China "no lack of successors."

The Tenth Central Committee continued 204 members from the previous committee; only 115 were newly seated. About 100 seats are said to be assigned to representatives of the masses—that is, outstanding workers, peasants, soldiers, and leaders of the recently reconstructed mass organizations. The current Central Committee includes a number of rehabilitated cadres who served on the Eighth Central Committee but not on the Ninth. Nine provincial leaders who were purged during the Great Proletarian Cultural Revolution (GPCR) are on the Tenth Central Committee. The committee has a greater representation of central government officials than did the Ninth, but their numbers are below levels known before the GPCR. Officials involved in foreign affairs are prominently present. In addition to those continued from the Ninth Central Committee (including Huang Chen, head of the PRC Liaison Office in Washington, D.C.) are the Chi P'eng-fei, who was foreign minister until November 1974; Chiao Kuan-hua, who was deputy foreign minister and became foreign minister in November 1974; ambassador to the U.N. Huang Hua; China-Japan Friendship Association head Liao Ch'eng-chih; and rehabilitated former vice-foreign minister Wang Chia-hsiang.

Effective policy-making power within the party rests with the Central Committee and at higher levels, particularly the Politburo and its Standing Committee. Mao Tse-tung is chairman of the Central Committee. The vice-chairmen are Chou En-lai, Wang Hung-wen, K'ang Sheng, Yeh Chien-ying, and Li Teh-sheng. Standing Committee members are Mao Tse-tung, Wang Hung-wen, Yeh Chien-ying, Chu Teh, Li Teh-sheng, Chang Ch'un-ch'iao, Chou En-lai, K'ang Sheng, and Tung Pi-wu (listed in the order of the number of strokes in their surnames, as are those below). Other members of the Political Bureau elected in August 1973 are Wei Kuo-ch'ing, Liu Po-ch'eng, Chiang Ch'ing, Hsü Shi-yu, Hua Kuo-feng, Chi Teng-kuei, Wu Teh, Wang Tung-hsing, Ch'en Yung-kuei, Chen Shi-lien, Li Hsien-nien, and Yao Wen-yuan. Teng Hsiao-p'ing was added as a member in January 1974, at which time his name was listed in terms of rank immediately after the members of the Standing Committee (John Burns, *Christian Science Monitor*, 17 January 1974). The alternate members of the Political Bureau are Wu Kuei-hsien, Su Chen-hua, Ni Chih-fu and Saifudin. All of the 16 surviving members of the previous Politburo retained their seats; the three former alternates among them were promoted to full membership. Thus, the Politburo added to its ranks in August 1973 five new full members and four alternates. All of these had been on the Ninth Central Committee except for Su Chen-hua, a rehabilitee of the Eighth Central Committee. Three Politburo members are labor heroes: Ch'en Yung-kuei, head of Tachai; Ni Chih-fu, a Peking worker-inventor; and Wu Kuei-hsien, a woman textile worker from Sian. Four of the newest members were provincial party first secretaries.

Below the Central Committee there is a network of party committees at the provincial special district, county, and municipal levels. A similar network of party committees exists within the PLA, from the level of the military region down to that of the regiment. According to the party constitution, primary organizations of the party, or party branches, are located in factories, mines, and other enterprises, people's communes, offices, schools, shops, neighborhoods, PLA companies, and elsewhere as required.

Except within the PLA, the national structure of party organization was shattered in the course of the GPCR. Reconstruction began in late 1969 and by mid-August 1971 the last of the provincial-level party committees was reestablished. Reconstruction at the lower and intermediate levels was probably completed during 1973. The "revolutionary committees," which were created at all levels during the GPCR in order to provide leadership in the temporary absence of regular party and government organizations, remain a party of the still emerging institutional structure of China. However, the revolutionary committees are now subordinate to reconstituted party committees.

The year 1974 began with dramatic developments in the PLA. On 1 January the New China News Agency gave details on sudden, surprising shifts in assignment that affected eight of China's eleven military regions. The shifts which began in December 1973 signal a further consolidation of party authority over the military. The PLA, which played a dominant role in the GPCR and was so prominent on revolutionary committees and at the Ninth Party Congress, and in the party organization established by that congress, had been receding into the background ever since. In 1972, PLA participants on civilian revolutionary committees were operating under a slogan of "learning form the people," a new complement to the prevailing "learn from the PLA." Through 1973, PLA participation on such committees seemed to be reduced. The sudden shift at the end of 1973 of so many top leaders among the military regions underscored this trend.

The following regional military commanders were moved: Ting Sheng, from Canton to Nanking; Hsü Shih-yu, from Nanking to Canton; Tseng Ssu-yu, from Wuhan to Tsinan; Yang Te-chih, from Tsinan to Wuhan; Han Hsien-ch'u, from Foochow to Lanchow; P'i Ting-chun, from Lanchow to Foochow; Ch'en Hsi-lien, from Shenyang to the vacant Peking command. Li Teh-sheng, a vice-chairman of the party and formerly head of the PLA's General Political Department, was given the Shenyang Regional Military Command. The other three regional military commanders remained where they were: Ch'in Chi-wei in Chengtu, Wang Pi-ch'eng in Kunming, and Yang Yung in Sinkiang. These three were only recently posted, and none simultaneously holds a top party position. Wang and Yang are party second secretaries; but Ch'in is not known to hold a high party post. Significantly, none of the transferred regional commanders was given a top party post in his new command, although seven of the eight had simultaneously held the top party post at their old commands (*Current Scene*, February 1974). Thus, the net result of the shifts seems to suggest that the military's role in civilian party affairs has been further reduced. It also suggests a significant reassertion of Peking's authority over long-suspected centrifugal tendencies in the military regions.

Some prominent military leaders were attacked in *ta tzu pao* (wall posters) during the spring of 1974, apparently as part of the current Anti-Lin, Anti-Confucius campaign, which at times aimed particularly at the "sworn followers" of the late Lin Piao. Li Teh-sheng, member of the Politburo's Standing Committee and commander of the Shenyang Military Region, was the most prominent target. Tseng Ssu-yu, commander of the Tsinan Military Region, was another (ibid., May). However, nothing seems to have come of such attacks. Whereas the 1973 Army Day went relatively uncelebrated, the reception on the eve of this year's Army Day (1 August) saw an unusual turnout of major political figures. These included ailing Chou En-lai, who made his first public appearance in two months on this occasion. Chou had not attended the previous year's celebration. The implication of such attention to the military might be that it was a conciliatory gesture to the generals who have been moved about by civil authority and steadily removed from participation in civil administration. The gathering was marked also by the reappearance of two more senior military leaders after several years' absence. These were former acting chief of the general staff Yang Cheng-wu and a former air force political commissar, Yu Li-chin. Both had lost their positions in March 1968 while under Red Guard attack. On National Day, 1 October, among those who reappeared was Hsiao Hua, who served as director of the PLA's General Political Department from 1964 to 1968 (*Washington Post*, 3 October). A new air force commander, Ma Ning, was announced in June (*NYT*, 11 June).

The urban militia, which was created so suddenly in late 1973, continued to receive publicity. Through much of 1974 the country was encouraged to emulate the Shanghai militia. The latter model was regarded as a "three-in-one combination for safeguarding social order, fire prevention and civil defense." It appears that priority is being placed in such units on the preservation of law and order. It has been speculated that because the urban militia units have been successful in this regard there had been little disorder throughout much of the otherwise often heated Anti-Lin, Anti-Confucius campaign in 1974 (Leo Goodstadt, *Far Eastern Economic Review*, 30 August).

State organization continued to have several significant vacancies in 1974. No appointments were yet made to the top positions in either the Ministry of Defense or the Ministry of Finance. It is uncertain that the Ministry of Fuel and Chemical Industries has a head. There is as yet no new Ministry of Education. Altogether there are only 18 known ministries, 4 commissions of the State Council, and 20˙ groups and special agencies under the State Council (*Current Scene*, August). This compares with the 40 ministries, 11 commissions, and 21 special agencies before the GPCR. There are only five vice-premiers (including the addition of rehabilitated Teng Hsiao-p'ing in 1973) under Premier Chou En-lai. This compares with the 15 vice-premiers up to the GPCR. Thus, Mao's call for "better troops and less administration" during the GPCR has resulted in a streamlining of government that remains evident today.

Rumors were rife once again in the fall of 1974 that the convening of the long-awaited and often-expected Fourth National People's Congress was imminent. Japanese newspapers reported in September that a new constitution had been drafted. One of the provisions of the new constitution was said to be the naming of Mao Tse-tung to the position of chief of state (John Roderick, Associated Press, 20 September). The post at present is occupied by aged Tung Pi-wu on an acting basis. The previous holder of the position, Liu Shao-ch'i, who as principal target of the GPCR was removed from all positions both inside and outside the party, was belatedly confirmed to be deceased by a communist newspaper in Hong Kong in late October (*Washington Post Service*, 1 November 1974).

Mass organizations were not particularly prominent in the news in 1974, but they are a significant component of socio-political life in China, especially since their reconstruction which took place basically during 1973. The Communist Youth League ostensibly has become more involved in education. The Women's Federation has been active in the Anti-Lin, Anti-Confucius campaign. The trade unions are the most important of the mass organizations. This is reflected by the prominent trade union representation in the Tenth Central Committee, in which they have one-ninth of the regular and one-sixth of the alternate membership. Twenty-two of the chairmen and vice-chairmen of the 28 known trade union committees are members of the Central Committee, and 19 are alternate members. Their top representative in the CCP is Wang Hung-wen, who is regarded as the number three man of the party. This representation contrasts with that of the Women's Federation, which has only three top officers among its local committees who are members of the Central Committee, and only eight are alternate members. Of top officers from Communist Youth League local committees, seven are members of the Central Committee, and only one is an alternate member.

Domestic Party Affairs. The year 1974 saw the continuing consolidation of the party's position vis-à-vis the PLA, and it was marked by widespread, unusually intensive, and apparently inconclusive criticism campaigns. The shifting of the eight (of eleven) regional military commanders and the divesting of them of simultaneous top party positions, already noted above, clearly signaled a reassertion of party control, as well as of the authority of Peking over the military regions.

The campaigns reached levels of intensity unknown since the GPCR of 1966-69. Early in the year, Chekiang Province was lauded as a model for its undertaking of rural reforms. Authorities in the province were praised for seeking to continue and to complete the Socialist Education Movement, a campaign which had reached no firm conclusion in the early 1960s. Other provinces reportedly joined in this rural reform effort, but little else was heard of the campaign later in the year (Leo Goodstadt, *Far Eastern Economic Review*, 14 January). However, many thousands of young people and cadres continued to be sent to rural districts in the course of the year (e.g., *Peking Review*, 10 May).

The campaign atmosphere led to a temporary coolness toward foreigners in some quarters and to the criticism of specific Western cultural expressions early in the year, all of this contrasting with the relative cosmopolitanism of the previous two years. Beethoven and Schubert were attacked, for example, even though in the preceding year no less a figure than Chiang Ch'ing requested that Beethoven's Sixth Symphony be performed by the visiting Philadelphia Orchestra. A new radical journal, *Study and Criticism*, published in Shanghai since late 1973, attacked a current American best-seller, *Jonathan Livingston Seagull*, as being an example of "subjective idealism." The moral of the article: "In societies which are rotten to the core, no efficacious medicine of idealism can save them from death." (*Current Scene*, April.) Also severely criticized was a travelogue film on China produced by Italian director Michelangelo Antonioni two years previously. The film was termed a "wild provocation against the Chinese people." The *People's Daily* criticism specified that the "three-and-a-half-hour film does not at all reflect the new things, new spirit and new face of our motherland, but puts together many viciously distorted scenes and shots to attack Chinese leaders, smear socialist China, slander China's great proletarian Cultural Revolution and insult the Chinese people. Any Chinese with a modicum of national pride cannot but be greatly angered on seeing this film." (*Peking Review*, 1 February.)

Scathing criticism was directed at a number of Chinese theatrical productions as well. One such opera, *Three Trips to Taofeng*, produced in Shansi and performed at a drama festival in Peking in January, was initially praised. By the end of January the work was denounced with intense vituperation. It was alleged to be a sly effort to revive an earlier opera which had glorified the discredited Liu Shao-ch'i. Furthermore, it was suggested that senior members of the Shansi provincial administration had compelled unwilling actors and public alike to perform the opera. The attack on *Three Trips to Taofeng* spread to other works, including: *Case Number 302*, in Kiangsi, which reportedly was the same work attacked in Shantung under the name *Turbulent Beach*; *Returning the Ox* and *The Song of the Gardener*, both in Hunan; and *San Miang Teaches Her Son*, in Kwangtung (Leo Goodstadt, *Far Eastern Economic Review*, 4 October).

But the major effort of the year, to which the above activities were variously related, was the Criticize Lin, Criticize Confucius (or Anti-Lin, Anti-Confucius) campaign. Continuing since the previous fall, the originally separate campaigns were joined together in January. The two men, Lin Piao and Confucius, whose lives were separated by so many centuries, were said to have had one overridingly common characteristic: each in his own day had tried to restore an outmoded social system. The joint campaign had periods of peak intensity in February-March and again during the summer. On 2 February, following months of relatively academic discussions in the press, a campaign was launched on a mass basis with the warning that it was a "matter of first importance for the whole party, the whole army, and the whole nation." Within days there were calls for a large-scale renewal of the Cultural Revolution (*NYT*, 5 February). "Criticism groups" were set up, with which to spearhead the "people's war" (ibid., 6 February). There were even hints of impending violence when the party journal *Red Flag* (*Hung Ch'i*) announced Mao's dictum that "without destruction there can be no construction" (ibid., 7 February). The campaign was accompanied by the usual posters and an avalanche of criticism articles in the press. Targets other than Lin and Confucius emerged in the course of the campaign. Some of these are noted above. The late Hu Shih, a well-known educator-thinker of the May Fourth Movement, was once again attacked (ibid., 20 February). The principal target for a time was thought to have been Chou En-lai. All of the living targets who were publicly identified at one time or another seem to have survived; Chou En-lai did so despite serious illness, hospitalization, and convalescence. Speculation was rife, and remained so near year's end, as to just what the campaign ultimately was all about, as to the complete identity and composition of the engaging factions, and as to what Mao's role was from month to month. Some of the confusion about purpose may be attributed to the diversity of objectives toward which it was turned. Managers were attacked for placing production ahead of ideology (ibid., 6 March). In general, the campaign was aimed at any and all remnants of "feudal" ideas and behavior, and against corruption and backsliding from revolutionary ideals. There does appear to have been opposition. Claims were articulated often that "reactionaries at home and abroad" were striving to "attack, slander and sabotage" the movement which was supposed to be reviving the values of the GPCR (ibid., 25 March). Posters in Peking were removed by authorities, and this drew attacks. Worker Propaganda Teams, which were used during the GPCR to stabilize the schools, and which had begun to fade away over the last couple of years, were again called to action. Their purpose, it appeared, was to put new life into a campaign that was apparently dying out (ibid., 11 June). Violence was reported at times in a number of places, but it was on a much smaller scale than during the GPCR (Leo Goodstadt, *Far Eastern Economic Review*, 1 July). By September the Chinese press issued strong appeals to close ranks politically and to prevent a "troublemaking minority" from upsetting national unity (*Christian Science Monitor*, 12 September).

The theme of unity was stressed again on 1 October, China's national day and this year the twenty-fifth anniversary of the establishment of the PRC. The word "unity" and similar words expressing the concept of unity were used repeatedly in the national day joint editorial of the *People's Daily, Red Flag*, and *Liberation Army Daily*. Mao again called for unity and internal order in December (*Washington Post*, 18 December 1974). This contrasted with the exhortations to "go against the tide" that prevailed late the previous year and at the outset of the 1974 campaign against Lin Piao and Confucius. On the other hand, the editorial indicated the campaign would "broaden and deepen" and continue "for a long time." Mao did not appear at public festivities marking the day. Chou En-lai, once again after several weeks of apparently recuperating, made an appearance at a reception on the eve of the national day. Despite the uncertainty engendered by the age and frail health of China's two principal leaders, and despite the inconclusive character of the year's massive political campaign, the Chinese leadership was obviously in a jubilant mood on the occasion. The entire Politburo, except for Mao, Chou, and Li Teh-sheng, appeared in a public show of unity. They could look back over a quarter-century of accomplishment. Statistics were available in abundance to demonstrate how much better the Chinese people fared now, as compared with the pre-communist period. Among the rehabilitees—other than Hsiao Hua, noted above—who made an appearance on this occasion were: Sung Jen-chiung, former first secretary of the party's Northeast China Bureau; Fu Chung-pi, who was dismissed as commander of the Peking Garrison in March 1968; Chiang Nan-hsiang, former minister of higher education and president of Tsinghua University; Fan Chin, former editor of the *People's Daily,* and deputy mayor of Peking; and Hu Chiao-mu, a leading party propagandist.

International Views and Positions. "Chairman Mao's revolutionary line in diplomacy" continued its initiative through 1974. This policy began in May 1969, and continues to contrast with the diplomacy of the GPCR period, in the course of which ambassadors were withdrawn from all posts except Cairo. Diplomatic relations were exchanged with six more countries in 1974. There are now diplomatic ties with 93 countries. The accompanying three tables provide a comprehensive overview of China's diplomatic relationships:

I.   Countries which established diplomatic relations with China before 1970,
     exclusive of those which later suspended relations (44):

Afghanistan	Iraq	Southern Yemen (P.D.R.)
Albania	Kenya	Sri Lanka
Alberia	Korea (North)	Sudan
Bulgaria	Laos	Sweden
Burma	Mali	Switzerland
Congo	Mauritania	Syria
Cuba	Mongolia	Tanzania
Czechoslovakia	Morocco	Uganda
Egypt	Nepal	U.S.S.R.
Finland	Netherlands	United Kingdom
France	Norway	Vietnam (North)
Germany (East)	Pakistan	Yemen Arab Republic
Guinea	Poland	Yugoslavia
Hungary	Rumania	Zambia
India	Somalia	

II.   Countries which have established diplomatic relations with China since 1970,
      listed chronologically with date of establishment of diplomatic relations (49):

Canada	13 October 1970	Greece	5 June 1972
Equatorial Guinea	15 October 1970	Guyana	27 June 1972
Italy	6 November 1970	Togo	19 September 1972
Ethiopia	3 December 1970	Japan	29 September 1972
Chile	15 December 1970	Germany (West)	11 October 1972
Nigeria	10 February 1971	Maldives	14 October 1972
Kuwait	22 March 1971	Malagasy Republic	6 November 1972
Cameroon	26 March 1971	Luxembourg	16 November 1972
Austria	26 May 1971	Zaire	19 November 1972
Sierra Leone	29 July 1971	Jamaica	21 November 1972
Turkey	4 August 1971	Chad	28 November 1972
Iran	16 August 1971	Australia	21 December 1972
Belgium	25 October 1971	New Zealand	22 December 1972
Peru	2 November 1971	Dahomey (resumed)	29 December 1972,
Lebanon	9 November 1971		(first est. 12 Nov. 1964)
Rwanda	12 November 1971	Spain	9 March 1973
Senegal	7 December 1971	Upper Volta	15 September 1973
Iceland	8 December 1971	Guinea-Bissau	15 March 1974
Cyprus	12 January 1972	Gabon Republic	20 April 1974
Mexico	14 February 1972	Malaysia	31 May 1974
Argentina	19 February 1972	Trinidad and Tobago	20 June 1974
Malta	25 February 1972	Venezuela	28 June 1974
Ghana (resumed)	29 February 1972,	Niger	20 July 1974
	(first est. 5 July 1960)	Brazil	15 August 1974
Mauritius	15 April 1972	Gambia	17 December 1974
Netherlands (resumed)	16 May 1972,		
	(first est. 19 Nov. 1954)		

III.   Countries which do not have diplomatic relations with China (47):

   A.   Countries which have diplomatic relations with Taiwan (32):

Barbados	Libya
Bolivia	Malawi
Botswana	Nicaragua
Central African Republic	Panama
Columbia	Paraguay
Costa Rica	Philippines
Dominican Republic	Portugal
El Salvador	Saudi Arabia
Guatemala	South Africa
Haiti	Swaziland
Honduras	Thailand
Ivory Coast	Tonga
Jordan	United States
Korea (South)	Uruguay
Lesotho	Vatican
Liberia	Vietnam (South)

   B.   Countries which have diplomatic relations with neither China nor Taiwan (15):

Bahamas	Ireland
Bahrain	Israel
Bangladesh	Oman
Bhutan	Qatar
Cambodia	Rhodesia
Ecuador	Singapore
Fiji	United Arab Emirates
Indonesia	

A steady succession of important visitors and many others continued to visit China in 1974, despite the higher-than-usual level of domestic political campaigning. U.S. senator Henry Jackson visited China in July, and secretary of state Henry Kissinger in late November. Senator Mike Mansfield visited China for the second time in December. Other prominent foreign government visitors included the presidents of Zambia, Algeria, Tanzania, Senegal, Cyprus, Togo, Nigeria, Mauritania, Gabon, the People's Democratic Republic of Yemen, and Zaire; the vice-presidents of Niger and Equatorial Guinea; the prime ministers of Pakistan, Malaysia, Denmark, and Trinidad and Tobago; the deputy prime minister of Australia; the deputy premiers of the Royal Government of the National Union of Cambodia and the Democratic Republic of Vietnam; and the foreign ministers of Japan, Austria, Tinisia, Turkey, Romania, and Rwanda. The king of Nepal paid a visit. Mrs. Imelda Romualdez Marcos represented her husband, the president of the Philippines, on 20-29 September. There were many others. Chairman Mao continued to indicate his support for this brand of diplomacy by meeting personally with no less than 19 of these visitors during the year.

China's international trade pattern also continued to reflect the increasing global intercourse, although because of the delay in getting statistics we must shift our focus primarily to the previous year. In 1973, three major new developments characterized foreign trade: there was a resumption of whole plant imports on a scale that went far beyond that of the early 1960s; huge contracts were negotiated for agricultural imports; and there was a sudden overall expansion in both exports and imports. From late December 1972 until the end of 1973, China purchased a total of 62 plants from Japanese, French, Dutch, American, West German, Italian, and British suppliers for an estimated value of U.S. $1.2 billion. This included the largest single plant purchase ever made by China, a 16-plant French petrochemical complex valued at $300 million. These contracts are valued at roughly six times as much as the total value of contracts undertaken for the same purposes during the 1960s. Thirty-four of the plants were obtained on a five-year deferred payment basis from Japanese, Italian, and French suppliers. Machinery purchases also increased during 1973. PRC purchases of agricultural commodities, in response to poor harvests in 1972, reached an estimated $1.1 billion in 1973. It is estimated that some 7.6 million metric tons of grain were in all likelihood imported in 1973 as compared with the 4.8 million tons in 1972 and the record 6.6 million tons in 1964. The 1973 imports consisted of wheat shipments of 2.8 million metric tons from Canada, 0.8 million metric tons from Australia, and 2.6 million metric tons from the United States; also 1.4 million metric tons of corn came from the United States. Thus the United States emerged as the principal supplier, with 1973 sales estimated at $580 million, including sales of wheat, corn, soybeans, soybean oil, cotton, tobacco, and hides. Overall imports and exports increased several-fold in the first six months of 1973. It is estimated that China's trade deficit could increase to about $735 million in 1974 (*Monthly Economic Letter*, First National City Bank, December 1974). These are impressive increases, and if the import program, particularly for whole plants, is to be sustained over a period of years as would be desirable for continued economic growth, the wherewithal to pay for the imports must be found beyond the substantial gold reserves China possesses and the capacity of its agricultural economy, subject as that is to the vagaries of weather, to produce the needed capital. There is the possibility that China may make more use of international banking facilities for credit. However, by 1974 a major source of needed capital appears destined to be China's petroleum and petroleum products, if its promising reserves are exploited properly in the years to come (see *Current Scene*. March 1974). Indeed, it is estimated that at its present growth rate, annual output of oil may reach 120 million tons a year by 1977 (*Monthly News Letter*, December 1974).

All of this continued open diplomacy and increasing trade, sanctioned as it appears to be by Chairman Mao himself, suggests that China is gaining an even keel and is attempting to be a stable force in the international community while trying to promote its own economic growth. There remain, however, the uncertain implications of the internal criticism campaigns and also the memory of Chou En-lai's statement to the Tenth Congress, in August 1973, that "Relaxation is a temporary and superficial phenomenon, and great disorder will continue." This sentiment was echoed in the twenty-fifth anniversary joint editorial of the *People's Daily, Red Flag*, and the *Liberation Army Daily*, which maintained that the "international situation characterized by great disorder under heaven is developing in a direction favourable to the people of all countries." Chou had explained, and this line has often been repeated since the Tenth Party Congress, that "such great disorder is a good thing for the people, not a bad thing. It throws the enemies into confusion and causes division among them, while it arouses and tempers the people, thus helping the international situation develop further in the direction favourable to the people and unfavourable to imperialism, modern revisionism and all reaction." This interpretation provides ideological bearings for the Chinese people during a period of policies that might otherwise appear to compromise revolutionary resolve. In the meantime, China continues adroitly to make the most of the temporary relaxation.

Relations with the Soviet Union. Sino-Soviet relations continued to remain tense in 1974, but there also remained contradictory elements in this relationship, and there appeared to be possible conciliatory signals from both sides toward the end of the year. But the year began with rather harsh accusations. On 19 January, the Chinese expelled five Russians from the Soviet Embassy in Peking (two diplomats, their wives, and a translator), charging them with espionage. They were said to have been caught red-handed making contact with a "Soviet-sent" agent of Chinese nationality who also made a confession (*Peking Review*, 25 January). The Russians countered less than a week later by expelling a Chinese diplomat who was alleged to have been caught while aboard the trans-Siberian train obtaining espionage information (Associated Press, Moscow, 24 January). The Chinese responded with a protest charging that their envoy, who was returning to Peking after six years in the Soviet Union, was framed (ibid., Tokyo, 25 January). The nineteenth regular meeting of the Sino-Soviet Joint Commission for Navigation on Boundary Rivers met 5 February-21 March but failed to reach an agreement (*Current Scene*, April). On 23 March the Chinese protested that the Soviet Union had sent a reconnaissance helicopter into Sinkiang on 14 March. The Chinese took the three-man Soviet crew captive and charged that there had been 61 such incursions into Sinkiang since January 1973. (Ibid.) On 23 May the Soviet government issued an ultimatum which warned of "inevitable consequences" if the Soviet crewmen were not returned. The Chinese, it was warned, would be cut off from use of Siberian inland waterways unless they began showing "respect" for Russian rights and territory. The Chinese rejected this note and did not return the crewmen. (Agence France-Presse, Peking, 1 June.) The Soviet Union has not pursued the issue publicly. In fact, it has been reported that a Soviet lecturer told an audience at a foreign policy forum later in the year that the crew was being treated humanely (Washington Post Service, Moscow, 2 October). Of course, polemics on a number of other issues continued throughout most of the year, and this is discussed below.

On the other hand, there appeared to be signs at times of improving relations, or at least of the prospects of improved relations. A healthy trade continued between the two countries ($300 million in 1973). Each country has an ambassador in the other's capital. On 30 February the Civil Aviation Administration of China (CAAC) inaugurated its first non-stop Peking-to-Moscow flight, following the signing in July 1973 of a protocol to the 1954 Sino-Soviet Civil Aviation Agreement. Previously, Chinese flights were limited to Irkutsk. On 25 June, Soviet deputy foreign minister Leonid Ilichev, the chief delegate at the Sino-Soviet border talks, arrived back in Peking after an absence of almost a year. This did not necessarily mean that talks were to begin again right away, and nothing has been heard of negotiations since, if they have been renewed. Interestingly, on the occasion of the twenty-fifth anniversary of the PRC, 1 October, the Soviet Union called for improved relations between the two countries, although indicating at the same time that such improvement was not likely. However, the Soviet statement on this occasion contained no threats, in contrast to statements earlier in the year. (Ibid.) On the Chinese side, also early in October, came the revelation during discussions with a group of visiting Canadian journalists that the Chinese leadership no longer considers that China is in imminent danger of attack from the Soviet Union. This belief, it was said, proceeded from the assumption that the Soviet Union regarded the United States as its main enemy, and in any case would not attack China until it had secured its rear by establishing domination over Europe and the Middle East. This analysis held that the one million Soviet troops poised along the Sino-Soviet border were actually a bigger threat to the United States and Japan than to China. The Chinese explained that one million troops would not be enough in any attack upon China. They pointed to recent Soviet naval activity near Midway Island and in the vicinity of Hawaii. This and "other signs" made it clear, it was reported, that the Soviet Union regarded the United States as its main enemy. (John Burns, *NYT*, 5 October.) Then, on the occasion of the anniversary of the Bolshevik Revolution, the Chinese announced what appeared to be a major shift in policy. China told the Soviet Union that it was interested in a non-aggression pact, but this was linked to the idea of a pull-back of forces from along the disputed frontier. The pull-back qualification made the proposal's acceptance by the Soviet Union unlikely, and in fact, it was soon rejected as a propaganda move. Two earlier proposals by Soviet leader Leonid I. Brezhnev (on 15 January 1971 and again in mid-June 1973) were similarly ridiculed by the Chinese as propaganda. (Hedrick Smith, *NYT*, 8 November.)

Aside from the developments just noted, there were in the course of the year the usual acrimonious verbal exchanges. The Chinese rarely spared an opportunity to criticize the Soviet Union on a wide range of issues. They depreciated Soviet aid to Arab countries, claiming that Soviet revisionist social-imperialism was an "out-and-out merchant of death," and that the small quantities of weapons provided by the Soviets to the Arabs were "intended to control the battles waged by the Arab and Palestinian people and to force them once again to accept a 'no war, no peace' situation" (*Peking Review*, 11 January). The Chinese claimed that the Soviet leaders were a "renegade clique, the new tsars," and that they were "sitting in a volcano," inasmuch as the Soviet Union today was "filled with sharp class antagonisms, national contradictions and social upheavals." (ibid., 25 January). Soviet aid to India was termed "bait," with which the Russians were "plundering India economically through gross inequality in trade" (ibid., 29 March). As for Soviet activities regarding the Cyprus crisis, the Chinese asserted that the Soviet Union was "again poking its nose and fishing in troubled waters there, in an attempt to extend its sphere of influence in the Mediterranean region," and they warned others to "beware" of the Soviet revisionists, who were "out to rob the owner while his house is on fire" (ibid., 9 August). Ridiculing Soviet "so-called 'good-neighbourly friendship'" with Japan, the Chinese asked if the Russians are not "merely turning the heat on that country to commit expansion in order to dominate Asia" (ibid., 16 August). Hitting again at the domestic situation in the Soviet Union, the Chinese charged that "Soviet working people have again become wage-labourers who must sell their labour to eke out a living." This was because of the "serious fluidity of manpower in the Soviet Union," a "dire consequence of the all-round restoration of capitalism" in that country (ibid., 27 September). Similarly, the Chinese, asking "who is to blame for Ukraine's economic trouble" ridiculed the Soviet leadership's effort to "palm off" responsibility on Ukrainian officials as another example of Russian big-nation chauvinism (ibid., 27 September). Many other charges were made by Chinese spokesmen at various meetings of the United Nations Organization during the year, which will be discussed below.

For their part, the Russians also kept up a verbal barrage through much of the year. Basically, they tried to portray China as an imperialist power that was ambitious for hegemony in Asia, that was acting in collusion with Japanese and U.S. imperialists in expansion, and that was also subverting the independence of Asian nations by supporting insurgents. Chinese occupation of the Paracel Islands provided an opportunity to drum upon this theme. The Russians claimed that the islands "have very little value except as a convenient jumping-off ground for Peking's expansion toward the

Indian Ocean." Another claim was that the occupation was important in establishing Chinese paramountcy in the South China Sea (Denzil Peiris, *Far Eastern Economic Review*, 25 March). The death in March of Wang Ming (Ch'en Shao-yu), an erstwhile rival of Chairman Mao who had been living in exile for many years, gave the Russians opportunity to give some prominence to the publication of Wang Ming's posthumous work (Theodore Shabad, *NYT*, 28 March, and *FBIS*, 3-20 June).

Relations with the United States. Sino-American relations proceeded apace in 1974, although with a certain degree of awkwardness. It was widely believed earlier in the year that relations were actually becoming strained because of alleged foot-dragging on the part of the United States in furthering the implementation of the terms of the Sino-American Shanghai communiqué of February 972. It was suspected that part of the reason for any U.S. reneging on extending recognition was President Richard Nixon's anxiety not to alienate further the conservative senators whose votes might be needed in what appeared at the time to be an inevitable impeachment showdown in Congress. Those who advocated close ties with the PRC were surprised by the speed with which veteran diplomat Leonard Unger was appointed as ambassador to Taiwan, (United Press International, Key Biscayne, 16 February 1974), and they were concerned about the implications of the opening of new Taiwan consulates in the United States (AP, Washington, D.C., 12 August). The Chinese did seem cooler toward the United States earlier in the year, during the intensity of the earlier peak period of the current Anti-Lin, Anti-Confucius campaign. This apparent anti-foreignism has been noted above. The scholar Owen Lattimore was singled out for criticism as a "reactionary historian and international spy" during this period (AP, Tokyo, 8 February). A minor campaign was promoted again recalling U.S. and Japanese atrocities in pre-liberation times (Henry Bradsher, *Washington Star-News*, 28 March). Senator Henry Jackson, often regarded as a likely Democratic presidential candidate, visited China in July and called for U.S. recognition of the PRC (Washington Post Service, 9 July). On the other hand, Alfred S. Jenkins, who retired from his post as senior deputy chief of mission in the U.S. Liaison Office in Peking in mid-year, wrote later that the "scenario so far has been carried out with refreshing forthrightness." He advised that "On balance, enlarging the functions of the liaison offices appears to be the best course for now, based on what can be known publicly." He acknowledged, however, that "No one else . . . has quite as many pieces to the complex Chinese puzzle as does Kissinger." (Los Angeles Times Service, 24 November). Whatever might be the best course, the Chinese did not appear to be particularly anxious regarding either Taiwan or the diplomatic recognition issue, which in part depends upon the decision of the United States on Taiwan. And specifically with regard to Taiwan, the Chinese position stiffened during the year. Apparently related to the change of policy vis-à-vis the Soviet Union, as discussed with the Canadian journalists in October, it was revealed that negotiation with Chiang Ching-kuo, Chiang Kai-shek's son, was not possible. While a long-term peaceful settlement was still anticipated, a military solution, however, could not be ruled out if a peaceful one was not forthcoming (John Burns, *Toronto Globe and Mail*, 11 October).

Certainly in other respects the relationship was smooth and productive. An American captured during the Chinese taking of the Paracel Islands from South Vietnam was returned without incident (AP, Clark Air Force Base, 31 January). The Chinese expressed polite regret at the resignation of Richard Nixon from the presidency, for they had respected the bold diplomacy that had brought him to Peking and that established the détente. The Chinese were gratified by the assurances of the new president, Gerald Ford, who himself had visited China in 1972, that the new China policy of the United States would be continued. They must have been bemused by his call, during an Ohio State University speech, for the opening of U.S. college doors to workers in a "great new partnership of labor and academia" (Washington Post Service, 31 August). Henry Kissinger remained on as secretary of state. David Bruce, chief of the U.S. Liaison Office in Peking, was replaced by George Bush in

September. Bush was chairman of the Republican Party and formerly the U.S. chief delegate to the United Nations. Ironically, it had been Bush who argued against the entry of the PRC into the U.N. on the basis of Taiwan's expulsion. At the time of the vote which admitted the PRC, Bush had lamented the decision, calling it "a disappointment for all those who wish to see the U.N. promote the goals of peace and progress" (*NYT*, 5 September).

Following the summit meeting between President Ford and Soviet leader Leonid Brezhnev in Vladivostok in late November, Secretary Kissinger journeyed on to Peking (his seventh such visit), where he presumably briefed the Chinese leaders on the Vladivostok meeting. Kissinger paid a call on ailing Chou En-lai, who remained at a rest home, and engaged in more substantive discussions with Foreign Minister Chiao Kuan-hua and Vice-Premier Teng Hsiao-p'ing. He did not meet with Chairman Mao. The four days of talks, which included a Thanksgiving Day dinner during which a Chinese army band played "Turkey in the Straw," did not produce any dramatic results, and none had been expected. However, it was announced that President Ford would visit China in the next year, and progress was made toward an understanding on assets that had been frozen after 1949 in each of the two countries. Also, as Secretary Kissinger stated in a farewell toast, the two sides have "deepened [their] common understanding," and he added that they had committed themselves to "continuing the process of normalization." (AP, Peking, 28 November.) The fact that Chairman Mao's niece, Wang Hai-jung (age 36), was appointed to supervise the division of the Foreign Ministry that manages relations with the United States was regarded as auspicious (John Burns, *Toronto Globe and Mail*, 12 September). A similar reading was given Chiao Kuan-hua's promotion to foreign minister in November.

Already noted above was the greatly increasing trade between the United States and China in 1973. This trend continued into 1974, so much so that by March the United States had become China's third-ranking trading partner, behind Japan and Hong Kong (*NYT*, 22 March). A U.S. Commerce Department estimate of the total 1974 Sino-American trade figure held that it would reach $1,350,000,000, which would represent nearly an 80 percent increase over 1973. This was expected to be a highly imbalanced trade, with the Chinese deficit expected to be as much as $1,150,000,000 (*National Observer*, Washington, D.C., 31 August).

In addition to the U.S. governmental visitors to China already mentioned above (Kissinger, Jackson and Mansfield), Senator William Fulbright led a U.S. Congressional delegation in September. This delegation included Senator Hiram Fong of Hawaii, the only Chinese-American senator. During the first seven months of the year, seven groups of U.S. professionals visited China, representing such fields as aeronautics, meteorology, acupuncture anesthesia, architecture, pharmacology, and plant sciences. The plans of the International Longshoremen Warehouseman's Union to visit China had to be canceled in April, following the withdrawal of an invitation by the Chinese (*Honolulu Star-Bulletin*, 8 April). A group of Chinese commercial specialists visited the United States in August. A Chinese Medical Association organ replantation delegation was the only professional group to visit the United States. In the cultural exchange field, a Chinese *wushu* (martial arts) troupe performed in four U.S. cities in June and July. A large 385-item art and archeological exhibition from Peking was scheduled to open in Washington, D.C. in December. The campaign against Western culture earlier in the year in China may have had something to do with an absence of U.S. cultural delegations to China during 1974.

Relations with Japan. The year began with Japanese foreign minister Masayoshi Ohira's visit to Peking, 3-6 January, during which he met with Chairman Mao. On 5 January, China and Japan signed a full-scale international trade agreement, the first pact between the two countries since they normalized relations 15 months earlier. During the ceremonies in Peking the two countries also agreed to upgrade press exchanges by allowing eleven permanent correspondents from each side. The three-year agreement provided for the extension of most-favored-nation treatment by each side and established a joint committee to review any problems that might arise (Washington Post Service, 6 January). The trade agreement formalizes the significant commercial relationship that has developed between the two countries. Japan is China's most important trading partner. Two-way trade in 1973 was around $2 billion, and this brisk trade continued into 1974. In April the two countries agreed to lay underseas cables for mutual telecommunications. Installation of the cables was to have started shortly afterward, eventually to connect Kyushu with Shanghai. The cables will be capable of handling 480 telephone circuits; the project is to be completed in 1976 (Agence France-Presse, Tokyo, 8 April). In April, an air transport agreement was signed in Peking which inaugurated direct flights between Peking and Tokyo. These began on 29 September. Japan is thus the only Pacific air gateway to the PRC, and the only country to have a reciprocal aviation service with China (*Japan Times Weekly*, Tokyo, 5 October). The cost of this agreement was suspension of Japan Air Lines service to Taiwan, which had had 37 flights a week carrying an average of 30,000 passengers a month (Fox Butterfield, New York Times Service, Tokyo, 15 April). Japan was concerned about China's thirteenth nuclear detonation on 17 June, and noted heavy radiation over Kyushu (UPI, 19 June).

Relations with Southeast Asia. Conflicting images emerged in 1974 out of Chinese relations with Southeast Asia. On the positive side was Chou En-lai's endorsement of the proposal to make the area a "zone of peace and neutrality." (*Washington Post*, 29 May). Likewise, the Chinese premier assured the visiting Thai defense minister that China had ended her support for communist insurgents in Thailand (*FBIS*, 19 February). China agreed to supply the Philippines with a million tons of crude oil, beginning October 1974 and though 1975 (Agence France-Presse, Manila, 2 October). Malaysia exchanged diplomatic relations with China in the course of Prime Minister Tun Abdul Razak's visit to Peking in May. Mrs. Imelda Marcos, wife of Philippine president Ferdinand Marcos, visited China in October and met with both Chairman Mao and his wife, Chiang Ch'ing, with whom she seems to have got along nicely (Joseph Lelyveld, New York Times Service, Manila, 22 October). President Marcos has indicated that he would normalize relations between the Philippines and the PRC.

It is not clear that other Southeast Asian countries will quickly follow the lead of Malaysia in recognizing the PRC. In Thailand, the caretaker civilian government that replaced a military dictatorship in 1973 indicated that it would improve relations with China, but little has been done to follow up on this intention in 1974. Neither Singapore nor Indonesia seems disposed to recognized the PRC in the near future. In fact, Prime Minister Lee Kuan Yew of Singapore has reportedly said that his country will be the last ASEAN (Association of Southeast Asian Nations) member to open diplomatic ties with China (UPI, Bangkok, 29 November).

The brief military encounter with South Vietnam and forcible occupation of the Paracel Islands in January was regarded by the Chinese as the assertion of China's rights over its own territory Conceivably others in Southeast Asia may wonder about this penetration deeper into the South China Sea by their sizable northern neighbor. Reports also that China had sent troops into Burma while withdrawing them from Laos gave rise to some apprehensions. Some estimates of the number of Chinese troops inside Burma in March ran as high as 9,000. Journalists were taken on a conducted tour of Burma's northern Shan State and shown graves marked with Chinese characters which were supposed to indicate that Chinese had been involved in recent fighting with Burmese forces. The Chinese troops have not penetrated deeply into Burma. (Daniel Southerland, Christian Science Monitor Service, 27 March).

United Nations. On 12 April 1974 Vice-Premier Teng Hsiao-p'ing traveled to New York and gave a speech at the Sixth Special Session of the U.N. General Assembly on raw materials. The speech was a modest one, devoid of apparent ethnocentrism, and it refrained from presuming leadership of the Third World, to which it appealed. Teng praised the Arabs, who had shown how political weapons could be forged out of natural resources. "The oil battle," he said, "has broadened people's vision."

Teng described the U.S. notion of "interdependence" as actually meaning an exploitative relationship. He called upon the Third World countries to seek for self-reliance—without suggesting China as a model—and urged them to take into their own hands the production, sale, and transport of raw materials. He condemned the superpowers for their plunder and attacked the Soviet Union, which sided with the United States on the issue of cartels. (*Peking Review*, 12 April).

Vice-Minister Chai Shu-fan led the Chinese delegation to the Third United Nations Conference on the Law of the Sea, held in Caracas on 20 June-29 August. The Chinese called for a united front against the superpowers' maritime hegemony and gave support to the following positions: a 200-mile exclusive economic zone; joint exploitation of sea-bed resources in the international area; the right of coastal states to regulate passage through straits; and peaceful use of the ocean floor (*Peking Review*, 26 July).

At the U.N. World Population Conference in Bucharest, 19-30 August, the Chinese maintained their position that the causes of poverty are imperialism, colonialism, and superpower hegemony, not population growth. The Chinese position did not oppose population control, but maintained that different situations require different solutions and that these are best determined by the government of each country (*Peking Review*, 30 August).

Hao Chung-shih, vice-minister of agriculture and forestry, addressed the U.N. World Food Conference, held in Rome on 5-16 November. The Chinese position was similar to that maintained at the World Population Conference: it is not oil prices and population growth that cause food shortages; instead, the culprits are imperialism, colonialism, and hegemonism. The developing countries were enjoined to try to be self-reliant and self-sufficient, and the superpowers were criticized for overspending on the arms race (NCNA, 9 November).

Chiao Kuan-hua, chairman of the Chinese delegation, addressed the U.N. General Assembly session on 2 October, providing a comprehensive review of China's policies, strongly supportive of Third World issues (*Peking Review*, 11 October).

Publications. The official and most authoritative publication of the CCP is the newspaper *Jen-min jih-pao* ("People's Daily"), published in Peking. The theoretical journal of the Central Committee, *Hung ch'i* ("Red Flag") is published approximately once a month. The daily paper of the PLA is *Chieh-fang-chün pao* ("Liberation Army Daily"). The weekly *Peking Review* is published in English and several other languages. It carries translations of important articles, editorials, and documents from the three aforementioned publications. The official news agency of the party and government is the New China News Agency (Hsinhua; NCNA).

University of Hawaii   Stephen Uhalley, Jr.

India

Indian communists give December 1925 as the founding date of the Communist Party of India (CPI). Although the Western sources usually put the founding in December 1928, there were regional Marxist groups in various parts of India earlier.

After the death of CPA Secretary General Ajoy Ghosh, in 1962, and the Sino-Indian border conflict of the same year, the struggle between the right and left factions within the party intensified. This culminated in a formal split in 1964, when two separate congresses were held, each claiming to be the Seventh All-India Party Congress. Since that time, two parties have existed independently. One is commonly referred to as the "right" or pro-Soviet party, and the other as the "left" or "independent" party. They call themselves, respectively, the Communist Party of India—the CPI, and the Communist Party of India (Marxist)—The CPI(M). In 1969 a new, Maoist communist party, the Communist Party of India (Marxist-Leninist)—the CPI(M-L)—was created, largely by defectors from the CPI(M). This group derives its inspiration from the peasant revolt it instigated in 1967 in Naxalbari, West Bengal; and its members, along with other numerous but smaller Maoist organizations, continue to be referred to popularly as Naxalites.

On a nationwide basis the two large parties, the CPI and the more militant CPI(M), have competed against each other on more or less equal bases of strength. Active membership is probably between 80,000 and 100,000 in each, although the parties themselves claim a much higher figure. The population of India in 1974 was estimated at about 590 million.

While the strength of the CPI(M) is concentrated heavily in Kerala, West Bengal, that of the CPI is more widely distributed—in Bihar, Andhra Pradesh, Kerala, West Bengal, Uttar Pradesh, and Tamilnadu.

The March 1971 parliamentary elections gave the CPI and CPI(M) almost equal shares (about 4 percent for each) of the seats in the Lok Sabha. The CPI has 24 MPs in the Lok Sabha, compared with CPI(M)'s 25. In the fifth general elections for the state and union territory legislative assembly seats, held in March 1972, the CPI won a total of 112 seats while the CPI(M) won only 34 (as against CPI's 110 seats and CPI(M)'s 160 at the end of 1971). This marked a drastic decline in the electoral support and strength of the CPI(M). The February 1974 state legislative elections in four states and one union territory saw the CPI gaining additional seats through electoral arrangements with the ruling Congress. And in India's August presidential election, the CPI helped ensure a large victory margin for Congress candidate Fakhruddin Ali Ahmed by instructing its electors to abstain from voting for either Ahmed or the CPI(M)—backed opposition candidate, T. K. Chaudhury (see below).

The CPI(M-L), the most militant of the three communist parties, opposes parliamentary methods and does not participate in any elections. Its membership (estimated at 10,000 in 1972) has declined sharply during the last two years due to the government's armed campaign and detention policy against it, the increased popularity of Prime Minister Mrs. Indira Ghandhi's regime, and the emergence of Bangladesh which as East Pakistan was believed to provide a sanctuary and a channel for arms for the Naxalites. Current estimates put the membership at 1,000.

There are a number of smaller communist parties—generally to the left of CPI. These include the various Naxalite factions which are scattered throughout the country, and several parties (such as the Revolutionary Communist Party of India, West Bengal) with limited significance and purely local influence.

The CPI and the CPI(M) operate legally, although members of both parties have been arrested or detained from time to time. The intense government campaign against members and followers of the CPI(M-L), which went underground shortly after its establishment in April 1969, has resulted in detention or incarceration of thousands of Naxalities.

Other national parties in India are: the Indian National Congress or the Congress(R), the moderate socialist party led by Indira Gandhi; Congress(O), the breakaway conservative ("Syndicate") faction of the Indian National Congress; Bharatiya Lok Dol (BLD, a new rightist party formed in August 1974 by a merger of Swatantra and 6 regional parties); Bharatiya Jan Sangh (often referred to as the Jan Sangh), a militant Hindu-Nationalist and conservative party; the Socialist Parry (SP; formed out of the merger of the Praja Socialist Party and the Samyukta Socialist Party in August 1971), seeking to develop the image of a moderate socialist party; and the Dravida Munnetra Kazhagam or the DMK, an ardently sub-nationalist party of Tamilnadu which has now split into two factions, the breakaway faction calling itself Anna-DMK (Anna, for the ex-leader of the party, Annadurai who died recently). The conservatives within the congress(R), the Congress(O), Swatantra, and the Jan Sangh have consistently been the targets of severe criticism from the communist parties in India.

The CPI. Estimates of active membership in the Communist Party of India vary so much as to be of limited significance. The active membership of the party is probably between 80,000 and 100,000. During the meeting of the party's Central Executive Committee in March 1974 new membership figures of about 340,000 were announced.

Leadership and Organization. The central leadership of the CPI, elected at its Ninth Congress in 1971, includes the party chairman, Sripad Amrit Dange; the general secretary, C. Rajeswara Rao; the Central Secretariat (chairman, general secretary, and 7 secretaries), the Central Executive Committee (25 members), the Control Commission (9 members), and the National Council (101 full members and 10 candidate members). There are also party secretariats and state councils in each state in India. Bhupesh Gupta is the party's spokesman in the Parliament.

Chief among the CPI's major fronts is the All-India Trade Union Congress (AITUC), in which the CPI and the CPI(M) exercised joint leadership until the two parties' differences led to a formal split of the AITUC in 1970. The CPI retained control of the original AITUC, leaving the CPI(M) to form a new organization. CPI chairman S. A. Dange is the secretary-general of the AITUC as well; its president is S. S. Mirajkar. Its membership is claimed to be 1,984,778 (*New Age*, 4 February 1973).

Another important front, the All-India Kisan Sabha (Peasants' Association; AIKS) split in 1969 into two separate organizations—one controlled by the CPI and the other (the larger one) controlled by the CPI(M), both continuing the IKS name. The AIKS of the CPI is led by A. A. Ahmed, the organization's secretary-general, who is also a nember of the CPI's Central Executive Committee. Other major mass organizations dominated by the CPI include the All-India Youth Federation (AIYF); the All-India Student Federation (AISF); the National Federation of Women; and for agricultural laborers, the All-India Khet Mazdoor Union.

Domestic Attitudes and Activities. The party's long-range goal is the establishment of a "national democracy" composed of a coalition of "left and democratic forces" led by the communist party and based on worker-peasant alliance. This coalition would be composed of the "patriotic" elements of the national bourgeoisie, the intelligentsia, the peasants (including the "rich peasants"), and the workers, with the working class gradually rising to a position of leadership under the guidance of the communist party, ultimately forming a "genuinely socialist" society.

The coalitions envisaged by the CPI have been only partly successful and only at the state level. At the national level, the CPI has not yet been able to form a single alliance with another party, despite constant appeals for a coalition of "progressive" parties in the Lok Sabha. On 5-6 April 1974 the CPI and CPI(M) met on a national basis—for the first time since 1965—with six other leftist parties, including the Socialist Party. A charter of minimum demands and plans for a jointly-sponsored protest on 3 May against "anti-people policies" of the government were adopted by the meeting. Efforts to create a coalition party spanning the non-Congress left failed, however, due to the CPI's refusal to move into total opposition to the Congress(R). (*The Hindu*, 6 April.) The CPI seeks to utilize parliamentary methods as well as extra-parliamentary devices such as mass struggles, including "bandhs" (moratoriums), "hartals" (strikes), and demonstrations, in achieving its goal.

To help bring about a shift toward the left in India and to simultaneously create a "left and democratic unity," The Ninth Congress in 1971 put forth a 27-point "broad program" providing the basis for a mass movement. Among the salient demands of this program were those for nationalization of "monopoly concerns," expansion of the public sector of the economy, radical land reforms, repeal of "repressive laws," great autonomy to the states, abolition of privy purses and privileges for the ex-rulers of princely states, a moratorium on foreign debts, and stronger links with communist countries (not including China).

The CPI has been critical of the ruling Congress(R) party for pursuing "the futile path of capitalistic development" rather than taking the "national democratic path of non-capitalistic development"—which would end "monopolies, landlordism, and imperialist loot." It has called for nationalization of various sectors of the economy (including the 75 "monopoly houses"), radical land reforms, ceilings on property-holdings, minimum "need-based" wage, unemployment insurance, free education up to 14 years of age, and development of close relations with the Soviet Union and other socialist states. (See *YICA, 1974*, pp. 456-57.)

Election Campaigns and Results. The CPI's 1974 electoral hopes were raised by a surprise victory in a January by-election in a traditionally Congress Lok Sabha constituency in Bombay. The winning candidate (S. A. Dange's daughter) polled 79,653 to the Jan Sangh candidate's 74,677 and the Congress's 70,851. Party leader Dange interpreted the result as a sign of the readiness of democratic masses to take the country's destinies in their hands. In fact, however, the very low turnout (38 percent of the electorate) provided clear evidence that the CPI victory stemmed not so much from its own appeal as from voter apathy and disgust with the Congress candidate's acceptance of endorsement by the neo-fascist Shiv Sena.

The February legislative elections in four states—including the most populous, Uttar Pradesh (UP)—and the Union Territory of Pondicherry drew widespread attention as a test of Prime Minister Gandhi's continuing popularity in the face of rampant inflation and spreading disillusionment over official corruption. A defeat for the ruling Congress party—especially in UP, where Mrs. Gandhi campaigned vigorously—would have been viewed as a sign of the collapse of the "Indira wave" and Congress's vulnerability in the coming national elections.

In both UP and Orissa the main challengers to Congress came from right-wing national and regional parties. Preferring Congress rule to a rightist victory, the CPI made electoral arrangements with the Congress in four of the five elections—a strategy which probably resulted in larger gains than the CPI could have achieved in isolation. In UP, where Mrs. Gandhi's party won a decisive victory (215 of 425 seats, with 32.2 percent of the vote) and an assembly majority for the first time in 12 years, the CPI's strength rose from 4 seats to 16, though its relative vote (2.4 percent) was lower than it had received in two decades. The four major right-wing parties captured over 47 percent of the votes, but their disunity caused them to capture only 178 seats among them.

In Orissa, Congress fell just short of a majority (with 69 of 147 seats, and 37.5 percent of the vote), while the CPI gained 3 seats, for a total of 7 (and 4.9 percent of the vote). Regional parties dominated the seats in Nagaland, Manipur, and Pondicherry. In the latter territory, the Anna DMK and the CPI, with 12 and 2 seats respectively, formed a minority government in the 30-seat assembly. The government fell, and President's Rule was imposed, within a month after the election.

In both UP and Orissa, the Congress was reportedly resentful of CPI betrayal of electoral arrangements. In the former state, the CPI had been given 22 districts with no Congress candidate (13 of which it won) and permission to challenge a Congress candidate in ten others, but it had unilaterally decided to run candidates in another 10 and supported over a dozen independents, resulting in Congress losses. In neither state did the victorious Congress invite the CPI to join the government, though the latter promised its support to "progressive" socio-economic reforms.

Further strains in the Congress-CPI alliance were evident in West Bengal, where the CPI deputy leader of the joint Progressive Democratic Alliance resigned in February. The Alliance itself, which had existed since 1972, was jettisoned by the CPI in June. The Congress state government, which has its own solid majority, was accused by the CPI of domination by rightists and repressive actions against striking workers. At the same time, however, the Communists, indicating continuing support for the government's "progressive" policies, declared their refusal to join other left parties in whipping up "blind anti-Congressism." (*New Age*, 23 June.)

At the time of the August Presidential election, the CPI made another gesture of simultaneous non-support of the Congress and refusal to join "right reactionaries" and "left adventurists" in open opposition. The Congress candidate, the Moslem former food minister Fakhruddin Ali Ahmed, was assured of victory by the indirect electoral system, featuring weighted voting by the Congress-dominated national parliament and state assemblies. The only other candidate—Tridib Kumar Chaudhury, veteran leader of the tiny leftist Revolutionary Socialist Party—was supported by the Hindu-chauvinist Jana Sangh and the left-wing Socialist Party and CPI(M). A statement issued by the CPI National Council on 11 August blasted the Congress's "shift to the right" in economic policies and its "brutal suppression" of the working class during India's "worst crisis since independence," and refused to give support to Ahmed. Yet at the same time the CPI condemned the effort of "right reaction" to use Chaudhury's campaign to carry on the "counter-revolutionary offensive," and it accused the other leftist parties of playing along with this scheme. (Ibid., 11 August). Thus, CPI electors were directed to abstain in the voting, ensuring an even larger victory margin (765,587 votes, or 80.2 percent) for Ahmed. (Chaudhury received 189,196 votes, or 19.8 percent.)

Attitudes toward the Government. Despite its reluctance (clearly endorsed by the Soviet party) to break completely its ties with the ruling Congress, the CPI engaged in steadily sharper criticism of government policies as the economic crisis of 1974 intensified. At the 23-26 March session of the CPI National Council, a resolution was passed which pointed to the "utter bankruptcy" of the centrist policies of the government. Despite the CPI's pleasure at the defeat of "right-wing" forces in the election, General Secretary Rajeswara Rao warned of a renewed rightist offensive, supported by the "imperialists" and rightist politicians within the Congress, in the face of which the Congress leadership appeared to be retreating. Citing the government's recent de-nationalization of trade in wheat as an example of Congress backsliding, the National Council called for leftist unity in the struggle to defeat the reactionary forces and to compel Congress to take radical steps to alleviate the growing economic misery. Included in the CPI's demands was a call for reconstitution of the central government. (*The Hindu*, Madras, 29 March.)

Such talk alarmed Congress centrists, who attended a seminar the following month "In Defense of Democracy and Socialism." Organized by INTUC, the Congress's trade union affiliate, and attended by Mrs. Gandhi and senior cabinet ministers, the session noted its grave concern over CPI efforts to divide Congress ranks.

The CPI attacks escalated in May as the government took harsh measures to break a national strike by railway workers. For the first time in years, the CPI joined other opposition parties in voting in the Lok Sabha for a censure resolution against the government. With a delay which was probably embarrassing to the CPI, the government incarcerated leaders of its trade union affiliate together with almost 700 union leaders from other parties.

In the wake of the strike, the CPI called a special session of its Central Executive Committee to assess its meaning. The government's "war on working class people," denationalization of coal and the wheat trade, virtual abandonment of the new five-year plan, and growing receptivity to investment by foreign capital were cited by the committee as evidence of a definite shift to the right which had both accentuated the struggle within the Congress and opened new opportunities for strengthening the left-democratic movement. But the solution was not, as the Socialist Party and CPI(M) were urging, an all-out struggle in "blind opposition" to the Congress. (Ibid., 25 May.) It was necessary to draw "progressive Congressmen" into the battle against the rightward shift, and to join with them and other left forces in launching mass movements in favor of government takeover of the grain trade and food distribution system, dehoarding of food stocks, and further nationalization in the economy (*New Age*, 2 June).

In August the party's press issued directives for a month-long "All-India Struggle against Price-rise, Hoarding, Wage Freeze and Victimization of Railwaymen." Focused on the growing food crisis in the wake of the failure of the monsoon, the new campaign reflected the earlier-expressed intention of the CPI to force the government to give up its policy of "surrender to reactionary vested interests." Still, however, the CPI hesitated to engage in an all-out struggle; it reiterated its goal of compelling the CPI(M) and the Socialist Party to give up their collaboration with "reactionary" and "chauvinist" elements and to forge "unity in action of progressive sections inside the Congress and outside" (ibid., 11 August).

The CPI's expressed objective of demarcating its movement from those "conducted by reactionary forces" (who were said to "use the discontent of the people to spread anarchy and chaos" and subvert India's democracy) was an outgrowth of its determined opposition to the growing protest movement headed by the veteran Gandhian leader Jaya Prakash Narayan. This movement grew out of the student-led protests and demonstrations which toppled the blatantly corrupt Congress-majority Patel government in normally conservative Gujarat in March. When Narayan sought to achieve the same end through massive non-violent protests against the similarly inept Congress government of Abdul Ghafoor in the backward, caste-ridden state of Bihar, Mrs. Gandhi took up the challenge as a major test of Congress's ability to hold on to the power it had won at the ballot box. The CPI, though it hailed the "justified discontent and anger" of the people and condemned the Bihar government for creating a situation which "fascist elements" could exploit, stood by Mrs. Gandhi and Ghafoor in resisting the demand for dissolution of the Bihar assembly. As other right- and left-wing opposition parties began to line up behind Narayan—whose vision of a "partyless democracy" seemingly placed him above partisan struggle—the CPI moved to the forefront of the campaign to discredit the aged Gandhian as a counter-revolutionary and to deflect his popular following in a shift to the left. In the CPI's view, India's massive problems could not be solved without "basic changes . . . in the socio-economic set-up, putting our country firmly on the path to national democracy" (ibid., 17 March). But the party's reaction to Narayan's movement showed that it continued to regard mass movements under the control of alleged "reactionaries" as far more dangerous than the continued rule of an admittedly imperfect Congress government. For the CPI's party congress, scheduled to be held in

Uttar Pradesh late in the year, reappraisal of this assessment would undoubtedly constitute a major agenda item.

International Views and Attitudes. CPI leaders in 1974 continued their undeviating support and praise for the Indo-Soviet treaty of 1971, the Soviet campaign for a "system of collective security in Asia," the help rendered by the Soviet Union to India, and the Soviet foreign policy of peaceful coexistence and détente flowing from the "peace program" adopted by the Twenty-fourth Congress of the Communist Party of the Soviet Union (CPSU). In June, on his sixtieth birthday, Rajeswara Rao was presented the Order of Lenin by the Soviets for his "active participation in the struggle for peace, democracy and social progress" and his great contributions in "strengthening friendship between the Soviet and Indian peoples" (*FBIS*, 18 June). Rao took advantage of the occasion to declare the CPI's support for convening a new international meeting of communist and workers' parties.

In October, CPI secretary M. K. Krishnan was received in Moscow by B. N. Ponomarev, CPSU Central Committee secretary in charge of relations with non-ruling parties. In a "warm, friendly atmosphere," the two exchanged views on the situations in their parties and in the international arena, including the need for "further rallying the international communist movement on the basis of Marxism-Leninism and proletarian internationalism." Not surprisingly, the resulting TASS account reported that the two parties had reaffirmed "identity of views on all matters discussed." (Ibid., 8 October.)

A number of high-level visits were also exchanged between the CPI and the ruling parties of Eastern Europe. In April, a delegation of the Polish United Workers Party visited India at the CPI's invitation. In June, CPI secretary Yogindra Sharma traveled for a "fact-finding visit" to the German Democratic Republic. In July, Central Executive Committee member and Kerala chief minister Achuta Menon visited Czechoslovakia for several days. And CPI chairman S. A. Dange, who turned 75 in October, spent 8-28 September in Bulgaria, where he was awarded the Dimitrov Prize by party leader Zhivkov.

The chief foreign targets of CPI polemics continued to be the People's Republic of China and the United States. "Imperialist circles" and "Maoist forces" were said by Rajeswara Rao to be joined in support of "reactionary" and "chauvinist" groups who were engaging in "hackneyed slanderous fabrications" against the Soviet Union (ibid., 8 October).

A pamphlet written by party chairman Dange in May, *What Is Passed over in Silence in Peking*, attacked the Chinese party for departure from the principles of Marxism-Leninism and betrayal of the international movement (ibid., 21 May). An article by CPI secretary N. K. Krishnan blasted China's "expansionist" policies and "subversive" activities aimed against the governments of India and Bangladesh (*Pravda*, 20 September).

The United States drew increasing criticism as the Indian government moved toward closer relations with Washington. A particular target of the CPI was the U.S. plan to expand its naval facility in the Indian Ocean; a 4 September by Rajeswara Rao called on the Indian government to oppose more firmly "the evil designs of U.S. imperialists and their plans to proceed with the expansion of the Diego Garcia base" (*New Age*, 8 September). Also objectionable to the general secretary were U.S. offers to resume concessional food aid to India. Pointing to the danger of "strings" on "imperialist" aid, Rao in October urged the government—to no avail— to refuse to accept the offer. (*Hindustan Times*, New Delhi, 4 October).

*   *   *

The CPI(M). The Communist Party of India (Marxist) claimed a membership of 106,841 at its Ninth Congress in Madurai in mid-1972. More realistically, the party membership is probably between 80,000 and 100,000.

Leadership and Organization. The CPI(M) is led by P. Sundarayya as general secretary and Jyoti Basu as chairman, and by its Politburo (which includes, in addition to the above, B. T. Ranadive, M. Basavapunniah, E. M. S. Namboodiripad, A. K. Gopalan, Promode Das Gupta, Harkishan Singh Surjeet, and P. Ramamurthy), the party Central Committee (31 members), and state secretariats and committees.

The CPI(M) acquired its own trade union federation in May 1970 when a CPI(M)-dominated "All-India Trade Union Conference" created a new organization, the Center of Indian Trade Unions (CITU) and elected B. T. Ranadive and P. Ramamurthy (who were leaders in the undivided AITUC) as its president and general secretary, respectively. In 1971, a new General Council of CITU, consisting of 191 members, was elected at the second conference of the organization, held at Cochin on 18-22 April. The conference confirmed Ranadive and Ramamurthy in their offices and elected seven vice-presidents (Jyoti Basu, Mohammad Ismail, Sudhin Kumar, S. M. Chowdhury, S. Y. Kolhatkar, E. Balanandan, and K. Ramani), four secretaries, a treasurer, and a Working Committee of 32—which was elected by the new General Council. The CITU (with more than 2,000 affiliated unions) probably has a membership of about a million (see *People's Democracy*, 6 May).

The CPI(M) has been somewhat stronger than the CPI in organizing the peasantry. The party's AIKS probably has about a million members, with close to two-thirds of the membership in West Bengal. The leadership includes the Politburo member A. K. Gopalan as president and Central Committee member Harekrishna Konar as general secretary. The CPI(M) also controls an agricultural laborers' union which probably has a membership of about 300,000. The CPI(M)'s former student organization (All-India Student Federation; AISF) was reorganized in December 1970 as the Students' Federation of India.

Domestic Attitudes and Activities. The CPI(M) emerged from the split of the CPI in 1964. Initially it was more militant than its parent organization in supporting armed revolts by workers and peasants, and was oriented toward, but not a partisan of, China. In the first year of its existence it had no agreed-upon ideology. In 1966 the Chinese Communist Party (CCP) attempted unsuccessfully to have at least a strong minority of CPI(M) leadership adopt the Maoist line and break away from the parliamentary tradition of the CPI.

With the adoption in 1967 of the "Madurai line," the CPI(M) assumed an internationally "independent" policy—abandoning its pro-Chinese sentiments and the ramifications of these domestically. It has adopted a stance in recent years which has been "anti-revisionist," "anti-dogmatist," and against "left-wing opportunism."

The CPI(M) has constantly criticized the CPI for the latter's willingness to form coalitions with various "reactionary parties." However, the CPI(M)'s practice in making alliances has not been inflexible; consequently, it has had to face counter-criticism from the CPI on this issue.

The CPI(M)'s long-range goal is the establishment of a "people's democracy" in India. The views and positions of the party with regard to this central concept are still evolving. In the political resolution adopted at the Ninth Congress, the CPI(M) took the position that "the traditional Marxist concept of self-determination by nationalities was not applicable in the Indian context and that in the interests of the working class the unity of the country should be preserved." According to this resolution, the party would oppose secessionist and separatist trends. However, it had deemed that the real threat to unity arose from the increasing centralization of powers by the present Congress government. Thus the party would also support "real autonomy," for all nationalities—aimed at strengthening the unity of the people and based on the party's perception of the voluntary character of the Indian Union: "real equality and autonomy" for various nationalities that have found expression in the form of linguistic states, combined with the party's opposition to centralization and its repudiation of separatism. Clarifying the concept of autonomy further, the political resolution stated that except for defense, currency, foreign affairs, communications, centralized economic planning, and inter-state relations, all subjects should remain within the jurisdiction of the states. In terms of party tactics, the political resolution had proposed the continuation of the "parliamentary path," revival of united fronts, and, for the present, not an armed struggle. Sundarayya, summing up the achievements of the Ninth Congress, stated that the party had overcome threats from "right deviationism and left adventurism from within" and succeeded in projecting to other "left and democratic parties" in the country an "alternative line to the ruling classes." (See *YICA, 1973*, P. 463.)

In the various elections of 1974, the CPI(M) fared less well than did the CPI. Continuation of the party split undoubtedly harms both, yet the two groups have been unable to compromise their differences concerning election tactics. The CPI(M) sought to interpret Mrs. Deshpande's victory in Bombay as a lesson to the CPI that, since the people were emerging from the Congress's spell, the CPI ought to terminate its "alliance" with Mrs. Gandhi's party. But the CPI's refusal to adopt a stand of total opposition and its distaste for the CPI(M)'s occasional willingness to form tactical alliances with the right, which have kept the two parties apart, contributed to the failure of the April "left unity" meeting.

The CPI(M), whose electoral strength is more geographically concentrated than that of the CPI, failed to perform well in the February state elections. In Uttar Pradesh the CPI(M) increased its holdings in the assembly from one to two seats, winning 0.7 percent of the votes. In Orissa it managed to win three seats (with 1.2 percent) and in Pondicherry, one (with 1.2 percent), but it won no seats in Manipur or Nagaland. In the August presidential elections, the CPI(M), finding Congress rule more distasteful than cooperation with rightist parties, broke with the CPI's strategy and joined other opposition parties in supporting the losing candidate, R. K. Chaudhury.

The railway strike and food crisis were, for the CPI(M) like the CPI, major opportunities for demonstrating concern for the plight of the working masses and criticizing the "anti-people" policies of the government. In the former case, the left opposition parties managed to attain a rare degree of anti-government cooperation in parliament and in the streets, but the dismal collapse of the strike movement in the face of harsh government actions was a blow to leftist hopes.

The communist parties were again divided in their responses to the Bihar agitations of Jaya Prakash Narayan. Unlike the CPI, the leaders of the CPI(M) decided, after a meeting with Narayan on 20 September, to throw the party's support behind the anti-government demonstrations in the state.

The revival of Naxalite activities in West Bengal, a CPI(M) stronghold, renewed the internal stresses in the party's unit in that state. In April there were reports that young dissidents in West Bengal—with affinities for Peking—were in ideological revolt against the alleged passivity of the national and state CPI(M) leadership. The party's State Council was said to be engaged in a drive for renewal of memberships as a device for screening out these dissidents. (*Times of India*, Delhi, 18 April).

International Views and Attitudes. The CPI(M) maintains a policy of independence and refuses to be aligned with either the Chinese Communist Party or the CPSU, neither of which has accorded international recognition to it. Since 1967 the party has condemned with equal intensity Chinese "left-sectarianism" and Soviet "revisionism." The party in 1974 centered its efforts on establishing relations with "like-minded" communist parties in Cuba, North Korea, Romania, and North Vietnam. Unlike the CPI, the CPI(M) has not endorsed the Soviet campaign for a new international meeting of communist and workers' parties, and would not be likely to attend one.

The CPI(M) supports close Indo-Soviet relations, but also urges Sino-Indian rapprochement. It has criticized the CPI for "willy-nilly advocating that Soviet aid is a panacea for India's economic crisis" while failing to fight against the "exploiting ruling classes for misusing [such aid] for their narrow partisan interest." (*People's Democracy*, 16 December 1973.)

The CPI(M) has campaigned loudly against warming relations between India and the United States, and it participated in anti-U.S. demonstrations during Secretary of State Kissinger's visit to India in October. The CPI(M) has been far less circumspect than the CPI on the subject of harm to third-world interests arising from closer U.S.-Soviet relations. Like the CPI, the CPI(M) has been vigorous in condemning U.S. plans for expanding the naval facilities on Diego Garcia, though it has also engaged in broader criticism of all superpower naval activity in the Indian Ocean.

*   *   *

The CPI(M-L), or Naxalites. The Communist Party of India (Marxist-Leninist) was formed in 1969. It advocated the organization of peasants for armed struggle to seize power, condemning the CPI as "revisionist" and the CPI(M) "neo-revisionist." The Naxalite violence in rural and urban areas led to the government's armed campaign and strong detention policy against them. Following the death of their leader Charu Mazumdar in July 1972, the imprisonment or detention of most of their leaders, and persistent factionalism within their ranks, the Naxalities have generally been demoralized. The CPI and CPI(M) have campaigned for better treatment in prisons, grant of political status, and release of the Naxalite prisoners. Both parties supported the appeal of Amnesty International in the late summer for an investigation of charges of torture of Naxalites in the jails of West Bengal. The state government, denying the accusations, claimed that only 1,609 Naxalites remain in prison under preventive detention or awaiting trial.

During the year, Naxalite activity (particularly in eastern India) was again on the increase. A new "Lin Piao faction," under the leadership of Mahadev Mukherjee, was reported active in districts near Calcutta (*NYT*, 6 August.)

*   *   *

In May 1974 a new party, the Communist Liberation Front of India, held its founding convention in Kerala. Attended by 150 delegates, mostly former members of the CPI(M), the convention adopted a platform rejecting the parliamentary paty of struggle and elected P. Gangadharan as its secretary. (*The Hindu*, 26 May.)

*   *   *

Publications. The communist parties and groups in India publish dailies, weeklies, and monthlies, issued in English and various vernacular languages. The central organization of the CPI publishes the english weekly *New Age* in New Delhi (1971 circulation 7,500). It also publishes the weekly *Party Life*, in English. In 1973, it started publishing a daily, *Janyug* ("People's Era"), in Hindi; and a journal, *Problems of Peace and Socialism*, in English, in New Delhi. Moreover, it has dailies in five states: two in Kerala, and one each in Andhra Pradesh, West Bengal, Punjab, and Manipur.

The CPI(M)'s central organ is the weekly *People's Democracy*, published in Calcutta, in English (1971 circulation 10,000). The party also publishes dailies in Kerala, West Bengal, and Andhra Pradesh and weeklies in Tamilnadu, Karnataka, West Bengal, Punjab, and Jammu and Kashmir.

The CPI(M-L)'s publications (see *YICA, 1973*, p. 468) have virtually ceased to appear.

Vanderbilt University   Robert H. Donaldson

Indonesia

Communism in Indonesia is confined to small-scale underground and occasionally terrorist activity, the latter mainly in Western Kalimantan (Borneo). The Communist Party of Indonesia (Partai Komunis Indonesia; PKI), formally banned since 1966 in the aftermath of an abortive coup attempt the previous year, is split into two small rival factions. One, also with several score adherents in Moscow and other Central and East European capitals, and with contacts in India, Ceylon, and more recently also in Japan, follows a Soviet orientation in tactical and international political questions. The other faction, with an indeterminate following in Indonesia, but mostly domiciled in People's China and Albania, and more recently reportedly also with contacts in North Vietnam, calls itself the "Delegation" of the Central Committee of the PKI. This faction's principal publication, *Indonesian Tribune*, is published in Tirana, although some editing and writing appears to be done also by Indonesian Maoist exiles in the Chinese capital. Although, since 1966, Indonesian government spokesmen, civil as well as military, have as a matter of policy continued to stress a general threat of communist subversion in the country, there is no evidence that the government of President Suharto is in any danger from the scattered, exiled, or underground communist activity. Since 1972, both the Soviet Union and the People's Republic of China have considerably scaled down erstwhile sharp criticism of the Suharto regime and its domestic anti-communist policies.

History. The PKI is the oldest communist party in Asia, having been organized on 23 May, 1920. The party grew out of the so-called "Indies Social Democratic Association" founded by Dutch Marxists six years previously. Among these Dutch Marxists was Hendrick Sneevliet (Maring) who in the 1920s was active as the Comintern's agent in China. Later, Indonesian Marxists assumed control of the PKI.

Party history consists of three periods of intense activity, all culminating in failed attempts to seize power, followed in turn by underground activity or by efforts at legitimization and rehabilitation. In 1926-27, after extensive infiltration of the budding Indonesian trade union movement, and in the midst of a confused relationship with the Comintern (Third International), whose directives had proved of little practical benefit, the PKI launched its first abortive coup in parts of West Java and West Sumatra. There had been opposition to the coup even within the party leadership itself, and poor planning, as well as the well-coordinated police suppression of the Dutch colonial establishment, swiftly led to failure and the arrest, jailing, and confinement in a West New Guinea concentration camp of several hundreds of cadres and suspected coup participants and sympathizers. A number of party leaders escaped, taking up residence in the U.S.S.R., or acting for the Comintern in Asia.

Not until two months after Indonesians proclaimed their independence of Dutch rule on 17 August 1945, shortly before the formal Japanese surrender that ended the Second World War, was the

PKI legally and openly reorganized. There is no indication that communists in Indonesia during the Japanese Occupation period (1942-45) played any role of significance in the few instances of open resistance, unlike communists in Malaya, the Philippines, and elsewhere in Japanese-occupied Southeast Asia. After 1945, PKI relations with other parties soon polarized even as the fledgling Indonesian republic was struggling for its independence against the Dutch. The Communist Youth Conference in Calcutta, in February 1948, may have contributed to acceptance of a tactic of militancy, as tensions deepened between the communists and the government of President Sukarno over the control or disbanding of para-military communist organizations formed to fight the Dutch. A communist coup attempt on 18 September 1948, by a number of party, front group, and local Army commanders in Madiun, in East Java, was quickly nipped by forces loyal to Sukarno and the party's prestige and fortunes again plummeted, though there was no formal proscription of the PKI.

Under new, younger party leaders, among whom the Sumatran Dipa Nusantara Aidit was the most important, Indonesian communism made a quick, and in some respects even spectacular comeback, skillfully seeking a new legitimacy, disavowing its "coup-ist" past, stressing its national orientation, and skillfully participating in the developing new inter-party national political structure. In Indonesia's first general parliamentary elections, the PKI garnered the fourth largest number of seats and about 16 percent of the popular vote. By allying itself with Sukarno in the latter's complicated power struggle with the Army, and by adjusting party tactics to the Sukarnoist ideology of militant Third World nationalism that seemed to bring Indonesia also into a steadily growing partnership with People's China, Aidit and other party leaders steadily rose in influence. They even obtained minor cabinet posts, but also deepened anti-communist suspicion and resentment, particularly in military and Muslim political circles.

On the night of 30 September 1965, under circumstances that remain controversial and not altogether clear, a number of principal PKI leaders, among them party chairman Aidit, with the aid of Army and Air Force units led by dissident and reportedly "left progressive" officers, and with the support also of several hundreds of the party's women and youth front groups who had covertly been given military training and weapons, attempted yet another coup of Djakarta and nearly simultaneously in parts of Central and East Java. Although there is no agreement as to the precise foreknowledge of or direct or indirect involvement of President Sukarno in the coup attempt, which Indonesians usually referred to as the *Gestapu* affair (from "Gerakan September Tiga Puluh," or Thirty September Movement), some degree of implication came to be widely assumed in various Indonesian circles and also among some foreign commentators on the coup.

Within forty-eight hours, however, *Gestapu* was crushed, largely because of the actions of the commander of the Army's Strategic Reserve, General Suharto. Six top Army generals had been killed by coup assassin units, an event which spurred an accelerating anti-communist fury, in which tens of thousands of communists, suspected sympathizers, and innocents were killed in a wide-ranging purge inspired by the Army, groups of young Muslims, and other party enemies. The PKI was formally banned on 12 March, 1966, and on 5 July the dissemination of Marxist-Leninist ideology was proscribed, and its study confined to an academic context only, by action of the People's Constituent Assembly, the country's highest policy-making body.

Even so, underground communist activity continued, culminating in 1968 in a short-lived communist "Indonesian People's Republic" near Blitar, East Java. The "Republic" was supported by underground party "project committees" on the slopes of the mountains of Central Java, led by second- and third-echelon PKI leaders who had escaped the immediate post-*Gestapu* purges. New waves of arrests followed, including scores of military personnel, among them field and general grade officers accused of complicity in the original *Gestapu* incident.

Since 1966, warnings by high-ranking civilian and military officials, including President Suharto, Sukarno's successor, that communist subversion is continuing to threaten the country have been regular and frequent. Only in Western Kalimantan, however, near the border of the Malaysian state of Sarawak, has guerrilla activity, attributed to roving underground elements of the PKI in league with the Sarawak Communist Organization (see *Malaysia*) continued to be of some significance. There are also frequent reports of attempts to "revive" the party through new front groups in Java. Publications of rival PKI refugee groups in Moscow, Tirana, and Peking, and Indonesian government claims of latent or actual communist dangers, are, for the moment, the principal signs of life of what, until the *Gestapu* incident, was one of the largest if not the largest communist organizational complex in the non-Communist world.

Organization and Tactics. During the past two years there has been no evidence that, whatever the coordinated factional activity among its adherents in exile, the PKI inside Indonesia has any integrated organization or party leadership structure left. The party, now operating in small scattered underground cells, but as close to the surface of normal public life as possible, has had little success since the *Gestapu* affair in infiltrating such favorite targets as trade unions, student and Muslim groups, or the communities of resettled Javanese migrant farmers in southern Sumatra and parts of Sulawesi (Celebes). According to Indonesian Army intelligence sources, the total number of PKI activists and more latent supporters inside the country is estimated at about 4,000.

Indonesian military authorities, interpreting the student riots that broke out in Djakarta in mid-January 1974, during the visit of Japanese premier Kakuei Tanaka, have claimed that "New Left" elements were responsible. This "New Left," though "an organization without structure," is considered by the Indonesian government to be "on the same footing as the Communist Party," and its teachings or activities are therefore prohibited (Antara dispatch, Djakarta, 25 September). Whether or not the "New Left" phenomenon has been accurately assessed by the Indonesian government, it is probable that in university student circles and among youths of the Chinese ethnic minority in Indonesia (numbering some three million), where resentment of past indignities and discriminatory treatment remains alive, there is considerable, if covert, opposition to the policies of the Suharto regime along with some (by no means general) latent sympathy for Marxism and (to an even lesser extent) for a new legitimization of the Radical left, perhaps the PKI. Today there are no indications that the previous underground party structure of "project committees" (*kompros*) and even of a Politburo, or of regularly operating armed gangs of the self-styled Indonesian People's Liberation Army (Laskjar Pembebasan Rakjat Indonesia), still exist. Severe government surveillance, including periodic new arrests of suspected communists, has confined party activity to haphazard, widely dispersed, infiltration of greatly diversified organizations, including sports and religious associations, students, and trade union groups, and interest groups among lower-ranking military personnel.

Principal underground party tactics are first of all to stimulate, through infiltration and covert radicalization and propaganda, such groups and social strata as are dissatisfied, particularly over the government's economic policies. These policies appear to polarize them on the basis of income, as high prices for oil and other mineral exports primarily seem to benefit a corrupt civil and military bureaucracy, while the Indonesian mass remains poverty stricken (cf. William D. Hartley, "Money and Misery," *Wall Street Journal*, 26 February). Second, tactics call for the utilization of public incidents, usually demonstrations or other confrontations with public authority, in which the police or armed forces can be put into a bad light. The so-called Bandung incident of 5 August 1973 (see *YICA, 1974*, pp. 460-61) and the 15 January 1974 demonstration in Djakarta (see below) were instances of the latter and are exploited by the party for their obviously radicalizing value. Indonesian security officials (see below, "Domestic Developments") refer to these tactics as having "organization without form," in which most of the party structure or discipline is absent or invisible and maximum emphasis is placed on agitation and infiltration in separate contexts by individual activists or small groups of cadres. There are, however, no details on how underground party recruitment appears to be taking place, unlike the previous two years when local military commanders in Central Java and West Kalimantan publicly supplied data on covert communist proselytising among youths in their areas.

The extent to which the ideological split between pro-Msocow and pro-Peking PKI factions is affecting communist tactics in Indonesia itself can, at present, only be surmised. In a recent description of the pro-Moscow faction, appearing in the Soviet-oriented *World Marxist Review* (June 1974), it was asserted that, "unlike the Maoists," the adherents of this faction "regard resotration of the party on the principles of Marxism-Leninism and proletarian internationalism as their main task." This must apparently be taken to mean primary emphasis on political rather than armed revolutionary struggle (attributed by the Moscow-oriented group to the Maoist PKI faction) and on restoring the legitimacy of the party. In the same description one also reads that the PKI today "carries on political work among the masses, primarily among the workers and peasants, and strives to organise their struggle against the reactionary military regime and imperialism." In implementation of these objectives the party considers an urgent task to be the formation of a "national unity front" in order to give direction to strikes, demonstrations by students, and manifestations of "peasant unrest," which, it is claimed, are now becoming more frequent and widespread, and are involving more people. The PKI's ultimate objective, according to the same description is the establishment of a "national anti-imperialist, democratic government as the prelude to advancing to socialism." (Ibid.)

Apart from the shadowy operations of the pro-Moscow PKI faction in Indonesia itself, the center of this faction's operations appears to be in Moscow, although in Czechoslovakia and other East European countries, and in India, Ceylon, and Japan, the faction also has its representatives, some of them active in local media. Officially, the pro-Moscow PKI faction calls itself either the "Committee Abroad of the PKI" or explicitly identifies itself with "Marxism-Leninism" (e.g., "the Marxist-Leninists of the PKI"). It is estimated that there are now altogether about 60 persons in the group, comprising former foreign personnel of the Indonesian news agency "Antara" (which was heavily infiltrated by the PKI before the *Gestapu* incident), lesser former Indonesian diplomats who prefer exile, students, and minor PKI cadres who went (or escaped) abroad either before or after the anti-communist purges since 1965. Tomas Sinuraja, a Sumatran, and a minor PKI functionary, who was out of the country at the time of the abortive 1965 coup, has for the past three years been the principal spokesman of the PKI Marxist-Leninists in the Moscow-sponsored international media. During 1973-74 some thirty Indonesian students, who had been residing in Soviet-bloc countries since *Gestapu* and are known to be hostile to the Suharto regime began returning to Indonesia after Djakarta and Moscow had quietly worked out the mechanics of their repatriation, and after the Soviets had begun exerting pressure on the students to repatriate. Moscow's interest in improving its relations with the Suharto government was one reason for this development, and Djakarta's concern to minimize the volume of sharp criticism of the Suharto regime abroad, in deference to Indonesia's credit investments and trading needs, was another. Moscow appears interested in minimizing the significance of the PKI contingent on its soil, in favor of emphasizing the struggle of the party in Indonesia itself. Soviet-oriented communist media in 1973-74 gave much less space to signed statements by Sinuraja than in previous years.

Also in *World Marxist Review* (April), One Sudiman spoke for Indonesia in a discussion by an "international research group" on the function of the Army. According to Sudiman, communists in Indonesia, confronted by a "reactionary military regime" intent on persecuting the Left as well as "all democrats," were attempting to establish a new united national front composed of workers, peasants, and "progressive" bourgeois elements. Such a front would be directed against "anti-popular" elements in the Indonesian armed forces, a tactic that was pursued with some success in the late 1950s when the PKI and "progressive" organizations were able to influence even rightist Army elements to come out against separatist rebels then plaguing the country. The suggested tactic seems to rely on a gradually accelerating momentum of popular opposition to the Suharto government, on which the PKI underground could capitalize.

Comparatively, the Chinese-oriented PKI faction in exile, usually called the "Delegation of the Central Committee of the PKI," maintained the volume of its publicity in 1974, but not so much through the Chinese communist publications and broadcasts destined for foreign consumption as through its own Tirana-based publications.

Like the Moscow-oriented PKI "Marxist Leninist" group, so the Maoist PKI "Delegation" has since 1966 issued self criticisms and programmatic statements. On the occasion of the PKI's fifty-fourth anniversary, 23 May 1974, a lengthy statement was issued over the signature of Jusuf Adji-torop, usually identified as "Chief of the Delegation" of the PKI Central Committee. Adjitorop was a prominent PKI Politburo member before the *Gestapu* affair, with particular responsibility for the party's relationship with the academic and intellectual community. He was in China, reportedly for medical treatment, at the time of the *Gestapu* coup attempt and so escaped the anti-communist purges. The anniversary statement sharply attacked the "Suharto military fascist regime," charging it with transforming the country into a pawn of "U.S. and Japanese imperialism" as a handful of "national renegades," joining hands with "foreign monopolistic capitalists," who indulged themselves in luxurious living while unemployment exceeded "28 million," "social demoralisation" and crime became ever more serious, and dope addiction and problems of starvation were "rampant."

According to Adjitorop, Indonesia under the Suharto regime had become a "lackey" of U.S. "imperialism," supporting the "Lon Nol Traitorous clique" in Cambodia, for example, and, while Indonesia served on the International Commission for Control and Supervision in South Vietnam, slandering and boycotting the "patriotic struggle" of the South Vietnamese and serving the interests of the "puppet Nguyen Van Thieu clique." But, the statement went on, mass struggles were now developing against the Suharto regime, such as the mid-January 1974 demonstrations against the visit of Japan's premier Tanaka. As the "vanguard of the proletariat in Indonesia," the PKI would lead the Indonesian people to "real national liberation and socialism," and all efforts to destroy the party would fail.

Three tasks continued to confront the PKI, according to the statement by Adjitorop. First, the PKI must be built up into a "Marxist-Leninist party free from subjectivism, opportunism, and modern revisionism." Second, the party must advocate the "armed struggle of the people," basic to the "revolutionary struggle for land and against exploitation" and to be carried forward by "the armed peasants under the leadership of the working class." Third, the party must establish the "revolutionary united front" led by the working class and based on the alliance of workers and peasants. Meanwhile, the PKI was faced with a "handful of Indonesian revisionist renegades" who were being "manipulated by the Soviet modern revisionist clique." But the "objective situation" both internationally and within Indonesia was seen as favorable to revolution, and although the "people of the world" were supporting one another in their revolutionary struggle, the Indonesian revolutionaries would "resolutely rely on their own efforts," guided by "Marxism-Leninism-Mao Tse-tung Thought." ("Voice of the Malayan Revolution," clandestine broadcast in Mandarin, to Singapore and Malaysia, 23 May, *FBIS*, 6 June.)

Basic to the "Delegation's" tactics is continuous exposure of the allegedly massive penetration of foreign capital in Indonesia and of the dependence of the Indonesian economy on the U.S. "imperialists." As the principal periodical of the "Delegation" put it recently:

> The total external debts it (i.e., the Suharto government) has accumulated during the past seven years has swelled to U.S. $3,720 million, surpassing by far the $1 billion of total foreign debts incurred by the country over the period of 20 years before the advent to power of the Suharto regime. Of the $2.5 billion of foreign monopoly capital invested in Indonesia (until the end of 1972) in hundreds of mining, agricultural, and light industrial projects, $800 million represents U.S. capital, with Japanese capital holding second place. (*Indonesian Tribune*, Tirana, vol. 7 [1973] no. 3-4, p. 13.)

Concern over allegedly rapacious Japanese business methods and economic expansionism in Indonesia has particularly grown in the publications of the Maoist "Delegation" group:

> A case in point is the Toray Industry, Inc.–a giant textile concern–which has set up half a dozen enterprises in Indonesia. All of them are respectively engaged in specific activities related to textile production. . . . For this purpose they import machines, basic materials and semi-finished products . . . from Japan. Such a system has naturally boosted the already superior competitiveness of Japanese capital over national textile firms, making it easier for them to liquidate the latter. (Ibid., "Growing Japanese Economic Expansionism in Indonesia," vol. 8 [1974], no. 1, pp. 12-13.)

A related theme in the "Delegation's" publications is the skyrocketing jump in the cost of living in Indonesia attributed to "the lack of commodities and production." The "Delegation" continues periodically to affirm its ideological and tactical adhesion to the policies of People's China. The occasion of the Chinese party's Tenth Congress prompted a congratulatory message by Adjitorop on behalf of the "Delegation" group which declared that the congress's achievements were a "tremendous support" to the PKI as well as a means of strengthening the unity of the Chinese party with "fraternal Marxist-Leninist Parties on the basis of Marxism Leninism and proletarian internationalism" (*Peking Review*, 12 October 1973, supplement).

Both the shattered state of domestic Indonesian communism and the political climate in which it operates are revealed to a degree by the continuing problem of political prisoners and of new political arrests. The majority of the 55,000 prisoners estimated to be under detention (Amnesty International, *Annual Report, 1973-1974*, [London, 1974], p. 52) were arrested in the 1965-66 period on grounds of various degrees of involvement in the *Gestapu* affair or in other Communist activities, or for having subversive sympathies. International controversy has continued over the culpability and treatment of the prisoners (*YICA, 1973*, pp. 470-71; and *1974*, pp. 454-55). According to one authoritative U.S. journalist's analysis, there remain 2,500 so-called Class A prisoners, described as hard-core communists, about whom there is sufficient evidence for a trial (a number in this classification have received sentences from between five and ten years), and about 200 trials of this class are held a year (other sources report less than half this number) (Robert Shaplen, "Letter from Indonesia," *The New Yorker*, 1 April 1974, pp. 81-82). There are also at least 26,000 Class B prisoners (probably the actual number is more) who will not be tried because the evidence against them is considered not definite enough but about whose loyalty and past activities, in the present mind of the authorities, there nevertheless exist serious questions. About 10,000 of this class, along with about 4,000 members of their families, have been confined to the small island of Buru, in the Moluccas, eastern Indonesia, where they are presumably working toward their rehabilitation. The remaining 16,000 or more Class B prisoners will probably go to Buru also, or else eventually be released. There is additionally an unspecified "X" group of prisoners, neither A nor B, whose numbers are estimated to range between 7,000 and 15,000. The preliminary investigation of these is said not to have been completed. A final category of Class C prisoners has, according to the government, ceased to exist, all those formerly detained having been released. It may be, however, that an indeterminate number of them have been reclassified in the B or X categories, since relatively few actual releases of prisoners have occurred. (Amnesty International, op. cit., p. 53.)

In Indonesia, as well as abroad, the prisoners (usually called "tapol"–from *tabanan politik*, "political resisters"), have become objects of concern. In October 1974 a spokesman for the "Command for the Restoration of Security and Order" (KOPKAMTIB), which has become sensitive to foreign criticism, even denied that there were any political prisoners at all in Indonesia (since no one was presumably being held for political beliefs) and said that there were, instead, some 35,000 detainees who had been involved in rebellion against the government in connection with the abortive 1965 coup and other disturbances (*FBIS*, 2 October). The presence of the prisoners' colony on Buru has been described by the Indonesian government itself as creating a problem of social interaction between the local, less developed inhabitants of the island and the "tapol people, with their higher intelligence." The government therefore has felt constrained to "accelerate the socialization process of the local people so that they will ... attain a proportional level of civilization and welfare" (Antara dispatch, Ambon, Indonesia, 1 October). Criticism of the existence of prisoners has been particularly vociferous in the Netherlands, and has affected Dutch development assistance to the Suharto government. The Indonesian ambassador to The Hague has stressed that Indonesians, like Netherlanders, were "not happy" about the thousands of prisoners, and stated that "testing" of detainees was under way to determine whether they could be loyal to the country. He added that Indonesia was still experiencing the adverse consequences of the policies of President Sukarno, who allegedly had permitted too many Indonesian youths to study in communist countries, and that these students, when repatriated, were "more like communists than like Indonesians." (*Empat Lima*, Djakarta, 29 August; *Indonesian Current Affairs Translation Service Bulletin*, August, pp. 610-11).

Indonesian officials expressed concern over the "Campaign to Release Indonesian Political Prisoners," in Britain and Australia, reportedly organized by Carmel Suwondo Budiardjo. She has been described by official Indonesian sources as a former political prisoner who was released in November 1971 and who subsequently resumed her British nationality, and further as the wife of a former member of the PKI Central Committee, himself still a prisoner in Indonesia. She allegedly was at one time active in communist party affairs both in Britain and in Indonesia. (*Antara Daily News Bulletin*, 30 August; *Berita Yudha*, Djakarta, 29 August; see also Carmel Budiardjo, "Political Imprisonment in Indonesia," *Bulletin of Concerned Asian Scholars*, April-August 1974, pp. 20-23).

As of 26 April, the military commander of Eastern Indonesia banned foreigners from visiting or residing on Buru Island, and Chinese residents on the island for less than nine years were ordered expelled (*Asia Research Bulletin*, 30 June, p. 2803). This measure has only aggravated suspicions, and has tended to negate the value of earlier Indonesian assurances given to the Dutch Ministry of Foreign Affairs that the Indonesian Red Cross would be ready to provide information to the Dutch government on the status of the prisoners (*De Volkskrant*, Amsterdam, 28 January).

On 14 June the British newspaper *The Guardian* carried a report alleging that large numbers of Indonesian political prisoners were being sent from prison camps to distant labor gangs. This was denied by a spokesman for the government's security command (KOPKAMTIB), who added that, contrary to reports, no prisoners were being used in foreign-financed development projects, like the Japanese-financed cement plant, in Tjilatjap, Central Java (*FBIS*, 28 June). In December 1973, Amnesty International expressed its concern to the Indonesian government over reports of serious malnutrition and even deaths of starvation among prisoners. In April and May 1974, reports that prisoners were being sent to agricultural labor projects in Central Java prompted a new Amnesty International protest that the relocation of these detainees "represented a new and more permanent form of detention for these prisoners," none of whom had as yet been either tried or convicted (Amnesty International, op. cit., p. 53). By mid-October the government changed the name of the *Tempat Pemanfaatan* (political indoctrination center) on Buru Island to *Instalasi Rehabilitasi* (rehabilitation center) and called on the country to stop using the term *tapol*, in favor of the word "detainees" (Antara dispatch, Djakarta, 14 October).

Domestic Developments. During 1974 the Suharto government continued its policy of calling attention to the threat of internal communist subversion, linking such opposition to various expressions of public discontent. The exact nature of the threat, or its organizational context, apart from the West Kalimantan terrorist problem, was rarely defined. For instance, late in 1973 the minister of information, after a cabinet discussion of national security problems, declared that the "conspiring activities" still being conducted by "Communist remnants" were carried forward by "organisations of no form" (*Jakarta Times*, 28 November). That is, highly fluid, virtually structureless tactics of penetration and exploitation of public grievances were used. On 26 November 1973 the deputy commander of KOPKAMTIB, in a hurriedly called press conference, appealed to all segments of Indonesian society to "refrain from creating conditions which the communist remnants could easily exploit for their political ends," an exhortation which in some editorial circles was taken primarily as a warning to restive and protesting students in the capital (cf. editorial, "A Latent Danger," ibid.). He defined the communist remnants' alleged tactic of "organization without form" (*Organisasi Tanpa Bentuk*, or OTB) as akin to application of the "iceberg theory," in which "one-tenth of the PKI membership is visible, while nine-tenths of it operates secretly." The PKI was engaged in creating and enhancing "contradictions" in society. As instances he named the anti-Chinese riots in Bandung, on 5 August 1973 (*YICA, 1974*, pp. 460-61)—an incident which the Indonesian minister of defense and security affairs, General Maraden Panggabean, had already termed as "engineered by Gestapu-PKI remnants" (*Pedoman*, Djakarta, 20 September)—and various subsequent acts of "sabotage," such as damage to sugar kilns in Central and East Java and a fire in Tanjungpriok harbor (ibid., 28 November).

In the last few months of 1973 there was a steady drumfire of official warnings about the dangers of communist infiltration (e.g., the military commander in West Java, on 30 October warned against "communist infiltration of government and private universities": a warning echoed on 9 November by the commanding officer of the Armed Forces Academy), and reports of newly discovered nests of elements of the PKI (on 6 November it was reported that some 500 employees of state-owned pawnships had been dismissed "for having been members" of the PKI or of PKI fronts, while 450 employees of the state-owned pharmaceutical company Kimia Farma were dismissed for the same reason, and on 3 November, the military commander in the central Celebes was reported as saying that no less than "29,000 communists" were still being sought in his area) (*FBIS*, 30 October, 7, 16 November).

Around the turn of 1973 there were also continuing reports of new arrests and trials of old alleged PKI figures. In Sambas, West Kalimantan (Borneo), in early October, three "leaders of the underground PKI" were arrested after local villages engaged in an intensive coordinated search of the area called "Operation *pagar betis*" (human fence), while later that month the arrest was announced of 31 suspected "communist infiltrators" in Jayapura, capital of Irian Jaya (West New Guinea). In mid-February 1974, an intelligence unit of the South Sulawesi (Celebes) military command reportedly uncovered undefined "activities" of PKI "remnants," and the arrest of four alleged "remnant" leaders was announced. Earlier, the killing of PKI West Kalimantan leader S. A. Sofjan on 12 January by a special KOPKAMTIB unit in a clash near the town of Pontianak had merited a report by TASS (ibid., 16 January). Meanwhile there were the trials and sentencing of such PKI figures as Djadi Wirosubroto (former chairman of the PKI's principal Peasants' Front, the Barisan Tani Indonesia or BTI); Tati Hartati, the party's former women's leader in West Java; and Suhadi, one of the PKI's principal leaders in the Riau Islands, who was accused of aiding figutive communists after the failure of the *Gestapu* coup in attempts to rebuild the party in the Riau area. (Ibid., 15, 25, 30 October, 16 November 1973, 3 November 1974, 15, 16, 29 January, 1, 15 February 1974.)

Dahlan Rivai, alleged PKI activist in West Java, was given a life prison sentence in a Bandung, West Java, court on 2 April for having spread "false rumors" about an Army generals' plot against the state on the eve of the *Gestapu* coup. Bahrum Muin was given a life sentence in a Medan, Sumatra, court on 11 July for making contact with "underground subversive militants" in a coup attempt. Also in Medan, at about the same time, the former PKI Medan secretary received a life sentence for alleged involvement in the *Gestapu* coup affair. (Ibid., 12 April, 12 July.)

Most of these trials provided little new insight into past and present PKI tactics. Of more than passing interest, however, was the trial of Ruslan Widjojosastro, described as the chairman of the PKI

Central Committee during the revival of PKI activities in the Blitar area of East Java around the middle of 1967. During the course of the trial, which began on 2 May, the prosecution provided considerable detail about the extent to which top PKI leaders, two days before the 30 September 1965 coup, were given instructions by Politburo member Sudisman for the purpose of implementing the planned coup in various parts of Indonesia. Other details were provided on the course of PKI tactics after the party was formally banned in March 1966, particularly the underground struggle in East Java. (*Berita Buana*, Djakarta, 3 May; *Indonesian Current Affairs Translation Service Bulletin*, Djakarta, May, pp. 363-65.)

The effect of all these developments on Indonesian public opinion can only be surmised. There appeared to be some skepticism in public circles that the threat posed by continuing communist subversion was as serious as official warnings and arrests would suggest; on the other hand, there could be little question of persistent underground PKI activity in the country as a whole and of its interaction with the developing dynamics of political criticism and opposition to the Suharto regime— as, among students and some intellectuals. Often the sequence of government revelations about alleged communist activity was contradictory and confusing, buttressing charges that the Suharto regime was counting on a "Red scare" tactic to maintain itself in power. An example would be the official announcements about the communist problem in West Kalimantan. In mid-February the West Kalimantan military commander, Lieutenant General Widodo, reportedly announced categorically that the "entire organization and leaders of the underground communist movement in West Kalimantan" had been eliminated, in consequence of the killing of PKI regional leader Sofjan and his cohorts a few days earlier. Subsequent weeks, however, brought reports of continuing security operations against communist guerrillas in the Sarawak and Sabah border areas and of the elimination of various "subversive organizations," such as a "Front for the Independence of North Kalimantan" which was not further identified. In mid-April and again in mid-June 1974 military spokesmen in West Kalimantan still maintained that with the killing of Sofjan there was no longer any link in the chain activating communist terrorists in West Kalimantan," and that Indonesian West Kalimantan was now "free of communist activities." (*FBIS*, 26 February, 13 March, 9 April; *Sarawak Tribune*, Kuching, 14 June; *Indonesian Current Affairs Translation Service Bulletin*, April p. 262.)

By the middle of July Widodo seemed to be retreating from his earlier confidence. After joint Indonesian-Malaysian military discussions on the Sarawak-Kalimantan border problem, Widodo reportedly declared that Indonesia was now intensifying its operations against the "remaining few terrorists" still operating along the border. The threat along the border was "always present," it was now conceded, although Widodo added that "almost all" communist underground elements had been destroyed "on our side." (*FBIS*, 19 July.) On 22 August an official report on the settlement of new migrants in West Kalimantan (as part of the security stabilization efforts of the government) declared that the settlers would go to a "security belt" where large numbers of security troops had been stationed to fight "communist rebels in the border areas" (*Antara Daily News Bulletin*, 22 August).

Meanwhile, in North Sumatra the commander of the Bukit Barisan military command declared that although "practically all" communist activity had been banned or destroyed, community alertness should be maintained, because communist tactics "never changed," including the "playing off of one group against another" (Antara dispatch, Medan, 24 June). Presumably he was speaking generally about the situation in the entire country. On 8 May, armed forces sources in Djakarta announced that an "all out" military offensive had been launched by government forces against "communist remnants" in central and southern Sulawesi (Celebes), the military commander of the area declaring that communists were still "active" and existed "within the ranks of the military and civilian authorities" (*FBIS*, 8 May.) By early August, KOPKAMTIB commander Admiral Sudomo, after a conference with President Suharto, announced that a network of underground PKI activists had been discovered in Ngawi, East Java, and in Kendall, Central Java. Ten former Class C prisoners who had been released from detention earlier, had been rearrested, Sudomo said, because they had admitted to having committed robberies following their release in order to raise funds with which to revive the PKI. (Radio Djakarta, domestic service, 5 August [*FBIS*, 6 August].) Later reports by police indicated that in the attempted revival effort of the PKI in Ngawi, eighteen suspects, including a former member of the armed forces, had been arrested; they had been engaged in robberies, presumably to finance the local communist underground.

As was the case in the past five years, purges within the Indonesian armed forces themselves continued in 1974. Defense minister Panggabean said at the close of June, that during the nation's first five-year development plan, recently ended, the Indonesian Navy had successfully cleared itself of communist and *Gestapu* affair "remnants." In early August a similar claim was made for the armed forces as a whole by the then second territorial defense commander for Java and Madura, Lieutenant General Widodo, who said that purges had also taken place within "the ministries and social organizations," presumably connected with the armed forces establishment. Trials of former military personnel accused of communist activity and/or *Gestapu* involvement underscored a problem which the Indonesian government seemed loath to discuss, namely the extent to which members of the Indonesian armed forces had been involved in the 30 September 1965 coup attempt and in alleged PKI activity before and since. Skepticism about the exact nature of alleged military complicity in communist activity has seemed to some observers as justified as that about such alleged activity by civilians.

Taking a leaf from the policies of the Marcos regime in the Philippines, Indonesia in the middle of 1974 embarked on a policy of rounding up unauthorized firearms, presumably in the context of general anti-subversion efforts. Between 18 July and 18 August, KOPKAMTIB commander Sudomo announced, 170 firearms were confiscated. It was not disclosed where the weapons had been found; security was said, however, to have been "improved" as a result of "frequent" raids for weapons conducted by the armed forces (Antara dispatch, Djakarta, 12 September.)

By far the most troubling single event in the context of the Suharto government's security concerns were the violent student demonstrations in Djakarta against visiting Japanese premier Kakuei Tanaka in mid-January. For weeks before the visit there had been anti-Japanese unrest among students. Toward the close of November 1973, hundreds of them demonstrated in front of the Japanese Embassy, staging a mock play, reciting satirical poems, and giving vent generally to anger about the allegedly nefarious influence of Japanese capital, said to be in league with corrupt Indonesian officials. The Embassy, Japan's officials, and Japan itself clearly were becoming a common symbol in the minds of youths of all the things wrong with the Suharto regime, from rising prices to the unequal benefits and other dangers flowing from the government's economic policies, particularly from its accommodation of foreign capital. In mid-November, editorials warned the Suharto government to mend its ways lest an "undesired event" result (editorial, "What Goes Wrong" *Jakarta Times*, 14 November, also 26, 27 November, and 1 December 1973; *NYT*, 2 January 1974). Mixed with the students' criticisms of the economy were attacks on the Suharto government's allegedly repressive political policies. In a public petition addressed to the government on 24 October 1973, University of Indonesia students had asked for an end to "legal uncertainty and legal violations" as well as an end to "abuse of power" and "rampant corruption" by and among those in authority.

Tanaka's visits to other Southeast Asian capitals had been marred by student demonstrations, and his arrival in Djakarta led to similar outbursts on 15 January 1974, as students made street bonfires out of Japanese cars, motorcycles, and other products; vandalized Japanese business offices; and engaged police in bloody clashes. By the end of the following day the rioting had led to at least 13 dead and 49 wounded. Some 200 persons were arrested, among them a principal student leader, Hariman Siregar; university lecturers; and prominent civil rights spokesmen. (*De Volkskrant*, 18 January; *Jakarta Times*, 19 January).

As arrests continued in subsequent weeks, government spokesmen publicly mooted communist instigation of the riots and asserted that non-students as well as armed forces personnel were among those recently detained (*Antara Daily News Bulletin*, 6 February). Further, government reaction to the riots had ranged from a ban on all political activities in the universities and new measures (announced on 24 January) to give a greater share to ethnic Indonesians in the operations of foreign business enterprises, to the removal from office by President Suharto of his four personal assistants (*Aspris*), all of them high-ranking generals who had long been targets of student criticism (*Asia Research Bulletin*, 28 February pp. 2449-50). Seeming government sensitivity to the students' criticism of government policies that preceded the mid-January riots came to be intertwined, however, with political infighting and power plays in the president's own circle of confidants and among the major political interest groups. New warnings were issued by military and other spokesmen that the riots had been "master-minded" by "remnants" of the Socialist and Masjumi parties (anti-communist groups banned by the Sukarno regime more than a decade before) (*FBIS*, 21 March). According to defense minister Panggabean, an investigation of the 15 January riots revealed that "in addition" to "subversive movements" directed by the PKI, "another movement" supported by "some elements of political parties" (not further defined) had attempted to topple the Suharto government (*Antara Daily News Bulletin*, 16 February).

By mid-February KOPKAMTIB commander Sudomo was able to reveal preliminary results of the government's investigation of the riots. Eventually a total of 820 persons had been arrested, among them four members of parliament, but 778 had already been released, though a number of these were required to report to police daily. The riot, said Sudomo, was designed to implement "well prepared and coordinated plans" by a group of people "dedicated to the concept of socialism" and ready to use "radical means" to replace the government; this clearly indicated "subversion" within the meaning of the 1963 anti-subversion law. Long before the incident, according to Sudomo, preparations had been under way to create "opposition" and stir up "controversies" in economic, social, and cultural life and over the role of the armed forces. (*Antara Daily News Bulletin*, 26 February; *FBIS*, 22 February.)

Indonesian officials also disclosed that "underground leaflets" attacking the government were being circulated in Djakarta, and that "false rumors" were being disseminated (Reuter's dispatch, Djakarta, 6 February). Shortly, President Suharto even felt it necessary to warn against coup attempts, declaring that those threatening the safety of the nation were now not only remaining members of the PKI but also "other social forces" (not further defined) who were allegedly undermining the state (Antara dispatch, Djakarta, 21 February). In May, Suharto announced that the government did not consider the "subversive activities" connected with the 15 January riots to have ended, and that "people in general should remain alert." Suharto noted in this connection not only the domestic dissemination of what he called "blackmail circulars" designed to put the government in a bad light, but also adverse press accounts abroad about the Indonesian government. The latter, he said, had been inspired by "certain elements at home." (*Antara Daily News Bulletin*, 7 May.) Military commanders like Army chief of staff General Surono stressed that national development and maintenance of security were inseparable, and warned against "subversive elements" (not further defined) who were trying to disturb conditions, also from abroad (Antara dispatch, Djakarta, 7 May).

On 8 July the attorney-general forewarded the dossiers of three alleged leaders of the January riots to the courts for trial. But the subsequent trial of Hariman Siregar on the capital charge of planned "subversion," within the meaning of the anti-subversion law, was soon overshadowed by widespread public speculation that the January riots either had occurred spontaneously without "planning" or had in fact been "engineered by men engaged in a power struggle within the government" itself (*Far Eastern Economic Review*, 16 August). Certainly the Siregar trial, and the projected trials of a businessman and a member of parliament on similar charges, did not enhance the government's credibility, particularly in respect to its persistent claims of continuing threats of subversion.

The deeper causes of the disquiet among students, intellectuals, and even among some parliamentary deputies of the government party have been reported to lie in the continuing polarization of wealth, the prevalence of corruption in the restrictions on the press and on dissenting political opinions (see, e.g., *NYT*, 22, 27 January; *Wall Street Journal*, 26 February) and the planned "stricter regulations within the universities" (Antara dispatch, Djakarta, 30 January)—not easily to be dismissed by official denunciations of and vaguely formulated prohibitions against what government spokesmen call the "New Left movement" in the country (ibid., 25 September).

International Aspects. Indonesia professed to be unmoved officially by the Sino-Malaysian mutual diplomatic recognition at the end of May 1974, or by the announcements of impending Sino-Philippine mutual diplomatic exchanges in September. Indonesia reportedly had warned Malaysia before the May diplomatic exchange with China about the dangers inherent in such a move (*Sarawak Tribune*, Kuching, 26 July; *South China Morning Post*, Hong Kong, 23 July). In early October, Indonesian foreign minister Adam Malik declared that although he had met with the Chinese representative at the United Nations in New York, there had been no progress in restoring normal relations with Peking. Sino-Indonesian diplomatic relations, though not formally broken, were suspended in 1967, in the aftermath of rising hostility between the two governments stemming from official Indonesian suspicion of Chinese involvement in the 1965 coup attempt and from the treatment of the Chinese minority in Indonesia. Over the years Indonesia has given various explanations why it does not wish to normalize its relations with People's China (it has no diplomatic relations with Taiwan), among them a claim that time will be needed to educate the Chinese minority to be loyal to the Indonesian Republic and a demand that Peking stop its anti-Suharto propaganda in its media.

According to a prominent Indonesian parliamentary deputy, Imron Rosjadi, chairman of the parliament's Foreign Affairs Committee, impending Sino-Philippine mutual diplomatic recognition would not have an immediate effect on Indonesia, because Indonesia "wants to maintain its internal security and stability in order to be able to concentrate on the implementation of its national development plans" (*Antara Daily News Bulletin*, 12 October). The statement reflects a fear allegedly found in particular in upper Indonesian military, Muslim, and business circles that normalization of diplomatic relations with Peking would intensify the danger of a "fifth column" of Chinese residents and their Indonesian allies, or else strengthen Chinese business interests in Indonesia at the expense of Indonesian merchants.

Such concerns are amplified and, presumably, legitimized by official reports of alleged ongoing Chinese subversive burrowing in Indonesia. The spokesman for the First Defense Territorial Command in Medan, Northeast Sumatra, warned the local population in February 1974 against Chinese Indonesians who had gone to China recently and then returned illegally to Indonesia; returning Chinese youths were believed to have had cadre training in China and to be assisting in the revival of the PKI (*FBIS*, 2 February). Other military information officers seem to make it a point to reveal the ethnic Chinese identity of guerrillas in West Kalimantan. In June, Indonesian immigration officials announced that a total of 170 illegal Chinese immigrants had been arrested during the first four months of the year. Most of those detained had been arrested for "suspected subversive activities" and alleged involvement in illegal drug trafficking. The majority of the arrested, it was further disclosed, were Chinese who had left Indonesia eight years ago when the Indonesian government tightened citizenship laws and restrictions on the residence of Chinese in rural areas. Immigration officials also expressed concern over the recent influx of illegal Chinese immigrants from Portuguese Timor following the announcement of de-colonialization policies by the new Portuguese government. (Ibid., 7 June.)

In August, it was reported from North Sumatra that during the trial of a local underground PKI leader the existence of an underground "Chinese communist ring" had been revealed. An unspecified number of Chinese in the Karo area of North Sumatra were arrested in connection with the alleged ring, among them two Chinese who claimed to be members of the Chinese People's Liberation Army and who had helped the PKI leader in reviving the party. The incident took another turn when, as the arrested Chinese were being transported to Medan, the provincial capital, five other Chinese in a jeep overtook the convoy of prisoners and attempted to rescue them, without success. (Ibid., 30 August; *Free China Weekly*, Taipei, 8 September.) Fear of illegal Chinese activity had lead earlier to a recommendation by one North Sumatran politician that all telephone communications in Chinese be prohibited, and that, also in order to accelerate their integration into the Indonesian environment, all Chinese speak only in the Indonesian language when using the telephone (*FBIS*, 29 November).

Despite the frozen state of diplomatic relations and the climate of suspicion and hostility, Sino-Indonesian trade has continued, although the balance of such trade heavily favors Peking and there is no confidence that diplomatic normalization would necessarily benefit Indonesia, given the limited range of Peking's export products. Chinese exports to Indonesia grew from U.S. $27.6 million in 1971 to $54.7 million in 1973, and in the first five months of 1974 had already reached $106.2 million (*Far Eastern Economic Review*, 4 October). Official trade statistics show no Indonesian exports destined for People's China.

Relations with the U.S.S.R., also strained in the post-*Gestapu* period, have comparatively improved much more, although diplomatic ties were never suspended, as was the case with China. The December 1973 visit of the late Ekatrina A. Furtseva, Soviet minister for culture and the highest Russian official to come to Djakarta since the 1965 coup attempt, marked a new high in the slowly improving diplomatic climate between the two countries (Justus M. van der Kroef, "Recent Trends in Indonesian-Soviet Relations," *Pacific Community*, Tokyo, July 1974, pp. 590-613). Still, official Indonesian suspicions that the U.S.S.R. has been covertly attempting to rebuild the PKI—and particularly the reported dissemination of Soviet propaganda in Central Java, where communist remnants have been active—have tended to freeze economic cooperation (*FBIS*, 9 October).

Improvement of Soviet-Indonesian trade relations is further impeded by the huge Indonesian debt, now estimated at $500 million, still owed the Russians from the days of the Sukarno era, and by Russian criticism of the Western-oriented investment policies of the Suharto government. Soviet commentators have warned that reliance on "large-scale foreign capital investments" from the United States and "other capitalist countries" will not accomplish necessary developments projects in Indonesia; but they also note that recently there has been a "growing tendency" toward "expanding cooperation" between Indonesia and the "socialist countries," and that improving relations with the U.S.S.R. "would at least give Indonesia more room to maneuver" (*Current Digest of the Soviet Press*, 13 March). Soviet press comment is also relatively mildly critical of the Suharto government's domestic anti-communist policies.

The Soviets appear to see possibilities in Indonesia's proclaimed independence in foreign policy. Moscow media quoted with approval an Indonesian press comment criticizing the continuation of SEATO as standing in the way of "the struggle of Asian nations to free themselves from colonial domination and to determine their own future." Soviet reaction to this comment (which is not typical of most Djakarta press or official Indonesian views on the matter) included the observation that "Indonesia also wishes to expand its relations with the Soviet Union and other socialist countries," and that for its part the U.S.S.R. was ready to "broaden and strengthen its relations with developing countries" (Radio Moscow, in Indonesian, 17 September [*FBIS*, 19 September]).

In mid-March, Indonesian foreign minister Malik reviewed relations with the U.S.S.R. He said that generally speaking there were "no big problems" between the two countries, and quoted Soviet deputy foreign minister Nikolai P. Firyubin as saying that the U.S.S.R. "would always be prepared to aid Indonesia in its development efforts" (Antara dispatch, Djakarta, 16 March). Malik also claimed that the Soviet official respected Indonesia's position on a twelve-mile territorial waters limit, a matter of earlier controversy. As for the Soviet "collective security" concept for Asia introduced by Soviet party secretary Leonid Brezhnev five years ago, Malik said that Indonesia would not want to reject the Russian position, but felt that more time was needed to study the matter. On 23 March a new Indonesian-Soviet trade agreement was signed in Djakarta, under which Indonesian rubber, pepper, copra, and leather goods would be traded for Soviet cement, road-building equipment, chemicals, optical instruments, and machinery. Visiting Soviet deputy minister for trade I. T. Grishin declared that the U.S.S.R. by using 300,000 tons annually of natural rubber was the world's biggest consumer of that commodity, and that Indonesia could supply larger quantities to Russia than in the past.

The new trade agreement was followed by Indonesian efforts to cement relations with the East European countries generally, not least in order to offset (*a*) growing ASEAN-Chinese diplomatic and commercial interaction and (*b*) continuing domestic criticisms of the Suharto government's reliance on Western and Japanese development capital. In the first two weeks of July, Malik briefly visited several East European countries, and the Indonesian minister for research declared that Rumania, Hungary, and Poland had all indicated a willingness to cooperate more closely with Indonesia in science and technology. The Soviet chargé in Djakarta somewhat earlier had emphasized that conditions of Soviet aid for Indonesia "had always been more favorable" for the Djakarta government than aid from other countries. (Ibid., 20 June, 13 July.) By December a new Soviet-Indonesian agreement was expected to be formalized, specifying Soviet assistance for Indonesia's second national development plan, now under way.

It has been speculated that Indonesia's "opening to East Europe" may be connected with new difficulties for the Suharto regime in acquiring a continuing flow of credits from the IGGI (Intergovernmental Group on Indonesia), the international consortium of major Western powers and Japan which has been underwriting the country's development effort with credits and other assistance amounting to nearly $5 billion in recent years. In May there had been reports that the Indonesian delegation at the IGGI conference in the Netherlands was informed that IGGI would reduce its aid to Indonesia because of the latter's growing economic stability (*Straits Times*, Singapore, 11 June).

However, political considerations appear to have been significant also in the Suharto government's search for a new rapprochement with East European countries. While Malik before leaving for Eastern Europe had stressed the economic prospects opened by the trip (e.g., he hoped for Polish and Yugoslav assistance in the development of dockhards—Antara dispatch, Djakarta, 3 July), the agreement signed between Poland and Indonesia at the end of Malik's official visit to Warsaw was noteworthy for its political clauses and its few specifics on the "intensification" of economic cooperation, such as a proposed civil air transport agreement. Support for Soviet-U.S. détente, for the recent Nixon-Brezhnev talks, for "preservation and consolidation of world peace and security of all nations," for peaceful coexistence between states with different "social systems," for limitations of arms and the prevention of nuclear war, for compliance by all sides with the Paris accords on Vietnam, for the withdrawal of Israel from all occupied Arab lands, and for a "prompt and peaceful settlement" of the problems of Cambodia—all these gave a rather distinctive character to what official Indonesian news sources kept calling the "trade agreement" (ibid., Warsaw, 12 July).

How successful the Suharto government's East European gambit will be remains to be seen; the same powerful military and religious circles in domestic Indonesian politics that oppose a normalization of relations with China remain only a little less hostile to a warming of Soviet-Indonesian relations. Criticism in Indonesian Muslim circles of the plight of Islamic minorities in the U.S.S.R. and alleged distortions and errors concerning the Prophet Muhammad and Islamic doctrine in Soviet books have long been obstacles to an improvement in relations between Djakarta and Moscow. In this context it was noteworthy that on 17 July the Indonesian religious affairs minister, Mukti Ali (traditionally an official who has been acceptable to the most orthodox and politically conservative Muslim religious leaders in Indonesia), left for a visit to the U.S.S.R. at the invitation of the Great Mufti for southern and central asia, Daankhanov, and of the Soviet government. Ali and two Indonesian Muslim scholars visited Uzbekistan, Kazakhstan, and Azerbaidjan, and upon their return spoke graciously but in cautiously general terms about the conditions of the Muslim community they had observed. Additional Indonesian ulamas (Islamic scholars of the writ) have been invited for an "orientation tour" of the U.S.S.R.

Regular conferences were held between Indonesian and Malaysian military officials on conditions along the Sarawak-Indonesian border in Kalimantan (Borneo) in an effort to stamp out lingering communist guerrilla activity. At the close of May, "joint security operations" conducted in the border area were reported to have made "considerable progress" (*FBIS*, 31 May).

The announced "de-colonization" of its overseas empire by the new Portuguese government resulted in political stirrings in Portuguese Timor that are of growing concern to Djakarta, since Indonesia controls the western half of Timor Island. Early speculation that Eastern (Portuguese) Timor would seek union with Indonesia was later qualified by the activity of a local Portuguese Timor independence movement. At the close of September the Indonesian daily *Berita Yudha*, a medium of the Indonesian armed forces, reported that four Chinese residents in the town of Dili (Portuguese Timor), all of them allegedly nationals of People's China, had been stirring up anti-Indonesian and pro-independence demonstrations on behalf of the Frentili Party, which seeks a free Portuguese Timor. The Apodeti Party in Portuguese Timor, however, is pro-Indonesian. (*FBIS*, 27 September.) Official concern is rising in Indonesia that polarizations of political opinion in Portuguese Timor, aided by communist agitation, may eventually create a serious security problem on the country's doorstep, including communist infiltration into Indonesia by Peking-oriented Chinese in Eastern Timor.

Publications. PKI factions and underground groups inside Indonesia lack regularly appearing publications, nor can they rely (as Burmese, Thai, and Malaysian communists can) on a friendly, if clandestine, radio transmitter. Since 1971 there have been no issues of *Mimbar Rakjat* ("People's Forum"), at one time the principel regular PKI underground publication. In West Kalimantan differently titled and signed mimeographed leaflets continue to appear; some of these, like *Front Rakjat* ("People's Front") attempt to give the appearance that they are the sole, authoritative media of the local communist underground. The Soviet-oriented "Marxist Leninist" group of PKI exiles has relied particularly on the Prague-based *World Marxist Review* and *Information Bulletin* in the past, but during 1974 there was a drop in the space accorded this group as compared with previous years. *Tekad Rakjat* ("People's Will") has been the Moscow-oriented faction's principal remaining publication, but in 1974, as in the previous year, its appearances were quite irregular.

In contrast, the PKI Maoist faction in exile, the "Delegation of the Central Committee of the PKI," continues to publish its Tirana-based journal, *Indonesian Tribune*, five or six times a year. The Maoist faction's student and youth publication, *API* (*Api Pemuda Indonesia*—"The Fire of Indonesian Youth"), also issued from Tirana, now appears only once or twice a year. The Peking-based *Suara Rakjat Indonesia* ("Voice of the Indonesian People"), issued by the "Indonesian Organization for Afro-Asian Solidarity," also headquartered in the Chinese capital, is published infrequently. Coverage in the Soviet and Chinese media of the positions and statements of the rival PKI factions in exile has dropped notably in the past two years.

University of Bridgeport

Justus M. van der Kroef

Japan

The Japan Communist Party (JCP) was founded in 1922 and its activities were carried out until the end of World War II. Permitted by order of General MacArthur to organize openly in 1945, the party grew rapidly and managed in 1949 to elect 35 members to the House of Representatives. However, condemnation by the Cominform in 1950 and a series of "red purges" carried out by Allied Occupation authorities resulted in defeat for all JCP candidates in the elections of 1952 and reduction of the party's popular vote from 9.7 percent in 1949 to 2.5 percent in 1952. In 1955 the party was reorganized and under a policy of "power through parliamentary means" it began a steady ascent in membership and seats in the Diet.

Party membership was estimated in 1974 to be 330,000. This total was slightly under that of November 1973, the date of the Twelfth Congress. Membership expansion campaigns were not particularly successful, and party authorities have been prudent in expelling members for infractions of rules and regulations, treating each case individually rather than carrying out automatic separations. The circulation of *Akahata* ("Red Flag"), the JCP's principal organ, kept its 1973 level of 600,000 for the daily and 2,200,000 for the Sunday edition until 1 September, when the price was raised and it is believed that the circulation dropped somewhat.

Japan's population was reported by the Statistics Bureau of the Prime Minister's office to have reached 110 million by 28 September 1974, a gain of 2 million over 1973, making the country the sixth most populous in the world after China, India, the Soviet Union, the United States, and Indonesia.

Parliamentary Strength. As a result of the July 1974 elections, the JCP increased its seats in the (upper) House of Councillors from 11 to 20 (out of 252). With 38 seats (out of 491) in the House of Representatives won in the election of December 1972, the party now holds a total of 58 seats in the two houses of the Diet, or parliament. The JCP is the third party in each house, after the Liberal Democratic Party (LDP) and the Japan Socialist Party (JSP).

The JCP won the right to initiate legislation in the upper house as a result of a by-election in 1973 and is now entitled, through the 20 seats it occupies, to the chairmanship of one of the 16 committees of the House of Councillors. As a consequence, a JCP member of the upper house is now chairman of the Disciplinary Committee.

In 1974 the JCP won 65 additional seats in prefectural, city, town, and village assemblies. It thus holds 135 seats in prefectural assemblies, 1,373 in city and district (*ku*) assemblies, and 1,301 in town and village assemblies, making a grand total of 2,809. Local elections are due to be held in April 1975, and elections for the House of Representatives also will probably take place sometime in 1975.

Leadership and Organization. The affairs of the JCP are directed by the Central Committee, whose 168 members (120 regular and 48 alterate) were elected by the Twelfth Congress. Elected by the Central Committee is the 38-member Presidium, whose 14-member Standing Committee exercises controlling power over the party. The most senior party official is Nosaka Sanzo, 83 years old, who holds the honorary position of chairman of the Central Committee. Miyamoto Kenji, the effective leader of the party, is chairman of the Presidium; he is assisted by three deputies (for names of the deputies and of the members of the Standing Committee, see *YICA, 1974*, pp. 465-66 and *YICA, 1972*, p. 516). The second most powerful organ after the Standing Committee of the Presidium is the 15-member Secretariat, headed by Fuwa Tetsuzo, the third-ranking party official after Nosaka and Miyamoto. Other important party organs are the Control Committee (6 members), the Audit Committee (6 members), and the Central Party Organ Publications Committee (21 members). In addition there are some 22 special committees; the most important of these runs the newspaper *Akahata*, which maintains full-time correspondents in Moscow, Berlin, Prague, Bucharest, and Hanoi. Other committees are charged with responsibility for such varied matters as: party policy, international affairs, party theory, mass movements, sports, culture, propaganda, party construction, education, magazine publishing, elections, military bases, and policy toward nuclear weapons and the U.S.-Japan security treaty. In addition the party maintains a "Research Institute for Social and Scientific Problems." The 58 Diet members are organized into caucuses in each of the parliamentary houses.

Party and Front Organizations. National organizations directly controlled by or supportive of the JCP include peace movements, cultural societies, and international friendship associations, and relate to youth, labor, students, women, businessmen, doctors and nurses, lawyers, consumers, writers, journalists, scientists, athletes, and many other professions and interests. Outside of the party itself, the youth movement probably receives the greatest attention and is considered by JCP leaders to be the most important of the many JCP-affiliated organizations.

The Youth Movement. The Democratic Youth League (Minseido), dating from 1923, came under tightened control of the JCP during 1974. Obviously determined not to let the insurgency which almost disrupted the organization in 1971 and 1972 occur again (see *YICA, 1973*, p. 480), party leaders saw to it that no dissidence would be allowed. This control was so clearly in evidence at the Minseido congress on 24-26 February that the organization can now be considered a "youth branch" of the JCP.

Minseido rules stipulate that a national congress shall be held once every two years. The 1972 congress was held in September but because of the important Kyoto prefectural governorship and House of Councillors elections set for April and July respectively, the 1974 congress was moved up to February. Since more than half of the Minseido members were eligible to vote for the first time, the congress was utilized to mobilize support for the party's candidates. Delegates to the congress numbered 1,129. Their average age was 22.6 years, and 30 percent were women (twice the percentage in 1972). A new Central Committee of 91 members was elected whose average age of 26 years was about a year and three months below that of the previous committee. Nineteen of the members, or 21 percent, were women, compared to 12 percent previously.

Miyamoto Kenji exhorted those attending the congress to work hard for the expansion of the membership, still estimated at "more than 200,000" as in previous years. He complained that this was too few, that in fact Minseido membership should be two or three times that of the party. Among the specific goals set forth at the congress were: more recruiting among industrial and non-unionized young workers, establishment of local branches in the 1,202 cities, towns and villages still lacking any Minseido organization, and expanding units in universities and high schools, especially large private universities.

Two representatives from North Vietnam were welcomed at the congress. The Japan Socialist

Party was not invited to send delegates, reflecting the serious rift which has developed between the JCP and the JSP because of factional disputes and competition for leadership in trade union youth groups.

Reports approved by the fourth meeting of the Central Committee in August noted that the number of drop-outs from Minseido was disturbing and attributed this to the lack of training of Minseido members in the nature and purposes of the organization. The committee decided that the JCP would assist Minseido in improving or developing educational materials for use by members. For examples, the classic texts of Marxism-Leninism were removed from reading lists and tracts by contemporary JCP leaders were substituted. The justification was that younger readers could not understand Marx and Lenin, and their education would be better served by writings which dealt with the realities of the present-day world.

In October a Minseido "Autumn Study Assembly" was held, with a reported attendance of 13,000. The purpose of the meeting was to indoctrinate members of the youth league in JCP objectives and policies. Secretariat Chief Fuwa criticized the league's educational materials, pointing out the need for books and pamphlets which could be readily understood by fifteen-year-olds.

Labor. The four-day annual congress of Sohyo (General Council of Trade Unions), 19-22 August, 1974, was characterized by the most heated confrontation between the JSP and the JCP yet to occur on the issue of "freedom of political party choice." Each year the JCP has striven to revise Sohyo's regulations which provide for support of the Socialist Party by member unions. The communists base their stand on the unconstitutionality of regulations that abridge the fundamental rights of freedom of thought and expression. The JSP charges the JCP with presenting a false issue of constitutionality to hide a selfish desire to win union support for the Communist Party. Furthermore, the JSP argues, "freedom of choice" could also mean support of the Liberal Democratic Party (LDP), which stands for reaction and monopoly capitalism, the opposite of the principles of Sohyo. To meet this accusation, the JCP this year argued for the first time that one need not adhere to a "mistaken decision" by one's union. The press reported that the discussion of this issue took up an inordinate amount of time and waxed so hot that at one moment the secretary-general of Sohyo was constrained to remark, "I would like it recognized that the JSP and the JCP are not in a hostile relationship with each other." (*Asahi*, Tokyo, 23 August). When the vote was taken on the last day of the congress, supporters of the "freedom of party choice" resolution numbered only 71 out of 613 delegates to the congress. Observers agreed that the intensity of the arguments between the two parties resulted partly from the ill will created by the July elections to the House of Councillors. The newspaper *Asahi* expressed disappointment over the accomplishments of the congress and noted that many important issues, outside of organizational ones, had been almost totally neglected by the delegates (ibid.).

Peace Movement. The peace movement received an impetus after the Bikini Island nuclear test incident in 1954 and two organizations were formed the following year: the Japan Peace Committee and the Japan Council Against Atomic and Hydrogen Bombs (Gensuikyo), both sponsored by the JCP. Later the anti-nuclear bomb movement split over the attitude to be taken toward Soviet and Chinese nuclear test explosions and in recent years two rival organizations have existed in addition to the JCP-supported Gensuikyo, one formed by the JSP and Sohyo (Gensuikin) and another with allegiance to the DSP (Kakkin). Over the past ten years repeated efforts have been made to reunite the movement but without success. In 1974 a meeting was held attended by representatives of all three organizations but union again proved impossible to achieve. As usual, the organizations held their rallies on or near the dates of the bombings of Hiroshima and Nagasaki (6-9 August). Observers commented in 1974 that young people were showing declining interest in the anti-bomb demonstrations as the images of Hiroshima and Nagasaki faded. (*Asahi*, 12 August).

International Friendship Associations. The three most important international friendship associations affiliated with the JCP are the Japan-Korea Association (Ni-cho Kyokai), the Japan-Soviet Association (Nisso Kyokai), and the Japan-China Friendship Association (Ni-chu Yuko Kyokai).

The Japan-Korea Association, with approximately 14,000 members, is directly allied with the General Federation of Korean Residents in Japan (Chosen Soren), which in turn is an arm of the Korean Workers Party of the Democratic People's Republic of Korea. Although there have been differences in the past between Chosen Soren and the JCP, the latter has consistently supported the Ni-cho Kyokai. In August the organization representing the Koreans in Japan loyal to South Korea openly accused Chosen Soren of responsibility for the assassination of the wife of President Park Chung Hee of the Republic of Korea. Officers of Chosen Soren hotly denied the charge, blaming "military-fascist elements within the Park group itself" for maneuvering to connect the slaying to Chosen Soren.

Although a Soviet-Japanese friendship society was founded in 1949, the present pro-JCP Japan-Soviet Association has existed only since 1965 when JSP and anti-JCP members bolted to form a competing Japan-Soviet Friendship Association. The societies have been affected by the changing relationships between the JCP and the CPSU and Soviet officials have handled the two groups gingerly. The Japan-Soviet Association, which held its eighteenth congress in February 1974, has about 10,000 members, as contrasted with the 4,000 who affiliate with the pro-JSP Japan-Soviet Friendship Association.

Societies promoting friendly relations with China are likewise divided. The Japan-China Friendship Association, originally formed in 1950, followed the JCP in its quarrel with the CCP in March 1966. As a result, the supporters of the PRC withdrew to form a Japan-China Friendship Association (Orthodox) in October, 1966. Membership in the pro-JCP Japan-China Friendship Association is estimated at 35,000, compared to 7,000 members of JCFA (Orthodox). Meeting in March, 1974, leaders of the pro-JCP association affirmed that it was a mistake to conclude that political problems had been resolved by the normalization of relations between Japan and China and that the PRC was still taking an "unprincipled attitude" by calling the Soviet Union its first enemy and by condoning the U.S.–Japan security treaty. (*Chugai Tokuho*, Tokyo, May, 1974).

Other Fronts. The following are examples of other JCP-affiliated interest groups.

The New Japan Women's Association (Shin Fujin), founded in 1962, has a reported membership of 143,000, with branches at prefectural and local levels.

The JCP-affiliated National Federaton of Students Self-Governing Associations (Zengakuren) embraces more than half of the organized university students in Japan, amounting to almost 600,000 persons. During 1974 the principal concern of the JCP-oriented student leaders was how to combat the opposition of the "Trotskyites" and radical New Leftists who were posing a threat to the internal security of Zengakuren.

The Federation of Democratic Commerce and Industry Associations (Zenshoren) was founded in 1951 and claims a membership of 300,000 with more than 320 branches throughout the country. This organization aims its appeal at the interests and grievances of small and medium-sized businesses.

The Federation of Democratic Medical Institutions (Zen-i-ren) has a reported membership of approximately 10,000 with 380 affiliated institutions.

Party Internal Affairs. During the first half of 1974 party energies were focused on the upper house elections, which took place on 7 July. Subsequently and during the rest of the year, the JCP leadership set about drawing lessons from the election results and exhorting party members to redouble their efforts to achieve the goals of party membership and circulation of *Akahata* established by the 1973 congress. Immediately party heads began to urge preparation for the local elections scheduled for the spring of 1975 and lower house elections expected sometime during 1975. On 2-5 August, the Central Committee, meeting for the fourth time since the 1973 congress, established four "pillars" to guide the activities of the membership: mass movements, elections, party building, and party defense. Although the party now had 20 seats in the House of Councillors, it had fared badly in the national constituencies and had slipped in the number of votes received in several of Japan's largest cities. Priorities were placed on membership drives, on increasing the circulation of *Akahata*, which had dropped since the Twelfth Congress, and on the education and training of party adherents. Increasingly, the leadership became concerned over attacks on the JCP, not only from the LDP, but also from other opposition parties, and especially from the radical Left. Consequently, "defense of the party" became a burning issue.

The Central Committee's second meeting in February approved three reports submitted by the Presidium: on mass action for the defense of people's livelihood, on party advancement through the forthcoming House of Councillors elections, and on party construction and the three-year plan. The first report called upon the membership to oppose the LDP's "economic miracle" achieved at the expense of low wages, low income, a continuous rise in consumer prices, heavy taxes, pollution, traffic accidents, scarcity of housing, and exploitation by monopoly capitalists of Prime Minister Tanaka's super-growth policy through cornering land. On the elections, the committee reminded JCP members of their opportunity to pass judgment on the LDP-generated livelihood crisis and held out the possibility of ending the LDP's majority in the upper house. The third report extolled the three-year plan established by the Twelfth Congress to run through 1975, emphasizing that the plan was aimed at both qualitative and quantitative improvements; that the first half of the plan's first year would coincide with the July elections, and that the goals for the Thirteenth Congress in 1975 were more than 400,000 party members and an *Akahata* daily circulation of more than 4 million.

At the third meeting of the Central Committee, in May, the last opportunity to mobilize a drive for seats in the July elections was fully exploited. The principal reports were delivered by the two prominent brothers, Fuwa Tetsuzo and Ueda Koichiro, who expounded policies for victory in the upper house elections and stepped-up party expansion. Ueda enunciated "four fundamental policies": democratic reform of the economy, protection of freedom and democracy, democratization of education and culture, and independence and neutrality for Japan to bring about true peace in Asia. Fuwa announced that the loss of 200,000 subscribers to *Akahata* since the 1973 congress had been made up; at the same time, more than half of the prefectures were not yet back to the 1973 subscription level.

The fourth meeting, in August, indulged in soul-searching over the results of the upper house elections. The fact that votes in the national constituencies were down 800,000 from the 1972 House of Representatives elections was a shock to the party. In 15 (out of 47) prefectures, the JCP was lowest in votes among five contesting parties—the others being the JSP, the LDP, the Komeito (Clean Government Party), and the Democratic Socialist Party (DSP)—while in 24 it was in fourth place. Furthermore, votes for the JCP had decreased in several local constituencies, including Tokyo. Members were admonished that they must immediately begin political activities looking toward the spring elections of 1975, when 17 prefectural governors, 193 mayors of cities, and most local assemblies and town and village heads would be up for election. It was not too early also to begin to think about the next lower house elections; in at least 20 new districts, JCP candidates could be successful.

Party Policy. Miyamoto Kenji outlined at the beginning of the year the policies to be followed by the party during 1974. His "three tasks" for the year were: defending the people's livelihood, surmounting obstacles to the united front (see below), and facing the new international situation (see below).

Noting the severity of the economic situation, the slowdown in production and the rise in inflation, Miyamoto blamed the government's high growth policy and the exhorbitant profits of private enterprise. He recommended that in facing the oil crisis, Japan should break ties with multi-national corporations, meaning the U.S.-controlled "majors" which supplied most of Japan's oil. The government should instead deal directly with the oil producers, including socialist countries. The JCP had already proposed the establishment of a national energy corporation and had set up within the joint JCP and reformist Diet group a committee for countermeasures to deal with inflation, materials shortages, and the oil crisis. Miyamoto criticized the government for having allowed Japan's economic structure to become subordinate to the United States. The country was now dependent on foreign sources, largely U.S.-controlled corporations, for more than 86 percent of its energy needs, whereas in 1955 dependence was only 23 percent. Self-sufficiency in grain, 85 percent in 1934-36, was now only 48 percent. Furthermore, because "our country is a military base for America which is encouraging the aggressor Israel with arms and aid, Arab nations have made Japan an object of their oil strategy." The conclusion was that Japan should abrogate the security treaty with the United States, which had become a problem inseparable from the defense of the people's livelihood. (*Akhata*, 1 January.)

Aiming at the July elections, party leaders pursued the above positions vigorously during the first half of the year, using every means of propaganda available. Especially during February and March, JCP Diet members played prominent roles in attacking the Tanaka government and the industrialists for policies which had produced inflation and violations of the anti-monopoly act. Fuwa Tetsuzo was a particularly persistent questioner of the prime minister in budget committee hearings of the lower house, taking issue with Tanaka's contention that Japan's troubles were due largely to outside influences. Communist party members were also prominent in bringing accusations against top business executives for price fixing and for organizing cartels.

The JCP early in the year stepped up its anti-LDP barrage, focusing personally on the prime minister, Tanaka Kakuei. Just before the House of Councillors elections, the party addressed two open letters to Tanaka, denouncing his "reactionary politics" and demanding answers to a series of detailed questions. The first letter concentrated on economic questions: commodity prices, energy, and agriculture; the second took up political issues, accusing Tanaka of supporting aggressive war and military dictatorships. By the latter the JCP meant principally the government of South Korea, which it said was bolstered by the U.S. military establishment and the Japanese yen. (*Akahata*, 25 June, 4 July.) The secretary-general of the LDP refused to reply to the open letters on the grounds that such questions could be discussed in the forum of the Diet and that the prime minister was dealing with the problems raised by the JCP in press conferences given during the election campaign.

Playing on the theme that the "LDP and Big Business are one," party propagandists scored some success in attacking Tanaka and the LDP for the large financial contributions they had received from corporations. The term "money-power politics," which became current before and after the upper house elections, was thoroughly publicized by the JCP but was not a communist monopoly. As the campaign to oust Tanaka, in which all opposition parties joined, became more intense, JCP publicists competed with non-communist journalists in exposing and condemning the tangled financial history of the Tanaka "empire." When one of Japan's leading monthly magazines, *Bungei Shunju*, published in its November issue a detailed exposé of Tanaka's machinations, *Akahata* promptly claimed credit for having publicized the "black mist" of corruption surrounding the prime minster as early as 1972, the year he took office. After the appearance of the *Bungei Shunju* article, the JCP organized its own team of researchers to compile a report on Tanaka which, after appearing in large part in *Akahata*, was published on 12 November in a 32-page pamphlet, replete with detailed statistics and charts, entitled "This Is the 'Tanaka Family': Exposure of the Black Mist Surrounding the 'Money-Power' Prime Minister."

The JCP policy for the establishment of a "democratic coalition government," announced at the Twelfth Congress in November 1973, came in for a biting attack in an article published in the June issue of *Bungei Shunju*, attributed to "Group 1984," an anonymous assemblage of specialists and scholars reputedly representing no particular political party. The 53-page monograph examined the JCP's foreign policy, economic policy, and the "essence" of its program for "democratization," concluding that a look behind the verbiage of the JCP's vision of a "rose-colored Japan" revealed outdated concepts (the "cold war," for example), misleading propositions, and dangerous proposals. The magazine extended the right of reply to the JCP and the July issue carried a refutation written by Ueda Koichiro, chairman of the party's policy committee, and Kudo Akira, chairman of the economic committee. These authors called the treatise "slanderous," insisted that the anonymous authors were adamantly hostile to the JCP and that they completely misunderstood the nature of the proposed democratic coalition government, confusing it with the JCP itself. Ueda and Kudo went into considerable detail to meet the arguments of "Group 1984." The exchange of polemics continued in August and September with the group's reply to the JCP and the JCP's reply to the reply. The series was unusual in Japanese journalistic history; seldom before have two opposing viewpoints, especially on such an explosive issue as communism, been so fully debated for the benefit of the Japanese reading public.

In an effort to test popular response to the proclaimed policies of the JCP, the newspaper *Sankei* in July took an opinion poll on the "image" of the JCP. Of the respondents, 58 percent affirmed that the JCP "cannot be trusted" while only 11 percent found the party reliable. Fifty-six percent believed that a socialist government was not likely to be established in Japan. The most pro-JCP responses came from youths in their teens, 40 percent of whom held a "plus" image of the JCP while for 30 percent the image was unfavorable (*Sankei Shimbun*, Tokyo, 11 July).

"Freedom of Speech" Issue. The JCP found itself on the defensive on the issue of "freedom of speech" through both the expulsion from the Soviet Union of Nobel-prize-winning author Aleksandr Solzhenitsyn and the "*Sankei* controversy" which arose over an advertisement placed by the LDP in the newspaper.

During the campaign for the House of Councillors elections, the LDP candidates made the most of the slogan "Preserve Free Society." They were aided in this effort by the extensive publicity given to the anti-Soviet statements and eventual expulsion from the Soviet Union of Solzhenitsyn. To the LDP this presented proof for all to see of the lack of freedom in a socialist state. The JCP, at once on the defensive, took up the Solzhenitsyn question in a series of articles in *Akahata*: among them, a three-part polemic (3-5 March) and a major full-page presentation (20 March) entitled: "Scientific Socialism and the Freedoms of Speech and Expression." Miyamoto and other high-ranking party officials made numerous statements and delivered lectures that were widely publicized in JCP publications. The principal arguments used by the party propagandists were: (1) the LDP campaign was intended to distract public attention from Big Business politics by trying to make capital out of *any* event in a socialist country; (2) the JCP was the *only* party that had been fighting consistently for freedom of speech for fifty years; (3) the JCP disapproved of the Soviet action and in fact few communist parties had unconditionally supported it (Miyamoto stated in a press conference on 21 February, "In Japan we would never do such a thing"); (4) since the Soviet Union by its history was a one-party system which permitted no anti-government newspapers, radio, or television, its expulsion of an anti-revolutionary person was harmful more to the working classes than to the ruling classes of capitalist nations; (5) Solzhenitsyn, moreover, went too far by denouncing Marxism, and while his criticism, based on personal experiences in concentration camps was justifiable (at least two prominent JCP members had disappeared in the Soviet Union without a trace), his denunciation of the socialist system could not be condoned—Solzhenitzyn's ideal was the old Russia; (6) the Solzhenitsyn matter, unlike the Soviet invasion of Czechoslovakia, did not represent the intervention of one state in the affairs of another—the JCP therefore did not attack the Soviet Union for its special point of view, though it disapproved of the action in this case— and the JCP itself would never accept the intervention of another state, especially the effort of one communist party to lead others. One of the most categorical statements on the Solzhenitsyn affair appeared in *Akahata* on 21 February: "The JCP, whether in charge of the government or a participant in a coalition, would permit the publication of works by an author with thoughts and opinions contrary to those of the JCP." (Quoted in Sakaki Toshio, "The Solzhenitsyn Question and Socialism," *Zenei*, June.)

On 2 December 1973, the *Sankei* and *Nihon Keizai* newspapers published identical paid advertisements signed by the Liberal Democratic Party and bearing the headlines: "Japan Communist Party, Explain yourselves clearly! Many citizens look at you with apprehension." The text printed parallel excerpts from the JCP's party platform and its "Program for a Democratic Coalition Government," and expressed the opinion ("we think") that the two documents were inconsistent. The advertisement asked whether, in considering both programs, the plan for a democratic coalition government did not represent a take-off point for proletarian dictatorship and a step toward revolution. The JCP reacted promptly and sharply, denouncing the advertisement in *Sankei* as slander, abuse, and an example of "fascist information manipulated by money power." While other newspapers ignored the controversy, the editor of *Sankei* jumped to the defense of his paper, citing the principle of freedom of information and referring to the precedent of the *New York Times*, which publishes paid political advertisements. On 8 February, which happened to be four days before Solzhenitsyn was expelled from Russia, the JCP brought suit in the Tokyo district court, charging the *Sankei* with "damage to reputation." The confrontation between the *Sankei* and the JCP became more than just a controversy between a newspaper and a political party; together with the Solzhenitsyn case, it acquired major significance as a test of the principles of freedom of information and democratic practice. (See *Koan Joho* [Public Safety Report], a monthly magazine utilizing material from government security agencies, July.)

In addition to instituting legal action, the JCP mobilized its affiliated organizations, including labor unions and women's, youth, student, and cultural groups, to pressure the *Sankei* in every possible way, particularly through mass communications. The JCP attacked the motives of the LDP, accusing it of attempting to perpetuate one-party rule by stopping the expansion of the JCP, and of exploiting newspapers, which are "public organs," in order to slander another political party under the guise of a "campaign to preserve a free society." The motive of the LDP, according to JCP spokesmen, was to crush the ethical principles of newspapers and newspaper advertising in order to blemish the honor of a public party. Party propagandists quoted the publisher's code established soon after the war and claimed that a newspaepr is a public enterprise which should not permit exploitation for propaganda purposes. Although the *Sankei* offered the JCP the opportunity to reply by a paid advertisement, the party refused, asserting that acceptance of such an offer would mean assent to the very practice the party abjured.

On the question of a contradiction between party documents. JCP spokesmen denied the charge but were vague in their specific responses: "The LDP tries to make a contradiction out of no contradiction, to show that the JCP is a wolf in sheep's clothing and thus to deceive the public." Miyamoto Taro, chief of the Central Committee's Information Section, in an article in the June issue of the party magazine *Zenei*, "The *Sankei* Problem and Freedom of Speech," quoted Miyamoto's statement at the Twelfth Congress that there were no inconsistencies between JCP policies and the party platform. "At the same time the JCP has never hidden from the public the fact that it looks toward a revolution to free Japan from the control of the U.S. and Japanese reactionary forces and to establish a democratic, independent Japan. . . . Such an aim, exactly opposite to the LDP's image of a 'frightening revolution' and a 'dark dictatorship,' is a dream full of hope."

Domestic Attitudes and Activities. *United Front.* Miyamoto Kenji in his 1974 New Year's statement listed two principal obstacles to the formation of a renovationist united front of the JCP, JSP, DSP, and Komeito. One was the insistence of the JSP that joint action be agreed upon by all four of the opposition parties; the other was the Komeito's proclaimed principle of "absolute pacifism" (see *YICA, 1974*, p. 474). Appealing for cooperation from the other opposition parties to make 1974 "a year of fruitful advance toward a united front," Miyamoto emphasized that joint struggles and controversy are not contradictory. While calling for discussions to solve mutual problems, Miyamoto took occasion to characterize an article by a JSP leader as "mere repetition of scorn in total disregard of JCP arguments." (*Akahata*, 1 January.)

Although in isolated elections of mayors and members of local legislatures the opposition-party cooperation had been successful, the only candidate for a national office who won a seat in the upper house through support by a "united front" was an independent, not a member of the JCP, from Okinawa prefecture. In one other case, in Kochi prefecture, on the island of Shikoku, the JCP and JSP reached agreement to support each other's candidates. The JCP backed a socialist to fill a vacancy in the House of Councillors in May, in return for which the JSP endorsed a JCP contender in the July elections for that house. In each case the LDP won the seat.

In spite of much talk and meetings among representatives of the various opposition parties (the JCP even assented to a four-party conference on the assumption that the DSP would not join), little if any progress was made during the year toward the achievement of a viable united front which could win elections. The JCP seemed as far away from the others as ever and mutual criticisms and denunciations were exchanged throughout the year. JCP readers realized that agreement with the Socialists was of first priority, since they represent the largest opposition party, but rejected JSP insistence on "waiting for the DSP" as a "phantom argument." The JSP, in fact, seemed to be attacking the JCP in more strident terms than those it used for its principal enemy, the LDP. Moreover the results of the July elections gave the Socialists confidence which made them less inclined to enter into coalitions with the Communists, which so often benefitted only the latter. In July, during the campaign for the upper house elections, the JCP addressed to each of the other three opposition parties an open letter or questionnaire similar to the one sent to Prime Minister Tanaka. According to a JCP pamphlet, the JSP did not reply but published a "refutation," which the Communists termed "not the sincere act of a public political party." Instead of directly meeting the issues, the Socialists had, according to the JCP, retorted by characterizing the open letter as "missing the mark," "a posture of opposing unity," and "a stimulus toward hostility among the opposition parties." (*Open Questionnaires to Prime Minister Tanaka, the DSP, Komeito, and JSP*, Japan Communist Party, 5 September.)

With the Komeito, the JCP carried on a running exchange of polemics, beginning with a JCP "Appeal" (published 17 December 1973), continuing with a reply from the Komeito (8 February 1974), and a JCP reply to the reply (16 April). Although the JCP expressed gratification over the change in the Komeito position on the U.S.-Japan security treaty from one of "gradual dissolution" to "immediate dissolution," the JCP found that Komeito policy was conservative and pro-status quo. The Komeito's propagation of "absolute pacifism" came in for special abuse. Such a policy of "non-resistance" was inconsistent with the Komeito's announced support of a "national police force" if it should come to power. The Komeito did not answer the July open letter but reference to it by a party official in a press conference was described by the JCP as "no serious reply." JCP leaders were particularly irritated at the stance taken by the Komeito in the Kyoto gubernatorial election. By refusing to endorse the long-term renovationist candidate, Ninagawa Torazo, and leaving the choice to party members, the Komeito in fact threw its support to the LDP-supported candidate. This, in JCP eyes, was treason to the concept of a united front.

Communist contempt for the DSP continued to be enunciated. This party was regarded as a collaborator of the LDP, fundamentally anti-communist, and only posing as renovationist in order to gain advantage at the polls.

Elections. For more than a year, the JCP, like all other political parties in Japan, had been preparing for the crucial upper house elections of 1974 which were to "Reverse Conservatives and Renovationists." During the latter part of 1973 and early 1974, LDP politicians seriously feared that their party might for the first time lose its majority in one of the houses of the national parliament. Serious observers for some time considered the chances for such an upset to be fifty-fifty. All parties exerted the most vigorous campaigning efforts in many years of election history. As the year 1974 wore on, however, the LDP began to gain confidence, strengthened largely by the split in the renovationist camp revealed by the Kyoto gubernatorial election of 7 April and local elections held on 21 April.

In Kyoto, Ninagawa Torazo, continuously governor since 1950, was expected from the beginning easily to win election for his seventh term, supported as in the past by both the Socialist and the Communist parties. This time, however, a split developed within the JSP because of dissatisfaction over Ninagawa's alleged decidedly pro-communist policies. In the end, the central JSP organization backed Ninagawa while the Kyoto branch of the JSP endorsed his opponent, Ohashi Kazutaka, who ran with the open support of both the LDP and the DSP. The Komeito, by refraining from an open endorsement of Ninagawa, in fact threw its weight to Ohashi. The result of the election was a very close win by Ninagawa, by only 4,000 votes. Although the JCP hailed the reelection of its candidate as a "beacon for reformism," the wounds caused by the split in the JSP and the defection of the Komeito seriously damaged the chances for the formation of any viable united front among the parties of the opposition.

The LDP was cheered by its success in local elections on 21 April. Out of 23 mayoralty elections, the LDP captured 22. The exception was a city in Osaka prefecture which reelected for the third time a candidate backed jointly by the JSP, JCP, Komeito, and DSP. Furthermore in the May by-election for the House of Councillors in Kyoto prefecture the LDP candidate defeated by nearly 30,000 votes a candidate endorsed by the JSP, JCP, and Komeito.

By the time the House of Councillors elections occurred on 7 July, the LDP no longer feared for its majority. Still party officials and candidates campaigned tirelessly, spending enormous sums of money (which later became a controversial issue) and aimed their attacks at the JCP, using such slogans as: "Protect free society," "Stop the democratic coalition government which threatens the destruction of free society," "Beware of the two-faced JCP," "Don't be fooled by the pose of the JCP," and "Stop is red." Both the DSP, which had officially decided on "anti-communism" as a policy, and the Komeito campaigned against the JCP; the Komeito used such slogans as "JCP: Mouth and heart are different" and "JCP: Liars good at deceit." Against this opposition and in the face of its much touted proposal for a "people's democratic coalition government" to win support from other parties, the JCP put Marxism-Leninism in the background and harped on "people's issues" symbolized by "livelihood and economics." Inflation, aggravated by the oil crisis, received major attention. Candidates stressed the problem of education with warnings against LDP-sponsored "militaristic" course content and defended teachers, in words unusual for communists, as members of a "sacred" profession. Foreign policy issues, such as abolition of the security treaty, were relegated to second priority. To fight the well-financed LDP, the JCP made extraordinary efforts to raise funds, claiming that the party would take no money from Big Business and would neither assess its members nor accept contributions from the poor. Intensive efforts were made to raise money through the various JCP-affiliated organizations and through constant appeals in *Akahata*; in June, however, the party announced that it had attained only 30 to 40 percent of its set goal. After the enormous expenditures of money and energy for the House of Councillors elections, the party leadership urged members to contribute from ten to thirty thousand yen to meet rising costs due to inflation.

The 7 July elections, characterized by the highest voting average in history (73.2 percent), did not wipe out the LDP's majority, which it retained by a margin of seven seats, but did, as noted earlier, increase JCP representation from 11 to 20, advancing the party to third place, after the LDP and the JSP, in both houses of parliament. Communist candidates contested eight out of 54 seats in the national constituency and 46 out of 76 seats in the local constituencies; at the second plenary session of the Central Committee in February, goals were set at all 8 seats in the national and 10 seats in the local constituencies, seeking a popular vote of 6 million in the former and 10 million in the latter. The party met its objective of eight seats in the national constituency but elected only half of its candidates to the local constituencies. These 13 seats, added to the seven not up for election this year, brought the JCP's total to 20. In popular votes, the JCP failed to reach its goals, polling 4.9 million in the national and 6.8 million in the local constituencies, or 9.4 percent and 12.8 percent respectively, of the total vote, amounting to 1.3 percent and 10.7 percent over the 1971 elections. Compared with the House of Representatives elections in 1972, the JCP increased its percentage of the popular vote by only 1.9%.

Although growth for the JCP was demonstrated by the July elections (the party polled approximatley 18 votes for every member), the rate of increase slowed down somewhat. For example, in percentage increases of the popular vote, the JCP jumped by nearly four percentage points in the local constituencies from 1968 to 1971, whereas the figure in 1974 was less than a percentage point above that of 1971. The JCP also surprisingly failed to meet expectations in cities where its polling power has always been strongest. In Tokyo, for example, the party expected to gain more than a million votes and to become the second party after the LDP. In fact, however, the JCP came out fourth, trailing not only the LDP and JSP, but even the Komeito. Its 810,000 votes were 100,000 more than those won in the 1971 elections but down from the 980,000 of the 1972 lower house elections and the 960,000 of the July 1973 municipal assembly contests. In percentage terms, this meant 15.2 percent as compared with 16.2 percent in 1971 (upper house), 19.7 percent in 1972 (House of Representatives), and 20.2 percent in 1973 (Tokyo Municipal Assembly). The JCP captured fewer votes in 1974 than in 1972 in four prefectures in the national and eight in the local constituencies; percentages of the total vote decreased in 19 of the local constituencies over 1971. Three of the four prefectures in which national constituency losses were registered were Tokyo, Aichi (in which Nagoya is located), and Kyoto. At the same time, the prefectures in which losses for local constituency candidates were suffered were not those including large metropolitan areas. Local constituency candidates in Tokyo, Kyoto, and Osaka, who expected to win top place in their areas on the basis of previous records, were in fact elected by small margins.

As a result of the loss of eight seats by the LDP and gains by the JSP and JCP (the Komeito increased its seats by one), a realignment of committee chairmen and memberships was carried out in the House of Councillors. As noted earlier, the JCP now holds the chairmanship of one of the 16 committees, the Disciplinary Committee. In eight of the committees, LDP members now occupy only half of the seats. Some commentators have suggested that the LDP has already lost its "stable majority" in the upper house.

Fuwa Tetsuzo, director of the Central Committee Secretariat, admitted in June before the elections that the reversal of the conservative-renovationist forces could not be brought about in 1974. He severely criticized the JSP, stating that it faced the clear choice between a renovationist united front with the JCP and an anti-communist JSP-Komeito-DSP alliance. He believed that the best chance to accomplish the united front would be to strengthen the JCP so that the JSP would be forced to come into close cooperation with it. (*Akahata*, 9 June.)

International Views and Policies. The JCP world view still focuses on détente as a delusion and on the United States as the leader of imperialism. U.S. foreign policy is seen as exploiting the

Sino-Soviet conflict to pursue militaristic aggression through aiding hostilities in Vietnam, intervening in the Middle East, and maintaining military bases and forces in East Asia. Meanwhile Japanese monopoly capital and LDP governments fall in line with the U.S. strategy. So far as the communist world is concerned, the JCP continues to reject emphatically the leadership of the Communist Party of the Soviet Union (CPSU) in the world communist movement and to castigate both the Chinese Communist Party (CCP) and the CPSU for unacceptable intervention in the internal affairs of the JCP. Nearer home, the JCP has attacked the Japanese government's policy of placating the "fascist, dictatorial" administration of President Park Chung Hee in South Korea. As the JCP leaders look around the world, they find they have more in common with their confreres in the capitalist nations, such as Italy and France, than they do with those in socialist countries. Ueda Koichiro, head of the JCP s publishing empire, noted in a recent panel discussion that the JCP and the communist parties of Italy and France share the line that the protection and the strengthening of freedom of speech and political democracy are integral parts of the prospective development of socialism. He admitted that the three parties faced similar difficulties in convincing their respective electorates of the sincerity of this line. ("The Political Situation and the United Front," *Zenei*, January 1975.)

Relations with the CCP. Although relations between the JCP and the CCP did not improve during 1974, there seemed to be a slackening off of public polemics. Miyamoto in his New Year's policy statement referred to the usefulness of controversy between parties and insisted that friendly inter-party relations should not be obstructed by differences of opinion, if these do not "lose moderation." Still, no normalization of relations between the Japanese and Chinese parties appeared likely in the near future.

Just before the beginning of the year, *Akahata* was chafing over statements made in Peking to a Japanese Diet delegation, in which the JCP was not included, to the effect that Japan's maintenance of the security treaty with the United States was understandable as defense against the menace of the Soviet Union. From such assertions the JCP concluded that Chinese leaders, "who should spearhead the anti-imperialist forces, are prettifying the U.S. nuclear umbrella and are supporting the maintenance of the Japan-U.S. security treaty and the presence of the Self Defense Forces" (*Akahata*, 17 December 1973.) This theme was emphasized in JCP propaganda during the year.

The JCP continued to be excluded from delegations traveling to mainland China and from meetings with People's Republic of China delegations coming to Japan. In January, JCP representatives did not join in a reception committee to greet a Chinese youth group which spent a month in Japan at the invitation of 28 Japanese youth organizations. In April, the Chinese embassy in Tokyo invited the president of the Tokyo Metropolitan Assembly to send a good-will delegation to China, and specified that members of all political parties should be included *except* the JCP. The Communists were particularly irritated that a representative of the anti-JCP Japan-China Friendship Association (Orthodox) was invited by the Chinese. An editorial in *Akahata* (11 April) characterized the action as "China's flagrant great-power chauvinistic infringement on and intervention in the autonomy of the Tokyo Metropolitan Assembly." It also reproached the four parties for accepting this "unwarranted" invitation and the municipal assembly for "throwing away its independence" by agreeing to the mission and dispatching it to China at the expense of Tokyo taxpapers. The editorial saw in the Chinese action clear evidence that the JCP was still regarded as one of China's "four enemies." Moscow radio (21 April) gleefully reported that "such discrimination was unparalleled in the history of international relations."

Two additional instances of deliberate exclusion of the JCP by the Chinese occurred during the year. In July, JCP members of the prefectural and municipal assemblies of Osaka were not invited to the opening there of a Chinese trade exhibition. A member of the JCP Central Committee protested this discrimination as "flagrant Big Power intervention" and "an attempt to cause a split among local organs of authority" (*Akahata*, 14 July). In September, Japan Air Lines invited Diet representatives from each of the five political parties to fly on its inaugural flight to Peking. The Chinese, however, refused to grant a visa to the JCP member of the House of Councillors who had been selected to go. The party officially protested the refusal, terming it inconsistent with the development of normal relationships between Japan and China on the basis of equality and non-intervention in domestic politics (ibid., 20 September).

In line with its condemnation of Chinese-U.S. rapprochement as false détente, the JCP described the communiqué issued in Peking after the November visit there of U.S. secretary of state Kissinger as another "beautification of American imperialism" (ibid., 1 December).

Relations with the CPSU. Relations between the JCP and the CPSU, which have had their ups and downs over the years, appeared to worsen during 1974. Except for the Solzhenitsyn case, already noted, the contentious issues were not new and were further from resolution than ever. Among the issues which continue to concern spokesmen of the two parties are (1) differences in approach toward the problem of U.S. imperialism, (2) attitudes toward the Sino-Soviet conflict, (3) evaluation of the role of the Soviet Union in the international communist movement, (4) the question of a world conference of communist and workers' parties, and (5) the Kurile Islands.

The most comprehensive treatise on CPSU-JCP relations in 1974 appeared in *Akahata* on 15 September as an answer to a lengthy article in Moscow's *Party Life* (13 May). The Soviet magazine had reprinted an essay written by Athos Fava, secretary of the Central Committee of the Argentine communist party, for his party's journal *Nueva Era*. Fava strongly criticized JCP policies as manifest in the Twelfth Congress, held in 1973, which he had attended. *Akahata* suggested that the Argentine article, if not written in Moscow, parroted the Soviet party line a hundred percent, even to spelling Japanese names in the Russian fashion. The article, as it appeared in *Party Life*, accused the JCP of ignoring in its Twelfth Congress the role played by the socialist countries in effecting relaxation of tension and strengthening peaceful coexistence among states with different social systems. Peaceful coexistence was defined as a form of class struggle whose principles U.S. imperialism had been forced to recognize. Fava denounced JCP leaders for failing to differentiate between Soviet and Chinese policies, the former aimed at détente and the latter at anti-Sovietism. The JCP was called "revanchist" for its support of claims to the Kurile Islands. Referring to the resolutions of the congress, Fava stated that there was no precedent in the history of the international communist movement for the advancement in such a forum of territorial claims against a socialist state.

The *Akahata* "rebuttal" put forth the JCP's usual arguments about the "beautification of American imperialism," criticizing at length the Soviet role in the Vietnam war. *Akahata* went on to attack the Soviet and Chinese parties alike for their support of the Nixon Administration, asserting that coexistence as a form of class struggle does not mean "cooperation and détente with American imperialists who pursued aggression in Indochina." The "rebuttal" found that the intervention by the CCP and the CPSU in the affairs of the JCP differed in no essential way. Particularly contemputuous, according to *Akahata*, was the fostering by the Soviet party of the anti-JCP Shiga splinter party, "Voice of Japan." Moreover, the Sino-Soviet confrontation, including competition between these two socialist nations for the favors of the United States, had obstructed the unity of the anti-imperialist forces and enormously benefited U.S. imperialists.

In a lengthy section on the Kurile Islands question, *Akahata* reiterated the JCP position that Japan's title to the islands was legally established, that the Soviet Union should immediately return the Habomais and Shikotan and negotiate a peace treaty with Japan, and that, after a democratic coalition government was set up, the remaining islands should be ceded to Japan by the Soviet Union. To support the JCP claim that the CPSU had promised that the Soviet government would change its policy toward the islands, *Akahata* included in the article the text of an agreement said to have been reached by the Soviet and Japanese parties in Moscow in January 1959 at the time of the Twenty-first Extraordinary Congress of the CPSU. After admitting that the presentation to the Soviet Union of a territorial demand by the Japanese government was not supported on legal grounds (which appears contrary to the present position of the JCP), the document affirmed that Japan's main task was to obtain complete independence from U.S. "rule," including the removal of military bases and forces: once a "truly popular and democratic" government is established in Japan, "there will appear the possibility of the taking of a new attitude toward the problem of the South Kurile Islands." According to *Akahata*, no objection was expressed by the CPSU to this agreed statement until ten years after it was signed; further, it was apparently reconfirmed at a meeting between representatives of the two parties in March 1971. Although the 1959 statement mentions the possibility of a "new attitude" toward the territorial question, it appears far from a promise to settle the question by returning the islands, which is the meaning that the JCP has given to it. (*Akahata*, 17 September.)

On the question of the role of the Soviet party in the world communist movement and its desire to convoke a world conference of communist and workers' parties, the JCP has repeatedly stressed its firm position. It will never accept the leadership of Moscow as the "vanguard" of world communism and it adamantly refuses to participate in a world conference which, in its view, would confirm the Sino-Soviet split and create wider rifts among the various parties in the international communist movement.

The United States. JCP policy statements issued periodically during the year revealed clearly that party spokesmen felt on the defensive in regard to the traditional socialist concepts of "American imperialism." The very stridency of their warnings over the threat of U.S. imperialism betrayed deep concern that the increasingly accepted world view of détente between communist and non-communist nations was damaging to JCP interests. They protested that certain "anti-imperialist forces" (an obvious reference to the Chinese and Russians) had let themselves be convinced that Nixon's imperialism had changed. To demolish such a theory JCP leaders detailed American imperialistic designs and actions: continuing a war in Indochina, engineering a coup in Chile, carrying on aggressive maneuvers in the Middle East, blocking the unity of Korea, and backing such machinations with 3,000 military bases and 560,000 military men stationed around the world. Lined up on the anti-imperialist side were three revolutionary forces: the socialist countries, the national liberation movements, and the working masses in capitalist nations. With a deliberate slap at the Chinese and Soviet communist parties, the JCP publicists often pointed out that socialist countries alone could never take the place of the struggles of other revolutionary forces nor could they determine by themselves the general state of the world situation. (See *Akahata*, 4 April, for a comprehensive statement, "American Imperialism's Strategy and the Great Cause of the Anti-Imperialist Forces in the Present Phase of the International Situation.")

The JCP found fault with every phase of U.S. policy. SALT was a delusion since the agreements reached between the United States and the U.S.S.R. failed to restrict warheads and new weapons and placed no restraints whatsoever on U.S. plans to develop nuclear weapons and plot nuclear war. While NATO was the main threat to Europe, Kissinger tried to link Japan and Europe into American imperialistic strategy. The Sino-Soviet conflict was a boon to the United States, which had taken full advantage of it in seeming to ease tensions while at the same time strengthening U.S. military power. (Ibid.)

The principal specific attacks against the United States during the year were related to the energy crisis, military policy and actions, and the presidential visit to Japan.

The United States was seen consistently as the evil genius in the oil crisis, seeking (1) to boost the dollar by "taking advantage of the oil-plagued economies of Japan and Western Europe," and (2) to prevent these oil-consuming nations from making direct deals with the oil producers (ibid., 8 February). The JCP supported Arab policies, finding nationalization of resources a natural "trend of the times." The United States was portrayed in the role of an imperialist power supporting reactionary forces in Israel who were waging a war of aggression against the Arab states. A threat to the Arabs was discerned in the statement that the United States would not resort to armed force even if Arab oil producers did not respond to its demand for lower crude oil prices (ibid., 29 September). Secretary Kissinger's energy speech of 14 November was described as a "political declaration of war" (ibid., 17 November).

Several military issues involving the United States engaged JCP attention, among them the long-standing problem of the entry of nuclear-powered submarines into Japanese ports. Fuwa Tetsuzo, chief of the JCP Secretariat, announced to the Budget Committee of the House of Representatives on 29 January that the monitoring system established to check levels of radioactivity at Japanese ports had been faulty, that the Japan Analytical Chemistry Research Institute, entrusted with this task, had issued inaccurate reports. Fuwa demanded that the entry of all U.S. nuclear-powered submarines into Japanese ports be prohibited at once. Government spokesmen later acknowledged that the data obtained had indeed been incorrect, and agreed to effect changes. Meanwhile JCP representatives carried on inspections at the sites of the monitoring systems and denounced the government for its lax measures and again called for the termination of the security treaty with the United States.

In August a Communist member of the Foreign Affairs Committee of the House of Representatives charged that the United States was violating the security treaty by maintaining the Over-the-Horizon Radar (OTH) which was designed to detect by radar missiles which might be fired against the United States from the Soviet Union or China. He contended that the installation of such a system had no relation to the defense and security of Japan; it would only furnish a vulnerable target in case of war and thus threaten Japan's being drawn into America's wars. A special JCP Survey Mission visited the three sites where such equipment was installed, in Okinawa, Saitama, and Hokkaido prefectures. In spite of the government's denials that OTH violated the security treaty, JCP Diet members and publicists made the most of the matter and reported in detail the results of their surveys. (*Tokyo Shimbun*, 19 August.)

By far the most sensational and profitable issue to fall into the lap of the Communists since the reversion of Okinawa was the statement by retired U.S. Rear Admiral Gene R. La Roque before a sub-committee of the Joint Congressional Committee on Atomic Energy to the effect that U.S. warships bearing nuclear weapons did not offload these weapons before entering ports in Japan or other countries. First published in Japan on 6 October, this story, with elaborations, was spread across the front pages and in the editorial columns of every principal daily newspaper in the country. JCP journalists, officials, and Diet members were quick to exploit the reported testimony, the first of its kind from such a credible source as a retired admiral who had once commanded the flagship of the Seventh Fleet. Fuwa Tetsuzo called the La Roque testimony the most important of all current problems. (*Akahata*, 26 October.) JCP spokesmen boasted that their repeated warnings about the violation of Japan's three non-nuclear principles (not to make, possess, or bring in nuclear weapons) had been confirmed by an unimpeachable source. An enterprising *Akahata* reporter tracked down the admiral at a hotel in Moscow, where he was a guest of the Institute of U.S. Studies of the Soviet Academy of Sciences. In an interview, Admiral La Roque reportedly admitted that he had never called at a Japanese port aboard a U.S. ship which was then carrying nuclear weapons; he suggested, however, that the Japanese government query the U.S. government about the validity of his testimony. He carefully explained that he had not referred to the presence of nuclear weapons in Japan but had stated that nuclear-armed ships usually carry their weapons wherever they are in the world and do not unload them. (Ibid., 13 October.) A member of the Standing Committee of the Presidium announced that the JCP would submit to the two houses of the Diet at the next session a resolution calling for the prohibition of the entry into Japan of planes or ships armed with nuclear weapons, even though such entry might be only temporary or mere passage through Japanese territory (ibid., 20 November).

Immediately after the first of the year the JCP repeated its firm opposition to a visit to Japan by President Nixon, which would only "reinforce the U.S.-Japan military alliance in every aspect, politically, economically, and militarily" (Tokyo Joint Press Service, 5 January). In August when President Ford took office and the invitation was renewed, the JCP launched a campaign to stop the visit which continued in unremitting and accelerating intensity until the President came to Japan (18-22 November). The same themes were embroidered throughout the period, that the Ford visit would demonstrate the subordination of Japan to American imperialist policy, that the Ford Administration was continuing the Nixon "policy of power" intended to forge an anti-communist alliance and to violate Japanese sovereignty by the maintenance of military bases and forces. The Emperor's statement of welcome to the President was denounced as "political" and therefore unconstitutional, and Prime Minister Tanaka was berated for trying to bolster his own crumbling regime by raising the image of Japan as a "Big Power."

The JCP and the JSP joined in October in calling for opposition to the Ford visit. The JSP, however, later made it clear that it would not *block* the visit, that the party was only opposed to the Japan-U.S. military alliance and hoped that general relations between the two countries would not be impaired. Plans were made for a mammoth rally on "Anti-War Day," 21 October, and for a series of demonstrations in November, to culminate at the time President Ford would be in Tokyo. Although the organizers of the rallies—the JCP, JSP, Komeito, Sohyo, and various labor and peace organizations—claimed a total turnout of more than two million in 458 places throughout Japan, police authorities placed the figure at less than 300,000. The leader of the mass meeting in Tokyo (estimated at 70,000) affirmed that the aim was to create an atmosphere which would cause President Ford to cancel his visit. The *New York Times* correspondent questioned whether it would be possible for the demonstrators to generate and sustain enough vocal opposition to achieve their stated goal. "With the rather light-hearted, carnival atmosphere that prevailed tonight, it seemed doubtful that they had made much headway toward that objective." (*NYT*, 22 October.)

The Komeito and the DSP decided not to protest the visit. Thus the JCP and the JSP were left to organize the anti-Ford movement. On 13 November, some 90 leftist organizations sent representatives to a meeting which decided on rallies for later in the month. On 17 November about 85,000 protesters met in Tokyo to present double demands, for the ouster of Prime Minister Tanaka and for the cancellation of the Ford visit. On the day of the President's arrival, 18 November, rallies took place in Tokyo, including separate demonstrations by New Leftists, 188 of whom were arrested. The National Police Agency estimated that a total of 3,900 persons gathered in Tokyo, and 11,325 at 60 places in other parts of Japan. The meetings and marches were characterized as "generally subdued." (Kyodo News Service, Tokyo, 18 November.) After the joint Ford-Tanaka communiqué had been issued at the end of the visit, Ueda Koichiro, chairman of the JCP policy committee, declared on behalf of the party that the Ford visit had aimed at strengthening and making permanent the Japan-U.S. military alliance, that it had advanced the aggressive plans of a solidified Japan-U.S.-South Korea military combination, and, by the President's evasive attitude on the subject of nuclear weapons had provided proof that such weapons were actually being brought into Japan. Non-communist observers concluded that the JCP had failed to muster sufficient opposition strength to obstruct the visit because of the general good-will felt for the President by the great majority of Japanese citizens. (*K. D. K. Information*, monthly newsletter published by K. D. K. Kojimachi Institute, Tokyo, 1 December).

International Party Contacts. In January 1974, five members of the JCP, including three members of the Presidium, attended a conference in Prague to discuss the magazine *Problems of Peace and Socialism*. In August a member of the Presidium and of the House of Representatives, Yonehara Itaru, represented the JCP in Bucharest at the celebrations of the Thirtieth anniversary of the liberation of Romania.

The most publicized visit of the year was the dispatch to Hanoi of a JCP delegation headed by Fuwa Tetsuzo which spent a week in North Vietnam, 9-16 March. After inspecting various economic and cultural institutions, including a mining area and a farm machinery plant and conducting discussions with top leaders of the Vietnamese Workers' Party, the JCP visitors issued jointly with their hosts a communiqué which expressed the fraternal solidarity of the two parties, condemned serious violations by the United States of the Paris agreements to settle the Vietnam war, and pledged the JCP to seek recognition by the Japanese government of the Provisional Revolutionary Government of the Republic of South Vietnam.

On 24-27 February, representatives of the League of Communists of Yugoslavia visited Japan at the invitation of the JCP. After mutual discussions, a joint statement was issued 27 February which confirmed the developing relations between the two parties "on the basis of the principles of self-reliance, independence, and non-interference in each other's internal affairs" (*Akahata*, 28 February). In October, officers of the JCP received in the party's Tokyo headquarters members of delegations from Italy and North Korea who were attending the conference of the Inter-Parliamentary Union then being held in Tokyo.

Several exchanges of visits with Vietnamese delegations took place during the year. On 31 March a good-will group left Tokyo for Vietnam at the invitation of the National Front for the Liberation of South Vietnam and the Vietnam-Japan Friendship Association. The group spent fifteen days in communist-controlled areas in South Vietnam, after which they traveled to Hanoi. Return visits were paid in September by two delegations attending the twenty-fourth meeting of the Japan-Vietnam Friendship Association, one a group from the South Vietnam Peace Committee and another representing directly the Japan-Vietnam Friendship Association. Talks were held at the JCP headquarters in Tokyo. In the meantime, in May, a parliamentary delegation from the Democratic Republic of Vietnam (DRV) called on the JCP Diet representatives at the Diet building in Tokyo. The chief delegate from the DRV lauded the solidarity between the Japanese and Vietnamese people and called on the JCP to play a bigger role in developing diplomatic, trade, and economic relations between North Vietnam and Japan (ibid., 22 May).

Splinter Parties. The two principal splinter parties which oppose the JCP are the Voice of Japan (Nihon no Koe), formed in 1964 when the JCP broke with the CPSU over the partial nuclear test ban treaty, and the Japan Communist Party (Left), which came into existence in 1966 as a result of the quarrel which started at that time between the JCP and the CCP.

The Voice of Japan was founded by Shiga Yoshio, one of the leaders of the postwar JCP who was expelled from the party after he had cast his vote in the House of Representatives in favor of the partial nuclear test ban treaty which the JCP had opposed. Shiga and his small group of followers have never been able to expand their organization into one of influence; they have been a constant irritant for the JCP by their consistently pro-Soviet policies and by the sporadic assistance they have obtained from the Soviet Union. The party membership is estimated at 450; the total number of supporters may reach 600. The party issues two publications, a weekly: *Voice of Japan*, and a monthly; Flag of Democracy (*Minshushugi no Hata*). An affiliated student group is called Student Alliance for Democracy (*Minshushugi Gakusei Domei*).

The JCP (Left) was organized in Yamaguchi prefecture by pro-Peking dissidents who defected after the split between the JCP and the CCP in 1966. The founder of the group is Fukuda Masayoshi. The official membership is estimated at 500 with a possible 1500 supporters. The party is said to maintain 22 branches. Its publications include: People's Star (*Jinmin no Hoshi*) and *Choshu Shimbun*, both issued twice weekly. The party claims to have supporting youth groups in universities and high schools. The JCP (Left) is given frequent publicity in the Peking press, often because of anti-Soviet articles which appear in People's Star.

JCP Publications. Carrying out Lenin's dicta on the power of the party press, the JCP maintains an extensive publishing organization. In addition to *Akahata*, the party's national daily newspaper which is now attempting to compete on a commercial basis with Japan's leading dailies, the JCP and its affiliated organizations issue a continuing stream of periodicals, books, pamphlets, and tracts, aimed at the party membership in general or at particular segments of the party. Listed below are some of the principal nationally distributed periodicals with their current circulation figures.

Party organs: *Akahata*, daily, 600,000; Sunday 2.2 million; reduced edition, monthly, 6,000; Vanguard (*Zenei*), monthly magazine, 110,000; Documents of World Politics (*Sekai Seiji Shiryo*), semi-monthly, 30,000; Problems of Peace and Socialism (*Heiwa to Shakaishugi no Sho Mondai*), monthly, 10,000; Parliament and Self-Governing Organizations (*Gikai to Jichitai*), monthly, 15,000; Students' News (*Gakusei Shimbun*) weekly, 26,000; Studies Monthly (*Gekkan Gakushu*), guidance for new party members, 110,000; Cultural Critique (*Bunka Hyoron*), monthly, 20,000; Akahata Picture News (*Akahata Shashin Nyusu*), every 10 days, 7,000.

Semi-party organs: Economics Monthly (*Gekkan Keizai*), 30,000; New Women's News (*Shin Fujin Shimbun*), weekly, 160,000; Democratic Youth News (*Minshu Seinen Shimbun*), 300,000; Youth Movement (*Seinen Undo*), monthly, 20,000; Friend of Learning (*Gakushu no Tomo*), monthly, 120,000; The Farming Village Worker (*Noson Rodosha*), semi-monthly, 10,000; The Workers and Farmers Movement (*Rodo Nomin Undo*), monthly, 20,000; Democratic Literature (*Minshu Bungaku*), monthly, 20,000. (1974 circulation figures are taken from *Nikkyo, Minsei*, Handbook on JCP, Minseido, published by Japan Institute for Politics and Economics, Tokyo, October 1974).

Hoover Institution   John K. Emmerson
Stanford University

Korea: Democratic People's Republic of Korea

The Korean Communist Party (Choson Kongsan-dang; KCP) was formed at Seoul in 1925 during the time of the Japanese rule; in 1928, due chiefly to suppression, it ceased to function. Shortly after World War II, a revived KCP appeared briefly in Seoul. Control of the communist movement in Korea soon shifted to the northern part of the country, then occupied by Soviet forces, where the "North Korean Central Bureau of the KCP" was formed in October 1945 under Soviet auspices. The three major factions of the movement—comprising Korean communists who during the Japanese period had gone to China, or to the Soviet Union, or had remained in Korea—subsequently merged, and on 24 June 1949 the Korean Workers' Party (Choson Nodong-dang; KWP) was established. The KWP is today the ruling party of the Democratic Republic of Korea (DPRK).

Kim Il-song, Korean-born but Soviet-trained, who had been an anti-Japanese communist guerrilla leader in southern Manchuria in the 1930s, consolidated his power by eliminating rival factions, and today his Manchurian partisan group (the Kapsan faction) holds unassailable supremacy in the North Korean leadership.

The number of the KWP members is estimated at 2,000,000. (This figure was given in an editorial in *Nodong Shinmun*, 29 August 1972.) The population of the DPRK is about 14,700,000.

Leadership and Organization. North Korea has a typical communist administrative structure. The center of decisionmaking is in the KWP, and the government merely executes party policy. All important leaders hold concurrent positions in the party and government.

The present top leadership of the DPRK, as elected at the KWP's Fifth Congress on 13 November 1970, includes the following:

KWP Political Committee (In order of rank in November 1970)	Other Positions Held Concurrently
Kim Il-song	KWP secretary-general; DPRK president; Supreme commander of armed forces
Choe Yong-gon	KWP Central Committee (CC) secretary; DPRK vice-president; member of Central People's Committee
Kim Il	KWP CC secretary; premier of State Administration Council; member of Central People's Committee
Pak Song-chol	Deputy premier of State Administration Council; member of Central People's Committee
Choe Hyon	Minister of defense; colonel general; vice-chairman of National Defense Commission of Central People's Committee

Kim Yong-ju	Kim Il-song's younger brother; KWP CC secretary; deputy premier of State Administration Council; member of Central People's Committee
O Chin-u	KWP CC secretary; Armed Forces chief of General Staff; lieutenant general; vice-chairman of National Defense Commission of Central People's Committee
Kim Tong-gyu	KWP CC secretary; director of KWP International Affairs Department; vice president
So Chol	Lieutenant general; vice-chairman of Presidium of Supreme People's Assembly
Kim Chung-rin	KWP CC Secretary; director of KWP Liaison Bureau (General Bureau on South Korea); member of Central People's Committee
Han Ik-su	KWP CC secretary; director of General Political Bureau of Armed Forces; colonel general
Yang Hyong-sop	KWP CC secretary; member of Central People's Committee
Yi Yong-mu	Deputy director of (North) Korean People's Army's General Political Bureau

Candidate (Non-voting) Members

Hyon Mu-gwang	KWP CC secretary; member of Central People's Committee; chairman of Transportation and Communications Committee of Administration Council
Chong Chun-Taek	Deputy premier of State Administration Council; member of Central People's Committee
Kim Man-gum	Deputy premier of State Administration Council; member of Central People's Committee
Yu Chang-sik	Deputy foreign minister and vice director of KWP International Department

The 17-member Political Committee (created during the Fourth Party Congress, 1961) and the 10-member Secretariat constitute the core of important decision-makers in the DPRK and act as a controlling nucleus for the Central Committee (117 regular and 55 alternate members).

The present central government structure consists of three pillars of power: the 25-member Central People's Committee (which is basically a policy-making and supervisory body under the KWP guidance); the 29-member State Administration Council (an organ to execute policies already made by the Central People's Committee); and the 18-member Standing Committee of the Supreme People's Assembly (a symbolic and honorific body which functions as a legislative branch).

The KWP controls the following mass organizations: the two-million-member General Federation of Trade Unions of Korea (GFTUK); the 2.7-million-member League of Socialist Working Youth of Korea (LSWY); the Union of Agricultural Working People; the Korean Democratic Women's Union; and the General Federation of Korean Residents in Japan (Chongnyon or Chosen Soren).

At least two subordinate political movements under the tight KWP control exist in North Korea: the Korean Democratic Party (Choson Minju-dang) and Young Friends' Party of the Chondogyo Sect (the sect being the Society of the Heavenly Way—Chondogyo Chong-u-dang). No membership figures are available on these movements. Their function is to enhance acceptance of the United Democratic Fatherland Front (Choguk Tongil Minjujuui Chonson), created by 71 political and social organizations in June 1949, which is assigned the task of uniting "all the revolutionary forces of North and South Korea" under the leadership of the KWP, in order to implement the "peaceful unification and complete independence of the country." The KWP also controls the "Committee for Peaceful Unification of the Fatherland," established in May 1961 and consisting of representatives from the KWP, the subordinate "democratic" parties, and the mass organizations.

According to unconfirmed reports coming from the 26 February 1974 issue of the *Tongil Ilbo* ("Unification Paper"), a newspaper published by Korean residents in Tokyo, Japan, the DPRK's power hierarchy was realigned in February 1974. The paper said that the DPRK leaders who were involved in the dialogue with the South had been demoted. Military leaders instead advanced in the power rank.

Kim Yong-ju, younger brother of president and party secretary-general Kim Il-song and Pyongyang's co-chairman of the South-North Coordinating Committee, was demoted from 6th to 13th in rank; Pak Song-chol, Politburo member and deputy premier, from 4th to 7th; Kim Chung-rin, Politburo member and head of the KWP bureau responsible for operations against South Korea, from 10th to 12th.

Choe Hyon, Politburo member and defense minister, was promoted from 5th to 4th in the ranking system; O Chin-u, general chief of staff of the (North) Korean People's Army and also a Politburo member, from 7th to 5th; Kim Tong-gyu, Politburo member and director of the KWP Central Committee's International Affairs Department from 8th to 6th; So Chol, Politburo member, from 9th to 8th; and Han Ik-su, Politburo member and chief of the army's General Political Bureau, from 11th to 9th.

According to the paper, there was at least a coincidence in timing between the promotion of these military leaders in the ranking order and the DPRK's increasingly aggressive attitude toward the South (i.e., the North Korean attack on two South Korean fishing boats at sea on 15 February 1974). The first three top-ranking figures—Kim Il-song, Choe Yong-gon, and Kim Il—were not affected.

What was most significant in this power realignment, if true, was the apparent demotion of Kim Il-song's younger brother, Kim Yong-ju, who was believed to have been slated to be the successor to his brother. During the same month of February he was also relieved of his influential party post—directorship of the KWP Organization and Guidance Department that he had held for 12 years—and moved to the relatively powerless position of deputy premier of the State Administration Council.

Pak Su-dong, the first deputy director of the KWP Organization and Guidance Department, was promoted to head the department. Pak's ranking was 17th as he attended the so-called national industrial congress in Pyongyang in late February. His previous ranking status in the KWP Central Committee was 65th.

Interestingly enough, the demotion of Kim Yong-ju was accompanied by the rapid ascendancy of Kim Il-song's son, Kim Chong-il, to powerful posts in the DPRK regime. This may indicate that Kim Il-song is trying to groom his son as his future successor, as the *Tongil Ilbo* hinted on 9 April. The move to make Kim Chong-il his father's future successor began last year, the paper said, quoting reliable sources on Pyongyang affairs. It said further that the changes in early 1974 in the ranking order of the DPRK officials reflected a move involving the succession problem.

Kim Chong-il is Kim Il-song's only surviving son and is now in his thirties. (His mother was his father's first wife, Kim Chong-suk, who died in 1949.) Kim Il-song's other (elder) son died while swimming in the Taedong River before the Korean War. While in his twenties, Kim Chong-il acted as his father's personal secretary, and also worked under Pak Su-dong, when Pak was a deputy chief of the KWP Organization and Guidance Department. In the 1970s he appears to have been promoted to influential posts in the Pyongyang regime. In 1972 he reportedly became the director of the KWP Propaganda and Agitation Department, and in 1973 he was said to have been appointed a member of the KWP Secretariat. Since February 1974, it is reported, he has been in overall charge of the DPRK's operations toward South Korea and Japan. His personal coterie is now believed to include O Chin-u, Politburo member and defense minister; Yi Yong-mu, Politburo member and deputy director of the army's General Political Bureau; Pak Su-dong, director of the KWP Organization and Guidance Department; Yi Kun-mo, deputy premier; Yu Chang-sik, candidate Politburo member and deputy foreign minister and vice-director of the KWP International Department; and Yon Hyong-muk, KWP Central Committee member and chief secretary of a provincial committee.

At the 4th session of the 5th Supreme People's Assembly, held in late November, Kim Tong-gyu, a member of the Political Committee and secretary of the KWP Central Committee, was elected vice-president of the DPRK.

Domestic Attitudes and Activities. The 8th plenum of the 5th KWP Central Committee was held in Pyongyang on 11-13 February 1974. The plenum decided to send a letter from the party Central Committee to all party members asking them to mobilize every effort in the grand construction work of socialism. In this connection, the North Korean people were urged to finish the current six-year plan in 1975, one year ahead of the original schedule.

The plenary meeting also decided to refer the question of completely abolishing taxes to the Supreme People's Assembly, which was to be held in March, and also to refer the question of sharply reducing the prices of industrial goods to the Central People's Committee for deliberation.

The 3rd session of the 5th Supreme People's Assembly was held in Pyongyang on 20-25 March. On 22 March a law of the Supreme People's Assembly on complete abolition of taxation in the DPRK as of 1 April 1974 was adopted. North Korea probably thus became the first tax-free country in history. The DPRK press hailed the move as an advance toward true communism.

For the average North Korean household, according to a report to the session by Yi Kun-mo, deputy premier of the State Administration Council, the abolition of taxes and a 30 percent average reduction in the prices of manufactured goods in March would mean an additional 28 won (U.S. $14) a month in real income—6 won ($3) from abolishing taxes and 22 won ($11) from cutting prices. (The exchange rate of won to U.S. dollars is estimated to be 2.05 to 1.) As a result, Yi said, the real income of the working people in 1974 would jump 50 percent above 1970 for the factory and office workers and 60 percent for the peasants.

With the abolition of the taxes and the reduction of the prices of goods, according to Yi, the state would bear an additional financial burden running into 900 million won ($450 million) in 1974 and more than 1,300 million won ($750 million) in 1975. The state revenue from 1 April 1974 on will come completely from what Pyongyang calls "state accumulation," or income from state enterprises. Yi said at the session that the funds needed for "revolution and construction" in the DPRK could be fully covered with the revenues from the socialist state economy and, furthermore, the state could assume responsibility for the people's life, its funds being scores of times larger than the taxes formerly paid by them.

Even with the abolition of taxes, however, the delegates to the Assembly were told that the DPRK still had fundamental economic problems. Deputy premier Yi said that the most important task today was to "narrow down the distinction between the workers and the peasants in their living standards and distinctions between the urban and rural inhabitants in their living conditions."

On 25 March the session approved a letter from the Supreme People's Assembly to the U.S. Congress in which Pyongyang proposed talks with Washington on a "peace" accord to replace the 1953 Korean armistice agreement. (See the section dealing with the DPRK's relations with the United States.)

Finally, the session passed the 1974 state budget, set at 9,801,210,000 won ($4,781,080,000), an increase of 14 percent over last year. Defense spending for 1974 was set at $764,970,000 or 16 percent of total expenditure. (The actual defense budget spending would be higher because the DPRK regime makes it a rule to hide defense expenditure in other sectors.) Total active armed forces in 1974 were believed to number around 450,000 (including 26,000 security units).

The 4th session of the 5th Supreme People's Assembly was held from 27 to 30 November in Pyongyang. The session adopted the following agenda: (1) the summing up of the implementation of the "theses on the socialist rural question" set forth by President Kim Il-song and future tasks; and (2) election of vice-president (see the section on Leadership and Organization).

South Korea. There were growing signs in 1974 that the much-hailed dialogue between the two Koreas was dead and that the level of tension and animosity between them had in fact reached a new peak. The *New York Times* reported on 23 February, quoting Pentagon officials, that North Korean forces had been redeployed toward South Korea "in a major way" and had stepped up their military preparedness over the last few months.

The relations between North and South Korea, already strained since the rapprochement talks were suspended in August 1973, plunged into a new crisis when the North Korean navy sank a small South Korean fishing boat and captured another in the Yellow Sea on 15 February. Shortly after this first shooting incident at sea between the two sides since their détente announcement of 4 July 1972, Seoul publicly resumed calling Pyongyang a "northern puppet."

North Korean gunboats sank a South Korean maritime patrol vessel in the East China Sea on 27 June, and the two governments quickly exchanged charges and threats.

No full-dress Political Coordinating Committee talks between North and South Korea have been held since June 1973. For several months, the North refused to meet as long as the then director of the South's Central Intelligence Agency, Lee Hu-rak, remained as a co-chairman of the committee—in protest over Lee's alleged role as mastermind in the Tokyo kidnaping of a South Korean opposition leader, Kim Dae-jung.

Lee Hu-rak was dropped from office in December 1973, but still Pyongyang would not agree to resume formal Coordinating Committee meetings. During 1974 the meetings were stalled over the North's demand for a grand national conference of some 1,400 participants, which the South resists as a ploy for a propaganda sounding board.

The two governments were also deadlocked over separate proposals for some sort of "friendship" treaty between them—South Korean president Park's 18 January call for a "non-aggression pact" countering the DPRK's earlier proposals for a "peace agreement."

In the fall of 1974 North Korea increased its denunciations of the South Korean government in reaction to charges from Seoul that it was responsible for the attempted assassination of President Park on 15 August by Mun Se-kwang, a Korean resident of Japan. The North emphatically denied South Korean accusations that the attack, in which Park's wife was killed, had been directed by President Kim Il-song. The South Korean allegation that North Korea was responsible for the attack on President Park and the angry North Korea response seemed to have virtually eliminated any chance for a dialogue between the two regimes for the present.

North and South Korean troops fought a gun battle on 15 November when South Korean soldiers discovered a tunnel dug by northern forces to a point about 1,000 yards south of the military demarcation line.

International Views and Positions. Following the détente mood between the United States and the two major communist powers in 1971, the DPRK began gingerly opening windows and doors to make contact with the outside world.

During 1974 Pyongyang supplemented its efforts on the reunification issue by becoming extremely active on the foreign policy front, partly to undermine the international position of its rival in South Korea and partly to develop world support for North Korean policies. Parliamentary, trade, and other good-will missions were dispatched abroad and invited to North Korea, and friendly diplomatic gestures were made to every corner of the earth, particularly the Afro-Asian "third world."

On 1 June the DPRK obtained membership in the Universal Postal Union, where South Korea was already a member. Since the UPO is a United Nations affiliate, the North's admission was a diplomatic leap forward. When the U.N. General Assembly opened its annual session in the fall of 1974, with the question of divided Korea as one of the important issues on its agenda, representatives from Pyongyang were quite active in trying to line up votes of the group of communist and more militant third-world countries that joined forces to suspend South Africa from the Assembly session on 12 November and ten days later pushed through a resolution, sought by the Palestine Liberation Organization, declaring that the Palestinian people had a right to independence and sovereignty

In relations with the communist bloc, North Korea continued to avoid leaning toward either the Soviet Union or China, in accordance with the *chuch'e* principle, and to maintain or seek warm, friendly relations with all of the communist bloc countries and all leftist revolutionary groups of the world.

Relations with the Soviet Union and China. Currently, the DPRK's *chuch'e* policy in communist-bloc affairs is exemplified by its opposition to both Soviet "revisionism" and Chinese "left opportunism" or "dogmatism." But relations with the Soviet Union and China continued in 1974 to be warm and cordial. The Soviets and the Chinese gave a matter-of-fact support to the DPRK's positions both in its détente talks with the South and in the U.N. debate on the Korean question. But military assistance from the two major communist powers to the DPRK (also from the United States to South Korea) was reported to have declined substantially in recent months.

In November mainland China opened another front in its propaganda war against the Soviet Union by accusing Moscow of betraying North Korea. An article in the 10 November issue of Peking's *People's Daily* claimed that the Soviets did not dare explicitly support the North Korean program for reunification of the Korean peninsula. The article also said that Moscow had recently had low-level contacts with the South Korean government and individual South Koreans. The Soviet government emphatically denied the Chinese allegations. The *People's Daily* article was ostensibly written to counter a report by the Soviet news agency TASS that China had agreed to sell about 1,000 tons of red peppers to the South Koreans. The article described the report as a fabrication.

Relations with Japan. While highly critical of the growing Japanese stakes in the South, the Pyongyang regime has been openly bidding for Japanese diplomatic recognition and closer economic ties. Suspicions and hostility toward Japan are still profound in the DPRK. Pyongyang views Tokyo as being excessively partial to Seoul, pursuing a policy of two-Koreas and hostility toward North Korea, although the degree of antagonism was reduced under the cabinet of Tanaka Kakuei. During 1974 North Korea was actively trying to loosen Japanese ties with South Korea or to have Tokyo pursue a more even-handed posture toward the rival Korean states.

Relations with the United States. The Pyongyang regime has been vigorous and a good bit more shrill in demanding the removal of all U.S. troops from South Korea, pointing out that its own Chinese allies have long since departed. It has contended that the 38,000 U.S. troops stationed in South Korea are a source of tension and potential conflict, and an obstacle to peace in the divided country.

In the 25 March letter from the Supreme People's Assembly to the United States Congress, the DPRK made a proposal for a bilateral "peace" agreement with Washington, without the participation of Seoul. The letter proposed: (1) that each agree not to invade the other, and each avoid all the danger of direct armed conflict; (2) that each stop introducing weapons, combat equipment, or war supplies into Korea; (3) that the United States remove the U.N. insignia from U.S. troops stationed in the South and withdraw the troops "at the earliest date"; and (4) that each refrain from making Korea an operational base of any foreign country after the withdrawal of foreign troops.

In Washington, the State Department reacted coolly to the North Korean appeal. A department spokesman affirmed the U.S. position that the Korean problem should be resolved directly by the two Koreas.

In testimony before the Senate Armed Services Committee in early 1974, the U.S. secretary of defense, James Schlesinger, supported the need for U.S. forces in South Korea, maintaining that the troop presence was essential for deterring another outbreak of hostilities in the Korean peninsula.

In April, the U.S. government turned down a request by North Korea's chief U.N. delegate, Ambassador Kwon Min-joon, to attend a seminar at Harvard.

But in June three North Korean diplomats broke diplomatic ground by attending a five-day U.N.-sponsored conference on food hygiene in Washington, D.C., becoming the first DPRK officials permitted to venture beyond New York City since the Korean War.

State Department officials said that the United States had an obligation to allow persons attached to the United Nations to travel to U.N.-connected meetings. The officials categorically denied that there was any political significance in the presence of the three in Washington, though one official said that North Korea was "interested in a broader relationship."

United Nations. The Korean question was brought up again in the fall session of the U.N. General Assembly. The Seoul government was expected to seek again the simultaneous admission into the world organization of South and North Korea, and the Pyongyang regime to stick to its previous proposal that the two sides join the United Nations as a single unified body after the abolition of the U.N. military command in Korea and the withdrawal of all U.S. troops.

Opening a debate on the Korean issue in the General Assembly's Political Committee in November, DPRK deputy foreign minister Yi Chong-mok said: "Mr. Ford's trip to South Korea [in November 1974] was, indeed, a trip for war expansion and a trip for aggression." The minister generally reiterated the previous year's demand by North Korea that the U.N. General Assembly call for the withdrawal of the 38,000 U.S. troops in South Korea and for dismantling of the U.N. Command.

Acting on behalf of the DPRK, which is a non-member but has observer status at the United Nations, 36 countries submitted a draft resolution calling for the withdrawal from South Korea of all foreign forces under the U.N. flag. The sponsors of the motion included the Soviet Union, China, the communist bloc, and Algeria and other members of the Arab, African, and Asian group of the third-world countries.

The United States, Great Britain, and 25 other countries mostly Western, countered with a proposal saying that tension persist in the Korean peninsula and that the United Nations has a "continuing responsibility" there, leaving it to the Security Council to decide about the U.N. Command when conditions improve.

On 9 December the General Assembly's Political Committee approved, 61 votes to 42 with 32 abstentions, the pro-Seoul resolution. Once again, the resolution spoke of the need for continuing dialogue between the two Koreas.

In the same meeting, the Committee rejected, by a 48-to-48 vote with 38 abstentions, the pro-Pyongyang resolution.

Publications. The KWP publishes a daily organ, *Nodong Shinmun*, and a journal, *Kulloja*. The DPRK government publishes *Minju Choson*, the organ of the Supreme People's Assembly and the cabinet. The *Pyongyang Times, People's Korea*, and *Korea Today* are weekly English-language publications. The official news agency is the Korean Central News Agency.

Washington College   Tai Sung An

Laos

The communist party of Laos, under its cover of the Lao Patriotic Front, found itself in 1974 a full participant in its country's government and even had one of its prominent members as acting prime minister. While continuing to exhort its cadres in the "liberated zone" to further efforts in the struggle to achieve the party's aim of complete victory of the revolution, it experimented successfully with the pursuit of a more gentle revolution through its official positions within the government, advocating police measures to control gambling and crime, and announcing plans for the development of agriculture, industry, and trade.

Leadership and Organization. The Lao People's Party (Phak Pasason Lao; PPL) operates in semi-secrecy. Its overt activities occur through the medium of the Lao Patriotic Front (Neo Lao Hak Xat; NLHX—sometimes NLHS). So far as is known, the Central Committee of the PPL comprises the following 11 members: Kaysone Phomvihan, secretary-general; Nouhak Phoumsavan, deputy secretary-general; Prince Souphanouvong, first committee member (and chairman of the NLHX Central Committee); Phoumi Vongvichit, foreign affairs; Sisomphone; PPL organization and membership; Samseun, PPL internal security; Sanan; General Khamtay Siphandone, commander in chief of the Lao People's Liberation Army (LPLA, better known as the Pathet Lao); General Sisavat, chief of staff, LPLA; General Saman, chief of staff, political affairs, LPLA; Khamsouk, first secretary, South Laos (Joseph J. Zasloff, *The Pathet Lao*, Lexington, Mass.; Heath, 1973, p. 33).

Historically the furtherance of the party's clandestine efforts by political and military means has been facilitated by its consolidation of control over a base area in strategic proximity to the border of Laos with Vietnam. This fact has given the leaders first of the Indochinese Communist Party and later of the Vietnamese Workers' Party a deciding voice in the PPL's policies and actions enjoyed by no other foreign country with which the PPL maintains friendly relations. Thus, while (on the evidence of a former Polish member of the International Control Commission in Laos) the Russian and Chinese representatives in the PPL base area were frequently kept in the dark as to the PPL's intentions during the crucial period leading up to the party's decision to enter the second coalition government in 1962, the North Vietnamese representatives spoke with an authority about Laos affairs suggesting that it was they who set the line. In fact, it was North Vietnam which was able to provide guidance and support to the PPL to a degree which allowed it to exercise a considerable degree of control over it. Thus, it is a development of more than passing interest that 1974 saw the emergence of a new "base of the LPF Central Committee in the liberated zone" (Pathet Lao News Agency, 23 August) at Viengsay, 20 miles east of Sam Neua near the North Vietnam border. Sam Neua had served as the headquarters of the Lao communist movement ever since the 1950s and was still so used as late as 1973. Its buildings had been almost totally destroyed in recent years, however, as a result of U.S. bombing.

Precise information on the personalities of the leaders of the Lao communist party is extremely difficult to obtain. However, an official announcement broadcast over Radio Pathet Lao on 28 July stated that Sot Phetrasi, who had represented the NLHX in Vientiane following the collapse of the second coalition in 1963, and who is considered certain to be a member of the PPL, was replaced in this capacity by Sanan Soutthichak. Sot Phetrasi is minister of economy and planning in the new government; he also holds the important position of head of the Central Joint Commission for the implementation of the Vientiane Agreement and Protocol.

Broadcasts from Radio Pathet Lao spoke of the largely ceremonial activities of the two top leaders of the PPL, Kaysone and Nouhak, who have remained in the liberated zone and not been chosen to join the coalition government. The activities of Prince Souphanouvong during the year were reported in much greater detail, since he has assumed an important role as chairman of the National Consultative Political Council (NCPC), the body which, at NLHX insistence during the prolonged negotiations leading to formation of the government, enjoys co-equal authority with the cabinet in deciding matters of government policy. At its first session the NCPC approved an 18-point domestic and foreign program that reflected the lead given by the NLHX in suggesting and obtaining assent to statements of how the government should tackle the urgent problems facing Laos.

Domestic Attitudes and Activities. While NLHX broadcasts during 1974 continued a drumfire of demands for acceptance of communist positions on many matters both domestic and foreign, the NLHX ministers within the government showed a moderate line in day-to-day government business that surprised many observers in Vientiane, where the outward routine of government appeared to have varied very little. The question of the rightist-dominated National Assembly (elected in the non-NLHX-controlled areas in 1972), for instance, which threatened to come to a head in July, was eventually skirted with typical Lao deftness. The Assembly was not dissolved, but it did not meet, and its fate was put on the shelf, despite the loud protests of some members. Realization that formal dissolution implied fresh elections within 90 days compelled moderation on both sides on this issue: participation in such elections by the NLHX would imply acceptance of existing election laws, something the NLHX refused, but the NLHX was not yet ready to have the formulation of new election laws discussed by the NCPC and cabinet, as prescribed by the signed agreements. Meanwhile, the NLHX was creating a favorable image and discretely propagandizing among the populations of Vientiane and Luang Prabang, the two towns in which it had a sizable representation (including security forces of its own) under the agreements.

A heart attack in July removed the prime minister, Prince Souvanna Phouma, from the political scene while he underwent treatment in Vientiane and convalescence in France. In this situation, Phoumi Vongvichit, the senior of the two deputy prime ministers in terms of age and the highest-ranking NLHX minister in the cabinet, was appointed acting prime minister (Radio Vientiane, 9 August). In his concurrent capacity as foreign minister, Phoumi also traveled to New York to head Laos's delegation to the U.N. General Assembly.

The apparent willingness to compromise on issues that threatened a head-on collision with the rightists was evidenced by the NLHX ministers on the question of recognition of the Provisional Revolutionary Government of South Vietnam and Prince Norodom Sihanouk's government of Cambodia. Decisions on both were put off by the cabinet, while NLHX broadcasts from its liberated zone continued to demand recognition of these governments as the sole representatives of the people of South Vietnam and Cambodia. The NLHX appeared to be putting the survival of the coalition before all else during 1974, when the peace agreement in Laos was still fragile.

In an interview with a Polish correspondent, Prince Souphanouvong expressed the following view when asked if the establishment of the coalition represented a victory for the NLHX:

I have already said that this was a victory of all the Lao people, a people who have fought against neocolonialism and who have begrudged no suffering and sacrifices in this struggle. In our talks with the Vientiane side we never say that we have won. Everyone has won, all the people. Only a small minority of those who have lived from war were on the losing side.

(Question:) This means that today there are no victors and no vanquished in Laos?

Exactly. Both sides agreed to a compromise. After all, if the Vientiane side did not agree to a compromise we would have no peace in Laos today. Both sides accepted the conditions of peace and the program adopted by our council. The most important task now is to implement this program. (*Trybuna Ludu*, Warsaw, 14 August.)

International Activities. The NLHX continued in 1974 to receive delegations from friendly socialist countries in its liberated zone, and to exchange messages of greetings in conformity with past practice. Also welcomed to Viengsay were two high-ranking functionaries of the communist movement in Cambodia, Khieu Samphan and Ieng Sary. A long-time sympathizer of the NLHX, Khamphay Boupha, was approved in the key position of ambassador of Laos to North Vietnam ("Radio Pathet Lao," 5 July).

University of Maryland

Arthur J. Dommen

Malaysia

Communism in Malaysia is confined (*a*) to one major underground organization, the Communist Party of Malaya, (CPM), whose organizational jurisdiction is limited to West Malaysia but also includes Singapore, and (*b*) to a number of local revolutionary and/or guerrilla groups in Eastern Malaysia in the states of Sarawak and Sabah on Borneo, usually collectively designated by such terms as the Sarawak Communist Organization (SCO) or the North Kalimantan Communist Party (NKCP). None of these groups recognizes the legal or constitutional existence of the Malaysian Federation, established in 1963, and hence there is no single official communist organization that encompasses the entire country. Since 1948, and the upsurge of guerrilla communism in Western Malaysia, communist organizations have been illegal. Before World War II illegality generally also tended to be the rule.

History. The roots of communism in Western Malaysia lie in local radical trade union, educational, and other groups formed by Chinese in Singapore, Penang, and other major cities during the 1920s. Under the direction of the Comintern a "Communist Party of the South Seas" was organized in 1928, but it presumably included Thai, Malayan, Philippine, and other Southeast Asian communist groups, and offered little coordination. The CPM was formally established on 28 April 1930 to direct communist activities both on the Malay Peninsula and in Singapore. Indonesian communists who had fled after an unsuccessful coup attempt in their country in 1926-27 were active in the early CPM, and also acted as liaison with Comintern leaders in Moscow and their agents in the Far East. During the early 1930s the effect of the economic depression enhanced Communist appeals among tin mining and rubber estate workers, and in the predominantly Chinese labor organizations among them. A party constitution in 1934 provided additional organizational stability. (Gene Z. Hanrahan, *The Communist Struggle in Malaya*, Kuala Lumpur, University of Malaya Press, 1971, pp. 43-46.)

Communism on the Malay Peninsula before, during, and, indeed, even after World War II was and has remained largely a Chinese affair, with only minimal participation of the Malayan and Indian population groups. During World War II, communism in Malaya, as in other areas of Southeast Asia, acquired significant prestige because of communist initiatives in the organization of the anti-Japanese guerrilla resistance. CPM efforts to effect linkages with the budding Malayan nationalist movement during the war period proved largely unsuccessful, however, although some measure of de facto solidarity developed between Chinese and other population groups in the common struggle against Japan.

After World War II, as the British took initiatives toward eventual independence for Malaya, the CPM again lost support and in 1948 launched a protracted guerrilla war against British rule from jungle strongholds in the heart of the peninsula. The "Emergency" which thus began was not officially proclaimed to have been ended until twelve years later. But well before then the CPM's revolutionary "people's war" tactics had proved ineffective. (See Edgar O'Ballance, *Malaya: The Communist Insurgent War, 1948-1960*, Faber and Faber, London, 1966, esp. pp. 143-76). Virtually all population groups in Malaya, except segments of the Chinese community, refused to join in the gerrilla war, and deep-rooted anti-Chinese racial hostilities in the Malayan community continued to block communist appeals for "democratic" interrracial unity. Government counterinsurgency tactics, particularly those imposing logistical isolation on the guerrillas, gradually became more varied, sophisticated, and effective (Richard Clutterbuck, *Riot and Revolution in Singapore and Malaya, 1945-1963*, Faber and Faber, London, 1973, pp. 211-29). Above all, the proclamation of Malaya's independence on 31 August 1957 undercut the nationalist appeal in the guerrillas' struggle.

By the early 1960s the remnant of the CMP's "people's" forces, numbering perhaps no more than a hundred, had regrouped along the Thai-Malayan frontier. Now called either the Malayan National Liberation Army (MNLA) or Malayan Revolutionary Liberation Army (MRLA), the guerrillas in the past decade have solidified their organization, engaging in ambushes and other hit-and-run attacks on government posts and patrols, as meanwhile their underground network of cadres, training schools, and camps, and the creation of new cells of followers in the rural areas as well as major cities, including Singapore, continues.

By August 1974 there was official Malaysian government confirmation of a three-way split in Malayan communism. A rival party, calling itself the Communist Party of Malaya (Marxist-Leninist), or CPM-ML, had broken off from the CPM and claimed to have its own fighting force, the "Malayan People's Liberation Army" (MPLA). Before this, yet another group had seceded from the CPM, this one calling itself the Communist Party of Malaya (Revolutionary Faction), or CPM-RF. The last group, which began operating in February 1974, seems to be composed mainly of the MNLA's "Eighth Regiment," while the CPM(ML) is said to be made up of the "2nd district" unit of the MNLA's "Twelfth Regiment." Serious questions about the loyalty of recruits in the MNLA had erupted as early as 1970, and appear basic to the present three-way split. (*New Straits Times*, Kuala Lumpur, 2 November; *FBIS*, 8 November.) The ideological and tactical differences between these three factions, and the relative strengths of each faction, have not as yet become clear.

Organized communism in Eastern Malaysia has been primarily concentrated in the state of Sarawak. Before and During World War II, particularly in the Sarawak towns of Sibu and Miri, underground communist activity was centered in a virtually entirely Chinese "Sarawak Liberation League" and later in the "Sarawak Anti-Fascist League," which was active in the resistance movement during the Japanese occupation. In 1951 supporters of these leagues identified themselves with a new complex of covert communist organizations, of which the "Sarawak Overseas Chinese Democratic Youth League," which recruited its adherents among teachers and students of Chinese schools in Sarawak, and the "Sarawak Farmers' Association" were the most important. Since 1963 the underground communist complex, usually referred to by government and press as the Sarawak Communist Organization, seized much of the initiative in the opposition, especially among Sarawak's 460,000 Chinese inhabitants, to the creation of the Malaysian Federation. In the later 1960s and early 1970s this opposition crystallized in "people's war" guerrilla attacks, comparable to those in Western Malaysia, and involved small insurgent groups operating under different names on both sides of the Indonesian-Malaysian border. Despite Indonesian-Malaysian counterinsurgency coordination, and the continuous arrests and periodic surrenders of guerrillas under promised government rehabilitation schemes, resistance has persisted, and small, largely isolated bands of insurgents—some still aided by a handful of Chinese dissidents and underground cadres of the banned Indonesian Communist Party in Indonesian Kalimantan (Borneo)—have remained active.

Organization and Tactics. In July 1974 Malaysian police sources estimated that the CPM in the Malay Peninsula had about 3,000 core followers, with an informal "emotional support" following among Chinese, and in much smaller measure also among Malays and Indians, of about twice that figure. CPM-ML and CPM-RF strengths are not known but are estimated about 100 to 200 for each. Officially banned since 1948, the CPM's organization in the immediate aftermath of its defeat during the "Emergency" tended to become haphazard, but since the later 1960s greater formality and regularity in leadership structure have become apparent. Daily decisions are in the hands of a four-member Politburo, with a twelve- to twenty-member Central Committee composed of Chinese, Indians, and Malays providing overall direction. A general party congress has not been held since 1947. Chin Peng, the CPM's principal leader during the "Emergency," remains as secretary-general (in some accounts, chairman). Some sources have associated the Malay communist Musa Ahmad with this office. The vice-chairman's position has been held by another Malay, Abdul Rashid bin Maidin, the CPM's major guerrilla commander, in recent years, but his present position is unclear. These titles appear to have largely an honorific meaning, being used mainly in dealings with foreign communist movements and countries.

The furtive, underground position of the CPM at present puts maximum emphasis on an extremely fluid pattern of loosely linked localized party and guerrilla organizations. (The present party constitution, adopted in 1972, does not in fact provide for the positions of chairman and vice-chairman.) The constitution stresses the necessity of completing a "new democratic revolution" committed to the ultimate establishment of "socialism and communism" in Malaya, and using the tactic of "encircling the cities from the countryside."

The achievement of political power "by armed force" is emphasized as the "only correct line" in the CPM constitution, and this directive appears to have created some dissension in party ranks and in the MNLA-MRLA. In May and June 1974 CPM statements began to stress the need to develop "other forms of struggle to coordinate with the armed struggle," meaning that political as well as armed revolutionary tactics should be implemented. The directive appears to have reflected the prominence of an anti-Chin Peng faction, more Malay than Chinese in racial character, which presumably has not forgiven Chin Peng for the alleged failure of his "people's war" tactics during the Emergency and feels that a more "moderate" policy should be pursued, utilizing the left and center opposition to the present National Front coalition government of premier Tun Abdul Razak, rather than further militant extra-constitutional isolation. Reportedly, the dissension affected two of MNLA-MRLA's "regiments," the 8th, which operates in and near the Sadae district of southern Thailand, and the 12th, which is in the Betong region of Malaysia's Upper Perak state, a major focus of insurgent activity. (M. G. Pillai, "The Problems of Chin Peng," *Far Eastern Economic Review*, 24 December 1973.) As indicated, the CPM-RF arose out of dissident elements in the 8th, and the CPM-ML in the 12th MNLA "regiments."

Other major CPM leaders, whose role in the present leadership controversy is unclear, are Agit-prop section chairman Chen Tien, the CPM's principal liaison with Peking, and Control Commission chairman Li On, in charge of party discipline. The clandestine radio transmitter "Voice of the Malayan Revolution," which is financed by, and located in southern Yunnan Province of the People's Republic of China, has a small resident staff of CPM cadres who also assist in the New China News Agency.

According to a "Voice of Malayan Revolution" broadcast on 27 April 1974, the CPM is "a revolutionary party armed with Marxism-Leninism-Mao Tse-tung thought," and it has "persisted in following the road of having the countryside envelop the cities and seizing political power by armed force," thus creating a "victorious future for the new democratic revolution" in Malaya. Claiming that the MNLA-MRLA during the past year had "smashed" the enemy's "sabotage and interference," and that "revolutionary base and guerrilla war areas" had been further expanded, the "Voice" broadcast characterized the general strategic condition of the CPM as follows:

The situation at home and abroad during the past year has continuously developed in favor of the people. Internationally, countries want revolution. This has become an irresistible historical trend. The Chinese people have won brilliant victories in their socialist revolution and construction. The peoples of Asia, Africa and Latin America have won a series of new victories in opposing colonialism, imperialism and especially hegemonism. The unity among the Third World countries and peoples has been strengthened daily and the power of the Third World has grown ever stronger. Imperialism—especially the two super-powers: The United States and the Soviet Union—is declining daily. (*FBIS*, 30 April. All "Voice" broadcasts cited were in Mandarin, directed to Malaysia and Singapore.)

Whatever its interest in alternative, and presumably more moderate, political tactics in winning adherents, formally the CPM remains committed to a policy of "intensified struggle." "Voice of Malayan Revolution" broadcasts during 1974 repeatedly emphasized that "without armed struggle the proletariat, the people, and the Communist Party will lose their footing," and that "no matter what tricks the enemy may play we will never give up armed struggle" (*FBIS*, 3 September). "Struggle" is viewed by the CPM in a number of different contexts, however. In a broadcast of 30 April commemorating 1 May, "International Labor Day," a "Voice" broadcast declared that "only through a protracted struggle for wage increases and improved working conditions" could workers' unity be strengthened, and that the working classes also had to realize in this connection that in order to alter their condition "fundamentally," and realize their complete economic and political emancipation, they had to lead the "everyday economic struggle toward overthrowing the reactionary rule of imperialism and its lackeys and establishing the people's political power" (*FBIS*, May 2).

Given its acknowledgment of (1) "Mao Tse-tung thought" in its doctrine, (2) the "brilliant victories" of the Chinese people in their "socialist revolution," and (3) the tactical primacy of armed struggle, the CPM's hostility to the U.S.S.R. is perhaps not surprising. "Voice" broadcasts assert, for example, that the "Soviet revisionist renegade clique" has joined the "imperialist rank" in contending for hegemony in the Malaysian area, and that, using Sinapore as a base, "Soviet social imperialism is accelerating its infiltration of Malaysia and other countries using its embassies, branches of the Moscow People's Bank, and other channels for various nefarious 'secret activities' " (3 January, 6 April; *FBIS*, 8 January, 11 April).

According to its 1972 constitution, the CPM has the responsibility of building a united front, based on the workers' and peasants' alliance, but including all revolutionary classes under party leadership. This explicitly means racial equality in a common struggle against the government of Malaysian premier Tun Abdul Razak, whose "national oppression" policy is said by the CPM to be predicated on discrimination against ethnic Chinese and Indians in the country. Even the Malayan working masses, however, according to the CPM, are realizing that the Razak policy means nothing but special privileges for the "Malayan bureaucratic capitalists and big landlords." Hence, in the view of the CPM, the "national struggle is a class struggle," in which Malayans of all ethnic backgrounds seek to overthrow the "Razak and [Singapore premier] Lee Kuan Yew cliques and their imperialist masters." To be sure, "big comprador bougeoisie of both Chinese and Indian nationalities" also have joined with Razak in a government that is a "new counterrevolutionary alliance," but, according to the CPM, they face increasing difficulties. "People of all nationalities" are urged by the CPM to develop a "people's war" and use the villages to surround the cities and seize power by armed force. (Broadcast of 11 May; *FBIS*, 11 May.) It is also stipulated by the CPM constitution that a National Congress (which has yet to meet in a generation) is the party's supreme leadership. But in recognition of the impossibility of maintaining prescribed decision-making functions in the party's present under-ground and insurgent condition, the constitution provides too (art. 25) that, if required, the Central Committee has authority to draw up regulations "in accordance with the Party's Constitution." At least three party members, in any place of work, and also in schools and in the MNLA, can form a party branch and CPM basic unit.

The hard core of the party organization today, however, is in the MNLA, most if not all of whose 1,500 members must be considered CPM members. Officially, there are four MNLA "regiments" based on the Malaysian side of the border with Thailand but operationally accustomed to moving back and forth across the frontier. The MNLA's "8th regiment" of some 300 to 400 men operates on the western side of the frontier, in and near the Malaysian states of Kedah and Perlis. The "regiment" is only minimally known to be involved in actual guerrilla strikes and seems more concerned with developing a political underground and popular united-front support structure in the rural areas. In early February, as a result of the dissension over CPM tactics in the party's leadership noted earlier, it was reported that a split had occured in the 8th, with a faction in the Sadae district of the Thai province of Songkhla disavowing Chin Peng and following its own leader, identified as "E. Chiang." Chin Peng, reportedly, was recruiting new local Chinese in Sadae to supplement his forces (*The Nation*, Bangkok, 22 February). The Betong salient, near Kroh in northern Perak State, is the MNLA's core region of operations, and this is where the insurgents' 12th regiment is active. Despite the defection of its "2nd district unit," which went over to the CPM-ML, the core of the 12th remains untouched. The 12th has from 700 to 750 men under arms and its units also serve as guards for the CPM and MNLA's shifting headquarters in the Betong region. Along the eastern part of the Thai-Malaysian border, with an operational area largely based in northern Kelantan State, there is the MNLA's 10th regiment, of about 450 to 500 troops. Like the 8th, so the 10th has major responsibility for the development of a local rural support base and CPM front infrastructure. Additionally, from 200 to 250 troops are in various MNLA "support" or reserve units, strung along the frontier, but their exact function is not clear; it is assumed that intelligence and courier duties preoccupy much of their time, and Malaysian intelligence sources assert that some reserve units are, in fact, composed of hard-core CPM cadres with field experience and are used as instructors or in agitation and propaganda work.

"Voice of the Malayan Revolution" broadcasts during the year reflect the pivotal importance accorded by the CPM to the "liberation army." The twenty-fifth anniversary of the MNLA-MRLA's founding, according to a "Voice" broadcast, found the army's "assault troops" pushing south and "winning one victory after another." At the same time, "in commemoration," army personnel and "masses of all nationalities" at revolutionary bases and in guerrilla areas were "jubilantly engaged in all sorts of celebrations." Meanwhile the "Voice" upheld the principle (in which "we must persist . . . under all circumstances") of "using the countryside to circle the cities" which would permit the opening of "vast battle areas in the northern and central parts of our country" and frustrate the efforts of the Malaysian government to "check the victorious advance of our army." (Broadcasts of 2 March, 21 June; *FBIS*, 13 March, 26 June.)

In Eastern Malaysia, guerrilla communism is centered on two armed groups, the North Kalimantan People's Army (Pasokan Rakyat Kalimantan Utara; Paraku), and the Sarawak People's Guerrilla Force (Pergerakan Gerijla Rakyat Sarawak; PGRS), both of them together usually referred to as the North Kalimantan People's Armed Forces (KNPAF). Two years ago Malaysian and Indonesian government spokesmen claimed that the PGRS had been destroyed. Insurgent leaders have denied this and today refer to the existence of yet another guerrilla organization, the North Kalimantan People's Guerrilla Force (NKPGF) (*Sarawak Tribune*, Kuching, 10 July 1974). The fluid leadership and organizational structure of the guerrilla communist movement in Malaysian Borneo over the years make it difficult to determine whether the NKPGF is the successor to the PGRS, or has a distinctive existence apart from Paraku (which continues to be named as a separate organization by guerrilla commanders), or is, in fact, but a catch-all term for the whole Sarawak insurgent force today and thus in effect but another name for the NKPAF. Malaysian security officials, when queried by the author, appeared themselves uncertain upon this point.

The confusion has been further increased because of the claim of the government, on 4 March

1974, that "75 percent of the entire communist fighting force in Sarawak" (482 militant communists), including the "director and polotical commissar of Paraku," Bong (or Wong) Kie Chok, an employee of the Chinese Embassy in Djakarta in the 1960s, had laid down their arms since the launching of the government's "Sri Aman" (Peace) campaign on 21 October 1973. By June 1974, however, Sarawak's acting chief minister, Stephen Yong, announced that "more or less" 50 armed NKPGF members remained active in Sarawak's First Division, and that additionally 120 Paraku members had not surrendered (*Sarawak Tribune*, 5 March, 21 June). Meanwhile, statements by the North Kalimantan Communist Party (NKCP) on these developments alluded not to the NKPGF or to Paraku, but, instead, to the "People's Armed Forces of North Kalimantan," presumably the NKPAF (*Peking Review*, 26 April). Just before the "Sri Aman" campaign the total communist guerrilla force in Sarawak was estimated at about 1,000 active and armed guerrillas, virtually all Chinese (about 20 percent women) between the ages ot seventeen and thirty years, operating in small bands on and drawing recruits from both sides of the Indonesian-Malaysian border. Since the "Sri Aman" campaign's official termination on 4 July 1974 and the resumption of full-scale military action by the government against the remaining insurgents, the total guerrilla force may be estimated at about 200 (still some 500 hundred according to the NKCP), most of them considered to be formal members of the NKCP.

The guerrillas remain at the heart of the loosely structured SCO complex, which also includes underground and proscribed affiliates like the Sarawak Advanced Youths Association (SAYA) and the Sarawak Farmers' Association (SFA). The surrender (on or shortly after 21 October 1973) of Bong Kie Chok, age 39, generally described as chairman of the NKCP's Central Committee, and a number of his key party division and district committee members (for their names and careers see *Sarawak Tribune*, 5 March 1974) was kept secret by the government until March, reportedly at Bong's request (*FBIS*, 4 March). But well before then the surrender had thrown the SCO complex, and particularly the NKCP leadership structure, into further serious disarray. On 30 March 1974 the "Voice of the Malayan Revolution" broadcast a statement by one Wen Ming Chuan, described as chairman of the NKCP Central Committee. The statement referred to the recent surrender of NKPAF insurgents to the Malaysian government as a "serious incident betraying Marxism-Leninism-Mao Tse tung thought." Those who had laid down their arms were said to have been "forced or deceived" into taking this road, and they had caused "a grave setback" in the "revolutionary struggle of our country." But the "Voice" went on to say:

> Comrades we have not been destroyed. So long as one single soldier remains, we will continue to fight. The revolutionary red flag will flutter forever. Instead of being destoryed our party still leads a fairly strong armed force. We will continue to use armed struggle as the main form of struggle. We will persist in guerrilla warfare and continue to develop it in the vast countryside. We will continue to unfold mass movements and carry on revolutionary propaganda and organization, and build up our strength and wait for the opportune moment. (Broadcast of 30 March; *FBIS*, 3 April.)

Wen Ming Chuan's statement was criticized in the Sarawak press by unidentified "former leaders" of the SCO, Paraku, and the NKPGF. According to them, Wen had not himself experienced the "hardships suffered by the Communist guerrillas and had never given any active support to the NKCP" (*Sarawak Tribune*, 10 July). Wen's direct connection with the Sarawak insurgency, according to government sources, had been spasmodic. Little was known of him until his arrest in Kuching on 22 June 1962 on grounds of subversive activity, and he was then deported to People's China five days later. Sometime early in 1963 he infiltrated back into the Sarawak-Indonesian border area and until shortly before the abortive 30 September 1965 coup attempt of Army dissidents and communists in Indonesia, he was, according to the Malaysian government, the principal leader (title or rank unspecified) of the NKCP in West Borneo. At the time of his departure, just before the coup attempt, he appointed Bong Kie Chok and Lim Ho Kuei (Lam Woh Kai) as his successors. (Ibid.) The latter has on occasion been identified in the Sarawak press as "the head of the SCO" (ibid., 20 August 1973) and as a leader of the NKGPF (ibid., 10 July), and like Bong Kie Chok he has surrendered to the government. Since 1965, Wen Ming Chuan has lived abroad reportedly mostly in China.

The composition and, indeed, the present location of the NKCP's Central Committee can only be surmised, although an informal leadership structure of other organizations in the SCO complex, like SAYA and SFA, reportedly had continued intact after the recent surrender of Bong and his insurgents. Since 1972, according to a statement in early July 1974 by the chief minister of Sarawak, Abdul Rahman Ya'Kub, 1,124 "unarmed Communists and pro-Communists" mostly members of the SFA, SAYA, "illegal SCO study cells," and other front and insurgent groups have voluntarily surrendered to the government, making use of the government's "liberal policy" of modified amnesty and rehabilitation of communists and front-group adherents (ibid., 4 July). Meanwhile, the predominantly Chinese Sarawak United People's Party (SUPP), whose left wing was considered communist infiltrated and oriented, and which before 1971 was perhaps the SCO's principal, if muted, aboveground and parliamentary sympathizer, has now all but divested itself of its erstwhile aura of radicalism and has stressed its political loyalty in anti-communist terms and joined the coalition of government parties at both the Sarawak and national Malaysian levels.

Even so, the SCO probably retains a high degree of sympathy among a majority of Sarawak's 400,000 Chinese today, not least because communist tactics in the state were always closely responsive to a prevalent Chinese sense of being discriminated against in Malaysian education, economic, and other public policies. Wounded Chinese ethnic pride, especially among the politicized students of Chinese schools in Sarawak, has not been altogether assuaged by government efforts to integrate loyal Chinese more fully into the state's political life and economy. A recent survey of 16 insurgents between the ages of 19 and 35 years, described by the Sarawak government as members of the NKPGF who spurned the government's offer of rehabilitation and a return to normal civilian life, preferring to resume their jungle struggle, almost all appear to have been educated in Chinese primary and secondary schools, either in Sarawak or in neighboring Indonesian West Kalimantan (Borneo) (ibid., 6 July).

It is difficult to predict what success the government's resumed campaign against the remaining insurgents will have. Less than a week after Operation "Sri Aman" (under which the insurgents could surrender with hope of rehabilitation and de facto amnesty) terminated, after a four months' lull in the fighting, Sarawak security forces reportedly discovered a guerrilla camp accommodating about 50 persons in the Matang/Batu Kawa area only 15 miles from the capital, Kuching, and Sarawak's chief minister, Abdul Rahman Ya'kub, announced that five jungle food dumps, consisting of a "large quantity" of rice, sugar, soya beans, flour, and cooking oil had also been discovered in the same area. The food caches also suggested connivance of the local population, to whom Ya'kub appealed for full cooperation with the government forces in their effort to eliminate the insurgents. (Ibid., 11 July.) Shortly afterward the "Voice of the Malayan Revolution" declared that despite the government's attempt to use the "surrender of renegades" to destroy the "revolutionary armed struggle" in Sarawak, the "people's armed forces," though reduced in numbers, were "finer and stronger now" and, as they upheld the "spirit of revolutionary heroism," were continuing to advance (broadcast 27 July; *FBIS*, 2 August).

The circumstances and effects of the surrender of former insurgents have begun to raise some questions in Sarawak political circles. It has been noted that when Bong Kie Chok and his followers came out of the jungle they brought only homemade weapons, not the sophisticated arsenal which reportedly the insurgents possess and which, some security circles believe, remains with the guerrilla remnant (M. G. Pillai, "Sarawak: After Peace, the Inquest," *Far Eastern Economic Review*, 15 April). Then, too, the future political role of the surrendered guerrillas is viewed with some concern, in the light of assurances given by Sarawak's chief minister that the former rebels will be entitled to vote in elections and run for office if they wish, even though organized communism remains proscribed. Bong has denied, however, that he will join the SUPP. (Ibid.) The opposition Sarawak National Party (SNAP) made it a particular point to welcome the surrendered rebels and called on the government not to disillusion them but to make sure that "the democratic process of our nation is carried out fairly and justly" (*Sarawak Tribune*, 8 March 1974). While the Malaysian government's policy of attempting to rehabilitate and integrate the insurgents has been hailed as a progressive and stabilizing move, it is also clear that the long-term effect on the Sarawak and Malaysian political environment of a continuing communist insurgency, along with the parliamentary and partisan activities of a political-ly unpredictable but presumably still left-oriented former guerrilla force, cannot be foreseen.

Domestic Developments. Even as communist insurgents were coming out of the Sarawak jungle, CPM and MNLA-MRLA terrorists and guerrillas remained active. Early in January 1974 yet another Special Branch police officer was assassinated by terrorists, the third to be killed within six months, as meanwhile clashes between police and MNLA bands continued in the states of Kedah and Perak. "Large" rebel food dumps were discovered in the state of Pahang, where armed insurgents had been sighted, and, reportedly, CPM commander Rashid bin Maidin stepped up propaganda efforts in the states of Kelantan, Trengganu, and Pahang, centers of Malay cultural and religious traditionalism (M. G. Pillai, "The Red Watch," *Far Eastern Economic Review*, 14 January). The upsurge of CPM activity led Malaysian home affairs minister Ghazali Shafie to issue a public warning that communists were attempting a comeback and were trying to "create chaos in the country" (*FBIS*, 15 January) and, subsequently, to promise that all possible aid would be channelled to people's volunteer guard units in those rural settlements and areas where renewed CPM activity had been discovered (Kuala Lumpur radio, domestic service in English, 2 February; *FBIS*, 4 February). Intensified anti-guerrilla "sweeps" through Perak State in the following months led to several clashes, in one of which, at Chemor, five insurgents were killed and later a well-camouflaged terrorist camp, complete with a rifle range and accommodating 50 people, was discovered in the Perak jungle (Bernama dispatch, Pekan, Malaysia, 1 April; *Asia Research Bulletin*, 31 May, p. 2735).

Throughout the first half of 1974 Malaysian government spokesmen stressed the futility of the CPM struggle in view of aroused public sentiment, and called on the insurgents to surrender. In early February, Malaysian police inspector-general Abdul Rahman Hashim estimated the guerrilla strength in the states of Perak, Kedah, and Pahang at 200, with operational support of another 1,500 commu-nists along the Thai-Malaysian border. Even so, he termed the situation as "not at all serious." Malaysian Army and police forces, along with armored units, were hunting down the rebels, who now were said to have had split into small groups of 20 and 30. (*FBIS*, 13 February.)

Despite appeals to surrender and intensified government sweeps, resistance continued. Near the end of April, the home affairs minister issued instructions to all police stations to be vigilant in the face of possible attacks by communists, who, he charged, wanted to "bring their terrorism out of the jungle," where their morale had been deteriorating because of losses suffered at the hands of govern-ment forces (Reuters' dispatch, Temerloh, Malaysia, 28 April). A few weeks later, the head of the Malaysian Police Intelligence branch in Kedah-Perlis, Superintendent Ibrahim Shawal, was quoted as saying that "certain youths" had gone into the jungles to join the insurgents and that others were acting as "terrorist agents" in their home localities; some of the latter, Shawal said, had been trained in the use of weapons and their task was "to infiltrate into society in the rural areas" (*Straits Times*, Singapore, 10 June). Other reports noted that Malaysian communists were building their comback attempt on "befriending the civilian population" and might also be seeking more secure base areas in Malaysia, as compared with their present jungle sanctuaries (Reuter's dispatches cited in *Christian Science Monitor*, 19 March).

Confronted with the impending establishment of diplomatic relations between People's China and Malaysia, the CPM seemed determined to appear undaunted in its revolutionary policies. On 30 May, police inspector-general Rahman Hashim issued a statement that the forthcoming conclusion of Sino-Malaysian diplomatic relations would not stop the Malaysian government's policies of eradicating the CPM and that the battle against the communist insurgents would continue (UPI dispatch, Kuala Lumpur, 30 May). A week later, Hashim was shot dead by two unidentified gunmen in broad daylight in the very heart of the Malaysian capital, and while government spokesmen did not formally blame the communists, the assassination followed a pattern of similar killings of seven top Malaysian security officers, all closely involved in anti-guerrilla operations, during the past year. Premier Tun Abdul Razak declared Hashim's murder to have been the work of "anti-national and extremist elements," the current euphemism used by the government to refer primarily to communist terrorists. (*Bangkok Post*, 8 June; *The Nation*, Bangkok, 9 June.)

The extent to which the Hashim assassination was part of a calculated policy of CPM defiance, in the face of the normalization of Sino-Malaysian relations formally concluded on 31 May during the visit of Malaysian premier Razak to Peking, became a matter of considerable speculation. Already on 23 May, just before Razak's journey to the Chinese capital, communist insurgents had destroyed 63 bulldozers and tractors near Grik, along the east-west highway near the Thai border, now under construction, a project which the CPM had earlier vowed would never be permitted to reach completion. The destruction of the road equipment led to a temporary halt in construction, and to a decision by the Malaysian government to arm the road construction workers. Defense minister Hamzah Abu Samah attributed the attack to a 100-man force belonging to the MNLA's 12th regiment (*Asia Research Bulletin*, 30 June, p. 2765, and 31 July, p. 2889).

During his talks in Peking, Razak said on 2 June, the Chinese leaders had assured him that China would not interfere in Malaysia's internal affairs and that Malaysia could deal with the insurgents as it deemed best. Razak said that in turn he had stated that the Malaysian government was ready to discuss a "political settlement" with the CPM, provided the guerrillas would lay down their arms. The government was prepared to offer the CPM the same terms it had offered the communists in Sarawak: official aid to help the insurgents to rehabilitate and find their places in society, and the right to join existing political parties, with the explicit proviso, however, that communism was and would remain banned. Chinese readiness to permit Malaysia to handle the insurgents' problem in its own way was interpreted by Malaysian officials to mean that China had withdrawn its support from the CPM. (*Bangkok Post*, 9 June; *The People*, Dacca, 4 June.)

CPM statements, both before and after the Razak visit to Peking and the normalization of diplomatic relations, sought to create the impression that this normalization, far from heralding a change in China's policies, including support for external revolutionary movements, was instead occasioned by the "bankruptcy" of the "Razak clique's" previous policies toward Peking, in view of China's soaring international prestige and the failure of "U.S. imperialism and Soviet social imperialism" to isolate and frustrate China. China's pursuit of a policy of peaceful coexistence with countries with differing social systems, including presumably Malaysia, was in harmony with "the interests of the revolutionary struggle carried out by the peoples of various countries." Moreover, the establishment of Sino-Malaysian diplomatic relations had "not changed a bit" the "nature of the Razak clique," or its role as "lackeys of the imperialists." Another "voice of the Malayan Revolution" broadcast commemorating the twenty-fifth anniversary of the MNLA was, according to the "Voice," "repeatedly transmitted in different languages by Radio Peking," thus showing the continued "vigorous support of the Chinese Communist Party and the Chinese masses for the CPM and its guerrilla struggle." The Peking rebroadcasts, according to the "Voice," had brought "tremendous happiness and emotion" to CPM members. (Broadcasts, 25 May, 8 June; *FBIS*, 28 May, 11 June; also *The People*, Dacca, 4 June 1974).

After the Hashim assassination, little was heard at first from Malaysian officials about possible amnesty and rehabilitation offers to the CPM. Instead, government spokesman vowed intensified efforts to eradicate the insurgents. On 10 June, home affairs minister Ghazali Shafie vowed relentless pursuit of what he termed the "jungle rats," declaring: "We shall, if we must, search every tree and look behind every rock in the mountains" [in order to find and] annihilate [the communist] scourge" (Bernama dispatch, Kuala Lumpur, 10 June). The next day a communiqué issued by Thai and Malaysian officials at their border meeting for mutual consultation and anti-guerrilla action declared that communist insurgent activity along the border was intensifying, and hence security operations were being stepped up also (Radio Singapore, in English, 11 June). On 25 June in a raid by government security forces on what was described as an insurgents' "nest" at Jinjang village, on the outskirts of Kuala Lumpur, 16 alleged members of the CPM were arrested, and unspecified quantities of firearms, explosives, and "subversive documents" were seized (*FBIS*, 25 June), and four days later Premier Razak said that the communist insurgents were continuing to get assistance from the village population. Such support, he said, had even come from some inhabitants of "new villages" (special communities constructed in northwestern Malaysia by the government in recent years for the resettlement of the rural population in guerrilla-infested areas); the insurgents also had had civilian help when they sabotaged and destroyed road construction equipment along the east-west highway (Bernama dispatch, Kuala Lumpur, 29 June). By early September, in the face of continuing guerrilla activity along the Thai-Malaysian border, there appeared to be small likelihood that a Sarawak-style mass surrender consequent upon a de facto amnesty and rehabilitation scheme could or would be implemented in West Malaysia in the near future.

In Sarawak, Paraku director Bong Kie Chok, in a letter to Sarawak's chief minister Ya'kub dated 13 October 1973 (but not released by the Sarawak government until 4 March 1974), had notified the latter that he was sending two Paraku members to "negotiate with your representatives for making arrangements for a peace talk." Bong and Ya'kub held fruitful discussions at a government resthouse (named "Sri Aman") at Simanggang on 20 October 1973. In a public announcement on 4 March 1974 Ya'kub said that "since 18 October 1973" 482 insurgents, Bong Kie Chok among them, had "laid down their arms" and come out of the jungle. The government's "Sri Aman" plan officially took effect on 20 October when Bong and Ya'kub at their Simanggang meeting had signed a "Memorandum of Understanding" regulating the citizenship of Paraku members and providing Paraku members with opportunities to participate in "legitimate" political activities in Sarawak but noting that the NKCP would not be legitimized.

On 4 March 1974, Ya'kub announced that "for the time being" there would be a suspension of all government military action against the Sarawak insurgents "in the operational areas" of the state (between October 1973 and March 1974, operations had continued even as Bong and his Paraku insurgents began surrendering), in yet another effort to demonstrate the government's bona fides to the communist rebels. On 4 July this suspension ended, and Malaysian home affairs minister Ghazali Shafie at that time announced resumption of "all operations to eliminate the remaining elements who have refused to come out." According to Ghazali Shafie, a total of 585 communist guerrillas had laid down their arms between 4 March and 4 July. But in respect of the 4 March date this description was contradicted by acting chief minister Stephen Yong, who on 20 June said in Kuching that 585 insurgents had come out of the jungle "since the launching of Operation Sri Aman on October 21, 1973" (*Sarawak Tribune*, 21 June, 5 July 1974). Even as Paraku insurgents were surrendering between October and March, moreover, clashes had continued: on 7 February 1974, for example, three guerrillas were killed and twenty-one were captured by a police patrol vessel which exchanged fire with a boatload of communists in a coastal encounter off Muara Tebas, in Sarawak's First Division (*Sunday Tribune*, Kuching, 10 February). Before temporarily halting military operations against the guerrillas in March, the government took precautions: on 14 February it was announced, for example, that a total of 628 had enlisted as members of an armed rural "vigilante corps" in Sarawak established by the government, and the Sarawak state minister for land and natural resources said on this occasion that the "enthusiastic response" of the population to participation in the vigilante corps must be regarded by "subversive elements" as meaning that the latter were "totally rejected by the people" (Kuala Lumpur, domestic service in English, 14 February, *FBIS*, 15 February).

Throughout the year prominent captured Paraku figures were released from detention. Described by the government as "self renewed," groups of several scores of former guerrillas were set free from the Centers of Protective Custody in Kuching and Sibu, all of them having pledged, according to an official statement, their loyalty to king and country and declared that the SCO now was "shattered" (*Sarawak Gazette*, Kuching, 31 January). Some of those released had been in detention, without trial, for as long as 10 to 12 years (*Sarawak Tribune*, 13 July), but upon gaining their freedom had declared: "Communist ideology is totally irrelevant to our society and therefore can never be accepted by the people" (ibid.) As the 4 July deadline approached, the government continued to urge the CPM-NKPG-NKPAF-Paraku remnants in the jungle to surrender, disseminating some 40,000 leaflets bearing a message from former Paraku commander Lam Woh Kwai (Lim Ho Kuei), some of these leaflets also being distributed through Indonesian military commanders on the other side of the border (ibid., 26 June). But while as early as 4 March the government's Radio Malaysia transmitter in Sarawak had confidently asserted that "peace had returned to Sarawak" (*Sarawak Gazette*, 31 March), in subsequent months neither Malaysian nor Indonesian military men were so sanguine. By mid-May it was authoritatively reported from Kuching that the armed forces and security services there did not appear convinced that the emergency was "all but over," although possibilities for a more rapid economic development in the state were now seen as more promising (M. G. Pillai, "Sarawak: The Fruits of Peace," *Far Eastern Economic Review*, 13 May). In June, Indonesian security chief Admiral Sudono said in Pontianak, Indonesian West Kalimantan, that the surrender of communists in Sarawak had not ended the communist threat in the area, and that the recent agreement between Bong and Ya'kub "called for strict vigilance" (*FBIS*, 12 June).

Meanwhile, a number of the former Paraku insurgents that had come out of the jungle proved unassimilable. On 5 July the Sarawak government announced that six former guerrillas (of the 585 who surrendered during operation "Sri Aman") had been "repatriated" to the People's Republic of China during the previous week and that preparations were being made for the "repatriation" of two others (*Berita Harian*, Kuala Lumpur, 5 July; *FBIS*, 18 July).

On 24 August, general parliamentary elections were held in Malaysia, and the government's National Front (Barisan Nasional) coalition led by Premier Razak scored a lopsided victory, winning 135 out of the 154 parliamentary seats, with some 64 percent of the four million eligible voters casting ballots. While a number of smaller opposition parties, including some left-wing groups, fared very badly (e.g., the Malaysian People's Socialist Party, or Partai Sosialis Rakyat Malaysia, did not win a single seat), and the candidates of the more conservative Malay parties in the government coalition (e.g., the United Malays National Organization, and the Party Islam) all were successful, the left-of-center Democratic Action Party (DAP), the principal opposition group before the election, kept its nine-man parliamentary delegation. Indeed, though its parliamentary delegation did not increase, the heavily Chinese DAP increased its share of the popular vote to more than 20 percent of the total. In Sarawak, the opposition Sarawak National Party increased its national parliamentary delegation from seven to nine (it also won 18 of the 48 seats in the Sarawak state assembly). Although the government's National Front coalition won majorities in all the fifteen state assemblies (in three such assemblies—Pahang, Kelantan, and Perlis) the opposition failed to win a single seat), there is no question that the size of the popular vote for the opposition was surprising. Especially in West Malaysia, the DAP's strength was an indication that the National Front government had continued to fail to attract non-communist but left-oriented younger Chinese. Authoritative warnings that the

Chinese element continued to be discriminated against, and that the non-communist Chinese left in Western Malaysia had become severely alienated from the established Malaysian political and constitutional process, suggest a developing political dynamic that may well eventually affect the Razak National Front's continuing struggle against the CPM. (*Asia Research Bulletin*, 31 May, p. 2733; *Far Eastern Economic Review*. 6 September, p. 10, and 27 September, p. 13; *NYT*, 26 August).

While a call by the "Voice of the Malayan Revolution" on all "nationalities" to "obstruct the puppet clique's general election" (*FBIS*, 7 August), had little or no effect, there is not inconsiderable dissatisfaction, particularly in academic and professional circles, with the Razak regime's allegedly high-handed of even non-communist political opinions of which it disapproves. Expulson from Malaysia in the first half of the year of two foreign scholars, Dr. Shirle Gordon and Professor Ernst Utrecht, the former on alleged grounds of security, the latter presumably because of pressure from official Indonesian quarters which resented Utrecht's outspoken opposition to the Suharto regime, are cases in point (*De Volkskrant*. Amsterdam, 16 April; *Far Eastern Economic Review*, 6 May, p. 24).

The plight of political prisoners in Malaysia held in detention camps at Batu Gajah and Taiping under Malaysia's Internal Security Act aroused renewed concern when, on 29 December 1973, prisoners began a hunger strike. Fighting between prisoners and security units in the camp broke out, and one prisoner reportedly committed suicide. The government agreed in March 1974 to an inquiry into camp conditions after requested to do so by Amnesty International (Amnesty International, *Annual Report, 1973-1974*, London, n.d., p. 55). The case of Khoo Ee Liam, a Malaysian student in New Zealand and Australia who upon his return to Kuala Lumpur was arrested for activities while a student abroad (e.g., active participation in the pro-Peking New Zealand-China Friendship Society, alleged study of "communist literature" in Melbourne, and supposed attempts, while in New Zealand, to join the Malayan National Liberation Army—activities which Khoo's solicitors assert were quite legal in the countries concerned, even if true), has further polarized student opinion against the Razak regime's security policies (on Khoo's case see *Far Eastern Economic Review*, 30 August, p. 6).

International Aspects. Even before Premier Razak's historic visit to Peking at the end of May, there was official anticipation of the effect on domestic Malaysian communism of impending improvements in Sino-Malaysian relations. Indeed, former Malaysian premier Tunku Abdul Rahman, in April, was quoted as saying that the planned establishment of diplomatic ties had resulted in a subsiding of communist activities in Malaysia "of late" (*Bangkok Post*, 10 April; *FBIS*, 10 April. The 31 May communiqué issued by Chinese premier Chou En lai and Malaysian premier Razak not only provided for mutual diplomatic recognition, but also for Malaysian recognition that Taiwan is an "inalienable part" of China's territory and for the closing of the Malaysian consulate in Taipeh in return for Chinese recognition of the Malaysian government's independence and sovereignty. The last-named provision cuts the ground from under the MNLA's claim that the Razak "puppet clique" is not the legitimate government of Malaysia.

In the communiqué the Chinese and the Malaysians both also repudiate dual nationality, and the Peking government recognizes that those Chinese in Malaysia who, of their own free will, have acquired Malaysian nationality shall be considered as having forfeited Chinese nationality, and that those Chinese in Malaysia who have retained their Chinese nationality are enjoined to abide by Malaysian laws, although the "proper rights and interests" of these Chinese nationals "will be protected by the Government of China and respected by the Government of Malaysia" (*Asia Research Bulletin*, 30 June, p. 2829). Considering Malaysian fears of Chinese aid to external insurgents, perhaps the most important provision of the joint communiqué was the clause which asserted that both Malaysia and China considered "all foreign aggression, interference, control and subversion" to be impermissible.

Although Premier Razak at a banquet in his honor in Peking on 28 May had stressed that China could play a constructive role in promoting peace and harmony in Southeast Asia (Bernama dispatch, Peking, 28 May), and although, according to Malaysian sources, Peking supported in principle the idea, long touted by Malaysia, that Southeast Asia should be "neutralized" and free from big-power rivalries, informed quarters expressed concern that People's China would never wholly disavow the various Mao-oriented insurgent groups operating in Malaysia, Burma, the Philippines, Indonesia, and elsewhere in Southeast Asia. The same quarters also wondered whether or not the new official cordiality between Kuala Lumpur and Peking existed, in keeping with Chinese policy, at the government-to-government level only, thus leaving the "Chinese people" or the Chinese Communist Party as such free to continue to aid the CPM and the MNLA.

Reaction to the communiqué in the ASEAN region was generally, if guardedly, positive, with Singapore premier Lee Kuan Yew declaring that "if there are no untoward developments" China would likely have its diplomatic representatives throughout Southeast Asia in the next few years" (*Asia Research Bulletin*, 30 June, p. 2764). Especially in Indonesia, skepticism remained, however, while other ASEAN sources speculated on the implications of a developing Chinese as well as Soviet presence in the region (J. M. van der Kroef, "The Malaysian Formula: Blueprint for Future Sino-Southeast Asian Relations?" *Asia Quarterly*, 1974, no. 4). The question as to how long Peking would or could remain indifferent to internal Malaysian developments was also raised by commentators in Malaysia, in the light of Chinese premier Chou En lai's banquet speech during Razak's Peking visit, in which Chou said that China remained "internationalist" and felt duty-bound to support consistently the "just struggle of all oppressed nations and peoples" (Political Observer, "Chou's Speech: An Analysis," *Sarawak Tribune*, 31 May).

During the year, Indonesian-Malaysian cooperation in joint action against the communist insurgents in Sarawak continued and further solidified. On 6 December 1973, *nota bene*, some five weeks after Bong and Ya'kub had held their discussions to regularize the surrender of Paraku and other SCO elements, Indonesia and Malaysia reached agreement on new but undisclosed details of joint military cooperation against the guerrillas; according to a joint statement, the guerrillas still posed a threat to the security of both countries. By the following May, however, the Malaysian government's policies pursued in connection with the "Sri Aman" operation were beginning to give Indonesian border commanders considerable concern. Because of the Malaysian government's new attitude toward the guerrilla problem, the Indonesian commander of the West Kalimantan (Borneo) military district, Brigadier General Seno Hartono, complained on 29 May that the task of guarding the 1,800-kilometers-long frontier between Indonesia and the Malaysian states of Sabah and Sarawak "was becoming more difficult." Hartono said that the Malaysian government currently was not taking action against the guerrillas, provided they were not engaged in insurgent activity, and indeed was permitting guerrilla leaders to enter into politics as one of the conditions governing their return to regular society. Release of all political prisoners and Malaysian willingness to grant Malaysian citizenship even to communist guerrillas operating in Indonesian territory of the guerrillas surrendered to Malaysian authorities would make it additionally difficult to guard against future border infiltrations, Hartono added. (*FBIS*, 31 May.) It is unlikely that such Indonesian complaints will affect future anti-insurgency border cooperation between the Djakarta and Kuala Lumpur governments, not least because at the conclusion of the "Sri Aman" operation, and also in light of continuing CPM-MNLA activity in West Malaysia, the Razak government's decision to move ahead in suppressing remaining communist insurgent activity throughout the country has been repeatedly affirmed in recent months and has been reassuring to the Indonesian government. Hartono's complaint may well reflect fears of the Indonesian military about the implication of Malaysian policies for the rehabilitation of Indonesian political prisoners (see *Indonesia*).

Malaysia maintains diplomatic and/or growing commercial relations with the U.S.S.R. and most Central and East European governments. During the year, the official cordiality in these relations, the

Soviet demand for Malaysian rubber, and the Polish and Romanian interest in forging firmer shipping links with Malaysia were reviewed in knowledgeable Malaysian academic and political circles as an appropriate counterbalance to the new Sino-Malaysian rapprochement.

Lingering British, Australian, and New Zealand military commitments to the strategic defense of Malaysia and Singapore, in the context of a steadily scaled-down and modified Five Power Commonwealth Defense Agreement, continued to provide grist for CPM propaganda mills. CPM media, in the face of renewed British determination in the course of 1974 to reduce its military personnel and operations in Malaysia portrayed the "Razak clique" as "shamelessly" begging "British imperialism not to reduce or withdraw its troops" ("Voice of the Malayan Revolution," 27 July, *FBIS*, 27 July).

Publications. "The Voice of the Malayan Revolution," the clandestine radio transmitter believed to be located in China's southern Yunnan Province, has become the principal CPM medium of communication with the outside world, although Malaysian security sources claim also the regular discovery of MNLA mimeographed leaflets and propaganda brochures for local use. Both "Voice" broadcasts and MNLA materials utilize Malay and Hindi, although Mandarin Chinese is most commonly employed. There are no CPM or SCO dailires or periodicals, and *The Malayan Monitor & General News*, which used to be issued almost monthly by CPM sympathizers in London, during 1974 appeared even less regularly. In Sarawak, the NKCP has irregularly issued special appeal leaflets in Chinese, but the one-time more frequently appearing SCO publications like the newspaper *Masses News* and the monthly *Liberation News* have not appeared since 1972. People's China media occasionally relay broadcasts of the "Voice of the Malayan Revolution."

University of Bridgeport   Justus M. van der Kroef

Mongolia

A fusion of two revolutionary groups in 1921 produced the Mongolian People's Party, which held its First Congress in March of that year at Kyakhta, in Soviet territory. It became known as the Mongolian People's Revolutionary Party (MPRP) in 1924.

Fiftieth-anniversary celebrations in November 1974 marked the shift to "socialism" in 1924. Russian dominance had already been established in 1921. But in 1924 the "Mongolian People's Republic" (MPR) name was adopted, as was the present name of the capital city, Ulan Bator (formerly Urga), and the non-capitalist and anti-bourgeois line was announced by the party's Third Congress and First Great Khural (structural equivalent of the U.S.S.R.'s Supreme Soviet).

In 1971 the MPRP claimed 58,048 members, or about 4 percent of the population of the MPR, recently estimated at just under 1,400,000. The city of Ulan Bator accounts for about 300,000 of that total.

Organization and Leadership. The MPRP is organized approximately along the same lines as the Communist Party of the Soviet Union.

The party's long-time first secretary, Tsendbal, has served also as premier of the MPR, but in June 1974 a major domestic political change raised Jambyn Batmunkh to the latter office. Batmunkh (b. 1926) is, like Tsedenbal, an economist trained in the U.S.S.R. From the comparatively obscure position of head of a department of the party Central Committee, he was appointed a deputy premier in May, and premier and full Politburo member in June.

Tsedenbal, continuing as first secretary, took the position of "president" by becoming chairman of the Presidium of the Great Khural, a post vacant since Sambu's death in 1972.

Besides Tsedenbal and Batmunkh, full members of the Politburo are Jagvaral, Jalan-ajav, and Molomjants (secretaries of the Central Committee), Luvsanravdan (chairman, Commission on Party Control), Maidar (first deputy premier, chairman of the State Committee for Science and Technology), and S. Luvsan (first deputy chairman of the Presidium of the Great Khural). Candidate members are Altangerel (first secretary of the Ulan Bator city committee, or "gorkom") and Ragcha (first deputy premier). Chimiddorj is secretary of the Central Committee.

Domestic Attitudes and Activities. The general pattern of Mongolian political and economic events continued with little change in 1974. The number of livestock, the country's most important economic resource, remained about 23 million head (see *YICA, 1973*, p. 520).

In the most significant economic development in many years, construction actually began in July-August on the important Erdenet copper-molybdenum mining operation, which has long been planned as a joint Mongolian-Soviet project and is oriented toward the Soviet economy. Its product is destined for the U.S.S.R., Soviet construction and operations plans direct the project, and it is situated only a short distance south of the Soviet-MPR border, where on the Soviet side, in the Buryat Autonomous Republic, is the Zakamensk wolfram-molybdenum mining and processing complex. For many years the U.S.S.R. has sent substantially more exports to the MPR than it has received in imports, the latter in recent years representing a ruble value of about one-third the value of the exports. Erdenet copper and molybdenum alone is projected to double the value of MPR exports to the Soviet Union.

International Views and Activities. Soviet party chief Brezhnev met with Tsedenbal in Moscow in April and June 1974. In November, Brezhnev paid a visit to Ulan Bator (his second, the first being in 1966), en route to the Vladivostok summit meeting with U.S. President Ford. Mongolian television broadcasted parts of the visit live to Moscow through the Soviet MARS satellite system. The Soviet ambassador to the MPR is A. I. Smirnov.

Two Soviet Red Army divisions reportedly continue to be stationed in the MPR, and the Mongols continue to pursue a strong pro-Russian and anti-Chinese line in the Sino-Soviet dispute. They protested China's 17 June nuclear test, complained often during the year about Chinese "pressure" on Mongolia, and vigorously attacked Mao Tse-tung and developments in China. At the United Nations in November, the MPR representative appeared to act as a U.S.S.R. surrogate in calling on China to endorse a Soviet proposal for renunciation of the use of force. A new Chinese ambassador, Chang Wei-lieh, arrived in Ulan Bator in October; his predecessor, Hsu Wen-i had left in February.

Although U.S. recognition of the MPR appeared imminent in 1973, it did not take place then or in 1974. In August 1974, however, an unprecedented visit by a U.S. sports team opened what is planned to be a regular exchange, with a Mongolian team to come to the United States in 1975.

Diplomatic relations were established during the year with West Germany and Iceland, bringing the total of official recognizers to 65. The MPR now trades with about twenty countries, although the U.S.S.R. accounts for some 90 percent of Mongolia's total international trade. In March the "Asian Committee of Buddhists for Peace" met in Ulan Bator. Unusual public mention of Tsedenbal's Russian wife occurred when the couple paid a visit to Tito in Yugoslavia in September.

Publications and Communications. Principal MPRP publications include *Unen* ("Truth"), *Namyn Amdral* ("Party Life"), the Russian-language *Novosti Mongolii* ("News of Mongolia"), and a Chinese-language weekly, *Meng-ku Hsiao-hsi Pao* ("News of Mongolia"). Beginning 1 January 1975, the Central Committee is to publish *Ediyn Djasag* ("Economics"). The Ministry of Agriculture issues *Shine Hodoo* ("New Countryside"). The MPR assigns a representative to the editorial board of the international communist organ *Problems of Peace and Socialism*.

Mongolian radio now broadcasts in Mongolian, Russian, English, Chinese, and Kazakh. Television broadcasting was begun in 1970.

University of North Carolina   Robert A. Rupen
Chapel Hill

Nepal

The Communist Party of Nepal (CPN) was formed in 1949. All political parties have been banned since 1960 when the late King Mahendra dissolved the Nepali Congress party (NC) government headed by B. P. Koirala. CPN membership is estimated at about 5,000.

Leadership and Organization. During the 1950's differences emerged within the leadership on the issue of party policy toward Nepal's monarchy. The moderate faction, led by General Secretary Keshar Jung Raimajhi, would work within the system to gain power. Pushpa Lal Shrestha's minority faction, however, advocated a revolutionary overthrow of the King.

Following the King's actions in 1960, this disagreement developed into an open split. Raimajhi retained party control; Pushpa Lal Shrestha, Tulsi Lal Amatya, and their supporters fled to India where they formed a parallel CPN organization at the May 1962 "Third Party Congress." Although the Sino-Soviet dispute did not cause the CPN split, Raimajhi supports the Soviet position, while the "revolutionary" elements are pro-Chinese.

Both organizations operate within Nepal, concentrating their activities in the Kathmandu Valley and in the Tarai, the southern plains adjoining India. Communist sympathies seem strongest among students, educators, and urban elements. Among the active student groups, the pro-revolutionary CPN All Nepal National Independent Students' Union (ANNISU) competes with the National Student Union, sponsored by the moderate CPN. Their major non-Communist rival is the NC student organization, the Nepal Students' Union. (*YICA, 1973*, p. 507.)

Through its pro-monarchy stance and support of "progressive" government measures such as land reform, the Raimajhi CPN and its sympathizers have gained positions in government and officially-sponsored political organizations. (Ibid.)

The policies and views of the moderate CPN as outlined at its own "Third Party Congress" in 1968, however, did contain criticism of the present political system. The Congress criticized the ban on parties, demanded the release of all political prisoners, and proclaimed the need for restoring democratic rights, with the ultimate aim of establishing a national democracy. Immediate targets in this task were "workers, peasants, students, youth, traders, and professionals." (*New Age*, 12 January 1969.)

Further factionalization has developed in the revolutionary CPN. Pushpa Lal Shrestha remains in India, but Man Mohan Adhikari, a CPN founder who was imprisoned for several years, now leads an extremist faction in Nepal. The extremist CPN has called for reinstatement of political parties, restoration of parliamentary democracy, and distribution of surplus land among the peasants. Pushpa Lal Shrestha, however, advocates a more militant strategy than Adhikari in their campaign against the monarchy.

Current Domestic Activities. Beginning in late 1972 terrorist activities in Nepal, particularly its southeastern region, have increased. A series of violent incidents, including assassinations, occurred at that time in Jhapa district. A group of extremists led by Chandra Mohan Adhikari, Man Mohan Adhikari's nephew, was allegedly responsible. Chandra Mohan Adhikari was later arrested and, in April 1974, sentenced to life imprisonment for murder. (*Gorkhapatra*, 17 April.)

The Jhapa violence led to intensified anti-subversive measures by the government. In April 1973 King Birendra denounced the activities of "anti-social and anti-national elements," stating that they "will never be tolerated." (*YICA, 1973*, p. 510.) Some of the "elements" responsible may have ties with Indian Naxalites, but many are believed to be followers of NC leader B. P. Koirala or Pushpa Lal Shrestha. Head of the NC dissidents in India, Koirala has threatened to launch an armed revolution. According to some reports, he and Pushpa Lal are "working in harmony" and "jointly supervising the bomb explosions in different parts of Nepal." (*Arati Weekly*, 25 April, and *Charcha Weekly*, 20 May.) Among these continuing incidents was a grenade explosion in Biratnagar during the King's visit in March.

The government's anti-terrorist campaign has resulted in numerous arrests and frequent confiscation of explosives as well as Nepali Congress and Maoist literature. It was officially reported in August that 155 suspects were in detention under the Public Security Act. Members of the revolutionary CPN and its student affiliate, the ANNISU, were among those arrested. (*Matribhumi Weekly*, 5 February and 6 August.) Others were NC supporters, some of whom said that the explosives were smuggled from India. (*Gorkhapatra*, 31 August.)

Nepalese political activity has also increased during the year, focussed mainly on demands for reform of the "partyless" Panchayat system of government. In August the King held a meeting with several former Prime Ministers to discuss possible reforms. The pro-Raimajhi *Samiksha Weekly* expressed satisfaction August 30, saying that the meeting had "initiated the process of formulating long-term solutions" to Nepal's problems.

In October, one of the ex-Ministers convened a meeting of various political groups. Man Mohan Adhikari and Shambu Ram Shrestha, another pro-Chinese figure, were among those attending. They expressed support for the announced goal of devising solutions for existing problems through "collective efforts on the basis of nationalist and democratic ideas." (*Nabin Khabar*, 6 October.) Raimajhi did not participate, however, reportedly because it was dominated by "one bloc." (*Samiksha Weekly*, 11 October.)

International Views and Attitudes. Under Nepal's foreign policy of non-alignment, it maintains good relations with all the major powers. Its balanced policy toward neighboring India and the People's Republic of China was highlighted in late 1973 by King Birendra's visits to both countries.

The moderate CPN is recognized and given financial assistance by the Soviet Union. The Raimajhi party Congress in 1968 praised the U.S.S.R. as a "bulwark of peace, Socialism and national liberation," while criticizing China's views. (*New Age*, 12 January 1969.) The moderate faction would prefer closer Nepal-Soviet relations, and in November the pro-Raimajhi paper criticized the "present low level" of these relations. (*Samiksha Weekly*, 8 November.) In May *Samiksha* had strongly supported the Soviet Asian Collective Security proposal in the wake of India's nuclear explosion. During the year the Nepal-Soviet Friendship Association hosted several visiting Soviet delegations.

Competing factions of the revolutionary CPN have appealed to China for closer working relationships, but Chinese involvement appears limited to some financial support. In addition to continuing its substantial economic assistance to Nepal, recent cultural activities included the participation of a Chinese table tennis team in a Nepalese tournament.

Publications. The weekly *Samiksha* reflects the views of the moderate CPN. The Pushpa Lal Shrestha revolutionary faction reportedly publishes *Nepal Patra*.

Barbara Reid

New Zealand

The Communist Party of New Zealand (CPNZ) was founded at a conference in Wellington in 1921 which brought together representatives of earlier socialist groups and Marxist clubs. The party has enjoyed legal status throughout its history but its membership has remained small, rising to a peak of 2,000 at the end of the Second World War, since when there has been a steady decline. Current estimated membership is about 100. New Zealand has a population of 3 million.

The CPNZ took the Chinese side in the Sino-Soviet dispute (the only "Western" communist party to do so), but this led to the defection of the Moscow supporters, who formed the New Zealand Socialist Unity Party (SUP) in 1966. Both parties have maintained their separate identiy, with SUP estimated membership also in the vicinity of 100. While the SUP has made some small gains over the years, especially in the trade unions, the CPNZ has been plagued by further defections and expulsions—almost the entire Wellington District (the so-called Manson-Bailey clique) was expelled in 1970, while 1974 saw the announcement of the expulsion of W. P. G. McAra and his supporters.

The only other Marxist group of note is the Socialist Action League (SAL), a Trotskyist organization founded in 1969, with an approximate membership of 40.

Organization and Leadership. The CPNZ has its headquarters and the bulk of its membership in Auckland. Elsewhere there are only small branches, notably in Wellington and Christchurch. The current leadership comprises V. G. Wilcox, national secretary since 1951, R. J. Taylor, national organizer, and two members of the National Secretariat, R. C. Wolf and A. G. Rait. The National Conference, which according to the constitution must be held triennially, has not met since 1966, and even the National Committee, in theory the highest party body between conferences, meets most infrequently. Its membership has eroded through deaths and defections, and the committee did not meet at all in 1971 or 1972, being called together in October 1973 primarily to ratify the expulsion of McAra.

This expulsion—the culmination of a three-year conflict in the leadership—was announced in March 1974. McAra, for long the foremost figure in the CPNA next to Wilcox, had already resigned from the Political Committee and later from the National Committee, and had gone to live out of Auckland. The charges brought against him were "big-shotism," intrigues, self-interest, and refusal to practice democratic centralism (*People's Voice*, 6 March), but from documents circulated later there emerged a story of a deep personality clash between McAra and Wolf, coupled with political differences over whether New Zealand is a junior imperialist partner of Britain and the United States, or whether it is itself a "neo-colony of imperialism" (as maintained by McAra)—in other words, whether New Zealand is part of the world's "cities" or of the world's "countryside." On this question of imperialism the current policy of the CPNZ is at odds with that of its nearest ideological partner, the

Communist Party of Australia (Marxist-Leninist). In 1973 inner-party distribution of certain issues of the *Australian Communist* was allegedly banned by the CPNZ.

McAra's supporters included R. G. Hegman, a former National Secretariat member who had left the CPNZ in 1973, and F. W. N. Wright, former secretary of the CPNZ in Wellington, whose expulsion was announced in the *People's Voice* of 13 November. In 1969-70 McAra had been the main opponent of the party group led by Nunes, Ostler, and McLeod in Auckland, and by Manson and Mrs. Bailey in Wellington. It is now revealed that at a Political Committee meeting in March 1969, with Wilcox absent on sick leave, this group had gained a 4-to-3 majority. Vigorous counteraction initiated by McAra and/or Wolf (here the accounts differ) led to their defeat at the next meeting of the committee in April, and forced the resignations of Nunes and Ostler from the National Secretariat. Thereafter McAra had insisted on carrying this conflict to the bitter end—the expulsions of 1970—while Wilcox apparently would have preferred some sort of compromise. McAra's fall was thus the logical signal for the expelled members—the Manson-Bailey group—to put out feelers for their reinstatement. Confidential talks are said to have taken place and some of the former Wellington members have apparently applied individually for readmission, but officially the CPNZ has rejected all attempts at reconciliation and has denounced the Manson-Bailey group as "renegade Communists" who are trying to split the party. (*People's Voice*, 28 August 1974.)

The SUP also has its headquarters in Auckland, where the party now has five branches, as well as branches in other centers. Its leadership has shown great stability, with G. H. ("Bill") Andersen as president, Mrs. E. Ayo as vice-president, and G. E. Jackson as national secretary. The National Committee comprises Mrs. Ayo and J. Brinklow, P. Cross, K. G. Douglas, J. L. Marston, F. E. McNulty, E. J. S. Miller and A. B. Skilton. The party's main power base is in the trade unions: 52 percent of its members are active in unions, and one third are union delegates, executive members, or officials. More than a quarter of SUP members (26 percent) are women, and the triennial conference in September 1973 was told that the average age of members was 47 years, with 16 percent below the age of 30 (*Socialist Politics*, December 1973).

The Socialist Action League has its national office in Wellington, with branches there, in Auckland, and in Christchurch. The membership is young, with few if any members above the age of 30. Its most prominent leaders are K. Locke and G. Fyson. Following an established pattern, the SAL and its associated Young Socialists held several educational conferences during the year, and it celebrated the fifth anniversary of its journal *Socialist Action* with public dinners in three cities. The Young Socialists are the only nationwide socialist youth organization in the country. The Progressive Youth Movement, linked with CPNZ, and the Democratic Youth Front (SUP) are confined to Auckland. They have been only sporadically active during the year. The Young Socialists now have branches in the four main centers of population; they have announced plans to hold their first national conference next year and to launch their own journal. The SAL will hold its next national conference in January 1975.

Some indication of the relative support for the three communist organizations can be gained from the results of their fund drives in 1974. The SAL collected $4,841 for its journal (of which $2,103 came from Wellington), while the SUP collected $4,504 (with $1,928 coming from Auckland). The *People's Voice* of the CPNZ collected $3,901 in two half yearly fund drives, of which $1,852 came from Auckland, but to this must be added weekly donations which amounted to $1,874.

Domestic Views and Activities. One of the most dramatic events of 1974 was the jailing of the secretary of the Northern Drivers' Union, "Bill" Andersen (who is also national president of the SUP) on 1 July for defying a court injunction against his union. Spontaneously thousands of Auckland workers downed tools and marched on the Supreme Court, and a threatened general strike was averted only through a hurriedly reached compromise whereby Andersen was released, his union promised to obey the court order, and the government allegedly undertook to change the law relating to industrial injunctions. The publicity surrounding this incident made Andersen into a national figure, and it undoubtedly helped to promote the extension of SUP influence in the trade union movement. The party failed again to elect one of its members to the executive of the N. Z. Federation of Labour (the national trade union body) but in October Andersen was elected unopposed to represent Auckland, the largest Trades Council in the country, on the National Council of the Federation. The second largest Trades Council, Wellington, has as secretary K. G. Douglas, also of the SUP.

The triennial municipal elections were held in October 1974 throughout New Zealand and, as in 1971, the SUP put forward candidates in Auckland (6) and Dunedin (2). Where it had no candidates, the SUP urged its supporters to vote for Labour Party candidates. The SAL, which did not contest the elections, also urged support for the Labour Party (but not for the SUP), though it criticized the absence of revolutionary demands from Labour policy. The CPNZ boycotted the elections altogether, denouncing them as a fraud. The results were disappointing for the SUP, whose votes fell significantly from levels reached earlier. The two Dunedin candidates polled 1,405 and 1,193 votes, compared with a poll of 5,663 and 2,486 in 1971, while in Auckland Andersen received 2,539 votes (as against 3,579 in 1971, and 4,596 in 1968) and Jackson 1,757 (2,515 in 1971, and 4,443 in 1968). The remaining SUP candidates fared even worse. In 1944, when communist influence was at its peak in New Zealand, Jackson gained 7,045 votes as a CPNZ candidate for the Auckland City Council.

On 2 November a parliamentary by-election was held in Sydenham (Christchurch) to fill the seat left vacant by the sudden death of the prime minister, Norman Kirk. The SAL decided to contest this election (for the first time since 1969), and it put forward as candidate Kay Goodger, women's liberation editor of *Socialist Action* and national coordinator of the Women's National Abortion Action Campaign. Ms. Goodger conducted election meetings throughout New Zealand, putting the emphasis on feminist issues. She gained 181 votes in a total poll exceeding 10,000.

The Labour Party executive had decided in May 1972 that membership of the SAL was incompatible with membership of the Labour Party. Party branches were expected to enforce this ban, but as they failed to take action, the executive took the initiative in 1974 by ordering the expulsion of K. Locke in Wellington. One of the reasons given for the ban was that the SAL was a separate political party which had stood candidates in opposition to official Labour Party candidates. This had happened only once, in 1969, but the fact that the SAL has now again opposed an official Labour Party candidate in Sydenham will probably lead to a much stricter enforcement of the ban in future. Ms. Goodger, who was a member of both the SAL and the Labour Party, has already forfeited her membership in the latter.

Little can be said about the activities of the CPNZ because they were minimal, apart from the production of a weekly journal. The Manson-Bailey group in one of its publications commented that because of its sectarianism "the Communist Party's lead has been rejected, its vanguard role lost. Its influence has been reduced, its members have become disheartened and thereby less active. Its publications have less and less appeal. Its members who lead the Progressive Youth Movement have seen the organization and its influence on the wane. When there is an upsurge of radical thought and action among the young people and ever widening circles, the Communist Party, by its 'closed door' policies and methods, is causing only a sterile turning of these radicals to the more active revisionists in the Socialist Unity Party—and to the Trotskyists! " (*Draw Lessons from the Past*, Wellington, 1974. p. 19a)

International Positions and Contacts. The international alignment of the three communist organizations remained unchanged in 1974, and the pattern of overseas visits and exchanges was predictable. V. G. Wilcox visited Peking for several weeks in August-September at the invitation of the Central Committee of the Chinese Communist Party, but no information has been released about the topics he discussed with Chinese leaders. These visits have taken place annually ever since 1959, with the exception of 1972 and possibly also 1960. H. W. Crook, a member of the Political Committee, represented the CPNZ in Tirana in November at celebrations to mark the thirtieth anniversary of Albania's liberation.

George Meyers, a member of the Political Committee of the Communist Party, USA, came to New Zealand in August at the invitation of the SUP to give a series of lectures. This was the first such visit by a leading U.S. communist. Meyers also lectured in Australia, and his discussions with party leaders led to a lengthy joint statement by the SUP, the Socialist Party of Australia, and the CPUSA, in which they welcomed advances made toward dçetente, called for an end to all nuclear testing, the destruction of nuclear stockpiles, and the dismantling of military bases on foreign territory, urged the establishment of peace zones in the Indian and Pacific oceans, and demanded the fulfillment of the Vietnam Paris peace accords. The three parties also condemned the policies of the Chinese leaders, whose "rabid chauvinism and rabid nationalism" they denounced as "a betrayal of the forces for peace and socialism" and "outright assistance to imperialism" Maoist and Trotskyist ultra-"left" groups were to be opposed as divisive and disruptive elements, and the three parties supported an early convening of an international meeting of communist and workers' parties "as soon as adequate preparations have been completed." (*New Zealand Tribune*, 4 November.)

Mrs. Ayo traveled to Russia in October, and I. Tucker represented the Democratic Youth Front at the Ninth Assembly of the World Federation of Democratic Youth in Varna, Bulgaria, in November. The SAL invited U.S. and Australian Trotskyists to take part in its educational conferences and it sent delegates, including K. Locke, to the Tenth World Congress of the Fourth International which met in Sweden in February. At this congress the SAL was granted official recognition as the New Zealand section of the Fourth International of which it had previously been a sympathizing organization.

The U.S.S.R. and China Friendship Societies continued their activities at an increased level, and a new society was formed in August, following a visit from a North Korean delegation, to promote friendship between New Zealand and the Democratic People's Republic of Korea. Vietnam was much less in the news than in previous years, but campaigns were conducted for medical aid and the release of political prisoners in the South. Late in the year the Committee on Vietnam launched a campaign for New Zealand recognition of the Provisional Revolutionary Government. Another international issue was solidarity with Chile, coupled with demands for the admission of Chilean refugees to New Zealand. Here there was some unacknowledged cooperation between the SUP and the SAL, while the CPNZ virtually ignored this campaign.

Publications. The official journals of the three communist organizations are all similar in size (8 pages) and format. The CPNZ publishes the weekly *People's Voice* in Auckland, and a monthly theoretical journal, *New Zealand Communist Review*. The SUP journal, *New Zealand Tribune*, is also published in Auckland. It used to appear monthly, but has come out every three weeks since March 1974, with a special supplement to mark the 100th issue in October. The party also revived its theoretical journal, *Socialist Politics*, which has appeared quarterly since September 1973. The SAL journal *Socialist Action*, which is published fortnightly in Wellington, also reached its 100th issue during the year, in May. An independent radical journal, called *The Paper*, is published monthly in Wellington with the assistance of members of the Manson-Bailey group. The circulation within New Zealand of these journals is probably between 1,000 and 2,000 copies each.

University of Auckland   H. Roth

Pakistan

The Communist Party of Pakistan (CPP) was declared an illegal organization in 1954. Its current legal position, however, is unclear because of subsequent constitutional developments and court decisions which overturned the 1954 ruling. Whatever vitality which the party might still have had was dealt a mortal blow when the former province of East Pakistan achieved independence as Bangladesh in December 1971. With the separation of the two wings, the more active and better organized East Pakistani branch of the party and its front groups apparently went their own way.

A resurgence of regional nationalism as the focus of domestic politics in post-separation Pakistan has tended to deprive the CPP of even the limited appeal which it once had for the various elements which have supported it over the years. Moreover, much of the radical rhetoric and some of the ideologues who gave the party its characteristic appeal during the past have been co-opted by Prime Minister Zulfikar Ali Bhutto and his ruling Pakistan People's Party (PPP). As a result, the CPP's membership is negligible and it has for all practical purposes virtually disappeared, although some individuals still consider themselves communists. Strong pro-communist biases are reflected in the writing of a number of Pakistani journalists, some of whom have achieved important editorial positions with leading Pakistani newspapers. An example is the PPP party organ, the Urdu daily *Musawaat* published from Karachi, Lahore, and Lyallpur; many of its editorial staff make little effort to hide their pro-communist views.

The National Awami Party (NAP)—which is a party in its own right, not a front, although at times it has provided an institutional haven for communists who could not function politically with open CPP identification—is now more than ever before basically a regionalist group. Despite its status as leading element of the small opposition in Pakistan's National Assembly, the NAP is not really an all-Pakistan party. Although its election manifesto included socialist rhetoric, its primary objective is the achievement of increased autonomy for the Pathan and Baluch peoples who dominate the country's two western border provinces abutting on Afghanistan.

The NAP is poorly organized in the Punjab, where it has little following, except among a few of the old communists and "progressive" intellectuals, plus some factory-level trade union leaders. The Punjab provincial NAP vice-president, Falek Sher Bharwana, left the NAP in July 1974 to join the PPP. Similarly, the NAP is weak in the Sind; its primary support there is drawn from lawyers and students in Karachi and Hyderabad, Kaneez Fatima's labor union in the Karachi Port Trust, and possibly some of the 500,000 to 1,000,000 Pathan laborers in the Karachi area.

Although the basic focus of NAP attention is the Pathan homeland in the North-West Frontier Province (NWFP), it has been drawn in recent months to the arid and inhospitable Marri and Mengal Baluch tribal lands in north-central Baluchistan. A protracted and still unresolved war between the military and paramilitary forces of Bhutto's central government and the Baluch tribal sirdars (chieftains) of the two clans only now seems to be drawing to an uneasy close. During the course of the conflict, NAP leader and veteran oppositionist Khan Abdul Wali Khan and his principal lieutenants have been the targets of a highly publicized campaign by the federal authorities.

This antagonism grows to some extent from Bhutto's fears—or at least often repeated allegations—that Wali Khan and the NAP are the domestic agents of an anti-Pakistan plot masterminded by the Soviet Union and eagerly supported by the governments of Afghanistan and India. This anxiety stems in part from a war of words which has its roots in the past, but has gained in intensity since the July 1973 coup through which Afghan president Mohammad Daud seized power from his cousin, the former king. Daud's vocal support for the creation of Pashtunistan, an autonomous Pathan (and Baluch) nation-state, has both angered and perturbed a Pakistan which is only now recovering from the trauma of the 1971 secession of Bangladesh.

These fears are not allayed by Wali Khan's frequent attacks on the Bhutto government and regular visits to Kabul, supposedly for treatment of a chronic eye ailment. Moreover, a series of bombings and minor sabotage incidents in the NWFP, Punjab, and Sind in October and November have resulted in the arrest of scores of NAP party faithful. The Pakistan government has accused the NAP and the Afghans of complicity in these developments, but Wali has denied these charges.

Despite such problems as the tribal insurgency in Baluchistan; a religious conflict involving the small but influential Ahmadiyya sect; border troubles with Afghanistan; slow progress toward normalization of relations with India against a background of continuing tension; and nagging but not yet unmanageable domestic economic pressures, Bhutto continues to dominate the new Pakistan without any significant challenger. There is, however, dissatisfaction among the educated elite and other elements of the society over his occasionally high-handed approach to problem solving and the way in which he has manipulated such democratic principles as freedom of the press in order to stifle criticism of his policies and programs.

This has not prevented Bhutto from mounting an effective campaign for economic assistance from such traditional sources as the United States and Iran. The Shah, despite improved ties with India and Afghanistan, has recently promised Pakistan a loan of $580 million over the next three years. This should ease the country's balance of payments problem during the current period of economic strain aggravated by inflation and the world energy and food crises. Although the United States has not agreed to resume full-scale military assistance to Pakistan, the door is still open. During Secretary of State Kissinger's visit to Islamabad in October 1974, the United States promised to furnish Pakistan with about 100,000 tons of wheat on long-term, low interest credit and to give "careful consideration" to the country's "additional requirements." As it is, Pakistan remains a recipient of significant amounts of U.S. economic assistance while other such programs are shrinking drastically.

Pakistan continues to have close relations with the People's Republic of China, which remains an important source of planes, medium tanks, and naval patrol boats, although not the sophisticated new equipment and replacements which the Pakistanis would like to acquire on concessional terms from the United States. This close relationship was underlined during Bhutto's state visit to Peking in May, when the Chinese were understood to have promised to expedite the unused $100 million portion of $230 million in economic assistance committed in 1972.

At the same time, reversing the trends of the Bangladesh war period, Pakistan has mended its fences with the U.S.S.R., or at least ended signs of outward hostility to the Russians. During Bhutto's visit to Moscow in October, he discussed the problem of Pakistan's relations with Afghanistan and asked the Soviets to try to dissuade the Afghans from pursuing their current border policy. He was unable, however, to gain any Soviet support for Pakistan's efforts to have the United Nations declare South Asia a zone free of nuclear weapons, following India's successful explosion of a nuclear device in May.

Washington, D. C.   Joel M. Woldman

Philippines

Philippine Communism revolves around two parties, one oriented toward Peking, the other toward Moscow, but both claiming to speak for national interests. Both parties are underground, with dispersed leaderships, but the Peking-oriented group is more actively involved in a guerrilla insurgency, which, according to the Philippine government, is also meshed with the uprising of Muslim groups on the island of Mindanao and other southern islands in the country. Elements of the Moscow-oriented faction appear to have made their peace with the Marcos government.

History. Chinese and Indonesian communists had been proselytizing in the Philippine islands all during the 1920s, but the PKP, or Partido Komunista ng Pilipinas (Philippine Communist Party), was not officially born until 7 November 1930, although it had been organized some six weeks before on 26 August. From the start the PKP drew its support from the budding Philippine trade union movement, including such Marxist-oriented labor federations as the KAP, or Katipunan ng mga Anakpawis sa Pilipinas ("Association of the Sons of Sweat of the Philippines"). The PKP's first general secretary, Crisanto Evangelista, had been a major KAP leader, and both KAP and PKP, after instigating a minor wave of strikes and anti-government agitation, were formally banned on 14 September 1931.

Even before this proscription, however, and at the apparent direction of the Comintern, the Communist Party, USA had provided much of the policy guidance for the PKP, and in Comintern councils and statements relating to the Philippines U.S. communists played a major role. Realizing the difficulty of achieving political legitimacy, the PKP relied largely on a variety of informal or formal front organizations, such as the "League for the Defense of Democracy" and on 7 November 1938, in conformity with Comintern united-front directives, merged with the legal but small Socialist Party of the Philippines and its labor arm, the "General Union of Workers." The merger occurred in a context of rising demands for independence by non-communist Philippine nationalist organizations, and as early as 31 December 1936 the president of the Commonwealth of the Philippines government, Manuel Quezon, in an effort to unify Philippine public opinion, had granted clemency to a number of detained PKP leaders.

It was not until the Japanese invasion of the Philippines during World War II that significant new tactical opportunities presented themselves to the communists. The communists, allied with others, took the lead in the formation of a "National Anti-Japanese United Front," and on 29 March 1942 this front's military committee spearheaded the creation of an "Anti-Japanese People's Army" (Hukbo ng Bayan Laban sa Hapon, or Hukbalahap—"Huks" for short) which became a major focal point of the national resistance movement. A separate "squadron" of Chinese communists operated with the Huks. Communists clearly hoped that the Huks' prestige would legitimize their own objectives in the post-war period. Refusing to surrender their arms, the Huks were outlawed on 6 March 1948, as throughout Southeast Asia meanwhile communists moved toward confrontation of established governments or even of other nationalist movements with which they had earlier collaborated. The PKP technically was not included in the ban on the Huks, but most party leaders identified themselves with the reconstituted Huk organization, the "People's Liberation Army" (Hukbo ng Mapagpalaya ng Bayan, or HMB) formed on 7 November 1948 and nominally led by Luis Taruc, who later was to say that he had never been a communist.

Using the HMB as its armed force, the PKP, internally restructured, urged a general rising against the Philippine government and set 1 May 1952 as the date of the latter's overthrow. But the government did not fall, and on 18 October 1952 most of the PKP's Politburo, including secretary-general José Lava, fell into government hands. Initial Huk military successes, which had helped boost a combined PKP-HMB membership to about 25,000 at the beginning of 1950, now came to naught with effective, U.S.-assisted counter-insurgency tactics implemented under Philippine defense secretary and later president Ramon Magsaysay. On 17 June 1957, Philippine Republic Act 1700 formally outlawed both the PKP and HMB, but by this time effective Huk resistance and PKP organization had long since been broken, though neither wholly disappeared.

Limited until the early 1960s to scattered marauding by small bands, which often engaged in extensive racketeering and mere criminal activities, underground PKP leaders eventually embarked on a reconstruction of their organization, stressing "parliamentary" tactics, developing front groups, and capitalizing on a rising nationalist restiveness in youth, intellectual, and the more radical labor circles, impatient with the manifestations of deep economic inequalities, extensive corruption, inefficiency, partisan political and parliamentary haggling, and horse-trading that characterizes public life. Some elements of the Huks also identified with vaguely Marxist and radical-populist reform ideologies, or occasionally cultivated a rough Robin Hood-style image of rural justice appealing to the exploited tenant farmer. But most of the new impetus came from new urban front organizations, all strongly nationalistic, with generally "progressive" or socialistic and anti-U.S. leanings. The Kabataang Makabayan ("National Youth," or KM), the Lapiang Manggagawa ("Labor Party," or LM), the "Movement for the Advancement of Nationalism" (MAN), and the "Free Peasants Union" (Malayang Samahang Magsasaka, or Masaka) were among the most important of these organizations, which also attracted a broad spectrum of non-communists, from intellectuals, students, and some prominent business figures to agricultural and industrial workers. The arrest on 12 May 1964 of PKP secretary-general Jesús Lava, who had succeeded his brother, José, in that party post, did not impede development of the new united-front tactic. Overlapping memberships further strengthened the emergence of other fronts, like the reconstituted "Socialist Party of the Philippines" (SPP) in 1967. (Justus M. van der Kroef, "Communist Fronts in the Philippines," *Problems of Communism*, March-April 1967, pp. 65-75).

The tactical value of the new front-group strategy increasingly came to be questioned by younger Philippine radicals, ideologically attracted by Maoist doctrine and by militant "people's war" tactics, and disturbed over the PKP's continuing relationship with the discredited HMB and its crude brigandage. During 1966-67 came a break within the PKP leadership over this tactical question, and from 26 December 1967 (Mao Tse-tung's seventy-fifth birthday) to 7 January 1969 a "Congress of Reestablishment of the Communist Party of the Philippines" convened near the town of Capas, in southern Tarlac Province, Luzon. This congress formally established a new rival communist party, the "Communist Party of the Philippines-Marxist-Leninist (CPP-ML). The new party formally identified itself with "Mao Tse-tung thought" and on 29 March 1969, probably also after a meeting near Capas, CPP-ML cadres, veterans, and militants, some with old Huk or HMB backgrounds, and calling themselves "Red Commanders and Soldiers of the People," formed a new fighting force, the "New People's Army" (NPA). The Moscow-oriented rump PKP core, denouncing the Maoists' breakaway and their irresponsible "cowboy ideology," eventually broke with the old Huk organization, forming its own "liberation" force, the "National Army" (Army ng Bayan, or AB). Although some Philippine authorities claim the AB to be a viable force, in reality the more militant guerrilla confrontations with the government since 1970 have mainly involved the NPA and their Masaka allies in the rural areas and veteran KM student activists in Manila.

During 1971-72, as partisan wrangling over a new Philippine constitution and reports of attempts by the government of President Ferdinand Marcos to perpetuate itself in power deepened public uncertainty and the domestic political crisis, the NPA and its allies, according to the government, engaged in running clashes, terrorism, and violent disturbances with Philippine security forces. On 22 September 1972 President Marcos proclaimed martial law throughout the country and in a nation-wide address blamed a "state of rebellion" in the country on the CPP-ML and the NPA which, he asserted, were controlling "33 municipalities" and had established "communal farms and production bases."

By the beginning of 1973, however, while clashes with the NPA continued to be reported by government spokesmen, the NPA threat seemed to have abated notably, leading to speculation among informed observers that the danger of Maoist subversion had been magnified in order to justify the Marcos regime's proclamation of an emergency by which it was enabled to perpetuate itself in power. The same speculation applied also to the regime's subsequent implementation of constitutional, agrarian, and other reforms, and the temporary arrest of hundreds of its more vocal political and media critics. (Justus M. van der Kroef, "Communism and Reform in the Philippines," *Pacific Affairs*, Spring 1973, pp. 29-58, and "The Philippine Maoists," *Orbis*, Winter 1973, pp. 892-926.)

As in the course of 1973-74 fighting between Muslims and Christians in the Southern Philippines intensified, amplifying threats of secession of the Islamic South, government spokesmen also professed to see NPA influence in this conflict. Periodic assertions in the middle and toward the end of 1973 that the NPA forces were declining, and that the Muslim problem was on the way to solution, appeared to be contradicted by reports in September 1974 that rebel Muslim and NPA forces were continuing their activities, and that clashes were occurring with combined Muslim and Maoist insurgent bands in Cotabato and elsewhere in the South (*NYT*, 22 September).

Organization and Tactics. The rivalry between the two communist parties, as well as their lack of legitimacy, seriously impedes their effectiveness, although both parties, during 1974, benefited somewhat from the fact that, as a result of Marcos's foreign policies, establishment of diplomatic relations with both the U.S.S.R. and People's China is considered to be but a matter of time. The Moscow-oriented PKP, whose leadership has been trying to project the party in terms of a nationalist, progressive, but responsible and parliamentary policy, opposed to the militant "adventurism" of the CPP-ML and the NPA, is likely to gain most from the impending Philippine diplomatic recognition of the chief communist world powers. There remains military opposition to such recognition, however. Estimates have put the PKP's hard-core strength at 1,200 to 1,500 members, including 100 or so in the AB with probably an additional several hundred fringe supporters and sympathizers in various front organizations now reduced to paper status, dormant, or wholly inoperative since the martial law declaration of 1972. Among these front groups are or were trade union federations like the "National Workers Federation" (Pambansang Kilusan ng Paggawa), student groups like the "Democratic Union of Filipino Youth" (Malayang Pagkakaisa ng Kabataang Pilipino, or MKPK, founded in 1967 as an offshoot of the KM), leftist nationalist and pacificist groups like MAN and the "Bertrand Russell Peace Foundation" (founded in 1964), and self-help groups of the industrial proletariat like the "Brotherhood for Our Development" (Ang Kapatrian Sa Ikauunlad Natin, or AKSIUN). The peasant organization Masaka, where the PKP also has supporters, nominally still exists, but according to Philippine security sources it is tightly supervised by police and military authorities; its leaders are under continuous direct surveillance.

Some prominent former PKP Politburo figures like the Lava brothers have been released from detention and are said to be playing an unspecified intermediary role in the movement toward the establishment of diplomatic relations with the Soviet Union, including visits to Moscow, but the Marcos government has not publicly acknowledged this. Because of strict martial-law supervision, participation in erstwhile PKP fronts has all but become impossible. Party supporters have surrendered (see below), gone underground, or gone abroad—particularly to India and Ceylon, where pro-Moscow communist parties are both legitimate and influential. PKP "cells" are still known to exist among trade union supporters and probably also in the Masaka organization, but such leadership hierarchy as exists beyond this level is both fluid and deeply hidden.

In a background essay on the PKP appearing recently in the principal international medium of Moscow-oriented parties, the basic unit of the PKP is described as "the nucleus," organized in factories and schools, on plantations and estates, in the offices of the government and in the mass media, in prisons and in the villages and streets of the cities (*WMR*, April 1974, p. 44). Highest authority is vested in a party congress (the Fifth Congress, according to the PKP, met in February 1973; see *YICA, 1974*, pp. 522-23), which elects the Central Committee. The latter in turn elects the Politburo and the Secretariat. There are "intermediate leading organs" varying in "accordance with time and place."

The overall political condition in which the PKP now must operate was described in the "Political Resolution" adopted by the Fifth Congress. According to this document, the Philippines is "a neo-colonial country of dynamic capitalist development," distorted in growth by "colonial plunder" and underdevelopment and subjected to survivals of feudalism in the rural areas and to the hegemony of finance capital, directed by "U.S. imperialism" (*IB*, no. 13, 1973, p. 25). Under the present martial-law regime the Philippines is said to have been transformed into a manufacturing base of labor-intensive products for the benefit of U.S. and Japanese monopoly interests, and even the country's educational system is being changed into a vocational training system providing skills for the "neo-colonial industrialization" process now taking place. Especially in agriculture the transformation of the economy into a tool of "imperialist" interests is said to be evident. Processing industries are to be expanded with a corresponding reduction in the land and labor concerned with corn and rice production so that available resources can be harnessed to new processing industries, including vegetables and fruit, meat and poultry products. These new processing industries will, however, be but "adjuncts" of "multi-national companies" and such land reform as is now being undertaken is merely paving the way for the development of the new foreign-owned raw material and food processing industries according to this "Political Resolution." A strong bourgeois class is being promoted by "pro-imperialist policy makers" and a "petty bourgeois mentality" is being encouraged. The grievous consequences of this process are said to be already apparent in the impoverishment of tenants and in the rise of the sisantes, or landless rural semi-proletariat. Meanwhile, the "CIA forces" have been using the "ultra-revolutionary phraseology" of "Maoist adventurism" in order to sponsor anarchism and counterrevolution and so break up the unity of "the anti-imperialist movement." Hence, according to the "Political Resolution," a new identification with the masses is necessary so that the party will not be dragged into "left adventurist policy" and "infantile" revolutionary sloganizing. (Ibid., pp. 17-35.)

On 11 October 1974 the PKP's commitment to a parliamentary course of action, designed to re-legitimize the party, took a new turn with the surrender of Felicisimo Macapagal, described as the PKP secretary-general, and 26 armed followers, among them three Politburo members. The surrender took place in the presence of President Marcos, and Macapagal said that it had occurred in response to the president's call for national unity and out of the PKP's desire to begin a "patriotic and socially conscious participation" in nation building. The Philippine government claimed that the surrender "marked the end of the CPP's 44-year illegal and underground existence." (*FBIS*, 15, 17 October.) Doubts were expressed whether Macapagal necessarily spoke for the entire PKI Politburo, in view of continued underground opposition to the government by other PKP cadres and followers, although the government subsequently claimed surrender of hundreds of other "communist rebels" (ibid., 18 November). Nor was there any formal repudiation by Macapagal of the PKP's "Political Resolution" or its other programs. After the surrender, Philippine armed forces sources said that the PKP might win government recognition in the near future—at least if a "normal peace situation" prevailed, with a corresponding lifting of martial law (ibid., 18 October). There was skepticism, however, about the government's taking such a step at any time soon. Subsequently the rank and importance of Macapagal came to be questioned and the whole surrender incident, and the government publicity surrounding it, was seen as not unrelated to the warming trend in Soviet-Filipino relations.

The PKP Fifth Congress also laid down a specific party program, based on the implementation of a "national democratic revolution," which was defined as the rising of the broad masses of people, organized into a united front of all "patriotic and democratic forces" and led by the "working class" (*IB*, no. 17-18, 1973, p. 17). This program presumably is still operative despite Macapagal's surrender. It rejects the paths of schism, coup d'état, and "foco guerrillaism or anarcho-terrorist revolutionism that stands apart from the sentiment of the masses." The PKP affirmed, rather, that it is in the masses' interest that the "road to revolution" be without bloodshed. But the people's right to use force against those who use force against the people was also supported.

The party program favors a united front of all revolutionary forces, including the proletariat, peasants, working intellectuals, and "progressive" students, and notes that a "progressive outlook" is also developing among the big bourgeoisie not connected with foreign monopoly capital. Even among young officers and servicemen a "patriotic and anti-imperialist consciousness" is said to be developing, while, unlike the "landlord leadership of the Church," the "patriotic young members" of the Filipino clergy sense the need for the "social liberation" of workers and peasants. Bearing the interests of the revolutionary forces in the country in mind, the PKP's "immediate demands" include (1) termination of the martial law condition, (2) restoration of freedom of the press, the right to strike, and other "liberties of the people," and (3) release of all political prisoners. Other demands include: removal of U.S. military bases; expulsion of CIA agents, Peace Corps volunteers, and the Asia Foundation; severance of relations with the World Bank and the International Monetary Fund; recognition of the PKP as a legal organization; promotion of public education in the context of "mass political education"; distribution of land to tenants and cancellation of tenant debts; transformation of sugar and other plantations into cooperative farms managed by the workers and other employees; nationalization of banks, foreign trade, foreign estates, and the mining industry; promulgation of autonomy for the Muslim population, which "shall set up its own government" (with exclusive powers over all internal Muslim affairs such as family, property, and religious laws). Further, the PKP program calls for the inauguration of an anti-colonialist and anti-imperialist foreign policy committed to breaking the control of "U.S. imperialism"; withdrawal from the Southeast Asia Treaty Organization (SEATO); establishment of diplomatic relations with the U.S.S.R. "and other socialist countries," including the Democratic Republic of Vietnam; and "friendship and close cooperation" with the Arab countries. (Ibid., pp. 14-28.)

The organizational structure of the CPP-ML follows that of the PKP, with the National Congress exercising supreme leadership, vested in an elected Central Committee, which in turn elects the Politburo and the party chairman and his deputies (Southeast Asia Treaty Organization, *The Maoist Communist Party of the Philippines*, Short Paper, 1971, Bangkok, 1971, pp. 10-11). The CPP-ML's chairman and head of its Politburo is José Maria Sison, former teacher at the University of the Philippines. Overall command of the NPA, nominally entrusted to the party's military commission, is reportedly in the hands of Victoriano Corpus, a Philippine Army lieutenant who deserted. Former

HMB commander Bernabe Buscayno ("Commander Dante"), because of tactical and ideological differences with Sison, was previously reported to be inactive, although still considered a behind-the-scenes NPA strategist by some Philippine security sources. Other sources still describe Buscayno as the chief NPA commander, with Corpus occupying a minor position as "training officer."

The total NPA force, in the middle of 1974, was estimated by some Philippine military intelligence sources at about 1,400. Only perhaps a fourth of these are considered well-armed, disciplined regulars. Additional supporters in such Maoist-infiltrated youth organizations as the "Democratic Youth Association" (Samahang Demokratiko ng Kabatang, or SDK), and in other fronts like the "Movement for a Democratic Philippines" (MDP), now both shattered and underground, are believed to number less than 2,000. Because of the mobility of the NPA organization and dissension within the ranks of the insurgents, the CPP-ML leadership structure gives an impression of serious instability.

The program and tactical norms of the CPP-ML and of the NPA are doctrinaire Maoism, but said to be adapted to Philippine conditions. One of the most recent tactical statements of the party was issued by the CPP-ML Central Committee on 26 December 1973 and subsequently printed in the party's publication *Ang Bayan* (for an earlier statement see *YICA, 1974*, p. 525). According to this statement, the party sees itself as the "vanguard of the revolutionary proletariat," concerned with forming a "broad national united front" and developing the "basic unity of the workers and peasants." The statement asserts that "there is no substitute for a protracted people's war," and declares it to be altogether proper that armed units of the people's revolutionary forces are engaged in tactical strikes in the rural areas as meanwhile the underground in the cities "bides its time" gathering strength and generating revolutionary propaganda (*Peking Review*, 22 February 1974). The statement holds that the party's struggle against "the Lava revisionist renegades" (the Moscow-oriented PKP) and the "gangster clique" of the old Huks has improved "the weapons of revolution," and that the worsening domestic economic condition of the Philippines is coupled with a brightening international situation—for example, the Indochinese people "have brilliantly proven that a small country can defeat such a superpower as U.S. imperialism" if the people are united and are prepared to take their destinies in their own hands.

As for the NPA, its "area of operations," according to an NPA release on 29 March 1973, had grown from four provinces in 1969 to thirty-four by the beginning of 1973. It was engaging in successful ambushes of government troops and generally "raising high the banner of armed resistance in the face of the Marcos rightist coup." (*Indonesian Tribune*, Tirana, no. 1, 1973, p. 26). Despite "unprecedentedly large campaigns of encirclement" by government forces numbering 10,000 men, the NPA nevertheless was able to defeat the enemy and also raise to 25 the number of U.S. military personnel it had killed. Meanwhile, and along with its military activity, the NPA was carrying forward its work of "agrarian revolution" and "base building," mobilizing men and women in the villages in support. The NPA also claimed to be implementing a land reform program and, as the result of its appeal to the people, to have established local organs of government in "several thousands" of villages, aside from its own political organizing committees' in "the guerrilla zones." These committees in turn were supported by local "mass organisations" of peasants, youths, women, children, and "cultural activists." The overthrow of "the fascist dictatorship of the U.S.-Marcos clique"; the arrest and trial of Marcos before a people's court; the nullification of and fight for the abrogation of all "unequal treaties" with the United States, especially those relating to direct investment, military bases, and U.S. assistance; and the reestablishment of "the democratic rights" of mass media, political parties, religious organizations, and others, remained the immediate objectives of the CPP-ML.

Under the pseudonym "Amada Guerrero," CPP-ML chairman José Sison has written *Philippine Society and Revolution* (Pulang Tala Publications, Manila, 1971, 296 pp.) to "present in a comprehensive way" Philippine history and the main problems of the Filipino people "from the standpoint of Marxism-Leninism-Mao Tse-tung Thought." The most important doctrinal statement by a CPP-ML leader, this book is studied and considered authoritative by party cadres and applicant members. It envisages the establishment of a "new democratic republic" in the Philippines, which, harmonizing the interests of all revolutionary classes, will be neither a "bourgeois dictatorship" or a "dictatorship of the proletariat," but rather a "joint dictatorship of all revolutionary classes and strata under the leadership of the proletariat" (p. 287). To achieve this objective "revolutionary bases" must be established even though the reactionary "landlords-bureaucrat state" has not as yet been wholly eliminated. Such bases should be created in the rural areas first, since the guerrilla forces will be drawn mainly from the peasantry. "Guerrero" cites the well-known Maoist adage that "political power grows out of the barrel of a gun" (p. 288). As for the course of the Philippine revolution, the Filipinos are very fortunate to be so close to the center of the "world proletarian revolution"— People's China, the "iron bastion of socialism" (p. 296).

If government sources as well as insurgent claims are to be believed, the year 1974 witnessed new highs in guerrilla activity. In mid-January the armed forces announced that communists were regrouping and were again posing a main threat to national security. Despite release of detainees previously arrested, new communist recruitment, especially at the universities, was said to be continuing, and students who went underground after the imposition of martial law were said to have increased the number of communist regulars from 1,710 to 2,266 by late 1973. NPA activity was also reported to have expanded to the Visayas and Mindanao. (*NYT*, 13 January 1974.)

Two months later, Philippine Armed Forces chief of staff General Romeo Espino declared that the communist movement was still "very much alive," though the nation was not in immediate danger, and there had been "an interesting tempo of insurgent, subversive and guerrilla activities" in preparation for another effort to overthrow the government (*FBIS*, 20 March). By July it became apparent that NPA activity had spread to the island of Samar in the Eastern Visayas, as a Philippine Constabulary unit ran into an NPA ambush there and the existence and tactics of a local Maoist organization were revealed. Led by a former radio announcer, Prudencio Calubid ("Commander Eliot"), NPA cadres in the area were reported to have been organized for training, political activity, and supply work, while local farmers were approached by cadres offering instruction in better cultivation methods and medical aid. Several local villages were reported to be completely NPA-organized. (Bernard Wideman, "A New Front for the Insurgents," *Far Eastern Economic Review*, 15 July.)

By September defense secretary Juan Enrile was saying that new clashes were taking place with either NPA or other, presumably Moslem, rebel forces in southern Mindanao, and that there were indications that a united front, involving all those opposed to the Marcos regime, was being established (*NYT*, 22 September). Enrile's statement followed by three weeks an official announcement of the discovery of an alleged communist plot, linked to a recent and much publicized breaking-up by government forces of an arms smuggling ring. The plot had been designed, according to the Defense Department, to establish a "national democratic front," bringing together all those against the martial law regime of President Marcos, on the basis of a ten-point revolutionary action program. Forming of a coalition government under communist leadership was presumably envisaged. (*FBIS*, 3 September.)

The report on the new "national democratic front" plot underscored a seeming intensity of underground NPA and CPP-ML organizational efforts during the year. By the close of August, Philippine security forces, in an operation named "Sea Hawk," had arrested 38 "high-ranking" communist cadres, seized a number of motor vehicles and "assorted sea craft," and uncovered a number of communist bases used for arms smuggling and transportation. Three motor vessels, in size ranging from 30 to 60 tons, had been seized and were reported to have been used for transporting firearms and ammunition from a "foreign source" to designated "drop sites" where frogmen would later recover the arms and bring them to private beach resorts aboard smaller vessels for later distribution. According to the Defense Department, the "Sea Hawk" operation disclosed that the communists had acquired two private beach resorts in the northern province of La Union, facing the South China Sea, and had equipped them with underground arms-storage facilities. Trucking services had been acquired for distribution of the weapons from there. The unnamed "foreign source" had financed this smuggling network to the amount of 2 million pesos (about $285,714). (*FBIS*, 28 August.)

The revelations of Operation "Sea Hawk," like similar reports of arms smuggling to the NPA via small coastal vessels supplied by a "foreign source," have aroused some public skepticism. At the same time, reports of foreign arms supplies to the NPA have been too persistent and have come from too many different sources to be ignored altogether. If the revelations of Operation "Sea Hawk" and of the related plot of a "national democratic front" are even partially correct they suggest the continuation of communist organizational infrastructure two years after the proclamation of a national emergency designed to stamp the Communists out. There can also be little question that at least *operationally* NPA and some Muslim rebel units in the southern Philippines find it possible on occasion to join in common attacks against the government, thus repeated a pattern of tactical cooperation similar to that existing between orthodox Malay Muslim secessionist insurgents and Mao-oriented ethnic Chinese guerrillas in the Thai-Malayan frontier area (see *Malaysia*).

The extent of NPA tactical cooperation with the Philippine Muslim insurgents is a matter of controversy, however. Anti-Marcos sources have claimed that the mere fact that one of the leaders of the anti-government rising in Marawi City in Mindanao in October 1972 had a past association with the Kabataang Makabayan probably led the Philippine president to designate the insurgents as "Maoist-Muslims" even though the Marawi group was not part of any organized Muslim resistance force, let along associated with the NPA (*Journal of Contemporary Asia*, 1974, vol. 4, no. 1, p. 125). NPA infiltration of the Muslim rebels continues to be claimed by the government, with Defense Secretary Enrile, for example, blaming a mortar attack on the town of Jolo, in the Sulu islands, on "Maoist Moslem rebels" numbering some 300 armed men who also according to local officials control about eight towns in the area (*FBIS*, 7 February). By mid-April 1974 the government claimed that "all remnants of the Maoist rebellion" in the Sulu islands, a strongly Muslim area, had been eliminated (ibid., 19 April).

Whatever the reverses presumably suffered by the NPA in the Southern Philippines in the course of 1974, military operations during the year revealed the Maoist guerrilla force and its party organizational structure to be a nationwide force, committed tactically to erode government strength in widely scattered areas throughout the country as its attempts to establish secure rural bases. In June a reign of NPA terror briefly struck three towns some 125 miles northeast of Manila where public officials were beheaded by the communists; in mid-September sharp clashes took place with NPA forces in Matnog, Sorsogon Province, 230 miles southeast of Manila, and the following month four covert NPA camps were reportedly discovered in Bulan, Sorsogon. On 11 October military authorities reported they had killed ten communist guerrillas and captured 49 others on the island of Panay, in the Central Philippines, in operations during July-September. (Ibid., 25 June, 17 September, 16, 23 October.)

Particularly noteworthy has been a new pattern of urban-rural interaction in NPA-CPP-ML tactics. On 28 August the Defense Department announced, in connection with recent arrests of 57 persons allegedly engaged in smuggling arms and in making explosives for anti-government actions, that two business establishments and seven residences in Manila were involved in the illegal manufacture of the explosives. "Detonation teams" had been trained in Manila by the CPP-ML's "Military Commission" for work in outlying areas. The government claimed also that prominent intellectuals, including three college professors and two writers, had been involved in and had been arrested for arms smuggling (*NYT*, 29 August). In an address to officers of the National Philippine Defense College, Secretary Enrile claimed on 30 September that the NPA was now engaged in "subtler" activities than in the past, that it was operating outside its usual fighting zones, and was establishing new urban front groups to "subvert" civic, religious, business, and other interest groups, playing up economic problems and "distorting other national issues (*FBIS*, 1 October).

Domestic Developments. Despite continuing opposition from communists, Moslem insurgents, some elements of the Catholic clergy, prominent intellectuals, segments of the Philippine community in the United States and other groups, there was no indication in 1974 that the Marcos regime, and its Martial-law-based power structure, could be effectively challenged in the near future. On 17 September the Philippine Supreme Court upheld as constitutional the assumption of emergency powers by Marcos two years previously, a majority of the court stressing that an insurgency condition had in fact existed in the country and that the president had not acted arbitrarily in applying a constitutional provision giving him the right to declare martial law. The legality of the martial law proclamation had originally been challenged by a group of 31 prominent journalists and politicians who had been arrested under the president's emergency powers, and all but one of whom (Senator Benigno Aquino, a long-time political enemy of Marcos) had since been released. (*NYT*, 19 September.)

The court's decision came shortly after two top-ranking Catholic prelates, Julio Cardinal Rosales and Archbishop Jaime Sin, had addressed a petition to Marcos requesting him to lift martial law because of the "climate of fear" which it allegedly was creating in the country. Tensions between Marcos and some church leaders had abruptly peaked at the close of August when government forces entered a Jesuit novitiate in a Manila suburb, acting on reports that CPP-ML leader José Sison was there (he wasn't), and arrested a priest and some youths on charges of subversion. Those arrested were soon released, but Archbishop Sin called for "prayers of reparation" to be said for the alleged injustice of the raid on the novitiate.

Cardinal Rosales and Archbishop Sin were subsequently in attendance at a Philippine armed forces loyalty parade on 10 September, at which Marcos revealed that at the time martial law had been declared, two years before, the chiefs of the Philippine armed forces had made a pact with him (Marcos) that they would always submit to a civilian head of state. Defense secretary Enrile and twelve top-ranking officers had sworn loyalty to him as a civilian leader. Marcos said he was revealing the matter at this time because of speculation that he would be deposed by the armed forces. Earlier in the year Marcos had already indicated that a presidential decree, which is presently being kept secret, provides for his successor, since the succession stipulated by the 1935 constitution became inoperative when Marcos assumed martial law. (Ibid., 4, 11 September.)

Several factors explain the continuing viability of the Marcos regime despite internal and external opposition. One is that the pre-Marcos political system, with its deep corruption is still fresh in mind and a consensus exists that, for the moment, "there is no acceptable alternative to Marcos and his martial law" (Clayton Fritchey, *Washington Post*, 29 December 1973). Another is the significant economic advance which the country has been making, although there is serious doubt as to how much this has benefited the mass of Filipinos. The new national development plant fo4 1974-75 has projected an annual Gross National Product increase of 7 percent, which seems realistic enough since by the end of 1973 the real growth rate had reportedly already reached 10 percent. Some $1,440 million, or 75 percent of the 1974 total budget, has been allocated for social and economic development, and liberalization of regulations has had the result that the "flow of foreign investments into the country [has] increased tremendously since late 1972," with U.S. companies investing the greater part. ("The Philippine Progress," *Insight*, Hong Kong, June 1974, pp. 51-56.)

At the same time, the Philippine inflation rate this year is estimated at between 40 and 50 percent (*NYT*, 24 October). Increased fuel costs and sharp declines in U.S. and Japanese imports have adversely affected the Philippine wood products industry, a top foreign-exchange earner; the resulting jump in joblessness has been viewed by one regional military commander as a boost for the communist insurgents, with every jobless man becoming an easy target for the "moneyed rebel recruiters" (Associated Press dispatch, Manila, 28 August). Marcos has become particularly vulnerable because of what are alleged to be special privileges for U.S. economic interests. The formal expiration of the Laurel-Langly Agreement on 3 July has not affected U.S. land rights acquired under the agreement and related compacts, and a decision on the future status of these landholdings has been postponed until 27 May 1975. American corporate holdings in the Philippines have an estimated value of $1 billion to $1.5 billion, ranging "from just a plot for a small factory to a rubber plantation of several thousand acres" (*Far Eastern Economic Review*, 1 July, pp. 38, 39-42), and foreign investment regulations are said to be favorable to continung massive inputs of U.S. capital.

Questions continue to be raised about the extent and effectiveness of the regime's land reform measures. Land transfer certificates have now reportedly been given to 30 percent of the nation's 1.5 million tenant farmers, according to the government, but according to others most of the certificates have only been earmarked and not actually issued (ibid., 4 October, p. 5). On the other hand, veteran Philippine social reformers like one-time Huk commander Luis Taruc have publicly professed confidence that Marcos's "peaceful revolution" in the rural society can succeed and that the peasant masses will have no one to blame but themselves if it fails (*Christian Science Monitor*, 8 April). Marcos himself appears confident of his position, indicating in a BBC interview in July that his martial law administration would continue for at least another five years, and adding that martial law should have been implemented "as far back as immediately after the war" (*Asia Research Bulletin*, 31 July, p. 2889). Marcos also has claimed that major aspects of the martial law restrictions on civil liberties have been moderated, including the reestablishment of the rights of the courts to issue warrants of arrest, and the proper filing of sworn charges (*Far Eastern Economic Review*, 27 September, p. 37). At the same time reports have persisted of the use of torture on political opponents and of no attempts being made to control such practices (*Amnesty International Newsletter*, September). Opposition figures have estimated that there were 5,000 political prisoners in the Philippines (*Asia Research Bulletin*, 31 July, p. 2889). This estimate has not been substantiated by other quarters.

Not the least of the continuing sources of opposition to the Marcos regime is composed of elements of the Philippine community in the United States, which numbers about 500,000 persons, mostly on the east and west coasts. Because of their frequent travel to the Philippines, and the interaction of their social contacts, these elements in effect constitute an extension of the domestic opposition to the Marcos government. Some of the expatriate Filipino groups, like the Katipunan Demokratikong Pilipino, organized on 27 September 1973 in California, appear to be distinctively leftist in outlook, advocating a "national democratic revolution" in the Philippines, as well as "socialism" in the United States, and believing that the struggle for economic and political liberation in both countries should be joined together. In October 1973 the "Friends of the Filipino People" was organized in New York City. Another anti-Marcos group, the "Movement for a Free Philippines" (MFP), led by former Philippine senator and foreign secretary Raul S. Manglapus, is also headquartered in New York City. It has basically remained free from more radical influences, unlike the "National Committee for the Restoration of Civil Liberties in the Philippines," founded in 1972 and reportedly with chapters in major eastern and midwestern cities, which came under leftist direction from the start, drawing inspiration avowedly from a CPP-ML's front, the "Movement for a Democratic Philippines," and describing the three major enemies of the Filipino people as "U.S. imperialism, domestic feudalism, and bureaucrat capitalism" (Bradford Lyttle, "The Philippines—An Overview," *Win*, New York, March 1974, cited in *Terrorism*, staff study, committee on Internal Security, U.S. House of Representatives, Washington, D.C., 1 August 1974, pp. 74-75).

Some Philippine media published in the United States and catering to the interests of the resident Philippine community, like the semi-monthly *Philippine Times*, of Chicago, generally also articulate an anti-Marcos line. The acknowledged leader of the opposition remains Raul Manglapus, who repeatedly has castigated President Marcos as a dictator and usurper who rules without legal succession, but also has stressed that his MFP is not advocating the violent overthrow of the Marcos government but rather is attempting to bring about "a peaceful return of the country to democracy" (*Philippine Times*, 14 July). The Marcos government is known to be exerting pressure on the U.S. State Department to exercise greater control over the expatriate Philippine opposition groups, and has mounted a counter-propaganda effort of speaking tours by prominent Filipinos in the political and publishing fields. The repeated offers of amnesty to Moslem and communist rebels and the surrender in October of Felicisimo Macapagal apparently have had little effect on the expatriate opposition groups.

Continuous reports by regime spokesmen and Philippine news media relating to the capture or surrender of insurgents tend to be devalued and discounted by the Philippine public in part because they seem to go on and on, and partly because tactically their aggregate effect seems so slight: the fighting against the NPA and their Huk or Moslem allies continues as well. (See *FBIS*, 15, 28 February, 22 May, 13 June, 6 August, 12 September and *Bulletin Today*, Manila, 13 June.) The occasional killing by NPA units of a U.S. businessman or landowner, like that of landowner Peter James Grant in Castilla, in Southern Luzon, in October, scarcely draws greater public Filipino attention (*NYT*, 24 October).

Notwithstanding evidence of attempts by some NPA military commanders, or of former members of the CPP-ML and its front groups, to identify themselves with or infiltrate the Moslem insurgent movement, the latter is essentially a non-communist phenomenon. One report from the insurgent area in the Southern Philippines notes, for example, that if there are really "Maoist insurrectionaries" there, then "they are the first Maoists who attend Mosque regularly, and honestly believe that the United States is their real hope in winning their war against authority" (Harry Rolnick, in the *Sunday Magazine* of the *Bangkok Post*, 3 February). On the other hand, NPA elements are definitely known to have been active among some of the Moslem rebels, and an attack on Troli, South Cotabato, on 10 September was reportedly staged by a Moslem-NPA force (*NYT*, 22 September).

Rooted in the long-standing difficulties between Southern Filipino Christian and Moslems over landownership, in acute Moslem distress over alleged discrimination in employment and education, and in the continuing competitive influx of Northern (and Christian) immigrants into the South, and aggravated by covert supplies of arms and training for the rebels from the Malaysian state of Sabah, and possibly from Libya, the present stage of the Moslem conflict with Manila, now in its third year, shows no signs of abating. The Moro National Liberation Front (MNLF), with its mountain headquarters in Bato Pubih and led by Nuruliaji Misuari, former University of Philippines professor and KM activist, wants a completely independent state for the Muslims in the South, the "Bangsa Moro Republik" (*Far Eastern Economic Review*, 11 March, p. 15). Periodic reports of the reaching of agreements of cooperation between the government and rebel Muslim leaders, (e.g., last December, *FBIS*, 6 December 1973), have proved to be of as little lasting value as the equally frequent government offers of amnesty, after which fighting erupts again. On 8 November 1974, for example, President Marcos ordered a cease-fire in two Moslem-populated provinces, Lanao del Sur and Laneo del Norte, in an effort to make peace with the Moslem bands. But fighting broke out again within hours, just as on the previous 28 June, when a presidential offer of amnesty was followed within twenty-four hours by a Moslem attack on Marantaw (*Asia Research Bulletin*, 31 July, p. 2859).

Fighting between government forces and the MNLF has frequently been heavy; half the town of Jolo was burned, and scores of civilian, government, and rebel casualties resulted when Moslem rebels raided the town on 7-8 February (*FBIS*, 12, 19 February). The continuing intensity of fighting at such places as Jolo adds to mutual animosity in the same way as the massacre of the Moslem village of Mala, 28 miles northeast of Zamboanga, by armed Christians, in retaliation for a bush ambush by Moslem rebels in which two scores of Christians were killed (AP dispatch, Zamboanga City, 6 September).

In an effort to promote Southern development, a total of 406 million pesos (about $58 million) has been authorized by the Philippine government for Reconstruction and Development (RAD) programs for Mindanao, including irrigation and communication projects, new housing, and extension of agricultural loans and relief assistance to thousands of refugees from the continuing fighting (Government of the Philippines, Bureau of National and Foreign Information, *Economic Development of Muslim Mindanao*, 12 June, Manila, pp. 1-2). Marcos has been officially successful in winning international Moslem support for his development efforts. The International Islamic Organization, meeting in Djakarta on 1 June, voiced support of the economic rehabilitation program for the Southern Philippine Moslem areas (Agence France Presse, Djakarta, June 2, 1974), but it has not been possible, according to Philippine intelligence sources, to persuade strongly Moslem top public officials in the Malaysian state of Sabah to end their covert aid to the MNLF.

The extent of tactical cooperation between MNLF and NPA units in the Southern Philippines is not known, but appears to be relatively infrequent and uncoordinated. Fundamentally, the antagonism between Islam and Marxism-Leninism, including the Maoist variety, remains present among more articulate and politically conscious Southern Filipino Moslems. This dues not preclude, however, a readiness to join in common strikes against government forces if the opportunity arises. While the CPP-ML's program offers all distinctively religious and ethnic communities of Philippine society a high degree of cultural and legal autonomy, neither the NPA nor the CPP-ML has officially endorsed the MNLF aim of an independent Moslem republic.

International Aspects. According to Philippine foreign secretary Carlos P. Romulo, the government has now embarked on a new foreign policy which includes among other objectives "the widening of relations with the Socialist world" (*Asia Research Bulletin* 30 April, p. 2637). In the first instance this new policy has meant the forging of diplomatic ties with both the People's Republic of China and the U.S.S.R. In May 1974 President Marcos reportedly send a special envoy to Taipei to inform the Republic of China government on Taiwan that Philippine recognition of the mainland Chinese government was imminent and that the president would shortly visit Peking. A high-ranking Philippine official was quoted in early June as saying that Manila-Peking negotiations were "almost complete" (*FBIS*, 3 June). Later in June, Marcos seemed a good deal more hesitant. The Philippines would first have to solve the problem of "foreign support" for leftist insurgents, he said, adding that China was one of the countries that has been supporting them (*Asia Research Bulletin*, 30 June, p. 2799). Also, relations with "friends and allies" would have to be considered, Marcos said, as would the effect on other members of the Association of Southeast Asian Nations (ASEAN).

Clearly Manila was not going to be stampeded into a diplomatic rapprochement with the Chinese communists, even though the Peking media were taking note of the allegedly changing popular political orientation of the Philippine people, who, it was said, were anxious to end their dependency through "unequal treaties" on the United States (*Peking Review*, 19 July, p. 22). Yet the dynamics of mutual diplomatic recognition were becoming irresistible, whatever the remaining hesitations in Philippine government and, especially, military circles about the effects of such recognition on the regime's struggle against the Maoist NPA and CPP-ML. By early September something of a compromise had been found: not Marcos himself, but his wife, Imelda, a political power in her own right, would make the journey to Peking.

Even as he was seeing Mrs. Marcos off on her flight to Peking, on 20 September, the president seemed to put the exchange of diplomatic recognition into a longer time perspective. The "next step" following his wife's visit would be "formal negotiations for diplomatic relations" (*FBIS*, 20 September). This raised the question of just what had been happening during commercial, cultural, and other contacts in preceding months, including yet another visit of Marcos's personal emissary, Benjamin Romualdez, to Peking on 5-9 August (*Far Eastern Economic Review*, 23 August, p. 26). In the event, the visit of Imelda Marcos to Peking was quite successful; a photograph of Mrs. Marcos and her son, Ferdinand Marcos, Jr., with Chairman Mao on 27 September conveyed unusual warmth and cordiality (*Peking Review*, 4 October) and may well have marked the first time that Mao had posed for an official and widely disseminated picture with the wife of a head of state.

Mrs. Marcos was reported to have been invited to stay an extra five days in China so that she might observe festivities in connection with the celebrations of "National Day" on 1 October 1. At a banquet in her honor on 20 September, Chinese vice-premier Li Hsien-nien declared that between the Chinese and Philippine peoples there exited a "traditional friendship of long standing" and noted that the increasing friendly relations between Peking and Manila was further evidence that countries with "different social systems" can develop relations on the basis of mutual respect and respect for each other's territorial integrity (ibid., 27 September, p. 3). Reportedly relations and discussions between Imelda Marcos and Chiang Ching, Mao's wife, were particularly cordial, due to a reportedly shared identity of "Orientalness" between the two women (*NYT*, 22 October). The Chinese media also took good note of assessments in the Philippine press that Mrs. Marcos's visit to China had been a success (*FBIS*, 10 October).

Since 1971, when the first formal commercial exchanges began, Philippine exports to China have amounted to $42 million and Chinese imports into the Philippines to $26 million (*Far Eastern Economic Review*, 4 October, p. 48). On 23 September, Philippine industry secretary Vicente Paterno, who accompanied Mrs. Marcos to Peking, signed an agreement with Chinese trade minister Lin Chiang providing for shipments of one billion barrels of crude Chinese oil to the Philippines in the future, and by mid-October the first shipment of 125,000 barrels had already arrived; most of the remainder was to be shipped during 1975 (*FBIS*, 26 September 16 October). Philippine sugar exports to China are to be stepped up as part of the agreement (*NYT*, 25 September).

Although President Marcos announced on 8 October that the Philippines would establish diplomatic relations with China first, in contradiction to official earlier statements that relations would be established simultaneously with the U.S.S.R. (*Asia Research Bulletin* 31 October, p. 16), there remains resistance to the exchange of diplomatic recognition, among military commanders, aware that NPA spokesmen by their own admission have been getting arms from Chinese sources (*Far Eastern Economic Review*, 18 October, p. 24). There is also a fear that it will be difficult to hold up the NPA as a danger to the nation of Peking and Manila exchange diplomatic recognition. Official, particularly military, suspicion of the loyalties of some half million Chinese residents in the Philippines, in the event diplomatic relations are established, has also become more apparent.

In 1972, diplomatic relations were established with Yugoslavia and Romania, and in 1973 with Poland, Hungary, Bulgaria, Czechoslovakia, and the German Democratic Republic. In May 1972 the Philippine Congress provided funds for the opening of a Philippine Embassy in Moscow and by December 1972 the establishment of official Soviet-Filipino relations seemed but a matter of time when an "agreement of intent" was reached with a visiting Soviet trade mission which provided for reciprocal air services, exchanges of commercial missions and films, and expansion of tourism (*Asia Research Bulletin*, 31 October 1974, p. 16). The new government offering of amnesty on 3 November 1974 to all ideological "subversives" was prompted in large part by the surrender in October of KPK leader Macapagal and a score of other Moscow-oriented Philippine communists and was considered another gesture toward improving Soviet-Filipino relations. Recent Soviet radio commentaries do not gloss over Philippine involvement with "the American imperialists," but appear to emphasize more the machinations of "the Mao Tse-tung group" in the country and indeed in all of Southeast Asia (*FBIS*, 18 June). References in Russian media to "Maoist interference" in the Philippines, such as the recent alleged discovery of a "network for supplying anti-government rebels with Chinese-made weapons," occur periodically (*FBIS*, 6 September).

While in the Western press Marcos's martial-law regime has come in for often sharp criticism, the

Soviet press generally has carried much more flattering accounts and, while stressing the plight of the small producer, has found praise for Marcos's attempted agrarian reforms (*World Affairs Report*, Stanford, vol. 4, 1974, no. 1, p. 73, and no. 3, p. 265). The visit of a group of Philippine industrialists to the Soviet Union in September 1974 was described by a *Pravda* commentator as having not only "great economic but also political significance," and it was noted that in recent years "Philippine Soviet contacts have become increasingly frequent and regular" (*Pravda*, 22 September, *Current Digest of the Soviet Press*, 16 October). Allegedly changing anti-communist attitudes in the Philippines have also been noted in the Soviet media. Toward the end of March, Moscow's "Radio Peace and Progress" stated that the Filipino public was now demanding that the "Anti-Communist League of the Philippines," which it described as "one of the most reactionary organizations in the country" be outlawed. Quoting a Manila paper, the *Bulletin*, it described the League as CIA-financed. (*FBIS*, 27 March.)

Although relations between Manila on the one hand and Peking and Moscow on the other are improving, there has been no change in official Philippine attitudes toward other communist regimse (such as those in North Korea and North Vietnam) in Asia, or toward communist parties in the Asian continent. Philippine membership in SEATO is continuing and, despite muted criticism in some intellectual circles, there is no immediate prospect that the government will leave the organization.

In November, the head of the Southwest Mindanao military command revealed that a border patrol agreement had been reached with the Indonesian government to enhance security in southern waters so that the flow of weapons and other contraband to Mindanao could be checked (*NYT*, 13 November). Earlier, Indonesian president Suharto had attempted to mediate the Philippines-Malaysia dispute involving the status of Sabah and the Moslem insurrection in the Southern Philippines. There is widespread official Philippine belief that the prime minister of the Mayalsian state of Sabah has been encouraging the Philippine Moslem rebels, affording them training sites and weapons. Malaysian prime minister Tun Abdul Razak has claimed that there are "22,000 Philippine refuges" now residing in Sabah (*Sarawak Tribune*, Kuching, 18 April). At the Indonesian-Philippine discussions in Menado, North Sulawesi, Indonesia, in May, agreement was reached that "Sources of conflict in Southeast Asia should not be exploited by forces outside the region" (Agence France Presse dispatch, Menado, 31 May), a possible reference to support for the Moslem insurgents from Arab countries.

As for the anti-Marcos opposition in the Philippine community in the United States, Manila's official position today is that a so-called "government in exile" has been formed by a Filipino "rightist group" of expatriates. Notwithstanding the "rightist" complexion of this group, whose leaders, other than former senator Raul Manglapus, have not been identified, it has linked itself nevertheless with the NPA, and the "rebel government" is veering closer to the left "with the aim of forming a united front" (*FBIS*, 24 January).

Publications. The CPP-ML's main publication is *Ang Bayan* ("The Nation"), in English and Tagalog. Its contents are occasionally excerpted in *Peking Review* and in the publications of other Maoist-oriented communist parties throughout the world, such as *Indonesian Tribune* (Tirana), the mouthpiece of the Peking-based faction of the underground Indonesian communist party (see *Indonesia*). During 1974 the PKP's main organ, *Ang Komunista* ("The Communist"), appeared but rarely. Both parties occasionally issue mimeographed leaflets, usually over the names of their front organizations. The KM's principal organ, *Progressive Review*, has not been published for nearly four years. NPA and CPP-ML policy statements, or reports of NPA victories still appear, if infrequently, in the Chinese media, including *Peking Review* and the New China News Agency Reports.

University of Bridgeport

Justus M. van der Kroef

Singapore

The Communist Party of Malaya (CPM) is the major underground organization embracing communists in Singapore, who have no separate party and are compelled to operate mainly through a front, the Barisan Sosialis Malaya, usually called Mariasan Sosialis or the Barisan. Additionally Singapore communists have operated in the island republic through the "Malayan National Liberation Army" (MNLA), the fighting arm of the CPM mainly active in the Malay Peninsula (see *Malaysia*). In 1974 the MNLA, after a lull of several years, identified itself with a number of protest and incipient urban guerrilla activities in Singapore. During 1974 the Barisan engaged in little overt partisan activity, and a party spokesman with whom the author talked at the Singapore Barisan headquarters in early June alleged that intensive and "repressive" policy surveillance, as well as government refusal to issue permits for regular party publications, severely hampered all party activities. Government security laws and regulations inherited from the British colonial rule remain, be it in modified form, and arrest for political reasons, in effect, is legal under Singapore statutes. In the past fifteen years the application of security laws has all but neutralized even the underground communist leadership in Singapore.

However, the principal reason for the absence of a regular Singapore communist party organization is political-ideological. The CPM and the Singapore communists both regard constitutional developments in Malaya and Singapore since 1963 to have been arbitrary, unlawful, and merely a dimension of British and U.S. "imperialist" strategy in the region. In that year, Malaya, Singapore, and the Borneo territories of Sarawak and Sabah (North Borneo) merged into the Federation of Malaysia. In 1965, Singapore seceded from the federation, becoming an independent republic but remaining in the Commonwealth. Recognizing neither the merger nor the subsequent secession, Singapore communists, like their CPM counterparts, remain committed to a unification of the states on the Malay Peninsula (i.e., Malaya proper) with Singapore only, permitting Sabah and Sarawak, which unlike Singapore have remained in the original Malaysian Federation, to go their own way. The Barisan Sosialis has been consistently committed to a "democratic Malaya" (*YICA, 1974*, p. 530), comprising the Malay Peninsula and Singapore, and according to party spokesmen remains so today.

During 1974, in view of renewed speculation concerning an eventual return of Singapore to the Federation of Malaysia, some elements within the Barisan begin to suggest a program for the preservation of Singapore's independence, in an attempt also to solidify support in leftist but non-communist circles in opposition to the present government of Singapore premier Lee Kuan Yew.

Though both the Barisan and the CPM emphasize their interracial appeals and organizational structure, communism in Singapore, in keeping with the ethnic composition of the population of the island republic, is overwhelmingly Chinese in character. According to population data supplied the author by the Singapore Ministry of Social Affairs in June 1974, the total population was then estimated at about 2.13 million, of whom approximately 76 percent were Chinese, 15 percent Malays, and nearly 8 percent Indians, Pakistanis, or Bangladeshi. From its development in the early 1920s, and particularly during the 1950s and early 60s when communist-directed or -inspired labor unrest, street unrest, and strikes reached new highs, a number of Chinese schools, labor unions, and newspapers tended to articulate Chinese communist influence and, later, the influence of the CPM.

Organization and Tactics. The Barisan Sosialis Malaya, founded on 26 July 1961, has been the most important of the communist front groups in Singapore. Originally established by dissenting radicals within the ruling People's Action Party (PAP), the Barisan has remained a formally legal organization and has been permitted to participate in local and general elections. But in a political environment in which even relatively mild partisan rhetoric easily can become the basis for a prosecutor's charge of incitement to violence or defamation of character, the Barisan, like other more ephemeral front groups employed by Singapore communists, has not constituted any significant threat to the PAP-dominated government for nearly a decade. This is not to say, however, that the opposition as a whole to the Lee Kuan Yew government is nugatory. Rather it is that communists do not dominate that opposition.

Other, now almost wholly inactive or dissolved, groups like the Partai Rakyat (People's Party), founded in 1956, or the more moderate "People's Front" active in 1971-72, at one time accommodated varying degrees of Barisan and/or CPM influence. But the principal strength of both the Barisan and the Singapore communist underground today generally is derived from about a dozen smaller trade unions of clerical and service workers, shop assistants, and street hawkers, backed by a few scores of militants in the Chinese secondary schools, journalists, or other young professionals. In the 1972 Singapore parliamentary elections Barisan strength was particularly evident in the Industrial Workers Union (IWU), three of whose officials ran on the Barisan ticket.

While opposition to the ruling PAP and the Lee Kuan Yew government must be estimated at from one fifth to one fourth of the total electorate, Singapore's single-member parliamentary constituencies do not accurately reflect the significance of that opposition. Government surveillance and controls have tended to hollow out the Barisan over the years, and internal party leadership squabbles have made the party unattractive to the few score remaining Malay radicals, once the core of such organizations as the Partai Rakyat. At the same time, the Barisan's following among younger Chinese intellectuals and students, especially at the Nanyang University and other Chinese schools and professional interest groups, evident particularly in the 1950s and early 60s, has been greatly attenuated, although opposition as such to the PAP-dominated Lee Kuan Yew regime in these circles remains quite significant. As Singapore politics remains in the throes of finding a meaningful Leftist alternative to the Barisan, the latter continues to see its organization and strength erode, limiting support to hard-core militants, and is unable to reach out in order to develop an effective united front.

In early July 1974, a Barisan cadre claimed to the author that the party had about 6,000 members, but the Barisan's solid base probably comprises less than a tenth that number. Not all of even this base can be considered completely committed to, or under the discipline of, the CPM, although one authoritative estimate (U.S. Department of State, Bureau of Intelligence and Research, *World Strength of the Communist Party Organizations* 1973 edition, Washington, D.C., 1973, p. 95) refers to "Communist Party membership" (i.e., CPM membership) in Singapore as comprising possibly only 200.

Daily leadership of the Barisan is in the hands of a 14-member Central Executive Committee (CEC), led by Dr. Lee Siew Choh, a 56-year-old physician and the principal founder and the party's preeminent leader since 1961. The Barisan has been plagued by serious factional disputes over the years. In 1974 reports circulated widely that party chairman Lee Siew Choh and his principal lieutenants, vice-chairman Chen Kiong and party treasurer Tai Cheng Kang, were confronted by an organized ouster demand from younger IWU and other trade union leaders. Around younger CEC members Ng Ah Chue and Ng Yang Choe, both 31, reportedly a faction has crystallized demanding a change toward a more flexible, less overtly radical, CPM-oriented policy, designed to capture support from non-communist Left and Liberal opposition to the Lee Kuan Yew government.

In the September 1972 Singapore national parliamentary elections, a number of Barisan cadres urged a boycott of the polls, thereby in effect disavowing some of the party's own candidates. In the event, the Barisan won 4.5 percent of the votes cast, and none of the seats at stake, while the People's Action Party won 69.2 percent of the votes and all 65 seats at stake. The more moderate, centrist Workers' Party and the non-communist leftist People's Front garnered 12 percent and 3 percent of the votes respectively. Younger, flexibility-oriented tacticians of the Barisan appear to believe that efforts should be made to win a following for a more moderate united front from among the adherents of the two other major opposition groups. Dr. Lee Siew Choh is believed to be mildly sympathetic to this tactic, which, however, is contrary to the view of some of his senior fellow CEC officers. Barisan spokesmen, in conversation with the writer in early June 1974, insisted that due to the allegedly autocratic policies of the Lee Kuan Yew government, political polarization is steadily accelerating, with new radical currents stirring the restive student community in the University of Singapore, and that, in consequence, the Barisan's popular "support base" as distinct from its membership must now be considered as from seven to eight thousand.

A major dynamic in broadening this support base is the problem of Singapore's political prisoners. Before the 18 June arrests (see below), one authoritative source estimated the probable number of political prisoners in Singapore as fewer than 40 (*Amnesty International Report, 1973-1974*, London, p. 56). Other, more controversial estimates, which include some allegedly political detainees formally held on other criminal charges, go as high as 100. On 13 December 1973 a former assistant secretary-general of the Barisan, Dr. Poh Soo Kai, was released from a ten-year prison confinement, along with six other detainees, at least two of whom, Lan Ah Lek and Tan Kim Siar, were also formal Barisan members. The others were trade union activists sympathetic to the Barisan cause. Upon his release Dr. Poh declared that he rejected the government's statement accompanying his official release to the effect that the released prisoners were not to associate with "pro-Communist elements" on pain of possible rearrest as a "threat to the security of Singapore" (Hong Kong, Agence France Presse dispatch, 14 December; *FBIS*, 14 December). In a joint statement describing their confinement and issued on 13 December, Dr. Poh and his former fellow detainees, according to an undated Barisan leaflet, accused the government of subjecting them to "threats of perpetual and indefinite imprisonment," cuts in food rations, censorship, and restrictions of movements and activities within the prison, and even of periodic solitary confinement in "secret holding centers." A government statement, issued at the time of the release of the seven detainees, accused them of having been "actively involved in Communist-directed activities" in political, labor, and student organizations, but also said that they could now be released because "the capacity of these seven men to cause damage to the security and stability of Singapore" had been considerably reduced owing to the considerable "progress" made by the republic (*Asia Research Bulletin*, 31 January 1974, p. 2409). By 25 January 1974, all seven political detainees had challenged the government to rearrest them, denying that they had signed any agreement that would restrict their political activities. One of the detainees also declared on this occasion that other remaining political prisoners were then on a hunger strike to protest "persecution in prison"; he estimated the total number of detainees to be about 300 (Hong Kong, Agence France Presse dispatch, 25 January; *FBIS*, 6 February).

Poh's statements, and the alleged plight of political prisoners in the island republic, had an initially radicalizing effect on segments of the University of Singapore student community. In July an "anti-repression week" was organized at the university, during which Dr. Poh addressed a packed audience. Poh charged that the government's grounds for his detention had not only been "flimsy" but also "lent themselves to embarrassing refutation" (*Far Eastern Economic Review*, 2 August, p.

20). Poh's address had all the more impact because it came in the midst of new, quietly conducted, arrests of alleged political dissidents by the Lee Kuan Yew government. Singapore foreign minister S. Rajaratnam, in an indirect comment on the student "anti-repression" agitation, declared that a minority of students seemed to be wasting their talents and energies in contesting "imaginary wrongs and wrestling with fabricated oppression" (ibid., p. 21).

It would appear, however, that not only has the government become concerned over the issue of the political prisoners, but that, because of it, the Barisan is acquiring a measure of new sympathy in the younger, restive Singapore electorate. However, compared with the 1950s, student political activism remains in a low key. A recent editorial in a University of Singapore student publication still complained of a "lack of student participation in national affairs" and of the fact that steps still have not been taken toward the formation of a National Youth Council (editorial, "Student Inaction," *Commentary*, Singapore, new series, no. 8, March/April, 1974, p. 8).

As a dimension of its tactic to win a broader united-front-type following, Barisan statements during 1974 concentrated on the effects of steady price rises on the poorer social strata, blaming the Lee Kuan Yew government for having financed its much touted development policies through ruinous inflation, and through the imposition of taxes that fall heaviest on the average consumer (e.g., new rises in bus fares, in electricity and gas rates, and higher gasoline taxes). The proposed solution advanced by the Barisan is "to struggle for genuine independence in a unified Malaya." Additionally, the following measures were proposed in a mimeographed leaflet headed "Raise Wages and Reduce Taxes," issued by the Barisan on 2 March: (1) a "substantial" increase in the wages of workers, and a repudiation of the policies of the National Wages Council, which, it is alleged, "is completely dominated by the bosses"; (2) the abolition of the Employment Act and the Industrial Relations Amended Act, so that workers can be allowed "to take legitimate industrial action to improve their working conditions"; (3) a demand that wage agreements include "cost-of-living escalation clauses"; (4) abolition of the "numerous" indirect taxes and so-called protective duties, especially reduction of taxes on gasoline and cigarettes, and of bus fares and rates for water and electricity; (5) abolition of charges of treatment in government out-patient clinics and the institution of free medical care for the poor in hospitals; (6) abolition of direct taxes on lower and middle incomes, an increase in taxes on "all large incomes," and the imposition of appropriate capital gains taxes; (7) a check on the price increases initiated by "big monopolies"; and (8) a cut in government expenditures on "non-essentials," particularly in the armed forces. The leaflet concludes with the following:

> Big monopolies squeeze huge profits from the people. As they are confronted with economic and monetary crises, one after another, the big monopolies now try to use inflation as a weapon to further exploit the people and to increase profits. The people must therefore unite and struggle against these big monopolies and their local agents in the LKY [Lee Kuan Yew] government—they are those who have caused the big price hikes and pushed inflation and caused sufferings and hardships to the people!

The tenor of this statement had been heard in previous Barisan publications. Charges that the PAP government of Lee Kuan Yew is imposing heavy taxation on those least able to afford it, and allegations that it is committed to provide "everything" for "the big capitalists," had been made before ("Five Years of Taxation and Suppression," *Plebeian*, Singapore, 29 October 1972, pp. 1-2), but earlier the bite of inflation had not been as sharp. During 1974, however, a population which, thanks to the policies of the PAP-dominted regimes of the past decade had come to rely on and take for granted more and more the social services development encouraged by these policies, felt far more threatened and deprived than in years past. Hence the Barisan's "proletarian appeal," as one party theorist once put it to this writer, has now found a more sympathetic sounding-board. Already the year 1973, in the judgment of one authoritative account, had probably gone down as the first in Singapore's history "in which inflation overtook all economic growth," and while Gross Domestic

Product during the year might well even have exceeded even the government's expectation of 15 percent, there was also "widespread belief that the cost of living for the average Singaporean had increased by 35 to 40 percent during the year (*Asia 1974 Yearbook*, Hong Kong: *Far Eastern Economic Review*, 1974, p. 274). These trends were aggravated during 1974.

There was less evidence than in the previous year of the influence of younger, Maoist-oriented Barisan activists (*YICA, 1974*, pp. 531-32), although controversy over Dr. Lee Siew Choh's leadership, and criticism that no full party congress had been held in four years, persisted. Six prominent Barisan cadres who because of disagreement with chairman Lee's policies had been ousted from the party in the aftermath of the 1972 national elections, were all reinstated by early 1974, according to a party spokesman. An apparently maturing consensus within the Barisan leadership that the present political polarization process in Singapore and the slowly rising disquiet with the Lee Kuan Yew leadership in the long run promise the best practical prospects for the building of a national united front is likely somewhat to further internal dissension.

Little is known of the MNLA organization inside Singapore. Singapore, along with the Malay states of Negri Sembilan, Malacca, and Johore, falls within the "South line" area of CPM operations (*Asia Research Bulletin*, 30 September 1974, p. 3, Political Supplement). There had been no overt MNLA activity in the republic for several years until 1974 (see below), and the extent to which the upsurge of such activity suggests a new tactic of Singapore communists to operate independently from the Barisan front complex, or suggests dissatisfaction with the Lew Siew Choh leadership, can at this point only be speculated upon. Some knowledgeable government sources assume that renewed MNLA activity in Singapore just before, and in the weeks after, the Sino-Malaysian diplomatic agreement of 31 May 1974 may have been a gesture of encouragement on the part of CPM leaders to the Singapore radical Left generally. The gesture presumably was designed to counter expectations that after such a diplomatic agreement no more political, moral, or other assistance would be forthcoming from Peking and further opposition to the Lee Kuan Yew government would become futile.

Domestic Developments. Even as the Lee Kuan Yew government seemed to be continuing a policy of offering conditional release to political prisoners, there were new crackdowns on opponents of the government, including Barisan members, during 1974, as meanwhile caches of alleged communist propaganda materials and arms were also said to have been discovered by government security forces. On 29 April and 4 June, flags and signs said to be containing communist slogans were reportedly found in more than a score of hiding-places throughout the island, and some of the banners reportedly had simulated booby traps attached to them, suggesting that they had been meant to be discovered by opponents. A banner discovered on 19 June at an overhead bridge, near a popular modern shopping complex, had in fact a live booby trap attached to it. The following day a 40-foot-long banner was found strung across an overhead pedestrian crossing in a busy downtown shopping section. On it, in Chinese, was written: "Help the Liberation Army. Join the Liberation Army and successfully expand the people's war." When police came to take the banner down the booby trap reportedly exploded, but there were no injuries. A government announcement on the incident stated that the booby-trapped banner and the three flags discovered at the same time (one red and bearing the hammer and sickle, the other two said to be flags of the MNLA) were designed to call attention to the fact that 20 June marked the twenty-sixth birthday of the outbreak of the "liberation struggle" waged by the MNLA against the British in Malaya (an episode usually referred to as "the Emergency"). The official statement went on to emphasize that the communist underground, having apparently reorganized itself, was now ready to create disturbances in order to bring about uncertainty and economic decline. According to the government, the communists' aim was to bring about "increasing unemployment, declining living standards, and increasing misery to make people amenable to revolutionary violence." (*Asia Research Bulletin*, 31 July, p. 2858; *Far Eastern Economic Review*, 1 July, p. 14.)

On 12 July a Singapore daily had reported that the Singapore government had monitored a clandestine broadcast by the CPM in which the party claimed responsibility for the planting of the booby-trapped banners (*New Nation*, Singapore, 12 July; *FBIS*, 12 July). According to this report, the planting of homemade bombs and booby-trapped posters was claimed by the CPM to be the work of both the "revolutionary masses" and of the Malayan National Liberation Front (MNLF) in commemoration of the birthday of the armed struggle launched by the CPM shortly after the close of World War II. The alleged claim was made at a time when new tensions had risen between the Lee Kuan Yew government and Singapore Leftists as a result of a new wave of arrests. On 18 June, after what the government asserted was a prolonged period of surveillance, 30 persons, described either as members of the MNLF or the CPM, or both, were apprehended in island-wide raids. Reportedly, quantities of small arms, ammunition, and explosives were also seized in these raids. Among the arrested were prominent figures associated with the Barisan Sosialis, among them Chan San Choy and Nge Tek Nam, both journalists connected with the Singapore Chinese-language daily *Sin Chew Jit Poh*, and T. T. Rajah, a former attorney for the Barisan, who has retained active connections with the organization. There was no formal government statement as to why, specifically, the thirty were apprehended, though the government did allege connection with the communists' new policy of armed struggle. The arrests were the most extensive since the government's "Operation Cold Storage" in February 1963, which had netted the detention of 113 persons, most of them within the Barisan orbit. It was also noted that the Singapore government was acting with a new openness in combating its allegedly communist opponents; previous arrests had been made with little publicity, but on 18 June the arrests occurred "in broad daylight, and in many instances those arrested were plucked from their air-conditioned offices" (*Far Eastern Economic Review*, 1 July, p. 14; *Asia Research Bulletin* 31 July, p. 2858).

Reactions to the arrests, adverse to the government in nature, came from various directions. On 26 June the Barisan Sosialis condemned the detentions as arbitrary and as intended to suppress "the struggle of the people" against spiraling inflation and the cost of living (*FBIS*, 26 June). On 27 June the student union organizations of the University of Singapore and the Singapore Polytechnic Institute criticized the government in a joint statement which asserted the arrests to be "a part of the government strategy to eliminate political opposition and a blatant violation of basic democratic principles." The statement demanded that the arrested be tried in open court and that there be a full disclosure of their names. The statement also asked the government to explain "why there is this sudden crisis" when only a few months ago the government itself had indicated that "stability and progress in Singapore" had now made communism "irrelevant" and "no threat to the nation." (*Bangkok Post*, 27 June; *Asia Research Bulletin*, 31 July, p. 2859).

In the weeks following this statement tensions between the students and the government appeared to be mounting, particularly after the University of Singapore vice-chancellor, and concurrently the science and technology minister, Dr. Toh Chin Chye, asserted that the leadership of the Student Union at the university was not representative of the students and that a recent $100 tuition increase was being used to stir up trouble. In a statement on 8 July the Student Union repudiated these charges, emphasizing that the majority of the executive officers of the organization were native Singaporeans. (*Asia Research Bulletin*, 31 July, p. 2850.) The incident was perhaps reflective of what the government's critics called the insensitive paternalism of a regime whose members have made it evident that "popularity is their last concern, effectiveness their first" (Ilsa Sharp, "Pragmatism versus Hypocrisy," *Far Eastern Economic Review*, 9 August, p. 20).

Both the recent arrests of dissidents and the growing realization of the adverse consequences of the absence of a meaningful parliamentary opposition have been a boon to Barisan theorists who are counting on the eventual success of a tactic founded on the steady radicalization and polarization of political attitudes in the island republic.

Meanwhile, the CPM was increasingly reaching out to the student dissidents. On 1 August in a broadcast in Mandarin to Singapore on the subject of the republic's educational policies, the clandestine "Voice of the Malayan Revolution" relayed the substance of a report presented to a forum on higher education in Asia by a delegation of Singapore students in Hong Kong on 21-25 March. The report claimed that the Lee Kuan Yew government was deliberately denigrating Chinese-language education, and asserted that "People who have received a Chinese-language education have been given unequal treatment, both politically and economically, as compared with those who received an English-language education." The report, according to the broadcast, also claimed that parents were being discouraged from sending their children to Chinese-language schools and that the government had "reedited" Chinese-language textbooks and had constructed far fewer Chinese- than English-language schools during the past decade. The English-language educated were viewed by the government as "obedient people" occasionally permitted to be heard, while the Chinese-language educated were considered to be a "potential menace." The students' report, according to the broadcast, also said that students of the social sciences in Singapore were under particular official pressure and were in fact warned by the government not to become involved in "social activities" that might arouse the government's displeasure. (*FBIS*, 1 August.)

The broadcast of this report by Singapore student dissidents was perhaps particularly noteworthy for its reaffirmation of a theme current among Singapore's radical leftists in the past, that is, the difficulties said to be faced by the Chinese-educated and the Chinese schools because of allegedly discriminatory government policies that favor English-medium institutions. It seems likely that as, under the aegis of the Barisan and the CPM underground, student discontent with the PAP-dominated government of premier Lee Kuan Yew is nourished further, the allegedly "anti-Chinese" cast of government policies will be accentuated also.

On 31 January 1974 four men, three reportedly Japanese and one an Arab, attempted to blow up a Shell refinery about one mile and a half off Singapore (one storage tank was set on fire, and small damage done to two others) and subsequently seized five Singapore citizens aboard a ferry, threatening to kill themselves and their hostages unless they were given safe conduct to an Arab country and were accompanied by the Japanese ambassador in Singapore. The four men claimed to be members of a Japanese guerrilla organization calling itself "the Red Army" and of the Marxist-oriented Popular Front for the Liberation of Palestine. Members of "the Red Army" were responsible for the massacre at Lod Airport in Israel in 1972, in which 26 victims perished. The incident strengthened the Singapore government's subsequent claim concerning the need for vigilance against communist infiltration in the state. At the same time the incident seemed to give added impetus to the strengthening of Singapore's coastal defense system, particularly the republic's maritime command base at Pulau Brani in Singapore harbor (*NYT*, 1 February; *Washington Post* 1 February; *Far Eastern Economic Review*, 11 March, pp. 17-18).

Relations with Communist Countries. The long-expected formal mutual diplomatic recognition between Malaysia and the Chinese People's Republic on May 31 1974 reportedly had as disturbing an effect on the communist movement in Singapore as in Malaysia. Barisan chairman Dr. Lee Siew Choh, commenting on the mutual diplomatic recognition, was quoted in the Singapore press as believing that "one section" of the Barisan was attempting to "rationalise" what had happened by saying that it "would increase contacts between the peoples of the two countries as well as trade and cultural exchanges." The "other section" of his party, according to Dr. Lee, viewed the diplomatic recognition as "a great setback" in the "struggle against the reactionaries." Dr. Lee himself appeared to hold to the latter opinion, declaring: "As far as I can see 'normalisation' would not help the people's 'struggle' because it would strengthen the Malaysian government's position." Dr. Poh Soo Kai, as previously noted a former assistant secretary-general of the Barisan, released from political detention on 13 December 1973, was said to have commented that normalization of Sino-Malaysian diplomatic relations would and could have no effect on the "liberation" struggle of communists, because that struggle was indigenous in nature and had nothing to do with Peking or the Chinese communists. (*New Nation*, Singapore, 2 July; *Asia Research Bulletin*, 31 July, p. 2839.)

The Sino-Malaysian diplomatic rapprochement has made no perceptible difference in the Singapore government's calculated slowness in moving toward improved formal relations. Singapore government spokesmen on repeated occasions have stressed that while normalization of China's relations with Southeast Asian countries was inevitable, they saw no reason for Singapore to accelerate the process. In an official comment on the May 1974 Sino-Malaysian diplomatic agreement, the Singapore government strove for non-committee blandness, declaring that "subsequent developments" following the agreement would "influence" the response of other countries in the region (*Far Eastern Economic Review*, October, p. 48). In August, Singapore's foreign minister, S. Rajaratnam, answered with an unqualified "yes" a press interview question as to whether his government remained committed to "letting the other Southeast Asian countries go ahead first" in establishing relations with China. As for the Bank of China branch in Singapore, Rajaratnam indicated that the policy of having a Singaporean in charge of the branch, rather than a citizen of People's China, would also remain unchanged, although if and as diplomatic relations between the two countries developed "we may have to see what is advantageous to Singapore" (ibid., 9 August, p. 6). Relations between Singapore and a number of East European states remained cool but correct during 1974 with modest but steady increases in trade levels.

It has been a pivoted assumption in the conduct of Singapore's external relations that whatever the advantages a regional "neutralization" are eventually likely to bring, Southeast Asia will remain a cockpit of big power rivalries. In respect specifically of the island republic's relations with the communist states, Singapore's position was perhaps most clearly formulated in a response made by Rajaratnam to a question in the previously cited press interview. Asked then about the presence of the big powers in the Indian Ocean area, Singapore's foreign minister replied: "Either all should be present or none should be present here. The latter is a very impractical proposition. Therefore, we say, let all the great powers be here." (Ibid., p. 7.) It is apparent, however, from Singapore's readiness to grant refueling and repair facilities in its harbor to Soviet vessels now on patrol in the Indian Ocean, that the Lee Kuan Yew government believes that a pattern of watchful rivalry between the major powers will likely guarantee the republic's and the region's safety the longest. But such a mutual balancing strategy is constantly in danger of being upset by security imbalances resulting from the erosion or the departure of one of the major participants from the region. For example, the future of the Five Power Commonwealth Defence Agreement, involving Malaysia, Singapore, the United Kingdom, Australia, and New Zealand, and concurrently the future military commitments of the last three named powers to Singapore's and Malaysia's defense, has been uncertain for some five years. By the close of July 1974, however, the British Labour Government of prime minister Harold Wilson was said to be seriously considering keeping a British naval and air presence in Singapore in view of the Soviet naval buildup in the Indian Ocean area. On 12 July, Singapore defense minister Dr. Goh Keng Swee said that Singapore's defense forces were "adequate" and that further reduction of allied military forces, including probable reductions in the British ground, naval, and air force personnel, would not harm Singapore's economy or affect the climate of confidence." (*Asia Research Bulletin*, 31 July, p. 2891, and 31 August, p. 2954.)

Although there is little published evidence, knowledgeable sources in Singapore believe that Barisan cadres today continue, as in the past, to go to China via Hong Kong contacts. Barisan or underground communist Singapore contacts with Moscow and with Soviet-oriented centers or organizations are believed to be so minimal as to be virtually non-existent. Because Singapore communists are formally members of the CPM, they do not function independently of the latter in the issuance of policy statements, or in official messages or at international gatherings. The mutual diplomatic recognition of Malaysia and People's China, and the awareness in the Singapore government that it too will have to move eventually toward such recognition, has raised as yet unanswered questions about their future tactics for Singapore's communists and their Barisan front complex, but there has been no indication that their essentially pro-Peking orientation is likely to change in the near future.

Publications. Except for mimeographed leaflets infrequently issued by the Barisan or the MNLF, Singapore communists had no publications in 1974. The Barisan's biweekly *Plebeian* has not been published since 1972, and neither has the Barisan's Chinese-language *Chern Sian Pau* because, as Barisan spokesmen claimed to the author in June 1974, no permit to publish could be obtained from the government. The CPM's major means of communication to Singapore is its clandestine radio transmitter "Voice of the Malayan Revolution," believed to be located in Yunnan Province, southern China; public awareness in Singapore of the "Voice's" messages appears to be minimal. The CPM's principal international publication, *Malayan Monitor & General News*, issued from London, has little or no circulation in Singapore. It purports to speak also for Singapore communists. References to Singapore in this publication tend to be very brief and relatively scarce, however; for example, in a recent issue (April 1974) Singapore is merely mentioned, along with Malaysia, as an area where anti-inflation "austerity measures" have become necessary. The Chinese government disclaims official involvement in the "Voice's" broadcasts, declaring that the latter are the work of "Malayan friends."

University of Bridgeport   Justus M. van der Kroef

Sri Lanka (Ceylon)

Sri Lanka's oldest Marxist party, the Lanka Sama Samaja Party (Ceylong Equal Society Party; LSSP), was formed in 1935. From the original LSSP, a number of parties and groups have emerged. The present Trotskyist LSSP, still led by N. M. Perera, Colvin R. de Silva, and Leslie Goonewardena, is the country's major Marxist party.

The Ceylon Communist Party was formed in 1943 by an LSSP founder, S. A. Wickremasinghe. This party split in 1963 into pro-Soviet and pro-Chinese factions led by Wickremasinghe and N. Sanmugathasan, respectively. Membership in the pro-Soviet Sri Lanka Communist Party (SLCP) is estimated at 2,000. That in the now divided pro-Chinese group is probably less than 1,000. According to the 1971 census, Sri Lanka's population is 12,800,000.

In 1968 the LSSP and the SLCP subordinated their mutual antagonism and joined in the "United Front" (UF) with the social-democratic Sri Lanka Freedom Party (SLFP). Following the May 1970 general elections, the three parties formed a coalition government headed by the SLFP leader, Mrs. Sirimavo Bandaranaike. In the elections the LSSP won 19 of the 151 seats contested and 8.7 percent of the popular vote. The SLCP won 6 seats and 3.4 percent of the vote.

Leadership and Organization. *The LSSP.* In its party structure the LSSP followes the Leninist model, as do the Communist parties. The general secretary is Bernard Soysa. The following LSSP leaders hold cabinet positions in the UF government: N. M. Perera, finance minister; Colvin de Silva, minister of plantation industries and constitutional affairs; and Leslie Goonewardena, minister of communications.

The labor movement has long been identified politically with the Marxists, and the LSSP is a major influence in trade unionism. The party controls the Ceylon Federation of Labor and also receives support from the Government Workers' Trade Union Federation and the Government Clerical Service Union. (See *YICA, 1974*, p. 543.)

The LSSP seeks extensive political and economic reforms, some of which have been achieved in government actions such as land reform, an income ceiling, greater press regulation, and the 1972 constitution. The younger, more militant party members consider the UF government's progress toward socialism too slow, however, and question the party's cooperation with the SLFP. The resulting strains between these dissidents and the established leadership persist.

The Pro-Soviet SLCP. Internal divisions within the SLCP over the party's attitude toward the coalition had by 1973 split the party. The "hard-line" faction led by S. A. Wickremasinghe has long criticized the government's failure to take over all foreign banks, industries, and plantations, and has also opposed Pieter Keuneman's participation in the Cabinet. Keuneman, head of the "soft-line" faction, remains minister of housing, and the party's internal crisis has now been resolved (see below). Its reunification also applies to factionalism which had emerged in the party's Youth League and Women's Organization, and in the Ceylon Federation of Trade Unions.

Wickremasinghe is general secretary, and Pieter Keuneman the party President. The 14-man Politburo includes both men (*Times of Ceylon*, Colombo, 3 July).

The Pro-Chinese Communist Parties. Factionalism within N. Sanmugathasan's pro-Chinese SLCP has led dissidents to form a separate party. In July 1972, Central Committee member Watson Fernando attempted unsuccessfully to have Sanmugathasan expelled during the latter's visit to China, and later broke away to establish the Communist Party of Sri Lanka (Marxist-Leninist). Sanmuga-thasan's faction is now called the Ceylon Communist Party (CCP) and has retained support of the Ceylong Trade Union Federation.

Sanmugathasan has consistently advocated violent overthrow of the government, but Fernando is apparently willing to support the UF's "progressive" measures.

The Revolutionary JVP. In April 1971 the traditional Marxist parties found themselves challenged by a young radical movement—the Janatha Vimukthi Peramuna (JVP), or People's Liberation Front. Rohana Wijeweera and other JVP leaders had been members of the orthodox communist parties. Although their armed attempt in 1971 to overthrow the government failed, sporadic violence has continued. On 20 December 1973, Wijeweera was sentenced to life imprisonment. Most of the 18,000 suspects originally detained had been released earlier.

Current Domestic Activities. The year 1974 was marked by reunification of the pro-Soviet SLCP and by increased strains within the UF. An internal struggle has preoccupied the SLCP since early 1972. Wickremasinghe's faction gained control of the party's organization at its Eighth Congress, in August 1972, and he replaced Keuneman as general secretary. The formal split occurred in September 1973 when Keuneman established a rival party organization.

Reunification was finally achieved in July, reportedly with the help of Soviet mediation. On 3 July the SLCP issued a communiqué announcing the reunification and affirming its commitment to the UF "while seeking to win mass support for its programme" (*WMR*, September).

Increasing strains in the coalition, exacerbated by the Ceylonese economic crisis and the Marxists' internal tensions between moderates and radicals, were apparent, particularly between the LSSP and Mrs. Bandaranaike's SLFP. In September Prime Minister Bandaranaike stated that the government would continue the social-democratic policies of her late husband, despite leftist pressures for more drastic policies. The LSSP's N. M. Perera had claimed in December 1973 that the government had failed to "respond fully to the aspirations of the masses." He said that more steps were necessary to "smash the capitalist system." (*Asian Analysis*, November 1974.)

An LSSP youth rally on 11-12 August reportedly included "ultra-red" slogans and a call for Mrs. Bandaranaike to give way to Perera. On 16 November the party's Ceylon Federation of Labor defied a government ban on demonstrations, resulting in a clash with police. Finally, the University of Sri Lanka's Colombo and Vidyalankara campuses were closed 12 December following student agitation for guaranteed employment in which the pro-LSSP Ceylon Students Federation was involved.

International Views and Attitudes. The Marxist parties operate within the context of Sri Lanka's non-alignment and Mrs. Bandaranaike's maintenance of relatively balanced relations with China, the Soviet Union, and the United States. Both China and the U.S.S.R. were among the nations which came to her aid after the 1971 insurrection.

Although the LSSP rejects Soviet domination (for example, it condemned the Soviet-led invasion of Czechoslovakia), it has supported the "socialist" U.S.S.R. against "imperialism" and "capitalism."

Both the pro-Soviet SLCP and the pro-Chinese CCP have recently commented on the Soviet Asian collective security proposal. The SLCP supports the proposal, and Politburo member D. W. Subasinghe said in May that the "significance of Asian security is not sufficiently understood" in Sri Lanka, but that the party will "clarify" the matter. He also supported détente. (*World Marxist Review*, May.) In contrast, the Tamil-language daily, *Tolilali*, believed to be pro-Sanmugathasan, said that the Soviet plan aimed to "establish hegemony in Asia" (*Peking Review*, 15 March).

Publications. SLCP publications include *Aththa* and *Forward*. The current orientation of pro-Chinese Communist Party publications, such as *Kamkaruwa, Tolilali*, and *Red Flag*, is not clear. LSSP newspapers include *Samasamajaya*.

Washington, D.C.   Barbara Reid

Thailand

The Communist Party of Thailand (CPT) was organized in 1942 largely as an "anti-Japanese" party. It grew out of several divergent communist groups that had negligible impact on the citizenry or the functioning of the government. Partly because the Soviet Union insisted that the CPT be allowed to function as a legitimate party as a quid pro quo for Thailand's becoming a member of the United Nations, and partly because of the liberal ideas of the civilian Prime Minister Pridi Panomyong, the CPT in 1946-47 openly proclaimed a comprehensive program that was decidedly mild in tone. Even then, the CPT members, mostly Sino-Thai, were ineffective and wielded little influence.

Since the ouster of Pridi Panomyong, Thailand has been ruled by a succession of military generals all of whom supported anti-communist legislation that forced the CPT underground. The party increasingly turned to the People's Republic of China and the Democratic Republic of Vietnam for ideological, training, and logistical support. In the early 1960s the CPT intensified its activities in the impoverished and ethnically Lao Northeast with terrorist and propaganda campaigns. In 1965 the various communist groups began to merge into the Thailand Patriotic Front, an organization calling for the overthrow of the regime in power, an end to U.S. "imperialism," and a drastic restructuring of the society to give power to the peasants. Communist insurgency became both politically and militarily more sophisticated and geographically more diversified as insurgents began operating in hill tribe areas and the southern provinces, yet by the standards of other Southeast Asian nations, the level of insurgency remained comparatively low.

In response to what the Thai government perceived as a growing threat to the internal stability of the nation and in response to the urging of U.S. authorities, Marshall Thanom Kittikachorn established the Communist Suppression Operation Command (CSOC) in 1965. CSOC's purpose was to coordinate the communist suppression operations of the army, police, and civilian sectors. Nevertheless, the number of CPT members and followers appeared to increase each year despite sporadic strong Thai government counter-insurgency operations, so that by October 1974 the number of armed insurgents involved in the CPT armed struggle was estimated at between 7,800 and 8,800. This figure included the party soldiers, local soldiers, and armed village militia of the Thai People's Liberation Armed Forces (TPLAF), established by the CPT on 1 December 1968. The figure represents about a 10 percent increase over a comparable date in 1973 but remains still only a miniscule 0.02 percent of the total 36,000,000 Thai population (estimated 1972).

Estimates of the number of armed insurgents and CPT members are not reliable. The above figures differ slightly from those cited in the *YICA, 1973* article on Thailand, which states that the number of communist terrorists had declined from between 6,000 and 7,000 (in 1972) to about 3,700 hard-core insurgents. In May 1973 General Saiyud Kerdphol, the director of CSOC, estimated the total guerrilla force at about 6,000. One of the reasons for the disparity between U.S. and Thai government estimates of the number of armed insurgents is the criterion used in determining what constitutes an "armed insurgent." In some areas, the Thai government analysts do not include village militia in their strength estimates even if armed and serving as members of the jungle force of the TPLAF. Additionally, U.S. estimates include the CPT insurgents located in Laos adjacent to the Thai-Lao border, while some Thai government agencies do not consider them a part of the armed insurgent strength even though they frequently cross into Thailand for operations.

On 14 October 1973 the military government led by Marshall Thanom was overthrown and replaced by a civilian regime with Sanya Thamasak as prime minister. The major underlying causes of the revolt included the political and economic mismanagement of the military regime itself, the perception that the military was increasingly ruling in their own self interest, factionalism within the military, and the rise of an organized and aroused student population supported by the citizenry and the king. Sanya's government was immediately besieged by problems, including labor strikes, a rise in crime, rampant inflation, and a discouraged student-intellectual coalition that saw the prospects for democracy diminishing as the government often ineffectively tried to cope with unprecedented strains.

Government and counter-insurgency leaders in Bangkok announced that the CPT was taking advantage of the instability of the transitional period following the overthrow of the military. Prime Minister Sanya indicated that the communist threat had increased dramatically since the October revolt. Lieutenant General Vitoon Yasawat, assistant director of the Police Department, reported that the CPT was more aggressive because of the new democratic freedoms. He commented that since the October revolt the CPT seemed to have widened its range of operations, concentrating chiefly on political activities (*Bangkok World*, 23 March).

Military attacks were also reported to have increased following the October revolt. The Internal Security Operation Command (ISOC, formerly CSOC) announced that during the four months following the revolt there were 64 incidents of either attacks or ambushes in the North, compared with 30 incidents in the preceding four months. In the Northeast, 117 clashes were reported during a four-month period since October, compared with 64 during the previous four months. ISOC reported an increase in the number of communist terrorist incidents in the South as well. In an overall assessment, General Saiyud reported a 50 percent increase in terrorist activity following the change to a civilian government. However, the third quarter of the year (which includes most of the rainy season months) has traditionally reflected lower levels of CPT armed activity than other quarters. A comparison of figures for the period from July to October with November to February does not accurately reflect the increase in CPT armed activity as a result of the October revolt, although the CPT certainly took advantage of Thai government indecisiveness whenever possible in the months following the revolution.

A high-ranking official of ISOC noted that pro-communist elements were infiltrating the ranks of students, the press, labor, and other urban groups (*Siam Rath*, Bangkok, 30 March). However, no evidence has been provided to prove the allegations of CPT complicity in the large number of urban strikes, demonstrations, violent crimes, and riots that have occurred in Bangkok following the October revolt. Many politicians denounced such allegations as a return to the days when the specter of the "third hand" of communism was blamed for every ill besetting the society. As the year ended there was not enough reliable information or time perspective to assess adequately the differing interpretations concerning communist involvement in urban political affairs.

Communist Party of Thailand. The overall policies of the CPT are made at infrequent meetings of the Central Committee, which still consists predominantly of the 55 Sino-Thai and other CPT members who gathered at the Marx-Lenin Institute in Peking in the early 1950s and after several years of study returned to Thailand to form the backbone of the CPT. There has been a slow but deliberate effort to increase ethnic Thai participation in the top leadership of the CPT, and the overall ethnic distribution is increasingly Thai. The Secretariat supervises the daily routine work of the party and oversees the military, propaganda, training, organization, finance, and front organization sections.

The party is organized into geographic branches. The Northeast branch is the most elaborately organized, most active, and most competent in both political and military programs. The Northern branch is limited to certain minority hill tribe groups and is oriented towaard military operations, although low-level efforts to expand into the lowlands of North Thailand have been attempted, albeit without success thus far. In the South, the CPT is not well organized although in 1974 there were reports of CPT contact with the Muslim Separatist Movement, whose goal is separate autonomous states for the three southernmost Thai provinces. Unsubstantiated reports by high-ranking ISOC officers indicated that local Thai communist insurgents in the South were also collaborating with members of the factionalized Malayan National Liberation Army (communist terrorist organization) led by Chin Peng. The insurgents were said to have helped train Muslim rebels in springing ambushes and laying land mines against Thai government forces.

The Central branch is the least active, with almost no instances of armed insurgency during 1974. Fewer than 200 persons are thought to be working for the CPT in the Central Region. Bangkok-Thonburi is a separate branch, but thus far there is no reliable information on CPT activities in that area.

The main political activity of the CPT is propaganda. The four basic themes stressed by the CPT during 1974 were that the Thai government is a lackey of American imperialism, that the U.S. Central Intelligence Agency (CIA) and the U.S. Air Force bases must be routed from the country, that the government is fascist and corrupt, and that the government rules in its own interest without regard for the peoples' interests. The major propaganda organ is the "Voice of the People of Thailand" (VPOT) radio, which broadcasts 46 hours per week. Reception is clearest in the North, Northeast, and Central regions, and weakest in the South.

The CPT in 1974 continued its pro-China position, its Maoist doctrine of peoples' war, and its denunciations of Soviet "revisionism" and of collusion between the two principal "imperialist powers," the United States and the Soviet Union. During the year, the Thai government sanctioned various cultural and trade missions to the People's Republic of China. The most notable trip was made in February by the defense minister, who negotiated a contract for China to sell 75,000 tons of diesel oil to Thailand. He quoted PRC premier Chou En-lai as saying that Chinese support for local insurgents was "now a thing of the past." In October the deputy foreign minister confirmed that there was no Chinese involvement in the insurgency in Thailand. He stated that Radio Peking had stopped attacking Thailand and that the VOPT was now emanating from Hanoi rather than from China. However, the *Bangkok Post* (21 November) reported that the VOPT was continuing to transmit from a site several kilometers southwest of the city of Kunming, the capital of Yunnan Province in China.

Counter-insurgency Activity. The mission of the ISOC has been to coordinate all areas of counter-insurgency from the village level to the highest echelons of government. Military and paramilitary tactics, border surveillance, psychological warfare, and welfare programs were the basic means used to counter communist activities, with emphasis on military strategy. In 1974 approximately 47,300 persons were attached to ISOC, including 3,000 civilians, 9,000 police, 17,500 military, 9,000 paramilitary, 400 township and village chiefs, 4,400 people's volunteers, 2,700 community development workers, and 600 in various other positions.

ISOC serves as a coordinating and budgeting center for the Royal Thai Army (RTA), police, and civilian elements involved in counter-insurgency. In the field, the RTA commanders also serve as the regional commanders of ISOC, thus technically having control of all counter-insurgency elements within their region. Throughout the year spokesmen for ISOC increasingly stressed the importance of using psychological and political warfare rather than military suppression against communist terrorists. General Saiyud pointed out on numerous occasions that the most important way to win over rural villagers should be through development aid.

In 1974 the success of counter-insurgency programs in Thailand was threatened by a number of serious problems. CSOC troops were alleged to have systematically killed villagers suspected of being communist and then looted their town at Ban Na Sai in Northeast Thailand. CSOC spokesmen denied the allegations and the prime minister ordered a committee to investigate. Although student leaders have continued to protest Thailand's "mini My Lai" the investigators' findings have never been made public.

Adding to CSOC's problems in 1974 was a confused transitional period during which the command was reorganized. The newly named ISOC continued to be directly subordinate to General Krit Sivara in his capacity as "director of internal security and peace-keeping." General Siyud charged that communist suppression activities had ground to a halt as a result of the "indecisive attitude" of the Sanya Thamasak government. General Saiyud claimed also that his position has been eroded of power and authority to act. His authority was restored in June, when in addition to his position at the Supreme Command he was named chief of staff of ISOC with supervisory control over counter-insurgency activity.

During the transitional period a high ranking CSOC official claimed that control over the movement of hill tribes in the North was impossible and that about 5,000 hill tribe persons had illegally migrated from Burma to Thailand in a two-month period. Under the former military regime Generals Thanom Kittikachorn and Prapat Charustiara had been able to issue orders directly to CSOC commanders. Under the civilian government, the chain of command assigned to carry out the government's counter-insurgency policy was in such disarray that for some six months during the transitional period the government had no set counter-insurgency policy.

A further problem concerned the publication of a book, *Com Theerak* ("Dear Communist"), written by officers of CSOC, which criticized the government's anti-insurgency work. The main point of the book was that a strictly military solution to insurgency does not work. In figures from CSOC itself, the authors showed that the ratio of government officials killed to insurgents killed dropped from 1:2.8 in 1967 to 1:0.7 in 1972. The authors charged that the nearly $200 million that had been spent on communist suppression during the last eight years had been a waste.

CSOC became embroiled in still another dispute when the Central Intelligency Agency came under attack by student groups, politicians, and newspapers. The controversy involved a letter written to the prime minister and varous newspapers. The letter, purportedly written by a communist insurgency leader, called for a one-month truce in insurgency operations to be observed by both sides. The letter in fact was traced to a CIA branch office in Sakhon Nakhon. CSOC chief Saiyud criticized the "American interference" in Thai affairs, stating that such interference adversely affected anti-communist operations (*Bangkok Post*, 8 January). However, no official action was taken by the Thai or U.S. governments to eliminate or reduce the CIA presence in Thailand.

In summary, CPT-sponsored insurgency continued to affect a small proportion of the countryside where for ethnic or economic reasons the citizenry felt most alienated from the Thai government. The fall of the military regime in October 1973 brought about a transitional era with ineffective central leadership and with a rise in political and economic demands which had been suppressed by the prevous military government. Counter-insurgency operations were temporarily muddled because of the military's loss of influence and the consequent restructuring of the government's communist suppression command.

Northern Illinois University   Clark Neher

Vietnam: Democratic Republic of Vietnam

In May 1929, the Association of Young Revolutionary Vietnamese Comrades (Viet Nam Thanh Nien Cach Mang Dong Chi Hoi), a Marxist organization founded four years earlier by Ho Chi Minh (who was then 35 years old), met in Hong Kong. The meeting ended in disagreement over the advisability of establishing a political party on a mass basis to replace the smaller, increasingly less effective Association. By the end of 1929, three separate communist parties (Indochinese Communist Party, Annam Communist Party and New Vietnam Revolutionary Party) had been formed. Ho Chi Minh, who had been curiously absent from the Hong Kong congress, was directed by the Comintern to effect a merger of the fragmented movement. At a clandestine "congress" in Kowloon on 3 February 1930, Ho met with representatives of the rival parties and formed the Vietnam Communist Party. Eight months later the name was changed to the Indochinese Communist Party (ICP–Dang Cong San Dong Duong), a more accurate reflection of the role the Vietnamese communists envisioned for themselves on the Indochinese Peninsula.

The ICP was born out of the complex social and economic situation existing in the five political entities which then made up French Indochina—the protectorates of Tonkin, Annam, Cambodia and Laos, and the colony of Cochinchina—but its roots reached far back into an intense nationalist tradition. The extent to which late 19th and early 20th century efforts to oust the French influenced the founders of the ICP may never be fully known. Ho Chi Minh, at least, is said as a young boy in Nghe An province to have sat at the feet of the last of the great Vietnamese scholar-nationalists, Phan Boi Chau, and listened to stories of earlier efforts at resistance. It is unlikely that many other early ICP members escaped similar indoctrination in Vietnamese traditions of resistance to foreign rule, and most probably thought themselves as much a part of that tradition as a part of the broader, worldwide communist movement.

The French conquest of Vietnam in the latter half of the 19th century and the failure of royalist and mandarin-inspired rebellions to oust the French had discredited the Nguyen Dynasty and created something of a domestic power vacuum. In the turmoil of the 1920's in Vietnam, a variety of nationalist organizations appeared and attempted to fill that vacuum. Some, like the Constitutionalist Party, were unabashedly collaborationist. Others were mildly reformist. All demonstrated organizational and intellectual impotence in the face of adamant French refusal to adopt effective political and social reforms. Their failure made it clear to other nationalists that violence was the only tool which was likely to oust the French. Reformism was replaced by extremism. Two years after Ho Chi Minh founded the Association of Young Revolutionary Vietnamese Comrades, the noncommunist VNQDD (Viet-Nam Nationalist Party) established itself as the banner-carrier of the new extremism. The organizational successes of the VNQDD probably did much to convince the Vietnamese communists that the time was right for a broad-based organization. The possibility that the VNQDD might just succeed certainly was an additional spur to action.

The early years of the ICP were less than heartening for Party activists. In a classic understate-ment, the official history published on the occasion of the Party's 40th anniversary in 1970, stated that in 1931 "the movement temporarily faltered." Aroused by an abortive VNQDD rebellion in February 1930, and by widespread, ICP-led peasant uprisings in the central Vietnamese provinces of Nghe An and Ha Tinh, the French colonial administration launched a massive program of political repression. By the middle of 1932, the White Terror had all but destroyed the ICP (as well as the VNQDD). Six of the Party's current Politburo members (including First Secretary Le Duan) were jailed in 1931 or 1932. The then Secretary-General of the ICP, Tran Phu, either was beaten to death by French police or more formally executed.

The establishment of the Popular Front Government in France in 1936 opened prison doors in Vietnam. Another of the ICP's early organizers, Le Hong Phong, was directed by the Comintern to return to Vietnam to take over the leadership of the resurgent party organization. Phong brought with him the new Comintern line: the fight against fascism was to take precedence over the fight against capitalism and imperialism. Dutifully, the ICP established the Indochinese Democratic Front and went semi-legal. Over the next three years, the Party rebuilt and expanded, although much of its potential strength in the southern part of the country was co-opted by an active and politiically successful Trotskyite movement. In November 1939, at the direction of the Comintern, the ICP once more adopted an anti-imperialist stance. As it had in 1930, the Party again misjudged domestic conditions and once more moved faster than circumstances warranted. In what Party historians now admit was a mistake—but which they blame on communications failure—the Party's Cochinchina Regional Committee ordered an uprising in the Mekong Delta in November 1940. The French were prepared and the uprising smashed. In the repression which followed, the ICP was once again almost destroyed. Virtually the entire Cochinchina Regional Committee was wiped out. Other regional apparati suffered to lesser, but still devastating, degrees. The Party Secretary-General, Nguyen Van Cu, was executed in August 1941, along with several Central Committee members. Many of the Party leaders who survived fled to China. Looking for a brighter side to events, the survivors probably noted that their Trotskyite rivals had suffered even more.

In early 1941, Ho Chi Minh returned to Vietnam and, in a demonstration of the organizational genius that eventually defeated the French and co-opted noncommunist competition, created the Viet-Minh (Viet Nam Doc Lap Dong Ming Hoi), an ostensibly noncommunist front organization of all anti-French and anti-Japanese elements in the country. Although Ho's role as the personification of the Vietnamese revolution is undisputed from this point on, his part in the Party's early years is coming under increasing scrutiny. Gathering around him several key advisers (including Vo Nguyen Giap and Pham Van Dong), Ho directed the Viet Minh movement from secure bases in the Viet Bac mountains (the Party continued to operate from clandestine locations in the Red River Delta and, at times, even on the outskirts of Hanoi). With the collapse of the Japanese, who had conveniently brought an abrupt end to almost a century of French rule in Indochina some months earlier, Ho's forces entered Hanoi in August 1945 and declared the independence of the country and the establish-ment of the Democratic Republic of Vietnam.

French intentions fell somewhat short of Ho's vision of a unified, independent and communist Vietnam, and in December 1946 the party abandoned Hanoi for a return to the resistance bases in the northern mountains. Although the ICP had been declared "dissolved" in November 1945 as part of an effort to gain domestic support for the new government and to undermine the position of non-communist rivals, by 1951 Ho was ready to make the communist role in the resistance public again. At the ICP's Second National Congress, held February 11-19, 1951, the Party's name was changed to the Viet-Nam Workers Party (VWP—Dang Lao Dong Viet Nam) and a Party platform was adopted and publicized. Ho was named Party Chairman and Truong Chinh Secretary-General.

By 1951, Party membership had grown from approximately 5,000 in August 1945 to almost a half million. Although little growth was recorded between 1951 and 1960, probably as the result of wartime losses and the land reform upheavals of the mid-1950's, the Party's undisputed power in the North after 1954 demanded an expansion of Party ranks. The Third Party Congress in 1960 called for such expansion as a necessary tool to effect the "socialist transformation" of the North. The steady escalation of North Vietnam's commitment to the completion of the revolution in the South also necessitated a larger pool of Party cadres. Between 1960 and 1963, Party membership increased from 500,000 to 700,000. By 1966, membership had risen to 900,000. The rate of increase was accelerated after 1965 and by the end of 1970, there were some 1,100,000 Party members.

Although as fraught with problems as any large organization, the VWP's control of the Democratic Republic of Vietnam has not been seriously challenged.

The Position in 1974. The year 1974 in the Democratic Republic of Vietnam (DRV) was unremarkable in that it witnessed no historic events, or traumatic experiences, or any discernible fundamental change. It was a year in which not much was new. In the areas of chief concern here—leadership and organization, party internal affairs, domestic attitudes and activities, and international views and activities—developments largely were straight-line continuations of conditions and trends fixed during the previous year which, unlike 1974, was something of a watershed in North Vietnamese history.

This continuity and steadiness was not unexpected, for the DRV has been more consistent in behavior, more constant in purpose, than almost any other nation in modern times. And, for reasons not entirely clear, it has been less buffeted by the winds of change than most other countries, communist and non-communist alike.

Certain major constants of the DRV scene thus remain. They can be stated briefly. (*a*) The DRV intends to control the South or, in its parlance, reunify the Fatherland; this long ago ceased to be mere state policy, is now holy crusade. (*b*) The DRV rigidly opposes all social and political liberalization, for itself or for any other communist country that it can influence. (*c*) The DRV strongly opposes détente or peaceful coexistence with the capitalist world, and unashamedly embraces the primitive view that the capitalist world must be destroyed (and that the best means is by revolutionary guerrilla war). (*d*) The DRV tenaciously adheres to the once orthodox Marxist dogma of proletarian monolithism and its corollary that there can be but "one Rome" for communism. (*e*) The DRV asserts, in a barbed way, its right of non-dependent (and in some ways non-reciprocal relations) with its two chief allies, China and the Soviet Union. All five of these concepts have long existed as building blocks in Politburo thinking, and remain so at this writing.

The year 1974 must be viewed in context of the years and events which preceded it. The failure of the DRV's 1972 Easter offensive—a high technology big-unit war campaign once and for all to win militarily in the South—set the course of events. By the summer of 1972 the DRV could no longer sustain the level of combat that it had reached. Doctrinal pressures within the Politburo grew against such lavish warfare. The Chinese and the Soviets grew restive and increasingly critical. Punitive blows were being rained on North Vietnam by U.S. planes. The Politburo, faced with several unattractive alternatives, procrastinated for a time and then acted decisively. The result was that the campaign ended, the Paris Agreements were signed, and the DRV resigned itself to an indefinite period of restoration and reexamination of its basic doctrines.

The subsequent DRV behavior—which was logical and should have been anticipated—now stands out clearly, in historical terms. The next three years were devoted to a search for a formula for victory. It became a time of doctrinal experimentation, not only militarily but politically (in the South) and diplomatically abroad. Various battle tactics were tested in the South, including use of the augmented sapper team (the "super guerrilla concept"). Offers and gestures were made in various international forums. National Liberation Front (NLF) cadres in the South experimented with new uses for the old communist-front device. Tests were made to determine how best the Paris Agreements might be put into service for the DRV and its instrument in the South, the Provisional Revolutionary Government (PRG). In every sphere there was testing, improvising, trying first one approach and then another, always done cautiously with great conservatism in risk taking, with consistent refusal to accept any high-stakes gamble. When collated and viewed in retrospect this activity has the clear stamp of a systematic search for a grand strategy, some new mix of old doctrine which would delivery victory. No such winning formula was found as of the end of 1974, but the search continued.

During the year, it is imperative to note, there was no reduction in military capability by the People's Army of Vietnam (PAVN) in the South or by proxy force, the People's Liberation Armed Force (PLAF). Strategists may have been uncertain as to how to proceed, but the logisticians knew exactly what they were doing. Military supplies were steadily pumped southward. Fresh manpower arrived daily. New transportation and communication routes were opened, new airfields and encampments built. By December 1974 military stocks were more than adequate for a return to big-unit war. PAVN-PLAF had the military capability, beyond doubt. What was in question was intent: would the Politburo order a return to big-unit warfare, either in the form of a limited campaign with limited objectives or in an all-out "go for broke" campaign? In December 1974 no one could be sure. The best judgment seemed to be that the Politburo's decision would turn on its estimate of the probability of success in such a move. Probability must be considered high. If it was (particularly if raised by some momentous development such as economic collapse in the South, a coup d'état in Saigon, or U.S. abandonment of the RVN), then PAVN divisions owuld be ordered into action. But, on the other hand, if the Politburo saw the RVN as reasonably strong and unified, its various economic and political problems still manageable, with support continuing by the United States, and thus its estimate of PAVN's probability of success was not high, then the marching orders would not be given. In the latter case, the DRV would continue mounting great pressure—military, political, economic, and diplomatic—against the GVN while the doctrinal hunt continued.

Several factors appeared to militate against the idea of a high-risk military campaign: the strain it would put on the DRV internal system; the possible reaction of its allies; the backlash effects of failure; and most of all, the Politburo's implicit belief that in the long run the RVN cannot and will not survive, hence high risks need not be taken. The crucial factor was the course of events in Saigon, not so much the truth of it as the Politburo's perception, which was most difficult to determine.

Party Leadership and Organization. The eleven men of the Dang Lao Dong Politburo have more unchallenged control of their society than virtually any other ruling group on earth. Their tenure, unchanged since the 1940s save for two deaths, certainly is one of the most durable.

During 1974 the leadership saw no personnel change and, by all evidence, remained united in action although still divided in doctrine (For discussion of the doctrinal disputes see "Party Internal Affairs," below).

For still another year the leadership failed to face the question of generational political succession and thus the matter grew one year more crucial. The average age of the Politburo was 65 (the Central Committee, 64). The country is run by old men; virtually all power holders are of the older generation. Soon these men must arrange an orderly transfer of power or time will intrude to preempt a decision. At year's end, speculation was rife in Hanoi that the Lao Dong's Fourth Congress (ten years overdue; the last one was in 1960) would be held in mid-1975, at which time announcement would be made on the pattern for passing the mantle of power (retirements, vacancies filled in the Central Committee and Politburo) to the next generation. Similar rumors circulated in late 1973, predicting a party congress in mid-1974. None eventuated, possibly because the Politburo was unwilling or unable to decide when, how, and to whom the power should be shifted.

Ferment relating to the leadership, apparently significant, occurred during the year in the military establishment, suggesting but not clearly establishing, certain civilian-versus-military tension. There were assignment changes and a large number of high-level promotions, some of them overdue. Stepping down from a fully active role as defense minister was Senior General Vo Nguyen Giap, who was reported as having spent several months in a Moscow cancer ward with Hodgkin's disease; other reports said he had a gallstone operation. PAVN's second ranking officer, Van Tien Dung was promoted to senior general and unofficially became acting minister of defense and PAVN commander in chief. (The highest rank in PAVN is senior general, carrying four stars; only three men have held this rank: General Giap, the later General Nguyen Chi Thanh, and now General Dung). Promoted to colonel general (three stars) were Song Hao, the PAVN political commissar, and Hoang Van Thai (who thus ended this year an eight-year absence from DRV public reference); they join at that rank Chu Van Tan, a Montagnard. Promoted to lieutenant general (two stars) were Bang Giang, Le Quang Dao, and Tran Sam, thus joining the rank with lieutenant generals Phan Kiet, director of the Public Armed Security Corps; Nguyen Don, vice-minister of national defense; and Tran Van Tra and Tran Do, line commanders. New major generals (one star) include Hoang Minh Thi and Do Trinh (other major generals are Phung The Tai, Cao Van Khanh, Mai Chi Tho, and Nguyen Quyet).

A second development within PAVN suggested changes in thinking in fundamental military science. In part this appeared to be an effort to explain to field-grade officers and others why the Tet 1968 and the Easter 1972 military offensives were unsuccessful. Much of this thinking was outlined candidly at a series of high-level military conferences. For example, at a June conference General Dao listed a series of doctrinal and technical problems: finding the proper role of the party within PAVN; lowered soldier morale, what was called "the post-war mentality"; lack of standardization in military hardware; a generally inadequate military logistics system; basic military units insufficiently skilled in the use of modern infantry weapons; and poor relations between North Vietnamese soldiers in Cambodia and their Khmer insurgent allies. Much of this trouble, General Dao indicated turned on the long-standing Red-versus-expert argument whether ideological and motivational factors were more important than military technology and skill in producing a first-class fighting man.

A third development in PAVN, reflection of the first two, was a massive emulation movement, which is a form of intensified troop-indoctrination. Its direct objective was to alter attitude and opinion of the rank-and-file soldier. Indirectly it appeared to be an effort to eliminate many myth-ridden notions which surround guerrilla warfare, replacing them with faith in high-technology big-unit warfare.

On the civilian side of the government much attention was paid to overhauling and streamlining the managerial and administrative system at the ministerial level. Various ministries and commissions were combined into what came to be called "super ministries," investing special powers in four newly appointed vice-ministers acting as "economic czars." Le Thanh Nghi was given the key role of overall economic planner. Nguyen Con, as vice-minister of machinery and metallurgy, was to insure that mechanization of agriculture proceeded at proper pace. Dan Viet Chau, vice-minister of finance, trade, and banking, was to develop a comprehensive economic monitoring and auditing system. Pham Trong Tue, vice-minister of transportation and communication, was to integrate and upgrade the nation's transportation system. And Tran Huu Duc, vice-minister of the "internal bloc" (a deliberately obscure term), was to tackle the socio-psychological problems related to the economy, such as reasserting state control of grain (an estimated 25 percent of the rice harvested in the DRV does not go through government hands enroute to the consumer), and to the misallocation or embezzlement of state property.

Hoang Anh was relieved of the chairmanship of the all-important Central Agriculture Commission and replaced by Nguyen Tho Chan, a relative unknown in the agriculture sector. Also relieved of their posts were Nguyen Huu Khieu, minister of labor; Nguyen Huu Mai minister of power and coal; and Dang Viet Chau, minister of finance. Most of these changes appeared to be technical rather than political.

Tran Quoc Hoan, minister of public security, was conspicuously absent from public functions that required his attendance. This led to speculation that he was in semi-disgrace because of failure by his service to maintain the law and order desired and believed possible by the Politburo.

Party Internal Affairs. Doctrinal disputes continued to range within the Lao Dong Party and represented the most significant ongoing internal development of 1974. These ideological clashes— there were three major ones—reached as in years past into the Politburo itself. Evidence of continued doctrinal dispute was overwhelming, but it was not safe to conclude, as did some French observers, that the prospect was great for some hostile action or even preemptive power grab, particularly in the event of several deaths in the Politburo. All available evidence indicated that the collective leadership system continued and was adhering to its operational code that no decision would be taken if it were not acceptable to all 11 members. The three doctrinal disputes, however, were genuine and offered the best single means of reviewing Party activity.

First, there was the doctrinal dispute over proper strategy to achieve unification of Vietnam— that is, victory in the South: whether primary emphasis should be put on political struggle (that is, politics with guns) or on armed struggle, and, if the latter, whether by regular force strategy (either big-unit warfare, high-technology warfare, or some variant) or by protracted conflict (either orthodox people's war or some form of neo-revolutionary guerrilla warfare such as the so-called super guerrilla concept).

Through the war years the goal of unification was never challenged either by the leaders or by the rank and file. None questioned Ho Chi Minh's dictum that no price was too high, no sacrifice too great, to achieve this goal. However, this year DRV theoretical journals attacked certain unidentified elements within the party who question this no-limit assumption. The position of these oppositionists can be extrapolated from the rationale of the attack: they believe in unification but think there is a price beyond which the DRV should not go; and they consider lavish military expenditure, as in high-technology warfare, to be unnecessary; it appears that they also advocate unification by means of political struggle in the South and certain diplomatic moves abroad.

The second doctrinal dispute, on which the first obviously impinges, concerns economic policy, chiefly the principles which the Politburo should follow in allocating resources (especially manpower) to the war in the South and to nation building in the North; and, within the latter, the proper division of resources between the agricultural sector and industrial development. It is here that the heresy noted in the first dispute has its most meaning. If an essentially non-military strategy is pursued for unification, it follows that fewer resources need be allocated to the South and that of course would sharply reduce PAVN's military credibility. Some observers doubt that the military logistical expenditure in the South drains much from the DRV economy, holding that war supplies simply transit North Vietnam, from communist-nation supplier to PAVN units in the field (the obvious exceptions being manpower and transportation).

It is clear there is little support in the Politburo for the idea of cutting the costs of warfare, although it does have appeal to middle- and upper-level party members and bureaucrats for whom a reduction would facilitate their work assignment, speed national development, and raise the standard of living.

To the degree that economic problems are also psychological, the second doctrinal dispute impinges on the third, the question of how best to eliminate the various socio-psychological troubles in North Vietnam collectively known as the "quality of life problem." This was seen as a general social malaise, ennui, *Weltschmerz*, a sour-outlook world view accompanied by a letdown in fervor and a lessening of social responsibility and resulting in indifference to party call or, even worse, use of prerogative of office for immoral or illegal personal gain. It is social pathology compounded of many symptoms: self-aggrandizement by party cadre and government bureaucrat; "official" corruption by economic managers (the scheme by a candy factory to sell half its output on the black market and divide the money among the workers and management); anti-social activity by disgruntled veterans and members of the "war-widow bloc"; worker absenteeism; petty graft; ethnic disturbances; public disorders; sabotage; theft of state property; juvenile delinquency. In short: the manifestation in individuals of a cynical selfishness which corroded or touched ambitious government schemes and bright party dreams.

That this alienation of spirit existed, no one would dispute; nor that it must be dissipated before there could be true progress. The quarrel was over remedy. On the one hand were the ideologues, who advocated a communicational approach: appeals to altruism, moral exhortation, lecturing, increased use of the *khiem thao* (self-criticism), and party officials setting selfless examples (together with some purging of party members with poor "revolutionary ethics"). The ideologues sought to harness social pressure and put it to work. Doctrinally opposite were what might be called the pragmatists, who sought to lessen the pressure on the individual and offer him new or increased individual incentives such as bonuses for over-production, larger private-plot holdings on the commune, increased privilege of rank, and other such "capitalist" devices. The pragmatists did not simply advocate materialism. Rather they considered that the quality of life in North Vietnam had deteriorated and anti-social activity had increased because of the extraordinary strain which the war had put on the society. Reduce the strain, they argued, and the situation would correct itself; add material incentive and it would improve.

What divided ideologue and pragmatist was their differing philosophic view on the basic nature of man and, within this, on whether Marxism could be more than an icon for North Vietnam, whether it was a workable guide offering sound advice to solve problems. As such, this third doctrinal dispute, in the long run, could prove far more significant than the first two.

Domestic Attitudes and Activities. Economics dominated the consciousness of the individual North Vietnamese again during the year if for no other reason than the subject nearly monopolized mass-media attention.

The government, more by word than deed, sought to convince the population that the country's economic prospects were very bright indeed. In two years, it indicated, the back would be broken on present major economic ills. Then the country would move into a series of five-year plans which would turn North Vietnam into something of an economic utopia. Since the DRV is dedicated to the idea of a totally planned society, the bulk of what was communicated consisted of announcements on plans—large and small, general and specific, realistic and grandiose plans.

Meanwhile, life for the average North Vietnamese continued to be as harsh as in previous years. Rice, meat, sugar, and cloth continued to be tightly rationed and often were unavailable. The fifth-month rice crop was poor and the tenth-month crop below average, so rice production for the year was somewhat below recent years. The DRV continued to depend on outside sources for some 20 percent of the food it consumed (but distribution was equitable and above the 1,600 calories per day minimum).

In February came an official announcement: a full-scale communist-style five-year plan, the country's second (1960-65 the first) would begin in 1976 and run through 1980. In the interim the country would operate on a one-and-a-half-year plan (what was left of the three-year plan drafted in early 1972 but never fully implemented).

As outlined in the Hanoi press, the major objectives of the second five-year plan would be these:

(1) The agricultural sector would be rationalized, and both productivity and absolute production increased. Communes would be fully mechanized. Protein production would be improved, and the country finally would "solve the grain problem"–that is, become self-sufficient in grain production.

(2) A modern, technically based managerial system would be created for both agriculture and industry. This would involve reorganization of the administrative structure down into the most basic-level units; it would involve new labor-discipline methods and worker-incentive programs. It would require vast new research and development work.

(3) The DRV's economy's physical infrastructure–plant facilities, for example–would be greatly expanded through large-scale construction projects.

(4) The transportation and communication matrices–now restored to pre-war level–would be upgraded and expanded to meet the needs of the new semi-industrialized economy.

(5) Heavy industry, including mining, would be enlarged or developed: coal production by a factor of three, steel production by a factor of ten, chemical fertilizer by a factor of six. Textile production would be doubled. Shipbuilding, tractor manufacture, and plastics, soda, cement, and paper production would be developed or greatly expanded.

(6) Light industry (consumer goods) production capacity would be vastly expanded.

(7) New capital investment in great amounts would be generated, partly through foreign aid but chiefly through internal borrowing.

(8) A commodity export trade would be developed, with emphasis on production of industrial crops, sugar, and fish.

Such were the rough outlines of the initial draft of the plan. While the parameters were fixed in 1974, the planning work was only well begun, since what was involved was not simply setting down specific objectives with governing guidelines, but totally planning all economic activity for all North Vietnamese, excluding nothing. The second five-year plan represented a vast, mind-boggling venture, one which would test the managerial limits of the most advanced computer-based economic system. It required nothing less than planning the day-by-day activity, for five years, of eleven million North Vietnamese workers. The plan would assure that all equipment, supplies, and materials were procured and delivered to the right place at the right time. Every single act of production, each phase of distribution, would be programmed. End use and final consumption would be prearranged. An omnipresent administration would be required, since no one was to do anything on his own initiative, only under supervision and in accordance with The Plan. For five years literally each individual economic act in North Vietnam–and there would be billions upon billions of them–would be scheduled sequentially and supervised at every point to insure that it correctly jibed with every other act. Whether the DRV was equal to such a task–whether it could even plan the plan–was highly questionable. But politics were in command. The omnipotence of the party was to replace the logic of the market. The result could prove as disastrous for North Vietnam as was the "great leap forward" for China.

The five-year plan, announced in February, received much public attention until July, when, unaccountably, official references to it began to taper off. Possibly this was because serious differences had arisen in the Politburo, making any comment difficult; or because uncertainty in direction has arisen among the planners; or because for some reason the plan was cancelled or indefinitely postponed.

North Vietnam's present economic condition stems from years of neglect, in capitalist terms from lack of plant investment. For more than a decade and a half the country's resources were poured into the war in the South, with little allocated to nation building in the North. The economic sector declined not spectacularly but steadily year after year. The result was a stagnant, anachronistic economy, inadequate to the steadily growing needs of an ever-expanding population.

North Vietnam is an agrarian country and to speak of its economy is virtually the same as to speak of its agricultural sector. For example, by developed-nation standards there are only six heavy industry plants in the entire country. Hence, until the present at least, all emphasis was on the commune, under the major slogan: "First of All Agriculture."

Basic improvement of DRV agriculture requires mechanization and technological development—bringing to the commune the necessary tools, machines, and chemical additives, the new seed varieties. If this is done, productivity will increase, as will absolute farm yields. This requires industrialization. But industrialization in the service of agriculture requires tremendous inputs of money. As all developing nations know, the money must come from somewhere, either borrowed from abroad or extracted as "surplus" from the people.

North Vietnam is an extremely poor country—a gross national product of about U.S. $1.6 billion, which gives it a per capita income of about $68. Half of its GNP is generated by agriculture. Since a labor shortage exists in the agricultural sector, to remove manpower from it would further reduce production. In order to remove manpower from agriculture and transfer it to industry without loss of production it is necessary to increase agricultural productivity. And this in turn, cannot be done without industrialization. Hence the North Vietnamese dilemma.

To absorb one million of the North Vietnamese agrarian labor force of nine million into the industrial sector would cost about U.S. $2.3 billion (based on a U.N. world-wide study which indicated it costs about $2,500 to absorb a worker into industry. To provide the plant capacity for this industrial support of agriculture would require another $5 billion. Finally the DRV must import about one million metric tons of food per year to make up its deficit in food production. This amounts to somewhat more than one-fourth billion dollars per annum, with the figure growing yearly since increased production has not kept pace with population growth. (The DRV population according to the 1 April 1974 census, which apparently does not include overseas Chinese, was 23,878,375. The growth rate was fixed at 2.9 percent per year.

What these figures add up to is this: some $14 billion is needed to "solve the grain problem"—not to industrialize North Vietnam but to make it self-sufficient in food. And $14 billion is seven times the country's GNP. The problem of the DRV planners is, where is this money to come from? And beyond this, if industrialization under the five-year plan is to be achieved, what will be the source of the money required, sums so staggering that they cannot yet even be estimated?

International Views and Activities. Contradictory as it might appear, the DRV's imperative economic need was of limited influence on its external behavior during 1974. Although foreign friends were generous, the Politburo knew that the sort of money it required was not to be forthcoming. Had there been genuine prospect of vast sums, quite probably DRV external behavior would have radically altered. But there was not, so the DRV could afford a haughty and even hostile posture abroad while at the same time garnering such economic aid as it could demand, cajole, or entrap.

Economic aid arrived at Haiphong in 1974 at an unprecedented rate. Both communist and non-communist countries poured in assistance. France sent a bicycle factory; Sweden, a paper factory and a hospital; Cuba, a hotel; Finland, prefabricated houses; Hungary, bauxite-mining equipment; UNICEF, school buildings; the U.S.S.R., a hospital; China, public housing. While symbolically important and certainly welcome, this aid was marginal when thinking in terms of an economic quantum jump costing billions. Such appears to have been the Politburo's estimate, for clearly it did not permit economics to condition its foreign policy.

Military aid, by all available evidence, dropped during the year, at least in total tonnages. This may have been because of deliberate restraint on the part of the two major suppliers—China and the U.S.S.R.—seeking to serve their own respective interests (and over DRV objections), or it may simply reflect the fact that armament stockpiles were extraordinarily high in the pre-Paris Agreement period and that logistic expenditure since then had diminished sharply.

Much DRV diplomatic activity during the year was conditioned by its peculiar relationship with the Provisional Revolutionary Government. The DRV sought to increase the PRG's world-wide prestige and acceptance by setting as its price for improved relations with such countries as Japan, Great Britain, the Netherlands, and Italy, the official acceptance by those countries of the PRG. As a result diplomatic forward movement with many non-communist countries slowed. The DRV objective in this appeared to be to keep the southern communist elements loyal and in line, and the conditions set down may have been stage posturing for their benefit, which would mean that after a period the DRV would drop such demands.

DRV relations with communist countries, however, were another and far more important matter. Here the DRV posture was correct and cool, warming somewhat perhaps towards China and at the same time pursuing what might be called the principle of non-dependency, balancing ideological ties with DRV national interest. The Politburo clung to its fundamentalist views of our times, that the capitalist world must be ruined, that this can be done only by revolutionary guerrilla warfare conducted by the united international proletariat. Once this idea had been orthodoxy, but now it isolated the DRV from the rest of the communist world and from the rest of the world.

The communist nations of the world, the DRV believes, are guilty of two sins. The first is the sin of commission, called détente or peaceful coexistence. Here the DRV finds the U.S.S.R. somewhat more guilty than China, and says so publicly. The second sin is one of omission, lack of communist solidarity or proletarian unity—that is, the monolithism that at one time marked the international communist world's outward appearance. The genesis of this condition, of course, is the Sino-Soviet dispute. While the DRV condemns both parties it tends to regard Peking rather than Moscow as more contributive to the continuing breach and less willing to seek an improvement in relations.

Communist world unity has become something of a ploy for the North Vietnamese. It throws into the face of communist leaders some of the most sacred texts in the Marxist catechism, there being virtually nothing prior to workers of the world uniting. The DRV sees the issue as a struggle between international proletarianism and national selfishness, and as a problem in reconciliation of patriotism (defined as DRV national interest) with the common interests of the communist world. The DRV holds that small nations themselves must distinguish between their international obligations to the proletariat and their own national interests, and never have that determination forced on them by larger communist nations. Small nations have the right to demand the support of big nations, but also must always be free to determine their own course of action. Thus a claim is staked for the best of both worlds: Moscow and Peking must support Hanoi in the name of international proletarianism. But neither—in the same spirit—may levy requirements on North Vietnam, for this would violate the principle of national self-determination.

What is involved is conflicting national interests among countries which happen to be allies and communists. But it is small wonder that neither Moscow nor Peking welcomes, or even takes seriously, these criticisms from its small associate.

Publications. VWP policy statements, Politburo resolutions, Secretariat directives and major speeches by principal Party figures usually appear in *Nhan Dan* ("The People"), the VWP Central Committee's daily newspaper, *Hoc Tap* ("Studies"), the Central Committee's monthly theoretical journal, *Quan Doi Nhan Dan* ("People's Army"), the armed forces daily, and *Tap Chi Quan Doi Nhan Dan* ("People's Army Magazine"), a monthly. Policy statements of special significance frequently are published in two or more of these publications. Other major publications include *Tien Phong* ("Vanguard"), twice-weekly organ of the Central Committee of the Ho Chi Minh Working Youth Union, *Lao Dong* ("Labor"), the journal of the Viet-Nam General Federation of Trade Unions, *Cuu Quoc* ("National Salvation"), weekly organ of the Central Committee of the Viet-Nam Fatherland Front, and *Nghien Cuu Kinh Te* ("Economic Studies"), which carries major articles on economic planning and development.

Major VWP statements also are aired by "Voice of Vietnam"—Radio Hanoi—in both Vietnamese and English. Radio Hanoi also broadcasts in some 10 other languages. The most recent addition to Hanoi's language services is Malay. Radio Hanoi is supplemented domestically by regional and provincial radio outlets, which generally repeat Radio Hanoi broadcasts and add items of local interest. Similarly, most of North Vietnam's provinces publish daily or weekly newspapers.

Washington, D.C.   Douglas Pike

U.S. Information Service   James Haley
Saigon

Vietnam: Republic of Vietnam

In late December 1961, remnants of the badly decimated southern organization of the Vietnam Workers' Party (Dang Lao Dang Viet-Nam; VWP), newly arrived cadres ("regroupees") from North Vietnam, and other "progressive" individuals attended a meeting of the Association of Former Resistance Fighters at which the decision was taken to form the People's Revolutionary Party (Dang Nhan Dan Cach Mang; PRP). The date 1 January 1962 was chosen as that of the founding.

A special announcement issued shortly after the formation of the PRP affirmed that the party would "carry on the glorious and historic work of [its] revolutionary predecessor parties" (Liberation Press Agency [LPA], 13 January 1962). One of the predecessor parties was indicated to be the Indochinese Communist Party (ICP), which existed from 1930 until 1945, when it went underground, functioning under the cover of the Indochina Marxist Studies Association. It reemerged as the VWP in 1951. If the creation of the PRP did not signal the formation of a new and independent communist party, neither was it done for "propaganda reasons" (YICA, 1973, p. 567, relies on a 1961 document "captured" in Ba Xuyen Province; it has now been established that this document was in fact forged by Republic of Vietnam [RVN] authorities.)

The PRP was created in recognition of the fact that Vietnam was divided into "two regions having different social regimes" and that the party would have to carry out "two different revolutionary tasks" (LPA, 13 January 1962). At the VWP Third National Congress, held in Hanoi in September 1960, these different revolutionary tasks were defined as socialist construction in the north and "the people's national democratic revolution in the south."

According to the party's analysis, South Vietnam was under the control of "imperialists and feudalists" (meaning the Diem government and its U.S. backers) and at that time priority was given to the overthrow of the "U.S.-Diem clique" above all other considerations, including proletarian revolution. Thus the party, as the vanguard group of the workers, peasants, and laborers, was to "unite and cooperate closely with all democratic parties, religions and patriotic people's organizations." For this purpose party leaders and other dissident groups met in December 1960 at an organizing congress where agreement was reached to form the National Front for the Liberation of South Vietnam (Mat Tran Dan Toc Giai Phong Mien Nam Viet Nam; NFLSV, or NFL). In 1969, partly for reasons connected with the legitimacy of the NFL's position as one of four negotiating parties at the Paris peace talks, the NFL (having joined with the Vietnam Alliance of National Democratic Peace Forces [VANDPF]), declared itself the Provisional Revolutionary Government of the Republic of South Vietnam (PRG RSVN, or PRG). Today the political resolution of the VWP's Third National Congress still remains the most authoritative statement of party policy. The PRP is still committed to bringing about a "national democratic revolution" in the South. In effect this means a submerged, low-profile role for the PRP. Within the NFL and the PRG the party has made a deliberate choice to share power, at the national level at least, with as wide a range as possible of groups and individuals who oppose having a government in Saigon dependent on foreign (that is, U.S.) support.

The PRP retains connections with the VWP through a specially created Central Committee Directorate for Southern Vietnam (Trung Uong Cuc Mien Nam, known popularly as COSVN), originally set up in October 1961. Provision for this organizational structure was incorporated in the new party statues (art. 24) drawn up at the Third National Congress. The creation of COSVN allows the entire region of South Vietnam to be treated separately and under the close supervision of senior party leaders.

The PRP has drawn up its own rules, statutes and by-laws. Its most senior cadres are high-ranking members of the VWP who were either born south of the seventeenth parallel or who have had extensive experience there. Membership of the subordinate echelons has been filled by recruitment in the South as well as the integration of several thousand cadres from north of the seventeenth parallel. Although there has been some friction reported between these groups, it has been resolved by giving preference to native southerners. According to P. J. Honey:

> The solution adopted to resolve this difficulty [of rebuilding a depleted reserve of cadres] was to employ only southerners in high-level positions and to select for preference, those who had spent some time as regroupees in the North and who were too old for active combat duties. Because of the dearth of suitable southerners, some northerners would have to be used, but only men who had served for at least three years in the South might be chosen, and they would be restricted to low level positions. (*China News Analysis* [CNA], Hong Kong, no. 973, 13 September 1974.)

Any assessment of the PRP's role in 1974 must take into account the fact that the party is banned under the present constitution of the Republic of Vietnam. Its operations and activities in areas under the control of the RVN are covert. In areas under the control of the PRG RSVN, the party still maintains a very low profile. There was virtually no mention of the PRP by the LPA or by Liberation Radio (as monitored by the *FBIS*) this year. Therefore in order to present as complete a picture as possible of communist activities in Vietnam it is necessary to consider in addition to the PRP the activities of both the NFL and the PRG-RSVN.

Size and Strength. The PRP has never released precise membership figures. According to estimates by U.S. officials, the strength of the communist movement is "roughly 50,000 guerrillas and about an equal number of political cadre. The total Viet Cong troop strength numbers an additional 75,000 of whom about 30,000 are considered combat forces" (*Vietnam: May 1974*, Moose-Meissner report prepared for the Committee on Foreign Relations, U.S. Senate). Since communists are banned from participating in RVN elections it is impossible to determine from past performance how many votes they are capable of attracting. General Westmoreland, however, has written that "even the most critical observers [of the Saigon government] would give the Communists no more than 25 percent of the vote" (*NYT*, 18 April 1974).

In mid-July 1974, the RVN conducted a national poll to elect 478 municipal and provincial councillors. Despite attempts by communists to harass the voters (causing the number of "Viet Cong" incidents recorded by the Saigon Military Command to rise to the highest level in 17 months), *Vietnam Press*, Saigon, reported that 5,732,654 registered voters out of a total of 7,228,736 went to the polls. This represented a 79.3 percent turnout. According to one foreign observer, the election results "demonstrated yet again the unsurprising fact that Saigon remains in firm control of much of the country and a high eprcentage of the population" (*Far Eastern Economic Review* [FEER], 2 August).

PRG spokesmen have never given precise figures on the numbers of people or the extent of area under their control. Nguyen Thi Binh, PRG foreign minister, in an interview with the Swedish newspaper *Dagens Nyheter*, stated:

In general, our vast liberated zone covers more than three quarters of South Vietnam's territory, stretching from Quang Tri to the point of Ca Mau, with different strategic points, rich natural resources, fertile and populous areas. The situation being still unstable, there are as yet no official data about the population in the liberated zones. It is safe, however, to say that the population of the liberated zones has increased unceasingly. (Vietnam News Agency [VNA], 7 February.)

However, captured documents make it clear that PRG officials do in fact run a rigorous accounting system in which land and population are classified into two categories: "Liberated areas" (free of RVN presence, with functioning revolutionary committees and a local PLAF [People's Liberation Armed Forces] self-defense unit) and "contested areas" (where the RVN has only a static presence and offers no organized military opposition, and where PLAF armed propaganda teams can operate). According to extrapolations made from PRG documents, 10 percent of the land is considered "liberated." The PRG, using an even more rigorous system, estimates that 12 percent of the total population of 18,000,000 in South Vietnam is under its control, or 2.2 million (Peter Collins, *FEER*, 2 August).

Both the United States and the RVN maintain their own complicated systems of population classification. According to one estimate, the RVN has "dominant access" to 94 percent of the population. If this were so, the PRG would control only 1.2 million people out of an estimated total of 19.6 million people. (The RVN and PRG do not agree on the total population figures in South Vietnam). The PRG maintains that the RVN controls only 1.2 percent of the countryside (*The Australian*, Canberra, 20 September).

Leadership and Organization. *The PRP.* The PRP has never released publicly a list of its Central Committee members. Intelligence analysts who have long studied the relationship between the PRP and COSVN are unsure if a PRP Central Committee in fact exists separately from COSVN. Only a handful of individuals have been identified as PRP members in open sources since 1962. These include Vo Chi Cong (chairman), Nguyen Van Linh (secretary-general), Tran Nam Trung (assistant secretary-general), Pham Xuan Thai, and Tran Bach Dang. Vo Chi Cong was allegedly made a member of the VWP Central Committee in 1960. Nguyen Van Linh is thought to have operated under the following aliases: Nguyen Van Cuc, Nguyen Van Muoi, Muoi Cuc, Muoi Ut, Pham Cuc. Tran Nam Trung is thought to be a pseudonym used over the course of time by various VWP members involved in military affairs; it is allegedly used currently as an alias for PAVN Major General Tran Luong. Pham Xuan Thai is thought to have operated under a variety of cover names, including Hai Van, Nguyen Van Dang, Nguyen Van Dong, Pham Xuan Vy, Van Han Hau, Vo Han Hau, Phan Xuan Thai, and Xuan Vy.

According to British and U.S. biographic summaries, other members of the PRP Central Committee may include: Dang Tran Thi, Hai Viet, Hoang Son, Huynh Van Nghi, Le Thanh Nam, Nguyen Don, Nguyen Trung Thua, Nguyen Van Chi, Pham Hung, Pham Thi Yen, Pham Trong Dan, Pham Van Co, Phung Van Cung, Tran Do (alias Cuu Long), Tran Hoai Nam, Tran Van Binh, Tran Van Thanh, Tran Van Tra, and Truong Cong Thuan.

COSVN. The PRP is considered a special regional branch of the VWP. The organizational tie-up between the VWP Central Committee and the PRB is maintained through COSVN. According to U.S. government sources, there are at least 16 committees comprising COSVN, the two most important of which are the Current Affairs Committee, headed by Nguyen Van Linh (a member of the VWP Central Committee), and the Military Affairs Committee, headed by Major General Hoang Van Thai. The highest ranking VWP member in the South and secretary of COSVN is Pham Hung, a Politburo member.

Other members of COSVN include: Lieutenant Genral Tran Van Tra; Major Generals Le Trong Tan, Tran Do (alias Tran Quoc Vinh), Dong Van Cong, and Tran Nam Trung; Senior Colonels Le Duc Anh, Nguyen Thi Dinh, Le Chan (alias Le Van Tuong) and Le Huu Xuyen; Dao Son Tay; and Nguyen Van Xe (alias Hai Gia, Hai Xe Ngua) (*Vietnam Documents and Research Notes*, no. 111, p. 91-92).

The PLAF. The People's Liberation Armed Forces high command is headed by Lieutenant General Hoang Van Thai. His deputy is Lieutenant General Tran Van Tra. Deputy commanders of the PLAF include Senior Colonels Le Duc Anh, Nguyen Thi Dinh, and Le Huu Xuyen. The PLAF political department is staffed by Major Generals Tran Do and Hoang Anh Tuan, Senior Colonel Le Chan, and Do Xhanh Van.

The PRP structure, from COSVN downward, parallels that of the NFL and consists of regional, provincial, district, and village committees. The most basic unit is the three-man cell. Members of the PRP occupy positions in the NFL structure at all levels.

The NFL. At the top of the NFL organizational structure are the Central Committee, Presidum, and Secretariat. At the NFL's Second Congress, 1-8 January 1964, the Central Committee had a membership of 64 persons, the Presidium 7, and the Secretariat 5. Several of these individuals have since died and others have been appointed to membership. For these reasons, and in the absence of a later congress, the exact membership of these bodies is unknown. In 1974, however, the following individuals were specifically identified by official NFL sources as Presidium members: Nguyen Huu Tho (president), Ibih Aleo, Phung Van Cung, and Tran Nam Trung (vice-presidents), Huynh Tan Phat (vice-chairman and secretary-general), Nguyen Thi Dinh, Thich Thien Hao, Nguyen Van Ngoi, Pham Xuan Thai, Nguyen Huu The, Dang Tran Thi, Nguyen Van Hieu, and Huynh Van Tri. Ho Xuan Son was the only member of the Secretariat to be so identified (although it probably includes Huynh Tan Phat, Ho Thu, Le Van Huan, and Ung Ngoc Ky).

Other members of the Central Committee mentioned officially included: Ho Hue Ba, Ho Thu, Hoang Bich Son, Huynh Cuung, Le Quang Chanh, Le Van Huan, Nguyen Thi Binh, Nguyen Van Quang, Nguyen Van Than, Tran Hoai Nam, and Vo Van Mon.

Perhaps significantly, two known PRP members who also serve on the NFL Presidium failed to receive any publicity: Vo Chi Cong and Tran Bach Dang. Tran Buu Kiem, a Presidium member and former NFL representative at the Paris peace talks in 1968, also escaped attention.

The NFL organizational structure consists of regional committees (for central, eastern, and western Nam Bo, southern and western Trung Bo, the Highlands, and the Saigon-Cholon-Gia Dinh Special Zone), provincial, district, and village-level committees. In addition, the NFL works through a variety of mass organizations. During 1974 the following functional organizations were active:

Liberation Federation of Trade Unions
  Chairman, Tran Hoai Nam; deputy chairman, Dang Tran Thi; members Ngo Quy Can, Lam The Vu, Le Hai, and Trung Binh.
Liberation Peasants' Association
  Chairman, Nguyen Huu The; members Nguyen Xuan Trinh and Nguyen Van Quyen
Liberation Students' and Pupils' Association
  (a distinction is sometimes made which indicates that there might be two separate groups, one for university students and the other for high school students)
  Members Nguyen Thi Chau, Ho Thanh Yen
Liberation Women's Association
  Chairman, Nguyen Thi Dinh; vice-chairman, Le Thi Xuyen; Executive Committee member Nguyen Bach Tuyet; Central Committee members Luu Thi Lien, Ma Thi Chu, Nguyen

Ngoc Dung, Tran Thi Hung, Bui Thi Me, and Mrs. Huynh Tan Phat
Liberation Youth Union
Vice-chairman, Tran Le Dung; Central Commitee members Le Phuong and Nguyen Thi Chau

Other organizations associated with the NFL in 1974 whose activities received news coverage included:

Movement for the Autonomy of the Central Highlands
Chairman: Ibih Aleo
Patriotic and Democratic Journalists' Association
Executive Committee members Huynh Van Ly and Nguyen Trung Trinh
Liberation Writers' and Artists' Association
Chairman, Luu Huu Phuoc; secretary-general, Ly Van Sam; vice-president, Thanh Loan; member, Thanh Nghi
Liberation Red Cross Society
Presidents Phung Van Cung (February), Nguyen Van Thu (August)

Among the most active of the NFL-connected organizations are those associated with external relations. These include:

South Vietnam Afro-Asian Solidarity Committee
Leading members Le Tri, Le Than, Tran Hoai Nam, Truong Binh (vice-chairman)
South Vietnam Committee for the Defense of World Peace (linked to the World Peace Council)
Le Hai, secretary; members: Ibih Aleo, Luu Phuong Thanh, Tran Hoai Nam, Nguyen Ngoc Dung
South Vietnam Committee for the Release of Patriotic and Peace-Loving People Still Detained by the Saigon Administration
Chairman, Thich Thien Hao; leading members: Vo Dong Giang (secretary-general), Ton That Duong Ky, Tran Quang Nghiem, Tran Hoai Nam, Nguyen Dinh Chi, Van Trang, Luu Phuong Thanh (secretary), Le Thi Do
South Vietnam Committee for Solidarity with the American People
Leading members: Tran Hoai Nam, Van Trang, Luu Phuong Thanh (secretary), Le Thi Do
South Vietnam Committee for Solidarity with the Latin American People
Chairman, Le Van Huan; leading members: Vu Trieu Phong, Le Van Quynh (mentioned as president in September)
South Vietnam Peace Committee.
Leading members: Le Hai, Nguyen Ngoc Dung, Nguyen Van Than

The PRG RSVN. The governmental structure of the PRG RSVN consists of elected people's revolutionary committees at the village, district, and provincial levels, topped by a national government composed of the Council of Ministers and the Advisory Council. There appears to be an intermediate, regional-level "PRG representation" which from mid-year was being merged with its counterpart NFL regional committee into a regional people's revolutionary committee.

The PRG RSVN is headed by Huynh Tan Phat as president and Nguyen Don and Nguyen Van Kiet as vice-presidents. They are asissted by the president's office, in which Ho Xuan Son appears to be the most active member. It was thought that the Council of Ministers was composed of eight ministries, but recent information suggests that there are three other ministries, not yet publicly identified (according to reports from the liberated areas brought back by a member of a visiting Australian peace movement delegation).

The present ministerial leadership consists of Nguyen Van Kiet (education and youth), Nguyen Thi Binh (foreign affairs, assisted by deputy ministers Le Quang Chanh and Hoang Bich Son), Luu Huu Phuoc (information and culture, assisted by deputy Thanh Nghi), Phung Van Cung (interior), Truong Nhu Tang (justice), Tran Nam Trung (defense), and Duong Quynh Hoa (public health, social affairs, and war invalids (assisted by deputy minister Bui Thi Me). Also, on 10 August the LPA announced that Duong Thanh Long had been appointed deputy minister for economy and finance; it was assumed that Nguyen Van Trieu continued as acting minister. Nguyen Van Hieu was identified as a minister of state without portfolio.

The following were identified as members of the Advisory Council: Nguyen Huu Tho (president), Trinh Dinh Thao (vice-president), Ibih Aleo, Huynh Cuong, Thich Don Hau, Le Van Giap, Pham Ngoc Hung, Nguyen Dinh Chi, and (*VNA*, 10 January) Nguyen Thi Dinh, who appears to be the only addition. (Nguyen Cong Phuong was erroneously included in last year's list [*YICA, 1974*, p. 563]; it has now been confirmed that he died on August 21, 1972.) No mention was made of the following individuals or their activities who have in the past been identified as members of the Advisory Council: Huynh Van Tri, Lam Van Tet, Vo Oanh, and Huynh Thanh Mung.

The VANDPF. The Vietnam Alliance of National Democratic Peace Forces, formed in April 1969, joined with the NFL in June of that year to form the PRG. It consists of urban-based intellectuals. During 1974, with the rise of an urban-based anti-thieu movement, the VANDPF was given increasing prominence. Its national leadership was identified as follows: Trinh Dinh Thao (chairman), Thich Don Hau (vice-chairman), Ton That Duong Ky (secretary-general), Thanh Nghi and Le Hieu Dang (deputy secretaries-general), and Nguyen Van Kiet (member of the Standing Committee).

The leadership of the Saigon-Cholon-Gia Dinh committee consisted of Le Van Giap (chairman), Truong Nhu Tang (vice-chairman), Nguyen Thi Trang and Van Trang (deputy secretaries-general), and Nguyen Thi Cam and Pham Ngoc Hung (members of the Standing Committee. Le Van Hao was identified as chairman of the Hué VANDPF committee.

Domestic Attitudes and Activities. *Attitudes.* According to senior PRG officials, the PRP is just another party among several comprising the NFL. Asked by UPI correspondent Tracy Wood to point out the "influence of the People's Revolutionary Party on the resolutions of the NFLSV and the PRGSV," President Huynh Tan Phat replied: "Together with the other political parties [Democratic Party, Radical Socialist Party] and organizations affiliated with the NFLSV [listed above] the Vietnamese People's Revolutionary Party, which is also a component of the NFLSV, strives to implement the NFLSV's political action program." (Liberation Radio, 12 December 1973).

While Phat's observation may be true, it is only partly so. Overall guidance for communist activities in South Vietnam is set by the VWP's Central Committee meeting in plenary session. Southern leaders play an intimate role in drawing of the broad policy resolutions. The VWP Politburo issues specific directives, based on Central Committee resolutions. These resolutions and directives are then forwarded to COSVN, which produces even more specific guidelines. According to P. J. Honey, who had access to defectors' testimony, sometime in late June 1973 a group of high-level COSVN leaders journeyed to Hanoi "to study the definitive plan for South Vietnam drawn up by the Party leadership and to make any amendments which might seem necessary in the light of the southern situation before the plan was finalized" (CNA, no. 973, 13 September 1974, p. 5). Honey also states that this "master document" was still in effect as late as September 1974, although it was subject to certain modifications. In summary, VWP leaders were said to have held out slight hope that a political settlement, based on the 1973 peace agreement, would be reached as long as Richard Nixon remained U.S. President. With this in mind, they drew up a new policy geared to the 1976 U.S. presidential elections, by which time they hoped to see the establishment of a "National Council for National Reconciliation and Concord." In the meantime they built up massive stocks of military supplies and improved their communications network so that they had at least the capacity to defend themselves and the capability to launch a crushing attack against the Army of the Republic of Vietnam (ARVN).

Honey summarized the new policy in this way:

> The plan therefore called for increased military pressure in South Vietnam designed to win more territory there for the communists and to put them in a strong position to demand further concessions from the U.S. and South Vietnam. The overall plan governing such military operations called for the employment of small regular military and guerrilla units everywhere, coupled with stronger action by larger main-force units in a few selected areas chosen to enable the communists to expand their territorial and population control.
>
> Alongside this military campaign there would be a programme of political action regarded by some, at least, of the communist leaders as no less important. The first and most essential part of the programme would have to be the rebuilding of the cadre structure in South Vietnam. . . .
>
> Also in the political programme is a campaign to improve the somewhat bedraggled image of the [PRG] both within the country and abroad. A second "People's Convention" would be held . . . probably toward the end of 1974 . . . at which the name of the PRG would be changed to "government of the People's Republic of Vietnam." (Ibid.)

However, there is other evidence of the VWP's intentions which can be added to this view. Shortly after the 20 December 1973 meeting between Henry Kissinger and Le Duc Tho in Paris, the VWP Politburo convened and decided not to exercise its military capabilities for an all-out attack on the RVN. It should be recalled that the final quarter of 1973 was marked by repeated predictions that the communists would launch a massive conventional offensive (*YICA, 1974*, p. 566). Unfortunately no clear picture has emerged at this time from the contradictory press accounts, based on leaked information from U.S. intelligence sources. It will, therefore, be necessary to summarize the information at hand.

The most authoritative report on the new VWP policy line appeared four days after the Kissinger-Tho discussions (Philip McCombs, *Washington Post* 24 December 1973). McCombs wrote: "Hanoi has apparently decided against a major offensive in South Vietnam for the next six months, but may then turn to an all-out offensive if it finds progress toward victory slow." A careful reading of this account, especially its references to a series of articles in the November issues of *Quan Doi Nhan Dan* and to "COSVN Resolution 4," makes it appear that these decisions were taken before the Kissinger-Le Duc Tho meeting, possibly in the autumn of 1973.

This impression is strengthened by the confused reporting of two columnists (*Boston Globe*, 10 April 1974), who obviously relied on leaked intelligence information. They stated that the VWP decision to postpone a military offensive was taken at the 21st Plenum, held in either November or December of 1973, and that this new strategy was incorporated in "COSVN Resolution 13," drawn up in December. The existence of a "COSVN Resolution 13" was inferred from a document captured in Binh Thuan Province. Yet the excerpts cited are identical with passages of a document published that month (April) in Saigon (*Vietnam Documents and Research Notes*, no. 117). According to an introduction attached to the document in question ("Guidelines for Binh Thuan Province," dated 5 February 1974), it was a distillation of the latest VWP resolutions "probably taken from COSVN Resolution 12."

The picture is further complicated by a report by James Markham (*NYT*, 28 February), which stated that a "Resolution 21" of the VWP's Central Committee was drafted after the 20 December Kissinger-Le Duc Tho talks. According to Markham, this resolution contained a "respectful" analysis of ARVN strength, urged a heightening of the political struggle movement against ARVN incursions and foresaw no major military initiatives in the South.

From all the evidence presented so far it seems fairly certain that a major policy statement, perhaps a COSVN resolution, was drawn up in December 1973 (Charles W. Corddry *Baltimore Sun*, 3 January 1974). It is also known that the VWP Politburo met after 20 December and decided to convene the 22d Plenum, which was held in either late January or early February 1974 (*CNA*, no. 953). According to Corddry, captured directives indicated that COSVN had decided (in December) on a strategy of "increased but limited military pressure on Saigon's forces in widely separated parts of the country," to be accompanied by other measures. These were: to maintain an unhindered supply route to the Mekong Delta, to intensify attacks in selected areas in RVN-controlled territory, to continue to harass ARVN base areas and communication lines, and to undermine the ARVN's strength so as to cause the balance of forces to shift in favor of the PLAF.

To date, the most detailed explanation of party policy to emerge in print is the Binh Thuan Province document, dated 5 February and entitled "Political Reorientation and Training Materials for Infrastructure Cadres and Party Members." Since the document was drawn up at the province level it is only an abridged version of a COSVN resolution (whether number 12 or 13 is not clearly known), whose text is only circulated at the regional level. The document is divided into three parts: reasons for victory, the current situation and missions, and some principal missions. Of interest is the list of shortcomings and weaknesses enumerated in part two where the admission is made that "the enemy is still able to control populated areas and communication routes and to utilize manpower and property of their area of control." Other faults include:

- Our liberated areas are large, but have few people.
- Our Party Chapters are not yet close to the masses and have so far failed to become the nucleus to guide the in-place movements.
- Our in-place forces are still weak and undermanned; the guerrilla warfare movement is not yet strong.
- Our three-pronged offensive is still weak and uneven.

Part three of this document reaffirmed that the basic mission of the revolution was still the national democratic revolution aimed at the "U.S. imperialists and the ruling capitalists, bureaucrats, militarist fascists, and active lackeys of the U.S. imperialists." In order to accomplish this basic mission successfully, the document listed five "immediate missions and tasks" and six "principal tasks":

Five immediate missions and tasks:

(a) Use the slogan of peace, independence, democracy, improved living conditions and national concord in order to accomplish national reunification . . .

(b) Push our attacks strongly in all areas; combine the three types of forces in three areas in a three-pronged offensive; foil all enemy mopping-up and land-grabbing operations designed to seize liberated areas . . . Regain areas occupied by the enemy . . .

(c) Strongly promote the political struggle in order to gradually reach the high tide of revolution in urban areas . . .

(d) Strengthen our three-pronged offensive of military, political, and military-proselytizing activities, coordinating with the legality of the agreement . . .

(e) We should grasp the standpoint: The revolution in South Vietnam can only be won by means of armed violence in close coordination with the political violence of the masses.

Six principal tasks:

1. We must maintain the armed forces and strongly develop our militia and guerrilla forces . . .

2. We should concentrate our efforts in the contested and weak hamlets and villages and carry out comprehensive attacks . . .

3. Strive to motivate the masses to build revolutionary bases and broaden the struggle movement . . . in order to create conditions for promoting the rising struggle in cities and towns.

4. Strive to develop the liberated areas (including base areas) and safeguard and protect large and small liberated areas and penetration and base areas.

5. Increase motivation and organization.

6. We should intensify the operations of the party and groups on two fronts: ideology and organization.

Later in the year the RVN's Political Warfare Agency claimed to have acquired the text of COSVN Resolution 12 (Agence France Presse, Hong Kong, 12 June). According to a summary, this document contained a call for the formation of a "people's unified front" (*Vietnam Press*, morning edition, 15 August). This front was to attract specifically the bourgeoisie, intellectuals, and members of other political parties and religious communities who were not members of the NFL. The RVN summary provided these further details:

> Resolution No. 12 of the communists defines that the front would adopt a program of action in conformity with the mottos of struggle and advocate a government of freedom, democracy, coalition and neutrality in South Vietnam which would establish diplomatic relations with and receive aid from all world countries (without any political conditions). This front would also work to build a self-sufficient economy, to encourage capital development in the country and to improve the people's living standards with a view to strengthening the political force in the coming phase of political struggle to isolate and weaken the RVN Government.

Two other indications of the PRP's attitudes emerged in 1974. In May there were reports of another COSVN resolution, no. 6, which barred trade and movement between the PRG and RVN areas of control and also restricted movement within PRG areas. According to Peter Collins (*FEER*, 2 August, pp. 10-11) these new regulations were adopted to keep people in the liberated areas. If this report is correct, and there must be some doubt that it is, it represents a change from the present pattern whereby the PRG has seemingly encouraged trade and has paid handsomely to keep it going.

In October the PRG finally responded to the growing movement of urban non-communist opposition to the Thieu government by issuing a major policy statement which, for the first time since the cease-fire, demanded the overthrow of the Thieu regime. In the words of the PRG's 8 October statement:

> The Provisional Revolutionary Government of the Republic of South Vietnam highly appreciates any statements, any actions truly favorable for peace, independence, and democracy in South Vietnam, now invites all political forces, regardless of their political and religious character, and all individuals who, regardless of their past, genuinely wish the war be ended, peace and national concord be achieved to join one another in unity and in concerted actions to [push] for an end to the United States' military involvement and interference in South Vietnam, the overthrow of the Nguyen Van Thieu [administration] and his clique and the establishment in Saigon at an early date of an administration willing to implement the Paris Agreement seriously. This is the most correct way to put a stop to all the sufferings and disasters that have been brought upon our people. (LPA, 8 October; distributed by DRVN Embassy, Canberra, Australia.)

Activities. Locating any reportage on PRP activity has proved as elusive as in previous years. Virtually no mention was made of the PRP by either Liberation Radio or the LPA in 1974, although the activities of the Ho Chi Minh People's Revolutionary Youth Union (PRYU), a PRP affiliate, did receive some coverage. Prominent members of the PRP are identified by the titles or positions they hold in other organizations associated with either the NFL or PRG, and only rarely by their PRP positions.

This lack of visibility does not mean that the PRP does not exist. A careful reading of reporting on the activities of NFL-affiliated groups reveals the presence of senior party-members. Occasionally direct mention of the party is made in a public speech. Such was the case with Lieutenant General Tran Van Tra's remarks at a ceremony marking the founding of the PLAF (15 February). According to excerpts broadcast by Liberation Radio (30 March), Tra said, in discussing a recently launched PLAF emulation movement: "The Political Bureau has issued concrete instructions." Later in his address he spoke about the political tasks entrusted "by the party and people."

The Ho Chi Minh PRYU has been described as "the revolutionary assault force and the reserve unit of the party [PRP]" (Hanoi radio, 5 august 1973). Sometime in January 1974 it was reported that three provinces had held conferences of provincial delegates to review the activities of the previous year and to set forth the new tasks for the coming year, and to elect new executive committees (Liberation Radio, 10 January). The provinces included: Khanh Hoa (20 delegates), Quang Da (sixth) congress; 200 representatives) and Quang Nam. Later, it was announced that the Kontum province Ho Chi Minh PRYU had "recently" held its fourth congress, with 160 representatives in attendance (ibid., 1 March).

In mid-May, the Ho Chi Minh PRYU of Eastern Nam Bo held its third conference, attended by "hundreds" of delegates from province and district levels, as well as by representatives of local PLAF units and by members of the PRYU's Central Committee. A report was given on achievements scored by young people since January 1973, new tasks were set, and a new executive committee was elected. There were no further details. (Ibid., 14 May.)

On the forty-third anniversary of the PRYU (which obviously dates itself from the founding of the ICP's youth organization) two public statements were broadcast: a set of instructions and an appeal. The instructions comprised a three-point guideline:

1. Launch a political activity drive [and] give attention to the experience in building the group . . .
2. Review the achievements, offer commendations and rewards, and hold congresses on the village, district, and province level to greet the achievements of the youths in defeating the U.S. aggressors . . .
3. Launch an emulation drive to score achievements. . . . The contents of this emulation drive are: strive to frustrate the enemy's pacification and encroachment scheme; consolidate and expand the liberated areas; win and protect the people, including the youths; train oneself to acquire the ethics and behavior for a new way of life; admit new members into the youth group, and organize the study of the group's statute and five tasks to help improve the quality and behavior of youth group members and overcome the failure to get closer [to] the masses. (Ibid., 20 March.)

The appeal of the PRYU's Central Committee broadcast for the anniversary on 26 March (ibid., 24 March), stated in part:

The youths in the liberated areas, in the armed forces, and in the various organs must stand ready for combat, actively engage in productive labor, practise thrift, study hard, train themselves, improve their standards and contribute to building the liberated areas. In this way they will become strong politically and in national defense, prosper economically, and contribute to building a new civilized life, in solidarity, order, and discipline They must stand ready to welcome the youths coming from the areas under temporary enemy control or from the ranks of the Saigon army, who come to build the liberated areas.

The PLAF. On 1-6 February 1974 the PLAF held the fourth "South Vietnam Heroes' and Emulation Combatants' Congress." This congress was attended by the most senior officials on the insurgent side: Huynh Tan Phat (PRG president), Tran Nam Trung (PRG defense member), Thanh Nghi (VANDPF), Tran Van Tra (PLAF, Central Committee member of the VWP), Tran Quoc Vinh (alias for Major General Tran Do, an alternate member of VWP Central Committee), Senior Colonel Le Chan (PLAF; alias Le Van Tuong), Phung Van Cung (PRG interior minister), Nguyen Huu The (Liberation Peasants' Association, senior PRP member), Phan Min Tan (secretary of the Central Committee of the PRYU), Truong Thi Hue (Standing Committee member of PRYU Central Committee), and Ly Van Sam (secretary-general of the Liberation Writers' and Journalists' Association).

According to Tran Nam Trung, the congress was being convened to "implement all the directives and resolutions issued recently by the higher echelons." He was undoubtedly referring to the December resolutions discussed previously, as well as decisions taken at the VWP 22d Plenum (see *Vietnam: Democratic Republic of Vietnam*).

The most important speeches were given by Le Chan (a seven-part report) and Tran Van Tra. The two most significant decisions undertaken were to launch a "determined-to-win" emulation movement and to proceed with the thorough modernization of the PLAF (that is, turning it into a conventional army). Tran Nam Trung set forth four "major tasks" to be undertaken by the PLAF following the congress:

1. Constantly heighten the spirit of revolutionary vigilance and sharpen their determination to fight.
2. Positively participate in the revolutionary movement and in building local revolutionary forces, serve as core elements in the people's struggle movement, and develop the impetus of the three-pronged offensive aimed at frustrating the enemy's nibbling schemes and pacification plans . . .
3. Make strenuous efforts to develop their strength in all respects and consolidate and increase the combat strength of the three troop categories by intensifying the organizational tasks, studies, and training, satisfactorily carrying out the rear base and logistical tasks, and intensifying the political task among the armed forces . . .
4. Participate in building and firmly strengthening the liberated zone in all respects, protect the lives and property of the people, accelerate production to achieve self-sufficiency and improve living conditions, build revolutionary bases, and implement all front and government lines and policies in an exemplary manner. (Liberation Radio, 3 March.)

The Peace Agreement. No progress has been achieved toward reaching agreement on any political provisions in the 1973 Paris peace agreement in the bilateral talks between representatives of the PRG and the RVN, held at La Calle Saint-Cloud near Paris. On 22 March 1974 the PRG tabled a major six-point proposal which served as their basic position for the remainder of the year. These six points are, in summary:

1. Immediate end to the shooting and strict observance of the cease-fire throughout South Vietnam
2. Return of all captured and detained Vietnamese civilians and military personnel
3. Full democratic liberties to be ensured immediately to the people
4. Prompt establishment of the National Council for National Reconciliation and Concord
5. The organization of truly free and democratic elections
6. Settlement of the question of armed forces
(Distributed by NFL Permanent Mission in Djakarta, Indonesia)

The PRG delegation to the bilateral talks was headed by Nguyen Van Hieu, and during his absence (10 January-1 April; 17 May-   ) by Ambassador Dinh Ba Thi. Duong Dinh Thao, transferred from duties in Saigon, served as official spokesman.

In Saigon, the year was marked by the resumption of prisoner exchanges between the PRG and the RVN, suspended since July 1973. They were carried out in three phases during February and March, with the RVN releasing 31,502 persons and the PRG 5,942. Unfortunately this auspicious start was not duplicated, as fighting around South Vietnam (in particular the RVN "loss" of Tong Le Chan) resulted in a suspension of the activities of the Two-Party Joint Miliatry Commission (JMC) in May. These sessions were briefly resumed in June when the RVN restored privileges and facilities to the PRG delegation (which it had suspended earlier). On 22 June, after a DRVN vessel (LC-174) was sunk in the Cua Viet estuary, the sessions were again suspended. This was the last forum still functioning under the 1973 peace agreement. Later in the year the PRG halted all activity of the Four-Party Joint Military Team (JMC), accusing the United States of continued involvement in South Vietnam's internal affairs (and frustrating U.S. efforts to recover the bodies of certain missing-inaction soldiers). The PRG also refused to meet its share of the expenses (23 percent) for the running costs of the International Commission for Control and Supervision (ICCS).

In September the PRG accused the Iranian and Indonesian delegations on the ICCS of bias in "unilaterally investigating alleged cease-fire violations."

The PRG delegation to the Two-Party JMC is headed by Major General Hoang Anh Tuan, who is assisted by Colonel Vo Dong Giang. The PRG delegate to the Four-Party JMT is Lieutenant Colonel Vo Tho Son.

According to the PRG, the total number of RVN cease-fire violations committed between 28 January 1973 and 20 October 1974 was 459,979 (VNA, 21 October).

Relations with the North. A tangled web of party, military, and government interaction quickly confuses any discussions of North-South relations. It is known that the PRP is considered a regional (and hence subordinate) branch of the VWP. Yet as a regional branch headed by a special Central Committee directorate, it also exercises a certain amount of autonomy. It is also known that senior cadres in the South participate in the highest-level party decisions. Part of the confusion arising from a study of North-South relations is embedded in this paradox: on the one hand, party members assert that Vietnam is one country and that all Vietnamese have a sacred right to defend the fatherland anywhere on Vietnamese soil, on the other hand, party policy apparently has been to insist that organizations in the south are autonomous and independent entities.

In the case of military forces, for example, DRVN officials usually respond to questions about the presence of PAVN units in the South by avoiding an outright denial of their presence and by quickly referring to the 1973 peace agreement as evidence that there are none in the South (they are not mentioned as either North Vietnamese or foreign troops). PRG officials respond to questions about the presence of PAVN forces in the South by terming the question as "impertinent" or a "slander." Despite this obfuscation there can be no doubt that there are PAVN forces south of the 17th parallel, and that they have been reinforced by infiltration from the North since January 1973.

Estimates of PAVN forces in the South are "notoriously unreliable" (*FEER*, 22 July 1974). For example, last year (*YICA, 1974*, p. 560) an estimate of 270,000 to 300,000 PAVN soldiers was given. This was based on RVN sources and was reached by totaling the maximum estimates of infiltrators to existing strength and by adding on the maximum estimates of the "Viet Cong infrastructure." A more realistic estimate for late 1973, according to U.S. sources, would be in the range of 120,000 to 170,000. Another analysis, drawing on figures issued as late as February 1974, concluded that a net reduction of PAVN forces had occurred if repatriation figures (40,000 to 50,000 returned to the North) and attrition rates (RVN) claims as killed 38,630 enemy soldiers) were figured in (*Stockholm International Peace Research Institute Handbook, 1974*). A similar conclusion was reached in the Moose-Meissner Report cited above. The authors concluded:

> Since the Paris Agreement was signed, the North Vietnamese have sent between 100,000 and 120,000 men to the south. Their casualties during this period have been substantial, however, and these losses, together with the sizeable totals of men exfiltrated, reduce the net increased in Communist forces in the South since the cease-fire to about 30,000 men ... but in the last few months (April-May 1974) North Vietnamese strength has actually been dropping and in April 1974, the North Vietnamese and Viet Cong total was estimated to be about 184,000 men.

These conclusions are also consistent with subsequent estimates of PAVN troops for August 1974 which put the total number at 140,000 to 160,000 (information supplied privately to the author by a U.S. government official). These men are organized into 15 fully operational main-force divisions, in addition to several smaller, autonomous units, such as anti-aircraft regiments operating in the South. These units are dispersed as follows (using RVN designations):

Military Region I	6 PAVN divisions, 4 artillery regiments, and 1 anti-aircraft regiment
Military Region II	3 PAVN divisions, 1 artillery division, and elements of the PAVN 7th and 9th divisions
Military Region III	3 PAVN divisions plus elements of the PAVN 7th and 9th divisions
Military Region IV	1 PAVN division, the 1st
Above DMZ	2 PAVN divisions, the 304th and 308th

These military units are supplemented by support, logistics, and engineering units totalling an additional 40,000 to 70,000. There is some evidence that the DRVN has sponsored a settlement scheme in the central Highlands and in PRG-controlled Quang Tri Province. Estimates of the total numbers involved vary enormously: 6,000 (David Shipler, *NYT*, 31 March), 40,000 (Peter Collins, *FEER*, 2 August), and 70,000 (George McArthur, *Los Angeles Times*, 13 February). These figures may include a small portion of Vietnamese who had regrouped north of the 17th parallel during the war (Collins, *FEER*, 2 August; Shipler, *NYT*, 31 March).

Other sources have commented on the repatriation of PAVN soldiers back to the DRVN (Michael Parks, *Baltimore Sun*, 10 April). The numbers involved, also varied, range from 40,000 to 50,000 (*International Herald Tribune*, Paris, 14 February).

In order to maintain this number of men in the South, it has been necessary to develop a communications-logistics system to bring in supplies, materials, and petrol. There are about fourteen airfields which have been reconstructed since the 1973 cease-fire: Dong Ha, Khe Sanh, and Ai Tu (in Quang Tri Province), Camlo, Dak Tho, Duc Tho, Ben Het, Polei Kleng, and Phuong Hoang (in the central Highlands); Bo Duc, Loc Ninh, Katum, Minh Thanh, and Thien Ngon (northwest of Saigon). Khe Sanh is heavily defended by SAM anti-aircraft missile batteries, and both it and Dong Ha airfields are judged capable of handling up to MIG-21 jet fighters (*FEER* 11 March; *Aviation Week and Space Technology*, 25 February).

Since the 1973 peace agreement some 20,000 engineering troops and civilian laborers have succeeded in building more than 1,000 miles of roads in South Vietnam, the most impressive being so-called Corridor 613, a 375-mile, two-lane, crushed rock all-weather road which runs from the DMZ to Dar Lac Province in the Highlands. This route potentially replaces the Ho Chi Minh Trail. This system is supplemented by at least three hard-surfaced, pressed crushed-rock, all-weather roads in Quang Tri, Kontum, and Tay Ninh provinces, as well as by lesser trails.

Corridor 613 is paralleled by a system of fuel pipelines and pumping stations which were expected to reach the vicinity of Loc Ninh by October 1974. This entire logistics complex has made it much easier for the DRVN authorities to continue the infiltration of military supplies and equipment to the south. During 1974 it was estimated that 27 anti-aircraft regiments (totaling 1,600 AA guns) and 4-5 battalions of SA-2 missiles were moved south, some elements as far as the Iron Triangle (Collins, *FEER*, 30 August). Other equipment sent south includes 400-600 T-34, T-54, and PT-76 tanks; over 200 130-mm. artillery pieces, as well as a very sophisticated array of other weapons: SAM-2, SAM-3, SAM-6, Strela SA-7 missiles; 23-mm., 85-mm., and 100-mm. radar-controlled anti-aircraft guns; 85-mm. and 122mm. artillery pieces; 82-mm. and 120-mm. mortars; 107-mm. and 122-mm. rockets; 75-mm. recoilless rifles; AT-31 wire-guided missiles; and so on.

This enormous involvement by the DRVN in sending soldiers and equipment must inevitably raise questions of political control. One foreign correspondent who visited the liberated areas of the RSVN reported: "They [PRG officials] were also careful to avoid any suggestion that North Vietnamese units were in the area or that northerners might have any kind of an influential role in the Vietcong political and administrative setup." (Philip McCombs, *Washington Post*, 6 August). Another correspondent has described the relationship this way: "North Vietnam has made no attempt to bring Vietcong-controlled areas of South Vietnam under northern governmental control, with the exception of the northern areas of Quang Tri Province bordering the demilitarized zone, one American official reported. That part of the province has been annexed by Hanoi, he said, and governing officials there are North Vietnamese." (David Shipler, *NYT*, 31 March). This observation is reinforced by Peter Collins's report that "although Dong Ha is normally under the control of the PRG, intelligence sources say the town and areas north and west of it have been integrated into the administrative structure of North Vietnam" (*FEER*, 2 August). Other observers have reported that whereas the Saigon piastre is used as legal tender elsewhere in the liberated areas, DRVN currency is used in Quang Tri Province. These reports of DRVN-PRG control in Quang Tri are in contrast with the impressions of sympathetic visitors who must present visas on crossing the Ben Hai river (and this includes U.S. peace movement personalities as well as touring Russian artists).

International Relations. The PRP made no public statements on international affairs nor did it send or receive any delegations in 1974. The PRP's twelfth anniversary went unheralded by foreign communist parties, thus reinforcing the observation that "the international communist movement does not recognize the independent existence of the PRP" (*YICA, 1973*, p. 567). During the year messages of greeting sent to the congresses of the Austrian, Australian, and Portuguese communist parties were signed by the NFL Central Committee. The French Communist Party (November 1973), the Italian Communist Party (March 1974) and the All-Union Lenin Young Communist League from Russia (May) all sent delegations to the liberated areas of the RSVN. No mention was made that they were received by or had held talks with PRP officials. During April a delegation from the Liberation Youth Union (led by Tran Le Dung) attended the congress of the Lenin Young Communist League in Moscow (LAP, 22 April).

The PRG was recognized by five countries during 1974, thus raising to 42 the total number of countries granting diplomatic recognition: Guinea-Bissau (20 May), Malagasy Republic (10 June), Mauritius (14 June), Mauritania (14 June), and the Arab Republic of Yemem (13 September). Both Sweden and France raised the level of their relations with the PRG by allowing the PRG's Bureau of Information to be converted into a "general delegation" (*tong dai dien*) and a "permanent delegation" (*phai doan thuong truc*) respectively. In August it was rumored that India was preparing to grant formal recognition to the PRG (Vietnam Press, 2 August).

During the year a number of high-level foreign delegations were received by PRG officials in Quang Tri Province, including: Swedish parliamentarians and government officials (4-7 January), China-Vietnam Friendship Association members (9-11 January), a Bulgarian Committee for Solidarity with Vietnam group (7 March), a delegation of the Hungarian Peace Council (19 May), a delegation from the Emilia Romagna area, Italy, (408 June), a joint delegation of the National United Front of Cambodia-Royal Government of National Union of Cambodia, led by Khieu Samphan (11-13 June), a second Swedish delegation, comprising government aid officials (16-18 August), an Australian Peace Movement delegation (October). There was also a visit by the deputy premier of Hungary (31 October-1 November).

A number of PRG and NFL delegations made overseas trips. Nguyen Huu Tho, president of the PRG's advisory council, accompanied by senior government officials, visited India, the U.S.S.R., Poland, and Hungary during December 1973, and during 1974 visited the liberated areas of Laos in January, North Korea in August, Bangladesh, East Germany, Czechoslovakia, Albania, and Bulgaria in September, Mongolia in September-October, and Syria, Iraq, and the DRVN in October.

PRG foreign minister Nguyen Thi Binh kept up an intense mid-year schedule, attending the Organization of African Unity's summit conference in Somalia (12-16 June), after which she visited the People's Democratic Republic of Yemen, Malagasy Republic, Mauritius, Egypt, Algeria, Republic of Guinea, and East Germany. Nguyen Thi Dinh, president of the South Vietnam Liberation Women's Association, led delegations of her organization to conferences in the DRVN, Laos, China, Poland, the U.S.S.R., East Germany, Hungary, and Cuba. Other Women's Union delegations visited Algeria,

Bangladesh, and Senegal.

PRG minister of health Duong Quynh Hoa led an important series of delegations overseas, stopping in the DRVN, Sweden, East Germany, the Netherlands, Belgium, Italy, Hungary, France, and England, from February through June.

Other NFL-affiliated organizations sent delegations abroad, the most significant of which were: a tour of India, Nepal, and Afghanistan by the South Vietnam Afro-Asian Solidarity Committee in May-July and a subsequent stop in the U.S.S.R. in August; a visit to Australia by members of the Liberation Students' Union in September-October, a visit to Japan by a PRG table tennis team in September-October, and a visit to China by a People's Delegation from South Vietnam led by Thich Thien Hao in August.

Publications. The PRP produces two major publications for use by its members: the official party weekly *Nhan Dan* ("The People"), and a monthly theoretical journal, *Tien Phong* ("Vanguard"). The "central organ" of the NFL's Central Committee is *Giai Phong* ("Liberation"). The PLAF produces *Quan Giai Phong* ("Liberation Army"). The official paper of the VANDPF is *Lien Minh* ("Alliance"). PRG diplomatic posts and information bureaus distribute *South Viet Nam in Struggle* in both English and French for external consumption. Other news coverage is carried by Liberation Press Agency (sometimes abbreviated GPA for Giaiphong Press Agency) and by Liberation Radio.

The Australian National University   Carlyle A. Thayer

THE AMERICAS

Argentina

The Communist Party of Argentina (Partido Comunista de Argentina; PCA) originated from the Internationalist Socialist Party (Partido Socialista Internacionalista), a split-off from the Partido Socialista. It was established in 1918 and its present name was taken in 1920.

The PCA in early 1974 claimed to have 126,000 members. Non-communist sources put the party membership at a considerably lower figure. The population of Argentina is about 24,350,000 (estimated 1970).

PCA membership, two thirds of which is said to be concentrated in the Federal Capital (city of Buenos Aires) and in Buenos Aires Province, is drawn mainly from the urban middle and lower classes. Although no such data seem to have been issued for the 1973 congress, the class distribution of delegates to the previous congress, in March 1969, gives some idea of the social composition of the membership: 72 workers, 10 members of the liberal professions, 6 teachers, 6 writers and journalists, 4 peasants, 2 housewives, and one student. The party claims to have made substantial gains among peasants and students between 1969 and 1974. The PCA is believed to be financially well off through its indirect participation in various commercial and banking enterprises. In June-July 1974 the party carried out a drive to raise a billion pesos, and at the time of launching this campaign it announced that in 1973 it had been able to raise 700 million pesos. (Radio La Opinion, 25 June.)

The PCA was legalized by President Héctor Cámpora in one of his first acts after assuming the presidency in late May 1973. The PCA congress in August of that year was the first legal one in 27 years and only the second held under legal conditions since 1930.

In addition to the PCA, which is pro-Soviet, communist parties in Argentina include the Revolutionary Communist Party (Partido Comunista Revolucionario; PCR), and the Communist Vanguard (Vanguardia Comunista; VC), both of which are pro-Chinese, and a Trotskyist movement, split into various factions, at least one of which is dedicated to terrorism and guerrilla war.

In recent years, other small leftist groups (composed of Castroite or Peronista extremists, or both) have emerged. While most of these do not espouse communist ideologies, they have a shared strategy of armed struggle to seize power. Their total membership, reportedly distributed in as many as 15 different organizations, has been estimated at between 6,000 and 7,000. After the assumption of power by Peronista President Cámpora in May 1973, the avowedly Peronista terrorist groups generally threw their support behind the new government and denounced the continuation of guerrilla activities by Trotskyist groups. However, in the latter part of 1974 some of these groups, including the most important of them, the Montoneros, resumed guerrilla activities, this time against the government of President María Estela (Isabel) Martínez de Perón.

The PCA. Leadership and Organization. The PCA is led by Gerónimo Arnedo Alvarez as secretary general. Other leading figures in the party were indicated by those named to the presiding board of the National Congress in August 1973: Rodolfo Ghioldi, Rubens Iscaro, Alcira de la Peña, Héctor P. Agosti, and national deputies Jesús Mira and Juan Carlos Domínguez. Orestes Ghioldi is also a leading figure in the party. The PCA is organized pyramidally from cells, neighborhood committees, and local committees on up to provincial committees and the Central Committee, Executive Committee, and Secretariat.

The PCA youth movement, the Communist Youth Federation (Federación Juvenil Comunista; FJC) is organized along the same lines as the party. It claims 40,000 members. It provided 50 of the 510 delegates to the PCA 1973 congress. The FJC's strength is concentrated largely in the student movement, and it has benefited to some degree from the radicalization of the students in recent years, although it is vastly overshadowed by the Peronista student groups.

The PCA is weak in the labor movement despite the presence of party units in many unions. The major trade union body, the General Confederation of Labor (Confederación General del Trabajo; CGT) is completely controlled by Peronistas who are very powerful and generally reject communist interference. The communists are strongly opposed to the CGT leadership. However, they have little influence in the principal area of resistance to the national CGT, the province of Córdoba, where the dissident faction is led by pro-Maoist and pro-Trotskyite elements, as well as by left-wing Peronistas.

The PCA controls the Movement for Trade Union Unity (Movimiento de Unidad y Coordinación Sindical; MUCS), which represents some small regional unions, mostly those centered in Córdoba and Mendoza provinces. PCA Central Committee member Rubens Iscaro is secretary-general of the MUCS, as well as being closely associated with the World Federation of Trade Unions, although the only Argentine elected to the General Council of that organization at its 1973 congress was Susana Errasti (*World Trade Union Movement*, November-December 1973, p. 67).

Although peasant organizations are mostly grouped under the non-communist Argentine Agrarian Federation (Federación Agraria Argentina; FAA), the PCA claims to be active in the Union of Agrarian Producers of Argentina (UPARA), formed in 1969. UPARA is composed of small and medium farmers, and claims to have 60,000 members.

Most PCA fronts, such as the Argentine League for the Rights of Men, the Union of Argentine Women (UMA) and the Argentine Peace Council, were illegal for many years until 1973. There is, however, also communist participation in the Argentina Women's League, in MODENA (a group of civilians and retired military seeking to protect national resources).

PCA National Meetings. There were three national meetings of the PCA of some consequence during 1974. One was a plenum of its Central Committee, another a national conference of the party, and the third a congress of its youth organization.

In theory at least, the second-highest body within the PCA, after the party congress, is the plenum of its Central Committee, composed of members of the committee and representatives of various provincial organizations. There was apparently one plenum meeting during 1974, late in June. It featured a speech by Secretary-General Arnedo Alvarez, in which, according to TASS, he said that the political situation was "characterized by a sharpening of contradictions between those who defend the interest of the nation on the one hand, and foreign monopolies and the oligarchy on the other." Arnedo Alvarez also expressed PCA support of "all the measures of the present government aimed at intensifying the process of liberation of Argentina," and noted that "there are conditions for the unification of the popular political parties on the basis of a single platform." He added that "such a unification would make it possible to strengthen in near future the unity of action of all the patriotic forces and form a popular unity government, reflecting the interests of the majority of the Argentine People." (Radio Moscow, 26 June.)

At an unstated date in the first half of the year a national conference of the PCA was held particularly to consider organizational matters. There it was reported that 27,950 new members had joined the party since April 1972 and that the party membership stood at 126,000. Organizational secretary Athos Fava announced a goal of a party membership of 200,000 and an FJC membership of 100,000. He reported that there were 3,216 party cells, and that the party was aiming to establish 3,000 new cells, of which 2,000 would be organized in industrial plants, 500 among farm workers, and 800 among women. (*WMR*, June.)

On 4-7 June the FJC held its Tenth Congress, the first in ten years to meet legally, with 600 delegates in attendance, along with fraternal delegates from 18 foreign countries. The delegates were received and addressed by President Juan Perón in the presidential palace at Olivos.

Domestic Attitudes and Activities. The political situation of Argentina was particularly unstable in 1974. President Juan Peron, who had been elected in October 1973 after having been out of office and a virtual pariah for more than 18 years, died on 1 July. He was succeeded by his widow, the vice-president. With the succession of María Estela (Isabel) Martínez de Perón, the existing split within the Peronista ranks grew to critical proportions, as a result of which former Peronista guerrilla groups returned to terrorist activities. During the last months of the year, the country's most serious immediate problem was a wave of assassinations of Left, Right, and Center political figures, which threatened to undermine the fabric of society.

Throughout the year, the PCA expressed its support for the maintenance in power of the Perón administration, although also noting disagreements with certain government actions. The PCA had supported Juan and Isabel Perón in the 1973 election.

On 23 January, the PCA Executive Committee issued a statement in connection with the attack by the Trotskyite ERP guerrillas (see below) on the Azul military garrison in Buenos Aires Province. This statement noted that "the PCA reaffirms its acknowledged position of categorically rejecting such attempts which are, in fact, against the masses since they favor the plans of reactionaries and imperialism." After expressing doubts about some recent government measures, the statement added: "If General Perón's government wants to push forward the liberating process, it will have the backing of the overwhelming majority and will be able to defeat the conspiracy plotted by the Central Intelligence Agency. However, anything that goes against the people's will will aggravate the atmosphere of social unrest and political instability." (Radio FRELA, Buenos Aires, 23 January).

On 25 February the Executive Committee issued another statement which pointed to "the danger of terrorism unleashed in the country by the ultra-right elements with which extremist actions of the ultra-left elements merge." It claimed that there was "a vast plot of the reactionary circle backed by large imperialist monopolies and the CIA." (Radio Moscow, 25 February.)

About a month later, on 19 March, the PCA newspaper *Nuestra Palabra* extensively praised a statement by the leader of the Peronista bloc in the Chamber of Deputies, Ferdinando Pedrini, who had said: "What I demand as an Argentine and as a defender of institutions is a constructive opposition which will be at the service of the country and which will establish a pattern so that all of us, Peronists, Radicals, Communists and whoever else it may be, may definitely liberate and construct the country, in order that we never again have coups d'état."

On 8 April a PCA delegation consisting of Rubens Iscaro, Orestes Ghioldi, and Fernando Nadra, met with General Perón. After this session, it was reported that "the Communist Party . . . stated its support for the national government with regard to its handling of the institutional policy" (Radio Telam, Buenos Aires, 8 April).

An interview with Nadra, in the Italian communist daily *L'Unità* (23 April) gave some indication of the basis of PCA support of the Perón administration. After noting that Presidents Cámpora and Perón both had promised "national liberation," Nadra commented: "Perón and his government have implemented a few important measures with respect to our national liberation. For example: the upholding, from many viewpoints of foreign policy and national sovereignty in the face of imperialism, the development of broad diplomatic and trade relations with the U.S.S.R. and the socialist world and the contribution made to the running of the blockade against Cuba by the drawing up of important trade agreements with Havana and the visit of a large delegation of Argentine entrepreneurs to the island. . . . What is lacking—and there is a delay in this respect—is a series of measures of a domestic nature which will uphold and consolidate this foreign policy."

On 3 May, "sources close to the Central Committee of the Communist Party" reported to the newspaper *La Opinión* that the PCA approved of Perón's message to Congress on the morning of 1 May, but considered his speech of that afternoon as having a "negative context which contradicts everything that was said in the morning." It was "important to point out these mistakes to the government," because they contributed to "frustrating the process of profound change which we all desire." An article by Iscaro in *World Trade Union Movement* (May) indicated some of the government policies with which the PCA disagreed. These included the "social compact" signed the year before by the CGT and the employers' Confederación General Económica to maintain wage and price stability, and the threats by the Ministry of Labor to withdraw legal recognition from unions which broke the social compact.

Early in June the PCA Executive Committee issued another attack on "political terrorism, from the far left as well as the far right." It said that terrorism suits the reactionary forces of the country, and urged the government to take steps to counter popular unrest arising from shortages and inflation. (Radio EFE, Madrid, 5 June.)

On 13 June the PCA sent a delegation to meet with interior minister Benito Llambi to tell him of their support for a speech by Perón. It was noted that the delegation, consisting of Nadra, Iscaro, and Rodolfo Ghioldi, had said that the time had come "for all political parties, for all democratic and anti-imperialist forces to unite and share a common stand to defend the constitutional regime" (Radio TELAM, Buenos Aires, 13 June).

On 25 June the PCA made the first statement of a desire to participate in the Perón government, which it was to repeat at various times later in the year. Nadra urged the formation of a coalition cabinet "made up of all the country's progressive forces who are against coups and who support national liberation" (*La Opinión*, 25 June).

When Juan Perón fell fatally ill at the end of June, the PCA Executive Committee immediately expressed its support for vice-president Isabel Perón, who had taken over the presidential duties. The statement warned that reactionary elements might try to take advantage of the confused situation to carry out a coup. (Radio Moscow, 30 June.) Upon the death of Perón, the PCA reiterated its support. The Executive Committee on 12 July pledged the party to "make an earnest effort to establish a National Democratic Front or a Coordinating Center in defense of the constitutional regime under María Estela Martínez de Perón, against the offensive of the rightists" (*IB*, no. 16).

The PCA took part in the Second National Unity Assembly, on 29 July. This was a meeting of virtually all political parties, to rally support for the constitutional regime.

Obviously perturbed by the maneuvers of right-wing Peronista elements to control the administration of Isabel Perón, the PCA Executive Committee issued a statement on 1 September entitled "The Decisive Moment Draws Nearer." After again warning of a coup by reactionary elements, the statement attacked "the right wing Peronists," who "support those in the federal police who collaborated with the dictatorship, facilitate subordination of autonomous provincial government bodies, and interfere in the affairs of militant trade unions." The statement ended with this assertion:

> The Communist Party declares its readiness to share responsibility for carrying out the following tasks:
> 1. Resolutely oppose the plotters against the people and the country; prevent a reactionary coup from destroying the established order; protect human and civil rights.

2. Consistently apply, with broad participation of workers and other people, the law against the disruption of supplies.

3. Ensure the holding of a Constituent Congress which should adopt a modern constitution, as well as orderly elections in 1977.

4. Ensure implementation of the minimum common program of all parties and democratic and anti-imperialist forces sharing the aspirations and just demands of the working people and oriented on progressive changes in the socio-economic structure of the country. (*IB*, no. 18.)

About two weeks later, the PCA, through Athos Pava, again emphasized its concern for the constitutional regime. Pava commented that "the party is seeking to promote the union of the democratic forces of Argentina so as to defend constitutional development, so that an insuperable barrier can be set up to prevent the reaction from carrying out a coup."

However, symptomatic of the cooling of relations between the government of Isabel Perón and the PCA was the fact that the party was not among those invited to the multi-party consultative meeting on 8 October.

International Views and Contacts. During 1974 the PCA continued its traditionally pro-Soviet attitudes. Various PCA delegations visited Eastern Europe and the Soviet Union. In July the PCA was a host to a delegation of the Communist Party of the Soviet Union. On the occasion of his 75th birthday, PCA leader Alvarez was awarded the Order of the October Revolution by Soviet president Podgorny (Radio Moscow, 24 September).

Publications. The PCA's *Nuestra Palabra* appears weekly. *Nueva Era* is the party's monthly theoretical journal. It publishes also the bimonthly *Cuadernos de Cultura*, catering mainly to intellectuals, and (since August 1970) the *Boletín de Informaciones Latinoamericanos*, a fortnightly report. The FJC has a fortnightly, *Juventud*.

*　　*　　*

The PCR. The Revolutionary Communist Party (originally the Communist Party of Revolutionary Recovery) was created in January 1968 by dissidents from the PCA, especially the youth organization, who rejected the PCA's attempted "broad democratic front" as an effort at "class conciliation" and "conciliation with imperialism." César Otto Vargas is the PCR secretary-general; another leading figure is Guillermo Sánchez. Several PCR leaders held important positions in the FJC before expulsion from the PCA in 1967.

The PCR tends to be pro-Maoist, advocates armed struggle, and believes that leadership in the revolutionary movement must be held by the party. It favors only urban guerrilla struggle, contending that the "wide plains" of Argentina and the "highly developed agriculture of the coast" would not permit successful operations. There is no evidence of any recent participation in guerrilla activities.

In August 1974 a PCR Central Committee delegation, led by Sánchez, visited China at the invitation of the Central Committee of the Chinese Communist Party (*Peking Review*, 16 August).

The PCR fortnightly paper *Nueva Hora* was clandestine until 1973, since when it has appeared legally.

The VC. The Communist Vanguard, probably founded in 1964, is pro-Chinese and reportedly has some influence among student and worker groups. Since 1973 its fortnightly newspaper *No Transar* has been appearing legally. During 1974 the VC was hostile to the Perón government and very critical of the Soviet Union. *Peking Review* (31 May) saw fit to praise articles critical of the Soviet Union in *No Transar* (and also the PCR *Nueva Hora*).

*   *   *

Trotskyism is represented in Argentina by varied groups. The Socialist Workers Party (Partido Socialista de Trabajadores; PST), and the Revolutionary Workers Party (Partido Revolucionario de los Trabajadores; PRT) both have, or have had, affiliation with the United Secretariat of the Fourth International. The PRT has spawned the so-called People's Revolutionary Army (Ejército Revolucionario del Pueblo; ERP), a guerrilla group. In 1973 the PRT and the ERP split into factions, and PRT-ERP leaders said that they no longer considered themselves Trotskyists.

The Trotskyist Labor Party—Partido Obrero (Trotskista)—is aligned with the International Secretariat of the Fourth International headed by J. Posadas, an Argentine. Politica Obrera is apparently an independent group. Another element of Trotskyist origins, the Partido Socialista de la Izquierda Nacional, has formally foresworn allegiance to Trotskyism, while still revering Trotsky.

The PRT-ERP. The PRT was founded in 1964 and divided in 1968, when two thirds of the members espoused the tactic of armed struggle. The views of the majority faction are expressed in *El Combatiente*, which still appears clandestinely, and those of the minority in *La Verdad*.

The "armed branch" of the majority faction is the ERP, in existence since August 1970. The ERP was at first particularly strong in Córdoba and Rosario, with some influence in Tucumán and Buenos Aires, and in recent years it has operated in virtually all parts of the country.

The principal ERP leaders, Mario Roberto Santucho Juárez and Enrique Harold Corrianán Merlo, are members of the 11-man Executive Committee of the PRT. The ERP follows a cellular type of organization; a political commissar in each cell is appointed by the PRT.

During 1974, ERP terrorist activities reached an unprecedented level, both in frequency and boldness. Late in 1973, Santucho wrote in *El Combatiente* that the ERP was "increasing its power constantly and at an ever faster pace," and went on:

> In the present circumstances of a rapid change from a pre-revolutionary situation and a political awakening of the masses, the role of the revolutionary vanguard takes on enormous weight and significance. The content and pace of the development of a new conscience of the masses depends directly on the clarity, sobriety, the energy and the political initiatives—as well as the military initiative—of the revolutionary vanguard. (Radio Prela, 1 November.)

On 20 January 1974, the ERP sent 60 men in army uniform against the army base at Azul, 170 miles south of Buenos Aires. Fighting lasted for five hours, and at least five persons, including the commander of an army tank regiment and his wife, were killed. Lieutenant Colonel Jorge Roberto Ibarzabal was kidnaped. (*NYT*, 21 January.) President Juan Perón used this incident to win passage of a very strong anti-guerrilla law a week later. Eight Peronista members of the Chamber of Deputies resigned because they were unwilling to vote for the law. On 14 February three ERP leaders held a clandestine press conference, attended by foreign journalists and representatives of some local papers, to demand release of two captured ERP members, and threatened to kill Ibarzabal if they were not freed.

On 13 April the ERP kidnaped Alfred Laun, head of the U.S. Information Service in Córdoba, whom they accused of being an agent of the U.S. Central Intelligence Agency. They claimed they wanted to "interrogate" Laun. Ten days later it was announced that another victim of ERP kidnapping, Victor Samuelson, manager of the Exxon refinery at Campana, had been released after being held for seven weeks, in return for a record ransom payment of $14.2 million. On 30 May, apparently in response to a police raid on an ERP training camp in Tucumán Province ten days earlier, 40 ERP terrorists occupied the town of Acheral.

In mid-June the ERP announced the establishment of its first rural guerrilla front. At the same time it announced that it was giving $5 million to help guerrilla groups of Bolivia, Chile, and Uruguay (Radio Latin, Buenos Aires, 12 June), with whom it had formed a Revolutionary Coordinating Committee (JCR) earlier in the year (see *Chile*, "Appendix" on JCR).

Following the death of Juan Perón there was a two-week "truce" between the ERP and the government. This was ended by the ERP with the kidnapping and murder of the editor of the La Plata newspaper *El Día*.

In August, ERP terrorists launched simultaneous attacks on army installations in the provinces of Córdoba and Catamarca. In the former, 60 men seized the army's explosive factory in Villa María and succeeded in getting away with substantial quantities of arms and munitions. In the latter, an attack on the 17th Airborne Infantry Regiment resulted in a substantial defeat for the ERP, with 19 members killed and 20 captured. (*Christian Science Monitor*, 2 August.) Among those killed was Antonio del Carmen Fernández, first military chief of the ERP.

Subsequent to this major showdown, which involved not only the Federal Police, who had hitherto dealt with guerrilla activities during the Perón regime, but also the Argentine Army, the ERP announced its intention of killing "army officers indiscriminately" in revenge for the guerrillas who had died in Catamarca. In the weeks that followed, various military leaders were assassinated by ERP units. In a strong denunciation of the terrorist group, President Isabel Perón accused the ERP of "trying to provoke a military coup" (*NYT*, 7 September).

For reasons which remain unclear, early in October the ERP issued a proposal, in the name of Santucho, for a "truce" with the government, offering to call off military operations if captured ERP leaders were released, repressive legislation was repealed, and legalization of the ERP was enacted (*Washington Post*, 8 October). The government seems to have paid little attention to this.

ERP guerrilla activities continued, but there were some indications by the end of 1974 that the terrorists had been substantially crippled by the police and army offensive during the last months of the year.

Estimates of the number of ERP activists have varied considerably. The *New York Times* (24 January) estimated that there were 2,000 guerrillas and a further 12,000 supporters, organized in "political cells." The *Washington Post* (4 October) reported an ERP claim of 10,000 guerrillas. There were no indications of a persistence of the three-way split in the PRT and ERP that took place in the previous year. The guerrilla operations were apparently the work of the major ERP faction headed by the guerrilla group's founder, Mario Roberto Santucho.

The PST. A veteran Trotskyist, the aforementioned Nahuel Moreno, headed the faction of the original PRT that was opposed to guerrilla activities. At the end of 1971 it joined with a faction of the Socialist Party headed by Juan Corral to form the Socialist Workers Party (PST). During 1974 the PST remained very critical of the Perón government while doing its utmost not to be declared illegal and having no ostensible contacts with the ERP.

Late in 1973 the PST had held a special congress, which gave some indication of its size. There were 371 delegates present, each of whom was said to have represented 10 members. Guests reportedly were present from neighboring countries and from the Socialist Workers Party of the United States. Corral and Moreno were the principal speakers. (*Intercontinental Press*. New York, 21 January 1974.)

The PST criticized President Juan Perón's introduction of a bill for repressive action against the guerrillas in January, but added: "We believe that the kidnappings and executions have done nothing to develop the struggles and independent organization of the workers" (ibid., 4 February). As the government's efforts to repress terrorist activity gained momentum, the PST suffered. In March, Corral was arrested for a short while. In May a PST militant in the Metal Workers Union was killed, presumably by right-wing terrorists. In June three other PST members were assassinated. In November the PST headquarters in Buenos Aires was raided by the police. (Ibid., 22 April, 27 May, 18 November.)

Some of the European groups associated with the United Secretariat of the Fourth International criticized the PST for participating in meetings of various parties with the Presidents Perón, and accused it of tendencies towards compromise and "reformism" (ibid., 15 July). It seems likely that this muted controversy was part of a broader polemic going on within the United Secretariat over the question of guerrilla warfare as the road to power.

The organ of the PST is the weekly newspaper *Avanzada Socialista*.

Other Trotskyist Groups. The Partido Obrero (Trotskista) of J. Posadas concentrated most of its activities during the 1974 on its periodical *Voz Proletaria*. It tended to have a more friendly attitude toward the government than did the PRT or PST. The Partido Socialista de la Izquierda Nacional continued to give critical support to the Peronista regime.

*   *   *

Peronista Extremist Groups. During most of the year the Peronista terrorist groups gave support to the government. The most important of these terrorist formations are the Montoneros, the Peronista Armed Forces (Fuerzas Armadas Peronistas; FAP) and the Revolutionary Armed Forces (Fuerzas Armadas Revolucionarias; FAR). However, even while Juan Perón was still alive, the terrorists were becoming increasingly critical of the Administration. In September the Montoneros, the most important Peronista guerrilla group, announced that they were returning to armed opposition to the government of Isabel Perón, which they accused of being "anti-popular." They claimed the backing of Peronista youth groups in this struggle. (Radio Latin, 7 September.)

Rutgers University   Robert J. Alexander

Bolivia

The Communist Party of Bolivia (Partido Comunista de Bolivia; PCB) was founded in 1950 and is pro-Soviet in orientation. A pro-Chinese splinter group became the Communist Party of Bolivia, Marxist-Leninist Partido Comunista de Bolivia, Marxista-Leninista; PCB-ML) in 1965. The Trotskyist Revolutionary Workers' Party (Partido Obrero Revolucionario; (POR) is currently split into three factions. The National Liberation Army (Ejército de Liberación Nacional; ELN) was founded in 1966. The Movement of the Revolutionary Left (Movimiento de Izquierda Revolucionaria; (MIR) was formed in mid-1971 and reorganized after the 21 August 1971 coup in which rightist Colonel Hugo Banzer overthrew the government of leftist General Juan José Torres and seized the presidency for himself.

All of these parties were illegal during 1974. The PCB and PCB-ML are estimated to have 300 and 150 members, respectively (*World Strength of the Communist Party Organizations 1974*, p. 151). The population of Bolivia is 5,000,000 (estimated 1972).

In recent years many Bolivian leftist parties and organizations in the country and in exile have called for the formation of a united opposition to the Banzer government, the most important being the Anti-Imperialist Revolutionary Front (Frente Revolucionaria Anti-imperialista; FRA) founded in November 1971. Among the original members were the PCB, the PCB-ML, the MIR, the ELN, and two factions of the POR. During 1973 the Alliance of the National Left (Alianza de la Izquierda Nacional; AIN) reportedly was formed. In June 1973 a "Call to the Bolivian People" was issued by leaders of the PCB, the PCB-ML, the Revolutionary Party of the Nationalist Left (PRIN) and the Leftist Revolutionary Nationalist Movement (MNRI) to overthrow the "fascist" Banzer government and its North American and Brazilian supporters (see *YICA, 1974*, pp. 282-83). Pressure on the Bolivian left increased after the military coup in Chile in September 1973 when plots against the Bolivian government were reportedly discovered. During 1974 efforts to unite the left were apparently unsuccessful, in large part due to power and other rivalries within and among the parties in Bolivia and in exile.

The PCB. Leadership and Organization. The first secretary of the PCB is Jorge Kolle Cueto. Others prominent in the party include Mario Monje Molina, a former first secretary, and Central Committee members Simón Reyes, Arturo Lanza, and Carlos Alba. Luis Padilla, a member of the Central Committee, is on the editorial board of the Prague-based *Problems of Peace and Socialism (World Marxist Review)*.

The basic organization of the PCB is the cell, which consists of no fewer than three party members. District committees, elected at National Congresses (the most recent in June 1971), exist in each department and in most important mining centers. The National Congress elects the Central

Committee, the latter guiding the party between congresses. The Central Committee elects the Political and Control-Auditing Commissions and the first secretary, and convenes National Conferences to discuss current organizational and political affairs not requiring the convocation of the National Congress. District committees may hold district conferences with the approval of the Central Committee. (*WMR*, September 1973.)

The PCB's youth organization, the Communist Youth of Bolivia (Juventud Comunista de Bolivia; JCB) is illegal. Among the JCB leaders are Jorge Escalera and Carlos Soria Galvarro. At an international conference sponsored by the *World Marxist Review* in mid-1974, Lanza noted that left extremism in Bolivia was closely associated with the social behavior of students as part of the middle strata. He added that despite the ideological vagueness of the Bolivian student movement, there was a clear pattern: ingrained individualism, avant-guardism, voluntarism, anarchic terrorism, and other attributes of leftism. Though the students negate theory, they theorize about the absolute character of action. The youth struggle was acquiring a class dimension, according to Lanza, under the ideological influence of the proletariat. This new development was supported by the PCM while the party intensified its struggle against the "pseudo-left." (*WMR*, August 1974.)

The PCB's main labor leader, Simón Reyes, an officer in the outlawed Bolivian Mineworkers' Federation (FSTMB) spent the year in exile.

Domestic Attitudes and Activities. Bolivia is a victim of predatory imperialist exploitation, according to Luis Padilla. Foreign monopolies, attracted by the country's vast natural resources, act hand in glove with the local oligarchy to destroy Bolivia's unity, promoting so-called "frontier zones of inter-ethnic development" and striving to establish a separatist state in Santa Cruz department. National capitalists, "hanging on to the apron strings of international imperialism," are openly hostile to Bolivian national interests. The strategic objective of the working class, the defense of national sovereignty, is occupying an increasingly decisive place in the political struggle of the Bolivian people. The PCB is firmly convinced that there must be an alliance of all democratic and revolutionary forces against the Banzer government, U.S. imperialism, and Brazilian fascist intervention in Bolivia. Such an alliance "will lead the country to independence, facilitating the establishment of a peoples' government and paving the way to socialism." (*WMR*, September 1974.)

While the PCB encourages the formation of a united revolutionary front, it condemns "ultra-leftism." A Bolivian writer in the *World Marxist Review* (June 1974) maintained the 1971 coup in Bolivia was one element in the U.S. plot to overthrow the Allende government elected in Chile in late 1970. Rehearsing in La Paz its conspiracy against Allende, the secret services of Brazil and the U.S. united the right wing groups, neutralized all progressive and patriotic elements in the armed forces, and incited "leftists"—Maoists, Trotskyists, anarchists—to "superrevolutionary demands and acts of terrorism" on the theory: "Encourage ultra-leftist action to bring ultra-rightists to power." After the Bolivian coup, the CIA and its Brazilian counterpart busily transferred ultra-leftists to Chile from other Latin American countries. Some were misguided while others were on direct instructions from the imperialist secret services. All helped to discredit the Popular Unity government and provoke a military coup.

Publications. The PCB published an irregular, clandestine paper, *Unidad*.

*   *   *

The PCB-ML. The Communist Party of Bolivia, Marxist-Leninist, is headed by its secretary-general, Oscar Zamora Medinacelli. It has suffered from internal disputes in recent years. The youth group of the PCB-ML bears the name of its pro-Soviet counterpart, the JCB.

Domestic and International Attitudes and Activities. In September 1973, Oscar Zamora described the Banzer government as a "heinous military-fascist dictatorship imposed by U.S. imperialism [and] its gendarme for Latin America, the military dictatorship which oppresses the Brazilian people." According to Zamora, the PCB-ML is working for the Unity of the Bolivian people to overthrow the Banzer government by means of revolutionary action as a first step toward national liberation and ultimately socialism. The party remains an unshaken admirer of Mao Tse-tung and the Chinese Communist Party. Its expressed positions on international issues have paralleled those of the Chinese communists. (See *Peking Review*, 12 October 1973.)

Publication. The PCB-ML organ is *Liberación*.

*   *   *

The ELN. The National Liberation Army was founded in 1966 and became internationally famous under the leadership of Che Guevara. The chief leader of the ELN in 1974 was evidently Osvaldo "Chato" Peredo. Many ELN members have been lost by desertion or killed by the government in recent years.

Early in 1974 the ELN announced that it had joined an international Revolutionary Coordinating Committee (Junta de Coordinación Revolucionaria; JCR) with the Uruguayan National Liberation Movement (MLN: Tupamaros), the Chilean Movement of the Revolutionary Left (MIR), and the Argentine People's Revolutionary Army (ERP). A JCR statement issued on 13 February 1974 criticized both bourgeois nationalism and reformism, "two tendencies in thought and action that gravely obstruct the revolutionary efforts of Latin Americans." The JCR's program stated that "the only viable strategy in Latin America is one of revolutionary war . . . a complex process of both armed and unarmed, peaceful and violent, mass struggle in which all forms develop harmoniously, converging around the axis of armed struggle." (Trans. in *Intercontinental Press*, New York, 11 March; also see *Chile*, "Appendix" on JCR.)

*   *   *

The MIR. The Movement of the Revolutionary Left was formed in 1971 by the Revolutionary Christian Democracy (DCR), the Spartacus Revolutionary Movement (MRE), independent Marxist groups, and others. It seeks to organize the people politically and militarily and to prepare for revolutionary violence.

*   *   *

The POR. The Revolutionary Workers' Party is divided into three factions: the first, under Hugh González Moscoso, is aligned with the Trotskyist Fourth International—United Secretariat; the second faction, headed by the well-known political figure and historian of the Bolivian labor movement, Guillermo Lora, and by Philemon Escobar, were aligned with the French Internationalist Communist Organization (see *France*); the third faction, the POR-Trotskyista (PORT), aligned with the Fourth International—International Secretariat (Posadas branch), is led by Amadeo Vargas.

Hoover Institution   William E. Ratliff
Stanford University

Brazil

In recent years the prospects for organized communist groups in Brazil have been dismal. Even the relative political relaxation following the inauguration of a new president, General Ernesto Geisel, in March 1974, does not seem to have greatly changed this situation, since the effectiveness of repression of far-Left activities by police and military authorities does not appear to have changed.

The original Communist Party of Brazil (Partido Comunista do Brasil), which remains the nation's leading Marxist-Leninist organization, was founded in March 1922. During the 1930s several groups broke away or were expelled from the party, and these formed a Trotskyist movement, which still exists although split into several factions.

In 1960 the original, pro-Soviet party, in an effort to gain legal recognition and to give itself a more national appearance, changed its name to Brazilian Communist Party (Partido Comunista Brasileiro; PCB). A pro-Chinese element broke away the following year and in February 1962 adopted the original party name, Communist Party of Brazil (Partido Comunista do Brasil; PCdoB). Still another source of present far-Leftist groups was Popular Action (Ação Popular; AP), a left-Catholic group originating in the Catholic student movement in the late 1950s, which in the following decade proclaimed itself to be Marxist-Leninist.

Dissidence within the ranks of these parties after the military coup of 1964 led to the formation of numerous splinter groups, predominantly of Castroite tendency, that strongly advocated the use of armed violence to overthrow the government. Some of them, employing urban guerrilla tactics, gained considerable notoriety for a time, but between 1969 and 1972 the death of their most prominent leaders, the wholesale arrests of militants, and continued public indifference or hostility drastically reduced the number and effectiveness of the terrorist groups.

In February 1973 four extremist organizations—the National Liberation Action (Ação Libertadora Nacional; ALN), Marxist-Leninist Popular Action (Ação Popular Marxista-Leninista; APM-L), the Revolutionary Brazilian Communist Party (Partido Comunista Brasileiro Revolucionário; PCBR), and the Palmares Armed Revolutionary Vanguard (Vanguarda Armada Revolucionária-Palmares; VAR-Palmares)—issued a joint statement recognizing the defeat of the guerrilla movement, at least in the short run. Although they called for a long "people's war," there is no evidence that any of the revolutionary leftist groups have had any role in leading sporadic guerrilla outbursts, particularly in the Amazon region. However, in 1974 the PCdoB expressed its support for these armed efforts and some underground Marxist-Leninist publications carried news about them.

The communist movement has been illegal in Brazil throughout most of its existence. Except for one year in the 1920s and for the years 1945-47 (when it reached its largest membership, about 150,000), the PCB has been outlawed. However, from 1947-64 the PCB was allowed to function with varying degrees of freedom, and its members ran for office on tickets of other parties. During the presidency of João Goulart (1961-64), the PCB succeeded in infiltrating and controlling important labor, student, political and bureaucratic bodies. At that time, its membership was estimated at 30,000. In this period other far-Left groups, although not enjoying legal recognition, were also able to operate freely.

The military regime which came to power in March 1964 drove the PCB and other far-Leftist groups underground and banned the existing communist-influenced organizations. Since 1969 certain acts of subversion have been punishable by banishment or death. In practice the death penalty has not been applied by the courts though several dozen Brazilian terrorists have been exiled and others have been killed in shootouts with the police and military.

Estimates of PCB membership have dropped from about 13,000 in 1972 to about 6,000 in 1974. In the latter year the PCdoB was said to have about 1,000 members (*World Strength of the Communist Party Organizations*, 1974). Little is known of the membership of the other Marxist-Leninist groups. The population of Brazil was estimated at 100,000,000 in 1972.

The PCB. Organization and Leadership. The PCB apparatus includes the 21-member Executive Commission (some of whose members reside abroad), the Central Committee (which appears to function chiefly in Brazil, although several of its members also reside abroad), state committees, municipal committees, and local cells in residential districts and places of employment. The Sixth Congress of the PCB, its latest, took place in December 1967. The PCB paper *Voz Operária* (July 1974) said the government had "unleashed brutal repressions" against the party—killing, kidnaping, and torturing its members (*IB*, Prague ed., no. 19).

However, in spite of such statements published abroad, there is little recent information about the party apparatus. The last known plenum of its Central Committee took place in November 1973; it is not clear whether this meeting was held in Brazil or abroad. The limited evidence indicates that defections and police repression have taken progressively heavier tolls at the lower echelons of the PCB organization. There appears to be a full complement of state committees, an incomplete roster of municipal committees, and only a partial and poorly coordinated collection of cells or branch organizations. The November 1973 plenum stressed that "a task of key importance is to build up Party organizations at major enterprises." (*IB*, no. 4, 1974.)

The PCB secretary-general has resided in Moscow since March 1971. In his absence, the party is led by Assistant Secretary Giocondo Alves Dias, said to live in Rio de Janeiro. Other prominent leaders include Zleika Alembert, Agilberto Vieira de Azevedo, Sabino Bahia, Roberto Morena, Augusto Bento, Abel Chermont, David Capistrano da Costa, Armênio Guedes, Luís Tenório de Lima, Olga Maranhão, Felipe Rodrigues, Oto José Santos, Jorge Villa, and Armando Ziller.

The PCB has consistently drawn its leadership and members from the ranks of students, intellectuals, and organized labor. The sentencing of Carlos Eduardo Fernandes Silveira, a 22-year-old student to a year in jail in September 1973 for attempting to reorganize the PCB would seem to indicate that young intellectuals still are playing a role in seeking to reestablish the party.

Domestic Attitudes and Activities. The PCB is an orthodox pro-Soviet party which upholds the theory of the role of the masses in obtaining power and opposes the "reckless ventures" advocated by extremist elements. Its avowed aims are traditional Marxist-Leninist goals, couched in language reflecting the orthodoxy that has characterized the party during most of its existence.

The current thinking and position of the PCB was presented in a resolution of the November 1973 plenum (*Voz Operária*, December 1973; *IB*, no. 4, 1974). This statement started out with the assertion that "the regime has evolved from a reactionary military dictatorship into a military dictatorship of an overtly fascist type." Its main features are: "a semblance of representative democracy involving a regular succession of dictators; all-out efforts to isolate the people, the working class in the first place, from political life; use of the armed forces as a tool of political repression and direct support of the regime; a marked increase in the number of so-called security bodies which play a basic part in the state machinery and the life of the country; terror as the main method of government; mounting control over the structure of the trade unions, which are imbued with the spirit of corporativism and are 'tied' to the state machinery . . . ." The resolution denounced the "Brazilian miracle," saying that it is "based on fierce exploitation of the working class and the toiling people in general," that it "infringes on the interests of even some sections of the bourgeoisie and throws open the doors for foreign monopoly plunder and domination; it thus gives rise to a profoundly anti-democratic political superstructure."

On various occasions, Brazilian communist leaders have stressed the aggressive designs which they attribute to their country's military regime, and view these as converting Brazil into a "sub-imperialism" under the United States. Prestes has accused the regime of "rejecting the possibility of maintaining national sovereignty [and advancing] the thesis of so-called 'interdependence,' that is, total subordination to the higher interests of the imperialist protector" (*WMR*, November 1973).

In *World Trade Union Movement* (April 1974), PCB founder and veteran trade union leader Roberto Morena wrote:

> Brazil is arrogating to itself the right to intervene in any Latin American state whose internal policies threaten the interests of the oligarchies and of imperialism.
> The "theoreticians" of expansionism have conjured up the spectre of "subversive aggression" to justify the conception preached by the Brazilian military dictatorship; they are calling for "living space" (of sad memory) and advocate "preventive war" with the aim of hindering the revolutionary processes and holding back and containing the untiring struggle of the workers and peoples of Latin America for real political and economic independence.

The November 1973 resolution called on "all forces suffering from the fascist military dictatorship to unite in a broad anti-fascist patriotic front comprising all segments of the population—workers, peasants, urban petty bourgeoisie, those sections of the bourgeoisie that are at odds with the regime, political opposition forces, and the ARENA groups rejecting the regime's fascist character."

A statement by the PCB Executive Committee in mid-1974, published in *Voz Operária* (July), outlined the prime political tasks of the party in promoting its policies, particularly in uniting all democratic forces in a patriotic front against fascism:

> (1) Struggle for immediate demands of the working class, all working people, civil servants, etc., at their places of work, in urban and rural trade unions, with the objective of securing wage increases;
> (2) Struggle against high prices and shortages of primary products, which will enable us to expose the financial and economic policies of the dictatorship and step up the struggle against government wages policies;
> (3) Struggle against torture, killings, and kidnappings, for solidarity with political prisoners and the persecuted;
> (4) Promote tasks in connection with the campaign for electing deputies to the Parliament in November, raising the banner of working-class, popular demands, the demands of democratic freedoms. (*IB*, Prague ed., no. 19.)

The Paris daily *Le Monde* (18 December) reported that the PCB considered the substantial gains made by the country's only official opposition party, the Movimento Democrático Brasileiro (MDB), in the 15 November congressional elections, the "starting point of an anti-fascist patriotic" front, in the urban if not the rural areas. The PCB says the party emerged strengthened from the battle. (AFP, 18 December.)

The major political change during 1974 was the advent to power of General Ernesto Geisel in March. He promised a relaxation of the dictatorship and the November elections were reasonably free. The relaxation was perhaps also reflected in the considerable increase in the number of labor conflicts. Although there is no direct evidence that comunists were involved, one of the most important disputes involved the Metallurgical Workers Union of São Paulo, which had been largely controlled by the PCB before 1964.

International Views and Positions. The PCB's strongly pro-Soviet position was reaffirmed in 1974 by publication in Brazil and abroad of the November 1973 plenum resolution, which stated:

> Internationally, the Communist movement is growing stronger. Its unity is more solid, despite all the problems, notably the splitting anti-Soviet policy of the Chinese Communist Party leadership. The socialist camp's successes in building the new society and in foreign policy, and especially the achievements of the CPSU in implementing the Program of its 25th Congress, are of tremendous significance. Our Party declares its firm determination to help fortify the unity of the world Communist movement and promote the struggle for peace, democracy, national liberation and socialism.

Brazilian communists continued to participate during international gatherings of pro-Soviet parties. For example, the conference on "Youth Activity in Society and the Communists," in Prague, 6-8 May, was attended by a delegation representing Brazil (*WMR*, July). Brazilian communists resident abroad comprised the PCB delegations to conferences and ceremonies in communist countries. Among these were Luís Carlos Prestes, resident in Moscow since 1971; Tenório de Lima, who lives in Prague; and Sebastiao Pereira, a candidate member of the Executive Bureau of the World Federation of Trade Unions, also living in Prague.

A significant number of other high PCB leaders and members live permanently outside Brazil, where they serve in the international communist bureaucracy or are assigned as representatives to foreign communist parties. This pattern, as well as the identity of several PCB expatriates, was revealed by a defector, Adauto Alves dos Santos, in December 1972. He pointed out that David Capistrano da Costa and Roberto Morena (who frequently publishes articles on Brazil in WFTU publications) lived in Prague, presumably as officers of the WFTU, while Ana Montenegro and Silval Bumbirra resided in Berlin and Agilberto Vieira do Azevedo served as the contact with the French Communist Party in Paris. Adauto dos Santos also said that three PCB Central Committee members were serving in Latin America. (*O Globo*, Rio de Janeiro, 8 December.) Among members of the General Council of the WFTU elected in October 1973 were Orlando Morgado and Roberto Silvoz, both presumably resident outside Brazil.

Publications. The PCB's clandestine newspaper, *Voz Operária*, the party's central organ, appears irregularly but with reasonable frequency in central and southern Brazil, less frequently elsewhere. The party also publishes a theoretical journal, *Estudos*, and Portuguese-language translations of international communist periodicals, as conditions permit, primarily for distribution to party members. To reach wider audiences the PCB occasionally distributes leaflets.

*   *   *

The PCdoB. Organization and Leadership. The organizational structure of the PCdoB, which was formed by men who had long held leadership positions in the PCB, is believed to be patterned after that of the parent party. Little is known about the number or distribution of currently functioning units, but they are believed to exist in São Paulo, Rio de Janeiro, Espírito Santo, Bahia, and the Northeast.

The PCdoB top leadership has been much reduced in recent years in clashes with police (see *YICA, 1974*, p. 291).

Domestic Attitudes and Activities. As in the recent past, the PCdoB in 1974 appears to have devoted most of its energies to recruitment and the organization of its ranks. University students played a major role in its activities and direction. There is no information as to the degree of its participation in and leadership of the guerrilla fighting which took place along the Araguaia River along the southern border of the Amazon area in the state of Pará. However, on the second anniversary of the outbreak of the struggle, the PCdoB Central Committee issued a message hailing the rebels and underscoring the party's principled adherence to guerrilla warfare: "The appearance of guerrilla groups and detachments as well as the Freedom and People's Rights Union demonstrate in a clear fashion that the crimes of the fascist military have had an effect contrary to what they were trying to achieve. Those facts are an unprecedented development and the great success of armed resistance." In spite of these claims, it should be noted that the Araguaia fighting had little or no impact on general politics in Brazil, or on the rhythm of life in the country.

International Views and Positions. The PCdoB was the first pro-Chinese communist party founded in Latin America, and it has long joined the Chinese Communist Party in condemning "Soviet revisionism." Since the easing of Sino-U.S. relations, however, the PCdoB has been less outspoken in its praise of China and apparently has dropped Mao Tse-tung from its list of giants of international communism. For their part, the Chinese appear to have ceased giving publicity to the PCdoB.

Publications. The PCdoB publishes an irregular clandestine newspaper, *A Classe Operária*, and an occasional journal, *Resistencia Popular*. Its statements were until recently carried by Chinese and Albanian publications.

*   *   *

Castroite Organizations. Like many other Latin American countries, Brazil has seen the emergence of various small subversive groups holding communist and left-nationalist views and advocating "armed struggle" tactics as the means to establish a socialist system. Organizations of this type proliferated in the late 1960s under the leadership of men such as Carlos Marighella, Joaquim Camara Ferreira, and Carlos Lamarca. They functioned chiefly at the regional and local levels, since they were not organized on a national basis, and drew their following mainly from students, and to a lesser extent from workers, former soldiers, and elements of the Catholic church. The revolutionary groups received verbal and, sometimes, material support from Cuba. At one point there were 16 or more terrorist groups operating in Brazil, frequently joining forces to carry out sensational acts of political violence. However, they failed to capture the public imagination. Since the death of their outstanding leaders and under the stress of persistent persecution by security agencies they have steadily declined in strength. Those that still exist probably average fewer than 100 members each. Only seven Castroite groups—the ALN, Marxist-Leninist AP, MOLIPO, MR-8, PCBR, VAR-Palmares, and VPR—are known to have survived, and most of these appear to be under life-and-death pressure from government repressive agencies.

The ALN. The strongest of the terrorist groups has been the National Liberation Action, founded by Carlos Marighella, a one-time PCB member of the Chamber of Deputies, who quit the party in 1967. Subsequently, Marighella became the principal theoretician of urban guerrilla activity in Latin America. Since his death, the ALN has not been able to engage in any major terrorist activities.

Although the ALN was not notably active in 1974, there was a report of its participation in an attempt to reorganize the People's Liberation Movement (Movimento Popular de Liberação; MPO). São Paulo police arrested those involved in this attempt in April.

Other Castroite Groups. Several other extremist groups on the revolutionary left still exist at least in name. Late in 1973, shootouts of members of the PCRB with the police were reported in São Paulo, Rio de Janeiro, and Pernambuco. Several of those who were killed and injured were identified as having participated in bank robberies assassinations, and other terrorist activities.

*   *   *

Trotskyist Groups. At least two Trotskyist groups exist in Brazil. One of these is the Partido Operário Revolucionário (Trotskyista), affiliated with the International Secretariat of the Fourth International headed by J. Posadas. It occasionally issues an illegal periodical *Frente Operária*, largely filled with articles or speeches by Posadas. The other is the Partido Operário Comunista, more or less aligned with the United Secretariat of the Fourth International. It has been officially committed to the strategy of guerrilla war although there is no evidence that it has undertaken any serious guerrilla activities. It published in the Belgian Trotskyist paper *La Gauche* (19 April 1974) a denunciation of other leftist groups which had recently given up commitment to guerrilla activities.

Rutgers University   Robert J. Alexander

Canada

The Communist Party of Canada (CPC) was founded in 1921. It functions legally and has a membership of between 2,000 and 3,000. Canada has a population of about 22 million.

While most of the CPC members are elderly, there is some suggestion of a slight influx of younger members which the *Canadian Tribune* (22 May 1974) noted at the party's convention—the result of an intensive recruitment campaign this year. The membership continues to be composed mostly of old-age pensioners, manual and white-collar workers, and a disproportionate number of people of East European extraction.

The CPC has no representation in the Federal Parliament or in any of the ten provincial legislatures. The party nominated candidates in 69 of the 264 constituencies in the 8 July federal election. As a result, and after some negotiation with broadcasting authorities, for the first time in its history the party was granted free-time political broadcasting in an election campaign. Party secretary William Kashtan and two other candidates appeared on 27 June for six and a half minutes beginning at 8:30 p.m. on the English national television network of the Canadian Broadcasting Corporation and for the same amount of time on the French network at 11:00 p.m. On 29 June, Kashtan was heard for three minutes on both French and English radio of the government-owned network. Nine minutes of free television time was given to the party in both Toronto and Montreal by the Canadian Broadcasting Corporation. The Vancouver station of the privately owned Canadian Television network granted 30 minutes.

The party obtained 12,074 votes in the election, only 0.13 percent of the total cast. Several party members or sympathizers, however, were elected to municipal councils and school boards across the country.

The United Fishermen and Allied Workers Union, on the West Coast, and the United Electrical, Radio, and Allied Workers Union are run by party members. Communists are influential on several district and town labor councils and in the British Columbia Federation of Labour. The CPC controls a half dozen ethnic organizations of Canadians of East European origin.

Leadership and Organization. There was no change during 1974 in the leading personnel of the party or in its organization. William Kashtan is national secretary, Alfred Dewhurst is national organizer, Bruce Magnusson is labor secretary, and William Sydney is treasurer. The party has committees in all provinces except the four Atlantic provinces. An attempt is under way to set up a club in Halifax.

The Parti Communiste du Quebec (PCQ) continues to enjoy a certain autonomy within the CPC.

Domestic Attitudes and Activities. About 200 CPC members attended the Twenty-second Congress of the party, held in Toronto on the weekend of 18-20 May 1974. They passed resolutions urging abolition of provincial sales tax, supporting a federal minimum wage of $3 an hour, cost-of-living escalator clauses in union contracts, and reduction of interest rates on working peoples' home mortgages to a maximum of five percent. The delegates welcomed the creation of the Canadian Petroleum Corporation as "the cornerstone of an integrated energy policy embracing all energy resources and based on public ownership." (*Canadian Tribune*, 22 May; also see *IB*, Prague ed., no. 17.)

The party sent observers to the second annual conference of the Ontario Anti-Poverty Coalition, held in Toronto in February, and delegates to the Canadian Peace Congress in Toronto in April.

Kashtan undertook three national tours, two during the federal election campaign and the third in the last two weeks of November.

The Young Communist League (YCL) held its fourteenth annual convention in Toronto on the weekend of 28 June-1 July.

International Views and Positions. The CPC and its publications continued to favor the strict implementation of the Paris agreements on Vietnam and Canadian withdrawal from the North Atlantic Air Defence Agreement, and urged recognition of the Palestine Liberation Organization as the "legitimate expression of the Arab people of Palestine" (*Canadian Tribune*, 23 October 1974).

International Party Contacts. During 1974 Kashtan made two trips abroad. In January he headed the delegation of the CPC to a conference in Prague sponsored by the periodical *Problems of Peace and Socialism*. He met with Gustav Husák, secretary-general of the Communist Party of Czechoslovakia on 16 January and with Jozef Lenárt, secretary-general of the Slovak Communist party and member of the Presidium of the Czechoslovak party, on 18 January. A week earlier, he met with Yugoslavia's president, Josip Broz Tito, in Brdo.

On 2 August, Kashtan met with Boris N. Ponomarev, member of the Central Committee of the Soviet party in Moscow and then spent the next ten days vacationing in Bulgaria, meeting near Varna with party and state leader Todor Zhivkov on 10 August.

Publications. The CPC publishes the theoretical journal *Communist Viewpoint* six times per year and two weeklies: *Canadian Tribune* (Toronto) and *Pacific Tribune* (Vancouver). The PCQ issues the fortnightly *Combat* (Montreal). The organ of the YCL, *Young Worker* (Toronto), appears irregularly and has a circulation of 5,000. Party members edit pro-communist weeklies in eight languages other than English and French.

The North American Edition of the Prague-based *Problems of Peace and Socialism* is printed in Toronto as the *World Marxist Review*. The fortnightly *Information Bulletin* is its companion publication.

*   *   *

The Communist Party of Canada (Marxist-Leninist), or CPC(M-L), which is Maoist, nominated candidates in 101 constituencies for the 1974 federal election and obtained 16,281 votes, 0.17 percent of the total cast. Compared with the CPC, they were especially visible in the province of Quebec, where they were nominated in 38 of the 74 constituencies while the CPC was nominated in only 14. This presence in Quebec reflects the decision taken in 1973 to move party headquarters from Toronto to Montreal.

The theoretical organ of the CPC(M-L), *Mass Line*, continues to appear irregularly, while the *People's Canada Daily News* (Toronto) republishes news items supplied by the New China News

Agency. The editor, Hardial Bain, is chairman of the CPC(M-L).

The League for Socialist Action/Ligue Socialiste Ouvriere, or LSA/LSO, is the most important Trotskyist organization in Canada in spite of splits which took place in its ranks in 1972 and 1973.

The LSA/LSO publishes the bimonthly *Labor Challenge* (Toronto) and the monthly *Liberation* (Toronto). *The Young Socialist* (Toronto) is the organ of its youth wing, the Young Socialists. All these newspapers engage in polemics with those of other Trotskyist groups and the CPC.

The Revolutionary Marxist Group (RMG) consists of those who broke away from the LSA/LSO, the Red Circle composed of some left-wing members of the New Democratic Party, and the Old Mole, a student group at the University of Toronto. The Groupe Marxiste Revolutionnaire (GMR) is the RMG's "sister organization in Quebec." Its founders were French Canadian Trotskyists who broke away from the LSA/LSO in the summer of 1972.

The Workers League of Canada, which is the Canadian section of the International Committee of the Fourth International in Paris, confines its activities to Montreal. Its monthly, *Labor Press*, appears in English and French and is printed in the United States.

The Canadian Party of Labour (CPL) was founded by some of those who broke away from the Progressive Workers Movement, the first Maoist organization in Canada. Like the Progressive Labour Party in the United States, the CPL followed a pro-Maoist line until the improvement in Sino-U.S. relations. Its monthly, *Worker* (Toronto), publishes articles in English, French, and Italian.

University of Rochester

Peter Regenstreif

Chile

The Communist Party of Chile (Partido Comunista de Chile: PCCh) was first established as the Socialist Workers' Party in 1912 by Luis Emilio Recabarren. The name PCCh was adopted in January 1922 following the party's decision in 1921 to join the Communist International. The party was declared illegal between 1948 and 1958. A pro-Chinese party, the Revolutionary Communist Party of Chile (Partido Comunista Revolucionario de Chile; PCRCh) was established in May 1966, primarily by a group of communists expelled from the PCCh in 1963. The Movement of the Revolutionary Left (Movimiento de Izquierda Revolucionaria; MIR) brought together several leftist groups in 1965 and soon developed an affinity for the form of revolutionary struggle advocated during the late 1960s by Che Guevara and Fidel Castro.

All of these groups were illegal throughout 1974. Alluding to the PCCh, the PCRCh, the MIR, and some other parties, the president of the constitutional commission in Chile late in the year said that the new constitution being drafted for the country "will establish that those parties which, through ideology or the behavior of their members, are opposed to the democratic regime, will be against the Constitution and the law" (*Christian Science Monitor*, 13 November 1974).

The PCCh, which reported a membership of 60,000 at the time of its last congress in 1969, claimed 200,000 members in early 1973. A prominent party leader has written that more than 12,000 members of the PCCh and the Communist Youth (see below) were killed during the first year of military rule (Rodrigo Rojas, in *Pravda*, 10 September). At its height before the military coup the PCRCh probably had several hundred active members. The MIR, which may have had 5,000 members in mid-1973, began to suffer serious losses at the end of 1974 (see below).

The Anti-fascist Alliance. Between 1956 and 1969 the PCCh allied itself for electoral purposes with the Socialist Party of Chile (Partido Socialista de Chile; PSCh) in the Popular Action Front (Frente de Acción Popular; FRAP). In 1969 the PCCh played a leading role in founding the FRAP's successor, the Popular Unity (Unidad Popular; UP), whose presidential candidate, PSCh leader Salvador Allende, was elected president of Chile in 1970. This fluctuating coalition of six or more leftist parties and movements dominated by the PCCh and the PSCh held the executive branch of government in Chile between November 1970 and September 1973 and sought to lay the foundations for socialism amidst ever more widespread national dislocations and, during the last year in particular, rapidly increasing popular disillusionment.

On 11 September 1973 the Chilean military ousted the UP from power and shortly thereafter declared the participating parties and movements illegal. Operating on two levels—as exiles abroad with wide international support, and underground in Chile—the groups immediately began to reestablish their alliance and to work for an even more broadly-based coalition, a national anti-fascist front.

Representatives of seven former UP and other leftist organizations signed joint statements in December 1973 (Rome), February 1974 (Paris), and August 1974 (Budapest). The signatories were mostly old members of the UP, including the PCCh, the PSCh, the Radical Party (PR), the Christian Left (IC), the Movement of United Popular Action (MAPU), and a MAPU splinter group calling itself the Worker-Peasant MAPU (MAPU-OC). Also signing was the MIR, at times an ally but often a rival of the UP before and during the Allende term of office.

The Rome statement (in *L'Unita*, Rome, 12 December 1973) was chiefly a condemnation of the military coup, the ensuing government, and a general call for a united opposition front. Similarly, the Budapest statement (*Granma*, weekly English ed., Havana, 15 September 1974) castigated the government after its first full year in power, pointing to political and economic problems faced by an ever larger percentage of the population and predicting an increasingly broad front against the "fascist dictatorship" in the future. The most important exile declaration was the Paris statement (complete in *L'Unita*, 13 February; summarized in *Granma*, English, 24 February). After condemning the barbarous fascist regime, the statement said national discontent with the government existed among the working class, the peasants, and the residents of the shanty towns; opposition was even erupting among small property owners, traders and industrialists. Of particular significance were the increasingly anti-fascist sentiments within the Christian Democratic Party (PDC), the military, and the Christian church. The popular forces had already had their first successes—survival and reorganization. Their present task was to consolidate the anti-fascist alliance between the proletariat and all the other discontented sectors of society, making it potentially the broadest movement in Chilean history. The ultimate objectives were the overthrow of the dictatorship, the elimination of the institutional and ideological bases for its domination, and the destruction of the real masters of the system—national monopoly capitalism and imperialism. The forms of struggle, to be chosen by those residing in Chile, were to be determined by the conditions of the moment.

The first joint statement by the reformed UP coalition in Chile appeared on 1 May (published in *L'Unita*, 15 June). This more comprehensive document denounced the coup instigated by a privileged minority in league with foreign imperialism. The dictatorship had flouted the democracy, liberty, and individual rights it purported to defend. Control over the national economy was being turned over to the monopolies and foreign capital. The vast majority of Chileans now opposed the government and an anti-fascist front was on the way with immediate and longer-term objectives. The former were the recovery of the rights of man and democratic rights, the struggle to defend employment and the standard of living, the resistance to the pauperization of the small and medium farmers, the businessmen and manufacturers, and the defense of national independence. The latter objectives were the fall of the dictatorship and the police state it had created, and the construction of a new, democratic, national, pluralist, people's state. The chief difference between this domestically-produced document and the exile statements was the former's analysis of leftist mistakes made during the 1970-73 period which reflected the guiding hand of the PCCh. The people's movement and its leaders bear the major historical responsibility for the fall of the Allende government. The UP was unable to give unified political leadership which would have enabled the majority of the Chilean people to unite to successfully isolate the absolute minority who actively opposed the UP policies. Indeed, the leadership suffered from ultra-leftist and right revisionist tendencies which led to the increasing isolation of the workers from the majority of the population. This was above all the result of ultra-leftist attacks on the UP and its policies which played into the hands of and significantly strengthened the most reactionary forces. The UP also misunderstood the Armed Forces and failed to strengthen the patriotic over the reactionary sectors. Right wing opportunism was reflected in inadequate demands for radical change in the bourgeois state structure, in too little reliance on the workers in the exercise of power, in administrative corruption, in insensitivity of some officials to mass demands, in extensive economism in some sectors of the workers' movement, in toleration of fascist attacks, and in the failure to adequately mobilize mass support for government policies. Thus the coup was not above all a military defeat, but rather a political defeat for which the leftists themselves were ultimately responsible. By self-criticism, it was hoped that the Chilean left would learn from its mistakes of the past. Many of these same problems were raised—from misunderstanding the army to ultra-leftism and "revolutionary phrase-mongering"—by a prominent UP member in an interview with the Paris daily *Le Monde* on 17 September (see *Intercontinental Press*, New York, 21 October).

Leadership and Organization. The secretary general of the PCCh is Luis Corvalán. The party has a 75-member Central Committee, a 9-member Political Commission, and a 7-member Secretariat. At the time of the September 1973 coup the Political Commission was composed of Corvalán, Víctor Díaz (deputy secretary general), Orlando Millas, Gladys Marín, Mario Zamorano, Volodia Teitelboim, José Cademártori, Rafael Cortés, and Jorge Insunza, with alternates Mireya Baltra and Rodrigo Rojas. The Secretariat was made up of Corvalán, Díaz, Cortés, Zamorano, Riquelme, Julieta Campusano, and Carlos Jorquera. At least four Central Committee members were killed in the first days after the coup, according to Rojas. It is not known how many more party leaders were among the 12,000 communists allegedly killed during the year that followed. (See *Pravda*, 10 September 1974.) Corvalán was captured in late 1973 and remained in prison, still apparently without trial, at the end of 1974. Prominent party spokespersons in exile included Volodia Teitelboim, Orlando Millas, Rodrigo Rojas, Luis Figueroa, Manuel Cantero, and Gladys Marín. According to Millas in August, a majority of the Central Committee members were still active in their positions in Chile, while only a small number of top officials had been given assignments abroad. A limited number of intermediate-level cadres had also been given permission to leave Chile. (*L'Unita*, 4 August.) The party claims to have regrouped since the coup and to be operating underground through all its leading organs and branches (*WMR*, September). Another leader reports that the party circulated 10,000 copies of an appeal in Santiago and that young communists painted 1,000 slogans on walls in one industrial area in a single week. The party meets with other groups of the UP and in particular claims to be strengthening mutual understanding with the PSCh. (*Ankahata*, Tokyo, 12 September.) An alleged secret document from Volodia Teitelboim and other PCCh members in exile (intercepted and released by the military government) calls for the establishment of a party military organization and says that the exiled PSCh leader Carlos Altamirano is "expensive," ideologically infirm, and "does not like to speak together with Volodia." (*FBIS*, 6 September.)

The PCCh-affiliated youth movement is the Communist Youth of Chile (Juventud Comunista de Chile; JCCh). The organization, once strong in most of the nation's universities and among youth generally, has been banned by the present government. JCCh Central Committee member Carlos Ortega acknowledged at an international conference that communist youth had failed to win over a substantial part of the Chilean youth between 1970 and 1973, adding to the isolation of the workers from their potential allies (*WMR*, August). Gladys Marín, JCCh secretary general, visited many conferences and countries during the year.

The PCCh was long the dominant force in the Single Center of Chilean Workers (Central Unica de Trabajadores de Chile; CUTCh), which claimed one million members in 1973, the only important labor confederation in Chile prior to the coup. PCCh Central Committee member Figueroa was reelected CUTCh president in 1972. CUTCh was banned by the military government late in 1973. Its leaders and activists have reportedly adapted to the new conditions and are working underground for the most part, though not neglecting the few legal openings which still exist, such as within the federations recognized by the government (Figueroa, in *Flashes*, Prague, 23 August). Figueroa travelled widely during the year, appearing particularly at international meetings, seeking statements of support for the Chilean anti-fascist struggle. The typical "program of solidarity" sought by the CUTCh envisaged: (1) breaking diplomatic and trading relations with the existing government of

Chile; (2) active denunciation of its representatives wherever they appear; (3) total boycott of arms to Chile; (4) a partial boycott, with practical and achievable aims, of Chile's foreign maritime trade; and (5) concrete forms of material assistance to the trade union movement. In addition he sought international solidarity behind the following immediate demands: (1) an end to the state of war; (2) the freeing of political and trade union prisoners; (3) the reestablishment of human rights and trade union liberties; and (4) an end to tortures and executions. (*World Trade Union Movement*, Prague, September 1974.)

Domestic Attitudes and Activities. Exiled members of the PCCh criss-crossed the world giving speeches and publishing articles with their party's views on the military government, conditions in Chile, essential strategy and tactics for the present time, and analyses of the lessons to be learned from the 1970-1973 period.

The military government, wrote Rene Castillo in a major two-part article entitled "Lessons and Prospects of the Revolution," is a "vengeful, ruthless, reactionary regime uninhibited by the constitution or by law and maintained by force of arms." It has destroyed all forms of democracy: the only pre-coup institutions remaining are a "decrepit judiciary and a puppet Controller-General." Junta policies have nothing in common with bourgeois reformism. The economy is a mess, with inflation, unemployment, instability, and corruption of gigantic proportions. The worst hit are the workers, though the peasants and even the middle strata find life increasingly difficult. The government represents only the "united forces of the imperialists, the monopoly and landed oligarchy." Its policies "dutifully respond to U.S. imperialist diktat." (*WMR*, August; also see Teitelboim, ibid., March; Millas, ibid., September.)

During 1974 conditions became ever more ripe for the formation of the broad united front. Whereas Castillo notes the majority of the Chilean people were not prepared for defense of the Allende government in September 1973, the acceptance of the military began to disintegrate within its first six months in power. The anti-imperialist and anti-oligarchic front of recent years has taken on the form of an anti-fascist front. The participation of the PCCh and PSCh remain essential to the unity of the working class, the UP forces and the politically-minded sectors. The democratically-minded Christian Democrats (those who do not follow former Chilean president Eduardo Frei) must be brought into the front as well as unaffiliated left organizations. Building the front will not be easy. Common viewpoints will have to be identified and practical solutions found for a variety of problems. Contradictions are a logical development but must not become antagonistic. Decisive is the ability of the working class to follow an independent and principled policy which will rule out all right and left opportunism. The party has made efforts to split the existing military by urging "patriotic" elements to join the ranks of the people in the anti-fascist struggle (*IB*, Prague ed., no. 19). In time the front will have to draft a government program for the "destruction of the dictatorial police state and for the creation of a new, law-governed, democratic, anti-fascist, national, popular, representative state."

The PCCh insists that the 1970-1973 experience did not prove that victory in the socialist revolution had to come by armed struggle as claimed by the "reactionaries and the representatives of petty-bourgeois revolutionism who echo them." Though non-armed victory would now be more difficult, the party refused to insist at this point on any unquestioned road to power. It did insist that the anti-fascist front reject individual terror, adventurism, and conspiracy. When the people return to power they will adopt a new constitution and new laws, establish new government departments and institutions. "The new anti-fascist state will guarantee a multi-party structure and the normal activity of all democratic parties." It will carry out a "fundamental reform of the armed forces and the carabineer corps." (*WMR*, August; also see ibid., March; ibid., September.)

Lessons of the Allende Years (1970-1973). For several months after the September 1973 coup the PCCh refused to undertake serious public analyses of leftist shortcomings during the years of Salvador Allende's presidency, arguing that such analyses would "prejudice the popular parties' unity" during a period when unity was essential (see *IB*, 1973, no. 20; and *YICA, 1974*, p. 301). During 1974 the analyses began to appear, however, clearly indicating that the PCCh believes the Chilean left must learn from the failures of the Allende years. In these analyses, the party mentions the obvious resistance put up by "foreign capital and the local oligarchy," but emphasizes the many ways in which the left not only failed to isolate the reactionaries but even played into their hands and strengthened them. (1) The UP was too slow in eliminating old state institutions, even when the reactionaries were misusing those institutions to rebuild their positions; the parties did not fully understand or deal with the problems in the essential terms of class struggle. (2) The UP was unable, in part due to missed opportunities, to gain a dominant position in the press, radio, television, cinema, and schools, through which it could have made a deep political and ideological impact on the masses. (3) The UP was unable to resolve many economic problems which were, on the contrary, aggravated by the reactionaries. (4) The UP was unable to unite the majority of the people behind it and to isolate the main enemies. In Chile during those years it was necessary to win over the "non-monopoly bourgeois groups" (the middle and petty bourgeoisie) in addition to the workers and peasants. (5) "The Popular Unity parties and movements believe that the defeat was due mainly to the absence of a united leadership pursuing a principled policy and avoiding the pitfalls of Left and Right opportunist deviations." One especially important factor which worked against united leadership was the "ceaseless subversion of the ultra-Left elements," what the PCCh has for years labeled "petty-bourgeois pseudo-revolutionary groups," such as the MIR, the PCRCh, and some individuals and groups within the UP, which did "grave damage to the popular movement." (*WMR*, July: also see *YICA, 1974*, pp. 299-300.) The ultra-left groups provoked clashes with potential allies and drove them into the enemy camp; they rejected all compromise and alliances; they rejected any work with progressive Christian Democrats or patriotic members of the military. Ideologically, their dogmatism found expression in virtual disregard of the gains of popular rule. Finally, concluding the longest section of his article, Castillo wrote: "The Chilean experience has reaffirmed that ultra-leftism is a boon for imperialism and reaction." One of the most pronounced features of Right deviation was economism among the more politically backward workers. (6) There were manifestations of bureaucracy. Finally, Castillo concluded:

> The September coup was possible because imperialism and internal reaction had built up a broad anti-government front. This was its class composition: the monopoly bourgeoisie and agrarian oligarchy made up its core and it included the vast majority of the middle and petty bourgeoisie, most of the middle strata, the backward elements of other social groups . . . . We assess our defeat primarily as a political one and only after that as a military one. The isolation of the working class from its allies enabled the reactionaries to launch their coup. Isolation ruled out the possibility of the working class and the people taking up arms. (*WMR*, July.)

International Attitudes and Activities. Prior to the 1973 coup, the PCCh was extraordinarily interested and active in international affairs; during 1974 the party had much more pressing problems. Proletarian internationalism meant chiefly international support for Chileans. Several PCCh leaders travelled ceaselessly, particularly in Europe and the Soviet Union, promoting international opposition to the Chilean military government and support for the anti-fascist front. Their activities were in part responsible for a variety of international meetings and declarations, such as the international Chilean Solidarity Week in September (*IB*, Prague ed., no. 17).

Publications. The PCCh printed some handouts and underground papers during 1974. Abroad, PCCh statements were published in numerous countries, especially in pro-Soviet communist party papers, and in the publications of international front organizations, in particular *World Trade Union Movement* and *Flashes*, of the World Federation of Trade Unions. The PCCh radio station "Radio Magallanes," shut down in September 1973, reappeared in August with political programs twice a week for Chileans on Moscow "Radio Peace and Progress."

* * *

The PCRCh. The Revolutionary Communist Party is a small organization, founded in 1966, with some contacts among students, workers, and peasants. Party statements are made anonymously.

Domestic Lessons and Views. The PCRCh, which has for years argued that revolution could come to Chile only by armed struggle and peoples' war, was not surprised by the military coup of September 1973 which brought an end to the Popular Unity experiment. As an exiled party leader said in December 1973, the party had examined the armed forces carefully in 1971—the results were published in the group's unofficial journal *Causa Marxista-Leninista*, no. 21—and thus knew what to expect. The leader acknowledged, however, that the PCRCh lacked adequate communication with the people and thus had not been able to prepare most Chileans for the events of 11 September. The PCRCh was particularly critical of the PCCh, charging the latter with having spread all sorts of illusions and false hopes among the masses regarding the possibility of peaceful transition to socialism. Though the spokesman discussed the negative role played by the United States and the U.S.S.R., he insisted that internal causes were decisive. The peaceful Road had been tried and failed. Speaking before the PCCh had made any serious analysis of the failures of the Allende period (see above), the PCRCh leader insisted the pro-Soviet party was trying to conceal its responsibility—by refusing to talk about the mistakes of the past and by issuing only vague general programs for the future. (*Clarte et L'Exploite*, Burssels, 27 December 1973-2 January 1974.) An analysis in the party's clandestine paper (*El Pueblo*) at mid-year referred to the fascist repression and imperialist exploitation which marked the Chilean scene. This had driven classes from the poor peasants to the non-monopolist big bourgeoisie into varying degrees of opposition to the government. The situation was painful but provided a good opportunity for forging popular unity. The article mentioned the popular front the party sought, an instrument of unity and struggle, supported by all patriotic citizens, and gave the minimum program of that front: the struggle to defeat the dictatorship and exploitation, to attain university autonomy, to defend the small and middle businessmen, to abolish restitution of expropriated enterprises, and to develop agrarian reform. The program, according to the PCRCh, enables the party to unite all sectors hit by the dictatorship, concentrating all forces in a single broad popular front whose vanguard must be the working class led by the PCRCh. The article condemned the PCCh and its "peaceful road." (*Nuova Unita*, Rome, 6 August 1974.)

* * *

The MIR. The Movement of the Revolutionary Left was formed in 1965 and in December 1967 became an avowedly "Castroite" organization advocating the armed road to power enunciated at the Latin American Solidarity Organization (OLAS) conference held in Havana in August of that year. Early in 1969 the MIR went underground and did not surface again until after Salvador Allende's inauguration as president of Chile in November 1970. The MIR was not a member of the UP alliance, preferring to operate outside of the "bourgeois" constitutional system within which UP leaders repeatedly pledged to work. Supporters and detractors of the MIR alike agree that the organization played an important part in heightening the "class struggle" in Chile throughout the UP period, and particularly during 1973 (see *YICA, 1974*, pp. 301-305). The MIR went underground again on 11 September 1973.

At the time of the coup Miguel Enríquez was secretary general. Other prominent leaders, most of them on the Political Commission, included: Edgardo Enríquez, Bautista van Schouwen, Humberto Sotomayor, Nelsón Gutiérrez, Andrés Pascal Allende, Roberto Moreno, Arturo Villavela, Alejandro Alarcón, and Víctor Toro. Van Schouwen had been arrested by the end of 1973; Moreno, Villavela, Toro, and several other members of the Central Committee were under arrest by mid-1974. Miguel Enríquez was killed in a shootout with government authorities in early October 1974. Sotomayor, Enríquez's successor, immediately sought refuge with his family in the Italian Embassy, a violation of the strict MIR code of revolutionary ethics and thus a source of uncertainty and reportedly of serious dissension within the group. By the end of the year, the MIR, for so long an effective and unified underground organization, seemed to be in serious disarray. Sotomayor's successor, Pascal Allende, was reportedly confirmed as the new secretary-general in late December. Alejandro de la Barra, José Bordaz Paz, and other emerging leaders were killed. Several MIR sub-organizations, such as the People's Revolutionary Command (Comando Revolucionario del Pueblo) were broken up and arsenals were discovered around the country by the police.

   Domestic Attitudes and Activities. MIR views on the military government and conditions in Chile after September 1973 were not remarkably different from those of the PCCh (see above; some MIR positions are found in *Granma*, English, 29 September 1974). As has been the case for many years, however, the MIR proposed a more militant road to socialism than the PCCh and some other leftist groups. At mid-year, the Political Commission sent Edgardo Enríquez abroad to explain MIR tactics, which he did in an interview in Cuba in late June. The military government could only be overthrown, he said, by a "long and difficult people's war, full of sacrifices." The MIR was engaged in "preparing the conditions for starting this war." The immediate objectives of the MIR were: (1) setting up a political front for popular resistance, including the UP parties, progressive Christian Democrats, and the MIR; (2) "setting up the movement of people's resistance as a mass organization and a base for the political front, with the participation of all those workers who are not affiliated with any political party and want to fight"; and (3) "setting up the first embryonic units of the People's Revolutionary Army, the military organization of the resistance" which should enlist all persons willing to fight militarily against the regime. Enríquez added, in an allusion to the PCCh and some others, that the MIR realized not all parties of the Chilean left were in agreement with this immediate program. He added: "We are not going to give up defending our program, but, at the same time, we think it would be a serious mistake, if not a criminal omission, to give priority to these discussions rather than the urgent need of uniting all the forces of the Chilean left." (*Granma*, English, 7 July; also see MIR analysis in ibid., Spanish, 18 February.) The Political Commission elaborated on MIR relations with the PCCh in a statement signed 10 September: "There were important differences between us and the Communist Party and its policies during the Popular Unity Government, and still today we have differences with them, but they are our allies in the struggle against the dictatorship, they are comrades on the same path" (ibid., English, 29 September).

   In September the Political Commission charged that beginning in July the Chilean Intelligence Service of the Armed Forces (SIFA) had tried to work out an agreement with the MIR whereby: the MIR would surrender its weapons, give up its political work in the Armed Forces, and send its members abroad (with government assistance); the government would release all MIR prisoners, study which ones could remain in Chile, and consider the possibility that the MIR could continue functioning in Chile if in the next two or three years it did not carry out "active political opposition" to the government. The MIR rejected this proposal publicly on the first anniversary of the coup.

   On 7 July the Paris daily *Le Monde* reported on an interview with Edgardo Enríquez in which the MIR leader acknowledged that resistance to the junta up to that time seemed modest. "But there will soon be spectacular and effective action." Enríquez added that the main thing about the united front, whatever it might be called, was "quickly to reach the stage of armed propaganda and then the armed struggle in the cities and the countryside." (*Intercontinental Press*, New York, 22 July.) A bank robbery at the end of September, probably considered one of the first "spectacular and effective actions," led the police to Miguel Enríquez and several comrades (including Sotomayor) resulting in the death of the organization's top leader on 5 October, the defection of its next-in-command, and evidently considerable demoralization within the leadership and ranks. Though the MIR took the initiative several times during the remainder of the year, for the first time since the coup the security forces increasingly had the upper hand.

Early in the year the MIR, together with the Bolivian National Liberation Army (ELN), the Uruguayan National Liberation Movement (MLN; Tupamaros), and the Argentine People's Revolutionary Army (ERP), formed a Revolutionary Coordinating Committee (see below). In his Havana interview, Edgardo Enríquez gave his special thanks to these groups, as well as the Argentine Montoneros, for their solidarity with the Chilean struggle.

Publications. The MIR released several statements abroad and circulated some fliers in Chile. In September the MIR started a clandestine news service, scheduled to be available to the international press at lease once each week; its bulletins were called *El Rebelde*, the name of the MIR's weekly paper before the September coup.

*   *   *

Appendix

The Revolutionary Coordinating Committee. On 13 February four guerrilla organizations announced the formation of the Revolutionary Coordinating Committee (Junta de Coordinación Revolucionario; JCR). The four were the Chilean Movement of the Revolutionary Left (MIR), the Argentine People's Revolutionary Army (Ejército Revolucionario del Pueblo; ERP), the Uruguayan National Liberation Movement (Movimiento de Liberación Nacional; MLN), the Tupamaros, and the Bolivian National Liberation Army (Ejército de Liberación Nacional; ELN). The four founding members called on other revolutionary organizations in Latin America to join them in their continental struggle.

The JCR, according to the founding declaration, was a "response to a deeply felt need, the need to offer our peoples organizational cohesion, to unite the revolutionary forces against the imperialist enemy, to achieve a greater effectiveness in the political and ideological struggle against bourgeois nationalism and reformism." This was the concrete realization of "one of the main strategic conceptions of Comandante Che Guevara, the hero, symbol, and pioneer of the continental socialist revolution." For the past century Latin Americans have borne the colonial and neocolonial yoke of the imperialists and the native ruling classes. The triumph of the Cuban Revolution marked the beginning of the move toward true national independence and well-being for the Latin American peoples. In recent decades the majority of the hemisphere's communist parties fell into reformism so that the masses were deflected from their revolutionary course and fell under the influence and leadership of bourgeois nationalism, the latter being a "clever demagogic device the ruling classes resorted to in order to prolong the reign of the neocolonial capitalist system through deception." The Cuban victory in 1959 encouraged other Latin Americans, and the decade of the 1960s "saw an uninterrupted succession of great popular struggles, violent guerrilla combat, and powerful mass insurrections." Millions of workers began the march toward revolutionary socialism. The "cruelty and power of imperialism make it necessary, as Comandante Guevara foresaw in a general way, to mount a fierce and prolonged revolutionary war that will transform the Latin American continent into the world's second or third Vietnam."

Two tendencies in thought and action "gravely obstruct" the revolutionary efforts of Latin Americans: bourgeois nationalism, an outright enemy, and reformism, a "false conception in the people's camp." The bourgeois nationalists use anti-imperialist rhetoric, and speak of a "third road," but actually prepare the way for new and more subtle forms of foreign economic imperialism. Reformism, rooted in the toiling population, "reflects the fear that petty-bourgeois sectors and the labor aristocracy have of confrontation." But the Latin American workers "will unleash the irresistible energies of the masses in all their intensity and thus win happiness for our peoples." The JCR program follows:

> We are united by our understanding that the only viable strategy in Latin America is one of revolutionary war. This revolutionary war is a complex process of both armed and unarmed, peaceful and violent, mass struggle in which all forms develop harmoniously, converging around the axis of armed struggle.
>
> In order for this whole process of revolutionary war to be carried out victoriously we have to mobilize the entire people under the leadership of the revolutionary proletariat. Proletarian leadership of the war must be provided by a Marxist-Leninist combat party of a proletarian character that can centralize, direct, and combine all aspects of popular struggle in a single powerful cutting edge, a party that can provide the proper strategic guidance. Under the leadership of the proletarian party, we must organize a mighty people's army, the iron core of the revolutionary forces. Developing progressively from small beginnings, this people's army will rise up as an impenetrable wall against which all the military assaults of the reactionaries will shatter and which will have the material capacity to assure the total annihilation of the counterrevolutionary armies.
>
> At the same time, we must build a broad, mass workers and people's front that can mobilize all the progressive and revolutionary people, the unions and other similar organizations—in short the broadest masses, whose struggle parallels and continually converges with the military activity and strategy of the people's army and the clandestine political activity of the proletarian party.
>
> A clear response is needed to the present challenge and the only possible one is armed struggle. This must be the main factor in political polarization and agitation, and ultimately in defeating the enemy; it is the only road to victory. This doesn't mean that we will not utilize every possible form of organization and struggle, legal and clandestine, peaceful and violent, economic and political. All converge with increased effectiveness in *armed struggle*, which will be waged in accordance with the peculiarities of every region and country.
>
> The continental character of the struggle is determined fundamentally by the presence of a common enemy. American imperialism is carrying out an international strategy to halt the socialist revolution in Latin America. It is no accident that fascist regimes have been imposed in countries where a rising mass movement has threatened the stability of oligarchic power. The international strategy of imperialism requires a continental strategy on the part of revolutionists.
>
> The road to be traveled in this struggle is not a short one. The international bourgeoisie is determined to prevent revolution by any means, even if it arises in a single country. It has every kind of official and unofficial means, both military and propagandistic, that can be used against the people. Therefore, in its first phases, our revolutionary war is one of wearing out the enemy until we are able to form a people's army stronger than the enemy force. This process is a slow one, but paradoxically, it is the shortest and least costly road to achieve the strategic objectives of the disadvantaged classes.

The JCR document closes with a "call on the exploited toilers of Latin America, on the working class, the poor peasants, the urban poor, the students and intellectuals, the revolutionary Christians, and all elements of the exploiting classes ready to support the just cause of the people to take up arms resolutely, to join actively in the revolutionary struggle against imperialism and for socialism that is being waged on our continent following the banner and the example of Comandante Guevara." (*Intercontinental Press*, New York, 11 March 1974.)

Hoover Institution   William E. Ratliff
Stanford University

Colombia

The communist movement in Colombia began within the ranks of the Socialist Revolutionary Party (Partido Socialista Revolucionario; PSR) shortly after the party's formation in December 1926. Contacts between the PSR and the Communist International during 1929 and 1930 inspired a group of PSR members to proclaim publicly the creation of the Communist Party of Colombia (Partido Comunista de Colombia; PCC) on 17 July 1930. The party has retained this designation ever since except for a short period (1944-47) during which it was called the Social Democratic Party (Partido Social Democrático). In July 1965 a schism within the PCC between pro-Soviet and pro-Chinese factions resulted in the latter's becoming the Communist Party of Colombia, Marxist-Leninist (Partido Comunista de Colombia, Marxista-Leninista; PCC-ML). Only the PCC has legal status.

The PCC is estimated to have 10,000 to 12,000 members and exercises only marginal influence in national affairs. The population of Colombia is 25,000,000 (estimated 1974).

The PCC participated in the 1974 general elections as a member of the leftist coalition National Opposition Union (Unión de Oposición Nacional; UNO), founded in September 1972. The other parties comprising UNO are the pro-Chinese Independent Revolutionary Workers Movement (MOIR), and the Broad Colombian Movement (MAC), from whose ranks the Coalition's presidential candidate, Hernando Echeverri Mejía, was selected. UNO presented joint electoral lists, winning two seats in the 112-member Senate (Antioquia, Cundinamarca), and 5 seats in the 199-member Lower Chamber (Antioquia, Cauca, Cundinamarca 2, and Santander). Of these, PCC members occupy one of the Lower Chamber seats from Cundinamarca and the seat from Cauca. In addition, UNO gained two seats on Bogotá's 20-member Municipal Council, one of which is held by a member of the PCC. Voting in the 1974 presidential election is shown in the accompanying table (page 488).

Guerrilla warfare, although not a serious threat to the government, has been a feature of Colombian life since the late 1940's, the current wave beginning in 1964. The three main guerrilla organizations are the PCC-controlled Revolutionary Armed Forces of Colombia (FARC), the pro-Chinese People's Liberation Army (EPL), and the Castroite National Liberation Army (ELN). Although isolated units of these groups were active in 1974, defections and heavy casualties inflicted by the Colombian military kept the scope of their operations at its lowest level in nine years. Estimates of membership at midyear ranked the ELN first with 150-200 men, followed by the FARC and the EPL with fewer than 100 and 50 members respectively. Kidnappings and other acts of violence are frequently carried out by criminal elements who profess membership in either the ELN or FARC. One such band operating in southern Santander had carried out 42 kidnappings by mid-year, and was charged with the deaths of at least two landowners who refused ransom payment (*El Tiempo*, 13 July 1974).

COLOMBIA, National (Presidential) Election 21 April 1974

Name of party	Votes cast	Percent of total votes cast
Communist-Leftist Coalition:		
(National Opposition Union; UNO)		
Communist Party of Colombia (PCC)		
Broad Colombian Movement (MAC)		
Independent Revolutionary Workers Movement (MOIR)		
Hernando Echeverri Mejía	137,054	2.6
Non-Communist Left:		
Christian Democratic Party (PDC)		
Hermes Duarte Arias	5,718	0.1
National Popular Alliance (ANAPO)		
María Eugenia Rojas de Moreno	492,166	9.4
Liberal Party		
Alfonso López Michelsen	2,929,719	56.2
Conservative		
Conservative Party		
Alvaro Gómez Hurtado	1,634,879	31.4
Other		
Blank or null	16,574	0.3
Total	5,212,110	100.0

Source: Official results sanctioned by the Electoral Tribunal on 14 July. The 1974 elections were the first in 16 years in which competition for elective offices at the national level was opened to all parties. The National Front agreement implemented in 1958 had provided for strict parity between the Liberal and Conservative parties, and alternation in the presidency. Competition in municipal and departmental elections was opened to all parties in 1970. In the concurrent 1974 congressional elections, the Liberals won a clear majority in both the Senate and the Lower Chamber: Senate (112 members); Liberals 66, Conservatives 37, ANAPO 7, UNO 2; Lower Chamber (199 members); Liberals 113, Conservatives 66, ANAPO 15, UNO 5.

The PCC. Leadership and Organization. The PCC is headed by its 12-member Executive Committee and 45-member Central Committee. The highest party authority is the Congress, convened by the Central Committee at four-year intervals. The XI Congress was held in December 1971. Gilberto Vieira is general secretary of the party. Members of the Executive Committee include, besides Vieira: Alvaro Vásquez, Joaquín Moreno, Jesús Villegas, Roso Osorio, Hernando Hurtado, Julio Posada, Gustavo Castro, Gustavo Osorio, Juan Viana, Manlio Lafont, and Manuel Cepeda Vargas.

A major source of the PCC's influence lies in its control over the Trade Union Confederation of Workers of Colombia (Confederación Sindical de Trabajadores de Colombia; CSTC), which claims a membership of 160,000-170,000. The CSTC was granted legal status by the Colombian government in August 1974. CSTC president, Pástor Pérez, declared that legal recognition would contribute significantly toward efforts to unite the Colombian working class (WFTU, *Flashes*, no. 35, 30 August 1974). In October, the CSTC withdrew its representation on the National Wage Council, established by the government to review problems related to Colombia's minimum wage. Prior to the walkout, Pérez had called for an increase in the daily minimum wage to $60 pesos, along with a general wage adjustment of 50 percent "to compensate for recent inflation spurred by the government's economic policy" (*El Tiempo*, 3 October). The PCC continues to oppose any merger between Colombia's two largest labor organizations—the Union of Workers of Colombia (Unión de Trabajadores de Colombia; UTC) and the Confederation of Workers of Colombia (Confederación de Trabajadores de Colombia; CTC). In turn, UTC and CTC officials frequently denounce efforts by the PCC to increase its influence in the labor movement. At midyear the CSTC announced plans to organize a National Trade Union Congress for December to promote greater unity within the trade union movement. The CSTC sent delegates to national trade union congresses held in Peru (March) and Cuba (November). The CSTC was also represented at the 25th meeting of the General Council of World Federation of Trade Unions (WFTU) in Havana on 15-17 October. In addition to Pérez, prominent leaders in the CSTC are Gustavo Osorio (general secretary), Hernán Sabogal, Luis Carlos Pérez, Julio Poveda, and Alcibiades Aguirre.

PCC efforts to expand its influence within the 900,000-member National Peasant Association of Land Users (Asociación Nacional de Usuarios Campesinos; ANUC) achieved no visible success in 1974. Although founded by the government to encourage peasant participation in the development and implementation of agrarian reform, the ANUC established a militantly independent policy under its first president, Jaime Vásquez. It is expected to retain its autonomous position under a new president, Jesús Pérez, elected at ANUC's Third Congress held in early September. PCC initiatives to create a peasant movement more amenable to its influence continue to be hampered by ideological, sectarian, and personalist differences within the peasant leadership. The PCC's principal agrarian leaders affiliated with ANUC are Víctor Merchán and Gerardo González.

The PCC's youth organization, the Communist Youth of Colombia (Juventud Comunista de Colombia; JUCO) has an estimated membership of 2,000. JUCO has its own National Directorate, Executive Committee, and Central Committee. The general secretary is Carlos Romero, a member of the PCC's Central Committee. Other members of the Executive Committee elected in 1973 are Jaime Caicedo, Leonardo Posada, Jaime Miller Chacón, Eduardo Martínez, Enrique Sierra, Lucio Lara, and Alvaro Oviedo. In addition to supporting the PCC's role within UNO, JUCO was active in 1974 in attempting to expand its influence at the university and secondary levels, especially through the National Union of University Students. JUCO leadership continues to be critical of disunity among the Left in university politics, which it blames on "the ideological struggle precipitated by Maoist and Trotskyite elements" (*Voz Proletaria*, 9 May).

The PCC has controlled a peasant guerrilla group since 1966, the Revolutionary Armed Forces of Colombia (FARC). Although party spokesmen continue to hold that "armed revolutionary struggle is a necessary factor of the revolution in Colombia," the importance of guerrilla warfare has been deemphasized in recent years in accordance with Soviet policy (*WMR*, February). FARC guerrilla units incurred heavy losses in late 1973. Its inactivity in early 1974 prompted speculation that FARC's principal leader, Manuel Marulanda Vélez, had left the country (*El Tiempo*, 3 March). In a subsequent editorial appearing in *Resistencia*, the illegal FARC information publication, Marulanda vowed to continue the armed struggle "until the system that oppresses the Colombian people is brought down" (*Resistencia*, April). In May, FARC guerrillas were reportedly attempting to join an

ELN unit operating in Huila. In August, FARC units operating in northern Antioquia were rumored to be willing to surrender under conditions of general amnesty, although the rumor was denied by official military sources (*El Tiempo*, 30 August). Following sporadic actions in September, including the ambush of a military patrol, the Army began to express some concern over the reappearance of FARC guerrilla activity in southern Santander (ibid., 6 October).

Domestic Attitudes and Activities. The PCC's domestic policy in early 1974 was guided by its efforts to strengthen coalition activity with other leftist parties through the National Opposition Union (UNO). At a plenary meeting of the Central Committee on 8-9 December 1973, it was agreed to present joint electoral slates with MOIR and MAC. While the political resolution adopted stressed that electoral agreements would be made with a view to preserving the independence of the PCC, UNO was praised as "the initial stage of popular unity in Colombia ... and the only consistent unitary and revolutionary force which the masses see as a new alternative—a frontal opposition to the oligarchical system and Yankee imperialism" (*IB*, 31 April 1974).

In defending the practice of coalition politics, PCC spokesmen have emphasized that the unity of the parties comprising UNO is "political and not ideological" (*Voz Proletaria*, 4 April). The unity which exists has been achieved largely on the basis of a joint political program which includes support for a radical agrarian reform, improved living and working conditions, educational reform, free medical and hospital assistance, elimination of economic, political and cultural domination of imperialism, and the establishment of an "independent" foreign policy (ibid., 18 April).

At the 17-20 May plenum Vieira spoke of "the growing influence of the party among the masses" and assessed UNO's participation in the April elections as "an extremely important development which favors democratic change" (*IB*, no. 12, 1974). During UNO's convention held on 13 July, Vieira strongly criticized the predictions of "the right and the extreme left" that UNO was "merely a temporary electoral alliance" that would not survive the elections. He stated that UNO would provide a "democratic and revolutionary opposition" to the López administration, while at the same time suggesting that the movement would support legislation which coincided with the reforms advocated by UNO's political program. The dominant note of the convention was an appeal to combat sectarian interests within the coalition and to broaden the base of the movement by "opening the doors to the revolutionary faction of ANAPO and Liberals of the Left" (*Alternativa*, no. 12, 22 July). UNO elected a new 15-member National Directorate at midyear with Manuel Bayona Carrascal of MOIR as president and Carlos Romero as general secretary. Other PCC members on the Directorate besides Romero are Hernando Hurtado, Manuel Cepeda, Gustavo Osorio, and José Cardona Hoyos (*El Tiempo*, 7 July).

The PCC and UNO face their strongest challenge for opposition leadership from ANAPO, headed by former dictator Gustavo Rojas Pinilla and his daughter, María Eugenia Rojas de Moreno. Despite internal factionalism arising in part over the presidential candidacy of María Eugenia, ANAPO's program of "Colombian-styled socialism" and its broad organizational base should ensure the party's survival in the immediate future as the country's largest opposition movement to the traditional Liberal and Conservative parties. In addition to periodic attacks against ANAPO, the PCC continues to wage an ideological struggle against Maoist and Trotskyite groups who oppose the party's line and tactics.

In a statement drawn up at the May Plenum, and published in *Voz Proletaria* (6-12 June), the PCC declared that Colombians were entering a "new stage of the struggle, with conditions favouring the broad expansion of mass action." The party called for the use of "enthusiasm and political flexibility" in the campaign to achieve popular unity. The best way was to make rallying points of the popular demands put forward by the UNO and PCC program. Those points were:

1. Against Yankee imperialism and for national liberation.
2. Solidarity with the peoples fighting for freedom, the fraternal people of Chile in the first place.
3. Against high prices, inflation and growing poverty, for a general increase in wages and incomes.
4. Against latifundia, for land, work and higher reimbursement of the labour of peasants and farm workers.
5. Against rising rent and services rates.
6. Against the crisis in all levels of the educational system; for a democratic and popular educational reform.
7. Against the government's pro-American policy in international relations and for the establishment of relations and rapprochement with all peoples.
8. Against the reactionary, anti-democratic character of the ruling system; for expanding freedoms and democratic guarantees for workers, employees, peasants and students. (*IB*, Prague ed., no. 16.)

International Views and Positions. The PCC closely follows the Soviet Union with respect to its international views. At the December 1973 plenary meeting the Central Committee adopted a resolution stressing the importance of strengthening the present tendencies toward peaceful coexistence and détente. The resolution cited the contribution made by the CPSU in "furthering unity within the international communist and working class movement," while criticizing the Peking leadership for "betraying the ideas of proletarian internationalism" (*IB*, 31 April 1974). On 4 July *Voz Proletaria* carried a long attack on the Maoist attitude toward Latin America (*IB*, Prague ed., no. 16). At the May Plenary session Vieira reaffirmed PCC support for Soviet international policies and spoke of the "new achievements and mounting international prestige of the Soviet Union and other countries of the socialist community" (*IB*, no. 12, 1974). The PCC continued in 1974 to support an expansion of trade and increased cultural, technical, and scientific exchange between Colombia, the Soviet Union, and other members of the socialist bloc.

Hemispherically, the PCC adopted statements of solidarity with the communist parties of Cuba, Chile, and Uruguay, concluding that "the machinations of imperialism in Latin America which brought on a military coup in Chile cannot hold back the development of the revolutionary process in the continent" (TASS, 11 December 1973). In May Vieira stated that the main task of Colombian communists was "to support the struggle of the Chilean people and to defend the lives of political prisoners" (TASS, 23 May 1974). At UNO's convention in July, PCC delegates sponsored resolutions calling for the establishment of diplomatic and commercial relations with Cuba and support for demonstrations of solidarity with Chile on 17-18 September (*Alternativa*, no. 12, 22 July 1974).

Party Contacts. A PCC delegation headed by Vieira visited East Germany in June, followed by trips to Leningrad and Moscow where talks were held with members of the CPSU Central Committee. A joint communication on 5 July expressed the desire to "further broaden friendly ties between the U.S.S.R. and Colombia" (*Pravda*, 6 July 1974). Julio Posada of the PCC's Executive Committee visited Romania in September at the invitation of the Central Committee of the RCP.

Publications. The PCC publishes a weekly newspaper, *Voz Proletaria*, founded in 1957 with a circulation of 25,000; a theoretical journal, *Documentos Políticos*, with a circulation of 5,000; and a Colombian edition of *Problems of Peace and Socialism*. The FARC publishes a clandestine bulletin, *Resistencia*.

*   *   *

The PCC-ML. The Communist Party of Colombia Marxist-Leninist is firmly pro-Chinese. Although its leadership hierarchy is not clearly known, important positions have been held in recent years by Francisco Garnica, Pedro Vásquez, and Pedro León Arboleda. The party has an estimated membership of 1,000. In terms of national political life, the party's impact is insignificant.

Unlike the PCC, the PCC-ML has not attempted to obtain legal status. The party was virtually inactive in 1974 and is believed to be suffering from divided leadership and financial difficulties. Within the labor movement, the PCC-ML has exercised some influence in the past over the Bloque Independiente, a small trade union organization with an estimated membership of 20,000.

The Independent Revolutionary Workers' Movement (MOIR), established in 1971, also follows a pro-Chinese orientation. In September 1973 a faction of the MOIR headed by Francisco Mosquera and Ricardo Samper joined the National Opposition Union.

The PCC-ML's guerrilla arm, the EPL, was the first attempt to stage a revolutionary "people's war" in Latin America. The EPL suffered critical setbacks in late 1973 which led to predictions of its "imminent elimination" by Army spokesmen. In March 1974, 21 EPL members surrendered in Antioquia and reports circulated that the remaining guerrillas had joined FARC (*El Tiempo*, 3 March). Although the movement may be approaching total disintegration, in August four guerrilla units affiliated with the EPL were reportedly still operating in isolated regions of Antioquia, Córdoba, and Bolívar (ibid., 30 August).

Publications. The organ of the PCC-ML is *Revolución*. PCC-ML statements are sometimes found in Chinese Communist publications and those of pro-Chinese parties in Europe and Latin America.

*   *   *

The ELN. The National Liberation Army was formed in Santander in 1964 under the inspiration of the Cuban Revolution. It undertook its first military action in 1965.

Military operations carried out against ELN guerrilla units operating in the middle Magdalena River region were extremely successful in late 1973. The confirmed deaths of Antonio and Manuel Vásquez Castaño on 18 September was followed by the capture of the movement's principal ideologue, Ricardo Lara Parada, on 23 November 1973. Lara was quoted by military sources as predicting an end to the ELN "because of the existing ideological conflicts within the guerrilla hierarchy" (*El Tiempo*, 27 November). The ELN's political leadership was further weakened in February with the capture of José Martínez Quiroz, one of the original founders, and the death of Domingo Laín, a former Spanish priest who joined the ELN in 1970 (ibid., 23 March 1974). Laín's death left Fabio Vásquez Castaño as the only surviving leader. In July reports of executions and defections within the ELN accompanied intensified anti-guerrilla operations in the Central Magdalena region in an effort to liquidate the remnants of units attempting to regroup in southern Bolívar (ibid., 14 July). In September military sources confirmed the death of ex-university student Jaime Andrade Sosa, reportedly the only ideologue left following the deaths of Manuel Vásquez and Laín (ibid., 3 September). Sixteen additional members of the ELN were captured in late September (*El Siglo*, 1 October). With a price on his head of $1,000,000 pesos, rumors persisted at year's end that Fabio Vásquez Castaño had abandoned the guerrilla struggle and fled to Cuba. In December, a statement attributed to Vásquez denied a report appearing in *El Tiempo* that "an understanding with the guerrillas is imminent" (*Times of the Americas*, 11 December). With the collapse of the ELN's urban network and the death of capture of its principal leaders except Fabio Vásquez, the ELN appears to be on the verge of extinction.

Washington College   Daniel L. Premo

Costa Rica

The Communist Party of Costa Rica (Partido Comunista de Costa Rica) was founded in 1931 and accepted as a full member of the Communist International in 1935. In 1943, following the wartime policy of many Latin American communist parties, the Costa Rican communists reorganized under a new name, the Popular Vanguard Party (Partido Vanguardia Popular; PVP).

The PVP was illegal between 1948 and mid-1974, though in recent years it had operated with considerable freedom. Prior to regaining its legality, the PVP participated in the February 1974 elections by running its members as candidates of the Socialist Action Party (Partido de Acción Socialista; PASO), a legal, leftist coalition party. PVP secretary general Manuel Mora Valverde, the PASO presidential candiate, came in near the bottom of the slate:

3 February 1974 Presidential Election Results

National Liberation Party (PCN)	42.58 percent
National Unification Party (PUN)	30.20 percent
National Independent Party (PNI)	11.03 percent
Democratic Renewal (RD)	9.73 percent
PASO and three other parties	6.46 percent

The PASO won two seats in the 57-seat Legislative Assembly.

The PVP is the best organized and most sophisticated communist party in Central America, but its small size, aging leadership, and illegal status, as well as Costa Rican conditions, long prevented it from becoming a significant force in Costa Rican politics. The membership of the PVP is estimated at 1,000 (*World Strength of the Communist Party Organizations, 1973*, p. 158). The population of Costa Rica is 1,800,000 (estimated 1972).

Leadership and Organization. Manuel Mora Valverde, founder of the PVP, has been secretary general of the party from its beginning. The assistant secretary general is his brother, Eduardo Mora Valverde. The organizational secretary is Arnoldo Ferreto Segura ("Oscar Vargas").

The PVP is active in the labor movement through the General Confederation of Costa Rican Workers (Confederación General de Trabajadores Costarricenses; CGTC) which it controls. The CGTC is believed to have about 2,500 members out of some 24,000 unionized workers in the country. The secretary general of the CGTC was last reported to be Alvaro Montera Vega. In 1972 the CGTC began publishing a newspaper, *El Orientador*, which it hoped would encourage the workers to adopt more revolutionary positions. The PVP also sponsors the United Agricultural Workers' and Peasants' Federation (FUNTAC) and claims to be actively engaged in organizing peasants in all the provinces of the country. PVP work among youth is carried out through its affiliate, Vanguard Youth (Juventud Vanguardia de Costa Rica; JVCR) and its university organization, the University Action Front (Frente de Acción Universitaria; FAU). The secretary general of the JVCR is Luis Orlando Corrales. The FAU, whose organ is *Unidad*, is small and represents only a minor percentage of the university students. The PVP claims to be active in the organization of women and circulates a monthly publication concerned with women's affairs.

Party Internal Affairs. The PVP Central Committee held its 8th plenum in two sessions (20-21 April and 4-5 May) during 1974. The meetings were devoted chiefly to self-criticism, to a critique of the party's "sectarian" political line during the February election. The party acknowledged numerous mistakes made during the 1973-74 election campaign, including a failure to unite the forces of the left and mobilize the masses, inadequate financing, and errors in parliamentary activity (the responsibility of the party's Political Commission). The Central Committee instructed the Political Commission to convene a special plenum to discuss party policy for the present day and ordered an immediate start be made on preparations for the 12th party congress.

Domestic Views and Attitudes. Prior to the February election the PVP maintained that only the PASO represented the interests of the people and the working class and would struggle against the exploiters, thieves, and speculators for a more truly revolutionary program (see *YICA, 1974*, p. 312). The poor PASO performance in the election forced the party to reexamine its line. At the 8th plenum the PVP concluded that its political line during the election had been sectarian; its slogan "For Popular Power" had come to mean immediate struggle for popular power. The party had not adequately planned for or attempted to form the "anti-imperialist agrarian, popular, democratic front" called for by the 11th party congress in 1971. During the campaign all slogans were abandoned which would have won the support of groups which, though progressive, did not think the elections could establish this popular power. The party had been wrong in thinking that objective or subjective conditions existed which would have made possible the formation of a new type of government devoted to deep-going social revolution under the leadership of the communists. There was no national crisis in Costa Rica, and no united front of revolutionary and popular forces to provide the political and social support for such a new type of government. The PVP slogans and line did not attract, but merely confused, the politically less developed sectors of the people who should have been susceptible to communist appeals. In the end, the party had contested the election with the support of only a few small, very militant groups. Whereas the party should not renounce its long-term objectives, the plenum concluded that sectarianism, and the adventurism which flowed from it, had to be rejected. The Central Committee called for better and more systematic work among the masses, centered on developing all forms of class struggle. Organizational efforts should be directed toward trade unions, students, women, and youth. The PVP had to promote mutual understanding between the "new political democratic movements so as to lay the ground for an "anti-imperialist and democratic front." (*IB*, Prague edition, no. 14.)

The Costa Rican communists accomplished one of their main short term objectives late in July when the national congress approved a constitutional amendment which repealed part of article 98 of the Constitution, thereby making possible the legalization of the PVP.

International Affairs. The PVP attended the preparatory meeting for the 9th conference of Communist and Workers Parties of Mexico, Central America, and Panama in December 1973-January 1974, and the conference itself toward the end of May 1974. With the other parties, the PVP reaffirmed its pro-Soviet stance, condemned the military coup in Chile which overthrew the Popular Unity government of Salvador Allende, attacked those who seek to provoke further military conflict in Central America, and called for a meeting of all Communist and Workers parties of Latin America to explore the possibility of a conference of all parties of the region and to discuss its organization, agenda, and related matters. (*IB*, no. 3; ibid., Prague ed., nos. 14 and 16; also see *Mexico.*)

Publication. The PVP publishes the weekly paper *Libertad.*

Hoover Institution
Stanford University

William E. Ratliff

Cuba

The Communist Party of Cuba (Partido Comunista de Cuba; PCC), Cuba's ruling party, was founded in August 1925. For decades the Party followed closely the Moscow political line and adapted to the prevailing political situations in the country. Communist leaders collaborated with the regime of President Gen. Fulgencio Batista (1940-44), and in 1944, Carlos Rafael Rodriguez, one of the leaders, today one of Fidel Castro's deputy prime ministers, became Batista's minister without portfolio, with special responsibility for education. In 1944, the Party changed its name to the People's Socialist Party (Partido Socialista Popular; PSP). It retained this name until July 1961, when it merged with Premier Fidel Castro's victorious 26th of July Movement and the Revolutionary Directorate to form the Integrated Revolutionary Organizations (Organizaciones Revolucionarias Integradas; ORI). In 1962, the ORI was transformed into the United Party of the Socialist Revolution (Partido Unido de la Revolución Socialista; PURS). On 5 October 1965, PURS was dissolved and in its place the present ruling Communist Party of Cuba (PCC) was formed along orthodox communist lines.

In recent years, the PCC has grown rapidly in membership. While in August 1973, Fidel Castro stated that the Party had more than 100,000 members, the *World Marxist Review* (March 1974) stated that by late 1973 the PCC had 170,000 members. This number is believed to have grown to close to 200,000 by the end of 1974. Cuba has a population of over 9 million (estimated 1974).

Party Organization and Leadership. Since late 1972, when a reorganization of the Cuban top governmental structure took place, political power and the decision-making process have slowly been acquiring a collective character. While disproportionately hugh power continued to be vested in Fidel Castro by virtue of his three positions: first secretary of the PCC; prime minister; and commander-in-chief of the Armed Forces, other leaders—notably his brother Raúl Castro, President Osvaldo Dorticós Torrado, Deputy Prime Minister Carlos Rafael Rodríguez, were visibly sharing major responsibilities and exercising a degree of independence and self-condifence. During 1974, significantly, Fidel Castro's speeches, while still being invariably policy-setting pronouncements, were less frequent, shorter and usually read from a prepared text—a departure from the premier's habit of oral improvisation. What Castro read appeared to have been carefully thought out, possibly discussed with associates and modified in the process by some kind of intra-party collective. The PCC's pyramidal organizational model remained unchanged in 1974. At the top of the pyramid was the eight-member Political Bureau, which included Fidel and Raúl Castro, Dorticós, Juan Almeida Bosque (who holds the unique title of the major of the revolution), Ramiro Valdés Menendez, Armando Hart Dávalos, Guillermo García Frías and Jorge del Valle Jiménez. The Party Secretariat had 12 members: Fidel and Raúl Castro, Dorticós, Blas Roca Calderio, Faure Chomón Mediavilla, Carlos Rafael Rodríguez, Armando Hart Dávalos, Jorge Risquet Valdés, Antonio Pérez Herrero, Isidoro Malmierca Peoli, Raúl

García Pelaez and Pedro Miret Prieto. Both the Politburo and the Secretariat (and the later's eight special commissions) are supposed to be elected by the party's Central Committee of some 100 members. (The exact size of the Central Committee is not known because Cuba has not updated its membership since 1967.) About two thirds of Central Committee members are military commanders, either on active duty or holding civilian governmental posts. This body is not known to be meeting regularly, thus relinquishing effective power to the Secretariat and the Politburo. Below the top party structure, party secretariats exist in each of Cuba's six provinces, which in turn supervise secretariats in counties, cities and city districts. Party cells exist in practically all centers of work and in larger military units. Party membership is usually a reward for outstanding production performance and enthusiastic acceptance of party directives. *Granma*, the official PCC newspaper, said the party "directs and guides at all levels of economic and social activity . . . . [it] carries out its work, for the most part, by means of its nuclei, the Party guides, directs and controls the general system of education, the organization in charge of cultural and educational centers and the mass organizations." (*Granma*, Weekly Review, English, 17 March 1974).

The Soviet role in party affairs in Cuba is considerable, and aimed principally at "guiding" the PCC along the Soviet communist party lines. This role is expected to be enhanced in late 1975 when the PCC is scheduled to hold its First National Congress, an institutional landmark for Communist parties all over the world. In addition to party matters, the First Congress is expected to approve the drafts of the country's first Five-Year Economic Plan (for 1976-1980) and, more important, of the new Constitution of Socialist Cuba. In October 1974, Blas Roca became chairman of a 19-member PCC commission responsible for preparing the constitutional draft. According to Castro, the new Constitution, which will replace the 1940 Constitution in force only in parts, "will allow us to put an end to the provisional character of the Revolutionary State." Castro said that the draft, to be ready by 24 February 1975, would be "discussed by the masses . . . analyzed by the Party's Political Bureau and the executive Council of Ministers . . . then submitted to the country congress and finally to a referendum in which all the people will participate." (*Granma*, 24 October 1974.)

The Cuban Government is made up of the Executive Committee of the Council of Ministers, whose nine members are responsible for individual "sectors" of the country's life and who supervise 27 ministries and 17 independent agencies on sub-ministerial levels. Premier Fidel Castro, chairman of the Executive Committee, is in charge of the Defense, Security and Non-Sugar Agriculture responsibilities he shares with First Deputy Premier Raúl Castro.

President Dorticós is in charge of planning, banking and trade relations with non-communist countries.

Deputy Premier Ramiro Valdés is in charge of the Construction Sector.

Deputy Premier Guillermo García is in charge of the Transportation and Communication Sector.

Deputy Premier Flavio Bravo Pardo is in charge of the Consumer Goods and Domestic Commerce and Industry Sector.

Deputy Premier Belarmino Castilla is in charge of the Education, Culture and Science Sector.

Deputy Premier Carlos Rafael Rodríguez is in charge of the Foreign Affairs Sector.

Deputy Premier Diocles Torralba González is in charge of the Sugar Sector.

Also described by Havana as an important step toward the institutionalization of the Cuban State was the process of electing "organs of the People's Power" in Matanzas province in the summer of 1974. If successful, the Matanzas experiment of electing provincial and regional State governing bodies will be carried out in the remaining five provinces in late 1975. Cuba also introduced new military ranks and demilitarized government and PCC officials. Since 1 December 1973, Cuba has begun using military ranks to describe only officers on active duty in the Armed Forces and the Ministry of Interior. The new Cuban military ranks (until December 1973 the Cuban Armed Forces had had three basic officer ranks: major, captain and lieutenant) conform generally to those of the

Soviet armed forces. The highest rank, held by Fidel Castro, is commander-in-chief. It is followed by Army commander, or general of the army, and Corps commander (colonel general). Neither of these two ranks was occupied at the end of 1974. Defense Minister Raúl Castro was "promoted" on 3 December 1973 to the rank of division commander (lieutenant general), and is the only officer who has been awarded that insignia.

The Soviet military mission in Cuba was large and high ranking. Its head in 1974 was Lt. Gen. Dmitri Krutsky, whose title was "chief of Soviet military specialists" in the Cuban Armed Forces.

Mass Organizations. During 1974, Cuba's mass organizations were: the Confederation of Cuban Workers (Central de Trabajadores de Cuba; CTC), the National Association of Small Farmers (Asociación de Agricultores Pequeños; ANAP), the Committees for the Defense of the Revolution (Comités de Defensa de la Revolución; CDR), and the Federation of Cuban Women (Federación de Mujeres Cubanas; FMC). The other four groups: the Union of Young Communists (Unión de Jóvenes Comunistas; UJC), the Union of Cuban Pioneers (Unión de Pioneros de Cuba; UPC), the University Student Federation (Federación Estudiantil Universitaria; FEU), and the Federation of High School Students (Federación de Estudiantes de la Enseñanza Media; FEEM), are not really regarded as mass organizations. Rather, they are institutional stepping stones in the selection process of the ruling elite: the Communist Party and the governmental officialdom.

The CTC. The Confederation of Cuban Workers was headed by Roberto Veiga González, secretary general of its National Committee. Veiga was chosen in place of Lázaro Peña, an old guard communist labor leader who died in March 1974 in Havana. Throughout 1974, implementing directives adopted at the 13th CTC Congress held in November 1973, the Cuban government continued its attempts to revitalize the labor unions, whose membership totals 2.2 million. (*New York Times*, 1 December 1975). The main objective of the CTC continues to be improving productivity and reducing waste in agriculture, industry and the services. Unpaid "voluntary labor" is stressed as one means of achieving ¬roduction goals. The CTC has been particularly entrusted with forming the so-called "micro-brigades," which, on a crash basis, build public housing. Slowly, the labor movement is adjusting to a policy of material incentives, which was at least partially introduced by the Cuban government at the CTC's 1973 Congress. Material rewards for "exemplary workers" are being distributed by the unions. The CTC not only offers scarce appliances (such as refrigerators or television sets) at reduced prices to those who get the highest production (and political) marks, but also sells these goods on installment payments. Trade unions also control space at various vacation resorts around the country as well as tickets to entertainment places and sports events, reserved for "vanguard" workers.

The ANAP. The National Association of Small Farmers is headed by José ("Pepe") Ramirez Cruz, a member of the PCC Central Committee. It exercises strict control over the activities of independent farmers, whose farms represent about 20 percent of the land under cultivation. ANAP membership in 1974 was about 180,000. In contrast to the situation in most Soviet bloc countries, private farmers in Cuba have no officially-sponsored outlets to sell their products, and sales to citizens who visit their farms are discouraged. While official figures are lacking, there are indications that their output continues to be decisive in specialized crops like tobacco, coffee and tubers.

The CDR. The Committees for the Defense of the Revolution are headed by Jorge Lezcano, who holds the title of CDR national coordinator. Lezcano is directly responsible to the PCC Central Committee. In 1974, there were 4,751,963 members of CDR in 73,604 committees, organized in 446 municipalities in the country, in every city, factory, and place of work. CDR members perform a variety of tasks. In addition to their original vigilance of "counterrevolutionary activities," they collect empty glass containers, used paper and even postage stamps, clean the streets, check on school attendance and make blood donations. "Today," Lezcano said at a ceremony commemorating the CDR's 14th anniversary, "we are combating the enemy in all its manifestations; we are acting to bolster the unity of the entire nation around the line of the Communist Party of Cuba .... We are striving for the masses' active participation in support of the plans of the Revolution, thus contributing to the exercise of Socialist democracy." (*Juventud Rebelde*, Havana, 29 September 1974.) With over 4,700,000 members, the CDR includes over 70 percent of the country's adults and over 50 percent of Cuba's total population.

The FMC. The Federation of Cuban Women was headed in 1974—as it has been since its inception in 1960—by Vilma Espín Villoy, the wife of Defense Minister Raúl Castro. (Since Premier Castro is not married, his sister-in-law has also functioned, albeit unofficially, as Cuba's First Lady.) In 1974 the FMC claimed about 2,000,000 members, most of whom also belonged to the CTC and, especially, to the CDR. In November, the FMC held its Second Congress. Speaking at its closing ceremony, Premier Castro said that out of the total of 2,331,000 persons working in Cuba 590,000 were women. Castro called attention to what he called a "low" percentage of women who occupy positions of authority in the country and of "low" female membership in the party. "Cuba is still behind in women's equality . . . and for that reason it is necessary to wage a continuous battle against the mentality of discriminating women in their job opportunities," he said. He added that in the local elections held in Matanzas province, only 3 percent of women were elected to posts in local government. (*Granma*, English, 8 December 1974.)

The UJC. The Union of Young Communists is the Cuban equivalent of the Soviet Komsomol. An elitist group, with a membership of 200,000 (*New York Times*, 1 Decmeber 1974), the UJC in 1974 was headed by Luis Orlando Rodríguez, its first secretary, who was responsible directly to the PCC's Central Committee. Cuban youth can become members of the UJC at 14, and at 27 they are entitled to become full-fledged PCC members if they pass through the party's selective admission process. The UJC has many functions, but its principal task is to watch over the ideological formation of youth, directly in the case of the Union of Cuban Pioneers, and indirectly in those of the University Student Federation (FEU) and the Federation of High School Students. The UJC, particularly, coordinates production effort of the Cuban youth, which is mandatory for every young Cuban in school from the elementary to the university levels.

The UPC. The Union of Cuban Pioneers was founded in 1961 and incorporates most school-age children from the age of 5, when they start school, to the age of 14. It is estimated that over 80 percent of all Cuban school children up to the age of 14 belong to the UPC.

The Revolutionary Armed Forces. The FAR (Fuerzas Armadas Revolucionarias) according to Castro numbered about 100,000 regular troops with 150,000 on active reserve. Although the FAR has reduced its ranks by 40 percent in comparison with 1970, "the power of our armed forces has not weakened in the least, it becomes stronger every day," Castro said. "But even if one day there should be economic and even diplomatic relations with the U.S.A. that would not give us the right to weaken our defense, because our defense can never depend on the imperialists' good faith. As long as imperialism exists, our defense will depend on our strength, on our fighting capacity, on the fighting capacity of the whole socialist camp and all revolutionary peoples." (*Granma*, 1 December 1974.) The Cuban armed forces, equipped exclusively with modern Soviet weapons, including Mig 21 fighter planes and ground-to-sea and ground-to-air missiles, are regarded as the best trained military force in Latin America. Since the FAR has a very weak Navy and limited helicopter capacity, this force is primarily a defensive one. It represents a heavy drain on the nation's resources, despite the soldiers' regular participation in production tasks.

Domestic Affairs. Called "The Year of the 15th Anniversary" (of Fidel Castro's ascent to power) 1974 was characterized internally by a governmental effort to put the country's economy in order. The economy was still recovering from near chaotic conditions caused by the upsetting, all-out drive in 1970 to attain a record sugar production of 10 million tons. There were indications that the country was being better run, even though no dramatic changes occurred during the year. While nobody starved in the country, Cuba's most serious problem continued to be food. All basic goods, and industrial consumer goods, were strictly rationed, and there was an active black market, especially in clothing, shoes and appliances. The distribution of rationed goods did not improve perceptively, according to government news media. Prices of rationed items continued to be heavily subsidized, but those that were not rationed (and restaurant meals) were very expensive—as a matter of governmental policy aimed at syphoning excess currency from the market. There were long queues for everything, including paying for electricity, telephone or water at the banks, a cumbersome activity in Cuba as the Government does not allow personal checking accounts. Rationing has continued virtually unchanged since 1963 when it was established. Rations per person were: Meat, three-quarters pound every 9 days; sugar, 4 pounds per month; rice, 6 pounds per month; coffee, 1.5 ounces per week; cooking fat, 1.5 pounds per month; cigarets, 2 packs per week for adults; cigars, 2 per week for men only; eggs, 15 per month; milk, 1 liter daily, for children and elderly; milk, 6 liters per month, for adults. At the end of the year Cuban workers approved a monthly reduction of one pound of sugar per person during 1975 to enable the government to obtain an additional $50 million in foreign exchange.

The 1974 sugar harvest was estimated at 5.6 million tons, slightly higher than that of 1973. But because of higher prices of sugar on the international market, Cuban hard currency earnings in 1974 were close to $2 billion, twice those of 1973. Soviet aid did not diminish; if anything it exceeded $650 million during the year, or $1.5 a day. There were efforts at decentralizing the economy (according to Defense Minister Raúl Castro the establishment of the "People's Power" in Matanzas province was intended as a means to decentralize the state apparatus at all levels), but main decisions were still made in Havana by ministry heads and the highest PCC bodies. Very little was done to improve the quality of Cuban products made for domestic consumption, and a nation-wide effort to build new dwellings made hardly a dent in a severe shortage of housing. But the mass transportation system improved throughout the country, and good social services were maintained for the unemployment-free population.

Internally, there were no signs of opposition to the government, and police control over the population continued to be pervasive. Despite the absence of internal opposition, the PCC urged relentless struggle against what it regarded as "dangerous influences of western ideas." Cuban youth "must never coexist with any of the alienated and anti-social attitudes with which they [the Westerners] try to infiltrate us," said Raúl Castro at the April 1974 congress of the UJC in Havana. "There will be neither individualism nor pseudo-intellectualism" among the youth, he declared, calling the incidence of truancy among youths between the ages of 13 and 16 a "grave problem." (*Granma* 16 April 1974.) Control over the arts also continued to be tight. "The most important thing is that the artist, through his work, expresses the links between that work and the masses and (rejects) individualism," was a party directive given artists at the First Council of the Arts and Entertainers held in Havana in September.

International Position. Cuba made progress in the process of rejoining the family of American nations. She also moderated her previous hard-line posture toward the United States. In January, a Cuban diplomat in Mexico stated that the Havana government would be willing to talk with Washington if the United States lifted its ban on trading with Cuba. The same diplomat, Cuban Ambassador to Mexico L. López Muino, stated that the United States' use of the Guantanamo Naval Base in Cuba was "not important to us" and would not be an obstacle to talks between Washington and Havana. (*New York Times*, 9 January 1974.) Cuba's effort to project internationally an image of businesslike reasonableness was perhaps influenced by the Soviet Communist Party leader, Leonid I. Brezhnev, who visited the island late in January.

Brezhnev, who held talks in Havana with Cuban leaders and several leading Latin American communists, reportedly tried to persuade Fidel Castro that Communism can be achieved only from within a country and not by revolutions exported from the outside, the latter view for years the cornerstone of the Cuban leader's revolutionary credo. Principally because of the commanding size of Soviet aid to Cuba, Brezhnev was apparently successful in making Castro sound more conciliatory as far as Cuba's Latin American relations were concerned, and decidedly pro-Soviet in his pronouncements related to the Soviet-Chinese dispute. At a rally honoring Brezhnev, Castro referred to the Chinese obliquely by attacking "renegades of the revolutionary left who criticize the Soviet Union." In the same speech, he stated that Cuba supports Soviet efforts to end the arms race. (*Baltimore Sun*, 30 January 1974.)

Cuba broadened her trade relations with Latin countries, having made her first large-scale commercial deal with Argentina in 1973, under which she received a credit of $1.2 billion to finance purchases of Argentine manufactured and farm products at the rate of $200-million annually for six years. Trade delegations from Peru, Panama, Mexico and Venezuela traveled to Havana to establish guidelines for expanding commerce. In December, Venezuela and Colombia announced they would begin negotiations for the reestablishment of relations with Cuba. Relations between Caracas and Havana were expected to have important implications for Cuba, reducing her isolation in hemispheric affairs and obtaining a source for imports of oil. The announcement came in the wake of a refusal by the Organization of American States at a November meeting in Quito, Ecuador, to lift the 1964 hemispheric sanctions against the Cuban government. Venezuela, with Colombia and Costa Rica, spearheaded a drive in Quito to lift the Cuban sanctions. They mustered 12 votes, a simple majority, but fell short of the necessary two-thirds majority.

Although OAS sanctions against Cuba remain in force, seven countries maintain ties with Cuba despite them: Argentina, Barbados, Trinidad and Tobago, Jamaica, Peru, Panama and Mexico. Canada, Guyana and the Bahamas, which have an observer status in the OAS, also maintain relations with Cuba. Perhaps indicating a change in the U.S. attitude toward Cuba, the American delegation to the Quito conference did not vote against lifting the anti-Castro sanctions, but abstained. Even if it had been allowed to rejoin the OAS, the Cuban government was not expected to have done so, at least not immediately. In a series of speeches during 1974, Castro and other Cuban leaders stated that they were not interested in the OAS. They advocated the creation of a new regional organization, without the participation of the United States.

International Contacts. Cuba was visited by many foreign dignitaries during 1974, and Cuban leaders made a series of trips abroad. Brezhnev visited Cuba on 28 January-3 February. The February visitors were Erich Honecker, first secretary of the Socialist Unity Party of East Germany; Santiago Carrillo, secretary general of the Communist Party of Spain; and Peruvian and Argentine trade delegations. Phan Van Dong, prime minister of the Democratic Republic of Vietnam, visited Cuba in March, and Algerian President Houari Boumedienne in April. The June visitors were Juan Mari Bras, secretary general of the Socialist Party of Puerto Rico, and Roland LeRoy, secretary of the French Communist Party. Julius K. Nyerere, President of Tanzania went to Cuba in September; October visitors were U.S. Senators Jacob Javits and Clairborn Pell and French Socialist leader François Mitterand. In November, Yasser Arafat, leader of the Palestine Liberation Organization, flew from New York to Havana to meet Fidel Castro, as did Gen. Francisco Morales Bermudez, chief of the general staff of the Peruvian Armed Forces.

Cuban travelers abroad included Defense Minister Raúl Castro, who visited the Soviet Union, Czechoslovakia, Yugoslavia and Bulgaria in February; Deputy Prime Minister Carlos Rafael Rodríguez, who went to South Yemem, Syria and Bulgaria in May, to the World Food Conference in Rome in November (where he urged oil-rich nations to invest in developing countries like Cuba), and to Mexico in December, where he discussed the Cuban-Mexican position on Latin American problems with President Luis Echeverria and top government ministers. In December, Cuban Foreign Minister Raúl Roa met with Venezuelan President Carlos Andres Pérez in Caracas, apparently to discuss future bilateral diplomatic, trade and cultural relations. The Cuban position on the OPEC countries was stated in September when Fidel Castro said it was "unjust to blame the oil-producing countries for the world inflation and the world monetary crisis."

Publications. *Granma* is the daily organ of the Central Committee of the PCC; it appears also in weekly editions in Spanish, English and French. Its editor is Jorge Enrique Mendoza and it has a daily circulation of 600,000. Every province except for Havana province has its own party daily. The UJC publishes *Juventud Rebelde*, with a national circulation of 200,000 copies. *Verde Olivo*, a weekly, is the organ of the FAR, and *Bohemia* is a general news weekly magazine.

University of Miami   George Volsky

Dominican Republic

Intense disagreement over leadership and policy issues, especially since the civil war of 1965, has led to the fragmentation of the communist movement of the Dominican Republic. There are three principal organizations: the Dominican Communist Party (Partido Comunista Dominicano; PCD), which enjoys more or less official recognition by the Soviet Union; the Dominican Peoples Movement (Movimiento Popular Dominicano; MPD), which has been pro-Chinese; and the Revolutionary Movement of 14 June (Movimiento Revolucionario 14 de Junio; MR-1J4), which is also pro-Chinese, but is the group most sympathetic toward the Castro regime. Splits within these groups have created several new factions and parties. These include the Popular Socialist Party (Partido Socialista Popular; PSP), the Communist Party of the Dominican Republic (Partido Comunista de la Republica Dominicana; PCRD or PACOREDO); and the Red Flag (Bandera Roja) and Red Line (Linea Roja) factions of the MR-1J4, and Proletarian Voice (Voz Proletaria). Only the PCD appears to enjoy recognition within the international communist movement.

Until 1974 Communism was completely proscribed in the Dominican Republic, under laws covering propaganda and subversive activities. However, the present government of President Joaquin Balaguer allowed communist parties to issue statements in the mass media and communist student groups to operate more or less uninhibitedly, while maintaining strict surveillance of their activities.

In 1974 several of the Communist groups tried to acquire a respectability which they had not had before. The MPD condemned terrorism; the PCD continued to seek legal recognition, and was supported by a bill which President Belaguer sent to Congress to legalize it.

Estimates concerning the membership of the Dominican Marxist-Leninist groups vary widely. Late in 1974 the *New York Times* (2 October) reported that the MPD, which was rated the largest of the Communist groups, had some 2,000 members, and Reuters Agency in May credited the PCD as having 300 members (*Christian Science Monitor*, 31 May). However, the U.S. State Department estimated all of the leftist groups had only about 1,400 members. These were said to include 460 in the PCD, 385 in the MPD, 300 in MR-1J4, 145 in the PCRD, 65 in the VP, and 40 in the PSP (*World Strength of the Communist Party Organizations*, 1974, p. 162). The population of the Dominican Republic is about 4,300,000 (estimated 1970).

Politically motivated murders became an established feature of the Dominican scene after the 1965 civil war. Although the victims were of all political colors most were members of communist groups or of the major opposition party, the Dominican Revolutionary Party (Partido Revolucionario Dominicano; PRD). The killings were attributed both to feuds among communist groups and to actions by paramilitary groups reportedly organized by the military and police, particularly the latter. During 1974 political terrorism declined, perhaps reflecting the concentration of political attention, even among extremist groups, on the presidential election campaign.

Sources of support for the communists include the universities, secondary schools, and labor unions, and reflect the fragmentation of the movement. At the university level, the student movement is divided into the following organizations: "Fragua," led by the Red Line of the MR-1J4; Juventud Comunista, led by PCRD members; the Comité Universitario "Julio Antonio Mella," led by PCD members; and the Comité Flavio Sucre," led by MPD members. The powerful Federation of Dominican Students (Federación de Estudiantes Dominicanos; FED), which is said to enroll about 200,000 university and secondary school students, was after 1969 in the hands of non-communist but left-wing students of the PRD. The communist movement at the secondary school level is represented by the Union of Revolutionary Students (Unión de Estudiantes Revolucionarios; UER).

Within the labor movement, which generally has been weak since the 1965 civil war, communist support is more limited. The "Foupsa-Cesitrado" labor confederation, reportedly in the hands of MPD members, is only one of several central labor bodies. The largest is the Confederación Autonoma Sindical Cristiana, more or less associated with the Revolutionary Social Christian Party (Partido Revolucionario Social Cristiano; PRSC). The powerful "Unachosin" chauffeurs' union includes communist members, mostly of the MPD.

The PCD. The PCD was founded clandestinely in 1942. As the Popular Socialist Party (Partido Socialista Popular), it came into the open for a short while in 1946, but it was again suppressed by the Trujillo dictatorship. During the military-civilian revolt in April 1965, the party took the PCD name, which it has used since. Although in 1967 the PCD adopted (verbally but not in practice) a Castroite line, advocating the concept of armed struggle in most Latin American countries, it soon abandoned that position. In recent years it has advocated the kind of popular front which has been characteristic of the pro-Soviet parties in Latin America. In 1974 the party both cooperated with the major parties opposing the Balaguer government, while seeking friendly relations with the administration.

Leadership and Organization. Narciso Isa Conde is the PCD secretary general. Other leaders include Dr. Julian Pena and Mario Gonzalez Cordova. The party claims to be organized on a national scale, with cells in almost every city and in various regions of the countryside. It has a committee operating in New York City among persons of Dominican origin.

Domestic Attitudes and Activities. During 1974 the PCD continued its efforts to enter into the mainstream of Dominican politics. They were aided by a bill which President Joaquin Balaguer sent to Congress on 27 February, suggesting that the PDC be granted legal recognition. (Radio Santo Domingo, 27 February). In his speech, the president commented:

> We have here the legalization of the communist party. It is another bill of particular interest which I today present to this Congress and which seeks to lift the legal ban which weighs upon the Dominican Communist Party.
> The nation's constitution guarantees freedom of association for political objectives, as long as this freedom is not used for purposes contrary to or disruptive of public order, national security or good habits. The legislative act issued on 8 October 1963, which forbids the activities of communist groups in the country, has undoubtedly been healthy because most of those groups are not composed of persons who believe communist ideas of their own conviction. They are individuals who use these ideas as a pretext to carry out illicit activities with subversive aims.
> Because of [the] institutional viewpoint in the past years, I think the time has come to make a distinction between those groups and parties which really follow the communist line because they sincerely believe the doctrines of Marx and Lenin, hoping to establish them in their fatherland through legal and essentially peaceful means, and these groups which, to the contrary, disguise themselves as communists so as to perpetrate political crimes and immoral acts in violation of the nation's laws.

In accordance with what I have just said, the bill which I submit to Congress seeks to legalize the activities of the Dominican Communist Party, an organization largely composed of young intellectuals who profess Marxist-Leninist ideas and who so far have not carried out any unconstitutional or illegal acts.

The bill provoked considerable protest. One of those who objected was Lucas Rojas, general secretary of the PRSC, who compared the move to dictator Trujillo's legalization of the same party in 1946, and was an effort to make the people believe that there was democracy in the Dominican Republic. He said that the PRSC favored legalization of all of the far-Leftist groups.

The process of discussing this bill was slow. At one point, PCD secretary general Narciso Isa Conde appeared before the Senate Committee on Interior and Police to testify in favor of the measure. He made the rather surprising confession that "we admit certain deficiencies and failures in the Communist system," and that one of those was restrictions on freedom of speech. He noted that "if our party is legalized, we shall use such legality to disseminate our ideas." (El Caribe, 27 March). During this discussion the PCD joined other far Left organizations to urge Congress to legalize all those groups (Radio Santo Domingo, 8 March).

After the reelection of President Balaguer in May, interest in the bill to legalize the PCD revived. The Reuter news agency attributed President Balaguer's interest in the idea to the growing strength of the MPD (Christian Science Monitor, 31 May).

The PCD had a somewhat equivocal position during the campaign leading to Balaguer's reelection. They did not join the coalition of right and left wing opponents known as National Dignity which was established late in 1973 to name a single candidate of the opposition. When it broke up with the withdrawal of the Partido Revolucionario Dominicano and several others in January 1974, the PCD issued a statement to the effect that the failure of the bloc was due to the "antihistoric nature of the bloc and its harmful effects on the popular forces" (Radio Santo Domingo, 5 January).

However, the PCD also did not join the more limited "Agreement of Santiago" signed after the split in the National Dignity group. The PRD was the axis of this group and one of its principal leaders, Antonio Guzman, was named as candidate against Balaguer. However, in the showdown, neither opposition coalition remained in the race, charging that Balaguer had rigged the election. However, the refusal of the PCD to contribute to the efforts to create a united opposition to Balaguer won it the condemnation of much of the rest of the far Left. Thus, in an interview in April, two left-wing faction leaders, Ivan Rodríguez of the Red Line of the 14th of June and Juan B. Mejia of the Red Banner group, referred to "the Balaguerista agents of the PCD" (Ahora, 1 April).

Publication. The PCD publishes a clandestine weekly, El Popular. Its declarations are also published from time to time in the daily press of Santo Domingo.

*   *   *

The PSP. When the PCD adopted Castroite views and tactics—mostly limited to verbal declarations—in 1967, a split occurred within the party. The more moderate members, proclaiming their support for the Soviet Union and "peaceful coexistence," formed a new party, using the PCD's former name, the Popular Socialist Party (Partido Socialista Popular; PSP). Despite its pro-Soviet stance, the PSP has not been recognized by the Soviet Union, but it seems to maintain friendly relations with some other pro-Soviet parties in Latin America.

The PSP was apparently relatively inactive during 1974.

*   *   *

The MPD. The MPD was formed by Dominican exiles in Havana in 1956, and originally included among its leaders many persons who did not have communist sympathies. However, after the death of Trujillo in 1971 and the return of the founders to Santo Domingo, it quickly took on a Marxist-Leninist orientation, and those who were opposed to this left the party.

The MPD became a formal party only in August 1965. It was then pro-Chinese, and was one of the most active and violent leftist groups, with considerable support among students and slum dwellers and some following in organized labor. However, more recently it, like the PCD, has sought to acquire a more respectable image, a development which has led to the desertion of its ranks by more violence-prone elements.

Leadership and Organization. Among the leaders of the MPD is Julio de Peña Valdés who has been secretary general of the trade union group "Foupsa-Cesitrado." Others include Rafael Tavares and Rafael Enrique Rivera Mejia. (For other names of MPD leaders see *YICA, 1972*, pp. 363-64).

Domestic Attitudes and Activities. The MPD proclaims its intention to bring about a seizure of power by the proletariat, peasantry, and other "progressive" forces in order to install a "people's democratic dictatorship." Until recently, it maintained that "the only road . . . is armed violence" (*Tricontinental Bulletin*, Havana, August 1971).

The MPD was reported as enjoying substantial growth during 1974. The party was said by Reuter's Agency to be "finding disgruntled adherents in the countryside despite the economic boom that President Balaguer has engineered in the Dominican Republic in the last five years" (*Christian Science Monitor*, 31 May).

The MPD played a minor role in the presidential election campaign. It first joined the anti-Balaguer coalition known as National Dignity. However, when that group split early in the year, the MPD apparently abandoned it, and urged a more limited alliance against the president's attempt to be reelected for a third term.

The MPD was accused by the PCD of forming an alliance with the major opposition party, the Partido Revolucionario Dominicano. There was some additional evidence that, in spite of earlier attacks by the MPD on the theory of "Dicatorship with Popular Support." first enunciated by Juan Bosch, the PRD founder, and subsequently endorsed by the PRD, the two parties were moving closer together in 1974. This was perhaps facilitated by Juan Bosch's abandonment of the PRD in 1973, and his founding of his own party, the Partido de Liberación Dominicana.

The change in party policy was demonstrated when a break-away group from the MPD held hostages they had seized in the Venezuelan consulate. The MPD denounced the kidnapers, and an unidentified U.S. official commented: "The Left here is maturing. The MPD is trying hard to be a legitimate political party, as legitimate as any other party. It realizes it can't engage in terror if it hopes to become an elected party in this society." (*NYT*, 2 October.)

Publications. The MPD publishes an irregular clandestine weekly, *Libertad*.

*   *   *

The 12 January Liberation Movement. As the MPD has sought a more respectable and recognized position in the national political spectrum, some more extremist elements have abandoned it. One such group formed the 12 January Liberation Movement. Late in November 1973 the principal leader of this group, Dr. Plinio Matos Moqueto, was captured by the police (*Ahora*, 12 November).

The capture of its leader did not end the 12th of January group. This was demonstrated late in September, when some of its members kidnaped Barbara A. Hutchinson, local director of the United

States Information Service, took her to the Venezuelan Consulate, and seized it by force. For close to two weeks negotiations continued before the release of the hostages and the granting of permission to the guerrillas to leave the country. The leader of this guerrilla group was Radamés Mendez Vargas.

* * *

The PCRD. The Communist Party of the Dominican Republic was formed by dissidents of the MPD, after the 1965 civil war and is considered very extreme. The secretary general is Luis Adolfo Montes González. The membership is limited mostly to the city of Santo Domingo. The PCRD defines itself as a Marxist-Leninist party, "created in conformity with the thoughts of Mao Tse-tung." The party proclaims its major objective to be to install socialism and then communism, through a "democratic revolution." (Statement of Montas Gonzalez, Radio Continental, Santo Domingo, 17 January 1971.) The PCRD seems to have been relatively inactive during 1974.

The PCRD's official organ is *El Comunista.*

* * *

The MR-1J4. The Revolutionary Movement of 14 June derives its name from an unsuccessful attempt to overthrow the late dictator Trujillo on that day in 1959. Although the 1959 invasion came from Cuba and was helped by Castro, many of the early leaders of the MR-1J4 felt that the Cuban leaders had betrayed them, and the party was not pro-communist until October 1963, when the government of President Juan Bosch was overthrown. Soon thereafter, the MR-1J4 attempted a military uprising, which resulted in the death of the original leaders of the movement. Those who took over evolved quickly in the communist direction, particularly towards the Castro version of Marxism-Leninism. The MR-1J4 has subsequently split into several factions. Aside from the main body, there now exist the so-called Red Flag, Red Line and Voz Proletaria groups.

Like the rest of the extreme Left, the various factions of MR-1J4 moved towards legal and less violent activities during 1974. They participated as minor elements in the presidential election campaign. The Red Line (Linea Roja) faction led by Ivan Rodríguez, the Bandera Roja (Red Banner) faction led by Juan B. Meijia, as well as the Voz Proletaria and the otherwise unidentified left-wing factions known as New Course, Revolutionary Action and Advanced Revolutionary Action Nucleus, formed part of the National Dignity coalition formed late in 1973 to oppose the reelection ambitions of President Joaquin Balaguer. When that coalition broke up early in 1974 these far Left elements stayed with the National Dignity alliance. They were particularly critical of the MPD for abandoning it. (*Ahora*, 1 April, p. 4.)

Somewhat earlier, in November 1973, the Bandera Roja group had strongly attacked the Balaguer government for allegedly seizing control of the Port Workers Union for the administration's Partido Reformista. A statement of Bandera Roja claimed that "the government wants to seize control of all labor unions to convert them into yellow organizations that support its and imperialist interests instead of those of the working class" (Radio Santo Domingo, 1 November).

Another small far-Left group, known as Patria Roja (Red Fatherland), was reported to have joined in March with a party of the same name in Peru for the summoning of a meeting of Latin American Communist groups of their orientation. There is no indication that any such meeting took place during the year.

Rutgers University   Robert J. Alexander

Ecuador

The communist movement in Ecuador began in 1926 with the founding of the Socialist Party of Ecuador. In 1928 the party became a member of the Communist International, and in 1931 changed its name to the Communist Party of Ecuador (Partido Comunista del Ecuador; PCE). A pro-Chinese splinter group, the Marxist-Leninist Communist Party of Ecuador (Partido Comunista Marxista-Leninista del Ecuador; PCMLE) dates from 1963.

The PCE is estimated to have 500 members and the PCMLE 100 (*World Strength of Communist Party Organizations 1973*, p. 163). The population of Ecuador is 6,300,000 (estimated 1974).

The military junta that assumed power in July 1963 declared the PCE illegal, but the party was able to remain intact through clandestine activities and its representation in various mass organizations. After 1966, when the government returned to civilian control, the party again began to function openly. In 1971 the PCE and several other small leftist organizations formed the Popular Unity bloc in anticipation of elections promised for June 1972. Their efforts were halted when the government was overthrown in a military coup led by General Guillermo Rodríguez Lara on 15 February 1972 and the elections were canceled. The PCE was legalized in 1973.

Organization and Leadership. The PCE elected a new Central Committee of 27 full and 15 alternate members at its 9th congress (see below), and at the Central Committee plenum after the congress reelected Pedro Saad General Secretary (*IB*, 1973, no. 23-24).

The party's youth organization is the Communist Youth of Ecuador (Juventud Comunista Ecuatoriana; JCE). The party waged a constant struggle against the influence of "Maoist terrorist groups" in the universities, particularly the so-called ATALA group, sometimes known as the Student Struggle Front (Frente de Lucha Estudiantil; FLE). The PCE controls the Confederation of Ecuadorean Workers (Confederación de Trabajadores Ecuatorianos; CTE), which until recently was the largest labor organization in the country, with a claimed membership of 60,000. The CTE, a member of the World Federation of Trade Unions, is led by Leonidas Córdova and Bolívar Bolanos. The party has condemned "desperate attempts by pro-Peking adventurers to sow discord in the ranks of the revolutionary democratic forces of the people" (*El Pueblo*, 20 October 1973), particularly in the CTE affiliate Guayas Provincial Workers Federation (Federación Provincial de Trabajadores de Guayas; FPTG) in Guayaquil. Peasant organizations under PCE influence are the Coastal Farm Workers Federation (Federación de Trabajadores Agrícolas del Litoral; FTAL) and the Ecuadorean Federation of Indians (Federación Ecuatoriana de Indias; FEI). According to PCE leaders, party influence on peasants is great and growing. Calls are repeatedly made for the formation of a single national peasant organization.

Party Internal Affairs. The PCE held its 9th congress in Guayaquil on 15-18 November 1973. (The conclusions of this congress, not available when the *YICA, 1974* went to press last year, are reported below.) The "Political Resolution" of the congress stated: "the essential condition for the victory of our [Ecuadorean] people is the ideological, political, and organizational strengthening" of the PCE. While noting party growth, the resolution indicated that the "main weaknesses" of the PCE were "a low ideological level" and inadequate organization. The party needed to preserve its unity "at all costs," fighting any signs of anti-communism, factional activity, and sectarianism. A systematic campaign for the recruitment of new members for the PCE and JCE was essential. A beginning had already been made to transform the PCE into a "great party of the masses." The ideological level had to be raised, in part by strengthening the Marxist-Leninist education of PCE members. (See *IB*, Prague ed., no. 7, 1974.) The Central Committee held a plenum on 2-3 February 1974 in Guayaquil (ibid., no. 5-6).

Domestic Views. The "Political Resolution" of the 9th congress states that "the sole way to freedom, well-being and progress is the national-liberation, anti-imperialist, anti-feudal and democratic revolution with its subsequent progress towards socialism." There is economic growth in the country, capitalism is advancing alongside remnants of feudalism and the domination of imperialism. This growth is dependent on foreign factors and is still profitable to the "ruling minority." Some policies of the military government are constructive, or partially so, while others are not. The "Resolution" states that "support must be given to the positive aspects and activities of the military government," while the PCE must "combat anti-popular attitudes, actions, and ideas within the government." Agrarian reform, oil policies and defense of off-shore rights had some positive elements. (Ibid.; and *El Pueblo*, 5 January 1974; *El Tiempo*, Quito, 28 April.) The agrarian reform bill adopted by the government at the end of 1973, which drew extensive comment from the PCE, had positive as well as simple reformist and even adventurist aspects. Among the latter was the provision to set up agricultural cooperatives when the consciousness of the peasant masses was only ready for individual land holding and utilization. (Saad, *Zemledelsko Zname*, Sofia, 21 April.) At the same time the government has displayed weakness and vacillation in some domestic policies and at times has acted against the people. However, an anti-imperialist, anti-feudal and democratic consciousness is developing among workers, peasants, students, civilians and military men, and distrust of the ruling classes is growing. In the face of this, reactionary forces are joining forces with imperialists to preserve the decaying system, hatching reactionary plots and trying to "deflect the masses from their aims." (*IB*, Prague ed., no. 7.)

The PCE's program calls for revolutionary changes to achieve the party's "basic aims": (1) eradication of economic and political causes of imperialist rule; (2) a democratic agrarian reform; (3) democratization of public life; (4) development of the national industry, particularly the state sector; (5) raising the people's standard of living; and (6) an independent peaceful foreign policy towards all countries. By taking this path, a "revolutionary people's democratic and patriotic government" may be established. More specifically, the immediate struggle needs to be intensified in the following ways: (1) nationalization of oil; (2) defense of 200-mile territorial waters; (3) campaign for electrification of the country; (4) nationalization of exports and establishment of strict controls on imports; (5) nationalizaton of all banking operations; (6) full utilization of Andes Pact; (7) immediate action on agrarian reform; (8) all-round increase in wages and establishment of a sliding wage scale; (9) freezing of prices on primary necessities and lower rent and medicine charges; (10) preservation and extension of democratic rights. (Ibid.)

The main slogan of the 9th congress was: "Unity of the Anti-Imperialist, Democratic, and Patriotic Forces of Ecuador in the Struggle for National and Social Liberation." According to the PCE, the communists need to work with peasants and workers, forming a closer alliance between them, and appeal to the "middle sectors of the population," adding that "here our weaknesses have been chronic." The party maintains that "a national-liberation front must be created as the main tool of our revolution." (Ibid.)

International Views. At its 9th congress the PCE expressed its admiration for the Communist Party of the Soviet Union and hailed its unceasing work to safeguard world peace, build communism, and help the world's workers and national liberation movements. It also praised the example and stimulation offered by the Communist Party of Cuba, and proclaimed its solidarity with the Communist Party and people of Chile. The PCE supports the convening of a conference of Latin American communist parties to discuss common problems. (*IB*, Prague ed., no. 7; also see *El Pueblo*, 8 February.)

Publications. The PCE publishes the weekly *El Pueblo* in Guayaquil as well as pamphlets, books and other papers.

*   *   *

The PCMLE. The Marxist-Leninist Communist Party of Ecuador was first established in 1963. As a result of ideological disputes and personal rivalries, the PCMLE itself split into three factions by 1968. One of these, led by Rafael Echeverria, has been regarded by the Chinese as the authentic PCMLE. In recent years, the party has directed its attentions primarily toward students and secondarily toward workers and peasants. The party's long-term objectives are an anti-feudal and anti-imperialist national liberation revolution led by the working class in close alliance with the peasants, and with the cooperation of all revolutionary elements of society. (*En Marcha*, Quito, 30 April-6 May 1972.)

Hoover Institution   William E. Ratliff
Stanford University

El Salvador

The Communist Party of El Salvador (Partido Comunista de El Salvador, established in 1925, is an outlawed group of around two hundred, with its most recently reported secretary general Jorge Shafik Handal.

The upsurge of communist and related guerrilla activity during 1974 must be understood against the background of the deteriorating socio-economic situation of the country. Since 1971, unemployment has hovered around twenty percent, with a much greater portion of the population under-employed. Inflation, by mid-1974, had reached an annual rate of sixty percent. Because of cost pressures, many landlords have turned to cattle raising and consequently evicted large numbers of rural peasants who swell the urban population at the very time the government is attempting to get rid of street peddlers and shanty towns around the capital. In January, President Colonel Arturo Armando Molina announced a new rural minimum wage of a dollar ten a day, plus rations, but this ineffective gesture simply signified that his vaunted land reform program had been permanently shelved.

One major problem of the faltering economy has been the disruption of the Central American Common Market, due to the border conflict between El Salvador and Honduras. The most recent provocations and clashes occurred in December 1973. This conflict has not, however, driven any wedge between the communist parties of the two countries, which have, indeed, found the conflict a fertile source of propaganda. At the preliminary meeting for the Ninth Congress of Communist and Workers' Parties of Mexico, Central America and Panama, held in December 1973, the parties affirmed their solidarity and declared that "the differences between the governments of Honduras and Salvador . . . should under no circumstances become the pretext for an armed conflict." They urged all democratic social and political forces to work together to prevent war. (*Libertad*, 12 January 1974.) At a joint meeting of the two parties in February, as reported by TASS, they blamed the conflict on "ultra-reactionary ruling circles of El Salvador, and the reactionaries of Honduras, with direct encouragement of U.S. Imperialism." The Mexican and Central American parties met again in May and again attacked the regime of President Molina specifically on the border question and the fraudulent elections of March 1974. (*IB*, Prague ed., no. 14; also see *Mexico*).

The flurry of meetings mentioned above indicates a considerable resurgence of activity among Salvadoran Communists. The Federación Unida de Sindicatos Salvadoreños (FUSS), the communist-backed labor organization long thought moribund, has revived remarkably during the year, due to economic unrest. At a june 1974 workers' congress, FUSS demanded a general price freeze, a law providing for automatic wage and salary adjustments and an immediate fifty percent wage increase. One reason for this new stridency is the fact that FUSS is being challenged by the non-communist left-wing organization known as Frente de Acción Popular Unida (FAPU). With a less orthodox and more dynamic approach, FAPU has succeeded in organizing large numbers of hitherto unorganized rural and urban workers. FUSS characterizes the new movement as "petty bourgeois," and the bickering between the two has so far played into the hands of Colonel Molina and the ruling Partido de Conciliación Nacional (PCN) (*Latin America*, 9 August).

While a revived FUSS may be a problem for the government, the major challenge appears to come from groups of guerrilla terrorists operating mostly in the cities. The most active groups appear to be the Ejército Revolucionario Popular (ERP), which, like FUSS, is Moscow-oriented, and the Fuerzas Populares de Liberación (FPL), said to be "Maoist-Guevarist."

This guerrilla activity first became a major problem in the summer of 1973 when four guerrillas robbed the Bank of London and Montreal in San Salvador, shot a policeman and escaped with nine thousand dollars. With much greater affrontery, a group of fifteen, belonging to the ERP, sealed off the Twenty-Ninth of August Avenue in the capital on 24 November 1973. They then proceeded to rob one store of fifty pistols and automatic weapons, although the store was only a short distance from police headquarters. Three persons were killed.

The ERP followed this up with an attack on two San Salvador radio stations, YSKT and YSR, on 3 March. Before withdrawing, the group broadcast a recording calling on the people, "especially peasants" to launch an armed struggle. This was probably designed to embarrass the municipal and legislative elections to be held on 10 March. To underscore this point the same group raided the Central Electoral Council, which tabulates votes, on the sixth. In this raid two police guards were killed and several more wounded. A group of eight guerrillas, including one woman, then proceeded to destroy the council's records with fire bombs and attempted unsuccessfully to kidnap the General Secretary of the Electoral Council.

Not to be outdone, a band calling itself the Farabundo Martí Group of the FPL (named for a communist martyr of the 1932 uprising), assassinated the private secretary of the Presidency, Raymundo Pineda Rodrigo in early April. On 5 April this caused the Interior minister, Juan Antonio Martínez Varela, to admit the presence of communist guerrillas. On 29 April, the ERP seized a radio station in Santa Ana. The next day the FPL planted a bomb which shattered the Chilean Embassy in San Salvador.

By 1 July, President Molina was publicly decrying "professional agitators who, on orders from other quarters, are trying to weaken our institutions." However, despite government promises of a crackdown, bombings continued to occur at North American owned firms throughout the summer and fall.

Paradoxically, this upsurge in communist activity has coincided with better relations between El Salvador and the Soviet Union. In January the two countries agreed to trade relations, although they have no diplomatic ties.

Eastern Connecticut State College   Thomas P. Anderson

Guadeloupe

The Guadeloupe Communist Party (Parti Communiste Guadeloupéen; PCG) originated in 1944 as the Guadeloupe Federation of the French Communist Party, which in March 1958 transformed itself into the present autonomous party. In recent years the PCG has been plagued by conflict and expulsions, and the communist left in Guadeloupe is now represented by several diffuse groups in addition to the PCG.

The PCG is legal. It claims to have 1,500 members (*WMR*, April 1972). The United States State Department has estimated its membership as 3,000 (*World Strength of the Communist Party Organizations*, Washington, D.C., 1973, p. 145). The population of Guadeloupe is 335,000 (estimated 1970).

The PCG is an active and effective participant in Guadeloupe's political life, on both local and departmental levels, in spite of its internal dissension. (As one of France's overseas departments, Guadeloupe is an integral part of the French Republic.) With one seat in the French National Assembly (Hégésippe Ibéné) and 10 of the 31 seats in the Guadeloupe General Council, the PCG is the strongest single party on the council and the most powerful communist party in any of the French overseas departments (see *L'Humanité*, Paris, 2 October 1973). Ibéné, who was defeated in the March 1973 elections for the National Assembly only to win the seat after the CPG successfully challenged the legality of the election, was faced with a rematch also as mayor of Sainte-Anne when his defeated opponent challenged the legality of his election to that body. Municipal elections on 29 September reinstalled Ibéné and the rest of the Sainte-Anne Council.

Leadership and Organization. The PCG is headed by Guy Daninthe as first secretary. Other prominent leaders include René Georges, Bernard Alexis, Henri Bangou, Jérôme Cléry, H. Ibéné, P. Lacave, R. Baron, Serge Pierre-Justin, Hermann Songeons, Diniéres Talis, and Pierre Tarer. Bangou is mayor of Point-a-Pitre, the largest city of Guadeloupe. Cléry is mayor of Basse Terre, its capital. Ibéné and Lacave are also mayors.

The PCG, according to Guy Daninthe, is organized in 11 "sections" and 50 "nuclei." None of its officers are full-time party workers. A large number of its members are said to be workers, many of whom are engaged in the growing of sugar cane, the island's main economic activity. (*WMR*, April 1972.)

The PCG has strong influence in Guadeloupe's largest trade union, the General Confederation of Labor of Guadeloupe (Confédération Générale du Travail de la Guadeloupe; CGTC), which has some 5,000 members. The party's youth front, the Union of Communist Youth of Guadeloupe (Union de la Jeunesse Communiste de la Guadeloupe; UJCG), has limited influence among young people. The party is influential also within the Union of Guadeloupe Women (Union des Femmes Guadeloupéenes; UFG), which is affiliated with the Soviet-controlled Women's International Democratic Federation.

Departmental and National Views and Positions. In 1974 the PCG was concerned primarily with the issues of Guadeloupe's independence from France, the island's deteriorating economy, and the French presidential elections in May. The party organ, *L'Etincelle*, reported frequently on interventions by PCG members on the General Council, presenting grievances or proposals relating to the economy of Guadeloupe. The year's first such report related that the PCG representatives had voted against the proposed departmental budget for 1974: 1) because additional taxes would be imposed on the working people who would not benefit from their expenditures; 2) because much of the revenue would be used to diminish the consequences, on the social level, of the deterioration of the economy, instead of contributing to the establishment of a "new economy from which the consequences of the colonial regime can be extirpated"; and 3) because much of the disbursement would be to those who have "no relation to the vital needs" of Guadeloupe; and 4) because the prevailing attitudes and the substance of the budget provide a "powerful means of pressure and blackmail, used by the power of the colonialists, against the workers, unemployed persons, young persons, and a majority of elected officials." (Ibid., 26 January.)

The CGTG and other trade union organizations organized a "Great Assembly of Protest" on 30-31 March, at which Daninthe presided and Ibéné, one of the four founding members of the CPG, was principal speaker. Reporting on the event, *L'Etincelle* stated that it had been motivated, in part, by the fact that 27 percent of Guadeloupe's working force is unemployed.

A Politburo communiqué on 2 February termed the rise in price of petroleum by the oil-producing nations "legitimate." It called on the French government, however, not to pass on this increase by raising taxes, but rather to absorb at least a portion of it, while at the same time attacking the "enormous profits" of the oil companies. The communiqué added that it was an unfortunate situation in which the "colonial regime [would] never permit the Guadeloupe people to resolve the problems with which they are confronted." (Ibid., 2 February.)

The PCG expressed increased optimism about the autonomy movement. Whereas in 1971 it had been the lone representative from Guadeloupe at the autonomy convention at Morne-Rouge (Martinique), it now appeared that the concept was gaining greater currency in Guadeloupe. The leftist unity, forged by the presidential election and campaign, indicated that the positions of various leftist parties had shifted somewhat toward favoring autonomy. These included the Socialist Federation of Guadeloupe, the Progressive Party, and the Guadeloupe Socialist Movement. (Ibid., 13 July.) Whenever it could, the party pointed to examples, such as Papua and Malta, of newly acquired independence by very small countries with small populations to demonstrate the feasibility of such an action.

As mentioned above, the presidential elections tended to strengthen the bonds among Guadeloupe's leftist parties. All the major leftist parties, with the PCG in the forefront, supported François Mitterand, who won an easy plurality in the first round of the election on 5 May, but lost to Giscard d'Estaing by a very narrow margin in the final round. In Guadeloupe, However, Mitterand polled 56 percent in the final vote, a figure that was often used by the CPG to remind adversaries of the trend of popular sentiment on the island.

International Views and Positions. The PCG is a strong supporter of the Soviet Union, and although most of its attention outside of Guadeloupe was given to France and its possessions, it reported frequently on developments of communist parties throughout the world.

On 19 January, *L'Etincelle* responded to attacks by the People's Republic of China (PRC) on the Soviet proposal for collective security in Asia and a "zone of peace" in the Indian Ocean. These attacks, according to *L'Etincelle*, belonged to a "worn out theme, long ago pulverized by reality."

They were reminiscent of the "exercises of Western propaganda during the time of the cold war." On the occasion of the twenty-fifth anniversary of the PRC, *L'Etincelle* wished the Chinese people "prosperity and success in the building of the socialist society founded on the Leninist principles of proletarian internationalism."

Publications. The PCG publishes a weekly newspaper, *L'Etincelle*, with a claimed circulation of 5,000 (occasionally reaching 15,000 during special events).

*   *   *

In addition to the PCG there are at least two other Marxist-Leninist parties in Guadeloupe: The Combat Ouvrier (Worker Combat) and the G.O.G. (Guadeloupe National Organization Group). Both created interference in CGTC strike activities in April this year. Combat Ouvrier, which *L'Etincelle* identified as Trotskyist, and two trade unions attempted unsuccessfully to disrupt a strike of banana workers during the first week of April (*L'Etincelle*, 20 April). Combat Ouvrier, according to a *L'Etincelle* report, appealed to the workers to abandon the CGTC leadership in the strike and "direct themselves" in their own strike (interpreted by *L'Etincelle* as meaning "directed by Combat Ouvrier"). The G.O.N.G., also with two unions, sought to expand a building trades strike and disrupt negotiations during the first two weeks in April. Neither were successful but *L'Etincelle* attempted to justify the rather moderate position of the CGTC by stating: "For the serious union organizations the strike is not a goal, but rather a means of satisfying a claim against the bad will of the employer" (ibid.).

A new Trotskyist group, the Socialist Revolution Group, representing the Fourth International in the Antilles, held its founding congress on 28-30 December 1973 in Fort-de-France, Martinique (See *Martinique*).

Mountain View, California   Eric Stromquist

Guatemala

The communist party in Guatemala, which since 1952 has been called the Guatemalan Party of Labor (Partido Guatemalteco del Trabajo; PGT), originated in the predominantly communist-controlled "Socialist Labor Unification," founded in 1921. This group became the Communist Party of Guatemala (Partido Comunista de Guatemala; PCG) in 1923 and joined the Communist International in 1924. Increasing communist activities among workers during the mid-1920s were cut off by the end of the decade and were kept at a minimum throughout the dictatorship of Jorge Ubico (1931-44). In 1946-47 new Marxist groups appeared in the trade union and student movements, organized in the clandestine "Democratic Vanguard." At an underground Congress held in 1949 this group took the name PCG. A prominent communist labor leader founded a second and parallel communist party in 1950, called the "Revolutionary Workers' Party of Guatemala." The two groups merged into a single PCG in 1951. In 1952 the PCG adopted the name PGT, which it has continued to use. The PGT was legal between 1951 and 1954 and played an active role in the administration of Jacobo Arbenz. The party was outlawed and has worked underground since the overthrow of Arbenz in 1954. Although the party has some influence among students and intellectuals, it does not play any significant role in national affairs. Voting in the latest national election, March 1974, is shown in the accompanying table.

The PGT is estimated to have 750 members. The population of Guatemala is 5,310,000 (1970 census).

Three guerrilla groups have operated in Guatemala in recent years; the Revolutionary Armed Forces, which is the military arm of the PGT; the Rebel Armed Forces (Fuerzas Armadas Rebeldes; FAR); and the 13 November Revolutionary Movement (Movimiento Revolucionario 13 de Noviembre; MR-13). The FAR and M-13 are believed to have fewer than 100 members each, plus several hundred sympathizers. The relative inactivity of all three groups in 1974 is attributed to the long war of attrition against the guerrillas waged by the Guatemalan military, especially effective during the "law-and-order" administration of General Carlos Arana Osorio (1970-74). In January, Arana charged that "antipatriotic forces" composed of discredited politicians, guerrilla remnants, and the PGT had infiltrated the capital's municipal government, the University of San Carlos, and various professional and labor organizations (*Prensa Libre*, 14 January).

Assassinations, kidnapings, and other acts of violence, especially by clandestine organizations of the right, intensified during the first half of the year, disrupting domestic tranquility in Guatemala City and the surrounding countryside. Previous rightest groups such as the Organized Anti-Communist Movement (MANO) and the "Eye for an Eye" ("Ojo por Ojo") were superseded by the self-named "Death Squadron," which began operations in February by announcing its intention to "execute all types of criminals without mercy" (*El Imparcial*, 1 February). By mid-April the organiza-

516

Guatemala, National (Presidential) Election, 3 March 1974

Name of party	Votes Cast	% of Total Votes
Communist:		
Guatemalan Labor Party (PGT)	(Outlawed)	– –
Non-Communist Left:		
Christian Democratic Party (PDC)		
General Efraín Ríos Montt	228,067	31.1
Center:		
Revolutionary Party (PR)		
Col. Ernesto Paiz Novales	143,111	19.9
Conservative:		
Institutional Democratic Party (PID)		
National Liberation Party (MLN)		
Gen. Kjell Laugerud García	298,953	41.1
Other:		
Blank or null	57,059	7.9
Total	727,190	100.0

Source: Official count released by Guatemalan Electoral Commission on 11 March. Amid widespread charges of electoral fraud, the Guatemalan Congress elected MLN-PID candidate Kjell Laugerud president on 13 March.

---

tion claimed 28 victims, among them trade union and political leaders, students, and journalists (ibid., 27 April). The murder of newsman and militant Christian Democrat Mario Monterroso Armas on 27 March prompted the influential Association of Guatemalan Journalists (APG) to appeal to the Defense and Interior ministers for stronger guarantees of freedom of the press and personal safety for newspapermen (ibid., 20 April).

The most prominent political victim claimed by the violence was Edmundo Guerra Theilheimer, 46-year-old director of a people's legal counseling bureau of the Association of University Students and outspoken critic of the government. Guerra, who was gunned down at his office on 11 March, had written a political advertisement that appeared in Guatemala's leading newspapers on 2 March. The document called for "the revolutionary seizure of power by the extreme Left" and denounced the "anticipated electoral fraud of the bourgeoisie and the three parties which represent it" (ibid., 2, 12 March). Interior minister Roberto Herrera charged that leftist groups, specifically the FAR and PGT, had assassinated Guerra "in order to create a martyr" (ibid., 13 March).

Leadership and Organization. Little information is available on the leadership and organization of the PGT. Six Central Committee members, including Mario Silva Jonama, Hugo Barios Klee, Carlos Alvarado Jérez, Carlos René Valle, and Bernardo Alvarado Monzón (who had been general secretary of the PGT since 1954, were killed in late September 1972, apparently by the police or the army. In November 1972 a plenum of the Central Committee elected a new leadership. Miguel Rodríguez became general secretary of the party. Other prominent members of the Central Committee are Humberto Alvarado Arrellano, Pedro Gonzales Torres, and Otto Sánchez. On 26 December the Yugoslav news agency, Tanjug, reported that Alvarado, identified as the PGT secretary general, was assassinated by "fascist gangs under Government protection." The PGT publishes an illegal newspaper, *Verdad*.

A PGT Central Committee statement issued on 31 August 1974 described the party as a "political tool of the workers and peasants," a "profoundly revolutionary" party of a "new type." It speaks for the working people of town and country, employees, students, and intellectuals, and its aim is to "tackle the problems of the broadest middle sectors of the population." To many, the statement asserts, the PGT is "the only party capable of freeing the people from the yoke of exploitation and capitalist oppression." It is understandably opposed by the ultra-right and the imperialists, but also by the "so-called ultra-revolutionary elements, with their ill-conceived objectives." The latter "attack the Party, slander it, question its role, fight [it] with the full malice of their empty, demagogic rhetoric and, in violation of all the standards of ideological struggle, vilify it and act virtually as informers and agents-provocateurs." The PGT wages a tireless struggle against reaction, imperialism, and these pseudo-revolutionaries. (*IB*, Prague ed., no. 18.)

The PGT has a youth auxiliary, the Patriotic Youth of Labor (Juventud Patriótica del Trabajo). Delegates attended an international conference on communist youth activity held in Prague on 6-8 May 1974. The PGT also controls the clandestine Guatemalan Autonomous Federation of Trade Unions (Federación Autónoma Guatemalteca), a small and relatively unimportant labor organization. The federation was approved as an affiliated member of the World Federation of Trade Unions in October at the 25th meeting of the WFTU General Council, in Havana (*Granma*, English ed., 27 October).

Domestic Attitudes and Activities. Since the PGT's last illegal congress, in December 1969, the main strategic aim of the party has been to carry out an "agrarian anti-imperialist people's revolution" (*WMR*, January 1974). The PGT did not openly support the actions of any party in the March 1974 elections. In assessing the domestic situation in January, the Political Commission of the Central Committee denounced the ruling coalition parties—the National Liberation Movement (MLN) and the Institutional Democratic Party (PID)—as the "chief enemy of students, workers, peasants, and intellectuals" (*IB*, no. 5-6, 1974). The PGT was equally critical of the leadership of reformist parties, namely, the Revolutionary Party (PR), the Christian Democratic Party (PDC), and the Revolutionary Democratic Unity Front (RDUF), whom the party accused of "seeking military and imperialist support at all costs." The PGT viewed itself "passing through a period of revolutionary decline when the alignment of forces is favorable to counter-revolution [and] the main danger the likelihood of a still more authoritarian and repressive fascist regime." (Ibid.)

In a post-election declaration adopted on 15 March, the Political Commission of the Central Committee issued a call for Guatemalans to "resort to revolutionary violence against reactionary violence." The strong vote for Ríos Montt was interpreted as "a demonstration of the determination of broad sectors of the population to end the rule of the ultraright" (*Granma*, English edition, 28 April). The declaration further predicted a deepening social and economic crisis in Guatemala, which the party attributes to "imperialism's increasing dominion in the country, the preservation of an outmoded social structure, and domination by the bourgeois-landowning oligarchy which openly betrays national interests" (*Pravda*, 29 September).

Writing in the *World Marxist Review* (September), Miguel Rodríguez stated the party would seek more effective organizational forms of joint worker, peasant, and student actions against the government, "using every form and method and bringing into struggle all the social forces interested in barring the way to neo-fascism." The Central Committee statement in August called upon the whole people to rise in mass struggle "against the reactionary policies which bring Guatemalans high living costs, low wages, flagrant violations of democratic rights, foreign domination, systematic repression in the villages, and constant threat on the part of urban reactionaries, who are ready to clamp down with a new wave of repression." The statement added that "mass insistence on immediate demands will open the way to greater action for democracy, which will lead to an increasingly resolute, head-on struggle between the reactionaries, small in numbers, and the democratic and revolutionary forces with whom the majority sides." (*IB*, Prague ed., no. 18.)

International Positions and Contacts. The PGT's positions on international issues follow those of the Soviet Union. Delegates attended the Ninth Conference of Communist and Workers' Parties of Panama, Mexico, and Central America, held in Mexico City in May 1974. The conference's final declaration defined "U.S. imperialism" as "the main enemy of our peoples and the biggest obstacle to the struggle for democracy, national sovereignty and socialism in the area" (*Granma*, English ed., 16 June). The document condemned the "Yankee-supported, fascist coup" in Chile and appealed to "all parties and democratic social and political forces in Central America to act in a way that will prevent internecine war between El Salvador and Honduras." (*IB*, Prague ed., no. 14; also see *Mexico*.)

In a recent statement, Rodríguez reaffirmed the PGT's support for "peoples fighting for national liberation," its opposition to "capitalist tyranny," and its affinity with "the peoples who are in the front ranks of building socialism and communism, notably the Soviet Union" (*WMR*, September). Rodríguez and other PGT leaders were planning to visit the Soviet Union and several Eastern European countries during late 1974 and early 1975.

Washington College   Daniel L. Premo

Guyana

The People's Progressive Party (PPP) of Guyana was founded in 1950. At its first congress, in 1951, it declared itself a nationalist party, committed to socialism, national independence, and Caribbean unity. During the nearly two decades following, the leadership of the PPP claimed to be Marxist-Leninist, but the party was not officially affiliated with the international communist movement. In 1969 the leader of the party, Cheddi Jagan, moved unequivocally to align the PPP with the Soviet Union. In turn, the PPP was recognized by the Soviet leaders as a bona fide communist party.

The PPP is a legal organization and represents the major opposition to the ruling People's National Congress (PNC), a party led by one-time PPP member, the present prime minister, Forbes Burnham. Particularly after Burnham's break with the PPP in the mid-1950s, Guyanese politics followed closely the ethnic differences in the country—roughly half of the population is East Indian (and supported the PPP) while the other half is black (and supported the PNC). In the July 1973 elections, however, Forbes Burnham was reelected for his third team and the PNC obtained a two-thirds majority in the parliament. When the PPP received only 26 percent of the vote (and 14 out of the 53 seats in parliament), Jagan and his party protested that fraud and illegal maneuvers had prevailed. The PPP presently boycotts the parliament and all other official government bodies.

PPP membership, including members of the Progressive Youth Organization and the Women's Progressive Organization, is slightly over 20,000, though active Marxist-Leninists are believed to be only about 100 (*World Strength of Communist Party Organizations*, 1973, p. 168).

Leadership and Organization. The leadership of the PPP includes Cheddi Jagan, reelected general secretary at the party congress in August (see below), Ranji Chandisingh, vice-chairman, Ram Karran, member of the general council and Janet Jagan (Cheddi's wife). The congress elected a new Central Committee.

The Progressive Youth Organization (PYO) is the official youth group of the PPP. It has traditionally been the source of strong personal support for Cheddi Jagan. The general secretary of the PYO is Feroze Mohamed. The PYO held its 8th congress in Allandale on 13-15 April. The PYO's Central Committee report to the congress (portions of which are published in *Thunder*, April-June) was highly critical of the PBC, aiming particularly at the government's educational policies, which it considered disastrous. Outlining its future tasks, the PYO expressed its determination to help transform the PPP into a "more disciplined Marxist-Leninist party, to heal the racial wounds exacerbated by the PNC, to oppose the national service program (see below), to forge links between the working people and youth of the country, and to increase the effectiveness and discipline of the PYO. (*Thunder*, April-June.)

The PPP also sponsors the Women's Progressive Organization and the Guyana Agricultural Workers' Union, the latter made up primarily of workers from the sugar industry.

Party Internal Affairs. The PPP held its 18th national congress in a Georgetown suburb on 3-5 August. It was attended by 479 delegates and 170 observers from Guyana, and by representatives from fraternal parties and organizations in Venezuela, Guadeloupe, Surinam, and French Guiana.

PPP leaders consider the party the vanguard, founded on a scientific Marxist-Leninist ideology and anti-imperialist program, for leading the Guyanese revolution (*Thunder*, January-March). The party plays a vanguard role firstly in educating the masses by explaining "why things are bad, why they will get worse, and what must be done to make them better; and secondly, in organizing the people to take power—anti-imperialist, pro-democratic and pro-socialist power" (*Thunder*, April-June). At the August congress, Jagan spoke on the need for increased party work in the mass organizations and improved ideological work among party members. Particular attention had to be devoted to exposing the ideological trends designed to sow confusion in and weaken the front for anti-imperialist struggle, namely Maoism, neo-Trotskyism, neo-pan-Africanism, black capitalism, and national communism. (*IB*, Prague ed., no. 17.)

Domestic Attitudes and Activities. According to Cheddi Jagan, the PNC heads a "corrupt, anti-working class, pro-imperialist and racist" government. It is responsible for the economic crisis facing Guyana, with its soaring prices, rising taxes, perpetual shortages, unemployment, balance of payments deficit, and declining production. (*Thunder*, April-June.) In Guyana, methods of political struggle were being replaced by military-bureaucratic methods of suppressing political opposition and fundamental civil rights were being violated (*IB*, Prague ed., no. 17). Jagan was particularly critical of PNC trade policies which tied Guyana in with the capitalist world. Imperialist pressure had "hitched Guyana to the Caribbean" through relations with the Caribbean Free Trade Area, the Caribbean Common Market, and the foreign imperialists. (*Thunder*, April-June.)

The PPP believes that only a socialist system based on the principles of Marxism-Leninism can free the people of Guyana from poverty, hunger, unemployment, and proposes a program it says is aimed at drawing the masses into the struggle for fundamental social and economic change, for democracy and socialism, and against imperialist monopoly domination. (*WMR*, July.) The August congress called for far-reaching structural reforms, including the nationalization of key industries, establishment of state control over mines, factories, banks, plantations, foreign trade, and agrarian reform (*IB*, Prague ed., no. 17). All imperialist interests—the bauxite and sugar companies, the banks, the insurance companies—must be nationalized (*Mirror*, 17 October). However, nationalization alone cannot bring either democracy or socialism. Commenting on PNC nationalization policies at mid-year, Jagan said that nationalization was just one aspect of social change (*Daily Gleaner*, Kingston, Jamaica, 1 July). The PPP strongly opposed the PNC proposal of compulsory national service of a year or more for all young people after they finish school. Janet Jagan rejected Burnham's suggestion that the system would be similar to that employed in Cuba. According to Mrs. Jagan, Burnham failed to point out that Cuba had a revolutionary government with full popular support, whereas Guyana had a "minority government which usurped power by fraud and has failed to get people's support or consent." (*Thunder*, January-March.) PPP leaders frequently turned to what it considered the racist nature of the PNC government. The party recognized that there was a "racial problem" in Guyana, but insisted that this problem "will increasingly play a minor secondary role as the national liberation, class and ideological struggles sharpen." (Ibid.) The PPP, the vanguard of the working class, recognized that there were other classes and strata which had an anti-imperialist position—the farmers, intellectuals, students, and petty-bourgeoisie. Thus the party states that it is "willing and anxious to cooperate and work with other parties, groups, and even progressive individuals" who oppose the PNC and its imperialist supporters. (*Thunder*, April-June.)

International Relations. At the 18th congress, Cheddi Jagan stated that International socialism has launched an historic offensive and the balance of world forces has changed in its favor. This increased might of the socialist world is what compels imperialism to restrain its aggressive aspirations and move away from its cold war policies of containing communism to peaceful coexistence. This was so in spite of the fact that the imperialists were actively engaged in the suppression of revolutionary forces in Chile, Uruguay, Bolivia and other countries. (*IB*, Prague ed., no. 17.) Cheddi Jagan condemned the military coup which overthrew the Popular Unity government in Chile in an article charging that the CIA had been similar active in undermining his position in Guyana a decade earlier (*WMR*, June). At the height of the oil crisis in early 1974, the party called upon the Guyanese people to throw their support behind the oil producing countries, especially the Arab world (*Mirror*, 6 January). Jagan repeatedly denounced the imperialists and the Chinese Communists for promoting the reactionary and anti-socialist doctrine of the "two superpowers" (the U.S. and the U.S.S.R.). At mid-year Jagan gave his support to the proposal to convene a new conference of world communist and workers parties (TASS, 19 June).

Publications. The PPP daily newspaper is *Mirror*, edited by Janet Jagan, and its quarterly theoretical and discussion journal is *Thunder*, edited by Ranji Chandisingh.

Hoover Institution   William E. Ratliff
Stanford University

Haiti

The United Party of Haitian Communists (Parti Unifié des Communistes Haitiens; PUCH) was formed in 1969 by the merging of the Party of the Union of Haitian Democrats and the People's Entente Party. (For background on these parties, see *YICA, 1973*, p. 356.) The membership of the PUCH is unknown, but presumed to be less than several hundred persons. The population of Haiti is 5,400,000 (estimated 1974).

All political parties in Haiti have been proscribed since 1949. In April 1969 a law was passed declaring all forms of communist activity crimes against the state, the penalty for which would be both confiscation of property and death. The government's anti-communist campaign which followed, under François Duvalier (until his death in April 1971) and his son Jean-Claude, has decimated the ranks of the PUCH. Much PUCH activity has been carried on outside Haiti among exiles in Europe (especially the Soviet Union) and Cuba. PUCH Central Committee member Jacques Dorcilien claimed at mid-year that exiles in the United States were increasingly anxious to join the popular movement. The PUCH says it is disseminating revolutionary ideas, starting more cells in industry and agriculture, and forging links between the party and the workers, peasants, and other sectors of the population. (*WMR*, May.) In recent years, PUCH statements have been issued by Dorcilien, Jean Gerard, and Casal Dumercier.

Domestic and International Positions. According to the PUCH, the Duvalier power structure is in a state of crisis, plagued by infighting, plots and counterplots. The party claims to be working to unite all the anti-dictatorial forces and directing actions by workers and others against the dictatorship, imperialism, and reaction. The continued penetration of the Haitian military by the U.S. Pentagon and CIA merely invigorates the revolutionary movement and brings the day closer when the movement will confront the Duvalier regime, the imperialist monopolies, and the big landed interests. (*WMR*, May.)

The PUCH is firmly pro-Soviet in its international orientation (*Pravda*, 13 November).

Hoover Institution   William E. Ratliff
Stanford University

Honduras

The Communist Party of Honduras (Partido Comunista de Honduras; PCH) was organized in 1927, disbanded in 1932, and reorganized in 1954. In 1967 a dispute over strategy and tactics led to a division of the PCH into rival factions. Since 1971 there has been a self-proclaimed pro-Chinese Communist Party of Honduras/Marxist-Leninist (PCH-ML). A later division within the PCH led to the formation of the Honduran Workers' Party (Partido de los Trabajadores Hondureños; PTH).

The PCH has been illegal since 1957. In December 1972 the armed forces of Honduras overthrew the government of President Ramón Cruz in a non-violent coup. Under the leadership of General Oswaldo López Arellano the situation in Honduras has relaxed and the PCH, though still formally illegal, has been able to operate more openly than before. The membership of the PCH is estimated at 350. The PCH-ML and the PTH have estimated memberships of 100 and 150 respectively.

Leadership and Organization. The secretary general of the PCH is Dionisio Ramos Bejarano; Rigoberto Padilla is a prominent member of the Political Commission. Though the PCH remains a minor factor in Honduran politics, due to internal dissension and national conditions, the party is slowly increasing its strength and influence among Honduran workers and in the country in general.

Domestic Views. According to the PCH, a reactionary oligarchy maintained control in Honduras until the military coup of December 1972. The reactionary oligarchs lost their political power in the coup, but retained their economic influence. During 1974 the PCH charged that the oligarchs, who still held most of the peasants in a state of "semi-slavery or semi-serfdom," attempted to regain their positions through the traditional Liberal and National parties. By mid-year, in the most recent documents available at this writing, the PCH was critical of what it called the "vacillation" of López's government in the face of "ultra-rightist plots," to reestablish what the land-owning oligarchy called "constitutional order."

Overall, however, the PCH defended the policies and actions of the military government as was evident in the discussions at the 15th enlarged plenum of the PCH Central Committee in early 1974. Progress was being made for the Honduran people within the framework of bourgeois reformism. The National Development Plan (NDP) announced by General López in January 1974 envisaged the capitalist road of development under the influence of the reformist bourgeoisie. The NDP provided for measures in many fields, including mining, industry, the social sphere, and taxation, but its main object was bourgeois agrarian reform to break the back of the existing semi-feudal production relations. The National Agrarian Reform plan, which the PCH supported, sought to reduce the traditional latifundia and minifundia and replace them by modern, productive estates using up-to-date techniques, all in order to speed up capitalist development in the countryside. The PCH favored the establishment of asentamientos, joint rural enterprises the party felt would improve the conditions of the peasants and make them more progressive-minded. Fulfillment of the NDP, according to the PCH, might have the following economic and political results: 1) increase class struggle, especially in rural areas; 2) strengthen and expand mass organizations; 3) increase political consciousness in the masses; 4) increase bourgeois legality; and 5) further discredit the traditional parties. (*IB*, no. 12.)

This program, the NDP, was as constructive a program as possible under the objective and subjective conditions in Honduras during 1974, according to the PCH. Thus the party repeatedly called for a united front of Hondurans which would give explicit and firm support to the positive aspects of the NDP and actively oppose all "ultra-reactionary actions" originating in Honduras or organized abroad (*El Dia*, Tegucigalpa, 28 March; *Pravda*, Moscow, 7 June). The democratic content of the domestic political situation, the PCH argued, would be determined mainly by the resolve of the masses rather than by the government's programs *per se*. Thus it was essential to form a worker-peasant alliance which could serve as the pivot of a broad front of the masses. And, in order to assure the ultimate goal of the proletarian revolution, the independence of the working class had to be maintained. (*IB*, no. 12.)

The effectiveness of the united front and the PCH line was challenged by the ultra-right, as indicated above, and by the "ultra-left," the latter falling into three more or less different currents: the Maoists, the neo-anarchists, and the social nationalists. All of these groups held that no changes had occurred in Honduras since December 1972, maintaining that the country was still ruled by a dictatorship of the traditional oligarchy and that the military government's apparently progressive policies were "sheer demagogy." The Maoists, the PCH-ML, called for protracted warfare. The neo-anarchists and the social nationalists, members of the PTH, according to the PCH, advocated "guerrilla war ... as the catalyst for revolutionary struggle," and the "Honduran road to socialism," respectively.

International. The PCH and the Communist Party of El Salvador issued a joint statement in February saying that a very tense situation existed between their two countries because of the maneuvers of reactionaries in Honduras and El Salvador who received direct encouragement from U.S. imperialism. Whereas the reactionaries sought a new armed conflict in order to prevent progressive change, all true democrats should assume the task of upholding peace. (TASS, 14 February.) This position was also maintained at the preparatory meeting for the Ninth Conference of Communist and Workers' Parties of Central America and Mexico in December 1973 (*IB*, no. 3). the parties added that Honduras and El Salvador should reestablish diplomatic relations after negotiating bilateral agreements which recognize the conditions under which Honduras would return to the Central American Common Market and also reestablish borders which existed before the 1969 "Soccer War" (Prensa Latina, 9 February).

The PCH evidently did not participate in the Ninth Conference of Communist and Workers' Parties of Central America and Mexico, held somewhere in Central America in May (see signatories of the Declaration of the conference, in *IB*, Prague ed., no. 14).

Publications. The PCH publishes *El Trabajo*, a theoretical, political, and informational journal, and the paper *La Vanguardia Revolucionaria*. Party statements are often found in the *World Marxist Review* and that journal's *Information Bulletin*.

Hoover Institution   William E. Ratliff
Stanford University

Martinique

The Martinique Communist Party (Parti Communiste Martiniquais; PCM) traces its founding to July 1921. In September 1957 it became the autonomous PCM. The party is legal.

The PCM is estimated to have 1,000 members. The population of Martinique is 335,000 (estimated 1970).

The PCM is an active participant in Martinique's political life, on both local and departmental levels. (As one of France's overseas departments Martinique is an integral part of the French Republic.) Its following, however, has generally been declining over the past fifteen years, partly because one of its leaders, Aimé Césaire, withdrew in 1956 to create the left-wing non-communist Martinique Progressive Party (Parti Progressiste Martiniquais; PPM), and partly as a consequence of the PCM's policy of autonomy for Martinique, which has not enjoyed mass support, although there was a resurge in the autonomy movement in 1974. The PCM controls several municipal governments in Martinique and holds 4 seats on the 36-member Municipal Council. The PCM has no representatives in the French National Assembly.

Leadership and Organization. The PCM's Fifth Congress was held in late December 1972. A Central Committee of 35 members and Control Commission of 3 members were elected, and Armand Nicolas was reelected secretary-general. In January 1973 the Central Committee elected a new 13-member Political Bureau: Armand Nicolas, Luc Bourgeois (propaganda secretary), René Bramban, Philibert Dufeal (organization secretary), Mathurin Gottin, Georges Gratiant, Walter Guitteaud, Victor Lamon, Gabriel Lordinot, Georges Mauvois, René Menil, Edgar Nestoret, and Albert Platon.

The PCM controls the General Confederation of Labor of Martinique (Confédération Générale du Travail de la Martinique; CGTM), which has some 4,000 members and is the largest trade union organization in Martinique. The party's youth organization is the Union of Communist Youth of Martinique (Union de la Jeunesse Communiste de la Martinique: UJCM).

Departmental and National Views and Positions. In 1974 two developments had profound effects on the PCM: a challenge from the left in the form of a nascent but threatening Trotskyist party, and the creation of a united left that included the CPM, the PPM, and seven other organizations.

On 28-30 December 1973 the Socialist Revolution Group (GRS) held its founding congress in the capital city of Fort-de-France. Professing to represent the Antilles in the Trotskyist Fourth International, the GRS began early in the year to make serious verbal attacks on the PCM. On 31 January the PCM organ *Justice* launched its counter campaign against the GRS by stating, first, that it had identified the GRS as Trotskyist almost two years ago, and its adherence to the Fourth International, allegedly decided at the founding congress should have been a surprise to no one (see also

Intercontinental Press, 4 February). The PCM statement continued:

> According to the GRS orators, to be internationalist, it is necessary to adhere to an international [organization], that is to say to a planning system above the national parties and which would be enabled to impose its command .... [But] one does not stimulate a revolution in a country by foreign intervention .... After having, without any analysis, chosen independence as the solution for Martinique, they have advanced the line of a "socialist federation of the islands of the Caribbean."

The article ended with the observation that there was a common desire between the GRS and the Gaullist Union of Democrats for the Republic (UDR); they both wanted to "replace the PCM, which exists, with the shadow of a communist party which does not exist."

The French presidential elections in May were supported by an intense publicity campaign by the PCM in support of François Mitterand. The first round of elections on 5 May, demonstrated a "certain disorientation of public opinion under the influence, principally, of UDR propaganda massively diffused by the official means of radio and television." The second round on 19 May, gave Mitterand 49.3 percent nationally, and 43 percent in Martinique. This percentage was seen as significant of a new trend toward the left on the island. In several municipalities (including Fort-de-France) the left regained a majority lost since 1958.

Most important, the temporary leftist unity created during the election campaign developed an impetus for the formation of a more lasting union. On 3 July the "Permanent Committee of the Martinique Left" was established by nine leftist parties and labor organizations, including the PCM, PPM, Socialist Federation of Martinique, and the CGTM. With an inventory of those issues on which all could agree, a "common declaration" was drafted (see *IB*, Prague ed., no. 17). On the issue of self-determination, it was agreed that the people of Martinique would have the exclusive right to determine, if they so desired, a statute for self-determination. However, the participating organizations explicitly did not envisage a statute placing Martinique completely outside French purview. (*Justice*, 11 July.) This was in line with the PCM's past position that sought control for the island of its own legislative and executive functions, while maintaining cooperation with France through a body comprising equal representation from Martinique and France, primarily for the purpose of administering financial and technical assistance for Martinique.

Early in the year there were numerous strikes affecting all sectors of the economy. At the call of the CGTM and other leftist labor organizations, a 24-hour general strike was held on 12 February. Described as the "most powerful strike in 15 years," it reportedly involved 1,000 strikers and violent episodes resulted in two deaths and several serious injuries. Some of the basic demands included a minimum wage equivalent to that of France, financial aid to families of unemployed persons, and financial aid for housing. (Ibid., 21 February.)

International Views and Positions. The PCM position on international affairs coincides in all important respects with that of the French Communist Party, which it praises as its chief ally in the struggle against "anticolonialism." The party condemns the leaders of the People's Republic of China and carries articles on pro-Soviet or non-aligned communist parties on major occasions. In 1974 it continued its coverage of the aftermath of the military coup that overthrew Allende in Chile in 1973.

Publications. The PCM publishes a weekly newspaper, *Justice*, and an irregular theoretical journal, *Action*.

Mountain View, California   Eric Stromquist

Mexico

In analyzing the development of Communist and Marxist parties and groups, one should consider the environment in which these elements operate. The environment determines the strategy and tactics of political parties and groups in the continuous effort to increase their influence and power. In 1974, two significant components formed part of the Mexican environment: further efforts of the Echeverría government to realize a "democratic opening" in the country, and a noticeable increase in violence.

The government continued its policy of slowly moving toward a more open society. It did not discourage the press from openly criticizing governmental policies and even the president himself. President Echeverría asked the students and intellectuals to form legal opposition parties and groups to express their dissent. He also tried to "democratize" the ruling Institutional Revolutionary Party (PRI) by allowing younger talented people to attain positions of leadership.

The real confrontation appeared in the economy, where the government has been trying to change the country's wealth structure. But the efforts to increase taxes on the wealthy, and adjust priorities to favor the poorer elements, have caused unprecedented strain among traditional political relationships and alliances. The powerful and conservative private sector has been vehemently opposing the government's efforts. Added to this is the worst inflation in 20 years, over 30 percent by some accounts.

The president's attempt to broaden the political system and PRI itself has not succeeded. By awakening expectations on the left and fears on the right, the government found itself in a crossfire. The left is discouraged because no meaningful reforms have been forthcoming. As a result, some have joined existing guerrilla bands and formed new ones because they believe the system is unwilling or unable to reform itself. The right wants law and order, and the private business sector has been holding back on investment and sending money abroad.

The increase in violence is a symptom of the growing disillusionment of some with the Mexican political system. Some of the incidents included clashes between students and the police and army; others were the result of attacks by various guerrilla groups. Violent outbreaks have occurred in many parts of the country. In Mérida, the death of a student leader resulted in the bombing of the regional Military Zone headquarters and PRI headquarters. In Tlaxcala, a state capital 115 km. from Mexico City, 2,500 demonstrators protested the appointment of 9 municipal mayors by taking over the government palace and causing the governor to flee. Approximately 1,500 peasants occupied farmland in Cuernavaca and clashed with the police. The Cuban Action group, made up of anti-Castro Cuban exiles, has been making plans to attack Castro sympathizers in Mexico. The Cuban Embassy was bombed several times, with considerable damage resulting.

Several developments have emerged from this environment. First, we see a growing polarization between the right and left. The army and police have been called out more frequently to put down violent outbreaks. Anti-communist groups are now operating. "Los Halcones" have been joined by a group called "Sangre." The latter has been charged with torturing and murdering 20 to 30 guerrilla sympathizers, particularly in the state of Guerrero. Students and guerrillas have increasingly resorted to bombings and street demonstrations; several kidnap victims have been assassinated. A second development involves the reaction of the government. With the apparent failure of the "democratic opening," the Echeverría administration decided to take a stronger hand. Besides more frequent utilization of the police and army, the left-wing magazine *Por Que?* was closed down. It had been sympathetic to guerrilla movements and generally published their communiqués. The police were said to have arrested the entire staff and confiscated the magazine's machinery. The director, Roger Menéndez Rodríguez, was kidnapped the previous day by four unknown persons who, according to his brother, were police agents. Third, there are indications that elements in the military are concerned about these developments.

This is the environment, then, in which the communists and Marxists operate. Their organizations include the Mexican Communist Party (Partido Comunista Mexicano; PCM), the Popular Socialist Party (Partido Popular Socialista; PPS), the Trotskyite groups, and various guerrilla groups. Mexico has a population of 52,640,000 (estimated 1972).

The PCM. The membership and leadership of the Mexican Communist Party have not varied much over the last few years. The estimate of the party's membership continues to be approximately 5,000. Although the PCM is a legal political party, it has not been able to meet the legal membership requirement of 75,000 to enter candidates in national elections. Arnoldo Martínez Verdugo, a leader in the party since the 1940s, is the secretary-general. Some of the other leaders are J. E. Pérez and Arturo Martínez Nateras (members of the Executive Commission of the Central Committee), Reynaldo Rosas, Pablo Gómez, and Liberato Terán Olguin.

Since its inception in 1919, the PCM has never been a party of the workers and peasants, although its leaders have long exhorted their followers to broaden the base of the party. In 1974 the problem was restated by Fernando G. Cortez, commenting bitterly on his expulsion after 43 years: "[The party] is at present made up primarily of petty-bourgeois intellectuals and students, when the base should be the working class."

The PCM takes a somewhat independent position. Although careful not to take sides in the Sino-Soviet dispute and critical of the Soviet-led invasion of Czechoslovakia in 1968, the party continues to have friendly relations with the Communist Party of the Soviet Union (CPSU).

There is tension between the PCM and its youth group, the Mexican Communist Youth (JCM), over the party's control of the JCM and the degree of support to be given to student activism. In October 1973, during the PCM's Sixteenth Congress, the party formally expelled Manuel Terrazas Guerrero, former second secretary of the party and leader of the pro-Soviet faction.

The party has several publications, including a weekly newspaper, *La Voz de México*; a magazine, *Oposición*; and a theoretical journal, *Nueva Epoca*. It also publishes the resolutions and results of communist regional conferences and party congresses.

The Sixteenth PCM Congress. In October 1973, the PCM's Sixteenth Congress summed up the results of the party's work in the past six years, endorsed the work of the Central Committee, defined tasks for the coming period, and adopted a program and statutes.

The report of the congress states that Mexico is controlled by national and international capitalism. Within the country the large bourgeoisie, formed after the Cárdenas administration in the decade of the 1940s, is seen as dominating every avenue of economic life through their monopolies, control of banking, and domination of commerce and agriculture. They are joined by the oligarchy and imperialist monopolies of the United States to make the program of "Mexicanization" a farce. The communists also refer to the Leninist theory of the stage of monopoly capitalism— "intervention of the state to save the capitalist structure and impel it to a superior stage: the predominance of monopolies in the economy"—which Mexico is said to be approaching (Partido Comunista Mexicano. *Programa y Estatutos*, México: Ediciones de Cultura Popular, 1974, p. 37). The analysis does not follow Lenin's theory to its final step, that monopoly capitalism within the country must lead to Mexican imperialism, though the implication may be that Mexican imperialism is integrated with that of the United States.

According to the PCM, the promises of the Mexican Revolution have not been realized. On the contrary, a bloc of large bourgeoisie and large landowners has triumphed over the original democratic-revolutionaries leading to the further development of capitalism and a worsening of the condition of the masses. This in turn has led to "presidentialism," which guarantees the large bourgeoisie's dictatorship. This development particularly worries the PCM, because "it may lead, unless prevented by the revolutionary and democratic movement, to a terroristic, military and police dictatorship of big capital like the one established in Brazil" (*Political Resolution of the 16th National Congress of the Mexican Communist Party*, p. 4). The congress was very critical of President Echeverría and his government. The PCM maintains that already the political regime is a despotic presidentialism which is not restricted by law. It controls elections and the judiciary, and has created a fascist system. It is supported by U.S. penetration not only of the military and police, but also in the broader ideological and political areas.

According to the congress, the only way to change the system is through armed struggle in the form of a new revolution. This will be led by the workers and will be supported by the peasants, students, and progressive elements of the Church and the small bourgeoisie. Expanding on a concept defined in the party's *Bulletin for Discussion* (May 1973), it is described as a democratic and socialist revolution and part of the present world-wide revolutionary movement. This is a change from the party's analysis of the Mexican Revolution. In the earlier period, through the Cárdenas administration, the PCM called for completion of the Mexican Revolution under communist leadership. The current position is that the Mexican Revolution is dead and must be replaced by a new communist-led revolution.

The PCM divides its revolution into two phases, democratic in the first and socialist in the second. In phase one, the property of the medium and small capitalists will be respected. Through government regulation, they will adapt to the general revolutionary process. In phase two, the medium and small capitalists will be incorporated into socialist production. (The congress did not stipulate how long phase one will last). Thus we witness the democratic and socialist revolution: "a revolution which resolves democratic tasks and is oriented toward socialism in its first phase, which forms part of the cycle of socialist revolution and which opens for our country the perspective of a society without exploited or exploiters" (*Programa y Estatutos*, p. 46).

The PCM is consistent with the Marxist dialectic in stating that under the new state, the working class will be converted into the organ of the dictatorship of the proletariat. Sovereignty will be in a Popular Assembly which will combine legislative and executive powers. Under the new order, there will be religious freedom, encouragement to form trade unions, and the right to strike. In regard to private property, the congress repeated the program originally spelled out by the party in 1972. In the first phase of the revolution, private ownership of from 20 to 50 Hectares (1 hectare = 2.47 acres) will be permitted as production is incorporated into the revolutionary process. The same will hold true for those who own from 50 to 100 head of cattle. The congress spelled out a detailed program for the future revolutionary government. It dealt with such areas as urban reform and housing, education, health, rest and recreation. It called for the cooperation of the school, factory and farm to "stimulate the formation of a new man in Mexican society."

In the foreign policy field, the revolutionary government will work with revolutionary states world-wide. It will reject force and threats of force; military blocs also will be rejected (implicitly both NATO and the Warsaw Pact). It will support the revolutionary movement in the United States and the struggle of the Chinese people. It will denounce all treaties and international covenants between the Mexican government and the United States.

And finally, the State will begin to wither away in socialism and will be extinguished in communism. The communist party will also disappear because it will have completed its historic mission. But communism in Mexico will only be assured with the international revolution of the proletariat. Only then will capitalist aggression against the socialist countries be impossible. (Ibid., pp. 65-67.)

In spite of the call for a new revolution, the PCM supports the concept of peaceful coexistence. It also criticizes the various guerrilla movements for using violent methods at this time. In a sense they reject the Guevara-Debray thesis that the time is right for violent revolution whenever there is a guerrilla *foco*. According to the PCM, "the main weakness of guerrilla groups is not the lack of contact with the masses, nor shortcomings in their technical training, which makes them vulnerable to government repression. It is the fact that they are based on a strategic misconception to the effect that revolutionary conditions are ripe enough for resolute action to win power. . . . In the opinion of the Communist Party, it is political and not armed forms that play this role today. Now is the time for a political offensive." (*Political Resolution of the 16th National Congress*, pp. 8-9.) The same point was made by the Central Committee at the party's 6th plenum at mid-year with specific reference to the guerrilla activities of Lucio Cabañas (*Oposición*, 10 July, trans. in *IB*, Prague ed., no. 17).

The Ninth Conference of Communist and Workers' Parties of Mexico, Central America, and Panama. At the end of May 1974, following two preparatory meetings, the PCM met with representatives of communist and workers' parties of Central America and Panama in their Ninth Conference. One of the concerns at the meeting was the coup d'etat in Chile. The United States was accused of direct involvement, its "shift from cold war to détente" being "only a change of tactic meant to retain control over Latin America." The United States was trying to establish "fascist governments in Latin America to compensate for the collapse of [its] rule in other parts of the world." The representatives expressed support for their comrades in Chile, Guatemala, and Uruguay.

The conference also expressed concern that war might break out again between El Salvador and Honduras. The representatives called on the people and political groups of Latin America to do all they could to prevent a new war, which would only benefit the military and the reactionary right. (*IB*, no. 3.)

The conference recognized the leading role of the CPSU in the world revolutionary struggle. Thus, although the PCM maintains that there is no international communist organization, and that each communist party is responsible for the revolutionary movement in its country and before the international working class (*Programa y Estatutos*, p. 12), it does pay homage to the Soviet leaders. "The revolutionary movement is gaining in strength and scope by following the path charted by Marx and Lenin. Led by the U.S.S.R., the socialist camp is developing in progressively closer unity and has become a decisive force in the world. . . . The Communist Party of the Soviet Union is the vanguard of the revolutionary struggle of our era." (*IB*, no. 3.)

The report of the conference also recognized a need to coordinate the efforts of the various organizations and groups in a "democratic front." This would include workers, peasants, and "other patriotic strata [struggling] for liberation from imperialism and for democracy." The conference called for an "intensified struggle to free Mexican political prisoners, particularly the two outstanding peasant leaders, Ramón Danzos Palomino, General Secretary of the Independent Peasant Center, and

Samuel Sánchez, member of its Central Committee." (*IB*, Prague ed., no. 14.)

Fear of the Right. A persistently expressed fear in 1974, noted by the PCM congress and the above-mentioned Ninth Conference, was repression by right wing governments. As a result of the fall of Allende and increased repression of the post-Allende government in Chile, as well as the dictatorships in Brazil and Uruguay, the PCM expressed fears of the possible spread effect in Mexico. On 8 July the plenum of the PCM Central Committee published a document which stated: "The country's labor and democratic movement should be careful not to underestimate the threat of the extreme right, which is made up of the most authoritarian tendencies and semifascists as well as of U.S. imperialism. . . . Fear that the people's discontent will burst out and fear of a revolution, along with the influence of the Chilean military coup, is pushing the most reactionary sectors of the bourgeoisie to use all their influence to control more government posts in order to give it an antidemocratic direction and to benefit themselves in the next presidential term. . . . Due to a political crisis of such dimensions it is necessary to find ways for the left to take part in the activities of the nation and to make every possible effort to change the correlation of forces on behalf of the working classes and democratic sectors. Otherwise, the most repressive reactionary forces will benefit from the logical consequences of a setback for the revolutionaries. We have the proper conditions to prevent this from happening. We have the common duty to stop the advance of the recalcitrant right."

*   *   *

The PPS. The Popular Socialist Party, founded by the late Vicente Lombardo Toledano, continues to be the largest organization on the left of the Mexican political spectrum, claiming 75,000 members. Certain of its leaders are allegedly communist, but the rank and file is, for the most part, non-communist. Since Lombardo died in 1968, the PPS has been under the leadership of its present secretary-general, Jorge Cruickshank. Other members of the Central Committee include Francisco Ortiz Mendoza, Deputy Miguel Hernández González and Lázaro Rubio Felix. With the PRI, the conservative National Action Party (PAN) and the Authentic Party of the Mexican Revolution (PARM), the PPS in recent years has been able to meet the minimum legal number for registration to have candidates on the printed ballot. In the congressional election of 1 July 1973, the PPS received 483,647 votes (3.5 percent) and 10 seats in congress (4.4 percent). The leaders continue to be strong supporters of the Soviet Union, a position established by Lombardo at the party's founding in 1948. Throughout the years, political analysts have considered the PPS to be part of the recognized establishment, acceptable to the PRI as a voice on the left with seats in the congress and some representation on the state and municipal levels. The party has carefully refrained from advocating violence or opposing the goals of the Mexican Revolution, and there is evidence that this cooperative attitude has resulted in a favorable response from the PRI, including an opening up of opportunities for government employment. The PPS has endorsed the PRI presidential candidate (while running its own congressional candidates) since 1958, and in the last presidential election supported the candidacy of Luis Echeverría. Unlike the PCM, the PPS did not oppose the Soviet invasion of Czechoslovakia. However, recent PRI-PPS tension indicates that periodic reassessments are necessary.

In December 1973, four PPS members were killed in disorders when authorities intervened to evict some 5,000 members of the PPS who had seized the city hall in Jaltipan (Veracruz) to protest the fact that the alleged victory of their candidate for mayor of Jaltipan was not recognized by the counting board. When the army forced them to leave, the PPS members demonstrated along the main streets of the town and committed acts of vandalism, including setting fire to the homes of some 20 prominent members of the PRI.

For the next few days, military patrols guarded the streets against new disorders. Reports stated that security agents of Veracruz raided several private homes at night and arrested over 140 persons presumably implicated in the events. Those arrested were charged with attacking the communications media, since they seized a local radio station from which they appealed to the citizens of Jaltipan for support.

Not only did the events strain PPS-PRI relations—they also caused a crisis within the PPS and between the PPS and other groups. Various worker and peasant organizations in Veracruz publicly condemned the PPS secretary-general, naming him as the principal instigator and agitator of the incidents in Jaltipan. These included the Confederation of Mexican Workers (CTM) and its regional organizations. They condemned "the acts which were planned by the eternal enemies of the revolution who are entrenched in the PPS." The local youth group of the PPS demanded that Jorge Cruickshank resign as secretary-general. But he did not resign and the PPS weathered the crisis.

The CPM and the PPS disagree on their attitude toward President Echeverría. Cruickshank stated "... this is the fourth year of President Echeverría's administration and the United States does not want the positive results that he has achieved to continue. They want a president who will change his work and insure that Mexico will serve the imperialist policy and that our country will not be a driving force in behalf of Latin American liberation." But on some other matters, the positions and actions of the CPM and the PPS coincide. In March, Cruickshank accused the United States ambassador, John Joseph Jova, of participating in plans for a coup in Mexico "which would close the circle of anti-democratic regimes on the continent." The Central Committee of the PPS issued a resolution calling for "revolutionary and anti-imperialist unity and militant solidarity with the heroic Chilean people." The resolution also condemned those who were allegedly carrying out a campaign against the Soviet Union. These included anti-communists and Trotskyites. Also like the CPM, the PPS attempted to show some independence vis-à-vis the Soviet Union by announcing that several of its delegates would attend the Tenth Congress of the League of Communists of Yugoslavia. According to the Central Committee, the PPS was extended a special invitation, and the congress was considered to be of "great importance because, in the opinion of the Yugoslavs, it will strengthen the structure of socialism based on self-management."

In July, the PPS was forced to admit that one of its leaders had worked as an agent of the U.S. Central Intelligence Agency (CIA). Charges and counter-charges, caused by statements made in England by former CIA agent Philip B. Agee, proved to be politically embarrassing to the party. According to the PPS, the party leaders instructed Lázaro Rubio Felix and other members of the party to infiltrate the CIA to get proof of its activities in Mexico. They accused their accusers and stated that PAN and the Mexican police were the real agents of the CIA and imperialism.

*   *   *

Socialist and Trotskyite Groups. In 1972 several student leaders of the 1968 movement met with Demetrio Vallejo, a leader of the Movimiento Sindical Ferrocarrilero (MSF), to discuss the possibility of forming a new workers' party. The discussions continued for approximately one year, but eventually they split into two groups and two political parties emerged: the Partido Socialista de los Trabajadores (PST) and the Partido Mexicano de los Trabajadores (PMT). The latter, formed in September of 1974, claims a membership of approximately 45,000. The president of the PMT is Heberto Castillo. In its Declaration of Principles, the PMT states that it will elaborate the ideas of the Mexican revolutionaries from Flores Magón to Lázaro Cárdenas. It criticizes imperialist industries which operate in Mexico without helping the people. Point 5 of the Declaration states: "Human labor is the origin of all wealth. Therefore, that wealth should pass to the power of the manual and intellectual workers, of the field and the city, who are the true proprietors."

Two Trotskyite groups have been operating in the country for several years: the Liga Socialista, which publishes *El Socialista*, and the Grupo Comunista Internacionalista, which publishes *Bandera Roja*.

* * *

The Guerrilla Movements. Mexico has an extensive list of self-proclaimed guerrilla groups. Some of these may simply issue a pamphlet and declare their existence, while others have been carrying on extensive operations for several years. The less prominent groups include the Union of the People, the Independent Popular Front, and the Maramillista Front.

Other groups have carried on very limited activities. The Spartacus Leninist League, formed in 1971, was responsible for the 1973 murder of Monterrey's industrial patriarch, Eugenio Garza Sada, age 82. The Salvador Allende Urban Guerrilla Command kidnaped Guadalajara industrialist Pedro Sarquis, age 70, who apparently died of a heart attack. The National Revolutionary Civic Association, formerly led by the late Genaro Vázquez Rojas, still operates in the state of Guerrero. In April, the People's Revolutionary Armed Vanguard kidnaped the son of Rafael Camacho Salgado, head of the Acapulco transporters' union. They held the boy for 16 days and released him after his father paid an undisclosed ransom.

Three other groups were somewhat more active during 1974. The Movimiento de Acción Revolucionaria (MAR), formed in 1971, continued its operations as an urban guerrilla group. There are indications that several of its members have been involved in armed robberies in Mexico City. The police captured more than 50 MAR members during the last few months of 1973 and early 1974. In February the Attorney General denounced the Fuerzas Armadas de Liberación Nacional, which is known to be operating in Monterrey (Nuevo León), Nepantla (Mexico) and Ocotillo (Chiapas). The leader of the organization is César Yañez, "Brother Pedro." Several of its members were captured at the time the American foreign ministers were meeting in Mexico City. Those arrested included Napoleon Bulnes, "Carrerto"; Mario Sandoval, "Luis"; Nola Rivera Rodríguez, "Asandra"; Raúl Sergio Morales, "Renal Martín"; Orestes Cardenal, a university teacher whose arrest was widely publicized because he teaches at the National University and is the author of the book *New Mexico*. Also in February the 8 October Proletarian Liberation Movement (Movimiento de Liberación Proletaria; MLP), emerged for the first time claiming responsibility for an attack on the 8th Naval Zone arms depot in Acapulco (Guerrero). The group claimed that it seized a large quantity of arms and ammunition. In the same communiqué the MLP praised Che Guevara and two other guerrilla groups: the Party of the Poor and the People's Revolutionary Armed Forces. The MLP also kidnaped a local deputy and demanded three million pesos and the release of 49 political prisoners from the Acapulco prison.

Four other guerrilla groups were active during 1974 and received a great deal of notoriety. On 22 March a commercial officer of the U.S. Consulate-General in Hermosillo (Sonora), John Patterson, was kidnaped. Patterson, the 31-year-old vice-consul, wrote a note stating that the kidnapers demanded $500,000 ransom. The note did not have any political content and made only monetary demands. Patterson's wife raised $250,000 and was preparing to meet the demands but further communication ceased. While she was waiting to negotiate, a group calling itself the People's Revolutionary Army of Mexico claimed credit for the kidnaping. On 7 July the body of John Patterson was found in the Sonora desert.

Another sensational kidnaping occurred on 28 August. The 83-year-old father-in-law of President Echeverría, José Guadalupe Zuno Hernández, was kidnaped in Guadalajara (Jalisco) by the People's Revolutionary Army Forces (Fuerzas Revolucionario Armado del Pueblo; FRAP), an urban guerrilla group. This kidnapping presented the president with a test of his policy of not negotiating with kidnappers. (That policy was adopted in 1973 after the U.S. consul-general in Guadalajara, Terrence

G. Leonhardy, was abducted by the "23 September Communist League" and then exchanged for 30 Mexican political prisoners. The prisoners were flown to Cuba and a ransom of $80,000 was paid by Mrs. Leonhardy.)

Zuno's eldest son said that U.S. imperialism was indirectly responsible for the kidnaping of his father. A similar charge was made in Mexico City by Jorge Cruickshank of the PPS, who said the kidnaping demonstrated the provocative attitude of the right, the reactionary forces, the oligarchy and imperialism. He accused the U.S. ambassador of being involved. Meanwhile, President Echeverría stated emphatically that the government would not deal with the kidnapers, who demanded a ransom of $1.6 million and the release of 100 political prisoners. After 11 days in captivity, Zuno was released in downtown Guadalajara. He said his kidnapers were "good boys, but mixed up. They want to change the world but don't know how to do it." Zuno then proceeded to criticize the Mexican government. He said that his son-in-law's administration "sided with capitalist reaction." He predicted that "the revolutionaries will win power in Mexico" and stated that their final objective was "the well-being of the people." Zuno also attacked the church, accusing it of being "a blind instrument used by the government to enslave the people." He had strong praise for guerrilla leader Lucio Cabañas (see below). Zuno gave his opinion that the government "will not overcome the economic, political and social crisis" in Mexico, "because it has sided with capitalist reaction, and this, of course, diminishes its merits, creditability, and strength before public opinion." The following month, 14 members of the FRAP were arrested and charged with the kidnaping. Although other members of the FRAP were still at large, the government claimed to have dealt the organization a final blow.

One of the strongest and most active urban guerrilla groups is the "23 September Communist League," which takes its name from an abortive 1967 guerrilla attack on a Chihuahua army post. In October 1973 the League kidnaped Guadalajara industrialist Fernando Aranguren and the honorary British consul in Guadalajara, Anthony Duncan Williams. When the government did not agree to its demands, including ransom and a plan to leave for North Korea, the industrialist was killed and the consul was released. In the spring of 1974, the League held up banks and dynamited factories and monuments throughout the state of Jalisco and its capital city, Guadalajara. During the period, the police and army cracked down and arrested and killed several League members. In January, the state attorney-general of Jalisco announced that League leader Pedro Orozco Guzman was killed in a shootout with police. The same month, four members of the League were arrested, including Peruvian physician Pedro Miguel Morón who operated a League hospital in San Juan de Aragón (Mexico City). In February, three other members were arrested in Torreon (Coahuila). Arrests continued throughout the year, but did not prevent the League from participating in various acts of violence.

In January some 300 youths clashed with army and police forces for 11 hours in the city of Culiacán (Sinaloa). The clashes resulted in 5 dead, 10 or more injured, and 14 arrested for possessing stolen arms. At the outset, authorities attributed the violence to an increase in local transportation rates. But the governor stated that outside agitators had entered the state to cause the disturbances, and the government announced that members of the League were the perpetrators of criminal acts that included kidnaping, hijacking of vehicles, shootings, armed holdups, and damaging of property. The army virtually occupied the city.

In March the League left a note in a school in Acapulco to report they had killed 73-year-old Raymunco Soberanit Otero "for being a bourgeois." The victim, a wealthy landowner, was the uncle of the governor of the state of Guerrero. He had been held by the guerrillas for more than a month. Later in the spring the League attacked Culiacán again. One member was killed and 12 others were captured after they had staged a series of synchronized attacks. The youths, numbering more than 50, stole several cars and busses, some of which they burned. Others staged robberies in various parts of the city. In June, 6 League members were arrested in Guadalajara: a doctor and 5 members of the League and the Student Revolutionary Front. Dr. Ramiro Vázquez Gutiérrez had run an underground clinic in the city.

On 10 December, five policemen were killed by 15 stocking-masked terrorists who raided two Mexico City banks. Three women were reported among the gunmen who grabbed $200,000, scattered notes in the banks signed "Commando Alfonso Rojas Díaz, 23 September Communist League," and escaped in two black automobiles. Members of the police department vowed to avenge the deaths of their fallen colleagues.

The strongest and most active rural guerrilla group is the "Party of the Poor" (Partido de Los Pobres). Unlike the League, which has been active in several states, it operates primarily in the state of Guerrero. The organization, which has existed since 1967, is led (or was led, if recent reports of his death are accurate; see below) by 34-year-old former schoolteacher, Lucio Cabañas Barrientos. It went practically unnoticed for five years, overshadowed by the actions of the band led by Cabañas's predecessor, Jenaro Vázquez Rojas. When Vázquez died in February 1972, Cabañas and his men collected their forces and became the only organized rural guerrilla band in Mexico. Over the past two years they have staged several ambushes of army patrols, leading to more than 60 deaths.

During 1974 the government issued periodic announcements listing the names of guerrillas who were captured or killed in shootouts. The guerrilla band also issued its own communiqués. At the beginning of the year, for example, the newspaper *El Día* received a document signed by Lucio Cabañas and others, who announced various attacks against army troops in the Sierra de Guerrero in which several people were killed. A controversy developed over the alleged death of Cabañas. Periodically police and army officials claimed he was dead but the guerrillas denied the reports (see below). In the spring, the PRI announced its intention to nominate Senator Rubén Figueroa as its candidate for governor of the state of Guerrero. After his nomination, he satated: "Guerrero is not ungovernable; the major task is to bring peace to the state and toward that end, I will meet with Lucio Cabañas to offer him total amnesty." The magazine *Por Que?* was highly critical of the senator's offer. After the official backing for his candidature, Figueroa apparently received a letter dated 9 May from Cabañas and others on behalf of the Brigada Campesina de Ajusticiamiento del Partido de los Pobres "Party of the Poor," proposing a meeting on 25 May. This eventually took place on 30 May, when the senator was met by Pascual Cabañas and Luis Cabañas Ocampo, the uncle and first cousin of Lucio Cabañas, who took him to a point some 50 miles inland from Acapulco. Three days later the guerrillas announced that Figueroa, his secretary, and his nephew were in the Brigada's hands. They demanded that police and army troops be removed from several towns in the mountainous area where their camp was located. President Echeverría ordered the police and troops removed. A few days later the PRI nominated Figueroa, still missing, as their candidate for governor.

The guerrillas held Figueroa for 12 weeks. In one communiqué the guerrillas made certain demands which were rejected by the government: release of federal political prisoners, and of all prisoners—political and criminal—from the jails of Guerrero; a payment of 50 million pesos; delivery to the group of 100 M-1 rifles and 50 Browning pistols, with ammunition; nationwide TV and radio broadcast of statements from the guerrillas; turning over of all land and property of the Mexican Coffee Institute to the workers' cooperatives; peasants on illegally occupied land to be given title to those lands and sufficient credit to work them; and the immeidate favorable settlement of a long list of local disputes.

The army never did withdraw all of its troops. Some of their intelligence agents remained in the area dressed in civilian clothes, and in July infantrymen and paratroopers supported by helicopters moved into the area. The president stated that "the people and the government do not negotiate with criminals" and ordered the army to free the senator. Some 16,000 soldiers, about a third of the Mexican Army, were mobilized in the region.

The kidnapings of Zuno Hernández and Rubén Figueroa were a setback for the government. Approximately 24 hours after the FRAP released the president's father-in-law, the army attacked a large band of Cabañas's guerrillas on a ranch near Acapulco and freed Figueroa. There were many casualties on both sides, with at least twelve soldiers killed. On 2 December, the Army announced that Cabañas and ten of his followers had been killed in a battle on the Otatal Ranch, 88 miles north of Acapulco.

The political advantages handed to the government by the military victory in Guerrero were more than offset by the acute embarrassment suffered by the government in Guadalajara. Despite the president's remarks about the kidnapers being "delinquents, criminals, homosexuals, or adventurers," his refusal to negotiate gave him much-needed public sympathy. But when the president's father-in-law denounced the government and praised the guerrillas upon his release, the government badly lost in prestige. Zuno Hernández is an old-guard revolutionary with a long history of loyalty to the original ideals of the Mexican Revolution. No one questions his revolutionary qualifications. The most obvious beneficiaries were the conservatives, both inside and outside the PRI, and the army.

Most political analysts believe the guerrilla movements do not endanger the government because the various bands operate in different parts of the country, lying quiet for a while, with membership apparently changing rather regularly. They are not perceived as coordinated groups such as Uruguay's Tupamaros had been. However, in November 1974 guerrillas set off at least 15 bombs over a two-day period. They damaged banks, department stores, and government offices in Mexico City, Guadalajara, and Oaxaca, some U.S.-owned. In Guadalajara, where the police accused the FRAP of organizing the attacks, one of the blasts rocked the state attorney-general's office, another went off near the military hospital, one at the offices of the Confederation of Mexican Workers, and one at a factory in the suburbs.

Grand Valley State Colleges   Donald L. Herman

Nicaragua

The Socialist Party of Nicaragua (Partido Socialista de Nicaragua; PSN) was founded in 1937 and held its first official congress in 1944. A year later it was declared illegal and has been a clandestine organization ever since.

The PSN is a pro-Soviet party. In 1967 an internal struggle resulted in the expulsion of some party leaders who then organized an anti-Soviet Communist Party of Nicaragua (Partido Comunista de Nicaragua; PCN).

The communist organizations in Nicaragua have a negligible effect on the national political situation. This is due to their small, scattered membership, internal splintering and the thorough suppression of such groups by the government of Anastasio Somoza. A slight rise in communist activities followed the disastrous earthquake of December 1972. The PSN did not participate in the 1 September presidential and legislative elections, in which incumbent President Anastasio Somoza and his followers won an overwhelming victory.

Leadership and Organization. The leadership of the PSN has undergone numerous changes in recent years. Luis Domingo Sanchez Sancho is presently believed to be the head of the party.

According to the main resolution of the 10th congress of the PSN (October 1973), the most recent substantive document available at this writing, the party recognizes its own weakness and has set out to strengthen its organizations both qualitatively and quantitatively. This entails opposition to all "distortions of Marxism-Leninism," whether coming from the right or from the left. The mission of the PSN consists in organizing and leading the working class through the various phases and periods of the revolutionary struggle. At present the PSN influences only a few small labor groups, among them the Independent General Confederation of Workers, and recognizes that both the workers and the people generally in Nicaragua are poorly organized and lack proper social consciousness. (*IB*, no. 1-2.)

The Nicaraguan Socialist Youth (Juventud Socialista Nicaraguense) is the official young peoples' organization of the PSN.

Party Internal Affairs. Typical of the confusion and uncertainty surrounding most meetings of the PSN (and many other Latin American Marxist-Leninist organizations) was the time and place of the 10th congress of the party (see *YICA, 1974*, p. 346). It is now apparent that the congress was held in October 1973, probably in Managua, and attended by more than 90 delegates. (*IB*, 1973, no. 23-24; ibid., 1974, no. 1-2.)

Domestic Views. At its 10th congress the PSN concluded that the severe economic crisis in

Nicaragua was due to the survival of antiquated forms of land tenure and agricultural production, strong dependence on foreign imperialism, the underdeveloped state of domestic capital and productive forces, the disastrous earthquake of December 1972, and the protracted drought of 1973. According to the PSN, the main issues of Nicaraguan government policy are decided by the U.S. Embassy and military mission. The "despotic, autocratic character of the oligarchic Somoza clan" prevents even the traditional parties from functioning significantly; lesser organizations, and the people, are poorly motivated and will remain powerless until they become organized and work together against the regime.

The PSN calls for a united front incorporating all labor unions, students, peasant organizations, committees for defense and improvement of the people's conditions, democratic political parties, elements of the middle class, progressive Christians, democratically-minded military, and all others who oppose the Somoza government. Only thus will it be possible to create a broadly-based popular movement capable of overthrowing the regime and bringing down its oligarchic, imperialist mainstays. (*IB*, no. 1-2.)

According to the PSN resolution, every patriot, democrat, humanist, and revolutionary in Nicaragua is duty bound to fight for the creation of a democratic opposition front, repeal of repressive laws, full democratization of the country, nationalization of national wealth, implementation of an anti-latifundist agrarian reform, higher wages for workers, and democratic and patriotic reform in the universities. Its long-term objectives remain the establishment of a socialist society, the elimination of social classes and privileges, and the construction of a society of working people free from exploitation, poverty, ignorance, and all other social evils of the capitalist system. (Ibid.)

International Attitudes. The PSN attended the preparatory meeting for the ninth conference of Communist and Workers Parties of Mexico, Central America, and Panama in December 1973-January 1974, and the conference itself toward the end of May 1974. With the other parties, the PSN reaffirmed its pro-Soviet stance, condemned the military coup in Chile which overthrew Salvador Allende, attacked those who seek to provoke further military conflict in Central America, and called for a meeting of all Communist and Workers parties of Latin America to explore the possibility of a conference of all parties of the region and to discuss its organization, agenda, and related matters. (*IB*, no. 3; ibid., Prague ed., no. 14; also see *Mexico*.)

*   *   *

The FSLN. The Sandinist National Liberation Front (Frente Sandinista de Liberación Nacional; FSLN), is a small guerrilla organization founded in 1961 by Carlos Fonseca Amador. After the exile of Fonseca to Cuba in 1970, the group became virtually inactive. During 1974 several operations were carried out resulting in occasional shootouts with the army, several casualties, and the liberation of several thousand dollars for revolutionary purposes. On 27 December the group broke up a Christmas party in Managua, killed several persons and kidnaped more than a dozen prominent politicians and business leaders. All were subsequently released in exchange for the freedom of several imprisoned revolutionaries. Released prisoners and kidnapers were given safe conduct to Cuba.

Hoover Institution
Stanford University

William E. Ratliff

Panama

The Communist Party of Panama (Partido Comunista de Panamá) was founded in 1930 through the unification of communist groups and the left wing of the Labor Party. Internal dissension led to the party's dissolution in 1943 and the formation in the same year of the People's Party of Panama (Partido del Pueblo de Panamá; PDP). The party has been illegal since 1953 though its activities have been tolerated to some degree by the government which followed the October 1968 National Guard coup.

The PDP, which claims to have grown substantially in recent years, is still estimated to have approximately 500 members (*World Strength of Communist Party Organizations 1973*, p. 176).

Leadership and Organization. Rubén Darío Souza has been general secretary of the PDP since the party's third congress in 1951. Other leaders include Hugo Víctor, Miguel Porcell, and Luther Thomas.

The PDP's supreme authority is the national congress, which is supposed to meet every four years. The congress elects a central committee, the highest body between congresses, and the central committee elects from its own members a Political Bureau, a general secretary, and a Secretariat, making up the national executive committee. Party branches (cells and *activos*) are found in urban and rural enterprises and residences. The *activo* is comprised of party members and those who have decided to join the PDP; it may be transformed into a cell. (*WMR*, March 1974.)

The PDP university-student affiliate is the University Reform Front (Frente Reformista Universitaria; FRU); its labor affiliate, disbanded by the government in 1968, is the Trade Union Federation of Workers of the Republic (Federación Sindical de Trabajadores de la República de Panamá; FST).

Party Internal Affairs. The fact that the PDP has been operating openly has given rise to some dissension in its ranks. A party statement issued in mid-1974 reported that "right-wing deviationists . . . see everything through rose-colored spectacles," imagining that the party enjoys full legality and is in power; the "left deviation" is unable to adapt to the new conditions and take advantage of them for solid, revolutionary purposes. According to the statement, party members must fight uncompromisingly against: attempts to bring division into the Party; renunciation of class independence; nationalism and chauvinism as incompatible with proletarian internationalism; factional activity, passive contemplation, liquidationism, anarchism, and petty-bourgeois individualism. Particular stress is laid upon improving education and propaganda, and on increasing party membership by going over from spontaneous to conscious growth controlled through well-organized campaigns. It should strengthen its ties with other revolutionary and progressive forces and, above all, seek to recruit new members from among the active and sound forces of the working class and peasantry. (*IB*, Prague edition, no. 14.)

Domestic Views and Activities. According to the PDP, the Panamianian oligarchs (the landed and house-owning bourgeoisie, the commercial bourgeoisie, and the bureaucratized officialdom) ruled Panama until the 1968 coup, an action the party now considers revolutionary. They still seek to defend the old order, as do the foreign private monopolies, the colonial administration of the Canal Zone, and Yankee imperialism. The present government is petty-bourgeois, members of the petty-bourgeoisie heading the key ministries. The PDP regards these leaders as anti-oligarchic, but at times maintains they are "doing nothing to undermine the foundations of the oligarchy's economic power," and claims that though they have made increasing demands against U.S. colonialism, they still allow "imperialism fully to carry on its neocolonialist policy." (See *IB*, Prague edition, no. 14.) At other times the PDP analysis of the present government is more positive. Darío Souza commented late in the year that important changes were taking place in the structure and superstructure of the country. The PDP general secretary pointed to the increasing power of the national assembly of *corregimiento* representatives, a large majority of whom are peasants, and commented favorably on boards operating at provincial, municipal, and local levels. He praised the nationalization of electrical energy and the banana export tax which affected the interests of the transnational companies. (Moscow radio, 19 October.) In June the PDP pointedly recognized the "decisive role" of General Omar Torrijos in the struggle of banana plantation workers (*IB*, Prague edition, no. 16). Darío was enthusiastic about recently formed worker and peasant cooperatives. While nothing that not all of these positive changes had been planned by the government, Darío explained that many had simply evolved during the course of the struggle against imperialism and the oligarchy. The military led by General Torrijos has opened the way for all social forces interested in national democracy and independence to implement their ideals of national liberation and development. The Panamianian military's interest in creating a free fatherland which could independently determine its own development had won the support of the workers, peasants, progressive intellectuals, professionals, and other democratic segments of the population. (Moscow radio, 19 October.) A PDP document published in February stated that there was a "new balance of forces [in Panama] in favor of national liberation, progressive democracy, and the anti-imperialist and anti-oligarchic struggle" (*IB*, Prague edition, no. 5-6).

As for the future, it was essential as never before for all patriotic and progressive forces to rely on the masses, thus to form a united front of the workers, peasants, intellectuals, students, small proprietors, national industrial bourgeoisie, and military based on a program of national liberation (ibid.). The party stresses the need for the organization and unity of workers who will protect, expand, and control the public property in the economy. The peasants, who constitute the majority of the population, have formed a national movement. The National Confederation of Peasant Asentamientos (CONAC) should be transformed into a national movement for all laborers in the countryside. It is also necessary to develop national organizations of women and young people. (*IB*, Prague edition, no. 14.) As the revolutionary process develops, some of the petty-bourgeoisie will draw nearer to the big employers, and some move closer to the workers. The PDP is particularly pleased with the "progressive trend" in the National Guard, warning that on the whole the military is distrustful of the revolutionary forces. Progressive tendencies are growing stronger in the Church though support for the old order is dominant. On the other hand, ultra-leftists attack both the government and the PDP; these groups are "objectively reactionary because their activity plays into the hands of imperialism and the oligarchy, with which they are at one in striving to check the current process." (*IB*, Prague edition, no. 14.)

International Views and Contacts. The most important international issue for the PDP during

1974 was the status of the Canal Zone. A Politburo document published on 7 February, referring to the "agreement in principle" signed that day by representatives of the governments of Panama and the United States, stated that the Panamanian government had "given voice to the best wishes of the Panamanian people about the Canal Zone." A new balance of forces had been reached in the country, as noted above, but the Politburo warned that the success was merely temporary. "With the destruction of colonialism, imperialism here, as elsewhere, will not entirely relinquish its domination, but will change from direct colonial force to neo-colonialist domination." (*IB*, Prague edition, no. 5-6.) This government support for popular interests, according to Darío Souza, had brought on an "open confrontation" with imperialism (Moscow radio, 19 October). The party agreed with the government decision to impose a $1 tax per box of exported bananas in order to recover part of the wealth taken over by foreign monopolies (*IB*, Prague ed., no. 16). Darío Souza strongly supported the reestablishment of diplomatic relations between the governments of Panama and Cuba, a step which supported the world struggle for peace and democracy against imperialism (Moscow radio, 19 October).

The PDP attended the preparatory meeting for the 9th conference of Communist and Workers Parties of Mexico, Central America, and Panama, in December 1973-January 1974, and the conference itself toward the end of May. With the other parties, the PDP reaffirmed its pro-Soviet stance, condemned the military coup in Chile, attacked those who sought to provoke further military conflict in Central America, and called for a meeting of all Communist and Workers parties of Latin America to explore the possibility of a conference of all parties of the region and to discuss its organization, agenda, and related matters. (*IB*, no. 3; ibid., Prague ed., no. 14; also see *Mexico*.)

Publications. The PDP publishes the monthly newspaper *Unidad*, as well as books, pamphlets, and information bulletins (*WMR*, March 1974).

Hoover Institution   William E. Ratliff
Stanford University

Paraguay

The Paraguayan Communist Party (Partido Comunista Paraguayo; PCP) was founded in 1928. It has been illegal since that time except for the August 1946-January 1947 period. The PCP, which was torn by disputes during the 1960s, seems to be increasingly effective in its recent efforts to attract Paraguayan communists to its ranks. The party is pro-Soviet in orientation.

The membership of the PCP, including all factions and sympathizers, is estimated at between 3000 and 4000 persons (*World Strength of Communist Party Organizations 1973*, p. 177). The party claims a six-fold increase in membership between June 1972 and January 1974 (*WMR*, April). The population of Paraguay is 2,500,000 (estimated 1974).

Leadership and Organization. Miguel Angel Soler heads the PCP; other party leaders include Pedro Vásquez, who serves on the editorial council of the Prague-based journal "Problems of Peace and Socialism" (*WMR*), Mario Bruno, Carlos Masiel, and, among those imprisoned for more than 15 years, party chairman Antonio Maidana.

In a special study made at its Third Congress (1971), the PCP recognized its previous inadequate program for young people. According to Vásquez, the congress approved a number of concrete demands expressive of the aspirations of young workers, peasants, and soldiers (e.g., shorter conscription terms, and loans to young peasants returning to civilian life after military service). The PCP stated its support for Lenin's idea that the communist youth must have its own independent organization. (*WMR*, April.) The party claims to be reestablishing relations with students and with workers. The PCP argues that the peasants are becoming more politically aware and active in demanding and seizing land; it notes the formation of "one more militant and organized detachment against the dictatorship," but claims no peasant organization of its own (*WMR*, May).

Party Internal Affairs. In accordance with a decision of its fourth plenum, the Central Committee of the PCP, elected at the Third Congress in 1971, convened a secret national conference in January 1974 (reportedly in Paraguay) attended by 14 members of the Central Committee, 16 delegates from party organizations, and a representative of the Communist Party of Argentina. The conference unanimously approved the Central Committee report on domestic, international, and intraparty work. (*IB*, Prague ed., no. 5-6.) The party claims that the moral and political prestige of the Central Committee is rising, conscious party discipline is taking root, democratic centralism is being advanced, a mass party is being developed, plans are underway to eliminate educational deficiencies of party cadres, and a successful fund-raising campaign has been completed. The congress in 1971 launched an ideological and political offensive against "right-opportunist" and "liberal" conceptions, and against "left-sectarianism" and "adventurist" views, reflected in bourgeois nationalist and anti-

Soviet positions, respectively. (*WMR*, April; and *FBIS*, 18 March.) In response to the statements by some PCP dissidents, the national conference proclaimed "the party is open to anyone who wants to rejoin the PCP in a spirit of genuine unity." The party promised that two of the main opposition leaders of the dissidents would be welcomed on the Central Committee, and on the Political Commission, and that all former party members would be readmitted as soon as the existing extra-party groups were dissolved. (*IB*, Prague ed., no. 5-6.) Preparations are reportedly underway for the Fourth Congress of the PCP, to be conducted under the guidelines—cohesion, common outlook, unity of organization and action, and no concession to factionalism. The forthcoming congress will be convened by the Central Committee elected at the Third Congress, and if a special preparatory commission is formed, it will consist of only those party members who have firmly defended the PCP's Marxist-Leninist principles and proved their loyalty to the program, constitution, political theses, and other documents of the 1971 congress. (*WMR*, April.)

Domestic Views and Activities. The PCP argues that Paraguayan president Alfredo Stroessner (in office since 1954; reelected in 1973) is a spiritual descendant of Hitler, a hatchetman subservient to the CIA, the Pentagon, and the Brazilian militarists. He is selling out much of the country to the U.S. monopolies and threatening to turn Paraguay into an "associated state" (indeed, a province) of Brazil. The degree of prosperity which seems to have hit Paraguay has not touched the bulk of the population whose standard of living continues to fall. (*WMR*, April.)

Paraguay's problems are due to the "triple evil" of latifundism, imperialism, and dictatorship. According to the PCP, the country's obsolescent social, economic, and political system, combined with the radicalization of all sections of society, is bound to produce an unprecedented national political crisis fraught with revolution. The Stroessner government will not collapse on its own, however, but must be pushed by the Paraguayan people in a national, anti-dictatorial front. The PCP argues that it must play a decisive part in the building of the united front, and stresses that unity must be achieved on the basis of a minimum program of democratization. The front should incorporate the workers, peasants, petty and middle bourgeoisie, students, intellectuals, white-collar workers, and many members of the military, the church, and the existing political parties, all of whom have turned in varying degrees against the dictatorship. The front will fail, however, if it adopts a bourgeois-nationalist or anti-communist posture, whether of the right or of the "left." Any form of mass struggle which extends the organization and unity of the masses and promotes their demands and political education, which helps to isolate the enemy and build up the revolutionary movement, can be regarded as revolutionary. But, when the time of decision comes, "none but the most effective forms of struggle for working-class and popular power are revolutionary." Thus, the PCP's policy of alliances must be tactically flexible while it is firm in principle, particularly toward the national bourgeoisie since that class (witness the Frei forces in Chile) frequently turns against democracy and supports fascism. (*WMR*, April.)

International Positions. The PCP equates support for the Soviet Union with proletarian internationalism (see *Pravda*, 13 November; *WMR*, September). It supports the idea of convening a new world meeting of communist and workers' parties to study collectively international developments and set new tasks, and it resolves to help in holding a conference of Latin American communist and workers' parties in the near future (*IB*, Prague ed., no. 5-6). The party condemns United States policies throughout Latin America and maintained at the time of the January conference that the U.S., having overthrown the Popular Unity government in Chile, was conspiring against the popular movements in Argentina, Peru, and Panama.

Publications. The PCP monthly newspaper, *Adelante*, was reportedly published in Paraguay during 1974, for the first time in recent years; a new political and theoretical journal, *Bases*, appeared during the year.

Hoover Institution
Stanford University

William E. Ratliff

Peru

The Peruvian Communist Party (Partido Comunista Peruano; PCP) had its origins in the Peruvian Socialist Party founded by José Carlos Mariategui in 1928. As a result of orders from the Communist International it took its present name in 1930. Since 1964 the movement has been divided into a pro-Soviet party and several pro-Chinese splinter groups, some of them using the PCP name.

There also exist in Peru various Marxist-Leninist organizations to the left of the PCP. These include the Castro-oriented Movement of the Revolutionary Left (Movimiento de Izquierda Revolucionaria; MIR) and Army of National Liberation (Ejército de Liberación Nacional; ELN), and the Trotskyite Revolutionary Left Front (Frente de Izquierda Revolucionaria; FIR), Partido Obrero Revolucionario (Trotskista), and Revolutionary Vanguard (Vanguardia Revolucionaria; VR).

Membership of the pro-Soviet and pro-Chinese PCP groups has been estimated at 2,000 and 1,200 respectively (*World Strength of the Communist Party Organizations*, 1974). This perhaps overestimates the pro-Chinese following. Other Marxist-Leninist groups are small, the FIR and VR having perhaps the largest memberships. The population of Peru is about 14,460,000 (estimated 1972).

Communist membership is predominantly urban, mainly drawn from workers, students, and professional groups. Pro-Chinese elements seem to have the strongest hold in the universities. Communist influence in the trade union movement is exercised mainly by the pro-Soviet PCP, which controls the General Confederation of Workers of Peru (Confederación General de Trabajadores del Peru; CGTP). The FIR and MIR at one time had some influence among the peasants, although in recent years that has largely dissipated. The pro-Soviet PCP, through the CGTP, has gained more influence among the peasants in recent years than it had had in the past.

A constitutional provision prohibits communist parties from participating in Peruvian elections, which are not being held in any case under the present military government; but the communists have been allowed to operate under various degrees of police surveillance and harassment. The present government led by President Juan Velasco Alvarado has permitted the pro-Soviet PCP to function freely, but has kept considerable control over other leftist groups, and has deported several pro-Chinese and Trotskyist leaders. On 1 December 1971 a law was passed providing for the death penalty or 25-year prison terms in cases of terrorist attacks causing death, serious injury, or property destruction. The Velasco government has also sought to co-opt leaders of various Marxist-Leninist groups.

The Pro-Soviet PCP. Leadership and Organization. The highest organ of the pro-Soviet PCP is officially the national congress, which is supposed to meet every three years. Its Sixth Congress, the most recent, met in November 1973. The principal party leaders include Jorge del Prado, secretary-general, and Raúl Acosta Salas, undersecretary-general. Prominent Central Committee members include Félix Arias Schreiber, Jorge Bejár, Alfredo Abarca, Segundo Collazos, Andrés Paredes, José Reccio Gutiérrez, Pompeyo Maras, Magno Falcón, Mario Ugarte Hurtado, and Juan Caceres. Central Committee member Gustavo Espinoza is secretary-general of the General Confederation of Workers of Peru (Confederación General del Trabajadores del Peru; CGTP).

The pro-Soviet party is organized from cells upward through local and regional committees, to its Central Committee. Regional committees exist in at least 22 cities (see *YICA, 1972*, p. 411). Lima has the largest number of local committees, concentrated in low-income neighborhoods and in the slum areas which the government now refers to as "new towns."

A report delivered at the PCP's Sixth Congress stated that 56 percent of the party members were urban workers. The rest included 8 percent peasants, 21 percent intellectuals, 4 percent students, and 9 percent undifferentiated. It was also reported that the average party member had belonged for 9½ years, and the average age was 34 years (*WMR*, January 1974).

The pro-Soviet PCP has a youth group, the Peruvian Communist Youth (Juventud Comunista Peruana; JCP) which is small and operates mainly in the universities. It also controls several front organizations, including the Popular Union of Peruvian Women (Unión Popular de Mujeres Peruanas.)

The CGTP. The most influential organization under the control of the pro-Soviet PCP is the CGTP. Enjoying legal recognition granted by the military government, it expressed strong support during 1974 for the Velasco regime. Thus, in January the CGTP applauded the regime's decision to take over the Cerro de Pasco corporation, a U.S.-owned mining firm (*Unidad*, 4 January). At the end of the same month, it called on people to be on guard against attempts to overthrow the government, such as that which had overthrown Salvador Allende in Chile.

Early in March the CGTP held its Third Congress. Its officials claimed that 46 national federations and approximately 300 local unions were represented. The congress adopted resolutions expressing support of the revolutionary government, urging it to provide for representation of the "labor communities" on the boards of directors of private firms, and advocating the merger of all of the existing Peruvian central labor organizations.

Another important effort of the CGTP during the year was that of launching a peasant confederation, the Confederación Nacional Agraria. A convention held in May, reportedly attended by 200 delegates from ten departments, formed this organization to compete with other peasant groups controlled by the Partido Aprista, the far-Left, and SINAMOS.

Although the pro-Soviet communists firmly control the CGTP, they have faced considerable opposition within some of its affiliates. This was particularly the case in the CGTP's miners' federation (Federación de Trabajadores de la Industria Mineral del Peru; FETIMP). Elections were held in that union late in January and the vituperation with which the communist paper *Unidad* attacked the opposition slates would seem to indicate some fear of the opponents' being successful. The pro-Soviet slate headed by José Chávez Canales was successful against List No. 2 backed by FIR, Patria Roja, and the MIR, and List No. 3 supported by Vanguardia Revolucionaria. The PCP accused the far-Left groups of seeking to organize a new central labor group to confront the military government.

Throughout the year, the CGTP was faced with the rivalry of the government-sponsored Central Organization of Workers of the Peruvian Revolution (Central de Trabajadores de la Revolución Peruana; CTRP). The CTRP paid no apparent attention to the CGTP's invitations to establish "trade union unity," in spite of claims by CGTP leaders in November that "rapprochement" between it and the CTRP was "progressing." Neither did the other two trade union groups, the Confederación de Trabajadores del Peru, controlled by the Partido Aprista, and the Confederación Nacional de Trabajadores, under Catholic leadership.

Party Internal Affairs. The pro-Soviet PCP held its Sixth National Congress on 2-5 November 1973. Present were more than 200 delegates, and also fraternal delegations from 19 foreign parties, including that of the Soviet Union. The congress adopted a new party program, called for a national conference to discuss party development, and elected a new Central Committee of 40 full and 5 alternate members. Jorge del Prado was reelected secretary-general, a post he had held for almost thirty years.

Several national PCP meetings were held during 1974. One was a conference of the leaders of ten regional committees with national leaders on 26 May, the principal purpose of which was to launch a party recruiting campaign to celebrate the 80th anniversary of the birth of José Carlos Mariategui. Another was a congress of the secondary school members of the JCP in March. The Central Committee met in August (see *IB*, Prague ed., no. 17) to discuss the newly announced "Inca Plan" of the government, which the communists were said to see as a "program of anti-imperialist and anti-oligarchy actions aimed at building socialism" (Moscow radio, 5 September).

Domestic Attitudes and Activities. The Peruvian government has been undertaking since October 1968 various measures of economic and social reform to the benefit of the workers and peasants, and the pro-Soviet PCP has maintained a policy of virtually total support, which was reiterated during 1974. The Sixth Congress of the party had declared in November 1973: "We have a profound respect for the Revolutionary Government as far its ideology and politics."

In its New Year's message, the PCP Political Committee urged all revolutionary forces, the workers, and the people in general to rally behind the military regime. It also urged that all should be "alert and vigilant in the face of the counter-revolutionary plot."

In February, Jorge del Prado, in a speech at Trujillo in northern Peru, reiterated the PCP's support of the regime, saying: "Those who beleive this is not a revolution because it is being carried out by military men are wrong." Two months later the PCP weekly, *Unidad* (25 April), asserted: "The communists fight responsibily and on a principled basis, in defense of and for the deepening of the revolutionary process."

The communists were particularly enthusiastic about the confiscation of the remaining independent newspapers in July. This was indicated by *Unidad* on 11 July when it commented: "Press freedom begins with the revolution, which is the fundamental freedom. The rest is all humbug." Earlier, on 27 June, the PCP paper had expressed support for banning the Leftist but critical magazine *Caretas*, by saying that it was "impossible to tolerate any longer the insolence of those who traffic with the right to disagree. . . . The Peruvian revolution does not deny this right to anyone, but it does deny the right to attack the revolution."

PCP and SINAMOS. However, in spite of constant communist proclamations of support for the military regime, relations between the PCP and the Velasco administration were not without difficulties. For one thing, rivalry was clear between the government-oriented CTRP and the communists' CGTP. For another, the communists were still unhappy about the government's overall agency for social mobilization, known by its Spanish initials as SINAMOS.

The 6 December 1973 issue of *Unidad* carried an article ostensibly praising SINAMOS. It mentioned the good work that SINAMOS was doing in the cooperative field and in certain economic activities. However, the article notably left out any mention of SINAMOS activities in the labor movement, which centered on the CTRP.

The clearest conflict between the communists and SINAMOS took place in August in the form of a polemic between SINAMOS director-general Carlos Delgado, and the PCP. Delgado, the most important civilian in the Velasco government, asserted: "We maintain policies different from those of the communists. We have different ideas, defend incompatible goals, and follow irreconcilable political matters. If under these conditions the communists decide to support a revolution, that will mean their historical destruction. That is their business. No one has said the last world about the hidden motives of conduct leading to personal or political suicide." (Agence France Press, 7 August.)

The communists replied to Delgado's attack. Jorge del Prado denied any opportunistic motives behind the party's support of the government, and said: "[The PCP] supports the Peruvian regime because it fights against dependency, underdevelopment and the type of social justice which characterizes national reality. . . . Communism, like the Peruvian revolution, defends the transfer of power by means of popular organizations." (*Estado de Sao Paulo*, 13 August.)

A new element in the relations between the PCP and the Velasco government was introduced in 1974 when Peru received for the first time a substantial shipment of Soviet arms, including missiles, tanks, and other heavy equipment. These were put on exhibition in July in the annual Independence Day parade.

International Views and Positions. The PCP continued in 1974 to maintain a very close pro-Soviet alignment. In February and March a high-level delegation, headed by Jorge del Prado, visited Eastern Europe and the Soviet Union. Except in Poland, the delegation was not received by the heads of the national communist parties, although high-ranking party figures did meet with the Peruvians. In the U.S.S.R. they were received by B. N. Ponomarev, candidate member of the Politburo and first deputy chief of the Central Committee's International Section. Delegates from fraternal parties and trade union groups attended the PCP's Sixth Congress in November 1973 and the CGTP's Third Congress in March 1974.

Publication. The official organ of the pro-Soviet PCP is the weekly newspaper *Unidad*. It claims a circulation of more than 10,000.

*   *   *

The Pro-Chinese Communists. Leadership and Organization. The PCP organ *Unidad* asserted on 31 January 1974 that there were as many as 30 far-Left groups in Peru. Most of these, certainly, were tiny organizations with little more than a name, a handful of members and a rubber stamp for their stationery. However, some of the more important ones fell into more or less easily identifiable categories. One of these consists of pro-Chinese parties.

Virtually from their inception, the pro-Chinese communists have experienced internal dissension and splits. There are at least three factions of the pro-Chinese PCP. The one which enjoys more or less official recognition from the Chinese Communist Party is headed by Saturnino Paredes Macedo and, from its somewhat sporadic periodical, *Bandero Roja,* is generally known as the Bandera Roja, PCP. The so-called Sotomayor faction has its principal center of influence in the southern city of Arequipa. The Red Fatherland faction, so called because of its periodical *Patria Roja*, is said to have the largest following of all pro-Chinese groups among the students. All these factions oppose the military regime.

The pro-Chinese parties had limited activity during 1974. They had some influence in the metal workers federation of the CGTP, and the teachers unions. The Patria Roja faction was reported in March to have joined with a party with the same name in the Dominican Republic in a call for a meeting of Latin American communist parties of their orientation. No date or place was suggested for such a conference, and there is no indication that it was held during the year.

The several Marxist-Leninist parties and groups of Castroite and Trotskyist orientation in Peru that reached their apogee in the early 1960s are now small in membership, although they have some ideological influence among young people, particularly students. The Castroite groups include the MIR, ELN, and a faction of the VR. The Trotskyists encompass the FIR, POR(T), and POMR.

In November 1973 several far-Leftist groups met in La Oraya to try to forge a common policy. The FIR, MIR, POMR, and VR were among those represented. Reportedly a common strategy was agreed upon to try to take control of the CGTP away from the pro-Soviet communists. (*Caretas,* 8-16 November.) There is no indication that they made substantial progress towards this objective, although they did provoke some violent diatribes from the PCP.

*   *   *

The MIR. The Movement of the Revolutionary Left was first organized as the Partido Apra Rebelde in the late 1950s by a group of young people who felt that the country's traditional democratic leftist group, the Partido Aprista, had abandoned its early militancy. After the Cuban Revolution it came under Castroite influence and adopted its present name. In 1965 it launched a major guerrilla war effort, in which its then leader was killed, and the membership suffered many casualties. The extent of current membership is not known, but the MIR has some influence in the universities. Ricardo Gadea, brother of Che Guevara's first wife, is the principal leader. The MIR has consistently opposed the military regime since 1968.

The ELN. The ELN, founded in 1962 by former PCP members, participated in the peasant guerrilla movement of 1965. Its main leader, Héctor Béjar, was released from prison in December 1970 in a general political amnesty. In 1974 he was head of the Youth Section of SINAMOS, and in a New Year's Message urged the youth to organize in defense of the revolution, to thwart the "little groups" which were opposing it. Angel Castro Lavarello is now president of the FLN; Genaro Carnero Checa, Hernán Altamirano, Maruja Roque, and José Roma Galván are national secretaries.

*   *   *

The VR. The VR is a Marxist-Leninist party founded by former Aprista Party members in 1965. It advocates armed confrontation as a means of achieving socialism, but holds that its members should have theoretical and practical training before engaging in actual struggle. Although composed primarily of intellectuals, it includes some workers. In 1974 it was reported that it was the most important political element among the mining workers of the central part of Peru, centering on the former holdings of the Cerro de Pasco corporation.

The VR split in 1971. A faction led by Ricardo Napuri formed the Marxist Revolutionary Workers Party (Partido Obrero Marxista Revolucionario; POMR). The party leaders describe it as "Leninist-Trotskyist," but it has no affiliation with any of the international factions of Trotskyism.

The FIR. The FIR is a Trotskyist party associated with the United Secretariat faction of the Fourth International. Its principal figure is Hugo Blanco, who in 1962 led a movement of peasants near Cuzco to seize land, culminating in an armed uprising. He was captured and kept in prison until December 1970, when he was released in a general amnesty. Because of his criticisms of the military government, he was deported in September 1973.

The FIR has a youth group, the Vanguard Socialist Youth (Juventud Avanazada Socialista; JAS). It also published a fortnightly periodical, *Palabra Socialista*.

During 1974 the FIR carried on a campaign for the merger of all of the country's central labor organizations. It also attacked the pro-Soviet PCP and other groups which were claiming that there was a danger there might be a move against the Velasco regime similar to that against the Allende government in Chile in September 1973.

The POR(T). The POR(T) is a Trotskyist faction associated with the International Secretariat of the Fourth International, Posadas faction. It has supported the government since 1968. As in previous years, the POR(T) concentrated most of its efforts in 1974 on distributing its periodicals and pamphlets, most of them written by J. Posadas.

Rutgers University   Robert J. Alexander

Puerto Rico

The Puerto Rican Communist Party (Partido Comunista Puertorriqueño; PCP) is closely associated with the Communist Party, USA (CPUSA) and shares its pro-Soviet orientation. The Puerto Rican Socialist League (Liga Socialista Puertorriqueña; LSP) has close ties to the Progressive Labor Party (PLP) of the United States, and like the PLP, dropped its pro-Chinese orientation in 1971. Together the PCP and LSP probably have fewer than 200 members.

The Puerto Rican Socialist Party (Partido Socialista Puertorriqueño; PSP), formerly the Pro-Independence Movement (MPI), with close ties to Cuba, is independent in the Sino-Soviet dispute. It claimed to have about 6,000 members at the beginning of 1972 and implied approximately 15,000 to 18,000 followers one year later.

The PCP. The Puerto Rican Communist Party was founded in 1934, dissolved in 1944, and founded again in 1946. Little is known of its organizational structure, except that it appears to operate both in Puerto Rico and in New York City. Among its leaders are its secretary general, Félix Ojeda Ruiz, and Politburo-member Manuel Méndez del Toro. The party is organized in residential and working areas, with branches united in territorial organizations led by municipal committees. The party congress, held once every five years, elects a central committee, which in turn elects a political commission. The party says its social composition is: wage-earners (70 percent), peasants (5), salary-earners (20), and other categories (5). Women constitute 15 percent and persons under 30 years of age constitute 60 percent. (*WMR*, July.)

Domestic and International Views. The domestic and international views of the PCP mirror those of the CPUSA, as reflected in a published report on a 27-28 March 1973 meeting between Ojeda and CPUSA general secretary Gus Hall in Puerto Rico. The U.S. delegation hailed the achievements of the PCP as the Marxist-Leninist vanguard in the Puerto Rican struggles for socialism. The conference condemned U.S. imperialism for using Puerto Rico as a nuclear base and as a storage place for gas and oil supplies. The continued use of Culebra as a military target calls for ever greater demands for an end to all military occupation by U.S. forces in Puerto Rico. The meeting called for greater popular unity in the struggle against the rising cost of living, racism, and war, and for united strength for the working class in the class struggles for peace and socialism. (*IB*, no. 7, 1973.)

The PCP publishes a monthly paper, *El Pueblo*, with a claimed circulation of 3,000, and an irregular information bulletin, *El Proletario*.

*   *   *

The LSP. The Puerto Rican Socialist League, apparently operating in both Puerto Rico and New York City, is led by its secretary general, Juan Antonio Corretjer. The LSP still calls for "people's war" in Puerto Rico. Its organs, which appear irregularly, are *Pabellón* and *El Socialista*. Information on the LSP is found in the PLP paper *Challenge/Desafío*.

* * *

The PSP. The Puerto Rican Socialist Party was formed in November 1971 at the Eighth National Assembly of the MPI. Juan Mari Bras is secretary general and Julio Vives Vásquez is president or chairman. Among the members of the 12-person political commission are Mari Bras, Vives, Pedro Baigés (secretary of international relations), Alberto Márquez (secretary of political education), and, until his death in a car accident in December, Raúl González Cruz, editor of the party paper, *Claridad*.

Domestic and International Views and Activities. The PSP holds that Puerto Rico is an exploited colony and that the present political structure serves only the interests of U.S. imperialism and Puerto Rican reactionaries. In September Raúl González said the political situation in Puerto Rico could be summarized under two basic headings: (1) the economic crisis, and a crack in the long-standing colonial political structure, and (2) an increasing awareness and restlessness among the masses which encourages revolutionary change. The masses are beginning to see the nature and effect of the political superstructure of colonialism and they are now striking out against it, as in the PSP-organized boycott of light bills at mid-year. (*Granma*, Havana, 17 September.)

Mari Bras presented a new PSP strategy in San Juan in early March. Labeled "the socialist alternative," approved by an extraordinary congress of the party, the main point of the new line was that political sovereignty should no longer be sought through Washington's recognition. In the future the independence movement would have to develop all existing forms of struggle to overthrow the colonial regime and proclaim a Workers' Democratic Republic, whether or not the United States wants to recognize it. Under the leadership of its vanguard party, the Puerto Rican people will have to organize several power institutions, including their own armed forces. According to Mari Bras, the successes of the PSP in the independence struggle are what allows the PSP "to undertake, in a realistic way, the organization of the people so that they, without previous consultations or negotiations with Washington, will be able to proclaim the Workers' Democratic Republic and move on to organize the life of the society." (*Granma*, English, 17 March.)

The PSP has actively and apparently effectively recruited members among Puerto Ricans in the United States. The party has a mission in Cuba, in large part to facilitate the presentation of its views in the international community. Mari Bras condemned U.S. birth control policies in Puerto Rico before the United Nations special committee on decolonization on 30 October.

The organ of the PSP is *Claridad*, described in González's obituary in December as "the number-one daily in support of Puerto Rican workers and independence" (*Granma*, English, 29 December).

Hoover Institution
Stanford University

William E. Ratliff

United States of America

Communism in the United States includes parties with quite different ideologies, ranging in membership from a few dozen to 16,000. The two most important are the Communist Party, USA and the Socialist Workers Party. The latter is Trotskyite. Some Maoist sects, such as the October League and the Revolutionary Union, have recently been attempting to form a new nationwide organization. The Progressive Labor Party, formerly Maoist, is now Stalinist. Numerous splinter groups and small sects look to some variant of Marxism-Leninism for inspiration.

The CPUSA. The Communist Party, USA (CPUSA), is the oldest and largest of the Marxist-Leninist movements in the United States. It traces its lineage to the Communist Labor Party and the Communist Party, both formed in 1919. The CPUSA claims to have around 16,000 members (*Saturday Review World*, 23 February 1974).

Organization and Leadership. Only minor changes occurred within the CPUSA leadership during 1974. Gus Hall and Henry Winston continued as general secretary and national chairman respectively. Danny Rubin resigned as national organizational secretary for health reasons and was replaced by Arnold Bechetti. Among the other party leaders are Helen Winter (international affairs secretary), James Jackson (national education director), Alva Buxenbaum (chairwoman, National Women's Commission), George Meyrs (chairman, National Labor commission), Victor Perlo (chairman, Economics Commission), Arnold Johnson (legislative director), Betty Smith (national administrative secretary, Roscoe Proctor (co-chairman, Black Liberation Committee), William L. Patterson (co-chairman, Black Liberation Committee), Charlene Mitchell (national secretary, Black Liberation Committee), Grace Mora Newman (chairwoman, Puerto Rican Commission), Lorenzo Torres (chairman, National Chicano Commission), Hyman Lumer (editor, *Political Affairs*), Alex Kolkin (chairman, Jewish Commission), Conrad Komorowski (chairman, Nationality Groups Commission), William Fugate (chairman, National Coal Commission), Carl Bloice (editor, *People's World*), Si Gerson (executive editor, *Daily World*), Carl Winter (editor, *Daily World*), and Claude Lightfoot, Angela Davis, and Herbert Aptheker (Central Committee members).

Among the party leaders in important states were Al Lima and William Taylor (California), James Kling and Ishmael Flory (Illinois), James West (Ohio), Thomas Dennis (Michigan), Rasheed Storey and Ken Newcomb (New York), Joelle Fishman (Connecticut), and Sondra Patrinos (Pennsylvania).

The CPUSA has no official auxiliary bodies. A number of organizations, however, while lacking official party ties, are largely led by party members. These organizations cooperate closely with the party, hold the same views, and receive wide coverage in the party press. The most important is the Young Workers Liberation League (YWLL). Jarvis Tyner, who was the CPUSA candidate for the U.S.

vice-presidency in 1972, is national chairman. Other YWLL leaders include Judy Edelman (national labor secretary, and editor of *Young Worker*), Victoria Missick (national student secretary), Mike Zagarell (education director, and CPUSA Political Committee member), Victoria Stevens (student secretary), Roque Restorucci (New York state chairman), Susan Borenstein (organization secretary), Danny Spector (organizational secretary), and Jeff Schwartz (international affairs secretary). Among its other activities the YWLL was active in the movement to impeach U.S. President Nixon, endorsing a Washington impeachment rally in April. The YWLL also publicly attacked police tactics in San Francisco as "martial law in the black community" (*Daily World*, 24 April) and urged young people to fight racism. At its convention in Philadelphia in December the YWLL focused on support for unity in the youth movement and for job creation and training for all youth, against racism, and for quality, desegregated education. YWLL student leaders attacked a ruling of the U.S. Immigration Service barring foreign students from holding summer jobs (ibid., 10 May). A number of YWLL members were candidates for public office. YWLL membership is approximately 4,200.

The National Co-ordinating Committee for Trade Union Action and Democracy (TUAD), founded in 1970, has been the CPUSA's instrument for increasing its influence in the trade union movement. In a report to the party Central Committee, George Meyers stated that TUAD was "winning respect as the outstanding proponent of class-struggle trade unionism," but pointed to local weaknesses: "in a number of cities, promising TUAD chapters have floundered." Meyers attributed the difficulties to insufficient work within local unions, lack of attention from local CPUSA groups, and failure to oppose united fronts with "Trotskyites, Revolutionary Union disrupters, Staughton Lynd types, and similar anti-working class, anti-Communist elements." (*Political Affairs*, August.) At a TUAD emergency conference in September, delegates from 28 unions called for a stepped-up fight against inflation and for improvement in workers' standards of living.

The National Alliance against Racist and Political Repression (NARPR) emerged during 1974 as the CPUSA's major united-front organization (see *YICA, 1974*, p. 374). The NARPR has attracted support from groups and political figures on the left. A number of its leading figures are prominently identified with the CPUSA. The national chairmen are Angela Davis, Carl Braden (Southern Conference Education Fund), and Clyde Bellecourt (American Indian Movement). Charlene Mitchell, CPUSA Political Committee member and party candidate for the U.S. presidency in 1968, is executive secretary. A conference in North Carolina, in February, attended by 350 persons, called for an end to repression in that state (ibid., 26 February). At a conference in April, in Washington, 300 delegates urged the termination of funding for "racist research" and passed a strong pro-busing resolution (ibid., 23 April). The CPUSA called for an all-out mobilization for an NARPR-sponsored march on 4 July in Raleigh, North Carolina, and described it as the first national demonstration in the South since M. L. King's funeral in 1968. According to the party, 10,000 persons marched and listened to Ralph Abernathy (Southern Christian Leadership Conference) and Angela Davis call for the release of political prisoners, the end of repression against the Tuscarora Indians, the abolition of the death penalty, and the closing of a prison behavior-modification center. (Ibid., February 26, 15 June.)

Party Internal Affairs. A December 1973 meeting of the CPUSA Central Committee expelled two long-term party leaders in California, Dorothy Healey and Al Richmond, who had both previously announced their resignations. They were denounced for their continued opposition to the Soviet-led invasion of Czechoslovakia and the "fundamental organizational principle of democratic centralism." (Ibid., 10 January, 1974.)

A March 1974 party conference on "work among women" urged that a party periodical on women be issued. The conference also proposed a "women's Bill of Rights"—to protect women from requirements detrimental to their health and to recognize their special needs—as an alternative to the

Equal Rights Amendment (ERA) to the U.S. Constitition. (Ibid., 7 March.) Interpreting the ERA to mean that "any law now on the books which applies only to women would become immediately unconstitutional" and asking if it is "wise to give up protection for half the workers if there is no guarantee we will ever win it back," the party declared opposition to the ERA "as it now stands," (*Political Affairs*, July), since, "by itself, the ERA is inefficient to deal with the whole range of sex discrimination in American life" (*Daily World*, 14 June).

At a Central Committee meeting in July, Henry Winston argued that for the party to "lead the fight for democracy," workers in basic industry had to be recruited: "When the workers . . . move, they can change America." He announced a four-month recruiting drive and foresaw "the party's resurgence in basic industry across the nation." (Ibid., 5 July.) Gus Hall stated that the party had "made some significant progress in many areas," but warned against the danger of neglecting to continue united-front work (ibid., 20 July). He later declared: "This Party has mastered the art of combining the two aspects of struggle—the independent activities and positions of the Party and the policy of simultaneously taking part in and leading united front movements of people" (ibid., 7 September).

The year saw a number of party victories on the legal front. Maurice Braverman, a Maryland lawyer convicted in a Smith Act trial in the 1950s, was reinstated to the bar after 19 years (ibid., 20 March). When Judge John Sirica struck down the last two sections of the McCarran Act as unconstitutional, Hall and Winston hailed it as a "victory for the democratic rights of the people of this country," since "This Act provided the scheme for the threat of a Fascist take-over" (ibid., 1 June). A number of states lifted restrictions that had kept the CPUSA off the ballot. In Indiana, for example, the party was able to run candidates for the first time since World War II (ibid., 21 June).

Party leaders called for a break with the two-party system and support for a third party of labor (ibid., 24 May). A large number of CPUSA candidates ran for state and federal offices. Jack Kurzweil, running for county tax assessor in San Jose, California, received 30,000 votes, just under 15 percent of the total. Candidates for state governor were on the ballot in Michigan, Minnesota, Wisconsin, and New York, and party members ran for other offices ranging from the U.S. Senate to state boards of education. Congressional candidates in New Jersey and Connecticut received about 1.4 percent of the vote. Low voter turnout showed massive discontent with government policies (ibid., 7 November).

The CPUSA continued to be a steady critic of other radical groups. In addition to frequent attacks on Maoism for its international role as an opponent of the Soviet Union, there was a call to strengthen the fight against Maoism in the U.S. ("its divisive effects hang on"), though its influence was waning (ibid., 24 February). The *Guardian*, a Maoist paper, was attacked, and "ultra leftists" were criticized as "propaganda sects" (ibid., 4 June). The Trotskyite Socialist Workers Party was attacked for its position on the Middle East (ibid., 12 January), and its support of Solzhenitsyn and defense of Soviet political prisoners (ibid., 24 January).

The party press devoted relatively little attention to the Symbionese Liberation Army (SLA) and its abduction of Patricia Hearst. A columnist commented that "acts of individual terrorism such as kidnaping are directly contrary to Marxist principles and tactics" (ibid., 5 April), since giving food to the poor (as demanded by the SLA) would not change capitalism (ibid., 16 February). The police chief of Los Angeles was criticized for referring to the SLA as communist (ibid., 21 June). There was a suggestion later that the entire affair was a police or FBI provocation against the radical movement, and that the SLA was "made up of a combination of lumpen police agents and wealthy youths." The CPUSA paper also charged that the episode came "at an opportune time for the Nixon Administration and the Right wing" (ibid., 10 May).

The CPUSA continued to denounce sharply the National Caucus of Labor Committees (NCLC), a small radical sect tracing its lineage to the Students for a Democratic Society. The NCLC had in the past distinguished itself by physical attacks on party members and disrupting meetings of other left-wing groups. The group believes that a conspiracy including the U.S. Central Intelligence Agency, the Soviet KGB, and the Rockefeller family is attempting to brainwash radicals. Its organ, *New Solidarity*, claimed (14 August) that "Nelson Rockefeller has destroyed the last vestige of the American democratic tradition with the removal of Richard Nixon."

A December plenum in New York scheduled the twenty-second CPUSA congress for 26-29 June 1975, in Chicago.

Domestic Affairs. The CPUSA attitude toward the Watergate Affair and the downfall of President Nixon was complicated by Nixon's role in establishing détente with the Soviet Union. While vigorously supporting impeachment and calling for full disclosure of all the President's alleged crimes, domestic and foreign, the CPUSA found it disturbing that the attack on the President was being led by Democratic Party opponents of détente (*Daily World*, 3 May). Early in the year a CPUSA columnist warned that Maoism,—"this anti-Soviet strategy"—was "at the center of all monopoly's maneuvers including, for example, the current Watergate controversy" (ibid., 27 February). On the other hand, an editorial called the President "a menace to the democratic process itself," and remarked that "even Nixon's stand on détente" was "undercut by his connivance" in continuing to support a high military budget and U.S. aid to Cambodia and South Vietnam (ibid., 27 February). The solution proposed by Gus Hall was "an independent movement outside the two-party system that is for détente and impeachment" (*Political Affairs*, March). Party leaders saw the roots of Watergate in the crisis of monopoly capitalism. Gus Hall suggested that the growth of a strong presidency and claims for executive privilege were signs that as the capitalist crisis deepened, democratic structures were being undermined (*Daily World*, 28 February).

After Nixon's assistants Haldeman and Ehrlichman were indicted by a federal grand jury, the CPUSA linked its call for impeachment with an attach on Vice-President Ford, insisting that new elections were in order (ibid., 2 March). At an April meeting of party leaders in New York, Hall noted "tremendous mass disillusionment" and "distrust of all institutions—the Presidency, the Congress and the two-party system," and called for a "united front against Watergate and for détente" (ibid., 10 April).

While the party supported impeachment, it objected to the narrowing of the issues so as to exclude racism and war crimes. Consequently, Hall indicated that he was uninterested in the White House tape recordings of "gossip between Nixon and his thugs of executive privilege," and wanted information about "Cambodia, the dismantling of the anti-poverty program, and police-state tactics" (ibid., 3, 7 May). Winston believed that "when the full crimes of both parties are revealed, then there will be a drive for an independent party based on labor" (ibid., 27 April). At the end of the House Judiciary proceedings, the CPUSA charged that the "narrowing of issues and total rejection of major abuses of power" had "weakened the impeachment proceedings and their democratic content" (ibid., 1 August).

Hall called Nixon's resignation a "historic step in the right direction," and declared: "An evil, anti-working class, racist, bigoted force has been discarded into the garbage can of history. . . . But the forces behind the conspiracy remain in their positions of power. . . . The election fraud can be undone only by an immediate, unprecedented, new midterm election." (Ibid., 9 August.) Vice-President Gerald Ford, in the CPUSA view, was just as immoral as Nixon; he was "backed by the corporate interests which have been behind Nixon" (ibid., 3 May). After he succeeded to the Presidency, Ford was called "a consistent foe of the legitimate interests of the Afro-American people and the poor." His inaugural speech "adhered to the Nixon-big business pattern," and his pledge of continuity in foreign affairs elicited a charge that the Nixon Administration had "dragged its feet on many aspects of détente, such as SALT and [the] European Conference on Security and Cooperation (ibid., 14 August). Ford's proposed budget cuts in social programs were attacked, and his anti-inflation plan was called "rank deception" (ibid., 10 October). Vice-Presidential nominee Nelson Rockefeller was castigated as "not a gunman or lieutenant for the money syndicate but the boss himself . . . a direct spokesman for the decisive section of monopoly capital." While noting his support of détente, the party commented that "he seeks to apply détente on an aggressive position of strength by increasing U.S. military power" (ibid., 22 August), and opposed his nomination. The new President's pardon of Nixon brought the charge that it was a "continuing cover-up of Nixon's criminal deeds" and the suggestion that Ford deserved "immediate impeachment" (ibid., 12 September).

At mid-year the CPUSA declared: "The ghost of a serious depression is now haunting the capitalist world" (*Political Affairs;* July). Inflation and the energy crisis were blamed on big business and its governmental allies. Consumers were warned that they would "be victimized until they join[ed] together in a mighty people's anti-monopoly coalition to compel nationalization of energy resources and to shackle the power of the trusts" (*Daily World,* 20 March), and the energy crisis was said to have been "planned 10 years ago by the oil monopolies" when they declined to increase refinery capacity (ibid., 28 March).

To help workers deal with the economic crisis, the CPUSA proposed the "elimination of all income tax for incomes of $15,000 or less" (ibid., 24 April). The inflationary surge was occasioned by the growing freedom of monopolies, and the solution for it was a "rollback of monopoly prices, profits and military spending (ibid., 15 August). Other proposals called for "expansion of social programs" and the launching of public works (ibid., 29 August).

At a June Central Committee meeting Gus Hall stated that "objective conditions" were "more ripe than ever for class struggle trade unionism," and lamented that unions had never before been led "by a worse mob of totally case-hardened reactionary toadying bootlickers"; these leaders were "more completely class collaborationist, racist, red-baiting and corrupt than any in the history of the AFL-CIO" (ibid., 20 July). Party labor leaders attacked the Experimental Negotiating Agreement (ENA) in the steel industry as an example of how union leaders were assisting employers in a "dangerous assault on the rights of workers" by taking away their right to strike (ibid., 25 April, 2 May).

Roscoe Proctor argued that the Nixon Administration had attacked the gains made by U.S. blacks in the 1950s and 60s. He applauded the growing number of black elected officials but argued that this would not solve poverty in black areas or racism. He urged attention to the labor movement, noting particularly that "white workers living in the suburbs must receive more attention from [the] Party in the struggle against racism," lest they become tools of reaction. (*Political Affairs,* February.) The violence in Boston resulting from school busing for racial balance was laid to President Ford and other politicians who gave "political encouragement to the hoodlums" and had "fascist tendencies." The CPUSA called for federal troops to protect black children. (*Daily Worker,* 11 October.) Two articles attacked the Black Panther Party for its glorification of the lumpen-proletariat (*Political Affairs,* May, June). Party spokesmen attacked the ideas of genetic factors in intelligence advanced by William Shockley, arguing that "racist views should be outlawed" (*Daily World,* 2 July).

On amnesty for Vietnam War resisters and deserters, the CPUSA declared that "general, unconditional amnesty" was the "only democratic solution," on the grounds that the war was illegal and immoral (ibid., 21 August).

International Affairs. In international politics the CPUSA continued in 1974 its strong, unvarying support for the Soviet Union. The Maoist leadership of China, according to Gus Hall, was "totally counter-revolutionary," and the U.S.-Chinese relationship was an entente cordiale (ibid., 26 February). China was charged with having long since withdrawn from the socialist camp: "The Maoists reject coordination with the socialist camp and instead mesh China's economy with imperialism. . . .

Monopoly capitalism is united in promoting Maoism as a weapon of imperialism in the class struggle." (Ibid., 1 March.) Further, Maoism was charged with serving imperialism in the underdeveloped world by suggesting that the primary social conflict was not socialism versus capitalism, but developed versus underdeveloped nations (ibid., 2 March).

The party's defense of the Soviet Union led to a series of attacks on Alexander Solzhenitsyn and the justification of his exile. He was denounced as "a piece of Tsarist flotsam" (ibid., 28 February) and "an instrument of the psychological warfare of imperialist interests in continuing an unarticulated cold war" (ibid., 5 March). The party also noted that the Soviet Union translated and published many more U.S. books than vice versa (ibid., 11 July), and charged that Western publication of Solzhenitsyn's *Gulag Archipelago* was an effort to sabotage détente (ibid., 2 January). Other Soviet dissidents were also criticized, including Andrei Sakharov (ibid., 8 March). When Soviet police disrupted an abstract art show, Gus Hall commented that "a socialist society has the right to ask its artists in every field to reflect the reality of that society and to enrich and inspire [the] people," but admitted that "how to struggle for the correct guidelines in the art field has always been a thorny question" (ibid., 21 September).

Détente continued to receive strong support. It was noted that détente meant increased trade and jobs for U.S. workers (ibid., 28 February). While supporting détente, the party noted that as a "policy of retreat and maneuver" it had been "forced on imperialists" and represented "a further shift in the balance of world forces against imperialism" (ibid., 6, 27 April; *Political Affairs*, July). While "new relationships of world forces had brought the United States to terms, the "basic decision about détente had not yet been made," even though the trend toward détente was "irreversible," the Vladivostik agreement was an "important step . . . for peace" (*Daily World*, 9 May, 5 July, 26 Nov.).

The CPUSA saw part of the opposition to détente as stemming from "the Defense Department and its allies in Congress and the Administration" who were "working feverishly to block agreement with the Soviet Union on arms limitation" (ibid., 11 April). To Hall, the Nixon Administration was trying to "ride two horses moving in opposite directions" on détente (*Political Affairs*, July). He also commented: "The campaign against détente is gaining some momentum. If not challenged by the people it can switch U.S. policy back to the cold war rails." The campaign united war industrialists, "George Meany, top Zionists, [and] Right-wing social democrats" (ibid., March). The CPUSA called for a united front in support of détente, linking it with domestic spending and increased trade (*Daily World*, 15 June).

In early May, Gus Hall, Henry Winston, James Jackson, Dan Rubin, and Helen Winter visited Moscow and met with Soviet leaders including Brezhnev and Suslov. They noted with satisfaction the relaxation of tensions and the importance of the 1973 summit meeting's contribution to détente. They jointly "reiterated the need for most resolute struggle against all distortions of Marxism, against Maoism which has become an outspoken enemy of the Communist and national liberation movements." While in Moscow, Hall and Winston called for a new conference of world communist parties. (Ibid., 8, 11 May.) The delegation went on to meet with government and party leaders in Hungary, Poland, and East Germany.

The party considered that the movement for the United States to end the boycott of Cuba and normalize relations was "swelling irresistably" (ibid., 26 February). Betty Smith and Claude Lightfoot represented the CPUSA at Cuba's May Day Celebrations (ibid., 12 May). With regard to Chile, the party sent Henry Winston and John Pittman to a meeting in Prague where representatives of 67 communist and workers' parties denounced the Chilean junta (ibid., 11 January). The CPUSA also called for the release of all political prisoners in Chile (ibid., 22 February) and charged: "The Chilean fascist coup bears the stamp 'made in America' " (*Political Affairs*, February).

The overthrow of the dictatorship in Portugal was applauded as symbolic of "the inner decay and the instability of the imperialist world" (ibid., July) and support was announced for the program of the Portuguese communist party, "the main force in the struggles against the fascist dictatorship." The CPUSA also endorsed freedom for Portugal's African colonies and the admission of Guinea-Bissau to the U.N. (*Daily World*, 7, 9 April.)

The CPUSA's position on the Middle East closely adhered to that of the Soviet Union. The peacemaking efforts of U.S. secretary of state Kissinger were criticized as distracting attention from U.S. policy, which had "abetted the Israeli warmakers," and support was expressed for the positive role of the U.S.S.R. in negotiations (ibid., 16 April). The Syrian-Israeli pact, like the Egyptian-Israeli agreement before it, was called "an important step towards peace," but final peace was said to depend on implementation of U.N. Resolution 242, calling for full Israeli withdrawal from occupied territory (ibid., 1 June). Israel and the United States were accused of "refusing to deal with the Palestinians" (ibid., 11 July). While Arab terrorist raids were condemned as Maoist and Trotskyite provocations, Israeli reprisals were condemned as "unjustifiable and reprehensible" since they were acts of state policy and strengthened Arab extremists (ibid., 14 May, 10 August).

The Palestine Liberation Organization (PLO) was criticized for demanding an end to Israel, but the U.N. decision to hear the PLO was hailed. Hyman Lumer, while supporting the legitimate struggle of the Palestinians, noted that public statements by PLO leaders envisaged separate Palestinian and Israeli states despite the official program, and insisted: "no support can be given to solve the problem at the expense of the national rights of the Israeli people" (ibid., 10 August). The tensions engendered by the party's Jewish members and sympathizers over the Middle East issue could be seen in a dispute over whether a May Day speaker had called for Israeli withdrawal from all or most of the territory conquered in 1969. Sensitive to charges that Jews faced discrimination in the USSR, party leaders reported assurances from Brezhnev that applications to emigrate were drying up and that many Jews who had left now wanted to return. (Ibid., 9 May.)

The CPUSA urged support of the Makarios government in Cyprus and charged that U.S. "imperialists" were keeping the Greek junta in power (ibid., 17 July). Seeing the crisis as a threat to world peace, the party claimed that "U.S. imperialism gambled and lost in trying to acquire Cyprus to guard its Middle Eastern oil interests" (ibid., 24 July). Support was expressed for a U.N. proposal to withdraw all foreign troops and restore Makarios to power (ibid., 16 August). An editorial applauded India's nuclear explosion, which "serves to remind us that the peril of nuclear war arises in U.S. imperialism" (ibid., 21 May). Hall and Winston called for the end of U.S. support to the Park government in South Korea, "a brutal fascist dictatorship" (ibid., 23 August). The party press, while not focusing much attention on the food crisis in the underdeveloped world, observed in one article that "the basic cause of the crisis and the famine is neocolonialism," not drought (*Political Affairs*, July). The U.S., Australian, and New Zealand parties called for disarmament and an end to NATO (*Daily World*, 8 Nov.).

Publications. The CPUSA's major publications are the *Daily World*, published five times a week in New York, and *Political Affairs*, a monthly theoretical journal. Other party-linked papers include *People's World*, a San Francisco Weekly; *Freedomways*, a black quarterly; *Labor Today*, a bimonthly publication of TUAD; *New World Review*, a bimonthly journal on international affairs; and *Jewish Affairs*, a bimonthly newsletter. The Black Liberation Committee announced a fund-raising effort for a party journal devoted to blacks (*Daily World*, 1 March).

SWP. The Socialist Workers Party (SWP), founded in 1938, traces its descent to 1928, when James Cannon returned from Moscow to break with the CPUSA over the issue of Trotskyism. It is the largest and most influential of the Trotskyite groups in the United States, which also include the Workers' League and the Workers' World Party. The SWP has around 2,500 members. Its youth affiliate, the young Socialist Alliance (YSA), claims 3,000.

Leadership and Organization. Jack Barnes continued in 1974 to hold the position of national secretary and Barry Sheppard remained organizational secretary. Other national leaders include Maceo Dixon, Debby Bustin, and Frank Boehm (heads of the National Campaign Committee), George Novack, Joseph Hansen, Peter Camejo, Linda Jenness (the coordinator of the party's Women's Liberation Activities), Jeff Mackler, Nat Weinstein, Tony Thomas, Elizabeth Stone, Frank Lovell, Carol Lipman, Mary Alice Waters, Derrick Morrison, Lew Jones, and Gus Horowitz (National Committee members). James Cannon, the founder and for many years leader of the SWP, died 21 August at the age of 84. The announcement of his death, made at a party conference in Ohio, brought $50,000 in pledges to the "Cannon Party-Building Fund," to go toward publishing Cannon's writings, supporting the *Militant*, and aiding teams of YSA recruiters who travel around the country. (*Militant*, 6 September.)

The largest and most important party auxiliary is the Young Socialist Alliance. Andrew Pulley is national chairman, Rich Finkel is national secretary, and Delphine Welch is national organization secretary (ibid., 11 January). The YSA held its Thirteenth National Convention in Chicago during late December and early January 1973. Just before the Fourteenth Convention held in St. Louis in December 1974, the YSA announced that Peter Camejo and Willie Mae Reid would be its candidates for president and vice president, respectively, in the 1976 national election (*NYT*, 28 December). The National Committee met in New York in June. Finkel, reporting on the political situation of young people in the United States, argued that the decline of political activity on campuses did not signify a return to 1950-like apathy. The dampening of political activity was laid to the withdrawal of U.S. troops from Vietnam and the decline of the black movement. Issues related to Watergate and to the economy, particularly inflation, had increased student distrust of capitalist government. "As a result," said Finkel, "more young people today are willing to listen to our ideas, to consider socialist solutions." Inflation and decreasing support for higher education were seen as part of a general attack on higher education. The YSA reaffirmed its belief that the "greatest opportunities to win young people to socialist ideas lie on the college and high school campuses." (Ibid., 2 August.)

Internal Affairs. The SWP insisted that only an independent third party could resolve the capitalist Watergate schemes (ibid., 1 March). In 1974 more than 100 candidates ran for office under the party label, including candidates for governor in Massachusetts, Pennsylvania, Colorado, California, Texas, New York, Ohio, Michigan, Minnesota, and Georgia. In Portland, Oregon, SWP candidates for local office received about 3 percent of the vote.

The SWP was not enthusiastic about new laws regulating campaign spending, charging that one such law in California was fraudulent and a threat to democratic rights. The major objection to the laws was their forcing the disclosure of contributors, who might be subjected to harassment. In several states the party sought to obtain exemption from naming its contributors (ibid., 21 June). Jack Barnes charged that "phony election reform laws" were a capitalist ploy to reinspire faith in government (ibid., 12 July). Larry Siegel noted that the SWP's fight against the government "put the SWP in the center of the fight against Watergate-style harassment of the socialist movement, Black movement and labor movement" (ibid., 12 July).

The SWP held a special national convention in Chicago late in December 1973 to discuss issues being debated in the world Trotskyite movement, such as the revolutionary experience in Bolivia and Argentina, the building of revolutionary parties in Europe, and the world political situation (ibid., 11 January 1974).

The 50-member SWP national committee met in New York in June 1974 and laid plans for an educational conference for party activists. In August, 1,250 persons attended the conference which was devoted to "assessing the current stage of revolutionary struggles around the world and discussing how socialists can participate in them" (ibid., 13 September).

The SWP filed a suit against the federal government, which admitted spying on the SWP and the YSA. The government's activities included electronic surveillance, mail covers, and investigation of members (ibid., 25 January). Activities of the Federal Bureau of Investigation against the SWP included establishing a file on a teen-ager who had written to the party, requesting information for a term paper. A federal court ordered the file destroyed. A "Political Rights Defense Fund" was set up by the SWP to raise money to prosecute the suit. A large number of liberal and radical groups and individuals gave it their support. (Ibid., 25 January.) When other government documents were released which indicated federal efforts to disrupt black and radical groups, the SWP demanded a reopening of the question of an FBI role in the assassination of Malcolm X (ibid., 22 March).

The SWP remained extremely critical of the CPUSA because of its support of Stalinism in Russia and its domestic activities. While willing to participate in joint programs with the CPUSA, the SWP bitterly protested communist efforts to exclude Trotskyite leaders in Chile from a list of political prisoners being supported at a rally (ibid., 26 April). The CPUSA was also criticized for its support of the Soviet persecution of political dissenters. The publication of *The Gulag Archipelago* was called a "heavy blow to the Soviet bureaucracy" and a "moving and forceful personal statement by one of the greatest Soviet writers." To those, like the CPUSA, who attacked Solzhenitsyn, the SWP replied that "the responsibility for giving the imperialists this weapon lies not with Solzhenitsyn but with the bureaucracy that has carried out the crime" (ibid., 18 January). The SWP also called for the release of Pyotr-Grigorenko from a Soviet psychiatric hospital (ibid., 10 May).

There was also a series of attacks on the CPUSA for supporting "the narrow interests of the Soviet bureaucracy" in Israel (ibid., 28 December 1973) by arguing that Israel had a right to exist. Linda Jenness, the SWP candidate for the Presidency in 1972, attacked the CPUSA for opposing the Equal Rights Amendment, which the SWP fully supported (ibid., 1 February 1974). Henry Winston's call for an anti-monopoly coalition was derided as non-revolutionary and class collaborationist (ibid., 12 April).

The Symbionese Liberation Army kidnaping of Patricia Hearst could "do nothing but harm to the revolutionary movement," in the view of the SWP, which suggested that the kidnaping might be a police provocation (ibid., 22 February) and SLA leader Cinque a police informer (ibid., 14 June). However, the Los Angeles police were criticized for overreacting in the shoot-out that killed most of the SLA members. Among the critics was YSA member Gary Atwood, whose wife was killed in the attack. (Ibid., 31 May, 7 June.)

The National Caucus of Labor Committees was attacked as a right-wing organization and for its hooligan tactics (ibid., 2 August).

Domestic Affairs. The SWP saw the Watergate affair as a manifestation of normal behavior by capitalist government. What was unusual was that the conspiracy had been uncovered. When the White House tapes were released, it was seen as "a heavy blow to the sanctity of capitalist government" (ibid., 17 May). The Judiciary Committee was attacked for voting to impeach President Nixon but ignoring his "attacks on Blacks, socialists, anti-war activists and others," and was accused of perpetuating the Watergate cover-up (ibid., 21 June). The ensuing debate over resignation and impeachment was seen as a way to preserve the illusion of democracy. The "rulers" were "trying to use impeachment to shore up sagging confidence in their capitalist two-party system" by demonstrating the soundness of bourgeois democratic procedures. The system of checks and balances was an effort to prevent majority rule. (Ibid., 21 June, 2 August.) Jack Barnes claimed that the roots of Watergate lay in protest over the Vietnam War, economic decline, and growing radicalization, and that Nixon's downfall would not cause those facts to disappear (ibid., 13 September).

An SWP writer insisted that the energy crisis was contrived by the oil companies to resolve harassment at home and a threat from the growing nationalism of Arab countries (*International*

Socialist Review, June). The SWP called for nationalization of the energy industry. In his political report to the national committee Jack Barnes commented that the fuel crisis highlighted the irrationality of monopoly capitalism, providing major profits for corporations and shortages for consumers. While the fuel shortage had assisted the ruling-class struggle against other imperialist powers, it had also provoked the workers to struggle, showing them that "present union officials [were] incapable of fighting for the needs of the working class as a whole." These officials were castigated as racist, chauvinist, and class-collaborationist. The party "took note of the significant increase in opportunities for socialists in the trade-union movement" in the recent period and Barnes noted that labor needed new allies, particularly in the black community (*Militant*, 13 September). Other planks in the SWP domestic program called for cost-of-living escalators in wages and all social benefits such as social security, a shortened work-week with no cut in pay, a large public-works program, elimination of the military budget, the end of taxes on incomes under $15,000 a year and a 100 percent tax on those above $30,000, independent trade unions, and "equal pay and preferential hiring for Black, Chicano, Puerto Rican and women workers" (ibid., 8 February).

The SWP was active in campaigns to prevent deportation of Haitians and Mexicans. It opposed any restrictions on immigration and criticized Cesar Chavez's United Farm Workers union for supporting stepped-up efforts to deport illegal aliens (ibid., 15 March). The party called the U.S. offer of political asylum to Alexander Solzhenitsyn hypocritical because such aid was not extended to Haitians or Chileans, and declared: "U.S. imperialism justly deserves its reputation as the greatest enemy of freedom and democracy around the world" (ibid., 1 March).

Barnes was optimistic about the potentiality for growing radicalization despite the decline of the campus movement and the absence of national struggles. His optimism flowed from the great number of local conflicts, ranging from opposition to police methods in black communities to struggles for community control of schools in New York. These were all signs of a "deepening radicalization" which was affecting young workers. He foresaw a "deepening of antireactionary trends in U.S. politics, a perspective of spontaneous explosions, of bigger struggles to come, and no fundamental reversal of the radicalization process." (Ibid., 13 September.)

Derrick Morrison charged that the difficulties faced by the black movement stemmed from the ties that existed between black leaders and the Democratic Party. The "key to the struggle for Black Liberation" was the "building of a revolutionary Marxist Party." (Ibid.)

International Affairs. Unlike the CPUSA, the SWP gave unqualified approval to the policies of no nation. The communist regimes were criticized for having abandoned their revolutionary heritage. The SWP charged that détente was an effort by the capitalists to avert the breakdown of their system: "The Kissingers and the Rockefellers of the world are relying on the Brezhnevs and Maos to lead the workers into the deadly trap of class collaboration." Détente also provided the "Stalinist bureaucrats" with technological assistance to help them placate the increasing demands of their own people and stave off a political revolution. (Ibid., 13 September 1974). Maoism was described as a "variant of Stalinism adapted to the requirements of preserving bureaucratic power in China" (*International Socialist Review*, June).

The SWP attributed the difficulties encountered by a number of revolutionary movements to the restraints imposed on them by the policy of détente and great-power cooperation. In Cyprus, it was claimed, the communist party's adherence to détente and support for the Makarios government had weakened the workers (*Militant*, 13 September).

Similarly, the Portuguese communists were accused of being Stalinists, acting as strikebreakers, joining a coalition government with reactionaries, and failing to support immediate independence for Portugal's African colonies (ibid., 7 June). General Spínola had been installed by Portugal's ruling class to transform the country from a colonial to a neocolonial power, yet communists and socialists "eagerly took posts in [the] coalition government, giving full support to the capitalist regime and siding with Spínola against the rising popular movement" (ibid., 14 June).

The SWP also charged that the Allende government in Chile was "the latest in a series of bourgeois nationalist governments toppled by U.S. imperialism and its native allies." By failing to arm the workers or accelerate the development of socialism—both a consequence of the united front—the opportunity for fascism was left open. (Ibid., 11 January.)

The SWP strongly supported the Palestinian guerrillas in the Middle East and called for the destruction of the state of Israel and its replacement by a binational Palestinian state. "There will be no peace in the Middle East as long as the area is dominated by imperialism, as long as the Israeli settler-state is maintained, as long as the Palestinian people are denied their homeland" (ibid., 28 December 1973). Even though Arab terrorism was tactically wrong, Israel was "to blame for large-scale acts of inhumanity in the Middle East." Since any act implying recognition of Israel was seen as perpetuating oppression of the Palestinians, disengagement agreements such as the one with Egypt were setbacks for the Arab people. (Ibid., 1 February 1974.) Responding to attacks by the CPUSA, one writer argued that Jews were entitled to national rights within a Palestinian state but not self-determination (ibid.).

A report to the national committee in June by Gus Horowitz noted that developments in Southeast Asia and the Middle East confirmed that détente had not led to a lessening of the class struggle but had encouraged imperialism and increased the danger of war. Horowitz also noted that the growth of imperialist rivalry had not shaken the United States from its position as the leading imperialist power. The revolutions in Ethiopia and Portugal illustrated the speed with which class struggles could break out in unlikely places despite détente. (Ibid., 12 July.)

Publications. The SWP publishes *The Militant*, a weekly newspaper, and the *International Socialist Review*, a monthly journal. The Fourth International publishes the monthly *Intercontinental Press*.

The PLP. The Progressive Labor Party (PLP) was formally organized in 1965. It began as the Progressive Labor Movement when Milt Rosen and Mort Scheer were expelled from the CPUSA in the early 1960s. PLP was generally considered Maoist, and until 1971 it followed a pro-Chinese line. Its present ideological orientation is rigidly Stalinist. It does not publish information about its organizational structure or its leading cadres. The PLP membership goal for 1974 was 1,000.

Domestic Views and Policies. The Workers Action Movement (WAM) is the PLP's arm for work within the labor movement. WAM's fourth convention was held in Chicago in October 1974 and was attended by 700 persons. Paul Foster, a black hospital worker, was elected international chairman. WAM sees its goal as uniting all workers around the issues of more jobs and opposition to speed-ups on the assembly line, forced overtime, and racism. Its major goal is the institution of "30-40": thirty hours' work for forty hours' pay (*Challenge*, 7 November). The PLP, which has pushed for better safety conditions, rank-and-file control of unions, and preferential hiring of minorities and women (ibid., 20 June), also announced: "We welcome and support open rebellion and strikes at the factories against lay-offs" (ibid., 10 October). Often in opposition to regular union leaderships, WAM and PLP claimed credit during 1974 for leading a number of strikes around the country. They generally favored all-out militancy, as when they urged members of the American Federation of State, County, Municipal Employees to "defy all non-strike laws as an instrument of government fascist-like control" (ibid., 20 June).

Another organization connected to PLP was the Committee against Racism (CAR). The PLP and CAR were active in efforts to prevent "racist research" and urged students to "shut Shockley up."

They also supported efforts to fire faculty members accused of racism, such as Edward Banfield, claiming they were "fighting against racist professors' text books and the open manifestation of their racist ideology." The PLP argued that racial integration was impossible under capitalism and claimed that the busing issue and "vicious racism" were being used by local governments to "prevent working class unity." (Ibid., 10 October.)

The PLP called the Watergate and impeachment controversy a "bitter internal struggle" between two sections of monopoly capital "taking place in the context of U.S. imperialism's worldwide decline." Sections identified with "new" and "old" money were struggling over a shrinking pie, but, the workers had "nothing to gain from the impeachment merry-go-round." (Ibid., 15 August.)

The resignation of President Nixon brought the charge that "the bosses have changed managers not to help us but to help themselves" (ibid., 29 August). The pardon of Nixon by new President Ford proved "once again that the bosses' system of justice works well for their class." Meanwhile the PLP urged workers not to be distracted from their revolutionary task by false arguments over pardon. (Ibid., 10 October.)

The U.S. leadership was seen as the "most vicious, most criminal and most degenerate in the history of capitalism." The PLP's stance was resolutely revolutionary: "We welcome ghetto and prison rebellions against police terrorism. . . . This militancy is a sign of health: the health and strength of the working class." (Ibid.) The party boasted that it had attempted to prevent speeches by Nelson Rockefeller and remarked that "when we, the workers, hold power, there won't be just protests against Rockefeller. He won't speak at all." (Ibid., 6 June.)

The PLP did, however, criticize terrorism. "You can't kill the ruling class and its profit system with individual or small group terrorist attacks." The real terrorists were the ruling class. Small-scale terror like that of the SLA invited repression and gave radicalism a bad image. "They want to picture left-wingers as losers, unable to win." Revolutionaries needed to establish a base in the working class and prepare for a long struggle. Also, "violence by the working class must be collective." (Ibid., 20 June.)

International Views and Policies. The PLP called détente a sham. The Cyprus situation illustrated the growth of inter-imperialist rivalry: "The Soviets are now trying to replace U.S. bosses as the top imperialist power. Behind all the talk about détente is wheeling and dealing to carve up the world." The PLP went on to charge that the United States had dumped Archbishop Makarios, "this slob [who] did nothing for the Cypriote people," while the Soviets backed the "Turkish bosses." (Ibid., 15 August 1974.)

China was regarded only slightly more positively: "Socialism has been reversed in China, while capitalism has been restored to the Soviet Union under Khrushchev." The PLP insited that "more than any other recent Communist leader, Stalin stands out to millions as the symbol of revolutionary working-class militancy and of uncompromising struggle against the imperialists." Criticism of him in *The Gulag Archipelago* represented a "nauseating attempt to portray counter-revolutionaries as heroes" by "Soldsomeshitsin." (Ibid., 20 June; *Progressive Labor*, March-April.)

The PLP charged that "the peaceful transition line of Allende and the Chilean CP led the workers towards fascism" (*Challenge*, 10 October). In the Middle East, "U.S. Gunboat diplomacy and reliance on the Zionist fascists to maintain profits was a disaster for all workers concerned" (ibid., 4 July), and the PLO was criticized for "rotten nationalism" (ibid., 24 October).

Publications. The PLP's English-Spanish newspaper *Challenge/Desafio* was issued every two weeks in 1974. Plans were announced for a weekly edition in November. The party's *Progressive Labor* is a bimonthly journal.

Emory University   Harvey Klehr

Uruguay

The Communist Party of Uruguay (Partido Comunista del Uruguay: PCU) dates its formation from September 1920, when the congress of the Socialist Party voted in favor of joining the Communist International. The present name was adopted in April 1921. On 1 December 1973 the PCU was declared illegal for the first time in its history. It is firmly pro-Soviet.

The Movement of the Revolutionary Left (Movimiento de Izquierda Revolucionaria; MIR) and the Revolutionary Communist Party (Partido Comunista Revolucionario; PCR) are small pro-Chinese organizations. The Revolutionary Workers' Party (Partido Obrero Revolucionario; POR), originally founded in 1944 as the Revolutionary Workers' League, is Trotskyist and is aligned with the International Secretariat (Posadas faction) of the Fourth International. Numerous other leftist organizations operate in Uruguay and display Soviet, Chinese, Cuban, or nationalist leanings or combinations thereof. Among the most important are the Uruguayan Revolutionary Movement (Movimiento Revolucionario Oriental; MRO), the Socialist Party of Uruguay (Partido Socialista del Uruguay; PSU), the Uruguayan Revolutionary Armed Forces (Fuerzas Armadas Revolucionarias Orientales; FARO), and the National Liberation Movement (Movimiento de Liberación Nacional; MLN)–better known as the Tupamaros.

Except for the PCU all these organizations are apparently small though no precise membership figures are known. The PCU is estimated to have 30,000 members, with workers accounting for about 73 percent of the total. The population of Uruguay is 2,900,000 (estimated 1974).

The Broad Front. The electoral strength of the PCU long resided in the Leftist Liberation Front (Frente Izquierda de Liberación; FIDEL), founded by the PCU in 1962 and composed of some ten small political and cultural groups. In an extremely complex electoral system which discourages voting for minority party candidates, FIDEL had never done very well, winning less than 6 percent of the vote in the 1966 election. In 1971 FIDEL took part in the national election as part of a much larger coalition, the Broad Front (Frente Amplio; FA), made up of 17 leftist and anti-government parties and groups, including, in addition to FIDEL, the PCU, PSU, POR, the Christian Democratic Party (Partido Demócrata Cristiano; PDC), a faction of the liberal Colorado Party led by Senator Zelmar Michelini, a faction of the conservative National (Blanco) Party led by Senator Francisco Rodríguez Camusso, and independent leftists. The Broad Front won 18 percent of the vote. From 1 March 1972 until 27 June 1973, the FA had 18 of its members in the Chamber of Deputies and 5 in the Senate. Backed by the military, on 27 June President Juan Bordaberry by decree dissolved the Congress, charging the FA congressmen with "criminal actions of conspiracy against the constitution."

The PCU. Organization and Leadership. The PCU's national headquarters administers provincial subdivisions of the party within each of the republic's 19 territorial departments (provinces). The PCU Central Committee has 48 regular members and 27 alternates. The Secretariat has five members: Rodney Arismendi (first secretary), Enrique Pastorino, Jaime Pérez, Enrique Rodríguez, and Alberto Suárez. The Executive Committee totals fifteen, consisting of the five Secretariat members and Alberto Altesor, Leopoldo Bruera, Félix Díaz, José L. Massera, Rosario Pietrarroia, César Reyes Daglio, Gerardo Cuesta, Jorge Mazzarovich, Wladímir Turiansky, and Eduardo Viera. Díaz and Viera, editor of the PCU daily newspaper *El Popular*, were already in prison when the PCU was outlawed in 1973. At the beginning of the year, Arismendi had asserted that most of the PCU leadership remained intact underground (*Granma*, Havana, 23 December 1973).

On 8 May 1974, the PCU First Secretary, Rodney Arismendi, was arrested by police in Pocitos, a suburb of Montevideo. He had been in hiding since the 1 December 1973 ban on all Marxist parties. From inside the house of a university professor, Arismendi had been directing the clandestine PCU activities until the police raid (*United Press International*, Buenos Aires, 29 May). One PCU Executive Committee member, Enrique Rodríguez, indicated at least a temporary exile for himself in Czechoslovakia, in an interview in Prague (*Prensa Latina*, Prague, 15 January).

Six second-level and third-level PCU leaders, part of the party's intermediate hierarchy, were convicted 18 April by a military court in Montevideo of trying to incite Uruguayans to attack the armed forces through circulation of propaganda calling for disobeying any governmental authority. Evelio Oribe, one of those arrested, had been adviser from the PCU for the Federation of University Students of Uruguay (Federación de Estudiantes Universitarios del Uruguay; FEUU) before the FEUU was outlawed in December 1973. Six years earlier, Oribe had been FEUU secretary general.

The PCU's youth organization, the Union of Communist Youth (Unión de la Juventud Comunista; UJC) was founded in 1955. It claimed a membership of 22,000 when outlawed in 1973. The UJC had dominated the FEUU, an affiliate of the Soviet-front International Union of Students. Until December 1973, the UJC and the FEUU had joined together to battle the anti-communist Uruguayan Youth on the March (Juventud Uruguaya en Pie; JUP) on and off each campus.

The PCU Executive Committee called on Uruguayans to struggle for the regaining by the party of its legal status, in a communiqué circulated from Buenos Aires 5 March into Uruguayan provincial cities and towns (*Prensa Latina*, Buenos Aires, 5 March).

The National Convention of Workers (Convención Nacional de Trabajadores; CNT), established in 1966 as the largest federation of labor unions, has been led by officials of the PCU, including Pastorino, Díaz, Turiansky, and Antonio Tamayo. In 1973 the CNT called a general strike to protest the government's dissolving of Congress. On 30 June 1973 the government responded by suspending all CNT activities. CNT leaders vowed to operate from underground but during 1974 no evidence of any CNT activity has manifested itself in public life. CNT official Pastorino remains the head of the pro-Soviet World Federation of Trade Unions (WFTU).

Domestic Attitudes and Activities. During January and February the PCU clandestinely circulated its views via leaflets printed on an underground press, with UJC teenagers in predawn operations painting "El Partido Vive" ("The Party Lives") on walls of buildings in various neighborhoods of Montevideo (*Unidad Internacional*, Lima 21 February).

The first issue of the clandestine weekly newspaper of the PCU, the *Carta Semanal del Partido Comunista*, appeared on 7 March. *Carta* takes the place of the outlawed PCU daily newspaper *El Popular*. Page one featured an editorial headlined "No respite for the dictatorship," calling for Third World public opinion to pressure the Bordaberry regime, to condemn it for arresting novelist Juan Carlos Onetti (*Unidad Internacional*, Lima, 28 March).

On 9 February, the government suspended the Marxist intellectual weekly *Marcha* for two issues for publishing Onetti's short story "The Bodyguard," which sympathetically portrayed the killing of a police inspector by Tupamaros. Government censors labeled the story pornographic. Arrested with Onetti were *Marcha* editor Carlos Quijano and feature editor Mercedes Rein. On March 4, the government suspended *Marcha* for ten issues, and on June 8 suspended *Marcha* for twenty issues. Quijano and Onetti were released from jail 14 May.

Carta Semanal charged that in March Mercedes Rein was jailed in a hospital for mental patients in the provincial city of Carmelo in the western Department of Colonia. The PCU weekly denounced Minister of Labor Bugallo for cooperating with the anti-Communist moves against Uruguayan labor leaders by the Regional Inter-American Labor Organization (Organización Regional Interamericana de Trabajo; ORIT). The PCU called the ORIT liaison spokesmen "Nazis" (*Prensa Latina*, Havana, 21 March).

Several PCU communiqués during 1974 concerning retired General Liber Seregni, leader of the Broad Front coalition within which the party gained political leverage during 1971-73, circulated on the Cuban news wires of *Prensa Latina*. In February, Seregni (arrested in 1973) went on trial for inciting to riot (Agence France Presse, Montevideo, 14 February). The PCU charged that testimony against Seregni had been obtained by threatening a witness (*Prensa Latina*, Buenos Aires, 16 February). On 1 November, the government announced that Seregni had been released from jail, "having served his sentence."

"We demand the reopening of the Congress" headlined PCU leaflets after a change in membership on the Council of State, whose twenty-five members function in lieu of the traditional legislative body.

Montevideo police 8 April arrested PCU Deputy Héctor Rodríguez and Luís Michelini for libel of the government in Michelini's column in his weekly *Nueve de Febrero*. Publisher-editor Michelini is the son of Senator Zelmar Michelini, leader of a Colorado faction opposed to Bordaberry. When the senator was a candidate for president of the republic in the 1966 election, son Luís got some leftist youth group support for his father but only in 1974 did Luís directly work with the Communists, according to his own statements (*Le Monde*, Paris, 9 April).

Juan Pablo Terra, a leader of the Christian Democratic Party (Partido Demócrata Cristiano; PDC) ran an editorial in the weekly *Ahora* in April praising the 1973-73 cooperation of the PCU, the PDC, and Broad Front leader Liber Seregni. Terra was arrested 25 April on charges of encouraging outlawed rebel activities, and was released 5 June. The license of radio station *Radio Oriental* of Montevideo was suspended 29 May for airing PCU attacks on the government's economic programs. A song written by PCU and PSU members, "Viva F.A.," referring to the Broad Front, was broadcast over *Radio Sur* in Montevideo 16 August, causing the government to suspend the station from broadcasting for twenty-four hours.

The National Education Council (Consejo Nacional de Educación; CONAE) discharged 398 teachers during 1974 for Marxist activities, including announcements by some teachers that they were members of the PCU (*Associated Press*, Montevideo, 11 October). The government temporarily closed the medical college of the University of Montevideo on 10 November, after fifty-two professors refused to declare whether or not they belonged to the PCU, the PSU, or the MLN. Half of the group, twenty-six professors, resigned rather than appear before investigators at the university.

On 1 September the peso was devalued for the eighth time in 1974, in a series of minidevaluations of approximately 2 percent each. However, since the March 1972 inauguration of President Bordaberry, the peso has lost 400 percent of its purchasing power, the PCU charged in November (*Prensa Latina*, Havana, 14 November).

The PCU was criticized severely as being politically inept by a rival Marxist group, the Trotskyists of the Revolutionary Workers Party (Partido Revolucionario de los Trabajadores; PRT). The PRT pointed out that its own organ, *Prensa Obrera*, manages to publish each week despite the governmental ban on Marxist publications, and asked why the PCU's own underground weekly, *Carta*, does not publish some weeks. A PRT editorial asserted: "We remind the PCU that the word 'periodical' means a publication issued at regular periods." (*Prensa Obrera*, Montevideo, 22 July). Previously, the PRT had criticized the PCU for encouraging strikes by unions to obtain better working conditions from the "more progressive elements in power." A PRT editorial contrasting Uruguay with Peru asserted that "such a hope is a PCU delusion." (*Prensa Obrera*, Montevideo, 22 April).

International Views and Positions. In March, an unnamed member of the PCU Executive Committee established an office for Uruguayan Communists in East Berlin, approved by the German Democratic Republic. The office was described as "an information bureau." (*Neues Deutschland*, East Berlin, 20 March).

After going to the U.S.S.R. in 1973, Francisco Orasli, former leader of the Metal Workers Union and a member of the PCU, settled in Buenos Aires. In June, Argentine police arrested him with a false passport and other papers with the name Orlando Caballero. Montevideo police had furnished Orasli's fingerprints, which prompted Buenos Aires police to send for the prints of the real Caballero, who had died in Entre Rios. Inasmuch as he had been arrested in the Plata estuary, Orsali was turned over to the Uruguayan Navy's Shore Patrol (Agence France Presse, Montevideo, 21 June). Argentina and Uruguay have an agreement about arrests of each other's nationals in the international waterway whereby a prisoner is put in the custody of his own country's authorities.

Argentine police on 2 June arrested 98 Uruguayans at a Buenos Aires conference called by the PCU. The Uruguayans were charged with illegal planning of guerrilla and other violent actions.

Enrique Rodríguez, secretary of the Central Committee of the PCU, headed a delegation of Uruguayan Communists meeting in Moscow on 5 July with Mikhail Suslov, secretary of the Central Committee of the Communist Party of the Soviet Union (CPSU). Among several CPSU officials at the meeting was Boris Ponomarev, member of the Politburo of the CPSU (TASS, Moscow, 5 July).

Enrique Pastorino, member of the PCU Central Committee, visited Siberia in July in his capacity as an official of the Marxist labor organization, the World Federation of Trade Unions (WFTU). Russian officials of the WFTU attended meetings with Pastorino at Irkutsk, Bratsk, and Lake Baykal (TASS, Irkutsk, 29 July).

Ricardo Paseyro, Uruguayan consul in Le Havre, France, was discharged in October from the foreign service. After receiving refugee status from the French Foreign Ministry, Paseyro held a press conference for reporters from Communist bloc nations, denouncing military and civilians of the regime in Montevideo and expressing his sympathy with PCU exiles (Agence France Press, Paris, 14 October).

Publications. The principal PCU publications, the daily newspaper *El Popular* and the theoretical journal *Estudios*, outlawed by the government, did not publish during 1974. An underground weekly, *Carta Semanal del Partido Comunista*, begun in March, has appeared irregularly in clandestine distribution.

The MIR and the PRT. The MIR, which published *Voz Obrera*, remained inactive during 1974. Although also outlawed as a Marxist publication, the weekly *Prensa Obrera* of the PRT, did manage to publish and circulate clandestinely to a limited readership during 1974.

*   *   *

The MLN (Tupamaros). The idea of the MLN arose among Uruguayan leftists in the early 1960s. The organization made its first raid in July 1963. Since 1969 the MLN has carried out a series of dramatic exploits (e.g., kidnaping, robberies, occupations of small towns and radio stations, mass escapes from government jails) intended to call into question the ability of the Uruguayan government to effectively control the country. The Tupamaros attracted international attention between July 1970 and January 1971 by kidnaping a number of foreign nationals in Uruguay.

At the end of 1972, the Tupamaros whose organizational ability had been their hallmark showed signs of an internal split. Once the army took over from the police in pursuing the guerrillas, military counter-insurgent efficiency replaced the inefficient tactics of the police, who were not trained to combat guerrilla bands. Since conviction on charges of subversion in April 1973, the Tupamaro leaders have been imprisoned.

On 13 February in Buenos Aires, spokesmen for the Uruguayan Tupamaros (MLN) joined those from Argentine, Bolivian, and Chilean Marxist guerrilla groups in forming a joint committee, the Revolutionary Coordinating Committee (Junta de Coordinación Revolucionaria; JCR). Tupamaros met with leaders of Argentina's People's Revolutionary Army (Ejército Revolucionario del Pueblo; ERP), Bolivia's National Liberation Army (Ejército de Liberación Nacional; ELN), and Chile's Movement of the Revolutionary Left (Movimiento de Izquierda Revolucionario; (MIR). (See *Chile*, "Appendix" on JCR.)

In April, Montevideo police publicly displayed materiel seized in a raid on the Tupamaros. In addition to bombs, grenades, rifles, and radio transmitters, were documents from the JCR calling for class warfare (*EFE*, Montevideo, 30 April). Joint Security Forces in Montevideo on 9 March announced discovery of an attempt to smuggle arms to an MLN group in Colonia Department from JCR sources in Buenos Aires. Based on clues in the March raid, Uruguayan police in April released descriptions of Tupamaros thought to be at a JCR hideout in Catmarca Province, Argentina. Argentine army units captured a Tupamaro in August, along with a member of the ERP, two Europeans identified only as Marxists, and a Syrian naturalized Argentine citizen with ties to the Palestine Liberation Organization (PLO). (TELAM, Montevideo, 29 August.)

In Paris 19 December, an MLN group calling itself the "Raúl Sendic Brigade" (after the MLN founder) killed Colonel Ramón Trabal, Uruguay's military attaché to France. On 20 December, Montevideo police found five Tupamaros killed by a rightwing group called "Tripple M" in retaliation for the Trabal murder.

Arizona State University   Marvin Alisky

Venezuela

The Communist Party of Venezuela (Partido Comunista de Venezuela; PCV), the oldest of the extreme leftist groups in Venezuela, was founded in 1931. In recent years, the PCV has suffered two serious splits, which have greatly undermined its strength and influence. One of these took place in December 1970, when most of the Communist Youth and substantial elements in the adult party broke away to form the Movimiento al Socialismo (MAS); the other in the middle of 1974, when a group of party leaders split away to form the Vanguardia Comunista.

Another Marxist-Leninist group, the Movement of the Revolutionary Left (Movimiento de Izquierda Revolucionaria; MIR), originated in 1960 from a split in the Democratic Action Party (Acción Democrática; AD), which controlled the government from 1959 to 1969, and returned to power early in 1974. The other new elements on the far Left have appeared in recent years—a Maoist movement, and a Trotskyist group, established early in 1973. Finally, there remain some active remnants of the urban and rural guerrilla movement which had its high point in the early 1960s, when both the PCV and the MIR participated; it has had little more than nuisance value since the major elements of both of these parties withdrew from guerrilla activities in 1965-66.

It has been estimated that at the beginning of 1974 the PCV had approximately 3,000 members and the MAS also some 3,000 (*World Strength of the Communist Party Organizations, 1973*, 1974, p. 181). These figures probably overestimate the membership of the PCV and perhaps understate that of the MAS. No figures are available for the other Marxist-Leninist groups, although their membership is certainly smaller than that of the two major parties. The population of Venezuela is 10,970,000 (estimated 1972).

Much of the activity of the Venezuelan Marxist-Leninists in 1974 centered on studying and discussing the reasons for and results of the very bad showing of all of them except MAS in the December 1973 general election. It was these discussions which led to the split in the PCV. Much controversy also centered during the year on the attitude of the various groups towards the nationalist and progressive policies put forward by the new Acción Democrática president, Carlos Andrés Pérez.

In the 9 December 1973 election the three far-Left parties which participated received together only about 6.8 percent of the total vote. The Communist Party got 49,453 votes, about 1.1 percent of the total and received two seats in the lower house of Congress; the MIR received 41,106 votes, or 0.94 percent, and one seat in the Chamber of Deputies. Although the MAS did considerably better than its two rivals, receiving 216,473 votes (5.2 percent, taking nine seats in the Chamber, as well as one in the Senate, it did not nearly approach some pre-election estimates that it might receive as much as 15 percent of the votes cast. Nevertheless, the MAS did emerge as the third largest party, behind Acción Democrática (42.5 percent of the vote) and Copei (29 percent).

The PCV. Organization and Leadership. The top leadership of the PCV is its 13-member Politburo. The body includes, among others: Gustavo Machado, party chairman, Jesús Faría, secretary general, as well as Eduardo Mancera, Alonso Ojeda and Radamés Larrazábal.

Until the December 1970 split of the PCV, the party's Venezuelan Communist Youth Juventud Comunista Venezolana; JCV) was the largest political group in the student movement. The split deprived the JCV of most of its leaders and members and threw it into such confusion that it was not until February 1972 that the JCV held its Third National Congress. As a result of the 1970 split, the PCV influence in the student movement was reduced to minor proportions, its formerly leading position being taken by the youth group of the MAS.

The principal center of influence of the PCV in the labor movement is the United Workers Confederation of Venezuela (Confederación Unitária de Trabajadores de Venezuela; CUTV), established in the early 1960's, when the PCV lost virtually all influence in the majority Confederation of Workers of Venezuela (Confederación de Trabajadores de Venezuela; CTV). The CUTV represents only a tiny fraction of the total labor movement.

The CUTV did not give much evidence of activity during 1974. It held a May Day meeting, and in March issued a statement denouncing United States Senate criticisms of the oil producing countries' moves to restrict production and raise the price of petroleum. It accused the U.S. senators of serving the interests of the large multinational corporations.

Domestic Attitudes and Activities. The PCV held several Central Committee plenums during the year, in an effort to define the party's attitude towards the new circumstances created by its poor showing in the 1973 election, and by the return of Acción Democrática to power. The first post-election meeting was held during the last days of 1973. Before this session, Politburo member Héctor Mújica announced that "we will study the national political situation which has developed with the obvious and overwhelming victory of Carlos Andrés Pérez and the AD and the defeat of the New Force. It will be a thorough, frank, objective and unsentimental study." (Radio El Nacional, 20 December 1973.)

In spite of these brave words, this meeting seems to have sown the seeds for the split which took place in the PCV about six months later. A few weeks after the Central Committee plenum, Jesús Faría, Alonso Ojeda and Guillermo García Ponce, the first two representing the dominant faction, the last the dissidents, went to Moscow, apparently to lay their quarrel before the leaders of the Soviet party.

A further plenum of the Central Committee was held late in February. It was reported that this meeting "approved a political resolution on unity of all the anti-imperialist forces in defense of the national interests. It calls for immediate nationalization of oil, price curbs and higher wages and salaries. It stresses the need to strengthen Party unity to rebuff the forces that are seeking to divide the Party." (*IB*, no 5-6, 1974.)

Plenum resolutions to the contrary notwithstanding, the dissidence within the PCV continued, and began to be discussed by outsiders. Radio El Mundo reported on 27 February that dissidents grouped around Guillermo García Ponce were seeking to get the party to adopt a position of relative independence from the Soviet party similar to that of the Italian communists.

In the middle of May, secretary-general Jesús Faría took disciplinary action against six members of the Central Committee: Guillermo García Ponce, Eduardo Machado, Alcides Hurtado, Simón Correa, Clemente Castro and Aníbal Rodríguez. Although they appealed his ruling, it was upheld, leading directly to the new split in the PCV. On 14 June, the new party, the Vanguardia Comunista, was formally launched at a conference in Caracas.

All of the causes for this new division in the PCV are not entirely clear. However, the dominant faction accused the dissidents of having supported the Social Christian Copei candidate Lorenzo

Fernández in the 1973 election, in violation of the PCV's backing of Jesús Paz Galarraga. There were probably other differences on policies and personal power positions which also contributed to the split.

Two months after the schism, the PCV Central Committee held another plenum. It concerned itself particularly with the issue of nationalization of petroleum, which President Carlos Andrés Pérez had announced as one of the objectives of his government. He had appointed a committee of 60 to draw up plans for nationalization and the subsequent reorganization of the industry, and Radamés Larrázabal was the communist party's member of this commission. Within it, he advocated that there be no compensation for the oil companies.

The August plenum particularly attacked the business group Fedecámaras, whose president was also a member of the petroleum commission and as such had come out in opposition to immediate nationalization of petroleum. Radamés Larrázabal, addressing the plenum, accused Fedecámaras (the Federation of Chambers of Commerce) of "turning its back on the people and joining the campaign being waged in the United States and from the great centers of power by the petroleum enterprises and monopolies" (*El Nacional*, 18 August).

The PCV's Fifth Congress was held during the first week of November. It was attended by a sizable number of foreign fraternal delegates.

International Views and Positions. The PCV's loyalty to Moscow remained strong during the year. At various times the party praised the co-existence policy presumably being followed by the Soviet Union.

Publications. The principal organ of the PCV is the daily newspaper *Tribuna Popular*. It also issues a theoretical periodical, *Documentos Politicos*, which has had some difficulty in coming out since the MAS split. Another "theoretical" publication is *Teoria y Praxis*. For several months before the congress the PCV published "Boletin del V Congreso."

*   *   *

The Vanguardia Comunista. This new party, launched in June 1974, was significant for at least three reasons. For one, it represented a split in the Old Guard of the Venezuelan Communist movement. Particularly interesting was the presence in its leadership of Eduardo Machado. In all previous divisions of the communist party, the Machado brothers, Gustavo and Eduardo, had always been aligned together. In its attacks on Vanguardia Comunista, the PCV tended to concentrate its fire on Guillermo García Ponce, rather than on Eduardo Machado.

A second point of interest concerning Vanguardia Comunista is its modification of traditional "democratic centralism." As described by Carlos Villegas in *Ultimas Noticias*, 17 June), the statutes of Vanguardia Comunista were to include "democratic consultation of the party rank and file each time an important political decision [is] made; appropriate selection of members of the Central Committee; limitation of its function to 2 years; requirement of the presentation of a favorable report from the rank-and-file organizations and from regional leaders for the reelection of a leader; loss of membership in the Central Committee when excluded from any lower organization for bad work or when not a regular member in a cell."

The third thing of interest is its members' apparent revolt against what was characterized at the VC founding congress as the PCV's "ideological stagnation." One orator commented that "this is the reason for the rhetorical textbook ideology which prevails among communists and which has led this movement to turn its back on the far-reaching changes which have taken place in Venezuela in the last 25 years" (El Universal Radio, 14 June).

Although a small group, Vanguardia Comunista further undermined the already depleted ranks of the PCV. The new party's following seems to be largely confined to Caracas.

* * *

The MAS. The "Movement toward Socialism" was formed late in 1970 as the result of a split in the PCV. Its principal leaders include former PCV Politburo member Pompeyo Márquez, the MAS secretary-general, and Alexis Adam, Eleazar Díaz Rangel, Germán Lairet, Augusto León, Freddy Muñoz, Alfredo Padilla, Teodoro Petkoff, Tirso Pinto, Héctor Rodríguez Bauza, and Eloy Torres, the last one of the principal trade union leaders of the PCV after 1958. The MAS took with it a large part of the intermediary leadership cadres of the PCV; it seems certain that a majority of the former PCV rank-and-file and virtually all of the JCV joined the new party.

The MAS youth organization, made up at its inception largely of dissident members of the JCV, is Juventud Comunista-MAS (JC-MAS). Since its formation, JC-MAS has dominated most of the student bodies of Venezuelan universities. However, in 1974, it suffered a relative setback at the Universidad Central de Venezuela, when student elections there gave it only about 37 percent of the total vote, with the Acción Democrática Youth being a close competitor. The majority of the students abstained from voting.

The MAS had some influence at its inception in the CUTV trade union movement. Those who went with MAS first formed the CUT Clasista, as a rival organization. However, in July 1974 the MAS Central Committee, on the recommendation of Eloy Torres, decided to have its supporters enter the Confederación de Trabajadores de Venezuela, the majority union group. The party announced its readiness to have its members participate in the coming Seventh Congress of CTV.

Domestic Attitudes and Activities. The MAS change in trade union policy reflected a general shift of the party during 1974 toward a friendly attitude towards the government of President Pérez. This was shown, too, in the party's decision in May to support the request of Pérez for special powers to deal with the economic situation. Although Senator Pompeyo Márquez announced that the support of his party for the Pérez government policies would not be unconditional, he did indicate that it would support most of the economic program offered by the new AD chief executive.

In September MAS deputy Freddy Muñoz strongly attacked the suggestion of Fedecámaras that the oil industry be reorganized in a series of mixed companies in which the foreign firms would have some ownership. Muñoz argued that Fedecámaras was engaging in "ideological terrorism," and was seeking to limit the Venezuelan government's power to negotiate. He added that once the petroleum industry "is under the full power of decision of the state, it will have greater freedom to decide on a proper policy, to bring about government-to-government negotiations and to move with greater flexibility without impairing its profits, and giving a special deal to the underdeveloped nations which consume our petroleum."

Within the petroleum commission established by President Pérez to make recommendations about the future of the industry, the MAS representative supported the idea of compensation for the foreign firms. This was in conformity with the thinking of the Pérez government.

International Views. During 1974 the MAS continued to try to maintain contacts with a variety of different foreign political groups. It still continued to maintain relations with the Yugoslav and Romanian Communist parties, as well as with some left-wing socialist groups. A new twist was given to the MAS's international contacts when Central Committee member Teodoro Petkoff made an extended tour of the United States in November and December, visiting many universities and establishing personal contact with a variety of different kinds of political leaders.

Publication. The principal organ of publicity of the MAS is the afternoon newspaper *Punto,* edited by Senator Pompeyo Márquez.

*   *   *

The MIR. The MIR was established in 1960 by dissidents from the AD, including most of that party's youth movement. In 1962 it joined in launching a guerrilla effort which lasted for several years. A large element of the party leadership and rank and file, headed by Domingo Alberto Rangel, withdrew from guerrilla activities in 1965-66. The MIR officially foreswore participation in the guerrilla activities in 1969.

In February the MIR announced its willingness to accept a proposal of Jesús Paz Galarrage, secretary-general of the Movimiento Electoral del Pueblo, and that party's candidate in the 1973 election, for "activities . . . in order to achieve the unity of the various leftist forces in Venezuela." However, nothing concrete seems to have occurred to further this objective during the rest of the year.

Now fully legal once more, the MIR had one representative in the Chamber of Deputies as a result of the 1973 election. It officially protested that it was entitled to two seats and had been illegally deprived of one by the Supreme Electoral Tribunal, but its protests were overruled.

The MIR was active during the year in seeking to build a semblance of mass support. It had militants working in the trade union movement, and claimed some influence in the steel workers union and the Transport Workers Federation. The party was also active during the year in seeking to establish organizations among the shanty-town dwellers of Caracas.

The MIR held its fifth National Congress in June. It claimed an attendance by 250 delegates, elected at 22 regional conferences. Among those invited to the conference were Régis Debray, and representatives of the Cuban Communist Party and Arab Ba'th Socialist Party, as well as ex-Presidential candidate José Vicente Rangel, and various independent left-wing politicians.

*   *   *

The Maoists. Pro-Mao elements in Venezuela appear to be divided into two groups: the Patria Nueva movement and the Party of the Venezuelan Revolution (Partido de la Revolución Venezolana; PRV). The PRV, reportedly led by Douglas Bravo, one time Politburo member of the PCV, claimed responsibility for a number of guerrilla actions during the year.

The Trotskyists. A Trotskyist party was officially founded in Venezuela for the first time in 1973. This party, the Socialist Workers Party (Partido Socialista de los Trabajadores), is associated with the United Secretariat of the Fourth International. It publishes a fortnightly periodical *Voz Socialista.* During 1974 its periodical carried on several campaigns, including one for unification of the various factions of the trade union movement, and one in favor of nationalization without compensation of the petroleum industry. It centered much of its polemics on the MAS, accusing it of betraying Marxism-Leninism and entering on the road to reformism.

The Guerrillas. Isolated guerrilla groups continued sporadic activities during the year, although they had no noticeable impact on the country's general political situation. Perhaps most spectacular was the thirty-day kidnaping of Pedro and Julio Molino Palacios, wealthy businessmen, in March-April. The so-called Red Flag group claimed responsibility for this. Outbreaks of armed attacks, blowing up of pipelines, and other similar activities were particularly numerous just before the inauguration of President Carlos Andrés Pérez in March. Both the Red Flag and Fabricio Ojeda

Operational Campaign of the PRV, and the so-called Armed Forces of National Liberation, claimed to have perpetrated these activities.

Rutgers University   Robert J. Alexander

MIDDLE EAST
AND AFRICA

Egypt

The Communist Party of Egypt (al-Hizb al Shuyu'i al-Misri; CPE) was founded in 1921.

In 1965 the party decided to dissolve, and merged with the Arab Socialist Union (ASU)–the country's sole legal party organization. This arrangement has continued under the presidency of Anwar al-Sadat, despite the gradually rightist evolution of the government's domestic and foreign policies. Indeed, two CPE members were brought into the cabinet in 1972. In 1973, however, Sadat turned against the left. He blamed "the Marxists" for instigating the student riots of October 1972 and January 1973, and then purged the ASU of about 90 communists and Marxists. These anti-communist moves came in the wake of Sadat's eviction of Soviet troops stationed in Egypt.

After the expulsion from the ASU, a number of Egyptian communists began to consider the reestablishment of a communist party. At the time of the October war with Israel, communist agitation was muted in deference to the spirit of national unity that pervaded the country. When the prospects of peace improved in November 1973, activity was renewed with the reappearance of the former official CPE organ *al-Tahrir*, and the propagation of an official party line.

Leadership and Organization. The Egyptian left is divided. At the left-center of Egypt's ideological spectrum stands a socialist contingent which considers itself the defender of Gamal 'Abd al-Nasir's Arab Socialism, including the single-party framework centered on the ASU. Despite a Marxist orientation and amicable relations with the Moscow-oriented CEP, this group is not communist.

The traditional communist party, the CPE, is led by men such as Lutfi al-Khauli and Khalid Muhyi al-Din.

On the far left of the political spectrum, there are dissident communists who refused to obey Brezhnev's orders to join the ASU during the mid-1960s and attempted to form a new communist party. The Nasir government promptly jailed the leading members of this faction, who had begun to display Maoist leanings.

The Egyptian left as a whole has clearly continued to stand on the defensive, but, nevertheless, wields considerable power among workers, students, intellectuals, and some of the farmers.

Domestic Views and Activities. During the year, the communists have attacked economic liberalization, "excessive" departures from Arab Socialist ideology, and the government's break with the Nasirite past. The Egyptian left as a whole (including the CPE) has waged a bitter struggle against the right (including the Muslim Brotherhood). Thus, the Sadat government emerged as the ultimate arbiter between the two poles of the ideological spectrum.

CPE spokesmen were particularly concerned at the way in which the Egyptian Army's surprisingly effective performance in the October war was credited to the Egyptian right. Lutfi al-Khauli was eloquent in his defense of Nasir and Nasirism. Salah Hafiz, another left-wing leader, went further by issuing a "warning to the Egyptian right" to accept "the national coalition"—that is, communist participation in the ASU and the government in general. Hafiz insisted that the Egyptian left had fought and made sacrifices for democracy both before and after the revolution of July 1952—a clear reference to the periodic jailings of communists by the late President Gamal 'Abd al-Nasir.

Despite the government's attempts to limit the pace of liberalization and de-Nasirization, the rightist press continued to attack the left in general, and the communists in particular. The leftists feared that Egypt's rapprochement with the United States and Saudi Arabia might lead Sadat to dismantle the ASU, in which leftists had participated until 1973, and that without the ASU, the left would be isolated from the political process and eventually liquidated, as it had been in the Sudan in 1971. Hence the leftists offered vehement opposition to a recommendation made by the ASU parliamentary committee in 1974 calling for the restoration of a multi-party system. The CPE did not participate in the committee's deliberations. The ASU's political monopoly was defended instead by trade union leaders and student representatives. Despite Sadat's popularity, derived from the substantial success gained by Egyptian arms in 1973, there was a revival of the Nasir cult. Ironically enough, this was led by the Egyptian left, including the communists who had so frequently been suppressed during the Nasir era. Nevertheless, the left considered Nasir as symbolic of a political order in which the left had enjoyed a considerable measure of recognition and of political representation.

International Views and Activities. The communists continued to take a militant stand against Israel and its "Western imperialist" allies. Specifically, the communists vehemently opposed Egypt's rapprochement with the United States, the possible acceptance of a U.S.-imposed peace settlement with Israel, and the anti-Nasir campaign of the rightist press. In the final analysis the prospects for the Egyptian communist movement depend on the evolving shape of the Arab-Israeli conflict, Egypt's relations with the United States and the U.S.S.R., and the degree of the government's ability to effect a perceptible improvement in the lives of Egypt's multitudes.

Publications. The party publishes *al-Tahrir* ("Liberation") as its official organ.

State University of New York   R. H. Dekmejian
Binghamton

Iran

Although communist activity has been known in Iran since 1920, it was not until August 1944 that the present communist party held its First Congress. Meeting at that time in Tehran, it approved the program and constitution of the Hizb-e Tudeh Iran ("Party of the Masses of Iran," or "People's Party of Iran"–PPI) and elected a Central Committee and Control Commission. The Second Congress, in 1946, adopted a new constitution and defined the tactics of the party. In February 1949, after an unsuccessful assassination attempt on the Shah by a party member, the PPI was declared illegal. Since then it has operated underground and the Central Committee has been functioning in various Iron Curtain countries.

In 1960, a joint conference of the PPI and the Azerbaijanian Democratic Party, based in Iranian Azerbaijan, adopted a resulution which called for a single party of the working class.

The extent of PPI membership is unknown, but probably does not exceed a few hundred. The population of Iran is estimated at 30,550,000.

Leadership and Organization. Iradj Eskanderi has served as the PPI's first secretary since 1971. The party does not ordinarily publish the names of its leading members. In September 1974, however, it announced the expulsion of Abdol-Reza Azar and Nostratollah Jahan Shahlu for "betraying the party and surrendering to the enemy."

In November, Mohammad Zaman Pahlavan, a party member for thirty years and since the early 1960s a resident of Prague and consulting editor of the Arabic edition of *Problems of Peace and Socialism*, returned to Iran. He was fired from his job and expelled from the party on "ideological" grounds. In a press and television interview he denounced the aim as well as the methods of the party, and called its leader the puppet of "foreign powers."

The massive economic and social-development programs of the Iranian Government and the effectiveness of its security force Savak further jeopardized the activities of the PPI in Iran. During the year there were arrests of scores of party members, usually charged with terrorist activities. Also some members surrendered to the government authorities and publicly denounced their former association with the party.

There was no sign that the PPI might become a viable instrument for change in Iran in the near future. Neither is it likely to be legalized. In an interview the Shah stated that his government would not tolerate political parties inspired and directed from abroad, especially Marxist parties (*Ettela'at-e Hava'i*, Tehran, 16 October).

Domestic Views and Activities. The PPI had steadily opposed all military, economic, and political links between Iran and the "Western imperialists." At the same time, it has sought the support of other "popular" and revolutionary movements in a common cause. In April 1974, for example, the PPI sent a message to the Iranian People's Mujahidin, known as Islamic Marxists, calling for cooperation: "Our views as Marxists, no doubt, do not always agree with those of the Islamic revolutionary strugglers in all respects, [but in opposition to] the enslaving chains of neocolonialism [you are] pursuing the same path that true Marxist-Leninists have adopted." The PPI invited the Mujahidin to hold mutual discussions and "draw up a long-term cooperation program." ("Radio Iran Courier," 30 April.)

International Views and Activities. The PPI has steadily pursued a pro-Soviet policy. A broadcast on 2 July, 1974, by the party's clandestine "Radio Iran Courier" stated that the U.S.S.R. had helped Iran to break the two great "imperialist spells," the spell of steel and the spell of gasoline. The PPI, on the other hand, has strongly opposed the Chinese communist position. A broadcast transmitted on 5 March asserted:

> Some years ago, Peking was the center of aspiration for many young strugglers both in Iran and other countries and the extremist and anti-Marxist dogmas of Mao's group were revered like the Koran. Now, not only in the world communist movement but also in the movement of the anti-imperialist struggles of peoples of the Third World, the Maoist group has become isolated and is moving toward complete isolation more and more each day.

In the same broadcast the Maoists were blamed, along with other domestic and foreign enemies, for spreading "discord among national and anti-imperialist forces" by means of "venomous propaganda."

On the issue of independence for the Kurdish ethnic group in neighboring Iraq, the PPI sided with the Soviet Union (which provided arms that the Iraqi forces have used against the Kurds), and the Iraqi Communist Party. As conflict between the Kurds and the Iraqi forces intensified in 1974, the PPI blamed the government of Iran and the Chinese communists for the failure of Iraqi-Kurdish negotiations. On the other hand, the "Central Command," a pro-Chinese splinter group within the Iraqi Communist Party, backed the Kurdish cause.

Publications. The PPI Central Committee published two magazines: *Donya* ("World") and *Peykar*. In July 1974, the Committee decided "in view of the party's limited resources," to stop the publication of *Peykar*, which had been issued for the past three years. The Committee also felt that the format of *Donya* did not meet the party's requirements: "The Executive board of the party is of the opinion that a magazine with fewer pages and shorter articles dealing with the complex and urgent political, economic, social, and theoretical problems [and] published more frequently each year [i.e., monthly] would meet the urgent and increasing needs." The party's primary medium of propaganda is the clandestine "Radio Iran Courier," which broadcasts from Iraq.

Lewis and Clark College   Nosratollah Rassekh

Iraq

The Iraqi Communist Party (al-Hizb al-Shuy'i al-'Iraqi; ICP) came into existence on 31 March 1934 through the merger of the local communist organizations in Iraq. At the party's First Congress, in 1946, the ICP elected a central committee and adopted a national charter. Until 1973 the party lacked legal status and operated underground. Between 1934 and 1973 it passed through several periods of repression in which many party members were killed or jailed.

Today the ICP, with an estimated 2,000 to 3,000 members and 15,000 to 20,000 fellow travelers and sympathizers, is considered one of the most important communist parties in the Arab world.

Leadership and Organization. The ICP is pro-Soviet. Most of its leaders are intellectuals and professional people, such as doctors, lawyers, and teachers. Many of these, such as 'Aziz Muhammad (known as Nazim 'Ali), the secretary-general, and Karim Ahmad, a member of the Politburo and the ICP's second highest dignitary, are of Kurdish origin.

Despite previous setbacks, the communists have become a thriving segment of Iraq's social and political life. Reports from Iraq in 1974 indicate that since 1973 several ICP branch offices have sprung up in major towns and cities of Iraq. At present there are about fifteen branches, scattered throughout the country.

Domestic Views and Activities. Traditionally the relationship between the ICP and the ruling Ba'th Party was one of mutual distrust and suspicion, punctuated by violence and bloodshed. A turning point in the relationship between the two parties came in 1972, when both made a determined effort to show good will. Relations improved to the extent that two communists were appointed to the cabinet (see *YICA, 1974*, p. 245).

On 17 July 1973 the two parties joined in signed the National Action Charter, the basis for the National Front, making the ICP legal for the first time since its establishment. The charter called for sixteen seats on the Supreme Committee of the front, three of which were to be filled from the ranks of the ICP. In a letter congratulating President Ahmad Hasan al-Bakr on his reelection as secretary-general of the Iraqi Ba'th Party, ICP leader 'Aziz Muhammad declared that the two-party alliance was conducive to checking the resurgent reactionary movement and to curbing imperialist reactionary conspiracies (Iraqi News Agency, 14 January 1974). On 28 March 1974 radio Baghdad broadcast a letter by Shibli al-'Aysami, assistant secretary-general of the Ba'th Party, congratulating the ICP Central Committee on its fortieth anniversary. He expressed the hope that the struggle of the National Front would be consolidated to achieve steadfastness, to confront the "zionist imperialist alliance," and to improve the lot of the toiling masses. On March 29 both 'Aziz Muhammad and Shibli al-'Aysami reportedly were present at an ICP celebration in Baghdad (Iraqi News Agency,

March 29). The following day, the appointment of three ICP Central Committee members to the Iraqi Revolutionary Command Council was announced. The three were Dr. Nazihah al-Dulaymi, Dr. Rahim 'Ajinah, and Mahdi al-Hafiz. They were to work full time for the National Front. (Iraqi News Agency, 30 March.)

In an interview with *Népszabadság* (Budapest) on 30 August, 'Aziz Muhammad praised the positive achievements of the Iraqi government, especially the distribution of lands among 375,000 peasant families, the establishment of cooperatives among peasants, the nationalization of oil, and the establishment of the National Front.

Between 1972 and 1973 the ICP frequently clashed with the Kurdish Democratic Party (KDP), which it had previously supported. In November 1973 the two parties signed an agreement, but dissensions between them continued nevertheless. Throughout 1974 the ICP daily newspaper accused the KDP of attempting to destroy the ICP. It stated that ICP members and supporters were being assassinated, kidnaped, tortured, and jailed in Kurdistan *Tariq al-Sha'b*, 29 January and 29 July). The KDP denied the charges and issued counter-accusations to the effect that the ICP was continuing to maintain its own armed forces in Kurdistan and was opposing the Kurdish independence movement.

The ICP continued to criticize the KDP, especially the Barzani leadership. ICP secretary-general 'Aziz Muhammad on several occasions accused Barzani of being a reactionary leader representing the interests of both rightist and imperialist forces, and of not striving for autonomy, but aiming at setting up an independent Kurdistan." Allegedly, Barzani had refused to join the National Front for reactionary reasons and had objected to the Iraqi land reform law of 1970, the Iraqi-Soviet treaty of friendship and cooperation, and the nationalization of foreign oil companies. (*al-Balagh*, Beirut, 22 July.) 'Aziz Muhammad upheld the program of the National Front proposed by the Ba'th Party as a basic framework for solving Iraqi social problems, including the Kurdish minority.

International Views and Activities. The Persian Gulf and the Arab-Israeli conflict occupied a prominent place in ICP writings during 1974. In September, an ICP newspaper warned the Arab countries of the consequences of imperialist intervention through the agency of Iran and Israel. In an attempt to change the map and protect their oil interests, imperialist forces were said to be arming Iran and Israel to the hilt. Iran allegedly had replaced British forces in the Arab Gulf and the Indian Ocean, and, in collaboration with imperialist agents, especially King Husain of Jordan, subverted the revolutionary movement in southern Arabia and Oman. Furthermore, Iran was said to be seeking to weaken the progressive regime in Iraq through continuous border provocations and support for the Kurdish movement's rightist wing. Israel was said to have been assigned the task of isolating Egypt and liquidating Syria. (*Tariq al-Sha'b*, 23 September.)

ICP criticism was also aimed at Egypt's new policy of friendship with the United States. Egypt's defense of American foreign policy allegedly was intended to paralyze the activities of the masses and split the nationalist ranks in Arab countries. In June the ICP Central Committee published a statement in which it defined the aims of U.S. foreign policy as (1) to undermine the Arab liberation movement and implement imperialist plans for gaining control of Arab oil wealth, (2) to offer only a partial solution to the Arab-Israeli conflict and to perpetuate Israeli occupation of lands in Egypt, Syria, and Jordan, and (3) to subvert the Palestine resistance movement. The statement outlined three steps to counteract American designs by (1) increasing mass awareness of the campaign of deception, (2) uniting all Arab revolutionary parties and forces into one nationalist front and alliance of struggle, and (3) promoting cooperation with the Soviet Union and other socialist powers. (Ibid.)

Relations with Other Communist Parties. Throughout 1974 the ICP praised the achievements of foreign communist parties. Several delegates visited the Soviet Union, Hungary, Bulgaria, Poland,

Bangladesh, Romania, and East Germany. In turn, the ICP received delegates from the Syrian, Lebanese, and Soviet parties, among others. Additionally, ICP members attended the conference of representatives of communist and workers' parties in Prague, in January, and took active part in organizing the international scientific and ideological seminar held in Baghdad in early June. The seminar "reaffirmed the need for patriotic and national liberation movements to cooperate with the Soviet Union and the 'Socialist' countries" (*Baghdad Observer*, 13 June).

On his fiftieth birthday, in 1974, 'Aziz Muhammad was awarded the Order of Friendship of the People by the Soviet Union for his continuous efforts to promote communism in Iraq.

Publications. In August 1973, the Iraqi Information Ministry granted the ICP a license to publish the daily newspaper *Tariq al-Sha'b* ("People's Road"). This name was previously that of an ICP monthly. The chief editor is 'Abd al-Razzaq al-Safti, a member of the Central Committee of ICP. In addition, the ICP distributes with relative freedom a number of illegal publications: the daily *Ittihad al-Sha'b* ("People's Union"), which is circulated within the ranks of the party; the cultural weekly *al-Fikr al-Jadid* ("New Thought"), edited by Karim Ahmad, which puts emphasis on communist and Soviet literature but also carries articles on political issues; and the monthly literary and political journal *al-Thaqafah al-Jadidah* ("New Culture"). ICP information is also regularly disseminated through the publications of the Lebanese Communist Party, *al-Nida'* and *al-Akhbar*.

California State University　　　　　　　　　　　　　　　　　　　　　　Ayad Al-Quazzaz
Sacramento

Israel

The first communist party in the Middle East was established in Palestine in 1919 as the Socialist Workers' Party (Mifleget Poalim Sozialistim). It lasted less than a year. In 1922 a group of communists founded the illegal Palestine Communist Party, which in 1924 affiliated with the Comintern. In May 1943, after extended internal dissension, the party split into the Arab League of National Liberation, which adopted an Arab nationalist philosophy, a Jewish splinter group, and the Communist Educational Association, which leaned toward Zionism. Following the establishment of Israel in 1948, the various communist groups were united as the Communist Party of Israel (Miflaga Komunistit Yisraelit; MAKI). The party accepted the new state, but denied any bond between the Jewish people in Israel and the Diaspora. It supported the right of Palestinian refugees to return or receive compensation, and advocated the establishment of a Palestinian Arab State in the territory allocated to it by the United Nations partition plan of 1947. Soviet policy toward Jewish citizens and toward Israel and Arab countries increased dissension within the party. Consequently, in August 1965 the party split into two factions, one of which kept the party name while the other called itself the New Communist List (Reshima Komunistit Hadasha; RAKAH). The majority of Jewish communists gravitated toward the MAKI faction, which leaned toward Zionist views (such as the recognition of a bond between Jewish people in Israel and the Diaspora). The majority of Arab Communists, but also some Jewish communists, joined the RAKAH faction, which continued to adhere to old party views.

Both parties are very small, each having an estimated membership of under 1,500. In 1972 the population of Israel was approximately 3,300,000. Both parties are legal, but their role in Israeli political life tends to be marginal.

RAKAH. Leadership and Internal Affairs. Approximately thirty percent of RAKAH memberships are held by Jews, with Arabs in the majority. The party congress convenes every four years and elects the Central Committee and the Control Commission. The Central Committee in turn elects the Political Bureau and the Secretariat. Among the leaders of the party are three members of the Knesset (the Israeli parliament): Meir Vilner, secretary-general; Tawfiq Tubi, coordinator of the Secretariat; and Avraham Livernbaum, Politburo member. Tawfiq Ziyad is a new Knesset member, Wolf Ehrlich is chairman of the Central Control Commission and Ramzi Khuri the secretary. Others prominent in the party are Emile Habibi, Central Committee member and editor of *Al-Ittihad*; David Khenin, Politburo member and secretary of the Central Committee; Zahi Karhubi, Central Committee member; and E. Ungar, Central Committee member and chief editor of *Zo Ha' derekh*.

RAKAH extends guidance to the Young Communist League, Democratic Women's Movement, Israeli Association of Anti-Fascist Fighters and Victims of Nazism, and the Israel-U.S.S.R. Friendship Movement (*WMR*, March 1974).

Domestic Views and Activities. In the December 1973 elections for the Knesset, RAKAH polled 53,350 votes, an increase of 36 percent over the 38,827 obtained in 1969. Of these, about 43,000 were Arab votes, and the remainder Jewish. It was the first time since 1965 that RAKAH had polled more than 50,000 votes. Advances were marked in Nazareth, the largest Arab city in Israel, where the party received 59 percent (7,707) votes, as against 47 percent (5,578) in 1969. The increase in Arab votes for the party is attributable to the October war of 1973, which itensified national feeling among the Arabs. If it were not for the Bader-Ofer law favoring big parties, RAKAH would have gained yet another seat in the Knesset.

The October War. RAKAH blames the Israeli government for the October 1973 renewal of the war between the Arabs and the Israelis. On 15 October, while the war was still in progress, Meir Vilner issued a statement claiming that Egypt and other Arab states were prepared to recognize the right of Israel to exist as a sovereign state but that Golda Meir's government repeatedly rejected all peace initiatives. The adoption of the Galili Document (a blueprint for extending and perpetuating the policy of annexing the occupied area), premeditated aggressive military operations against Syria and Lebanon, and continuous denial of the lawful rights of the Arab people of Palestine were claimed to be the main causes of the October war (ibid., p. 96).

From the U.N. Security Council Resolutions 242 and 338 RAKAH derived a four-point peace program calling for the withdrawal of Israel from occupied territories, assurance of the sovereignty and territorial integrity of all countries of the area, including Israel, recognition of the lawful rights of Palestinians, and recognition of Israeli shipping rights through the Suez Canal and the Straits of Tiran (*Népszabadság*, Budapest, 25 August 1974). RAKAH rejected both Israel's claims to Arab territory and the terrorist acts carried out by Palestinian groups. It criticized the policy of the new government, headed by Yitzhak Rabin, a policy of secure territories and borders (in effect, a continuation of the annexation policy of Golda Meir), as one that would lead to more war (Moscow radio, 6 June). It further criticized the government for not recognizing the legitimate rights of the Palestinian people and for its opposition to the participation of the Palestine Liberation Organization (PLO) in the Geneva conference (*Pravda*, Moscow, 25 July). On the other hand, it applauded disengagement agreements with Syria and Egypt as positive steps (Moscow radio, Arabic, 3 June). It supported initially formation of the Rabin government as the lesser of evils, but did not vote for it.

RAKAH criticized the government's high military expenditures (from a budget of 35 billion Israeli pounds last year, 21 billion were spent for military purposes), which resulted in a 38.7 percent increase in prices and a foreign trade deficit of 2.5 billion. Increased tax burdens were said to have caused particular suffering for the population segment living on wages and salaries. (*Népszabadság*, 25 August.) Further, the weekly party newspaper accused the government of harassing RAKAH members and sympathizers (particularly Arabs), and published numerous articles regarding house arrest, detention, and other annoyances. A poem by the new Knesset member Tawfiq Ziyad entitled "The Great Crossing," in which he expressed pride over the initial successes of the Arab armies during the October war, caused quite a stir in the Knesset, where some members questioned Ziyad's allegiance to the state (*Jerusalem Post*, 29 October).

International Views. RAKAH is recognized by most foreign communist parties as the legitimate communist party in Israel. During 1974 RAKAH sent delegations to the East European and Soviet parties and received several visiting foreign communist party delegations. The party continually praised Soviet policy in the Middle East as being aimed toward peace and justice for all people of the area.

Publications. RAKAH publications included the Hebrew weekly *Zo Ha'derekh* ("This Is the

Way"), the Yiddish *Der Veg* ("The Way"), the Arabic *al-Ittihad* ("Unity"), the theoretical journals *Arakhim* ("Values") in Hebrew and *al-Darb* ("The Way") in Arabic, and a monthly *Information Bulletin*. The Communist Youth League publishes *al-Ra'id* in Arabic and *Inyan* in Hebrew.

MAKI. Leadership and Internal Affairs. MAKI leaders include Meir Peil, member of the Knesset; Yair Tsaban, editor of *Kol Ha'am*, the party magazine; Yair Zahan, chairman of the Politburo; and Shmuel Mikunis, former Knesset member and secretary-general of the party until 14 November 1974. Tension begun in 1974 between veteran leader and MAKI founder Mikunis and members of the younger generation moved from estrangement toward a total split. This tension centers on Mikunis's opposition to merger of MAKI with the Blue-Red Movement, which maintains close cooperation with the MOQED (see *YICA, 1974*, p. 248). Mikunis refused to take part in the work of the committee preparing for the second session of the party's seventeenth Conference. He wants to see MAKI an independent communist party whose mission is to defend the interests of the working people and to explain the just position of Israel in the international communist movement. On 14 November he resigned as secretary-general in protest against party decisions and actions with which he could not agree. In particular he specified party opposition to the government's activities in the administered area and to army reprisal raids into Lebanon (*Jerusalem Post*, 19 November).

MAKI seemed to be experiencing financial difficulties. Their monthly magazine *Israel at Peace* has appeared only irregularly as funds became available.

Domestic Attitudes and Activities. MAKI entered the election of December 1973 elections for the Knesset on the MOQED list in coalition with the Blue-Red Movement. The coalition received 22,470 votes (1.4 percent of the total), as against 15,712 (1.1 percent) in 1969, although it captured only one seat in the Knesset. Were it not for the Bader-Ofer law, MOQED would have gained a second Knesset seat.

MAKI criticizes government economic policy as enriching the wealthy and impoverishing the poor. Along with its partners in the coalition, MAKI distributes leaflets and posters in industrial areas demanding that the government

> "(1) Revoke the decision to partially cancel subsidies to vital basic foodstuffs, stop the soaring price spiral, and exercise an effective price control; (2) pay automatically a cost-of-living allowance whenever prices rise by 3 percent; (3) raise the minimum wage to 750 Israeli pounds monthly; (4) increase monthly payments to mobilized soldiers (also to 750 pounds); (5) control profits and prohibit profit levels from rising above the 1972 rate; (6) tax war profits; and (7) revoke the income tax reduction granted to capitalists" (*Israel at Peace*, March 1974).

MAKI and its partners oppose co-optation of the National Religious Party (NRP) into the government because the latter's policy towards converts and civil laws blocks efforts to bridge the social gap (*Jerusalem Post*, 12 September).

Arab-Israeli Conflict. On 17 November 1973 the MAKI Central Committee condemned Golda Meir's policy in the occupied area and her refusal to recognize the rights of the Palestinians for self-determination (*Israel at Peace*, March 1974). MAKI believes that Resolutions 242 and 338 provide a sound basis for resolving the conflict. It believes the government must make far-reaching concessions to the Arabs, including the return of nearly all the administered territories, or else will face an imposed solution or another war (*Jerusalem Post*, 12 September.) MAKI opposes the establishment of settlements in the occupied territories. It has threatened to use extra-parliamentary activities, including street riots, to stop further settlements on the West Bank. The party also opposes the co-optation of the National Religious Party into the government because it believes such a move would hamper peace initiatives.

The party has praised the disengagement between Israel and Egypt and Syria as a significant step toward peace in the area.

International Views and Activities. Since the split in 1965, MAKI has been isolated from communist parties abroad except for limited support from those parties at odds with Moscow. On 2 March 1974 the Central Committee, acting upon a resolution passed by the Seventeenth Conference, decided to join the World Jewish Congress (*Israel at Peace*, March). MAKI is critical of Soviet policy in the Middle East and toward Soviet Jews (Jerusalem radio, domestic service in Hebrew, 9 September). It condemns the deporation of Soviet writer Alexander Solzhenitsyn and the censorship of art and literature (ibid.). The party organ published several articles on the conference of communist parties from countries of capitalist Western Europe, held in January 1974 in Brussels, which was critical of Soviet policy. MAKI hopes to establish contact with similar conferences in the future (*Israel at Peace*, March).

Publications. MAKI's central organ, *Kol Ha'am* ("Voice of the People"), is published biweekly. The once monthly *Israel at Peace* (in English and French), is now, for financial reasons published irregularly. The party publishes occasional papers in various languages.

California State University
Sacramento

Ayad Al-Qazzaz

Jordan

The Communist Party of Jordan (al-Hizb al-Shuyu'i al-Urdunni; CPJ) was officially established in June 1951. However, communist activity on the West Bank of the Jordan River, annexed by the Hashemite Kingdom after the 1948 Arab-Israeli War, can be traced back to the founding of the Palestinian National Liberation League (PNLL) in September 1943, in Haifa. The partition of Palestine, supported by the Soviet Union, caused splits among local communists, the PNLL initially opposing Jordan's takeover of the West Bank and denouncing the "Hashemite army of occupation." Nonetheless, members of the PNLL ultimately joined with like-minded Jordanians to form the CPJ.

Under constant government pressure since the early 1950s, the party has operated under the guise of various popular front organizations. Its center of activity has been on the West Bank, where it drew support from students, teachers, professional workers, and the "lower middle classes." Although it had probably no more than 1,000 members at the time, mostly Palestinians, the CPJ was reportedly the strongest party in Jordan during the country's first decade of independence (from 1946). An anti-communist law adopted in 1953 failed to suppress the organization, and repressive tactics appeared to be counter-productive. The CPJ retained its image as an enemy of "feudalism" and "imperialism," and in October 1956 a communist-led front elected three CPJ members to the Jordanian parliament. The party exercised considerable political influence through alliance with the Ba'th Party and Sulaiman al-Nabulsi's National Socialists. A CPJ member was appointed minister of agriculture, the first communist in the Arab world to receive a ministerial portfolio.

In reaction to the party's growing power, King Husain warned the country in February 1957 of the dangers of communist infiltration and urged Prime Minister al-Nabulsi to eliminate "destructive propaganda." As a result, all local communist publications were banned, along with films and newspapers. On 25 April 1957, the king declared the CPJ illegal and disbanded all other parties, following an abortive attempt by "left-wing nationalists" to overturn the monarchy. Hundreds of communists were arrested, including the CPJ parliamentary deputies, who were sentenced to long prison terms.

The CPJ has been illegal since 1957, although the government's normally repressive measures have occasionally been relaxed. For example, two communist deputies were elected to parliament as "independents" in 1961. More significantly, under a political amnesty granted at the outbreak of the 1967 Arab-Israeli war, all communists were released from Jordanian jails, and the party's secretary-general, Fu'ad Nassar, was allowed to return from exile. For a time the CPJ operated as a "semi-legal organization" (*WMR*, March 1974). Repressive measures were resumed in 1972, and at present communist party membership is punishable by jail sentences of 3 to 15 years. Party membership is estimated by Israeli authorities at no more than 400 persons, out of a total Jordanian population of about 2,575,000 (including some 700,000 on the West Bank).

Leadership and Party Affairs. The CPJ is said to be a "tightly organized, well-disciplined network of small cells" (*NYT*, 23 August 1974). Secrecy is highly valued, and little information on party leadership is available. The current secretary-general, and only person to hold that position, is Fu'ad Nassar, a Palestinian of Christian origin without formal education. Other prominent party members reportedly include 'Abd al-Muhsin Abu Mayzar, also of the Palestine National Front (PNF), and Ishaq al-Khatib, both of whom accompanied Palestine Liberation Organization (PLO) head Yasir 'Arafat to Moscow in July 1974. 'Arabi 'Awad is a member of the CPJ's Central Committee and a PNF leader. Other members of the Central Committee include 'Isa Madanat and Na'im Ashhad.

Since its decline in the late 1950s, the CPJ has been known as a "passive political underground movement" confined to the West Bank (*NYT*, 23 August 1974). In recent years, however, party activities have increased, and the CPJ claims to be the only party really active in Jordan. Nonetheless, Fu'ad Nassar declared in an interview late in 1973 (Budapest radio, 29 December) that the party operates "under very difficult circumstances" on both sides of the river, pointing to the frequent arrests of CPJ members by the authorities in Amman and the difficulties imposed by the Israelis, who have regularly rounded up communists, among others, and deported them to the East Bank. In December 1973, for instance, the Israelis deported eight West Bank Palestinians, including 'Arabi 'Awad, who were accused of being "top figures" in the CPJ, in addition to being members of the PNF. Another Israeli security campaign began in late 1974 to counter the upsurge in activity by the PLO, whose supporters include CPJ and PNF members. On 4 November, four PNF officials were deported for circulating pro-PLO petitions and other "hostile activity," and on 21 November a group of five PNF members was deported. Among the latter group was the president of Bir Zeit College, Dr. Hanna Nasir, a strong Palestinian nationalist but apparently not a communist (*NYT*, 22 November).

The Palestine Question. The CPJ appears to be essentially a Palestinian party, both in membership (whether on the West or the East Bank) and in ideological orientation, and the Palestine issue has vexed the party since its inception. As a generally "pro-Soviet" organization, moreover, the CPJ evidently has not been entirely free to take an independent stand on Palestine, and consequently has lost support to more committed and radical Palestinian liberation movements. In March 1970, the CPJ took the initiative in forming the Quwwat al-Ansar (Partisan Forces) guerrilla organization, later joined by the communist parties of Lebanon, Syria, and Iraq. The al-Ansar organization was never an integral part of the CPJ, however. Although designed in part to give the Soviet Union access to the growing power of the commando organizations, the group remained isolated among Palestinians, and its active strength never totaled more than 300 to 400 men. Officially, in keeping with Soviet policy, it did not aim to destroy Israel but rather to implement the U.N. Security Council resolutions on Palestine. The group fought well on the side of the commandos during the Jordanian civil war of September 1970, but it became controversial within the CPJ. One faction accused Fu'ad Nassar of "outdoing others by proclaiming the establishment of the al-Ansar organization before completing the necessary preparations." As a result of these and other problems, it was disbanded early in 1972.

The CPJ's basic position on Palestine is similar to that of the main Palestinian liberation groups. In December 1973, Fu'ad Nassar called for the "liquidation of the [consequences of the] Israeli aggression" and a "just political settlement," both standard phrases. He also termed the opening of the Geneva peace conference a "significant step toward resolving the Middle East crisis." (Budapest radio, 29 December.) The party advocated recognition of the Palestine Liberation Organization as the sole representative of the Palestinian people, and its 1974 program emphasized the Palestinians' right to "determine their destiny freely, including the right to establish their independent national state on lands evacuated by Israel" (*The Arab World*, Beirut, 3 June 1974).

CPJ cooperation with the PLO broadened during 1974. Fu'ad Nassar, in his December 1973 interview, reported increased cooperation with the PLO. In May 1974, 'Arabi 'Awad praised the role of the PLO in the Palestinian revolution and armed struggle, and stressed the need for a unified Palestinian resistance (*The Arab World*, 14 May). 'Awad, along with other West Bank deportees labeled by Israeli sources as communists, was elected in June to the Palestine National Council, the Palestinian/PLO "parliament in exile." The fact that 'Awad was not elevated to the Council's Executive Committee has suggested to some observers that the PLO wished to keep its distance from committed pro-Soviet communists. Nonetheless, Abu Mayzar, one of the "communist" deportees, was elected to the Executive Committee and was subsequently identified as "one of the [PLO's] eight senior deputies" (*al-Anwar*, Beirut, 3 November 1974; *FBIS*, 6 November 1974). He was reportedly excluded from consideration as head of a projected Palestinian provisional government, in discussions after the Rabat summit conference.

On 15 August 1973, the Palestinian National Front, composed of professional and labor union representatives as well as "patriotic personalities," was established on the West Bank, evidently at CPJ instigation. The PNF generally follows the PLO line; it advocates creation of an independent Palestinian state on the West Bank and the Gaza Strip and urges Palestinian participation in the Geneva peace talks. Its program also includes mass political struggle and armed resistance in the occupied territories.

Not until after the October 1973 Arab-Israeli war did the PNF emerge as an "active pro-Palestinian organizatin." According to Israeli officials, the CPJ is the core of the group's strength, and Israelis have referred to the PNF as a "terrorist organization" (*NYT*, 23 August 1974). In a statement in late December 1973, the CPJ hailed the growing resistance against the Israeli occupation and called for increasing solidarity with the PNF, said to be leading the struggle in occupied Palestine. The party claimed that resistance in the occupied territories was not a transient phenomenon but was based on a genuine nationalism of the masses; moreover, the desire for liberation had been strengthened within a PNF framework. (*al-Nida'*, Beirut, 29 December; *FBIS*, 7 January 1974). In recognition of the PNF's role, PLO spokesmen indicated that representatives of the group would be included in a provisional Palestinian government. Despite Israel's increased concern with PNF activities, many West Bank Arabs have argued that the PNF's main target is King Husain, not Israel.

Domestic Views. As a party oriented more toward Palestine than toward Jordan, the CPJ apparently has devoted little attention to purely domestic issues. Like other anti-Husain Palestinians of whatever ideological persuasion, Fu'ad Nassar has denounced the "reactionary regime" in Amman and its links to "imperialism," and has called for the establishment in Jordan of "a democratic, independent state" whose goal is social development (Budapest radio, 29 December 1973). Similarly, 'Arabi 'Awad advocates a "liberated and nationalist" regime on the East Bank (*The Arab World*, 14 May 1974). Not surprisingly, the party's lagest program calls for a "national and liberated regime in Jordan which alone would be capable of ending the policy of subservience to imperialism that led to Jordan's isolation from its Arab brothers" (ibid., 3 June). This statement evidently represents a shift in policy toward the Hashemites, as the CPJ had previously advocated the formation of a national unity government in Amman. All political factions were to have been represented, and there was no suggestion concerning Husain's overthrow.

The year 1974 marked a new effort at CPJ cooperation with "progressive forces" in Jordan. In May, the formation of a "Jordanian National Front" was announced; it was said to be composed of elements of the CPJ, the Arab Ba'th Party, and various Palestinian guerrilla organizations, including Fath. Former nationalist Prime Minister Sulaimain al-Nabulsi was also reportedly associated with the group. (ibid., 2 May.) Agreement on a program for the CPJ-sponsored front was reportedly reached in October, although planning had begun early in the year. The program called for "democratic nationalist rule, the promotion of democratic freedom and the consolidation of political and unionist action to guarantee the needs of the Jordanian working masses." (*al-Safir*, Beirut, 5 October; *FBIS*, 15 October.)

Publications. The CPJ publishes a journal, *al-Jamahir* ("The Masses"), and a newspaper, *al-Watan* ("The Homeland"), both of which appear irregularly once or twice a month. It also issues a political and theoretical journal, *al-Haqiqah* ("The Truth"), and special pamphlets. These clandestine publications are distributed on both sides of the Jordan River. The Palestine National Front began publication, evidently in 1974, of its own newspaper, *Filastin* ("Palestine"). News of CPJ activities also appears in the organs of the Lebanese Communist Party, *al-Akhbar* and *al-Nida'*.

U.S. Department of Commerce   Norman F. Howard*
Washington, D.C.

* The views expressed in this article are the author's own and do not necessarily represent those of the Department of Commerce.

Lebanon

The Lebanese Communist Party (al-Hizb al-Shuyu'i al-Lubnani; LCP) was established in 1924. During the period of the French mandate it accepted members from both Lebanon and Syria. Khalid Bakdash (see *Syria*) was elected secretary-general of the party in 1932. What is generally considered its First Congress was held under his leadership in January 1944, after Syria and Lebanon gained independence. This congress decided to establish separate Lebanese and Syrian communist parties to be organized respectively by Faraj Allah al-Halu and Bakdash. Some Lebanese communists consider that the real independence of their party was not achieved until 1964, when the LCP ceased to be under Bakdash's indirect control.

In 1965 LCP decided to break from its policy of working independently of other Lebanese political groups. Since then, it has become a member party in the "Front of Progressive Parties and National Forces" under the leadership of the Progressive Socialists, a party headed by Kamal Jumblat. The LCP was banned until 13 August 1970, when it gained recognition along with other controversial parties, thus becoming the only legal communist party in the Arab world. It is also believed to be the first Arab communist party ever to have openly held a formal party congress. This, its Third Congress, was held in Beirut in January 1972, with delegates from more than 30 foreign communist parties.

Estimates of LCP membership range between 3,000 and 6,000 active and committed members. The population of Lebanon is 2,960,000 (estimated 1972). The social composition of the party is said to be as follows: workers, other employees, and poor peasants, 64 percent; teachers and instructors, 11 percent; students, 9 percent; intellectuals, 7 percent; housewives, 6 percent; and others, 3 percent (*WMR*, May 1973).

Leadership and Internal Affairs. The congress, which is to be convened every four years, is the supreme organ of the party. Between congresses authority is vested in the 24-member Central Committee, which in turn selects and invests authority in the 11-member Politburo and the 5-member Secretariat. The secretary-general, Niqula al-Shawi, and his second in command, George Hawi, who is head of the Secretariat, are both Greek Orthodox. Other members of the Secretariat include: Karim Muruwwah, Nadim 'Abd al-Samad, and Khalil al-Dibs.

The Central Committee held a plenary session in April 1974 to review the party's accomplishments since the Third Congress and discuss the present Lebanese, Arab, and international situations. It adopted a more aggressive course of action aimed at making the party's activities more public, establishing a stronger presence among industrial and agricultural workers, recruiting new members, opening new and effective party offices throughout the country, issuing membership cards, and enlarging and diversifying efforts to collect party funds (*Arab World*, Beirut, 7 May).

On 22 June the Central Committee held a reception to commemorate the fiftieth anniversary of the founding of the LCP. At this occasion the party launched a campaign to collect a half million Lebanese pounds to support party programs and to cover costs of anniversary celebrations. These celebrations continued through 24 October, the actual date of the anniversary, and included political exhibitions, rallies, and speeches, and entertainment by folkloric troups from the Arab world and the communist bloc.

Domestic Views and Activities. The communist party is not represented in the Lebanese parliament. It aligns itself with other Lebanese leftist parties in the Front under the leadership of Kamal Jumblat. In January 1974 the LCP presented what Niqula al-Shawi called the "first document of its kind in Lebanon to discuss the agricultural question from a Marxist-Leninist viewpoint." It noted that agriculture in Lebanon is accounting for a drastically decreasing proportion of the national income, that most of the principal food products are imported, that the area of cultivation is shrinking and that most of Lebanon's water is wasted instead of being used for irrigation. It charged that land rents and loans for farmers are exhorbitant and that prices for agricultural products barely cover production costs for most farmers. According to the report, middlemen reap tremendous profits at the expense of farmers and consumers. The report provided details concerning the relatively small number of hospital beds and doctors, to illustrate the backwardness of rural areas. To improve the situation, the LCP called for health and social insurance for agricultural workers. It also proposed that laws be passed to protect the interests of agricultural workers in regard to unions, rents, loans, and profits. (*al-Nida'*, 16 January.)

A report to the plenary session in April stated that during the last two years Lebanese authorities and particularly the government of Prime Minister Sa'ib Salam had tried to deal with economic, political, and social crises by means of increasing suppression and efforts to set up a civilian dictatorship. The government had supposedly been responsible for massacres of factory workers and tobacco farmers, dismissals of teachers, and suppression of students. The authorities were also said to have made efforts to isolate the LCP from other progressive parties and to isolate the progressives from the Palestinian resistance. While claiming that the party had successfully coordinated its actions with other progressives, the report stated that the LCP still had to struggle in order to "strengthen, consolidate, and expand democracy, obtain a democratic elections law, and ensure public, partisan, trade unionist, and journalistic freedoms." Other domestic goals included defending the interests of workers and peasants, and struggling for a sound national defense policy (*al-Akhbar*, 11 May). Statements made during the anniversary followed the same line. In particular, LCP opposition grew against Prime Minister Sa'ib Salam in October as he tried to form a new cabinet.

In September, leaders of the LCP and of the Ba'th Party of Lebanon held discussions. The meeting reflected the continuing efforts of the LCP to strengthen its relations and coordinate its actions with other leftist parties.

The LCP and the Arab World. In regard to the Arab-Israeli crisis, the LCP continued to follow the Soviet line. It maintained that lasting peace could only be achieved through a political solution, and expressed support for U.N. Security Council Resolutions 242 and 338. Early in 1974, certain Arab governments accused the U.S.S.R. of failing to honor its commitments to the Palestinians. In its desire to express greater support to the Palestinian resistance, the LCP sent a delegation to Moscow to discuss the matter. Soon after, Moscow and, in turn, the LCP issued statements giving full support to the Palestine Liberation Organization (PLO) as the sole legitimate representative of the Palestinian people. In May the LCP expressed support for the establishment of a Palestinian national authority on any party of Palestine which becomes liberated (*al-Nida'*, 4 May).

While Moscow reported the Egyptian-Israeli accord of January without comment, the LCP was extremely hostile to the agreement. Egypt was, in fact, a target of criticism throughout the year by the LCP, which accused the "right-wing Egyptian leadership" of granting needless concessions to achieve disengagement. It charged that this separate, partial settlement was obtained "at the expense of the Syrian front, the other occupied lands and of the rights of the Palestinians" (*al-Nida'*, as cited in *An-Nahar Arab Report*, Beirut, 28 January). Also the LCP attacked anti-Soviet press campaigns in Egypt and accused the government of capitulating to U.S. pressures.

The LCP strongly attacked the "reactionary Arab oil countries," particularly Saudi Arabia, for their role in supporting U.S. imperialist interests. On the other hand, it praised Syrian steadfastness in the face of aggression and other pressures as an embodiment of the will of the Syrian masses (*al-Nida'*, 4 May). It credited the persistence and pressure of the Soviet Union for the first U.S. recognition of the Palestinian people's legitimate interests (ibid., 6 July).

The LCP reaffirmed its support for Arab unity founded on a popular, democratic, progressive, anti-imperialist base. It expressed approval of the self-rule law for the Kurds in Iraq. It urged escalation of "the struggle against the oil monopolies with the aim of finally nationalizing all the oil resources and placing them in the service of Arab development and growth" (ibid., 4 May).

Other International Views and Activities. The new U.S. ambassador to Lebanon was described by the LCP as a "distinguished U.S. intelligence agent, particularly in the field of sabotage and criminal actions against national liberation movements," who had been appointed to Lebanon to use his experience against the Arab liberation movement and in particular against the Palestinian resistance (*al-Nida'*, 16 March 1974).

In July, the LCP condemned the coup in Cyprus as "fascist" and urged the Arab peoples to support the Cypriots against the coup leaders. The United States was accused of engineering the coup and encouraging Turkish attacks in order to control the island "even if the price was to drown it in a sea of blood." (Ibid., 20 August.)

In September, the LCP stated that Iran was preparing to incite communal strife in Iraq, Jordan, Syria, and Lebanon by arming and training volunteers from rightist parties in collaboration with Jordanian intelligence officers. (Ibid., 22 September.)

Publications. The LCP publishes a daily newspaper, *al-Nida'*, ("The Call") and a weekly magazine, *al-Akhbar* ("The News"). These organs also serve as general information media for the illegal communist parties of the Middle East. Both publications are sold on newsstands. There are committees throughout Lebanon in charge of circulating them and a large portion of each issue is distributed free. In addition to these two, the LCP publishes the literary and ideological monthly *al-Tariq* ("The Road"), and the monthly *al-Waqt* ("The Time"). The LCP periodicals are of good quality and are among the most inexpensive of Lebanese publications.

Hoover Institution   Michel Nabti
Stanford University

The Maghreb

ALGERIA

The Algerian Communist Party (Parti Comuniste Algérien; PCA) began its career in 1920 as an extension of the French Communist Party. After 1936 it existed independently. It participated in the Algerian nationalist struggle against France following World War II and supported Ahmad Ben Bella's position. In 1962, a few months after independence was achieved the new government of Ben Bella banned the PCA. The communists, however, quickly adapted themselves to the situation, established friendly relations with the ruling National Liberation Front (FLN), and continued to publish their organ, *Alger Républicain*, albeit in softened tone.

Severely circumscribed under the government of Houari Boumedienne following the military coup d'état of June 1965, the PCA clandestinely formed the Socialist Vanguard Party (Parti de l'Avant-Garde-Socialiste; PAGS), which is recognized in the communist world as the official Algerian party. Active membership in the PAGS is estimated at about 400.

Leadership and Party Affairs. The leading figures are Larbi Boukhali, who lives in exile, and Bashir Hadj 'Ali, who was released from detention in 1970.

Domestic Activities. During 1974 the position of the PAGS improved. The military government of Boumedienne released some communists from jail and the PAGS participated in some international conferences. The PAGS again compromised its position, apparently for tactical purposes, vis-à-vis the FLN, and improved relations between Algeria and communist countries also ameliorated the party's position in Algeria.

The PAGS fared better by moderating its stand, but at a price. Its policies do not appear to differ greatly from those of the Algerian government. For the moment, at least, the PAGS recognizes that while Algeria has committed itself to socialist development, it has not committed itself to Marxism-Leninism, and probably will not do so because of its traditional cultural and religious attachments.

International Activities. The PAGS has not had extensive contacts with Soviet-controlled communist parties, despite improved relations between the communist countries and Algeria. Officially, the Soviets enjoy a special relationship with the FLN and cannot maintain equally close bonds with other "progressive" parties. FLN leader Sharif Belkasem stated on 8 May 1974 that "there exists mutual trust and cooperation" between the FLN and the Communist Party of the Soviet Union (CPSU).

While the FLN enjoys single-party status in Algeria and "exclusive" relationships with the CPSU and other communist parties, the PAGS nevertheless took part in the conference of communist and workers' parties in Prague to discuss the work of the journal *Problems of Peace and Socialism* in January.

Publications. The PAGS issues *Sawt al-Sha'b* ("Voice of the People"), a clandestine journal.

MOROCCO

Founded in 1943 as part of the French Communist Party, the Moroccan Communist Party (Parti Communiste Marocain; PCM) initially had no Moroccan members. The membership consisted essentially of Frenchmen and Spaniards living in Morocco. The "Moroccanization" of the party which the Comintern began by training students and other Moroccans was further emphasized when 'Ali Yata became secretary-general in 1945. Outlawed in 1959, the PCM went underground in 1964 and resurfaced in 1968 as the Party of Liberation and Socialism (Parti de la Libération et du Socialisme; PLS), only to be banned again the following year. 'Ali Yata was temporarily imprisoned, and the PLS newspaper, *al-Kifah al-Watani*, was suppressed.

Since 1971 the government has allowed the PLS to lead a peaceful, albeit illegal and ineffective, existence. The PLS is estimated to have about 300 members.

Leadership. 'Ali Yata is secretary-general of the PLS, and 'Abd Allah Husain Layashi is organizational secretary. Another important member is 'Abd al-'Aziz Belay, an attorney.

Domestic Attitudes and Activities. In the wake of the plots to overthrow the monarchy, the Moroccan government has taken strong measures against opposition forces. On 30 August 1973 a military court sentenced 16 men to death and 70 to prison for plots to overthrow the government. On 28 January 1974 a military court condemned 62 men to death, in absentia, on similar charges. A few days later the government used force against a student strike.

Recognizing the danger signals, the PLS has avoided frontal attacks on the monarchy. The principal PLS publication, *al-Bayan*, has concentrated largely on theoretical treatments of "scientific" socialism. The PLS continued to operate within Morocco during 1974 in a greatly restricted fashion. The small size and the ineffectiveness of the party apparently make it too unimportant, from the king's standpoint, to be outlawed once again. The king's attention is given more to the army, which has attempted several coups d'état, and to the other opposition parties.

Basically neutral on domestic issues, with some minor exceptions, the PLS has translated foreign communist documents for Moroccan consumption. Leonid Brezhnev's speech at the World Congress of Peace Forces, in Moscow, entitled "For Just Democratic Peace, Security of People, and International Cooperation," was published on 29 December 1973 in both French and Arabic.

Although plagued by ideological dissension to a degree, the PLS maintains a pro-Soviet orientation. 'Ali Yata's earlier attempts at steering a neutralist course between the Soviet Union and China have ended in a pro-Soviet line. The attraction of Maoism has become very limited in the PLS.

International Activities and Attitudes. The role of the PLS in international activities increased during 1974, perhaps in part because of improved relations between the Soviet Union and Morocco. The PLS participated in a number of Soviet-sponsored conferences. Significantly for communist activities in the Middle East, Moroccan delegates took part in a seminar sponsored by the National Front of Iraq and the periodical *Problems of Peace and Socialism*, which was held at Baghdad in June. The meeting had a strong anti-Chinese orientation. Moroccan communists in an article for *Problems* *of Peace and Socialism* supported the development of the socialist system on the Soviet model.

The PLS has not committed itself strongly to the Arab side in the Arab-Israeli conflict. The PLS, for example, did not endorse the Palestine Liberation Organization's offer to the Moroccan government of guerrilla support against Spain.

Publications. The PLS publishes *al-Bayan* ("The Bulletin"), a weekly, at Rabat.

TUNISIA

The Communist Party of Tunisia (Parti Communiste Tunisien; PCT), founded in 1920, is the oldest communist party of the Maghreb. Originally a branch of the French Communist Party, it became independent in 1934.

Although the PCT concentrated its activities on national liberation, the Destour Party was in the vanguard of the Nationalist movement, and later the Neo-Destour Party, which took over the leadership. As the Neo-Destour Party increased in importance, the PCT declined.

After leading Tunisia to independence in 1956 and becoming president in 1957, Habib Bourguiba at first took pride in the fact that his leadership was strong enough to tolerate the existence of the PCT. After a right-wing plot in December 1962, however, Bourguiba banned all parties except the Neo-Destour (subsequently renamed the Destourian Socialist Party). The government also banned the PCT publications *al-Tali'ah* and *Tribune du Progrès*. Party membership thereafter steadily decreased from about 2,000 in 1965 to an estimated 100 in 1974. The leading figure of the PCT is the secretary-general, Muhammad Harmel.

Domestic Activities. Opposition forces in Tunisia, from both the right and the left, have not fared well against the prestige and personality of President Bourguiba, who was reelected for life in November 1974. Under the single-party system, the Destourian Socialist Party dominates Tunisian political life. The illegal PCT has had no media for communicating with the Tunisians since the banning of its publications.

In Tunisia are various other leftist organizations, including radical Marxists, representatives of Trotskyite organizations, and so-called socialist study-groups, such as the group headed by Ahmad ben 'Uthman Raddam, publisher of *Tunisian Perspective* and the *Tunisian Worker*. In July 1974 the student Marxist movement was charged with involvement in a plot against the government. In August, the courts sentenced 175 persons, mostly young students belonging to the "Socialist Study and Action Group," to prison terms ranging from 6 months to 10 years for subversion.

The militant character of these leftist groups presents a danger for the PCT, which is officially recognized by Moscow. In effect, the PCT remains aloof from these organizations. Both for tactical reasons and because of its internal problems, the PCT remained essentially inactive during 1974.

The PCT sought, during the first half of the year, to resolve differences within the party over domestic and international issues. In July the *World Marxist Review* (p. 59) published a document indicating that it favored clandestine activities. The PCT platform is now officially oriented toward appealing to the broad masses and the trade unions, rather than identification with the clandestine opposition groups.

International Activities. The Party's internal problems have had a negative impact on its international activities. The discovery in September 1973 of a Soviet spy ring in Tunisia naturally damaged relations between Tunisia and the Soviet Union and also besmirched the reputation of the PCT. The party failed to attend a number of international communist events. The assumption is, however, that with its unification of domestic and international goals and a possible improvement of relations between Tunisia and the Soviet Union, the PCT will now involve itself to a greater extent than before in the international communist scene.

Publications: The PCT has no official journal.

University of   Willard E. Beling
Southern California

Réunion

The Réunion Communist Party (Parti Communiste Réunnionais; PCR) was founded in 1959 by the transformation of the Réunion Federation of the French Communist Party into an autonomous organization.

The PCR is legal. In 1967 the party claimed 3,500 members. No new figures were released at the party's Third Congress, in July 1972. The U.S. State Department has estimated PCR membership at 800 (*World Strength of the Communist Party Organizations*, Washington, D.C., 1973, p. 127). Réunion has a population of 470,000 (estimated 1972).

The PCR is an active participant in Réunion political life, on both local and departmental levels. (As one of France's overseas departments, Réunion is an integral part of the French Republic.) The PCR is the only party with a local organization; elected candidates of other parties are normally French, without permanent organization in Réunion. In 1974 the PCR held 6 seats on the 36-member General Council. The PCR won none of the three contested seats for the French National Assembly in March 1973. It repeatedly charged fraud and unsuccessfully called for the annulment of the September 1973 election.

PCR secretary-general Paul Vergès is the mayor of the island's main city. Vergès was reelected secretary-general of the PCR at the Third Congress, but no other leadership positions were announced in the party organ. A special party conference, scheduled to occur on 21 April 1974 was indefinitely postponed because of a time conflict with presidential elections in France.

The PCR controls the largest trade union, the General Confederation of Labor of Réunion (Confédération Générale du Travail de la Réunion; CGTR), led by Bruny Payet, who is also a member of the General Council. The party is also influential in the Réunion Front of Autonomous Youth (Front de la Jeunesse Autonomiste de la Réunion; FJAR), headed by Elie Hoarau, and the Union of Réunion Women (Union des Femmes de la Réunion; URF). The CGTR held its Third Congress on 9-11 November 1974, the previous congress having been held four years earlier, and the PJAR held also its Third Congress on 8 June, its latest having been held in 1964; the URF indicated intentions of holding a congress, without fixing a date.

Departmental and National Views and Positions. Throughout 1974, as in previous years, the PCR continued to strive for public acceptance of its goal of self-determination. It concluded much of its propaganda through the Réunion Coordination Committee for Self-Determination (Comité Réunnionnais de Coordination pour l'Autodétérmination), comprising the PCR, UFR, CGTR, FJAR, the Réunion Socialist Party (Parti Socialiste Réunionnais), and the Christian Witness of Réunion (Témoignage Chrétien de la Réunion). But this and other issues were overshadowed during the year by the presidential election and the rapidly deteriorating economic situation.

On 18 February, following a period of intense publicity in the PCR organ, *Témoignages*, a "day of action" was held at the behest of the Réunion Coordination Committee and its representative organizations. The grievances aired in public concerned rising prices of basic commodities, including gasoline; shortages in consumers' goods; the decline in purchasing power; and rising production costs of agriculture. The organization demanded a flat increase of U.S. $30 per month for all workers in the private sector; free meals for all students; higher prices for cane sugar, the main source of revenue for the island; increased credit for the unemployed; and more employment opportunities. The first demand (the $30 monthly increase) met with success in the building trades in January, and subsequently in a few other trades; free meals were granted to students of lower levels in a partial success for the second demand; little was accomplished on the problem of unemployment.

The growing influence of the Réunion Coordination Committee for Self-Determination was further demonstrated at the Second Congress of the Réunion Socialist Party, on 31 March, to which delegates of the PCR and other groups were invited. On 2 April, *Témoignages* reported that the congress marked the "reinforcement of the union of the left and the autonomist current in Réunion."

During the French presidential election campaign, a "Liaison Committee for the Victory of the Only Leftist Candidate" (i.e., François Mitterrand) was created by the member groups of the Coordination Committee and by the Jean Jaurès Club and the Socialist Federation of Réunion. The Liaison Committee had its first meeting at the headquarters of the Socialist Party. After the first round elections on 5 May, these parties were able to boast that Réunion had polled the highest percentage of votes for Mitterrand in the French overseas departments and territories. In the second round Réunion gave Mitterand 50.5 percent of the vote, though the national result was 5.7 percent for Giscard d'Estaing (see *France*). Within Réunion, the capital city of Port consistently cast the highest number of votes to Mitterrand.

The PCR expressed considerable concern throughout the year for the fates of Réunion emigrants in France. The emigration program is overseen by the Bureau for the Development of Migrations Concerning the Overseas Departments (BUMIDOM). The Réunion emigrants have organized the General Union of Réunion Workers in France, headed by Roland Malet, who also directs its organ, *Combat Réunionnais*. Malet has continually attacked the BUMIDOM for its alleged poor treatment of the immigrants; in March he was brought to court by the chief of BUMIDOM. The PCR, while supporting efforts to improve conditions for the emigrants in France, is concerned about the drain of qualified young persons from Réunion and warns of problems faced by a prospective emigrant.

International Views and Positions. The PCR is a firm believer in "international solidarity," but concentrates on the island colonies and nations off the East Coast of Africa (especially Madagascar, Mauritius, and the Comores) and the two French Caribbean departments (Martinique and Guadeloupe).

During 1974 the PRC, in conjunction with the World Peace Council, called for the demilitarization of the Indian Ocean. In March, the Réunion Peace Committe (of which the PCR is a member) issued a declaration opposing the use of Diego Garcia by the U.S. Air Force and Navy for atomically armed submaries and bombers, the penetration of the Republic of South Africa into the Indian Ocean, and the testing of French nuclear weapons near Kerguelen (*Témoignages*, 28 March).

The PCR also objected to the proposed inauguration of a direct passenger air route between Johannesburg, South Africa, and Saint-Denis, Réunion. Despite "encouraging" initial delays, the party expressed concern that the influx of South African tourists and the resultant introduction of "racist ideology" might break the unity of the people of Réunion, and transform Réunion, the "garden of races," into a "theater of racial war" (ibid., 28 February).

Publications. The 4-page daily organ of the PCR is *Témoignages*. The FJAR publishes a weekly, *Jeune Réunion*.

Mountain View, California   Eric Stromquist

South Africa

The Communist Party of South Africa was founded in 1921. Outlawed in 1950, it was reconstituted underground in 1953 as the South Africa Communist Party (SACP). The Party operates mainly in exile, but claims that cadres are active in South Africa, where its clandestine publications occasionally appear. The SACP considers itself an integral part of "our national liberation front, headed by the ANC" (*African Communist*. no. 56, p. 44). The ANC is the African National Congress, historically the leading African independence organization and banned within South Africa since 1960. Other organizations in the liberation front are the South African Indian Congress (SAIC), the South African Coloured People's Congress, and the South African Congress of Trade Unions (SACTU). Some leaders of the SAIC are banned or in exile, but its main component in Natal, the Natal Indian Congress, was revived as a legal organization within South Africa in the early 1970s. Leaders of the other organizations are in exile, although it is claimed that SACTU has made efforts to regroup in recent years.

The party's membership is unknown but does not, at the most, exceed a few hundred. (South Africa's population in 1970 amounted to 21,448,000).

Both the SACP and the ANC ally themselves with the South West African People's Organization (SWAPO), Zimbabwe African People's Union (ZAPU), Frente de Libertação de Moçambique (FRELIMO), and Movimento Popular de Libertação de Angola (MPLA).

Leadership and Organization. The SACP sees the South African congresses, dominated by the ANC, as mass organizations in a national struggle to overthrow white domination and to establish majority (i.e., African) rule as a step toward socialism. The SACP itself, in accordance with a decision of 1970, aims to "direct its main efforts to the reconstruction of the Party at home as an organization of professional revolutionaries" (ibid., no. 43, p. 54).

Dr. Yusuf M. Dadoo, a 65-year-old Indian leader who was active within South Africa before 1961, has been chairman of the SACP since 1972. He is also vice-chairman of a "Revolutionary Council" established by the ANC in 1969, when the ANC decided to shift from a formal to an active policy of non-racialism in its membership. At the same time, the ANC has sought to strengthen its nationalist appeal and has maintained an all-African composition in its national executive committee.

Although a number of prominent South African communists are well known, the full leadership of the SACP, centered in London, is not publicized. Moses Kotane, an African who was secretary-general, has been ill in recent years. Michael Harmel, a European who used to write under the pseudonym of "A. Lerumo," died recently. Bram Fischer, a lawyer and 70-year-old descendant of a distinguished Afrikaans-speaking family, headed the underground party in the early 1960s, but is in prison for life and in poor health. The government has categorically rejected appeals within South Africa for his release on humanitarian grounds.

Domestic Activities and Attitudes. In applying Marxism-Leninism to the South African situation, South Africans have long found that color has complicated their class analysis. Thus, Dadoo, in a statement of October 1973 prepared for the Central Committee, noted the "special contradictions" that flow from "capitalist-race rule," which "at the moment," is supported by the white working-class (ibid., no. 56, pp. 22, 32, 43). The party became "Africanized" in membership in the late 1920s but its critics inside and outside continue to argue for a yet more thorough identification with African tradition and experience.

In the latter part of 1974, the SACP's journal reviewed anti-apartheid developments and concluded that, "for the first time in many years, there are signs that the tide is beginning to rise against apartheid" (*African Communist*, no. 58, p. 13). In particular, it welcomed the mass strikes by black workers. (An earlier statement by the Central Committee had noted that workers sang ANC songs and on one occasion carried the red flag. (Ibid., no. 55, p. 20). It also welcomed the "upsurge of militant 'black consciousness' " in South Africa, a development which Dadoo has said contributes to the "psychological liberation" of the African people (ibid., no. 58, p. 13, and no. 56, p. 41).

The SACP journal also noted "a startling about-face for the [white] Nationalists": the news in April 1974 stated that Africans were being trained and armed as police to fight guerrillas (ibid., no. 58, p. 15). This development, it said, was part of the propaganda battle and reflected the government's realization that military means alone cannot defeat a national struggle.

The party journal described as counter-revolutionary the anti-boycott efforts of opponents of apartheid such as Gatsha Buthelezi, leader of the Zulu "homeland," and the Progressive Party (ibid., pp. 9ff.). However, the party has always favored the exploitation of available platforms, and therefore praised the Coloured Labour Party's call for total rejection of apartheid (ibid., no. 56, p. 40) and would justify the participation in the system of men like Buthelezi if they made utterly clear their opposition to "Bantustans" and their support for majority rule.

International Views and Activities. A plenary meeting of the Central Committee in 1974 reaffirmed the SACP's long-standing pro-Soviet position and aligned the party with the Arab struggle against Israel. Once again it condemned "contemptible actions" by China, the Chinese "path of accommodation to imperialism," and the spread of "Maoism, especially in Africa." (Ibid., no. 57, pp. 34 ff.) At the end of the year, Alfred Nzo, general secretary of the ANC, called on Boris Ponomarev, secretary of the CPSU Central Committee.

Publications. The SACP publishes the quarterly *African Communist* in London, and distributes underground in South Africa *Inkululeko-Freedom*, a mimeographed journal. The South African press reported distribution of the latter at a time of the recent Natal strikes and also the clandestine circulation of Marxist literature, some of it in Xhosa translation.

The *African Communist* advertises the daily hour-long broadcasts from Lusaka of "Radio Freedom, the Voice of the ANC," whose broadcasts to South Africa (over transmitters provided in 1973 by the Chinese) are in four vernaculars, English, and Afrikaans (*African Review*, March 1974, pp. 1-3).

City College of New York   Thomas Karis

Sudan

The Sudanese Communist Party (SCP) traces its origins to 1944, although it was not until 1947 that communists formed a political party, the Sudanese Movement for National Liberation, with 'Abd al-Khaliq Mahjub as its secretary-general. The SCP as it was later named, operated clanestinely at times, and at times in relative freedom. Some of its members were elected as representatives to the national legislature. It gradually became a focal point of opposition, successfully infiltrating a number of professional, student, and labor groups. Implication in the abortive coup d'état of 19 July 1971 led to severe repression of the party (see *YICA, 1972*, pp. 290-292). Numerous SCP leaders were executed, including Mahjub. Thousands of party members were arrested and held without trial.

No reliable figures exist concerning present SCP membership which before the 1971 coup was estimated at 5,000 to 10,000 active members. An undisclosed number are continuing party activities in exile or clandestinely within Sudan.

Leadership and Organization. Names of party leaders have carefully been withheld from statements issued by the SCP. The leading figure is believed to be Muhammad Ibrahim Nuqud, who is in exile. Other leading personalities include Dr. 'Izz al-Din 'Ali Amir, Mahjub 'Uthman, Ibrahim Zakariya and al-Fayjani al-Tayyib. Several SCP leaders who fed from Khartoum in 1971 returned to Sudan in 1974. 'Uthman and al-Tayyib were listed as being among the SCP leaders taken into custody upon their arrival in Khartoum (*FBIS*, 8 October).

Domestic Views and Activities. In mid-December 1973 some students at Khartoum University declared a sit-in strike to achieve various university-oriented political objectives. The SCP reportedly was one of the political parties represented in the committee which organized the strike. (Iraqi News Agency, in *FBIS*, 13 December 1973.) Reports from Khartoum also indicated that the SCP had been behind demonstrations in the spring protesting the rising cost of living. Though its operations are necessarily clandestine the SCP is said to have reorganized and strengthened its presence in many provincial towns. According to a Lebanese journal, "the party is aiming at the formation of a wide front which would embrace all other parties hostile to the Numairi regime, with a platform based on the question of democratic liberties" (*An-Nahar Arab Report*, Beirut, 11 March 1974). Some believe that this concept of a united opposition came closer to realization through the visit of Libya's Premier Jalloud to the Soviet Union. This event was thought to have lessened the hostility between the pro-Libyan Nasserites of the Sudan and the SCP. Other reports, close to the Lebanese Communist Party, state that the SCP has entirely reconstituted its trade union organization and that this organization was largely responsible for the almost daily strikes staged in the fall in diverse economic sectors protesting a new tax (ibid., 4 November).

The statement issued by the Central Committee of the SCP on the third anniversary of the 1971 coup was clear evidence of the continued existence of the party. The statement called for an alliance of the popular movement and the democratic forces in the army to renew revolutionary efforts and eliminate the existing regime. It listed four goals: (1) to free civilians and soldiers imprisoned after the July 1971 events, (2) to have those workers who had been laid off from their jobs reinstated and to halt similar layoffs, (3) to free all political prisoners and ban precautionary arrest, and (4) to publish the trials of the "martyrs" of the 1971 revolution. The SCP claimed credit for successfully influencing the army officers to disobey orders to fire on demonstrators during disturbances in September 1973. The Central Committee declared that suppression of the SCP would not discourage the party, but rather would draw it together. The SCP does not seek to work within the Sudanese political system, since the "reemergence of Numairi left no room for peace and compromise." (*al-Hadaf*, Beirut, 3 August.)

Sudanese President Ja'far Numairi has not publicly recognized the apparent revival of the SCP. In an interview in November he declared that there was no opposition to his regime, "neither strong nor weak." He said that the communists had lost most of their bases in Sudan. In regard to his own attitudes, he stated: "The conflict between myself and the communists has reached the extent where there will not be communism or communists in Sudan . . . as long as I am in power." (*Arab World*, Beirut, 15 November.)

International Views and Activities. The SCP follows a pro-Soviet line, but seems to have made no significant statements regarding international politics.

Stanford, California   Patricia Nabti

Syria

The Syrian Communist Party (al-Hizb al-Shuyu'i al-Suri; SCP) is an offshoot of the Lebanese Communist Party (LCP), which was established in 1924 (see *Lebanon*). Under the French mandate all communist activity was proscribed in 1939. This ban was continued after Syria gained independence in 1944, when the separate SCP was formed. Despite illegality, the SCP has enjoyed several periods of considerable political freedom. The last began in 1966 when a communist was named to a cabinet post for the first time. The communist position improved even further after the bloodless coup of Lieutenant General Hafiz al-Asad in November 1970. As a result of changes brought about by al-Asad, two cabinet posts have been held by communists since 1971. In March 1972 the SCP gained de facto legality through its participation in the "National Progressive Front" formed by al-Asad. Plagued with internal dispute since early 1971, the SCP finally split into two parties in December 1973 (see *YICA, 1974* pp. 269-70).

Combined membership in the SCP is believed to range between 3,000 and 4,000. The population of Syria is 6,680,000 (estimated 1972).

Leadership and Internal Affairs. The two communist parties which resulted from the split late in 1973 both identify themselves as the SCP. For convenience they are here designated the Bakdash-SCP (B-SCP) and the Turk-SCP (T-SCP). The B-SCP is led by Khalid Bakdash, a Syrian Kurd who has been secretary-general of the SCP—except for a brief period in 1968—since the inception of the party. The B-SCP held its Fourth Congress on 26-28 September 1974 after two postponements occasioned by its lack of unity. Reportedly 170 members attended. Bakdash was reelected as secretary-general and Yusuf Faisal, who had been a leader of the dissidents, as deputy secretary-general, a new post created by the Congress. Elected to the new ten-member Politburo were: Bakdash; three former dissidents—Daniel Ni'mah, Dhahir 'Abd al-Samad, and Ibrahim Bakri; and five new members—Murad Yusuf, Ramu Shaikhu, 'Umar Siba'i, Maurice Salibi, and Khalid Hammami. Siba'i is minister of communications and Samad is minister of state in the Syrian cabinet, which so far only recognizes the B-SCP. Bakdash and Ni'mah are the SCP representatives in the National Progressive Front. The congress received greetings from 42 foreign communist parties. Leaders of the rival T-SCP were officially expelled from the party.

The T-SCP held its Fourth Congress at the end of December 1973. The Central Committee which was formed at that time met in January 1974 and elected a Politburo comprised of Riyad al-Turk, first secretary of the party; Badr al-Tawil, 'Umar Qashshash, Wasil Faisal, and Yusuf Nimr, Secretariat members; and Ahmad Fayiz al-Fawwaz, Michel Jirji 'Isa and Nuri Rifa'i.

Domestic Views and Activities. In an interview in April 1974, Yusuf Faisal outlined some of the domestic goals of the B-SCP. These included strengthening the role of the working class and of the peasantry, expanding the public sector of the economy, and struggling against foreign monopolies (*FBIS*, 10 April). A Central Committee·statement outlining the accomplishments of the SCP on its fiftieth anniversary claimed that the party had "invariably fought against all military dictatorships and for greater democratic freedoms for the workers, peasants, intellectuals and other working people," had always opposed every form of national or religious segregation and had supported women's rights (*IB*, no. 14, 1974).

When the Soviet Union stepped up military aid to Syria in the spring, it was said to have imposed a condition demanded by the B-SCP, that disengagement with Israel should not involve any change in the social or political make-up of the Syrian government. A subsequent statement by the B-SCP Central Committee on April 19 denounced the "rightist tendency" in Syria which threatened "progressive gains" and might lead Syria to imitate the example of Egypt. (*An-Nahar Arab Report*, Beirut, 29 April). In September, the Fourth Congress reaffirmed its commitment to work toward strengthening the Syrian government and the national front and to develop greater cooperation with the ruling Ba'th Party (*Pravda*, 22 October, in *FBIS*, 1 November).

While the T-SCP has not issued any significant statements regarding domestic issues, one of the reasons for the split was the dissidents' rejection of Soviet domination of the SCP, particularly in domestic matters. T-SCP first secretary al-Turk declared: "We refuse the claim that our Soviet comrades know about our country's conditions better than we do" (*Arab World Weekly*, Beirut, 12 January).

The SCP and the Arab World. The SCP was also split by the Arab-Israeli conflict. In harmony with Soviet policy, the B-SCP has endorsed U.N. Resolution 338 calling for a cease-fire in the October war and the implementation of Resolution 242. It affirms two prerequisites to peace—the liberation of all occupied territories and the securing of the rights of the Palestinian people—and maintains that these objectives can be achieved only in cooperation with the Soviet Union. The party supports Syrian participation in the Geneva conference with the goal of achieving a total solution to the conflict. In a statement on the fiftieth anniversary of the SCP, Bakdash deplored the Zionists' obvious attempts to postpone or foil the Geneva conference and to drag the Arab countries into individual half-solutions which are outside the comprehensive settlement of the issue (*FBIS*, 1 November). A resolution of the Fourth Congress of the B-SCP hailed the October war as a war of liberation, that had increased the Arab peoples' self-confidence, dispelled the myth of the invincibility of the Israeli army, increased Israel's international isolation and domestic crises, and showed the superiority of Soviet arms. The conflict also provided "clear proof of the falsehood of the illusions which tried to draw a line between U.S. imperialism on the one side and Israel and Zionism on the other (*An-Nahar*, Beirut, 5 October). The party claims to have lost more than 85 members in the October war.

The dissident T-SCP rejects moderation in regard to the conflict with Israel. It repudiates Soviet policy in the Middle East, denounces U.S. Resolution 242, and advocates the destruction of Israel. In addition, it bitterly criticizes the Soviet Union for having recognized Israel in 1948.

In regard to other Arab issues, the T-SCP advocates establishing a united Arab communist party, rather than maintaining parties confined to national boundaries. This it believes would pave the way for one of its goals—the eventual unity of the Arab world. In contrast, the B-SCP does not support a unified Arab communist party or Arab unity without preconditions (*Arab World Weekly*, 12 January). It does, however, advocate cooperation of Arab communist parties. Thus in February leaders of the B-SCP met with a delegation of the Iraqi Communist Party in Baghdad. The two parties stressed the identity of their views on the need to use political and other means to achieve an Israeli withdrawal from occupied Arab territories and secure the rights of the Palestinian people. At the same time, the parties stressed the need to strengthen the ties between the countries and governments of Syria and Iraq (*An-Nahar Arab Report*. 4 March).

International Views and Activities. Policy-making within the B-SCP is dominated by the Soviet Union. On numerous occasions during 1974 the party praised Soviet contributions to Arab success in the October war, Soviet military and developmental aid to Syria, and Soviet support and guidance to the party itself. In its April resolution the Central Committee reaffirmed its condemnation of Maoism. In June in accord with a recently adopted party decision, the SCP members in the Syrian cabinet and the National Front refused to participate in the reception for U.S. President Richard Nixon during his visit to Syria. The congress in September expressed support for an international congress of communist and workers' parties. The congress also declared solidarity with the communists and democrats in Chile and Uruguay and with the Cypriot people. (*FBIS*, 2 October.)

By its independent stance, the T-SCP may have created a precedent for other Arab communist parties. However, at present its position has assured its isolation from most of the communist parties of the world. Only the Yugoslav press has taken a somewhat sympathetic position toward it. The T-SCP apparently has so far been preoccupied with domestic and Arab issues and has issued no significant statements regarding other international concerns.

Publications. The party organ of the B-SCP is the semi-monthly newspaper *Nidal al-Sha'b* ("People's Struggle"). The paper is officially banned, but it has been circulated freely since the party joined the National Progressive Front. The party disseminates most of its news through the two legal publications of the Lebanese Communist Party, *al-Nida'* and *al-Akhbar*.

Stanford, California   Patricia Nabti

INTERNATIONAL COMMUNIST FRONT ORGANIZATIONS

International Communist Front Organizations

International communist front organizations of the post-World War II period represent an expansion and rebirth of identical movements originally established by the Third (Communist) International. During the years 1919-1923, seven such groups were launched for the purpose of mobilizing non-communists in broad "civic support" for communist aims and causes. Two of them disintegrated in the early 1930's due to lack of membership. The remaining five were dissolved by Moscow in order not to interfere with the "popular front" tactics of the mid-1930's by communist parties in particular countries. Finally, in 1943 Stalin liquidated the Third International as evidence of the Soviet Union's alleged intention not to interfere in the internal affairs of foreign countries through Moscow-directed communist organizations.

After 1945, when the communist movement in Europe emerged as a strong force which had opposed nazism and fascism, communists infiltrated national civic and professional associations. When representatives of these groups began to form international organizations, communists were able to obtain influential positions on their executive bodies. By the time of the Prague coup in February 1948, the communists dominated ten of the more important among these international organizations and accepted direction from Moscow. Thus, they became fronts supporting the policies of the Soviet Union through mobilization of various segments of society on a world-wide basis. Many non-communists, unable to restore these organizations to their former aims and goals, left the communist-dominated international fronts.

The international communist front organizations have continued to operate with the avowed purpose of aiding the various segments of society that each group most clearly reflects in its name and operational characteristics. The World Federation of Trade Unions works with labor, the International Union of Students with student groups, and so on. In reality, however, the aim of each of these fronts has been and continues to be to support the policies of the Soviet Union through the mobilization of various segments of society. Indeed, these efforts have been carried to the point where even the internal and ideological disputes within the communist camp found their reflection in front activities. The most striking example of this condition is the withdrawal of the People's Republic of China from all involvement with these organizations.

Afro-Asian Peoples' Solidarity Organization. The Afro-Asian Peoples' Solidarity Organization (AAPSO) was set up in Cairo in1958 as an "anti-colonial" off-shoot of the World Peace Council (WPC; see below). During the first few years of its existence it was jointly controlled by the Soviet Union, China and the United Arab Republic. The Sino-Soviet dispute led to disruption of AAPSO conferences in Moshi, Tanzania, in February 1963, and Winneba, Ghana, in May 1965, and finally to a split in the organization following the WPC meeting in Nicosia, Cyprus, in February 1967. The

Chinese boycotted the Nicosia meeting, which decided to hold the fifth AAPSO conference in Algiers in 1967 rather than in Peking as originally planned. Since then, Soviet domination of the AAPSO has continued.

Structure and Leadership. From the AAPSO's inception, its organizational structure has been relatively loose. Although Congress and Council meetings have been held during this period, in a practical sense the Secretariat has been the key organizational unit. At the 11th Council meeting, March 1974, a Presidium was established. It would appear that the Presidium will now bear primary responsibility along with the Secretariat for the development and execution of AAPSO policy.

Yusuf el-Sebai, the AAPSO's secretary-general since its foundation, was reelected to that position at the 11th Council. He was also elected chairman (president) of the Presidium. Since Yusuf el-Sebai is secretary-general not only of AAPSO but also fo AAWPB-Cairo (see below), these two organizations have in effect an "overlapping directorate." Additional linkages are noticeable if the AAPSO and AAWPB-Cairo are juxtaposed: both are headquartered in Cairo and both focus on problems of the same geographical area and thus to an extent have analogous functions. The AAPSO at present appears to be the most active and important of the two organizations.

Views and Activities. The AAPSO Secretariat meeting in Cairo in December 1973 discussed two forthcoming international conferences to be held in Baghdad: an "International Conference for Solidarity with the National Liberation Movements in the Arab Gulf and Arabian Peninsula," and an "Afro-Asian Women's Conference" (*Baghdad Observer*, 16 January 1974). Shortly after the Secretariat met, Aziz Sharif, secretary-general of the Iraqi Council for Peace and Solidarity, announced that 82 organizations from almost 100 countries would attend the 11th Council session, scheduled for late March. Between mid-January 1974 and the opening of the Council several preparatory meetings were held, the most important of which took place in Cairo the latter part of January (TASS, 14 January; Baghdad radio, 26-29 January). Prior to the Council meeting the Soviet Committee for Afro-Asian Solidarity and the Iraqi National Council for Peace and Solidarity issued a statement indicating that "there exists an identity of views on all matters" regarding the Council agenda (Iraqi News Agency, 4 February).

The 11th Council, held in Baghdad on 23-27 March, was attended by some 400 delegates representing 79 "world solidarity organizations and liberation movements" in 67 countries. The opening address was delivered by President Bakr of Iraq; messages of congratulations were received from a number of communist party leaders including Brezhnev (U.S.S.R.), Ceauşescu (Romania), Zhivkov (Bulgaria), and Honecker (German Democratic Republic). Brezhnev's message contained warm greetings to the participants and declared that the AAPSO's "fruitful activities" were "helping to mobilize public forces in Asia and Africa to deal with the current problems of national liberation and social progress." In looking to the future, Brezhnev stressed that "favorable conditions" are now arising for solving the historic problems facing the people of Asia and Africa, and that the socialist countries, which are the "natural allies" of the Afro-Asian peoples, will give total support to the resolution of these problems. The Soviet Union, he said, has given and will give all-round support to the movement of the Afro-Asian peoples for national liberation. (TASS, 23 March; ADN, East German news agency, 22 March.) In his main report, Yusuf el-Sebai condemned the "aggressive policy" of the "imperialist powers" and praised the important contribution of the World Congress of Peace Forces held in Moscow, October 1973; he then pointed to several issues which he considered critical—the need for the Soviet-proposed collective security system for Asia, Iran's aggression against Iraq, the Palestine question, and potential conflict in the Persian Gulf—and to general problems facing Asia and Africa (Iraqi News Agency, 24-25 March).

Resolutions adopted at the Council meeting condemned Iranian military aggression against Iraq; affirmed that the Palestine revolution was an indivisible part of the Arab and world liberation movement, demanded withdrawal of Israeli troops from Arab lands, spoke against Saudi influence in North Yemen, called for a collective security treaty in Asia, and urged the liquidation of foreign bases in the Indian Ocean (Baghdad radio, 27 March; TASS, 27-29 March). The AAPSO Working Program for 1974-75 included numberous seminars and conferences, among them an international seminar on the "Indian Ocean peace area," an international seminar on training national cadres in the developing areas, and a conference of Mediterranean states to draw up a program of peace in that area (Iraqi News Agency, 28 March).

The Council elected Aziz Sharif (Iraq) as deputy secretary-general, and Vasco-Cabral (Guinea-Bissau) and Vassos Lyssarides (Cyprus) as vice-presidents. New affiliates entering the AAPSO at the Council were the Council of Solidarity and Peace (Ghana), the National and Liberation Congress (Swaziland), the Social Development Movement of Black Africa (MESAN), the Afro-Asian Solidarity Committee (Upper Volta), and the Democratic Party of Botswana. (Ibid., 28 March.)

Shortly after the meeting an AAPSO delegation led by Aziz Sharif attended the 6th special session of the U.N. General Assembly on Raw Materials and Development. In an interview with U.N. secretary-general Kurt Waldheim, Sharif urged the elimination of colonial and racist regimes in Africa. Throughout its visit, the delegation firmly stressed the need for independence, equality, and social progress for the developing areas. (TASS, 26 April.)

In early June, the AAPSO held a seminar in Hungary on "The Role and Significance of Progressive Forces in the Anti-Imperialist Struggle and for Social Advancement." As the seminar ended, several participants spoke out on the impact of the fall of the Caetano regime in Portugal. All agreed that change would occur in Africa, and that the Portuguese colonies should win full independence. (*MTI*, Hungarian news agency, 12 June.)

An "Emergency Conference on Cyprus" took place in Cairo in late July, sponsored by AAPSO and attended by representatives from liberation movements and a number of international organizations. The conference issued a statement condemning the 15 July coup in Cyprus. It also indicated its approval of the support given Makarios by all non-aligned and socialist countries, and emphasized its objection to the partition of the island. (Cairo radio, 29 July.)

In late September, members of AAPSO attended a Soviet-sponsored meeting in Samarkand where they gave full support to the Soviet proposal for a collective security treaty for Asia (*Izvestiya*, 29 September). The main document adopted by the more than 30 Afro-Asian Solidarity Committees represented at the meeting reflected an emphasis on "cooperation": renunciation of the use of force, respect for sovereignty and territorial integrity, and non-interference in internal affairs were all seen as "in line with the aspirations of all Asian peoples and states (*Pravda*, 1 October). The first secretary of the communist party of the Uzbek S.S.R. criticized the Chinese leaders for their "hegemonic ambitions" in Asia and accused them of "working with the imperialists" against collective security in the region (Moscow radio, 26 September). From Albania came a comment that the conference was "another effort of the Kremlin clique to advertise the plan proposed by Brezhnev for the creation of the so-called system of collective security" (ATA, Albanian news agency, 26 September).

Afro-Asian Writers' Permanent Bureau. The Afro-Asian Writers' Permanent Bureau (AAWPB) was originally set up by the Soviets at an "Afro-Asian Writers' Conference" in Tashkent in October 1958. Following a second conference, in Cairo, February 1962, a "Permanent Bureau" was established with headquarters in Colombo, Ceylon. The Chinese communists gained control of the organization at a meeting of its Executive Committee in Bali, Indonesia, in July 1963, and established a new Executive Secretariat in Peking on 15 August 1966. Thus, while the AAWPB is still officially based in Colombo, it operates exclusively from Peking. A pro-Soviet faction—the AAWPB-Cairo—broke away after the Chinese began to dominate the organization. The AAWPB-Peking, which has not yet held a third conference, appears to have no activities outside its irregular publication, *The Call*, and occasional statements carried by the New China News Agency.

The AAWPB-Cairo. The pro-Soviet faction of the AAWPB was founded on 19-21 June 1966 at an "extraordinary meeting" attended by delegations from Cameroun, Ceylon, India, Sudan, the Soviet Union, and the U.A.R. Its relatively successful "Third Afro-Asian Writers' Conference," held in Beirut in 1967 and attended by some 150 delegates from 42 countries, was the first serious blow to the pro-Chinese AAWPB. Since then, the pro-Soviet organization appears to have consolidated and augmented its base of support.

The secretary-general of the AAWPB-Cairo is Yusuf el-Sebai (Egypt), who is also secretary-general of the Afro-Asian Peoples' Solidarity Organization and a member of the Presidential Committee of the World Peace Council. The assistant secretary-general is Edward el-Kharat (Egypt). The AAWPB-Cairo has a 10-member Permanent Bureau, with members from India, Japan, Lebanon, Mongolia, the Portuguese colonies, Senegal, South Africa, the Soviet Union, Sudan, and Egypt. There is also a 30-member Executive Committee.

The AAWPB-Cairo Permanent Bureau meeting in Cairo on 9-10 January 1974 decided to set up a publishing house for Afro-Asian publications. Tentative plans were also discussed for a second Bureau meeting in Moscow in the summer and a seminar on Afro-Asian literary magazines. (*Rose-el-Yussef*, Cairo, 14 January.)

AAWPB-Peking. The pro-Chinese AAWPB, the continuation of the original body, is led by Frederik L. Risakotta (Indonesia), a member of the Peking-based Delegation of the Communist Party of Indonesia's Central Committee, who is identified as "acting head ad interim" of the AAWPB Secretariat. (The former secretary-general, Rathe Deshapriya Sananayake, returned to his native Ceylon in mid-1968; Kinkazu Saionji, who was identified in April 1970 by the New China News Agency as "acting head ad interim," returned home to Japan the following August.) The AAWPB-Peking claim of affiliates in some 40 countries probably includes individual as well as organizational memberships.

Publications. The main organ of AAWPB-Cairo is a "literature, arts and sociopolitical quarterly," *Lotus* (formerly *Afro-Asian Literature*), which appears in English, French, and Arabic editions. In addition, books by various "Afro-Asian men of letters" have been published by AAWPB-Cairo in the Soviet Union.

The AAWPB-Peking bulletin, *The Call*, is issued from Peking at irregular intervals in English, French, and Arabic.

International Association of Democratic Lawyers. The International Association of Democratic Lawyers (IADL) was founded at an "International Congress of Jurists" held in Paris in October 1946 under the auspices of a para-communist organization, the Mouvement National Judiciaire and attended by lawyers from 25 countries. Although the movement originally included elements of various political orientations, the leading role was played by leftist French lawyers, and by 1949 most non-communists had resigned. The IADL was originally based in Paris but was expelled by the French government in 1950. It then moved to Brussels, where it remains; some organizational work has also been carried out from Warsaw.

Membership is open to lawyers' organizations or groups and to individual lawyers, and may be on a "corresponding," "donation," or "permanent" basis. Lawyers holding membership through organizations or individually are estimated to number about 25,000. The IADL claims to be supported by membership fees and donations; no details of its finances are published.

The IADL holds consultative status Category C, with the U.N. Economic and Social Council.

Structure and Leadership. The highest organ of the IADL is the Congress, in which each member organization is represented. There have been nine congresses to date, the latest in Helsinki in July 1970. The Congress elects the IADL Council, which is supposed to meet yearly and consists of the Bureau, the Secretariat, and a representative of each member organization. The leadership in 1974 remained unchanged from the previous year with Pierre Cot (France) as president and Joë Nordmann (France) as secretary-general.

Views and Activities. The latest IADL Congress, the ninth, took place in 1970. In January 1974 representatives of lawyers' organizations from Eastern Europe met in Warsaw to discuss the next Congress, but no decision was reached as to either time or place (PAP, Polish news agency, 30 January).

During the latter part of January, 150 lawyers from 18 European and African countries plus representatives from international organizations such as the WFTU (see below) gathered in Paris to discuss problems affecting migrant workers in Europe. Several specific resolutions were adopted dealing with employment, living conditions, trade union rights, and conditions for residence. The general resolution called for immigration policies that respected the principles of the Universal Declaration of Human Rights (WFTU *Flashes*, no. 6, 1974).

The IADL continued its investigations in Spain on behalf of those it considered jailed for political reasons. Several members of the IADL were in attendance at "political" trials held in 1973 in both Barcelona and Burgos. In the spring of 1974 two of these "investigators" led a debate at the Brussels Free University on "Struggle and Repression in Spain." (*L'Humanité*, Paris, 12 December, 1973; *Le Soir*, Brussels, 17-18 March, 1974.)

Two hundred lawyers attended the first "Inter-American Conference on the Legal Aspects of Economic Independence" in Lima in June. The conference decided to set up an inter-American legal body to coordinate the tasks of the IADL in that part of the world (*Granma*, Havana, 18 June).

Expressions of deep concern over the political situation in Chile were repeatedly issued by the IADL. In each case the organization denounced the "reactionary forces" and called for support of those Chileans working for "genuine democracy" (TASS, 13 September). Two IADL members, from Belgium and Argentina, visited Chile in the spring and subsequently presented at a meeting in Buenos Aires a report on the problems facing the Chilean people (*Nuestra Palabra*, Buenos Aires, 1 May). In a joint protest, the IADL and the International Movement of Catholic Lawyers demanded of the Conference of Latin American Foreign Ministers that action be taken against the military junta in Chile (*Neues Deutschland*, East Berlin, 24 February).

Like other front organizations, the IADL strongly backed the Arabs in their struggle against Israel. Particular attention was given to the "oppression" practiced by the Israelis against Arabs living in occupied lands. Typical of the statements issued was one released late in the summer: "The association is lodging a protest at the arbitrariness of the Israeli authorities and is calling on the international inquiry commission to send its representatives to Sarafand camp to familiarize themselves with the position of the political prisoners. This is the more necessary as the Israeli authorities lately intensified their repressions against different sections of Palestinians and in particular against the members of the Palestinian national front." (TASS, 8 July.)

Publications. The IADL's two principal publications are the *Review of Contemporary Law* and the *Information Bulletin*, which appear irregularly in English and French. The IADL also issues pamphlets on questions of topical interest.

International Federation of Resistance Fighters. The International Federation of Resistance Fighters (Fédération Internationale des Résistants; FIR) was founded in 1951 in Vienna as the successor to the International Federation of Former Political Prisoners (Fédération Internationale des Anciens Prisonniers Politiques). With the name change, membership eligibility was widened to include former partisans and resistance fighters, and all victims of Nazism and fascism and their descendants.

In 1959 the FIR had a membership of four million; no recent figures have been announced. On its twentieth anniversary, in 1971, the FIR claimed affiliated groups and representation in every country of Europe (*Resistance unie*, no. 14). The headquarters is in Vienna; a small secretariat is maintained in Paris. In 1972 the FIR was granted Category B status with the U.N. Economic and Social Council (ECOSOC).

Structure and Leadership. The organs of the FIR are the Congress, General Council, Bureau, and Secretariat. Until the Sixth Congress (Venice, 1969), the Congress was convened every three years. It was then decided that this body should meet every four years. The Congress elects the FIR president, vice-presidents, and members of the Bureau, and determines and ratifies members of the General Council after they have been nominated by national associations. The General Council is supposed to meet at least once a year. The Bureau supervises the implementation of decisions reached by the Congress and General Council; it is also responsible for the budget, and from among its members it elects the Secretariat.

Arialdo Banfi (Italy) has been FIR president since 1965. At the Seventh Congress, Paris, November 1973, Alex Lhote (France) replaced Jean Toujas as secretary-general and Henryk Korotynski (Poland) replaced Gustav Alef-Bolkowiak as deputy secretary-general. Vice-presidents elected or re-elected at the Congress were: Gerassimos Avgheropoulos (Greece), Jacques Debu-Bridel (France), Mme André De Raet (Belgium), Dimo Ditchev (Bulgaria), Otto Funke (East Germany), Nicolae Guina (Romania), Helge Kierulff (Denmark), Franciszek Ksiezarczyk (Poland), Alexei Maressiev (U.S.S.R.), Jaroslav Masek (Czechoslovakia), Mimaly Padanyi (Hungary), Joseph Rossaint (West Germany), Ludwig Soswinski (Austria), Umberto Terracini (Italy), and Pierre Villon (France). (For a list of Bureau members see *Der Widerstandskampfer*, no. 24, October 1973; for additional information on the leadership see *YICA, 1972*, p. 613).

Views and Activities. Three hundred delegates from 22 countries gathered in Paris in November 1973 for the FIR's Seventh Congress. Messages of congratulations were received from numerous public officials including Willi Stoph and Horst Sindermann of the East German government. Banfi spoke of the need for disarmament and reviewed his talks in October with the World Veterans' Federation (WVF). Several members called for full solidarity with imprisoned anti-fascists in Spain, Greece, and Chile. The Action Program adopted at the congress urged cooperation between resistance fighters and servicemen of all political views, advocated closer contacts with the WVF, and demanded a "peaceful" Europe. (ADN, East Berlin, 26 November; *L'Humanité*, Paris, 27-28 November.)

Shortly after the congress, an FIR delegation comprising new secretary-general Lhote, outgoing secretary-general Toujas, and treasurer T. Heinisch, held discussions in Paris with leading officials of the WVF. At the same time, new deputy secretary-general H. Korotynski and secretary G. Gaddi met in Geneva with the ECOSOC Special Committee on Disarmament and the secretary-general of the WVF to review problems relating to disarmament (*Informationsdienst*, no. 3).

The Presidium, with five vice-presidents and members of the secretariat, met on 7 February to implement the decisions reached at the congress. This meeting discussed measures to strengthen cooperation with all groups within the resistance movement, and actions for peace and security and against fascism and war criminals. The campaign for disarmament was placed in the forefront of future activities: the ECOSOC World Week for Disarmament was to be vigorously supported and a symposium on disarmament, co-sponsored with the WVF, was planned. Finally, the Presidium urged the FIR to inform all young people of the ideals of the resistance movement. (MTI, 6 February; *Informationsdienst*, no. 3.)

An FIR statement described the overthrow of the Caetano regime in Portugal as a victory against fascism and a step toward détente in Europe (*L'Humanité*, 31 May). Several protests were issued condemning the military junta in Chile (*Informationsdienst*, no. 11). The FIR approved of the cease-fire arrived at on Cyprus (*Voix Ouvriere*, Geneva, 3 August).

Publications. The FIR publishes a journal in French and German, *Resistance unie* and *Widerstandskampfer*. News reports are also disseminated occasionally through the French-language *Service d'Information de la FIR* and its German counterpart, *Informationsdienst der FIR*.

International Organization of Journalists. The International Organization of Journalists (IOJ) was founded in June 1946 in Copenhagen. Merging with it at that time were the International Federation of Journalists (IFJ) and the International Federation of Journalists of Allied and Free Countries. By 1952 all non-communist unions had withdrawn in order to refound the IFJ. Since 1955 the IOJ has made unsuccessful overtures to the IFJ for cooperation and for eventually forming a new world organization of journalists. It was for the purpose of bridging differences with the IFJ that the IOJ in 1955 founded the International Committee for Cooperation of Journalists (ICCJ). No IFJ member is known to have affiliated with the ICCJ—perhaps because most ICCJ officers are also leading members of the parent IOJ. The IOJ headquarters, originally in London, was moved to Prague in 1947.

In 1963 pro-Chinese journalists established a rival organization, the Afro-Asian Journalists' Association (AAJA; see below).

The IOJ was awarded consultative and information Category B status with UNESCO in 1969. It also holds consultative status, Category II, with the U.N. Economic and Social Council.

Structure and Leadership. National unions and groups are eligible for membership in the IOJ, as are also individual journalists. The organization has claimed to have some 150,000 members, representing 67 organizations in 58 countries (TASS, 14 June 1971).

The highest IOJ body is the Congress, which is supposed to meet every four years. The Congress elects the Executive Committee, made up of the Presidium (president, vice-president, and secretary-general), other officers (secretaries and treasurer), and ordinary members. Present leaders, elected by the 1971 Congress, include Jean-Maurice Hermann (France), president, and Jiří Kubka (Czechoslovakia), secretary-general (for other leaders and details on structure see *YICA, 1972*, pp. 615-16).

Views and Activities. The activities of the IOJ during 1974 were rather limited, with the primary focus apparently on Latin America. The Executive Committee meeting of September 1973 in Baghdad decided to establish a regional organization in Latin America, called the Latin American Information Center, or CIPAL, which was officially set up in April 1974 in Lima, Peru. The Center is supported by two Peruvian groups of journalists: the National Association of Journalists and the Federation of Journalists. Two immediate tasks were given the Center: the sponsorship of a Latin American journalists' seminar to seek solidarity on behalf of persecuted Chilean journalists, and a meeting of journalists in Ayacucho to celebrate the Battle of Ayacucho (*Expreso*, Lima, 29 January). In a more general sense, the Center is charged with coordinating trade union activities of Latin American journalists, publicizing the progress made by the Peruvian revolution, and developing support for journalists persecuted by anti-populist governments in Latin America (*Unidad*, Lima, 30 April).

Throughout its history, one of the most important aspects of the IOJ's work has been the training of journalists from the developing areas. Most of this training takes place in Eastern Europe. In January 1974 a six months' course opened in Budapest with 16 trainees in attendance, four from Ghana and the others from Iraq, Bangladesh, India, and Egypt (Ghana News Agency, 18 January; MTI, 25 January). In East Germany, the Association of Journalists' "School of Solidarity" held a similar six months' program for 21 journalists from Afro-Asian countries (ADN, 10 July). The next training course was scheduled for Budapest in November (MTI, 1 June).

The IOJ, like other fronts, continued its open opposition to the Chilean junta. Posters and a booklet, *Chile-September, 1973*, appeared in March in both Spanish and English (CTK, Czechoslovak news agency, 25 March). On 10 September, during the "world week of solidarity with Chile," the IOJ issued a statement aligning itself with a world-wide campaign against oppression in Chile.

Late in the spring secretary-general Kubka and two secretaries, H. Brauer and Juan Alvarez, visited Vietnam. While in North Vietnam they signed a special protocol on assistance for Vietnamese journalists and the broadening of bilateral cooperation (Vietnam News Agency, 7 May). Returning from Vietnam, they stopped in India and Bangladesh and talked with representatives of the Indian Federation of Working Journalists and the Bangladesh Federal Union of Journalists. All these discussions served as preparations for the Presidium meeting planned for the fall in Ulan Bator. (*Journalists' Affairs*, no. 11-13.)

In a series of statements dealing with international problems, the IOJ condemned the coup in Cyprus and asked that the situation be resolved on the basis of the recent U.N. resolution (CTK, 17 July), welcomed the granting of autonomy to the Kurds in Iraq (*Baghdad Observer*, 1 April), protested the persecution of "democratic forces" in South Korea (CTK, 31 May), and denounced acts of repression in Uruguay (ibid., 14 May).

Publications. The IOJ issues a monthly journal, the *Democratic Journalist*, in English, French, Russian, and Spanish. The IOJ's *Information Bulletin* apparently is no longer published. A new fortnightly publication, *Journalists' Affairs*, is being distributed in English, French, Spanish, and Russian.

The AAJA. The Afro-Asian Journalists' Association was set up in Djakarta in April 1963 with an Afro-Asian Press Bureau and a permanent Secretariat. Until the attempted communist coup in Indonesia (1965), the AAJA appeared to represent a possibly serious rival to the pro-Soviet IOJ, particularly in developing countries. At that juncture, AAJA headquarters were "temporarily" moved to Peking. Djawoto, the AAJA's Indonesian secretary-general, who was dismissed from his post as Indonesia's ambassador to China, has since headed the Secretariat in Peking, which has become the permanent seat of AAJA operations.

There is no indication that the AAJA has succeeded in winning over the allegiance of IOJ members or member organizations. Few journalists' organizations and governments have expressed open support for the AAJA or indicated that they would send delegates to an eventual AAJA conference. The AAJA devotes its energies mainly to propagating the Chinese line in international political affairs.

The AAJA's main publication, *Afro-Asian Journalist*, appears irregularly. Pamphlets on topical issues are published from time to time.

International Union of Students. The International Union of Students (IUS) was founded in August 1946 at a congress in Prague attended by students of varying political persuasions. This diversity of views lasted until 1951, when most of the non-communist students unions disaffiliated because of the IUS's domination by pro-Soviet groups. The 1960s were marked by bitter debates between pro-Soviet and pro-Chinese students. In the middle 1960s China withdrew from active participation.

The IUS has consultative Category C Status with UNESCO; applications for Category B status have been repeatedly deferred.

Structure and Leadership. The highest governing body of the IUS is its Congress. Constitutional amendments approved by the Tenth Congress (Bratislava, January 1971) changed the requirements regarding the frequency that the Congress assembles from once every two years to once every three years. The terms of representation remain the same: each affiliate or associate organization is permitted to send delegates to the Congress. The Tenth Congress also changed the requirements pertaining to the Executive Committee. Previously it was to meet twice a year; now it meets merely once a year. The Congress elects the national unions to be represented on the Executive Committee; the national unions then determine which individual(s) will represent them. At the Eleventh Congress (Budapest, May 1974), the number of national unions represented on the Executive Committee was increased from 47 to 51. Representation in the Secretariat, which is part of the Executive Committee, was also expanded, from 23 to 34 unions. It is clear that the decreased frequency of Congress and Executive Committee meetings will indirectly increase the power of the Secretariat.

Throughout 1974 the same leadership remained: Dusan Ulcak (Czechoslovakia), president; Fathi Muhammad al-Fadl (Sudan), secretary-general.

Views and Activities. At the beginning of December 1973, the IUS Secretariat received an offer from the National Committee of Hungarian Student Organizations (NCHSO) to act as host for the Eleventh Congress. The Secretariat accepted the invitation, and thereafter began preparations for the event (*IUS News Service*, no. 1, 1974). Two articles in *World Student News* (no. 4, 1974), "Approaching the Congress," by the IUS president and "The IUS between Bratislava and Budapest: Events, Dates, Activities," provide an interesting and complete review of IUS activities between the Tenth and Eleventh Congresses. They do not, however, provide a clear picture of the specific objectives of the Eleventh Congress. Indeed, the host group, NCHSO, speaks only in broad generalities: the Congress will "contribute to the further growth of the anti-imperialist unity of progressive students, to the intensification of their struggle against imperialism, colonialism, neo-colonialism, exploitation and fascism, and to the strengthening of their fight for the reform of education, democracy and social progress" ("Hungarian Students Prepare for the 11th IUS Congress," ibid.). If one theme can be detected in the various preparatory speeches and articles it is "student solidarity." In a final preparatory action, the IUS sent delegations to Latin America and the Middle East to seek support for the Congress (*Mlada Fronta*, Prague, 14 March).

Assembled in Budapest for the Congress were 195 delegates and 170 observers, including representatives of national student unions from 70 member countries, observers from 40 other national youth and student bodies and 30 international organizations, along with guests and delegates from liberation movements. The IUS president opened the Congress; the first secretary of the Central Committee of the Hungarian Communist Youth League gave the keynote speech. On 4 May the Congress approved the agenda, which had been adopted at an Executive Committee meeting in Prague. On 8 May the Executive Committee reported on the IUS's work over the past three years. The fight against imperialism, and the struggles for social progress and a democratic educational system were cited as particularly important areas of activity. The report also stressed the growing unity of action of the student movement and the increasing effectiveness of IUS policy as shown by the fact that during the last three years a number of organizations had applied for membership. Of special significance, the report said, were the actions taken by the IUS to foster solidarity with the peoples of Chile, the Middle East, and Indochina. Eight commissions were set up at the Congress to discuss the following: solidarity with Chile, the Arab countries, and Indochina; the reform and democratization of education; international security and cooperation; student culture, press, tourism, and sport; the future IUS program; and the fight against colonialism and neo-colonialism. (Ibid., 6-14 May.)

The Congress approved 50 resolutions, statements, and other documents analyzing the results of IUS activities since its Tenth Congress, defining its tasks for the coming period, and dealing with a wide range of international student questions. The dominant feature was the proclamation citing the "correctness" of the policy of the IUS, which had been confirmed by the more than 27 years of the IUS's existence. The documents also confirmed the solidarity of the world student movement with the people of Chile, Indochina, and the Middle East, and indicated support for the liberation movements. Finally, the anti-imperialist struggle for peace, security, cooperation, and national independence was given full backing. In a final act, a telegram was sent to Chilean authorities demanding the release of Luis Corvalán and the restitution of democratic rights in that country. (Ibid., 16 May.) During the Congress, the Mandates Commission examined applications for membership from 11 student organizations and accepted 9 as full members (MTI, 11 May).

One note of criticism emerged. The Yugoslav delegation said that while the IUS was to be applauded for its various initiatives, it was also to be criticized for failing to allow members equal say in policy development. In this connection, it said, the Yugoslav delegation had proposed changes in the Statutes which would have improved the Union's activity; however, despite the considerable interest expressed by a great many delegations, the proposals had not been adopted. In concluding its remarks, the Yugoslav pressed for a more "just" regional representation in the IUS, and deplored the absence of the Chinese students' organization. (Tanyug, Yugoslav news agency, 12 May.)

As noted earlier, the Congress made some organizational changes. The extent to which these changes are really significant is in debate, for there are those who argue that all power will continue to reside in the Secretariat, which is controlled by the Soviets. For example, it is claimed that only between a third and a half of the organizations elected to the Secretariat appoint representatives to the offices in Prague. This means that the communist countries, all of which normally are included in the Secretariat and all of which have high-level representatives in Prague, control the Secretariat. Indeed the "inner circle" of the Secretariat normally consists of the representatives from the Soviet Union and one or two other East European countries, and one or two hard-line communist representatives from the Third World. Of these the Soviet representative is by far the most important. Further examination of not merely the number of people participating in decisionmaking but also of their functions reveals something else about the concentration of responsibility within the organization. Under the constitution, the Finance Committee is charged with handling the finances, but this committee seldom meets. It is apparently the treasurer, operating in the Secretariat, who in fact oversees the monies. This means, of course, that the Secretariat controls both policy development and finances. (*Report: European Union of Christian-Democratic and Conservative Students*, London, 1974.)

During 1974 the IUS held or participated in numerous seminars, conferences, and visitations. All of these activities were aimed at developing an expanded public awareness of various political issues. In January, a seminar entitled "The Student and European Security" was held in Bucharest. Approximately 160 student representatives from European countries attended. The main theme of the seminar was security and cooperation on the European continent and how students could become more effectively involved in this issue (Bucharest domestic service, 10 January).

The Middle East problem captured substantial IUS attention. The former president of the General Union of Palestinian Students (GUPS) visited the IUS Secretariat in Prague late in 1973. He urged continued cooperation between the IUS and GUPS. (*World Student News*, no. 12, 1973.) The IUS declared that 15 January-21 February 1974 was the "International Month of Solidarity with the Arab Peoples and Students." In connection with this "Month," a delegation composed of members of GUPS and the National Union of Syrian Students and supported by the IUS visited Finland, Denmark, Iceland, and Ireland. The goal of the group was "further strengthening of solidarity with the Arab liberation struggle." When asked what forms of solidarity could be developed, the delegation cited several possibilities. First, the creation of permanent, strong relations with European unions; second, the distribution in Europe of publications devoted to the Arab and Palestinian cause; and third, visitations by union groups to the Middle East. In a final remark, members of the delegation expressed appreciation of the role of the IUS in support of "our" struggle for self-determination. In March a delegation from the national student unions of Finland, Norway, and the Federal Republic of Germany, along with a member of the IUS Press and Information Department, visited the Middle East. While in that area the group spent a considerable amount of time talking with members of the Palestine Liberation Organization (ibid., no. 7). In its January *News Service* the IUS called on all students in the universities and colleges to take various actions—establishing committees of solidarity with the Arab peoples, carrying out publicity campaigns, and sending delegations to protest at U.S. Embassies.

On the invitation of the Union of Students in Ireland and the Secretariat of the IUS, the second annual student press seminar on the "Aims and Tasks of Student Press and Information Activities" was held in Dublin, 28-31 January. The participants felt that "the main priorities of student press and information activities should be the development of socio-political education, the formation of a progressive political consciousness among students, and the defense of student rights (*News Service*, no. 2/3).

On 23-29 April a student delegation composed of representatives from the national student unions of the United Kingdom, the Federal Republic of Germany, and Argentina visited Chile. The report submitted later by the group indicated that the new government had imposed stiff controls on newspapers, expelled large numbers of students and faculty from the universities, and in general instituted a reign of terror throughout the country. In spite of these repressive measures, the delegation felt that progressive forces were gaining strength. (Ibid., no. 7/8.) Shortly before the delegation left for Chile, the IUS participated in an "International Commission of Enquiry in the Crime of the Military Junta." The Commission met in Helsinki, 21 March. The widow of former Chilean president Allende delivered the opening address. In a concluding statement, all individuals and organizations were urged to work world-wide to isolate the junta (*World Student News*, no. 7). Other than Chile, Latin America did not appear to be an area of significant IUS activity in 1974.

Publications. The principal IUS publications are a monthly magazine, *World Student News*, published in English, French, German, and Spanish, and a fortnightly bulletin, *IUS News Service*, in English, French, and Spanish. Published once a year is the *Magazine on the Democratization and Reform of Education.*

Women's International Democratic Federation. The Women's International Democratic Federation (WIDF) was founded in Paris in December 1945 at a "Congress of Women" organized by the communist-dominated Union des Femmes Françaises. The WIDF headquarters was in Paris until 1951, when it was expelled by the French government. It was then moved to East Berlin. The WIDF holds Category A status with the U.N. Economic and Social Council, and Category B with UNESCO.

Structure and Leadership. The WIDF's highest governing body is the Congress, which meets every four years. Next in authority is the Council; meeting annually and in control between Congresses, it elects the Bureau and the Secretariat. The Bureau meets at least twice a year and implements decisions taken by the Congress and the Council; it is assisted by the Secretariat. Hertta Kuusinen (Finland), president of the WIDF, died in the spring of 1974. No replacement has been named. Fanny Edelman (Argentina) remains as secretary-general. Julia Arevalo (Uruguay) became vice-president, and Connie Seifert (United Kingdom) moved from the Council to the Bureau (*Women of the Whole World*, no. 3, 1973).

Membership in the WIDF is open to all women's organizations and groups, and in exceptional cases to individuals. Total membership in 1971 exceeded 200 million, including 110 affiliated and associated organizations in 97 countries. In 1974 the WIDF announced unofficially that it has 117 affiliated organizations in 101 countries (ADN, 25 June). The WIDF seeks to maintain contact with non-affiliated women's groups through its International Liaison Bureau, which has its general headquarters in Copenhagen and a secretariat in Brussels.

Views and Activities. Hertta Kuusinen, WIDF president, honorary chairman of the Finnish Communist Party and member of the party's Central Committee, died on 18 March 1974 in Moscow, where she had come to receive the Soviet "Order of Friendship among Peoples" (TASS, 7 March, 1974).

Both the Bureau and Council met in Warsaw on 17-23 May. These were the two most important WIDF meetings of the year. Attending the Council meeting were representatives of 110 organizations in 97 countries. Perhaps the major item on the agenda was the one dealing with preparations for International Women's Year, which, according to the United Nations, would be observed in 1975. The session also considered a wide range of problems, notably preservation and strengthening of universal peace, international security, defense of women's rights, and the struggle for social progress. Numerous speakers pointed out that the world was witnessing significant changes contributing to the easing of international tensions, and that this change had been significantly helped by the "program of the 24th Congress of the Communist Party of the Soviet Union." Although acknowledging that the general changes were positive, secretary-general Fanny Edelman warned that, despite détente, forces of war and reaction were still trying to thwart various peace efforts (PAP, Polish news agency, 20-21 May; Warsaw radio, 20-22 May).

The Council adopted a series of resolutions dealing with international issues. On Chile, "U.S. imperialism" was denounced as the true architect of the coup, and women from all countries were urged to help end the terror of the fascist junta which had overthrown the Allende government. The Council stressed the necessity of achieving a just and lasting peace in the Middle East, and expressed its determination to mobilize public opinion against aggressive Israeli policy. The Vietnam issue was raised and the "sabotage" of the Paris agreement by the United States and the Saigon administration was strongly condemned. Thus, on these three major international issues the Council's positions were uniformly anti-U.S. and pro-Soviet. (PAP, 24 May.)

A declaration and program was drawn up by the Council for "International Women's Year" and the "World Congress of Women." The program called on the WIDF's national organizations to work out plans for the equal participation of women in the life of their countries. It also urged these national groups to publicize the achievements of women in communist countries and to attract new forces to the "democratic" women's movement. (Ibid., 23 May.)

Finally, the Council instructed the Secretariat to support the initiatives of national organizations and to cooperate with them in regional seminars. More specifically, the Secretariat was asked to investigate the holding of the following seminars: in Asia on the integration of women in society and the abolition of U.S. military bases; in Europe on disarmament and the education of youth in the spirit of peace; in Latin America on the condition of women and children; and in North America on disarmament. (Ibid.)

New affiliates endorsed by the Council were the Popular Unity Women's Front (Chile), the women's section of the Zambia Labor Union, the General Federation of Iraqi Women, the Women's Organization for Struggle against Illiteracy (Jordan), the Social and Cultural Women's Organization of Kuwait, the Organization of Democratic Women of Nicaragua, and the People's Front for the Liberation of Oman and the Arabian Gulf (*Women of the Whole World*, no. 3, 1974).

As early as the spring of 1973, the WIDF had begun to formulate plans for a World Congress of Women (see *YICA, 1974*, p. 590). In January 1974, WIDF vice-president Ilse Thiele attended in Geneva the first preparatory meeting (ADN, 25 January). At a press conference later in the spring, Fanny Edelman indicated that a series of regional seminars would be held by the WIDF to generate support for the planned congress. She further stated that the details of the congress would be discussed at the May Council meeting, and that in the meantime an international preparatory committee would be established to begin working on the congress's agenda. (PAP, 5 March.) A number of women's organizations from Africa, Asia, Europe, and Latin America as well as the WIDF and other international groups gathered at the UNESCO building in Paris in April and pledged their support for the congress. According to the British communist party publication *Comment* (27 July), about 200 delegates are expected to attend the congress. Also mentioned in *Comment* was the fact that the British party had a "special responsibility" to help set up a national preparatory committee.

Reacting to events in Chile, the WIDF proposed late in 1973 a fact-finding mission to Chile which would include representatives of women's organizations in various countries (TASS, 15 December 1973). Indeed, in January 1974 a small WIDF group led by Margot Mrozinski of West Berlin and including two Argentinian representatives and one representative from Spain visited Chile. Although they subsequently claimed that they were restricted in their travels, they reported on "acts of terror" by the new ruling junta. At a Berlin press conference the group stressed the need for international solidarity on behalf of the Chilean people. (*Nuestra Palabra*, Buenos Aires, 23 January; ADN, 29 January.) In the spring Mrs. Allende, widow of the former Chilean president, led a WIDF delegation before the U.N. Human Rights Commission. She denounced the junta's crimes and appealed for support against the new regime. After the U.N. address, Mrs. Allende began a tour of Latin America, where she in effect became the WIDF's leading spokeswoman in the organization's attempt to turn public opinion against the junta. (*Punto*, Caracas, 1 March; *El Nacional*, Caracas, 3-10 March.) On 8 March, International Women's Day, the WIDF announced the start of a new campaign of solidarity with the women of Chile (*Neues Deutschland*, East Berlin, 7-8 March).

Preparations for an Afro-Arab women's seminar on education were started in December 1973; the seminar itself took place in Algiers in March 1974. The event was co-sponsored by the WIDF and UNESCO (*Jeune Afrique*, Paris, 30 March). Later in the year Fanny Edelman attended the fourth meeting of the All-African Women's Conference (AAWC) in Dakar, Senegal. (The AAWC has subsequently changed its name to the Pan-African Women's Organization.) (ADN, 30 July; Dakar radio, 31 July.)

Throughout 1974 the WIDF continued its support of the Arabs in their struggle against Israel. On several occasions the organization spoke out in favor of the "national rights" of the people of Palestine (ADN, 21 June). On Vietnam, the WIDF protested against the violation of the Paris agreements, in particular charging the United States with supplying war materials to the Saigon regime (ADN, 13 August).

When the Cyprus crisis erupted, the WIDF asked the U.N. Security Council to enforce its resolution of 20 July calling for the withdrawal of all foreign troops from Cyprus. It fully approved the idea of an international conference within the U.N. framework to deal with the issue (TASS, 4 September).

Publications. The WIDF publishes an illustrated quarterly magazine, *Women of the Whole World*, in English, German, Spanish, French, and Russian, and issues pamphlets and bulletins on specific problems.

World Federation of Democratic Youth. The World Federation of Democratic Youth (WFDY) was founded in November 1945 at a "World Youth Conference" convened in London by the World Youth Council. Although the WFDY appeared to represent varying shades of political opinion, key positions were quickly taken by communists. By 1950 most non-communists had withdrawn and established their own organization, the World Assembly of Youth (WAY). Originally based in Paris, the WFDY was expelled by the French government in 1951. Its headquarters has since been in Budapest.

All youth organizations that contribute to the safeguarding of the activities of young persons are eligible for membership. A total membership of some 100 million persons in 200 organizations in 90 countries was claimed by the WFDY in 1970 (TASS, 12 October).

Structure and Leadership. The highest governing body of the WFDY is the Assembly, which convenes every three years and to which all affiliated organizations send representatives. The Executive Committee is elected by the Assembly and meets at least twice a year. The day-to-day work is conducted by the Bureau and its Secretariat. Late in 1973 Renzo Imbeni, national secretary of the Italian Communist Youth Federation (FGCI), announced that his organization was "replacing" WFDY president Roberto Viezzi with Piero Lapiccirella (Italy). It was subsequently learned that Viezzi would join the Italian Communist Party's regional committee in Venezia Giulia (*L'Unità*, Rome, 23 December 1973). Other changes in leadership positions included the departure of three Bureau members, Rene Martinek (East Germany), secretary; Alberto Mendoza (Argentina), treasurer; and Alvaro Oviedo (Colombia), secretary. These individuals were replaced, respectively, by Werner Voight (East Germany), Sergio Dubrovsky (Argentina), and Eduardo Martinez (Colombia) (*WFDY News*, no. 8/9, 1973).

WFDY subsidiaries include the International Committee of Children's and Adolescents' Movements (CIMEA), which organizes international camps and film festivals; the International Bureau of Tourism and Exchanges of Youth (BITEJ), charged with planning and supervising work camps and meetings; the International Sports Committee for Youth, which arranges special events in connection with the World Youth Festivals; and the International Voluntary Service for Friendship and Solidarity of Youth (SIVSAJ), which seeks to increase WFDY influence in developing countries by sending "young volunteers" to work with the people of these countries.

Views and Activities. On 17-20 December 1973 the Executive Committee met in Bucharest. In addressing the gathering, Romanian president and communist party chief Nicolae Ceauşescu pointed to the role that the WFDY plays in rallying the efforts of the younger generation for a better and just world. To achieve this, he stressed that a diversity of views must be recognized, accepted, and properly channeled:

> We must realize that under the conditions of the world today, diversity of views on the ways of developing the social struggle, the anti-imperialist struggle, is inevitable. This, after all, is right. It is a phenomenon mirroring the rising political awareness of youth, its developing thinking. Everything must be done for channeling these forces, the various youth organizations, to a single direction—to anti-imperialist and anti-colonialist struggle, for peace and social progress. (Agerpres, Bucharest, 20 December.)

Ceauşescu's emphasis on "unity" was to be reflected in all WFDY activities throughout 1974; it also appeared in the more specific proposals of the Executive Committee. On the question of European security, the committee called for cooperation between organizations of the most "varied orientations," and after reviewing the problems of Latin America and the Middle East came out for the "solidarity" of all anti-imperialist forces. At this session it was decided to hold the WFDY's Ninth Assembly in Bulgaria in 1974. (Ibid., 21 December.)

A four member delegation from the WFDY Bureau, headed by Lapiccirella and vice-president Valery Lordkipanidze (U.S.S.R.), visited Sofia in January to discuss preparation for the Ninth Assembly. When asked about WFDY activities, Lapiccirella replied that the prestige of the WFDY had risen over the years and that 1974 would be devoted to all-round achievements and the holding of the Assembly. He also said that discussions between the WFDY and the Council of European National Youth (CENYC) would continue, and that it was hoped that the two organizations would cooperate in support of peoples fighting against domination. In his final remarks to the press, he reviewed the coming work of the various special bureaus within the Federation. (BTA, Bulgarian news agency, 16-18 January; *Mlada Fronta*, 30 January). It appears from the information emanating from this gathering that the visit to Sofia laid the groundwork for not only the Assembly but also a variety of other WFDY activities.

In preparation for the Executive Committee meeting scheduled for Warsaw in June, a WFDY delegation visited Moscow in February. Key figures in the group were secretary-general A. Therouse (France), vice-president Lordkipanidze, treasurer Dubrovsky, and F. Leszczynski (Poland), secretary (BTA, 7 February). The June executive session opened with some 60 organizations from 54 countries represented. The participants talked of the WFDY's need to expand its constituency. Jose Fort (France) pointed to "new methods" of making youth more active in the work for progress and democracy, and then stressed that a "new model of the WFDY, now under way, should insure the possibility of greater participation in performing the tasks of the federation for all member organizations" (PAP, 11 June). The "new model" was not defined; however, one can assume that it referred to organizational changes designed to attract increased numbers of youth groups into the WFDY.

At the second plenary session of the Executive Committee, problems of the Third World were emphasized. Antonio Castro (Cuba) characterized the situation in Latin America as a "struggle against reactionary forces." Sergio Blanco, who claimed to represent "50 thousand young communists of Argentina," called for further strengthening of the progressive forces of the continent in defense of democratic freedoms. Within the discussions on Latin America, Chile received the most attention. The delegates from that country denounced the "terror reigning in their country"; in support of the Chilean position, the Polish member introduced a resolution demanding that "Luis Corvalán, Clodomiro Almeida and other progressive Chilean leaders be released from prison." (Ibid., 12/13 June.) After reviewing the question of the Middle East, the session asked for the withdrawal of all Israeli troops from Arab territories, the guarantee of Palestinian "nation's" rights, and the enforcement of the U.N. Security Council's resolution (ibid., 13 June). In all, the problems of the Third World received a considerable amount of attention. As for Europe, it was suggested that the leading task of the European youth movement should be the convening of an assembly of European youth and students in Poland in 1975 (ibid., 11 June).

The WFDY Assembly, which had been under preparation for many months, opened in Varna on 10 November. In the opening address Lapiccirella reviewed the "tasks facing the world democratic youth movement, tasks directed above all to the further rallying of the forces of the young people of all continents, as well as the involvement of more youth organizations with different political organizations in joint actions" (BTA, 11 November). The second report, by secretary-general Therouse, reviewed the work of the federation and outlined future activities related to Indochina, Chile, and the Middle East. Messages of congratulations were received from Edward Gierek, Gustav Husák, Erich Honecker, Yasir Arafat, and other political leaders (ibid., 11 November). Soviet party chief Brezhnev's message was read to the Assembly by Komsomol first secretary V. Tyazhelnikov. It praised the work of the WFDY and encouraged the organization to continue its support of progressive and democratic forces (Sofia domestic service, 10 November).

At the plenary session on the second day, Tyazhelnikov expressed full support for holding the Eleventh World Youth Festival in Havana. He stressed the favorable impact that this "decision" would have on the struggle of the Latin American peoples. He went on to emphasize the necessity of consolidating youth solidarity with the peoples of the Third World. (BTA, 11 November.) In subsequent remarks, Tyazhelnikov continued to talk of "solidarity" and "consolidation." This idea of bringing together the youth of the world was a theme which had run through both Executive Committee meetings and the presentations of the WFDY's president and secretary-general at the Assembly. It was evoked again and most succinctly by the French representative, who appealed for a united anti-imperialist front which would consist of not only communists but also "socialists, social democrats, atheists, Protestants, Catholics, and all young people and organizations with progressive and democratic orientations" (ibid., 12 November). He was supported in his call for a united front by the delegates from the United States, Poland, Argentina, Angola, and Japan (ibid.).

Three special sessions were held to deal with questions related to Palestine, Chile, and Indochina.

Messages were read to the session on Indochina from the National Front for the Liberation of South Vietnam and from the premier of the Democratic Republic of Vietnam. Speakers at the session denounced the Thieu government in Saigon and U.S. involvement in the area. On the Chilean situation, Tyazhelnikov reminded the meeting that the Seventeenth Congress of the All-Union Lenin Communist Union of Youth called for intensifying the struggle for solidarity with Chile. Gladys Marin of the Union of Communist Youth in Chile stated that the overthrow of the Allende government was part of a general imperialist plan for making the continent fascist; she called for an economic blockade and boycott of Chilean goods. Secretary-general Therouse, with the approval of the delegates, sent a telegram to the United Nations demanding the observance of individual rights in Chile. The Palestinian cause was fully supported. The Komsomol announced to the special session that it was prepared to send "youth building brigades to the Arab States" to help the victims of Israeli aggression. The session received messages from the premier of Iraq, the president of Egypt, and the head of the Palestine Liberation Organization. At the end of the gathering, a resolution was drawn up emphasizing the need for solidarity with the Palestinians' struggle for their national rights. (Ibid.)

Before the end of the Assembly, the "specialized organs" of the WFDY held their meetings. SIVSAJ developed a number of "concrete" proposals for sending international youth brigades to Somalia, Syria, Egypt, Iran, and the Palestinian territories; CIMEA moved to increase its children's camps; BITEJ planned to expand its youth exchange programs (ibid., 11, 12 November).

Overall, the work of the Assembly was tied together by the idea of expanded cooperation with youth organizations. Indeed, the proposed solidarity campaigns on behalf of the Indochinese, Chilean, and Palestinian peoples were designed to attract new recruits and would be dependent on "mass" support for their effectiveness. The whole thrust for expanded cooperation had been developing within the WFDY throughout the year and was consistent with the ideas and activities prevailing in other fronts.

The international youth brigades have been in operation for some time. In 1974 several East German doctors worked in Guinea-Bissau. A WFDY agricultural team helped improve growing methods in Sierra Leone. (ADN, 8 February.) In March, a youth brigade visited several countries in the Middle East (*Mlada Fronta*, 16 March). The "specialized organs" had also been active: CIMEA held a summer camp in East Germany for 1,200 children from 30 countries. The slogan of the camp was "For Anti-Imperialist Solidarity, Peace and Friendship—Always Ready." Shortly before the camp opened the CIMEA leadership met in Warsaw and decided to increase its efforts to recruit new members from Africa, Asia, and Latin America. (*Mlada Fronta*, 10 July; *Neues Deutschland*, 15-29 July.)

A consultative meeting of European affiliates of WFDY took place in Kladino, Czechoslovakia, on 9 July. Sixty representatives from 27 organizations in 21 countries attended. The communiqué affirmed that the ideas of the peace offensive of the U.S.S.R. and other socialist countries had the full support of all progressive European youth. A "European Conference on Youth and Student Tourism" was planned for 1975; other events would include a regional "Colloquium on the Environment" and seminars for young people interested in agriculture.

One of the overriding preoccupations of the WFDY was Chile and, as understood by the WFDY, the repressive regime in that country. In the spring, Therouse stated that the WFDY would continue a broad propaganda campaign to expose "the crimes perpetrated by the fascist junta." In support of the general effort, the WFDY began a large scale effort to obtain signatures on a petition of protest against conditions in Chile. (TASS, 10 March.) A three-member WFDY delegation—Lapiccirella, Jose Fort of the French Young Communist League, Jorma Ollila (Finland) as an IUS representative—toured Chile on a fact-finding mission early in March. Their report, critical of the junta, was submitted to the United Nations (*Mlada Fronta*, 21 March). The WFDY claimed success in its propaganda effort when it announced that pressure from progressive international opinion forced the junta to allow Gladys

Marin, secretary-general of the Chilean Communist Youth League, to leave the country. In June the WFDY called on youth and student organizations to join forces in a world-wide solidarity campaign to isolate the junta and restore democracy in Chile (MTI, 19 June). Late in July it was announced that the WFDY, the International Union of Young Christian Democrats (IUYCD), the IUS, the International Student Movement for the United Nations (ISMUN), the International Union of Socialist Youth (IUSY), the Christian Democratic Youth of Latin America, and the Latin American Continental Organization of Students (OCLAE) were co-sponsoring a solidarity conference on behalf of the Chilean people (*Tribuna Popular*, Caracas, 20-26 July). Besides the groups mentioned above, organizations tentatively scheduled to take part included the Permanent Congress of Latin American Trade Union Unity (CPUSTAL), the Russell Tribunal, the World Council of Churches, the AAPSO, the Pan African Youth Movement (PAYM), the Council of European National Youth Committees (CENYC), the European Federation of Liberal and Radical Youth (EUROFED), the All Africa Students' Union (AASU), and most of the international fronts. The conference itself was scheduled for 11 September in Caracas. (Ibid., 10-16 August.)

At the request of Panos Peonides, secretary-general of the Cyprus Peace Council, the WFDY moved to organize a solidarity campaign in support of the progressive forces in Cyprus. On 16 July the WFDY called on the progressive youth of the world to condemn the Greek junta's intervention and its accomplice, U.S. imperialism. Subsequently the WFDY appealed to the UN on behalf of a "free Cyprus." (MTI, 17-19 July.)

Leaders of EUROFED and the WFDY met in Budapest in August to discuss general cooperation between the two organizations and the scheduled meeting of European youth and student organizations in Hungary in September. It was also decided that the two groups would hold a joint meeting in 1975 and would work toward expanding youth and student tourism. (Ibid., 27-30 August.)

Publications. The WFDY publishes a bimonthly magazine, *World Youth*, in English, French, German, and Arabic. The monthly *WFDY News* appears in English, French, and Spanish. Other publications, directed to specific areas of interest, include special magazines and pamphlets to commemorate congresses, festivals, and other events.

World Federation of Scientific Workers. The World Federation of Scientific Workers (WFSW) was founded in London in 1946 at the initiative of the British Association of Scientific Workers, with 18 organizations of scientists from 14 countries taking part. Although it purported to be a scientific rather than a political organization, communists obtained most official posts at the start and have kept control since. The headquarters is in London, but the secretary-general's office is in Paris.

WFSW membership is open to organizations of scientific workers everywhere and to individual scientists in countries where no affiliated groups are active. The WFSW claims to represent 300,000 scientists in 30 countries; most of the membership derives from 14 groups in communist-ruled countries. The only large non-communist affiliate, the British Association of Scientific Workers, has 21,000 members. Scientists of distinction who do not belong to an affiliated organization may be nominated for "corresponding membership." The WFSW has a constitution and a "Charter for Scientific Workers" to which affiliates must subscribe (see *YICA, 1968*, p. 736).

Structure and Leadership. The governing body of the WFSW is the General Assembly, in which all affiliated organizations are represented. Ten General Assembly meetings have been held, the latest in September 1973 in Varna. Between Assemblies, the Executive Committee and its Bureau are responsible for the operation of the Federation.

The Commission on Amendments to the Constitution recommended to the Tenth Assembly several changes in the organizational structure. The number of vice-presidents was increased from three to five, and the membership of the Executive Council was enlarged to a maximum of thirty-three. Three permanent standing committees were created: the Science Policy Committee, the Socio-Economic Committee, and the Committee on Peace and Disarmament.

Elected or reelected to the Executive Council at the Assembly were the following: president and chairman of the Council, E. Burhop (United Kingdom; also a member of the WPC Presidential Committee); vice-presidents, I. Artobolevsky (U.S.S.R.), K. Wirzberger (German Democratic Republic), K. Bratanov (Bulgaria), S. Zaheer (India); vice-chairman of Executive Council, A. Ishlinsky (U.S.S.R.); Heads of Regional Centers, N. Gupta (India), S. Hedayat (Egypt), J. Kracik, (Czechoslovakia); chairman, Editorial Board, C. Penescu (Romania); Honorary treasurer, A. Jaegle (France); chairman, Socio-Economic Committee, Rene Le Guen (France; also chairman of WFTU Commission on Engineers); Individual members of the Executive Council, P. Boskma (Netherlands); K. Grigorov (Bulgaria); J. Lesso (Czechoslovakia); M. Stanojevic (Yugoslavia); J. Legay (France); N. Singh (India); T. Hirone (Japan); H. Tzerev, A. Sztetyllo, and N. Teodorescu (Romania); H. Aboujeid and A. Sier (United Kingdom); R. Rutman and V. Truhanovsky (U.S.S.R.).

The WFSW has Consultative Status Category A with UNESCO (*Scientific World*, no. 4, 1974).

Views and Activities. Writing early in 1974, WFSW president Burhop wrote that the Tenth Assembly (September 1973) marked an important stage in the development of the federation. He pointed to the contacts that had been opened with international trade union centers, and more specifically to the recent meeting in Paris between the WFSW and the World Federation of Trade Unions. The WFSW and the World Confederation of Labor also had discussions. (*Scientific World*, no. 4.)

The Bureau met in London in April. WFSW vice-president Wirzberger, chairman of the Standing Committee on Disarmament, reported on the WFSW's recent intensification of its work on disarmament problems. He also indicated that his committee would soon publish a brochure on chemical weapons. The Socio-Economic Committee's report described the latest developments in the preparation of the draft "Instrument on the Status of Scientific Research Workers" to be presented to the General Conference of UNESCO. The Bureau also worked toward the establishment of a committee on science policy.

D. Bliznakov (Bulgaria) provided some information on the activities of the Joliot-Curie House of Scientists, a WFSW conference facility. In its eight years of existence, 293 meetings, symposiums, and conferences have been held there for about 35,000 scientists from 68 countries. During 1974 there are planned 56 international scientific events for 600 scientific workers from 32 countries. (Ibid., no. 3.)

Publications. The official publication of the WFSW is *Scientific World*, issued bimonthly in English, French, Russian, German, Spanish, and Czech. The WFSW *Bulletin*, issued irregularly and only to members, is published in English, French, German, and Russian. "Science and Mankind" is the general title of a series of WFSW booklets that have appeared in several languages. The WFSW publishes pamphlets on particular subjects from time to time.

World Federation of Trade Unions. The World Federation of Trade Unions (WFTU), set up at the initiative of the British Trade Union Congress, held its founding congress in October 1945 in Paris, where its first headquarters was established. Expelled from Paris and next from Vienna for subversive activities, the headquarters has been in Prague since 1956. At Soviet insistence, Louis Saillant (France) was elected the WFTU's first secretary-general. He is generally considered responsible for bringing the WFTU Secretariat and other ruling bodies under communist control. Some non-communist affiliates in 1949 gave up their membership to found an alternative organization, the International Conference of Free Trade Unions (ICFTU).

Structure and Leadership. The highest authority of the WFTU is the Congress; it meets every four years and is composed of delegates from affiliates in proportion to the number of their members. The latest Congress was held in Varna in the fall of 1973. The Congress, which has no policy-making function and is too large to transact much specific business, elects the General Council, Executive Bureau, and Secretariat. The General Council is composed of approximately 66 regular and 68 deputy members representing the national affiliates and 11 "Trade Union Internationals" (TUI). The 1973 Congress reelected Enrique Pastorino (Uruguay) as president, and Pierre Gensous (France) as secretary-general. Two seats have been left vacant on the General Council for China and Indonesia. The Executive Bureau is the most powerful body of the WFTU. It has assumed much of the authority which before 1969 was enjoyed by the Secretariat. The Secretariat was revamped by the 1969 Congress and reduced to 6 members, including the secretary-general.

The Trade Union Internationals represent workers of particular trades and crafts. One of the main purposes of the TUIs is to recruit local unions which do not, through their national centers, belong to the WFTU. Though the TUIs are in theory independent (each TUI has its own offices and officials, holds its own meetings, and publishes its own bulletin), their policies and finances are controlled by the WFTU department having supervision over their particular areas. The WFTU General Council in December 1966 decided that each TUI should have its own constitution; this move, taken to bolster the appearance of independence, had also the purpose of allowing the TUIs to join international bodies as individual organizations.

In recent years the WFTU has moved vigorously to establish working relationships with non-communist trade unions and intergovernmental organizations. In this area of operation one of the most important structural linkages is the WFTU's "Special Commission on U.N. Agencies," created in 1967 to facilitate WFTU activities in the United Nations. The WFTU enjoys Category A Status with a number of U.N. agencies, and has permanent representatives at the United Nations in New York, the International Labor Organization (ILO) in Geneva, the Food and Agriculture Agency (FAO) in Rome, and UNESCO in Paris. At the FAO the WFTU is represented by G. Casadei (Italy). Carlos De Angeli (Brazil) is the representative at the ILO. Marius Delsal (France) and Jacqueline Levy (France) and Ernest Lange are the representatives at UNESCO.

Views and Activities. Louis Saillant, honorary president of the WFTU, died in Paris on 28 October 1974. He was one of the founders of the Union and was secretary-general from 1945 until 1969, when he retired for reasons of health.

On 17-18 January 1974 the Bureau met in Geneva to discuss the "work plan" adopted at the Congress the previous fall. Addressing the group were Pierre Gensous, secretary-general, and Bureau members Alexander Shelepin (U.S.S.R.), Lazaro Pena (Cuba), and W. Kruczek (Poland). Adopted in the work plan was a commitment to stress unity both within the WFTU and between it and non-member trade union organizations. The energy crisis and its impact on workers was reviewed; in noting the connection between the energy crisis and the Middle East conflict, the members called for increased solidarity with the Arab peoples. The problems in Chile, political trials in Spain, and the need for action against the multi-national companies also came under discussion. Plans were laid for WFTU-sponsored meetings in 1974, and specific regional activities determined. Since the WFTU wished to improve its working relationship with the EEC, the ICFTU, and the World Confederation of Labor (WCL), all of which have offices in Brussels, the Bureau considered placing a permanent representative in that city; it also decided to "make better use of its London office." As for Latin America, the Bureau determined to try to strengthen its cooperation with the Permanent Congress of Latin American Trade Union Unity (CPUSTAL). It decided to install representatives in the Congo and Somalia, and to set up an "unspecified body" in India. Finally, stronger and more decisive activity was envisaged within the ILO, FAO, and UNESCO. (WFTU Document; TASS, 17 January; CTK, 29 January; *Flashes*, nos. 3, 4.)

The 10th Session of the WFTU was held in Prague on 14-15 May. Gensous in his report stressed that the WFTU wanted to continue establishing, developing, and intensifying cooperation with all national, regional and continental organizations (CTK, 14 May). He pointed out that the need for a "class-based international common front" was obvious, given the growing strife and dissatisfaction in the working class of the capitalist countries (*Flashes*, 24 May). The Bureau subsequently released a statement on "Workers' Action in the Capitalist Countries" which expanded on the secretary-general's contention that unrest was spreading: "A vast movement of industrial action of unprecedented proportions is developing in all the countries of the capitalist world. The movement . . . expresses the workers' deep-seated discontent with the worsening of their living and working conditions. The present situation fully confirms the correctness of the analysis of the 8th World Trade Union Congress." The elimination of these conditions required international solidarity "among all workers and unions in both capitalist and socialist countries." (Ibid.) Declarations were also issued on the situation in Latin America, on raw materials and development, and on the Middle East. In a final move, the Bureau created an "Advisory Committee on Social and Economic Questions," whose functions "will be research and studies of certain contemporary phenomena connected with economic and social issues." (Ibid.)

The WFTU's twenty-fifth General Council met in Havana on 15 October. This was the first time the Council had held its meeting in Latin America. WFTU president Pastorino expressed the gratitude of the "153 million workers of the WFTU" for the hospitality shown by the Cuban people. In all, 200 delegates from 60 countries attended the meeting. Fidel Castro delivered the major address. Its focus was primarily on the adverse economic conditions facing capitalism, and on the implication of the energy crisis for not only the capitalist countries but also the developing world. He stressed repeatedly that the imperialists would continue to try and exploit the resources of the Third World but that they would fail if the working people maintained their solidarity. The tone of the conference, the attitude of the delegates, is clearly expressed in the following passage from Castro's speech:

> On the other hand, the raising of petroleum prices cannot be adduced as the determining factor of world-wide inflation, which came long before that measure and whose consequences the developed countries were the first to suffer. The imperialists did not have to wait for petroleum prices to raise outlandishly the prices of foodstuffs, petrochemical byproducts, equipment. . . . No imperialist ruler worried then about the situation into which those [developing] countries were plunged. (Havana domestic service, 19 October.)

Going a step beyond Castro's general remarks, Cruz Villegas, president of the United Workers Federation of Venezuela, proposed to the Council that a meeting of Latin American trade union federations be convened to discuss the oil problem. This meeting, he suggested, could be organized by Cuba, Peru, and Panama. Robert Prieto, secretary of CPUSTAL, supported Villegas's remarks when he said that in the face of the threats of the U.S. President the "governments, including those that are not known as progressive, must adopt a defensive attitude toward their natural resources. And in so doing, the battle in defense of oil becomes a battle . . . of all nations of Latin America." (Ibid., 17 October.) In an overall response to the economic problems facing the world, Gensous proposed a three-point plan: (1) the right of every country to nationalize firms, (2) the establishment of democratic control within trade unions which would allow intervention in the giant international capitalist companies, and (3) the development of increased international economic cooperation (*Flashes*, 18 October). In the final address by Pastorino, the Council took note that "this is the century of the working class, which has demonstrated a clear-cut awareness of its organization and unity." Resolutions were also adopted regarding Chile, Cyprus, and the struggle against multi-national companies. (Havana domestic service, 18 October.) If one can point to a particular attitude that dominated the Council, it was an "awareness" among the delegates that their countries, although poor, possessed resources that were critical to the economic well-being of the developed world, and that this "relationship" could provide organizations like the WFTU with leverage in dealing with the capitalist world and particularly its working class.

The WFTU's call for unity and efforts to expand its contacts outside of its present organizational framework (see below for more details on this latter point) had earlier moved the Central Council of Albanian Trade Unions to denounce the leaders of the WFTU for seeking to create a single world trade union organization which would only serve the "Soviet social-imperialists" (ATA, 5 December 1973). An additional commentary accused the WFTU of having betrayed the interests of the working class and allowed itself to become "a department of the Soviet Administration" (ibid., 30 January 1974). It can be assumed that behind these remarks lay Albania's and thus China's opposition to WFTU policies and activities.

Throughout 1974 the idea of trade union unity was a major preoccupation of the WFTU. Gensous, writing in *World Trade Union Movement* (May), argued that unity and cooperation among workers on an international level was possible, considering the crisis of capitalism. In order for workers to take advantage of these conditions, he suggested that the trend toward continental or regional organizations be accelerated. Although Africa and Latin America were discussed in this context, it was and is Europe where the WFTU has focused its main efforts in the drive to bring together the various national and regional groups. In seeking this goal of regional unity in Europe, the WFTU has had to deal with several interrelated factors: the newly formed European Trade Union Confederation (ETUC), relations with the ICFTU and the WCL, and the attitudes of its own national affiliates, particularly the communist-controlled Italian labor confederation, CGIL.

Creation in February 1973 of the ETUC posed problems and opportunities. On the one hand, the ETUC was a potential competitior for the WFTU in Europe; on the other hand, it provided the WFTU, or at least its affiliates, with an opportunity to join and thus influence a regional non-communist group. Indeed, the latter option appears to have been the choice of the CIGL, which at the WFTU's Eighth Congress had asked for and received a change in the WFTU Statutes allowing national affiliates to withdraw from full membership in the WFTU to "associate memberships." In effect, however, the "associate membership" permits on a paractical basis the WFTU affiliate to remain within the Union while linking itself with another body—in this case the ETUC. In the spring of 1974 the CGIL sought admission to the ETUC but was temporarily blocked by the opposition of the West German labor groups (*Christian Science Monitor*, 22 May). That tension exists between the CGIL and at least some members of the ETUC is not surprising of one reads the CGIL's comments made shortly after the change in the WFTU's Statutes:

> What must we do to accelerate the unitary process on an international level in the trade union field? In Western Europe we certainly have social-democratic partners, and they represent millions of workers, they direct great mass organizations. Moreover, the history of the trade union movement in Europe for the past century [is] in large measure the history of these organizations. To enter into discussions with them, to work with them—as we of the CGIL are doing with the ETUC—means entering into contact with these millions of workers, it means trying to awaken in them the class spirit, to involve them in anti-capitalist action. (*Avanti*, 18 October 1973.)

In its relations with the ICFTU and the WCL, the WFTU has pressed for a "formal and legitimate" dialogue. At Helsinki (1971) and Vienna (1973) national and international European labor groups talked informally about cooperation, and specifically about further "informal" discussions at the Second European Regional Conference of the ILO, which was scheduled for Geneva in January 1974. At the ILO meeting, Gensous spoke with O. Kersten of the ICFTU, and on 29 January Gensous held a press conference to announce that bilateral contacts of the WFTU and the ICFTU had been agreed upon and that officials of the two Secretariats would meet in Prague to decide on the form of future contacts (CTK, 29 January). Within days of this press conference, the ICFTU publication *International Trade Union News* (February) contained a statement by Kersten contradicting Gensous and stressing "that there could be no question of any agreement between his own organization and the WFTU regarding meetings between the two Secretariats." In broad terms, then, the ICFTU and the WFTU remain at a standoff.

Contacts between the WFTU and the WCL moved ahead in 1974. On 11-12 March in Prague, delegations from the two groups met "as part of the regular meetings between their Secretariats." A joint communiqué noted the progress made in the effectiveness of workers' struggles for better living and working conditions. The two agreed that their organizations should strive for working-class solidarity and trade union action—especially against apartheid and multi-national companies. (*Flashes*, 15 March.)

Throughout 1974 the WFTU worked vigorously to increase its influence in the various bodies of the United Nations. As already mentioned, Gensous attended the Second European Regional Conference of the ILO, as did other WFTU delegates; in June, Gensous led a WFTU group to the annual ILO Conference. Pimenov was elected a vice-president of the ILO's Workers' Group. During this meeting the WFTU asked the ILO to investigate the situation in Chile (ibid., nos. 24, 33). In March the WFTU sent a message to the U.N. Human Rights Commission reminding the group of its prevous complaint against Israel's "violation of human rights" in Arab territories. The WFTU was assured that ECOSOC would take up the matter. (Ibid., 8 February.) Gensous and Casadei, the WFTU permanent representative to the FAO, met in March in Rome with officials of the FAO. They noted the existing cooperation between the two organizations and suggested expanded contacts. During these discussions the WFTU asked to take part in the upcoming World Food Conference (ibid., no. 11). In May, R. Aubrac, director of general affairs and information at FAO, visited Prague and discussed WFTU participation in the planned Rome meeting (ibid., 29 May). At the meeting itself, the WFTU spoke out on key issues, particularly those touching on the Third World. The WFTU was also represented at, among others, UNESCO, the U.N. Industrial Development Organization, and the Economic and Social Commission for Asia (ibid.). In all, 1974 was a year in which the WFTU expanded its influence throughout the U.N. structure.

The WFTU focused on several major international political issues during the year. In May, Pastorino announced that the WFTU would hold an "international conference of solidarity in support of the struggle of the Chilean people" (*Bohemia*, Havana). Plans were laid for the conference to be held in Lisbon on 11-15 September. These dates corresponded with a world-wide international day of solidarity organized by the WFTU. In response to these initiatives, a series of demonstrations were held in numerous countries during the first part of September (*Flashes*, nos. 34-36). Shortly before the rallies on behalf of the Chilean people, the WFTU responded to events in Cyprus with a sereis of resolutions, all of which contained the following points: (1) respect for the Security Council's resolution, (2) withdrawal of all foreign troops, (3) guarantee of independence, and (4) return of Makarios (ibid., 16 August).

The one issue which preoccupied the WFTU more than anything else was the oil crisis and its impact on the economies of the capitalist countries. In almost every edition of *Flashes* there was some mention and analysis of the problem. Perhaps the most interesting and certainly the most sophisticated critique of the subject appeared in a long article in *World Trade Union Movement* (May). Entitled "Oil Crisis and Energy Policy Crisis in the Developed Capitalist Countries," it not only defined the position of the WFTU but also clearly argued the "reasons" behind the crisis. In the WFTU's view, the crisis is caused by structural shortcomings in the capitalist system: mass waste, excessive profits for the oil companies, and the years of exploitation of the developing lands have all led toward the current crisis of capitalism. The WFTU rejects the argument that the rapid rise in oil prices has brought on the crisis; indeed, the WFTU considers the price increase long overdue. The solution to the crisis lies in the restructuring of the system. This includes establishment of direct relationships between producing and consuming states, thus replacing the existing role of the multi-national companies; the increased involvement of unions in the development of national energy programs; and the immediate halt to the rise in prices resulting from decisions taken by the monopolies. Overall, the WFTU deems it important that the people understand the true nature of the problem, and that the capitalist system not be allowed to use the crisis for its own benefit. In this latter context, the WFTU rejected Kissinger's efforts for Western cooperation: "the ideology of all-round solidarity which the capitalist governments are calling for from their people must be fought, for it can contribute to strengthening the false idea that states and their monopolies have been forced to adopt the present austerity policy despite their wishes." In sum, the WFTU views the crisis facing the developed capitalist countries as one of their own making, and the solution to be a fundamental social and political adjustment to the realities of the historical moment.

Consistent with its attitude toward the problems existing in the Middle East, the WFTU extended its full backing to the struggle of the Palestinian people. In a statement issued to support the request of several countries that the Palestine Liberation Organization be invited to appear before the United Nations, the WFTU called on the U.N. General Assembly not only to respond affirmatively to the request but also to give a massive vote of approval to the Palestinian cause. It also indicated that it would seek to mobilize world-wide trade union support for a permanent and just peace in the Middle East.

The Trade Union Internationals were active during the year in implementing the general policies laid down at the Eighth Congress. At a meeting of the Executive Bureau of the Commercial, Office, and Bank Workers' TUI it was stressed that future activities should bear the stamp of the WFTU's unity policy (*Flashes,* no. 2). The Metal and Engineering Industries' TUI issued a declaration on the deteriorating situation in the car industry. In it the workers were urged to resist measures being adopted by the multi-national companies aimed at making labor suffer the consequences of the oil crisis. The TUI then put forward proposals for cooperation with the ICFTU and the WCL (ibid., no. 1). These unity proposals were apparently rejected by the ICFTU and the WCL (ibid., no. 5). Irina Tsikora (U.S.S.R.), secretary, represented the World Federation of Teachers' Unions (FISE) at the 44th International Congress on Secondary Education. On behalf of the FISE she called on the teachers' movements to promote joint action; she also announced that the FISE would hold a "World Teachers' Conference" in 1975 (ibid., no. 34).

Publications. The most important publication of the WFTU is an illustrated magazine, *World Trade Union Movement,* circulated in some 70 countries and in English, French, Spanish, German, Russian, and other languages. *Flashes,* published several times a month in four languages, is a four-to-five-page information bulletin containing brief reports and documents.

World Peace Council. The "World Peace" movement headed by the World Peace Council (WPC) dates from August 1948, when a "World Congress of Intellectuals for Peace" in Wroclaw, Poland, set up an organization called the "International Liaison Committee of Intellectuals." This committee in April 1949 convened a "First World Peace Congress" in Paris. The congress launched a "World Committee of Partisans of Peace," which in November 1950 was renamed the "World Peace Council." Originally based in Paris, it was expelled in 1951 by the French government, moving first to Prague and then, in 1954, to Vienna—where it adopted the name "World Council of Peace." Although outlawed in Austria in 1957, the World Council of Peace continued its operations in Vienna under the cover of a new organization, the International Institute for Peace (IIP). The IIP has subsequently been referred to by WPC members as the "scientific-theoretical workshop of the WPC" (CTK, Czechoslovak news agency, 16 December 1971). In September 1968 the World Council of Peace transferred its headquarters to Helsinki, while the IIP remained in Vienna. Although no formal announcement was made, the World Council of Peace has reverted to its original name, the World Peace Council.

Structure and Leadership. The WPC is organized on a national basis, with peace committees and other affiliated groups in some 80 countries. No exact figure is available on the total individual membership. At the Council meeting in February 1974 several significant changes took place in the organizational structure. Although the Council remains as the highest authority, an expanded Presidential Committee was established of 101 persons. This committee in turn elects the Bureau (24 persons) and the Secretariat (18). On the Bureau are representatives from peace movements in the following countries: France, Italy, Belgium, and Great Britain; the U.S.S.R., the German Democratic Republic (GDR), Poland, Hungary, and Bulgaria; Cuba, Chile, Panama, and Argentina; Madagascar, Egypt, and Ghana; Vietnam, Japan, India, and Bangladesh; Iraq/Syria, the United States, and Australia. The number is completed with a representative of FRELIMO. The Secretariat has representatives from Chile, the Federal Republic of Germany, Finland, Madagascar, India, the GDR, the U.S.S.R., Argentina, Iraq, Italy, Egypt, Hungary, France, Bulgaria, Poland, South Africa, the United States, and Panama. It should be noted that various international organizations such as the IUS, WFSW, WFTU, WIDF, and WFDY are represented on the Presidential Committee.

Amendments adopted at the 1974 Council require the Council hereafter to meet every three years instead of every two; the national peace movements are urged to meet annually. The Presidential Committee will now meet only once a year instead of twice. The newly created Bureau will normally meet three or four times a year to review international events and the Council's work, and to execute decisions of the Presidential Committee. It appears that the Bureau will have the authority to act independently on a wide variety of matters (BTA, 19 February). The executive bodies of the IIP—ostensibly independent of those of the WPC, but in fact elected by the WPC Council—are the 7-member Presidium and 30-member Executive Committee.

The 1974 Council created two new commissions: one on mass media and one on peace research (*Peace Courier*, No. 6).

Romesh Chandra (India) was reelected as secretary-general of the WPC. As secretary-general he not only heads the Secretariat but is also a member of both the Bureau and the Presidential Committee.

UNESCO's Executive Committee on 24 June voted to admit the WPC to the status of "Consultation and Association—Category A". Only 36 of some 330 non-governmental organizations have been admitted under this category. "The new status grants the World Peace Council a number of advantages, such as the right to send observers to UNESCO's General Conference and Commissions, to advise the Director General on matters pertaining to UNESCO's program, to attend meetings organized by UNESCO on matters within its competence, and to receive subventions from UNESCO for activities which make valuable contribution to the achievement of the World Organization's activities" (ibid., July).

Views and Activities. In pursuance of the decisions taken by the Presidential Committee in Warsaw in May 1973, the secretary-general circulated a note calling for a Council meeting in February 1974. Entitled "New International Climate, New Peace Movement, Stronger Organization and Structure of the World Peace Council," the note put forward a set of proposals for discussion at the Council meeting. Many of these proposals dealt with organizational changes; others, however, suggested expanding both the "contacts" and activities of the WPC (*Peace Courier*, January). In the dialogue preceding the Council, particular attention was given to charting a new "action program" to take advantage of the improved international climate. The key to success in a period when "peace and détente" have the growing support of millions "will be the unity of action of all peace forces throughout the world, a unity bringing together diverse political forces concerned with the future of mankind" (ibid., February). Immediately before the Council, the Presidential Committee finalized the agenda, drew up for approval proposals to amend the statutes, and prepared the lists of Council members for election (Conference Documents).

The Council opened in Sofia before nearly 600 participants representing 103 countries and 30 international and non-governmental organizations. Bulgarian state and party head Todor Zhivkov delivered the initial speech. He was followed by Chandra, who thanked both the Bulgarian people and the other socialist countries for their contribution in the struggle for peace. In talking of the future, he emphasized the need to take into account the growing desire of all peoples for peace and thus the opportunities available to the WPC. Chandra added that the WPC is prepared for the occasion: it is a mass movement with national organizations in all parts of the world, and increasingly enjoys the support of groups not only in the socialist countries but also in the capitalist and non-aligned ones; all movements struggling for national liberation have sided with the WPC. Chandra spoke again and again of the need for unity of all peace-loving forces. (Sofia radio, 16 February.)

Four general commissions met during the second day. In one, representatives from peace organizations reviewed the role of the WPC, and the previous WPC Congress, in the "struggle for victory of peace and the relaxation of international tension." Speaking in this commission, Chandra noted "that certain peace organizations should be watched because they had taken an anti-Soviet stance—they had stopped being genuine peace organizations." The second commission discussed cooperation between the WPC and international organizations. It was determined here to continue the practice by the WPC affiliates of taking a stand on important questions in the United Nations and its Committees. In the third, on disarmament, the delegates denounced the high expenditures on armaments and praised the Soviet proposal for a cutback in the military budgets. The Bangladesh delegates accused the imperialists—including China—of hampering the establishment of a lasting peace on the subcontinent. The fourth, on "Hotspots: the Middle East and Indochina," saw Israel's occupation of Arab lands as the source of extreme tension, and the continued U.S. support of the "puppet" regimes in Southeast Asia as dangerous and war-provoking. (BTA, Bulgarian news agency, 17 February.)

On the third day the regional commissions on Europe, Asia, Africa, and Latin America held their sessions. The main topic throughout was disarmament and the regulation of arms. All speakers referred to the decisive role played in the area of disarmament by the socialist countries, led by the Soviet Union. The European group reviewed progress on European security and the role public opinion could play in reducing tensions. The African, Asian, and Latin American Commissions argued on behalf of liberation struggles and for the creation of united anti-imperialist fronts on each continent. Future seminars and conferences, on topics such as "Problems of the Indian Ocean," were projected. (*Daily Bulletin*, 19 February; BTA, 18 February.) Resolutions called for the peace forces to rally behind the struggle to build the edifice of peace; to defeat fascism, particularly in Chile; to remove Israeli forces from Arab lands; and to wage a just struggle against the imperialists in Indochina (BTA, 19 February). (The full reports of these commissions were issued on 13 March and are contained in the *Peace Courier* of that month).

After the close of the World Congress of Peace Forces, October 1973, a delegation from the Congress visited the United Nations headquarters in New York. This organized post-Congress activity was consistent with the general directions issued at the Congress. The delegation delivered the "conclusions" of the Congress to the president of the U.N. General Assembly and then spoke with the secretary-general. Prior to its departure, the members met with various U.N. representatives to discuss the "urgent issues" raised at the Congress (*Peace Courier*, no. 11, 1973). In early 1974 Chandra announced that the "Steering Committee," which had been set up at the October Congress, would convene for the first time in Moscow in February. This committee was created to maintain post-Congress organizational direction over various "peace" activities. In making this announcement Chandra indicated that the committee would operate under the slogan "There is no Time to be Lost" and would discuss the mechanics of further strengthening cooperation with all organizations and parties which participated in the Congress and ways of realizing the decisions of the Congress and its 14 commissions. (TASS, 15 January.)

Representatives from 20 international and 34 national organizations took part in a meeting of the Steering Committee in Moscow on 9-10 February 1974. Participants reported on the broad support the decisions of the Congress had received in their respective countries. It was also noted that the Congress had sent representatives to the highest level in the United Nations and UNESCO and that these bodies had pledged their cooperation in the struggle for peace. The Steering Committee decided that it was necessary to establish a body to coordinate the activities of the international and national organizations represented at the Congress. This decision led to the formation of the Permanent Liaison Committee of the World Congress of Peace Forces. This new committee, headed by Chandra, acts as an international coordinating body for the WPC. Other executives of the committee are vice-chairman, Sean MacBride (Ireland; president of the International Peace Bureau); executive secretary, Oleg Kharkhardin (U.S.S.R.); Horace Perera from Sri Lanka (secretary-general of the World Federation of United Nations Associations); and Mikhail Zimyanin (U.S.S.R.; IOJ vice-president). In its first public statement, the Liaison Committee issued a letter on 12 March outlining an extensive list of activities that would be undertaken under the sponsorship of the WPC in the months ahead. (*Neues Deutschland*, East Berlin, 10-12 February; TASS, 11 February.)

The first meeting of the Working Commission of the Continuing Liaison Committee was held in London on 22-23 June with the All-Britain Peace Liaison Group as host and representatives from numerous international organizations on hand. Problems in Chile, Vietnam, and the Middle East were discussed; concern was expressed at the slow progress of the negotiations on European security; and special emphasis was placed on the need to increase the cooperation between non-governmental public organizations and the United Nations and other inter-governmental organizations (*Peace Courier*, no. 7).

The WPC Secretariat called for observance of a special month of celebration in honor of the "twenty-fifth anniversary of the World Peace Movement." This month, 25 April-25 May, was highlighted by a Presidential Committee anniversary meeting in Paris on 26 May, preceded by rallies held by national peace movements of such countries as Argentina, Norway, Senegal, Finland, and Bulgaria. On 28 May, more than 2,000 persons attended the commemorative meeting in the Salle Pleyel in Paris. (*L'Humanité*, Paris, 23, 27, 29 May; *Peace Courier*, nos. 4, 5.)

A consultative meeting on the Middle East was held by the WPC in Rome early in December 1973. Discussion was focused on possible initiatives by public opinion to pressure Israel to withdraw from occupied Arab territories and to recognize the legitimate rights of the Palestinian people. It was decided to hold another international conference on the Middle East and the Italian Peace Committee, given the responsibility of convening an international preparatory committee, organized a meeting in Rome on 23 February which was attended by representatives from the international fronts and from numerous national groups (*WFTU Flashes*, no. 10). A second preparatory gathering, in Rome on 1 June, decided to hold the conference no later than the end of October (*L'Unità*, Rome, 5 June).

On 15-19 October the WPC Bureau met in Panama. The session, devoted to problems of Latin America, ranged over a number of subjects, but the main stress was on the importance of the national liberation movements and the danger inherent in the "fascist dictatorship" in Chile. The rise of fascism in Chile and other areas of Latin America was blamed on imperialism, international corporations, and the machinations of local oligarchies. To combat the multi-national companies, it was decided to organize an "international week of mobilization of masses" that would bring public pressure against these business corporations. The Bureau also determined to establish a new regional organization in Latin America to "defend the interests of the peoples." (TASS, 19 October.) A week after the Bureau meeting, the "International Committee for Continued Actions and Contacts of the

World Congress of Peace Forces" met in Moscow, 25-27 October. More than 80 international and national organizations from almost 100 countries were represented. Vasily Isaev, vice-chairman of Moscow City Soviet, welcomed the participants. In his speech, Chandra indicated that the forces of cooperation and détente had begun to prevail; fascism had been routed in Portugal, Guinea-Bissau had been liberated, and a new government had been formed in Mozambique. The final communiqué stressed the need for the continued struggle against the menace of imperialism. (TASS, 25, 27, 28 October.)

In line with the general interest over population questions, the WPC sponsored with the "Congolese Association of Friendship among Peoples," a seminar on "Population and Development" in Brazzaville. Third World countries and international organizations were well represented. All points of the agenda linked population with economic, social, and racial issues; the concluding remarks noted that "false and confusing theories were being put forward" on the issue of population. (*Peace Courier*, no. 7). The report of this seminar was subsequently presented to the U.N.-sponsored Population Conference in Bucharest, where the WPC held a series of informal discussions with the delegates (ibid., no. 8/9).

The WPC was represented at an "International Conference of Non-Governmental Organizations against Apartheid and Colonialism," held at Geneva, 2-5 September and organized by the Sub-Committee on Racism and Decolonization of the Special NGO Committee on Human Rights. R. Chandra is the chairman of this sub-committee. In addition to the NGOs, governments and national liberation movements were also well represented. Indeed, the national liberation movements were the driving force behind much of the discussions. (Ibid., no. 10.) The fact that Chandra chaired the sub-committee which organized the gathering, that Sean McBride, commissioner of the Council for Namibia and executive of the WPC's new Steering Committee, chaired the opening plenary session of this gathering, and that other WPC members were prominent in the organizations and national liberation movements represented clearly indicated that the WPC has attained an influential position in this and other "peripheral" organizations of the United Nations. Indeed, the WPC's influence in the United Nations can no longer be discounted.

The WPC along with other international fronts and non-governmental organizations met in mid-September in Paris and called for "urgent implementation of the Resolution of the Security Council on Cyprus." The declaration issued at the end of the session accused NATO of trying to deny Cyprus its independence (TASS, 23 September). This action followed a special WPC Bureau meeting in July which had set in motion the machinery for the Paris gathering (*Peace Courier*, no. 8/9).

A "Second International Seminar on Oil and Raw Materials for Economic Development, Social Progress and Equitable Economic Relations" was planned for Baghdad in November, to be jointly sponsored by the AAPSO. Among the agenda items are nationalization, oil revenues in the service of development, and the use of oil as a weapon in the struggle against imperialism. (Ibid.)

Chandra addressed the "All-India Peace and Solidarity" meeting in August, a national preparatory committee gathering for the "Conference on the Indian Ocean Bases" to be held in New Delhi in November. It was decided at this meeting that during October there would be a broad-based campaign on the Indian Ocean issue and against monopolies, and that 1 November would be observed as Indian Ocean Day. (*New Age*, New Delhi, 1 September.) In Hyderabad, India, earlier in the year Chandra led a WPC delegation to a similar conference sponsored by the All-Indian Peace and Solidarity Organization. The delegates called then for the liquidation of U.S. and British military bases in the Indian Ocean, and proposed the Indian Ocean Conference (*Patriot*, New Delhi, 8 January).

Christian Peace Conference. The Christian Peace Conference (CPC) emerged in 1974 as a particularly active group. Since the CPC operates in tandem with the WPC, the CPC activities are discussed in this section. A few years ago *Le Figaro* (Paris, 10 October 1973) had the following comment: "After the 1968 events in Czechoslovakia deep repercussions have occurred within the CPC so that it has become an instrument of Soviet policy."

On 5-7 December 1973, the CPC Secretariat met in Prague and reviewed plans for 1974 (*CPC Information*, no. 143, 8 December). On 17-20 January 1974 more than 50 participants attended a meeting in Budapest of the CPC's Committee for International Affairs which discussed "peaceful coexistence and the tasks of churches and Christians" (MTI, 18 January). Shortly thereafter, in Moscow, CPC president Metropolitan Nikodim (U.S.S.R.) held general discussions with CPC secretary-general Karoly Toth (Hungary) and 16 other delegates. Preparations were made for several upcoming meetings. (Ibid., no. 146, 1974.)

In Prague on 4-8 March, the CPC Study Commission for Economy and Politics discussed threats to world peace and agreed that an essential part of Christian activity consisted of exposing the "warlike political-economic mechanism of imperialism." (ibid., no. 149, 11 March). On 12-15 March some 50 representatives of churches and Christian organizations gathered in Prague as a working commission to review means of cooperation of all peace forces and the tasks of the CPC. The debate ranged over problems connected with the Indian Ocean, European security, Chile and Vietnam; the results of the World Congress of Peace Forces were fully supported (Prague radio, 14 March).

The CPC Sub-Commission on the Middle-East met in Cairo on 23-27 April. H. Hellstern (Switzerland), Bishop Samuel (Coptic Orthodox Church), and Archbishop Filaret (Russian Orthodox Church) chaired the commission. A series of topics were discussed, all of which dealt in some fashion with the politics of the area; the general position of the participants was supportive of the Arab struggle against Zionism. Several speakers linked the Christian commitment to the liberation struggle of the Palestinians while others talked of oil and its impact on politics and peace. In the end the meeting adopted a statement of principles placing the CPC firmly behind the struggle against Zionism. (Ibid., no. 153, 20 April.)

Representatives from the WPC Secretariat and Finnish churches attended the CPC International Secretariat meeting in Helsinki, 4-8 June. The report of the secretary-general, K. Toth, focused primarily on European security and Chile. It also noted, however, that "new prospects" were opening up for cooperation with churches in Africa and Asia. Agreement was reached on Cuba as the site of the next meeting of the International Secretariat; plans were laid as well for an "Asian Christian Peace Conference" in India. (Ibid., no. 156, 10 June.)

Publications. The WPC issues a semi-monthly bulletin, *Peace Courier,* in English, French, Spanish, and German, and a quarterly journal, *New Perspectives*, in English and French. The WPC also distributes occasionally a *Letter to National Committees,* and a *Letter* to members. Two new publications appeared in 1973: *Middle East News Letter* and *Spotlight on Africa.* Documents, statements, and press releases are issued in connection with conferences and campaigns.

California State College   Paul F. Magnelia
Stanislaus

SELECT BIBLIOGRAPHY

General on Communism

Alexander, T. *Communism; Short Outline of General Theory.* New Delhi, 1973. 189 pp.

Avineri, Shlomo (comp.). *Marx's Socialism.* New York, Lieber-Atherton, 1973. 220 pp.

Arvon, Henri. *Marxist Esthetics.* Ithaca, Cornell University Press, 1973. 125 pp.

Badaloni, Nicola. *Lenin, ciencia y política.* Buenos Aires, Tiempo Contemporáneo, 1973. 109 pp.

Baumann, Carol Edler. *The Diplomatic Kidnappings: A Revolutionary Tactic of Urban Terrorism.* The Hague, Martinus Nijhoff, 1973. 182 pp.

Bevan, Ruth A. *Marx and Burke: A Revisionist View.* La Salle, Ill., Open Court, 1973. 197 pp.

Bochenski, Joseph M. *Marxismus-Leninismus: Wissenschaft oder Glaube.* Vienna, Olzog, 1973. 147 pp.

Boggs, James, and Grace Lee Boggs. *Revolution and Evolution in the Twentieth Century.* New York: Monthly Review Press, 1974. 266 pp.

Brown, Bruce. *Marx, Freud, and the Critique of Everyday Life toward a Permanent Cultural Revolution.* New York, Monthly Review Press, 1973. 202 pp.

Brunhoff, Suzanne de. *La Politique monétaire: un essai d'interprétation Marxiste.* Paris, P.U.F., 1973. 200 pp.

Bukharin, N. I., et al. *Marxism and Modern Thought.* Westport, Conn., Hyperion Press, 1973. 342 pp.

Caute, David. *The Fellow-Travellers: A Postscript to the Enlightenment.* New York, Macmillan, 1973. 433 pp.

Chandet, Elizabeth, and Jean-Michel Frézals. *Le Communisme.* Paris, Filipacchi, 1973. 157 pp.

Childs, David. *Marx and the Marxists.* New York, Barnes & Noble, 1973. 367 pp.

Cohen, Lenard J., and Jane P. Shapiro (eds.). *Communist Systems in Comparative Perspective.* Garden City, N.Y., Anchor Press, 1974. 530 pp.

Colletti, Lucio. *Marxism and Hegel.* London, New Left Books, 1973. 287 pp.

Crozier, Brian (ed.). *Annual of Power and Conflict, 1973-74.* London: Institute for the Study of Conflict, 1974. 171 pp.

Dunayevskaya, Raya. *Philosophy and Revolution.* New York, Delacorte, 1973. 318 pp.

Duncan, Graeme Campbell. *Marx and Mill: Two Views of Social Conflict and Social Harmony.* Cambridge, University Press, 1973. 386 pp.

Ellis, Harry B. *Ideals and Ideologies: Communism, Socialism, and Capitalism.* New York, World Publishers, 1973. 255 pp.

Ellis, John. *Armies in Revolution.* New York, Oxford University Press, 1974. 278 pp.

Evans, John L. *The Communist International, 1919-1943.* Brooklyn, N.Y., Pageant-Poseidon, 1973. 194 pp.

Flechtheim, Ossip K., and Ernesto Grassi (eds.). *Marxistische Praxis.* Munich, Fink, 1973. 221 pp.

Fleischer, Helmut. *Marxism and History.* New York, Harper & Row, 1973. 157 pp.

Franke, Klaus, and Horst Müller. *Marxismus-Leninismus und die Jugend unserer Zeit.* East Berlin, Dietz, 1973. 78 pp.

Fullat Genis, Octavio. *Marx y la religión.* Barcelona, Editorial Planeta, 1974. 215 pp.

Garaudy, Roger. *The Alternative Future: A Vision of Christian Marxism.* New York, Simon & Schuster, 1974. 192 pp.

Gorz, André. *Socialism and Revolution.* Garden City, N.Y., Anchor Books, 1973. 270 pp.

Greene, Thomas H. *Comparative Revolutionary Movements.* Englewood Cliffs, N.J., Prentice-Hall, 1974. 172 pp.

Gripp, Richard C. *The Political System of Communism.* New York, Dodd, Mead, 1973. 209 pp.

Guettel, Charnie. *Marxism & Feminism.* Toronto, Women's Press, 1974. 62pp.

Hagopian, Mark N. *The Phenomenon of Revolution.* New York, Dodd, Mead, 1974. 402 pp.

Helberger, Christof. *Marxismus als Methode.* Frankfurt/M, Athenäum, 1974. 228 pp.

Henderson, Gregory (ed.). *Divided Nations in a Divided World.* New York, McKay, 1974. 470 pp.

Hobsbawm, Eric J. *Revolutionaries, Contemporary Essays.* New York, Random House, 1973. 278 pp.

Hunt, Richard N. *The Political Ideas of Marx and Engels.* Pittsburgh, University of Pittsburgh Press, 1974. 384 pp.

Hymans, Edward S. *A Dictionary of Modern Revolution.* New York, Taplinger, 1973. 322 pp.

Ibáñez Langlois, José Miguel. *El Marxismo; visión crítica.* Madrid, Rialp, 1973. 351 pp.

Kemper, Max. *Marxismus und Landwirtschaft.* Offenbach: Verlag 2000, 1973. 117 pp.

Kuehnelt-Leddihn, Erik von. *Leftism: From de Sade and Marx to Hitler and Marcuse.* New Rochelle, N.Y., Arlington House, 1974. 653 pp.

Lens, Sidney. *The Promise and Pitfalls of Revolution.* Philadelphia, United Church Press, 1974. 287 pp.

Löbl, Eugen. *Marxismus; Wegweiser und Irrweg.* Vienna, Econ Verlag, 1973. 231 pp.

Looker, Robert (ed.). *Rosa Luxemburg: Selected Political Writings.* New York: Grove Press, 1974. 309 pp.

Lukács, György. *Marxism and Human Liberation.* New York, Dell, 1973. 332 pp.

Marxistisches Lesebuch. Vienna, Verband Sozialistischer Mittelschüler, 1973. 135 pp.

Merkel, Renate. *Marx und Engels über Sozialismus und Kommunismus.* East Berlin, Dietz, 1974. 311 pp.

Morishima, Michio. *Marx's Economics: A Dual Theory of Value and Growth.* Cambridge, University Press, 1973. 198 pp.

Novack, George Edward, Dave Frankel, and Fred Feldman. *The First Three Internationals.* New York, Pathfinder Press, 1974. 207 pp.

Oberndörfer, Dieter, and Wolfgang Jäger. *Marx, Lenin, Mao: Revolution und neue Gesellschaft.* Stuttgart, Kohlhammer, 1974. 146 pp.

Paul, Wolf. *Marxistische Rechtstheorie als Kritik des Rechts.* Frankfurt/M, Athenäum, 1974. 184 pp.

Poulantzas, Nicholas. *Faschismus und Diktatur: Die Kommunistische Internationale und der Faschismus.* Munich, Trikont Verlag, 1973. 398 pp.

Pryor, Frederic L. *Property and Industrial Organization in Communist and Capitalist Nations.* Bloomington: Indiana University Press, 1973. 513 pp.

Reisner, Will (ed.). *Documents of the Fourth International.* New York, Pathfinder Press, 1973. Vol. I.

Sloan, Pat. *Marx and the Orthodox Economists.* Totowa, N.J., Rowman & Littlefield, 1973. 181 pp.

Staar, Richard F. (ed.). *Yearbook on International Communist Affairs, 1974.* Stanford, Calif., Hoover Institution Press, 1974. 648 pp.

Rossanda, Rossana, et al. *Teoría Marxista del Partido Político.* Córdoba, Siglo XXI Argentina Editores, 1973. 134 pp.

Tieffemberg, Yaco (comp.). *Juventud, estudiantes y proceso revolucionario.* Buenos Aires, Ediciones de la Larga Marcha, 1973. 229 pp.

United States Department of State, Bureau of Intelligence and Research. *World Strength of the Communist Party Organizations*. Washington, D.C., Government Printing Office, 1974. 182 pp.

EASTERN EUROPE AND THE SOVIET UNION

General

Beeson, Trevor. *Discretion and Valour: Religious Conditions in Russia and Eastern Europe*. Glasgow, Collins, 1974. 348 pp.

Berend, Iván, and György Ránki. *Economic Development in East-Central Europe in the 19th and 20th Centuries*. New York, Columbia University Press, 1974. 402 pp.

Bondarenko, E. L. *Vyravnivanie ekonomicheskikh urovnei stran-chlenov SEV*. Moscow, Izd. Mosk. Un-ta, 1973. 80 pp.

Bouscaren, Anthony Trawick. *Is the Cold War Over? A New Look at Communist Imperialism*. Falls Church, Va., Capitol Hill Press, 1973. 265 pp.

Brabant, Jozef M. P. van. *Essays on Planning, Trade and Integration in Eastern Europe*. Rotterdam: Rotterdam University Press, 1974. 310 pp.

Brus, Włodzimierz. *The Economics and Politics of Socialism: Collected Essays*. London, Routledge, 1973. 117 pp.

Burling, Robbins. *The Passage of Power: Studies in Political Succession*. New York, Academic Press, 1974. 322 pp.

Dahl, Robert A. (ed.). *Regimes and Oppositions*. New Haven, Conn.: Yale University Press, 1974. 411 pp.

Dalton, George. *Economic Systems and Society: Capitalism, Communism and the Third World*. Baltimore, Penguin, 1974. 250 pp.

Gati, Charles (ed.). *Political Modernization in Eastern Europe: Testing the Soviet Model*. New York, Praeger, 1974. 389 pp.

Hewett, Edward A. *Foreign Trade Prices in the Council for Mutual Economic Assistance*. New York, Cambridge University Press, 1974. 196 pp.

Hundt, Martin. *Wie das "Manifest" enstand*. East Berlin, Dietz, 1973. 139 pp.

Institut für Gesellschaftswissenschaften beim ZK der KPdSU und beim ZK der SED. *Der gegenwärtige Antikommunismus–Politik und Ideologie*. East Berlin, Dietz, 1974. 513 pp.

Iuzufovich, German Karlovich. *Ekonomicheskie metody upravleniia nauchnymi issledovaniiami v stranakh–chlenakh SEV*. Leningrad, Izd. Leningr. Un-ta, 1973. 120 pp.

King, Robert R., and Robert W. Dean (eds.) *East European Perspectives on European Security and Cooperation*. New York, Praeger, 1974. 254 pp.

Kiss, Tibor (ed.). *The Market of Socialist Economic Integration: Selected Conference Papers*. Budapest, Akadémiai Kiadó, 1973. 234 pp.

Krammer, Arnold. *The Forgotten Friendship: Israel and the Soviet Bloc, 1947-53*. Urbana, University of Illinois Press, 1974. 224 pp.

Leonard, Wolfgang. *Three Faces of Marxism: The Political Concepts of Soviet Ideology, Maoism, and Humanist Marxism*. New York, Holt, Rinehart & Winston, 1974. 497 pp.

Marczewski, Jan. *Crisis in Socialist Planning: Eastern Europe and the USSR*. New York, Praeger, 1974. 245 pp.

Mensonides, Louis J., and James A. Kuhlman (eds.). *The Future of Inter-Bloc Relations in Europe.* New York, Praeger, 1974. 217 pp.

Nagorski, Zygmunt, Jr. *The Psychology of East-West Trade: Illusions and Opportunities.* New York, Mason & Lipscomb, 1974. 228 pp.

Paulu, Burton. *Radio and Television Broadcasting in Eastern Europe.* Minneapolis, University of Minnesota Press, 1974. 592 pp.

Sanakoev, Shalva Parsadanovich. *Teoriia i praktika vneshnei politiki sotsializma.* Moscow, Mezhdunar. Otnosheniya, 1973. 160 pp.

Steffens, Rolf. *Integrationsprobleme im Rat für gegenseitige Wirtschaftshilfe (RGW).* Hamburg: Verlag Weltarchiv, 1974. 295 pp.

Sviridova, Inna Nikolaevna. *Strany sotsializma: zakonomernosti, problemy i tendentsii razvitiia.* Moscow, Kniga, 1973. 114 pp.

Usenko, E. T. (ed.). *Mezhvedomstvennye sviazi v usloviiakh sotsialistichesko ekonicheskoi integratsii.* Moscow, Yurid. Lit., 1973. 175 pp.

Wilczynski, J. *Technology in Comecon: Acceleration of Technological Progress through Economic Planning and the Market.* New York, Praeger, 1974. 392 pp.

Albania

Kessel, Patrick. *Les communistes albanais contre le révisionnisme: de Tito a Khrouchtchev, 1942-1961.* Paris, Union générale d'édition, 1974. 429 pp.

Lange, Klaus. *Grundzüge der albanischen Politik; Versuch einer Theorie politischer Kontinuität von den Anfängen der albanischen Nationalbewegung bis heute.* Munich, R. Trofenik, 1973. 129 pp.

Bulgaria

Chernenko, G. A. (ed.). *Narodnaya Respublika Bolgariya.* Moscow, Nauka, 1974. 176 pp.

Mozerov, V. D. *Ekonomicheskaia politika Bolgarskoi kommunisticheskoi partii v promyshlennosti: vosstanovitl'nyi period (1944-1948 gg.).* Saransk, Mordovskoe Knizhnoe Izdatelstvo, 1973. 318 pp.

Zhivkov, Todor. *Ausgewählte Reden und Aufsätze.* Vienna, Globus Verlag, 1973. 368 pp.

Czechoslovakia

Pelikan, Jiri (ed.). *Ici Prague: l'opposition interieure parle.* Paris, Editions du Seuil, 1973. 426 pp.

Szulc, Tad. *The Invasion of Czechoslovakia, August, 1968: The End of a Socialist Experiment in Freedom.* New York, Watts, 1974. 66 pp.

Tchecoslovaquie 1973: dossier pour une action. Brussels, Editions "Vie ouvriere," 1973. 210 pp.

Germany: German Democratic Republic

Armstrong, Anne. *Berliners: Both Sides of the Wall.* New Brunswick, N.J., Rutgers University Press, 1973. 463 pp.

Baylis, Thomas A. *The Technical Intelligentsia and the East German Elite.* Berkeley, University of California Press, 1974. 336 pp.

Birnbaum, Karl E. *East and West Germany: A Modus Vivendi.* Lexington, Mass., Heath, 1973. 157 pp.

Buch, Günther. *Namen und Daten: Biographien wichtiger Personen der DDR.* East Berlin, Dietz, 1973. 332 pp.

DDR–Material zur Politischen Bildung. East Berlin, Oekumenisches Zentrum, 1973. 199 pp.

Honecker, Erich. *Die Rolle der Arbeiterklasse und ihrer Partei in der sozialistischen Gesellschaft.* East Berlin, Dietz, 1974. 389 pp.

Institut für Internationale Beziehungen an der Akademie für Staats- und Rechtswissenschaft der DDR. *Aussenpolitik der DDR–für Sozialismus und Frieden.* East Berlin, Staatsverlag, 1974. 301 pp.

Krisch, Henry. *German Politics under Soviet Occupation.* New York, Columbia University Press, 1974. 312 pp.

Merkl, Peter H. *German Foreign Policies, West and East: On the Threshold of a New European Era.* Santa Barbara, Calif., Clio Press, 1974. 232 pp.

Moore-Rinvolucri, Mina Josephine. *Education in East Germany.* Hamden, Conn., Archon Books, 1973. 141 pp.

Reinhold, Otto. *Mit dem Sozialismus gewachsen: 25 Jahre DDR.* East Berlin, Verlag die Wirtschaft, 1974. 240 pp.

Strauss, C. J. *Die Materialwirtschaft der DDR.* East Berlin, Verlag die Wirtschaft, 1973. 544 pp.

Tailleur, Michèle and B. Di Crescenzo. *La R.D.A., un pays hautement développé.* Paris, Editions Sociales, 1973. 256 pp.

Thälmann, E. *Geschichte und Politik: Artikel und Reden, 1925 bis 1933.* East Berlin, Dietz, 1974. 120 pp.

Tiedtke, Horst. *Marktarbeit im Aussenhandel der DDR.* Berlin, Verlag die Wirtschaft, 1973. 128 pp.

Wohlgemuth, Heinz. *Karl Liebknecht: Eine Biographie.* East Berlin, Dietz, 1973. 520 pp.

Zur Theorie des Sozialistischen Realismus. East Berlin, Institut für Gesellschaftswissenschaften beim ZK der SED, 1974. 913 pp.

Hungary

Barber, Noel. *Seven Days of Freedom: The Hungarian Uprising, 1956.* New York, Stein & Day, 1974. 266 pp.

Berend, Tibor Ivan. *Hungary: A Century of Economic Development.* New York, Barnes & Noble, 1974. 263 pp.

Kadar, Janos. *For a Socialist Hungary: Speeches, Articles, Interviews, 1968-1972.* Budapest, Corvina Press, 1974. 404 pp.

Shawcross, William. *Crime and Compromise: Janos Kadar and the Politics of Hungary since Revolution.* New York, Dutton, 1974. 311 pp.

Poland

Ciechanowski, Jan M. *The Warsaw Rising of 1944.* New York, Cambridge University Press, 1974. 332 pp.

Hammer, Richard. *Bürger zweiter Klasse: Anti-Semitismus in der Volksrepublik Polen und der UdSSR.* Hamburg, Hoffmann & Campe, 1974. 278 pp.

Hoensch, Jorg Konrad. *Sozialverfassung und politische Reform: Polen im vorrevolutionären Zeitalter.* Cologne, Böhlau, 1973. 500 pp.

Kellermann, Volkmar. *Brücken nach Polen: die deutsch-polnischen Beziehungen und die Weltmächte 1939-1973.* Stuttgart: Verlag Bonn Aktuell, 1973. 227 pp.

Matejko, Alexander. *Social Change and Stratification in Eastern Europe: An Interpretive Analysis of Poland and Her Neighbors.* New York, Praeger, 1974. 325 pp.

Piekalkiewicz, Jaroslaw. *Communist Local Government: A Study of Poland.* Athens: Ohio University Press, 1974. 200 pp.

Zielinski. Janusz G. *Economic Reforms in Polish Industry*. London, Oxford University Press, 1973. 333 pp.

Romania

Blanc, André. *La Roumanie: le fait national dans une économie socialiste*. Paris, Bordas, 1973. 143 pp.

Ceauşescu, Nicolae. *Der rumänische Standpunkt: Thesen zur nationalen und internationalen Politik*. Freiburg, Rombach, 1973. 262 pp.

Georgescu, Paul Alexandru. *Rumania*. Bucharest, Meridiane, 1973. 176 pp.

Spigler, Iancu. *Economic Reform in Rumanian Industry*. London, Oxford University Press, 1973. 176 pp.

U.S.S.S.R.

Apresyan, G. Z. *Filosofiia i voprosy kommunisticheskogo vospitaniia*. Moscow, Vysshaya shkola, 1973. 173 pp.

Armstrong, John A. *Ideology, Politics, and Government in the Soviet Union: An Introduction*. 3rd ed. New York, Praeger, 1974. 229 pp.

Barker, Enno. *Die Rolle der Parteiorgane in der sowjetischen Wirtschaftslenkung 1957-1965*. Wiesbaden, Harrassowitz, 1973. 252 pp.

Barron, John. *KGB: The Secret Work of Secret Soviet Agents*. New York, Dutton, 1974. 462 pp.

Bundesinstitut für ostwissenschaftliche und internationale Studien. *Sowjetunion 1973*. Munich, Carl Hanser Verlag, 1974. 198 pp.

Ciliga, Anton. *The Russian Enigma*. Westport, Conn., Hyperion Press, 1973. 304 pp.

Clement, Hermann. *Die Organisationsstruktur der sowjetischen Aussenwirtschaft*. Hamburg, Verlag Weltarchiv, 1973. 223 pp.

Communist Party of the Soviet Union. *Programma Kommunisticheskoi partii Sovetskogo Soiuza*. Moscow, Politizdat, 1973. 144 pp.

——. *Voprosy ideologicheskoi raboty KPSS: sbornik dokumentov (1965-1973)*. Moscow, Politizdat, 1973. 624 pp.

Confino, Michael, and Shimon Shamir (eds.). *The USSR and the Middle East*. New York, Wiley, 1973. 441 pp.

Dewhirst, Martin, and Robert Farrell (eds.). *The Soviet Censorship*. Metuchen, N.J., Scarecrow Press, 1973. 170 pp.

Donaldson, Robert H. *Soviet Policy toward India: Ideology and Strategy*. Cambridge, Mass., Harvard University Press, 1974. 338 pp.

Dornberg, John. *Brezhnev: The Masks of Power*. New York, Basic Books, 1974. 317 pp.

Feldbrugge, F. J. M. (ed.). *Encyclopedia of Soviet Law*. 2 vols. Dobbs Ferry, N.Y., Oceana Publications, 1974. 774 pp.

Gouré, Leon, Foy D. Kohler, and Mose L. Harvey. *The Role of Nuclear Forces in Current Soviet Strategy*. Coral Gables, Florida, Center for Advanced International Studies, University of Miami, 1974. 148 pp.

Gregory, Paul R., and Robert C. Stuart. *Soviet Economic Structure and Performance*. New York, Harper & Row, 1974. 478 pp.

Hammer, Darrell P. *USSR: The Politics of Oligarchy*. Hinsdale, Ill., Dryden Press, 1974. 452 pp.

Haupt, Georges, and Jean-Jacques Marie (comps.) *Makers of the Russian Revolution: Biographies of Bolshevik Leaders*. Ithaca, N. Y., Cornell University, 1974. 452 pp.

Hingley, Ronald. *Joseph Stalin: Man and Legend*. New York, McGraw-Hill, 1974. 482 pp.

Hodnett, Grey. *Leaders of the Soviet Republics, 1955-1972: A Guide to Posts and Occupants*. Canberra, Australian National University, 1973. 454 pp.

Holzman, Franklyn D. *Foreign Trade under Central Planning*. Cambridge, Mass., Harvard University Press, 1974. 436 pp.

Iudin, Ivan Nikolaevich. *Sotsial'naia baza rosta KPSS*. Moscow, Politizdat, 1973. 295 pp.

Jacoby, Susan. *Inside Soviet Schools*. New York, Hill & Wang, 1974. 256 pp.

Jelavich, Barbara. *St. Petersburg and Moscow: Tsarist and Soviet Foreign Policy, 1814-1974*. Bloomington, Indiana University Press, 1974. 480 pp.

Kanet, Roger E. (ed.). *The Soviet Union and the Developing Nations*. Baltimore, Johns Hopkins University Press, 1974. 302 pp.

Khruschchev, Nikita S. *Khrushchev Remembers: The Last Testament*. Boston, Little, Brown, 1974. 602 pp.

Kortunov, V. *Ideologia i politika: bitva idei i evolyutsia ideologicheskikh kontseptsii antikommunisma v 1950-1970 gg*. Moscow, Politizdat, 1974. 287 pp.

Kuper, Yuri. *Holy Fools in Moscow*. New York, The New York Times Book Co., 1974. 230 pp.

Kuusinen, Aino. *The Rings of Destiny: Inside Soviet Russia from Lenin to Brezhnev*. New York, Morrow, 1974. 255 pp.

Landis, Lincoln. *Politics and Oil: Moscow in the Middle East*. New York, Dunellen, 1974. 201 pp.

Lathe, Heinz. *Reicher Nachbar USSR: Dynamik und Probleme einer Weltmacht*. Düsseldorf, Econ Verlag, 1973. 450 pp.

Lederer, Ivo J., and Wayne S. Vucinich (eds.). *The Soviet Union and the Middle East: The Post World War II Era*. Stanford, Calif., Hoover Institution Press, 1974. 302 pp.

Lenin, KPSS o sotsialisticheskom sorevnovanii. Moscow, Politizdat, 1973. 438 pp.

Levytsky, Boris (ed.). *The Stalinist Terror in the Thirties: Documentation from the Soviet Press*. Stanford, Calif., Hoover Institution Press, 1974. 520 pp.

London, Kurt (ed.). *The Soviet Impact on World Politics*. New York, Hawthorn, 1974. 312 pp.

Lumer, Hyman (ed.). *Lenin on the Jewish Question*. New York, International Publishers, 1974. 155 pp.

Massell, Gregory J. *The Surrogate Proletariat: Moslem Women and Revolutionary Strategies in Soviet Central Asia: 1919-1929*. Princeton, N.J., Princeton University Press, 1974. 448 pp.

Matthews, Marvyn (ed.). *Soviet Government: A Selection of Official Documents on Internal Policies*. New York, Taplinger, 1974. 472 pp.

MccGwire, Michael (ed.). *Soviet Naval Developments: Capability and Context*. New York, Praeger, 1973. 555 pp.

McLane, Charles B. *Soviet-Third World Relations*. Vol. 2, *Soviet-Asian Relations*. New York, Columbia University Press, 1974. 150 pp.

McLellan, David. *Karl Marx: His Life and Thought*. New York, Harper & Row, 1974. 498 pp.

McNeal, Robert H. (ed.). *Resolutions and Decisions of the Communist Party of the Soviet Union, 1898-1964*. Toronto, University of Toronto Press, 1974. 4 vols.

Medvedev, Zhores A. *Ten Years after Ivan Denisovich*. New York, Knopf, 1973. 202 pp.

Miliukov, Pavel N. *Russia To-day and To-morrow*. Westport, Conn., Hyperion Press, 1973. 392 pp.

Moses, Joel C. *Regional Party Leadership and Policy-Making in the USSR*. New York, Praeger, 1974. 300 pp.

Osborn, Robert J. *The Evolution of Soviet Politics*. Homewood, Ill., Dorsey Press, 1974. 574 pp.

Osofsky, Stephen. *Soviet Agricultural Policy toward the Abolition of Collective Farms*. New York Praeger, 1974. 301 pp.

Piatnitskii, Osip Aronovich. *Memoirs of a Bol'shevik.* Westport, Conn., Hyperion Press, 1973. 224 pp.

Poljakow, A., et al. *Antikommunismus-ideologische Hauptwaffe des Imperialismus.* East Berlin, Staatsverlag, 1974. 268 pp.

Quigley, John. *The Soviet Foreign Trade Monopoly: Institutions and Laws.* Columbus, Ohio State University Press, 1974. 256 pp.

Razvitoe sotsiologicheskoe obshchestvo: sushchnost' kriterii zrelosti, kritika revizionistkikh kontseptsii. Moscow, Mysl, 1973. 422 pp.

Rosefielde, Steven. *Soviet International Trade in Heckscher-Ohlin Perspective: An Input-Output Study.* Lexington, Mass., Heath, 1973. 173 pp.

Ruban, Mikhail Vasil'evich. *V. I. Lenin o vospitanii sovetskikh voinov.* Moscow, Voenizdat, 1973. 200 pp.

Sakharov, Andrei D. *Sakharov Speaks.* New York, Knopf, 1974. 245 pp.

Salisbury, Charlotte Y. *Russian Dairy.* New York, Walker, 1974. 179 pp.

Saunders, George (ed.). *Samizdat: Voices of the Soviet Opposition.* New York, Pathfinder Press, 1974. 464 pp.

Schmidt, Wolf Dieter. *Zielkonformität der sowjetischen Betriebssteuern.* Berlin, Duncker & Humblot, 1973. 153 pp.

Seale, Patrick, and Maureen McConville. *Philby: The Long Road to Moscow.* New York, Simon & Schuster, 1973. 292 pp.

Senn, Alfred Erich. *Diplomacy and Revolution: the Soviet Mission to Switzerland, 1918.* Notre Dame, University of Notre Dame Press, 1974. 221 pp.

Shaffer, Harry G. *The Soviet Treatment of Jews.* New York, Praeger, 1974. 252 pp.

Short History of the Communist Party of the Soviet Union. Moscow, Progress, 1974. 374 pp.

Simon, Gerhard. *Church, State and Opposition in the U.S.S.R.* Berkeley, University of California Press, 1974. 248 pp.

Smirnov, Georgii Lukich. *Soviet Man: The Making of a Socialist Type of Personality.* Moscow, Progress, 1973. 311 pp.

Smolansky, Oles. *The Soviet Union and the Arab East under Khrushchev.* Lewisburg, Penn., Bucknell University Press, 1974. 326 pp.

Sokolovskiy, V. D. *Soviet Military Strategy.* 3 ed. New York, Crane, Russak, 1974. 550 pp.

Solzhenitsyn, Aleksandr I. *The Gulag Archipelago.* New York, Harper & Row, 1974. 660 pp.

Stepanyan, Ts. A. (ed.). *Leninizm i upravlenie sotsial'nymi protsessami pri sotsializme.* Moscow, Mysl, 1973. 438 pp.

Sulzberger, C. L. *The Coldest War: Russia's Game in China.* New York, Harcourt, Brace, Jovanovich, 1974. 113 pp.

Suvorov, K. I. *Geroicheskii put' KPSS.* Moscow, Politizdat, 1973. 232 pp.

Vaughan, C. James. *Soviet Socialist Realism: Origins and Theory.* New York, St. Martin's Press, 1974. 146 pp.

Wesson, Robert G. *The Russian Dilemma: A Political and Geopolitical View.* New Brunswick, N.J.: Rutgers University Press, 1974. 228 pp.

Yudin, I. I. (ed.). *Nekotorye voprosy organizatsionno-partiinoi raboty.* Moscow, Politizdat, 1973. 334 pp.

Yugoslavia

Ciliga, Ante. *Crise d'etat dans la Yougoslavie de Tito.* Paris, Denoel, 1974. 360 pp.

Perlman, Fredy. *Revolt in Socialist Yugoslavia, June 1968.* Detroit, Black & Red, 1973. 23 pp.

WESTERN EUROPE

France

Barjonet, André. *Initiation au marxisme*. Parks, Editions universitaires, 1973. 166 pp.

Gaucher, Roland. *Histoire secrete du Parti Communiste Français (1920-1974)*. Paris, Albin Michel, 1974. 704 pp.

Kriegel, Annie. *Communismes au miroir français: temps, cultures, et sociétés en France devant le communisme*. Paris, Editions Gallimard, 1974. 252 pp.

———. *The French Communists: Profile of a People*. Chicago, University of Chicago Press, 1973. 408 pp.

Le Braz, Yves. *Les Rejetés: l'affaire Marty-Tillon pour une histoire différente du PFC*. Paris, Table Ronde, 1973. 280 pp.

Manceaux, Michèle, and Jacques Donzelot. *Cours, camarade, le P.C.F. est derrière toi*. Paris, Editions Gallimard, 1974. 264 pp.

Mury, Gilbert. *On leur fera la peau*. Paris, Editions du Cerf, 1973. 177 pp.

Nania, Guy. *Le P.S.U. avant Rocard*. Paris, Editions Roblot, 1973. 256 pp.

Tiersky, Ronald. *French Communism, 1920-1972*. New York, Columbia University Press, 1974. 425 pp.

Germany: Federal Republic of Germany

Dean, Robert W. *West German Trade with the East: The Political Dimension*. New York Praeger, 1974. 269 pp.

Fichter, Tilman, and Eugen Eberly. *Kampf um Bosch: Sieben Jahre offensiver Kampf gegen das Kapital*. Berlin, Wagenbach, 1974. 191 pp.

Mammach, Klaus. *Die Berner Konferenz der KPD, 20 Januar bis 1. Februar 1939*. East Berlin, Dietz, 1974. 130 pp.

Greece

Kousoulas, George D. *Greece: Uncertain Democracy*. Washington, D.C., Public Affairs Press, 1973. 154 pp.

———. *Modern Greece: Profile of a Nation*. New York, Scribner's, 1974. 300 pp.

Italy

Caretti, Stefano. *La Rivoluzione russa e il socialismo italiano (1917-1921)*. Pisa, Nistri Lischi, 1974. 332 pp.

Cassano, Franco (comp.). *Marxismo e filosofia in Italia (1958-1971). Vol. 1, Dibattiti e le inchieste su rinascita e il contemporaneo*. Bari, De Donato, 1973. 400 pp.

Ferrario, Clemente. *Lettere a L'Unità, 1924-1926*. Rome, Editori Riuniti, 1973. 264 pp.

Li Causi, Girolamo. *Il lungo cammino: autobiografia 1906-1944*. Rome, Editori Riuniti, 1974. 224 pp.

Marchesi, Concetto. *Umanesimo e comunismo*. Rome, Editori Riuniti, 1974. 400 pp.

Mastroianni, Giovanni. *Da Croce a Gramsci*. Urbino, Argalia Editore Urbino, 1973. 252 pp.

Piemontese, Giuseppe. *Il movimento operaio a Trieste.* Rome, Editori Riuniti, 1974. 540 pp.
Secchia, Pietro. *I comunisti e l insurrezione, 1943-1945.* Rome, Editori Riuniti, 1973. 381 pp.
Togliatti, Palmiro. *Momenti della storia d'Italia.* Rome, Editori Riuniti, 1973. 362 pp.
Vacca, Giuseppe (ed.). *PCI Mezzogiorno e intellettuali: dalle alleanze all'organizzazione.* Bari, De Donato, 1973. 478 pp.

Spain
Alba, Victor. *El Marxismo en España (1919-1939): historia del B.O.C. y del P.O.U.M.* Mexico City, B. Costa-Amic Editor, 1973. 2 vols.

ASIA AND THE PACIFIC

General
Gouth Kathleen, and Hari P. Sharma (eds.). *Imperialism and Revolution in South East Asia.* New York, Monthly Review Press, 1973. 470 pp.
Lewis, John Wilson. *Peasant Rebellion and Communist Revolution in Asia.* Stanford, Calif., Stanford University Press, 1974. 364 pp.
Pye, Lucian W. *Southeast Asia's Political Systems.* Englewood Cliffs, N.J., Prentice-Hall, 1974. 116 pp.

Cambodia
Simon, Sheldon W. *War and Politics in Cambodia: A Communications Analysis.* Durham, N.C., Duke University Press, 1974. 186 pp.

China
Barnett, A Doak. *Uncertain Passage: China's Transition to the Post-Mao Era.* Washington, D.C. Brookings, 1974. 387 pp.
Berman, Paul. *Revolutionary Organization: Institution-Building within the People's Liberation Armed Forces.* Lexington, Mass., Lexington Books, 1974. 249 pp.
Bettelheim, Charles. *Cultural Revolution and Industrial Organization in China: Changes in Management and the Division of Labor.* New York, Monthly Review Press, 1974. 128 pp.
Braun, Otto. *Chinesische Aufzeichnungen (1932-1939).* East Berlin, Dietz, 1973. 390 pp.
Chao, Kang. *Capital Formation in Mainland China: 1952-1965.* Berkeley, University of California Press, 1974. 178 pp.
Chen, Theodore Hsi-en. *The Maoist Educational Revolution.* New York, Praeger, 1974. 295 pp.
Corr, Gerard H. *The Chinese Red Army: Campaigns and Politics since 1949.* New York, Schocken Books, 1974. 489 pp.
Fejtö, François. *Chine-URSS: de l'alliance au conflict, 1950-1972.* Paris, Seuil, 1973. 472 pp.
Fitzgerald, C. P. *China and Southeast Asia since 1945.* New York, Longman, 1974. 488 pp.
Friedman, Edward. *Backward toward Revolution: The Chinese Revolutionary Party.* Berkeley, University of California Press, 1974. 237 pp.
Gittings, John. *The World and China, 1922-1972.* New York, Harper & Row, 1974. 320 pp.
Hoffmann, Charles. *The Chinese Worker.* Albany, State University of New York Press, 1974. 252 pp.

Hsiao, Gene T. (ed.). *Sino-American Detente and Its Policy Implications.* New York, Praeger, 1974. 352 pp.

Johnson, Chalmers. *Autopsy on People's War.* Berkeley, University of California Press, 1973. 118 pp.

Karol, K. S. *La deuxième révolution chinoise.* Paris, Laffont, 1973. 563 pp.

Kataoka, Tetsuya. *Resistance and Revolution in China: The Communists and the Second United Front.* Berkeley, University of California Press, 1974. 336 pp.

Kau, Ying-mao. *The People's Liberation Army and China's National Building.* White Plains, N.Y., International Arts and Sciences Press, 1973. 407 pp.

Kim, Ilpyong J. *The Politics of Chinese Communism: Kiangsi under the Soviets.* Berkeley and Los Angeles, University of California Press, 1974. 248 pp.

MacFarquhar, Roderick. *The Origins of the Cultural Revolution.* Vol. 1, *Contradictions Among the People, 1956-1957.* New York, Columbia University Press, 1974. 439 pp.

Milton, David, Nancy Milton, and Franz Schurmann. *People's China.* New York, Random House, 1974. 673 pp.

Ogunsanwo, Alaba. *China's Policy in Africa, 1958-1971.* New York, Cambridge University Press, 1974. 310 pp.

Ronning, Chester, *A Memoir of China in Revolution: From the Boxer Rebellion to the People's Republic.* New York, Pantheon, 1974. 306 pp.

Taylor, Jay. *China and Southeast Asia: Peking's Relations with Revolutionary Movements.* New York, Praeger, 1974. 300 pp.

Thornton, Richard C. *China: the Struggle for Power, 1917-1972.* Bloomington, Indiana University Press, 1973. 403 pp.

Townsend, James. *Politics in China: A Country Study.* Boston, Little, Brown, 1974. 377 pp.

Tung, William L. *Revolutionary China: Personal Account, 1926-1949.* New York, St. Martin's Press, 1973. 431 pp.

Whyte, Martin King. *Small Groups and Political Rituals in China.* Berkeley, University of California Press, 1974. 288 pp.

Wilson, J. Tuzo. *Unglazed China.* New York, Saturday Review Press, 1973. 336 pp.

India

Bandypadhyaya, J. *Mao Tse-tung and Gandhi.* Calcutta, Allied Publishers, 1973. 156 pp.

Indonesia

Mortimer, Rex. *Indonesian Communism under Sukarno: Ideology and Politics, 1959-1965.* Ithaca, N.Y., Cornell University Press, 1974. 464 pp.

Widjanarko, Bambang S. *The Devious Dalang: Sukarno and the "Untung" Putsch, Eye Witness Report.* The Hague, Interdoc, 1974. 211 pp.

Japan

Krauss, Ellis S. *Japanese Radicals Revisited: Student Protest in Postwar Japan.* Berkeley, University of California Press, 1974. 192 pp.

Korea

Chung, Joseph Sang-hoon. *The North Korean Economy: Structure and Development.* Stanford, Calif., Hoover Institution Press, 1974. 212 pp.

Kim, Chong Ik Eugene (ed.). *Korean Unification: Problems and Prospects.* Kalamazoo, Mich., Korea Research and Publications, 1973. 190 pp.

Sichrovsky, Harry. *Koreareport: vom Bruderkrieg zur Wiedervereiningung?* Vienna, Europa Verlag, 1973. 183 pp.

Wales, Nym [Helen Foster Snow], and Kim San. *Song of Ariran: A Korean Communist in the Chinese Revolution.* San Francisco, Ramparts Press, 1973. 346 pp.

Malaysia

Barber, Noel. *The War of the Running Dogs: The Malayan Emergency, 1948-1960.* New York, Weybright & Talley, 1973. 284 pp.

George, T. J. S. *Lee Kuan Yew's Singapore.* London, André Deutsch, 1973. 222 pp.

Hanrahan, Gene Z. *The Communist Struggle in Malaya.* Kuala Lumpur, University of Malaya Press, 1971. 237 pp.

Mongolia

Korostovetz, Iwan Jakowlewitsch. *Von Cinggis Khan zur Sowjetrepublik.* Berlin, Walter de Gruyter, 1974. 351 pp.

Philippines

Lichauco, Alejandro. *The Lichauco Paper: Imperialism in the Philippines.* New York, Monthly Review Press, 1973. 470 pp.

Sri Lanka

Wilson, A. Jeyaratnam. *Politics in Sri Lanka, 1947-1973.* New York, St. Martin's Press, 1974. 347 pp.

Thailand

Tanham, George K. *Trial in Thailand.* New York, Crane, Russak, 1974. 175 pp.

Vietnam

Andrews, William R. *The Village War: Vietnamese Communist Revolutionary Activities in Dinh Tuong Province, 1960-1964.* Columbia, University of Missouri Press, 1973. 156 pp.

Berman, Paul. *Revolutionary Organization: Institution-Building within the People's Liberation Armed Forces.* Lexington, Mass., Lexington Books, 1974. 249 pp.

Committee of Social Sciences. *The Paris Agreement on Vietnam: Fundamental Juridical Problems.* Hanoi, Institute of Juridical Studies, 1973. 403 pp.

Fenn, Charles. *Ho Chi Minh: A Biographical Introduction.* New York, Scribner's, 1974. 144 pp.

Joiner, Charles A. *The Politics of Massacre: Political Processes in South Vietnam.* Philadelphia, Temple University Press, 1974. 346 pp.

Risner, Robinson. *The Passing of the Night: My Seven Years as a Prisoner of the North Vietnamese.* New York, Random House, 1974. 264 pp.

Thompson, Sir Robert. *Peace is Not at Hand.* London, Chatto & Windus, 1974. 208 pp.

THE AMERICAS

General

Alexander, Robert J. *Agrarian Reform in Latin America*. New York, Macmillan, 1974. 118 pp.

Lowy, Michael *The Marxism of Che Guevara: Philosophy, Economics, and Revolutionary Warfare*. New York, Monthly Review Press, 1973. 127 pp.

Marinello, Juan. *Creación y revolución*. Havana, Instituto Cubano del Libro, 1973. 230 pp.

Ramos, Jorge Aberlardo. *El Marxismo de Indias*. Barcelona, Editorial Planeta, 1973. 295 pp.

Rojo, Ricardo. *Mi amigo, el Che*. Buenos Aires, Merayo, 1974. 438 pp.

Sauvage, Léo. *Che Guevara: The Failure of a Revolutionary*. Englewood Cliffs, N.J., Prentice-Hall, 1973. 282 pp.

Theberge, James D. *The Soviet Presence in Latin America*. New York, Crane, Russak, 1974. 109 pp.

Argentina

Arevalo, Oscar. *Breve introducción al socialismo cientifico: siete temas básicos*. Buenos Aires, Ediciones Centro de Estudios, 1973. 235 pp.

Astesano, Eduardo B. *Manual de la militancia política*. Buenos Aires, Editorial Relevo, 1973. 153 pp.

Ciria, Alberto. *Parties and Power in Modern Argentina (1930-1949)*. Albany, State University of New York Press, 1974. 347 pp.

Galasso, Norberto. *¿Qué es el socialismo nacional?* Buenos Aires, Ediciones Ayacucho, 1973. 105 pp.

Giudici, Ernesto. *Alienación, Marxismo y trabajo intelectual*. Buenos Aires, Editorial Crisis, 1974. 163 pp.

Guérin, Daniel. *Para un Marxismo libertario*. Buenos Aires, Proyección, 1973. 153 pp.

Lebedinsky, Maruicio. *El Marxismo-Leninismo frente al revisionismo de "izquierda" e de derecho: en general y en la Argentina*. Buenos, Aires, Ediciones Centro de Estudios, 1973. 235 pp.

Bolivia

Debray, Régis. *Prison Writings*. New York, Vintage Books, 1973. 207 pp.

Gambini, Hugo. *El Che Guevara*. Buenos Aires, Paidós, 1973. 549 pp.

Brazil

Chilcote, Ronald H. *The Brazilian Communist Party: Conflict and Integration, 1922-1972*. New York, Oxford University Press, 1974. 361 pp.

Chile

Allende Gossens, Salvador. *Chile: historia de una ilusión–discursos, conferencias, entrevistas, programa Unidad Popular*. Buenos Aires, Edita La Senal, 1973. 256 pp.

——. *Chile's Road to Socialism*. Baltimore, Penguin, 1973. 208 pp.

——. *La conspiración contra Chile*. Buenos Aires, Corregidor, 1973. 412 pp.

——. *La revolución Chileña*. Buenos Aires, Editorial Universitaria de Buenos Aires, 1973. 209 pp.

Barraclough, Solon, et al. *Chile: reforma agraria y gobierno popular*. Buenos Aires, Ediciones Periferia, 1973. 244 pp.

Barrera, Manuel. *El conflicto obrero en el enclave Cuprifero.* Santiago, Instituto de Economia y Planificación, 1973. 109 pp.

Bartsch, Hans-Werner. *Chile: ein Schwarzbuch.* Cologne, Pahl-Rugenstein, 1974. 228 pp.

Blanco, Hugo, et al. *La tragedia chileña.* Buenos Aires. Ediciones Pluma, 1973. 163 pp.

Castro, Fidel. *Allende: combatiente y soldado de la revolución.* Lima, Editorial Causachun, 1973. 108 pp.

Evans, Les (ed.). *Disaster in Chile: Allende's Strategy and Why It Failed—An Anthology.* New York, Pathfinder Press, 1974. 272 pp.

Frei Montalva, Eduardo. *Un mundo nuevo: respuesta a una carta.* Santiago, Ediciones Nueva Universidad, 1973. 206 pp.

Garcia, Leon Roberto. *Chile: una traición al futuro.* Mexico City, Editorial Epoca, 1973. 201 pp.

Gayango, Ignacio. *Chile: el largo camino al golpe.* Barcelona, Editorial Dirosa, 1974. 257 pp.

Jarpa, Sergio Onofre. *Creo en Chile.* Santiago, Sociedad Impresora Chile, 1973. 272 pp.

Kramer, André M. *Chile: historia de una experiencia socialista.* Barcelona, Ediciones Peninsula, 1974. 214 pp.

MacEoin, Gary. *No Peaceful Way: The Chilean Struggle for Dignity.* New York, Sheed & Ward, 1974. 230 pp.

Millas, Hernan, and Emilio Filippi. *Chile 70-73: crónica de una experiencia.* Santiago, Editor Zig-Zag, 1974. 147 pp.

Moss, Robert. *Chile's Marxist Experiment.* New York, Wiley, 1974. 225 pp.

Najman, Maurice (ed.). *Le Chili est proche: révolution et contre-révolution dans le Chili de l'Unité Populaire.* Paris, Maspero, 1974. 309 pp.

Nohlen, Dieter. *Chile: das sozialistische Experiment.* Hamburg, Hoffmann & Campe, 1973. 431 pp.

Orrillo, Winston (comp.). *La verdad sobre Chile.* Lima, Editorial Causachun, 1973. 181 pp.

Santana, Alberto, et al. *La tragedia chileña: testimonios.* Buenos Aires, Merayo, 1973. 385 pp.

Sotomayor, Froilan. *Chile: el terremoto de setiembre.* Montevideo, Ediciones Mapocho, 1973. 201 pp.

Sweezy, Paul M., and Harry Magdoff (eds.). *Revolution and Counter-Revolution in Chile.* New York, Monthly Review Press, 1974. 169 pp.

Cuba

Bambirra, Vania. *La revolución cubana: una reinterpretación.* Mexico City, Editorial Nuestro Tiempo, 1974. 172 pp.

Bonachea, Ramón L., and Marta San Martín. *The Cuban Insurrection, 1952-1959.* New Brunswick, N.J., Transaction Books, 1974. 452 pp.

Cardenal, Ernesto. *In Cuba.* New York, New Directions, 1974. 340 pp.

Castro, Fidel. *El tercer mundo y el futuro de la humanidad.* Rosario, Argentina, Editorial Encuadre, 1973. 187 pp.

——. *Todos empezó en el Moncada: discursos y otros documentos, 1953-1958.* Mexico City, Editorial Diogenes, 1973. 281 pp.

Dumont, René. *Is Cuba Socialist?* New York, Viking, 1974. 159 pp.

Gonzales, Edward. *Cuba under Castro: The Limits of Charisma.* Boston, Houghton Mifflin, 1974. 241 pp.

Guevara, Ernesto. *El hombre y el socialismo en Cuba.* Buenos Aires, Ediciones Sintesis, 1973. 215 pp.

Huteau, Michel, and Jacques Lautrey. *L'éducation à Cuba.* Paris, F. Maspero, 1973. 250 pp.

Nikiforov, Boris Sergeevich. *Kuba: krakh burzhuaznykh politicheskikh partii (1945-1958).* Moscow, Nauka, 1973. 415 pp.

Suchlicki, Jaime. *Cuba from Columbus to Castro.* New York, Scribner's, 1974. 242 pp.
Tellería Toca, Evelio. *Congresos obreros en Cuba.* Havana, Instituto Cubano del Libro, 1973. 587 pp.

Mexico
Herman, Donald L. *The Comintern in Mexico.* Washington, D.C., Public Affairs Press, 1974. 187 pp.
Partido Comunista de México. *Nuevo programa para la nueva revolución.* Mexico City, Ediciones de Cultura Popular, 1974. 102 pp.

Peru
Paris, Robert, et al. *El Marxismo Latinoamericano de Mariátegui.* Buenos Aires, Ediciones de Crisis, 1973. 246 pp.

U.S.A.
Bacciocco, Edward J., Jr. *The New Left in America: Reform to Revolution, 1956 to 1970.* Stanford, Calif., Hoover Institution Press, 1974. 300 pp.
Carpozi, George, Jr. *Red Spies in the U.S.* New Rochelle, N.Y., Arlington House, 1973. 251 pp.
Conlin, Joseph R. (ed.). *The American Radical Press, 1880-1960.* Westport, Conn., Greenwood Press, 1974. 720 pp.
Davis, Angela. *Angela Davis: An Autobiography.* New York, Random House, 1974. 320 pp.
Fitzgerald, Richard. *Art and Politics: Cartoonists of the Masses and Liberator.* Westport, Conn., Greenwood Press, 1973. 254 pp.
Johnson, Oakley C. *Marxism in United States History before the Russian Revolution (1876-1917).* New York, Humanities Press, 1974. 196 pp.
Martin, Rose L. *The Selling of America.* Santa Monica, Calif., Fidelis Publishers, 1973. 298 pp.
Vogelgesang, Sandy. *The Long Dark Night of the Soul: The American Intellectual Left and the Vietnam War.* New York, Harper & Row, 1974. 249 pp.

MIDDLE EAST AND AFRICA

Abboushi, W. F. *The Angry Arabs.* Philadelphia, Westminster Press, 1974. 285 pp.
Allen, Sir Richard Hugh Sedley. *Imperialism and Nationalism in the Fertile Crescent: Sources and Prospects of the Arab-Israeli Conflict.* New York, Oxford University Press, 1974. 686 pp.
Berreby, Jean-Jacques. *Le pétrole dans la stratégie mondiale.* Tournai, Casterman, 1974. 211 pp.
Cabral, Alvaro. *Revolyutsia v Gvineye.* Moscow, Nauka, 1973. 280 pp.
Carré, Olivier. *Proche Orient entre la guerre et la paix.* Paris, Epi, 1974. 175 pp.
Constant, Jean-Paul. *Le relations maroco-soviétiques, 1956-1971.* Paris, Librairie Générale de Droit et de Jurisprudence, 1973. 136 pp.
Davidson, Basil. *Black Star: A View of the Life and Times of Kwame Nkrumah.* New York, Praeger, 1974. 225 pp.
Dobson, Christopher. *Black September: Its Short, Violent History.* New York, Macmillan, 1974. 179 pp.

Hatch, John. *Africa Emergent: Africa's Problems since Independence.* Chicago, Regnery, 1974. 233 pp.

Laqueur, Walter Z. *Confrontation: The Middle East War and World Politics.* London, Wildwood House, 1974. 244 pp.

Lartéguy, Jean. *Tout l'or du diable: guerre, pétrole et terrorisme.* Paris, Presses de la Cité, 1974. 234 pp.

Lee, Franz John Tennyson. *Südafrika vor der Revolution?* Frankfurt/M, Fischer, 1973. 188 pp.

Mahgoub, Mohamed Ahmed. *Democracy on Trial: Reflections on Arab and African Politics.* London, André Deutsch, 1974. 318 pp.

O'Ballance, Edgar. *Arab Guerrilla Power, 1967-1972.* Hamden, Conn., Archon Books, 1973. 246 pp.

O'Neill, Bard. *Revolutionary Warfare in the Middle East: The Israelis vs. the Fadayeen.* Boulder, Colo., Paladin Press, 1974. 140 pp.

Palestine Lives: Interviews with Leaders of the Resistance—Khalid al-Hassan, Fateh; Abu Iyad, Fateh; George Habash, PFLP; Nayef Hawatmeh, PDFLP; Sami al-Attari, Sa'iqa, A. W. Sa'id, Arab Liberation Front. Beirut, Palestine Research Center, 1973. 172 pp.

Pennar, Jaan. *The U.S.S.R. and the Arabs: the Ideological Dimension.* New York, Crane, Russak, 1973. 180 pp.

Schmidt, Dana Adams. *Armageddon in the Middle East.* New York, John Day, 1974. 269 pp.

Snetsinger, John. *Truman, the Jewish Vote, and the Creation of Israel.* Stanford, Calif., Hoover Institution Press, 1974. 208 pp.

Tophoven, Rolf. *Fedayin—Guerilla ohne Grenzen.* Frankfurt/M, Bernard & Graefe, 1974. 158 pp.

Venter, Al J. *Africa at War.* Old Greenwich, Conn. Devin-Adair, 1974. 185 pp.

Zohar, David M. *Political Parties in Israel: the Evolution of Israeli Democracy.* New York, Praeger, 1974. 193 pp.

INDEX

INDEX OF PERSONS

Aalto, Arvo, 153, 155-6
Aarons, Brian, 273
Aarons, Eric, 269, 272, 282
Aarons, Laurie, 267-74, 276-7, 279, 281
Abadzhiev, Ivan 13-4
Abarca, Alfredo, 547
'Abd al-Samad, Dhahir, 608
Abernathy, Ralph, 555
Aboukeid, H., 630
Abu Mayzar, 'Abd al-Muhsin, 591-2
Acosta Salas, Raúl, 547
Aczél, György, 42-4, 50
Adam, Alexis, 574
Adamson, Bob, 273
Adhikari, Man Mohan, 391-2
Adhikari, Chandra Mohan, 392
Adjitorop, Jusuf, 336
Agee, Philip B., 533
Agosti, Héctor P., 458
Aguirre, Alcibiades, 489
Ahmad, Karim, 583, 585
Ahmad, Musa, 377
Ahmed, A. A., 324
Ahmed, Fakhruddin Ali, 323, 326
Ahmed, Tajuddin, 291
Aidit, Dipa Nusantara, 333
'Ajinah, Rahim, 584
Ajtai, Miklós, 44
Alarcón, Alejandro, 483
Alauddin, Mohammad, 288
Alba, Carlos, 465
Alef-Bolkowiak, Gustaw, 618
Alegría, Manuel Diez, 242
Alembert, Zleika, 469
Alenius, Ele, 154-5
Alexandrov, V., 103
Alexis, Bernard, 513
Ali, Bachir Hadj, 597
Ali, Mukti, 345-6
'Ali, Nazim (pseud. for 'Aziz, Muhammad), 583
Alia, Ramiz, 3
Aliev, Geidar A., 81
Allende Gossens, Salvador, 75, 151, 212, 466, 477, 495, 526, 532, 547, 565, 623
Allende, Mrs. Salvador, 625
Almad, Muzaffar, 283
Almeida, Clodomiro, 627
Almeida Bosque, Juan, 496
Altamirano, Carlos, 479
Altamirano, Hernán, 550
Altangerel, 389
Altenkirch, Ernst, 27
Altesor, Alberto, 567
Alvarado Arrellano, Humberto, 517
Alvarado Jérez, Carlos, 517
Alvarado Monzón, Bernardo, 517
Alvarez, Juan, 620
Amadu Idissa, David, 63

Amatya, Tulsi Lal, 391
Ambatielos, Antonios, 199
Amendola, Giorgio, 211, 213
Amir, Dr. 'Izz al-Din 'Ali, 606
Andersen, G. H. ("Bill"), 394-5
Anderson, Sven, 128
Andhroutsopoulos, Adamantios, 198
Andrei, Ştefan, 68, 75, 125
Andropov, Yuri V., 17, 80-1, 86
Annadurai, 324
Ansart, Gustave, 159
Antonioni, Michelangelo, 282, 313
Apró, Antal, 42, 45, 124
Aptheker, Herbert, 554
Aquino, Benigno, 407
Arafat, Yasir, 39, 105-6, 128, 501, 591, 627
Arana Osorio, Carlos, 516
Aranguren, Fernando, 535
Arbatov, Georgi A., 86, 89, 94, 98
Arbenz, Jacobo, 516
Arboleda, Pedro León, 491
Arevalo, Julia, 623
Arias, Arnulfo, 240-1
Arias Schreiber, Félix, 547
Arismendi, Rodney, 567
Arnalds, Ragnar, 204-6
Arnedo Alvarez, Gerónimo, 457-8
Artobolevsky, I., 630
al-Asad, Hafiz, 16, 75, 105, 129, 608
Ashhad, Na'im, 591
Ataún, Antonio Añoveros, 240
Atwood, Gary, 562
Aubrac, R., 634
Aung Myint, 296
Avcioğlu, Değan, 261
Avgheropoulos, Gerassimos, 618
'Awad, 'Arabi, 591-2
Axen, Hermann, 28, 35
Aybar, Mehmet, 255
Ayo, Ella, 394, 396
al-'Aysami, Shibli, 583
Azar, Abdol-Reza, 581
Azcárate, Manuel, 242
Azevedo, Agilberto Vieira de, 469, 471

Ba Myint, 296
Baader, Andreas, 190
Babamento, Luan, 7
Babiuch, Edward, 56, 64, 126, 156
Bachmann, Kurt, 181
Bahia, Sabino, 469
Baholli, Sulejman, 7
Baibakov, Nikolai K., 84-5
Baigés, Pedro, 553
Bailey, Rona, 393-6
Bain, Hardial, 476
Bakalli, Mahmut, 123
Bakarić, Vladimir, 113, 116